MATHEMATICS

for SEG GCSE

Higher Tier

Tony Banks ● Tony Fisher ● Paul Newton
Peter Balaam ● Bruce Balden ● David Alcorn

CPL

Causeway Press Limited

Published by Causeway Press Ltd
P.O. B0x 13, Ormskirk, Lancashire L39 5HP

First published 2000

© Tony Banks, Tony Fisher, Paul Newton, Peter Balaam, Bruce Balden, David Alcorn

British Library Cataloguing-in-Publication Data.
A catalogue record for this book is available from the British Library.

ISBN 1-873929-86-2

Acknowledgements
Exam questions
Past exam questions, provided by Southern Examining Group, are denoted by the letters SEG and the year of the exam. Where specimen questions are used the letter S appears after the applicable year. The answers to all questions are entirely the responsibility of the authors/publisher and have neither been provided nor approved by SEG.

GCSE Mathematics Coursework
The authors and publisher wish to express their thanks and gratitude to Paul Metcalf and Graeme Wales for their contribution to this section of the book.

Page design
Alan Fraser
Billy Johnson

Reader
David Hodgson

Artwork
Alan Fraser
David Alcorn

Cover design
Waring-Collins Partnership

Typesetting by Bibliocraft, Dundee
Printed and bound by Scotprint, Musselburgh, Scotland

preface

Mathematics for SEG GCSE - Higher Tier has been written to meet the requirements of the revised National Curriculum in Mathematics and provides full coverage of all GCSE examination syllabuses for first examination in 2000 at the Higher Tier of entry.

The book is suitable for students preparing for assessment at the Higher Tier of entry on either a 1-year or 2-year course or as a revision text.

In preparing the text, full account has been made of the new requirements for students to be able to solve problems in mathematics both with and without a calculator. Whilst there has been no artificial division of subject content into calculator and non-calculator work, non-calculator questions and exercises have been incorporated throughout the book where appropriate.

The planning of topics within chapters and sections has been designed to provide efficient coverage of the syllabus. Depending on how the book is to be used you can best decide on the order in which chapters are studied.

Chapters 1 - 7   Number
Chapters 8 - 16   Algebra
Chapters 17 - 27   Shape, Space and Measures
Chapters 28 - 31   Handling Data

Each chapter consists of fully worked examples with explanatory notes and commentary; carefully graded questions, a summary of key facts and skills and a review exercise. The review exercises provide the opportunity to consolidate topics introduced within the chapter and consist of exam-style questions, which reflect how SEG intend to assess the work, plus lots of past examination questions (marked SEG).

Further opportunities to consolidate skills acquired over a number of chapters are provided with section reviews. There is a final exam questions section with a further compilation of exam and exam-style questions, organised for non-calculator and calculator practice, in preparation for the exams.

Some chapters include ideas for investigational, practical and statistical tasks and give the student the opportunity to improve and practice their skills of using and applying mathematics. The section on GCSE Mathematics Coursework, on page 534, is a useful reference when trying any of the ideas for investigation.

contents

CHAPTER 3 Approximation and Estimation

CHAPTER 4 Powers, Roots and Reciprocals

CHAPTER 5 Direct and Inverse Proportion

CHAPTER 6 Rational and Irrational Numbers

CHAPTER 7 Understanding and Using Measures

CHAPTER 8 Introduction to Algebra

CHAPTER 16 Transforming Graphs

CHAPTER 17 Angles, Parallel Lines and Polygons

CHAPTER 18 Circle Properties

CHAPTER 23 Volumes and Surface Areas

CHAPTER 24 Enlargements and Similar Figures

CHAPTER 25 Transformations

CHAPTER 29 Presentation of Data

CHAPTER 30 Measures of Average and Spread

CHAPTER 31 Probability

CHAPTER 1

Percentages, Fractions, Decimals and Ratio

The meaning of a percentage

'Per cent' means 'out of 100'.
The symbol for per cent is %.
A percentage can be written as a fraction with denominator 100.

> **Remember** (note)
> 10% means 10 out of 100.
> 10% can be written as $\frac{10}{100}$.
> 10% is read as '10 percent'.

Changing percentages to fractions and decimals

EXAMPLES

1 Write 38% as a fraction in its simplest form.

38% means '38 out of 100'.

This can be written as $\frac{38}{100}$.

$\frac{38}{100} = \frac{38 \div 2}{100 \div 2} = \frac{19}{50}$

$38\% = \frac{19}{50}$

2 Write 42.5% as a decimal.

$42.5\% = \frac{42.5}{100} = 42.5 \div 100 = 0.425$

> **Remember**
> To simplify a fraction divide the **numerator** (top number) and the **denominator** (bottom number) of the fraction by their highest common factor.

> **Remember**
> To change a fraction to a decimal divide the numerator by the denominator.

Changing fractions and decimals to percentages

EXAMPLE

1 Change $\frac{3}{5}$ to a percentage.

Method 1

Multiply the fraction by 100.

$\frac{3}{5} \times 100 = \frac{300}{5} = 60$

> Method 1 can be used when the denominator of the fraction is a factor or a multiple of 100.

Method 2

Change the fraction to a decimal and then multiply by 100.

$\frac{3}{5} = 3 \div 5 = 0.6$

$0.6 \times 100 = 60\%$

> Method 2 is useful when the denominator of the fraction is not a factor or a multiple of 100 and a calculator is available.

Fractions Decimals Ratio

EXAMPLE

2 Write $\frac{7}{12}$ as a percentage.

$\frac{7}{12} = 7 \div 12 = 0.58333\ldots$

$0.58\dot{3} \times 100 = 58.\dot{3}\%$

$\frac{7}{12} = 58.\dot{3}\%$

Remember

Some decimals have recurring digits. These are shown by:

a single dot above a single recurring digit.
For example: $0.\dot{3}$ means $0.3333333 \ldots$

a dot above the first and last digit of a set of recurring digits.
For example: $0.\dot{1}2\dot{3}$ means $0.123123123 \ldots$

Comparing fractions

Fractions can be compared by first writing them as percentages.

EXAMPLE

Ben scored 17 out of 20 in a Maths test and 21 out of 25 in a History test. Which is Ben's better mark?

Change each mark to a percentage.

Maths: $\frac{17}{20} = \frac{85}{100} = 85\%$ History: $\frac{21}{25} = \frac{84}{100} = 84\%$

So Ben's better mark is his Maths mark of 85%.

Exercise 1.1

Do not use a calculator in this exercise.

1 Change these fractions to a percentage.

(a) $\frac{4}{5}$ (b) $\frac{12}{25}$ (c) $\frac{13}{20}$

2 Change these percentages to fractions in their simplest form.

(a) 52%   (b) 12.5%   (c) 72.5%

3 Change these decimals to a percentage.

(a) 0.45   (b) 0.07   (c) 0.015

4 Change these percentages to decimals.

(a) 15%   (b) 47%   (c) 87.5%

5 Change these fractions to percentages.

(a) $\frac{2}{3}$ (b) $\frac{2}{9}$ (c) $\frac{17}{45}$

6 Write in order of size, lowest first.

$\frac{17}{40}$ 0.42 $\frac{13}{30}$ 43%

7 Write in order of size, lowest first.

$\frac{2}{7}$ 28% $\frac{57}{200}$ 0.2805

8 Change each of these marks to a percentage.
(a) Maths: 27 out of 30.
(b) French: 34 out of 40.
(c) Science: 22 out of 25.
(d) Art: 48 out of 60.

9 Rohima achieved the following results.
Geography: 32 out of 40
English: 21 out of 25
Maths: 17 out of 20
In which subject did she do best?

10 In an ice hockey competition Team A won 8 out of the 11 games they played whilst Team B won 5 of their 7 games.

Which team has the better record in the competition?

Ratio

Ratios are used to **compare** quantities.
They do not give information about actual values.

For example
A necklace is made using red beads and white beads in the ratio **3 : 4**.
This gives no information about the actual numbers of beads in the necklace.
The ratio **3 : 4** means that for every 3 red beads in the necklace there are 4 white beads.

For the ratio 3 : 2 say 3 to 2.

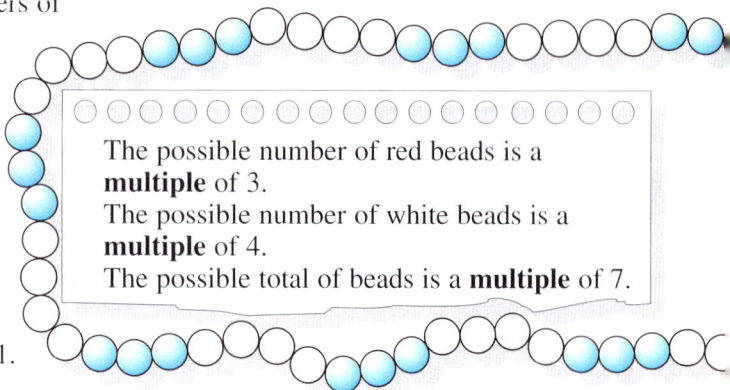

The ratios   3 : 4   6 : 8   9 : 12   ... are different forms of the **same** ratio.
They are called **equivalent** ratios.
They can be found by multiplying or dividing each part of the ratio by the **same** number.

A ratio in its **simplest form** has only whole numbers that have no common factor other than 1.

The possible number of red beads is a **multiple** of 3.
The possible number of white beads is a **multiple** of 4.
The possible total of beads is a **multiple** of 7.

EXAMPLES

1   Write the ratio 15 : 9 in its simplest form.

The highest common factor of 15 and 9 is 3. Divide both parts of the ratio by 3.
$15 \div 3 : 9 \div 3 = 5 : 3$
The ratio 15 : 9 in its simplest form is 5 : 3.

2   The ratio of boys to girls in a school is 3 : 4.
There are 72 boys.
How many girls are there?

$72 \div 3 = 24$
To find a ratio equivalent to 3 : 4 where the first number in the ratio is 72 multiply each number in the ratio by 24.
$3 \times 24 : 4 \times 24 = 72 : 96$
The number of girls = 96.

3   Write the ratio 2 cm : 50 mm in its simplest form.

This ratio compares two quantities with different units.
In its simplest form a ratio contains **only** whole numbers. There are **no units**.
In order to simplify the ratio both quantities in the ratio must be in the **same units**.

2 cm : 50 mm = 20 mm : 50 mm = 20 : 50
Divide both parts of the ratio by 10.
$20 \div 10 : 50 \div 10 = 2 : 5$
The ratio 2 cm : 50 mm in its simplest form is 2 : 5.

Exercise 1.2   Do not use a calculator in this exercise.

1   Give the simplest form of each of these ratios.

(a)   3 : 6
(b)   9 : 12
(c)   10 : 25
(d)   5 : 10 : 15
(e)   9 : 21
(f)   12 : 18 : 24
(g)   36 : 81
(h)   22 : 26 : 30

2   Each of these pairs of ratios are equivalent.

(a)   3 : 4 and 9 : n.
(b)   2 : 7 and 8 : n.
(c)   8 : n and 2 : 25.
(d)   25 : n and 5 : 4.
In each case calculate the value of n.

3 The heights of two friends are in the ratio 7 : 9.
The shorter of the friends is 154 cm tall.
What is the height of the taller of the friends?

4 Sugar and flour are mixed in the ratio 2 : 3.
How much sugar is used with 600 g of flour?

5 The ratio of boys to girls in a school is 4 : 5.
There are 80 girls.
How many boys are there?

6

I earn £800 per month.

I earn £720 per month.

The amounts Jenny and James earn are in the ratio of their ages.
Jenny is 20 years old.
How old is James?

7 Sam spends 45p a week on comics.
Tom spends £2 a week on comics.
Write the ratio of the amounts Tom and Sam spend on comics in its simplest form.

8 Denise draws a plan of the classroom.
On her plan Denise uses 2 cm to represent 5 m.
Write the scale as a ratio in its simplest form.

9 On a map a pond is 3.5 cm long.
The pond is actually 52.5 m long.
Write the scale as a ratio in its simplest form.

10 Write each of these ratios in its simplest form.
(a)   £2.20 : 40p   (b)   6 m : 240 cm
(c)   1 kg : 425 g   (d)   90 cm : 2 m
(e)   1500 mm : 2 m   (f)   3 litres : 600 ml
(g) $3 \, cm^2 : 75 \, mm^2$ (h)   20 seconds : 5 minutes

11 A hairdresser uses shampoo and conditioner in the ratio 5 : 2.

At the start of the day the hairdresser opens a 500 ml bottle of conditioner.
During the day she uses 1 litre of shampoo.
(a)   How much conditioner is left in the bottle at the end of the day?
(b)   Write the ratio of the amount of conditioner **used** to the amount of conditioner **left** in the bottle in its simplest form.

Sharing in a given ratio

EXAMPLES

1 Penny and Henry share £57.75 in the ratio 5 : 6.
How much do they each get?

Add the numbers in the ratio.
5 + 6 = 11
For every £11 shared:
Penny gets £5, Henry gets £6.
57.75 ÷ 11 = 5.25
Penny gets £5 × 5.25 = £26.25
Senry gets £6 × 5.25 = £31.50

2 A box contains red, white and blue buttons in the ratio 1 : 2 : 5.
There are 104 buttons in the box.
How many of them are blue?

Add the numbers in the ratio.
1 + 2 + 5 = 8
104 ÷ 8 = 13   5 × 13 = 65
There are 65 blue counters in the box.

1
(a) Share £81.90 in the ratio 11 : 3.
(b) Share £97.50 in the ratio 5 : 8.
(c) Share £111 in the ratio 7 : 5.
(d) Share £54.45 in the ratio 7 : 4.

2 A necklace contains 80 beads.
The ratio of red beads to blue beads is 5 : 3.
How many red beads are on the necklace?

3 What is the difference between the larger and smaller shares when £39 200 is shared in the ratio 7 : 9?

4 Jenny and Tim each have 40 counters.
Tim gives Jenny some counters so that the ratio of the number of counters they each have is 9 : 7.
How many counters does Tim give Jenny?

5 In the UK there are 240 939 km² of land.
The ratio of agricultural land to non-agricultural land is approximately 7 : 3.
Estimate the area of land used for agriculture.

6 In his will, a grandfather leaves his three grandchildren £8000 to be shared in the ratio 3 : 5 : 8.
How much does each grandchild get?

7 To make concrete a builder mixes gravel, sand and cement in the ratio 4 : 2 : 1.
The builder wants 350 kg of concrete.
How much gravel does the builder need?

8 The angles of a triangle are in the ratio 2 : 3 : 4.
Calculate the size of each angle.

9 The sides of a triangle are in the ratio 4 : 6 : 9.
The perimeter of the triangle is 38 cm.
Calculate the length of each side of the triangle.

10 A number of marbles are shared in the ratio 3 : 5.
5 marbles from the larger share are added to the smaller share.
The marbles are now in the ratio 7 : 9.
How many marbles are there altogether?

Types of fractions

Numbers like $2\frac{1}{2}$, $1\frac{1}{4}$ and $1\frac{2}{3}$ are called **mixed numbers** because they are a mixture of whole numbers and fractions.
Mixed numbers can be written as **improper** or 'top heavy' fractions. These are fractions where the numerator is larger than the denominator.

EXAMPLES

1 Write $3\frac{4}{7}$ as an improper fraction.

$3\frac{4}{7} = \frac{(3 \times 7) + 4}{7} = \frac{21 + 4}{7} = \frac{25}{7}$

2 Write $\frac{32}{5}$ as a mixed number.

$32 \div 5 = 6$ remainder 2.

$\frac{32}{5} = 6\frac{2}{5}$

Finding fractions of quantities

EXAMPLE

3 Find $\frac{2}{5}$ of £65.

$\frac{2}{5} \times 65 = \frac{130}{5} = 26$

So $\frac{2}{5}$ of £65 = £26.

Do not use a calculator in questions 1 to 4.

1 Change the following improper fractions to mixed numbers:

(a) $\frac{15}{4}$ (b) $\frac{23}{5}$ (c) $\frac{17}{8}$

2 Change the following mixed numbers to improper fractions:

(a) $1\frac{3}{5}$ (b) $5\frac{5}{6}$ (c) $4\frac{5}{9}$

3 Calculate:

(a) $\frac{3}{10}$ of 30   (b) $\frac{2}{3}$ of 39

(c) $\frac{3}{8}$ of 56   (d) $\frac{5}{6} \times 30$

(e) $\frac{4}{5} \times 85$ (f) $\frac{11}{5} \times 25$

(g) $\frac{17}{6} \times 42$ (h) $\frac{23}{7} \times 63$

4 A coat costing £138 is reduced by $\frac{1}{3}$. Find the new price of the coat.

5 A publisher offers a discount of $\frac{3}{20}$ for orders of more than 100 books.
How much would a shop pay for an order of 250 books costing £3.50 each?

6 In a sale of electrical goods all items are reduced by $\frac{3}{8}$.
What is the sale price of a microwave which was originally priced at £212?

7 Andy, Bill and Chris share two chocolate bars. Each chocolate bar has 30 squares.
Andy eats $\frac{2}{3}$ of one chocolate bar.
Bill eats $\frac{5}{12}$ of both chocolate bars.
Chris eats $\frac{2}{5}$ of one chocolate bar.

(a) (i) How many squares has Andy eaten?
    (ii) How many squares has Bill eaten?

(b) What fraction of **both** chocolate bars have Andy, Bill and Chris eaten altogether?
Give your answer as a fraction in its simplest form.

How to add and subtract fractions

Calculate $1\frac{7}{10} + \frac{5}{6}$

Change mixed numbers to improper ('top heavy') fractions. $1\frac{7}{10} = \frac{17}{10}$

The calculation then becomes $\frac{17}{10} + \frac{5}{6}$

Find the **lowest** common multiple of the denominators (bottom numbers).   Lowest common multiple of 10 and 6 is 30.

Change the original fractions to equivalent fractions using the lowest common multiple as the new denominator. $\frac{17}{10} = \frac{51}{30}$ and $\frac{5}{6} = \frac{25}{30}$

Add or subtract the new numerators. Keep the new denominator the same. $\frac{51}{30} + \frac{25}{30} = \frac{51+25}{30} = \frac{76}{30}$

Write the answer in its simplest form. $\frac{76}{30} = 2\frac{16}{30} = 2\frac{8}{15}$

Remember:
You can add or subtract fractions **only** when the denominators are the **same**.
*What happens if you use a common multiple that is **not** the lowest?*

EXAMPLE

Calculate $3\frac{3}{10} - 1\frac{5}{6}$

$3\frac{3}{10} = \frac{33}{10}$

$1\frac{5}{6} = \frac{11}{6}$

The lowest common multiple of 10 and 6 is 30.

$\frac{33}{10} = \frac{99}{30}$ $\frac{11}{6} = \frac{55}{30}$

$3\frac{3}{10} - 1\frac{5}{6} = \frac{99}{30} - \frac{55}{30} = \frac{44}{30}$

$\frac{44}{30} = \frac{22}{15} = \frac{15}{15} + \frac{7}{15} = 1\frac{7}{15}$

Exercise 1.5

Do not use a calculator in this exercise.

1 Calculate:

(a) $\frac{1}{2} + \frac{1}{8}$ (b) $\frac{1}{4} + \frac{1}{5}$

(c) $\frac{3}{8} + \frac{1}{4}$ (d) $\frac{3}{10} + \frac{1}{5}$

(e) $\frac{2}{5} + \frac{3}{7}$ (f) $\frac{3}{4} + \frac{2}{3}$

(g) $\frac{3}{10} + \frac{2}{3}$ (h) $\frac{5}{12} + \frac{7}{18}$

(i) $\frac{2}{3} + \frac{3}{4} + \frac{4}{5}$ (j) $\frac{2}{9} + \frac{2}{3} + \frac{1}{6}$

2 Calculate:

(a) $\frac{3}{4} - \frac{1}{8}$ (b) $\frac{5}{8} - \frac{1}{2}$

(c) $\frac{1}{3} - \frac{1}{4}$ (d) $\frac{13}{15} - \frac{1}{3}$

(e) $\frac{5}{6} - \frac{5}{24}$ (f) $\frac{7}{9} - \frac{2}{5}$

(g) $\frac{7}{8} - \frac{2}{3}$ (h) $\frac{13}{16} - \frac{5}{12}$

3 Calculate:

(a) $2\frac{3}{4} + 1\frac{1}{2}$ (b) $1\frac{1}{2} + 2\frac{1}{3}$

(c) $1\frac{3}{4} + 2\frac{5}{8}$ (d) $2\frac{1}{4} + 3\frac{3}{5}$

(e) $4\frac{3}{5} + 1\frac{5}{6}$ (f) $3\frac{3}{10} + 2\frac{3}{20}$

4 Calculate:

(a) $2\frac{1}{2} - 1\frac{2}{5}$ (b) $1\frac{2}{3} - 1\frac{1}{4}$

(c) $3\frac{3}{8} - 2\frac{3}{4}$ (d) $5\frac{2}{5} - 2\frac{1}{10}$

(e) $4\frac{3}{10} - 2\frac{5}{8}$ (f) $3\frac{3}{16} - 2\frac{5}{24}$

5 Both Billy and Mary have a packet of the same sweets.

Mary eats $\frac{2}{5}$ of her packet.

Billy eats $\frac{3}{4}$ of his packet.

(a) Find the difference between the fraction Mary eats and the fraction Billy eats.

Billy gives his remaining sweets to Mary.

(b) What fraction of a packet does Mary now have?

6 A school has pupils in Years 7 to 13.

$\frac{7}{12}$ of its pupils are in Years 7 to 9.

$\frac{3}{10}$ of its pupils are in Years 10 and 11.

What fraction of the pupils in the school are in Years 12 and 13?

7 Only Andy, Billy and Cathy are candidates in a school election.

Andy got $\frac{7}{20}$ of the votes.

Billy got $\frac{5}{16}$ of the votes.

(a) What fraction of the votes did Cathy get?

(b) Which candidate won the election?

8 In Jimmy's class:

$\frac{3}{10}$ of the pupils have blue eyes.

$\frac{7}{15}$ of the pupils have brown eyes.

What fraction of the pupils do not have blue or brown eyes?

How to multiply fractions

Calculate $2\frac{2}{5} \times 3\frac{1}{4}$

Change mixed numbers to improper ('top heavy') fractions. $2\frac{2}{5} = \frac{12}{5}$ $3\frac{1}{4} = \frac{13}{4}$

The calculation then becomes $\frac{12}{5} \times \frac{13}{4}$

Multiply the numerators.
Multiply the denominators. $\frac{12 \times 13}{5 \times 4} = \frac{156}{20}$

Write the answer in its simplest form. $\frac{156}{20} = 7\frac{4}{5}$

$\frac{156}{20} = \frac{156 \div 4}{20 \div 4} = \frac{39}{5}$

$7 \times 5 + 4 = 39$

Exercise 1.6

Do not use a calculator in this exercise.

1 Calculate:

(a) $\frac{1}{4} \times \frac{1}{3}$ (b) $\frac{1}{5} \times \frac{1}{6}$

(c) $\frac{2}{3} \times \frac{1}{2}$ (d) $\frac{2}{5} \times \frac{1}{7}$

(e) $\frac{3}{10} \times \frac{5}{6}$ (f) $\frac{5}{8} \times \frac{4}{15}$

(g) $\frac{2}{7} \times \frac{14}{15} \times \frac{5}{8}$ (h) $\frac{4}{5} \times \frac{10}{13} \times \frac{39}{56}$

2 Calculate:

(a) $1\frac{1}{2} \times \frac{3}{4}$ (b) $2\frac{1}{4} \times 1\frac{2}{3}$

(c) $2\frac{3}{4} \times 1\frac{2}{5}$ (d) $1\frac{1}{2} \times 3\frac{1}{4}$

(e) $1\frac{3}{5} \times 1\frac{1}{6}$ (f) $3\frac{3}{4} \times 3\frac{3}{5}$

(g) $2\frac{1}{4} \times \frac{7}{9} \times \frac{4}{21}$ (h) $2\frac{1}{3} \times 15 \times \frac{17}{100}$

3 Calculate:

(a) $\frac{4}{5}$ of $3\frac{1}{4}$ (b) $\frac{2}{3}$ of $5\frac{1}{4}$

(c) $\frac{3}{4}$ of $7\frac{1}{5}$ (d) $\frac{3}{8}$ of $3\frac{5}{9}$

(e) $\frac{5}{6}$ of $4\frac{2}{7}$ (f) $\frac{3}{10}$ of $4\frac{4}{9}$

4 Andy eats $\frac{1}{5}$ of a bag of sweets.

He shares the remaining sweets equally among Bob, Cathy and David.

(a) What fraction of the bag of sweets does Bob get?

(b) What is the smallest possible number of sweets in the bag?

How to divide fractions

The method normally used when one fraction is divided by another is to change the division to a multiplication. The fractions can then be multiplied in the usual way.

Calculate $\quad 1\frac{7}{25} \div 3\frac{1}{5}$

Change mixed numbers to improper ('top heavy') fractions.
$$1\frac{7}{25} = \frac{32}{25} \qquad 3\frac{1}{5} = \frac{16}{5}$$

Change the division to a multiplication.
$$\frac{32}{25} \div \frac{16}{5} = \frac{32}{25} \times \frac{5}{16}$$

Multiply the numerators.
Multiply the denominators.
$$\frac{32}{25} \times \frac{5}{16} = \frac{32 \times 5}{25 \times 16} = \frac{160}{400}$$

$$\frac{160}{400} = \frac{160 \div 80}{400 \div 80} = \frac{2}{5}$$

Write the answer in its simplest form.
$$\frac{160}{400} = \frac{2}{5}$$

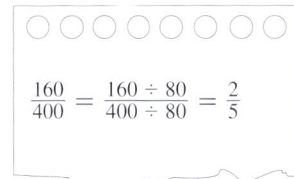

Exercise 1.7

Do not use a calculator in this exercise.

1 Calculate:

(a) $\frac{1}{5} \div \frac{1}{3}$ (b) $\frac{3}{5} \div \frac{1}{4}$

(c) $\frac{2}{5} \div \frac{3}{10}$ (d) $\frac{3}{8} \div \frac{9}{16}$

(e) $\frac{7}{12} \div \frac{7}{18}$ (f) $\frac{4}{9} \div \frac{2}{3}$

(g) $\frac{7}{10} \div \frac{3}{5}$ (h) $\frac{21}{25} \div \frac{7}{15}$

2 Calculate:

(a) $2\frac{3}{4} \div 4\frac{1}{8}$ (b) $1\frac{1}{2} \div 1\frac{1}{11}$

(c) $1\frac{3}{5} \div 1\frac{2}{5}$ (d) $6\frac{3}{10} \div 1\frac{7}{20}$

(e) $3\frac{3}{4} \div \frac{5}{18}$ (f) $1\frac{1}{4} \div 1\frac{9}{16}$

(g) $3\frac{1}{5} \div 2\frac{2}{15}$ (h) $2\frac{1}{4} \div 1\frac{4}{5}$

(i) $4\frac{2}{7} \div 1\frac{7}{8}$ (j) $5\frac{2}{5} \div 1\frac{2}{3}$

3 A shelf is $40\frac{3}{4}$ cm long.

(a) How many CD's of width $1\frac{9}{10}$ cm can be stored on the shelf?

(b) How many videos of width $1\frac{3}{4}$ cm can be stored on the shelf?

In each case how much space is left on the shelf?

4 (a) $3\frac{3}{4}$ is multiplied by a number to give $2\frac{2}{3}$. What is the number?

(b) The product of two numbers is 4. One of the numbers is $1\frac{2}{3}$. What is the other number?

5 A jug contains $1\frac{3}{4}$ litres of milk. Mrs Jones makes a rice pudding with $1\frac{1}{3}$ litres of the milk in the jug. What fraction of the milk in the jug does Mrs Jones use to make the rice pudding?

Fractions on a scientific calculator

Fraction calculations can be done quickly using the fraction button on a scientific calculator.
On most scientific calculators the fraction button looks like this … $\boxed{a^b/_c}$

1 Use a scientific calculator to calculate $4\frac{3}{5} \div 2\frac{1}{4}$

This can be calculated with this calculator sequence.

| 4 | a^b/c | 3 | a^b/c | 5 | $\div$ | 2 | a^b/c | 1 | a^b/c | 4 | = |

This gives the answer $2\frac{2}{45}$.

2 Calculate $\frac{7}{12}$ of 32.

This can be calculated with this calculator sequence.

| 7 | a^b/c | 1 | 2 | $\times$ | 3 | 2 | = |

This gives the answer $18\frac{2}{3}$.

Use a scientific calculator to check your answers to some of the questions in Exercises 1.5 to 1.7.

Problems involving fractions

Exercise 1.8

1 Ben spends $\frac{5}{8}$ of his pocket money.
He has £1.20 left.
How much pocket money did Ben get?

2 A cyclist travels from A to B in two stages.
Stage 1 is 28 km which is $\frac{2}{7}$ of the total journey.
How long is stage 2?

3

Music Sale
$\frac{1}{4}$ off all CD's

Billy pays £9.60 for a CD in the sale.
How much did he save?

4 Sara's hourly wage is increased by $\frac{1}{10}$.
Her new hourly wage is £5.50.
What was her original hourly wage?

5 A young tree is $\frac{3}{8}$ taller in August than it was in May.
In August it is 132 centimetres tall.
How tall was it in May?

6 A factory produced 231 sofas in May, $\frac{2}{9}$ more than the number of sofas it produced in April.
How many sofas did the factory produce in April?

7 Tom spends his wages as follows:
$\frac{3}{20}$ on tax, $\frac{1}{4}$ on rent and $\frac{1}{5}$ on fares.
He has £80 left. How much were his wages?

8 In jug X there is a litre of milk.
In jug Y there is a litre of water.
100 ml of milk is poured from X into Y.
Y is stirred thoroughly.
100 ml of the mixture in Y is then poured into X.
Which jug contains more of its original contents?

9 Is the value of $\frac{a+c}{b+d}$ always between the fractions $\frac{a}{b}$ and $\frac{c}{d}$?

Numerical calculations without a calculator

Order of operations in a calculation

What is $4 + 3 \times 5$?

It is not sensible to have two possible answers.
It has been agreed that calculations are done obeying certain rules:

First	Brackets and Division line
Second	Divide and Multiply
Third	Addition and Subtraction

1 $4 + 3 \times 5$ $= 4 + 15$ $= 19$

2 $10 \div 2 + 3$ $= 5 + 3$ $= 8$

3 $(5 + 6) \times 3 + 4$ $= 11 \times 3 + 4$ $= 33 + 4$ $= 37$

4 $\dfrac{12}{11 - 8} - 3$ $= \dfrac{12}{3} - 3$ $= 4 - 3$ $= 1$

This is the same as $12 \div (11 - 8) - 3$. So the division line is the same as brackets.

Exercise 1.9

1 Work these out without a calculator.

(a) $7 + 6 \times 5$　　　　(b) $7 - (6 - 2)$　　　　(c) $24 \div 6 + 5$

(d) $7 \times 6 + 8 \times 2$　　(e) $10 \div 5 + 8 \div 2$　　(f) $(5 - 2) \times 7 + 9$

(g) $4 \times 12 \div 8 - 6$　　(h) $9 \times 9 - 5 \times 5$　　(i) $(9 + 5) \times (9 - 5)$

(j) $\dfrac{22 - 4}{17 - 8} + 12 \div 3$　(k) $\dfrac{6 \times 3 - 2}{2 \times 2} + 3 \times 8$　(l) $\dfrac{(3 + 7) \times 10 - 19}{(2 + 1) \times (8 - 5)} - 3 \times 3$

2 Choose from the four signs $+$, $-$, $\times$ and $\div$ to make these sums correct.

(a) $5 \quad 6 \quad 7 = 37$　　　(b) $5 \quad 6 \quad 7 = 47$　　　(c) $15 \quad 8 \quad 9 = 87$

(d) $15 \quad 8 \quad 9 = 129$　(e) $15 \quad 8 \quad 9 = 111$　(f) $15 \quad 5 \quad 3 = 6$

(g) $5 \quad 24 \quad 6 = 1$　　(h) $19 \quad 19 \quad 7 \quad 0 = 1$　(i) $4 \quad 4 \quad 7 \quad 2 = 30$

3 Using all the numbers 6, 3, 2 and 1 in this order, brackets and the signs $+$, $-$, $\times$ and $\div$ make all the numbers from 1 to 10.

$6 - 3 \times 2 + 1 = 1$,　　　$6 - 3 - 2 + 1 = 2$,　　　and so on.

Numerical calculations with a calculator

Calculate the value of the following.

1 $\dfrac{326.4}{(5 - 3.3)} - 500$

This is the same as $326.4 \div (5 - 3.3) - 500$.
So the division line is the same as brackets.

To do the calculation enter the following sequence into your calculator.

$\boxed{3}\;\boxed{2}\;\boxed{6}\;\boxed{.}\;\boxed{4}\;\boxed{\div}\;\boxed{(}\;\boxed{5}\;\boxed{-}\;\boxed{3}\;\boxed{.}\;\boxed{3}\;\boxed{)}\;\boxed{-}$

$\boxed{5}\;\boxed{0}\;\boxed{0}\;\boxed{=}$　　　　　(The answer is -308)

2 $\sqrt{\dfrac{0.9 \times 8.1}{50 \times 0.0032}}$

To do the calculation enter the following sequence into your calculator.

$\boxed{\sqrt{\ }}\;\boxed{(}\;\boxed{(}\;\boxed{.}\;\boxed{9}\;\boxed{\times}\;\boxed{8}\;\boxed{.}\;\boxed{1}\;\boxed{)}\;\boxed{\div}\;\boxed{(}\;\boxed{5}\;\boxed{0}$

$\boxed{\times}\;\boxed{.}\;\boxed{0}\;\boxed{0}\;\boxed{3}\;\boxed{2}\;\boxed{)}\;\boxed{)}\;\boxed{=}$　(The answer is 6.75)

Use a calculator in this exercise.

1 Calculate these sums. Write down the full calculator display.

(a) $\dfrac{4.326 \times 0.923}{5.623 \times 9.123}$ (b) $\dfrac{4.326 + 0.923}{5.623 + 9.123}$ (c) $\dfrac{5.19 \times 37.2}{16.7 + 0.78}$

(d) $\dfrac{5.2 \times 2.5 + 6.3}{10.34 - 4.7}$ (e) $\dfrac{7.2^2 - 4.6^2}{5.9 \times 4.9}$ (f) $\sqrt{\dfrac{2.53^3}{1.7^2}}$

(g) $19.3 \div (5.7 - 2.3 \div 0.4)$ (h) $(5 - (5.6 - 4.1) \times 2.3) \div (6.9 + 3.1)$

2 (a) Find the value of $\dfrac{2.76 + 3.2}{1.25}$

(b) Write down the sequence of key presses that you made to work out (a).

3 (a) Work out $\sqrt{\dfrac{5.76 \div 3.6}{6.4}}$

(b) Write down a sequence of calculator keys that could be used to answer (a).

4 Jill used the following key sequences to answer the questions below.

A   5 . 4 2 ÷ 2 . 3 = + 5 . 7 5 =

B   5 . 4 2 + 5 . 7 5 = ÷ 2 . 3 =

C   5 . 4 2 + (5 . 7 5 ÷ 2 . 3) =

D   5 . 4 2 ÷ (2 . 3 + 5 . 7 5) =

(a) $5.42 + \dfrac{5.75}{2.3}$ (b) $\dfrac{5.42 + 5.75}{2.3}$ (c) $\dfrac{5.42}{2.3 + 5.75}$ (d) $\dfrac{5.42}{2.3} + 5.75$

Which key sequences can be used to answer the questions correctly?

5 (a) Write down a sequence of calculator keys that could be pressed to work out:

$$\left(\dfrac{2.6^2 + 2.48}{1.5}\right)^2$$

(b) Work out part (a), writing down the full calculator display of the answer.

6 (a) Use 1, 2, 3 and 4 to make all the numbers from 1 to 20.

e.g. $(2 + 3) \div (\ + 4) \quad = 1$

$2 \times 3 - 1 \times 4 \quad = 2$

and so on.

(b) What is the smallest number that you cannot make?

7 Solve these: (the solutions are whole numbers)

(a) $1^3 + 2^3 + 3^3 + 4^3 + 5^3 = m^2$

(b) $1^3 + 2^3 + 3^3 \ldots + n^3 = 55^2$

(c) The sum of which four consecutive square numbers is 534?

(d) $a^3 + b^3 = 1729$ and $c^3 + d^3 = 1729$ where a, b, c, and d are different positive whole numbers.

(e) $5000 < p^3 < 6000$

- 'Per cent' means 'out of 100'.
  The symbol for per cent is %.

- To change a percentage to a fraction, write the percentage as a fraction with denominator 100.
  Where possible simplify the fraction.
  $$38\% = \tfrac{38}{100} = \tfrac{19}{50}$$

- A fraction can be changed to a percentage using:

  Method 1: Multiply the fraction by 100.
  $$\tfrac{3}{5} = \tfrac{3}{5} \times 100 = \tfrac{300}{5} = 60\%$$

  Method 2: Change the fraction to a decimal, then multiply by 100.
  $$\tfrac{3}{5} = 0.6 \quad 0.6 \times 100 = 60 \quad \tfrac{3}{5} = 60\%$$

- The ratio 3 : 2 is read '3 to 2'.

- A ratio is used to compare quantities.
  A ratio does not give information about the exact values of quantities being compared.

- In its **simplest form**, a ratio contains whole numbers which have no common factor other than 1.
  All quantities in a ratio must have the **same units** before the ratio can be simplified.
  For example, £2.50 : 50p = 250p : 50p = 5 : 1.

- The top number of a fraction is called the **numerator**, the bottom number is called the
  denominator.

- To write **equivalent fractions**, the numerator and denominator of a fraction are multiplied (or
  divided) by the **same** number.
  $$\text{e.g. } \tfrac{3}{8} = \tfrac{3 \times 4}{8 \times 4} = \tfrac{12}{32}$$

- In its **simplest form**, the numerator and denominator of a fraction have no common factor,
  other than 1.

- $2\tfrac{1}{2}$ is an example of a **mixed number**. $\tfrac{5}{2}$ is an **improper** (or '**top heavy**') fraction.

- **Order of operations**. Calculations are done obeying certain rules.
First	Brackets and Division line
Second	Divide and Multiply
Third	Addition and Subtraction

IDEAS FOR INVESTIGATION

Choose any positive whole number   e.g. 20
On a calculator multiply 20 by several positive decimal numbers
e.g. 3.7, 0.24, 23.1, 0.98
$20 \times 3.7 = 74$ (bigger than 20)
$20 \times 0.24 = 4.8$ (smaller than 20)

Find a condition for a number to multiply 20 and make the answer **smaller** than 20.

Is the same condition true for any number other than 20?
*i.e. for a number to multiply 15 and make the answer **smaller** than 15.*

Now divide 20 by several positive decimal numbers e.g. 3.7, 0.24, 23.1, 0.98
$20 \div 3.7 = 5.405405 \ldots$ (smaller than 20)
$20 \div 0.24 = 83.33333 \ldots$ (bigger than 20)

Find a condition for a number to divide into 20 and make the answer **bigger** than 20.

Questions 1 to 9. Do not use a calculator.

1 Write in order of size, lowest first.

0.41 $\quad \frac{83}{200}$ $\quad 41.05\%$ $\quad \frac{2}{5}$ $\quad 0.405$

2 Each of these pairs of fractions are equivalent.
In each case find the value of n.

(a) $\frac{5}{8}, \frac{15}{n}$ (b) $\frac{n}{20}, \frac{5}{n}$ (c) $\frac{n}{20}, \frac{3}{15}$

3 $x = \frac{2}{5}$ $\qquad y = \frac{5}{7}$ $\qquad z = \frac{3}{14}$

Calculate the following giving your answer in its simplest form.

(a) xy (b) $y \div z$ (c) $x + y$
(d) $y - z$ (e) xyz

4 A shirt costing £15.30 is reduced by $\frac{1}{3}$.
Find the new price of the shirt.

5 The price of a coat is reduced by $\frac{2}{5}$ to £48.
What was the original price of the coat?

6 36 girls and 24 boys applied to go on a rock climbing course.
$\frac{2}{3}$ of the girls and $\frac{3}{4}$ of the boys went on the course.
What fraction of the 60 students who applied went on the course?
Write the fraction in its simplest form.

7 The length of a rectangle is $\frac{2}{3}$ m.
The width of the rectangle is $\frac{3}{8}$ m.
(a) What is the perimeter of the rectangle?
(b) What is the area of the rectangle?

8 During a money raising appeal for charity 367 290 metal cans were collected for recycling.
The ratio of steel cans collected to aluminium cans collected was 8 : 1.
How many steel cans were collected?

9 (a) Peter and Jane share £36 in the ratio 5 : 7.
What is Peter's share?
(b) A bag contains 5p coins and 1p coins in the ratio 2 : 3.
What percentage of the coins are 5p coins?

10 Sam and Anna share £94.50 in the ratio 11 : 4.
How much does each of them receive?
SEG 1998

11 Box A contains black counters and white counters in the ratio 3 : 5.
(a) What percentage of the counters are black?

Box B contains black counters and white counters in the ratio 7 : 5.
Box A and Box B each contain the same number of counters.
(b) What is the smallest possible number of counters in each box?
SEG 2000 S

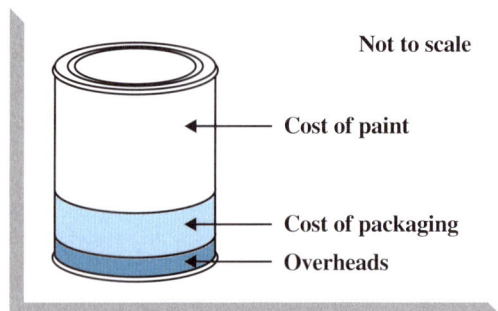

12 Selling price of a tin of paint = Cost of paint + Cost of packaging + Overheads.

Not to scale

Cost of paint

Cost of packaging

Overheads

When buying a tin of BRIGHTLY PAINT
$\frac{2}{3}$ of the price is the actual cost of the paint
and $\frac{1}{4}$ of the cost is packaging.
The rest is the amount needed for Fermats overheads.
(a) Calculate the amount needed for overheads on a $2\frac{1}{2}$ litre tin of paint which sells at £5.40.

Storage and transportation costs account for $\frac{2}{5}$ of Fermats overheads on any product.
(b) What fraction of the cost of a tin of paint goes towards transportation and storage?
SEG 1995

13 The price of an airline ticket to New York is £199 plus £14 for tax and £6 for airport security checks.

Douglas buys two tickets and calculates the cost as £418 by pressing the following keys on his scientific calculator.

| 1 | 4 | + | 6 | + | 1 | 9 | 9 | × | 2 | = |

Is Douglas correct? Give a reason for your answer.

SEG 1995

14 Gary is using a calculator to work out $\dfrac{241}{55.8 + 0.35}$. State the answer.

SEG 1997

15 Eric wanted to calculate $\left(\dfrac{4.8 + 1.27}{1.2}\right)^2$.

He pressed these keys to get his answer.

| (| 4 | . | 8 | + | 1 | . | 2 | 7 | ÷ | 1 | . | 2 |) | x^2 | = |

He got the answer 34.320069. This answer is wrong.
(a) Explain clearly what is wrong with Eric's method.
(b) Calculate the correct answer.

SEG 1997

16 Some students are using calculators to work out four questions.

Question 1. $\dfrac{2.34 + 1.76}{3.22 + 1.85}$

Question 3. $2.34 + \dfrac{1.76}{3.22} + 1.85$

Question 2. $\dfrac{2.34 + 1.76}{3.22} + 1.85$

Question 4. $2.34 + \dfrac{1.76}{3.22 + 1.85}$

(a) Tom presses keys as follows.

| 2 | . | 3 | 4 | + | 1 | . | 7 | 6 | ÷ | 3 | . | 2 | 2 |

| + | 1 | . | 8 | 5 | = |

For which of the four questions is this the correct method?

(b) Jayne presses keys as follows.

| 2 | . | 3 | 4 | + | 1 | . | 7 | 6 | = | ÷ | 3 | . | 2 | 2 |

| + | 1 | . | 8 | 5 | = |

For which of the four questions is this the correct method?

SEG 1995

17 The table below shows the daily cost of hiring three different cars from WEHIRE plc.
The total car hire charge includes a daily rate charge and a mileage charge for each mile over the daily free mileage allowance.

Model	Daily rate	Free miles per day	Mileage charge
Vauxhall Nova	£21	30	8.0p per mile
Ford Mondeo	£42	140	18.2p per mile
Ford Granada	£60	180	30.6p per mile

(a) Andrew hires a Nova for one day and drives 50 miles. He calculates the cost by pressing the following keys on his calculator.

| 5 | 0 | − | 3 | 0 | × | 0 | . | 0 | 8 | + | 2 | 1 | = |

Explain where and how Andrew has gone wrong.

(b) Stephanie lives in Leeds. She hires a Granada and drives to Bristol on Friday for a party. The journey is 220 miles each way. She drives back to Leeds on Sunday.
(i) What is the **total** hire charge?
(ii) How much would she save by driving back to Leeds on Saturday?

SEG 1994

CHAPTER 2

Percentages and Money

Finding a percentage of a quantity

Finding a percentage of a quantity is similar to finding a fraction of a quantity.
It can be done either by changing the percentage to a fraction or to a decimal.

EXAMPLES

1 Find 20% of £56.

Write 20% as a fraction.
20% of £56 is the same as $\frac{20}{100}$ of £56.
$56 \div 100 \times 20 = 0.56 \times 20 = 11.2$
20% of £56 is £11.20.

> To find $\frac{20}{100}$ of a quantity:
> find $\frac{1}{100}$ by dividing by 100,
> then multiply by 20 to find $\frac{20}{100}$.

Alternative method
Write 20% as a decimal.
20% of £56 is the same as 0.2 × £56.
$0.2 \times 56 = 11.2$
20% of £56 is £11.20.

> To multiply by 0.2:
> multiply by 2, then divide by 10.

2 A shirt normally priced at £24 is
reduced by 15% in a sale.
How much does this cost in the sale?

Reduction in price = 15% of £24
$\qquad\qquad\qquad = \frac{15}{100}$ of £24
$24 \div 100 \times 15 = 0.24 \times 15 = 3.6$
15% of £24 = £3.60
The shirt costs £24 − £3.60 = £20.40.

Alternative method
$15\% = \frac{15}{100} = 15 \div 100 = 0.15$
$1 - 0.15 = 0.85$
$0.85 \times 24 = 20.4$
The shirt costs £20.40.
Explain why this method works.

3 There are 440 g in a normal packet of Rice
Crunchies. A special offer packet contains
30% more than the normal packet.
How many grams of Rice Crunchies are
there in the special offer packet?

Extra contents = 30% of 440 g
$\qquad\qquad\qquad = \frac{30}{100}$ of 440
$\qquad\qquad\qquad = 132$ g
$440 + 132 = 572$
There are 572 g in a special offer packet.

Alternative method
$30\% = \frac{30}{100} = 30 \div 100 = 0.3$
$1 + 0.3 = 1.3$
$1.3 \times 440 = 572$
There are 572 g in a special offer packet.
Explain why this method works.

Exercise 2.1

Do not use a calculator in this exercise.

1 Find
  (a) 20% of £80   (b) 75% of £20
  (c) 30% of £220   (d) 15% of £350
  (e) 5% of £500   (f) 9% of 300 kg
  (g) 45% of £25   (h) 60% of 20 m

2 Increase:
  (a) £50 by 60%   (b) £10 by 30%
  (c) £15 by 10%   (d) £50 by 15%

3 Decrease:
  (a) £600 by 15%   (b) £55 by 90%
  (c) £42 by 20%   (d) £63 by 35%

4 There are 450 seats in a theatre.
60% of the seats are in the stalls.
How many seats are in the stalls?

5 Jenny gets a 15% discount on a theatre ticket.
The normal cost is £13.
How much does she save?

6 A mobile telephone company offers a 20% discount on calls made in March.
The normal cost of a peak time call is 50 pence per minute.
How much does a peak time call cost in March?

7 A dozen biscuits weigh 720 g.
The amount of flour in a biscuit is 40% of the weight of a biscuit.
What is the weight of flour in **each** biscuit?

8 A packet of breakfast cereal contains 660 g.
A special offer packet contains an extra 15%.
How many grams of breakfast cereal are in the special offer packet?

9 Abdul earns £200 per week.
He gets a wage rise of 7.5%.
What is his new weekly wage?

10 In a school of 1200 pupils 45% are boys.
(a) How many are girls?

30% of the girls are under 13.
(b) How many girls are under 13?

11 35% of a magazine is pictures.
In the magazine there are 60 pages.
Each page is 25 cm long and 16 cm wide.
What is the area of pictures in the magazine?

Expressing one quantity as a percentage of another

This involves writing a fraction and then changing it to a percentage.
The units of any quantities in the numerator and denominator of the fraction must be the same.

EXAMPLES

1 Express 30 p as a percentage of £2.

$$\frac{30\,p}{£2} = \frac{30\,p}{200\,p} = \frac{30}{200}$$

$$\frac{30}{200} = \frac{30 \div 2}{200 \div 2} = \frac{15}{100} = 15\%$$

This means that 30 p is 15% of £2.

2 A newspaper contains 48 pages, 6 of which are Sports pages.
What percentage of the pages are Sports pages?

6 out of 48 pages are Sports pages.

$$\frac{6}{48} = 6 \div 48 = 0.125$$
$$0.125 \times 100 = 12.5$$
12.5% of the pages are Sports pages.

Exercise 2.2

Do not use a calculator in questions 1 to 5.

1 What is
(a) 64 pence as a percentage of £2,
(b) 15 km as a percentage of 120 km,
(c) 30 cm as percentage of 600 mm,
(d) £3600 as a percentage of £4000,
(e) 18 pence as a percentage of £0.60?

2 A school has 800 pupils of which 160 are in Year 11.
What percentage of pupils are in Year 11?

3 James saved £30 and then spent £9.
What percentage of his savings did he spend?

4 240 people took part in a survey.
30 of them were younger than 18.
What percentage were younger than 18?

5 A bar of chocolate has 32 squares.
Jane eats 12 of the squares.
What percentage of the bar does she eat?

6 What is
- (a) £2 as a percentage of £6,
- (b) 80 km as a percentage of 120 km,
- (c) 20 cm as a percentage of 180 cm,
- (d) £1530 as a percentage of £3600,
- (e) £105.09 as a percentage of £186?

7 A new car costs £13 500.
The dealer offers a discount of £1282.50.
What is the percentage discount?

8 Billy earns £3.50 per hour.
He gets a wage rise of 28 pence per hour.
What is his percentage wage rise?

9 There are 600 pupils in Years 9 to 13 of a high school.
360 of the pupils are in Years 10 and 11.
15% of the pupils are in Years 12 and 13.
What percentage of the pupils are in Year 9?

More complicated percentage problems

Problems involving percentages can involve more complicated calculations.

Exercise 2.3

Use a calculator in this exercise.
Where appropriate give your answers to 3 significant figures.

1 Prices in a sale are reduced by 18%.
The normal price of a shirt is £22.50.
Calculate its sale price.

2
- (a) The price of a gold watch is £278.
  What does it cost with a 12% discount?
- (b) The price of a used car is £5200.
  What does it cost with a 9.5% discount?
- (c) The price of a new kitchen is £3650.
  What does it cost with a 35% discount?

3 A 5 litre can of paint covers an area of 28 m².
James buys 3 cans of paint to cover 70 m².
What percentage of the paint does he use?

4 A rectangle has length 12 cm and width 8.5 cm.
The length is increased by 8.5% and the width decreased by 13.5%.
- (a) Calculate the change in the area of the rectangle.
- (b) Find the change in area as a percentage of the original area of the rectangle.

5 Jane's salary of £14 050 is increased by 3.5%.
- (a) Calculate her new salary.

Jane pays tax at the rate of 23%.
- (b) How much extra tax does she pay as a result of her increase in salary?

6 A car was valued at £13 500 when new.
After one year it lost 22% of its value.
At the end of two years it was sold for £8200.
- (a) What was the value of the car after one year?
- (b) What percentage of its original value did the car lose in its second year?

7 There are 633 pupils in a school.
230 of the pupils walk to school, 212 travel by bus and 150 come by car.
- (a) What percentage walk to school?
- (b) What percentage come by car?

18% of the pupils who normally come by car start to travel on a new bus route.
- (c) What percentage of the pupils now travel by bus?

Hourly pay

Many people are paid by the hour for their work. In most cases they receive a **basic hourly rate** for a fixed number of hours and an **overtime rate** for any extra hours worked.

EXAMPLE

A car-park attendant is paid £3.20 per hour for a basic 40 hour week.
Overtime is paid at time and a half.
One week an attendant works 48 hours.
How much does he earn?

Basic Pay: £3.20 × 40 = £128.00
Overtime: 1.5 × £3.20 × 8 = <u>£38.40</u>
                Total pay = £166.40

Overtime paid at 'time and a half' means 1.5 × normal hourly rate. In this example, the hourly overtime rate is given by:
1.5 × £3.20

Common overtime rates are 'time and a quarter', 'double time', etc.

Commission

As an incentive for their employees to work harder some companies pay a basic wage (fixed amount) plus commission. The amount of commission is usually expressed as a percentage of the value of the sales made by the employee.

EXAMPLE

An estate agent is paid a salary of £11 000 per year plus commission of 0.5% on the sales of all houses.
In 1998 the estate agent sold houses to the value of £2 040 500.
How much did the estate agent earn?

Annual salary: £11 000
Commission: 0.005 × £2 040 500 = <u>£10 202.50</u>
               Total pay = £21 202.50

Remember:
$0.5\% = \frac{0.5}{100} = 0.005$

Exercise 2.4

1   A chef is paid £5.60 per hour for a basic 38 hour week.
Overtime is paid at time and a half.
How much does the chef earn in a week in which she works 50 hours?

2   A mechanic is paid £6.40 per hour for a basic 40 hour week.
Overtime is paid at time and a quarter.
One week the mechanic works 42 hours. How much does he earn?

3   A hairdresser is paid £4.80 per hour for a basic 35 hour week.
One week she works two hours overtime at time and a half and $3\frac{1}{2}$ hours overtime at time and a quarter.
How much is she paid that week?

4 A furniture salesperson is paid an annual salary of £9600 plus commission of 2% on sales.
In 1998 the salesperson sold £300 000 worth of furniture.
How much did the salesperson earn?

5 A car salesperson is paid an annual salary of £10 200 plus commission of 1.5% on sales.
How much does the salesperson earn in a year in which cars to the value of £868 000 are sold?

6 A double glazing salesperson is paid £480 per month plus commission of 5% on sales.
How much does he earn in a month in which he makes sales of £12 600?

7 A salesman earns a bonus which is calculated as a percentage of the value of his weekly sales.
He earns 3% on the first £1500 of his weekly sales and 4.5% on any sales more than £1500.
How much bonus does the salesman earn when his weekly sales are
(a) £1400, (b) £3455?

Income tax

The amount you earn for your work is called your **gross pay**.
Your employer will make deductions from your gross pay for
income tax, National Insurance, etc. Pay after all deductions
have been made is called **net pay**.

The rates of tax and the bands (ranges of income) to which they apply vary.

The amount of **income tax** you pay will depend on how much you earn.
Everyone is allowed to earn some money which is not taxed, this is called
a **tax allowance**. Any remaining money is your **taxable income**.

EXAMPLE

George earns £6800 per year. His tax allowance is £4195 per year
and he pays tax at 20p in the £ on his taxable income.
How much income tax does George pay per year?

An income tax rate of 20% is often expressed as '20p in the pound (£)'.

Taxable income: £6800 − £4195 = £2605
Income tax: £2605 × 0.20 = £521

George pays income tax of £521 per year.

Exercise 2.5

1 Lyn earns £8600 per year. Her tax allowance is £4195 per year and she pays tax at 20p in the
£ on her taxable income.
How much income tax does she pay per year?

2 Sam earns £10 140 per year. His tax allowance is £6095 per year and he pays tax at 20p in
the £ on his taxable income.
How much income tax does he pay per year?

3 Julie earns £685 per month. Her tax allowance is £4195 per year and she pays tax at 20p in
the £ on her taxable income.
How much income tax does she pay per month?

4 Jim is paid £156 per week for 52 weeks a year. His tax allowance is £4195 per year and he pays tax at 20p in the £ on his taxable income.
How much income tax does he pay per week?

5 Kay has an annual salary of £23 700. Her tax allowance is £4195 per year. She pays tax at 20p in the £ on the first £4300 of her taxable income and tax at 23p in the £ on the remainder.
How much income tax does she pay per year?

6 Les has an annual salary of £18 600. His tax allowance is £6095 per year. He pays tax at 20p in the £ on the first £4300 of his taxable income and tax at 23p in the £ on the remainder.
He is paid monthly. How much income tax does he pay per month?

7 Alex has an annual salary of £28 240. Her tax allowance is £6095 per year. She pays tax at 20p in the £ on the first £4300 of her taxable income and tax at 23p in the £ on the remainder.
She is paid monthly. How much income tax does she pay per month?

8 Alf's income is £19 850 per year.
He pays 9% of his gross income into a company pension scheme on which he does not pay tax.
Alf also has a tax allowance of £6420 per year.
He pays tax at 20p in the £ on the first £4300 of his taxable income and tax at 23p in the £ on the remainder.
Calculate how much income tax he pays per year.

Household bills

The cost of living includes many bills for services provided to our homes. Electricity, gas and telephone charges are all examples of **quarterly bills** which are sent out four times a year. Each bill is made up of two parts:
A fixed (standing) charge, for providing the service.
A charge for the quantity of the service used (amount of gas/electricity, duration of telephone calls, etc.)

Other household bills include taxes payable to the local council, water charges and the cost of the insurance of the house (structure) and its contents.

Exercise 2.6

1 Last year the Evans family received four quarterly gas bills.

March	£134.26
June	£52.00
September	£33.49
December	£80.25

(a) What was their total bill for the year?
(b) The family can pay for their gas by 12 equal monthly instalments.
How much would each instalment be?

2 Mrs Cotton uses 1064 units of electricity during one quarter.
Find the cost of her electricity bill if each unit costs 6.16 pence and the quarterly charge is £9.30.

3 Mr Jones receives an electricity bill for £59.20.
The bill includes a quarterly charge of £9.30 and the cost per unit is 6.16 pence.
Calculate to the nearest whole number, the number of units he has used.

4 Mrs Madan receives a gas bill for £179.53. The bill includes a standing charge and the cost of the gas used. During the quarter the gas used is equivalent to 13 377 kWh at 1.295 pence per kWh.
How much is the standing charge?
Give your answer to an appropriate degree of accuracy.

5 Mr Peters has an annual community charge of £1123.05.
He pays the community charge in 10 instalments.
The first instalment is £115.05 and the remaining amount is payable in 9 instalments of equal value.
How much is the second instalment?

6 Mrs Dear checks her water bill.
She has used 46 cubic metres of water at 77.76 pence per cubic metre and there is a standing charge of £11.
How much is her bill?

7 The table on the right shows the premiums charged by an insurance company to insure a house and its contents.

(a) Mrs Adams has a flat valued at £38 000. What premium would she pay to insure the flat?

(b) Jim has bought a house valued at £54 000. How much would he pay to insure the house?

(c) The cost for Mr Brown to insure his house is £124. What is the value of his house?

Buildings and Contents Insurance		
	Buildings	Contents
Annual premium for each £1000 insured.	£1.50	£5.00
	Minimum £20 per year	

(d) Mrs Crow insures the contents of her house for £18 500. What is the annual premium?

(e) Mr Rowe insures his house valued at £74 000 and its contents valued at £22 300. What is the total cost of the insurance premium?

(f) Andy insures his flat valued at £12 000 and its contents valued at £9500. Calculate the total cost of the insurance premium.

VAT

Some goods and services are subject to a tax called **value added tax**, or **VAT**, which is calculated as a percentage of the price or bill.
Total amount payable =
  cost of item or service + VAT

For most purchases the rate of VAT is 17.5%.
For gas and electricity the rate of VAT is 5%.
Some goods are exempt from VAT.

EXAMPLE

A bill at a restaurant is £24 + VAT at 17.5%.
What is the total bill?

VAT: £24 × 0.175 = £4.20

Total bill: £24 + £4.20 = £28.20

The total bill is £28.20.

Remember:
$17.5\% = \frac{17.5}{100} = 0.175$

1 A washing machine costs £340 plus VAT at 17.5%.
   (a) Calculate the amount of VAT charged.
   (b) What is the total cost of the washing machine?

2 A car service costs £90 plus VAT at 17.5%.
   (a) Calculate the amount of VAT charged.
   (b) What is the total cost of the service?

3 Jim buys a ladder for £145 plus VAT at 17.5%.
What is the total cost of the ladder?

4 A mountain bike costs £248 plus VAT at 17.5%.
What is the total cost of the bike?

5 Mrs Swan receives a gas bill for £179.53.
VAT at 5% is added to the bill.
   (a) How much VAT does she have to pay?
   (b) What is the total bill?

6 Joyce buys a greenhouse for £184 plus VAT. VAT is charged at 17.5%.
What is the total cost of the greenhouse?

7 James receives a telephone bill for £37.56 plus VAT at 17.5%.
How much is the total bill?

8 George buys vertical blinds for his windows.
He needs three blinds at £65 each and two blinds at £85 each.
VAT at 17.5% is added to the cost of the blinds.
How much do the blinds cost altogether?

9 Sarah hired a car when she was on holiday.

> **CAR HIRE CHARGES**
>
> £25 per day
> plus 10p for every mile driven.

She hired the car for two days and drove 90 miles.
VAT at 17.5% was added to the car charges.
How much did it cost to hire the car altogether?

Savings

Money invested in a savings account or a bank or building society earns **interest**, which is usually paid once a year.

With **Simple Interest**, the interest is paid out each year and not added to your account.
The amount of Simple Interest an investment earns can be calculated using:

Simple Interest = $\dfrac{\text{Amount}}{\text{invested}} \times \dfrac{\text{Time in}}{\text{years}} \times \dfrac{\text{Rate of interest}}{\text{per year}}$

Banks and building societies advertise the **yearly rates** of interest payable.
For example, 6% per year.

Interest, usually calculated annually, can also be calculated for shorter periods of time.

Compound interest

With **Compound Interest**, the interest earned each year is added to your account and also earns interest the following year.

For example, an investment of 5% per annum means that the amount invested earns £5 for every £100 invested for one year.

So, after the first year of the investment, every £100 invested becomes £100 + 5% of £100.
£100 + 5% of £100 = £100 + £5 = £105
So, after the second year of the investment, every £100 of the original investment becomes £105 + 5% of £105.
£105 + 5% of £105 = £105 + £5.25 = £110.25

This can also be calculated as: $100 \times (1.05)^2 = £110.25$
Explain why this works.

1 Find the Simple Interest paid on £600 invested for 6 months at 8% per year.

Simple Interest $= 600 \times \frac{6}{12} \times \frac{8}{100}$
$$= 600 \times 0.5 \times 0.08$$
$$= £24$$

The Simple Interest paid is £24.

Note:
Interest rates are given 'per year'. The length of time for which an investment is made is also given in years.

6 months $= \frac{6}{12}$ years.

Explain why.

2 Find the Compound Interest paid on £600 invested for 3 years at 6% per year.

1st year	Investment	$= £600$
	Interest: £600 × 0.06	$= £\ 36$
	Value of investment after one year	$= £636$
2nd year	Investment	$= £636$
	Interest: £636 × 0.06	$= £\ 38.16$
	Value of investment after two years	$= £674.16$
3rd year	Investment	$= £674.16$
	Interest: £674.16 × 0.06	$= £\ 40.45$
	Value of investment after three years	$= £714.61$

Remember:

$6\% = \frac{6}{100} = 0.06$

Compound Interest = Final value − Original value
$$= £714.61 - £600$$
$$= £114.61$$

This could also be calculated as follows:
$600 \times (1.06)^3 - 600 = £114.61$

Compound **decrease** can also be calculated.

3 A car is valued at £15 000 when new.
Its value decreases at the rate of 9% each year.
Find its value after 3 years.

Method 1
9% of 15 000 $= 15\ 000 \div 100 \times 9$
$$= 1350$$
$15\ 000 - 1350 = 13\ 650$
Value after 1 year $= £13\ 650$

9% of 13 650 $= 13\ 650 \div 100 \times 9$
$$= 1228.50$$
$13\ 650 - 1228.50 = 12\ 421.50$
Value after 2 years $= £12\ 421.50$

9% of 12 421.50 $= 12\ 421.50 \div 100 \times 9$
$$= 1117.935$$
$12\ 421.50 - 1117.935 = 11\ 303.565$
Value after 3 years $= £11\ 303.57$

Method 2
Value after 1 year
£15 000 − 9% of £15 000
$15\ 000 \times 0.91 = £13\ 650$

Value after 2 years
£13 650 − 9% of £13 650
$13\ 650 \times 0.91 = £12\ 421.50$

Value after 3 years
£12 421.50 − 9% of £12 421.50
$12\ 421.50 \times 0.91 = £11\ 303.57$

Method 3
After 3 years the car has the value:
£15000 × 0.91³ = £11303.57
Explain why this method works.

Do questions 1 to 5 without a calculator.
Where appropriate give your answers to
3 significant figures.

1 Tim invests £400 in a building
society.
He earns 5% interest per year.
How much interest does he get in
one year?

2 Find the simple interest paid on an
investment of £8000 at 7% per year
after
(a) 6 months,   (b) 1 year.

3 Jenny invests £200 at 10% per
annum compound interest.
What is the value of her investment
after 2 years?

4 Jenny invests £300 at 5% per
annum compound interest.
What is the value of her investment
after 2 years?

5 Which of the following investments
earns most interest?
(a) £200 for 3 years at 5%
compound.
(b) £300 for 2 years at 5%
compound.

6 Find the simple interest on:
(a) £1000 invested for 1 year at
7% per year,
(b) £800 invested for 9 months at
8% per year,
(c) £6000 invested for 6 months at
7.5% per year,
(d) £10 000 invested for 3 months
at 9% per year.

7 Find the compound interest on:
(a) £400 invested for 3 years at
5% per year,
(b) £3000 invested for 3 years at
7% per year.

8 A young oak tree gains 30% more
height each year.
It is 5 m tall.
How tall will it be in 3 years time?

9 A bouncy ball is dropped from the
top of a skyscraper 256 m high.
After each bounce it reaches a height
25% less than its previous height.
What is the height of the ball after
4 bounces?

10 A man buys a new car for £13 000.
The car loses value at the rate of
14% per annum.
(a) (i)   What is its value after
3 years?
(ii) Express its value after
3 years as a percentage of
its original value.
(b) Repeat (a) for a new car
originally valued at £20 000.
(c) What do you notice about your
answers to (a) and (b)?

11 Interest on a loan of £2000 is
charged at the rate of 21% per
annum. Interest is calculated on the
outstanding loan at the **start** of each
year.
(a) How much is owed immediately
the loan is taken out?
Repayments are £600 per year.
(b) How much is owed at the **start**
of the third year of the loan?

12 How long does it take £100 to double
in value at 9% per annum?

13 (a) A water lily doubles its leaf area
every day. It covers a pond after
50 days. How long does its take
to cover half of the pond?
(b) A frog jumps from the centre of
this pond to the edge. Each
jump he halves the distance
between himself and the edge of
the pond. How long does he
take to reach the edge?

Sadik and Chandni took Maths tests in October and June.

My mark went up from 54% to 72%.

My mark went up from 42% to 60%.

Who has made the most improvement?

They have both improved by a score of 18% so by one measure they have both improved equally.

Another way of comparing their improvement is to use the idea of a percentage increase.

$$\text{Percentage increase} = \frac{\text{actual increase}}{\text{initial value}} \times 100\%$$

Comparing percentage increases is the best way to decide whether Sadik or Chandni has made the most improvement. *Explain why.*

Remember
To calculate
% increase or % decrease
always use the initial value.

For Sadik
% increase = $\frac{18}{54} \times 100\% = 33.3\%$

For Chandni
% increase = $\frac{18}{42} \times 100\% = 42.9\%$

Both calculations are correct to one decimal place.

A percentage decrease can be calculated in a similar way.

$$\text{Percentage decrease} = \frac{\text{actual decrease}}{\text{initial value}} \times 100\%$$

EXAMPLES

1 A sample of soil is dried in an oven.
Its mass reduces from 65 g to 45 g.
Find the percentage decrease in the mass.

Actual decrease = $65 - 45 = 20$ g
% decrease = $\frac{20}{65} \times 100$
$= 30.8\%$, correct to one decimal place.

2 A shop buys pens for 15 pence and sells them for 21 pence.
What is their percentage profit?

Actual profit = $21 - 15$
$= 6$ pence
% profit = $\frac{6}{15} \times 100 = 40\%$

Exercise 2.9

Do questions 1 to 5 without a calculator.

1 A school buys calculators for £5 and sells them for £6.
Find the percentage profit.

2 Sara's wages of £7.50 per hour are increased to £9.00 per hour.
Find the percentage increase in her earnings.

3 A man buys a car for £3500 and sells it for £2625.
Find his percentage loss.

4 A book goes up in price from £5.99 to £6.99.
What is the percentage increase in the price?

5 In October, Sam scored 50% in an English test. In January he improved to 66%.
In the same tests, Becky scored 40% and 56%.
Who has made the most improvement? Explain your answer.

6 During 1998 the rent on Karen's flat increased from £80 to £90 per week.
(a) Find the percentage increase in her rent.
In the same period Karen's wages increased from £250 per week to £280 per week.
(b) Find the percentage increase in her wages.
Comment on your answers.

7 John's weekly wage rises from £150 to £168.
What is John's percentage wage rise?

8 The value of car A when new was £13 000.
The value of car B when new was £16 500.
After one year the value of car A is £11 200 and the value of car B is £13 500.
Calculate the percentage loss in the values of cars A and B after one year.

9 During 1995 the population of a village decreased from 323 to 260.
Find the percentage decrease in the population.

10 In a school the number of pupils increased as shown in the table:

Year	1995	1996	1997	1998	1999
Number	554	605	643	679	734

In which year is the percentage increase in the number of pupils the greatest?

11 At the start of May a flower was 12.3 cm high.
In May it grew by 14.5%.
At the start of July it was 16.7 cm high.
What was its percentage growth during June?

Reverse percentage problems

EXAMPLES

1 A 15% discount on a TV set is worth £82.50.
How much does the TV normally cost?

Method 1
15% of normal cost = £82.50
1% of normal cost = £82.50 ÷ 15
$\qquad$ = £5.50
So normal cost = £5.50 × 100
$\qquad$ = £550

Method 2
15% of normal cost = £82.50
0.15 × normal cost = 82.50
So normal cost = 82.50 ÷ 0.15
$\qquad$ = £550

2 A shop sells videos with a 20% discount.
Petra buys a video and pays £10.
How much does the video normally cost?

Method 1
Discount price is normal price less 20%.
So 80% of normal price = £10.
So 1% of normal price = £10 ÷ 80
$\qquad$ = £0.125
So normal price = £0.125 × 100
$\qquad$ = £12.50

Method 2
Discount price is 80% of normal price.
So £10 = 0.8 × normal price.
So normal price = £10 ÷ 0.8
$\qquad$ = £12.50

3 Tara gets a 5% wage rise.
Her new wage is £126 per week.
What was Tara's wage before her wage rise?

Method 1
New wage = old wage + 5%
So 105% of old wage = £126
1% of old wage is 126 ÷ 105 = £1.20
Old wage = 1.2 × 100 = £120

Method 2
105% of old wage is £126.
126 ÷ 1.05 = 120
Old wage = £120

4 A computer costs £1233.75 including VAT at 17.5%.
How much of the cost is VAT?

Method 1
Cost = cost without VAT + 17.5% VAT.
£1233.75 = 117.5% of cost without VAT.
1% of cost without VAT is given by
£1233.75 ÷ 117.5 = £10.50
VAT = 17.5% of cost without VAT.
So VAT = £10.50 × 17.5 = £183.75

Method 2
117.5% of cost without VAT is £1233.75
1233.75 ÷ 1.175 = 1050
1233.75 − 1050 **or** 1050 × 0.175
So VAT = £183.75

Do questions 1 to 4 without a calculator.

1 A special bottle of pop contains 10% more than a normal bottle.
The special bottle contains 660 ml.
How much does the normal bottle contain?

2 Tim saves 15% of his monthly salary.
Each month he saves £90.
What is his monthly salary?

3 Mary gets a 20% wage rise.
Her new wage is £264 per week.
What was Mary's wage before her wage rise?

4 Mary and Sam take a History and a Geography test.
(a)   Sam scored 60 marks in History.
Sam's score was 20% better than his score in Geography.
What was Sam's score in Geography?
(b)   Mary scored 72 marks in History.
Mary's score was 20% worse than her score in Geography.
What was Mary's score in Geography?

5 30 grams of a breakfast cereal provides 16.2 mg of vitamin C.
This is 24% of the recommended daily intake.
What daily intake of vitamin C is recommended?

6 VAT at 17.5% on a washing machine is £43.75.
What is the price of the washing machine including VAT?

7 Tom gets a 3% increase in his salary.
His new salary is £1462.60 per month.
What was Tom's salary before his wage rise?

8 Here is some data about the changes in the number of pupils in schools A and B.
School A's numbers increased by 4% to 442.
School B's numbers decreased by 6% to 423.
How many pupils were in schools A and B before the change in numbers?

9 A one year old scooter is worth £1344.
This is a decrease of 16% of its value from new.
What was the price of the new scooter?

10 These wage increases were announced by a company.
The managing director will receive 6% more and will now be earning £47 700.
The foreman will receive 4% more and will now be earning £31 200.
The skilled workers will receive 3.5% more and will now be earning £20 700.
The unskilled workers will receive 3% more and will now be earning £12 875.

(a)   Calculate the old wages for the managing director, the foreman, a skilled worker and an unskilled worker.
(b)   The company has 1 managing director, 1 foreman, 5 skilled workers and 9 unskilled workers.
Calculate the percentage increase in the total wage bill.

What you need to know

- **Hourly pay** is paid at a **basic rate** for a fixed number of hours.
  Overtime pay is usually paid at a higher rate such as time and a half, which means each hour's work is worth 1.5 times the basic rate.

- Everyone is allowed to earn some money which is not taxed.
  This is called a **tax allowance**.

- Tax is only paid on income earned in excess of the tax allowance.
  This is called **taxable income**.

- **Value added tax**, or **VAT**, is a tax on some goods and services and is added to the bill.

- Gas, electricity and telephone bills are paid **quarterly**. The bill consists of a standing charge plus a charge for the amount used.

- Money invested in a savings account at a bank or building society earns **interest**, which is usually paid once a year.
  With **Simple Interest**, the interest is paid out each year and not added to your account.

  $$\text{Simple Interest} = \frac{\text{Amount}}{\text{invested}} \times \frac{\text{Time in}}{\text{years}} \times \frac{\text{Rate of interest}}{\text{per year}}$$

  With **Compound Interest**, the interest earned each year is added to your account and also earns interest the following year.

- $\text{Percentage increase} = \dfrac{\text{actual increase}}{\text{initial value}} \times 100\%$ $\text{Percentage decrease} = \dfrac{\text{actual decrease}}{\text{initial value}} \times 100\%$

Review Exercise

1 A grandmother decides to share out £6000 among her 5 grandchildren.
Alex receives $\frac{5}{12}$, Brenda 15% and the remainder is shared in the ratio 6 : 4 : 3 between Christine, David and Ellie respectively.
How much does each grandchild receive?

2 In 1984, the total revenue of Portugal was 603 167 million Escudos, of which 8.2% was spent on health.
The population of Portugal was 10.25 million.
Calculate the expenditure per person on health.

SEG 1996

3 In January, Matthew has a new credit card. He uses it only once in that month, to buy a suit costing £125. When he receives his credit card statement at the end of January, Matthew pays £10. As he does not pay the full amount he owes, he is charged interest at the rate of 1.57% on the whole bill.
(a) How much is Matthew charged in interest?
Give your answer to an appropriate degree of accuracy.

Matthew does not use his credit card during the next month.
(b) What is the amount on his statement at the end of February?

SEG 1995

4 Jonathan is paid £4.20 per hour as his basic wage. In one week he works five hours twenty minutes overtime at time and a half and four and a half hours overtime at time and a quarter.
How much does Jonathan earn in overtime that week?

SEG 1994

5 A double-glazing salesman is paid a basic wage of £48 per week. He is also paid 6% commission on all his sales over £1600 in a week.
In a four week period his sales are:

> Week 1   £3040,
> Week 2   £1100,
> Week 3   £4500,
> Week 4   £9800.

Calculate his total pay for the four week period.

SEG 1997

6 Alex has an income of £518 per month. He has a tax allowance of £3525, and pays tax at the rate of 20p in the £ on his taxable income.
Calculate how much tax Alex pays per year.

SEG 1996

7 Dipak's income is £25 546 per year. He does not pay tax on a pension contribution of $17\frac{1}{2}\%$ of his income.
Dipak also has an allowance of £3155 on which he does not pay tax.
He then pays tax at 25% on the rest of his income.
Calculate the amount of tax which Dipak pays.

SEG 1996

8 An electricity bill is made up of three parts:

> (1) A fixed charge of £12.50;
> (2) A charge of 8.35 pence for each unit of electricity;
> (3) Value Added Tax (VAT) at $17\frac{1}{2}\%$ added on to the total of parts (1) and (2).

(a) Jasmin uses 1037 units of electricity.
Calculate her electricity bill.

(b) Next time Jasmin gets an electricity bill, it shows a cost of £172.49 before VAT is added.
Calculate how many units of electricity she used.

SEG 1997

9 Mrs Barker owns a car. For insurance purposes her car is in Group 8 and she lives in Area 5. The table shows the cost of basic premiums.

Area \ Group	4	5	6	7	8	9	10
1	597	650	702	760	819	912	1005
2	638	685	755	828	898	1001	1105
3	662	728	785	860	924	1034	1145
4	725	791	848	912	976	1088	1201
5	781	844	901	985	1066	1177	1288
6	873	942	1014	1070	1119	1241	1365

Mrs Barker receives a 30% no-claims discount and then a further 9% discount for agreeing to pay the first £250 of damage.
Calculate her net premium.

SEG 1996

10 Mr England insures his house for £68 000 and its contents for £17 000. The annual premiums for the insurance are

Buildings: 16p for every £100 of cover,
Contents: 98p for every £100 of cover.

What is the **total** annual cost for Mr England to insure his house and contents?

SEG 1994

11 An electrician makes the following labour charges when doing repairs:

£18 for the first 10 minutes then at a rate of £1.60 per 5 minutes.

He charges £67.60 for repairs.
How long does he spend on the repairs

SEG 1996

12 Leroy changes £475.60 into Guilders for a holiday in Holland.
The exchange rate is £1 = 2.68 Guilders.
There is a £5 charge for changing the money.

(a) How many Guilders should he receive?

(b) When he returns from Holland he has 84 Guilders left.
He changes these back into British money, and again £5 is deducted as a charge.
How much does Leroy receive?

SEG 1995

13 Claire needs to replace the glass in a broken window.
The area of the window is exactly 5.23 sq ft.
The shop sells the glass at £2.74 per sq ft, plus VAT at $17\frac{1}{2}$% and charges for the exact area which she needs.
How much does Claire pay for the glass?
Give your answer to an appropriate degree of accuracy.

SEG 1995

14 Kelly invests £5500 at an annual interest rate of 8%. After five months she withdraws all her money. How much does she receive?

SEG 1994

15 Sharon and Tim put £800 into a high interest account which pays compound interest at the rate of 1.1% per month.
After it has gained three months interest, they withdraw all their money.
How much do they receive?

SEG 1996

16 A car was bought for £7600.
It depreciated in value by 25% each year.
What was the value of the car after 3 years?

17 Charles buys an antique clock for £70 and sells it for £110, both costs being given to the nearest ten pounds.
Calculate the minimum percentage profit which Charles could have made.

SEG 1997

18 The population of a town increased by 20% between 1981 and 1991.
The population in 1991 was 43 200.
What was the population in 1981?

SEG 1994

19 In a sale all prices are reduced by 16%.
Alan is charged £21 for a shaver.
What is the reduction in its price?

SEG 1994

20 In a sale everything is reduced by 20% of the marked price.
Baljinder pays the sale price of £36 for a personal stereo.
How much does she save?

SALE
20% OFF
NOW ONLY £36

SEG 1995

21 A shop assistant earns £12 420 after a 3.5% pay rise.
What was her salary before the pay rise?

22 A gas bill of £33.60 includes VAT at 5%.
How much VAT is paid?

Approximation and Estimation

Approximation

In real-life it is not always necessary to use exact numbers. A number can be **rounded** to an **approximate** number. Numbers are rounded according to how accurately we wish to give details. For example, the distance to the Sun can be given as 93 million miles.

Can you think of other situations where approximations might be used?

Rounding to the nearest 10, 100, 1000

If there were 21 152 people at a football match a newspaper report could say, "21 000 at the football match".

Consider the number 7487.
The same number can be rounded to different degrees of accuracy depending on the situation.

Rounding to the nearest 10

7487 is between 7480 and 7490, but it is closer to 7490.
7487 rounded to the nearest 10 is 7490.

Rounding to the nearest 100

7487 is between 7400 and 7500, but it is closer to 7500.
7487 rounded to the nearest 100 is 7500.

Rounding to the nearest 1000

7487 is between 7000 and 8000, but it is closer to 7000.
7487 rounded to the nearest 1000 is 7000.

The number 7487 can be approximated as 7490, 7500 or 7000 depending on the degree of accuracy required.

It is a convention to round a number which is in the middle to the higher number.
75 to the nearest 10 is 80.
450 to the nearest 100 is 500.
8500 to the nearest 1000 is 9000.

EXAMPLES	Rounded to the nearest 10	Rounded to the nearest 100	Rounded to the nearest 1000
7547	7550	7500	8000
973	970	1000	1000
62 783	62 780	62 800	63 000
9125	9130	9100	9000

The number of visitors to the local museum was reported as 2600, to the nearest hundred.
What is the smallest possible number of visitors?
What is the greatest possible number of visitors?

The smallest possible number of visitors is 2550.
The greatest possible number of visitors is 2649.

Exercise 3.1

1 Copy and complete this table.

Number	Round to the nearest 10	Round to the nearest 100	Round to the nearest 1000
7613	7610	7600	8000
977			
61 115			
9714			
623			
9949			
5762			
7501			
7500			
7499			

2 Write down these figures to appropriate degrees of accuracy.
(a) There were 19 141 people at the football match.
(b) There were 259 people on the plane.
(c) Tom had 141 marbles.
(d) The class raised £49.67 for charity.
(e) There are 129 students in Year 7.
(f) The population of the town is 24 055.
(g) The land area of the country is 309 123 km².
(h) The distance to London is 189 km.
(i) Sarah spent £50.99 on CDs.
(j) There were 693 students in the school.

3 Write down a number each time which fits these roundings.
(a) It is 750 to the nearest 10 but 700 to the nearest 100.
(b) It is 750 to the nearest 10 but 800 to the nearest 100.
(c) It is 8500 to the nearest 100 but 8000 to the nearest 1000.
(d) It is 8500 to the nearest 100 but 9000 to the nearest 1000.

4 "43 000 spectators watch thrilling Test Match".
The number reported in the newspaper was correct to the nearest thousand.
What is the smallest possible number of spectators?

5 Carl has 140 postcards in his collection.
The number is given to the nearest ten.
What is the smallest and greatest number of postcards Carl could have in his collection?

6 "You require 2700 tiles to tile your swimming pool."
This figure is correct to the nearest 100.
What is the greatest number of tiles needed?

In a real-life problem a rounding must be used which gives a commonsense answer.

EXAMPLES

1 A Year group in a school are going to Alton Towers. There are 242 students and teachers going.
Each coach can carry 55 passengers.
How many coaches should be ordered?

$242 \div 55 = 4.4$
This should be rounded up to 5.

4 coaches can only carry 220 passengers $(4 \times 55 = 220)$.

2 Filing cabinets are to be placed along a wall.
The available space is 460 cm.
Each cabinet is 80 cm wide.
How many can be fitted in?

$460 \div 80 = 5.75$
This should be rounded down to 5.

Although the answer is nearly 6 the 6th cabinet would not go in.

Exercise 3.2

You may use a calculator.

1 49 students are waiting to go to the Sports Stadium. A minibus can take 15 passengers at a time. How many trips are required?

2 A classroom wall is 7 m long. How many tables 120 cm long could be fitted along the wall?

3 How many desks or tables in your classroom could be fitted along a suitable wall?

4 76 people are waiting to go to the top of Canary Wharf. The lift can only take 8 at a time. How many times must the lift go up?

5 A group of 175 people are going to Margate. Coaches can take 39 passengers. How many coaches should be ordered?

6 There are 210 students in a year group. They each need an exercise book. The exercise books are sold in packs of 25. How many packs should be ordered?

7 Car parking spaces should be 2.5 m wide. How many can be fitted into a car park which is 61 m wide?

8 A sweet manufacturer puts 17 sweets in a bag. How many bags can be made up if there are 500 sweets?

9 How many 26p stamps can be bought for £5?

10 How many grapefruits, each costing 29p can be bought for £1.50?

Rounding using decimal places

What is the cost of 1.75 metres of material costing £1.99 a metre?
    $1.75 \times 1.99 = 3.4825$
The cost of the material is £3.4825 or 348.25p.
This is a silly answer. After all you can only pay in pence.
A sensible answer is £3.48 correct to two decimal places (nearest penny).
This means that there are only two decimal places after the decimal point.

Often it is not necessary to use an exact answer.
Sometimes it is impossible, or impractical, to use the exact answer.

To round a number to a given number of decimal places

When rounding a number to 1, 2, 3 or more decimal places:
- (i) Write the number using one more decimal place than asked for.
- (ii) Look at the last decimal place and
  - if the figure is 5 or more round up,
  - if the figure is less than 5 round down.
- (iii) When answering a problem remember to include any units and state the degree of approximation used.

EXAMPLES

1 Write 2.76435 to 2 decimal places.
Write the number using one more decimal place. 2.76**4**
Look at the last decimal place. **4**
This is less than 5, so round down.
Answer 2.76

2 Write 2.76285 to 3 decimal places.
Write the number using 4 decimal places.
2.762**8**
The last decimal place is 5 or more, so round up.
Answer 2.763

3 Write 7.104 to 2 decimal places.
7.104 = 7.10 to 2 d.p.
The zero is written down because it shows the accuracy used, 2 decimal places.

4 5.98 = 6.0 to 1 d.p.
Notice that the next tenth after 5.9 is 6.0.

Notation
Often decimal place is shortened to d.p.

Exercise 3.3

1 Copy and complete this table.

Number	d.p.	Answer
2.367	1	2.4
0.964	2	
0.965	2	
3.9617	3	
3.9617	2	
3.9617	1	
0.056	2	
567.654	2	
567.654	1	
4.991	2	
4.996	2	

2 Carry out these calculations giving the answers correct to
(a) 1 d.p. (b) 2 d.p. (c) 3 d.p.

6.12 × 7.54   89.1 × 0.67
90.53 × 6.29   98.6 ÷ 5.78
67.2 ÷ 101.45

3 In each of these short problems decide upon the most suitable accuracy for the answer.
Then work out the answer. Give a reason for your degree of accuracy.

(a) 1.74 metres of cloth at £6.99 a metre.
(b) 1.74 metres of cloth at £2.05 a metre.
(c) 0.454 kg of cheese at £5.21 a kg.
(d) 7 equal sticks measure 250 cm in total when lying end to end. How long is each stick?
(e) A packet of 6 blank videotapes costs £7.99. How much does one cost?

Consider the calculation 600.02 × 7500.97 = 4500732.0194
To 1 d.p. it is 4500732.0, to 2 d.p. it is 4500732.02.
The answers to either 1 or 2 d.p. are very close to the actual answer and are almost as long.
There is little advantage in using either of these two roundings.
The point of a rounding is that it is a more convenient number to use.

Here is another calculation 12.34 ÷ 74830 = 0.000164907 . . .
To 1 d.p. it is 0.0, to 2 d.p. it is 0.00, to 3 d.p. it is 0.000
None of these answers is helpful.

Another kind of rounding uses **significant figures**.
The **most** significant figure in a number is the non-zero figure which has the greatest place value.
Noughts which are used to locate the decimal point and preserve the place value of other figures are not significant. For example, in the number 0.00328 the most significant figure is the 3 which represents 3 thousandths.

To round a number to a given number of significant figures

When rounding a number to 1, 2, 3 or more significant figures:

(i)   Start from the most significant figure and count the required number of figures.

(ii)   Look at the next figure to the right of this and

- if the figure is 5 or more round up,

- if the figure is less than 5 round down.

(iii)   Add noughts, as necessary, to locate the decimal point and preserve the place value.

(iv)   When answering a problem remember to include any units and state the degree of approximation used.

EXAMPLES

1   Write 4 500 732.0194 to 2 significant figures.

The figure after the first 2 significant figures **45** is 0.
This is less than 5, so round down, leaving 45 unchanged.
Add noughts to 45 to locate the decimal point and
preserve place value.
So 4 500 732.0194 = 4 500 000 to 2 sig. fig.

2   Write 0.000364907 to 1 significant figure.

The figure after the first significant figure 3 is 6.
This is 5 or more, so round up, 3 becomes 4.
So 0.000364907 = 0.0004 to 1 sig. fig.

Notice that the noughts before the 4 locate the decimal point and preserve place value.

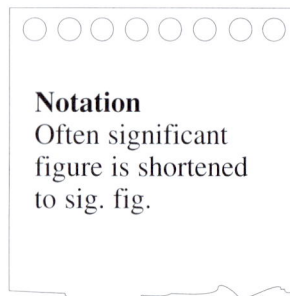

Notation
Often significant
figure is shortened
to sig. fig.

Choosing a suitable degree of accuracy

In some calculations it would be wrong to use the complete answer from the calculator.
The result of a calculation involving measurement should not be given to a greater degree of accuracy than the measurements given in the question.

EXAMPLE

What is the area of a rectangle measuring 4.6 cm by 7.2 cm?

$4.6 \times 7.2 = 33.12$
Since the measurements used in the calculation (4.6 cm and 7.2 cm) are given to 2 sig. fig. the answer should be as well.
33 cm^2 is a more suitable answer.

Exercise 3.4

1 Copy and complete this table.

Number	sig. fig.	Answer
456 000	2	460 000
454 000	2	
7 981 234	3	
7 981 234	2	
1290	2	
0.000567	2	
0.0937481	2	
0.0937481	3	
0.0937481	4	
0.010245	2	
0.02994	2	

2 Carry out these calculations giving the answers correct to
(a) 2 sig. fig.   (b) 3 sig. fig.   (c) 4 sig. fig.

672×123 6.72×12.3
78.2×12.8 $7.19 \div 987.5$
$124 \div 65300$

3 In each of these short problems decide upon the most suitable accuracy for the answer.
Then work out the answer, remembering to state the units.
Give a reason for your degree of accuracy.

(a) The area of a rectangle measuring 7.9 cm by 6.4 cm.
(b) The area of a rectangle measuring 13.2 cm by 11.9 cm.
(c) The area of a football pitch measuring 99 m by 62 m.
(d) The length of 13 tables was measured at 16 m. How long was each table?
(e) The area of a farmer's field measuring 320 m by 480 m.

Estimation

It is always a good idea to find an **estimate** for any calculation.
An estimate is used to check that the answer to the actual calculation is of the right magnitude (size).
If the answer is very different to the estimate then a mistake has possibly been made.

Estimation is done by approximating every number in the calculation to 1 significant figure.
The calculation is then done using the approximated values.

1 Without using a calculator find an estimate for the calculation 31.1×1.9.
Then, using long multiplication, find the actual value of the product. Compare your answers.

31.1×1.9
Approximating: $31.1 = 30$ to 1 sig. fig.
$\qquad\qquad\quad 1.9 = 2$ to 1 sig. fig.
$30 \times 2 = 60$ (estimate)
Now work out 31.1×1.9

$$
\begin{array}{r}
3\,1.1 \\
\times\ \ 1.9 \\
\hline
2\,7\,9\,9 \quad \leftarrow 311 \times 9 \\
+\ \ 3\,1\,1\,0 \quad \leftarrow 311 \times 10 \\
\hline
5\,9.0\,9 \qquad \text{(actual value)} \\
\hline
\end{array}
$$

Is 59.09 reasonably close to 60?   Yes.

> It is easy to make a mistake.
> If you thought the actual answer was 590.9 (because the decimal point was placed wrongly) then comparing 590.9 to 60 should point out the mistake.

2 Estimate $\dfrac{78.5 \times 0.51}{18.7}$

Approximating: $78.5 = 80$ to 1 sig. fig.
$\qquad\qquad\quad 0.51 = 0.5$ to 1 sig. fig.
$\qquad\qquad\quad 18.7 = 20$ to 1 sig. fig.

$\dfrac{80 \times 0.5}{20} = \dfrac{40}{20} = 2$ (estimate)

Using a calculator $\dfrac{78.5 \times 0.51}{18.7} = \dfrac{40.035}{18.7} = 2.140909\ldots$

Is 2.140909 reasonably close to 2?   Yes.

Exercise **3.5**

Questions 1 and 2.
Do not use a calculator. Show any working clearly.

1 By using approximations to 1 significant figure find estimates to these products.
Then carry out the calculations with the original figures.
Compare your estimate to the actual answer.
(a) 4.2×1.8 (b) 8.9×3.1 (c) 48.1×4.2 (d) 103.4×2.9

2 Find estimates to these divisions by using approximations to 1 significant figure.
Then carry out the calculations with the original figures.
Compare your estimate to the actual answer.
(a) $10.78 \div 4.9$ (b) $19.68 \div 4.1$ (c) $30.4 \div 3.2$ (d) $203.49 \div 5.1.$

Questions 3 to 10.
You may use a calculator to answer these questions.

3 Find estimates to these calculations by using approximations to 1 significant figure.
Then carry out the calculations with the original figures.
Compare your estimate to the actual answer.

(a) $\dfrac{7.9 \times 3.9}{4.8}$ (b) $\dfrac{400 \times 0.29}{6.2}$ (c) $\dfrac{81.7 \times 4.9}{1.9 \times 10.3}$

4 $\sqrt{35.4}$ is approximately equal to 6.

Use this to estimate the value of $\dfrac{7.91 \times \sqrt{35.4}}{5.2 \times 1.85}$

5 Find estimates to these calculations by using suitable approximations.
Then carry out the calculations with the original figures.

(a) $\dfrac{5.2 + \sqrt{51.1}}{6.3 \times 0.96}$
(b) $\dfrac{17.6 - 1.8^2}{\sqrt{23.4} - 2.76}$
(c) $\dfrac{\sqrt{3.87} + 4.6^2}{2.77 \times \sqrt{79.45}}$

6 Estate Agents sometimes quote the floor area of a flat in square metres.
They quote an estimate so that buyers can easily compare one flat with another.
Write down the lengths and widths of each room to 1 significant figure.

(a) Obtain an estimate of the total floor area of the two flats.

Meadow View Flat		**Park View Flat**	
Reception 1	4.1 m × 6.9 m	Reception 1	3.9 m × 5.1 m
Reception 2	3.9 m × 5 m	Reception 2	4 m × 3.8 m
Bedroom 1	3.2 m × 3.7 m	Bedroom 1	4.1 m × 3.9 m
Bedroom 2	2.9 m × 2.1 m	Bedroom 2	3.1 m × 2.9 m

(b) Work out the actual floor area of each flat. Compare the estimates.

7 Estimate the shaded area in the shape.
Take π to be 3.
Area of a circle $= \pi r^2$

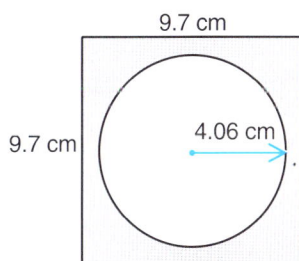

8 Estimate the shaded area.

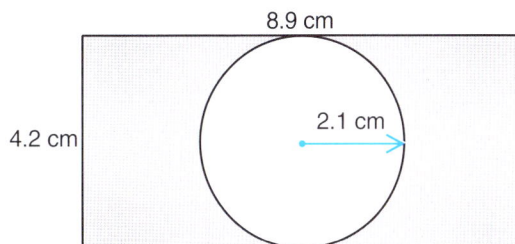

9 (a) Calculate $\dfrac{49.7 + 10.6}{9.69 \times 3.04}$

(b) Do not use your calculator in this part of the question.
By using approximations show that your answer to (a) is about right.

10 (a) Calculate $\sqrt{\dfrac{523}{19.6}}$

(b) By using suitable approximations check that your answer to part (a) is about right.

What you need to know

- A number can be rounded to an **approximate** number.

- How to approximate using **decimal places**.
  When rounding a number to 1, 2, 3 or more decimal places:
    (i)   Write the number using one more decimal place than asked for.
    (ii) Look at the last decimal place and
            if the figure is 5 or more round up,
            if the figure is less than 5 round down.

- How to approximate using **significant figures**.
  When rounding a number to 1, 2, 3 or more significant figures:
    (i)   Start from the most significant figure and count the required number of figures.
    (ii)   Look at the next figure to the right of this and
            if the figure is 5 or more round up,
            if the figure is less than 5 round down.
    (iii) Add noughts, as necessary, to locate the decimal point and preserve the place value.

- When answering a problem remember to include any units and state the degree of approximation used.

- Use approximation to **estimate** that the actual answer to a calculation is of the right magnitude (size).

Review Exercise

1 Two newspapers write about a rock concert.
Both newspapers estimate the number of people in the audience.

> According to *The Post*, 3000 fans attended.
> *The Post* make their estimate to **the nearest 1000**.

> *The Chronicle* said there were 2500 fans in the audience.
> Their estimate is to **the nearest 100**.

What are the largest and smallest possible sizes of the audience?

SEG 1997

2 A newspaper headline reads:

"250 000 shoppers at first day of Harrods sale"

The number given in the headline is correct to the nearest **ten thousand**.

(a) What is the **smallest** possible number of shoppers at the first day of Harrods sale?
(b) The exact number of people who watched the Wimbledon final on TV was 25 826 443.
   (i)   Choose a sensible rounded number to complete this headline.

". . . . . people watch the Wimbledon final on TV"

   (ii) To what is your number rounded?

SEG 1994

38

3 Calculate $72.5 \div 7.9$
  (a) to 1 decimal place,
  (b) to 2 decimal places,
  (c) to 3 decimal places.

4 Calculate $107.9 \div 72.5$
  (a) to 1 significant figure,
  (b) to 2 significant figures,
  (c) to 3 significant figures.

5 Liping and Sam use a calculator to work out

$$\frac{5.8^2 - 1.6}{3.2} + 1.96$$

Liping

I get 11.9725

John

Sam

My answer is different. I get 35.1

I am sure Liping is right. My estimate gives about 13

Without using a calculator, show how John makes his estimate.
You **must** show all your working.

SEG 1997

6 John uses his calculator to work out

$$\frac{0.39 \times 85.2}{5.8}$$

He gets an answer of 57.3.
Without using a calculator, use approximation to find whether John's answer is of the correct order of magnitude.
You **must** show all your working.

SEG 1996

7 (a) The exact width of a window is 2.7843 metres.
    Give this measurement to an appropriate degree of accuracy for a workman who is cutting a pane of glass for a replacement window.

  (b) A man lives 181.88 miles away from his daughter.
    Give this distance to an appropriate degree of accuracy when he is talking to a friend.

SEG 1997

8 Jane's classroom is rectangular. She measures the length and width of the floor. The length is 6.73 m. The width is 5.62 m.
  (a) Calculate the area of the classroom floor. Write down all the figures in the answer shown on your calculator.

  (b) (i) The classroom is to be carpeted.
        Give your answer to an appropriate degree of accuracy.
    (ii) Explain why you chose this degree of accuracy.

SEG 1994

9 Find estimates to these calculations by using approximations to 1 significant figure.
Then carry out these calculations with the original figures. Use a calculator.
Compare your estimate to the actual answer.

(a) $\dfrac{42.1 \times 2.97}{2.017 \times 31}$ (b) $\dfrac{38.2 + 60.17}{1.95 \times 5.12}$ (c) $\dfrac{61.4 \times 1.87}{49.2 - 28.8}$

10 (a) Calculate $\dfrac{89.6 \times 10.3}{19.7 + 9.8}$.

(b) Do not use your calculator in this part of the question.
By using approximations show that your answer to (a) is about right.
You **must** show all your working.

SEG 1999

11 Flour costs 48p per kilogram. Brett bought 205 kg and shared it equally among 14 people.
He calculated that each person should pay £0.72.

Without using a calculator, use a rough estimate to check whether this answer is about the right size. **You must show all your working**.

SEG 1994

12 Find the value of $\dfrac{1000}{3} + 18\pi$, giving your answer correct to three significant figures.

13 Ben buys 4 lb 4 oz of apples which cost £1.24 per kg.
453 grams is equal to 1 lb.

(a) Calculate the weight of the apples in kilograms, writing down all the figures shown on your calculator display.

(b) (i) For the purpose of calculating the cost, write this weight to an appropriate degree of accuracy.
(ii) Explain why you used this degree of accuracy.

SEG 1996

14 Fatima has used 208 units of gas during the last three months, at a cost of 32.5p per unit.
She calculates the cost as 67600 but does not note the position of the decimal point.
Use a rough estimate to check the position of the decimal point and give the cost of this gas in pounds and pence.
You **must** show all your working.

SEG 1994

15 Noreen insures her house for £91 000 and the contents for £18 000.
The annual premiums for the insurance are
        Buildings: 21p per £100 of cover;
        Contents: 98p per £100 of cover.
Noreen calculates the total annual cost of the premium to be £3675.
Use **estimation** to check Noreen's calculation to see if she is correct.
You **must** show all your working.

SEG 1996

16 The distance between Oxford and Banbury is 37 km.
Both Oxford and Banbury appear on the same map in a Road Atlas.
The scale is guessed at 1 : 20 000.
Is this likely?
You **must** show all your working.

SEG 1997

CHAPTER 4

Powers, Roots and Reciprocals

Index notation

$2 \times 2 \times 2 \times 2 \times 2 \times 2 \times 2 \times 2$ has the value of 256.

A short way of writing $2 \times 2 \times 2 \times 2 \times 2 \times 2 \times 2 \times 2$ is 2^8.

A short way of writing $a \times a \times a \times a \times a \times a \times a$ is a^7.

2^{10} is written using **index notation**.
2^{10} is read as "2 to the **power** 10."
2 is the **base**.
10 is the **index** or **power**.

Rules of indices

Multiplying

When multiplying:
powers of the same base are **added**.

In general: $a^m \times a^n = a^{m+n}$

Dividing

When dividing:
powers of the same base are **subtracted**.

In general: $a^m \div a^n = a^{m-n}$

Raising a power to a power

$(a^m)^n = a^{mn}$

Two special results

$a^1 = a$ $a^0 = 1$

EXAMPLES   Simplify each of these expressions.

(a) $2^9 \times 2^4 = 2^{9+4} = 2^{13}$

(b) $a^7 \times a^8 = a^{7+8} = a^{15}$

(c) $2^9 \div 2^4 = 2^{9-4} = 2^5$

(d) $a^5 \div a^4 = a^{5-4} = a^1 = a$

(e) $(4^9)^3 = 4^{9 \times 3} = 4^{27}$

(f) $(a^3)^2 = a^{3 \times 2} = a^6$

Powers on the calculator

Calculations with numbers written in index notation can be done on a scientific calculator using the $\boxed{x^y}$ button.

EXAMPLES

1   Calculate the value of 2.6^4

To do the calculation enter the following sequence into your calculator.

$\boxed{2}$ $\boxed{.}$ $\boxed{6}$ $\boxed{x^y}$ $\boxed{4}$ $\boxed{=}$

This gives $2.6^4 = 45.6976$

2   Calculate the value of $5^3 \times (2^4 + 2^3)$.

To do the calculation enter the following sequence into your calculator.

$\boxed{5}$ $\boxed{x^y}$ $\boxed{3}$ $\boxed{\times}$ $\boxed{(}$ $\boxed{2}$ $\boxed{x^y}$ $\boxed{4}$ $\boxed{+}$ $\boxed{2}$ $\boxed{x^y}$ $\boxed{3}$ $\boxed{)}$ $\boxed{=}$

This gives $5^3 \times (2^4 + 2^3) = 3000$

3   Find the value of x in: (a) $2^x \times 5 = 160$ (b) $5^x \times 4 = 2500$

(a) $2^x \times 5 = 160$
Dividing through by 5 gives:
$2^x = 32$
$2^5 = 32$ so $x = 5$.

(b) $5^x \times 4 = 2500$
Dividing through by 4 gives:
$5^x = 625$
$5^4 = 625$ so $x = 4$.

The **prime factors** of a number are those factors which are themselves prime numbers.
The prime factors of 12 are 2 and 3.

EXAMPLES

1 Write 60 as the product of its prime factors.

A **factor tree** can be used.

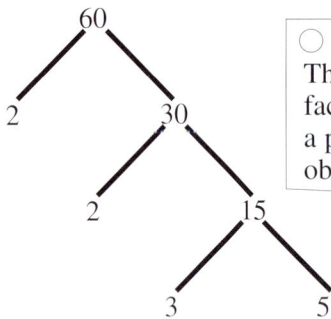

The branches of a factor tree stop when a prime factor is obtained.

The factor tree shows that:

$60 = 2 \times 30$
$60 = 2 \times 2 \times 15$
$60 = 2 \times 2 \times 3 \times 5$

Using index notation, 60 written as the product of its prime factors is $2^2 \times 3 \times 5$.

2 What is the lowest common multiple of 36 and 48?

Multiples of 36 are:
36, 72, 108, 144, 180, 216, …
Multiples of 48 are:
48, 96, 144, 192, …
The lowest common multiple of 36 and 48 is 144.

Alternative method
Write each number as a product of its prime factors.

$36 = 2^2 \times 3^2 \qquad 48 = 2^4 \times 3$

Circle the prime factor with the **highest** power for **each** prime factor.

$36 = 2^2 \times \boxed{3^2} \qquad 48 = \boxed{2^4} \times 3$

Multiply these numbers together.
$2^4 \times 3^2 = 16 \times 9 = 144$

3 What is the highest common factor of 36 and 48?

The factors of 36 are 1, 2, 3, 4, 6, 9, 12, 18, 36.
The factors of 48 are 1, 2, 3, 4, 6, 8, 12, 16, 24, 48.
The highest common factor of 36 and 48 is 12.

Alternative method
Write each number as a product of its prime factors.
$36 = 2^2 \times 3^2 \qquad 48 = 2^4 \times 3$
Circle the prime factor with the **lowest** power for prime factors **common** to both numbers.

$36 = \boxed{2^2} \times 3^2 \qquad 48 = 2^4 \times \boxed{3}$

Multiply these numbers together.
$2^2 \times 3 = 4 \times 3 = 12$

Remember
Multiples of a number are found by multiplying the number by 1, 2, 3, 4, …
For example, the multiples of 8 are
8, 16, 24, 32, 40, 48, 56, …

The **factors** of a number can be found from the multiplication facts that give the number:
For example:
$1 \times 12 = 2 \times 6 = 3 \times 4 = 12$
The factors of 12 are 1, 2, 3, 4, 6, 12.
Another method of finding the factors of a number is to find whole numbers that divide **exactly** into the number.

A **prime number** is a number with only two factors.
The first few prime numbers are
2, 3, 5, 7, 11, 13, 17, ...

The **Lowest Common Multiple** of two numbers is the smallest number that is a multiple of both numbers.

The **Highest Common Factor** of two numbers is the largest number that is a factor of both numbers.

Use a calculator for question 9 only.

1 Use index notation to simplify the following.

(a) $2 \times 2 \times 2 \times 2 \times 2 \times 2 \times 2 \times 2 \times 2$ (b) $2 \times 2 \times 2 \times 3 \times 3 \times 3 \times 3$

(c) $5 \times 5 \times 5 \times 5 \times 5 \times 7 \times 7 \times 7 \times 7$ (d) $\dfrac{3 \times 3 \times 3 \times 3 \times 7 \times 7 \times 7 \times 7 \times 7 \times 7}{3 \times 3 \times 7 \times 7 \times 7}$

2 Find x in each of the following.

(a) $2^x = 64$ (b) $3^x = 243$ (c) $5^x = 625$ (d) $4^x = 1024$

(e) $5^x = 1$ (f) $0.5^x = 0.25$ (g) $3 \times 2^x = 48$ (h) $5 \times 3^x = 405$

(i) $2^3 \times 5^x = 1000$ (j) $2^5 \times 5^x = 32$ (k) $3^3 \times 7^x = 189$ (l) $5^x \times 2^3 = 200$

3 Find x in each of the following.

(a) $2^3 \times 2^5 = 2^x$ (b) $3^5 \times 3^2 = 3^x$ (c) $7^2 \times 7^8 \times 7 = 7^x$ (d) $3^5 \div 3^2 = 3^x$

(e) $8^7 \div 8^6 = 8^x$ (f) $6^5 \div 6 = 6^x$ (g) $(2^3)^2 = 2^x$ (h) $(5^4)^5 = 5^x$

(i) $\dfrac{2^3 \times (2^2)^5}{2^8 \times 2^3} = 2^x$ (j) $\dfrac{(3^3 \times 3^2)^3}{3^7} = 3^x$ (k) $\dfrac{5^x \times 5^3 \times 5^4}{(5 \times 5^3)^3} = 5$ (l) $\dfrac{(3^x \times 3^2)^3}{(3 \times 3^5)^2} = 3^3$

4 In each of the following, find x and y, where x and y are integers.

(a) $5 \times 5 \times 7 \times 7 \times 7 \times 7 = 5^x \times 7^y$ (b) $2 \times 2 \times 2 \times 9 \times 9 \times 9 \times 9 \times 9 = 2^x \times 9^y$

(c) $2^x \times 3^y = 72$ (d) $2^x \times 3^y = 108$ (e) $2^x \times 5^y = 500$ (f) $3^x \times 5^y = 675$

5 In each of the following, find a and b, where a and b are prime numbers.

(a) $a^5 b = 96$ (b) $a^3 b^2 = 72$ (c) $ab^3 = 54$ (d) $a^2 b^3 = 500$

(e) $a^4 b = 80$ (f) $a^3 b^2 = 675$ (g) $a^4 b^2 = 324$ (h) $a^3 b^2 = 392$

6 (a) Express as the product of prime factors

    (i) 12,   (ii) 18,   (iii) 40,

    (iv) 30,   (v) 144,   (vi) 180.

(b) Find the lowest common multiple and the highest common factor of

    (i) 12 and 18,   (ii) 40 and 144,   (iii) 18 and 30,   (iv) 30, 144 and 180.

7 The diagram shows the starting position of a system of cogs A, B, C and D.

The cogs start to rotate.

How many revolutions does cog A make before the following sets of cogs all return to their starting positions (at the same time):

(a) A **and** B,

(b) A, B **and** C,

(c) A, B, C **and** D?

Cog A — 12 teeth

Cog B — 30 teeth

Cog C — 8 teeth

Cog D — 18 teeth

8 By first writing each number in the following sequences as the product of their prime factors, find the next term in each sequence.

(a) 6, 10, 14, 15, ...

(b) 12, 18, 20, 28, ...

(c) 72, 108, 200, 392, ...

9 Use a calculator to find the value of:

(a) $3^5 \div (3^7 - 3^5)$ (b) $(8^7 - 8^5) \div (4^7 - 4^5)$ (c) $2.4^5 \div 32^{0.6}$

(d) $0.25^{0.5} \times 0.5^2$ (e) $9^{1.5} \div 16^{0.75}$ (f) $4^{2.5} \times (6.25^{0.5} + 5^0)$

(g) $32^{0.4} \times (4^{0.5} + 64^{0.5})$ (h) $125^{\frac{2}{3}} \times (343^{\frac{2}{3}} + 5^0)$ (i) $0.04^{-\frac{1}{2}} \div 0.125^{-\frac{1}{3}}$

Negative powers and reciprocals

This section introduces negative powers and the term **reciprocal.**

Using the rules of powers

$\frac{1}{10} = 1 \div 10$

$\boxed{\begin{array}{l} 1 = 10^0 \\ 10 = 10^1 \end{array}}$

$\frac{1}{10} = 10^0 \div 10^1$

$\frac{1}{10} = 10^{0-1}$

$\frac{1}{10^1} = 10^{-1}$ $\boxed{a^m \div a^n = a^{m-n}}$

$\frac{1}{32} = 1 \div 32$

$\boxed{\begin{array}{l} 1 = 2^0 \\ 32 = 2^5 \end{array}}$

$\frac{1}{32} = 2^0 \div 2^5$

$\frac{1}{32} = 2^{0-5}$

$\frac{1}{2^5} = 2^{-5}$

$\frac{1}{625} = 1 \div 625$

$\boxed{\begin{array}{l} 1 = 5^0 \\ 625 = 5^4 \end{array}}$

$\frac{1}{625} = 5^0 \div 5^4$

$\frac{1}{625} = 5^{0-4}$

$\frac{1}{5^4} = 5^{-4}$

Using patterns of powers

This list shows the powers of two extended to include negative powers.

$2^3 = 2 \times 2 \times 2 = 8$

$2^2 = 2 \times 2 \qquad = 4$

$2^1 = 2 \qquad\qquad = 2$

$2^0 = 1 \qquad\qquad = 1$

$2^{-1} = \frac{1}{2} \qquad\quad = 0.5 \quad = \frac{1}{2^1}$

$2^{-2} = \frac{1}{4} \qquad\quad = 0.25 \quad = \frac{1}{2^2}$

$2^{-3} = \frac{1}{8} \qquad\quad = 0.125 = \frac{1}{2^3}$

All of the examples illustrate this general rule for negative powers.

$$a^{-m} = \frac{1}{a^m}$$

$\frac{1}{a^m}$ and, hence, a^{-m}, is called the **reciprocal** of a^m.

Using a calculator

Reciprocals can be worked out on a scientific calculator using the $\boxed{x^{-1}}$ button. Use this calculator sequence to work out 10^{-1}.

$\boxed{1}\ \boxed{0}\ \boxed{x^{-1}}\ \boxed{=}$

This gives $10^{-1} = 0.1$

$0.1 = \frac{1}{10}$ so $10^{-1} = \frac{1}{10^1}$

This calculator sequence, using the $\boxed{x^{-1}}$ button, can be used to work out 2^{-8}.

$\boxed{2}\ \boxed{x^{-1}}\ \boxed{x^y}\ \boxed{8}\ \boxed{=}$

Alternatively, this calculator sequence can be used:

$\boxed{2}\ \boxed{x^y}\ \boxed{8}\ \boxed{+/-}\ \boxed{=}$

These both give:
$2^{-8} = 0.00390625$

$0.00390625 = \frac{1}{256}$ so $2^{-8} = \frac{1}{2^8}$

EXAMPLES

1 Find the reciprocals of
  (a) 5,   (b) 3^2,   (c) 7^{-2},   (d) $\left(\frac{1}{6}\right)^{-2}$.

  (a) The reciprocal of 5 is $\frac{1}{5}$.
    This is equivalent to 5^{-1}.

  (b) The reciprocal of 3^2 is $\frac{1}{3^2}$ or $\frac{1}{9}$.
    This is equivalent to 3^{-2} or 9^{-1}.

  (c) The reciprocal of 7^{-2} is $\frac{1}{7^{-2}}$.
    This is equivalent to 7^2 or 49.

  (d) $\left(\frac{1}{6}\right)^{-2} = \frac{1}{6^{-2}} = 6^2$.
    The reciprocal of $\left(\frac{1}{6}\right)^{-2}$ is 6^{-2}.
    This is equivalent to $\frac{1}{36}$.

2 If $5x = \frac{1}{125}$ find the value of x.

  $125 = 5^3$
  $\frac{1}{125} = \frac{1}{5^3}$
  $\frac{1}{5^3} = 5^{-3}$
  This gives $x = -3$.

3 If $2^x \div 2^5 = \frac{1}{8}$ find the value of x.

  $\frac{1}{8} = \frac{1}{2^3} = 2^{-3}$
  $2^{x-5} = 2^{-3}$
  So $x - 5 = -3$
  This gives $x = 2$.

Exercise 4.2

Use a calculator for question 5(a) only.

1 Write down the reciprocals of
(a) (i) 2, (ii) 7, (iii) 20.

(b) (i) 7^3, (ii) 7^{-3}, (iii) 3^5.
Give your answers to (b) in index notation.

2 Write the following as fractions.
(a) 4^{-2} (b) 5^{-3} (c) 10^{-2}
(d) 2^{-4} (e) 3^{-1} (f) 20^{-2}

3 Calculate each of the following.
(a) $10 + 10^0 + 10^{-1}$
(b) $2 + 2^{-1} + 2^{-2} + 2^{-3}$
(c) $5^0 + 5^{-1} + 5^{-2}$
(d) $3^{-1} + 2^{-1}$
(e) $5^{-2} + 2^{-2}$
(f) $5^{-2} \times 2^{-2}$
(g) $5^{-2} \div 2^{-2}$
(h) $5 \times 6^{-1} + 2 \times 5^{-1}$

4 Find x in each of the following.
(a) $3^x = \frac{1}{81}$ (b) $5^x = \frac{1}{25}$
(c) $\left(\frac{1}{4}\right)^x = 16$ (d) $\left(\frac{1}{6}\right)^x = 216$
(e) $2^x = 0.5$ (f) $5^x = 0.04$
(g) $3 \times 10^x = 0.003$ (h) $2 \times 5^x = 0.4$

5 (a) Use a calculator to find the value of:
(i) $32^{0.2} \times 2^{-1}$ (ii) $25^{-0.5} \times 625^{0.25}$
(iii) $0.5^{-2} \div 16^{0.5}$ (iv) $0.25^2 \div 32^{-0.8}$

(b) Your answers in (a) can be confirmed by using the rules of powers. For example:
$32^{0.2} \times 2^{-1} = (2^5)^{0.2} \times 2^{-1} = 2^{5 \times 0.2} \times 2^{-1}$
$= 2^1 \times 2^{-1} = 2^0 = 1$

Use the rules of powers to confirm your other answers in (a).

Standard form

Standard index form is a shorthand way of writing very small and very large numbers.
Standard index form is often called **standard form** or **scientific notation.**

> In **standard form** a number is written as:
> $A \times 10^n$ where $1 \leqslant A < 10$ and n is an integer.
> For large numbers, greater than 10, n is **positive**.
> For small positive numbers, less than 1, n is **negative**.

EXAMPLES

1 Write the following numbers in standard form.

(a) 523 000
$= 5.23 \times 100\,000$
$= 5.23 \times 10^5$

(b) 0.007 12
$= 7.12 \times 0.001$
$= 7.12 \times 10^{-3}$

2 Write the following as ordinary numbers

(a) 7.25×10^2
$= 7.25 \times 100$
$= 725$

(b) 4.3×10^{-4}
$= 4.3 \times 0.000\,1$
$= 0.000\,43$

Try to find a quick method for changing ordinary numbers to and from standard form.

Exercise 4.3

Do not use a calculator.

1 Copy the table and fill in all of the different forms of each number.

Ordinary number	Power of 10	Standard form
300 000	3 × 100 000	3×10^5
75 000	7.5 × 10 000	
	8 × 100 000 000	
		3.5×10^{13}
62 300 000 000 000		

2 Write each of these numbers in standard form.
(a) 300 000 000 000
(b) 80 000 000
(c) 700 000 000
(d) 630
(e) 3 219 000 000

3 Change each of these numbers to an ordinary number.
(a) 6×10^5
(b) 2×10^3
(c) 5×10^7
(d) 3.7×10^9
(e) 2.8×10^1
(f) 7.1×10^4

4 Copy the table and fill in all of the different forms of each number.

Ordinary number	Power of 10	Standard form
0.000 03	3 × 0.000 01	3×10^{-5}
0.0075	7.5 × 0.001	
0.000 008 75	8.75 × 0.000 001	
0.000 000 003 5		
0.000 000 000 006 2		

5 Change each of these numbers to an ordinary number.
(a) 3.5×10^{-1} (b) 5×10^{-4}
(c) 5.5×10^{-6} (d) 6.25×10^{-8}
(e) 3.167×10^{-11} (f) 1.115×10^{-4}

6 Write each of these numbers in standard form.
(a) 0.007 (b) 0.04
(c) 0.000 000 005 (d) 0.000 8
(e) 0.000 002 3 (f) 0.000 000 045

7 (a) Distances from the Sun to some of its planets are:
Mercury 58 000 000 km
Venus 108 000 000 km
Earth 149 000 000 km
Mars 228 000 000 km
Write each distance in standard form.

(b) Distances from the Sun to the stars Alpha Centauri and Alpha Cygni are:
Alpha Centauri 4.035×10^{13} km
Alpha Cygni 1.053×10^{14} km
Write each distance as an ordinary number.

8 The smallest living cells are bacteria cells which have a diameter of 0.000 025 cm.

Here are some other very small numbers.
Blood cell: diameter 0.000 75 cm.
Hydrogen atom: diameter 0.000 000 2 mm.
Mumps virus: diameter 0.000 225 mm.
Write each of these very small numbers in standard form.

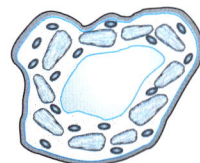

Calculations with large and small numbers can be done on a scientific calculator by:

    (i)   changing the numbers to standard form,

    (ii)   entering the numbers into the calculator using the [Exp] button.

If your calculator works in a different way refer to the instruction booklet supplied with the calculator or ask someone for help.

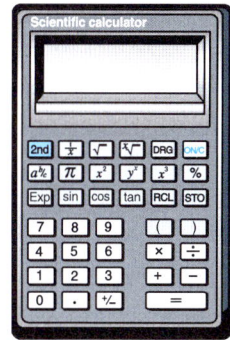

EXAMPLES

1 Calculate the value of 62 500 000 000 $\times$ 0.000 000 003

Give your answer both as an ordinary number and in standard form.

62 500 000 000 $\times$ 0.000 000 003 = $(6.25 \times 10^{10}) \times (3 \times 10^{-9})$

To do the calculation enter the following sequence into your calculator.

| 6 | . | 2 | 5 | Exp | 1 | 0 | $\times$ | 3 | Exp | 9 | +/- | = |

Giving:

6 250 000 000 $\times$ 0.000 000 03

= 187.5   (ordinary number)

= 1.875×10^{2} (standard form)

> Some calculators display this result as: 187.5
> Other calculators give this display: 1.875 *02*

Remember: The calculator display **must** be changed to either **standard form** or an **ordinary number**.

2 Calculate the value of $0.000\ 000\ 000\ 05^4$. Give your answer in standard form.

$(0.000\ 000\ 000\ 05)^4 = (5 \times 10^{-11})^4$

To do the calculation enter the following sequence into your calculator.

| 5 | Exp | 1 | 1 | +/- | x^y | 4 | = |

This gives the calculator display:

$0.000\ 000\ 000\ 05^4 = 6.25 \times 10^{-42}$ | 6.25   −42 |

3 The population of China in 1993 was 1.01×10^9.

The population of the USA in 1993 was 2.32×10^8.

By how much did the population of China exceed that of the USA in 1993?

> $1.01 \times 10^9 > 2.32 \times 10^8$
> The greater the power . . .
> . . . the bigger the number.

You need to work out $1.01 \times 10^9 - 2.32 \times 10^8$

To do the calculation enter the following sequence into your calculator.

| 1 | . | 0 | 1 | Exp | 9 | − | 2 | . | 3 | 2 | Exp | 8 | = |

Giving: $1.01 \times 10^9 - 2.32 \times 10^8 = 778\ 000\ 000 = 7.78 \times 10^8$

*Try this example **without** a calculator.*

You may use a calculator.

1 Give the answer to the following calculations in standard form.
   (a) $33\ 500\ 000\ 000 \times 2\ 800\ 000\ 000$
   (b) $0.000\ 000\ 000\ 2 \times 80\ 000\ 000\ 000$
   (c) $15\ 000\ 000\ 000\ 000^2$
   (d) $0.000\ 000\ 000\ 000\ 5^3$
   (e) $48\ 000\ 000\ 000 \div 0.000\ 000\ 000\ 2$
   (f) $25\ 000\ 000\ 000 \div 500\ 000\ 000\ 000$

2 Calculate each of the following.
   (a) $(5.25 \times 10^9) \times (7.12 \times 10^{-5})$
   (b) $(4.318 \times 10^9) \times (5.64 \times 10^{-5})$
   (c) $(8.1 \times 10^4) \div (2.4 \times 10^5 + 3 \times 10^4)$
   (d) $(8.45 \times 10^6) \div (1.29 \times 10^{-7})^2$
   (e) $(5.14 \times 10^{-3}) \div (2.46 \times 10^{-6} + 8.7 \times 10^{-5})$
   (f) $(4.5 \times 10^4)^3 \div (6.5 \times 10^{-2})^{-3}$
   Give your answers to 3 significant figures where appropriate.

3 In 1992, $1\ 400\ 000\ 000$ steel cans and $688\ 000\ 000$ aluminium cans were recycled.
   (a) Find the total number of cans that were recycled in 1992.
   (b) Express the number of aluminum cans recycled in 1992 as a percentage of the total number of cans that were recycled in 1992.

4 Alpha Centauri is $40\ 350\ 000\ 000\ 000$ km from the Sun.
   Alpha Cygni is $105\ 300\ 000\ 000\ 000$ km from the Sun.
   How much further is it from the Sun to Alpha Cygni than from the Sun to Alpha Centauri?

5 An oxygen atom weighs 2.7×10^{-23} g.
   An electron weighs 9×10^{-28} g.
   How may times larger than the weight of an electron is the weight of an oxygen atom?

6 The modern human appeared on the Earth about 3.5×10^4 years ago.
   The Earth has been in existence for something like 1.3×10^5 times as long as this.
   (a) Estimate the age of the Earth.

   Reptiles appeared on the Earth about 2.3×10^8 years ago.
   (b) Express the age of the modern human as a percentage of the age of the reptile.

7 The surface area of the Earth is approximately 5.107×10^{14} square metres.
   About 29.2% of the Earth's surface is land.
   What area is covered by water?

8 Approximate figures for the amount of carbon dioxide entering the atmosphere from artificial sources are shown below.

Total amount (world wide)	7.4×10^9 tonnes
Amount from the United Kingdom	1.59×10^8 tonnes

   (a) What percentage of the total amount of carbon dioxide entering the atmosphere comes from the United Kingdom?

   (b) Approximately 19% of the amount of carbon dioxide from the United Kingdom comes from road transport?
   How many million tonnes of carbon dioxide is this?

SEG 1999

EXAMPLES

1 Calculate the value of $(3 \times 10^2) + (4 \times 10^3)$.
Give your answer in standard form.
$3 \times 10^2 = 300 \qquad 4 \times 10^3 = 4000$
$(3 \times 10^2) + (4 \times 10^3) = 300 + 4000$
$= 4300$
$= 4.3 \times 10^3$

> When adding or subtracting numbers in standard form without a calculator change to an ordinary number first.

2 Calculate the value of ab where
$a = 8 \times 10^3$ and $b = 4 \times 10^5$.
$ab = (8 \times 10^3) \times (4 \times 10^5)$
$= 8 \times 4 \times 10^3 \times 10^5$
$= 32 \times 10^8$
$= 3.2 \times 10 \times 10^8$
$= 3.2 \times 10^9$

> When **multiplying** the powers are **added**.
> $10^3 \times 10^5 = 10^{3+5} = 10^8$
> $10 \times 10^8 = 10^{1+8} = 10^9$

3 Calculate the value of x^2 where $x = 7 \times 10^{-8}$.
$x^2 = (7 \times 10^{-8})^2$
$= 49 \times 10^{-16}$
$= 4.9 \times 10 \times 10^{-16}$
$= 4.9 \times 10^{-15}$

> **Remember:**
> $(7 \times 10^{-8})^2 = 7^2 \times (10^{-8})^2$
> $10 \times 10^{-16} = 10^{1-16} = 10^{-15}$

4 Calculate the value of $(1.2 \times 10^3) \div (4 \times 10^{-8})$.
$(1.2 \times 10^3) \div (4 \times 10^{-8}) = (1.2 \div 4) \times (10^3 \div 10^{-8})$
$= 0.3 \times 10^{11}$
$= 3 \times 10^{-1} \times 10^{11}$
$= 3 \times 10^{10}$

> When **dividing** the powers are **subtracted**.
> $10^3 \div 10^{-8} = 10^{3--8} = 10^{11}$

Exercise 4.5 Do not use a calculator.

1 $x = 3 \times 10^4$ and $y = 5 \times 10^{-5}$.
Calculate the each of the following.
(a) xy (b) x^3 (c) x^2y
(d) y^3 (e) $10y^4$ (f) $10\,000xy$

2 Calculate each of the following.
(a) $5.2 \times 10^6 + 3 \times 10^5$
(b) $5.031 \times 10^6 - 3.1 \times 10^4$
(c) $6.5 \times 10^{-3} - 3.5 \times 10^{-4}$
(d) $4.2 \times 10^5 + 1.28 \times 10^6$
(e) $6.25 \times 10^{-1} + 7.5 \times 10^{-2}$

3 Calculate each of the following.
(a) $8 \times (3 \times 10^7)$
(b) $5 \times (3 \times 10^4)$
(c) $200 \times (3 \times 10^9)$
(d) $400 \div (5 \times 10^6)$
(e) $(4 \times 10^5) \times (8 \times 10^3)$
(f) $(1.8 \times 10^3) \times (6 \times 10^{-7})$
(g) $(4 \times 10^5) \div (8 \times 10^3)$
(h) $(5 \times 10^{-5}) \times (6 \times 10^7) \div (3 \times 10^{-3})$

4 Calculate each of the following.
(a) $33\,500\,000\,000 \times 2\,800\,000\,000$
(b) $0.000\,000\,000\,000\,5^3$
(c) $48\,000\,000\,000 \div 0.000\,000\,000\,2$
(d) $2\,400\,000 \div 8\,000\,000\,000$
(e) $0.000\,000\,000\,000\,5^3 \times 200\,000\,000^4$
(f) $(0.005)^2 \div 0.000002$

5 $x = 4 \times 10^5$, $y = 8 \times 10^6$ and $z = 5 \times 10^{-2}$.
Calculate each of the following.
(a) $x + y$
(b) $y - x$
(c) $3 \times z$
(d) x^2
(e) $x \times y$
(f) $x \div y$
(g) z^3
(h) $x \times y \times z$
(i) $x \div z$
(j) $y \div z$

Powers and roots

The inverse (opposite) of raising to a power is finding a **root**.
The inverse of squaring is finding the **square root**.
The inverse of cubing is finding the **cube root**.
The inverse of raising to the power 5 is finding the **fifth root**.
For example:

The square root of 9 is 3 because $3^2 = 9$

The cube root of 64 is 4 because $4^3 = 64$

The fifth root of 32 is 2 because $2^5 = 32$

$\sqrt{6.25} = 2.5$ because $2.5^2 = 6.25$

$\sqrt[3]{1.728} = 1.2$ because $1.2^3 = 1.728$

$\sqrt[6]{15625} = 5$ because $5^6 = 15625$

The connection between powers and roots

If $a = b^n$, $\sqrt[n]{a} = \sqrt[n]{b^n} = b$

Using the rules of powers

$(b^n)^{\frac{1}{n}} = b^{n \times \frac{1}{n}} = b$

So $(b^n)^{\frac{1}{n}}$ is the same as $\sqrt[n]{b^n}$.

So $a^{\frac{1}{n}}$ is the same as $\sqrt[n]{a}$.

> The inverse of "raising to the power n" is finding the nth root.
>
> In general, finding the nth root of a number, a, can be written as:
> $$\sqrt[n]{a} \text{ or } a^{\frac{1}{n}}.$$

EXAMPLES

1 Calculate   (a) $25^{\frac{1}{2}}$ (b) $81^{\frac{1}{4}}$

(a) $25^{\frac{1}{2}} = \sqrt{25} = 5$
Because $5^2 = 25$.

(b) $81^{\frac{1}{4}} = \sqrt[4]{81} = 3$
Because $3^4 = 81$.

2 Calculate   (a) $25^{-\frac{1}{2}}$ (b) $16^{-\frac{1}{4}}$

(a) $25^{-\frac{1}{2}}$ is the **reciprocal** of $25^{\frac{1}{2}}$.

$25^{-\frac{1}{2}} = \frac{1}{25^{\frac{1}{2}}} = \frac{1}{\sqrt{25}} = \frac{1}{5} = 0.2$

(b) $16^{-\frac{1}{4}}$ is the **reciprocal** of $16^{\frac{1}{4}}$.

$16^{-\frac{1}{4}} = \frac{1}{16^{\frac{1}{4}}} = \frac{1}{\sqrt[4]{16}} = \frac{1}{\sqrt[4]{2^4}} = \frac{1}{2} = 0.5$

Roots on a calculator

Most calculators have a square root button and some also have a cube root button.
On most scientific calculators the yth root of a number can be calculated using the $\boxed{x^{1/y}}$ button.

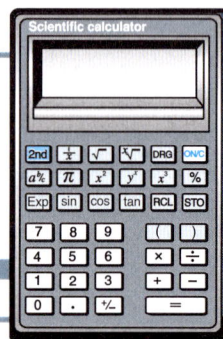

EXAMPLES

1 Calculate $\sqrt[5]{243}$.

Use this key sequence:

$\boxed{2}$ $\boxed{4}$ $\boxed{3}$ $\boxed{x^{1/y}}$ $\boxed{5}$ $\boxed{=}$

This gives $\sqrt[5]{243} = 3$

2 Calculate $512^{-\frac{1}{9}}$.

Use this key sequence:

$\boxed{5}$ $\boxed{1}$ $\boxed{2}$ $\boxed{x^{1/y}}$ $\boxed{9}$ $\boxed{+/-}$ $\boxed{=}$

This gives $512^{-\frac{1}{9}} = 0.5$

Harder fractional powers

This section deals with evaluating expressions of the form $a^{\frac{m}{n}}$ and $a^{-\frac{m}{n}}$.

In general, using the rules of indices:

$$a^{\frac{m}{n}} = \left(a^{\frac{1}{n}}\right)^m = \left(\sqrt[n]{a}\right)^m$$

$$a^{-\frac{m}{n}} = \frac{1}{a^{\frac{m}{n}}} = \frac{1}{\left(\sqrt[n]{a}\right)^m}$$

To find the value of $a^{\frac{m}{n}}$:
1. Find the nth root of a.
2. Raise the nth root of a to the power m.

To find the value of $a^{-\frac{m}{n}}$:
Carry out the first two steps as before.
3. Write down the reciprocal of $a^{\frac{m}{n}}$.

EXAMPLES

1 Find the value of $32^{\frac{4}{5}}$.

Find the 5th root of 32.
$32^{\frac{1}{5}} = 2$
Raise to the power of 4.
$2^4 = 16$
$32^{\frac{4}{5}} = 16$

2 Find the value of $27^{-\frac{4}{3}}$.

$27^{-\frac{4}{3}}$ is the reciprocal of $27^{\frac{4}{3}}$.
So first work out $27^{\frac{4}{3}}$.
$27^{\frac{4}{3}} = \left(27^{\frac{1}{3}}\right)^4 = 3^4 = 81$
The reciprocal of 81 is $\frac{1}{81}$.
So $27^{-\frac{4}{3}} = \frac{1}{81}$.

Exercise 4.6

Do not use a calculator.

1 Find the value of each of the following.
   (a) $\sqrt{400}$ (b) $\sqrt{25}$ (c) $\sqrt[3]{27}$ (d) $\sqrt[3]{1000}$ (e) $\sqrt[4]{16}$
   (f) $\sqrt{6.25}$ (g) $\sqrt[6]{64}$ (h) $\sqrt[3]{64}$ (i) $\sqrt[3]{0.125}$ (j) $\sqrt[3]{343}$

2 Find the value of each of the following.
   (a) $100^{\frac{1}{2}}$ (b) $36^{\frac{1}{2}}$ (c) $64^{\frac{1}{2}}$ (d) $64^{\frac{1}{3}}$ (e) $32^{\frac{1}{5}}$
   (f) $81^{\frac{1}{4}}$ (g) $8^{\frac{1}{3}}$ (h) $625^{\frac{1}{4}}$ (i) $64^{\frac{1}{6}}$ (j) $125^{\frac{1}{3}}$

3 Find the value of each of the following.
   (a) $100^{-\frac{1}{2}}$ (b) $9^{-\frac{1}{2}}$ (c) $49^{-\frac{1}{2}}$ (d) $27^{-\frac{1}{3}}$ (e) $128^{-\frac{1}{7}}$
   (f) $16^{-\frac{1}{4}}$ (g) $125^{-\frac{1}{3}}$ (h) $256^{-\frac{1}{4}}$ (i) $243^{-\frac{1}{5}}$ (j) $64^{-\frac{1}{3}}$

4 Find the value of each of the following.
   (a) $1000^{\frac{2}{3}}$ (b) $9^{\frac{3}{2}}$ (c) $16^{\frac{3}{4}}$ (d) $32^{\frac{2}{5}}$ (e) $4^{\frac{5}{2}}$
   (f) $9^{2.5}$ (g) $125^{\frac{2}{3}}$ (h) $16^{\frac{5}{4}}$ (i) $243^{\frac{4}{5}}$ (j) $36^{1.5}$

5 Find the value of each of the following.
   (a) $1000^{-\frac{2}{3}}$ (b) $16^{-\frac{3}{2}}$ (c) $8^{-\frac{2}{3}}$ (d) $32^{-\frac{3}{5}}$ (e) $4^{-\frac{3}{2}}$
   (f) $100^{-\frac{5}{2}}$ (g) $25^{-\frac{3}{2}}$ (h) $16^{-\frac{3}{4}}$ (i) $128^{-\frac{5}{7}}$ (j) $125^{-\frac{2}{3}}$

6 Find x in each of the following.
   (a) $\sqrt[x]{27} = 3$ (b) $\sqrt[x]{16} = 2$ (c) $\sqrt[x]{32} = 2$ (d) $25^x = 5$ (e) $27^x = 9$
   (f) $16^x = 2$ (g) $16^x = 8$ (h) $x^{\frac{3}{4}} = 64$ (i) $x^{\frac{2}{3}} = 25$ (j) $25^x = 125$

7 Calculate each of the following.
   (a) $2^{-1} + \left(\frac{1}{16}\right)^{\frac{1}{2}}$ (b) $\left(\frac{1}{32}\right)^{-\frac{1}{5}} \times 8^{-\frac{2}{3}}$ (c) $27^{\frac{2}{3}} \times 3^{-1}$ (d) $49^{-\frac{1}{2}} + 16^{-\frac{3}{4}}$ (e) $9^{\frac{3}{2}} \div 8^{\frac{2}{3}}$

8 Use the rules of powers to show that:
   (a) $0.25^{-\frac{7}{2}} = 16^{\frac{7}{4}}$ (b) $32^{\frac{3}{5}} \times 4^{-\frac{3}{2}} = 1$ (c) $25^{\frac{1}{2}} \times 36^{-\frac{1}{2}} = 8^{-\frac{1}{3}} + 3^{-1}$

Simplifying algebraic expressions

Remember

$a^m \times a^n = a^{m+n}$	$a^m \div a^n = a^{m+n}$
$a^0 = 1$	$a^1 = a$
$(a^m)^n = a^{mn}$	$a^{\frac{m}{n}} = \left(a^{\frac{1}{m}}\right)^m$ $= \left(\sqrt[n]{a}\right)^m$
$a^{-m} = \dfrac{1}{a^m}$	$\sqrt[n]{a} = a^{\frac{1}{n}}$

EXAMPLE Simplify these expressions.

(a) $x^3 \times x^{-8} = x^{3\,+\,-8} = x^{-5} = \dfrac{1}{x^5}$

(b) $\dfrac{2}{x^2} \times 5x^7 = (2 \times 5) \times (x^{-2} \times x^7)$
    $= 10 \times x^{(-2\,+\,7)} = 10x^5$

(c) $x^3 y^2 \times xy^{-4} = (x^3 \times x) \times (y^2 \times y^{-4})$
    $= x^{3\,+\,1} \times y^{(2\,+\,-4)} = x^4 y^{-2} = \dfrac{x^4}{y^2}$

(d) $\left(27x^6\right)^{\frac{2}{3}} = \left(27^{\frac{2}{3}}\right) \times \left(x^6\right)^{\frac{2}{3}}$
    $= \left(27^{\frac{1}{3}}\right)^2 \times \left(x^{6\,\times\,\frac{2}{3}}\right) = 9x^4$

(e) $\sqrt[3]{x^8 \div x^5} = \left(x^{8-5}\right)^{\frac{1}{3}} = \left(x^3\right)^{\frac{1}{3}} = x^{3\,\times\,\frac{1}{3}} = x$

(f) $6y^2 \div 2y^4 = (6 \div 2) \times (y^2 \div y^4)$
    $= 3 \times y^{2-4} = 3y^{-2}$
    $= \dfrac{3}{y^2}$

(g) $\dfrac{(4ab)^2 \times 3ab^3}{6a^3b^{-4}}$ $= (4ab)^2 \times 3ab^3 \div 6a^3b^{-4}$
    $= (4^2 \times 3 \div 6) \times (a^2 \times a \times a^3) \div (b^2 \times b^3 \div b^{-4})$
    $= 8a^{(2\,+\,1\,-\,3)}b^{(2\,+\,3\,-\,-4)} = 8a^0b^9 = 8b^9$

When multiplying or dividing expressions that include both numbers and powers:
multiply or **divide** the **numbers**, **add** or **subtract** the **powers.**
Deal with the powers of different bases **separately.**

Exercise 4.7

Do not use a calculator.
Give your answers using positive powers only.

1 Simplify each of these expressions.
   (a) $a^4 \times a^3$ (b) $x^{11} \times x^{-5}$ (c) $b^{-4} \times b$ (d) $t^5 \times t^{-2}$
   (e) $x^{-5} \times x^2 \times x$ (f) $4b^4 \times 2b^3$ (g) $3t^5 \times 2t$ (h) $4x^{-2} \times 2x^4$
   (i) $\dfrac{5}{y^5} \times 5y^3$ (j) $2x^{-1} \times 3x^5 \times 2x$ (k) $x^5y \times xy^4$ (l) $yz^3 \times y^{-3}z$
   (m) $x^2y^4 \times x^{-3}y^{-3}$ (n) $3r^5s \times \dfrac{2r^4}{s^3}$ (o) $3p^5q^{-4} \times p^2q^4$ (p) $(3x^2y)^3 \times 2x^2y^{-3}$

2 Simplify each of these expressions.
   (a) $(b^4)^2$ (b) $(x^2)^{-3}$ (c) $(5p^3q^4)^2$ (d) $\left(\dfrac{2}{x^4}\right)^{-3}$ (e) $(8y^3)^{-\frac{2}{3}}$
   (f) $(4a^2)^{\frac{3}{2}}$ (g) $\sqrt[3]{x^6y^3}$ (h) $\sqrt{9a^4b^2}$ (i) $\sqrt[3]{8x^6y^3}$ (j) $(5rs^{-2}t^3)^3$

3 Simplify each of these expressions.
   (a) $a^4 \div a^3$ (b) $x^{11} \div x^{-5}$ (c) $x^{-2} \div x$ (d) $x^{-11} \div x^{-11}$ (e) $\dfrac{1}{a^4} \div \dfrac{1}{a^2}$
   (f) $8b^5 \div 2b^2$ (g) $6y^3 \div 3y$ (h) $15z^3 \div \dfrac{3}{z}$ (i) $6x^6 \div 2x^{-2}$ (j) $\dfrac{16}{t^3} \div 4t^2$
   (k) $x^5y \div xy$ (l) $p^3q^6 \div \dfrac{p}{q}$ (m) $8r^5s^3 \div 2r^4s^{-3}$ (n) $6x^5y \div 2x^4y$ (o) $rs^{-3}t^3 \div \dfrac{s^{-3}}{t^{-3}}$

4 Simplify each of these expressions.
   (a) $\dfrac{8ab^2c^3 \times 6a^2bc^{-5}}{12a^2b^3c}$ (b) $\sqrt[3]{\dfrac{xy \times x^4y^5}{x^2y^{-3}}}$ (c) $\sqrt{\dfrac{8a^2b \times 5ab^2}{10a^3b^3}}$ (d) $\dfrac{(5xy^2)^3 \times 2xy^{-3}}{(25x^{-2}y^6)^{\frac{3}{2}}}$

One method of solving equations involving powers is to use the rules of powers to change each side of the equation to a single power with the **same base**.
Then make the powers equal.

1 Solve the following equations.

(a) $2^2 \times 2^x = 64^x$

$2^2 \times 2^x = 2^{2+x}$
$64^x = 2^{6x}$
$2^{2+x} = 2^{6x}$
$2 + x = 6x$
$5x = 2$
$x = \frac{2}{5}$

(b) $27^x \times 81^{\frac{1}{4}} = 243$

$27^x = 3^{3x} \qquad 81^{\frac{1}{4}} = 3 \qquad 243 = 3^5$
$3^{3x} \times 3 = 3^5$
$3^{3x+1} = 3^5$
$3x + 1 = 5$
$3x = 4$
$x = \frac{4}{3}$

Exercise 4.8

Do not use a calculator.

1 Solve the equations.

(a) $16^x = 2$
(b) $125^x = 25$
(c) $9^{-x} = 27$
(d) $8^{-x} = 4$
(e) $8^{\frac{x}{2}} = 32$
(f) $36^{-2x} = 216$
(g) $\left(\frac{1}{4}\right)^x = 16$
(h) $\left(\frac{1}{9}\right)^x = 27$

2 Solve the equations.

(a) $36^2 = \left(\sqrt{6}\right)^x$
(b) $8^2 = \left(\sqrt[3]{2}\right)^x$
(c) $27^x \times 3 = 9^x$
(d) $125^x \times 5 = 25^x$
(e) $16^{x-1} = 64$
(f) $27^{x-1} = 3^{x+1}$
(g) $4^{x+1} = 2^x$
(h) $4^{x-1} = 8^x$
(i) $16^x \times 4 = 8^x$
(j) $27^{x+1} = 9^x$

3 You are given the formula $y = 2x^n$.

(a) Use the formula to calculate
(i) y when $x = 5$ and $n = 0$,
(ii) y when $x = 8$ and $n = -\frac{4}{3}$,
(iii) x when $y = 8$ and $n = -\frac{2}{3}$,
(iv) n when $x = 8$ and $y = 64$.

(b) Rearrange the formula to give x in terms of y and n.

4 In an experiment on the growth of bacteria, a scientist finds the rule $N = B \times 25^t$, where N is the number of bacteria after t hours.

(a) What does B represent in this rule?

At the start of one experiment there are five bacteria.

(b) How many bacteria are there after 30 minutes?
(c) How long does it take for the number of bacteria to grow to 625?

5 R_t is the radioactivity of an isotope after t years.
It is given by $R_t = R_0 \times 0.81^t$
where R_0 is the radioactivity when $t = 0$.

(a) Does R_t increase or decrease with time?
How can you tell from the formula?

(b) Calculate the percentage change in R_t
(i) between $t = 0$ and $t = 0.5$,
(ii) between $t = 0.5$ and $t = 1$,
(iii) between $t = 1$ and $t = 1.5$,
Can you explain your answers?

What you need to know

- **Index notation**

  An expression such as $a \times a \times a \times a \times a$ can be written in a shorthand way as a^5.

  This is read as "a to the power 5".

  a is the **base** of the expression, 5 is the **power** or **index**.

  The inverse of raising to a power is finding a **root**.

- **The rules of indices**

Multiplying powers with the same base	$a^m \times a^n = a^{m+n}$
Dividing powers with the same base	$a^m \div a^n = a^{m-n}$
Raising a power to a power	$(a^m)^n = a^{mn}$
Raising any number to the power zero	$a^0 = 1$ (also $a^1 = a$)
Negative powers and reciprocals	$a^{-m} = \dfrac{1}{a^m}$ a^{-m} is the reciprocal of a^m
Fractional powers and roots	$a^{\frac{1}{n}} = \sqrt[n]{a}$ and $a^{\frac{m}{n}} = \left(a^{\frac{1}{n}}\right)^m = \left(\sqrt[n]{a}\right)^m$

- **Products of prime factors**

  Prime factors are the factors of the number which are themselves prime numbers.

  Powers can be used to help write any number as the product of prime factors.

  The **lowest common multiple** of two numbers is the smallest number that is a multiple of both numbers.

  The **highest common factor** of two numbers is the highest number that is a factor of both numbers.

- **Standard index form** (or **standard form**)

  Numbers in **standard form** use the powers of 10 to write very large and very small numbers in shorthand form.

  > In **standard form** a number is written as:
  > $A \times 10^n$ where $1 \leq A < 10$ and n is an integer.
  > For large numbers, greater than 10, n is **positive**.
  > For small positive numbers, less than 1, n is **negative**.

- **On a scientific calculator** …

  powers can be calculated using the $\boxed{x^y}$ button,

  reciprocals can calculated using the $\boxed{x^{-1}}$ button,

  numbers can be entered in **standard form** using the $\boxed{\text{Exp}}$ button,

  roots can be calculated using the $\boxed{x^{1/y}}$ button.

You should be able to …

- express numbers as products of prime factors,

- find highest common factors and lowest common multiples,

- calculate in standard form both with and without a calculator,

- solve problems with numbers given in standard form,

- use the rules of powers to evaluate numerical expressions involving powers,

- simplify both numerical and algebraic expressions involving powers,

- use the rules of powers to handle equations and formula that involve powers.

54

1 12 written as the product of its prime factors is $2^2 \times 3$.

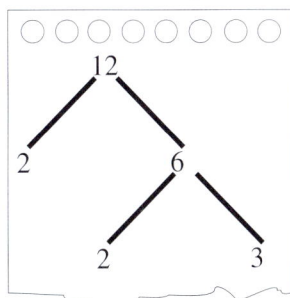

12 has 6 factors.
1, 2, 3, 4, 6, 12.

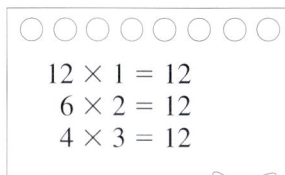

$12 \times 1 = 12$
$6 \times 2 = 12$
$4 \times 3 = 12$

Find the number of factors of some more numbers of the form $a^2 \times b$ where a and b are prime numbers.
What do you notice?

Investigate the number of factors of other numbers with just two prime factors.
What about numbers with any number of prime factors?

2 The squares and cubes of whole numbers can be written as the sum of consecutive odd numbers.

$1^2 = 1$
$2^2 = 1 + 3$
$3^2 = 1 + 3 + 5$

$1^3 = 1$
$2^3 = 3 + 5$
$3^3 = 7 + 9 + 11$

Continue these patterns.
Can you find general rules for n^2 and n^3?

Investigate the connection between other powers and the sum of consecutive odd numbers.

Review Exercise

Questions 1 to 8.
Do not use a calculator.

1 Find x in each of the following.
   (a) $2^x = 128$
   (b) $6^x = 1296$
   (c) $8^x = 1$
   (d) $0.2^x = 0.008$
   (e) $5 \times 3^x = 45$
   (f) $7 \times 2^x = 112$

2 Find x in each of the following.
   (a) $5^3 \times 5^2 = 5^x$
   (b) $2^5 \div 2^4 = 2^x$
   (c) $(5^2)^3 = 5^x$
   (d) $(7^3)^2 = 7^x$

3 (a) Write as a product of prime factors
      (i) 126   (ii) 90   (iii) 210
   (b) What is the smallest number that has both 90 and 210 as factors?
   (c) What is the highest common factor of 90 and 126?

4 (a) Find the value of p when $2^p \times 3 = 24$.
   (b) Write 56 as the product of prime factors.
   (c) A blue light flashes every 24 seconds and a red light flashes every 56 seconds. The two lights flash at the same time. After how many seconds will the lights next flash at the same time?

5 A number of counters can be grouped exactly into 5's, 6's and 9's.
Find the smallest possible number of counters.

6 (a) Write $2^{-2} \times 4$ as a single power of 2.
   (b) Write $2^3 \div \frac{1}{8}$ as a single power of 2.
   SEG 1998

7 (a) A lorry weighs 3.2×10^4 kg. A double decker bus weighs 6.4×10^3 kg. How many buses weigh the same as a lorry?
   (b) A stamp weighs 3×10^{-5} kg. A speck of dust weighs 1.5×10^{-7} kg. How many specks of dust weigh the same as a stamp?
   SEG 1995

8 (a) (i) Calculate the value of $(3 \times 10^{-4}) \times (7 \times 10^6)$. Give your answer in standard form.
      (ii) Give your answer to part (i) as a product of prime factors.
   (b) Write down the smallest value of n so that $(7 \times 10^6)^n$ is divisible by 5^{12}.
   SEG 1996

Questions 9 to 14.
You may use a calculator.

9 A number n, expressed in terms of its prime factors, is $2^6 \times 3^4 \times 11$.
  (a) Find the value of n,
  (b) Express $8n$ as a product of prime factors.
  (c) Find the value of $8n$, giving your answer in standard form.
                  SEG 1995

10 A packet of paper contains 5×10^2 sheets.
The packet is 4.8cm thick.

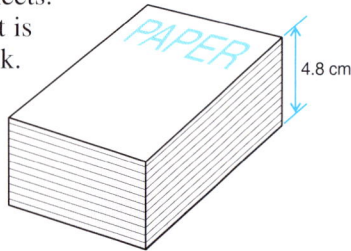

  (a) Work out the thickness of **one** sheet of paper in centimetres giving your answer in standard form.
  (b) A magazine is made from 36 sheets of paper.
     The number of magazines printed is 3.3×10^6.

    (i) Calculate how many sheets of paper are needed to print these magazines.
       Give your answer in **standard form.**
    (ii) If all the magazines were piled up on top of each other, how high would the pile be?
               SEG 1995

11 The planet Pluto is 5.914×10^9 km from the Sun.
The Earth is 1.496×10^9 km the Sun.
A model of the solar system uses a scale of 1 m to represent 2×10^8 km.
In the model, how much further is Pluto from the sun than the Earth is from the Sun?
               SEG 1998

12 An electron weighs 9.109×10^{-28} grams.
A proton weighs the same as 1836 electrons.
Calculate the weight of a proton.
Write your answer in standard form.
               SEG 1997

13 Calculate the value of each of these expressions.
  (a) $2^5 \times 3^8 + 5^0$
  (b) $2.5^5 \times (2.5^4 + 2.5^{-2})$
               SEG 1997

14 (a) (i) Evaluate 30^4.
    (ii) Give your answer to part (a) (i) in standard form.
    (iii) Evaluate $64^{\frac{1}{3}}$
  (b) Hence express $30^4 \times 64^{\frac{1}{3}}$ in standard form.
               SEG 1994

Questions 15 to 20.
Answer the questions without using a calculator.
Use a calculator to check your answers.

15 Evaluate: (a) $16^{\frac{1}{4}}$, (b) 2^{-4}, (c) $27^{-\frac{1}{3}}$
               SEG 1994

16 (a) Find the value of w in $2^w = 1$
  (b) Find the value of x in $2^x = \frac{1}{4}$
  (c) Find the value of y in $32^y = 2$
  (d) Find the value of z in $16^{z+3} = 2^z$
               SEG 1999

17 (a) Simplify the following
    (i) $x^{-5} \times x^2$, (ii) $(36x^{16})^{\frac{1}{2}}$,
    (iii) $3^a \times 3^{-b}$.
  (b) Express using index notation $\left(\sqrt{a}\right)^3$.
               SEG 1996

18 Find the value of each of the following.
  (a) $27^{\frac{2}{3}}$ (b) $25^{-\frac{3}{2}}$ (c) $81^{-\frac{3}{4}}$

19 You are given the equation $y = 5x^n$.
  (a) Find the value of y when $x = -4$ and $n = 0$.
  (b) Find the value of n when $y = 10$ and $x = 4$.
  (c) Rearrange the formula to express x in terms of y and n.
               SEG 1998

20 You are given that $y = ax^b$.
When $x = 1$, $y = 10$ and when $x = 8$, $y = 40$.
Find the values of a and b.

CHAPTER 5

Direct and Inverse Proportion

Activity

A car travels at constant speed.
The table shows the relationship between the time travelled, t, and the distance covered, d.

t (hours)	1	2	3	r	9	10
d (km)	50	p	q	300	450	s

(a) Find the values of p, q, r and s.
(b) What happens to d when t doubles?
What happens to d when t trebles?
(c) Copy and complete the table of ratios $d : t$.
Write each ratio in its simplest form.
(d) Compare the ratios:
    (i)   1 : 9 with 50 : 450,
    (ii) 2 : 3 with $p : q$,
    (iii) r : 10 with 300 : s.
What do you notice?
(e) Write down an equation connecting d and t.

Remember

$$\text{Speed} = \frac{\text{Distance}}{\text{Time}}$$

t	$d : t$		
1	50 : 1	=	50 : 1
2	p : 2	=	
3	q : 3	=	
r	300 : r	=	
9	450 : 9	=	

Direct proportion

If x and y are quantities such that $y : x$ is always constant, then y is said to vary **directly** with x.

In this table, $y : x$ in its simplest form is always 5 : 8.

x	16	32	80	96	160	800
y	10	20	50	60	100	500

So y **varies directly** with x.
This can be expressed in words as:
    y is **proportional** to x
and expressed in symbols as:
    $y \propto x$
where $\propto$ means "is proportional to".
The relationship between x and y can also be expressed as an equation.
    $y = kx$
where k is the **constant of proportionality**.
This equation can be rearranged to make k the subject of the formula.
    $k = \dfrac{y}{x}$

Look at the table of values of x and y:
What happens to y when x is doubled?
What happens to y when x is trebled?
What happens to y when x is multiplied by 10?

Remember
A ratio in its **simplest form** has only whole numbers that have no common factor other than 1.
To **simplify a ratio** divide each part of the ratio by the highest common factor of the numbers.
Equivalent ratios can be found by multiplying, or dividing, each part of the ratio by the **same** number.

Finding k
Corresponding values of the proportional quantities can be used to find the value of k.
From the table:
When $x = 16$, $y = 10$.
Substitute these values into the equation $y = kx$.
$10 = k \times 16$
Divide both sides by 16.
$k = 0.625$
The equation connecting x and y is $y = 0.625x$.

When two quantities are in direct proportion, as one quantity increases the other quantity **increases** at the **same rate**.

Examples of quantities in direct proportion are:

When a vehicle travels at constant speed … distance travelled (d) is proportional to time taken (t).

$$d \alpha t \qquad d = kt$$

For any circle … circumference (C) is proportional to radius (r).

$$C \alpha r \qquad C = kr$$

What is the constant of proportionality, k, in each of these examples?

EXAMPLES

1 The table shows values of x and y where y is proportional to x.
(a) Find an equation expressing y in terms of x.
(b) Find the values of a and b.

x	2	4.2	b
y	1.2	a	14.4

(a) $y \alpha x$
So $y = kx$
From the table:
When $x = 2$, $y = 1.2$
$1.2 = k \times 2$
Divide both sides by 2.
$k = 0.6$
The equation connecting x and y is $y = 0.6x$.

(b) $y = 0.6x$
When $x = 4.2$, $y = a$
$a = 0.6 \times 4.2$
$a = 2.52$

$y = 0.6x$
When $x = b$, $y = 14.4$
$14.4 = 0.6 \times b$
$b = \dfrac{14.4}{0.6} = 24$

Use corresponding values of the proportional quantities to find the constant of proportionality, k.
Then substitute known values into the equation connecting y and x to find the unknown values.

2 The age of a tree, A years, is proportional to the radius of its trunk, r mm.
When the tree is 5 years old the radius of its trunk is 22 mm.
(a) Find a formula connecting A and r.
(b) Find A when $r = 242$.
(c) Find r when $A = 80$.

(a) You are given that $A \alpha r$.
So $A = kr$
When $A = 5$ years, $r = 22$ mm.
$5 = k \times 22$
Divide both sides by 22.
$k = \frac{5}{22}$
The formula connecting A and r is $A = \frac{5}{22} r$.

(b) $A = \frac{5}{22} r$
When $r = 242$
$A = \frac{5}{22} \times 242$
$A = 55$

(c) $A = \frac{5}{22} r$
When $A = 80$
$80 = \frac{5}{22} \times r$
$A = 352$

3 The table shows values of l and m.

l	5	8	12.3
m	1.3	2.08	3.198

Show that m is proportional to l.

If $m \alpha l$ then each ratio $m : l$ is equivalent.
$1.3 \div 5 = 0.26$
$2.08 \div 8 = 0.26$
$3.198 \div 12.3 = 0.26$
So $m : l$ is always equivalent to $1 : 0.26$.
So $m = 0.26 \times l$ which also means $m \alpha l$.

4 The table shows values of p and q where p is proportional to q.

p	a	b
q	8	12

What is the ratio of $a : b$?

Ratios of values of p are equivalent to ratios of corresponding values of q.

$a : b = 8 : 12$
$a : b = 2 : 3$

Do not use a calculator.

1

a	2	5	10	30	50
b	5	12.5	25	75	125

c	4	8	20	60	200
d	0.2	0.4	1	3	10

e	10	25	40	55	70
f	2	3.5	5	6.5	8

g	10	20	40	60	80
h	0.35	0.7	1.4	2.1	2.8

Which of the following statements are true?
(a) $b \propto a$ (b) $d \propto c$
(c) $f \propto e$ (d) $h \propto g$
Give a reason for each answer.

2 In this table $w \propto x$, $x \propto y$ and $y \propto z$.

w	0.5	2	5	10	50
x	1.5				
y	0.45				
z	0.99				

(a) Copy and complete the table.
(b) Check whether or not:
   (i) $w \propto y$ (ii) $w \propto z$ (iii) $x \propto z$
   Give a reason for each answer.
(c) Find the constant of proportionality for each pair of proportional quantities.

3 In this table p varies directly with q.

p	1	a	12	c	70
q	5	10	b	40	d

(a) Find, in their simplest form, the following ratios.
   (i) $1 : a$ (ii) $c : 40$ (iii) $b : d$
(b) Calculate the values of a, b, c and d.

4 In this table p is proportional to q.

p	4	12	b
q	2.5	a	20

(a) Find an equation connecting p and q.
(b) Find the values of a and b.

5 In this table $y \propto x$.

x	25	100	b
y	1.25	a	20

(a) Find an equation expressing y in terms of x.
(b) Find the values of a and b.

6 The cost, £C, of building a wall is proportional to its area, $A \, \mathrm{m}^2$.
A wall of area $20 \, \mathrm{m}^2$ costs £210.
(a) Find a formula giving C in terms of A.
(b) Find the cost of a wall of area $55 \, \mathrm{m}^2$.
(c) A wall of height $1.6 \, \mathrm{m}$ costs £1155.
   How long is the wall?

7 The distance travelled by a fixed wheel bicycle, d, is proportional to n, the number of times the pedal rotates.
In a journey of $400 \, \mathrm{m}$ the pedal rotates 80 times.
(a) Find an equation expressing d in terms of n.
(b) How far does the bicycle travel if the pedal rotates 200 times?
(c) How many times does the pedal rotate if the bicycle travels $3 \, \mathrm{km}$?

8 (a) The extension, e, of a spring is proportional to w, the weight hung on the spring.
   When $w = 2 \, \mathrm{kg}$, $e = 60 \, \mathrm{mm}$.
   (i) Find an equation expressing e in terms of w.
   (ii) Find e when $w = 5.3 \, \mathrm{kg}$.
   (iii) Find w when $e = 96.6 \, \mathrm{mm}$.
(b) The extension of another spring is also proportional to the weight hung on it.
   Weights of $2.5 \, \mathrm{kg}$ and $8 \, \mathrm{kg}$ are hung on this spring and the extensions measured.
   What is the ratio of these two extensions in its simplest form.

Activity

Five cars travel the same distance.
The table shows the time taken, t, for different speeds, s.

(a) Find the values of a, b and c.
(b) What happens to s when t doubles?
    What happens to s when t trebles?
(c) Copy and complete the table of ratios $s : \frac{1}{t}$.
    Write each ratio in its simplest form.
(d) Compare the ratios:
    (i) $2 : 3$ with $150 : a$,
    (ii) $3 : 4$ with $a : b$.
    What do you notice?
(e) Write down an equation connecting s and t.

t		$s : \frac{1}{t}$	
2	$150 : \frac{1}{2}$	$=$	$300 : 1$
3	$a : \frac{1}{3}$	$=$	
4	$b : \frac{1}{4}$	$=$	

t (hours)	2	3	4	c
s (km/hours)	150	a	b	50

Remember
Distance $=$ Speed $\times$ Time

Inverse proportion

If x and y are quantities such that $y : \frac{1}{x}$ is always constant, then y varies directly with $\frac{1}{x}$.
y is also said to vary **inversely** with x.

In this table, $y : \frac{1}{x}$ in its simplest form is always $1 : 60$.

x	1	2	5	10	12	15
y	60	30	12	6	5	4

So y **varies directly** with $\frac{1}{x}$.

This can be expressed in words as:
    y is proportional to the reciprocal of x
or
    y is **inversely proportional** to x
and expressed in symbols as:
$$y \, \alpha \, \frac{1}{x}$$
The relationship between x and y can also be expressed as an equation.
$$y = \frac{k}{x} \quad \text{or} \quad xy = k$$
where k is the **constant of proportionality**.

Look at the table of values of x and y:
    What happens to y when x is doubled?
    What happens to y when x is trebled?
    What happens to y when x is multiplied by 6?

Finding k
Corresponding values of the proportional quantities can be used to find the value of k.
From the table:
When $x = 1$, $y = 60$.
Substitute these values into the equation $y = kx$.
$60 = k \times 1$
$k = 60$
The equation connecting x and y is $y = \frac{60}{x}$.

This equation can also be written as $xy = 60$.
Using these equations, known values can be substituted to calculate unknown values.

When two quantities are in inverse proportion, as one quantity increases the other quantity **decreases** at the **same rate**.

Examples of quantities in inverse proportion are:

For cars travelling the same distance …
average speed (s) is inversely proportional to time taken (t).
$$s \, \alpha \, \frac{1}{t} \qquad st = k$$

For rectangles of constant area …
length (l) is inversely proportional to width (w).
$$l \, \alpha \, \frac{1}{w} \qquad lw = k$$

EXAMPLES

1 The table shows values of p and q.

p	2	10	50
q	0.25	0.05	0.01

(a) Show that q is inversely proportional to p.
(b) Express q in terms of p.

(a) If q is inversely proportional to p then pq is constant.
$2 \times 0.25 = 10 \times 0.05 = 50 \times 0.01 = 0.5$
So q is inversely proportional to p.

(b) $q \alpha \dfrac{1}{p}$ so $q = k \times \dfrac{1}{p}$ and $pq = k$
From (a) $k = 0.5$. So $q = \dfrac{0.5}{p}$

2 In this table y is inversely proportional to x.

x	5	a
y	12.5	1.25

Express y in terms of x and find the value of a.

$y \alpha \dfrac{1}{x}$ so $y = \dfrac{k}{x}$ and $xy = k$
When $x = 5$, $y = 12.5$.
$k = 5 \times 12.5 = 62.5$
which gives $y = \dfrac{62.5}{x}$
When $x = a$, $y = 1.25$.
$1.25 = 62.5 \div a$
$a = 62.5 \div 1.25$
$a = 50$

Exercise 5.2

Do not use a calculator.

1

a	2	2.5	4	5	10
b	5	4	2.5	2	1

c	6	12	30	90	300
d	0.2	0.4	1	3	10

e	1	2	4	8	10
f	1.6	0.8	0.4	0.2	0.16

g	1	2	3	4	5
h	30	15	10	7.5	6

Which of the following statements are true?
(a) (i) $b \alpha a$ (ii) $b \alpha \dfrac{1}{a}$
(b) (i) d varies directly with c.
  (ii) d varies inversely with c.
(c) (i) e is proportional to f.
  (ii) e is inversely proportional to f.
(d) (i) h and g are directly proportional.
  (ii) h and g are inversely proportional.
Give a reason for each answer.

2 Copy and complete each of the following tables for the relationship given.
(a) $b \alpha a$

a	2	5	10	25	50
b	10				

(b) $b \alpha \dfrac{1}{a}$

a	2	5	10	25	50
b	10				

(c) $q \alpha p$

p	2	5	10	25	50
q				0.5	

(d) $q \alpha \dfrac{1}{p}$

p	2	5	10	25	50
q				0.5	

Find the constant of proportionality for each table.

3 In this table y is inversely proportional to x.

x	5	12	b
y	9.6	a	0.5

(a) Find an equation connecting x and y.
(b) Find the values of a and b.

61

4 In this table M varies inversely with L.

L	8	12	b
M	1.8	a	0.9

(a) Find an equation connecting L and M.

(b) Find the values of a and b.

5 (a) y is inversely proportional to x.
$y = 12$ when $x = 3$.
Find y when $x = 4$.

(b) s is inversely proportional to r.
$s = 20$ when $r = 5$.
Find r when $s = 4$.

6 The length of a rectangle, l, of constant area is inversely proportional to its width, w.
When $l = 20$ cm, $w = 10$ cm.
Find an equation expressing l in terms of w.
Find the value of the constant of proportionality.
What does it represent?

7 A building contractor uses teams of workers to build sheds.
The time, t, for a team to build one shed is inversely proportional to the number of workers, n, in the team.
A team of 2 take 6 days to build one shed.
(a) Find an equation expressing t in terms of n.
(b) Find the time it takes a team of 6 to build one shed.
(c) A team builds a shed in 4 days. How many workers are in the team?

Other forms of proportion

This section deals with direct and inverse proportion involving powers.

EXAMPLE

1 When $x = 4$, $y = 8$.
Find an equation for y in terms of x if:
(a) y is inversely proportional to x,
(b) y is proportional to x^2,
(c) y is inversely proportional to x^2,
(d) y is inversely proportional to x^3,
(e) y is proportional to the square root of x.

(a) $y \propto \dfrac{1}{x}$ so $y = \dfrac{k}{x}$

When $x = 4$, $y = 8$.

$8 = \dfrac{k}{4}$ which gives $k = 32$.

$y = \dfrac{32}{x}$ or $xy = 32$

(b) $y \propto x^2$ so $y = kx^2$

When $x = 4$, $y = 8$.

$8 = k \times 4^2$ which gives $k = \dfrac{1}{2}$.

$y = \dfrac{1}{2}x^2$

(c) $y \propto \dfrac{1}{x^2}$ so $y = \dfrac{k}{x^2}$

When $x = 4$, $y = 8$.

$8 = \dfrac{k}{4^2}$

$8 = \dfrac{k}{16}$ which gives $k = 128$.

$y = \dfrac{128}{x^2}$ or $x^2 y = 128$

(d) $y \propto \dfrac{1}{x^3}$ so $y = \dfrac{k}{x^3}$

When $x = 4$, $y = 8$.

$8 = \dfrac{k}{4^3}$

$8 = \dfrac{k}{64}$ which gives $k = 512$.

$y = \dfrac{512}{x^3}$ or $x^3 y = 512$

(e) $y \propto \sqrt{x}$ so $y = k\sqrt{x}$

When $x = 4$, $y = 8$.

$8 = k\sqrt{4}$

$8 = 2k$ which gives $k = 4$.

$y = 4\sqrt{x}$

2 This table shows values of p and q where q is proportional to p^3.
Calculate A and B.

p	2	5	B
q	16	A	54

Method 1

Find the equation connecting p and q.

$q \propto p^3$ so $q = kp^3$

When $p = 2$, $q = 16$.

$16 = k \times 2^3$

This gives $k = 2$.

So $q = 2p^3$

When $p = 5$, $q = A$.

$A = 2 \times 5^3$

$A = 250$

When $p = B$, $q = 54$.

$54 = 2 \times B^3$

$B^3 = 27$

$B = 3$

Method 2

The ratio $q : p^3$ is always the same.

$16 : 2^3 = A : 5^3 = 54 : B^3$

$16 : 2^3 = 16 : 8 = 2 : 1$

So $A : 5^3 = 2 : 1$

$A : 125 = 2 : 1$

$250 : 125 = 2 : 1$

So $A = 250$

Also $54 : B^3 = 2 : 1$

$54 : 27 = 2 : 1$

So $B^3 = 27$

and $B = 3$.

3 A magnet is at a distance, x cm, from a metal object.
The force, F Newtons, exerted by the magnet on the metal object is inversely proportional to the square of x.
When $x = 10$, $F = 2$.

(a) Find an equation expressing F in terms of x.

(b) Find F when $x = 20$.

(c) Find x when $F = 8$.

(a) $F \propto \dfrac{1}{x^2}$ so $F = \dfrac{k}{x^2}$

When $x = 10$, $F = 2$.

$2 = \dfrac{k}{10^2}$

$k = 10^2 \times 2$ which gives $k = 200$.

$F = \dfrac{200}{x^2}$ or $Fx^2 = 200$

(b) When $x = 20$. $F = \dfrac{200}{20^2} = 0.5$

(c) When $F = 8$. $8 = \dfrac{200}{x^2}$

$x^2 = \dfrac{200}{8} = 25$

$x = 5$

4 The time taken, t seconds, for a skier to slide from rest down a ski slope is proportional to the square root of the distance travelled, d metres.
When $d = 100$, $t = 16$.

(a) Find an equation for t in terms of d.

(b) Find the ratio of the values of t when $d = 100$ and $d = 25$.

(a) $t \propto \sqrt{d}$ so $t = k\sqrt{d}$

When $d = 100$, $t = 16$.

$16 = k \times \sqrt{100} = k \times 10$

$k = 16 \div 10 = 1.6$

$t = 1.6\sqrt{d}$

(b) When $d = 100$, $t = 16$.

When $d = 25$.

$t = 1.6 \times \sqrt{25} = 1.6 \times 5$

$t = 8$

The required ratio is $16 : 8$ which in its simplest form is $2 : 1$.

Use a calculator in this exercise.

1 Write each of the following statements in words.

(a) $V \alpha t^2$ (b) $L \alpha \dfrac{1}{a}$ (c) $y \alpha x^3$

(d) $p \alpha \dfrac{1}{q^2}$ (e) $L \alpha \sqrt{m}$ (f) $b \alpha \dfrac{1}{c^3}$

2 y is proportional to the square of x.
(a) What happens to y when x is doubled?
(b) y is multiplied by 25. What happens to x?

3 y is inversely proportional to the square of x.
(a) What happens to y when x is doubled?
(b) y is multiplied by 25. What happens to x?

4 The radius, r, of a cone of fixed volume is inversely proportional to the square root of its height, h.
(a) r is doubled. What happens to h?
(b) h is multiplied by 16. What happens to r?

5 y is proportional to the cube of x. The constant of proportionality is k.
(a) Write an equation for y in terms of x.
(b) Find the ratio of the values of y when $x = 1$ and $x = 4$.
(c) Find the ratio of the values of x when $y = 8$ and $y = 15.625$. Write the ratio in its simplest form.

6 y is proportional to the square root of x. The constant of proportionality is k.
(a) Write an equation for y in terms of x.
(b) Find the ratio of the values of y when $x = 0.25$ and $x = 4$. Write the ratio in its simplest form.

7 y is inversely proportional to the square of x. The constant of proportionality is k.
(a) Write an equation for y in terms of x.
(b) Find the ratio of the values of y when $x = 0.1$ and $x = 0.5$. Write the ratio in its simplest form.
(c) Find the ratio of the values of x when $y = 9$ and $y = 6.25$. Write the ratio in its simplest form.

8 Use the information given to find an equation connecting each of the following pairs of variables.
(a) V is proportional to the square of t. $V = 45$ when $t = 3$.
(b) R is inversely proportional to the cube of s. $R = 5$ when $s = 4$.
(c) y is proportional to the square root of x. $y = 40$ when $x = 16$.
(d) A is inversely proportional to b. $A = 20$ when $b = 5$.
(e) L is proportional to the cube of p. $L = 25$ when $p = 2$.
(f) Q is proportional to the square root of P. $Q = 100$ when $P = 64$.

9 y is inversely proportional to the square of x.
When $x = 2$, $y = 20$.
(a) Find the constant of proportionality.
(b) Find y when $x = 4$.
(c) Find x when $y = 5$.

10 Copy and complete each of the following tables for the relationships given.

(a) $b \alpha a^2$

a	1	2	4	10
b	3			

(b) $b \alpha \dfrac{1}{a^2}$

a	1	2	4	10
b	10			

(c) $b \alpha \dfrac{1}{a}$

a	1	2	4	10
b	10			

(d) $b \alpha a^3$

a	1	2	4	10
b	0.5			

(e) $b \alpha \dfrac{1}{\sqrt{a}}$

a	1	2	4	10
b	0.2			

11 (a) $y = \dfrac{k}{x^2}$.

When $x = 2$, $y = 0.4$.
  (i) Find the value of k.
  (ii) Find y when $x = 10$.

(b) $y = k\sqrt{x}$.

When $x = 0.16$, $y = 4$.
  (i) Find the value of k.
  (ii) Find x when $y = 40$.

12 The height, h m, that a stone reaches when it is thrown upwards varies directly with the square of its initial speed, s metres per second.

When $s = 10$, $h = 5$.
  (a) Find a formula expressing h in terms of s.
  (b) Calculate s when $h = 20$.
  (c) Calculate h when $s = 50$.

Two stones are thrown upwards.
The ratio of their maximum heights is $9 : 4$.
  (d) What is the ratio of their initial speeds?

13 y is proportional to the cube of x.
When $x = 10$, $y = 1$.
  (a) Find the constant of proportionality.
  (b) Find y when $x = 20$.
  (c) Find x when $y = 5$.

14 For each part of this question find an equation connecting the variables p and q. Also find the values of the letters a to f.
  (a) q varies inversely with the square of p.

p	4	10	b
q	2.5	a	0.1

  (b) q varies inversely with the cube of p.

p	4	10	d
q	2.5	c	20

  (c) q varies with the square of p.

p	4	10	f
q	2.5	e	10

15 y is inversely proportional to x.
z is proportional to the cube of y.
When $x = 4$, $y = 2$ and
when $y = 2$, $z = 10$.
Express z in terms of x.

16 y^3 is inversely proportional to x^2.
When $x = 8$, $y = 2$.
Calculate y when $x = 125$.

17 In cylinders of equal volume, the radius, r cm, is inversely proportional to the square root of the height, h cm.
When $h = 4$, $r = 8$.
  (a) Find h when $r = 4$.
  (b) What does the constant of proportionality represent?

18 A simple pendulum of length l cm, takes t seconds to swing from A to B.

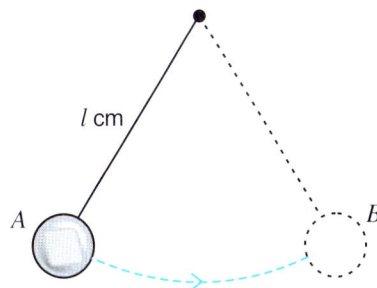

t is proportional to the square root of l.
When $t = 34$ seconds, $l = 72.25$ cm.
  (a) Express t in terms of l.
  (b) Find t when $l = 400$.
  (a) Find l when $t = 60$.

19 The weight of an object, W kg, is inversely proportional to the square of the distance of the object from the centre of the Earth, d km.
The radius of the Earth is 6400 km.
  (a) Mount Everest is 8846 m high. On the Earth's surface a mountaineer weighs 70.2 kg. How much does the mountaineer weigh on top of Mount Everest?
  (b) In a space station an astronaut weighs 58.7 kg. On the Earth's surface the astronaut weighs 72.3 kg. How far from the Earth's surface is the space station?

Proportion and graphs

The general form of the relationships dealt with in this chapter is $y \propto x^n$.
Values of $n > 0$ give **direct** proportionality.
Values of $n < 0$ give **inverse** proportionality.

When n is unknown, the graph of y plotted against x can be used to help find its value.

When $n = 1$ $y \propto x$ and $y = kx$.

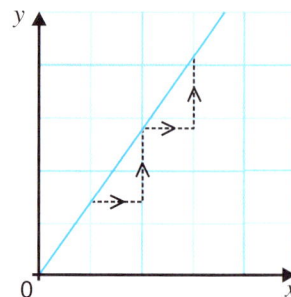

This relationship gives a straight line graph which passes through the origin.

As x increases by a constant amount, y increases by a constant amount.

k, the constant of proportionality, is given by the gradient of the graph.

When $n > 1$.

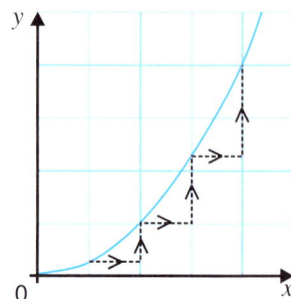

This relationship gives a curved graph which passes through the origin.

As x increases by a constant amount, y increases by amounts that increase.

As k increases the graph gets steeper.

When $0 < n < 1$.

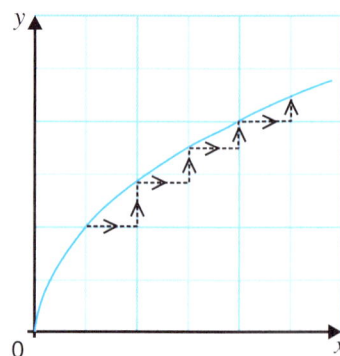

This relationship gives a curved graph which passes through the origin.

As x increases by a constant amount, y increases by amounts that decrease.

As k increases the graph gets steeper.

When $n < 0$.

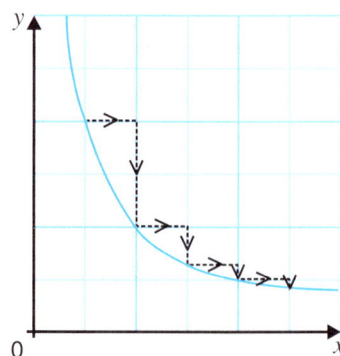

This relationship gives a curved graph, of the form shown.
The graph does not pass through the origin.

As x increases by a constant amount, y decreases by amounts that decrease.

As k increases the graph gets steeper.

1 The relationship 'y is inversely proportional to the square of x' is of the form $y \propto x^n$.
Find the value of n.

$$y \propto \frac{1}{x^2}$$

$$\frac{1}{x^2} = x^{-2} \quad \text{so} \quad y \propto x^{-2} \quad \text{and} \quad n = -2.$$

2 Use this table of values of x and y to find a formula connecting x and y where $y \propto x^n$.

x	1	2	4
y	12	3	0.75

Plot the points and sketch the graph.
$y \propto x^n \qquad$ so $\qquad y = kx^n$

> *How can you tell that both the graph and the table show inverse proportionality?*

Try $n = -1$.
This gives $k = xy$.

x	1	2	4
k	12	6	3

k is not constant so $n \neq -1$.

Try $n = -2$.
This gives $k = x^2 y$

x	1	2	4
k	12	12	12

k is constant.
So $k = 12$, $n = -2$ and $y = 12x^{-2}$.

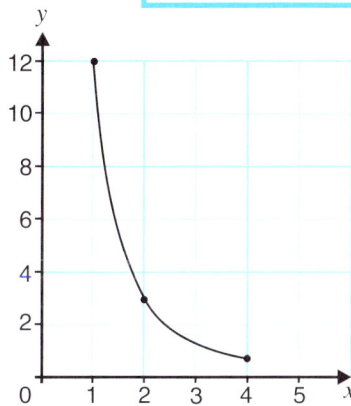

Alternative Method
$y = kx^n$
When $x = 1$, $y = 12$.
$\qquad 12 = k \times 1^n$ and $k = 12$.
So $\qquad y = 12 \times x^n$
When $x = 2$, $y = 3$.
$\qquad 3 = 12 \times 2^n$
Dividing both sides by 12.
$\qquad 0.25 = 2^n$
This gives $n = -2$.

Exercise 5.4

You may use a calculator.

1 (a) What is the value of n when $y \propto x^n$ and:
  (i) y varies directly with the cube of x,
  (ii) y varies inversely with x,
  (iii) y varies inversely with the square root of x?

In each of the relationships in (a) the constant of proportionality is 10.
  (b) Draw the graph of each relationship for positive values of x.
  (c) What happens to your graphs in (b):
  (i) when $k < 10$,
  (ii) when $k > 10$?

2 The graph of the relationship $y \propto x^n$ passes through the points $(0, 0)$, $(1, 0.25)$ and $(4, 4)$.
  (a) Find the value of n.
  (b) Find the constant of proportionality.
Repeat for a graph passing through the points $(1, 10)$, $(2, 2.5)$ and $(5, 0.4)$.

3 Use this table of values of p and q to find a formula connecting p and q where $q \propto p^n$.

p	1	2	5
q	0.2	1.6	25

4 Use this table of values of s and t to find a formula connecting s and t where $s \propto t^n$.

t	1	4	25
s	20	10	4

5 Match each graph to a relationship.

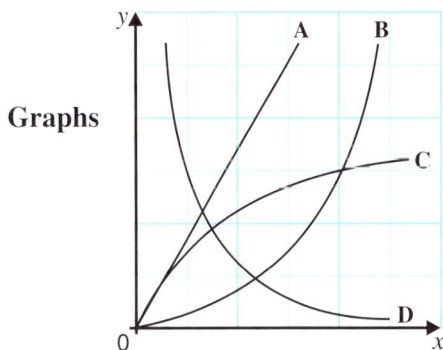

Graphs

Relationships

(a) y varies directly with the square of x.
(b) y varies directly with x.
(c) y varies inversely with the cube of x.
(d) y varies directly with the square root of x.

What you need to know

- **Direct proportion**
  If x and y are quantities such that $y : x^n$ is always constant, then:

  y varies **directly** with x^n,

  y is **proportional** to x^n,

  $y \propto x^n$,

  $y = kx^n$,

  $\dfrac{y}{x^n} = k$.

> The symbol α means 'is proportional to'. k is the constant of proportionality. k can be evaluated when corresponding values of x and y are known.

  The general form of a proportional relationship is $y \propto x^n$ or $y = kx^n$.
  The precise form depends on the value of n.

  Direct proportion, $n > 0$
  The graphical forms of $y = kx^n$ for direct proportion are illustrated below.

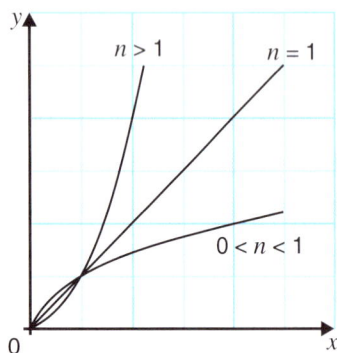

  As x increases at a constant rate:
  When $n = 1$:
  y increases at a constant rate.
  When $0 < n < 1$:
  y increases at rate that decreases.
  When $n > 1$:
  y increases at a rate that increases.

> When two quantities, x and x^n, are in direct proportion, as x increases x^n **increases** at the **same rate.**

- **Inverse proportion**
  If x and y are quantities such that $y : \dfrac{1}{x^n}$ is always constant, then:

  y varies **inversely** with x^n,

  y is **inversely proportional** to x^n,

  $y \propto \dfrac{1}{x^n}$,

  $y = \dfrac{k}{x^n}$,

  $x^n y = k$.

  Inverse proportion, $n < 0$
  The graphical forms of $y = kx^n$ for inverse proportion are illustrated below.

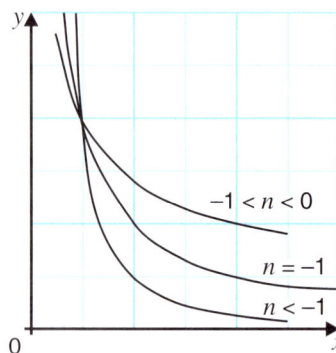

  As x increases at a constant rate:
  For all values of n:
  y decreases at a rate that decreases.
  When $n = -1$:
  the graph is symmetrical about the line $y = x$.

> When two quantities, x and x^n, are in inverse proportion, as x increases x^n **decreases** at the **same rate.**

1 Write each of the following statements in words.
(a) $q \propto p^2$ (b) $A \propto \dfrac{1}{b^3}$ (c) $y \propto x$

2 Describe what happens to y when x is:
(a) doubled, (b) trebled, (c) halved, when:
(i) $y \propto x^2$ (ii) $y \propto \dfrac{1}{x}$
(iii) $y \propto x^3$ (iv) $y \propto x$
(v) $y \propto \sqrt{x}$ (vi) $y \propto \dfrac{1}{x^2}$

3 Copy and complete each of the following tables for the relationships given.
(a) $q \propto p$

p	1	2	4	10
q	3			

(b) $q \propto \dfrac{1}{p}$

p	1	2	4	10
q	10			

(c) $q \propto p^2$

p	1	2	4	10
q	10			

4 The number, N, of square tiles needed to tile a floor varies inversely as the square of the length, L, of the side of the tile.
When $L = 0.4$ m, $N = 2000$.
(a) Find a formula connecting N and L.
(b) Calculate the number of tiles needed when $L = 0.6$ m.
SEG 1998 S

5 Given that y is proportional to x^2, copy and complete the table.

x	5		20
y	45	180	

SEG 1998

6 At constant temperature, the pressure, p, is inversely proportional to the volume, v.
Write this relationship as a mathematical equation.
SEG 1994

7 A man's weight, W, in kilograms is proportional to the square of his height, H metres.
The constant of proportionality is called the body mass index, B.
(a) Write down a formula connecting W, H and B.
(b) Ali is 1.8 m tall and weighs 81 kg.
Stephen is 2 m tall and has the same body mass index as Ali.
What is Stephen's weight?
SEG 1997

8 The increase in speed, V metres per second, at the lowest point of a "Big Dipper" ride is proportional to the square root of the vertical height, h metres, dropped.
(a) Write this relationship in mathematical terms.
(b) Use this relationship to find the ratio of the speeds obtained from heights 100 metres and 25 metres.
SEG 1996

9 The intensity of illumination, I, at a point varies inversely with the square of the distance, x, of the point from the light.
Express this in mathematical terms, and hence determine the ratio of the intensity of illumination produced by a light 8 m from the point, to the same light, 2 m from the point.
SEG 1996

10 In an oil leakage at sea, a circular slick of oil has a radius of 1 km at 0700 hours on the 20th March and a radius of 2 km at 0700 hours on the 21st March.
The area of the oil slick, A, varies with the time, t hours, since the oil first started leaking.
(a) Calculate the time when the oil first started leaking.
An island inhabited by a rare sea bird is 5 km from the centre of the oil slick.
(b) Calculate how long the authorities have to stop the slick reaching the island.

11 As a spherical balloon is inflated its volume varies directly with time.
At time T minutes the balloon has a radius of 24 cm.
4 minutes later the balloon has a radius of 30 cm.
Calculate the value of T and the time at which the radius of the balloon was 12 cm.
Give both answers to the nearest second.

12 The distance of the horizon at sea, d km, is proportional to the square root of the height, h m, of an observer above sea level.
When $h = 20$ m, $d = 16$ km.
(a) Find a formula for d in terms of h.
(b) Calculate the distance of the horizon at sea when an observer is 80 m above sea level.

SEG 1997

13 Two variables N and H are connected so that $N \propto \sqrt{H}$.
(a) Write down a formula connecting N and H and a constant k.
(b) When $N = 6$, $H = 9$.
Use these values to calculate the value of k.
(c) Use your value of k to calculate the value of N when $H = 6.25$.

SEG 1994

14 (a) Sketch each of the following graphs.

Graph 1
The graph passes through the point (0, 0).
As x increases by a constant amount, y increases by a constant amount.

Graph 2
The graph passes through the point (1, 10).
As x increases by a constant amount, y decreases by an amount that decreases.

Graph 3
The graph passes through the point (0, 0).
As x increases by a constant amount, y increases by an amount that increases.

Graph 4
The graph passes through the point (0, 0).
As x increases by a constant amount, y increases by an amount that decreases.

(b) Which of your graphs show inverse proportion?
(c) Give a possible equation for each graph.

15 In an electrical appliance, the power, P watts, is proportional to the square of the current, I amps, flowing through it.
Sketch a graph of P against I.

SEG 1994

16 (a) y varies inversely with the square root of x.
Sketch a graph of y against x.
(b) y is proportional to x^n.
Sketch a graph of y against x when:
(i) $n = -1$,
(ii) $n = 0.5$,
(iii) $n = \frac{2}{3}$.

17 The radius, r, and the value, v, of gold coins were measured and recorded.

r (cm)	0.5	1	1.5	2	2.5
v (£)	250	1000	2250	4000	6250

(a) (i) Which of these graphs represents this information?

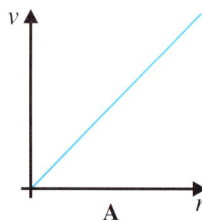

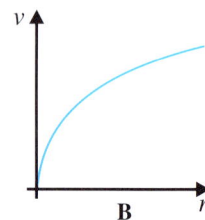

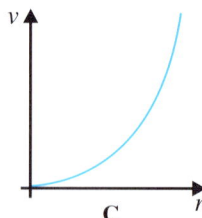

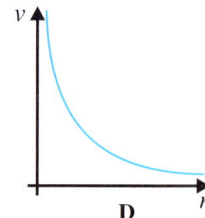

(ii) Which of these equations describes the graph you have chosen?
$$v = k\sqrt{r}$$
$$v = kr$$
$$v = kr^2$$
$$v = \frac{k}{r}$$

(b) Find the equation connecting the radius, r, and the value, v, of the gold coins.

SEG 1998 S

70

CHAPTER 6

Rational and Irrational Numbers

Rational numbers

Numbers which can be written in the form $\frac{a}{b}$, where a and b are integers (b $\neq$ 0) are **rational**. Examples of rational numbers are:

$$2 \qquad -5 \qquad \tfrac{2}{5} \qquad 0.\dot{6} \qquad 3.47 \qquad 1\tfrac{3}{4}$$

$\frac{a}{b}$ is a **proper fraction** if $a < b$.

$\frac{a}{b}$ is an **improper fraction** (top heavy) if $a > b$.

All fractions can be written as decimals.

$\frac{3}{4}$ can be thought of as $3 \div 4$ and is equal to 0.75.

Some decimals have recurring digits. These are shown by:
> a single dot above a single recurring digit,
> a dot above the first and last digit of a set of recurring digits.

For example:

$$\tfrac{1}{3} = 0.3333333 \ldots = 0.\dot{3}$$

$$\tfrac{123}{999} = 0.123123123 \ldots = 0.\dot{1}2\dot{3}$$

$$\tfrac{41}{70} = 0.5857142857142 \ldots = 0.5\dot{8}5714\dot{2}$$

$$\tfrac{3}{11} = 0.27272727\ldots = 0.\dot{2}\dot{7}$$

Changing recurring decimals to fractions

Recurring decimals can be converted to fractions.

Some are well known, such as $0.\dot{3} = \tfrac{1}{3}$ and $0.\dot{6} = \tfrac{2}{3}$.

To convert a recurring decimal to a fraction:

Let $x =$ the recurring decimal.
Multiply both sides by the power of 10 that corresponds to the number of digits in the recurring pattern.

E.g. by $10^1 = 10$ if only 1 digit recurs,
  by $10^2 = 100$ if 2 digits recur,
  by $10^3 = 1000$ if 3 digits recur,
  and so on.

Subtract the original equation from the new equation.

Solve the resulting equation for x.

Make sure that the answer is a fraction in its simplest form.

> **EXAMPLE** Write down the fraction, in its simplest form, which is equal to these recurring decimals.
> (a) $0.\dot{4}$ (b) $0.\dot{5}\dot{7}$ (c) $0.1\dot{2}3\dot{4}$

(a) $x = 0.444 \ldots$
Only 1 digit recurs so multiply both sides by 10.
$10x = 4.444 \ldots$
Subtract the original equation from the new equation.
$9x = 4$
Divide both sides by 9.
$x = \frac{4}{9}$
$0.\dot{4} = \frac{4}{9}$

(b) $x = 0.5757\ldots$
2 digits recur so multiply both sides by 100.
$100x = 57.5757\ldots$
Subtract the original equation from the new equation.
$99x = 57$
Divide both sides by 99.
$x = \frac{57}{99} = \frac{19}{33}$ (in its simplest form)
$0.\dot{5}\dot{7} = \frac{19}{33}$

(c) $x = 0.1234234 \ldots$
3 digits recur so multiply both sides by 1000.
$1000x = 123.4234234 \ldots$
Subtract the original equation from the new equation.
$999x = 123.3$
Divide both sides by 999.
$x = \frac{123.3}{999}$
A fraction should consist of whole numbers.
So multiply numerator and denominator by 10.
$x = \frac{1233}{9990} = \frac{137}{1110}$ (in its simplest form)
$0.1\dot{2}3\dot{4} = \frac{137}{1110}$

Exercise 6.1

1 Convert these recurring decimals to fractions in their simplest form.
   (a) $0.\dot{7}$ (b) $0.\dot{1}$ (c) $0.\dot{8}$ (d) $0.\dot{3}\dot{6}$ (e) $0.\dot{8}\dot{2}$
   (f) $0.\dot{1}3\dot{5}$ (g) $0.\dot{2}1\dot{6}$ (h) $0.\dot{4}2\dot{5}$ (i) $0.\dot{1}6\dot{2}$ (j) $0.\dot{2}8571\dot{4}$

2 Write each of these numbers as a fraction in its simplest form.
   (a) $0.1\dot{6}$ (b) $0.0\dot{3}$ (c) $0.6\dot{1}$ (d) $0.4\dot{6}$ (e) $0.2\dot{3}$
   (f) $0.8\dot{3}$ (g) $0.1\dot{8}\dot{2}$ (h) $0.1\dot{3}\dot{6}$ (i) $0.86\dot{1}$ (j) $0.77\dot{2}\dot{7}$

3 $0.\dot{1}176470588235294\dot{1}$
When the number above is written as a fraction the numerator and denominator are both less than 20. What is the fraction?

4 Look at the decimal expansions for the fractions $\frac{1}{a}$, where $1 < a < 21$ (a is a whole number).
For what values of a does the decimal not recur?
Find a condition so that a fraction with numerator 1 does not recur.

Irrational numbers

Numbers are either **rational** or **irrational**.
An irrational number **cannot** be written as a fraction.
Irrational numbers include:

square roots of non-square numbers,
cube roots of non-cube numbers.

Examples of irrational numbers are:

$$\sqrt{2} \quad \sqrt[3]{7} \quad \pi \quad \sqrt{13}$$

All numbers are either **real** or **imaginary**.
Real numbers are either rational or irrational numbers.
You will meet imaginary numbers, such as $\sqrt{-1}$, if you study Maths beyond GCSE.

EXAMPLES

1 Show that 0.425 and $0.\dot{2}$ are rational numbers.

0.425 is **a terminating decimal**.
$0.425 = \frac{425}{1000} = \frac{17}{40}$

$0.\dot{2}$ is a **recurring decimal.**

$x = 0.222\ldots$
$10x = 2.222\ldots$
$9x = 2$
$x = \frac{2}{9}$
$0.\dot{2} = \frac{2}{9}$

All terminating and recurring decimals can be written in the form $\frac{a}{b}$ so they are all rational numbers.

2 State whether each of the following are rational or irrational numbers.
Where a number is rational write it as a fraction in its simplest form.

$$0.6 \quad \pi \quad \sqrt[3]{7} \quad \sqrt{36}$$

$0.6 = \frac{6}{10} = \frac{3}{5}$ rational

$\pi = 3.141592654\ldots$ irrational

$\sqrt[3]{7} = 1.91293118\ldots$ irrational

$\sqrt{36} = 6$ rational

A rational number expressed in the form $\frac{a}{b}$ is in its simplest form if a and b have no common factor.

π is a non-recurring decimal and has no exact value.

$\sqrt[3]{7}$ is a non-recurring decimal and has no exact value.

Note: $\sqrt{36}$ means the positive square root of 36.

Exercise 6.2

1 These numbers are rational.
Write each number as a fraction in its simplest form. Do not use a calculator.

(a)   0.5   (b)   0.45   (c)   0.3   (d)   0.625   (e) $2\frac{1}{4}$

(f) -0.25 (g) $0.\dot{2}\dot{7}$ (h) $\sqrt{49}$ (i) $\frac{\sqrt{0.49}}{2}$ (j) $0.2\dot{2}\dot{5}$

(k) $\frac{\sqrt{64}}{\sqrt{16}}$ (l) $-\frac{\sqrt{0.16}}{2}$ (m) $\sqrt[3]{64}$ (n) $\frac{\sqrt[3]{27}}{4}$ (o) $0.1\dot{2}$

2 Which of these numbers are rational?

(a)   0.25   (b) $0.\dot{5}$ (c) $\sqrt{5}$ (d) $\sqrt{25}$ (e) $\sqrt{2.5}$

(f) $-\sqrt{0.25}$ (g) $\frac{\pi}{2}$ (h) $\frac{\sqrt{8}}{\sqrt{4}}$ (i) $\sqrt[3]{8}$ (j)   0.12

(k) $\frac{1.8}{3}$ (l) $2.\dot{1}$ (m) -2π

3 Which of these numbers are rational and which are irrational?

    (a) $\sqrt{2}$ (b) 3.14 (c) $\sqrt[3]{9}$ (d) $\sqrt{\dfrac{1}{4}}$ (e) $\dfrac{\sqrt{64}}{3}$

    (f) $\left(\dfrac{\sqrt{3}}{2}\right)^2$ (g) $\sqrt{\dfrac{1}{2}}$ (h) $\sqrt{1\tfrac{7}{9}}$ (i) $\sqrt{6\tfrac{1}{4}}$ (j) π^2

    Express each of the rational numbers in the form $\frac{a}{b}$, where a and b are integers.

4 Which of the following are rational and which are irrational?

    (a) $\dfrac{\sqrt{5}}{2}$ (b) $\left(\dfrac{\sqrt{5}}{2}\right)^2$ (c) $\sqrt{2\tfrac{1}{4}}$ (d) $\left(\tfrac{1}{3}\right)^2 + \tfrac{2}{3}$

    Express each of the rational numbers in the form $\frac{a}{b}$, where a and b are integers.

5 (a) Write down an irrational number that lies between 2 and 3.
    (b) Write down an irrational number that lies between 4 and 5.
    (c) Write down an irrational number that lies between 6 and 7.

6 (a) When p and q are both rational numbers, $p + q$ is also rational.
         Write down one example to show this.

    (b) When p and q are both irrational numbers, $p + q$ can be either rational or irrational.
         (i) Write down one example to show that $p + q$ can be rational.
         (ii) Write down one example to show that $p + q$ can be irrational.

7 m and n represent two different irrational numbers.
    In each case, write down one example to show

    (a) mn is rational,   (b) mn is irrational,

    (c) $\frac{m}{n}$ is rational,   (d) $\frac{m}{n}$ is irrational.

Surds

Roots of rational numbers which **cannot** be expressed as rational numbers are called **surds**.
A surd is an irrational number.
These are examples of surds:

$\sqrt{2}$ $\sqrt{0.37}$ $\sqrt[3]{10}$ $3 + \sqrt{2}$ $\sqrt{7}$

Numbers like $\sqrt{64}$, $\sqrt{0.25}$, $\sqrt[3]{27}$ are not surds
because the root of each number is rational.

$\left(\sqrt{64} = 8, \sqrt{0.25} = 0.5, \sqrt[3]{27} = 3.\right)$

Remember
$\sqrt{a}$ means the positive square root of a.

Manipulating and simplifying surds

Rules for surds.

$$\sqrt{ab} = \sqrt{a} \times \sqrt{b}$$
$$m\sqrt{a} + n\sqrt{a} = (m + n)\sqrt{a}$$
$$\sqrt{\dfrac{a}{b}} = \dfrac{\sqrt{a}}{\sqrt{b}}$$

To simplify surds look for factors that are square numbers.

EXAMPLE

Simplify the following leaving the answers in surd form.

(a) $\sqrt{32}$ (b) $\sqrt{8} + \sqrt{18}$ (c) $\sqrt{108} - \sqrt{75}$ (d) $\sqrt{\dfrac{72}{20}}$

(a) $\sqrt{32} = \sqrt{16} \times \sqrt{2} = 4\sqrt{2}$

(b) $\sqrt{8} + \sqrt{18} = \sqrt{4} \times \sqrt{2} + \sqrt{9} \times \sqrt{2} = 2\sqrt{2} + 3\sqrt{2} = 5\sqrt{2}$

(c) $\sqrt{108} - \sqrt{75} = \sqrt{36} \times \sqrt{3} - \sqrt{25} \times \sqrt{3} = 6\sqrt{3} - 5\sqrt{3} = \sqrt{3}$

(d) $\sqrt{\dfrac{72}{20}} = \dfrac{\sqrt{72}}{\sqrt{20}} = \dfrac{\sqrt{36}\,\sqrt{2}}{\sqrt{4}\,\sqrt{5}} = \dfrac{6\,\sqrt{2}}{2\,\sqrt{5}} = \dfrac{3\,\sqrt{2}}{\sqrt{5}}$

Exercise 6.3

1 Which of the following are surds?

(a) $\sqrt{2}$ (b) $\sqrt{4}$ (c) $\sqrt{9}$ (d) $\sqrt{10}$ (e) $\sqrt{40}$

(f) $\sqrt{1}$ (g) $\sqrt[3]{1}$ (h) $\sqrt[3]{8}$ (i) $\sqrt[3]{9}$ (j) $\sqrt[3]{27}$

(k) $\sqrt{0.4}$ (l) $\sqrt{0.09}$ (m) $\left(\sqrt{3}\right)^3$ (n) $\left(\sqrt{0.4}\right)^2$ (o) $\sqrt{54}$

2 Write the following surds in their simplest form.

(a) $\sqrt{8}$ (b) $\sqrt{18}$ (c) $\sqrt{12}$ (d) $\sqrt{27}$ (e) $\sqrt{45}$

(f) $\sqrt{20}$ (g) $\sqrt{48}$ (h) $\sqrt{32}$ (i) $\sqrt{50}$ (j) $\sqrt{54}$

(k) $\sqrt{24}$ (l) $\sqrt{98}$ (m) $\sqrt{75}$ (n) $\sqrt{72}$ (o) $\sqrt{80}$

(p) $\sqrt{63}$ (q) $\sqrt{200}$ (r) $\sqrt{128}$ (s) $\sqrt{112}$ (t) $\sqrt{175}$

3 Simplify.

(a) $\sqrt{2} + \sqrt{2}$ (b) $2\sqrt{5} - \sqrt{5}$ (c) $5\sqrt{3} + 2\sqrt{3}$

(d) $5\sqrt{2} - 3\sqrt{2}$ (e) $2\sqrt{5} + 3\sqrt{5}$ (f) $7\sqrt{3} - 3\sqrt{3} + \sqrt{3}$

(g) $\sqrt{18} + \sqrt{8}$ (h) $\sqrt{50} - \sqrt{32}$ (i) $\sqrt{45} + \sqrt{80}$

(j) $\sqrt{75} - \sqrt{12}$ (k) $\sqrt{300} - \sqrt{48}$ (l) $\sqrt{50} + \sqrt{18} - \sqrt{8}$

(m) $3\sqrt{20} + 2\sqrt{45}$ (n) $2\sqrt{48} + 3\sqrt{12}$ (o) $3\sqrt{45} - 2\sqrt{20}$

(p) $\sqrt{200} - 2\sqrt{18} + \sqrt{72}$ (q) $\sqrt{300} + \sqrt{48} - 3\sqrt{27}$ (r) $3\sqrt{18} - 2\sqrt{8} + \sqrt{2}$

4 Simplify the following.

(a) $\sqrt{\dfrac{9}{4}}$ (b) $\sqrt{\dfrac{25}{16}}$ (c) $\sqrt{\dfrac{18}{8}}$ (d) $\sqrt{\dfrac{24}{9}}$

5 Simplify the following.

(a) $\sqrt{3} \times \sqrt{3}$ (b) $\sqrt{3} \times 2\sqrt{3}$ (c) $3\sqrt{2} \times \sqrt{2}$ (d) $2\sqrt{5} \times 3\sqrt{5}$

(e) $\sqrt{2} \times \sqrt{8}$ (f) $\sqrt{18} \times \sqrt{2}$ (g) $\sqrt{12} \times \sqrt{3}$ (h) $\sqrt{5} \times \sqrt{10}$

(i) $\sqrt{3} \times \sqrt{6}$ (j) $\sqrt{3} \times \sqrt{15}$ (k) $2\sqrt{6} \times \sqrt{3}$ (l) $2\sqrt{5} \times \sqrt{10}$

(m) $\sqrt{8} \times \sqrt{18}$ (n) $3\sqrt{2} \times 2\sqrt{3}$ (o) $4\sqrt{3} \times 2\sqrt{2}$ (p) $\sqrt{27} \times \sqrt{32}$

6 Remove the brackets and simplify the following.

(a) $\sqrt{2}(\sqrt{2} + 1)$

(b) $\sqrt{3}(\sqrt{6} - \sqrt{3})$

(c) $\sqrt{2}(\sqrt{6} + \sqrt{2})$

(d) $\sqrt{5}(\sqrt{10} - \sqrt{5})$

(e) $(\sqrt{3} + \sqrt{2})(\sqrt{3} - \sqrt{2})$

(f) $(\sqrt{5} + \sqrt{2})(\sqrt{5} - \sqrt{2})$

(g) $(\sqrt{3} + \sqrt{2})(\sqrt{3} + \sqrt{2})$

(h) $(\sqrt{6} - \sqrt{2})(\sqrt{2} + \sqrt{6})$

(i) $(\sqrt{6} - \sqrt{2})(\sqrt{2} - \sqrt{6})$

(j) $(\sqrt{6} + \sqrt{3})(\sqrt{3} - \sqrt{6})$

Rationalising denominators of fractions

When the denominator of a fraction is a surd it is usual to remove the surd from the denominator. This process is called **rationalising the denominator**.

For fractions of the form $\dfrac{a}{\sqrt{b}}$, multiply both the numerator (top) and the denominator (bottom) of the fraction by $\sqrt{b}$ and then simplify where possible.

EXAMPLE

Rationalise the denominator and simplify where possible (a) $\dfrac{1}{\sqrt{2}}$, (b) $\dfrac{3\sqrt{2}}{\sqrt{6}}$.

(a) $\dfrac{1}{\sqrt{2}} = \dfrac{1}{\sqrt{2}} \times \dfrac{\sqrt{2}}{\sqrt{2}} = \dfrac{\sqrt{2}}{2}$

(b) $\dfrac{3\sqrt{2}}{\sqrt{6}} = \dfrac{3\sqrt{2}}{\sqrt{6}} \times \dfrac{\sqrt{6}}{\sqrt{6}} = \dfrac{3\sqrt{2}\sqrt{6}}{6} = \dfrac{3\sqrt{2}\sqrt{2}\sqrt{3}}{6} = \dfrac{6\sqrt{3}}{6} = \sqrt{3}$

Exercise 6.4

1 Rationalise the denominator in each of the following and then simplify the fraction.

(a) $\dfrac{1}{\sqrt{3}}$

(b) $\dfrac{1}{\sqrt{5}}$

(c) $\dfrac{1}{\sqrt{7}}$

(d) $\dfrac{2}{\sqrt{2}}$

(e) $\dfrac{5}{\sqrt{5}}$

(f) $\dfrac{4}{\sqrt{2}}$

(g) $\dfrac{6}{\sqrt{3}}$

(h) $\dfrac{14}{\sqrt{7}}$

(i) $\dfrac{3}{\sqrt{6}}$

(j) $\dfrac{15}{\sqrt{5}}$

(k) $\dfrac{9}{\sqrt{3}}$

(l) $\dfrac{5}{\sqrt{15}}$

(m) $\dfrac{18}{\sqrt{6}}$

(n) $\dfrac{35}{\sqrt{5}}$

(o) $\dfrac{7}{\sqrt{21}}$

(p) $\dfrac{11}{\sqrt{22}}$

(q) $\dfrac{10}{\sqrt{30}}$

(r) $\dfrac{21}{\sqrt{14}}$

(s) $\dfrac{14}{\sqrt{35}}$

(t) $\dfrac{15}{\sqrt{10}}$

2 Express each of the following in its simplest form with a rational denominator.

(a) $\dfrac{6}{\sqrt{8}}$

(b) $\dfrac{6}{\sqrt{12}}$

(c) $\dfrac{6}{\sqrt{24}}$

(d) $\dfrac{8}{\sqrt{32}}$

(e) $\dfrac{9}{\sqrt{18}}$

(f) $\dfrac{\sqrt{3}}{\sqrt{6}}$

(g) $\dfrac{\sqrt{15}}{\sqrt{5}}$

(h) $\dfrac{\sqrt{8}}{\sqrt{2}}$

(i) $\dfrac{\sqrt{12}}{\sqrt{3}}$

(j) $\dfrac{\sqrt{18}}{\sqrt{2}}$

(k) $\dfrac{\sqrt{5}}{\sqrt{20}}$

(l) $\dfrac{\sqrt{32}}{\sqrt{2}}$

(m) $\dfrac{\sqrt{75}}{\sqrt{100}}$

(n) $\dfrac{2\sqrt{3}}{\sqrt{12}}$

(o) $\dfrac{3\sqrt{5}}{\sqrt{15}}$

(p) $\dfrac{4\sqrt{6}}{\sqrt{12}}$

(q) $\dfrac{2\sqrt{8}}{\sqrt{32}}$

(r) $\dfrac{5\sqrt{7}}{\sqrt{35}}$

(s) $\dfrac{\sqrt{3}\sqrt{5}}{\sqrt{30}}$

(t) $\dfrac{\sqrt{2}\sqrt{3}}{\sqrt{18}}$

What you need to know

- **Rational numbers** can be written in the form $\frac{a}{b}$, where a and b are integers ($b \neq 0$).
  Examples of rational numbers are: 2, -5, $\frac{2}{5}$,   0.6,   3.47, $1\frac{3}{4}$.

- All fractions can be written as decimals.
  For example, $\frac{1}{3} = 0.3333333 \ldots = 0.\dot{3}$, $\frac{123}{999} = 0.123123123 \ldots = 0.\dot{1}2\dot{3}$

- **Irrational numbers** cannot be written as fractions.
  Irrational numbers include:
    square roots of non-square numbers,
    cube roots of non-cube numbers.
  Examples of irrational numbers are: $\sqrt{2}$, $\sqrt[3]{7}$, π, $\sqrt{13}$.

- All **terminating** and **recurring decimals** are rational numbers.

- A **surd** is the root of a rational number which is not rational.
  A surd is an irrational number.

- Rules for manipulating and simplifying surds:

$$\sqrt{ab} = \sqrt{a} \times \sqrt{b}$$
$$m\sqrt{a} + n\sqrt{a} = (m + n)\sqrt{a}$$
$$\sqrt{\frac{a}{b}} = \frac{\sqrt{a}}{\sqrt{b}}$$

- To **rationalise** the denominator of a fraction of the form $\frac{a}{\sqrt{b}}$ multiply both the numerator (top) and the denominator (bottom) of the fraction by $\sqrt{b}$.

IDEAS FOR INVESTIGATION

A sequence of triangles OPQ, OQR, ORS, … , etc is formed as shown.

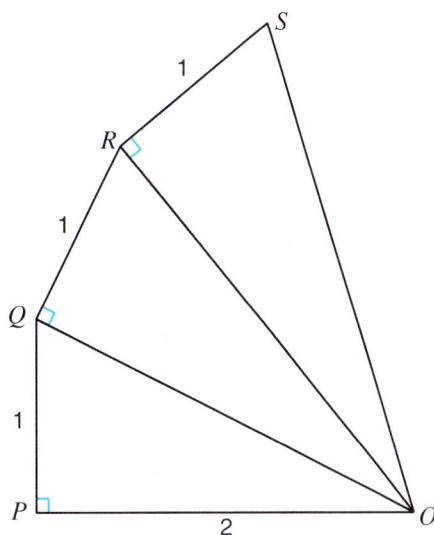

Calculate the lengths of OQ, OR and OS as surds in their simplest form.

Write in terms of n the hypotenuse of the n th triangle.
Investigate for different lengths of PO.

1 (a) Change $\frac{7}{9}$ into a decimal.

(b) Find the fraction, in its lowest terms, which is equal to $0.27\dot{7}$.

SEG 1994

2 (a) Change $\frac{2}{11}$ into a decimal.

(b) Find the fraction which is equal to $0.31\dot{8}1\dot{8}$. Give your answer in its simplest form.

SEG 1996

3 Write down the fraction, in its simplest form, which is equal to these recurring decimals.

(a) $0.4\dot{5}$ (b) $0.6\dot{4}\dot{5}$

SEG 1997

4 Say whether each of these numbers is **rational** or **irrational**.

$\sqrt{2}$ $(2.2)^3$ $\sqrt{16}$ π 0.66666

SEG 1994

5 (a) Write down **two** irrational numbers that multiply together to give a rational number.

(b) Which of the following numbers are rational?

$2^{\frac{1}{2}}$ 2^{-2} $4^{\frac{1}{2}}$ 4^{-2} $\pi^{\frac{1}{2}}$ π^{-2}

SEG 1995

6 (a) Write down a rational number between 5 and 6.

(b) Write down an irrational number between 5 and 6.

(c) Write down a rational number that has a rational square root.

(d) Write down a rational number that has an irrational square root.

(e) Write down an irrational number that has an irrational square.

(f) Write the number $0.4\dot{6}$ as a fraction in its simplest form.

SEG 1996

7 (a) Copy and complete the following table, writing YES if true and NO if false. The first line has been completed for you.

	Rational	Irrational
$\sqrt{2}$	NO	YES
$\frac{7}{3}$	…	…
π	…	…
$4\sqrt{2}$	…	…

(b) Write down an irrational number between 6 and 7.

(c) p is a non-zero rational number and q is an irrational number.

(i) Is $p \times q$ irrational or rational?

(ii) Is $p + q$ irrational or rational?

SEG 1994

8 (a) Write the following rational number as a fraction in its simplest form.

$3.27\dot{2}7\dot{2}7$

(b) Copy and complete the table below for the sum, $x + y$, where x and y are any two numbers.

Use a tick ☑ if TRUE and a cross ☒ if FALSE.

$x + y$	Always irrational	Always rational	Sometimes rational and sometimes irrational
x rational $\}$ y rational	....	....	....
x irrational $\}$ y rational	....	....	....
x irrational $\}$ y irrational	....	....	....

SEG 1996

9 (a) Consider the square roots of all whole numbers between 400 and 600.

$\sqrt{400}, \quad \sqrt{401}, \quad \sqrt{402}, \quad \ldots, \quad \sqrt{598}, \quad \sqrt{599}, \quad \sqrt{600}.$

Write down the numbers in this list which are rational.

(b) Consider the square roots of all whole numbers between 7 and 19.

$\sqrt{7}, \sqrt{8}, \sqrt{9}, \sqrt{10}, \sqrt{11}, \sqrt{12}, \sqrt{13}, \sqrt{14}, \sqrt{15}, \sqrt{16}, \sqrt{17}, \sqrt{18}, \sqrt{19}.$

Write down **two** different irrational numbers from this list which, when multiplied together, give a rational answer.

SEG 1997

10 (a) p and q are two different irrational numbers. Choose values to show that:

    (i) $p + q$ can be irrational;   (ii) pq can be rational or irrational.

(b) r is a non-zero rational number and s is an irrational number. Is the number rs 'rational', 'irrational' or 'could be either'?

(c) Which of the following are rational?

$$1 + \sqrt{2}, \quad \left(\sqrt{3}\right)^3, \quad \sqrt[3]{27}, \quad \pi^2, \quad \left(2^6\right)^{\frac{1}{3}}, \quad \left(\tfrac{1}{16}\right)^{-\frac{1}{4}}, \quad \sqrt{1000}$$

SEG 1996

11 (a) A square $ABCD$ of side 1 metre, contains a circle centre O, radius r.
A second circle centre O, radius R passes through the four vertices of the square as shown.
The length $AC = \sqrt{2}$ metres.

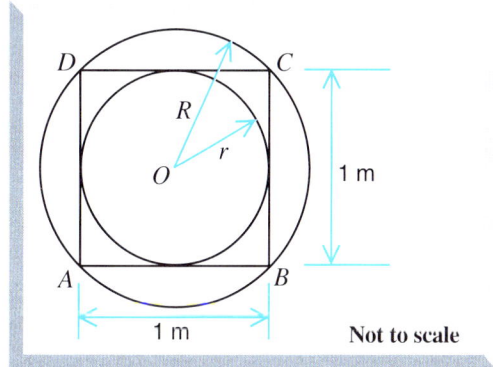

Not to scale

Write down answers to each of the following and say whether the true values are **rational** or **irrational**.

    (i)   The diameter of the circle radius R.
    (ii)   The diameter of the circle radius r.
    (iii)   The circumference of the circle radius R.
    (iv)   The area of the square $ABCD$.

(b) b is a positive integer greater than 2. $\sqrt{2} \times \sqrt{b}$ is rational.
Write down a possible value for b.

(c) Write the following recurring decimal as a fraction in its simplest form.

0.272727……

SEG 1995

12 The number x is given by the formula $x = \sqrt{a^2 + b^2}$.

(a) In each of the following cases, find x, and state whether it is a rational or irrational number.

    (i) $a = 5, b = 10$ (ii) $a = \sqrt{3}, b = \sqrt{6}$

(b) The numbers a and b satisfy $a^2 \leqslant 4, \quad 3 \leqslant b^2 \leqslant 5$.
Find two pairs of **positive** numbers, a and b, such that x is rational.

SEG 1997

13 Simplify the following expressions, leaving your answers, where appropriate, in surd form.

(a) $\dfrac{\sqrt{180}}{\sqrt{10}}$ (b) $\sqrt{108} + \sqrt{75}$

SEG 1998 S

14 Simplify the following expressions, leaving your answers, where appropriate, in surd form.

(a) $\dfrac{\sqrt{150}}{\sqrt{270}}$ (b) $\sqrt{27} + \sqrt{147}$

SEG 1998

15 Simplify the following expressions, leaving your answers, where appropriate in surd form.

(a) $\sqrt{\dfrac{50}{18}}$ (b) $\left(2 + \sqrt{3}\right)\left(3 + \sqrt{2}\right)$ (c) $\dfrac{5}{2\sqrt{10}}$

CHAPTER 7

Understanding and Using Measures

Units of measurement

There are two sorts of units in common use, **metric** units and **imperial** units.

Metric Units

Length
1 kilometre (km) = 1000 metres (m)
1 m = 100 centimetres (cm)
1 m = 1000 millimetres (mm)
1 cm = 10 mm

Mass
1 tonne (t) = 1000 kilograms (kg)
1 kg = 1000 grams (g)

Capacity and volume
1 litre = 1000 millilitres (ml)
1 cm³ = 1 ml
1 m³ = 1000 litres

Imperial Units

Length
1 foot = 12 inches
1 yard = 3 feet
1 mile = 1760 yards

Mass
1 pound = 16 ounces
14 pounds = 1 stone
2240 pounds = 1 ton

Capacity and volume
1 gallon = 8 pints

Conversions

Length
5 miles is about 8 km
1 inch is about 2.5 cm
1 foot is about 30.5 cm
1 m is about 39 inches

Mass
1 kg is about 2.2 pounds

Capacity and volume
1 litre is about 1.75 pints
1 litre is about 0.2 gallons

EXAMPLES

1 How many pints of milk are there in a 4 litre carton of milk.

1 litre is about 1.75 pints.
4 litres is about 4 × 1.75 pints.
4 litres is about 7 pints.

2 Convert 22.5 m² to square yards.

1 yard = 3 × 30.5 = 91.5 cm
91.5 cm = 91.5 ÷ 100 = 0.915 m.
An area of 1 square yard = 0.915 × 0.915 m².
22.5 ÷ 0.915² = 26.9 (to 3 significant figures).
22.5 m² is equivalent to 26.9 square yards.

Exercise 7.1

Do not use a calculator in questions 1 to 4.

1 How many 40 gram bags of sweets can Billy make with 3 kg of sweets?

2

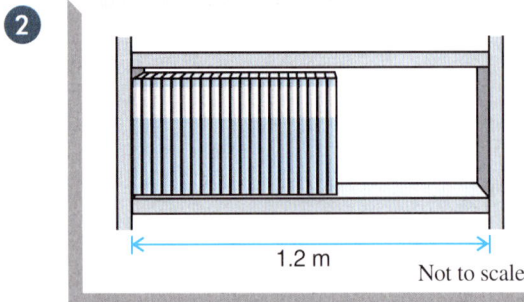

1.2 m   Not to scale

How many magazines, each 0.6 cm thick, will fit on a bookcase shelf which is exactly 1.2 m wide?

3 One glass of lemonade contains 300 ml. How many glasses of lemonade can be poured from three jugs each of which contains 2.5 litres?

4 How long is 400 km in miles?

5 A box contains 200 balls. Each ball weighs 50 g. What is the total weight in pounds?

6 James is 5 feet 8 inches tall. What is James' height in centimetres?

7 James weighs 10 stone 6 pounds. Estimate James' weight in kilograms.

8 Calculate:
  (a) the number of metres in 2000 feet,
  (b) the number of kilometres in 3 miles,
  (c) the number of feet in 170 centimetres,
  (d) the number of pounds in 1250 grams.

9 Concrete is sold by the cubic metre. A path, 31 feet long, 5 feet wide and 1 foot 6 inches deep, is to be made of concrete. How many cubic metres of concrete are needed?

10 30 g of grass seed is needed to sow 1 m² of lawn. What weight of grass seed is needed to sow a rectangular lawn measuring 40 feet by 30 feet?

Estimating with sensible units using suitable degrees of accuracy

EXAMPLES

1 The Great Wall of China, the longest man-made structure in the world, is about 2350 km long.
Degree of accuracy: nearest 50 km.

2 Earthquake shock waves travel through rock at a speed of approximately 25 000 km/hour.
Degree of accuracy: nearest 1000 km/hour.

3 The smallest mammal is the Kitti's hog-nosed bat.
It weighs about 1.5 g.
Degree of accuracy: nearest 0.1 g.

4 The current Olympic record for the men's 100 m is 9.92 seconds.
Degree of accuracy: nearest 0.01 seconds.

Exercise 7.2

1 Give a sensible estimate and an appropriate unit for the following measures:
  (a) the length of a matchstick,
  (b) the length of a football pitch,
  (c) the weight of a ruler,
  (d) the weight of a double decker bus,
  (e) the volume of drink in a glass,
  (f) the volume of water in a fish tank.
In each case state the degree of accuracy you have chosen for your estimate.

2 The diagram, which is drawn to scale, shows a man standing next to a tree.
Using an appropriate metric unit estimate the height of the tree.
State the degree of accuracy that you have used in making your estimate.

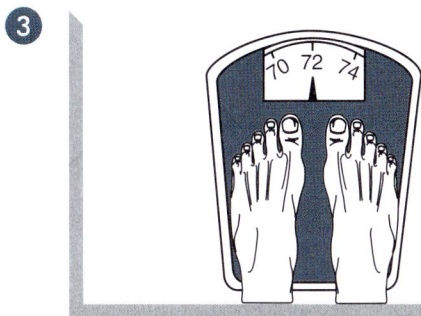

3

This scale shows a man's weight.
What is the man's weight?
Give your answer in an appropriate unit and state the degree of accuracy you have used.

④ How much milk is in this jug?
Give your answer in an appropriate unit
and state the degree of accuracy you have used.

⑤ "My teacher's height is about 1.7 mm",
This statement is incorrect.

It can be corrected by changing the unit:
"My teacher's height is about 1.7 m",
or it can be corrected by changing the quantity.
"My teacher's height is about 1700 mm".

Each of these statements is also incorrect.
"Tyrannosaurus, a large meat eating dinosaur, is estimated to have been about 12 cm long".
"The tallest mammal is the giraffe which grows up to about 5.9 mm tall".
"My car used 5 ml of petrol on a journey of 35 miles".
"The area of the school hall is about 500 mm²".

Correct each statement:
(a)   by changing the unit,
(b)   by changing the quantity.
For each statement give the degree of accuracy that is used.

Speed and average speed

Speed involves two other measures, **distance** and **time**. For this reason it is called a **compound measure**.

The formula for speed is:
$$\text{Speed} = \frac{\text{Distance}}{\text{Time}}$$

When the speed of an object is **constant** it means that the object doesn't slow down or go faster.
However, in many situations speed is not constant.
For example:
    A sprinter needs time to start from the starting blocks and is well into the race before running at top speed.
    Concorde changes speed as it takes off and lands.
In situations like this it is more common to use **average speed**.

The formula for average speed is:
$$\text{Average speed} = \frac{\text{Total distance travelled}}{\text{Total time taken}}$$

The formula linking speed, distance and time can be rearranged and remembered as:

(average) **speed** = (total) **distance** ÷ (total) **time**	S = D ÷ T
(total) **distance** = (average) **speed** × (total) **time**	D = S × T
(total) **time** = (total) **distance** ÷ (average) **speed**	T = D ÷ S

1 John runs from A to B and then from B to C.
The distance from A to B is 30 km.
John's average speed from A to B is 15 km/hour.
(a) Calculate the time it takes John to run from A to B.

John takes 30 minutes to run from B to C.
John's average speed from B to C is 10 km/hour.
(b) Calculate the distance John runs from B to C.
(c) Calculate John's average speed over the whole of the distance that he runs from A to B to C.

(a) Time = Distance ÷ Speed
Time = $30 ÷ 15 = 2$
John takes 2 hours to run from A to B.

(b) Distance = Speed × Time
Distance = $10 × 0.5 = 5$
The distance from B to C is 5 km.

(c) Total distance John runs = $30 + 5$
$= 35$ km.
Total time John takes = $2 + 0.5$
$= 2.5$ hours.
Average speed = $\dfrac{\text{Total distance travelled}}{\text{Total time taken}}$
Average speed = $\dfrac{35}{2.5} = 14$ km/hour

2 Angela, Ben and Cathy drive from London to Glasgow.
Angela takes 12 hours 30 minutes driving at an average speed of 64 km/hour.
Ben drives at an average speed of 100 km/hour.
(a) How long does Ben take?
Cathy takes 7 hours 12 minutes.
(b) At what average speed does Cathy drive?
Give your answer to 3 significant figures.

Angela takes 12.5 hours at 64 km/h.
Distance = Speed × Time
$= 12.5 × 64 = 800$
The distance from London to Glasgow is 800 km.
(a) Time = Distance ÷ Speed
$= 800 ÷ 100 = 8$
Ben takes 8 hours.

(b)
> 12 minutes = $\frac{12}{60}$ hours
> $\frac{12}{60} = 12 ÷ 60 = 0.2$
> 12 minutes = 0.2 hours

Speed = $\dfrac{\text{Distance}}{\text{Time}}$
$= \dfrac{800}{7.2}$
$= 111.111…$
Cathy drives at a speed of 111 km/hour to 3 significant figures.

Exercise 7.3

Give your answers to a suitable degree of accuracy.
Do not use a calculator in questions 1 to 6.

1 Billy drives for 40 km at an average speed of 60 km/h.
He starts his journey at 9.50 a.m.
At what time does his journey end?

2 Penny cycles to work at 18 km/h.
She takes 20 minutes.
How far does she cycle to work?

3 Bristol is 40 miles from Gloucester.
(a) How long does it take to cycle from Bristol to Gloucester at 16 miles per hour?
(b) How long does it take to drive from Bristol to Gloucester at 48 miles per hour?

4 The table shows details of 5 different journeys.

Journey	(a)	(b)	(c)	(d)	(e)
Total distance	200 m			200 km	250 m
Total time	25 secs	2 hours	10 min		
Average speed		50 km/h	1.2 cm/min	200 km/h	250 m/s

Copy and complete the table.
State the units of each answer.

5 Cars A, B, C and D travelled from London to Newcastle.
Details are given in this table.

Car	A	B	C	D
Time (hours)	5		6	4.2
Average speed (km/h)	84	105		

Copy and complete the table.

6 Jenny sets out on a journey at 10.20 a.m.
She completes her journey at 1.05 p.m.
She travels a total distance of 27.5 km.
Calculate her average speed in kilometres per hour.

7 Convert the following speeds to kilometres per hour.
(a) 30 miles per hour,
(b) 50 miles per hour,
(c) 30 metres per second.

8 Convert the following speeds to miles per hour.
(a) 60 kilometres per hour,
(b) 40 metres per second.

9 (a) A car does 40 miles to the gallon.
How many kilometres does it do per litre?
(b) A car does 9.6 kilometres to the litre.
How many miles does it do per gallon?

10 In a 4×400 metres relay the split times of the runners for each leg of the winning team were:

First leg   45.13 seconds.
Second leg   44.71 seconds.
Third leg   44.64 seconds.
Fourth leg   44.23 seconds.

Calculate, in metres per second,
(a) the average speed of each runner,
(b) the average speed of the relay team.

11 A car travels 140 km in 2 hours 30 minutes.
(a) What is its average speed in kilometres per hour?
The car takes 2 more hours to travel a further 130 km.
(b) What is its average speed for the whole journey?

12 Sally cycles 38 km at an average speed of 23 km/h.
She starts her journey at 9.30 a.m.
At what time does she finish?
Give your answer to the nearest minute.

13 Ron runs 400 m in 1 minute 23.2 seconds.
Calculate his average speed in metres per second.

14 Chandni runs from Newcastle to Whitley Bay and then from Whitley Bay to Blyth.
Newcastle to Whitley Bay
    Time taken: 1 hr 20 min.
    Distance: 20 km.
Whitley Bay to Blyth
    Average speed: 0.2 km/min.
    Distance: 12 km.
Calculate Chandni's average speed over the whole journey.

15 The distance from the Sun to the Earth is about 1.5×10^8 km.
It takes light from the Sun about 500 seconds to reach the Earth.
Calculate the speed of light in metres per second.

16 Coaches A and B are based in Leeds.
Coach A goes on a return trip to Scarborough.
Coach B goes on a return trip to Blackpool.
Here are details of the journeys.
Coach A
    Leeds to Scarborough
    Time taken: 1 hr 30 min.
    Average speed: 80 km/hour.
    Scarborough to Leeds
    Average speed: 75 km/hour.
Coach B
    Leeds to Blackpool
    Time taken: 1 hr 20 min.
    Distance: 135km.
    Blackpool to Leeds
    Average speed: 90 km/hour.
Which coach travels:
(a) for the longest distance and by how much,
(b) for the longest time and by how much,
(c) at the fastest average speed and by how much?

Density

Density is a compound measure because it involves two other measures, **mass** and **volume**.
The formula for density is:

$$\text{Density} = \frac{\text{Mass}}{\text{Volume}}$$

For example, if a metal has a density of $2500 \, \text{kg/m}^3$ then $1 \, \text{m}^3$ of the metal weighs $2500 \, \text{kg}$.

The formula linking density, mass and volume can be rearranged and remembered as:

$$\text{Volume} = \frac{\text{Mass}}{\text{Density}}$$

$$\text{Mass} = \text{Density} \times \text{Volume}$$

EXAMPLES

1 A block of metal has mass $500 \, \text{g}$ and volume $400 \, \text{cm}^3$.
Calculate the density of the metal.

Density $= \frac{500}{400} = 1.25 \, \text{g/cm}^3$.

2 Convert a density of 66 pounds/ft³ to kg/m³.

66 pounds $= 66 \div 2.2 = 30 \, \text{kg}$.
66 pounds/ft³ $= 30 \, \text{kg/ft}^3$.
1 foot $-$ 0.305 m.
1 ft³ $= 0.305^3 \, \text{m}^3 = 0.0284 \, \text{m}^3$.
$30 \, \text{kg/ft}^3 = 30 \div 0.0284 = 1056.3 \, \text{kg/m}^3$.
66 pounds/ft³ $= 1056.3 \, \text{kg/m}^3$.

3 Metal A has density $3 \, \text{g/cm}^3$ and metal B has density $2 \, \text{g/cm}^3$.
$600 \, \text{g}$ of metal A and $300 \, \text{g}$ of metal B are melted down and mixed to make an alloy which is cast into a block.
(a) Calculate the volume of the block.
(b) Calculate the density of the alloy.

(a) Volume of metal A $= \frac{600}{3} = 200 \, \text{cm}^3$.
Volume of metal B $= \frac{300}{2} = 150 \, \text{cm}^3$.
Total volume $200 + 150 = 350 \, \text{cm}^3$.

(b) Density $= \frac{900}{350} = 2.57 \, \text{g/cm}^3$.

Population density

Population density is a measure of how populated an area is.
The formula for population density is:

$$\text{Population density} = \frac{\text{Population}}{\text{Area}}$$

EXAMPLE

The population of the county of Cumbria is 4.897×10^5.
The area of the county of Cumbria is $6824 \, \text{km}^2$.
The population of the county of Surrey is 1.036×10^6.
The area of the county of Surrey is $1677 \, \text{km}^2$.
Which county has the greater population density?

The population densities are:

Cumbria $\frac{4.897 \times 10^5}{6824} = 71.8$ people/km².   Surrey $\frac{1.036 \times 10^6}{1677} = 617.8$ people/km².

Surrey has the greater population density.

Use a calculator for this exercise.

1 A block of concrete has dimensions
15 cm by 25 cm by 40 cm.
The block has a mass of 32 kg.
What is the density of the concrete?

2 A metal bar has a mass of 960 g and a
volume of 120 cm³.
Find the density of the metal in the bar.

3 A block of copper has a mass of 2160 g.
The block measures 4 cm by 6 cm by
10 cm.
What is the density of copper?

4 A silver necklace has a mass of 300 g.
The density of silver is 10.5 g/cm³.
What is the volume of the silver?

5 A rectangular can measuring 30 cm by
15 cm by 20 cm is full of oil.
The density of oil is 0.8 g/cm³.
What is the mass of the oil?

6 A rectangular pane of glass measures
60 cm by 120 cm by 0.5 cm.
The density of glass is 2.6 g/cm³.
What is the mass of the glass?

7 A bag of sugar has a mass of 1 kg.
The average density of the sugar in the
bag is 0.5 g/cm³.
Find the volume of sugar in the bag.

8 The table gives some information about
various materials.
Calculate the missing figures in the
table.
State the units of each answer.

Metal	Volume	Mass	Density
Steel	120 cm³	300 g	?
Foam	4000 cm³	?	0.05 g/cm³

9 Convert the density 50 g/mm³ to kg/m³.

10 A bottle holds 450 cm³ of water and has
a mass of 550 g.
The density of water is 1 g/cm³.
What is the mass of the empty bottle?

11 The population of Northern Ireland is
1.595×10^6.
The area of Northern Ireland is
13 483 km².
Calculate the population density of
Northern Ireland.

12 The table shows the total population,
land area and the population densities
for some countries in Europe.
Calculate the missing figures in the
table.

	Country	Area km²	Population	Population density
(a)	Belgium	?	9.97×10^6	326.6
(b)	France	543 960	5.67×10^7	?
(c)	UK	244 090	?	235.2

13 Brass is an alloy made from zinc and
copper.
The ratio of the volume of zinc to the
volume of copper in the alloy is 1 : 3.
The density of zinc is 2.5 g/cm³.
The density of copper is 3 g/cm³.

A block of brass in the shape of a
cuboid has dimensions 10 cm by 10 cm
by 40 cm. It is melted down and used to
make ornamental pyramids.

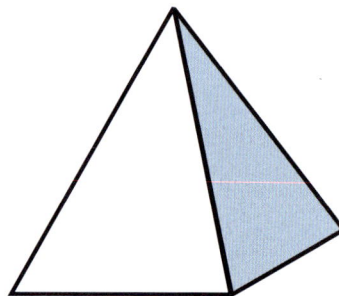

All of the brass is used to make
10 ornaments, which are of equal size.
Calculate the mass of each ornament.

Discrete and continuous measures

Discrete measures

Discrete measures can only take particular values.

For example:
    The number of people on a bus is 42.
    Two ice skating judges give scores of 5.1 and 5.2.
The number of people on a bus must be a whole number.
The ice skating scores show that a discrete measure does not need to be a whole number. They are discrete because scores are not given between numbers like 5.1 and 5.2.

Other examples of discrete measures
1. The number of pupils in a school is 630. This is a discrete measure because the number of pupils can only be a particular whole number.
2. The size of a pair of shoes. This is a discrete measure because the size can only take particular values like 5, $5\frac{1}{2}$, 6 …

Continuous measures

James was 14 on the day of his 14th birthday. He will still be called 14 years old right up to the day before his 15th birthday.
So, although James is 14, his actual age is any age within a range of 1 year.

I am 14.

I am 14 years and 3 months.

Jenny is **not** exactly 14 years and 3 months old.
However, Jenny's age is given to a greater degree of accuracy than James' age because the range of possible ages in her case is smaller.
What is the range of possible ages in Jenny's measurement of her age?

Measures which can lie within a range of possible values are called **continuous measures**.
The value of a continuous measure depends on the accuracy of whatever is making the measurement.

Other examples of continuous measures

1 Billy and Chandni stand against a scale on the classroom wall.

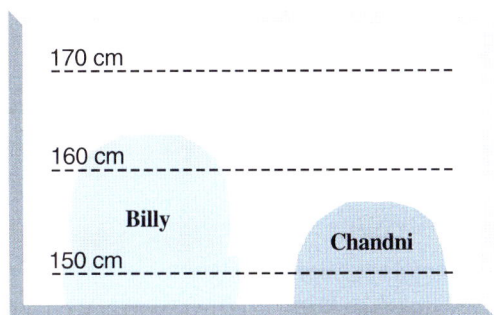

170 cm
160 cm
Billy
Chandni
150 cm

Billy is taller than Chandni but both of their heights are recorded as 160 cm because the scale only measures to the nearest 10 cm.
Make a copy of the scale.
Mark on it some more heights that would be recorded as 160 cm to the nearest 10 cm.

2 This diagram shows the first two runners in a 400 metre race as they cross the winning line.

Both runners were timed at 63 seconds. However, the winner has run faster than the runner who was second. So 63 seconds must represent different times.
What degree of accuracy do you think has been used to measure the time in the race?
Give some possible times for these runners if the time had been measured to the nearest one tenth of a second.

A closer look at measures

Continuous measures

Jane is 160 cm tall to the nearest 10 cm.
What are the limits between which her true height lies?

When rounding to the nearest 10:
The smallest value that rounds to 160 is 155.
155 cm is the smallest height that Jane can be.
The largest value that rounds to 160 is 164.$\dot{9}$ cm.
164.$\dot{9}$ cm is the largest height that Jane can be.

This can be written as an inequality:
$155 \leqslant$ Jane's height $\leqslant 164.\dot{9}$
This is usually written as:
$155 \leqslant$ Jane's height < 165

155 is the **lower bound** of Jane's height.
165 is the **upper bound** of Jane's height.

> Approximation, or rounding, was first covered in Chapter 3.

> All possible heights for Jane are shown on this number line.
>
>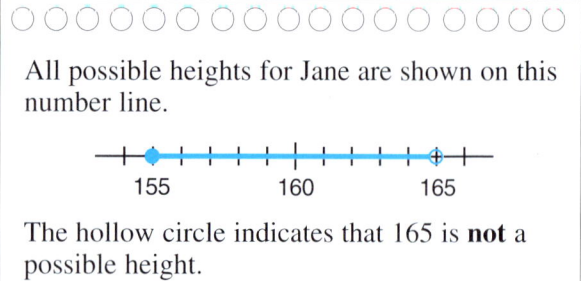
>
> The hollow circle indicates that 165 is **not** a possible height.

If a **continuous measure**, c, is recorded to the nearest x, then:	The **limits** of the possible values of c can be written as
Upper bound $= c + \frac{1}{2}x$ **Lower bound** $= c - \frac{1}{2}x$	$c \pm \frac{1}{2}x$

Discrete measures

160 students, to an accuracy of 2 significant figures, attend assembly.
What are the limits between which the number of students who attend assembly lie?

The attendance is measured to the nearest 10.
Explain why.
The smallest value that rounds to 160 is 155.
So the smallest attendance is 155.
The largest value that rounds to 160 is 164.
So the largest attendance is 164.

The limits between which the attendance lie
are given by the inequality:
$155 \leqslant$ attendance $\leqslant 164$

> All possible values for the attendance are shown on this number line.
>
>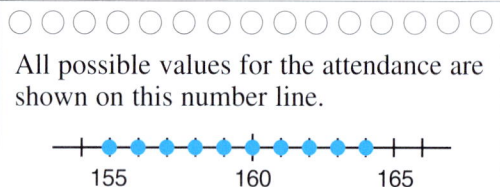

If a **discrete measure**, d, is recorded to the nearest x, then:
Largest possible value $= d + \frac{1}{2}x - 1$
Smallest possible value $= d - \frac{1}{2}x$

EXAMPLES

1 The number of words on this page is 400 to the nearest 100.
What is the value of the largest and smallest possible number of words on this page?

Largest possible value $= 400 + 50 - 1 = 449$
Smallest possible value $= 400 - 50 = 350$

2 The length of this page is 26 cm to the nearest centimetre.
What are the upper and lower bounds of the true length of this page?

Upper bound $= 26 + 0.5 = 26.5$ cm
Lower bound $= 26 - 0.5 = 25.5$ cm

1 State whether each of the following are discrete or continuous measures.
(a) The volume of a wine glass.
(b) The votes cast for a candidate in an election.
(c) The number of pages in a book.
(d) The time it takes to walk to school.
(e) The number of beds in a hospital.
(f) The weight of your best friend.

2 For each of the following measures state whether the value given is an exact value or give the limits within which it could lie.
(a) A book has 224 pages.
(b) A bus was 5 minutes late.
(c) Tom has two brothers.
(d) I weigh 63 kg.
(e) Judy is 153 cm tall.

3 Fifty flowers, to the nearest 10, each grow to a height of 50 cm, to the nearest 10 cm.

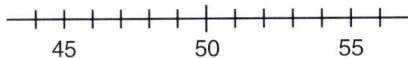

```
  +--+--+--+--+--+--+--+--+--+--+--+
    45         50         55
```

(a) Show on one copy of the number line the possible numbers of flowers.
(b) Show on another copy of the number line the possible heights of the flowers.

4 What are the slowest and fastest possible times:
(a) of Derek who runs exactly 100 metres in 13 seconds measured to the nearest second,
(b) of Jan who swims exactly 100 metres in 82.6 seconds measured to the nearest tenth of a second?

5 (a) What is the minimum weight of a 62 kg parcel measured to the nearest kilogram?
(b) What is the minimum length of a 2.3 m shelf measured to the nearest 0.1 m?
(c) What is the minimum time for a race timed at 12.63 seconds measured to the nearest one hundredth of a second?

6 Tina is 1.53 m tall.
(a) To what degree of accuracy is Tina's height given?
(b) What are the limits between which her true height lies?

7 What degree of accuracy has been used to make these estimates of the length of a corridor?
(a) About 120 m. The smallest possible length is 115 m.
(b) About 100 m. The smallest possible length is 75 m.
(c) About 200 m. The smallest possible length is 150 m.

8 Write down the largest and smallest values of the following discrete measures.
(a) 10 000 measured to the nearest 1000.
(b) 10 000 measured to the nearest 100.
(c) 10 000 measured to the nearest 50.
(d) 500 measured to 3 significant figures.
(e) 500 measured to 2 significant figures.

9 (a) In a swimming gala, Laura wins the girl's 100 metre breaststroke race.
Her time was 95 seconds to the nearest second.
What is the lowest possible time she could have taken?

(b) In 1994, the women's world record for 100 metres breaststroke was held by Samantha Reilly of Australia. The record was 67.69 seconds to the nearest $\frac{1}{100}$ second.
Give the lower and upper bounds for this world record.

(c) The boy's 100 metre race was won by Dan, a potential champion swimmer, with a time of 68 seconds, to the nearest second.
Dan said "I've already beaten Samantha Reilly's time."
Using the upper and lower bounds show whether Dan could be correct.

SEG 1996

Calculations involving bounds

EXAMPLES

1 Two strips of wood have lengths of 124 cm and 159 cm, to the nearest centimetre.
   (a)   What is the lower bound of the total length of the strips of wood?
   (b)   What is the upper bound of the difference between the length of the strips of wood?

Shorter strip
Lower bound = 124 cm − 0.5 cm = 123.5 cm
Upper bound = 124 cm + 0.5 cm = 124.5 cm

Longer strip
Lower bound = 159 cm − 0.5 cm = 158.5 cm
Upper bound = 159 cm + 0.5 cm = 159.5 cm

   (a)   To find the lower bound of the total length use the lower bounds of both strip lengths.
       Lower bound of the total length = 123.5 + 158.5 = 282 cm.

   (b)   The upper bound of the difference in lengths is found from:
           Upper bound of the longer strip − lower bound of shorter strip
           = 159.5 − 123.5 = 36 cm

2 The sides of a rectangle are measured to the nearest centimetre.
Calculate the smallest and largest possible areas of the rectangle.

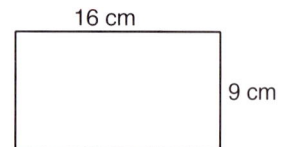
16 cm
9 cm

Length
Upper bound = 16 cm + 0.5 cm = 16.5 cm
Lower bound = 16 cm − 0.5 cm = 15.5 cm

Width
Upper bound = 9 cm + 0.5 cm = 9.5 cm
Lower bound = 9 cm − 0.5 cm = 8.5 cm

To find the largest possible area is found by using the largest length and largest width.
Largest possible area = 16.5 cm × 9.5 cm = 156.75 cm².

To find the smallest possible area is found by using the smallest length and smallest width.
Smallest possible area = 15.5 cm × 8.5 cm = 131.75 cm².

3 Gail's best time for running 100 metres is 12.7 seconds.
The length is accurate to the nearest metre.
The time is accurate to the nearest tenth of a second.
Calculate her maximum possible average speed.

Time
Upper bound = 12.7 s + 0.05 s = 12.75 s
Lower bound = 12.7 s − 0.05 s = 12.65 s

Distance
Upper bound = 100 m + 0.5 m = 100.5 m
Lower bound = 100 m − 0.5 m = 99.5 m

Gail's maximum possible average speed = $\dfrac{\text{greatest distance}}{\text{smallest time}} = \dfrac{100.5 \text{ metres}}{12.65 \text{ seconds}} = 7.944 \ldots$ m/s

Gail's maximum possible average speed = 7.94 m/s, correct to 3 significant figures.
What bounds should be used to calculate Gail's minimum possible average speed?

Calculation involving …	For upper bound calculate …	For lower bound calculate …
Adding measures	Upper bound + Upper bound	Lower bound + Lower bound
Multiplying measures	Upper bound × Upper bound	Lower bound × Lower bound
Subtracting measures	Upper bound − Lower bound	Lower bound − Upper bound
Dividing measures	Upper bound ÷ Lower bound	Lower bound ÷ Upper bound

Use a calculator for this exercise.

1 In the diagram, all angles are measured to the nearest degree.
Find the maximum possible size of angle a.

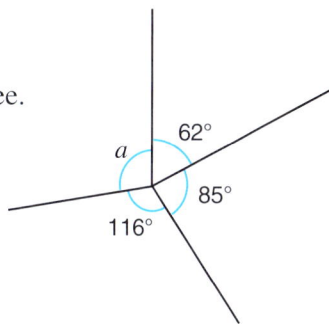

62°

a

85°

116°

2 Fiona measures a corridor as being 126 paces in length.
The length of her pace is 90 cm, to the nearest 10 cm.
What is the difference between the maximum and minimum possible lengths of the corridor?

3 George travels for 4 hours at an average speed of 50 miles per hour.
The time is given to the nearest hour.
The speed is given to the nearest 10 miles per hour.

  (a) What is the maximum possible distance George travels?
  (b) What is the minimum possible distance George travels?

4 A bag of potatoes weighs 5.0 kg to the nearest 100 g.
  (a) Find the upper bound of the weight of 100 bags of potatoes.

  1.5 kg of potatoes to the nearest 100 g are taken from a bag.
  (b) What is the lower bound of the weight of potatoes left in the bag?

5 The attendance at Newcastle's home game against Manchester United was 38 000.
When Newcastle played away to Manchester United the attendance was 49 000.
Both these attendances are accurate to the nearest 1000.

  (a) Calculate the largest and smallest possible total attendance at these games.
  (b) Calculate the largest and smallest possible difference in attendance at these games.

6 Books are packed into boxes for delivery.
The total weight of a box should **not exceed** 30 kg.
A book weighs 2.7 kg, to the nearest 0.1 kg.
What is the maximum number of books that can be packed in a box?

7 A cylinder has radius 5.2 cm and height 9.4 cm.
Both measurements are given to the nearest 0.1 cm.
Find the difference between the minimum and
maximum possible volumes of the cylinder.

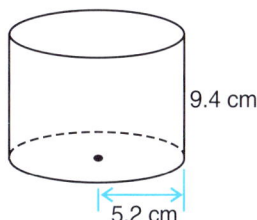

9.4 cm

5.2 cm

8 A metal block has mass 850 g and volume 550 cm³.
The mass is given to the nearest 10 g.
The volume is given to the nearest 50 cm³.
Find the difference between the greatest and smallest possible densities of the metal.

9 There are people queuing at two entrances, A and B, of a concert hall.
The number of people queuing at entrance A is 150 to the nearest 10.
The number of people queuing at entrance B is 300 to the nearest 100.
  (a) Calculate the largest possible total of the number of people queuing at entrances A and B.
  (b) Calculate the smallest possible difference between the number of people queuing at entrances A and B.

10 A water tank, in the shape of a cuboid, is full of water.
Water is drained from the tank at a rate of 8 litres per minute.
The dimensions of the tank are given to the nearest 10 cm.
The rate at which the water is drained from the tank is given to the nearest 0.5 litres per minute.

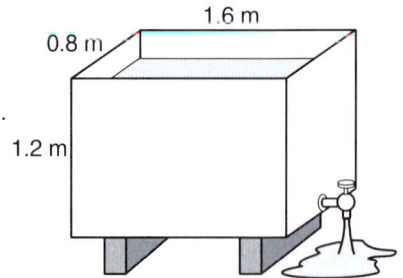

  (a) Calculate the smallest possible time to drain the tank.
  (b) Calculate the greatest possible time to drain the tank.

11 A rectangle has length 12.6 cm and area 93.20 cm².
The length is given to the nearest millimetre.
The area is given to the nearest 0.05 cm².
Calculate the upper bound of the width of the rectangle.

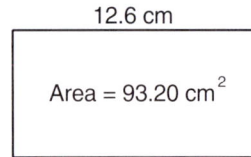

12.6 cm

Area = 93.20 cm²

12 The diameter of a concrete sphere is given as 20 cm, to the nearest centimetre.
The density of concrete is 2.2 g/cm³.
Calculate the minimum mass of the sphere.

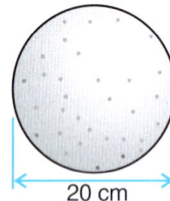

20 cm

13 The distance between A and B is 12.2 km to the nearest 100 m.
The distance between B and C is 14.34 km to the nearest 10 m.
  (a) Sam walks from A to B and meets Tom who walks from C to B.
      What is the upper bound of the difference in the distances that Tom and Sam walk?

  (b) James walks from A to B and then from B to C.
      He takes 8.5 hours to the nearest half an hour.
      (i) Calculate the upper and lower bounds of the total distance that James walks.
      (ii) Calculate the lower bound of James' average speed on the walk.

14 The diagram shows a rectangular flag, $ABCD$.
The flag is blue with a central white circle.
$AB = 3.2$ m and $BC = 2.1$ m, both accurate to the nearest 10 cm.
The diameter of the circle is 0.95 m to the nearest centimetre.
Calculate the lower bound of the area of blue on the flag.

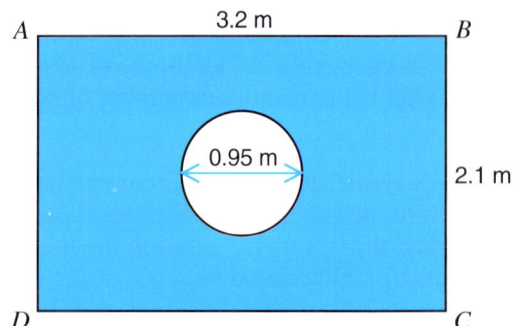

A 3.2 m B

0.95 m

2.1 m

D C

15 a, b and c are continuous measures.
$a = 7.6$ to an accuracy of 1 decimal place.
$b = 3.42$ to an accuracy of 3 significant figures.
$c = 23$ to an accuracy of 2 significant figures.
Calculate the upper and lower bound of:
  (a) $a + b + c$ (b) $a + b - c$ (c) abc (d) $ab - c$ (e) $a(b - c)$ (f) $\dfrac{a}{bc}$

Dimensions and formulae

Formulae can be used to calculate perimeters, areas and volumes of various shapes.
By analysing the **dimensions** involved it is possible to decide whether a given formula represents a perimeter, an area or a volume.

Length (L) has **dimension 1.**
Length (L) $\times$ Length (L) = **Area** (L^2) has **dimension 2.**
Length (L) $\times$ Length (L) $\times$ Length (L) = **Volume** (L^3) has **dimension 3.**

The size of this square based cuboid depends on:
    x, the length of the side of the square base,
    y, the height of the cuboid.

The total **length** of the edges of the cuboid is given by the formula:
    $E = 8x + 4y$
This formula involves:
Numbers: 8 and 4
Lengths(L): x and y
The formula has **dimension 1**.

The total **surface area** of the cuboid is given by the formula:
    $S = 2x^2 + 4xy$
This formula involves:
Numbers: 2 and 4
Areas (L^2): $x \times x$ and $x \times y$
The formula has **dimension 2**.

The **volume** of the cuboid is given by the formula:
    $V = x^2y$
This formula involves:
Volume (L^3): $x \times x \times y$
This formula has **dimension 3**.

EXAMPLE

In each of these expressions the letters a, b and c represent lengths.
Use dimensions to check whether the expressions could represent a perimeter, an area or a volume.
(a) $2a + 3b + 4c$ (b) $3a^2 + 2b(a + c)$
(c) $2a^2b + abc$ (d) $3a + 2ab + c^3$

Note
When checking formulae and expressions, numbers can be ignored because they have no dimension.
$\equiv$ means 'is equivalent to'.

(a) $2a + 3b + 4c$
Write this using dimensions.
L + L + L $\equiv$ 3L $\equiv$ L
$2a + 3b + 4c$ has dimension 1 and could represent a perimeter.

(b) $3a^2 + 2b(a + c)$
Write this using dimensions.
L^2 + L(L + L)
$\equiv$ L^2 + L(2L)
$\equiv$ L^2 + 2L^2
$\equiv$ 3L^2
$\equiv$ L^2
$3a^2 + 2b(a + c)$ has dimension 2 and could represent an area.

(c) $2a^2b + abc$
Write this using dimensions.
L$^2 \times$ L + L $\times$ L $\times$ L
$\equiv$ L^3 + L^3
$\equiv$ 2L^3
$\equiv$ L^3
$2a^2b + abc$ has dimension 3 and could represent a volume.

(d) $3a + 2ab + c^3$
Write this using dimensions.
L + L $\times$ L + L^3
$\equiv$ L + L^2 + L^3
The dimensions are **inconsistent**.
$3a + 2ab + c^3$ represents neither a perimeter, an area or a volume.

1 p, q, r and x, y, z represent lengths.
For each formula state whether it represents
a length, an area or a volume.

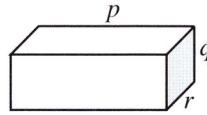

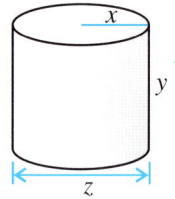

(a) pq (b) $2\pi x$ (c) $p + q + r$ (d) πz
(e) pqr (f) $2(pq + qr + pr)$ (g) $\pi x^2 y$ (h) $2\pi x(x + y)$

2 In each of the expressions below x, y and z represent lengths.
By using dimensions decide whether each expression could represent a perimeter, an area, a
volume or none of these.
Explain your answer in each case.

(a) $x + y + z$ (b) $xy + xz$ (c) xyz (d) $x^2(y^2 + z^2)$
(e) $x(y + z)$ (f) $\dfrac{x^2}{y}$ (g) $\dfrac{xz}{y}$ (h) $x + y^2 + z^3$
(i) $xy(y + z)$ (j) $x^3 + x^2(y + z)$ (k) $xy(y^2 + z)$ (l) $x(y + z) + z^2$

3 The diagram shows a discus.
x and y are the lengths shown on the diagram.
These expressions could represent certain quantities
relating to the discus.

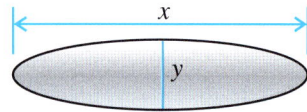

$\pi(x^2 + y^2)$ $\pi x^2 y^2$ πxy $2\pi(x + y)$

(a) Which of them could be an expression for:
 (i) the longest possible distance around the discus,
 (ii) the surface area of the discus.
(b) Use dimensions to explain your answers to part (a).

4 x, y and z represent lengths.
(a) $A = xyz + z(x - y) + 2y$
 This is not a formula for either
 perimeter, area or volume.
 Use dimensions to explain why.
(b) $P = 3z(x + y)$
 This could be a formula for area.
 Use dimensions to explain why.
(c) $V = x^2y + z^2(2x - y) + 2y^3$
 This could be a formula for volume.
 Use dimensions to explain why.

5 p, q, r and s represent the lengths of the
edges of this triangular prism.

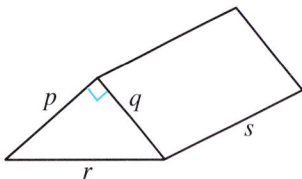

Match the formulae to the measurements.

Formulae

$\frac{1}{2} pqs$ $2(p + q + r + \frac{3s}{2})$ $s(p + q + r) + pq$

Measurements

Edge length Surface area Volume

6 These arrows are similar.

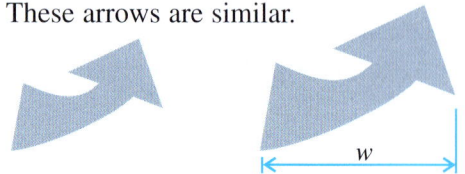

w represents the width of any arrow.
k and c are numbers.
H represents the height of the arrow and
A its area.
Which of the following statements could
be correct and which **must** be wrong.

(a) $H = kw$ (b) $H = ckw$
(c) $H = kw + c$ (d) $A = cw$
(e) $A = kw^2$ (f) $A = kw^3$

Give a reason for each of your answers.
Where you think the formula **must** be
wrong suggest what it might be for.

7 In these formulae a, b and c represent
lengths and A represents an area.

(a) $a = b + c$ (b) $a^2 = bc$
(c) $A = a^2 + bc$ (d) $c = A + ab$
(e) $Ab = a^3$ (f) $A = \dfrac{a^2}{c} + b^2$

Which of the formulas have consistent
dimensions?

You need to know:

- The common units, both **metric** and **imperial**, used to measure **length**, **mass** and **capacity**.

- How to convert from one unit to another. This includes knowing the connection between one metric unit and another and the approximate equivalents between metric and imperial units.

- **Speed** is a compound measure because it involves **two** other measures.

- **Speed** is a measure of how fast something is travelling. It involves the measures **distance** and **time**.

$$\text{Speed} = \frac{\text{Distance}}{\text{Time}}$$

- In situations where speed is not constant, **average speed** is used.

$$\text{Average speed} = \frac{\text{Total distance travelled}}{\text{Total time taken}}$$

- The formula linking speed, distance and time can be rearranged and remembered as:
  (average) **speed** = (total) **distance** ÷ (total) **time**
  (total) **distance** = (average) **speed** × (total) **time**
  (total) **time** = (total) **distance** ÷ (average) **speed**

- Two other commonly used compound measures are **density** and **population density**.

- **Density** is a compound measure which involves the measures **mass** and **volume**.

$$\text{Density} = \frac{\text{Mass}}{\text{Volume}}$$

- **Population density** is a measure of how populated an area is.

$$\text{Population density} = \frac{\text{Population}}{\text{Area}}$$

- A **discrete measure** can only take a particular value and a **continuous measure** lies within a range of possible values which depends upon the degree of accuracy of the measurement.

  If a **continuous measure**, c, is recorded to the nearest x, then:

  Upper bound $= c + \frac{1}{2}x$

  Lower bound $= c - \frac{1}{2}x$

  If a **discrete measure**, d, is recorded to the nearest x, then:

  Largest possible value $= d + \frac{1}{2}x - 1$

  Smallest possible value $= d - \frac{1}{2}x$

- By analysing the **dimensions** of a formula it is possible to decide whether a given formula represents a **length** (dimension 1), an **area** (dimension 2) or a **volume** (dimension 3).

IDEAS FOR INVESTIGATION

Shoe size is a discrete measure. Foot size is a continuous measure.
Investigate the connection between foot size and shoe size.

Questions 1 to 10.
Do not use your calculator.

1 One cake contains 0.2 pounds of butter.
How many cakes can be made with 5 kg of butter?

2 (a) Two girls are talking about their heights.

Clara

> I'm 5 foot 2 inches and I'm taller than Buki.

Buki

> I'm 157 cm and I'm taller than Clara.

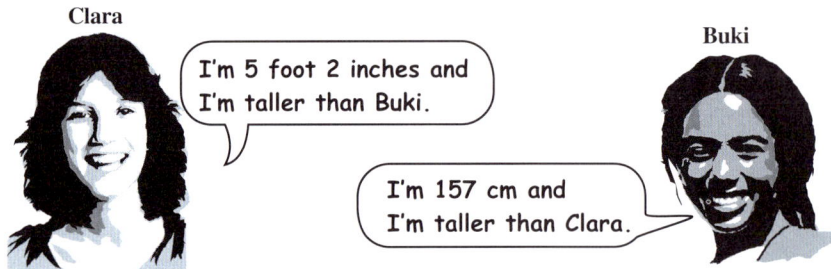

They cannot both be right.
Calculate who is taller.
You **must** show all your working.

(b) Buki's height is correct to the nearest centimetre.
What is the minimum height she could be?

SEG 1995

3 When measured to the nearest 100 ml the volume of a container was found to be 600 ml.
When measured to the nearest 10 ml the volume of the same container was found to be 650 ml.
Give an example of a volume that agrees with **both** of these measurements.

4 Write down the smallest and largest possible values of each of the following measures.
(a) 1 km measured to:
   (i) the nearest 100 m,
   (ii) the nearest 10 m,
   (iii) the nearest 1 m,
   (iv) the nearest 10 cm.
(b) 5000 gallons measured to:
   (i) the nearest 1000 gallons,
   (ii) the nearest 100 gallons,
   (iii) the nearest 10 gallons,
   (iv) the nearest gallon.
(c) 20 seconds measured to:
   (i) the nearest second,
   (ii) the nearest tenth of a second,
   (iii) the nearest hundredth of a second.
(d) 1000 kg measured to:
   (i) the nearest 500 kg,
   (ii) the nearest 50 kg,
   (iii) the nearest 5 kg,
   (iv) the nearest 20 kg,
   (v) the nearest 200 kg.

5 Erica measures the width of a room as 3.6 metres.
Asif measures the width of the same room as 3.60 metres.
Explain the difference in accuracy between the two measurements.

SEG 1996

6 A shot putt weighs 3.25 kg, to the nearest 10 g.
What are the upper and lower bounds for the actual weight of the shot putt?
Give your answers in grams.

SEG 1996

7 A runner completes a 100 m sprint in 11.61 seconds.
The time is recorded to the nearest one hundredth of a second.
What are the upper and lower bounds of the possible times?

SEG 1998

8 The height of a plant is measured as 1.20 m.
Write down the smallest possible value for the true height of this plant.

SEG 1996

9 The cost of a television is £320 to the nearest £10.
What is the maximum cost of the television?

SEG 1996

10 In her local supermarket, Joanna's shopping costs £92 to the nearest £.
(a) State the maximum and minimum possible cost of her shopping.

Joanna's friend spends £74 on her shopping, to the nearest £.
(b) Find the maximum difference in their spending.

SEG 1997

Questions 11 to 19.
You may use a calculator.

11 Jane cycles from *A* to *B* and then from *B* to *C*.
Details of each stage of her journey are given below.
  A to *B*   Distance 55 km.
           Average speed 22km per hour.
  B to *C*   Time taken 1 hour 30 minutes.
           Average speed 30 km per hour.
Calculate Jane's average speed over the whole of her journey from *A* to *C*.

SEG 1999

12 A light year is the distance travelled by light in 365 days.
The speed of light is 3.0×10^5 kilometres per second.
(a) Calculate the number of kilometres in one light year.
     Give your answer in standard form.
(b) The distance to the nearest star is 4.0×10^{13} kilometres.
     How many light years is this?
(c) Calculate the speed of light in miles per second.

SEG 1994

13 (a) Angus drives from Southampton to Durham, a distance of 310 miles.
         His average speed for the journey is 64 mph.
         How long does his journey take?
         Give your answer in hours and minutes.

(b) On a mountain walk it takes approximately:

> 1 hour for every 5 kilometres travelled horizontally,
> *plus*
> 1 hour for every 600 metres climbed vertically.

Ben goes on a mountain walk.
He estimates that he will travel 14.5 km horizontally and climb 750 m vertically.
He plans to stop once for 30 minutes.
Estimate how long he will take in hours.
Give your answer to an appropriate degree of accuracy.

SEG 2000 S

14 A ball bearing has mass 0.44 pounds.
  (a) (i) Calculate the mass of the ball bearing in kilograms.
      (ii) When the mass of the ball bearing is measured in kg and the volume is measured in cm³, what are the units of density?

  (b) The volume of a container is given by the formula $V = 4L(3 - L)^2$.
      Using **Mass** = **Volume** $\times$ **Density** calculate the mass of the container when $L = 1.40$ cm, and 1 cm³ of the material has a mass of 0.160 kg.

SEG 1994

15 Population density $= \dfrac{\text{Population}}{\text{Area}}$

Continent	Population	Area (km²)
Europe	6.82×10^8	1.05×10^{10}
Asia	2.96×10^9	4.35×10^{10}

Which of these two continents has the larger population density?
You **must** show all your working.

SEG 1996

16 A farmer has exactly 600 kilograms of potatoes. He fills a sack with 25.2 kilograms, to the nearest 100 grams.
  (a) What are the upper and lower bounds of the weight of potatoes in the sack?
  (b) Calculate the minimum weight of potatoes which the farmer could have left.

SEG 1994

17 A machine prints and cuts square tickets of side 6.3 cm.
The machine can cut to an accuracy of 0.1 cm.
The tickets are cut from square cardboard sheets of side 1 metre, measured to the nearest centimetre.
  (a) (i) What is the smallest possible size of the tickets?
      (ii) What is the largest possible size of the cardboard?
      (iii) Calculate the maximum number of tickets that it might be possible to cut from one sheet of cardboard.

  (b) Calculate the largest number of tickets you can be certain of cutting from one sheet of cardboard.

SEG 1997

18 The table gives some information about the three counties in East Anglia.

Counties in East Anglia	Land area (km²)	Population (people)
Cambridgeshire	3400	670 000
Norfolk	5400	759 000
Suffolk	3800	662 000

Each land area is given to the nearest 100 km² and each population to the nearest 1000 people.

$$\text{population density} = \frac{\text{population}}{\text{land area}}$$

Calculate the lower bound of the population density for the whole of East Anglia.

SEG 1999

19 A company makes rectangular sheets of tinplate for use in cans.

DIMENSIONS OF RECTANGULAR SHEETS

Thickness	Length	Width
0.15 mm	830 mm	635 mm

The length and width are given to the nearest mm, and the thickness to the nearest 0.01 mm.

Calculate the percentage saving in volume to the company if it produces the sheets to minimum dimensions rather than maximum dimensions.

SEG 1998 S

20 A solid has height h and length d.

   (a)   Explain why this could be a formula for the surface area of the solid: $A = \dfrac{d(5d + 4h)}{4}$

   (b)   Explain why the dimensions of this formula are not consistent: $V = \dfrac{d^2(d + 3h^2)}{12}$

   (c)   Make one change to the formula for V to make it dimensionally consistent with a volume formula.

21 In these expressions x and y are lengths.
$2(x + 3y)$, $3x^2y + 2y^2x$, $2x^2 + 2y(x + y)$
The expressions are for a length, an area and a volume. Which is which?

22 The letters a, b, h, l and r represent lengths.
Consider the following formulae.

$ab, \frac{2}{3}\pi r^3, \pi r, 4\pi rl, \frac{\pi r^2 h}{3}, \sqrt{a^2 + b^2}$

   (a)   Which of these formulae represent areas?
   (b)   Use dimensions to explain how you can tell which formulae represent areas.

SEG 1994

23 In this question only a, b and c represent length.
For each formula, state whether it could be a **length**, an **area** or a **volume**.

   (a) $(a + b)(b + c)$ (b) $\frac{1}{2}(a + b + c)$ (c) $(ab + bc + ca)^{\frac{3}{2}}$

SEG 1997

24 Which formula represents the total surface area of this hexagonal prism.

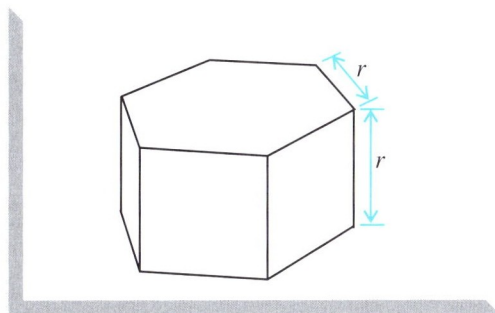

$11.2r^3$, $2\pi r^2 + 6r^2$, $11.2r$, $11.2r^2$.

Explain your answer.

Section Review - Number

1 The River Nile is 6 695 km long, measured to the nearest kilometre.
What is its shortest possible length, in metres?

SEG 1999

2 In 1990 a fruit corner yogurt cost 20p.

(a)   In 1991 a fruit corner yogurt cost 15% more
than in 1990.
How much more did one of these yogurts cost
in 1991?

(b)   In 1992 a fruit corner yogurt cost 24 pence.
Calculate the percentage increase in the price of
one of these yogurts from 1990 to 1992.

(c)   A fruit corner yogurt weighs 175 g altogether.
The ratio of the **weight of fruit** to the **weight of yogurt** is 2 : 5.
Calculate the weight of the fruit.

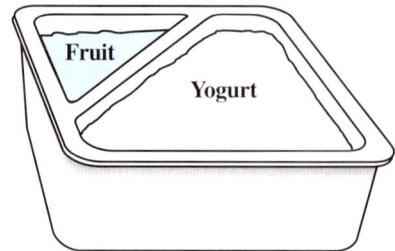

SEG 1995

3 Tim runs 100 m in 10 seconds.
What is his average speed?
Give your answer in kilometres per hour.

SEG 2000 S

4 Karen has just got a new job and has to move to a new flat.

(a)   Her old flat cost £480 per month to rent.
Her new flat costs 15% more to rent than her old flat.
How much does her new flat cost per month?

(b)   In her new job, Karen is paid a salary of £30 000 per year.
Her new salary is 25% more than her old salary.
What was her old salary?

SEG 2000 S

5 A number x written as the product of its prime factors is $2^3 \times 3^2 \times 7$.
A number y written as the product of its prime factors is $2^2 \times 3^3 \times 7$.

(a)   Calculate the values of x and y.
(b)   Write the number xy as the product of its prime factors.
(c)   Write the number $7x$ as the product of its prime factors.
(d)   Write the number $9y$ as the product of its prime factors.
(e)   Write $14x$ as the product of its prime factors and explain why it is a square number.

6 (a)   (i)   Write down the highest common factor of 10 and 15.
(ii)   Write down the lowest common multiple of 10 and 15.

p, q and r are prime numbers.
$x = pq$ and $y = qr$.
The prime numbers p, q and r have the following values:

$$1 < p \leqslant 4 \qquad 7 \leqslant q \leqslant 9 \qquad 10 \leqslant r < 15$$

(b)   Write down **all** the possible values of x and y.

SEG 1999

7 $A = 3 \times 10^4$

$B = 5 \times 10^{-2}$

(a) Calculate $A \times B$.

Give your answer in standard form.

(b) Calculate $A \div B$.

Give your answer in standard form.

8 The length of a rectangle is increased by 10%.

The width of the rectangle is decreased by 30%.

Calculate the percentage change in the area of the rectangle.

SEG 1998

9 (a) Use approximations to estimate $\sqrt{\dfrac{40\ 095}{(9.87)^2}}$.

(b) (i) Work out 3×10^5 times 5×10^{-2}, giving your answer in standard form.

(ii) Work out 3×10^5 divided by 5×10^{-2}, giving your answer in standard form.

SEG 2000 S

10 (a) Express 20 as the product of its prime factors.

(b) a and b are prime numbers.

(i) $\sqrt{20}$ can be written in the form $a\sqrt{b}$.

Calculate the values of a and b.

(ii) $\dfrac{1}{\sqrt{20}}$ can be written in the form $\dfrac{b^x}{a}$ where x is a rational number.

Calculate the value of x.

SEG 1999

11 (a) Evaluate 70^3 giving your answer in standard form.

(b) Evaluate $16^{\frac{1}{4}}$.

SEG 1997

12 Express each of the following as a fraction in its simplest form.

(a) 4^{-3} (b) $\left(\dfrac{27}{125}\right)^{\frac{1}{3}}$ (c) $256^{-\frac{1}{2}}$

SEG 1998

13 (a) State which of these numbers is irrational

$$\sqrt{5}, \quad \pi, \quad \sqrt{2.56}, \quad \left(\sqrt{3}\right)^3, \quad 2\tfrac{1}{7}, \quad 5, \quad \sqrt[3]{8}.$$

(b) Write down two different irrational numbers whose product is a rational number.

SEG 1995

14 (a) Which of the following are rational?

(i) $\pi\sqrt{3}$ (ii) $\sqrt{2} + 1$ (iii) $3^0 + 3^{-1} + 3^{-2}$

(iv) $\left(\sqrt{5}\right)^2$ (v) π^2

(b) When p and q are both rational numbers, $(p + q)$ is also rational.

Write down one example to show this.

(c) Write down a fraction which is equal to these recurring decimals.

(i) $0.555555\ldots$ (ii) $0.363636\ldots$

SEG 1994

15 (a) For each of the following, state whether it is rational or irrational.
When the result is a rational number, write the answer as a fraction in its simplest form.

   (i) 0.272727 …   (ii) $1 + \sqrt{2}$ (iii) $4^0 + 4^{-1} + 4^{-2}$

(b) b is a positive integer greater than 2.

   $\sqrt{2} \times \sqrt{b}$ is rational.
   Write down a possible value for b.

(c) $a^3 = 25$, $b^3 = 27$, $c^3 = 0.125$, $d^3 = 3\frac{3}{8}$.
   Which of the numbers a, b, c, d are irrational?

SEG 1995

16 (a) The mass of a plant on kitchen scales is 2.474 kg. What is the least possible mass of the plant?

(b) The mass of another plant on scientific scales is 1.6280 kg. What are the upper and lower bounds of the mass of this plant?

SEG 1994

17 Sections of a railway line are measured to the nearest metre as either 200 m or 80 m.
What are the bounds on the total length of 15 sections, consisting of eight 200 m sections and seven 80 m sections?

SEG 1995

18 The maximum clearance under a bridge is 4.1 m.
A bus is 12 feet 7 inches high.
Will the bus go under the bridge?
Use 1 m = 39 inches and 1 foot = 12 inches.
You **must** show all your working.

SEG 1997

19 When washing hair, a hairdresser uses shampoo and conditioner.
He uses 88% of a 660 ml bottle of conditioner.
The ratio of the amount of shampoo to the amount of conditioner used is 5 : 3.
How much shampoo is used?

SEG 1998

20 (a) Calculate the value of $\dfrac{6.73 + 4.23}{8.41 - \sqrt{9.71}}$.

(b) The cost, £C, of moving a load, M kilograms, a distance, D miles, is given by the formula $C = 22 + 0.47 (2M + D)$.
   (i) Find C when $M = 61.8$ and $D = 317$.
   (ii) Sarah calculates the value of C when $M = 53$ and $D = 198$.
        She gets an answer of £26.98.
        Use estimates to check whether Sarah's answer is of the correct order of magnitude.
        You **must** show all your working.

SEG 1997

21 (a) Calculate the value of 2×5^9.

(b) (i) Calculate $\dfrac{28.3 + \sqrt{0.512}}{(18.9 - 2.75)^2}$.

   (ii) Paul gives his answer to (i) correct to 5 significant figures.
        Give one reason why this is **not** an appropriate degree of accuracy.

(c) Calculate the value of $(2.34 \times 10^{-2})^{\frac{1}{2}}$.

SEG 1996

22 The formula for the population, P, of a country, with a growth rate of $r\%$ per year, in time t years, is given by

$$P = P_0 \left(1 + \frac{r}{100} \right)^t,$$

where P_0 is the population this year.
The population of Nigeria in 1994 is 66.2 million. The growth rate is 3% per year.
Calculate the population of Nigeria in five years time.

SEG 1994

23 Pamela wins £2 346 549 on the National Lottery.
(a) Write 2 346 549 in standard form.

Pamela invests some of her winnings.
The value of her investment, after t years, is given by the formula
Value (£) $= P(1 + 0.073)^t$
where P is the amount of money invested.

(b) Pamela invests two million pounds.
Calculate the value of her investment after 3 years.

SEG 1999

24 A plane flies from London to Naples at an average speed of 497 mph. The distance is 1413 miles.
(a) Find the time taken.
Give your answer in hours and minutes.

On one flight, the plane takes 2 hours 40 minutes for the journey from London to Naples.
(b) What is the average speed?
Give your answer correct to 3 significant figures.

SEG 1998

25 Light travels at 186 284 miles per second.
The planet Jupiter is 483.6 million miles from the Sun.
(a) Calculate how long light takes to travel from the Sun to Jupiter.
Give your answer to the nearest minute.
(b) Use approximation to check that your answer is of the right order of magnitude.
You **must** show all your working.

SEG 1998

26 On average, 5 litres of paint covers $22.5 \, \text{m}^2$.
A decorator buys 96 litres of paint to paint an area of $405 \, \text{m}^2$.
What percentage of the paint is used?

SEG 1999

27 (a) Simon invests £360 at 6.4% per annum simple interest.
How much interest does he get at the end of 6 months?
(b) Lucy invests £5000 at 6% per annum compound interest.
Calculate the interest on her investment at the end of 3 years.

SEG 2000 S

28 In the United Kingdom there are 28.7 million males of which 4.13 million are over 65.
Calculate the percentage of males in the United Kingdom who are over 65.
Give your answer to an appropriate degree of accuracy.

SEG 2000 S

29 Ben needs to insure his car. The gross premium is £1150 per annum.
There is a 15% reduction because he is the only driver.
He is then allowed a further 60% for his No Claim Bonus.
What premium does Ben pay?

SEG 1997

30 In a sale, everything is reduced by 17%. Charles pays £84.66 for a CD player in the sale.
How much money does Charles save by buying the CD player in the sale?

SEG 1999

31 The volume of a container is 1170 cu ft.
The weight of its contents is 59 500 lb.
Find the density of the contents.

SEG 1998

32 (a) Calculate the value of $2^a \times a^2$, when $a = -2$.

(b) Work out $\dfrac{2.7 \times 10^3}{4.3 \times 10^{-3}}$, giving your answer in standard form.

SEG 1999

33 In 1982, the electricity production in the United Kingdom was 2.8×10^{11} kilowatt hours.
The number of employees working in the electricity supply industry was 5.3×10^5.
What was the electricity production per employee? Give your answer in standard form.

SEG 1994

34 (a) A town has a population of 645 166 people.
The ratio of retired people to the rest of the population is 1 : 3.
How many people are retired?
Give your answer correct to three significant figures.

(b) In Britain there are 5.80×10^7 people.
The number of retired people is 1.04×10^7.
What percentage of people in Britain are retired?
Give your answer to an appropriate degree of accuracy.

SEG 1998

35 Some rectangles have diagonals whose lengths are irrational.
For each of these rectangles, calculate the length of the diagonal and state whether this
length is **rational** or **irrational**.

$$\text{Diagonal} = \sqrt{(a^2 + b^2)}, \text{ where } a \text{ and } b \text{ are the lengths of the sides}$$

(Diagrams not to scale)

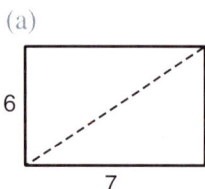

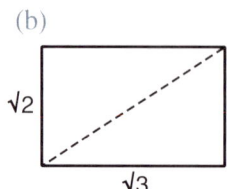

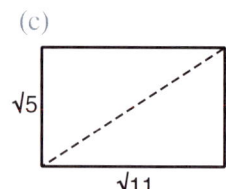

(a)

6

7

(b)

$\sqrt{2}$

$\sqrt{3}$

(c)

$\sqrt{5}$

$\sqrt{11}$

SEG 1995

36 (a) Find a fraction equivalent to the recurring decimal $0.2\dot{1}$.
(b) Hence, or otherwise, calculate a fraction equivalent to the recurring decimal $0.8\dot{2}\dot{1}$.

SEG 1998

37 (a) The sides of a rectangle have dimensions 20 cm and 30 cm each measured to the nearest centimetre.
Calculate the smallest possible area of the rectangle.

(b) The sides of a square have length x cm measured to the nearest centimetre.
Write down and simplify an expression, in terms of x, for the difference between the largest and smallest possible areas of the square.

SEG 1998

38 The contents of a packet of marzipan weigh 1.5 kg to the nearest 10 g.
(a) What is the largest number of grams it can contain?

Each packet of marzipan is sold at £4.20. This price is given to the nearest 20p.
(b) Find the maximum and minimum cost per 100 g of marzipan.
Give your answer correct to four significant figures.

SEG 1998

39 Rods are made to move up and down inside cylinders.
The radius of a rod is 5.50 cm, to the nearest hundredth of a centimetre.
The radius of a cylinder is 5.6 cm, to the nearest tenth of a centimetre.

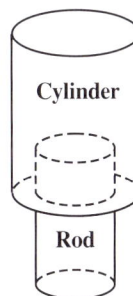
Cylinder
Rod

(a) What is the maximum gap between a rod and a cylinder when the rod is inside the cylinder?

(b) Will these rods always fit into these cylinders?
You **must** show all your working.

SEG 1997

40 The volume, V, of a regular tetrahedron of side length a is given by $V = \frac{\sqrt{2}}{12} a^3$.

The length of one side of a particular regular tetrahedron is measured as 5.20 cm to the nearest tenth of a millimetre.
(a) What is the range of possible values for V?

(b) Density is defined by density $= \frac{\text{mass}}{\text{volume}}$.

The mass of the tetrahedron is found experimentally to be 25 g to the nearest gram.
What is the minimum possible density of the tetrahedron?

SEG 1996

41 A car's stopping distance, d feet, is proportional to the square of its speed, v miles per hour (mph). For a car travelling at 30 mph, the stopping distance is 45 feet.
(a) Find the equation connecting v and d.
(b) Find the stopping distance when the car is travelling at 50 mph.
(c) Find the speed when the stopping distance is 210 feet.

SEG 1998

42 A gravitational force of F Newtons exists between two objects. This force is inversely proportional to the square of the distance, d metres, between them.
The force is 0.6673 Newtons when the distance is 10 metres.

(a) Find the equation connecting F and d.
(b) Find the force when the distance is 7.8 metres.
(c) Find the distance when the force is 0.38 Newtons.

SEG 1999

CHAPTER 8

Introduction to Algebra

Algebra is sometimes called the language of Mathematics.

Writing expressions and formulae

Algebra can be used in many situations.

> An **expression** is just an answer using letters and numbers.
>
> A **formula** is an algebraic rule. It always has an equals sign.

EXAMPLES

1 A fence is L metres long.
An extra 50 metres is put on one end.
Write an **expression** for the total length of the fence.

The fence is now $(L + 50)$ metres long.

2 Boxes of matches each contain 48 matches.
Write down a **formula** for the number of matches, M, in N boxes of matches.

$M = 48 \times N$

This should be written as $M = 48N$.

Exercise 8.1

1 Egg boxes hold 12 eggs each.
How many eggs are there in e boxes?

2 A child is making a tower with toy bricks. He has b bricks in his tower.

Write an expression for the number of bricks in the tower after he takes 3 bricks from the top.

3 I am a years old.
(a) How old will I be in 1 years time?
(b) How old was I four years ago?
(c) How old will I be in n years time?

4 John is h cm tall.
Sue is 12 cm taller than John.
Write down an expression for Sue's height in terms of h.

5 John has d CDs.
(a) Carol has twice as many CDs as John.
Write down an expression for the number of CDs that Carol has in terms of d.

(b) Fred has 5 more CDs than Carol.
Write down an expression for the number of CDs that Fred has in terms of d.

6 A packet of biscuits costs y pence.
Write down a formula for the cost, P pence, of another packet which costs
(a) five pence more than the first packet,
(b) two pence less than the first packet,
(c) twice the cost of the first packet,
(d) three pence more than twice the price of the first packet,
(e) a penny less than three times the cost of the first packet.

7 David is d years old.
Copy and complete this table to show the ages, A, of these people.

Name	Clue	Age
Alec	3 years older than David.	$A = d + 3$
Ben	2 years younger than David.	
Charlotte	Twice as old as David.	
Erica	Half David's age.	
Frank	5 years younger than three times David's age.	
Gillian	Next year she will be three times as old as David.	

Simplifying

Addition and subtracting terms

You can add and subtract **terms** with the same letter.
The process is sometimes called **collecting like terms**.

$w + 4w = 5w$
$5k + 3k - 2k = 6k$
$2a + 4b$ cannot be simplified.
$6 + a$ cannot be simplified.
$3p + 5 + p - 1 = 4p + 4$

Multiplying terms

$a \times b = ab$ $3x \times y = 3xy$
$a \times a = a^2$ $5c \times 4c = 20c^2$
$3a \times 2b = 6ab$ $b \times b \times b = b^3$

Dividing terms

Division is the opposite operation to multiplication.
Divide the numbers and then letters in alphabetical order.
The process is sometimes called **cancelling**.

$\dfrac{6ab}{2a} = 3b$

$\dfrac{4p^2q}{12pq^2} = \dfrac{p}{3q}$

EXAMPLE   Three girls were given this question.

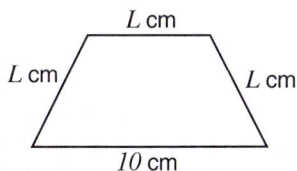

Write down the formula for the perimeter, P, of this shape in terms of L.

Their answers were:

Jaqui: $P = L + L + L + 10$
Fionna: $P = L \times 3 + 10$
Suzanne: $P = 3L + 10$

All three formulae are correct . . .
. . . but Suzanne's formula is the simplest.

Exercise 8.2

1 Write simpler expressions for the following.

(a) $c + c + c$
(b) $x + x + x + x + x$
(c) $p + p + p + p + p + p + p$
(d) $2y + 3y$
(e) $5g + g + 4g$
(f) $5z + 4z + z + 3z$
(g) $2m + 5m + m$
(h) $5r - 3r$
(i) $7t - 2t$
(j) $5j + 2j - 4j$
(k) $9c - 2c - 3c$
(l) $12w - 7w - 4w$
(m) $5d + 7d - 12d$
(n) $3x - 8x$
(o) $2a - 5a - 12a + a$

2 Write down the simplest possible expression for the perimeters of these shapes.

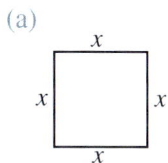

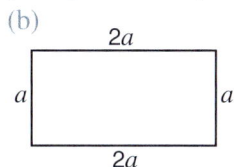

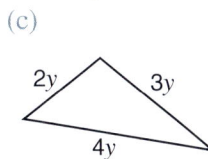

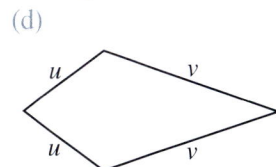

(a)   (b)   (c)   (d)

3 Simplify **where possible**.

(a) $a + 2a + 5$
(b) $3x + 5y - x - 2y$
(c) $m + 2m - n + 3n$
(d) $a + 6$
(e) $p + 2q + 2p + q$
(f) $2d + 5 - d - 2$
(g) $3a - 5a$
(h) $a - 2a + 7 + a$
(i) $2c + d + 4 - c - 2d + 7$
(j) $f + g - f - g$
(k) $2v + w - 3w + v$
(l) $7 - 2t - 9 - 3t$

4 Write down a formula for the perimeter, P, for each shape in terms of the other letters.

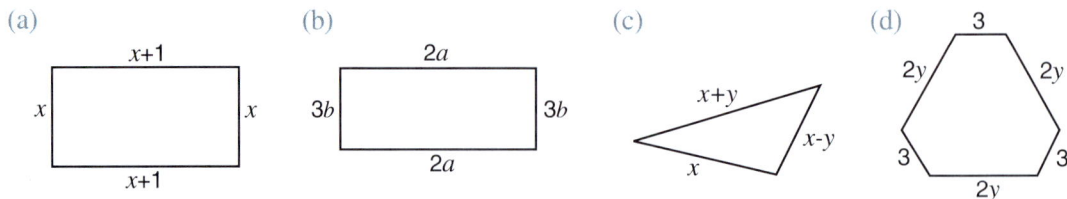

(a)

(b)

(c)

(d)

5 Simplify.

(a) $p^2 + 3p^2$
(b) $ab + ac - 2ab$
(c) $a^2 + 2a^2 + 3a^2$
(d) $a + 2a - a^2 + 3a^2$
(e) $8ab - 4ab$
(f) $x^3 + y^2 - x^3 - 2y^2$

6 Simplify.

(a) $3 \times y$
(b) $5 \times p$
(c) $x \times y$
(d) $a \times a$
(e) $2 \times a \times a$
(f) $4 \times a \times a$
(g) $h \times h \times h$
(h) $w \times w^2$
(i) $2 \times d \times d \times d$
(j) $2m \times m^2$
(k) $2x \times 3x \times x$
(l) $3a \times 2a$

7 Write the area of each shape in the simplest way.

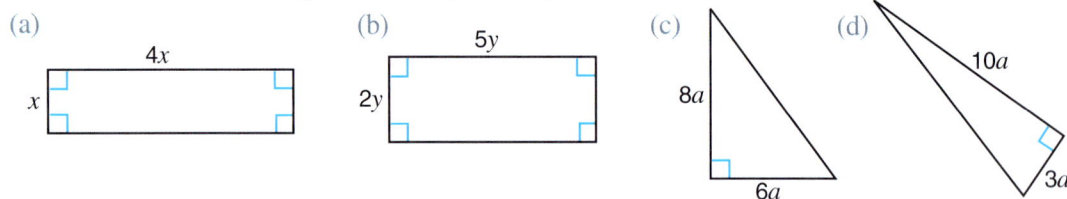

(a)

(b)

(c)

(d)

8 Find simplified expressions for the volumes of these cuboids.

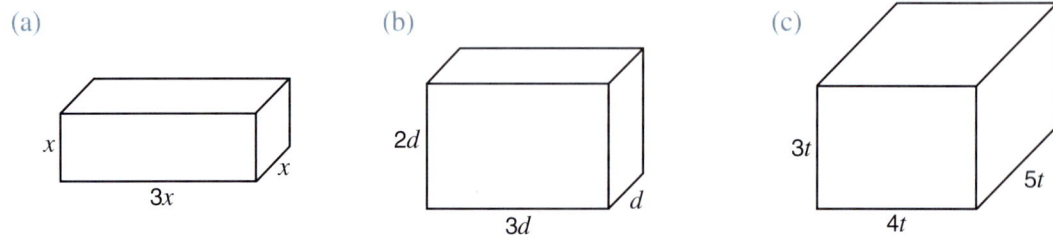

(a)

(b)

(c)

9 Simplify the following.

(a) $f \times g$
(b) $4 \times 5c$
(c) $4d \times e$
(d) $2 \times a \times b$
(e) $3x \times 4y$
(f) $4a \times 2b$
(g) $2h \times h \times j$
(h) $y \times 5w$
(i) $2m \times 7p^2$
(j) $2x \times 3y \times x^2$
(k) $3a^2b \times 7ab^2$
(l) $5e^2f \times 3f^3g^2$

10 Simplify the following by cancelling.

(a) $\dfrac{2uv}{u}$
(b) $\dfrac{12p^2}{3p}$
(c) $\dfrac{a^2bc^3}{2ab}$
(d) $\dfrac{20mn}{5m^2n}$
(e) $\dfrac{0.8w^3}{0.05w^5}$
(f) $\dfrac{3ab}{2ac} \times \dfrac{4bc}{6b^2}$

Brackets

Some expressions and formulae contain **brackets**.
You can remove brackets, either by using a diagram or by expanding (multiplying out).

Diagram method

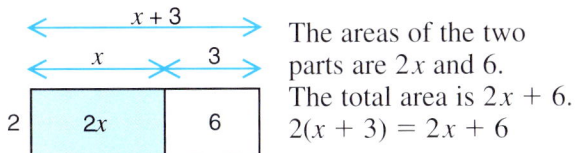

The areas of the two parts are $2x$ and 6.
The total area is $2x + 6$.
$2(x + 3) = 2x + 6$

Expanding

$2(x + 3) = 2 \times x + 2 \times 3$
$\qquad\qquad = 2x + 6$

EXAMPLES

1 Expand $x(x + 3)$ by multiplying out the brackets.

$x(x + 3) = x \times x + x \times 3$
$\qquad\qquad = x^2 + 3x$

2 Expand $3y(2x - 5y)$.

$3y(2x - 5y) = 3y \times 2x - 3y \times 5y$
$\qquad\qquad\qquad = 6xy - 15y^2$

3 Expand $2(3m + n) - 3(2n - m)$.

$2(3m + n) - 3(2n - m)$
$= 6m + 2n - 6n + 3m$
$= 9m - 4n$

Remember:
Always remove brackets first, then simplify by collecting like terms.

$3(t + 4) + 2$ — Remove the brackets
$= 3t + 12 + 2$
$= 3t + 14$ — Simplify

Exercise 8.3

1 Multiply out the brackets by expanding.

(a) $3(a - 4)$ (b) $b(c - 3)$ (c) $d(d + 2)$
(d) $3e(e - 1)$ (e) $2f(3 - 2f)$ (f) $g(2g + 3h)$
(g) $5j(3k - 4j)$ (h) $2m(3 - 4m)$ (i) $3p(2p + 3q - 4)$
(j) $rs(r + s + 2)$

2 Multiply out the brackets and simplify where possible.

(a) $2(x + 1) + 3$ (b) $3(a + 2) + 5$ (c) $6(w + 4) + 7$
(d) $4(z + 2) + z$ (e) $5(t + 3) + 3t$ (f) $3(c - 2) - c$
(g) $4(2a + 5) + 3$ (h) $2x + 4(x - 5)$ (i) $3(p - 5) - p + 4$

3 Remove the brackets and simplify.

(a) $2(x + 1) + 3(x + 2)$ (b) $3(a + 1) + 2(a + 5)$
(c) $4(y + 2) + 5(y + 3)$ (d) $2(3a + 1) - 3(a + 1)$
(e) $3(2t + 5) + 5(4t + 3)$ (f) $3(z + 5) + 2(z - 1)$
(g) $7(q - 2) - 5(q + 6)$ (h) $5(x + 3) - 6(x - 3)$
(i) $8(2e - 1) - 4(e - 2)$ (j) $2(5d + 4) - 2(d - 1)$

4 Simplify.

(a) $3(a + b) + 2(a - b)$ (b) $4(2x + 5) + 3(3x - 2)$
(c) $d(d + 2e) + 2d(2d + e)$ (d) $4(u + v) - 2(u - v)$
(e) $x(x + 3) - x(x + 2)$ (f) $x(2x + 1) - 2(x - 2)$

Factorising

Factorising is the opposite operation to removing brackets. For example, $x^2 + 4x = x(x + 4)$.

> **Common factors**
> The **factors** of a number are all the numbers that will divide exactly into the number.
> Factors of 6 are 1, 2, 3 and 6.
> A **common factor** is a factor which will divide into two, or more numbers.

EXAMPLES

> You can check that you have factorised an expression correctly by multiplying out the brackets.

1 Factorise $8ab + 12bc$.

Each term has a factor of 4 and a factor of b.
So the **common factor** of $8ab$ and $12bc$ is $4b$.
$8ab + 12bc = 4b(2a + 3c)$

2 Factorise $6d^2 - 3d^3$.

Each term has a factor of 3 and a factor of d^2.
So the **common factor** of $6d^2$ and $3d^3$ is $3d^2$.
$6d^2 - 3d^3 = 3d^2(2 - d)$

3 Factorise $e^3 + e$.

$e^3 + e = e(e^2 + 1)$
and $e(e^2 + 1) = e^3 + e$

4 Factorise $4f^3 + 6f^2 - 2f$.

$4f^3 + 6f^2 - 2f = 2f(2f^2 + 3f - 1)$
and $2f(2f^2 + 3f - 1) = 4f^3 + 6f^2 - 2f$

Exercise 8.4

1 Copy and complete the following.
   (a) $4a + 4b = 4(\ldots + \ldots)$
   (b) $5c - 5d = 5(\ldots - \ldots)$
   (c) $ef + eg = e(\ldots + \ldots)$
   (d) $hj + jk = j(\ldots + \ldots)$
   (e) $l^2 - l = l(\ldots - \ldots)$
   (f) $m + m^2 = m(\ldots + \ldots)$
   (g) $5n + 10p = 5(\ldots + \ldots)$

2 Factorise.
   (a) $2a + 2b$
   (b) $7c + 7d$
   (c) $8e - 2f$
   (d) $7g + 14h$
   (e) $24j - 16k$
   (f) $ab - a$
   (g) $cd + de$
   (h) $fg + fh$
   (i) $4jk + 2j$
   (j) $6l - 9lm$
   (k) $a^2 - a$
   (l) $b - b^2$
   (m) $cd^2 + cd$
   (n) $e^2f - e$
   (o) $gh^2 - g^2h$

3 Factorise completely.
   (a) $4a + 18ab$
   (b) $ab^2 - b^2c$
   (c) $20x + 4xy$
   (d) $a^3 + a^5 + a^2$
   (e) $2\pi r + \pi r^2$
   (f) $20a^2b + 12ab^2$
   (g) $4a^2 - 2a$
   (h) $3pq - 9p^2q$

Solving equations

Solving an equation means finding the numerical value of the letter which fits the equation.
If you do the same to both sides of an equation, it is still true.

EXAMPLES   Solve these equations. Explain what you are doing.

1 Solve $d - 13 = -5$.

$d - 13 = -5$
Add 13 to both sides.
$d = 8$

2 Solve $-4a = 20$.

$-4a = 20$
Divide both sides by -4.
$a = -5$

3 Solve $5 - 4n = -1$.

$5 - 4n = -1$
Subtract 5 from both sides.
$-4n = -6$
Divide both sides by -4.
$n = 1.5$

The aim is to find the numerical value of the letter, by ending up with **one letter** on one side of the equation and a **number** on the other side of the equation.

4 Solve $\frac{1}{2}x - 7 = -1$.

$\frac{1}{2}x - 7 = -1$
Add 7 to both sides.
$\frac{1}{2}x = 6$
Multiply both sides by 2.
$x = 12$

Look at the examples carefully.
The steps taken to solve the equations are explained.
Notice that:
Doing the same to both sides means:
  adding the **same number** to both sides.
  subtracting the **same number** from both sides.
  dividing both sides by the **same number**.
  multiplying both sides by the **same number**.

Equations with letters on both sides

In some questions letters appear on both sides of the equation.

EXAMPLES

5 Solve $2p + 3 = 4 + 5p$.

$2p + 3 = 4 + 5p$
Subtract 3 from both sides.
$2p = 1 + 5p$
Subtract $5p$ from both sides.
$-3p = 1$
Divide both sides by -3.
$p = -\frac{1}{3}$

6 Solve $\frac{1}{2}x - 7 = \frac{1}{4}x + 1$.

$\frac{1}{2}x - 7 = \frac{1}{4}x + 1$
Add 7 to both sides.
$\frac{1}{2}x = \frac{1}{4}x + 8$
Subtract $\frac{1}{4}x$ from both sides.
$\frac{1}{2}x - \frac{1}{4}x = \frac{1}{4}x$
$\frac{1}{4}x = 8$
Multiply both sides by 4.
$x = 32$

As you become more confident you will not need to write down the steps you use to solve equations.

1 Solve these equations. Explain what you are doing.
- (a) $4x + 3 = 11$
- (b) $3n - 1 = 8$
- (c) $2a + 7 = 7$
- (d) $2d - 7 = 8$
- (e) $8c + 3 = 15$
- (f) $3 + 2a = -17$
- (g) $-6p - 1 = 8$
- (h) $2w + 6 = 4$
- (i) $4m + 8 = 2$
- (j) $\frac{1}{2}z + 2 = 7$
- (k) $\frac{1}{4}t - 1 = 4$
- (l) $1 - \frac{x}{6} = 4$

2 Solve these equations.
There is no need to explain your working if you are confident of what you are doing.
- (a) $2p + 1 = 9$
- (b) $4t - 1 = 11$
- (c) $3h - 7 = 14$
- (d) $5d - 8 = 42$
- (e) $3 + 2b = 15$
- (f) $\frac{1}{2}x - 3 = 2$
- (g) $8y - 14 = 26$
- (h) $2.5z + 6 = 26$
- (i) $\frac{n}{4} + 1 = 7$

3 Solve these equations.
- (a) $p + 3 = -7$
- (b) $6a = 15$
- (c) $32 - 3t = 11$
- (d) $-3 = 17 - 5n$
- (e) $0.8c + 4 = 3.6$
- (f) $1.2h + 1.7 = -3.1$
- (g) $3 + 5x = 18$
- (h) $0.5y + 6 = 2$
- (i) $-\frac{1}{2}y + 13 = 7$
- (j) $-2 = 5m + 13$
- (k) $\frac{t}{3} + 21 = 15$
- (l) $12 - \frac{v}{3} = 15$

4 Solve:
- (a) $4x + 1 = x + 7$
- (b) $3a + 5 = a + 7$
- (c) $5p + 2 = p + 10$
- (d) $6m - 1 = m + 9$
- (e) $2y - 3 = 6 - y$
- (f) $3t - 5 = 7 - t$
- (g) $8n + 1 = 10 - n$
- (h) $2c + 1 = 8 + c$
- (i) $h - 2 = 2 - h$
- (j) $3d - 4 = 5 + d$
- (k) $7k + 3 = 3k + 7$
- (l) $x + 2 = \frac{1}{2}x + 5$
- (m) $4a + 3 = a$
- (n) $3x - 2 = x$

5 Solve:
- (a) $3c - 5 = c + 9$
- (b) $2p + 1 = 10 - p$
- (c) $3a + 1 = 16 - 2a$
- (d) $6t - 1 = 15 - 2t$
- (e) $6h - 16 = h + 4$
- (f) $13 + 2u = 7 + 5u$
- (g) $4b - 3 = 8b - 7$
- (h) $3 - 5d = d + 18$
- (i) $3n + 2 = n$
- (j) $7x = 12 + 3x$

6 Solve:
- (a) $4t + 3 = t - 12$
- (b) $3y + 1 = 9 - y$
- (c) $12s = 2s + 5$
- (d) $3q = 12 - q$
- (e) $6a - 2.5 = a + 6.5$
- (f) $8c + 0.7 = 1.8 - 2c$
- (g) $4 - 1\frac{1}{2}p = \frac{1}{2}p - 6$
- (h) $x = \frac{1}{2}x - 3$

Equations with brackets

Equations can include brackets.
Any brackets can be removed by multiplying out.
This is called **expanding**.

Remember:
$$2(x + 3) = 2 \times x + 2 \times 3$$
$$= 2x + 6$$
$$3(4a - 5) = 12a - 15$$

EXAMPLES Solve the following equations.

1 Solve $3(x + 2) = 12$.

$3(x + 2) = 12$
Expand the brackets.
$3x + 6 = 12$
$3x = 6$
$x = 2$

2 Solve $4(3 + 2x) = 5(x + 2)$.

$4(3 + 2x) = 5(x + 2)$
$12 + 8x = 5x + 10$
$8x = 5x - 2$
$3x = -2$
$x = -\frac{2}{3}$

EXAMPLE

3 Solve $5(x + 2) + 2(2x − 1) = 7(x − 4)$.

$5(x + 2) + 2(2x − 1) = 7(x − 4)$
Expanding.
$5x + 10 + 4x − 2 = 7x − 28$
Gather like terms.
$9x + 8 = 7x − 28$
Subtract 8 from both sides.
$9x = 7x − 36$
Subtract 7x from both sides.
$2x = −36$
Divide both sides by 2.
$x = −18$

Gathering terms
There are four terms in the expression.
$5x + 10 + 4x − 2$
The x terms are **like** terms.
$5x + 4x = 9x$
The number terms are **like** terms.
$10 − 2 = 8$
So, $5x + 10 + 4x − 2 = 9x + 8$

Equations with fractions

You have already met some equations with fractions in Exercise 8.5.
This section deals with harder equations involving fractions.
For example: $\frac{3}{4} x = \frac{2}{5}$
With equations like this, it is easier to get rid of the fractions first.
To do this multiply both sides of the equation by the lowest common multiple of the denominators of the fractions.

What part of the fraction is the denominator?

The multiples of 4 are: 4, 8, 12, 16, **20**, . . .
The multiples of 5 are: 5, 10, 15, **20**, . . .
The lowest common multiple of 4 and 5 is 20.
So, the first step is to multiply both sides of the equation by 20.

$$\frac{3}{4} x \times 20 = \frac{2}{5} \times 20$$
This is the same as:
$$x \times \frac{3}{4} \times 20 = \frac{2}{5} \times 20$$
$$15x = 8$$

Divide both sides by 15.
$$x = \frac{8}{15}$$

Remember:
$\frac{3}{4} \times 20$ is the same as $\frac{3}{4}$ of 20.
To find $\frac{3}{4}$ of 20:
$20 \div 4 = 5$ gives $\frac{1}{4}$ of 20.
$5 \times 3 = 15$ gives $\frac{3}{4}$ of 20.
So, $\frac{3}{4} \times 20 = 15$.

EXAMPLES

1 Solve $\frac{1}{4} x + 1 = 7$.

$\frac{1}{4} x + 1 = 7$
Multiply both sides by 4.
$4 \times \frac{1}{4} x = x, \quad 4 \times 1 = 4, \quad 4 \times 7 = 28$
$x + 4 = 28$
$x = 24$

2 Solve $\frac{2}{5} x = 6$.

$\frac{2}{5} x = 6$
Multiply both sides by 5.
$5 \times \frac{2}{5} x = 5 \times 6$
$2x = 30$
$x = 15$

113

3 Solve $\dfrac{x + 3}{4} = 2$.

$$\dfrac{x + 3}{4} = 2$$

Multiply both sides by 4.

$$4 \times \dfrac{(x + 3)}{4} = 4 \times 2$$
$$x + 3 = 8$$
$$x = 5$$

4 Solve $\dfrac{x - 1}{3} = \dfrac{x + 1}{4}$.

$$\dfrac{x - 1}{3} = \dfrac{x + 1}{4}$$

Multiply both sides by 12.
Explain why?

$$4(x - 1) = 3(x + 1)$$
$$4x - 4 = 3x + 3$$
$$4x = 3x + 7$$
$$x = 7$$

Exercise 8.6

1 Solve:
- (a) $2(x + 3) = 12$
- (b) $4(a + 1) = 12$
- (c) $6(c - 2) = 24$
- (d) $3(p - 2) = 9$
- (e) $4(2d - 1) = 20$
- (f) $5(4 + 2t) = 50$
- (g) $3(6 - a) = 15$
- (h) $2(2 - 3t) = 10$

2 Solve:
- (a) $3(n + 5) + n = 23$
- (b) $3(2z - 5) = z + 15$
- (c) $4(2w + 3) + 7 = 43$
- (d) $m + 2(m + 1) = 14$
- (e) $2(3h - 4) = 3(h + 1) - 5$
- (f) $2(3 - 2x) = 2(6 - x)$
- (g) $2(3w - 1) + 4w = 28$
- (h) $2(y + 4) + 3(2y - 5) = 5$
- (i) $3(2v + 3) = 5 - 4(3 - v)$
- (j) $5c - 2(4c - 9) = 5 + 5(2 - c)$

3 Explain how you could get rid of the fractions in each of these equations.
- (a) $\dfrac{3}{4} a = \dfrac{2}{3}$
- (b) $\dfrac{5}{8} = \dfrac{3}{4} b$
- (c) $\dfrac{2}{7} c + 4 = 5$
- (d) $\dfrac{x + 3}{5} = \dfrac{x - 7}{3}$

4 Solve these equations. Explain each step of your working.
- (a) $\dfrac{2}{3} x = 4$
- (b) $\dfrac{3}{4} w = 6$
- (c) $\dfrac{5}{6} n = 20$
- (d) $\dfrac{4}{5} a = \dfrac{3}{8}$
- (e) $\dfrac{3}{4} p = \dfrac{4}{7}$
- (f) $\dfrac{2}{3} b = \dfrac{5}{9}$

5 Solve these equations.
- (a) $\dfrac{1}{4} y - 2 = 5$
- (b) $\dfrac{a}{3} - 1 = 7$
- (c) $\dfrac{a}{4} - 1 = 5$
- (d) $\dfrac{1}{4} t - 1 = 5$
- (e) $\dfrac{h + 1}{4} = 3$
- (f) $\dfrac{7 - 2x}{3} = 5$
- (g) $\dfrac{2(4x - 3)}{5} = -6$
- (h) $\dfrac{a - 1}{2} = \dfrac{a + 1}{3}$
- (i) $\dfrac{x + 2}{5} = \dfrac{3 - x}{4}$
- (j) $\dfrac{(x + 2)}{3} - 2 = 0$
- (k) $3 - \dfrac{(1 - x)}{2} = 0$
- (l) $\dfrac{(x - 1)}{2} - \dfrac{x + 2}{5} = 0$
- (m) $\dfrac{(a + 2)}{3} + \dfrac{(a - 3)}{4} = 4$
- (n) $\dfrac{(x - 2)}{3} - \dfrac{(x - 3)}{2} = 1$

Writing equations

So far, you have been given equations and asked to solve them. The next step is to **write equations** (or **form equations**) using the information given in a problem.

The equations can then be solved in the usual way.

You may also be asked to use the solution to the equation to answer questions related to the initial problem.

Remember:
An **expression** is just an answer using letters and numbers.
An **equation** is similar to a formula. It always has an equal sign.

1

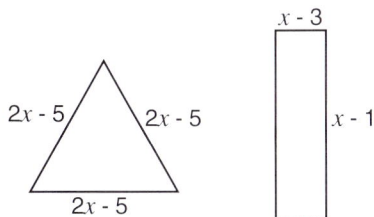

x - 3

2*x* - 5   2*x* - 5   *x* - 1

2*x* - 5

All measurements are in centimetres.

(a) Write down simplified expressions for the following, in terms of *x*.
   (i) The perimeter of the triangle.
   (ii) The perimeter of the rectangle.
(b) The perimeter of the triangle is equal to the perimeter of the rectangle.
   (i) Write down an equation in *x*.
   (ii) Use your equation to find the length of a side of the triangle.

(a) (i) The perimeter of the triangle is given by:
$$3(2x - 5)\text{ cm}$$
$$= 6x - 15\text{ cm}$$
   (ii) The perimeter of the rectangle is given by:
$$2 \times \text{length} + 2 \times \text{breadth}$$
$$= 2(x - 1) + 2(x - 3)\ \text{cm}$$
$$= 2x - 2 + 2x - 6$$
$$= 4x - 8\ \text{cm}$$

(b) (i) The perimeter of the triangle is the same as (equal to) the perimeter of the rectangle.
$$6x - 15 = 4x - 8$$
$$6x = 4x + 7$$
$$2x = 7$$
$$x = 3.5$$
   (ii) The length of a side of the triangle is given by:
$$(2x - 5)\text{ cm}$$
Substitute $x = 3.5$
$$2 \times 3.5 - 5$$
$$= 7 - 5$$
$$= 2$$
The length of a side of the triangle is 2 cm.

2 John has *x* CDs in his collection.
Sarah has five times as many CDs as John.
John and Sarah each collect another 12 CDs.
Now Sarah has twice as many CDs as John.

(a) Write down an expression, in terms of *x*, for the number of CDs Sarah has now.
(b) Form an equation and solve it to find how many CDs Sarah has now.

(a) John started with *x* CDs.
Sarah started with five times as many, 5*x* CDs.
After collecting another 12, Sarah now has 5*x* + 12 CDs.

(b) John started with *x* CDs.
He now has *x* + 12 CDs.
Sarah has twice as many CDs as John.
This means that:
$2 \times$ number of CDs John has now = number of CDs Sarah has now
$$2(x + 12) = 5x + 12$$
$$2x + 24 = 5x + 12$$
$$2x + 12 = 5x$$
$$12 = 3x$$
$$x = 4$$
The number of CDs Sarah has now is given by: 5*x* + 12
Substitute $x = 4$
$$5 \times 4 + 12$$
$$= 20 + 12$$
$$= 32$$
Sarah has 32 CDs now.

1 (a) Write down a simplified expression, in terms of x, for the perimeter of the triangle.
   (b) The perimeter of the triangle is 59 cm. Write down an equation and solve it to find the value of x.
   (c) Use your answer to find the length of each side of the triangle.

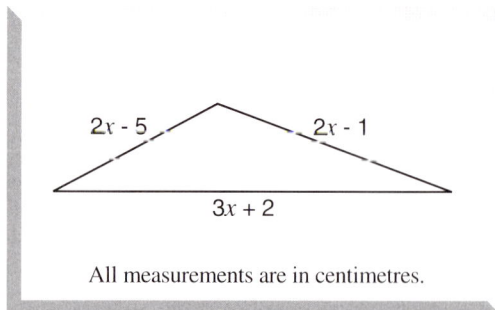

2x - 5   2x - 1   3x + 2

All measurements are in centimetres.

2 Geoffrey knows that the angles of a pentagon add up to 540°.
   (a) Write down an equation in x.
   (b) Use your equation to find the size of the largest angle.

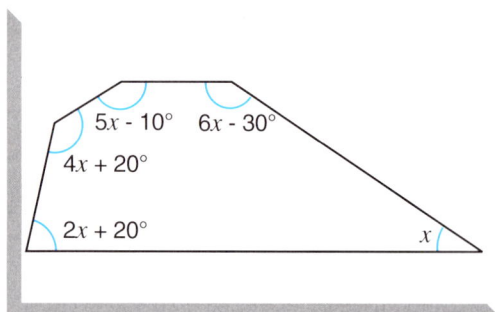

5x - 10°   6x - 30°   4x + 20°   2x + 20° x

3 (a) Write down an expression, in terms of x, for the perimeter of the rectangle.
   (b) The perimeter of the rectangle is equal to the perimeter of the square.
       Form an equation and find the value of x.
   (c) What is the perimeter of the rectangle, in centimetres?

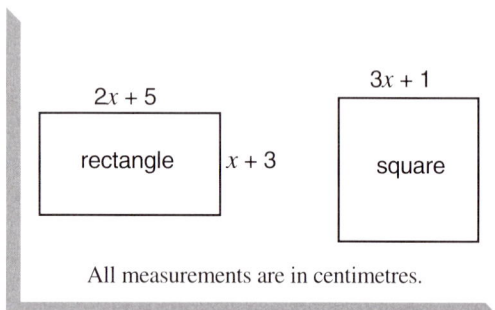

2x + 5   rectangle x + 3   3x + 1   square

All measurements are in centimetres.

4 Claire is x years old now. Her father is six times as old as Claire.
   (a) Write expressions for the following, in terms of x.
       (i) Claire's father's age now.
       (ii) Claire's age in 20 years time.
       (iii) Claire's father's age in 20 years time.
   After 20 years Claire's father will be twice as old as Claire.
   (b) Write an equation and solve it to find Claire's age now.

5 Alex has x marbles. Bert has 10 marbles fewer than Alex.
   Each boy wins two extra marbles.
   Alex then said to Bert, "I now have three times as many marbles as you have."
   (a) Write expressions for the following, in terms of x.
       (i) The number of marbles Bert had to start with.
       (ii) The number of marbles Bert has now.
   (b) (i) Using Alex's statement write down an equation.
       (ii) Solve your equation to find the number of marbles Alex had at the start.
       (iii) How many marbles does Bert have now?

What you need to know

You should be able to:

- Write simple algebraic expressions and formulae.

- Simplify expressions and formulae by collecting like terms together,
  e.g. $2d + 3d = 5d$ and $3x + 2 - x + 4 = 2x + 6$

- Multiply simple expressions together.
  e.g. $2a \times a = 2a^2$, $y \times y \times y = y^3$ and $2a \times 3b^2 = 6ab^2$

- Simplify expressions by **cancelling**. e.g. $\dfrac{6ab}{2a} = 3b$ and $\dfrac{4p^2q}{12pq^2} = \dfrac{p}{3q}$

- Multiply out brackets in expressions and formulae. e.g. $2(x - 5) = 2x - 10$

- Solve equations with unknowns on both sides of the equals sign. e.g. $3x + 1 = x + 7$

- Solve equations with brackets. e.g. $4(3 + 2x) = 5(x + 2)$

- Solve equations with fractions. e.g. $\dfrac{1}{4}x + 1 = 7$, $\dfrac{x + 3}{4} = 2$

- Write, or form, equations using the information given in a problem.

Review Exercise

1 (a) Aimee is n years old. Her brother Ben is two years younger.
Write down Ben's age in terms of n.

(b) Aimee's mother is three times as old as Aimee.
Write down her mother's age in terms of n.

(c) Aimee's father is four years older than her mother.
Write down her father's age in terms of n.

(d) Write an expression for the combined ages of all four members of the family.
Simplify your answer.

SEG 1994

2 Books of postage stamps contain n stamps.

(a) John buys a book of postage stamps. Each stamp costs 25p. Write an equation for the cost, in pence, of the stamps.

(b) Claire buys a book of postage stamps. Each stamp costs 19p. How much less than John did Claire pay for her n stamps?

SEG 1994

3

> I think of a number
> I call it x
> Multiply by 3
> Take away 5

> My answer is -2

(a) Write down an expression for
Sam's rule in terms of x.

(b) Find Sam's starting number.

SEG 1996

117

4 Solve these equations.

(a) $3 - 4q = 11$ (b) $2(s + 5) = 7$ (c) $3p - 2 = 6 - p$

(d) $4(2t - 3) + 4t = 6$ (e) $7 + 2(3p - 7) = 29$ (f) $\dfrac{2x + 9}{5} = 6$

5 Solve the equation $\frac{x}{4} + 7 = 12$.

SEG 1996

6 Solve these equations.

(a) $3x + 2 = 18 - 5x$ (b) $2(x + 3) = 18 - 6x$

SEG 1994

7 Solve the equation $2x - 1 = -2.6$.

SEG 1995

8 Solve the equation $5x - 3 = 7 - 3x$.

SEG 1996

9 The lengths of the sides of a triangle are x cm, $(x + 3)$ cm and $(x - 2)$ cm.

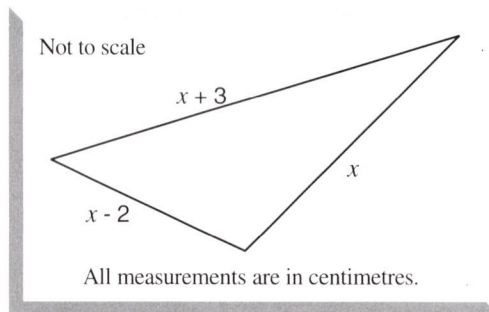

Not to scale

$x + 3$

x

x - 2

All measurements are in centimetres.

(a)   What is the perimeter of the triangle in terms of x?
(b)   The triangle has a perimeter of 22 cm.
    (i)   Write down an equation in x.
    (ii)   Use your equation to find the length of each side of the triangle.

SEG 1995

10 The angles of a triangle are $(2x - 3)°$, $(x + 4)°$ and $(x + 19)°$.

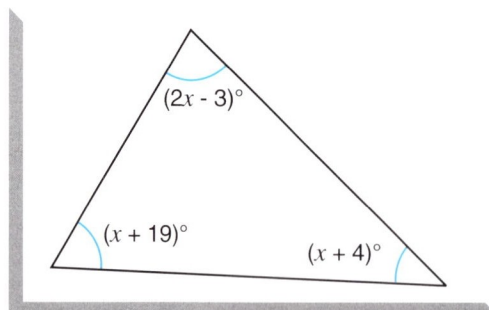

$(2x - 3)°$

$(x + 19)°$

$(x + 4)°$

(a)   Write an expression, in terms of x, for the sum of the angles.
    Write your answer in its simplest form.

The sum of the angles is 180°.
(b)   (i)   Write down an equation in x.
    (ii)   Solve your equation to find the size of the **smallest** angle in the triangle.

SEG 1998

11 P and Q are rectangles.
The dimensions are given in centimetres.

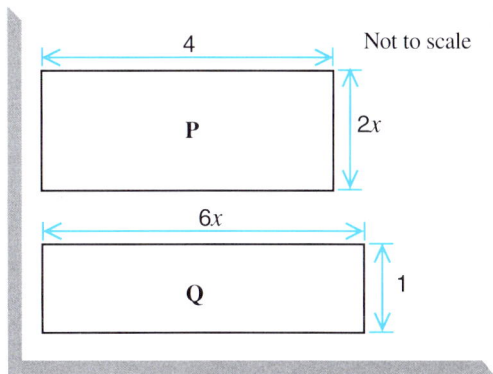

Not to scale

(a) Write down a simplified expression for the area of P.

The two rectangles have the same perimeter.
The perimeter of P is $4x + 8$.
The perimeter of Q is $12x + 2$.

(b) (i) Solve the equation $4x + 8 = 12x + 2$.
    (ii) What is the perimeter of P in centimetres?

SEG 1997

12 These rectangles are equal in area.
Solve $3(x + 2) = 2(5x - 4)$ to find the value of x.
Find the length and width of each rectangle.

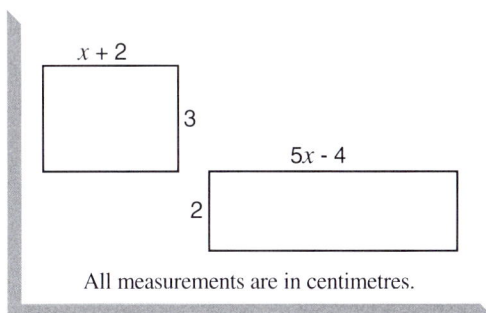

All measurements are in centimetres.

13 John is x years old now. His mother is three times as old as John.
(a) Write down expressions for the following, in terms of x.
    (i) John's age in 9 years time.
    (ii) John's mother's age in 9 years time.

After 9 years John's mother will be twice as old as John.
(b) Form an equation and solve it to find John's age **now**.

SEG 1995

14 A party cup costs three pence.
A party plate costs four pence.

(a) Write an expression, in terms of n, for the cost of n cups.

(b) Write an expression, in terms of n, for the cost of $n - 5$ plates.

(c) George buys n cups and $n - 5$ plates.
He pays 85 pence.
    (i) Form an equation in n.
    (ii) Solve your equation to find the number of cups bought.

SEG 1995

119

15 Suzi is wheeling two bags of compost in a trolley.
Mike is carrying five bags of compost in a basket.

An empty trolley weighs 10 kg and an empty basket weighs 1 kg.
A bag of compost weighs c kilograms.
Suzi's trolley and compost weigh $2c + 10$ kg.

(a)   Write down an expression for the weight of Mike's basket and compost.

Suzi's trolley and compost weigh the same as Mike's basket and compost.
(b)   (i)   Form an equation from the two expressions.
      (ii) Solve your equation to find the weight of a bag of compost.

SEG 1995

16 A bottle of lemonade costs x pence.
A bottle of cola costs 7 pence more than a bottle of lemonade.

(a)   Write down, in terms of x,
      (i)   the cost of a bottle of cola,
      (ii) the total cost of three bottles of lemonade and one bottle of cola.

(b)   The total cost of the three bottles of lemonade and one bottle of cola is £2.75.
      Form an equation in x and solve it to find the cost of a bottle of lemonade.

SEG 1997

17 The three-digit numbers in the following table are all divisible by 11.
They also have the property that the middle digit is the sum of the other two.

242	363	495
253	374	550
264	385	561
275	396	572

The value of the first digit is $100x$.
The value of the third digit is y.

(a)   Write down an expression in x and y for the value of the middle digit.

(b)   Write down an expression in x and y for the value of the three-digit number and show that it may be simplified to give

$$110x + 11y.$$

(c)   Factorise the expression in (b) and use your answer to explain why any three-digit number whose middle digit is the sum of the other two is divisible by 11.

SEG 1995

CHAPTER 9

Using Algebra

Number sequences

The first thing to consider when investigating a sequence is whether it is **linear** or **quadratic**.

> Numbers in a sequence are called **terms**.

Linear sequences

These increase (or decrease) by the same amount from one term to the next.
That is they have a **common difference**.
For example, terms in the sequence 2, 8, 14, 20, 26, … have a common difference of 6.
If a sequence is linear compare each term in the sequence with the counting numbers 1, 2, 3, 4, …

EXAMPLES

> Multiply the counting numbers by the common difference. In this example we multiply by 4.

① Find the nth term of the sequence 5, 9, 13, 17, …

First we have to decide whether the sequence is linear or quadratic.
It is linear because the numbers go up by 4 each time.
Compare each term with 1, 2, 3, …

1	2	3	4	… n
↓	↓	↓	↓	
4	8	12	16	
↓	↓	↓	↓	
5	9	13	17	…

$= 4 \times 1 + 1 \quad = 4 \times 2 + 1 \quad = 4 \times 3 + 1 \quad = 4 \times 4 + 1 … \quad 4 \times n + 1$

So the nth term is $4 \times n + 1$ or $4n + 1$.

② Find the nth term of the sequence 32, 26, 20, 14, …

This is a linear sequence because the numbers go down by 6 each time.
So multiply the counting numbers by -6.

1	2	3	4	n
↓	↓	↓	↓	↓
-6	-12	-18	-24	… $-6n$
↓	↓	↓	↓	↓
32	26	20	14	

$= -6 \times 1 + 38 \quad = -6 \times 2 + 38 \quad = -6 \times 3 + 38 \quad = -6 \times 4 + 38 \quad = -6 \times n + 38$

So the nth term is $38 - 6n$.

Quadratic sequences

Terms in a quadratic sequence do not have a common difference, **but** the change in the differences between terms increases (or decreases) by the same amount each time.
For example, the sequence 3, 4, 6, 9, 13, … has differences of 1, 2, 3, 4, … which increase by 1 each time.
If a sequence is quadratic compare each term with the square numbers 1, 4, 9, 16, …

1 Find the nth term of the sequence 2, 5, 10, 17, ...

This is not a linear sequence as the numbers do not increase by the same amount each time.
It is a quadratic sequence. The differences (3, 5, 7, ...) increase by 2 each time.
Compare each term with 1, 4, 9, 16, ...

1	2	3	4	n
↓	↓	↓	↓	↓
1	4	9	16 ...	n^2
↓	↓	↓	↓	↓
2	5	10	17 ...	
$= 1^2 + 1$	$= 2^2 + 1$	$= 3^2 + 1$	$= 4^2 + 1$ ...	$= n^2 + 1$

So the nth term is $n^2 + 1$.

2 What is the nth term of the sequence 3, 12, 27, 48, 75, ...

This is a quadratic sequence because the differences go up by 6 each time (9, 15, 21, 27, ...).

1	2	3	4	5	...	n
↓	↓	↓	↓	↓		↓
1	4	9	16	25	...	n^2
↓	↓	↓	↓	↓		
3	12	27	48	75		
$= 3 \times 1^2$	$= 3 \times 2^2$	$= 3 \times 3^2$	$= 3 \times 4^2$	$= 3 \times 5^2$ ...		$= 3 \times n^2$

So the nth term is $3 \times n^2$ or $3n^2$.

Exercise 9.1

1 The next number in this sequence is found by adding the last two terms.
1, 1, 2, 3, 5, 8, ...

(a) Write down the next **three** terms in the sequence.
(b) What is the 12th term of the sequence?

2 A sequence begins 4, 7, 13, 25, ...
The next number in the sequence can be found using the rule:
"Multiply the last term by 2 then subtract 1."

(a) Write down the next **two** terms in the sequence.
(b) The 11th term in the sequence is 3073.
Use this information to find the 10th term in the sequence.

3 Find the next term in each sequence and state whether the sequence is linear or quadratic?

(a) 1, 4, 7, 10, 13, ...
(b) 1, 3, 6, 10, 15, ...
(c) 1, 7, 13, 19, 25, ...
(d) 19, 16, 13, 10, 7, ...
(e) 5, 10, 17, 26, 37, ...
(f) 5, 9, 13, 17, ...

4 These sequences are linear.
Find the nth term of each sequence.

(a) 4, 8, 12, 16, ...
(b) 1, 3, 5, 7, 9, ...
(c) 7, 11, 15, 19, 23, ...
(d) 2, 7, 12, 17, 22, ...
(e) 8, 12, 16, 20, ...
(f) 6, 4, 2, 0, −2, ...

5 These sequences are quadratic. Find the nth term in each sequence by comparing it with 1, 4, 9, 16, …

   (a) 0, 3, 8, 15, 24, …

   (b) 4, 7, 12, 19, 28, …

   (c) 2, 8, 18, 32, 50, …

   (d) 2, 6, 12, 20, 30, …

   (e) $1, \frac{1}{4}, \frac{1}{9}, \frac{1}{16}, \ldots$

   (f) $\frac{1}{4}, \frac{4}{9}, \frac{9}{16}, \frac{16}{25}, \frac{35}{36}, \ldots$

6 Find the nth term in these sequences.

   (a) 5, 8, 11, 14, 17, …

   (b) 5, 8, 13, 20, …

   (c) 8, 14, 20, 26, …

   (d) 3, 12, 27, 48, …

   (e) 3, 8, 13, 18, 23, …

   (f) 3, 6, 11, 18, 27, …

   (g) 0, 2, 6, 12, 20, …

   (h) $\frac{1}{2}, \frac{2}{3}, \frac{3}{4}, \frac{4}{5}, \frac{5}{6}, \ldots$

Substituting into formulae

A formula is an algebraic rule.
Formulae can either be written in words or written using algebraic symbols.
For example,
$S = 2\pi r (r + h)$ is a formula used to find the total surface area,
$S\,\text{cm}^2$, of a cylinder that has radius, $r\,\text{cm}$ and height, $h\,\text{cm}$.
By **substituting** values for π, r and h you can calculate the value of S.

> You can find the value of any letter in a formula by substituting given values for all the other letters.

EXAMPLES

1 A joiner earns £W for working H hours. Her boss uses the formula
$W = 5H + 35$ to calculate her wage.
Find her wage if she works for 40 hours.

$$W = 5 \times 40 + 35$$
$$= 200 + 35$$
$$= £235$$

2 $H = 3(4x - y)$. Find the value of H when $x = 5$ and $y = 7$.

$$H = 3(4x - y)$$
$$= 3(4 \times 5 - 7)$$
$$= 3(20 - 7)$$
$$= 3(13)$$
$$= 39$$

3 The population density of a country is given by the formula:

$$\text{population density} = \frac{\text{Population}}{\text{Area}}$$

Find the population density of Greenland, which has an area of 840 000 square miles and a population of 56 000.

$$\text{population density} = \frac{56\,000}{840\,000}$$
$$= 0.0666 \ldots$$
$$= 0.067$$

Population of Greenland = 0.067 people per square mile, correct to 3 decimal places.

4 The height, h metres, of a bullet after t seconds, is given by the formula
$h = ut - \frac{1}{2} gt^2$, where $u\,\text{ms}^{-1}$ is the initial vertical speed and $g\,\text{ms}^{-2}$ is the acceleration due to gravity.
Find h when $u = 200$ and $t = 1\frac{3}{5}$.
Take $g = 9.8$

$$h = ut - \frac{1}{2} gt^2$$
$$= 200 \times 1.6 - \frac{1}{2} \times 9.8 \times 1.6^2$$

Notice that $1\frac{3}{5} = 1 + 3 \div 5 = 1.6$

$$= 320 - 12.544$$
$$= 307.456$$
$$h = 307\,\text{m, correct to 3 sig. fig.}$$

Questions 1 to 8.
Do not use a calculator.
Show your working clearly.

1 Find the value of $x + 3$ when
(a) $x = 2$ (b) $x = 12$ (c) $x = 25$

2 Find the value of $4a$ when
(a) $a = 5$ (b) $a = 14$ (c) $a = 2.5$

3 Find the value of $2p + 3$ when
(a) $p = 4$ (b) $p = 9$ (c) $p = 0$

4 Find the value of $7 - 2d$ when
(a) $d = 2$ (b) $d = -2$ (c) $d = 0.2$

5 $S = 2a^2$. Find the value of S when
(a) $a = 3$ (b) $a = -3$

6 $S = (2a)^2$. Find the value of S when
(a) $a = 3$ (b) $a = -3$

7 A simple formula for the motion of a
car is $F = ma + R$.
Find F when $m = 500$, $a = 0.2$ and
$R = 4000$.

8 The formula $F = \dfrac{mv^2}{r}$ describes the
motion of a cyclist rounding a corner.
Find F when $m = 80$, $v = 6$
and $r = 20$.

Questions 9 to 16.
You may use a calculator to answer these
questions.

9 $T = 45W + 30$ is used to calculate the
time in minutes needed to cook a joint
of beef weighing W kilograms.
How many minutes are needed to
cook a joint weighing $2.4\,\text{kg}$?

10 The formula $v = u + at$ gives the speed v of a
particle, t seconds after it starts with speed u.
Calculate v when $u = 7.8$, $a = -10$ and $t = \frac{3}{4}$.

11 The cost, £C, of n units of gas is calculated
using the formula $C = 0.08n + 3.5$
Calculate the cost of 458 units of gas.

12 Temperatures in °F can be changed into °C
using the formula: $C = \frac{5}{9}(F - 32)$.
(a) Calculate the value of C when $F = 59$.
(b) What temperature, in °C, is equivalent to
$5°F$?

13 Find y if $x = 8$ for:
(a) $y = 5x - 2$ (b) $y = 12 - \frac{1}{2}x$
(c) $y = 20 - 3x^2$ (d) $y = 4x^3 + 3x^2$

14 Find x given that $a = 4$, $b = 6$, $c = -2$ and
$d = 0.5$
(a) $x = a + b + c$ (b) $x = ab + c$

(c) $x = \dfrac{a + b}{c}$ (d) $x = a(c - d)$

(e) $x = \dfrac{b}{a} + \dfrac{c}{d}$ (f) $a + x = cd$

15 The time T, for a pendulum to make a complete
swing is given by the formula:

$$T = 2\pi\sqrt{\frac{l}{g}}$$

(a) Calculate the value of T when $l = 0.8$ and
$g = 9.8$
(b) Calculate the value of T when $l = 1\frac{1}{2}$ and
$g = 9.8$
Take π to be 3.14 or use the π key on your
calculator.

16 Use the formula $v = \sqrt{u^2 + 2as}$
to calculate the value of v when
(a) $u = 2.4$, $a = 3.2$, $s = 5.25$
(b) $u = 9.1$, $a = -4.7$, $s = 3.04$
Give your answers correct to one decimal place.

Rearranging formulae

Sometimes it is easier to use a formula if you **rearrange** it first.
The formula $k = \frac{8m}{5}$ can be used to change distances in miles to
distances in kilometres.
Rearrange this to give a formula which can be used to change
distances in kilometres into distances in miles.

$$k = \frac{8m}{5}$$

Multiply both sides by 5. $\quad 5k = 8m$

Divide both sides by 8. $\quad \dfrac{5k}{8} = m$

We say we have **rearranged the formula** $k = \frac{8m}{5}$
to make m the **subject** of the formula.

Here is a reminder of some operations and
their inverses.

Operation	Inverse operation
Addition $+a$	Subtraction $-a$
Subtraction $-a$	Addition $+a$
Multiplication $\times a$	Division $\div a$
Division $\div a$	Multiplication $\times a$
Squaring a^2	Square rooting $\sqrt{a}$
Square rooting $\sqrt{a}$	Squaring a^2
Cubing a^3	Cube rooting $\sqrt[3]{a}$
Cube rooting $\sqrt[3]{a}$	Cubing a^3

1 Make x the subject of $y = 2x + 8$.
$$y = 2x + 8$$
Subtract 8 from both sides.
$$y - 8 = 2x$$
Divide both sides by 2.
$$\tfrac{1}{2}y - 4 = x$$
So we rearranged $y = 2x + 8$
to get $x = \tfrac{1}{2}y - 4$.
y is the subject of $y = 2x + 8$.
x is the subject of $x = \tfrac{1}{2}y - 4$.

2 Make r the subject of $V = \tfrac{4}{3}\pi r^2$.
$$V = \tfrac{4}{3}\pi r^2$$
Multiply both sides by 3.
$$3V = 4\pi r^2$$
Divide both sides by 4π.
$$\frac{3V}{4\pi} = r^2$$
Take the square root of both sides.
$$r = \sqrt{\frac{3V}{4\pi}}$$
This can be written as $r = \tfrac{1}{2}\sqrt{\dfrac{3V}{\pi}}$

Exercise 9.3

1 Make x the subject of these formulae:
  (a) $y = x + 5$ (b) $y = x - 2$
  (c) $y = 4x$ (d) $y = \tfrac{1}{2}x$
  (e) $y = 2x + 6$ (f) $y = 3x - 9$
  (g) $4y = 2x - 5$ (h) $y = \tfrac{1}{2}(3x + 6)$

2 A formula for changing kilograms to pounds is
$P = 0.45K$.
Rearrange the formula to give K in terms of P.

3 $F = 1.8C + 32$ changes temperatures in °C
to °F.
Rearrange the formula to give C in terms of F.

4 Match the pairs:
$y = x + 3$ $x = 3y$ $y = 3x + 1$
$x = y - 3$ $y = \tfrac{1}{3}x$ $x = \tfrac{1}{3}y$
$y = 3x$ $x = \tfrac{1}{3}(y - 1)$ $y = 3x - 1$
$x = \tfrac{1}{3}y + \tfrac{1}{3}$

5 Make v the subject of each of these formulae:
  (a) $v + 3 = u$ (b) $v - u = r$
  (c) $2v = r$ (d) $vi = u$
  (e) $\frac{v}{x} = t$ (f) $v - u = at$
  (g) $p = mv + d$ (h) $mv^2 = F$

6 The cost, £C, of hiring a car for n days is
given by $C = 35 + 24n$.

  (a) Find the cost of hiring a car for 3 days.
  (b) A customer paid £251 to hire a car.
     Make n the subject of the formula and
     use your new formula to find for how
     many days the customer had hired the car.

7 The area of a trapezium is given by
$A = \tfrac{1}{2}h(a + b)$.
Make a the subject of this formula.

8 Make the bold letter the subject of these
formulae.
  (a) $\frac{\boldsymbol{V}}{I} = R$ (b) $E = \boldsymbol{m}c^2$
  (c) $y = a\boldsymbol{x}^2 + b$ (d) $e = \tfrac{1}{2}m\boldsymbol{v}^2$

9 Make a the subject of these formulae.
  (a) $b = a + c^2$ (b) $a^2 = b$
  (c) $4a = 8b + c$ (d) $6a = 2b$
  (e) $3a = \frac{4b}{5}$ (f) $b = \frac{2a}{3}$
  (g) $b = \tfrac{1}{4}a^2$ (h) $3b = 2a^2 - 5$

10 Make x the subject of these formulae.
  (a) $x + 2a = b$ (b) $2x + a = b$
  (c) $2(x + a) = b$ (d) $\frac{x}{2} + a = 3b$
  (e) $\frac{x}{a} = b + c$ (f) $x(a + 2) = b$
  (g) $a(x + b) = c$ (h) $a - x = \tfrac{1}{2}b$
  (i) $2a - \tfrac{1}{2}x = b^2$ (j) $\frac{a}{x} = b$
  (k) $\frac{a}{x + b} = c$

11 Make t the subject of these formulae.
  (a) $3t^2 = x$ (b) $at^2 = V$
  (c) $2t^2 + a = b$ (d) $a - t^2 = b$
  (e) $a + bt^2 = c$ (f) $a - bt^2 = c$
  (g) $\frac{a}{t} = \frac{t}{b}$ (h) $\frac{t + 1}{a} = \frac{b}{t + 1}$

12 (a) Make r the subject of the formula $F = \dfrac{mv^2}{r}$.

(b) Make c the subject of the formula $E = mc^2$.

(c) Make g the subject of the formula $T = \dfrac{1}{2\pi}\sqrt{\dfrac{l}{g}}$.

13 Make x the subject of each of these formulae.

(a) $\sqrt{x+3} = a$ (b) $\dfrac{\sqrt{x+2}}{3} = a$ (c) $\frac{1}{4}\sqrt{2x-a} = b$

14 Make a the subject of each of these formulae.

(a) $3a - x = a + 2x$ (b) $a - b = ax$ (c) $a - 2 = ax + b$

(d) $a + 2 = x(3+a)$ (e) $y = \dfrac{a-3}{5-a}$ (f) $x(a-1) = b(a+2)$

(g) $y(a-1) = 3(2-a)$ (h) $\sqrt{\dfrac{a+x}{a-x}} = 2$ (i) $\sqrt{\dfrac{a}{x-a}} = 2x$

What you need to know

- Numbers in a sequence are called **terms**.

- **Linear sequences** increase (or decrease) by the same amount from one term to the next, i.e. they have a **common difference**.

- **Quadratic sequences** do not have a common difference, but the change in the differences between terms increases (or decreases) by the same amount each time.

- A **formula** is an algebraic rule which can be **rearranged** to make another letter (variable) the **subject**.

IDEAS FOR INVESTIGATION

Harder quadratic sequences
Sometimes it is difficult to spot the rule for a quadratic sequence by comparing terms with square numbers.
In these cases it is necessary to the use the **difference method**.

1 Find the first 5 terms of these sequences:

(a) n^2 (b) $3n^2$ (c) $n^2 + 2n$
(d) $2n^2 + 3n - 1$ (e) $n^2 - 4$ (f) $6n - 3n^2$

2 Find the second differences in each case.

3 What is the relationship between the coefficient of n^2 and the second difference?

4 What should the second difference of $4n^2 - 3n$ be? Check your prediction.

5 Use what you learned above to find the nth terms of the following sequences.
(Hint: find the second difference first)

(a) 2, 6, 12, 20, 30, ... (b) 1, 6, 15, 28, 45, ... (c) 1.5, 3, 5.5, 9, 13.5, ...

1 (a) Sticks are arranged in shapes.

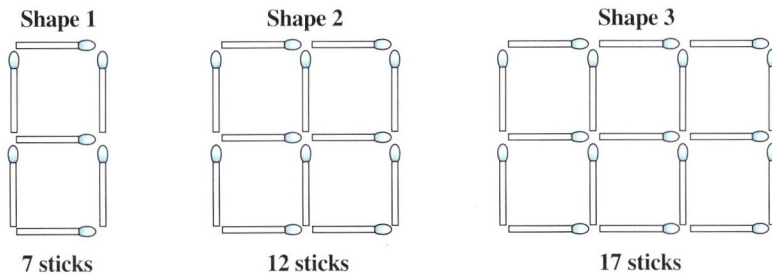

Shape 1	**Shape 2**	**Shape 3**
7 sticks	12 sticks	17 sticks

The number of sticks form a sequence.
Find a formula, in terms of n, for the number of sticks in the nth shape.

(b) Find a formula, in terms of n, for the area of the nth rectangle in this sequence.

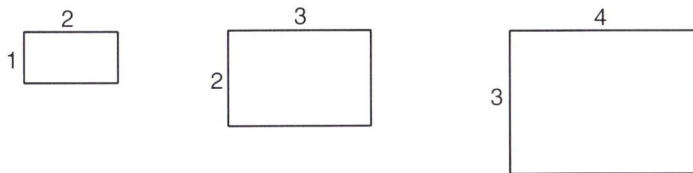

SEG 1994

2 Find the nth term for each of the following sequences.
   (a) 0.1, 0.2, 0.3, 0.4, …
   (b) 0, 3, 8, 15, …
   (c) 2, 4, 8, 16, …

SEG 1997

3 (a) The first four terms in a sequence are 4, 5, 6, 7.
      Find an expression, in terms of n, for the nth term of the sequence.
   (b) The first four terms in a sequence are 2, 8, 18, 32.
      Find an expression, in terms of n, for the nth term of the sequence.

SEG 1997

4 (a) A sequence of numbers is generated using only positive integers.

1st term	2nd term	3rd term	4th term	5th term	……
99	98	97	96	95	……

Write down a formula, in terms of n, for the nth term of the sequence.

(b) Another sequence is also generated using only positive integers.

1st term	2nd term	3rd term	4th term	5th term	……
$\frac{2}{99}$	$\frac{4}{98}$	$\frac{6}{97}$	$\frac{8}{96}$	$\frac{10}{95}$	……

Write down a formula, in terms of n, for the nth term of the sequence.

SEG 1995

5 (a) Write down the nth term of the sequence

$$2, \quad \frac{3}{2}, \quad \frac{4}{3}, \quad \frac{5}{4}, \quad ……$$

(b) (i) Write down the nth term of the sequence

$$1, \quad \frac{1}{2}, \quad \frac{1}{4}, \quad \frac{1}{8}, \quad \frac{1}{16}, \quad ……$$

   (ii) State what happens to the value of this nth term as n gets very large.

SEG 1997

6 The first five terms of two sequences A and B are

Sequence A	2	8	18	32	50
Sequence B	3	10	21	36	55

(a) The general rule for the nth term of sequence A is $2n^2$.
The nth term of sequence A is 450.
Form an equation and solve it to find the value of n.

(b) Write down the general rule for the nth term of sequence B.

SEG 1997

7 The first five terms in each of the three sequences A, B and C are

Term	1st	2nd	3rd	4th	5th
Sequence A	1	4	9	16	25
Sequence B	2	8	18	32	50
Sequence C	4	12	24	40	60

Write down the general rule for the nth term for each of the sequences.

SEG 1996

8 A number sequence is represented by these dot patterns.

Sequence	2	8	18	32

(a) Write down the nth term of the sequence.

The nth term of a different sequence is $\dfrac{3n^2 - n}{2}$.

(b) Form an equation and solve it to find n when the value of the nth term is 145.

SEG 1995

9 Equilateral triangles are combined together to form shapes.
The number of triangles in the shape form a sequence.

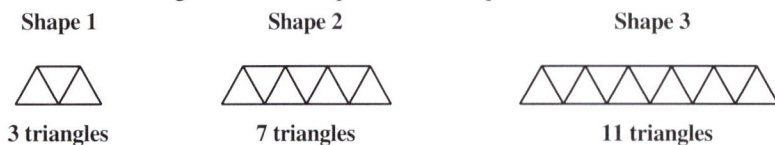

Shape 1	Shape 2	Shape 3
3 triangles	7 triangles	11 triangles

(a) Find a rule in terms of n for the number of triangles in the nth shape in the sequence.

(b) The triangles are now grouped together differently as shown below.

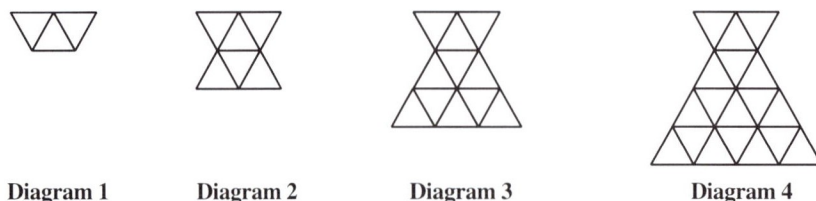

Diagram	1	2	3	4
Number of triangles	3	6	11	18

Find a rule in terms of n for the number of triangles in the nth diagram in the sequence.

SEG 1994

10 A sequence begins

Term	1st	2nd	3rd	4th
Sequence	$\frac{2}{3}$	$\frac{2}{9}$	$\frac{2}{27}$	$\frac{2}{81}$

What is the nth term of this sequence?
Give your answer in the form $a \times b^c$.

SEG 1996

11 (a) Write the nth term of this sequence.

    1   8   27   64   125   ...

(b) Write the rule for this sequence below in the form n^a, where a is an integer.

$$\frac{1}{1} \quad \frac{4}{8} \quad \frac{9}{27} \quad \frac{16}{64} \quad \frac{25}{125} \quad ...$$

SEG 1995

12 The formula for converting temperature from degrees Fahrenheit (F) into degrees Celsius (C)
is $C = \frac{5}{9}(F - 32)$.
Calculate the Celsius equivalent of -25 degrees Fahrenheit.

SEG 1994

13 The wind chill temperature, $T°C$, is given by the formula
$$T = 33 + (0.45 + 0.29\sqrt{v} - 0.02v)(t - 35).$$
Here $t°C$ is the air temperature and v mph is the wind speed.
Find T, to the nearest degree, when $t = -5$ and $v = 10$.

SEG 1994

14 Use the formula $u = \dfrac{2s}{t} - v$
to calculate the value of u when $s = 5.7$, $t = 7.9$ and $v = -5.3$.

SEG 1997

15 The following formula gives distance s, in terms of the acceleration a and speeds u and v.
$$s = \frac{v^2 - u^2}{2a}$$
(a) Find s when $a = 8$, $v = 1$ and $u = 15.5$.

The formula above may be rearranged to give $u = \sqrt{v^2 - 2as}$.

(b) Calculate the value of u when $a = 3\frac{1}{2}$, $s = 6\frac{2}{3}$ and $v = 18\frac{1}{2}$.

SEG 1995

16 The formula for the time for one swing of a pendulum is $T = 2\pi\sqrt{\dfrac{l}{g}}$
(a) Calculate T when $l = \frac{1}{2}$ and $g = 9.8$.
(b) Explain why the **exact** value of T calculated by this formula is irrational.

SEG 1995

17 The braking distance, D metres, of a car is shown by the formula $D = \dfrac{v^2}{252f}$

where v is its speed in kilometres per hour and f is the friction between the tyres and the road
surface.
(a) Calculate D when $v = 80$ and $f = 0.25$.
(b) After an accident, it was shown from the skid marks that $D = 50$ and $f = \frac{3}{8}$.
Use the formula to calculate v.

SEG 1997

18 When two resistors of R_1 ohms and R_2 ohms are connected in parallel the combined
resistance is R ohms, where $\dfrac{1}{R} = \dfrac{1}{R_1} + \dfrac{1}{R_2}$.
Calculate the value of R when $R_1 = 15$ ohms and $R_2 = 25$ ohms.

SEG 1994

19 This formula can be used to convert temperatures from degrees Celsius, °C, to degrees
$$F = \frac{9C + 160}{5}$$
(a) Use the formula to convert $-7°C$ to degrees Fahrenheit.
(b) Use the formula to find at what temperature $F = C$.
(c) Rearrange the formula to give C in terms of F.

SEG 1998

20 The formula for finding the total surface area of a cylinder is $A = 2\pi r^2 + \pi rh$.

Rearrange $A = 2\pi r^2 + \pi rh$ to make h the subject of the formula.

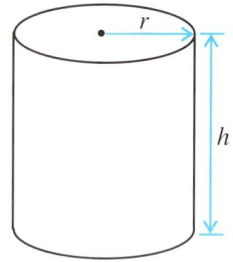

SEG 1995

21 You are given the formula $v = u + at$.
   (a) Work out the value of v when $u = 20$, $a = -6$ and $t = \frac{9}{5}$.
   (b) Rearrange the formula to give t in terms of v, u and a.

SEG 1998

22 You are given the equation $y = 5x^n$.
   (a) Find the value of y when $x = -4$ and $n = 0$.
   (b) Find the value of n when $y - 10$ and $x = 4$.
   (c) Rearrange the formula to express x in terms of y and n.

SEG 1998

23 The volume of a sphere is given by the formula $V = \frac{4}{3}\pi r^3$.
   (a) Rearrange the formula to give r, in terms of V.
   (b) Find the value of r when $V = 75$.

SEG 1995

24 When a person is 50 years old or more, the cost of joining the "Have Fun" Sports Club is calculated using the formula

$$C = \tfrac{1}{2}\sqrt{(75 - x)}.$$

C is the cost in pounds.
The age, in completed years, of the person joining is x.
Mary is more than 50 years old.
She paid £1.50 to join the club.
   (a) Calculate Mary's age.

When a person is younger than 50 years of age, the cost of joining the Sports Club is given by the formula

$$C = \tfrac{1}{3}\sqrt{(25 + y)},$$

where C is the cost in pounds and y is the age of the person joining.
   (b) Express y in terms of C.

SEG 1996

25 (a) The nth shape in this series has perimeter P.
     (i) Write down and simplify an expression for P in terms of n.
     (ii) Calculate the length of the **shortest** side of the first shape in this series for which $P > 150$.

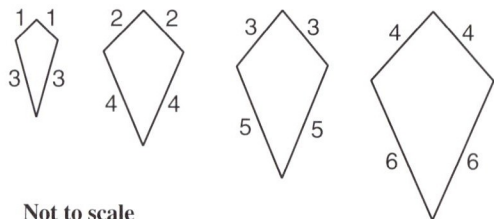

Not to scale

   (b) For a certain series of rectangles the area, A, of the nth rectangle is given by the formula $A = 5n^2 + 4$.
Make n the subject of this formula.

SEG 1996

CHAPTER 10

Graphs

Drawing a graph from a rule

To draw the graph of $y = 2x + 1$ we calculate the values of y for various values of x.

When $x = 1$, $y = 2 \times 1 + 1 = 3$.
This gives the point $(1, 3)$.

When $x = 2$, $y = 2 \times 2 + 1 = 5$.
This gives the point $(2, 5)$.

When $x = 3$, $y = 2 \times 3 + 1 = 7$.
This gives the point $(3, 7)$.

This is often shown in a table.

x	1	2	3
y	3	5	7

The diagram shows the coordinates plotted on a **graph**.
The points all lie on a **straight line**.
All points on the line obey the rule $y = 2x + 1$.

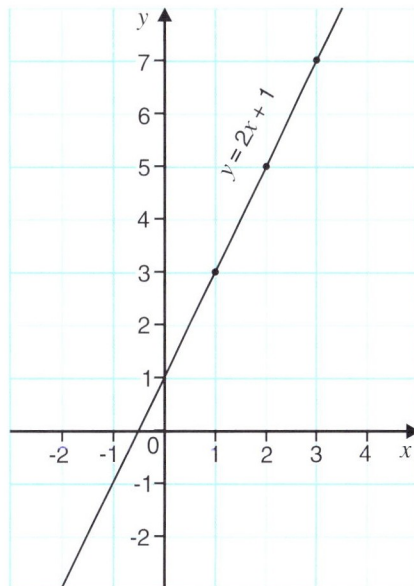

There is nothing magical about using $x = 1$, 2 and 3. We could have used any values for x.

It is only necessary to plot two points to draw a straight line. We usually plot a third point as a check.
Explain why.

EXAMPLE

Draw the graph of the equation $y = 3x - 4$.

If values for x are not given in the question you must choose your own.

When $x = 0$, $y = 3 \times 0 - 4 = -4$.
This gives the point $(0, -4)$.

When $x = 1$, $y = 3 \times 1 - 4 = -1$.
This gives the point $(1, -1)$.

When $x = 3$, $y = 3 \times 3 - 4 = 5$.
This gives the point $(3, 5)$.

Why do you think these values of x have been chosen?
Could other values have been chosen?

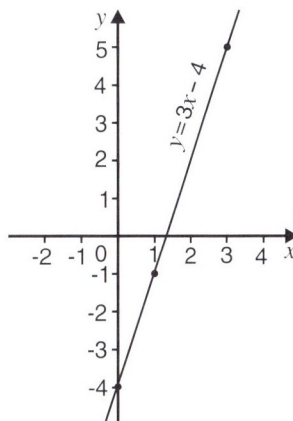

131

Special graphs

This diagram shows the graphs:

$x = 4$ $y = 3$
$x = -2$ $y = -5$

Notice that:
The graph of $x = 4$ is a **vertical** line.
All points on the line have x coordinate 4.

The graph of $y = 3$ is a **horizontal** line.
All points on the line have y coordinate 3.

$x = 0$ is the y axis.
$y = 0$ is the x axis.

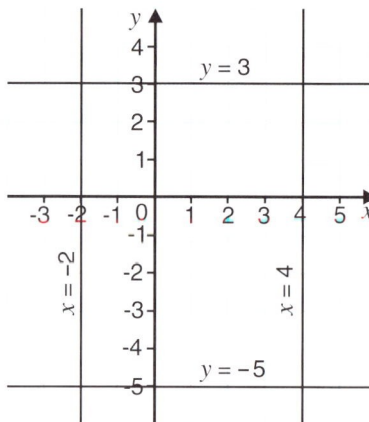

Exercise 10.1

1 Write down the equations of the lines labelled on this graph.

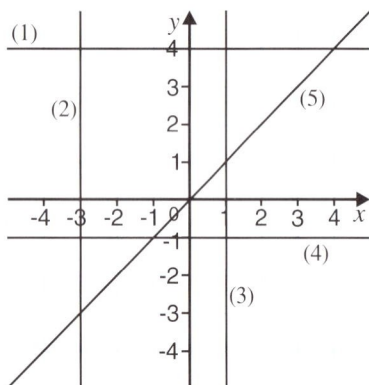

2

x	1	2	3
y			

Copy and complete a table like the one above for each of these equations.
(a) $y = x + 2$
(b) $y = 2x$
(c) $y = 6 - 2x$

3 On separate diagrams, draw graphs for each of the equations in Question 2.

4 Draw tables and use them to draw graphs of:

(a) $y = x - 1$
Draw and label the x axis from -2 to 3 and the y axis from -4 to 3.

(b) $y = 3x - 2$
Draw and label the x axis from -2 to 3 and the y axis from -10 to 10.

5 Complete this table and use it to plot the straight line graph of $y = 4 - x$.

x	-2	-1	0	1	2
y		5			2

Draw and label the x axis from -3 to 3 and the y axis from -1 to 6.

6 Draw the graphs of:
(a) $y = x - 3$ (b) $y = 2x + 1$
(c) $y = \frac{1}{4}x + 1$ (d) $y = 6 - x$
(e) $y = 10 - 2x$ (f) $y = 2(x - 1)$

7 (a) Draw these graphs **on the same diagram**:
(i) $y = x + 2$ (ii) $y = x + 1$
(iii) $y = x$ (iv) $y = x - 1$
Draw and label the x axis from 0 to 3 and the y axis from -1 to 5.

(b) What do they all have in common? What is different?

8 (a) Draw these graphs **on the same diagram**:
(i) $y = 2x + 2$ (ii) $y = 2x + 1$
(iii) $y = 2x$ (iv) $y = 2x - 1$
Draw and label the x axis from 0 to 3 and the y axis from -1 to 8.

(b) What do they all have in common? What is different?

9 (a) Draw these graphs **on the same diagram**:
(i) $y = 3x + 3$ (ii) $y = 2x + 3$
(iii) $y = x + 3$ (iv) $y = \frac{1}{2}x + 3$
Draw and label the x axis from -3 to 3 and the y axis from -6 to 12.

(b) What do they all have in common? What is different?

Gradient and intercept

Lines that are **parallel** have the same **slope** or **gradient**.

$$\text{Gradient} = \frac{\text{distance up}}{\text{distance along}}$$

The gradient of a straight line graph is found by drawing a right-angled triangle.

The gradient of a line can be positive, zero or negative.

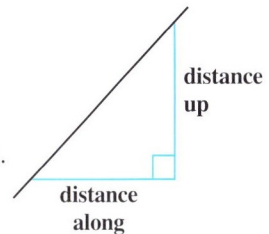

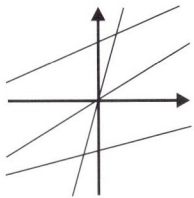

Positive gradients go "uphill".

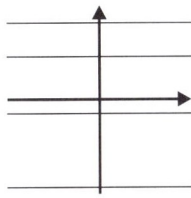

Zero gradients are "flat".

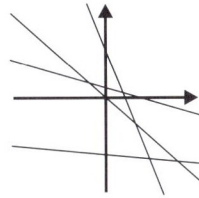

Negative gradients go "downhill".

In general:
the graph of $y = mx + c$ has **gradient** m and **intercept** c.

In Question 8 of Exercise 10.1, the graphs of
$y = 2x + 2$, $y = 2x + 1$, $y = 2x$, $y = 2x - 1$,
go 2 squares up for every 1 square along.
The graphs are all parallel and have a gradient of 2.

The point where a graph crosses the y axis is called the **intercept**.
In Question 9 of Exercise 10.1, the graphs of
$y = 3x + 3$, $y = 2x + 3$, $y = x + 3$, $y = \frac{1}{2}x + 3$,
all cross the y axis at the point (0, 3).
The graphs each have the same intercept, 3.

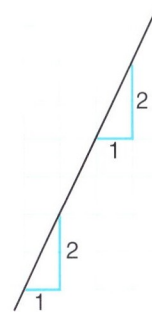

EXAMPLES

1 Write down the gradient and intercept for each of the following graphs.
(a) $y = 3x + 5$
(b) $y = 4x - 1$
(c) $y = 6 - x$

(a) Gradient = 3, intercept = 5.
(b) Gradient = 4, intercept = -1.
(c) Gradient = -1, intercept = 6.

2 Write down the equation of the straight line which has gradient -7 and cuts the y axis at the point (0, 4).

The general form for the equation of a straight line is $y = mx + c$.
The gradient, $m = -7$, and the intercept, $c = 4$.
Substitute these values into the general equation.
The equation of the line is
$y = -7x + 4$.
This can be written as $y = 4 - 7x$.

3

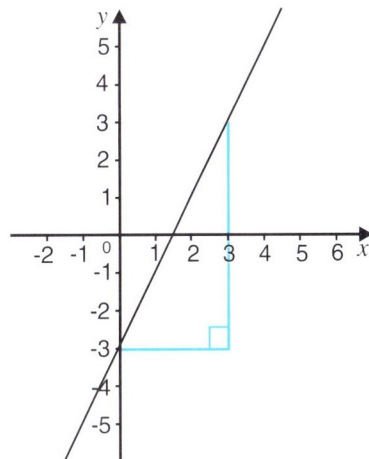

Find the equation of the line shown on this graph.

First, work out the gradient of the line.
Draw a right-angled triangle.

$$\text{Gradient} = \frac{\text{distance up}}{\text{distance along}}$$
$$= \frac{6}{3}$$
$$= 2$$

The graph crosses the y axis at the point (0, -3), so the intercept is -3.
The equation of the line is $y = 2x - 3$.

1 (a) Write down the gradient and intercept of $y = 3x - 1$.

(b) Draw the graph of $y = 3x - 1$ to check your answer.

2 Which of the following graphs are parallel?

$y = 3x$

$y = x + 2$

$y = 2x + 3$

$y = 3x + 2$

3 Copy and complete this table.

Graph	gradient	intercept
$y = 4x + 3$	4	3
$y = 3x + 5$	3	
$y = 2x - 3$		
$y = 4 - 2x$		4
$y = \frac{1}{2}x + 3$		
$y = 2x$		
$y = 3$		
$y = 4 - \frac{1}{2}x$		

4 Match the following equations to their graphs.

(1) $y = x - 6$

(2) $y = 6 - x$

(3) $y = 2x + 1$

(4) $y = 2x - 1$

A   B   C   D

5 (a) Write down the equation of the straight line which has gradient 5 and crosses the y axis at the point $(0, -4)$.

(b) Write down the equation of the straight line which has gradient $-\frac{1}{2}$ and cuts the y axis at the point $(0, 6)$.

6 Find the equations of the lines shown on the following graphs.

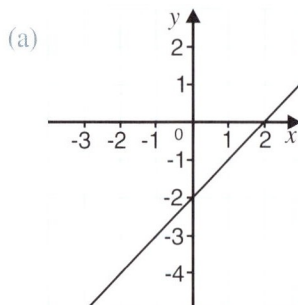

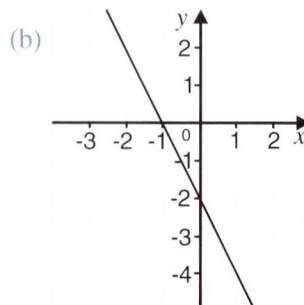

(a)

(b)

7 (a) Draw x and y axes from -8 to 8.
  (b) Plot the points A $(-2, -6)$ and B $(8, 4)$.
  (c) Find the gradient of the line which passes through the points A and B.
  (d) Write down the coordinates of the point where the line crosses the y axis.
  (e) Find the equation of the line which passes through the points A and B.

8 (a) Draw x and y axes from -8 to 8.
  (b) Plot the points P $(-2, 3)$ and Q $(3, -7)$.
  (c) Find the equation of the line which passes through the points P and Q.

Rearranging equations

The general equation for a straight line graph is $y = mx + c$.
When an equation is in this form the gradient and intercept are given by the values of m and c.

The equation for a straight line can also be written in the form $px + qy = r$.
To find the gradient and intercept of this line we must first **rearrange** the equation.

> Equations of the form $px + qy = r$ are used in simultaneous equations.

EXAMPLES

1 The graph of a straight line is given by the equation $4y - 3x = 8$.
Write this equation in the form $y = mx + c$.

$4y - 3x = 8$
Add $3x$ to both sides.
$4y = 3x + 8$
Divide both sides by 4.
$y = \frac{3}{4}x + 2$

The line has gradient $\frac{3}{4}$ and intercept 2.

2 The equation of a straight line is $6x + 3y = 2$.
Write down the equation of another line which is parallel to this line.

Write the equation in the form $y = mx + c$.
$6x + 3y = 2$
Subtract $6x$ from both sides.
$3y = -6x + 2$
Divide both sides by 3.
$y = -2x + \frac{2}{3}$

The gradient of the line is -2.
To write an equation of a parallel line keep the same gradient and change the value of the intercept.
For example: $y = -2x + 5$

Write the equations for two different lines which are parallel to this line.

3 Sketch the graph of the line given by the equation $4y - 3x = 12$.

Substitute $x = 0$ into the equation.
$4y = 12$
$y = 3$

The line crosses the y axis at $(0, 3)$.

Substitute $y = 0$ into the equation.
$-3x = 12$
Divide both sides by -3.
$x = -4$

The line crosses the x axis at $(-4, 0)$.

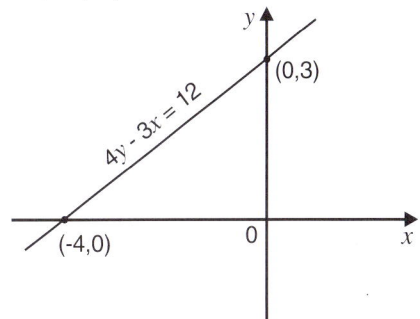

135

1　The graph of a straight line is given by the equation $2y - 3x = 6$.
Write this equation in the form $y = mx + c$.

2　Write equations for the following lines in the form $y = mx + c$.
　(a)　$5y + 4x = 20$　(b)　$2x - 7y = 14$　(c)　$4 - 3y = 2x$　(d)　$3(y - x) - 2$

3　The equation of a straight line is $2y + 3x = 4$.
Write down the equation of another line which is parallel to this line.

4　The equation of a line is given by $5y - 4x = 10$.
　(a)　Find the gradient of the line.
　(b)　Find the intercept of the line.
　(c)　Write down the equation of another line which has the **same** intercept but a **different** gradient.

5　A straight line has equation $3y + 5x = 15$.
　(a)　By substituting $x = 0$ find the coordinates of the point where the line crosses the y axis.
　(b)　By substituting $y = 0$ find the coordinates of the point where the line crosses the x axis.
　(c)　**Sketch** the graph of the line $3y + 5x = 15$.

6　Sketch the graphs of lines with the following equations, marking clearly the coordinates of the points where the lines cross the axes.
　(a)　$5y + 4x = 20$　(b)　$4x - y = 2$　(c)　$3y + 2x = 15$

Using straight line graphs

The equation $2x - 3 = 2$ can be solved **algebraically**.

$2x - 3 = 2$
Add 3 to both sides.
$2x = 5$
Divide both sides by 2.
$x = 2.5$

Graphs can be used to solve equations.
The diagram shows two graphs:
$y = 2x - 3$
$y = 2$

At the point where the lines cross,
both $y = 2x - 3$ and $y = 2$ are true.
The value of x at this point is the solution
to the equation $2x - 3 = 2$.
Reading from the graph, $x = 2.5$.

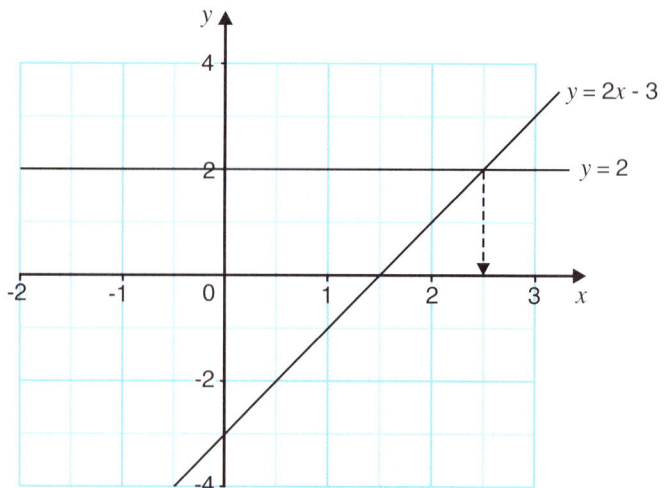

(a) Complete the tables for $y = x + 6$ and $y = 13 - x$.

x	1	2	3
$y = x + 6$			

x	1	2	3
$y = 13 - x$			

(b) Draw the graphs of $y = x + 6$ and $y = 13 - x$ on the same diagram.
(c) Use your graph to solve the equation $13 - x = x + 6$.

(a)

x	1	2	3
$y = x + 6$	7	8	9

x	1	2	3
$y = 13 - x$	12	11	10

(c) Reading from the graph.
$x = 3.5$

Check the graphical solution of the equation by solving the equation $13 - x = x + 6$ algebraically.

(b)

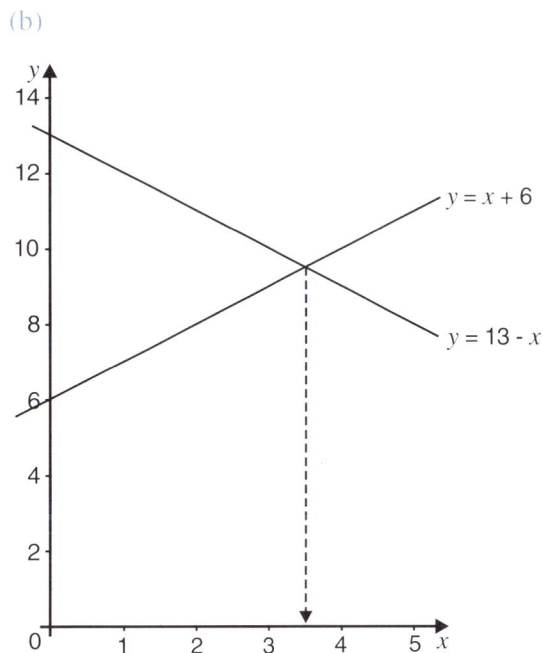

Exercise 10.4

1 (a) Copy and complete the tables for $y = x + 2$ and $y = 5 - x$.

x	1	2	3
$y = x + 2$			

x	1	2	3
$y = 5 - x$			

(b) Draw the graphs of $y = x + 2$ and $y = 5 - x$ on the same diagram.
(c) Use your graphs to solve $x + 2 = 5 - x$.

2 (a) Draw the graphs of $y = 3x + 1$ and $y = x + 6$.
(b) Use your graphs to solve the equation $3x + 1 = x + 6$.

3 Draw suitable graphs to solve the following equations:
(a) $x - 1 = \frac{1}{2}x + 3$ (b) $2(x + 1) = x + 4$ (c) $\frac{1}{2}(x - 1) = 4 - x$

4 (a) Draw the graph of $y = 3 + 2x$.
(b) What graph should be drawn to solve the equation $3 + 2x = 9$?
(c) Draw the graph and use it to solve the equation $3 + 2x = 9$.

5 A delivery firm charges £25 for delivering a package.
Another firm uses the formula $y = 10 + 2x$ to calculate the charge, in pounds, where x is the number of hours taken to make the delivery.

(a) Draw the graph of $y = 10 + 2x$.
(b) On the same axes draw another graph which could be used to solve the equation $10 + 2x = 25$.
(c) What does the solution to the equation in part (b) mean?

6 Two companies each use a formula to calculate the charge made for hiring out scaffolding.
Company A uses the formula $c = 20 + 5d$, Company B uses the formula $c = 8d + 2$, where c is the total charge, in pounds, and d is the length of the hire period, in days.

(a) Draw the horizontal axis for d from 0 to 8 and the vertical axis for c from 0 to 60.
(b) Draw the graph of $c = 20 + 5d$.
(c) Draw the graph of $c = 8d + 2$.

Use your graph to answer the following.
(d) From which company is it cheaper to hire scaffolding for 2 days?
(e) From which company is it cheaper to hire scaffolding for 8 days?
(f) For what number of days do both companies make the same charge?

Using graphs

Graphs are sometimes drawn to show real-life situations.
In most cases a quantity is measured over a period of time.

EXAMPLE

Craig drew a graph to show the amount of fuel in the family car as they travelled to their holiday destination. He also made these notes:

Part of Graph	Event
A	Leave home.
A to B	Motorway.
B to C	Car breaks down.
C to D	On our way again.
D to E	Stop for lunch.
E to F	Fill tank with fuel.
F to G	Country roads.
G	Arrive, at last!

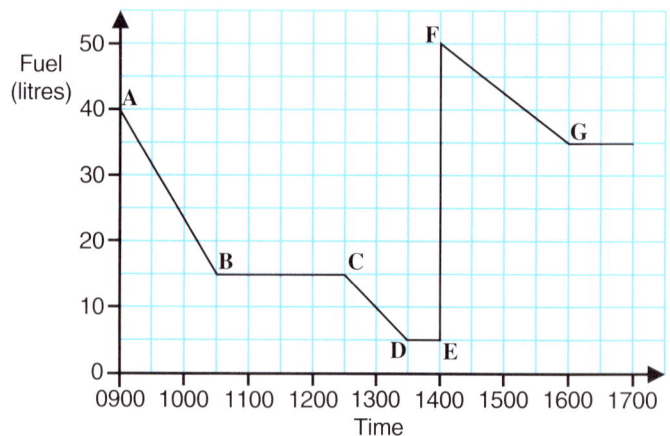

How much fuel was in the tank at the start of the journey?
At what time did the car break down?
How long did the family stop for lunch?
How much fuel was put into the tank at the garage?
At what time did the journey end?

138

Notice that in the previous example, and others involving graphs against time, the gradient of the line gives information about the quantity being measured.

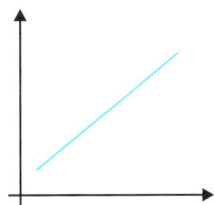

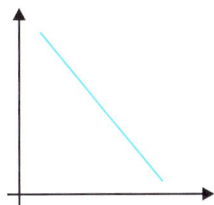

| A quantity increasing with time. | A quantity decreasing with time. | A quantity not changing, i.e. constant. | A quantity changing instantly. |

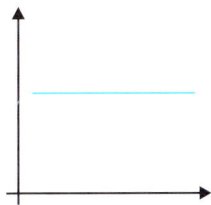

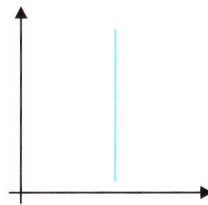

Exercise 10.5

1 A climber pulls a rucksack up a vertical cliff face using a rope.
Which of the graphs below could represent the motion of the rucksack against time?

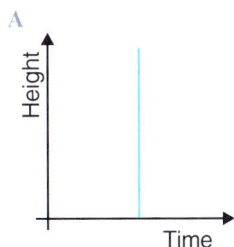

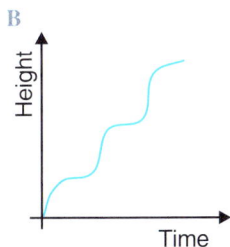

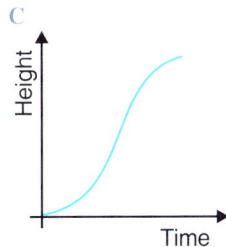

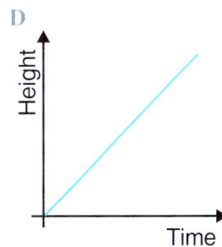

2 (a) Sketch a graph to show what is happening in this story:

"John leaves home at 8 am to go the shops. After walking for 5 minutes he sees the bus coming and runs for 2 minutes. The bus has broken down so he waits for 3 minutes. He then walks slowly home, which takes 10 minutes."

(b) Write a similar story about your journey to school and draw a graph for it.

(c) Write a story for this graph.

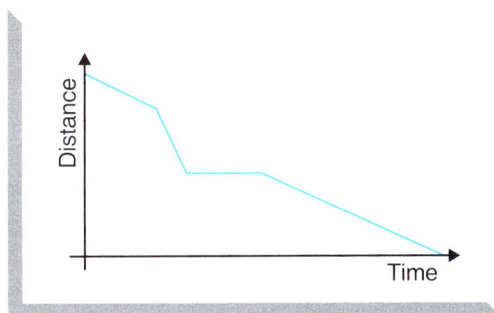

3 Cans of drink can be bought from a vending machine in the school canteen.
At the start of the day the machine is three-quarters full.
During break, from 10.45 to 11.00, drinks are bought from the machine at a steady rate.
By the end of the break the machine is one-quarter full.
At 12.00 the machine is filled.
The lunch break is from 12.30 to 1.30. Someone complains at 1.15 that the machine is empty.
The machine is filled at 2.00, ready for the afternoon break from 2.45 to 3.00.
At the end of the day the machine is three-quarters full.

Sketch a graph to show the number of drinks in the machine from 9.00 to 4.00.

4 Water is poured into some containers at a constant rate.
Copy the axes given and sketch the graph of the depth of the water against time for each container as it is filled.

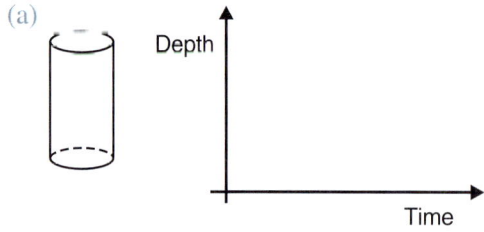

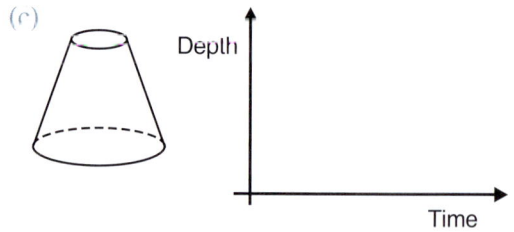

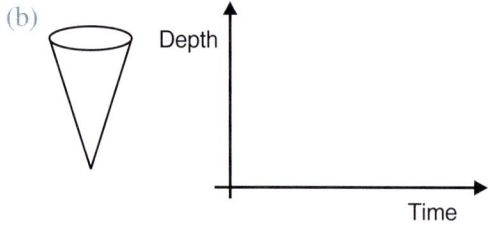

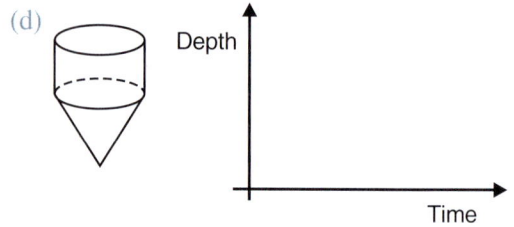

(a)

(b)

(c)

(d)

5 Water is drained from a hole in the bottom of a container.

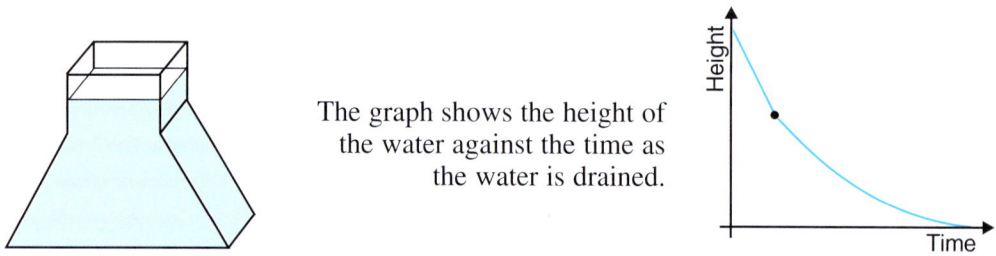

The graph shows the height of the water against the time as the water is drained.

Water is drained from these containers. Each graph shows the height of the water against time.
(a) Match the containers to the graphs.
(b) Draw a container for the graph which is not matched.

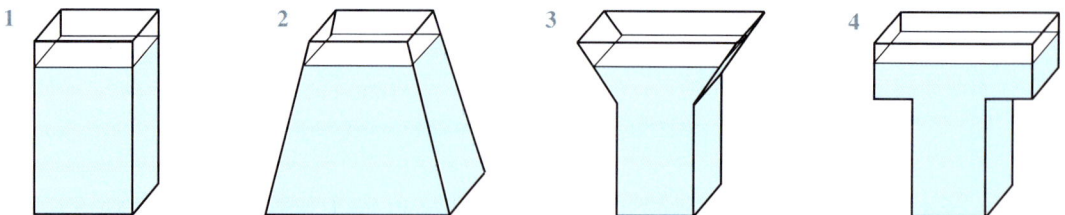

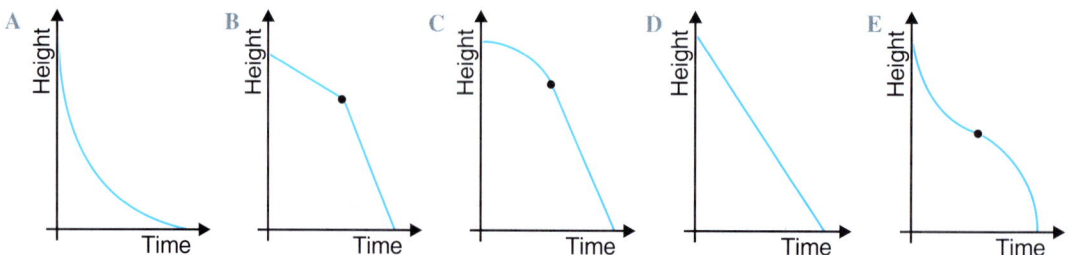

140

What you need to know

- **Coordinates** (involving positive and negative numbers) are used to describe the position of a point on a graph. For example, $A\,(-3, 2)$ is the point where the lines $x = -3$ and $y = 2$ cross.

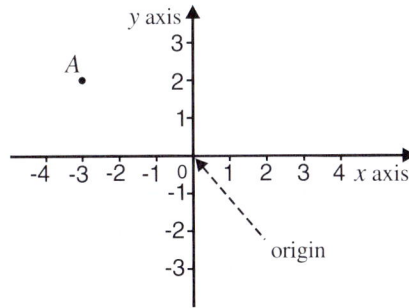

The x axis crosses the y axis at the origin.

- The general equation for a **straight line** graph is $y = mx + c$.
    where m is the **gradient** (slope) of the line,
    c is the **intercept**, the point $(0, c)$.

- The **gradient** of a line can be found by drawing a right-angled triangle.

    $\text{Gradient} = \dfrac{\text{distance up}}{\text{distance along}}$

    Gradient can be positive, zero or negative.

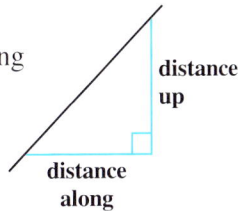

- The points where a line crosses the axes can be found:
    by reading the coordinates from a graph,
    by substituting $x = 0$ and $y = 0$ into the equation of the line.

- Equations of the form $px + qy = r$ can be **rearranged** to the form $y = mx + c$.

Review Exercise

1 Which of these diagrams shows the graph of $y = 2x$?

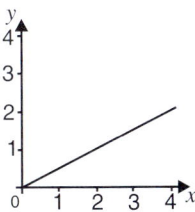

P

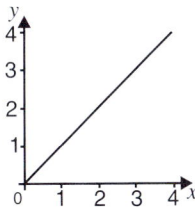

Q

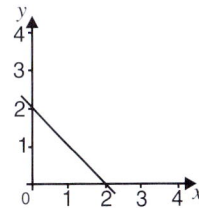

R

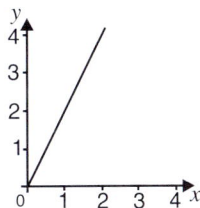

S

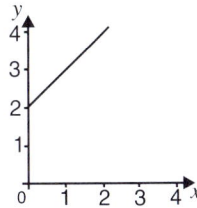

T

2 The graph of $y = 3 - x$ has been drawn. Copy the graph.

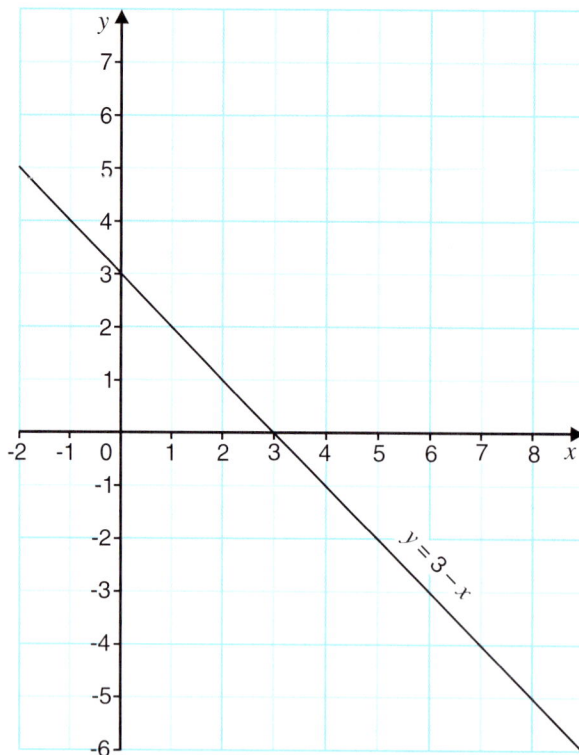

(a) Use your graph to solve the equation $3 - x = -1.2$
(b) On the same axes draw the graph of the equation $y = 2x - 3$.
(c) Use your graph to solve the equation $3 - x = 2x - 3$.

SEG 1994

3 (a) The graph of a straight line is given by the equation $y - 2x = 7$.
Write down, in the form $y = mx + c$, the equation of one other straight line which is parallel to this line.

(b) Write down the equation of one other straight line which crosses the y axis at the same point as $y - 3x = 5$.

SEG 1994

4 A graph of the equation $y = ax + b$ is shown.

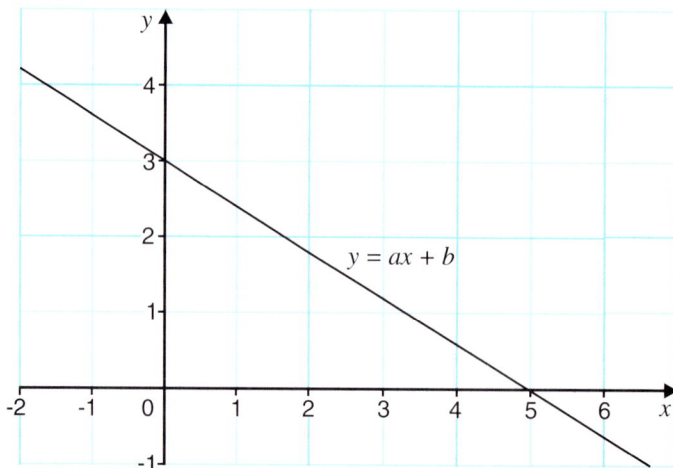

Find the values of a and b.

SEG 1998

5 (a) Helen entered the equation $y = 1\frac{1}{2}x + 3$ into the computer and obtained this graph.

Roy entered the equation $2y - 3x = 6$ and got the same graph.
Rearrange Roy's equation to show that it is equivalent to Helen's.

(b) (i) What is the gradient of the graph of $2x + y = 10$?
(ii) Sketch the graph of $2x + y = 10$.

SEG 1995

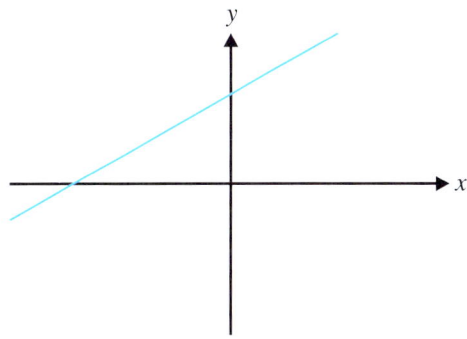

6 Television repair charges depend on the length of time taken for the repair, as shown on the graph.
The charge is made up of a fixed amount plus an extra amount which depends on the time.

(a) What is the charge for a repair which takes 45 minutes?
(b) (i) Calculate the gradient of the line.
(ii) What does the gradient represent?
(c) Write down the equation of the line.
(d) Mr Banks' repair will cost £84 or less. Calculate the maximum time which can be spent on the repair.

SEG 1994

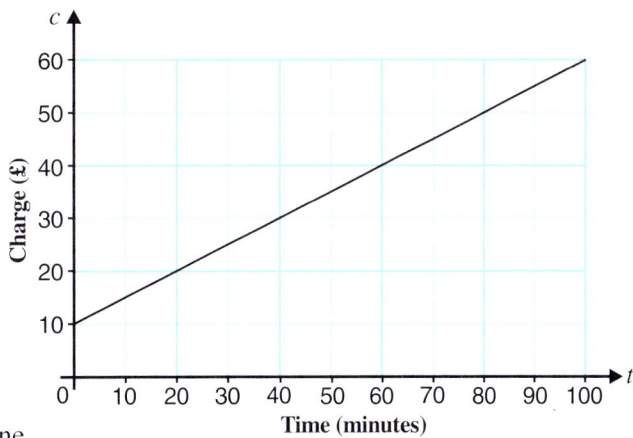

7 What is the equation of this line?

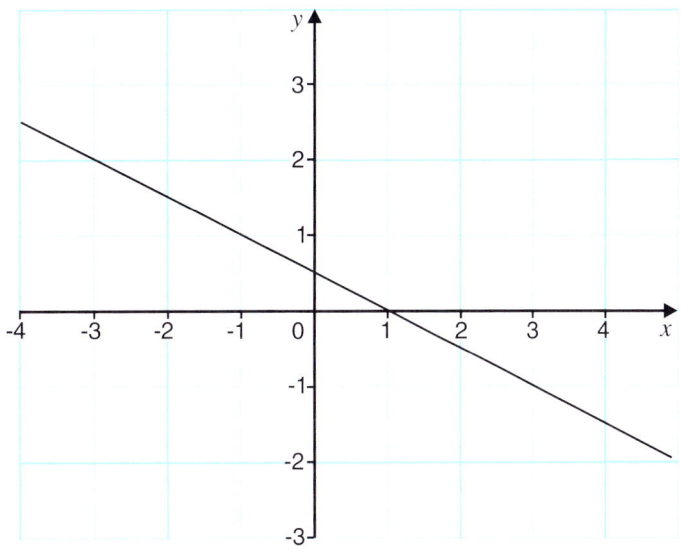

SEG 1996

8 Gail has two children, Amy and Ben.
The product of their ages is 30.

a	3	4	5	6	8	9	10
b	10						

(a) Given that Amy's age is a years and Ben's age is b years, copy and complete this table of possible values.
(b) Draw the graph of $ab = 30$.
(c) Amy is older than Ben and the sum of their ages is 12. Draw a suitable line on your graph and use it to find their ages to the nearest month.

SEG 1994

9 In an experiment, different weights are attached to a spring and the length of the spring is measured each time. The graph shows the result obtained.

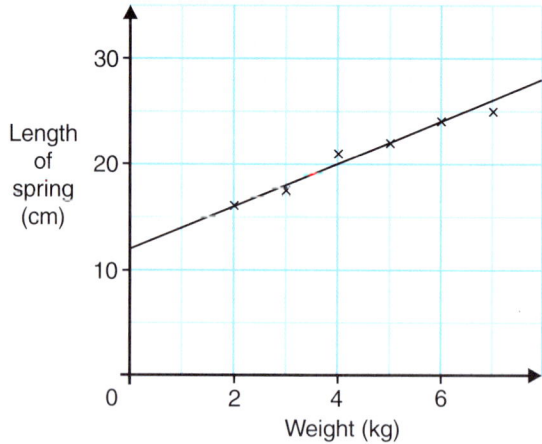

(a) Estimate the length of the spring when no weight is attached.
(b) Calculate the gradient of the line.
(c) Estimate the weight needed to **stretch** the spring by 20cm.

SEG 1999

10 Match the graphs to the situations. In each graph, the horizontal axis represents time and the vertical axis represents speed.

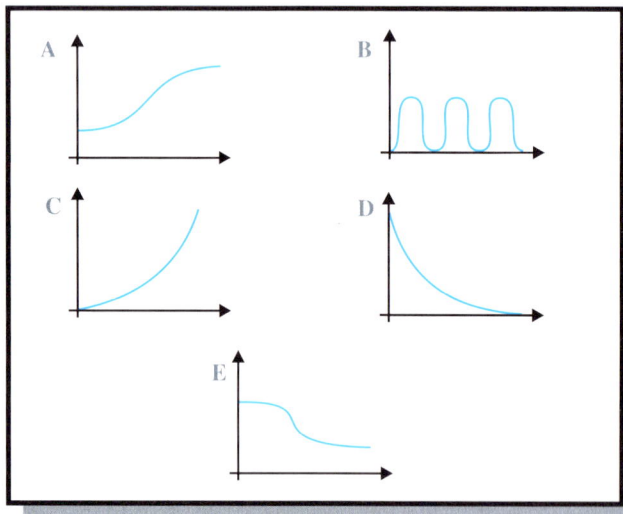

1 A runner starts from rest and begins to pick up speed.

2 A runner keeps having to stop and start.

3 A runner gets tired and has to slow down.

4 A runner sees the finish, builds up speed and sprints to the line.

11 Decide which graph matches each relationship.

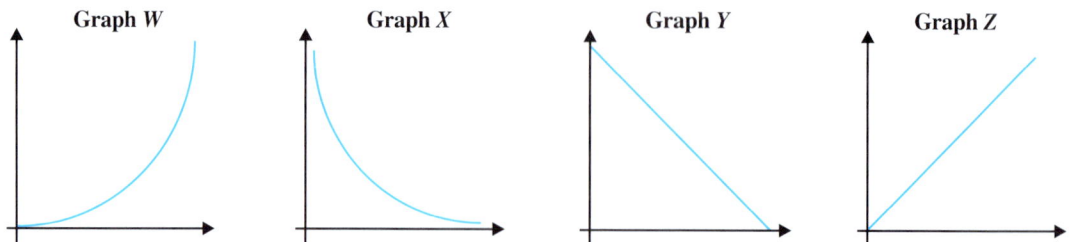

Graph *W*   Graph *X*   Graph *Y*   Graph *Z*

Relationships
A: The area of a circle plotted against its radius.
B: The circumference of a circle plotted against its radius.
C: The length of a rectangle of area 24 cm^2 plotted against its width.

SEG 1996

12 Water flows into some containers at a constant rate.

(a) Sketch the graphs of the depths of the water against time.

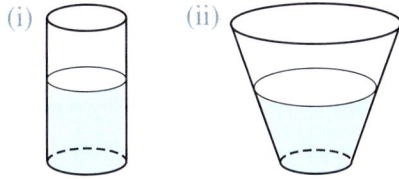

(i)   (ii)

(b) Sketch the cross-section of the container that generated this graph.

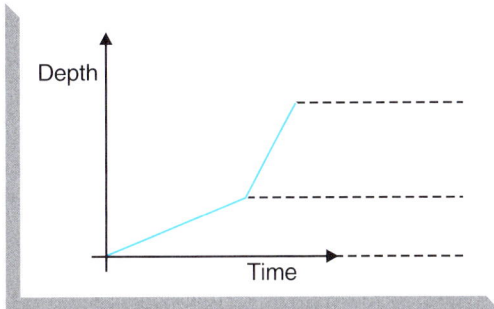

SEG 1995

13 (a) Water is poured at a constant rate into each of the four containers shown.

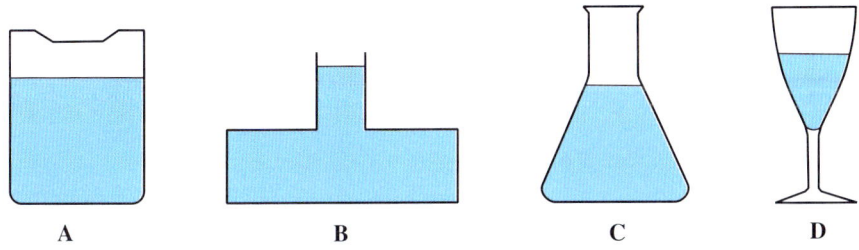

A   B   C   D

The graphs below show the height of water in the containers as they are being filled.

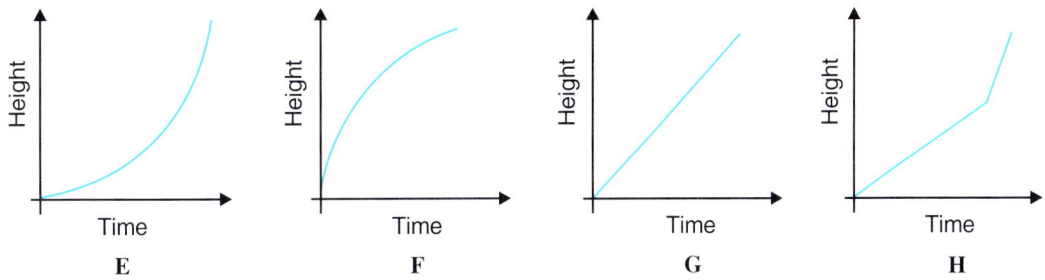

E   F   G   H

Write down the letter of the graph that matches each container.

(b) Draw similar graphs for each of the containers below.

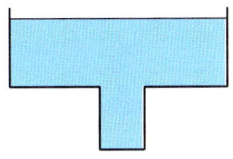

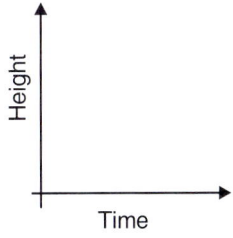

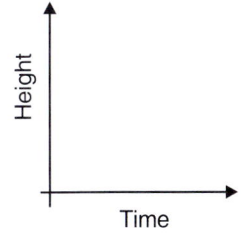

SEG 1994

CHAPTER 11

Simultaneous Equations

$x + y = 10$ is an equation with two unknown quantities x and y.
Many pairs of values of x and y fit this equation.
For example.
$x = 1$ and $y = 9$, $x = 4$ and $y = 6$, $x = 2.9$ and $y = 7.1$, $x = 1.005$ and $y = 8.995$, ...
$x - y = 2$ is another equation with the **same** two unknown quantities x and y.
Again, many pairs of values of x and y fit this equation.
For example.
$x = 4$ and $y = 2$, $x = 7$ and $y = 5$, $x = 2.9$ and $y = 0.9$, $x = -1$ and $y = -3$, ...

There is only **one** pair of values of x and y which fit **both** of these equations ($x = 6$ and $y = 4$).
Pairs of equations like $x + y = 10$ and $x - y = 2$ are called **simultaneous equations**.

To solve simultaneous equations you need to find values which fit **both** equations simultaneously.
Simultaneous equations can be solved using different methods.

Using graphs to solve simultaneous equations

Consider the simultaneous equations $x + 2y = 5$ and $x - 2y = 1$.

Draw the graphs of $x + 2y = 5$ and $x - 2y = 1$.

For $x + 2y = 5$:
When $x = 1$, $y = 2$.
This gives the point (1, 2).

When $x = 5$, $y = 0$.
This gives the point (5, 0).

To draw the graph of $x + 2y = 5$
draw a line through the points
(1, 2) and (5, 0).

For $x - 2y = 1$:
When $x = 1$, $y = 0$.
This gives the point (1, 0).

When $x = 5$, $y = 2$.
This gives the point (5, 2).

To draw the graph of $x - 2y = 1$
draw a line through the points
(1, 0) and (5, 2).

> Drawing straight line graphs was first covered in Chapter 10.

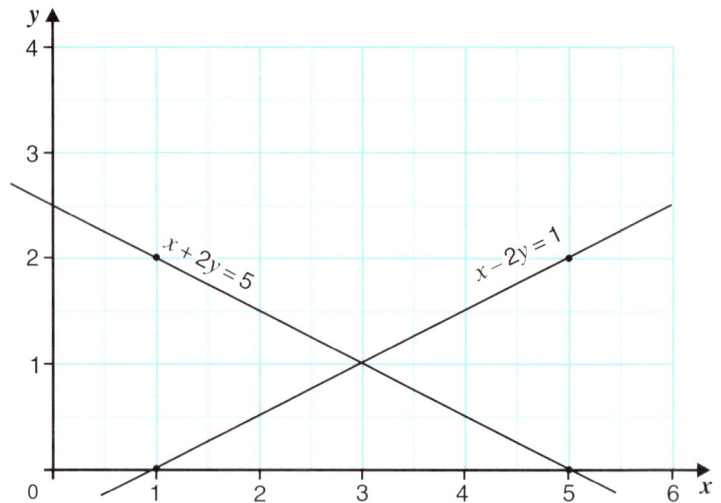

The values of x and y at the point where the lines cross give the solution to the simultaneous equations.

The lines cross at the point (3, 1).

This gives the solution $x = 3$ and $y = 1$.

To solve a pair of simultaneous equations plot the graph of each of the equations on the same diagram.
The coordinates of the point where the two lines cross:
- fit **both equations** simultaneously,
- give the **graphical solution** of the equations.

Use a graphical method to solve this pair of simultaneous equations:
$$5x + 2y = 20$$
$$y = 2x + 1$$

Find the points that fit the equations $5x + 2y = 20$ and $y = 2x + 1$.

For $5x + 2y = 20$:

When $x = 0$, $y = 10$.
This gives the point $(0, 10)$.

When $y = 0$, $x = 4$.
This gives the point $(4, 0)$.

For $y = 2x + 1$:

When $x = 0$, $y = 1$.
This gives the point $(0, 1)$.

When $x = 4$, $y = 9$.
This gives the point $(4, 9)$.

The lines cross at the point $(2, 5)$.
This gives the solution
$x = 2$ and $y = 5$.

Check
You can check a graphical solution by substituting the values of x and y into the original equations.
When $x = 2$ and $y = 5$
$$5x + 2y = 5 \times 2 + 2 \times 5 = 20$$
$$y = 2x + 1 = 2 \times 2 + 1 = 5$$

Exercise 11.1

Use a graphical method to solve each of these pairs of simultaneous equations.
For each question use the sizes of axes given.
All solutions are positive whole numbers.

Drawing and labelling axes
$0 \leqslant x \leqslant 8$ means draw and label the x axis from 0 to 8 inclusive.
What does $-3 \leqslant y \leqslant 7$ mean?

1 $x + y = 6$
   $y = x - 2$
   Axes $0 \leqslant x \leqslant 8$, $-3 \leqslant y \leqslant 7$

2 $x + y = 8$
   $y - x = 2$
   Axes $0 \leqslant x \leqslant 10$, $-3 \leqslant y \leqslant 10$

3 $x + 2y = 8$
   $2x + y = 7$
   Axes $0 \leqslant x \leqslant 10$, $0 \leqslant y \leqslant 8$

4 $3x + 2y = 12$
   $y = x + 1$
   Axes $0 \leqslant x \leqslant 5$, $0 \leqslant y \leqslant 8$

5 $x + 3y = 6$
   $y = 2x - 5$
   Axes $0 \leqslant x \leqslant 10$, $-6 \leqslant y \leqslant 4$

6 $3x + 4y = 24$
   $2y = x + 2$
   Axes $-4 \leqslant x \leqslant 10$, $-2 \leqslant y \leqslant 8$

Simultaneous equations with no solution

Some pairs of simultaneous equations do not have a solution.

EXAMPLE

Show that this pair of simultaneous equations do not have a solution.

$$y - 2x = 4$$
$$2y = 4x - 1$$

Method 1
Draw the graph of each equation.

$y - 2x = 4$
When $x = 0$, $y = 4$.
This gives the point $(0, 4)$.
When $y = 0$, $x = -2$
This gives the point $(-2, 0)$.

$2y = 4x - 1$
When $x = 0$, $y = -0.5$.
This gives the point $(0, -0.5)$.
When $x = 2$, $y = 3.5$
This gives the point $(2, 3.5)$.

The two lines are **parallel**.
This means they never cross
and there are no values of x
and y which fit both
equations.
So the simultaneous
equations have no solution.

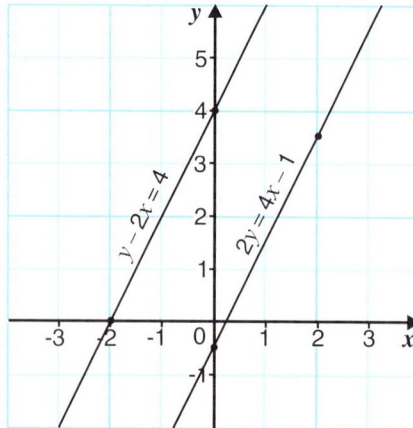

Method 2
Rearrange each equation to
the form $y = mx + c$.

$y - 2x = 4$
Add $2x$ to both sides.
$y = 2x + 4$
The graph of this equation
has a gradient (m) of 2 and
an intercept (c) of 4.

$2y = 4x - 1$
Divide both sides by 2.
$y = 2x - 0.5$
The graph of this equation
has a gradient (m) of 2 and
an intercept (c) of -0.5.

Both lines have the same
gradient (2) and different
intercepts which shows that
the lines are parallel.

Exercise 11.2

1 Draw graphs to show that each of these pairs of simultaneous equations have no solution.

(a) $x + y = 6$
$y = 2 - x$

(b) $y - 4x = 8$
$y = 4x + 2$

(c) $3x + 4y = 12$
$8y = 24 - 6x$

(d) $5y - 2x = 10$
$5y = 2x + 20$

2 By rearranging each of these pairs of simultaneous equations to the form $y = mx + c$ show that they do not have a solution.

(a) $2x + y = 6$
$y = 3 - 2x$

(b) $2y - 4x = 7$
$y - 2 = 2x$

(c) $5x - 2y = 8$
$4y = 10x + 7$

(d) $4y + 12x = 5$
$1 - 2y = 6x$

3 Two of these pairs of simultaneous equations have no solution.

(a) $5x + y = 6$
$y - 5x = 2$

(b) $5x = 8 + y$
$y - 5x = 2$

(c) $2y - 10x = 5$
$4y + 20x = 5$

(d) $y + 1 = -5x$
$2y + 10x = 5$

Use an appropriate method to find which ones.
Use a graphical method to solve the other two.

The graphical method of solving simultaneous equations can be quite time consuming.
Sometimes, due to the equations involved, the coordinates of the points where the lines intersect can be difficult to read accurately.
For these reasons, other methods of solving simultaneous equations are often used.

Consider again the simultaneous equations $x + 2y = 5$ and $x - 2y = 1$.
Both equations have the same number of x's and the same number of y's.
If the two equations are added together the y's will be **eliminated** as shown.

$$x + 2y = 5$$
$$x - 2y = 1$$

Adding gives $\quad 2x = 6$
So $\quad x = 3$

Remember
$+ 2y + -2y$
$= 2y - 2y = 0$

By **substituting** the value of this letter (x) into one of the original equations we can find the value of the other letter (y).

$$x + 2y = 5$$
$$3 + 2y = 5$$
$$2y = 2$$
$$y = 1$$

This gives the solution $x = 3$ and $y = 1$.

Remember:
If you do the same to both sides of an equation it is still true.

EXAMPLES

1 Use the elimination method to solve this pair of simultaneous equations:
$$2x - y = 1$$
$$3x + y = 9$$

Each equation has the **same number** of y's but the **signs** are **different**.
To eliminate the y's the equations must be **added**.

$$5x = 10$$
$$x = 2$$

Substitute $x = 2$ into $3x + y = 9$.
$$3 \times 2 + y = 9$$
$$6 + y = 9$$
$$y = 3$$

The solution is $x = 2$ and $y = 3$.

Check
Substitute $x = 2$ and $y = 3$ into
$$2x - y = 1$$
$$2 \times 2 - 3 = 1$$
$$4 - 3 = 1$$
$$1 = 1$$
The equation is true, so the solution $x = 2$ and $y = 3$ is correct.

2 Use the elimination method to solve this pair of simultaneous equations:
$$2x + 3y = 9$$
$$2x + y = 7$$

Each equation has the **same number** of x's and the **signs** are the **same**.
To eliminate the x's one equation must be **subtracted** from the other.

Subtract $2x + y = 7$ from $2x + 3y = 9$.
$$2y = 2$$
$$y = 1$$

Substitute $y = 1$ into $2x + y = 7$.
$$2x + 1 = 7$$
$$2x = 6$$
$$x = 3$$

The solution is $x = 3$ and $y = 1$.

Check
Substitute $x = 3$ and $y = 1$ into $2x + 3y = 9$.
Do this and make sure the solution is correct.

Use the elimination method to solve each of these pairs of simultaneous equations.

1 $3x - y = 1$
   $x + y = 3$

2 $2x - y = 2$
   $x + y = 7$

3 $4x + y = 9$
   $2x - y = 3$

4 $-x + 2y = 13$
   $x + y = 8$

5 $2x + y = 7$
   $x + y = 4$

6 $3x + y = 9$
   $2x + y = 7$

7 $2x + y = 12$
   $x + y = 7$

8 $x + 5y = 14$
   $x + 2y = 8$

9 $x + 2y = 13$
   $x + 4y = 21$

10 $x + 4y = 11$
   $x + y = 5$

11 $2x + 5y = 13$
   $2x + y = 9$

12 $5x + 3y = 26$
   $2x + 3y = 14$

13 $5x + 4y = 22$
   $5x + y = 13$

14 $2x - y = 10$
   $3x + y = 10$

15 $5x - 2y = 13$
   $3x + 2y = 3$

16 $x + 5y = 14$
   $-x + 2y = 7$

17 $2x + 3y = 8$
   $2x + y = -4$

18 $2x + y = 4$
   $4x - y = 11$

19 $3x + 4y = -8$
   $x + 4y = 4$

20 $3x + 2y = 6$
   $x - 2y = 6$

Further use of the elimination method

Look at this pair of simultaneous equations:
$$5x + 2y = 11$$
$$3x - 4y = 4$$

A useful technique is to use capital letters to label the equations.

$$5x + 2y = 11 \qquad \text{Equation A}$$
$$3x - 4y = 4 \qquad \text{Equation B}$$

These equations do not have the same number of x's or the same number of y's.

To make the number of y's the same we can multiply equation A by 2.

A × 2 gives $10x + 4y = 22$ Equation C
B × 1 gives $3x - 4y = 4$ Equation D

C + D gives $13x = 26$
                      $x = 2$

The number of y's in equations C and D is the **same** but the **signs** are **different**. So, to eliminate the y's the equations must be **added**.

Substitute $x = 2$ into $5x + 2y = 11$.
$$5 \times 2 + 2y = 11$$
$$10 + 2y = 11$$
$$2y = 1$$
$$y = 0.5$$

The solution is $x = 2$ and $y = 0.5$.

Check the solution by substituting $x = 2$ and $y = 0.5$ into $3x - 4y = 4$.

In this example eliminating the y's rather than the x's is less likely to produce an error.
Try to solve the equations by eliminating the x's.

Solve this pair of simultaneous equations:
$$3x + 7y = -2$$
$$4x + 9 = -3y$$

Rearrange and label the equations as necessary.

$3x + 7y = -2$ A
$4x + 3y = -9$ B

These equations do not have the same number of x's or the same number of y's.
So the multiplying method can be used.

> Both equations must be in the form $px + qy = r$ before the elimination method can be used.
> You may have to **rearrange** the equations you are given.
> $4x + 9 = -3y$ can be rearranged as $4x + 3y = -9$.

Method 1
Eliminating the x's.

A $\times$ 4 gives $12x + 28y = -8$ C
B $\times$ 3 gives $12x + 9y = -27$ D

C $-$ D gives
$$19y = -8 - -27$$
$$19y = -8 + 27$$
$$19y = 19$$
$$y = 1$$

Substitute $y = 1$ into $3x + 7y = -2$.
$$3x + 7 \times 1 = -2$$
$$3x + 7 = -2$$
$$3x = -9$$
$$x = -3$$

The solution is $x = -3$ and $y = 1$.

Method 2
Eliminating the y's.

A $\times$ 3 gives $9x + 21y = -6$ C
B $\times$ 7 gives $28x + 21y = -63$ D

D $-$ C gives
$$19x = -63 - -6$$
$$19x = -63 + 6$$
$$19x = -57$$
$$x = -3$$

Substitute $x = -3$ into $3x + 7y = -2$.
$$3 \times -3 + 7y = -2$$
$$-9 + 7y = -2$$
$$7y = 7$$
$$y = 1$$

Check the solution by substituting $x = -3$ and $y = 1$ into $4x + 9 = -3y$.

Exercise 11.4

Solve each of these pairs of simultaneous equations.

1 $3x + 2y = 8$
$2x - y = 3$

2 $x + y = 5$
$5x - 3y = 1$

3 $2x + 3y = 9$
$x + 4y = 7$

4 $x + 3y = 10$
$2x + 5y = 18$

5 $5x + 2y = 8$
$2x - y = 5$

6 $3x + y = 9$
$x - 2y = 10$

7 $3x - 4y = 10$
$x + 2y = 5$

8 $x + 6y = 0$
$3x - 2y = -10$

9 $2x + 3y = 11$
$3x + y = 13$

10 $2x + y = 10$
$-x + 2y = 9$

11 $2x + 3y = 9$
$4x - y = 4$

12 $2x + 3y = 8$
$3x + 2y = 7$

13 $3x + 4y = 23$
$2x + 5y = 20$

14 $2x - 3y = 8$
$x - 5y = 11$

15 $3x + 4y = 5$
$-2x + 5y = 12$

16 $3x - 2y = 4$
$x + 4y = 6$

17 $-3x + 2y = 5$
$4x + 3y = -1$

18 $3x + 4y = 6$
$3y = 7 - x$

19 $5x + 3y = 16$
$2y = 13 - x$

20 $5x - 4y = 24$
$2x = y + 9$

21 $2x + 3y = 14$
$8x - 5y = 5$

22 $4x - 7y = 15$
$5x - 12 = 2y$

23 $8x + 3y = 2$
$5x = 1 - 2y$

24 $9x = 4y - 20$
$5x = 6y - 13$

For some pairs of simultaneous equations a method using **substitution** is sometimes more convenient.

EXAMPLE

Solve this pair of simultaneous equations: $5x + y = 9$
$$y = 4x$$

$5x + y = 9$ Equation A
$\quad\quad y = 4x$ Equation B
Substitute $y = 4x$ into Equation A
$\quad\quad 5x + 4x = 9$
$\quad\quad\quad\quad 9x = 9$
$\quad\quad\quad\quad\quad x = 1$

Substitute $x = 1$ into $y = 4x$.
$y = 4 \times 1$
$y = 4$

The solution is $x = 1$ and $y = 4$.

Check the solution by substituting
$x = 1$ and $y = 4$ into $5x + y = 9$.

Exercise 11.5   Use the substitution method to solve these pairs of simultaneous equations.

1 $2x + y = 10$
$\quad\quad y = 3x$

2 $3x - y = 9$
$\quad\quad y = 2x$

3 $x + 5y = 18$
$\quad\quad x = 4y$

4 $x + 2y = 15$
$\quad\quad y = 2x$

5 $2x + y = 17$
$\quad\quad , y = 6x + 1$

6 $3x + 2y = 4$
$\quad\quad x = y - 2$

7 $5x + 6y = 34$
$\quad\quad y = x + 2$

8 $5x - 2y = 23$
$\quad\quad x = y + 1$

9 $5x - y = 12$
$\quad\quad y = 32 - 6x$

10 $x + 5y = 13$
$\quad\quad x = 3y + 9$

11 $5x - 3y = 26$
$\quad\quad y = 2x + 14$

12 $x + 4y = 32$
$\quad\quad x = 2y - 4$

Solving problems using simultaneous equations

EXAMPLE

Billy buys 5 first class stamps and 3 second class stamps at a cost of £1.93.
Jane buys 3 first class stamps and 5 second class stamps at a cost of £1.83.
Calculate the cost of a first class stamp and the cost of a second class stamp.

Let x pence be the cost of a first class stamp, and
let y pence be the cost of a second class stamp.
Billy's purchase of the stamps gives this equation.
$$5x + 3y = 193 \quad\quad \text{Equation A}$$
Jane's purchase of the stamps gives this equation.
$$3x + 5y = 183 \quad\quad \text{Equation B}$$
This gives a pair of simultaneous equations which can be solved using the elimination method.
$\quad\quad 5x + 3y = 193 \quad\quad$ A
$\quad\quad 3x + 5y = 183 \quad\quad$ B

A $\times$ 5 gives $25x + 15y = 965$ C
B $\times$ 3 gives $9x + 15y = 549$ D

C $-$ D gives $16x = 416$
$\quad\quad\quad\quad\quad x = 26$

Substitute $x = 26$ into $5x + 3y = 193$.
$5 \times 26 + 3y = 193$
$\quad\quad\quad 3y = 63$
$\quad\quad\quad\quad y = 21$

So the cost of a first class stamp is 26 pence and the cost of a second class stamp is 21 pence.

Check the solution by substituting the values for x and y into the original problem.

Exercise **11.6**

1   The "Durham" hotel charges £40 for a single room and £30 per person for a double room.
One night 44 people stay in the hotel. The hotel receives £1500.

Let s represent the number of people staying in single rooms.
Let d represent the number of people staying in double rooms.
The equation for the number of people staying in the hotel is $s + d = 44$.
   (a)   Write down an equation in terms of s and d for the amount of money received by the hotel.
   (b)   Solve these simultaneous equations.
                                                                          SEG 1994

2   Standard eggs cost x pence per dozen. Small eggs cost y pence per dozen.
10 dozen standard eggs and 5 dozen small eggs cost £13.60.
5 dozen standard eggs and 8 dozen small eggs cost £11.31.
Calculate x and y.

3   A group of children and adults went on a coach trip to a theme park.
Ticket prices for the theme park were £10 for adults and £5 for children.
Ticket prices for the coach were £5 for adults and £2 for children.
The total cost of the tickets for the theme park was £190.
The total cost of the coach tickets was £79.
How many children and adults went on the trip?

4   Jenny types at x words per minute. Stuart types at y words per minute.
When Jenny and Stuart both type for 1 minute they type a total of 170 words.
When Jenny types for 5 minutes and Stuart types for 3 minutes they type a total of 710 words.
Calculate x and y.

5   At a café, John buys 3 coffees and 2 teas for £2.30 and Susan buys 2 coffees and 3 teas for £2.20.
Calculate the price of a coffee and the price of a tea.

6   Standard coaches hold x passengers and first class coaches hold y passengers.
A train with 5 standard coaches and 2 first class coaches carries a total of 1040 passengers.
A train with 7 standard coaches and 3 first class coaches carries a total of 1480 passengers.

   (a)   Write down two equations connecting x and y.
   (b)   Solve these simultaneous equations to find the values of x and y.

What you need to know

- A pair of **simultaneous equations** are linked equations with the same unknown letters in each equation.

- To solve a pair of simultaneous equations find values for the unknown letters that fit **both** equations.

- Simultaneous equations can be solved either **graphically** or **algebraically**.

- Solving simultaneous equations **graphically** involves:
         drawing the graph of both equations,
         finding the point where the graphs cross.
  When the graphs of both equations are parallel, the equations have no solution.

- Solving simultaneous equations **algebraically** involves using either:
         the **elimination** method, or
         the **substitution** method (if it is more convenient).

1 Use a graphical method to solve each of these simultaneous equations.
For each question use the size of axes given.

   (a) $x + y = 10$
          $y = 2x + 1$
          Axes $0 \leqslant x \leqslant 11, 0 \leqslant y \leqslant 11$

   (b) $x + 3y = 9$
          $5y + x = 10$
          Axes $0 \leqslant x \leqslant 10, 0 \leqslant y \leqslant 5$

   (c) $5x + 6y = 30$
          $2y = x - 2$
          Axes $0 \leqslant x \leqslant 8, -3 \leqslant y \leqslant 8$

   (d) $3x - 2y = 18$
          $4x + y = 2$
          Axes $0 \leqslant x \leqslant 8, -10 \leqslant y \leqslant 3$

2 Use an algebraic method to solve each of these simultaneous equations.
You must show all your working.

   (a) $x + 3y = 5$
          $3x + y = 3$

   (b) $2x + y = 8$
          $x + y = 5$

   (c) $7x + 3y = 19$
          $2x + 3y = 14$

   (d) $6x + 5y = 28$
          $4x - 5y = 2$

   (e) $2x + 3y = 4$
          $x + 2y = 3$

   (f) $2x + y = 9$
          $x - 2y = 7$

   (g) $7x + 2y = 17$
          $3x + 4y = 1$

   (h) $9x - 4y = 20$
          $3x + 2y = 5$

   (i) $3x + 5y = 21$
          $2x + 7y = 25$

   (j) $9x - 4y = 31$
          $2x + 3y = 3$

   (k) $3x - 5y = 11$
          $2x + 7y = -3$

   (l) $3y - 5x = 1$
          $5y - 3x = 7$

   (m) $3x + y = 13$
          $y = 7 - x$

   (n) $x + 3y = 5$
          $y = 2x + 18$

   (o) $3x - 2y = 26$
          $x = 2y - 18$

   (p) $x + 5y = 3$
          $y = 3x + 7$

3
   (a) Show that the simultaneous equations $y = 2x - 2$ and $2y - 4x = 3$ have no solution.
   (b) Show that the simultaneous equations $4y = x + 1$ and $8y - 2x = 3$ have no solution.
   (c) The simultaneous equations $y = 3x + 2$ and $y = ax + b$ have no solution.
       What can you say about the values of a and b?
   (d) The simultaneous equations $y = 3x + 2$ and $py + qx = r$ have no solution.
       Find some possible values for p, q and r.

4 This graph shows the line $y - 2x = -1$.

Copy the graph.
By drawing another line, use the graph to solve
the simultaneous equations
       $y - 2x = -1$
       $x + 2y = 4$

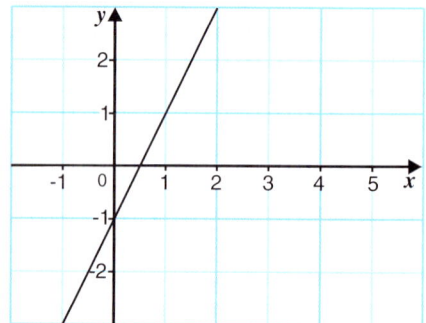

SEG 1997

5 A shop sells pens costing x pence each and pencils costing y pence each.
Sanjit pays 67 pence for 3 pens and 2 pencils.
Fiona pays 86 pence for 5 pens and 1 pencil.

   (a) Form two equations in x and y.
   (b) Use your equations to find the cost of a pen and the cost of a pencil.
       You must show **all** your working.

SEG 1995

6 Two adults and three children pay £10.75 to go to the cinema.
One adult and two children pay £6.00 to go to the same cinema.
Let an adult pay £x and a child pay £y.

   (a) Write down two equations connecting x and y.
   (b) Solve these simultaneous equations to find x and y.

SEG 1998

CHAPTER 12

More or Less

Activity

Poster Painting Competition
for all ages

- Child (Under 16)
- Adult

You must be at least 1.2 m. tall to go on this ride.

BARGAIN SUPERSTORE

ALL ITEMS £1 OR LESS

For all children who enter the competition we can say that
Age < 16 years

For anyone riding the Big Dipper we can say that
Height $\geqslant$ 1.2 m

For all items sold in the store we can say that
Cost $\leqslant$ £1

These are examples of inequalities.
Can you think of other situations where inequalities are used?

Inequalities

An **inequality** is a mathematical statement, such as $x > 1$ or $a \leqslant 2$.

In the following, x is an integer.

Sign	Meaning	Example	Possible values of x
<	is less than	$x < 4$	3, 2, 1, 0, -1, -2, -3, …
$\leqslant$	is less than or equal to	$x \leqslant 4$	4, 3, 2, 1, 0, -1, -2, -3, …
>	is greater than	$x > 6$	7, 8, 9, 10, …
$\geqslant$	is greater than or equal to	$x \geqslant 2$	2, 3, 4, 5, …

Inequalities are similar to equations.

An **integer** is a positive or negative whole number or zero.

Explain the difference between the meanings of the signs < and $\leqslant$.
Explain the difference between the meanings of the signs > and $\geqslant$.

Number lines

Inequalities can be shown on a **number line**.

$$-6 \quad -5 \quad -4 \quad -3 \quad -2 \quad -1 \quad 0 \quad 1 \quad 2 \quad 3 \quad 4 \quad 5 \quad 6$$

As you move to the right, numbers get bigger.
As you move to the left, numbers get smaller.

EXAMPLES

Draw number lines to show the following inequalities.

1 $x < 1.5$

The circle is **not filled** because 1.5 is **not included**.

2 $3 \leqslant x < 8$

The circle is **filled** because 3 is **included**.

Exercise 12.1

1 In this question x is an integer. Write down all the values of x which satisfy these inequalities.

(a) $1 < x < 5$ (b) $-2 < x \leqslant 3$ (c) $-4 \leqslant x \leqslant -1$ (d) $-1 \leqslant x < 3$

2 Write down a mathematical statement, using inequalities, for each of these diagrams.

(a)

(b)

(c)

(d)

3 Draw number lines to show the following inequalities. For each part, draw and label a number line from -5 to 5.

(a) $-2 \leqslant x < 3$ (b) $x > -4$ (c) $x < -3$ and $x \geqslant 1$

Solving inequalities

Solve means to find the values of x which make the inequality true.
The aim is to end up with **one letter** on one side of the inequality and a **number** on the other side of the inequality.

EXAMPLES

1 Solve the inequality $5x - 3 < 27$.

$5x - 3 < 27$
Add 3 to both sides.
$5x < 30$
Divide both sides by 5.
$x < 6$

This means that the inequality is **true** for all values of x which are less than 6.
Substitute $x = 5$ and $x = 7$ into the original inequality. What do you notice?

2 Solve the inequality $7a \geqslant a + 9$.

$7a \geqslant a + 9$
Subtract a from both sides.
$6a \geqslant 9$
Divide both sides by 6.
$a \geqslant 1.5$

This means that the inequality is true for all values of a which are equal to 1.5, or greater.
Substitute $a = 1.5$, $a = 2$ and $a = 1$ into the original inequality. What do you notice?

Exercise **12.2**

Solve the following inequalities. Show your working clearly.

1 $3d - 4 > 8$

2 $2e + 5 \geqslant 9$

3 $4 + 3f < -2$

4 $8g - 1 \leqslant 3$

5 $5h < h + 8$

6 $6j \geqslant 2j + 10$

7 $7k > 3k - 16$

8 $4m + 2 > 2m - 11$

9 $7n - 3 \leqslant 13 - n$

10 $3p - 2 > 6 + 2p$

11 $4q + 5 > 12 - 3q$

12 $6r + 1 \geqslant 4r - 2$

13 $2t - 10 > t + 3$

14 $2(u - 5) \leqslant 8$

15 $3(4v + 1) < -15$

16 $\frac{1}{2} w + 3 > 7$

17 $\frac{1}{4} x - 5 \geqslant -6\frac{1}{2}$

18 $7a - 2 < 4a + 5$

19 $3b + 5 \geqslant 10b - 3$

20 $6 - 4c > 3 + 4c$

21 $5 + 5x \leqslant 2 - 4x$

22 $3(x + 1) > 5x$

23 $8 + 2x \geqslant 3(4 - x)$

24 $8(3 + 2x) \leqslant 2 + 3x$

25 $\frac{4 - 3x}{2} > 3x$

26 $5 < \frac{2}{3}(x - 4)$

27 $\frac{x}{3} + \frac{5}{4} \geqslant \frac{3}{4}(2 - 3x)$

Multiplying (or dividing) an inequality by a negative number

Activity

$-2 < 3$

Multiply both sides by -1.
$-2 \times (-1) = 2$ and $3 \times (-1) = -3$

$2 > -3$

To keep the statement true we have to reverse the inequality sign.

Multiply both sides of these inequalities by -1.

1 $3 > 2$

2 $3 > -2$

3 $-3 < -1$

4 $5 \geqslant 4$

5 $-4 \leqslant 5$

6 $-4 \geqslant -5$

The same rules for equations can be applied to inequalities, with one exception:
When you **multiply** (or **divide**) both sides of an inequality by a negative number the inequality is reversed.

Remember:
Division is the inverse (opposite) operation to multiplication.

EXAMPLES

1 Solve $-3x < 6$.

Divide both sides by -3.
Because we are dividing by a negative number the inequality is reversed.
$x > -2$

2 Solve $3a - 2 \geqslant 5a - 9$.

Subtract $5a$ from both sides.
$-2a - 2 \geqslant -9$
Add 2 to both sides.
$-2a \geqslant -7$
Divide both sides by -2.
$a \leqslant 3.5$

Solve the following inequalities. Show your working clearly.

1 $-4a > 8$

2 $-5b \leqslant -15$

3 $-3c \geqslant 12$

4 $3 - 2d < 5$

5 $14 - 3e \leqslant 4e$

6 $-5f > 4f - 9$

7 $4g < 7g + 12$

8 $5 - 3h \leqslant h - 3$

9 $-5 - j \geqslant 12j - 18$

10 $3 - 5k < 2(3 + 2k)$

11 $3(m - 2) > 5m$

12 $3(2n - 1) < 8n + 5$

13 $3p \geqslant 5 - 6p$

14 $2(q - 3) < 5 + 7q$

Double inequalities

EXAMPLE

1 Find the values of x such that $-8 < 4x - 2 \leqslant 10$.

$-8 < 4x - 2 \leqslant 10$
Add 2 to each part of the inequality.
$-6 < 4x \leqslant 12$
Divide each part of the inequality by 4.
$-1.5 < x \leqslant 3$

Alternative method
Write the **double inequality** as two separate inequalities.
$-8 < 4x - 2$ and $4x - 2 \leqslant 10$
Solve each inequality.

$-8 < 4x - 2$
Add 2 to both sides.
$-6 < 4x$
Divide both sides by 4.
$-1.5 < x$

$4x - 2 \leqslant 10$
Add 2 to both sides.
$4x \leqslant 12$
Divide both sides by 4.
$x \leqslant 3$

So $-1.5 < x \leqslant 3$

The double inequality $-1.5 < x \leqslant 3$ gives **all** the possible values of x.
This means that the inequality $-8 < 4x - 2 \leqslant 10$ is true for all the values of x from -1.5 (not included) up to 3 (included).

Inequalities involving integers

EXAMPLE

2 Find the integer values of n for which $-2 \leqslant 2n + 6 < 13$.

$-2 \leqslant 2n + 6 < 13$
Subtract 6 from each part.
$-8 \leqslant 2n < 7$
Divide each part by 2.
$-4 \leqslant n < 3.5$

Alternative method
$-2 \leqslant 2n + 6$
Subtract 6 from both sides.
$-8 \leqslant 2n$
Divide both sides by 2.
$-4 \leqslant n$

$2n + 6 < 13$
Subtract 6 from both sides.
$2n < 7$
Divide both sides by 2.
$n < 3.5$

This can be written as the double inequality:
$$-4 \leqslant n < 3.5$$

Integer values of n which satisfy the inequality $-2 \leqslant 2n + 6 < 13$ are:
$-4, -3, -2, -1, 0, 1, 2, 3$.

Exercise **12.4**

1 Find the values of x such that:
(a) $5 < x + 4 \leqslant 9$
(b) $-3 \leqslant x - 2 < 7$
(c) $2 < 9 + x \leqslant 13$
(d) $2 < 2x \leqslant 6$
(e) $-6 \leqslant 3x < 12$
(f) $5 < 2x - 1 < 8$
(g) $-2 \leqslant 3x - 1 \leqslant 11$
(h) $12 < 5x + 2 \leqslant 27$
(i) $-9 \leqslant 4x + 3 < 27$
(j) $-16 < 7x - 2 < 12$
(k) $-1 \leqslant 3x - 10 < 8$
(l) $-4 \leqslant 5 + 2x \leqslant 3$

2 Find the integer values of n for which:
(a) $3 < n - 2 < 7$
(b) $-2 < n + 1 \leqslant 5$
(c) $-2 < 2n \leqslant 4$
(d) $5 \leqslant 2n - 3 < 13$
(e) $0 < 2n - 8 < 3$
(f) $5 < 4n + 1 \leqslant 13$
(g) $-4 \leqslant 5n + 6 < 11$
(h) $-4 < 3n + 2 \leqslant 11$
(i) $-5 \leqslant \frac{1}{2}n - 3 \leqslant 0$
(j) $-12 < 5 - n \leqslant -3$
(k) $-3 \leqslant 4 - 2n \leqslant 12$
(l) $-5 < 3(n + 5) < 0$

Inequalities involving x^2, n^2, etc.

EXAMPLES

1 Find the integer values of n such that $n^2 \geqslant 16$.

Obviously n can be 4, or 5, or 6, or ...
But there are some other answers.
Can you find them?

The square of a negative number is positive.
$(-4)^2 = 16$, $(-5)^2 = 25$, ...
So n can also be -4, -5, -6, ...

$n = 4, 5, 6, ...$ or $-4, -5, -6, ...$

2 Given that n is an integer, solve the inequality $n^2 < 8$.

The value of n can be 0, 1, or 2, but not 3 (because $3^2 > 8$).
It can also be -1 or -2.

$n = -2, -1, 0, 1, 2.$

3 Solve the inequality $x^2 > 36$.

$x < -6$ or $x > 6$

4 Find the values of x for which $x^2 \leqslant 4$.

The value of x must be 2, or less than 2.
It cannot be less than -2.
All the values from -2 to 2 satisfy the inequality.
We can write this as the double inequality:
$-2 \leqslant x \leqslant 2$

Exercise **12.5**

1 Find the values of x for which:
(a) $x^2 \geqslant 9$
(b) $x^2 < 36$
(c) $x^2 > 1$
(d) $x^2 \leqslant 25$
(e) $3x^2 < 12$
(f) $7 + x^2 \leqslant 56$
(g) $3x^2 - 8 > -5$
(h) $5 - 2x^2 \geqslant -3$

2 Find all the values of n, given that n is an integer, when:
(a) $n^2 \leqslant 3$
(b) $n^2 < 25$
(c) $n^2 > 9$
(d) $n^2 \geqslant 37$
(e) $n^2 + 3 < 12$
(f) $5n^2 > 23$
(g) $2n^2 - 6 \leqslant 66$
(h) $12 - 5n^2 \leqslant -31$

Activity

Line A has equation $y = 2$.

Describe the y coordinates of points **on** line A.
Describe the y coordinates of points **below** line A.
Describe the y coordinates of points **above** line A.

Above the line is the region $y > 2$.
Below the line is the region $y < 2$.

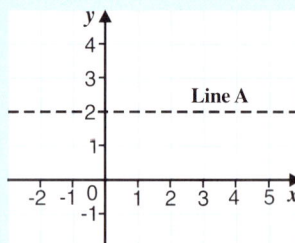

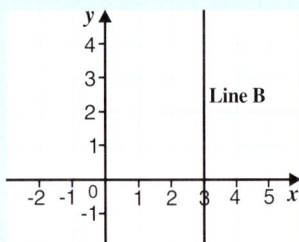

Use an inequality to describe the region to the right of line B.
Use an inequality to describe the region to the left of line B.

Regions

A line divides the graph into two **regions**.
The region $x \leqslant 2$ is to the **left** of the line $x = 2$,
including the line itself.
The region $x \geqslant 2$ is to the **right** of the line $x = 2$,
including the line itself.

The region $y < -3$ is **below** the line $y = -3$.
The region $y > -3$ is **above** the line $y = -3$.

A **solid line** is used when the points on the line are
included.
A **broken line** is used when the points on the line are
not included.

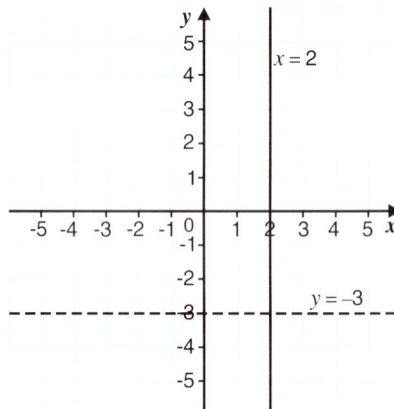

EXAMPLE

On a sketch, show the region where the inequalities
$x > -2$ and $y \leqslant 1$ are both true.
Label the region R.

To do this:
1   Draw the x and y axes.
2   Draw and label the line $x = -2$, using a broken line.
3   Show the region $x > -2$ by shading out the
    unwanted region.

4   Draw and label the line $y = 1$ using a solid line.
5   Show the region $y \leqslant 1$ by shading out the
    unwanted region.

6   Label the region, R, where $x > -2$ **and** $y \leqslant 1$.
    Note that the region R extends for ever to the
    right and downwards.

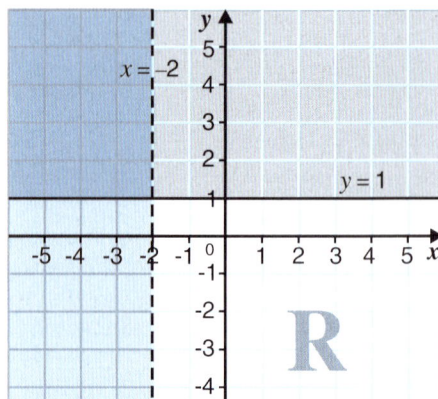

Shading regions on a graph
Unless you are told to do
otherwise, always shade out the
unwanted region.

Exercise 12.6

For each question, draw and label axes for x and y from -5 to 5. Shade the unwanted regions. Leave the given region unshaded and label it R.

1 $x > 2$ and $y \geqslant 1$

2 $x \geqslant -3$ and $y < 4$

3 $x \geqslant -2$, $x < 1$ and $y > 2$

4 $x < 5$, $x \geqslant -1$ and $y \leqslant 3$

5 $x \leqslant 2$, $x > -2$, $y < 3$ and $y \geqslant 1$

6 $x \geqslant -2$, $x \leqslant 0$, $y \geqslant 1$ and $y \leqslant 4$

7 $x \leqslant 1.5$, $y > -1$ and $y \leqslant 2.5$

8 $x > -2.5$, $x \leqslant 1.5$ and $y \leqslant 2.5$

Inequalities involving sloping lines

EXAMPLES

1 Show the region defined by the inequality $y \geqslant 2x - 3$.

First draw the line with equation $y = 2x - 3$.
When $x = 0$, $y = -3$. Plot the point $(0, -3)$.
When $x = 2$, $y = 1$. Plot the point $(2, 1)$.

Next, draw the line through the two points.
Use a solid line because the inequality sign is $\geqslant$.

Now test a point above the line and a point below the line.

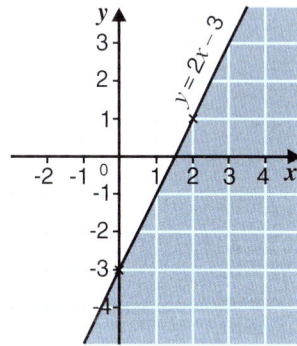

Point	Coordinates	Value of y	Value of $2x - 3$	Is $y \geqslant 2x - 3$?
Above	$(1, 3)$	3	-1	Yes
Below	$(4, -2)$	-2	5	No

The inequality $y \geqslant 2x - 3$ is true **above** the line, so we shade the unwanted region, below the line.

2 Show the region where the inequality $2x + 3y < 12$ is true.

First draw the line with equation $2x + 3y = 12$.
When $x = 0$, $y = 4$. Plot the point $(0, 4)$.
When $y = 0$, $x = 6$. Plot the point $(6, 0)$.

Next, draw the line through the two points.
Use a broken line because the inequality sign is $<$.

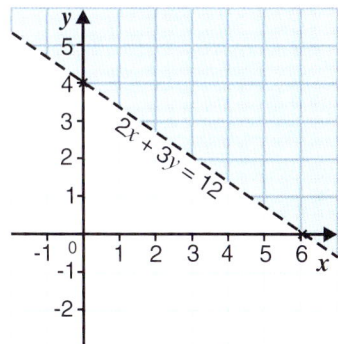

Point	Coordinates	Is $2x + 3y < 12$?
Above	$(3, 4)$	No
Below	$(2, 1)$	Yes

The inequality $2x + 3y < 12$ is true **below** the line, so we shade the unwanted region, above the line.

Exercise **12.7**

1 Draw graphs to show the following.
Leave unshaded the regions where the
inequalities are true.
(a) $y \geq x$
(b) $y < 2x$
(c) $y > x + 1$
(d) $y \leq 2x - 1$
(e) $y < 3x + 1$ and $x < 2$
(f) $y \geq \frac{1}{2}x + 2$, $x > -1$ and $y \leq 5$
(g) $y > -2x + 4$, $y < 5$ and $y \geq -1$
(h) $y \leq 5 - x$, $x \geq -1$ and $y < 3$
(i) $y < x + 5$, $y < 5 - 2x$ and $y > 1$
(j) $y > -3x - 4$,
$y < \frac{1}{2}x + 1$ and $y > -1$

2 Draw graphs to show the following.
Label with the letter R the region
defined by the inequalities.
(a) $2x + 5y \leq 10$
(b) $3x + 4y > 12$
(c) $4x + 3y \geq 6$ and $y > 2$
(d) $x + 3y < 6$, $x > -1$ and $y > 1$
(e) $2x + 3y > 9$, $x \geq 1$ and $x \leq 6$
(f) $4x + 5y < 10$, $x \geq -1$ and $y > 0$
(g) $3x + y < 9$, $y < 6x + 9$ and
$y > -1$
(h) $2x + 5y > 12$, $x + y < 6$ and
$x > 0$
(i) $3x + 2y \leq 8$, $2x + 3y > 6$ and
$x > -1$

3 The shaded area can be described by three
inequalities, one for each side of the shape.
One of the inequalities is $x < 3$.
Write down the other two inequalities.

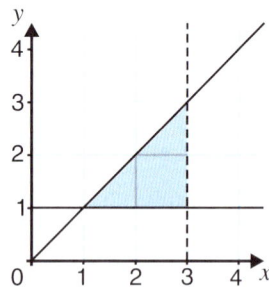

4 Use inequalities to describe the shaded
region in this diagram.

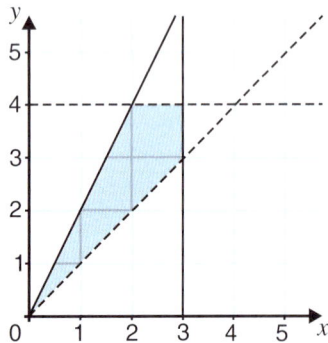

5 Use inequalities to describe the shaded
region in this diagram.

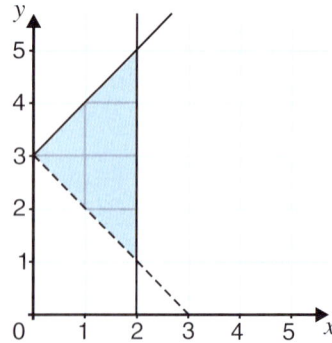

Forming inequalities

So far in this chapter you have been given inequalities and asked to solve them.
The next step is to **form inequalities** (or **write inequalities**) using the information given in a problem.

Problems often involve two, or more, inequalities and are best solved graphically.
This involves:
   drawing graphs of inequalities,
   identifying the region in which **all** the inequalities are satisfied.
You may also be asked to analyse the graph to answer questions related to the initial problem.

162

EXAMPLE

Mrs Jones needs to buy some copies of a textbook. The hardback version of the book costs £25 per copy and the paperback version costs £10 per copy.

Let the number of hardback books be x and the number of paperback books be y.

(a) Explain why $x \geqslant 0$.

(b) Mrs Jones needs to buy at least 7 copies, but she must spend less than £100.
Write down two more inequalities.

(c) Show these three inequalities on a graph.
Label, with the letter R, the region satisfied by all three inequalities.

(d) Given that at least one hardback copy is bought, find the possible combinations of books that could be bought and find the greatest number of books Mrs Jones could buy.

(a) The minimum number of books that can be bought is 0.
So $x \geqslant 0$.

(b) She has to buy at least 7 copies.
"At least" gives the inequality sign $\geqslant$.
$x + y \geqslant 7$

She has to spend less than £100.
"Less than" gives the inequality sign $<$.
One hardback book costs £25, so x will cost £25x.
One paperback book costs £10, so y will cost £10y.
$25x + 10y < 100$
Dividing throughout by 5 gives,
$5x + 2y < 20$

(c) For $x + y \geqslant 7$ the required region is above the line, so shade below the line.
For $5x + 2y < 20$ the required region is below the line, so shade above the line.
For $x \geqslant 0$ the required region is to the right of the line, so shade to the left of the line.
The region which satisfies **all** three inequalities is labelled R.

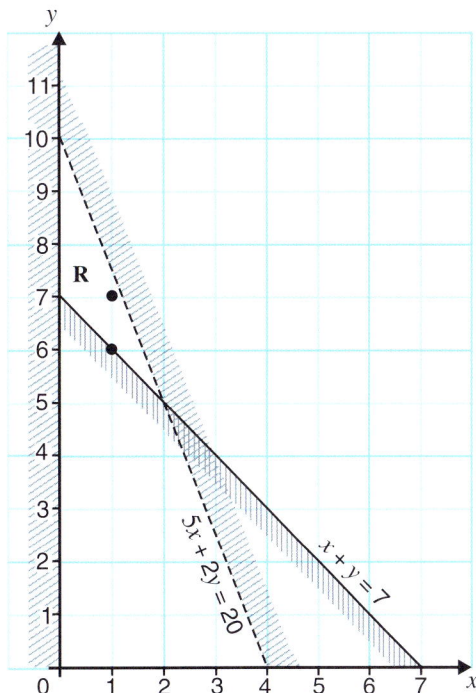

(d) From the graph the possible combinations with x at least 1, are (1,6) and (1,7).
She can buy:
one hardback and six paperbacks, or
one hardback and seven paperbacks.
The greatest number of books she can buy is eight.

Which is the cheapest combination?

1 A tram company has 40 tram units available for service. It can use them as 20 two-car trams or 40 single-car trams, or a combination of two-car and single-car trams.

Let x = number of two-car trams
   y = number of single-car trams
(a)   Explain why $2x + y \leqslant 40$.
(b)   There are at most 32 drivers available to drive each complete tram.
      Write down another inequality.

The numbers x and y must also satisfy $x \geqslant 0$ and $y \geqslant 0$.
(c)   Draw axes from 0 to 40 for both x and y.
      Leave unshaded the region defined by all these inequalities.
      Label this region R.

SEG 1997

2 As part of their Business and Finance course, a group of students have set up an Enterprise company to make and sell greetings cards. The Art department has designed two types of card, Type A and Type B. The cost of the materials and the time needed for the production of a batch of cards of each type are given in the table.

	Materials	Time
Type A	£12	2 hours
Type B	£8	3 hours

The total cost of the materials cannot exceed £100 and the total time taken cannot exceed 20 hours.

(a)   (i)   Write down an inequality for **Materials**.
            Shade on a graph where this inequality is not satisfied.
      (ii) Write down an inequality for **Time** and shade the region where this inequality is not satisfied.
(b)   What does the unshaded part of the graph represent?
(c)   What is the maximum number of Type B batches they can make?
(d)   What is the maximum number of batches they can make?

SEG 1995

3 A builder has 20 plots of land on which to build bungalows or houses.

A bungalow uses 1 plot and a house uses 2 plots.
A bungalow needs 1000 man hours to build, and a house needs 1500 man hours.

The builder estimates that he has 18 000 man hours available.
He builds x bungalows and y houses.

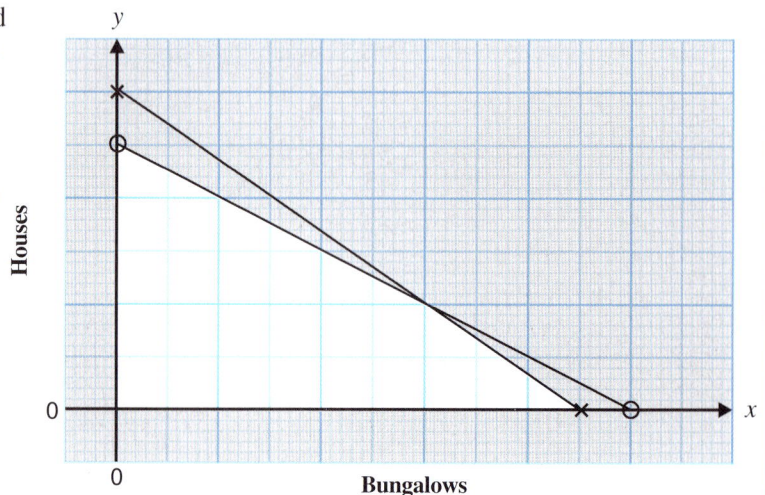

The graph shows the possible solutions.
(a)   Write down the **two** inequalities other than $x \geqslant 0$ and $y \geqslant 0$ which enclose the **unshaded** region.
(b)   If he builds 8 bungalows, how many houses can he build?
(c)   What is the largest number of dwellings he can build?

SEG 1994

4 Marc is making two types of biscuits for a fete.
He has 1.5 kg of sugar and 1 kg of butter.

A batch of cookies needs 150 g of sugar and 175 g of butter.
A batch of brownies needs 200 g of sugar and 75 g of butter.

(a) Marc makes x batches of cookies and y batches of brownies.
Use the amounts of butter to show that $7x + 3y \leqslant 40$.

The graph shows the line $7x + 3y = 40$.

Use the amounts of sugar to show that
$3x + 4y \leqslant 30$.

(b) Copy the diagram and draw the
line $3x + 4y = 30$ on the graph.
Label with the letter R, the region
where the following inequalities
are both true.
$3x + 4y \leqslant 30$, $7x + 3y \leqslant 40$.

(c) Marc makes 3 batches of cookies.
Use the diagram to find the largest number
of batches of brownies he can make.

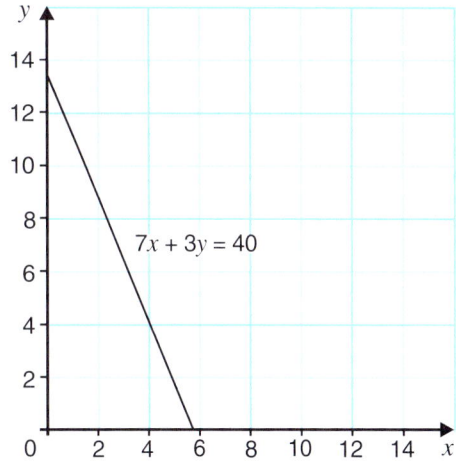

SEG 1998

Graph showing the line $7x + 3y = 40$, with y-axis from 0 to 14 and x-axis from 0 to 14.

What you need to know

- Inequalities can be described using words or numbers and symbols.

Sign	Meaning
$<$	is less than
$\leqslant$	is less than or equal to
$>$	is greater than
$\geqslant$	is greater than or equal to

- Inequalities can be shown on a **number line**.
The circle is:
  filled if the inequality is **included**
  (i.e. $\leqslant$ or $\geqslant$),
  not filled if the inequality is **not included**
  (i.e. $<$ or $>$).

$-2 < x \leqslant 3$

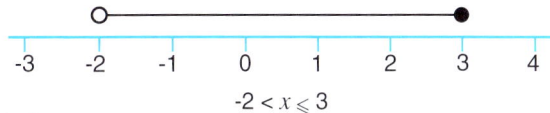

- Solving inequalities.
Solve means find the values of x which make the inequality true.
The same rules for equations can be applied to inequalities, with one exception:
  When you **multiply** (or **divide**) both sides of an inequality by a negative number the
  inequality is reversed. For example, if $-3x < 6$ then $x > -2$.

- Inequalities can be shown on a graph. Replace the inequality sign by '=' and draw the line.
For $>$ and $<$ the line is **broken**. For $\geqslant$ and $\leqslant$ the line is **solid**.
Test a point on each side of the line to see whether its coordinates satisfy the inequality.
Shade the **unwanted** region.

You should be able to:
- **Form inequalities** (or **write inequalities**) using the information given in a problem.
- Solve problems involving inequalities using graphical methods.

You should be able to do all these questions without a calculator.

1 Solve these inequalities.
(a) $3x \geqslant -15$ (b) $3x < x + 6$
(c) $5x - 4 \leqslant 2x + 14$ (d) $5 - 3x < 11$

2 Find the integer values of n such that:
(a) $-4 < 2n \leqslant 8$ (b) $-3 \leqslant 3n + 6 < 12$ (c) $-4 \leqslant 5n + 6 \leqslant 1$

3 Find the values of a which satisfy the following inequalities.
(a) $a^2 > 9$ (b) $a^2 \leqslant 100$ (c) $3a^2 - 5 \leqslant 43$

4 Given that p is an integer, solve the following inequalities.
(a) $p^2 \leqslant 16$ (b) $p^2 > 30$ (c) $2p^2 < 20$

5 (a) List the integers, x, such that $-3 \leqslant x < 2$.
(b) Solve the following inequalities.
(i) $17 < 2x + 3$
(ii) $15 + 2x \leqslant 12 - 2.5x$

SEG 1996

6 Solve the inequality $-1 \leqslant 3x + 2 < 5$.

SEG 2000 S

7 List the values of n, where n is an integer, such that $3 \leqslant n + 4 < 6$.

SEG 1998

8 Solve the inequality $5(a - 3) > 3a - 5$.

SEG 1996

9 (a) List all the possible values of x, where x is an integer, such that $-4 \leqslant x < 2$.
(b) Solve (i) $4x - 5 < -3$,
(ii) $y^2 \geqslant 25$.

SEG 1997

10 Find all pairs of **integer** values of x and y which satisfy all the inequalities.
$2 < x < 6$, $0 < y < 3$, $2 < x + y < 7$.

SEG 1997

11 (a) Solve the inequality $7x + 3 > 13x + 5$.
(b) Copy the diagram below.
Label with the letter R, the single region which satisfies all of these inequalities.
$$y < \tfrac{1}{2}x + 1, \quad x > 6, \quad y > 3.$$

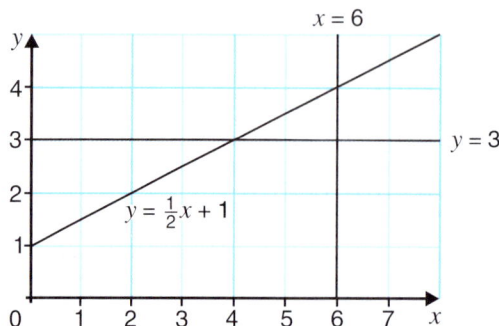

SEG 1994

12 Show, on a graph, the region where the following inequalities are true.

(a) $x \leqslant 2$, $y > -3$ and $y < 1$

(b) $2x + 3y < 6$, $x > -1$ and $y \geqslant 0$

(c) $3x + 4y \leqslant 12$, $3x + y > 3$ and $y > -1$

13 (a) Draw x and y axes from -5 to 5. Show the region which satisfies **all** the inequalities.
$$2y \leqslant x + 2, \qquad y \geqslant 1 - x, \qquad y \geqslant x - 1.$$
Label this region R.

(b) Write down the coordinates of any point (x, y) which has whole number values for x and y and which lies inside the region R.

SEG 1998

14 A bus company has been asked to transport some students on a trip.
The company has available 4 large buses, 5 small buses and a maximum of 7 drivers.
Let: x represent the number of large buses used;
y represent the number of small buses used.
Two inequalities which fit these conditions are:
$$0 \leqslant x \leqslant 4 \text{ and } x + y \leqslant 7.$$
These are shown on the graph with the regions **not** required shaded.

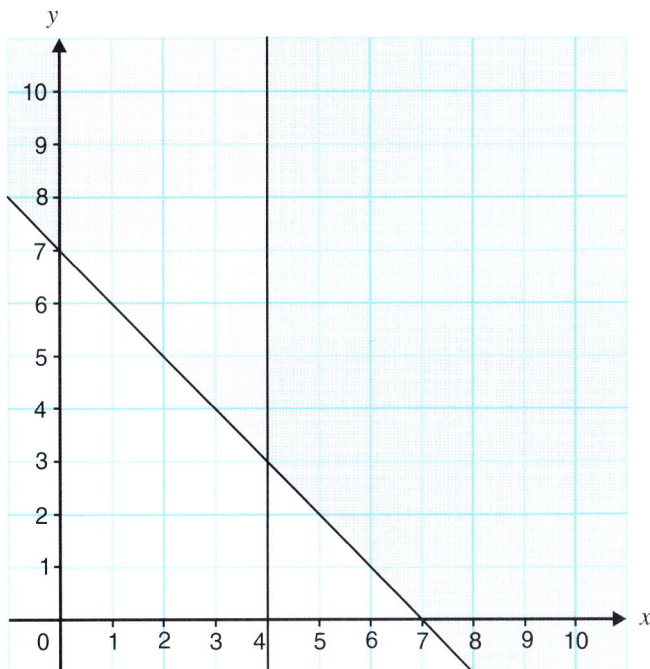

Copy the diagram.

(a) (i) Write down another inequality which fits these conditions and add this to your graph.

(ii) The large buses can transport 25 students.
The small buses can transport 15 students.
The company has been asked to transport a total of 90 students.
Write down an inequality that fits this condition and add this to your graph.

(b) What are the values of x and y which fit all of the bus company's conditions and leave no spare seats?

SEG 1998

CHAPTER 13

Quadratics

Brackets

You can multiply out brackets, either by using a diagram or by expanding.

Removing brackets was first covered in Chapter 8.

We can use a diagram to multiply out the bracket $x(x + 3)$.

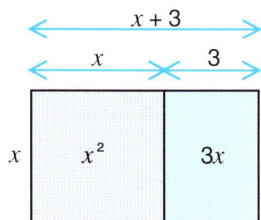

The areas of the two parts are x^2 and $3x$.
$x(x + 3) = x^2 + 3x$

This method can be extended to multiply out $(x + 2)(x + 5)$.

The areas of the four parts are:
x^2, $5x$, $2x$ and 10.

$(x + 2)(x + 5) = x^2 + 5x + 2x + 10$
Collect like terms and simplify (i.e. $5x + 2x = 7x$)
$\qquad\qquad = x^2 + 7x + 10$

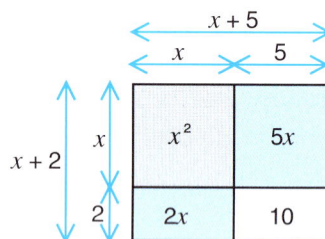

As you become more confident you should not need a diagram to expand brackets.

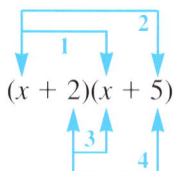

$(x + 2)(x + 5)$

1   $x \times x = x^2$
2   $x \times 5 = 5x$
3   $2 \times x = 2x$
4   $2 \times 5 = 10$

$(x + 2)(x + 5) = x^2 + 5x + 2x + 10$
$\qquad\qquad\quad = x^2 + 7x + 10$

EXAMPLES

1 Expand $(x + 3)(x - 5)$.

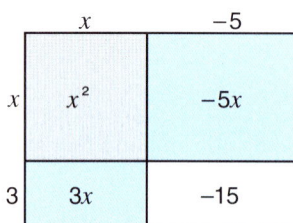

The diagram method works with negative numbers.
$(x + 3)(x - 5) = x^2 - 5x + 3x - 15$
$\qquad\qquad\quad = x^2 - 2x - 15$

2 Expand $(x - 1)(2x + 3)$.

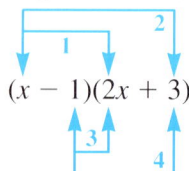

$(x - 1)(2x + 3)$

1   $x \times 2x = 2x^2$
2   $x \times 3 = 3x$
3   $-1 \times 2x = -2x$
4   $-1 \times 3 = -3$

$(x - 1)(2x + 3) = 2x^2 + 3x - 2x - 3$
$\qquad\qquad\qquad = 2x^2 + x - 3$

3 Expand $(2x - 5)^2$.

$(2x - 5)^2 = (2x - 5)(2x - 5)$
$\qquad\qquad = 4x^2 - 10x - 10x + 25$
$\qquad\qquad = 4x^2 - 20x + 25$

Questions 1 to 6.
Use diagrams to multiply out the brackets.

1 $(x + 3)(x + 4)$

2 $(x + 1)(x + 5)$

3 $(x - 5)(x + 2)$

4 $(2x + 1)(x - 2)$

5 $(3x - 2)(x - 6)$

6 $(2x + 1)(3x + 2)$

Questions 7 to 24.
Expand the following brackets. Only draw a diagram if necessary.

7 $(x + 8)(x - 2)$

8 $(x + 5)(x - 2)$

9 $(x - 1)(x + 3)$

10 $(x - 3)(x - 2)$

11 $(x - 4)(x - 1)$

12 $(x - 7)(x + 2)$

13 $(2x + 3)(x - 1)$

14 $(3x - 1)(x + 5)$

15 $(4x - 2)(3x + 5)$

16 $(x + 3)(x - 3)$

17 $(x + 5)(x - 5)$

18 $(x + 7)(x - 7)$

19 $(x - 10)(x + 10)$

20 $(x + 3)^2$

21 $(x + 5)^2$

22 $(x - 3)^2$

23 $(x - 7)^2$

24 $(2x - 3)^2$

Factorising quadratic expressions

$x^2 + 8x + 15$, $x^2 - 4$ and $x^2 + 7x$ are examples of
quadratic expressions.
You will need to be able to factorise such expressions
in order to solve quadratic equations in the next section
of this chapter.

> The general form of a
> quadratic expression is
> $ax^2 + bx + c$, where a
> cannot be equal to 0.

Common factors

A **common factor** is a factor which will divide into each term of an expression.
For example, $x^2 + 7x$ has a common factor of x.
$$x^2 + 7x = x(x + 7)$$

EXAMPLES

Factorise the following expressions.

1 $y^2 - 10y$

Common factor y.
$y^2 - 10y = y(y - 10)$

2 $5y + y^2$

Common factor y.
$5y + y^2 = y(5 + y)$

Difference of two squares

In the expression $x^2 - 4$,
$x^2 = x \times x$ and $4 = 2^2 = 2 \times 2$.

$x^2 - 4 = (x + 2)(x - 2)$
This result is called the **difference of two squares**.
In general: $a^2 - b^2 = (a + b)(a - b)$

> **Checking your work**
> To check your work, expand the brackets
> and simplify, where necessary.
> The result should be the same as the
> original expression.

Factorise the following.

1 $x^2 - 100$
$= x^2 - 10^2$
$= (x + 10)(x - 10)$

2 $25 - x^2$
$= 5^2 - x^2$
$= (5 + x)(5 - x)$

3 $s^2 - t^2$
$= (s + t)(s - t)$

Quadratics of the form $x^2 + bx + c$

The expression $x^2 + 8x + 15$ can be factorised.

From experience, we know that the answer is likely to be of the form:
$$x^2 + 8x + 15 = (x + ?)(x + ?),$$
where the question marks represent numbers.
Replacing the question marks with letters, p and q, we get:
$$x^2 + 8x + 15 = (x + p)(x + q)$$

Multiply the brackets out, using either the diagram method or by expanding, and compare the results with the original expression.

$px + qx = x(p + q) = 8x$
and $p \times q = 15$

1 $x \times x = x^2$
2 $x \times q = qx$
3 $p \times x = px$
4 $p \times q = pq$

$$(x + p)(x + q) = x^2 + qx + px + pq$$
$$= x^2 + (q + p)x + pq$$
$$= x^2 + 8x + 15$$

Two numbers are required which:
when multiplied give $+15$, **and**
when added give $+8$.
$+5$ and $+3$ satisfy **both** conditions.
$$x^2 + 8x + 15 = (x + 5)(x + 3)$$

1 Factorise $x^2 + 6x + 9$.

$x^2 + 6x + 9 = (x + 3)(x + 3)$
$= (x + 3)^2$
Because $3 \times 3 = 9$
and $3 + 3 = 6$.

2 Factorise $x^2 - 8x + 12$.

$x^2 - 8x + 12 = (x - 6)(x - 2)$

Because $-6 \times -2 = 12$
and $-6 + -2 = -8$.

3 Factorise $x^2 + 2x - 15$.

$x^2 + 2x - 15 = (x + 5)(x - 3)$

Because $+5 \times -3 = -15$
and $+5 + -3 = +2$.

4 Factorise $x^2 - 2x - 8$.

$x^2 - 2x - 8 = (x + 2)(x - 4)$

Because $+2 \times -4 = -8$
and $+2 + -4 = -2$.

Exercise **13.2**

1 Factorise these expressions.
  (a) $x^2 + 5x$
  (b) $x^2 - 7x$
  (c) $y^2 - 6y$
  (d) $5t - t^2$
  (e) $8y + y^2$
  (f) $x^2 - 20x$

2 Factorise.
  (a) $x^2 - 9$
  (b) $x^2 - 81$
  (c) $y^2 - 25$
  (d) $y^2 - 1$
  (e) $x^2 - 64$
  (f) $100 - x^2$
  (g) $36 - x^2$
  (h) $x^2 - a^2$

3 Copy and complete the following.
  (a) $x^2 + 6x + 5 = (x + 5)(x + \ldots)$
  (b) $x^2 + 9x + 14 = (x + 7)(x + \ldots)$
  (c) $x^2 + 6x + 8 = (x + \ldots)(x + 4)$
  (d) $x^2 + 9x + 18 = (x + \ldots)(x + 6)$
  (e) $x^2 - 6x + 5 = (x - 5)(x - \ldots)$
  (f) $x^2 - 7x + 10 = (x - 5)(x - \ldots)$
  (g) $x^2 - 7x + 12 = (x - \ldots)(x - 3)$
  (h) $x^2 + 3x - 4 = (x + 4)(x - \ldots)$
  (i) $x^2 + 5x - 14 = (x + 7)(x - \ldots)$
  (j) $x^2 - 4x - 5 = (x - 5)(x + \ldots)$

4 Factorise.
  (a) $x^2 + 3x + 2$
  (b) $x^2 + 8x + 7$
  (c) $x^2 + 8x + 15$
  (d) $x^2 + 8x + 12$
  (e) $x^2 + 12x + 11$
  (f) $x^2 + 9x + 20$
  (g) $x^2 + 10x + 24$
  (h) $x^2 + 13x + 36$

5 Factorise.
  (a) $x^2 - 6x + 9$
  (b) $x^2 - 6x + 8$
  (c) $x^2 - 11x + 10$
  (d) $x^2 - 16x + 15$
  (e) $x^2 - 8x + 15$
  (f) $x^2 - 10x + 16$
  (g) $x^2 - 12x + 20$
  (h) $x^2 - 11x + 24$

6 Factorise.
  (a) $x^2 - x - 6$
  (b) $x^2 - 5x - 6$
  (c) $x^2 + 2x - 24$
  (d) $x^2 + 5x - 24$
  (e) $x^2 - 2x - 15$
  (f) $x^2 + 3x - 18$
  (g) $x^2 - 3x - 40$
  (h) $x^2 - 4x - 12$

7 Factorise.
  (a) $x^2 - 4x + 4$
  (b) $x^2 + 11x + 30$
  (c) $x^2 + 2x - 8$
  (d) $x^2 - 4x - 21$
  (e) $x^2 + x - 20$
  (f) $x^2 + 7x + 12$
  (g) $x^2 + 8x + 16$
  (h) $x^2 - 2x + 1$
  (i) $x^2 - 49$
  (j) $t^2 + 12t$
  (k) $x^2 - 9x + 14$
  (l) $x^2 - 7x + 6$
  (m) $x^2 + 11x + 18$
  (n) $x^2 + 11x + 24$
  (o) $x^2 + 19x + 18$
  (p) $x^2 - y^2$
  (q) $x^2 + x - 6$
  (r) $y^2 + 4y$
  (s) $y^2 - 10y + 25$
  (t) $x^2 - 12x + 36$

Further factorising

When factorising, work logically.
  Does the expression have a common factor?
  Is the expression a difference of two squares?
  Will the expression factorise into two brackets?

EXAMPLE

1 Factorise $2x^2 - 14x$.

Common factor $2x$.
$2x^2 - 14x = 2x(x - 7)$

2 Factorise $25 - 4y^2$.

Difference of two squares.
$25 - 4y^2 = 5^2 - (2y)^2$
$= (5 + 2y)(5 - 2y)$

3 Factorise $8x^2 - 18y^2$.

Common factor 2.
$8x^2 - 18y^2 = 2(4x^2 \quad 9y^2)$
Difference of two squares.
$\qquad = 2(2x + 3y)(2x - 3y)$

4 Factorise $2x^2 + 11x + 15$.

First look at the term in x^2.
The coefficient of x^2 is 2, so the brackets start:
$(2x \ldots \ldots)(x \ldots \ldots)$
Next, look for two numbers which when multiplied give $+15$.
The possibilities are: 1 and 15 or 3 and 5.
Use these pairs of numbers to complete the brackets.
Multiply out pairs of brackets until the correct factorisation
of $2x^2 + 11x + 15$ is found.
$(2x + 1)(x + 15) = 2x^2 + 30x + x + 15 = 2x^2 + 31x + 15$
$(2x + 15)(x + 1) = 2x^2 + 2x + 15x + 15 = 2x^2 + 17x + 15$
$(2x + 3)(x + 5) = 2x^2 + 10x + 3x + 15 = 2x^2 + 13x + 15$
$(2x + 5)(x + 3) = 2x^2 + 6x + 5x + 15 = 2x^2 + 11x + 15$

$2x^2 + 11x + 15 = (2x + 5)(x + 3)$

Rather than expanding brackets fully it is only necessary to look at two terms.

$(2x + 5)(x + 3)$

Explain why.

5 Factorise $4x^2 + 19x - 5$.

$4x^2 + 19x - 5 = (4x - 1)(x + 5)$
The brackets contain different signs.
Explain why.

6 Factorise $4x^2 - 16x + 15$.

$4x^2 - 16x + 15 = (2x - 5)(2x - 3)$
The brackets contain two minus signs.
Explain why.

Exercise 13.3

1 Factorise.
(a) $7x^2 + 5x$
(b) $5x^2 - 4x$
(c) $x^2 + x$
(d) $y^2 - 2y$
(e) $10y - 5y^2$
(f) $9y - 6y^2$
(g) $6x^2 + 8x$
(h) $t + 5t^2$
(i) $-4x + 5x^2$
(j) $12x^2 - 8$

2 Factorise.
(a) $4x^2 - 1$
(b) $9y^2 - 49$
(c) $25 - 4x^2$
(d) $9x^2 - 16$
(e) $9t^2 - 4s^2$
(f) $100x^2 - 81$
(g) $121 - 16y^2$
(h) $s^2 - 4t^2$
(i) $50 - 2x^2$
(j) $12x^2 - 27y^2$

3

Find the value of $101^2 - 99^2$ without using a calculator.
Using the difference of two squares.
$101^2 - 99^2 = (101 + 99)(101 - 99) = 200 \times 2 = 400$

Without using a calculator, find the value of the following.
(a) $6.36^2 - 3.64^2$
(b) $7.5^2 - 2.5^2$
(c) $8.987^2 - 1.013^2$

4 Factorise.
(a) $2x^2 + 11x + 12$
(b) $2x^2 + 25x + 12$
(c) $4x^2 + 4x + 1$
(d) $6x^2 + 17x + 12$
(e) $11x^2 + 12x + 1$
(f) $3x^2 + 17x + 10$

5 Factorise.

(a) $2y^2 - 9y + 7$ (b) $4x^2 - 4x + 1$ (c) $3x^2 - 5x + 2$

(d) $2x^2 - 3x + 1$ (e) $2x^2 - 11x + 15$ (f) $9y^2 - 12y + 4$

6 Factorise.

(a) $2x^2 + x - 6$ (b) $3x^2 - 14x - 5$ (c) $3x^2 + 14x - 5$

(d) $2y^2 - 5y - 7$ (e) $9x^2 + 3x - 2$ (f) $10x^2 + 27x - 9$

7 Factorise.

(a) $3x^2 + 31x + 10$ (b) $64x^2 - 49$ (c) $3x^2 + 11x + 10$

(d) $6x^2 - 25x - 25$ (e) $5x^2 - 18x + 9$ (f) $8x^2 + 2x - 15$

8 Factorise.

(a) $13x - 20 - 2x^2$ (b) $1 + 9x^2 - 6x$ (c) $-10 - 7x^2 + 19x$

(d) $4x^2 + 22x + 24$ (e) $6x^2 + 3x - 18$ (f) $28x - 10 + 6x^2$

Solving quadratic equations

Activity

I am thinking of two numbers.
I multiply them together.
The answer is zero.

Write down 2 numbers which could be Jim's numbers.
Now write down **four** more pairs.
What can you say about Jim's numbers?

You should have discovered that at least one of Jim's numbers must be **zero**.
We can use this fact to solve **quadratic equations**.

EXAMPLES

1 Find x if

(a) $x(x - 2) = 0$
Either $x = 0$ or $x - 2 = 0$
Because one of them must be zero.
$x = 0$ or $x = 2$

(b) $(x - 3)(x + 2) = 0$
Either $x - 3 = 0$ or $x + 2 = 0$
Because one of them must be zero.
$x = 3$ or $x = -2$

2 Solve $x^2 - 18 = 3x$.

Rearrange the equation.
$x^2 - 3x - 18 = 0$
$(x - 6)(x + 3) = 0$
Either $x - 6 = 0$ or $x + 3 = 0$
$x = 6$ or $x = -3$

Check:
Does $6^2 - 18 = 3 \times 6$, **and**
$(-3)^2 - 18 = 3 \times (-3)$?

3 Solve $4x^2 + 3x = 0$.

$x(4x + 3) = 0$
Either $x = 0$ or $4x + 3 = 0$
$4x = -3$
$x = 0$ or $x = -\frac{3}{4}$

4 Solve $x^2 - 25 = 0$.

$x^2 - 25 = 0$
$x^2 = 25$
Take the square root
of both sides.
$x = \pm 5$

Alternative method
$x^2 - 25 = 0$
$(x + 5)(x - 5) = 0$
Either $x + 5 = 0$ or $x - 5 = 0$
$x = -5$ or $x = 5$

1 Solve these equations.
(a) $(x - 2)(x - 3) = 0$
(b) $(x + 4)(x + 6) = 0$
(c) $(x - 3)(x + 1) = 0$
(d) $x(x - 5) = 0$
(e) $x(x - 4) = 0$
(f) $3x(x + 2) = 0$

2 Solve.
(a) $x^2 - 3x + 2 = 0$
(b) $y^2 + 7y + 12 = 0$
(c) $m^2 - 2m - 8 = 0$
(d) $a^2 + a - 12 = 0$
(e) $n^2 - 5n - 36 = 0$
(f) $z^2 - 9z + 18 = 0$
(g) $k^2 + 8k + 15 = 0$
(h) $c^2 + 15c + 56 = 0$
(i) $b^2 + b - 20 = 0$
(j) $v^2 - 7v - 60 = 0$
(k) $w^2 + 8w - 48 = 0$
(l) $p^2 - p - 72 = 0$

3 Solve.
(a) $x^2 - 5x = 0$
(b) $y^2 + y = 0$
(c) $p^2 + 3p = 0$
(d) $4a - a^2 = 0$
(e) $t^2 - 6t = 0$
(f) $g^2 - 4g = 0$
(g) $x^2 + 7x = 0$
(h) $4x^2 = 3x$
(i) $20x = 100x^2$

4 Solve.
(a) $x^2 - 4 = 0$
(b) $y^2 - 144 = 0$
(c) $9 - a^2 = 0$
(d) $d^2 - 16 = 0$
(e) $x^2 - 100 = 0$
(f) $36 - x^2 = 0$
(g) $x^2 - 49 = 0$
(h) $2.25 - x^2 = 0$
(i) $2x^2 - 18 = 0$
(j) $3x^2 = 48$

5 Solve these equations.
(a) $2x^2 + 7x + 5 = 0$
(b) $2x^2 + 11x - 5 = 0$
(c) $3x^2 - 17x - 28 = 0$
(d) $6y^2 + 7y + 2 = 0$
(e) $3x^2 + 7x - 6 = 0$
(f) $3z^2 - 5z - 2 = 0$

6 Rearrange these equations and then solve them.
(a) $y^2 = 4y + 5$
(b) $x = 6x^2 - 1$
(c) $56 = 15x - x^2$
(d) $y^2 = y$
(e) $x^2 = 8x - 16$
(f) $19z = 6z^2 + 3$
(g) $6x^2 = 63 - 3x$
(h) $6x^2 = 2 - x$
(i) $10 + 3y = 4y^2$

Solving quadratic equations graphically

The graph of a **quadratic function** is always a smooth curve and is called a **parabola**. The general equation of a quadratic function is $y = ax^2 + bx + c$, where a cannot be equal to zero.

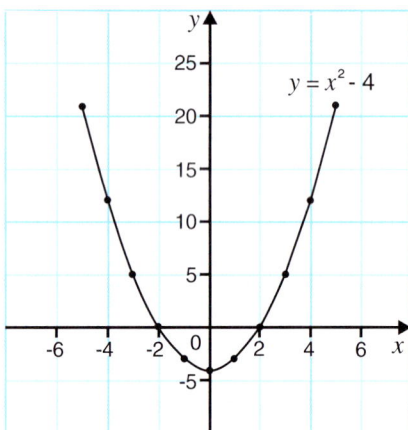

The graph of $y = x^2 - 4$ has a **minimum value** at the point $(0, -4)$.

The graph of $y = 6x - x^2$ has a **maximum value** at the point $(3, 9)$.

The values of x where the graphs of quadratic functions cross (or touch) the x axis give the **solutions to quadratic equations**.

At the point where the graph $y = x^2 - 4$ crosses the x axis the value of $y = 0$.
$x^2 - 4 = 0$
The solutions of this quadratic equation can be read from the graph. $x = -2$ and $x = 2$.

Remember:
• Your graphs should never be flat or pointed.
• Quadratic graphs are always symmetrical.
• Join plotted points using smooth curves and not a series of straight lines.

Find the solutions of the equation $6x - x^2 = 0$ from the graph of $y = 6x - x^2$.
Check the graphical solutions using the factorising method.

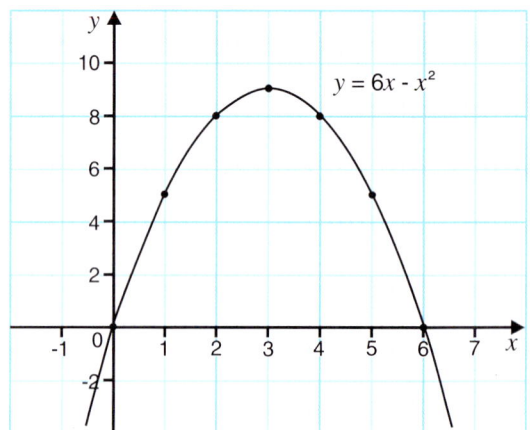

EXAMPLE

Draw the graph of
$y = x^2 + 3x - 2$ for values of x from -5 to 2.
Use the graph to find the solution of the equation
$x^2 + 3x - 2 = 0$.

First make a table of values for $y = x^2 + 3x - 2$.

x	-5	-4	-3	-2	-1	0	1	2
y	8	2	-2	-4	-4	-2	2	8

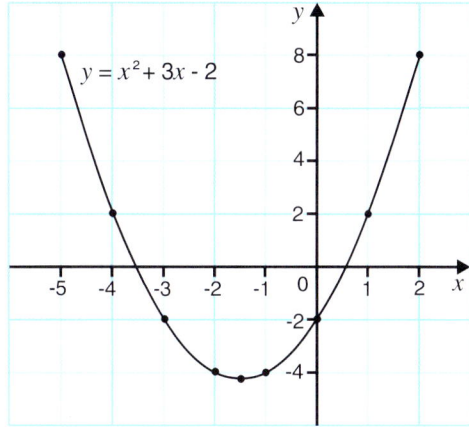

The graph has a **minimum value** between
$x = -2$ and $x = -1$.
To find this value substitute $x = -1.5$ into the
equation.
$y = (-1.5 \times -1.5) + (3 \times -1.5) - 2$
$\quad = 2.25 - 4.5 - 2 = -4.25$
Plot the point $(-2.5, -4.25)$.

$x^2 + 3x - 2 = 0$
To solve this equation, read the values of x
where the graph of $y = x^2 + 3x - 2$ crosses
the x axis.
$x = -3.6$ and $x = 0.6$, correct to 1 d.p.

Exercise 13.5

1   (a)   Copy and complete this table of values for $y = 2x^2$.

x	-2	-1	0	1	2
y					

     (b)   Draw axes marked from -2 to 2 for x and from -2 to 8 for y.
           Draw the graph of $y = 2x^2$ on your axes.
     (c)   Use your graph to solve the equation $2x^2 = 1.5$.

2   (a)   Copy and complete this table of values for $y = x^2 + x$.

x	-3	-2	-1	0	1	2
y						

     (b)   Draw axes marked from -3 to 2 for x and from -2 to 6 for y.
           Draw the graph of $y = x^2 + x$ on your axes.
     (c)   Use your graph to solve the equation $x^2 + x = 1$.
     (d)   Find the coordinates of the point at which the graph has a minimum value.

3   (a)   Copy and complete this table of values for $y = x^2 - x - 1$.

x	-2	-1	0	1	2	3
y						

     (b)   Draw axes marked from -2 to 3 for x and from -2 to 6 for y.
           Draw the graph of $y = x^2 - x - 1$ on your axes.
     (c)   Use your graph to solve the equation $x^2 - x - 1 = 0$.

4   (a)   Draw the graph of $y = x^2 + 2x - 2$ for values of x from -5 to 3.
     (b)   Use your graph to solve the equation $x^2 + 2x - 3 = 0$.

5 (a) Copy and complete this table of values for $y = 10 - x^2$.

x	-4	-3	-2	-1	0	1	2	3	4
y									

(b) Draw axes marked from -4 to 4 for x and from -6 to 10 for y.
   Draw the graph of $y = 10 - x^2$ on your axes.
(c) Use your graph to solve the equation $10 - x^2 = 5$.
(d) Find the coordinates of the point at which the graph has a maximum value.

6 (a) Draw the graph of $y = 15 - 2x^2$ for values of x from -3 to 3.
(b) Use your graph to solve the equation $15 - 2x^2 = -1$.

7 Draw suitable graphs to solve the following equations.
(a) $x^2 - 8 = 0$ (b) $5 - x^2 = 0$
(c) $3x^2 = 7$ (d) $12 - 2x^2 = 0$

Using the quadratic formula

Some quadratic expressions do not factorise.
Consider the equation $x^2 - 5x + 2 = 0$.
It is not possible to find two numbers which:
   when multiplied give $+2$, **and**
   when added give -5.

We could draw the graph of $y = x^2 - 5x + 2$ and
use it to solve the equation $x^2 - 5x + 2 = 0$.
One solution lies between 0 and 1.
Another solution lies between 4 and 5.
*Graphical solutions have limited accuracy and
are time consuming. Explain why.*

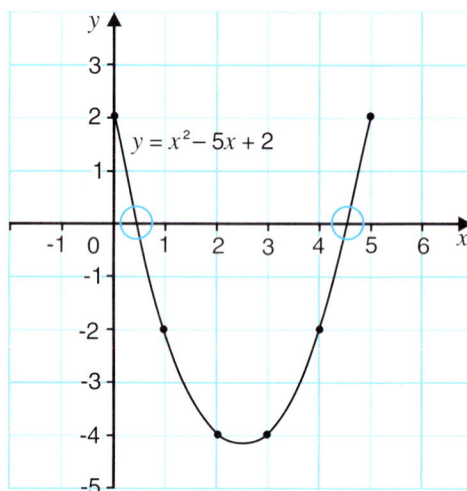

$y = x^2 - 5x + 2$

The solutions to a quadratic equation can be found using the **quadratic formula**.

If $ax^2 + bx + c = 0$ and $a \neq 0$

then $x = \dfrac{-b \pm \sqrt{b^2 - 4ac}}{2a}$

The quadratic formula can be used at any time, even if the quadratic expression factorises.

Solve $x^2 - 5x + 2 = 0$, giving the answers correct to three significant figures.

Using $x = \dfrac{-b \pm \sqrt{b^2 - 4ac}}{2a}$

Substitute: $a = 1$, $b = -5$ and $c = 2$.

$x = \dfrac{-(-5) \pm \sqrt{(-5)^2 - 4(1)(2)}}{2(1)}$

$x = \dfrac{5 \pm \sqrt{25 - 8}}{2}$

$x = \dfrac{5 \pm \sqrt{17}}{2}$

Either $x = \dfrac{5 + \sqrt{17}}{2}$ or $x = \dfrac{5 - \sqrt{17}}{2}$

$x = 4.5615\ldots$ or $x = 0.43844\ldots$
$x = 0.438$ or 4.56, correct to 3 sig. figs.

*Check the answers by substituting the
values of x into the original equation.*

EXAMPLES

1 Solve $2x^2 + 3x - 7 = 0$, giving the answers correct to three significant figures.

Using $x = \dfrac{-b \pm \sqrt{b^2 - 4ac}}{2a}$

Substitute: $a = 2$, $b = 3$ and $c = -7$.

$x = \dfrac{-3 \pm \sqrt{3^2 - 4(2)(-7)}}{2(2)}$

$x = \dfrac{-3 \pm \sqrt{9 + 56}}{4}$

$x = \dfrac{-3 \pm \sqrt{65}}{4}$

Either $x = \dfrac{-3 + \sqrt{65}}{4}$ or $x = \dfrac{-3 - \sqrt{65}}{4}$

$x = 1.2655 \ldots$ or $x = -2.7655 \ldots$

$x = -2.77$ or 1.27, correct to 3 sig. figs.

2 Solve $6x = 3 - 5x^2$, giving the answers correct to three significant figures.

Rearrange $6x = 3 - 5x^2$ to get $5x^2 + 6x - 3 = 0$.

Using $x = \dfrac{-b \pm \sqrt{b^2 - 4ac}}{2a}$

Substitute: $a = 5$, $b = 6$ and $c = -3$.

$x = \dfrac{-6 \pm \sqrt{6^2 - 4(5)(-3)}}{2(5)}$

$x = \dfrac{-6 \pm \sqrt{36 + 60}}{10}$

$x = \dfrac{-6 \pm \sqrt{96}}{10}$

Either $x = \dfrac{-6 + \sqrt{96}}{10}$ or $x = \dfrac{-6 - \sqrt{96}}{10}$

$x = 0.3797 \ldots$ or $x = -1.5797 \ldots$

$x = -1.58$ or 0.380, correct to 3 sig. figs.

Exercise 13.6

1 Solve the equations, giving answers correct to 3 significant figures where necessary.

(a) $x^2 + 4x + 2 = 0$

(b) $x^2 + x - 1 = 0$

(c) $3x^2 - 5x + 1 = 0$

(d) $2x^2 - 7x + 4 = 0$

(e) $3x^2 + 23x + 8 = 0$

(f) $3x^2 - 4x - 5 = 0$

(g) $2z^2 + 6z + 3 = 0$

(h) $3x^2 - 2x - 20 = 0$

(i) $\frac{1}{2}x^2 + 4x + 5 = 0$

2 Rearrange the following to form quadratic equations.
Then solve the quadratic equations, giving answers correct to 3 significant figures where necessary.

(a) $3x = 2x^2 - 4$

(b) $2 = x + 5x^2$

(c) $x(2x + 5) = 10$

(d) $3x(x - 4) = 2(x - 1)$

(e) $(3x - 2)^2 = (x + 2)^2 + 12$

(f) $\dfrac{5}{x} = 3x + 9$

3 (a) Draw axes marked from -3 to 2 for x and from -2 to 10 for y.
Using the same axes draw the following graphs:

$y = 2x^2 + 4x + 1$ $y = 2x^2 + 4x + 2$ $y = 2x^2 + 4x + 3$

Use your graphs to solve the equations:

$2x^2 + 4x + 1 = 0$ $2x^2 + 4x + 2 = 0$ $2x^2 + 4x + 3 = 0$

(b) Use the quadratic formula to solve the following equations:

$2x^2 + 4x + 1 = 0$ $2x^2 + 4x + 2 = 0$ $2x^2 + 4x + 3 = 0$

(c) Compare your answers to parts (a) and (b).

4 Find conditions involving a, b and c for $ax^2 + bx + c = 0$ to have:

(a) two solutions,

(b) one solution,

(c) no solutions,

(d) rational solutions (given that a, b and c are integers).

Some mathematical problems involve the forming of equations which are quadratic. The equation is solved and the solutions are analysed to answer the original problem.

The formation of **linear equations** to solve problems was covered in Chapter 8.

EXAMPLES

1 A rectangular lawn, 10 m by 8 m, is surrounded by a path which is x m wide.
The total area of the path and lawn is 143 m².
Calculate the width of the path.

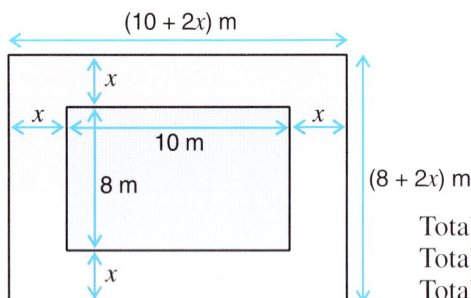

$(10 + 2x)$ m

x

x 10 m x

8 m

$(8 + 2x)$ m

x

Drawing a **sketch diagram**, to which labels can be added, may help you to understand and solve problems.

Total length $= (10 + 2x)$ m
Total width $= (8 + 2x)$ m
Total area $= 143$ m²

length $\times$ width $=$ total area
$(10 + 2x)(8 + 2x) = 143$
Expand the brackets.
$80 + 20x + 16x + 4x^2 = 143$
Rearrange to the form $ax^2 + bx + c = 0$.
$4x^2 + 36x - 63 = 0$
$(2x - 3)(2x + 21) = 0$
Either $2x - 3 = 0$ or $2x + 21 = 0$
$\quad\quad\quad 2x = 3$ or $2x = -21$
$\quad\quad\quad\quad x = 1.5$ or $x = -10.5$

The quadratic equation has two solutions.
However, $x \neq -10.5$ as it is impossible to have a path of negative width in the context of the problem.
So $x = 1.5$
The width of the path is 1.5 m.

Check:
Does $(10 + 2 \times 1.5) \times (8 + 2 \times 1.5) = 143$?

2 A canoe course is in the shape of a right-angled triangle.
The length of the course is 300 m. The longest leg of the course is 125 m. What are the lengths of the other two legs?
Let the length of one of the shorter legs be x m.
Then the length of the other shorter leg is given by:
$300 - 125 - x = (175 - x)$ m

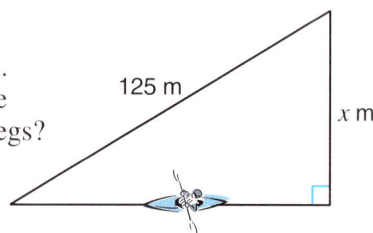

125 m

x m

Using Pythagoras' Theorem.
$x^2 + (175 - x)^2 = 125^2$
Expanding gives:
$x^2 + 30\,625 - 350x + x^2 = 15\,625$
Rearranging and simplifying gives:
$2x^2 - 350x + 15\,000 = 0$
Divide throughout by 2 (common factor).
$x^2 - 175x + 7500 = 0$
$(x - 75)(x - 100) = 0$
Either $x - 75 = 0$ or $x - 100 = 0$
$\quad\quad\quad\quad x = 75$ or $x = 100$

Using the solution $x = 75$.
The lengths of the shorter legs are 75 m and $175 - 75 = 100$ m.

Using the solution $x = 100$.
The lengths of the shorter legs are 100 m and $175 - 100 = 75$ m.
In this problem, both solutions to the quadratic equation are possible and both lead to the same answer to the problem.

Check:
Does $75 + 100 + 125 = 300$,
and $75^2 + 100^2 = 125^2$?

In this exercise form suitable equations and solve them using an appropriate method.
Give answers correct to three significant figures where necessary.

1 (a) The perimeter of a right-angled triangle is 40 cm.
The hypotenuse is 17 cm. What are the lengths of the other two sides?

(b) The perimeter of another right-angled triangle is 16 cm.
One of the shorter sides is 6 cm. What are the lengths of the other two sides?

2 Garden A consists of a lawn 8 m by 5 m with a path x m wide on all sides.
Garden B consists of a lawn 15 m by 14.5 m with a path x m wide on all sides.
Garden B is three times the area of Garden A.

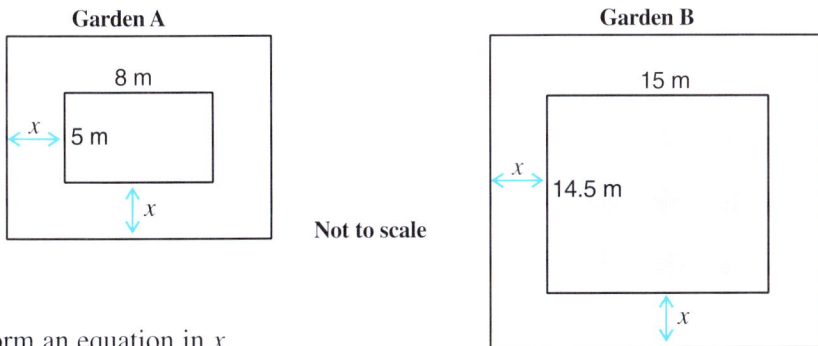

Garden A

8 m

x 5 m

x

Not to scale

Garden B

15 m

x 14.5 m

x

(a) Form an equation in x.
(b) Solve it to find x (the width of the path).
(c) Check that your value for x gives the area
for garden B as three times the area of Garden A.

3 The length of a rectangle is 5 cm greater than its width.
The area of the rectangle is 40 cm².
Calculate the length and width of the rectangle.

4 The perimeter of a rectangle is 62 cm.
The length of the diagonal is 25 cm.
Calculate the dimensions of the rectangle.

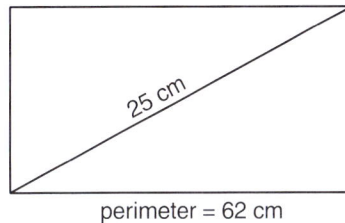

25 cm

perimeter = 62 cm

5 The perimeter of a rectangle is 20 m. The area is 20 m².
Calculate the dimensions of the rectangle.

6 (a) Two positive numbers differ by 5. Their product is 234.
What are the two numbers?

(b) The sum of two numbers is 12. Their product is 30.
What are the two numbers?

7 Three numbers are in this sequence: x, $x + 3$, $x + 6$.
The sum of the squares of the smallest two numbers is equal to the square of the largest
number.
What are the three numbers? (There are two solutions.)

8 Consider these numbers: x, $x + 1$, $x + 3$ and $x + 7$.
The sum of the squares of the smallest two numbers is equal to the product of the largest two numbers.
- (a) Form an equation and simplify it to a quadratic expression equal to 0.
- (b) Solve the equation to find the numbers (two solutions).

9 The nth triangle number is $\frac{1}{2} n(n + 1)$.
- (a) Which triangle number is equal to 66?
- (b) Which triangle number is equal to 120?

10 Two numbers differ by 5. Their squares differ by 55.
What are the two numbers?

Iteration

The solutions to a variety of equations can be found using a process called iteration.

The process of iteration has three stages.
1. Rearranging an equation to form an **iterative formula.**
   Sometimes the formula is given.
2. Choosing a **starting value**, x_1.
   Sometimes the starting value is given.
3. **Substituting** the value of x_1 into the iterative formula.
   This produces a value called x_2 which is then substituted into the iterative formula.
   Substituting a value for x_n produces the next value to be used, x_{n+1}.
   The process is continued, producing values x_3, x_4, … until the required degree of accuracy is obtained.

EXAMPLE

Find a solution to the equation $x^2 - 5x + 3 = 0$, correct to 3 significant figures, using **iteration**.
Use $x_1 = 4$ as a starting value.

$x^2 - 5x + 3 = 0$
$x^2 = 5x - 3$

Take the square root of both sides.

$x = \sqrt{5x - 3}$

Write the iterative formula.

$x_{n+1} = \sqrt{5x_n - 3}$

$x_1 = 4$ (this was given)
$x_2 = \sqrt{5 \times 4 - 3} = 4.1231 \ldots$
$x_3 = \sqrt{5 \times 4.1231 \ldots - 3} = 4.1970 \ldots$
$x_4 = \sqrt{5 \times 4.1970 \ldots - 3} = 4.2409 \ldots$
$x_5 = \sqrt{5 \times 4.2409 \ldots - 3} = 4.2666 \ldots$
$x_6 = \sqrt{5 \times 4.2666 \ldots - 3} = 4.2817 \ldots$
$x_7 = \sqrt{5 \times 4.2817 \ldots - 3} = 4.2905 \ldots$
$x_8 = \sqrt{5 \times 4.2905 \ldots - 3} = 4.2956 \ldots$
$x_9 = \sqrt{5 \times 4.2956 \ldots - 3} = 4.2986 \ldots$
$x_{10} = \sqrt{5 \times 4.2986 \ldots - 3} = 4.3003 \ldots$

To form an iterative formula, rearrange the equation so that one side has the variable on its own, e.g. '$x = \ldots$'

The efficient use of the memory facilities of a calculator can help to reduce greatly the time taken to perform lengthy calculations.

At this stage the answer is not changing from 4.30 (correct to 3 sig. figs.).

1 (a) Show how the equation $x^2 - 5x + 3 = 0$ can be rearranged to give:

$x = \dfrac{5x - 3}{x}$ and hence the iterative formula $x_{n+1} = \dfrac{5x_n - 3}{x_n}$.

(b) Starting with the value $x = 4$ find a solution to the equation using iteration, correct to 3 significant figures. Show all calculations.

(c) A solution to the equation $x^2 - 5x + 3 = 0$ was found in the example using a different iterative formula. Compare the two iterative processes.

2 (a) Show how the equation $6x^2 - 7x - 2 = 0$ can be rearranged to give:

$x = \sqrt{\dfrac{7x + 2}{6}}$ and hence the iterative formula $x_{n+1} = \sqrt{\dfrac{7x_n + 2}{6}}$.

(b) Starting with the value $x_1 = 1$ find a solution to the equation using iteration correct to 3 significant figures. Show all calculations.

(c) Show how this equation can also be rearranged to give: $x = \dfrac{7x + 2}{6x}$

and hence the iterative formula $x_{n+1} = \dfrac{7x_n + 2}{6x_n}$.

Use a starting value of $x_1 = 1$ and this formula.
Which is the more efficient iterative formula?

3 When finding a solution to $x^2 + 7x - 10 = 0$ the following iterative formula is used:
$x_{n+1} = \sqrt{10 - 7x_n}$. The starting value $x_1 = 1$ is used. What happens?

4 Find a solution to the equation $x^2 + 7x - 100$ (correct to 3 sig. figs.) by using iteration. Show your rearrangement giving an iterative formula and a good starting value.

5 Find a solution to the equation $x^2 + 3x - 8 = 0$ by using iteration. Give your answer to an appropriate degree of accuracy.

What you need to know

- Brackets, such as $(x + 2)(x + 5)$ can be multiplied out using:
  the **diagram method**,
  by **expanding**.

- **Factorising** is the opposite operation to removing brackets.
  When factorising, work logically.
  Does the expression have a **common factor**?
  Is the expression a difference of **two squares**?
  Will the expression factorise into **two brackets**?

$(x + 2)(x + 5) = x^2 + 5x + 2x + 10$
$= x^2 + 7x + 10$

- A **common factor** is a factor which divides into two, or more, numbers (or terms). For example: $x^2 + 7x = x(x + 7)$

- **Difference of two squares** $a^2 - b^2 = (a - b)(a + b)$

- **Quadratic equations** can be solved:
  by factorising, graphically, using the quadratic formula, by iteration.

- The general form for a **quadratic function** is $y = ax^2 + bx + c$, where a cannot be zero.
  The graph of a quadratic function is symmetrical and has a **maximum** or **minimum** value.

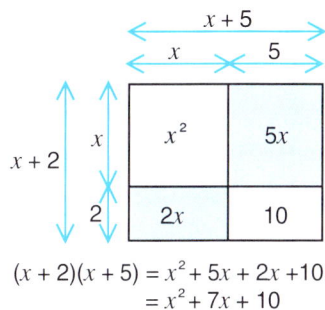

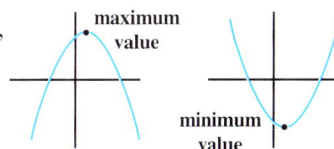

- The solutions to a quadratic equation can be found using the **quadratic formula**.

  If $ax^2 + bx + c = 0$ and $a \neq 0$ then $x = \sqrt{\dfrac{-b \pm b^2 - 4ac}{2a}}$

- The solutions to a variety of equations can be found using a process called **iteration**.
  The process of iteration has three stages.
  1   Rearranging an equation to form an **iterative formula**.
  2   Choosing a **starting value**, x_1.
  3   **Substituting** the starting value, and then values of x_n into the iterative formula.
       Continuing the process until the required degree of accuracy is obtained.

Review Exercise

1   (a)   Multiply out and simplify
              $(3p + 1)(p - 4)$.
         (b)   Simplify
              $3p^2 + 3p + 4 + 2(p - 2)$.
              Write your answer in fully
              factorised form.
              SEG 1997

2   (a)   Multiply out and simplify the
              expression $(x - a)(x + a)$.
              Hence, or otherwise, factorise
              $x^2 - 25$.
         (b)   Factorise fully $2x^5 + 4x^2$.
              SEG 1996

3   Factorise fully the expression $x^3 - 4x$.
              SEG 1994

4   Solve the equation $2x^2 + 5x - 3 = 0$.
        You **must** show all your working.
              SEG 1997

5   Triangle ABC has a base of length
        $(2x - 1)$ centimetres and perpendicular
        height of $(x + 1)$ centimetres.
        The area of triangle ABC is $52\,\text{cm}^2$.

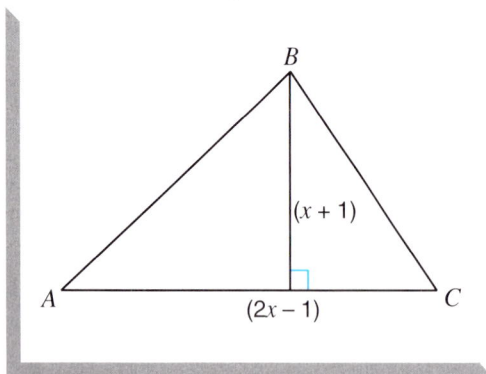

        Form an equation and solve it to find the
        perpendicular height of the triangle.
              SEG 1996

6   These two rectangles have the same
        area.

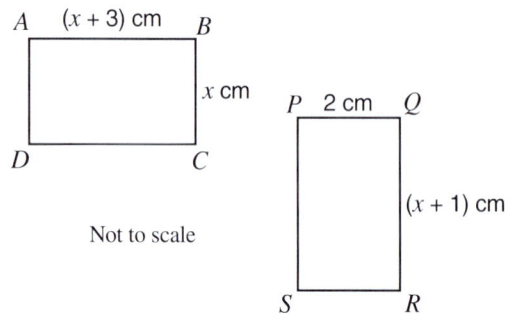

        Not to scale

         (a)   Form an equation in x and show
               that it can be simplified to
               $x^2 + x - 2 = 0$.
         (b)   Solve the equation $x^2 + x - 2 = 0$
               to find the length of BC.
              SEG 2000 S

7   A rectangular frame with two cross
        bars is to be made with 80 metres of
        metal.

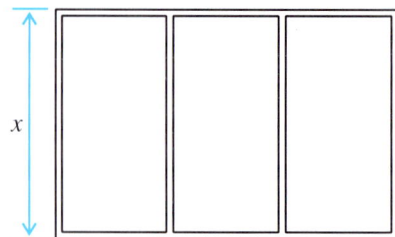

        The height of the frame is x metres and
        the total area inside the frame is $150\,\text{m}^2$.
         (a)   Show that x must satisfy the
               equation $x^2 - 20x + 75 = 0$.
         (b)   Find the values of x which satisfy
               this equation.
              SEG 1996

8 A farmer wants to build a fence to make a rectangular pen.
He is using his barn as one side of the pen, as shown.

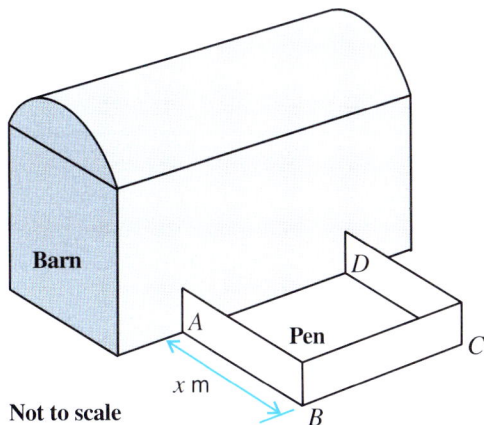

Not to scale

He has 60 metres of fencing and he wants the area of the pen to be $300\,m^2$.
The length of AB is x metres.

(a) Show that if the area is $300\,m^2$, x must satisfy the equation $x^2 - 30x + 150 = 0$.

(b) Solve the equation in (a) to find the two values of x that give the pen an area of $300\,m^2$.

SEG 1995

9 (a) Copy and complete the table of values for $y = x^2 - 2x - 2$.

x	-2	-1	0	1	2	3	4
y	6		-2			1	

(b) Draw the graph of $y = x^2 - 2x - 2$. Draw axes marked from -2 to 4 for x and from -4 to 6 for y.

(c) Use your graph to solve the equation $x^2 - 2x - 2 = 0$.

SEG 1998

10 The equation $x^2 - x - 7 = 0$ can be rearranged to give $x = \sqrt{x + 7}$.
This information can be used to obtain the iterative formula $x_{n+1} = \sqrt{x_n + 7}$.

(a) Starting with $x_1 = 4$ calculate the values of x_2, x_3 and x_4, giving all the figures on your calculator display.

(b) Find one solution of $x^2 - x - 7 = 0$ correct to 3 decimal places.

SEG 1995

11 A rectangle has a perimeter of 12 cm and an area of $7\,cm^2$.
Let the length of the rectangle be x cm.

(a) Show that $x^2 - 6x + 7 = 0$.

(b) (i) Complete the table of values for $y = x^2 - 6x + 7$.

x	0	1	2	3	4	5	6
y	7		-1			2	

(ii) Draw the graph of $y = x^2 - 6x + 7$.

(c) Use your graph to estimate the dimensions of the rectangle.

SEG 1998

12 A rectangular lawn has width x metres and length $2x$ metres.
The length is increased by 3 metres and the width by 1 metre.

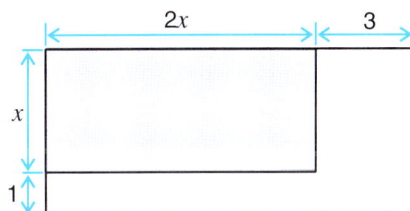

Not to scale

(a) Multiply out the expression $(2x + 3)(x + 1)$ to give the area of the new larger lawn.

(b) The new lawn has an area of $66\,m^2$. Form an equation and solve it to find the area of the original lawn.

(c) Another lawn is 3 metres longer than it is wide. Its area is $92\,m^2$.

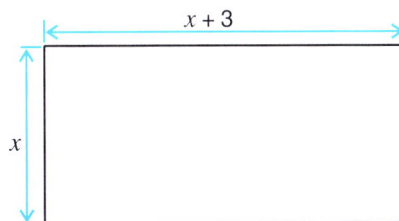

Not to scale

To find the width, x this iteration is used:
$$x_{n+1} = \frac{92}{x_n + 3}.$$

Starting with $x_1 = 8$, find the width, x, correct to **one** decimal place.

SEG 1996

CHAPTER 14

Algebraic Methods

When solving problems or simplifying expressions it is necessary to be able to manipulate algebra.

Simplifying expressions

EXAMPLES

The effect of a minus sign in front of a bracket is to change **all** signs inside the bracket.
Explain why.

1 Expand and simplify $(2x + 1)^2 - (x - 2)^2$.

$(2x + 1)^2 - (x - 2)^2$
Expand the brackets.
$= 4x^2 + 4x + 1 - (x^2 - 4x + 4)$
The second bracket was expanded and kept within a bracket because of the minus sign.
Remove the bracket.
$= 4x^2 + 4x + 1 - x^2 + 4x - 4$
Simplify.
$= 3x^2 + 8x - 3$

2 Expand and simplify $(x + 2y)^2 + (2x - y)^2$.
$= x^2 + 4xy + 4y^2 + 4x^2 - 4xy + y^2$
$= 5x^2 + 5y^2$
$= 5(x^2 + y^2)$ (In factorised form.)

Identities

A house has a front and a back garden.
The front garden consists of a square flower bed, 3 m by 3 m, surrounded by a path, x m wide.
The back garden consists of a rectangular lawn, 9 m by 5 m, surrounded by a path, x m wide.
Show that the total area of both gardens is given by: $2(4x^2 + 20x + 27)$.

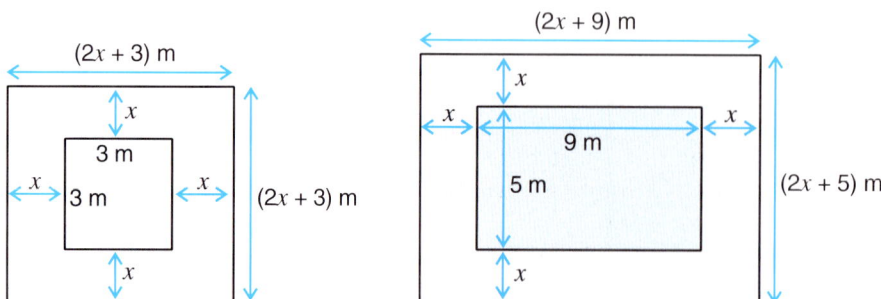

Sketch diagrams are drawn to help write expressions for the total length and total width of each garden.
Explain how each expression is obtained.

The area of the front garden is $(2x + 3)^2$.
The area of the back garden is $(2x + 9)(2x + 5)$.
The total area $= (2x + 3)^2 + (2x + 9)(2x + 5)$
$\qquad = (2x + 3)(2x + 3) + (2x + 9)(2x + 5)$
$\qquad = 4x^2 + 6x + 6x + 9 + 4x^2 + 10x + 18x + 45$
$\qquad = 8x^2 + 40x + 54$
$\qquad = 2(4x^2 + 20x + 27)$

This has shown that $(2x + 3)^2 + (2x + 9)(2x + 5) = 2(4x^2 + 20x + 27)$.
Although this looks like an equation it is called an **identity** because it is true for all values of x.
An identity is the same expression written in another form.

EXAMPLES

1 Show that $(x - 5)(x + 4) + (x - 3)(x - 2) = 2(x^2 - 3x - 7)$.

LHS $= (x - 5)(x + 4) + (x - 3)(x - 2)$
Expand the brackets.
$= x^2 + 4x - 5x - 20 + x^2 - 2x - 3x + 6$
Simplify.
$= 2x^2 - 6x - 14$
Factorise. Common factor 2.
$= 2(x^2 - 3x - 7)$
$=$ RHS

LHS $=$ RHS, so
$(x - 5)(x + 4) + (x - 3)(x - 2) = 2(x^2 - 3x - 7)$.

○○○○○○○○○○○

Abbreviations
LHS = left-hand side
RHS = right-hand side

To show that an identity is
true, either:
start with the LHS and show
that it is equal to the RHS,
or
start with the RHS and
show that it is equal to the
LHS.

2 Show that $(x + y)^2 - (x - y)^2 = 4xy$.

LHS $= (x + y)^2 - (x - y)^2$
$= x^2 + 2xy + y^2 - (x^2 - 2xy + y^2)$
$= x^2 + 2xy + y^2 - x^2 + 2xy - y^2$
$= 4xy$
$=$ RHS

LHS $=$ RHS, so
$(x + y)^2 - (x - y)^2 = 4xy$.

Exercise 14.1

1 Expand and simplify.
(a) $(x + 5)(x + 2) + (x - 4)(x - 6)$
(b) $(4x + 1)(x - 1) - (x + 2)(x - 3)$
(c) $(x - 5)(x - 5) - (x - 4)(x - 6)$
(d) $(2x + 3)(3x + 4) - (4x - 5)(5x - 6)$

2 Expand and simplify.
(a) $3(2x + 3y - 4z) - 4(3x - 5y + 3z)$
(b) $4(3x - 6y + 9z) - 3(4x - 8y + 12z)$
(c) $(x + 3y)^2 + (3x + y)^2$
(d) $(2x + 3y)^2 + (3x + 2y)^2$

3 Show that:
(a) $(x + 2)(x + 4) + (x - 3)(x - 4) = 2x^2 - x + 20$
(b) $(3x - 1)(x + 1) + (x + 4)(2x + 1) = 5x^2 + 11x + 3$
(c) $(x + 5)(x - 6) - (x - 4)(x - 3) = 6(x - 7)$
(d) $(2x + 1)(3x - 4) - (6x + 5)(x - 3) = 8x + 11$

4 Show that:
(a) $4(2x + 3y) - 2(3x - 4y) = 2(10y + x)$
(b) $3(s + 2t) + 2(3s + t) = 9s + 8t$
(c) $(x + y)^2 + (x - y)^2 = 2(x^2 + y^2)$
(d) $(x + 3y)^2 - (3x + y)^2 = 8(y + x)(y - x)$

5 Prove these identities.
(a) $(x + ay)^2 + (ax - y)^2 = (a^2 + 1)(x^2 + y^2)$
(b) $(x + ay)^2 - (ax + y)^2 = (a^2 - 1)(y^2 - x^2)$
(c) $(ax + by)^2 + (bx - ay)^2 = (a^2 + b^2)(x^2 + y^2)$

The graphs of **linear functions** are straight lines.
The general equation of a straight line is $y = mx + c$.
The graph of a **quadratic function** is always a smooth curve
and is called a **parabola**.
The general form of a **quadratic equation** is $y = ax^2 + bx + c$, where a cannot be equal to zero.
The general form of a **cubic equation** is $y = ax^3 + bx^2 + cx + d$, where a cannot be equal to zero.

> Solving equations of the form
> $ax^2 + bx + c = 0$ was covered in
> Chapter 13.

Consider the graph $y = x^3 + 2x^2 - 4x - 4$ for $-3 \leqslant x \leqslant 2$.
First make a table of values.

x	-3	-2	-1	0	1	2
y	-1	4	1	-4	-5	4

> The graph of $y = x^3 + 2x^2 - 4x - 4$
> has turning points at
> $(0.7, -5.5)$ and $(-2, 4)$.

Using the table of values and the information about turning
points, the graph of $y = x^3 + 2x^2 - 4x - 4$ can be drawn.
This graph can be used to solve the following equations.

Equation 1 $x^3 + 2x^2 - 4x - 4 = 0$
Equation 2 $x^3 + 2x^2 - 4x - 4 = 2$
Equation 3 $x^3 + 2x^2 - 4x - 4 = \frac{1}{2}x + 3$
Equation 4 $x^3 + 2x^2 - 2x - 8 = 0$

To solve equation 1:
At the points where the graph of $y = x^3 + 2x^2 - 4x - 4$
crosses the x axis the value of $y = 0$.
$x^3 + 2x^2 - 4x - 4 = 0$
The solutions of this cubic equation can be read from
the graph.
$x = -2.9$, -0.8 or 1.7, correct to 1 d.p.

To solve equation 2:
Draw the line $y = 2$.
Where the graph of $y = x^3 + 2x^2 - 4x - 4$
intersects (cuts) the graph of $y = 2$,
$x^3 + 2x^2 - 4x - 4 = 2$.
Solutions:
$x = -2.7$, -1.2 or 1.9, correct to 1 d.p.

To solve equation 3:
Draw the line $y = \frac{1}{2}x + 3$.

x	-2	0	2
y	2	3	4

Where the graph of $y = x^3 + 2x^2 - 4x - 4$
intersects (cuts) the graph of $y = \frac{1}{2}x + 3$,
$x^3 + 2x^2 - 4x - 4 = \frac{1}{2}x + 3$.
Solutions:
$x = -2.7$, -1.3 or 2.0, correct to 1 d.p.

To solve equation 4:
$x^3 + 2x^2 - 2x - 8 = 0$ can be rearranged as follows.
$x^3 + 2x^2 - 4x - 4 + 2x - 4 = 0$
$x^3 + 2x^2 - 4x - 4 = 4 - 2x$
Draw the line $y = 4 - 2x$.
Where the graph of $y = x^3 + 2x^2 - 4x - 4$
intersects the graph of $y = 4 - 2x$,
$x^3 + 2x^2 - 2x - 8 = 0$.
Solution:
$x = 1.8$, correct to 1 d.p.

> The equation to be solved is rearranged
> to get the equation of the given graph, in
> this case $y = x^3 + 2x^2 - 4x - 4$, on one
> side of the equation.
> *Explain why.*

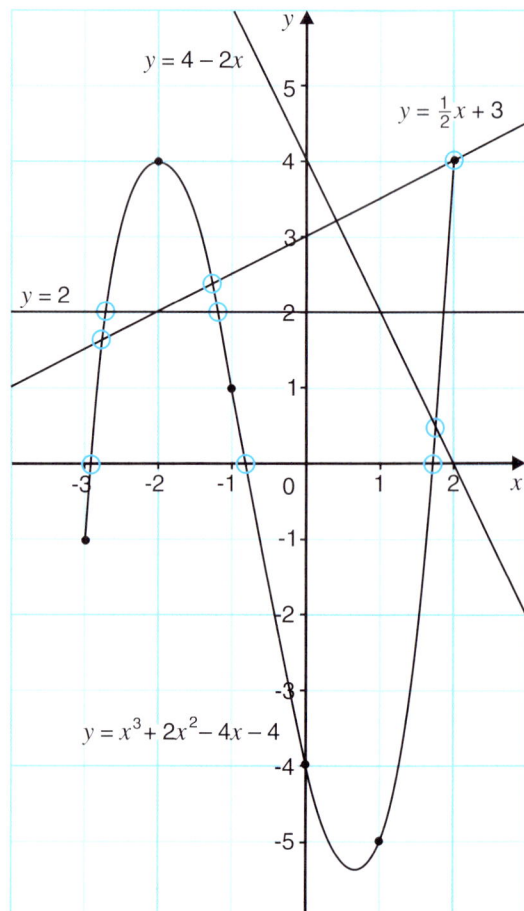
Graph showing $y = x^3 + 2x^2 - 4x - 4$ together with the lines $y = 4 - 2x$, $y = \frac{1}{2}x + 3$ and $y = 2$.

EXAMPLES

1 Given the graph of $y = x^3 + x^2 + x - 5$ what other graph would you draw to solve the equation $x^3 + x^3 + 2x - 10 = 0$?

$x^3 + x^2 + 2x - 10 = 0$
$x^3 + x^2 + x - 5 + x - 5 = 0$
$x^3 + x^2 + x - 5 = 5 - x$
Draw the graph of $y = 5 - x$.

2 Given the graph of $y = 2x^3 + 3x^2 - 7$ what other graph would you draw to solve the equation $2x^3 + 4x^2 - 10 = 0$?

$2x^3 + 4x^2 - 10 = 0$
$2x^3 + 3x^2 - 7 + x^2 - 3 = 0$
$2x^3 + 3x^2 - 7 = 3 - x^2$
Draw the graph of $y = 3 - x^2$.

Exercise 14.2

Having answered these questions you may wish to check your work using a graphical calculator.

1 Draw the graph of $y = 8 - x^2$ for $-3 \leqslant x \leqslant 3$.
Use this graph and any others you need to draw to solve these equations.
(a) $8 - x^2 = 0$
(b) $8 - x^2 = 4$
(c) $8 - x^2 = \frac{1}{2}x + 2$
(d) $8 - x^2 + x = 0$

2 Draw the graph of $y = x^3 - 5x + 6$ for $-3 \leqslant x \leqslant 3$.
Use this graph to solve the equation $x^3 - 5x + 6 = 15$.

3 Draw the graph of $y = 0.4x^3 - 1.6x$ for $-3 \leqslant x \leqslant 3$.
Use this graph and any others you need to draw to solve these equations.
(a) $0.4x^3 - 1.6x = 0$
(b) $0.4x^3 - 1.6x = 1$
(c) $0.4x^3 - 1.6x = x$
(d) $0.4x^3 - 0.6x - 3 = 0$

4 Given the graph of $y = 2x^3 + 3x^2 + 4x + 5$, what other graphs would you draw to solve the following equations?
(a) $2x^3 + 3x^2 + 5x + 6 = 0$
(b) $2x^3 + 4x^2 + 4x + 4 = 0$
(c) $x^3 + 3x^2 + 4x + 3 = 0$

5 Use a graphical method to solve the equation $x^3 = 6 - x$.

6 Use a graphical method to solve the equation $\frac{1}{x} = x^2 + 1$.

Algebraic fractions

Algebraic fractions have a numerator and a denominator (just as an ordinary fraction) but at least one of them is an expression involving an unknown.

e.g $\quad \dfrac{1}{x} \qquad \dfrac{x}{2} \qquad \dfrac{2}{x-5} \qquad \dfrac{x+1}{x-6} \qquad \dfrac{3}{x+7} \qquad \dfrac{x^2+2x+1}{x^2-1}$

These fractions can be simplified, added, subtracted, multiplied, divided and used in equations just as numerical fractions can be.

Simplifying algebraic fractions

Fractions can be simplified if the numerator and the denominator have a common factor.
In its **simplest form**, the numerator and denominator of an algebraic fraction have no common factor other than 1.

The numerator and denominator of $\frac{15}{25}$ have a highest common factor of 5.

$$\frac{15}{25} = \frac{15 \div 5}{25 \div 5} = \frac{3}{5}$$

3 and 5 have no common factors, other than 1.

$$\frac{15}{25} = \frac{3}{5} \text{ in its simplest form.}$$

Algebraic fractions work in a similar way.

To write an algebraic fraction in its simplest form:
- factorise the numerator and denominator of the fraction,
- divide the numerator and denominator by their highest common factor.

This is sometimes called **cancelling** a fraction.

EXAMPLES

Write the following in their simplest form.

1 $\dfrac{4x + 6}{2x + 8} = \dfrac{2(2x + 3)}{2(x + 4)} = \dfrac{2x + 3}{x + 4}$

4 $\dfrac{x^2 + 5x + 6}{x^2 - 2x - 8} = \dfrac{(x + 2)(x + 3)}{(x + 2)(x - 4)} = \dfrac{x + 3}{x - 4}$

2 $\dfrac{4x + 6}{6x + 9} = \dfrac{2(2x + 3)}{3(2x + 3)} = \dfrac{2}{3}$

5 $\dfrac{x^2 + 2x + 1}{x^2 - 1} = \dfrac{(x + 1)^2}{(x + 1)(x - 1)} = \dfrac{x + 1}{x - 1}$

3 $\dfrac{x^2y + 3xy^2}{xy - 2x^2y^2} = \dfrac{xy(x + 3y)}{xy(1 - 2xy)} = \dfrac{x + 3y}{1 - 2xy}$

6 $\dfrac{9 - 3y}{y - 3} = \dfrac{3(3 - y)}{y - 3} = \dfrac{-3(y - 3)}{y - 3} = -3$

Exercise 14.3

1 Simplify these algebraic fractions.

(a) $\dfrac{12}{3x - 9}$
(b) $\dfrac{5x + 10}{15}$
(c) $\dfrac{6x - 9}{3x + 15}$
(d) $\dfrac{51 - 3x}{3x + 9}$

(e) $\dfrac{2x + 4y + 6z}{4x - 6y + 2z}$
(f) $\dfrac{136x + 153}{51x + 34}$
(g) $\dfrac{-2x - 4}{-6x - 4}$
(h) $\dfrac{t - 5}{10 - 2t}$

2 Match the algebraic fractions with the values **A** to **E**.

(a) $\dfrac{3x + 6}{4x + 8}$
(b) $\dfrac{5x - 15}{2x - 6}$
(c) $\dfrac{8 - 4y}{6 - 3y}$
(d) $\dfrac{8x + 10}{4x + 5}$

(e) $\dfrac{-2x - 4}{-4x - 8}$
A 2
B $\frac{4}{3}$
C $2\frac{1}{2}$
D $\frac{1}{2}$
E $\frac{3}{4}$

3 Simplify these algebraic fractions.

(a) $\dfrac{x^2y + 5xy^2}{3xy + 4x^2y^2}$
(b) $\dfrac{x^2 + xy + 2xz}{2x^2 - 3xy + xz}$
(c) $\dfrac{a^2b^2 - 3ab}{ab^2 + a^2b}$
(d) $\dfrac{ax + ab + ay}{a^2b - 2ay}$

4 Simplify these algebraic fractions.

(a) $\dfrac{x^2 + 3x}{x^2 + 4x + 3}$
(b) $\dfrac{x^2 + 3x + 2}{x^2 + 4x + 3}$
(c) $\dfrac{x^2 - 2x}{x^2 + x - 6}$
(d) $\dfrac{x^2 - x - 20}{x^2 + 7x + 12}$

(e) $\dfrac{x^2 - 4x + 4}{x^2 - 5x + 6}$
(f) $\dfrac{x^2 - 5x}{x^2 + 4x}$
(g) $\dfrac{2x^2 - 7x - 15}{2x^2 - 5x - 12}$
(h) $\dfrac{6x^2 - 13x - 5}{9x^2 - 1}$

Arithmetic of algebraic fractions

The same methods used for adding, subtracting, multiplying and dividing numeric fractions can be applied to algebraic fractions.

> The arithmetic $(+, -, \times$ and $\div)$ of numeric fractions was covered in Chapter 1.

Multiplication

Numeric
$$\frac{8}{9} \times \frac{3}{14} = \frac{\cancel{2} \times 4}{3 \times \cancel{3}} \times \frac{\cancel{3}}{\cancel{2} \times 7} = \frac{4}{21}$$

Algebraic
$$\frac{2x + 2}{5x - 15} \times \frac{3x - 9}{4x + 4} = \frac{2(x + 1)}{5(x - 3)} \times \frac{3(x - 3)}{{}_2 4(x + 1)} = \frac{3}{10}$$

Division

Numeric
$$\frac{3}{7} \div \frac{9}{14} = \frac{3}{7} \times \frac{14}{9}$$
$$= \frac{\cancel{3}}{\cancel{7}} \times \frac{2 \times \cancel{7}}{3 \times \cancel{3}}$$
$$= \frac{2}{3}$$

Algebraic
$$\frac{7x - 7}{3x} \div \frac{4 - 4x}{x} = \frac{7x - 7}{3x} \times \frac{x}{4 - 4x}$$
$$= \frac{7(x - 1)}{3\cancel{x}} \times \frac{\cancel{x}}{-4(x - 1)}$$
$$= -\frac{7}{12}$$

Addition

Numeric
$$\frac{4}{11} + \frac{2}{5} = \frac{4 \times 5 + 2 \times 11}{11 \times 5}$$
$$= \frac{42}{55}$$

Algebraic
$$\frac{4}{x - 3} + \frac{2}{x + 2} = \frac{4(x + 2) + 2(x - 3)}{(x - 3)(x + 2)}$$
$$= \frac{6x + 2}{(x - 3)(x + 2)}$$

Subtraction

Numeric
$$\frac{4}{7} - \frac{2}{5} = \frac{4 \times 5 - 2 \times 7}{7 \times 5}$$
$$= \frac{6}{35}$$

Algebraic
$$\frac{4}{x - 3} - \frac{2}{2x + 1} = \frac{4(2x + 1) - 2(x - 3)}{(x - 3)(2x + 1)}$$
$$= \frac{8x + 4 - 2x + 6}{(x - 3)(2x + 1)}$$
$$= \frac{6x + 10}{(x - 3)(2x + 1)}$$
$$= \frac{2(3x + 5)}{(x - 3)(2x + 1)}$$

EXAMPLE

Simplify $\dfrac{x}{x - 1} + \dfrac{2 - x}{x + 2}$

$$\frac{x}{x - 1} + \frac{2 - x}{x + 2} = \frac{x(x + 2) + (2 - x)(x - 1)}{(x - 1)(x + 2)}$$
$$= \frac{x^2 + 2x + 2x - 2 - x^2 + x}{(x - 1)(x + 2)}$$
$$= \frac{5x - 2}{(x - 1)(x + 2)}$$

> It is common practice to leave the denominators of algebraic fractions in their factorised forms.

Exercise 14.4

1 Simplify.

(a) $\dfrac{4x - 2}{15 - 3x} \times \dfrac{5 - x}{2x - 1}$

(b) $\dfrac{5 + 5y}{y - 3} \times \dfrac{6 - 2y}{8y + 8}$

(c) $\dfrac{7}{y} \times \dfrac{y^2}{14}$

2 Simplify.

(a) $\dfrac{4x-2}{15-3x} \div \dfrac{2x-1}{5-x}$

(b) $\dfrac{4+y}{7-y} \div \dfrac{2y+8}{y-7}$

(c) $\dfrac{10-2x}{x^2} \div \dfrac{x-5}{x}$

3 Simplify.

(a) $\dfrac{3}{x+5} + \dfrac{4}{x-4}$

(b) $\dfrac{5}{2x+3} + \dfrac{6}{5x-3}$

(c) $\dfrac{x+4}{x+2} + \dfrac{2x-1}{x-3}$

4 Simplify.

(a) $\dfrac{4}{x+5} - \dfrac{3}{x-4}$

(b) $\dfrac{5}{2x+3} - \dfrac{6}{5x-3}$

(c) $\dfrac{2x-1}{x-3} - \dfrac{x+4}{x+2}$

5 If $\mathbf{p} = \dfrac{2}{x}$, $\mathbf{q} = \dfrac{3}{2x-6}$ and $\mathbf{r} = \dfrac{x-3}{2x}$, calculate

(a) $\mathbf{p} + \mathbf{q}$ (b) $\mathbf{p} - \mathbf{r}$ (c) $\mathbf{q} + \mathbf{r}$

(d) $\mathbf{p} \div \mathbf{r}$ (e) $\mathbf{q} \times \mathbf{r}$ (f) $\mathbf{r} \div \mathbf{p}$

Solving equations involving algebraic fractions

EXAMPLE

1 Solve the equation $\dfrac{7}{x} + \dfrac{6}{x+5} = 2$.

$\dfrac{7}{x} + \dfrac{6}{x+5} = 2$

Add the fractions.

$\dfrac{7(x+5) + 6x}{x(x+5)} = 2$

Simplify the numerator.

$\dfrac{7x + 35 + 6x}{x(x+5)} = 2$

$\dfrac{13x + 35}{x(x+5)} = 2$

Multiply both sides by $x(x+5)$.

$13x + 35 = 2x(x+5)$

Expand the bracket.

$13x + 35 = 2x^2 + 10x$

Rearrange into the form
$ax^2 + bx + c = 0$.

$2x^2 - 3x - 35 = 0$

Solve the quadratic equation.

$(2x+7)(x-5) = 0$

Either $2x + 7 = 0$ or $x - 5 = 0$

$\qquad 2x = -7 \quad$ or $x = 5$

$\qquad x = -\dfrac{7}{2}$

$\qquad x = -3\tfrac{1}{2}$

Solution: $x = -3\tfrac{1}{2}$ or 5

Alternative method:

$\dfrac{7}{x} + \dfrac{6}{x+5} = 2$

Multiply throughout by $x(x+5)$.

$\dfrac{7}{x} \times x(x+5) + \dfrac{6}{(x+5)} \times x(x+5)$
$= 2 \times x(x+5)$

$7(x+5) + 6x = 2x(x+5)$
$7x + 35 + 6x = 2x^2 + 10x$
$13x + 35 = 2x^2 + 10x$
$2x^2 - 3x - 35 = 0$

Solve as before.

○○○○○○○○○○○○○○○○

The final answers can always be
checked by substituting the
solutions, in turn, into the
original equation.

$\dfrac{7}{x} + \dfrac{6}{x+5} = 2$

Substitute $x = -3\tfrac{1}{2}$

Does $\dfrac{7}{-3\frac{1}{2}} + \dfrac{6}{-3\frac{1}{2}+5} = 2$?

Check the solution $x = 5$.

EXAMPLE

2 Henry took part in a sponsored walk between Aylestone and Bedrock.
He walked from Aylestone to Bedrock, a distance of 12 km, at a steady speed of x km/h.
His average speed for the return part of the walk was 2 km/h slower.

(a) Write down, in terms of x, the time taken for the whole journey.

(b) Henry walked for a total of $3\frac{1}{2}$ hours. Write an equation in x.
Show that the equation can be written as
$7x^2 - 62x + 48 = 0$.

(c) What was Henry's speed from Aylestone to Bedrock?

> Sometimes, questions are set in the form of a problem. Use the information given in the question to **form an equation.**
> **Solve** the equation.
> **Analyse** the solutions to answer the original problem.

(a) Using Time = Distance ÷ Speed

Total time $= \dfrac{12}{x} + \dfrac{12}{x-2}$

(b) $\dfrac{12}{x} + \dfrac{12}{x-2} = 3\frac{1}{2}$

Add the algebraic fractions.

$\dfrac{12(x-2) + 12x}{x(x-2)} = 3\frac{1}{2}$

Multiply both sides by $x(x-2)$.

$12x - 24 + 12x = 3\frac{1}{2}x(x-2)$

Simplify the left-hand side.

$24x - 24 = 3\frac{1}{2}x(x-2)$

Multiply both sides by 2.

$48x - 48 = 7x(x-2)$

Expand the right-hand side.

$48x - 48 = 7x^2 - 14x$

Rearrange into the form $ax^2 + bx + c = 0$.

$7x^2 - 62x + 48 = 0$

(c) $7x^2 - 62x + 48 = 0$
$(7x - 6)(x - 8) = 0$
Either $7x - 6 = 0$ or $x - 8 = 0$
$\qquad\qquad 7x = 6 \qquad$ or $x = 8$
$\qquad\qquad x = \frac{6}{7}$

The value of $\frac{6}{7}$ is a possible solution to the equation **but** it gives a negative speed for the return journey. So the solution which fits the problem is $x = 8$.
Henry's speed for the first part of the journey is 8 km/h.

Exercise 14.5

1 Explain each algebraic step in the solution to this equation.

$\dfrac{6}{x+1} - \dfrac{5}{x+2} = 2$

$\dfrac{6(x+2) - 5(x+1)}{(x+1)(x+2)} = 2$

$6x + 12 - 5x - 5 = 2(x+1)(x+2)$

$x + 7 = 2(x^2 + 3x + 2)$

$x + 7 = 2x^2 + 6x + 4$

$2x^2 + 5x - 3 = 0$

$(2x - 1)(x + 3) = 0$

$2x - 1 = 0$ or $x + 3 = 0$

$\qquad x = \frac{1}{2}$ or $x = -3$

2 (a) Show that the equation
$\dfrac{12}{x-3} + \dfrac{7}{x+1} = 5$
can be rearranged to give the equation $5x^2 - 29x - 6 = 0$.

(b) Solve $5x^2 - 29x - 6 = 0$ to find solutions for x.

3 Solve these equations, giving answers correct to 3 significant figures where necessary.

(a) $\dfrac{5}{x+1} + \dfrac{9}{x+2} = 8$

(b) $\dfrac{8}{x+4} - \dfrac{4}{x-2} = 5$

(c) $\dfrac{5}{2x+1} + \dfrac{4}{x+1} = 3$

(d) $\dfrac{10}{x-1} + \dfrac{12}{x+2} = 3\frac{1}{2}$

4 A car travels 60 km at a speed of x km/h.
It then travels a further 90 km at a speed 6 km/h faster.
The whole journey takes $5\frac{1}{2}$ hours.
   (a) Form an equation involving x.
   (b) Show that this equation can be written as $11x^2 - 234x - 720 = 0$.
   (c) Solve this equation to find the speed, x.

5 A rectangular photograph, 15 cm by 18 cm, is mounted on a larger rectangular piece of card so as to leave a border, x cm wide along both the top and bottom and y cm wide along each side.

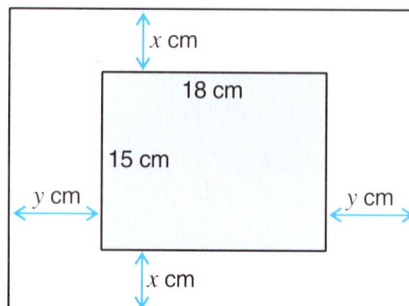

The perimeter of the mount is 102 cm.
The cost of mounting the photograph is £12.88.
   (a) Show that $x = 9 - y$.

The cost of mounting a photograph is
two pence per cm² of card.
   (b) Show that $(18 + 2y)(15 + 2x) = 644$.
   (c) Use the expression for x in part (a) to show that the equation in part (b) can be written as $2y^2 - 15y + 25 = 0$.
   (d) Solve this equation to determine the possible dimensions of the piece of card.   SEG 1993

Rearranging quadratics

Quadratics can be rearranged into a **square term** and a **constant value** (number).
This is sometimes called **completed square form** and can be used to solve quadratic equations and to determine the position of the quadratic graph.
The idea can also be used to derive the quadratic formula used in Chapter 12.

Consider the following.

$(x + 1)^2 = x^2 + 2x + 1$ $(x - 1)^2 = x^2 - 2x + 1$
$(x + 2)^2 = x^2 + 4x + 4$ $(x - 2)^2 = x^2 - 4x + 4$
$(x + 3)^2 = x^2 + 6x + 9$ $(x - 3)^2 = x^2 - 6x + 9$
$(x + 4)^2 = x^2 + 8x + 16$ $(x - 4)^2 = x^2 - 8x + 16$

In the expanded form the coefficient of x is always **twice** the constant in the brackets or, to put it another way, the constant in the brackets is **half the coefficient of x**.

$(x + a)^2 = x^2 + 2ax + a^2$ $(x - a)^2 = x^2 - 2ax + a^2$

> To write the quadratic $x^2 + bx + c$ in completed square form:
> write the **square term** as $(x + \frac{1}{2}$ the coefficient of $x)^2$
> and then adjust for the **constant value.**

$x^2 + 6x + 10$ can be written in the form $(x + a)^2 + b$. Find a and b.

The coefficient of x is 6. $\frac{1}{2}$ of 6 is 3.
The **square term** is $(x + 3)^2$.
    $(x + 3)^2 = x^2 + 6x + 9$
$x^2 + 6x + 10 = x^2 + 6x + 9 + 1 = (x + 3)^2 + 1$.
The **constant value** is $+1$.
So $a = 3$ and $b = 1$.

A sketch of $y = (x + 3)^2 + 1$ is shown on the right.
The bottom point (called the **minimum point** or **vertex**) is at $(-3, 1)$.

In general, the vertex of the graph $y = (x + a)^2 + b$ is at the point $(-a, b)$.

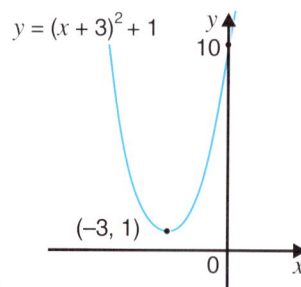

EXAMPLES

Put these quadratics into the form $(x + a)^2 + b$.

1 $x^2 + 10x + 7$

     $\frac{1}{2}$ of 10 is 5.
     $(x + 5)^2 \quad\quad = x^2 + 10x + 25$
     $x^2 + 10x + 7 = x^2 + 10x + 25 - 18$
                   $= (x + 5)^2 - 18$

2 $x^2 - 8x - 5$

     $\frac{1}{2}$ of -8 is -4.
     $(x - 4)^2 \quad\quad = x^2 - 8x + 16$
     $x^2 - 8x - 5 = x^2 - 8x + 16 - 21$
                   $= (x - 4)^2 - 21$

This change of form can still be done when the coefficient of x^2 is not 1.
Consider the following.

$(2x + 1)^2 = 4x^2 + 4x + 1$ $(2x - 1)^2 = 4x^2 - 4x + 1$
$(2x + 2)^2 = 4x^2 + 8x + 4$ $(2x - 2)^2 = 4x^2 - 8x + 4$
$(2x + 3)^2 = 4x^2 + 12x + 9$ $(2x - 3)^2 = 4x^2 - 12x + 9$
$(3x + 5)^2 = 9x^2 + 30x + 25$ $(4x - 5)^2 = 16x^2 - 40x + 25$

In general: $(px + q)^2 = p^2x^2 + 2pqx + q^2$
This can be used to change the form of quadratics.

$4x^2 + 20x + 31$ can be written in the form $(px + q)^2 + r$. Find p, q and r.

Using $(px + q)^2 = p^2x^2 + 2pqx + q^2$.
$4x^2 + 20x + 31 = p^2x^2 + 2pqx + q^2$.

Comparing the coefficients of x^2.
$p^2 = 4$
$p = \sqrt{4} = 2$

Comparing the coefficients of x.
$2pq = 20$
But $p = 2$.
So $4q = 20$
    $q = 5$

$(2x + 5)^2 = 4x^2 + 20x + 25$
$4x^2 + 20x + 31 = 4x^2 + 20x + 25 + 6 = (2x + 5)^2 + 6$
The constant value, r, is $+6$.

So p = 2, $q = 5$ and $r = 6$.

The vertex of the graph $y = (2x + 5)^2 + 6$ is at $(-\frac{5}{2}, 6)$.

In general the vertex of the graph
$y = (px + q)^2 + r$ is at $\left(-\frac{q}{p}, r\right)$.

EXAMPLE

3   Change $9x^2 + 24x + 5$ into the form $(px + q)^2 + r$.

Using $(px + q)^2 = p^2x^2 + 2pqx + q^2$.
$9x^2 + 24x + 5 = p^2x^2 + 2pqx + q^2$

$p^2 = 9$
$p = \sqrt{9} = 3$

$2pq = 24$
But $p = 3$.
So $6q = 24$
    $q = 4$

$(3x + 4)^2 = 9x^2 + 24x + 16$
$9x^2 + 24x + 5 = 9x^2 + 24x + 16 - 11 = (3x + 4)^2 - 11$

1 Change these quadratics into the form $(x + a)^2 + b$.
   (a) $x^2 + 6x + 20$ (b) $x^2 + 6x + 5$ (c) $x^2 + 10x - 4$
   (d) $x^2 - 4x + 5$ (e) $x^2 - 4x + 2$ (f) $x^2 - 4x - 4$
   (g) $x^2 - 6x + 4$ (h) $x^2 - 8x$ (i) $x^2 + 12x$

2 These quadratics can be put in the form $(x + a)^2 + b$.
   State the values of a and b.
   (a) $x^2 + 6x + 15$ (b) $x^2 + 10x + 5$ (c) $x^2 - 6x - 5$
   (d) $x^2 - 8x + 4$ (e) $x^2 + 12x + 4$ (f) $x^2 + 6x + 9$

3 Change these quadratics into the form $(px + q)^2 + r$.
   State the values of p, q and r.
   (a) $4x^2 + 16x + 5$ (b) $9x^2 + 12x + 3$ (c) $25x^2 - 40x - 3$
   (d) $16x^2 + 32x - 5$ (e) $100x^2 + 60x + 3$ (f) $16x^2 - 40x + 9$

4 Quadratic equations can be solved by completing the square.
   For example: Solve $x^2 + 6x + 7 = 0$, giving your answers correct to three significant figures.

   $x^2 + 6x + 7 = 0$
   $(x + 3)^2 - 2 = 0$
   $(x + 3)^2 = 2$
   Take the square root of both
   sides of the equation.
   $x + 3 = \pm \sqrt{2}$

   Either $x + 3 = \sqrt{2}$ or $x + 3 = -\sqrt{2}$
   $x = -3 + \sqrt{2}$ $x = -3 - \sqrt{2}$
   $x = -1.5857 \ldots$ $x = -4.4142 \ldots$
   Solutions:
   $x = -1.59$ or -4.41, correct to 3 s.f.

   Solve these equations the same way.
   (a) $x^2 + 2x = 5$ (b) $x^2 - 4x = 20$ (c) $x^2 - 6x = 16$
   (d) $x^2 + 8x + 12 = 0$ (e) $x^2 - 4x - 12 = 0$ (f) $4x^2 - 4x - 15 = 0$

5 Starting with $ax^2 + bx + c = 0$ prove the quadratic formula $x = \dfrac{-b \pm \sqrt{b^2 - 4ac}}{2a}$

Trial and improvement

Some equations cannot be solved directly (as quadratics can be). Numerical solutions can be found by making a guess and improving the accuracy of the guess by **trial and improvement**.
This can be a time consuming method of solving equations and is often used only as a last resort for solving equations which cannot be solved easily by algebraic or graphical methods.

A solution to the equation $x^3 - 4x = 7$ lies between 2 and 3.
Find this solution to 1 decimal place.

First guess: $x = 2.5$
$2.5^3 - 4(2.5) = 5.625$ Too small

Second guess: $x = 2.6$
$2.6^3 - 4(2.6) = 7.176$ Too big

The solution lies between 2.5 and 2.6,
but 2.6 gives an answer closer to 7.
The answer is probably 2.6, correct to 1 d.p.
To be certain, try $x = 2.55$.
$2.55^3 - 4(2.55) = 6.381375$ Too small

The solution lies between 2.55 and 2.6.
2.6 is the solution, correct to 1 d.p.

Because the solution lies between 2 and 3, notice that:
   when $x = 2$
   $2^3 - 4(2) = 0$ Less than 7

   when $x = 3$
   $3^3 - 4(3) = 15$ Greater than 7

We are trying to find a value for x which produces the answer 7.

EXAMPLE

A solution to the equation
$x^3 + 2x = 40$ lies between 3 and 4.
Find this solution to 2 decimal places.

The working can be shown in a table.

The solution lies between 3.225 and 3.23.
The solution is 3.23, correct to 2 d.p.

x	$x^3 + 2x$	
3.5	49.875	Too big
3.2	39.168	Too small
3.3	42.357	Too big
3.25	40.828125	Too big
3.22	39.826248	Too small
3.23	40.158267	Too big
3.225	39.992015	Too small

Exercise 14.7

1 A solution to the equation $x^3 + 5x = 880$ lies between 9 and 10.
Use trial and improvement to find this solution to 1 decimal place.
Show your trials.

2 Show that a solution to $x^3 - 5x^2 = 47$ lies between 6 and 7.
Use trial and improvement to find this solution, showing your trials,
   (a) to 1 decimal place,
   (b) to 2 decimal places.

3 This cuboid has dimensions: x, $x + 2$ and $2x$.

   (a) Write down an expression, in x, for the volume.
   (b) The volume of the cuboid is $400\,\text{cm}^3$.
       Form an equation and use trial and improvement to find x, correct to 1 d.p.

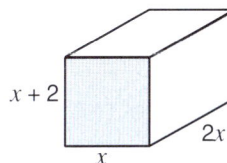

$x + 2$
$2x$
x

4 A solution to $x^4 + 5x - 20 = 0$ lies between 1 and 2.
Use trial and improvement to find this solution correct to 2 decimal places.
Show your trials.

What you need to know

- The effect of a minus sign in front of a bracket is to change **all** signs inside the bracket.
  For example: $-(3 - y) = -3 + y = y - 3$.

- An **identity** is true for all values of x.
  For example: $(2x + 3)^2 + (2x + 9)(2x + 5) = 2(4x^2 + 20x + 27)$.
  An identity is the same expression written in another form.
  To show that an identity is true, either:
     start with the LHS and show that it is equal to the RHS, or
     start with the RHS and show that it is equal to the LHS.

- The graph of a **linear function** is a straight line.
  The general equation of a straight line is $y = mx + c$.
  The graph of a **quadratic function** is always a smooth curve and is called a **parabola**.
  The general form of a **quadratic equation** is $y = ax^2 + bx + c$, where $a \neq 0$.
  The general form of a **cubic equation** is $y = ax^3 + bx^2 + cx + d$, where $a \neq 0$.

- The graph of a function can be used to solve a variety of equations.
  This may include drawing another graph and looking for points of intersection.

- **Algebraic fractions** have a numerator and a denominator (just as an ordinary fraction) but at least one of them is an expression involving an unknown.

- To write an algebraic fraction in its **simplest form**:
  factorise the numerator and denominator of the fraction,
  divide the numerator and denominator by their highest common factor.
  This is sometimes called **cancelling** a fraction.

- The same methods used for adding, subtracting, multiplying and dividing numeric fractions can be applied to algebraic fractions.

- Quadratic expressions, such as $x^2 + 8x + 20$, can be written in the form $(x + a)^2 + b$, where a and b are integers.
  In **completed square form**, $(x + a)^2 + b$:
  the value of a is half the coefficient of x,
  the value of b is found by subtracting the value of a^2 from the constant term of the original expression.
  For example: $x^2 + 8x + 20 = (x + 4)^2 + 4$

- Quadratic expressions, such as $4x^2 + 16x + 5$, where the coefficient of x^2 is not 1 can be written in the form $(px + q)^2 + r$.
  In completed square form, $(px + q)^2 + r$:
  the value of p is the square root of the coefficient of x^2,
  the value of q is the coefficient of x divided by $2p$,
  the value of r is found by subtracting the value of q^2 from the constant term of the original expression.
  For example: $4x^2 + 16x + 5 = (2x + 4)^2 - 11$

- **Trial and improvement** is a method used to solve equations. The accuracy of the value of the unknown letter is improved until the required degree of accuracy is obtained.

Review Exercise

1
(a) Multiply out the brackets $x(x + y)$.
(b) Multiply out the brackets.
     Write your answer in its simplest form.
     (i) $(x + 3y)(2x - y)$
     (ii) $(x + y)^2$

SEG 1994

2 Simplify as much as possible the expression
$5(x + 2y) - 2(2x + 4y)$.

SEG 1995

3 The graph of $y = x^2 - 1$ is drawn.
To solve the equation $x^2 = 2x + 2$ a line can be drawn on the graph.
What is the equation of the line?

SEG 1997

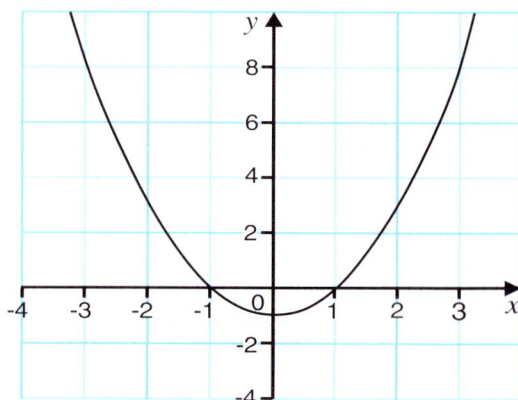

4 Draw the graphs $y = 20 - 5x$ and $y = x^3$ for $0 \leqslant x \leqslant 3$.
Use a scale of $2\,\text{cm} = 1$ unit on the x axis and $2\,\text{cm} = 10$ units on the y axis.
Use the graphs to estimate, correct to one decimal place, the solution of $x^3 + 5x - 20 = 0$.

SEG 1995

5 **Use a graphical method** to solve the equation
$$\frac{1}{x} = x^2 - 1.$$
You **must** show all your working.

SEG 1995

6 Simplify fully the following expression.
$$\frac{6x - 18}{x^2 - 5x + 6}$$

SEG 1998

7 Simplify the expression $\dfrac{6}{2x + 1} - \dfrac{3}{x + 1}$.

SEG 1995

8 Solve the equation $\dfrac{2}{x + 2} + \dfrac{3}{x} = 4$.

SEG 1997

9 This formula shows the relationship between x and A.
$$A = \frac{8}{2x - 1} - \frac{4}{x}$$

(a) Show clearly that this formula can be simplified to
$$A = \frac{4}{2x^2 - x}$$

(b) Find the values of x when $A = 2$.

SEG 1998

10 The formula for the stopping distance of a car, d feet, in terms of its speed, v miles per hour, is
$$d = v + \frac{v^2}{20}.$$

(a) Show that, when $d = 175$, the formula can be written as $v^2 + 20v - 3500 = 0$.
(b) Solve the equation $v^2 + 20v - 3500 = 0$.

SEG 1997

11 (a) Simplify the expression $\dfrac{2x^2 - 5x + 2}{x^2 - 4}$.

(b) The expression $x^2 - 8x + 17$ can be written in the form $(x - \text{p})^2 + q$.
Calculate the values of p and q such that
$x^2 - 8x + 17 = (x - \text{p})^2 + q$.

SEG 1998

12 (a) Write the expression $x^2 - 10x + 7$ in the form $(x - a)^2 + b$, where a and b are integers.
(b) Solve the equation $x^2 - 10x + 7 = 0$.

SEG 1998

13 (a) By writing the quadratic expression $x^2 - 4x + 2$
in the form $(x + a)^2 + b$, find a and b and **hence** find the minimum value of the expression.
(b) Solve the equation $x^2 - 4x + 2 = 0$,
giving your answers correct to 2 decimal places.

SEG 1995

14 The equation $x^3 + x = 20$ has a solution between 2 and 3.
Use a trial and improvement method to find the solution correct to two decimal places.
Show all your working.

15 A solution of the equation $x^4 + 2x = 200$ lies between $x = 3$ and 4.
Use the method of trial and improvement to find this solution.
Give your answer to one decimal place.
You **must** show all your trials.

SEG 1998

CHAPTER 15

Using Graphs

Activity

Look at the graph of $y = 2x^3$.

A is the point $(0, 0)$ and K is the point $(1, 2)$.
The line AK is called a chord.

Gradient $= \dfrac{\text{distance up}}{\text{distance across}}$

$= \dfrac{\text{difference in } y \text{ coordinates}}{\text{difference in } x \text{ coordinates}}$

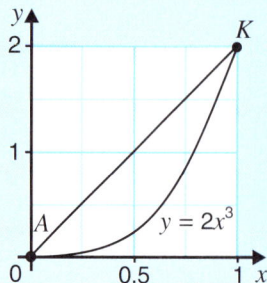

A **chord** is a straight line joining two points on a curve. The gradient of a straight line was first covered in Chapter 10.

So gradient of chord $AK = \dfrac{2 - 0}{1 - 0} = \dfrac{2}{1} = 2$

This table shows values of y for $y = 2x^3$ for values of x from 0 to 1.

Point	A	B	C	D	E	F	G	H	I	J	K
x	0	0.1	0.2	0.3	0.4	0.5	0.6	0.7	0.8	0.9	1
y	0	0.002	0.016	0.054	0.128	0.25	0.432	0.686	1.024	1.458	2

(a) On graph paper, draw and label axes for x and y using a scale of 10 mm for 0.1 units. Plot the points A to K and draw the graph of $y = 2x^3$.

(b) Draw the chords, AK, BJ, CI, DH and EG and calculate their gradients.

The points P (0.48, 0.221184) and Q (0.52, 0281216) lie on the graph of $y = 2x^3$.

(c) Calculate the gradient of the chord PQ.

The points P' (0.499, 0.248503) and Q' (0.501, 0.251503) also lie on the graph of $y = 2x^3$.

(d) Show that the gradient of the chord $P'Q'$ is 1.5.

(e) Comment on your results.

Finding the gradient of a curve

In the activity, the chord $P'Q'$ lies very close to the point F.
It also lies very close to the curve $y = 2x^3$.
So the gradient of $P'Q'$ is a very good estimate of the gradient of the curve at the point F.

A quicker method of finding the gradient at a point is by drawing the **tangent** at the point and calculating its gradient.
A tangent is a straight line **touching** a curve at a point.
The gradient of the curve at a point is equal to the gradient of the tangent at the point.

In practice, because it is difficult to draw an accurate tangent, this method only gives an **estimate** of the gradient.

To find the gradient at a point on a curve:
● draw the tangent to the curve at the point,
● find the gradient of the tangent.

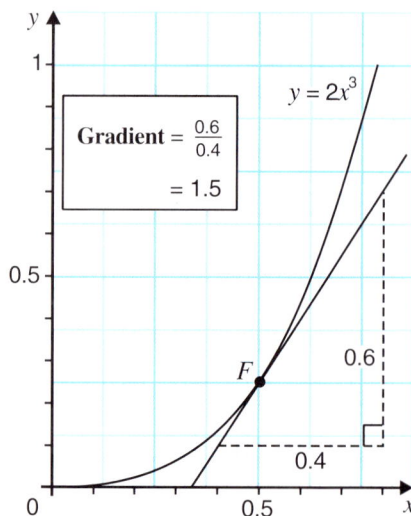

Gradient $= \dfrac{0.6}{0.4}$

$= 1.5$

The straight line is the **tangent** to the curve at $x = 0.5$.
The **gradient of the curve** at $x = 0.5$ is 1.5.

Drawing a tangent to a curve

To draw a tangent to a curve at the point P:

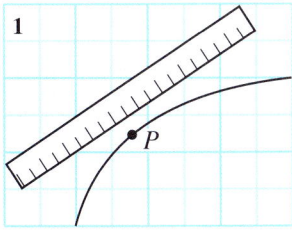

Put your ruler close to P. Make sure that your ruler does not cover the curve near P.

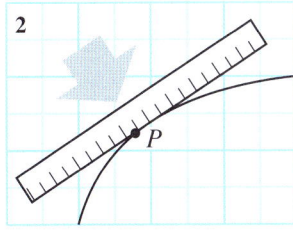

Slide your ruler towards the curve until it touches point P.

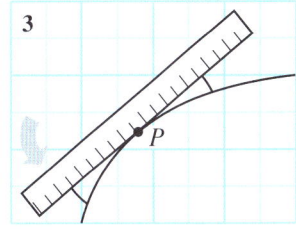

Rotate your ruler about P until the angle the curve makes with the ruler is approximately the same on both sides of P.

EXAMPLE

(a) Draw the graph of $y = x(6 - x)$ for $0 \leqslant x \leqslant 6$.
(b) Find the gradient of $y = x(6 - x)$ at the point (4, 8).
(c) What are the coordinates of the point where the gradient of $y = x(6 - x)$ is zero?

(a) Complete a table of values for $y = x(6 - x)$.

x	0	1	2	3	4	5	6
y	0	5	8	9	8	5	0

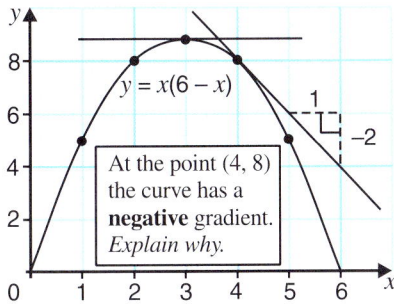

At the point (4, 8) the curve has a **negative** gradient. *Explain why.*

(b) **Step 1**
Draw a **tangent** at the point (4, 8).
Step 2
Find the gradient of the **tangent**.

Gradient $= \dfrac{-2}{1} = -2$

The gradient of $y = x(6 - x)$ at the point (4, 8) is -2.

(c) A horizontal line has zero gradient. So $y = x(6 - x)$ will have zero gradient at the point where the tangent is horizontal. This is at the point (3, 3).

Exercise 15.1

You may use a calculator.

1 Which of the lines a, b and c are tangents to the curve?

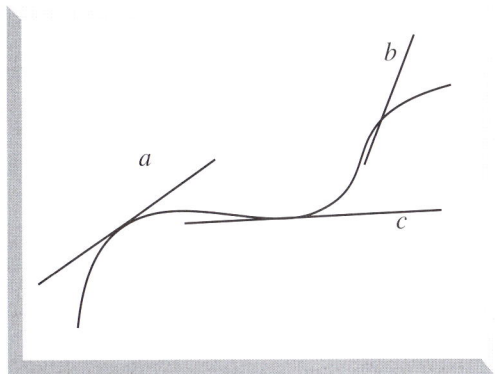

2 The diagram shows a curve on which the points *A* to *G* have been marked.

(a) At which points does the curve have a positive gradient?

(b) At which points does the curve have a negative gradient?

(c) At which points does the curve have a zero gradient?

(d) At which point does the curve have the greatest gradient?

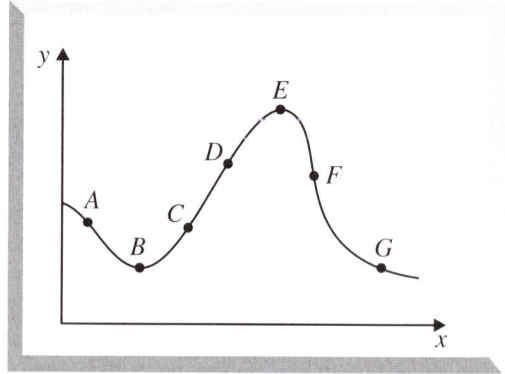

3 (a) Draw the graph of $y = x^2$ for $-3 \leqslant x \leqslant 3$.

(b) (i) On your graph draw a line passing through the point (2, 4) with a gradient of 4.

 (ii) Is the line you have drawn a tangent to $y = x^2$?

(c) Repeat parts (a) and (b) for:

 (i) a line passing through $(-2.5, 6.25)$ with a gradient of -5,

 (ii) a line passing through (3, 5) with a gradient of 2.

4 The diagram shows a curve and tangents to the curve at points *P*, *Q* and *R*.
Find the gradient of the curve at *P*, *Q* and *R*.

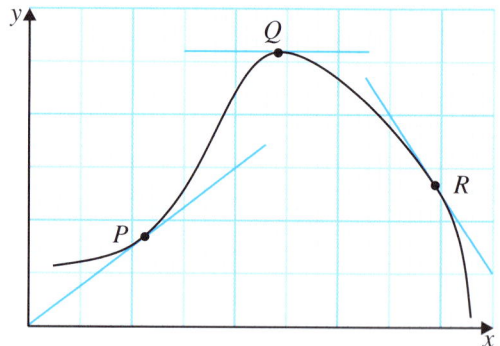

5 Draw a smooth curve through the points (0, 0), (1, 2), (2, 3), (3, 3.5) (4, 3.8) and (5, 3.9).
Estimate the gradient of the curve at the point (2, 3).

6 Draw a smooth curve through the points (0, 6), (1, 4), (2, 3.2), (3, 2.8), (4, 2.6) and (5, 2.5).
Estimate the gradient of the curve at the point (2, 3.2).

7 (a) Draw the graph of $y = x^2$ for $-1 \leqslant x \leqslant 5$.

(b) Estimate the gradient of the curve $y = x^2$ at the points where:

 (i) $x = 0$ (ii) $x = 1$ (iii) $x = 2$

 (iv) $x = 2.5$ (v) $x = 3$ (vi) $x = 4$

(c) What do you notice about your answers to part (b)?

8 (a) Draw the graph of $y = x^3$ for $-3 \leqslant x \leqslant 3$.

(b) Estimate the gradient of the curve $y = x^3$ at the points where:

 (i) $x = -2.5$ (ii) $x = -2$ (iii) $x = -1.5$ (iv) $x = -1$

 (v) $x = -0.5$ (vi) $x = 0$ (vii) $x = 0.5$ (viii) $x = 1$

 (ix) $x = 1.5$ (x) $x = 2$ (xi) $x = 2.5$

(c) What do you notice about your answers to part (b)?

Interpreting gradients

The graph shows how the length of a spring, l cm, varies when weights, w kg, are attached to it.

The line has a gradient of 4.5.
This means that whenever the weight attached to the spring increases by 1 kg, the length of the spring increases by 4.5 cm.

The **rate of increase** of the length of the spring is 4.5 cm per kg.

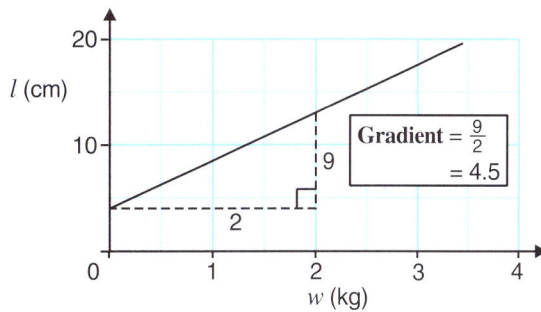

Gradient $= \frac{9}{2}$
$= 4.5$

A gradient measures the **rate of change** (increase or decrease) of one quantity with respect to another.

EXAMPLES

1 What is the rate of increase of y with respect to x in the graph of $y = 3x + 4$?

The graph of $y = 3x + 4$ is a straight line with a gradient 3.
So the rate of increase of y with respect to x is 3.
This means that when the value of x increases by 1, the value of y increases by 3.

2 A liquid at room temperature was heated for 15 minutes and was then allowed to cool. The graph shows the relationship between the temperature in °C and the time in minutes.

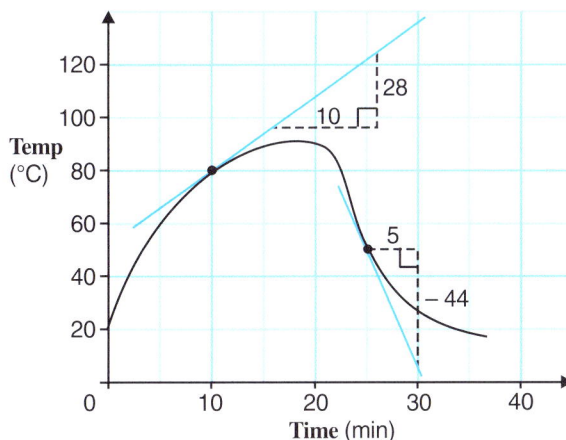

(a) Find the rate of increase of the temperature after 10 minutes.
(b) Find the rate of decrease of the temperature after 20 minutes.

Rates of change are found from the gradients of tangents.
(a) Gradient of the tangent after 10 minutes:
$$\frac{28}{10} = 2.8$$
Rate of increase of the temperature after 10 minutes is 2.8°C per minute.

(b) Gradient of the tangent after 20 minutes:
$$\frac{-44}{5} = -8.8$$
Rate of decrease of the temperature after 20 minutes is 8.8°C per minute.

Remember
Positive gradient − rate of increase
Negative gradient − rate of decrease

1 (a) Draw the graph of $y = x^2 - 2x$ for $-2 \le x \le 4$.
(b) For what values of x is the gradient of $y = x^2 - 2x$ negative?
(c) Find the rate of change of y with respect to x when:
(i) $x = -1$,   (ii) $x = 2$.

2 At birth, baby Jane weighed 3.2 kg. The table shows Jane's weight measured at various ages.

Age (weeks)	1	2	4	6	8	10
Weight (kg)	3.0	3.3	4.2	4.8	5.5	5.4

(a) Plot this information on a graph and join the points with a smooth curve.
(b) Find the gradient of your graph when Jane is 5 weeks old.
Explain the meaning of this gradient.

3 This table shows how the depth of water in a goldfish bowl varies with time as it is being emptied.

Time (seconds)	10	20	30	40	50
Depth (cm)	9.00	8.10	7.29	6.56	5.91

(a) Plot this information on a graph and join the points with a smooth curve.
(b) Use your graph to find the smallest rate of decrease in depth of water.

4 On bonfire night a rocket is fired into the air.
This table shows how the height of the rocket, in metres, varies with time.

Time (seconds)	0	10	20	30	40	50
Height (m)	0	9.00	17.6	25.4	32.5	35.9

(a) Plot a graph of the height of the rocket against time.
(b) Find the rate of change of height with respect to time after 7 seconds.

5 Water flows into a tank.
The depth of water, d centimetres, at time t minutes, is given by the equation $d = \dfrac{t^2}{4}$.
(a) Draw the graph of depth against time for $0 \le t \le 5$.
(b) Use your graph to estimate the rate of change of depth at $t = 4$.

6 A damaged oil rig leaks oil into the sea.
The graph shows how the area of the resulting oil slick varies with the time after the oil starts to leak.
(a) Estimate the gradient of the graph 10 hours after the oil starts to leak, stating the units.
(a) What does this gradient represent?

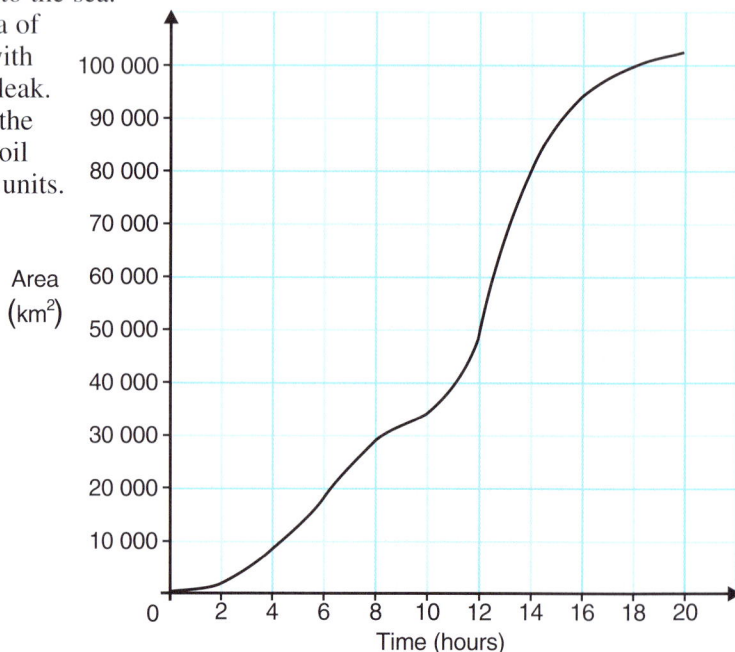

Speed and acceleration

Speed is the rate of change of **distance** with respect to **time**.
Speed can be calculated from the gradient of a **distance-time graph**.

Acceleration is the rate of change of **speed** with respect to **time**.
Acceleration can be calculated from the gradient of a **speed-time graph**.

EXAMPLE

1 The distance-time graph shows the journey of a bus between two bus stops, *A* and *B*.

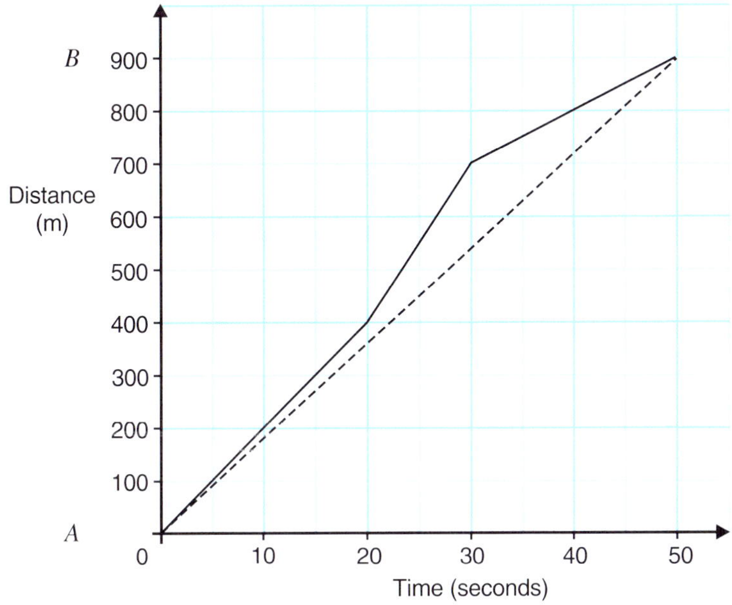

Remember
Gradients measure **rates** of change (increase or decrease).

Speed can be calculated from the gradient of a distance-time graph.

When the distance-time graph is **linear** the **speed is constant**.

When the distance-time graph is **horizontal** the **speed is zero**.

$$\text{Average speed} = \frac{\text{total distance}}{\text{total time}}$$

(a) (i) Calculate the gradient of the distance-time graph between $t = 0$ and $t = 20$.
(ii) What does this gradient represent?
(b) Calculate the fastest speed of the bus on its journey from *A* to *B*.
(c) Calculate the average speed of the bus on its journey between *A* and *B*.

(a) (i) Gradient $= \dfrac{400}{20} = 20$.

(ii) The gradient represents the rate of increase of distance with time, or speed in metres per second.

(b) The fastest speed of the bus occurs where the gradient is steepest. This occurs between $t = 20$ and $t = 30$.

$$\text{Speed} = \text{gradient} = \frac{300}{10} = 30 \,\text{m/s}$$

(c) Average speed is given by:

$$\frac{\text{Total distance travelled}}{\text{Total time taken}}$$

So the average speed of the bus between the bus stops is:

$$\frac{900}{50} = 18 \,\text{m/s}$$

The average speed can be calculated from the gradient of the dotted line on the graph.

2 The graph shows Jane's speed plotted against time during a run.

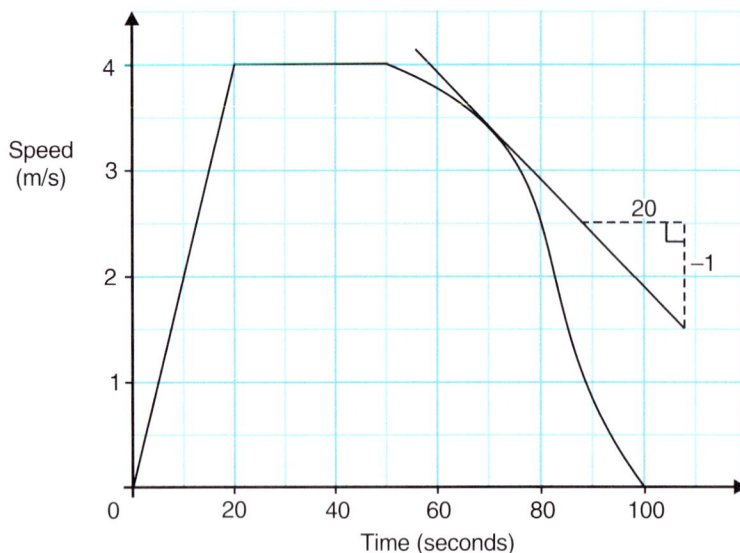

Remember
Gradients measure **rates** of change (increase or decrease).

Acceleration can be calculated from the gradient of a speed-time graph.

When the speed-time graph is **linear** the **acceleration is constant**.

When the speed-time graph is **horizontal** the **speed is constant** and the **acceleration is zero**.

(a) Give a brief description of Jane's run.
(b) Calculate Jane's acceleration:
  (i) during the first 20 seconds of her run,
  (ii) after running for 70 seconds.

(a) Jane accelerates at a constant rate for the first 20 seconds of her run.
She then runs at a constant speed of 4 m/s for 30 seconds before slowing to a stop after 100 seconds.

(b) Acceleration is calculated from the gradient of the speed-time graph.
  (i) Gradient during first 20 seconds $= \dfrac{\text{Change in speed}}{20}$
  So acceleration $= \dfrac{4}{20} = 0.2 \text{ m/s}^2$.

  (ii) The acceleration after running for 70 seconds is given by the gradient of the tangent to the speed-time graph at 70 seconds.
  So acceleration $= \dfrac{-1}{20} = -0.05 \text{ m/s}^2$
  A negative acceleration means that Jane is slowing down, or decelerating.

Units of measurement
Speed = distance ÷ time
Units: metres per second (m/s), kilometres per hour (km/h), etc.

Acceleration = speed ÷ time
Units: metres per second squared (m/s²), kilometres per hour squared (km/h²), etc.

Explain how these units are derived.

Try to do questions 1 to 4 without using your calculator.

1 Look at the points on this distance-time graph.

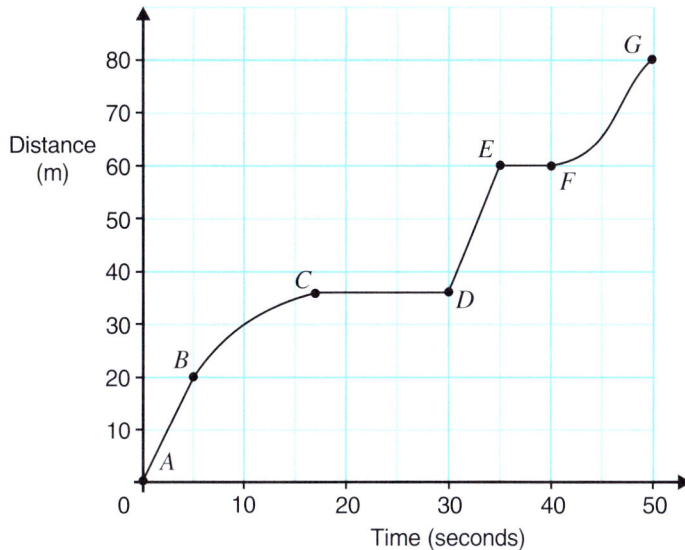

(a) Between which points is:
  (i)   the speed constant,
  (ii) the speed zero,
  (iii) the speed greatest,
  (iv) the acceleration zero?

(b) Find the average speed in metres per second between:
  (i)   A and D,
  (ii) D and G.

2 Look at the points on this speed-time graph.

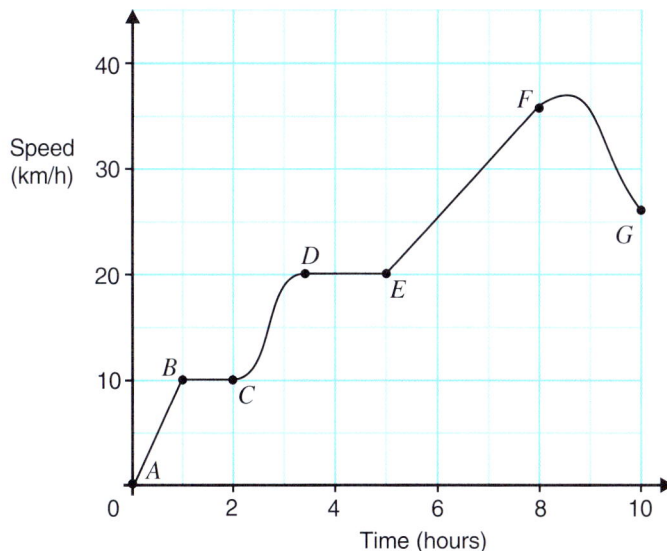

(a) Between which points is:
  (i)   the speed constant,
  (ii) the acceleration constant,
  (iii) the speed greatest,
  (iv) the acceleration greatest,
  (v)   the acceleration zero,
  (vi) the acceleration negative?

(b) Calculate the acceleration between points E and F, stating the units of your answer.

3 This graph shows the progress made by a runner during the first 20 km of a marathon race.

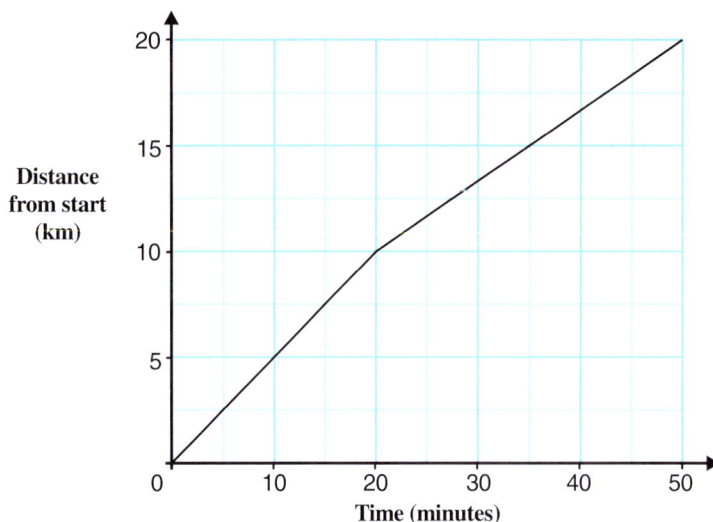

Find the average speed of the runner:
(a) during the first 10 km of the race,
(b) during the second 10 km of the race,
(c) during the first 20 km of the race.

4 The diagram shows a distance-time graph for a bus travelling between two bus stops.

(a) (i)   How long did the journey take?
    (ii) What is the distance between the bus stops?
    (iii) Calculate the average speed of the bus.
(b) Calculate the speed between $t = 0$ and $t = 15$.
(c) Estimate the speed when $t = 30$.

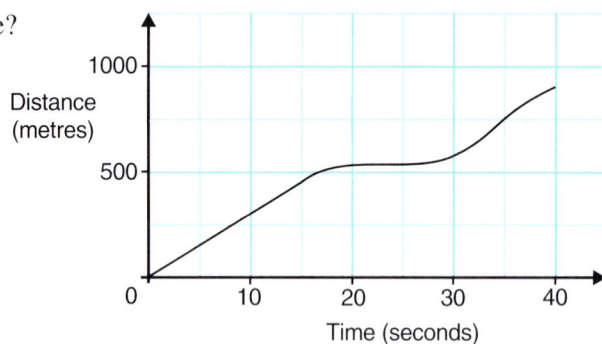

5 The diagram shows a speed-time graph for a train travelling between station A and station B.

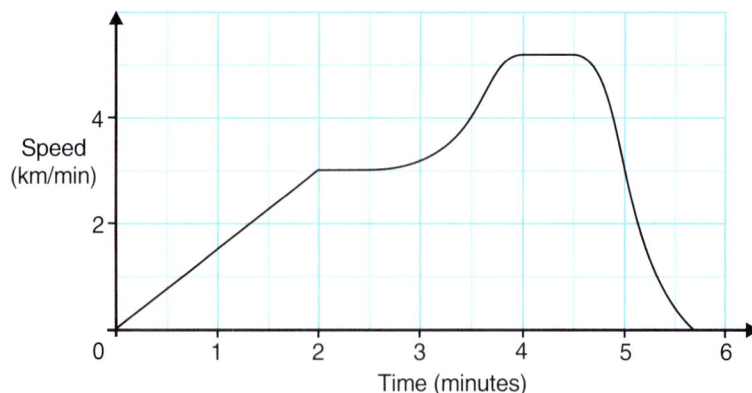

(a) For how long did the train accelerate at a constant rate at the start of its journey?
(b) What was the total time during the journey that the train was **not** accelerating?
(c) Estimate the acceleration 3 minutes after the train left station A, stating the units of your answer.

6 The distance-time graph shows part of the journey of a car on a motorway.

Draw a fully labelled speed-time graph for the same journey.

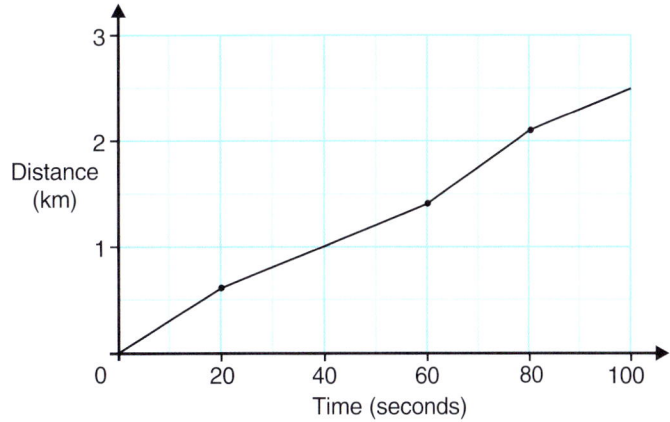

7 A parachutist jumps from a stationary balloon. The diagram shows the graph of his height above ground plotted against time.

Use the graph to find the approximate speed of the parachutist 10 seconds after the start.

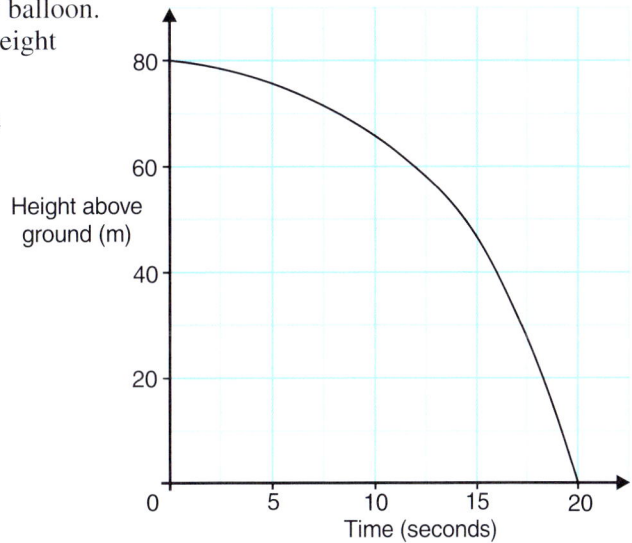

SEG 1997

8 Tom goes for a bicycle ride in the park.
The diagram shows the graph of his speed plotted against time.

(a) Describe Tom's ride.
(b) Calculate Tom's acceleration during the first minute of his ride?
(c) Estimate Tom's acceleration 2 minutes after the start of his ride.
(d) At what time did Tom start to slow down?

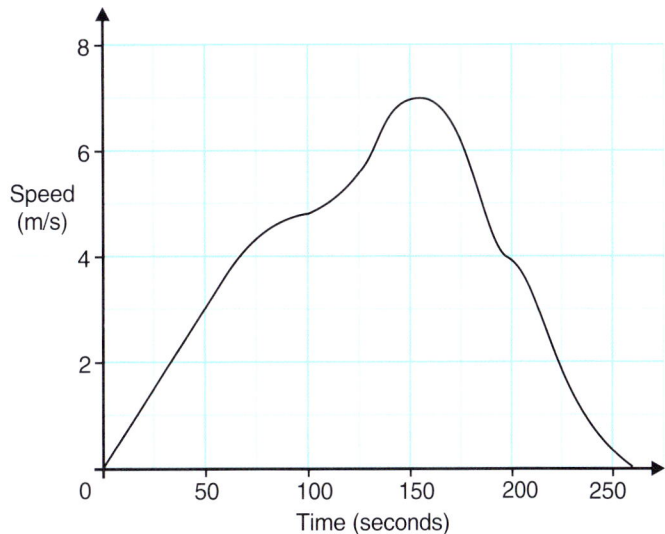

Area under a curve

The area under a curve can be estimated using trapezia.

EXAMPLE

Estimate the shaded area under this curve:
(a) by dividing the area into two trapezia,
(b) by dividing the area into four trapezia.

(a) The total width of the shaded area, measured along the horizontal axis, is 8 cm.
So the width of each trapezium is
8 ÷ 2 = 4 cm.

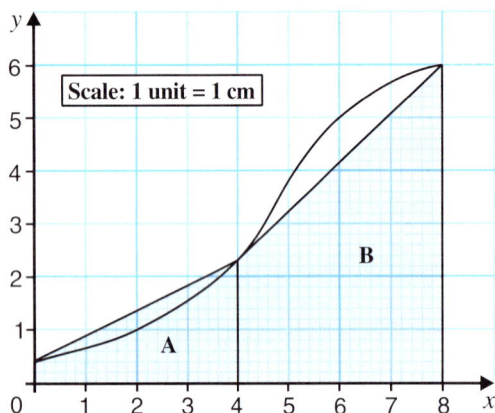
Scale: 1 unit = 1 cm

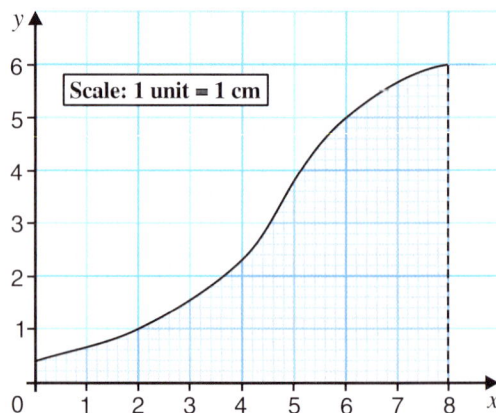
Scale: 1 unit = 1 cm

Trapezium A
Area = 0.5 × (0.4 + 2.3) × 4
    = 5.4 cm²

Trapezium B
Area = 0.5 × (2.3 + 6) × 4
    = 16.6 cm²

Estimate of shaded area = 5.4 + 16.6
                        = 22 cm².

Area of a trapezium

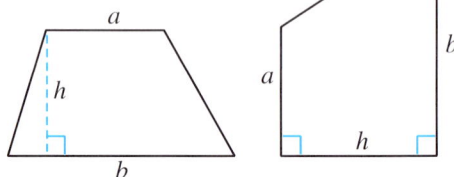

Area = $\frac{1}{2}(a + b)h$

h is the 'width' of each trapezium,
Values for a and b are taken from
the vertical axis of the graph.

(b) The width of each trapezium is 8 ÷ 4 = 2 cm.

x	0	2	4	6	8
y	0.4	1	2.3	5	6

Area P = 0.5 × (0.4 + 1) × 2 = 1.4 cm²
Area Q = 0.5 × (1 + 2.3) × 2 = 3.3 cm²
Area R = 0.5 × (2.3 + 5) × 2 = 7.3 cm²
Area S = 0.5 × (5 + 6)   × 2 = 11 cm²

Estimate of shaded area = 23 cm²

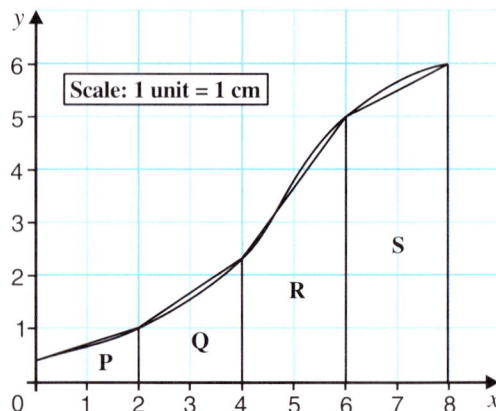
Scale: 1 unit = 1 cm

Which answer gives the better estimate? Why?

The trapezium rule

The **trapezium rule** is used to estimate areas beneath curves when a number of trapezia are involved.

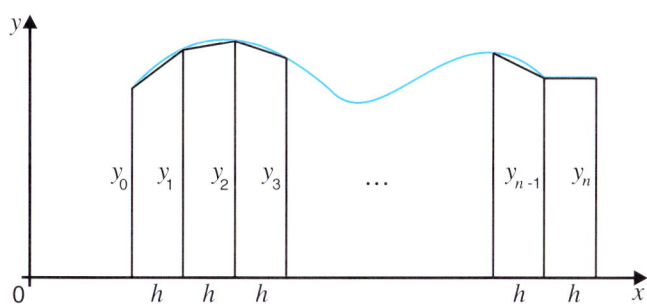

Estimated area $= \frac{1}{2}(y_0 + y_1)h + \frac{1}{2}(y_1 + y_2)h + \frac{1}{2}(y_2 + y_3)h + \ldots + \frac{1}{2}(y_{n-1} + y_n)h$

$\qquad\qquad = \frac{1}{2}(y_0 + y_1 + y_1 + y_2 + y_2 + y_3 + \ldots + y_n)h$

$\qquad\qquad = \frac{1}{2}(y_0 + 2y_1 + 2y_2 + 2y_3 + \ldots + 2y_{n-1} + y_n)h$

EXAMPLE

Estimate the area under the curve $y = 12 - (x - 5)^2$ between $x = 2$ and $x = 7$.

The table shows the values of y for $2 \leqslant x \leqslant 7$.

x	2	3	4	5	6	7
y	3	8	11	12	11	8

The required area has been divided into 5 trapezia each of width 1 unit.
So $n = 5$ and $h = 1$.
The values of y are:
$y_0 = 3$, $y_1 = 8$, $y_2 = 11$, $y_3 = 12$, $y_4 = 11$ and $y_5 = 8$.

Using the trapezium rule:

Estimated area $= \frac{1}{2}(y_0 + 2y_1 + 2y_2 + 2y_3 + 2y_4 + y_5)h$

$\qquad\qquad = \frac{1}{2}(3 + 2 \times 8 + 2 \times 11 + 2 \times 12 + 2 \times 11 + 8)$

$\qquad\qquad = \frac{1}{2}(3 + 16 + 22 + 24 + 22 + 8)$

$\qquad\qquad = \frac{1}{2} \times 95$

$\qquad\qquad = 47.5$ square units

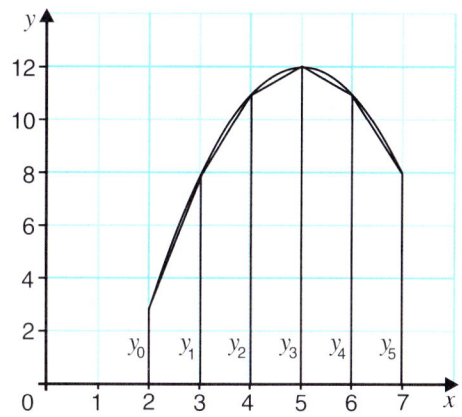

Is this estimated area likely to be more or less than the true area? Why?
Calculate another estimate of the area using 10 trapezia?
This is likely to be a more accurate estimate of the required area. Why?

You may use a calculator.

1   (a)   Draw a sketch showing the lines $y = 2x$, $x = 2$ and $x = 5$.
       (b)   Calculate the area bounded by these lines and the x axis.

2   Estimate the area beneath the curve $y = 10 - x^2$ between $x = -1$ and $x = 3$ using:
       (a)   2 trapezia,   (b)   4 trapezia,   (c)   8 trapezia.

3   Estimate the area between the curve $y = \frac{1}{2}x^2 + 2$ and the x axis between the y axis and the line $x = 4$ using:
       (a)   2 trapezia,   (b)   4 trapezia,   (c)   8 trapezia.

4   (a)   Draw a sketch graph showing $y = x^2$ and $y = 4x$, clearly showing the points where the curve and line intersect.
       (b)   Estimate the area between the curve, $y = x^2$ and the line, $y = 4x$.

5   Use the trapezium rule with 5 strips to estimate the area between the curve $y = x^2 - 5x$ and the x axis.

6   Estimate the area beneath the graph and the x axis between $x = 4$ and $x = 14$.

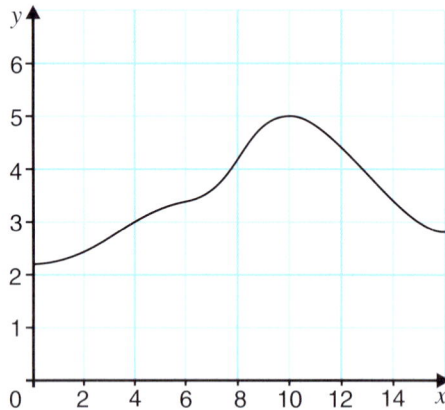

7   Use the trapezium rule to find the approximate area of the region between the curve, the x axis, the y axis and the line $x = 5$.

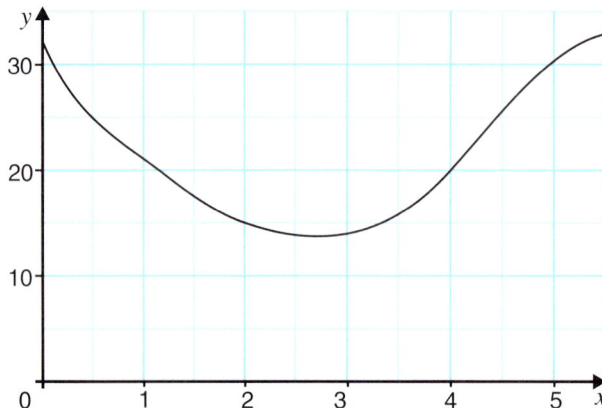

210

Interpreting the area under a graph

A pump delivers fuel at the rate of 2 litres per minute.
This graph shows the rate of delivery (flow) against time.

In the first 5 minutes the pump delivers $5 \times 2 = 10$ litres.
This is equivalent to the shaded area on the graph.

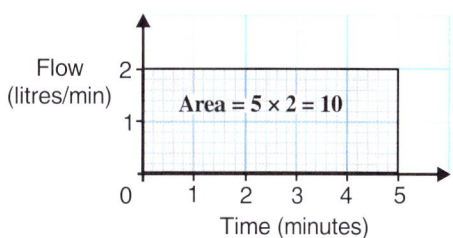

$$\frac{\text{litres}}{\text{minutes}} \times \text{minutes} = \text{litres}$$

Part of graph	Measure	Units
Vertical axis	rate of delivery	litres per minute
Horizontal axis	time	minutes
Area under graph	amount delivered	litres

The rate of delivery (flow) is the rate of change of **volume** with respect to time.
The area under the graph measures the **volume** delivered in litres.

A car travels at a speed of 20 m/s.
This graph shows speed against time.

In the first 10 seconds the car travels $10 \times 20 = 200$ metres.
This is equivalent to the shaded area on the graph.

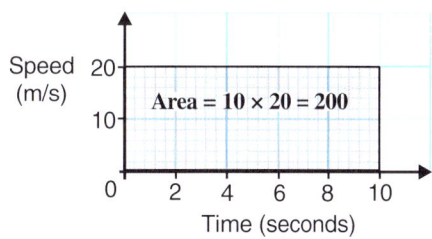

$$\frac{\text{metres}}{\text{seconds}} \times \text{seconds} = \text{metres}$$

Part of graph	Measure	Units
Vertical axis	speed	metres per second
Horizontal axis	time	seconds
Area under graph	distance travelled	metres

Speed is the rate of change of **distance** with respect to time.
The area under the graph measures the **distance** travelled in metres.

EXAMPLES

1 What is measured by the area beneath each of these graphs?

(a)

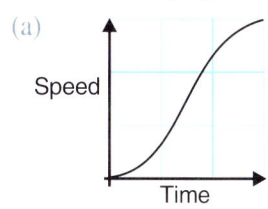

Speed is the rate of change of distance.
So the area under the graph is a measure of distance.

(b)

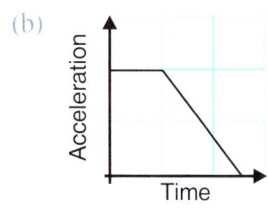

Acceleration is the rate of change of speed.
So the area under the graph is a measure of speed.

2 In a competition cyclists ride for exactly 5 minutes. This speed-time graph shows the journey of one of the competitors.

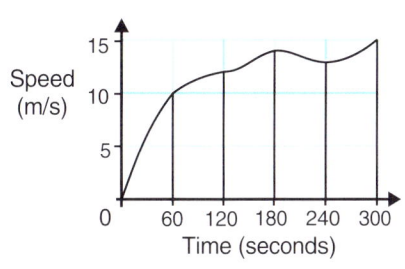

Estimate the distance this cyclist rides.

Distance = area under speed-time graph.
Divide the area into 5 strips each of width 60 seconds.
Using the trapezium rule, area
$= \frac{1}{2} (0 + 2 \times 10 + 2 \times 12 + 2 \times 14 + 2 \times 13 + 15) \times 60$
$= \frac{1}{2} (0 + 20 + 24 + 28 + 26 + 15) \times 60$
$= \frac{1}{2} \times 113 \times 60 = 3390$
So distance cyclist travels = 3390 metres.

1 (a) Calculate the shaded area in each of the following graphs.

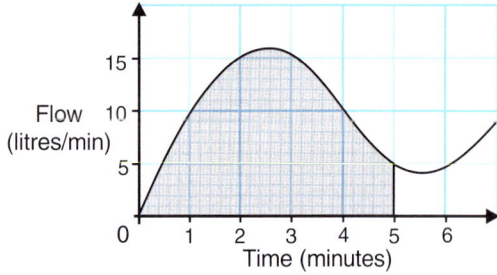
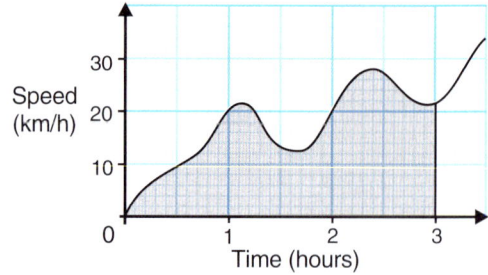

(b) For each graph in part (a):
    (i) state the measure the shaded area represents,
    (ii) state the units of the measure.

2 This is a velocity-time graph for a car which took 10 seconds to reduce its speed from 11 m/s to 0 m/s.

(a) Calculate, by a suitable method of estimation, the area under the curve between 0 seconds and 6 seconds.

(b) What does your answer to part (a) represent?

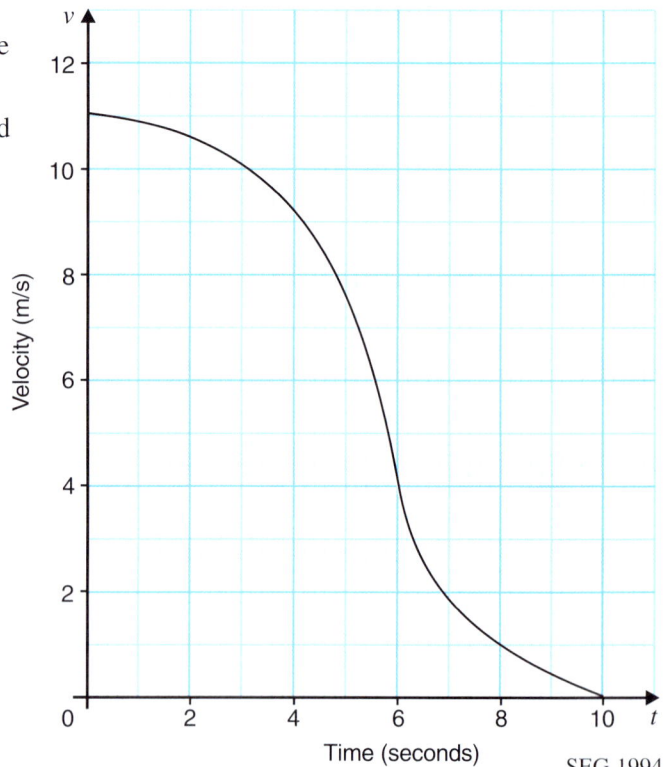

SEG 1994

3 This graph shows the speed of a bus plotted against time.

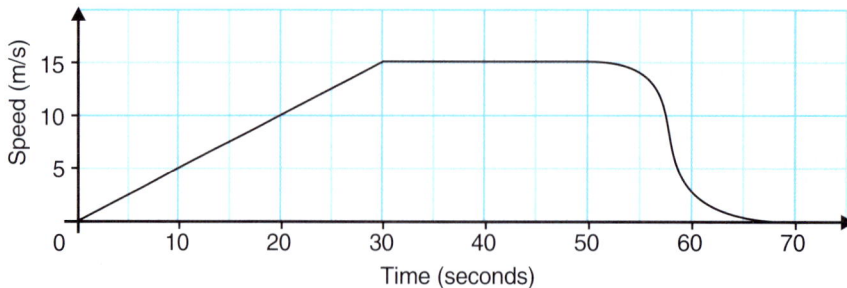

(a) Describe the motion of the bus for the **first 50 seconds** of the journey.
(b) Calculate the approximate **total** distance travelled by the bus over the 65 seconds.

SEG 1994

4 A velocity-time graph for a sports car as it accelerates from 0 to 30 metres per second in 8 seconds is shown.

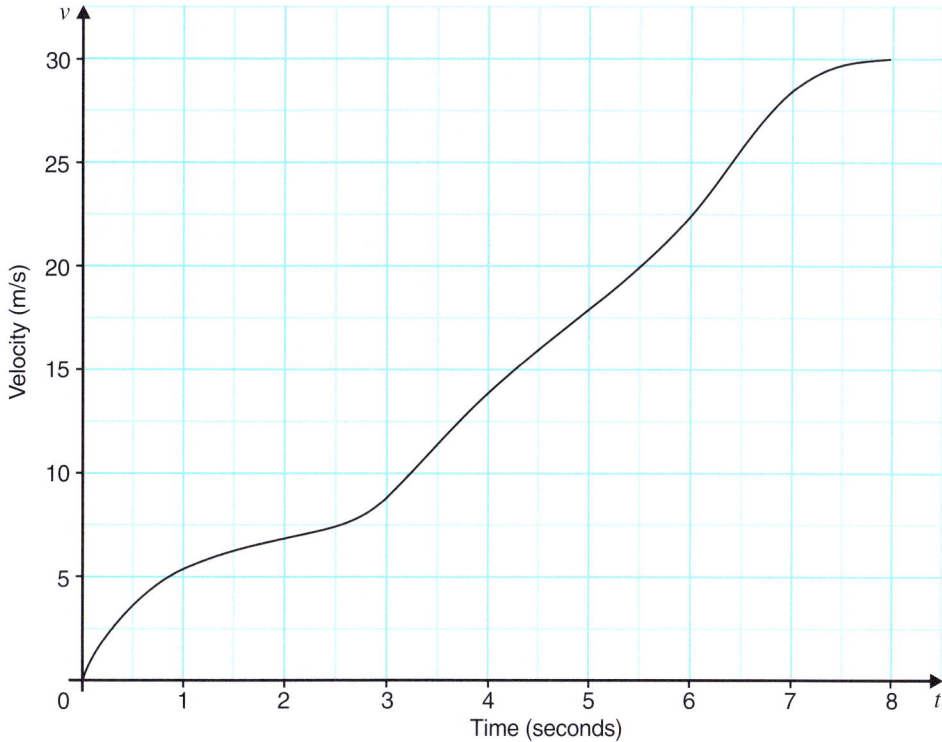

Use the graph to estimate the distance the car travels in the 8 seconds.

SEG 1996

5 The diagram shows the speed-time graph of a bus as its travels between two bus stops.
Calculate the time it takes to travel **half** the distance between the bus stops.

SEG 1998

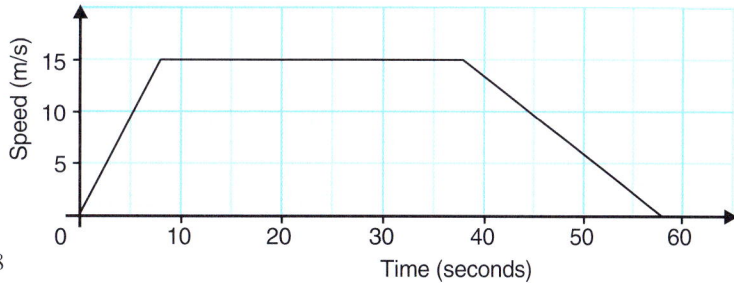

6 A firm manufactures a casting of a metal alloy which is then machined into part of a child's toy.
The casting is in the form of a prism.
The prism and its cross-section are shown in the diagram.

The firm receives an order for 2000 castings.
Assuming 5% wastage, calculate the volume of alloy required.

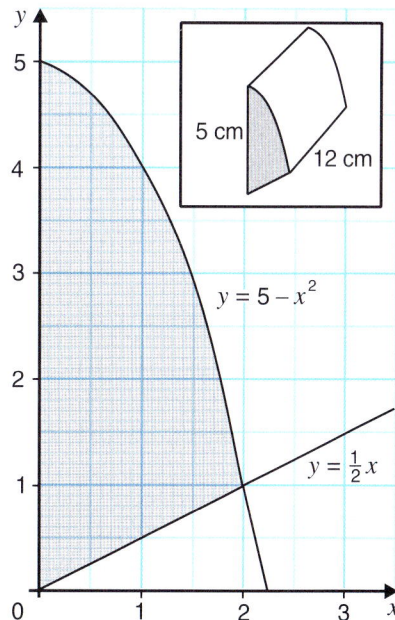

$y = 5 - x^2$

$y = \frac{1}{2}x$

7 An oil tanker is involved in a collision at sea.
After the collision oil leaks from the tanker into the sea.
This graph shows how the rate that the oil leaks varies with time.

Estimate the area under the curve between 0 and 5 hours after the collision.
What does this area represent?

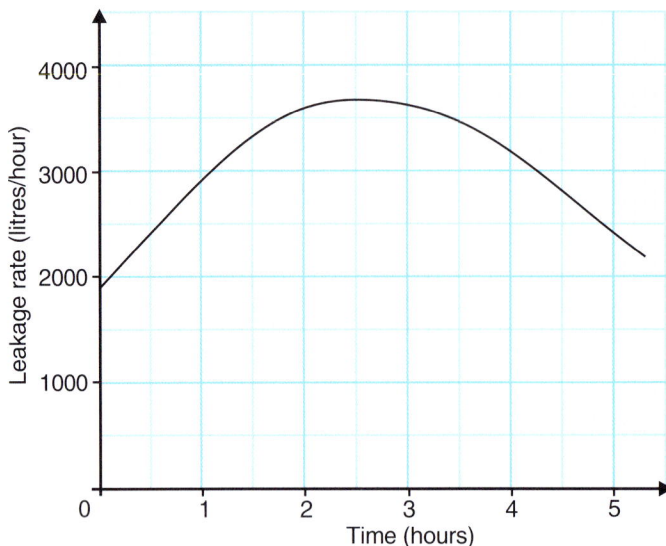

8 Water from a boiling kettle is poured into a bowl.
The rate that the water is cooling in °Celsius per minute at various times is shown in this table.

Time (min)	0	2	4	6	8	10	12	14
Rate of cooling (°C/min)	3.200	2.954	2.827	2.517	2.324	2.145	1.980	1.828

(a) Draw a graph of rate of cooling against time.
(b) Use your graph to estimate the area under the curve between 0 and 10 minutes after the water starts to cool.

The temperature of the water when it starts to cool is 100° Celsius.
(c) Use your answer to (b) to estimate the temperature of the water 10 minutes after it starts to cool.

9 (a) Areas (A) beneath the line $y = 2$ between the y axis and various values of x are shown below.

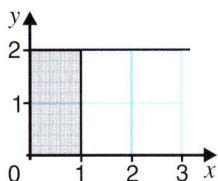
When $x = 1$, $A = 2$

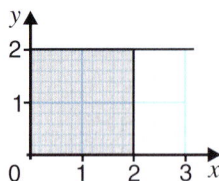
When $x = 2$, $A = 4$

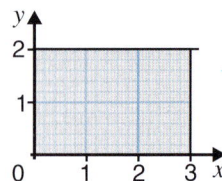
When $x = 3$, $A = 6$

(i) Find some more values for A for other values of x.
(ii) Draw a graph of A plotted against x and find an equation expressing A in terms of x.
(b) Repeat (a) for the following graphs:
(i) $y = 1$, (ii) $y = 3$, (iii) $y = 4$, (iv) $y = 10$.
What do you notice?
(c) Repeat (a) for the following graphs:
(i) $y = x$, (ii) $y = 2x$, (iii) $y = 3x$, (iv) $y = 4x$.
What do you notice?

214

- Gradient $= \dfrac{\text{distance up}}{\text{distance across}} = \dfrac{\text{difference in } y \text{ coordinates}}{\text{difference in } x \text{ coordinates}}$

  A **chord** is a straight line joining two points on a curve.

  A **tangent** to a curve at a point is a straight line which:

  touches the curve at the point,

  is parallel to an enlarged section of the curve close to the point.

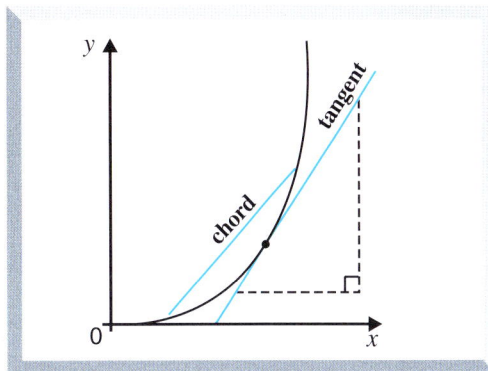

- The **gradient of a curve** at a given point can be **estimated** by:

  drawing a tangent to the curve at the point,

  calculating the gradient of the tangent.

- A **gradient** measures the **rate of change** of one quantity with respect to another.

  A **positive** gradient represents a **rate of increase**.

  A **negative** gradient represents a **rate of decrease**.

- The gradient of a **distance-time graph** gives the speed.

  Speed is the rate of change of distance with respect to time.

  When the distance-time graph is **linear** the **speed is constant**.

  When the distance-time graph is **horizontal** the **speed is zero**.

- The gradient of a **speed-time graph** gives the acceleration.

  Acceleration is the rate of change of speed with respect to time.

  When the speed-time graph is **linear** the **acceleration is constant**.

  When the speed-time graph is **horizontal** the **speed is constant** and the **acceleration is zero.**

- The **trapezium rule** is used to estimate the **area under a curve**.

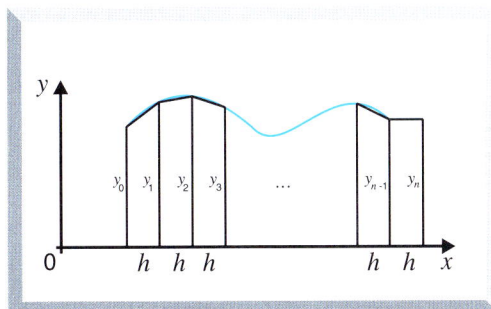

Estimated area $= \frac{1}{2}(y_0 + y_1)h + \frac{1}{2}(y_1 + y_2)h + \frac{1}{2}(y_2 + y_3)h + ... + \frac{1}{2}(y_{n-1} + y_n)h$

$= \frac{1}{2}(y_0 + 2y_1 + 2y_2 + 2y_3 + ... + 2y_{n-1} + y_n)h$

- The area under the curve on a speed-time graph measures distance.

  The area under the curve on a flow rate-time graph measures volume.

1 Aisha takes part in a race. The graph shows her distance from the starting line during the race.

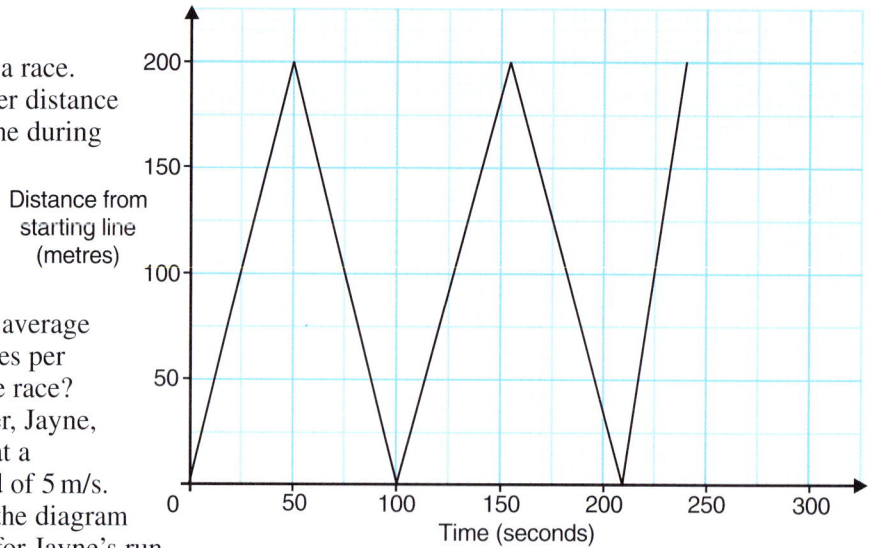

Distance from starting line (metres)

(a) What was her average speed, in metres per second, for the race?

(b) Another runner, Jayne, runs the race at a constant speed of 5 m/s. On a copy of the diagram draw a graph for Jayne's run.

Time (seconds)

SEG 1998

2 The graph represents a swimming race between Robert and James.

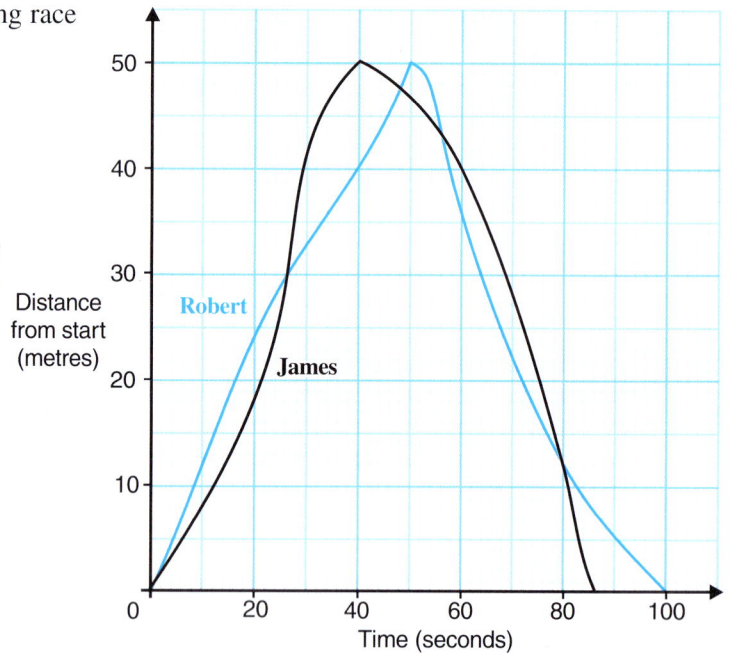

(a) At what time did James overtake Robert for the second time?

(b) What was the **maximum** distance between the swimmers during the race?

(c) Who was swimming faster at 56 seconds? How can you tell?

Distance from start (metres)

Robert

James

Time (seconds)

SEG 1995

3 The distance-time graph of a journey made on a bicycle is shown.

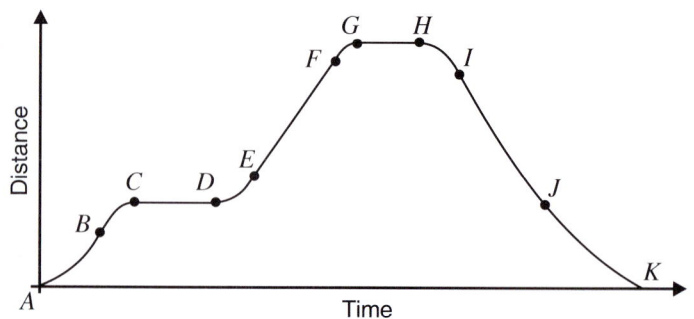

(a) Between which two points is the bicycle slowing down?

(b) Between which two points is the bicycle moving at a constant speed and travelling away from the starting point?

(c) Between which two points is the bicycle accelerating and travelling back to the starting point?

Distance

Time

SEG 1996

4 Water flows into a container.
The diagram shows the depth, d, plotted against time, t.

Find the rate of increase of depth when $t = 6$ seconds.

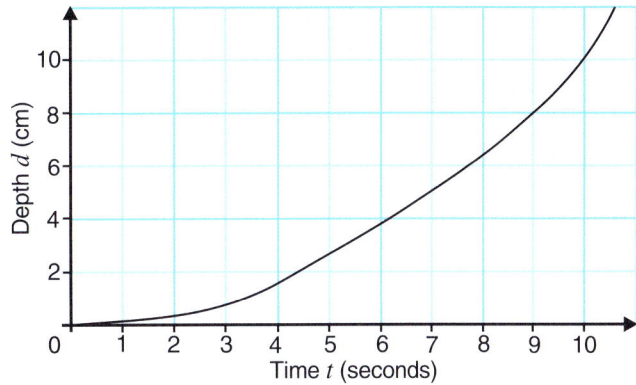

5 A rally car goes on a short time trial on a woodland track.
Its velocity-time graph is shown.

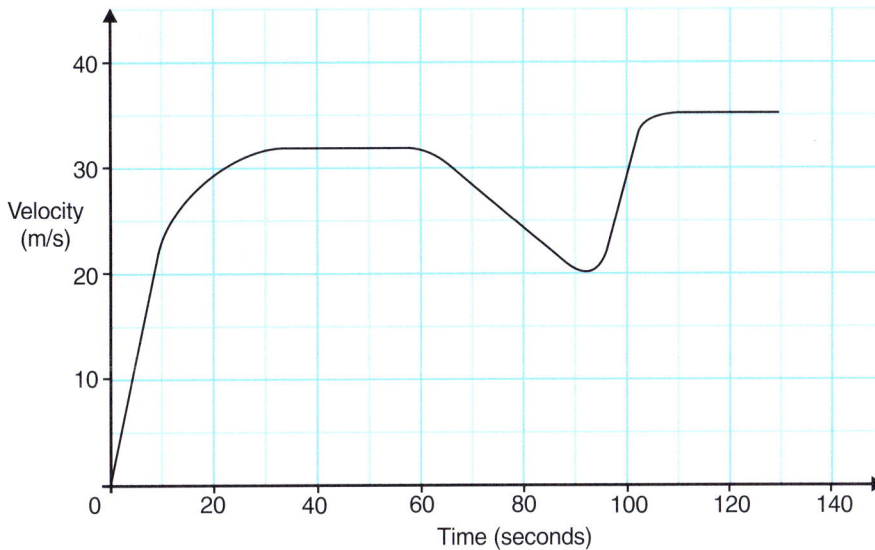

(a) Use the graph to find an estimate of the acceleration of the car 20 seconds after the start.
(b) Use an appropriate method to estimate how far the rally car has travelled in the first 80 seconds.

SEG 1998

6 A speed-time graph of a plane travelling between two airports is illustrated below.

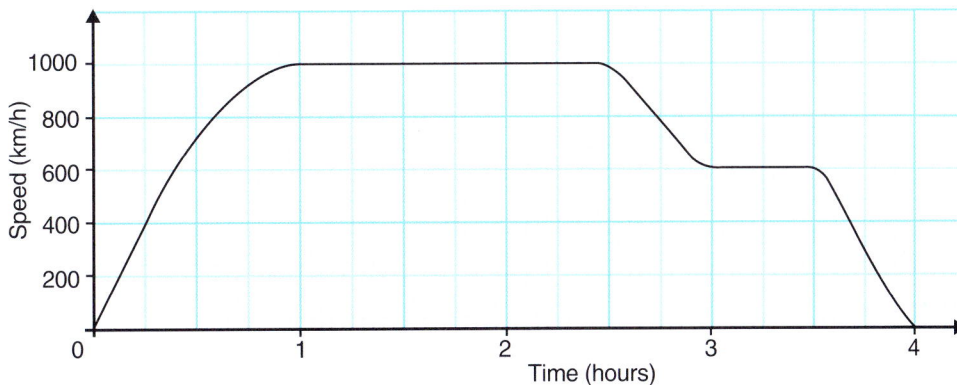

(a) What is the maximum cruising speed of the plane?
(b) Estimate the maximum acceleration of the plane.
(c) Estimate the distance travelled by the plane in kilometres.

SEG 1996

7 The graph represents the journey of a train between two stations.

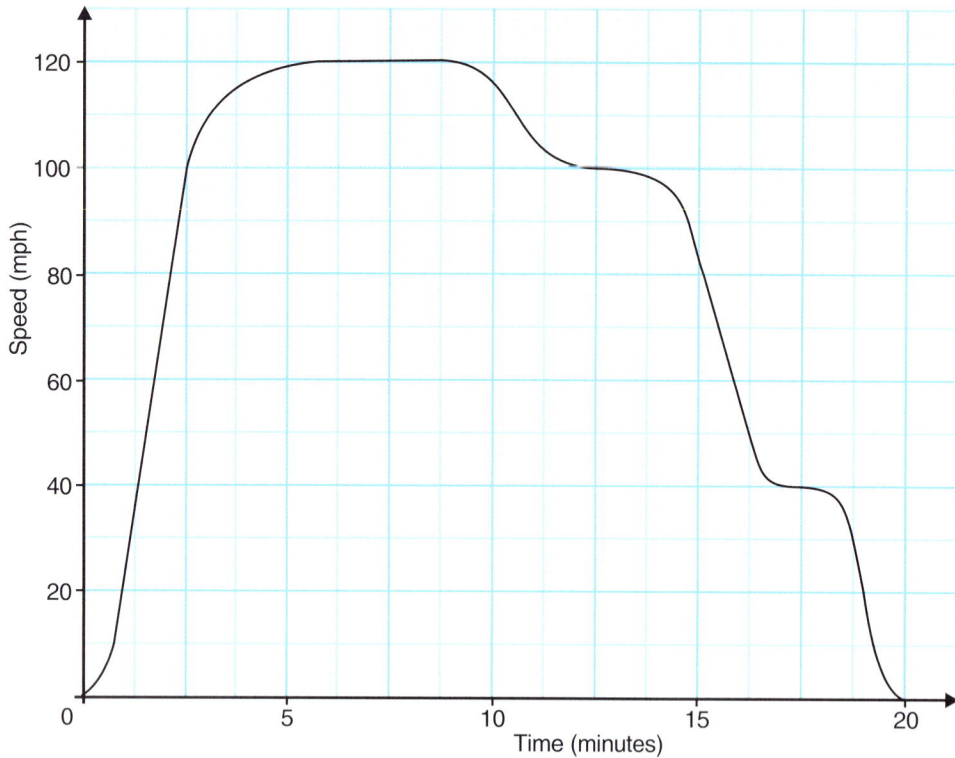

(a) How long did the train travel at its maximum speed?
(b) Describe the train's journey during the last five minutes.
(c) Use the graph to estimate the train's acceleration at three minutes.
(d) Calculate, by a suitable method of estimation, the distance, in miles, travelled by the train between 0 and 10 minutes.

SEG 1997

8 This diagram shows the speed-time graph of a racing car on the first lap of a race.

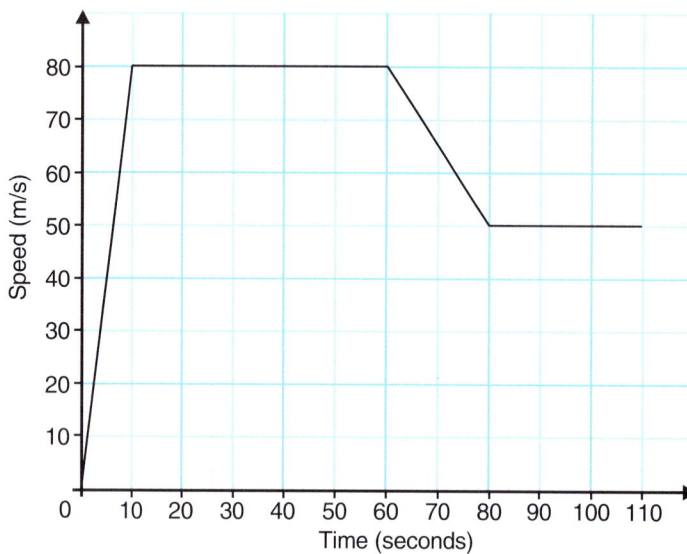

(a) What is the length of one lap?
(b) How long does it take the car to complete half the lap?

9 This graph shows the speed of a train between two stations. The journey takes 80 seconds.

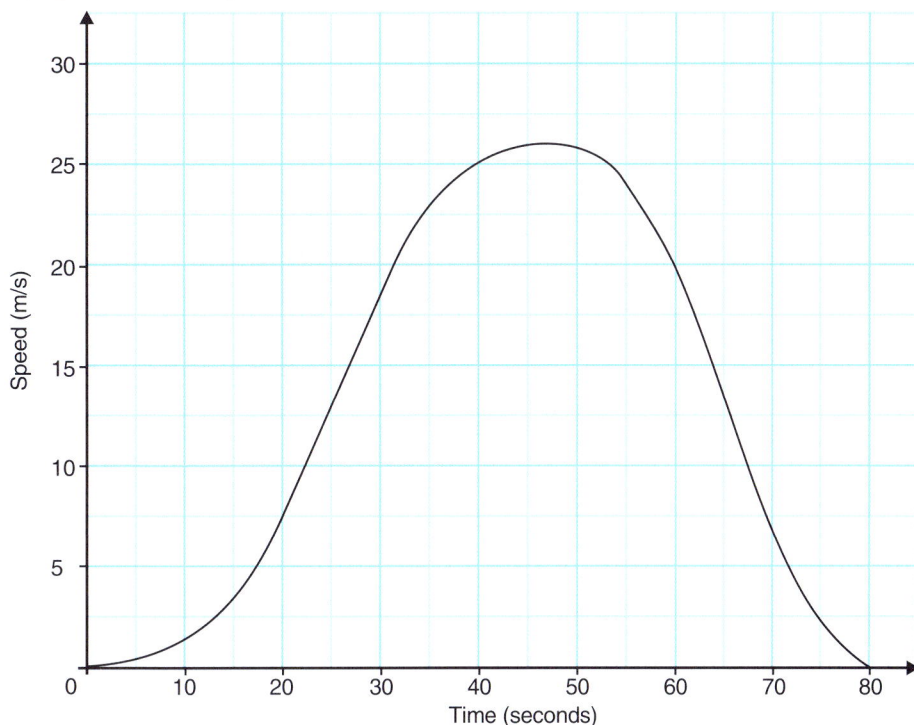

(a) Find the acceleration of the train 40 seconds after the start of its journey.

(b) Use an appropriate method, with intervals of 10 seconds, to estimate the distance between the stations.

SEG 2000 S

10 The graph below shows the velocity of a car over the time interval $0 \leqslant t \leqslant 20$, where t is time in seconds and v is velocity in metres per second.

(a) Use the graph to estimate the acceleration of the car at $t = 7.5$.

(b) (i) Estimate the area under the graph for the interval $0 \leqslant t \leqslant 10$.

(ii) What does this area represent?

SEG 1998

11 A spherical tank is filled with liquid gas at a constant rate.
The graph shows how the depth of the liquid gas in the tank varies with time.

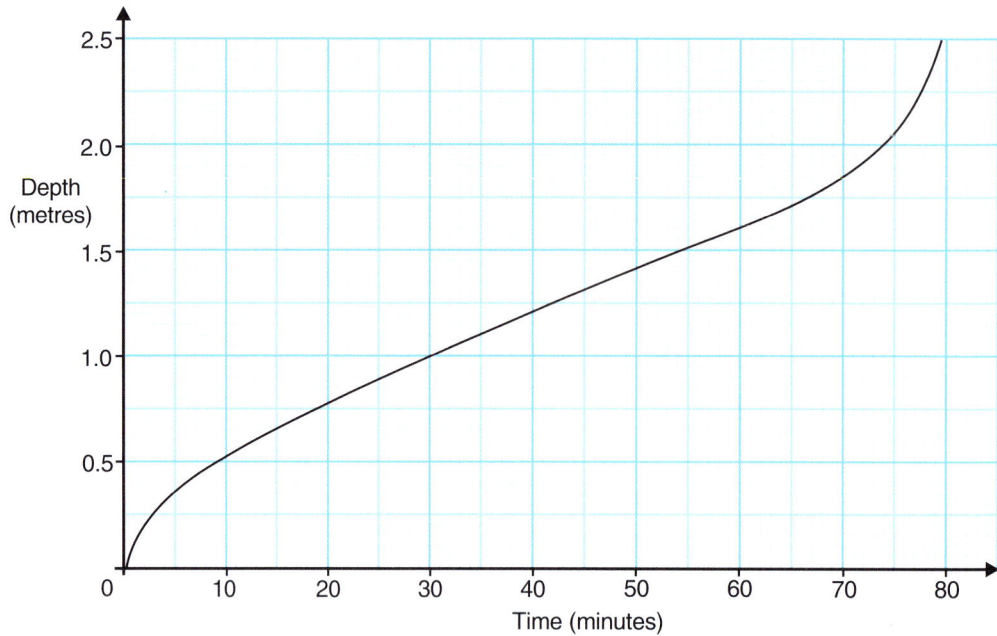

(a) Find the gradient of the curve at the following times:
   (i) 10 minutes   (ii) 40 minutes   (iii) 70 minutes
(b) What do these gradients represent?

12 A paddling pool is filled with water from a hose pipe.
The rate of increase of the depth of the water in the pool is plotted against time.

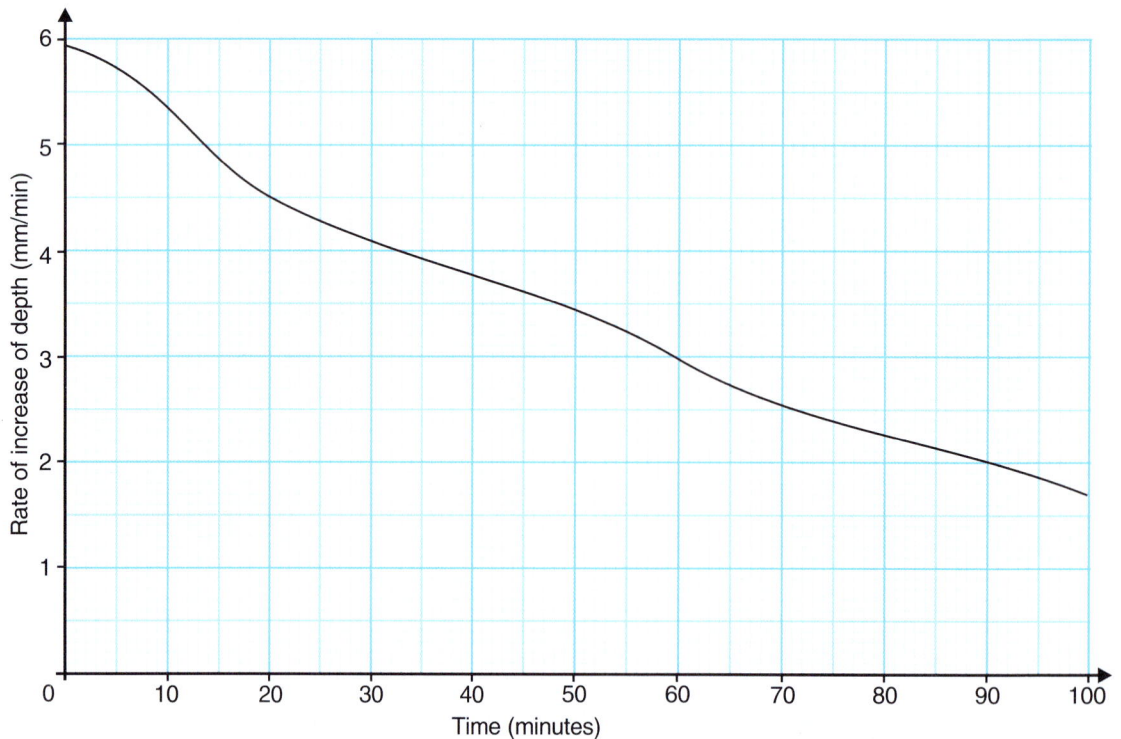

Use the graph to estimate the depth of water in the pool after 100 minutes.

CHAPTER 16

Transforming Graphs ●●●●●

Transformations, such as **translations** and **stretches**, can be used to change the position and size of a graph.
The equation of the transformed (new) graph is related to the equation of the original graph.

Transformations of geometrical shapes is covered in Chapter 25.

| Original graph | Transformation | New graph |

Translating a graph

The graph of $y = x^2$ is transformed to the graph of $y = x^2 + 2$ by a **translation**.

All points on the original graph are moved the **same distance** in the **same direction** without twisting or turning.

The translation has vector $\begin{pmatrix} 0 \\ 2 \end{pmatrix}$.

This means that the curve moves 2 units vertically up.

Draw the following graphs:
  $y = x^2$ for $-2 \leqslant x \leqslant 2$,
  $y = x^2 - 3$ for $-2 \leqslant x \leqslant 2$.
Describe how the graph of $y = x^2$ is transformed to the graph of $y = x^2 - 3$.

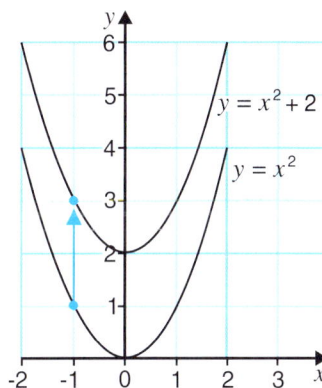

Original graph: $y = x^2$

Transformation: translation with vector $\begin{pmatrix} 0 \\ 2 \end{pmatrix}$.

New graph: $y = x^2 + 2$

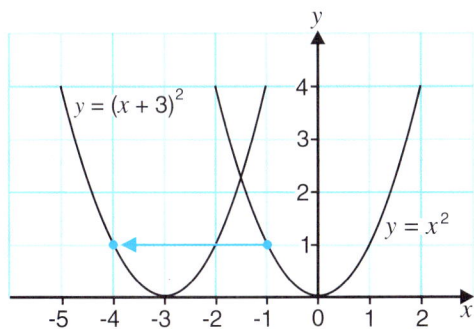

The graph of $y = x^2$ is transformed to the graph of $y = (x + 3)^2$ by a **translation**.

The translation has vector $\begin{pmatrix} -3 \\ 0 \end{pmatrix}$.

This means that the curve moves 3 units horizontally to the left.

Original graph: $y = x^2$

Transformation: translation with vector $\begin{pmatrix} -3 \\ 0 \end{pmatrix}$.

New graph: $y = (x + 3)^2$

Draw the following graphs:
  $y = x^2$ for $-2 \leqslant x \leqslant 2$,
  $y = (x - 2)^2$ for $0 \leqslant x \leqslant 4$.
Describe how the graph of $y = x^2$ is transformed to the graph of $y = (x + 3)^2$.

The graph of $y = x^2$ is transformed to the graph of $y = 2x^2$ by a **stretch**.

The stretch is **from** the x axis and is **parallel** to the y axis. The stretch has scale factor 2.

This means that y coordinates on the graph of $y = x^2$ are doubled to obtain the corresponding y coordinates on the graph of $y = 2x^2$.

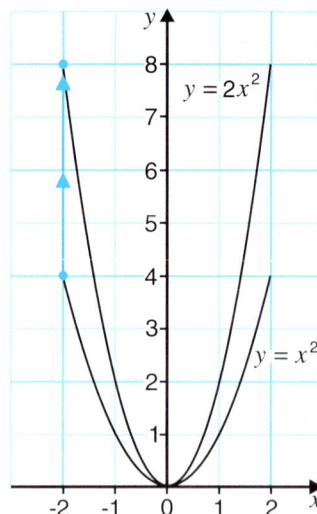

> *Draw the following graphs:*
> $\quad y = x^2$ *for* $-2 \leqslant x \leqslant 2$,
> $\quad y = 3x^2$ *for* $-2 \leqslant x \leqslant 2$.
> *Describe how the graph of* $y = x^2$ *is transformed to the graph of* $y = 3x^2$.

Original graph: $y = x^2$
Transformation: stretch from x axis, parallel to y axis, scale factor 2.
New graph: $y = 2x^2$

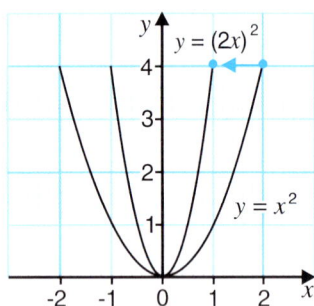

Original graph: $y = x^2$
Transformation: stretch from y axis, parallel to x axis, scale factor $\frac{1}{2}$.
New graph: $y = (2x)^2$

The graph of $y = x^2$ is transformed to the graph of $y = (2x)^2$ by a **stretch**.

The stretch is **from** the y axis and is **parallel** to the x axis. The stretch has scale factor $\frac{1}{2}$.

This means that x coordinates on the graph of $y = x^2$ are halved to obtain the corresponding x coordinates on the graph of $y = (2x)^2$.

> *Draw the following graphs:*
> $\quad y = x^2$ *for* $-2 \leqslant x \leqslant 2$,
> $\quad y = (4x)^2$ *for* $-0.5 \leqslant x \leqslant 0.5$.
> *Describe how the graph of* $y = x^2$ *is transformed to the graph of* $y = (4x)^2$.

In general

Original graph	New graph	Transformation
$y = x^2$	$y = x^2 + a$	**translation**, vector $\begin{pmatrix} 0 \\ a \end{pmatrix}$.
$y = x^2$	$y = (x + a)^2$	**translation**, vector $\begin{pmatrix} -a \\ 0 \end{pmatrix}$.
$y = x^2$	$y = ax^2$	**stretch**, from the x axis, parallel to the y axis, scale factor a.
$y = x^2$	$y = (ax)^2$	**stretch**, from the y axis, parallel to the x axis, scale factor $\frac{1}{a}$.

The general rules for translating and stretching the graph of $y = x^2$ apply to **all** graphs.

You may use a graphical calculator.

1 (a) Complete tables of values for:
(i) $y = x^3$ for $-2 \leqslant x \leqslant 2$,
(ii) $y = x^3 + 2$ for $-2 \leqslant x \leqslant 2$,
(iii) $y = (x - 3)^3$ for $1 \leqslant x \leqslant 5$,
(iv) $y = 2x^3$ for $-2 \leqslant x \leqslant 2$.

(b) Use your tables of values to draw graphs of each of the equations in (a).

(c) Describe how the graph of $y = x^3$ is transformed to:
(i) the graph of $y = x^3 + 2$,
(ii) the graph of $y = (x - 3)^3$,
(iii) the graph of $y = 2x^3$.

(d) Write down the equations of the graphs obtained when the graph of $y = x^3$ is transformed by:
(i) a translation with vector $\begin{pmatrix} 0 \\ -5 \end{pmatrix}$,
(ii) a translation with vector $\begin{pmatrix} 2 \\ 0 \end{pmatrix}$.

2 In this diagram, each of the graphs labelled **a**, **b**, **c** and **d** are transformations of the graph $y = x^2$.

What are the equations of graphs **a**, **b**, **c** and **d**?

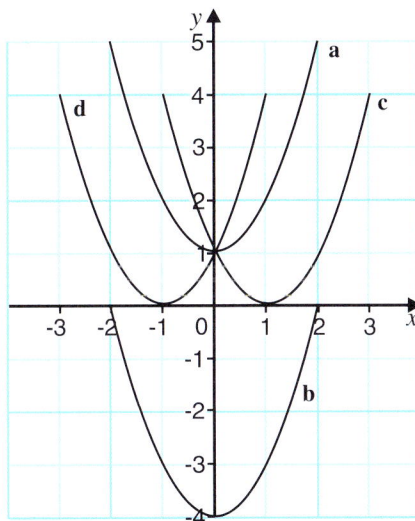

3 (a) Draw the graphs of:
(i) $y = x^2 + 2x$ for $-4 \leqslant x \leqslant 2$,
(ii) $y = x^2 + 2x + 3$ for $-4 \leqslant x \leqslant 2$.
Describe how the graph of $y = x^2 + 2x$ is transformed to the graph of $y = x^2 + 2x + 3$.

(b) Replacing x with $(x - 2)$ in $y = x^2 + 2x$ gives $y = (x - 2)^2 + 2(x - 2)$.
(i) Draw the graph of $y = x^2 + 2x$ for $-4 \leqslant x \leqslant 2$.
(ii) Draw the graph of $y = (x - 2)^2 + 2(x - 2)$ for $-2 \leqslant x \leqslant 4$.
Describe how the graph of $y = x^2 + 2x$ is transformed to the graph of $y = (x - 2)^2 + 2(x - 2)$.

(c) Draw the graphs of:
(i) $y = x^2 + 2x$ for $-4 \leqslant x \leqslant 2$,
(ii) $y = 2(x^2 + 2x)$ for $-4 \leqslant x \leqslant 2$.
Describe how the graph of $y = x^2 + 2x$ is transformed to the graph of $y = 2(x^2 + 2x)$.

(d) Replacing x with $\frac{1}{2}x$ in $y = x^2 + 2x$ gives $y = \left(\frac{1}{2}x\right)^2 + 2\left(\frac{1}{2}x\right)$.
Draw the graphs of:
(i) $y = x^2 + 2x$ for $-4 \leqslant x \leqslant 2$,
(ii) $y = \left(\frac{1}{2}x\right)^2 + 2\left(\frac{1}{2}x\right)$ for $-8 \leqslant x \leqslant 4$.
Describe how the graph of $y = x^2 + 2x$ is transformed to the graph of $y = \left(\frac{1}{2}x\right)^2 + 2\left(\frac{1}{2}x\right)$.

4 In this diagram, each of the graphs **a, b, c** and **d** are stretches of the graph of $y = x^2$.

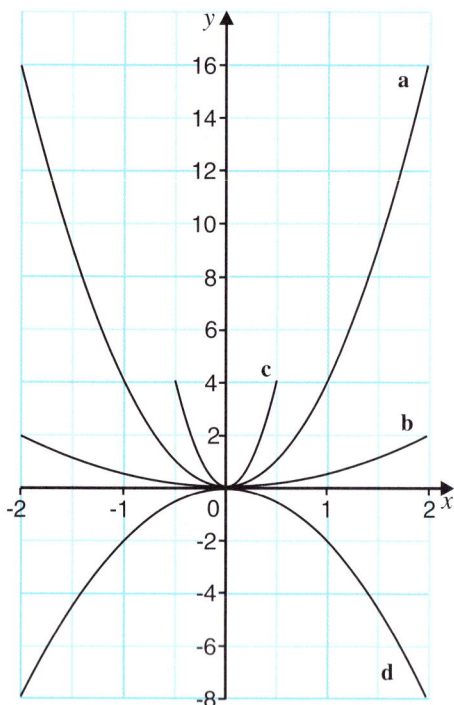

What are the equations of graphs **a, b, c** and **d**?

5 The graph of $y = 4 - x^2$ for $-2 \leqslant x \leqslant 2$ is transformed by:

(a) a translation of $\begin{pmatrix} 0 \\ 5 \end{pmatrix}$,

(b) a stretch from the x axis, parallel to the y axis, with scale factor 2,

(c) a stretch from the y axis, parallel to the x axis, with scale factor 2.

In each case draw the original graph and its transformation.

Write down the equation of each transformed graph.

6 The graph of $y = x^4 - x^3$ for $-2 \leqslant x \leqslant 2$ is transformed by:

(a) a translation of $\begin{pmatrix} 0 \\ -5 \end{pmatrix}$,

(b) a translation of $\begin{pmatrix} 3 \\ 0 \end{pmatrix}$,

(c) a stretch from the x axis, parallel to the y axis, with scale factor $\frac{1}{2}$.

(d) a stretch from the y axis, parallel to the x axis, with scale factor 2.

In each case write down the equation of the transformed graph.

Check each equation by drawing its graph.

Function notation

Function notation is an alternative way of expressing the relationship between two variables.

Using x and y

Input, x ⟶ | function (f) e.g. *square* | ⟶ Output, y

This notation gives $y = x^2$

Using function notation

Input (x) ⟶ | function (f) e.g. *square* | ⟶ Output, f(x)

This notation gives f$(x) = x^2$

f(x) means 'a function of x'. In general, $y = $ f(x).

For example:

The equation $y = x^5$ can be expressed in function notation as f$(x) = x^5$, where $y = $ f(x).

Letters other than f can be used.

For example:

The equation $y = \dfrac{1}{x^2 + 1}$ can be expressed in function notation as g$(x) = \dfrac{1}{x^2 + 1}$, where $y = $ g(x).

EXAMPLES

1 The function f is defined as $f(x) = x^2$.
Describe how each of the following graphs are related to the graph of $y = f(x)$.

(a) $y = f(x) + 2$ (b) $y = f(x + 2)$ (d) $y = 2f(x)$ (d) $y = f(2x)$

(a) Because, $f(x) = x^2$,
$y = f(x) + 2$ is equivalent to
$y = x^2 + 2$.
So the graph of $y = f(x)$ is
transformed to the graph of
$y = f(x) + 2$ by:
a **translation** with vector $\begin{pmatrix} 0 \\ 2 \end{pmatrix}$.

(b) Because $f(x) = x^2$,
$y = f(x + 2)$ is equivalent to
$y = (x + 2)^2$.

$f(x) = x^2$
Substitute $(x + 2)$ for x.
$f(x + 2) = (x + 2)^2$

So the graph of $y = f(x)$
is transformed to the graph of
$y = f(x + 2)$ by:
a **translation** with vector $\begin{pmatrix} -2 \\ 0 \end{pmatrix}$.

(c) $y = 2f(x)$ is equivalent to $y = 2x^2$.
So the graph of $y = f(x)$ is
transformed to the graph of
$y = 2f(x)$ by:
a **stretch** from the x axis, parallel
to the y axis, scale factor 2.

(d) $y = f(2x)$ is equivalent to $y = (2x)^2$.

$f(x) = x^2$
Substitute $(2x)$ for x.
$f(2x) = (2x)^2$

So the graph of $y = f(x)$
is transformed to the graph of
$y = f(2x)$ by:
a **stretch** from the y axis, parallel to the
x axis, scale factor $\frac{1}{2}$.

2 The diagram shows the graph of $y = f(x)$.
On separate diagrams show the graphs of:

(a) $y = f(x)$ and $y = f(x) - 2$,
(b) $y = f(x)$ and $y = f(x + 3)$,
(c) $y = f(x)$ and $y = 2f(x)$,
(d) $y = f(x)$ and $y = f(2x)$.

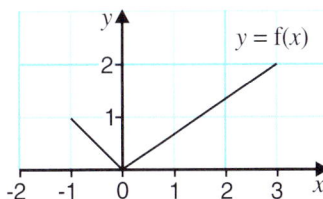

(a)
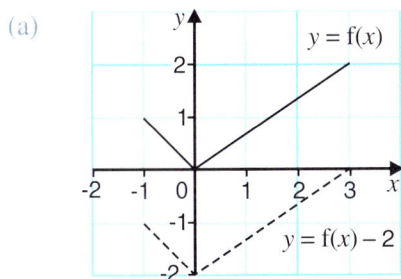

(b)
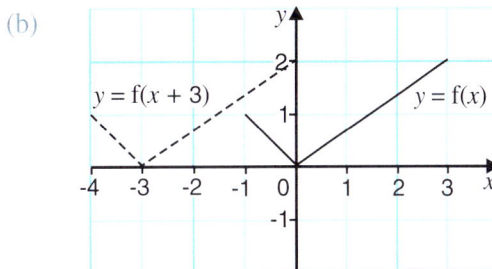

(c)
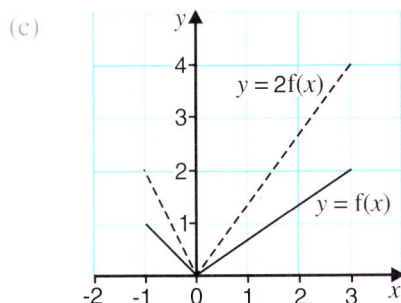

(d)
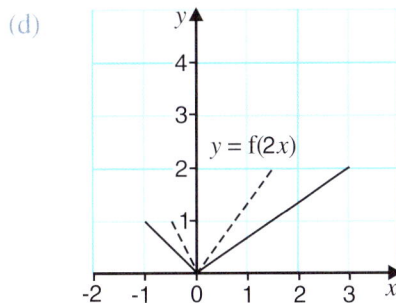

In general

Original	New graph	Transformation	Note
$y = f(x)$	$y = f(x) + a$	**translation**, vector $\begin{pmatrix} 0 \\ a \end{pmatrix}$.	If a is **positive**, curve moves a units **up**. If a is **negative**, curve moves a units **down**.
$y = f(x)$	$y = f(x + a)$	**translation**, vector $\begin{pmatrix} -a \\ 0 \end{pmatrix}$.	If a is **positive**, curve moves a units **left**. If a is **negative**, curve moves a units **right**.
$y = f(x)$	$y = af(x)$	**stretch**, from the x axis, parallel to the y axis, scale factor a.	The y coordinates on the graph of $y = f(x)$ are **multiplied** by a.
$y = f(x)$	$y = f(ax)$	**stretch**, from the y axis, parallel to the x axis, scale factor $\frac{1}{a}$.	The x coordinates on the graph of $y = f(x)$ are **divided** by a.

Reflecting a graph

The diagram shows the graphs of $y = f(x)$ and $y = -f(x)$.

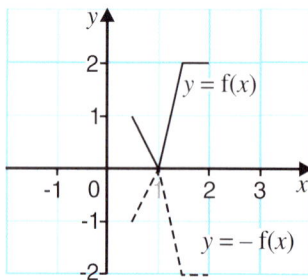

The graph of $y = f(x)$ is transformed to the graph of $y = -f(x)$ by:
a **stretch** from the x axis, parallel to the y axis, scale factor -1.
This transformation is equivalent to a **reflection** in the x axis.

The diagram shows the graphs of $y = f(x)$ and $y = f(-x)$.

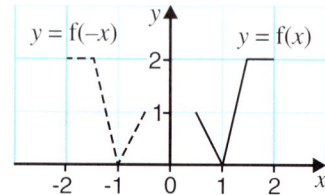

The graph of $y = f(x)$ is transformed to the graph of $y = f(-x)$ by:
a **stretch** from the y axis, parallel to the x axis, scale factor -1.
This transformation is equivalent to a **reflection** in the y axis.

EXAMPLE

1 The graph of the function f, where $f(x) = x^3 + 2$, is shown together with the graphs of two related functions g and h. Find equations for $g(x)$ and $h(x)$.

The graph of $y = g(x)$ is a reflection of the graph of $y = f(x)$ in the x axis.
This means that $\quad g(x) = -f(x)$
So $\quad\quad\quad\quad g(x) = -(x^3 + 2)$
So $\quad\quad\quad\quad g(x) = -x^3 - 2$

The graph of $y = h(x)$ is a reflection of the graph of $y = f(x)$ in the y axis.
This means that $\quad h(x) = f(-x)$
So $\quad\quad\quad\quad h(x) = -(-x)^3 + 2$
So $\quad\quad\quad\quad h(x) = -x^3 + 2$

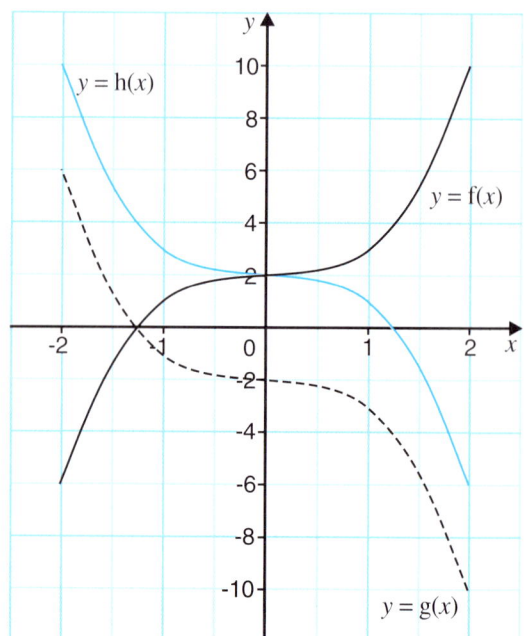

EXAMPLES

2 The diagram shows the graphs of the functions
$y = f(x)$, $y = g(x)$ and $y = h(x)$.
Express $g(x)$ and $h(x)$ in terms of $f(x)$.

The graph of $y = f(x)$ is transformed to the graph
of $y = g(x)$ by a translation with vector $\begin{pmatrix} -4 \\ 0 \end{pmatrix}$.
So $g(x) = f(x + 4)$.

The graph of $y = g(x)$ is transformed to the graph
of $y = h(x)$ by a translation with vector $\begin{pmatrix} 0 \\ 2 \end{pmatrix}$.
So $h(x) = g(x) + 2 = f(x + 4) + 2$.

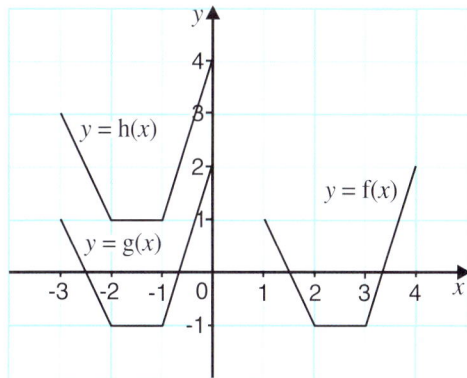

3 The diagram shows the graphs of $y = \sin x$ and
two related functions **a** and **b**.
Find equations for the functions **a** and **b**.

The graph of $y = \sin x$ is transformed to the
graph of function **a** by:
a **stretch** from the x axis, parallel to the
y axis, scale factor 2.
So the equation of function **a** is $y = 2\sin x$.

The graph of function **a** is transformed to the
graph of function **b** by:
a **translation** with vector $\begin{pmatrix} 0 \\ 1 \end{pmatrix}$.
So the equation of function **b** is $y = 2\sin x + 1$.

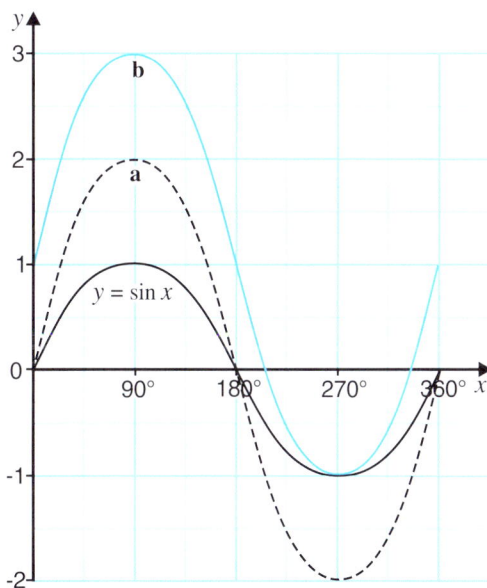

Exercise 16.2

1 The diagram shows the graph of the
function $y = f(x)$.
- (a) Copy the diagram, drawing axes
  marked from -4 to 4 for x and y.
  Draw the graph of the function
  $y = f(x) + 2$.

- (b) Describe fully how the graph of
  $y = f(x)$ is transformed to the graph
  of $y = f(x) + 2$.

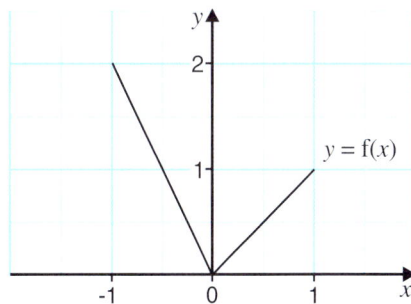

- (c) Repeat parts (a) and (b) for each of these functions:

(i) $y = f(x) - 1$	(ii) $y = f(x - 3)$	(iii) $y = f(x + 2)$
(iv) $y = 0.5f(x)$	(v) $y = 2f(x)$	(vi) $y = f(0.5x)$
(vii) $y = f(2x)$	(viii) $y = -f(x)$	(ix) $y = f(-x)$
(x) $y = f(2x) + 1$	(xi) $y = 2f(x + 1)$	(xii) $y = 1 - f(x)$

2 The graph of $y = f(x)$ is shown.

On separate diagrams sketch:
(a) $y = f(x)$ and $y = f(x) + 2$
(b) $y = f(x)$ and $y = f(x + 2)$
(c) $y = f(x)$ and $y = 2f(x)$
(d) $y = f(x)$ and $y = f\left(\frac{x}{2}\right)$
(c) $y = f(x)$ and $y = -f(x)$

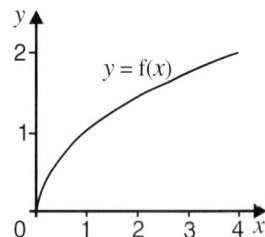

3 The graph shows $y = g(x)$.

On separate diagrams sketch:
(a) $y = g(x) - 2$
(b) $y = g(x - 2)$
(c) $y = \frac{1}{2} g(x)$
(d) $y = g(2x)$
(e) $y = -g(x)$

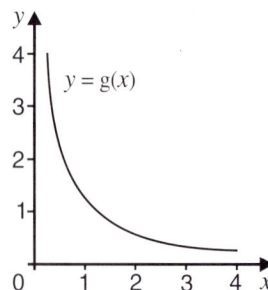

4 The graph shows $y = h(x)$.

On separate diagrams sketch:
(a) $y = h(x) + 1$
(b) $y = h(x - 90)$
(c) $y = h(2x)$
(d) $y = 2h(x)$
(e) $y = -h(x)$

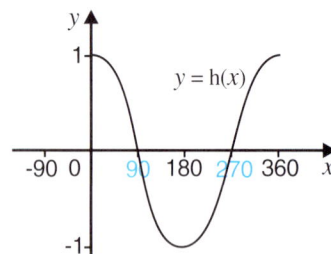

5 The diagram shows the graph of $y = f(x)$ for $-0 \leqslant x \leqslant 3$.

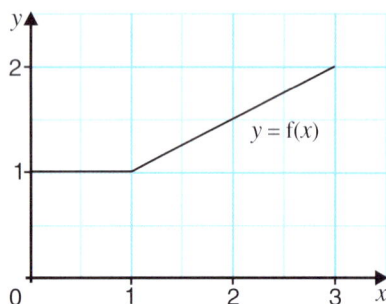

The graph of $y = f(x)$ is transformed to the graph of $y = g(x)$ by a stretch from the x axis, parallel to the y axis, scale factor 3.

The graph of $y = g(x)$ is transformed to the graph of $y = h(x)$ by a translation with vector $\binom{-3}{0}$.
(a) (i)   Draw the graph of $y = g(x)$.
     (ii) Express $g(x)$ in terms of $f(x)$.

(b) (i)   Draw the graph of $y = h(x)$.
     (ii) Express $h(x)$ in terms of $g(x)$.
     (iii) Express $h(x)$ in terms of $f(x)$.

(c) (i)   Draw the graph of $y = 2 - f(x)$.
     (ii) Draw the graph of $y = 2 + f(-x)$.

(d) Draw the graph of $y = 2 - g(x)$ and express the equation of this graph in terms of $f(x)$.

228

6 The graph of the function
$y = f(x)$ is transformed to each
of the graphs **a**, **b**, **c**, **d** and **e**.

Find, in terms of $f(x)$, equations
for the graphs **a**, **b**, **c**, **d** and **e**.

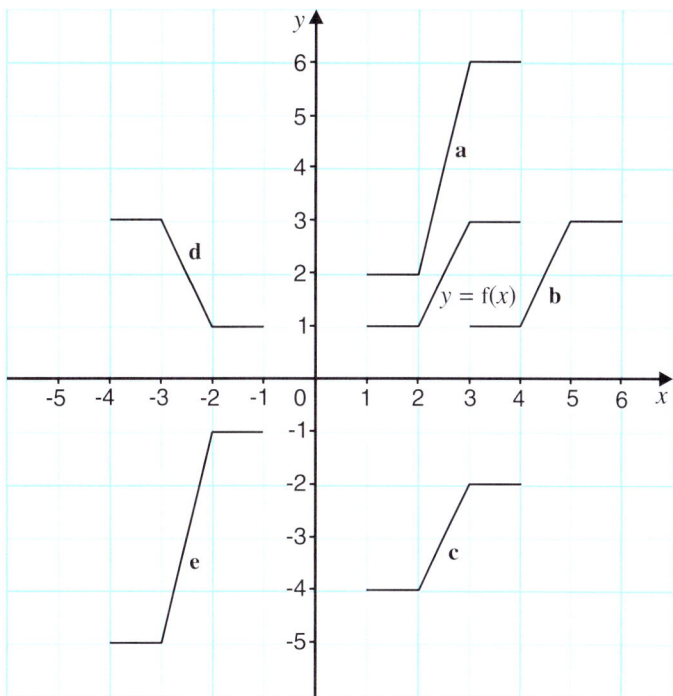

7 The diagram shows the graph of
the function $y = f(x)$ and the
graphs of three related functions
$y = A(x)$,
$y = B(x)$,
$y = C(x)$.

Express $A(x)$, $B(x)$ and $C(x)$
in terms of $f(x)$.

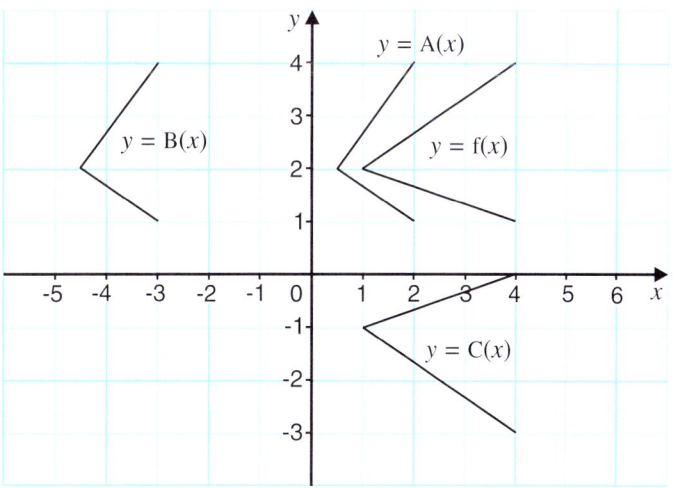

8 The diagram shows a sketch of $y = \sin x$
and three related functions.

Describe how the graph of $y = \sin x$ is
transformed to
(a) the graph of function **a**,
(b) the graph of function **b**.

(c) Describe how the graph of function **b** is
transformed to the graph of function **c**.
(d) Describe how the graph of $y = \sin x$ is
transformed to the graph of function **c**,
by using a combination of **two** transformations.

(e) What are the equations of the graphs **a**, **b** and **c**?

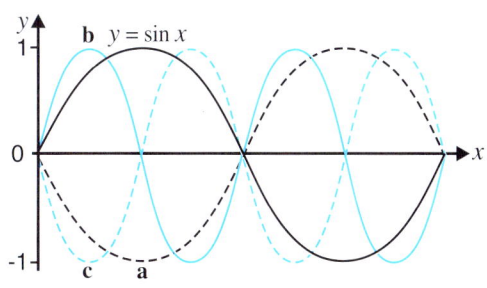

Graphs can be used to help find the relationship between two variables.
This is particularly useful when looking for rules to fit the results of scientific experiments.

Linear functions

Linear functions have straight line graphs.
Straight line graphs have equations of the form
$y = mx + c$, where m is the gradient and c is the intercept.

> Straight line graphs
> and $y = mx + c$ were
> first covered in
> Chapter 10.

EXAMPLE

The table shows the speed, v (m/s),
of a vehicle at various times, t (sec),
after it starts to decelerate.

t (sec)	10	20	30	40	50
v (m/s)	35	27	19	11	3

(a)   Find an equation connecting v and t.
(b)   Use your equation to find:
    (i) v when $t = 25$,   (ii) t when $v = 0$.

(a)   **Step 1**
Plot the data and draw a line of best fit,
by eye, to show the relationship between
the variables speed and time.

> Line of best fit is covered
> in Chapter 29.

Step 2
Find the equation of the line.
The equation is of the form
$v = m t + c$.
Find the gradient, m.
Draw a suitable right-angled
triangle.
$m = \dfrac{-16}{20} = -0.8$

Find the intercept, c.
The line passes through the
point $(0, 43)$.
$c = 43$.

Step 3
Substitute values for m and c
into $v = m t + c$.
$m = -0.8$ and $c = 43$.
So the equation connecting
v and t is:
$v = -0.8t + 43$.

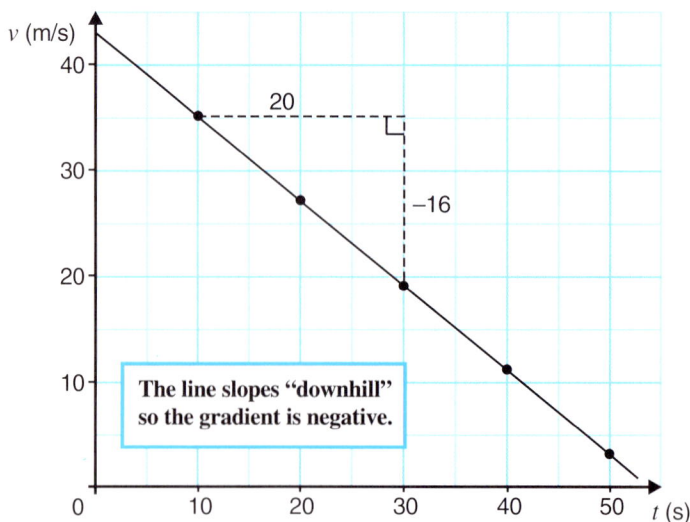

The line slopes "downhill"
so the gradient is negative.

(b)   (i)   Using $v = -0.8t + 43$.
When $t = 25$.
$v = -0.8 \times 25 + 43$
$v = 23$

(ii)   Using $v = -0.8t + 43$.
When $v = 0$.
$0 = -0.8t + 43$
$0.8t = 43$
Divide both sides by 0.8.
$t = 53.75$

Non-linear functions

This section looks at **non-linear functions** of the form $y = ax^n + b$.

To find the values of a and b:
1. Write $y = ax^n + b$ as the **linear function** $y = az + b$, by substituting $z = x^n$.
2. Draw the graph of y against z.
3. Use the graph to find:
   the gradient, a,
   the intercept, b.

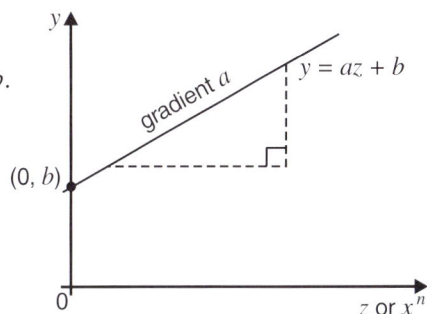

EXAMPLE

The table shows values of x and y which are connected by an equation of the form $y = ax^2 + b$.
Find the values of a and b.

x	0	0.5	1	1.5	2
y	-4	-3.25	-1	2.75	8

Substituting $z = x^2$ in $y = ax^2 + b$ gives the linear function $y = az + b$.
So draw the graph of y against z.
Since $z = x^2$, values of z are found by squaring the given values of x in the table.

This table shows the values of z and y.

$z (= x^2)$	0	0.25	1	2.25	4
y	-4	-3.25	-1	2.75	8

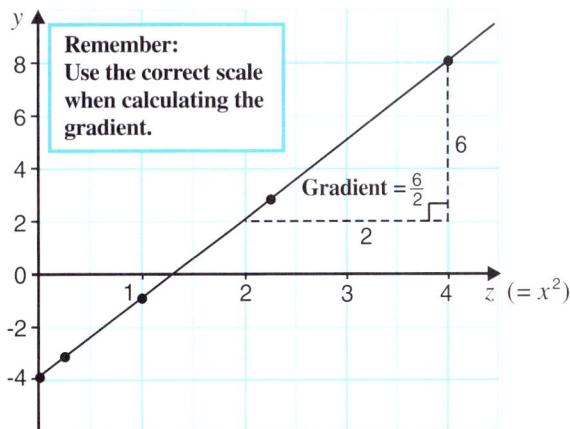

The graph has gradient 3 and intercept -4.
So $a = 3$ and $b = -4$.

Remember:
Use the correct scale when calculating the gradient.

Gradient $= \frac{6}{2}$

Exercise 16.3

You may use a calculator.

1 These tables show the data collected in two experiments.
(a) In each case assume that the variables are connected by a linear function and use a graphical method to find its equation.
(b) Use your equations to find:
   (i) y when $x = 2.7$
   (ii) p when $q = 7.6$

x	0.4	0.8	1.2	1.6	2
y	24.2	35.4	46.6	57.8	69.0

p	0.4	0.8	1.2	1.6	2
q	35.2	30.1	24.9	19.8	14.1

2 In an experiment, Kym hangs weights, w grams, on the end of a spring and measures its length, l centimetres.
This graph shows Kym's results.

(a) Find an equation expressing l in terms of w.
(b) Use your equation to find:
   (i) l when $w = 500$,
   (ii) w when $l = 55$.

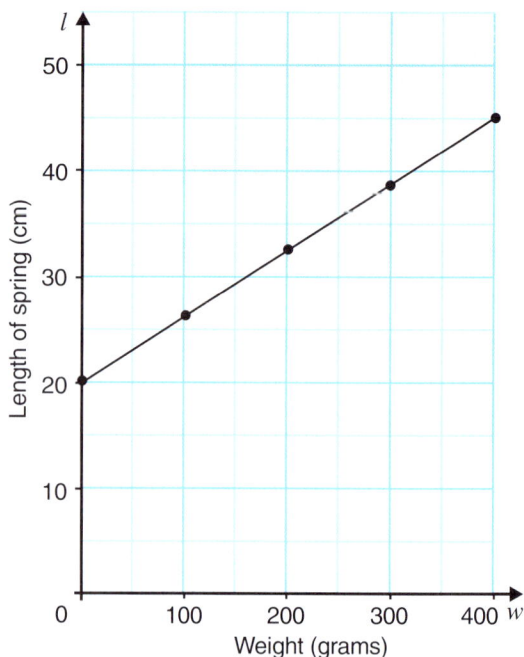

3 Two variables, x and y, are connected by the equation $y = ax^2 + b$.
Some pairs of values of x and y are shown in the table.
By drawing an appropriate graph find the values of a and b.

x	2	4	6	8	10
y	2.8	4	6	8.8	12.4

4 A vehicle starts from rest and accelerates with a constant acceleration of a m/s^2.
The formula $s = at^2$ gives the distance travelled, s metres, after time, t seconds.
The table shows pairs of values of s and t.
Use a graphical method to find the acceleration.

t	2	4	6	8	10
s	8.4	33.6	75.6	134.4	210

5 Tom and Sam perform an experiment.
The results are shown in the table.
Tom thinks that x and y are connected by a rule of the form $y = ax^2 + b$.
Sam thinks the rule is of the form $y = ax^3 + b$.

x	0.4	0.8	1.2	1.6	2
y	24.3	35.5	65.9	125.1	222.7

Tom uses the substitution $u = x^2$.

$u(=x^2)$	0.16	0.64	1.44	2.56	4
y	24.3	35.5	65.9	125.1	222.7

(a) Draw the graph of y against u and, if possible, use it to find the values of a and b.

Sam uses the substitution $v = x^3$.

$v(=x^3)$	0.064	0.512	1.728	4.096	8
y	24.3	35.5	65.9	125.1	222.7

(b) Draw the graph of v against y and, if possible, use it to find the values of a and b.

6 Two variables, x and y, are connected by the equation $y = ax^3 + b$.
Some pairs of values of x and y are shown in the table.
By drawing an appropriate graph find the values of a and b.

x	2	4	6	8	10
y	2.8	6.0	13.2	28.0	52.4

7 The diagram shows the graph of the function $y = ax^3 + b$.
By plotting an appropriate graph find the values of a and b.

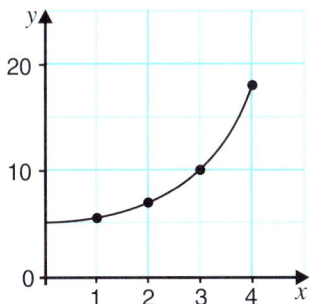

8 Two variables, q and p, are known to be connected by the equation $q = ap^n + b$.
The value of n is thought to be either 2 or 3.
The table shows some values of p and q.

p	1	1.5	2	2.5	3
q	10.1	9.6	8.7	7.2	4.9

Use a graphical method to find the values of n, a and b.

Finding the power

This section explores ways of finding the value of n in functions of the form $y = ax^n + b$.
Graphs of the form $y = ax^n$ were first covered in Chapter 5.

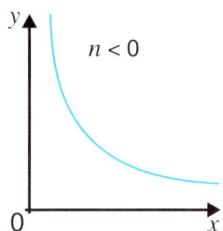
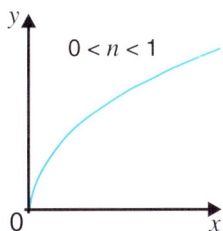
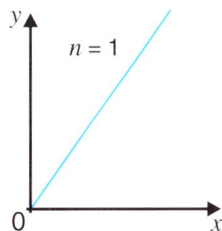
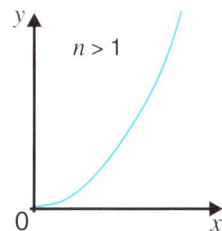

These graphs can be used to help find the value of n.

EXAMPLE

This set of data follows the rule $y = ax^n + b$.
Find the values of n, a and b.

x	1	2	3	4	5
y	14.5	10.4	9.0	8.4	7.9

Step 1: Draw the graph of y against x.
The shape of the graph suggests that $n < 0$.

Try $n = -1$. This gives the equation $y = \dfrac{a}{x} + b$.

Substituting $z = \dfrac{1}{x}$ gives $y = az + b$.

Step 2: Draw up a table of values of z and y.

$z \left(= \dfrac{1}{x}\right)$	1	0.5	0.33	0.25	0.2
y	14.5	10.4	9.0	8.4	7.9

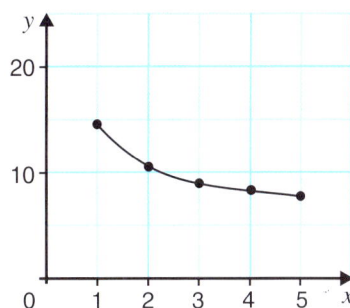

Step 3: Draw the graph of y against z.
This gives a straight line and confirms that $n = -1$.
The graph has gradient 8.2 and intercept 6.3.
So $a = 8.2$ and $b = 6.3$.

Passes through (0,6.3)

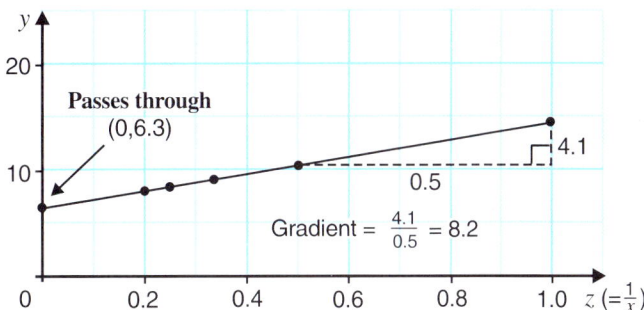

Gradient $= \dfrac{4.1}{0.5} = 8.2$

Some problems can be solved using the rules of powers. These were first covered in Chapter 4.

EXAMPLE

A sketch of the graph of $y = kx^n + 1$ is shown.
The graph passes through the points (1, 5) and (4, 3).
Find the values of k and n.

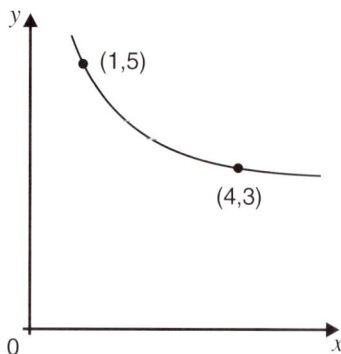

The shape of the graph suggests that $n < 0$.

To find the value of k:
The graph of $y = kx^n + 1$ passes through the point (1, 5).
So when $x = 1$, $y = 5$.
$5 = k \times 1^n + 1$
$5 = k + 1$ **Remember:** $1^n = 1$.
$k = 4$
So $y = 4x^n + 1$.

To find the value of n:
The graph of $y = 4x^n + 1$ passes through the point (4, 3).
So when $x = 4$, $y = 3$.
$3 = 4 \times 4^n + 1$
Subtract 1 from both sides.
$2 = 4 \times 4^n$
Divide both sides by 4.
$4^n = \dfrac{1}{2}$

Substitute values for x and y to give an equation involving the unknown power, n.

Method 1
Use your knowledge of powers to 'spot' the answer.

$4^{0.5} = 2$ so $4^{-0.5} = \dfrac{1}{2}$
So $n = -0.5$

Method 2
Write each side of the equation as powers of the same base.

$4^n = \dfrac{1}{2}$
Write 4^n and $\dfrac{1}{2}$ as powers of 2.
$4 = 2^2$ so $4^n = 2^{2n}$ and $\dfrac{1}{2} = 2^{-1}$
$2^{2n} = 2^{-1}$
Equate the powers.
$2n = -1$
$n = -0.5$

Exercise 16.4   You may use a calculator.

1 Match each of the following equations with the graphs.

Equations (1) $y = 10x^2 + 5$ (2) $y = \dfrac{10}{x} + 5$ (3) $y = 10\sqrt{x} + 5$

Graphs

(a)
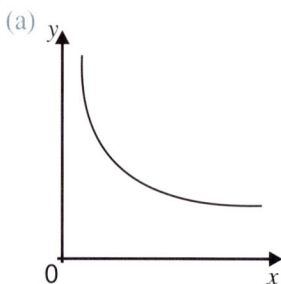

(b)
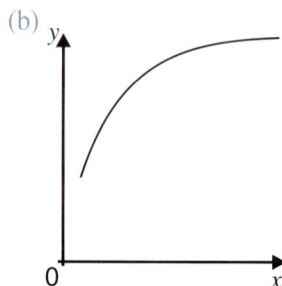

(c)
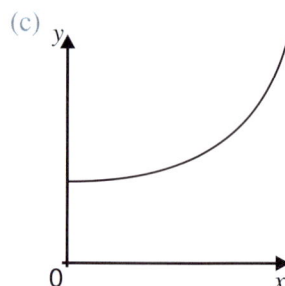

2 The diagram shows the graph of y against x^n, where $y = f(x)$.

Express $f(x)$ in terms of x when:

(a) $n = 2$ (b) $n = 0.5$
(c) $n = 3$ (d) $n = -1$
(e) $n = -2$ (f) $n = -0.5$

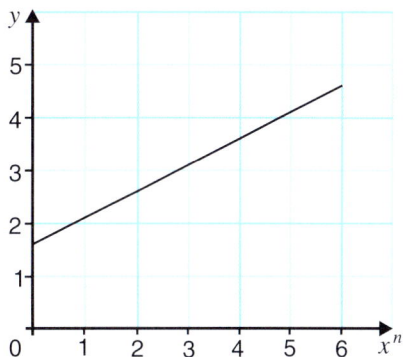

3 For each set of data the formula connecting x and y is of the form $y = ax^n + b$ where $-1 \leqslant n \leqslant 2$ and a and b are constants.

For each set of data:
Draw the graph of y against x and use it to help determine the value of n.
Confirm the value of n by drawing the graph of y against x^n.
Use the graph to find the values of a and b.

(a)

x	1	2	3	4	5
y	8.04	8.16	8.36	8.64	9.00

(b)

x	1	2	3	4	5
y	10.9	7.8	6.8	6.3	5.9

(c)

x	1	2	3	4	5
y	15.6	12.1	10.5	9.6	9.0

(d)

x	1	2	3	4	5
y	0.9	3.3	5.1	6.6	7.9

(e)

x	1	2	3	4	5
y	6.6	4.8	2.5	2.35	2.3

4 These sketch graphs each have an equation of the form $y = kx^n$.
Use the rules of powers to find k and n for each graph.

(a)

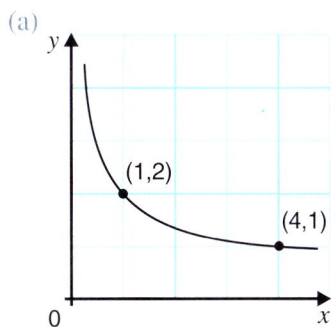

(b)

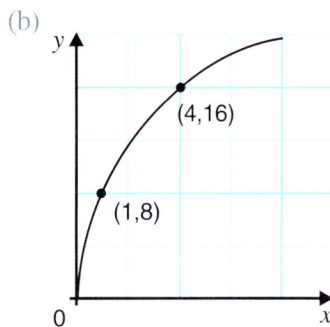

5 A sketch of the graph of $y = ax^n + b$ is shown.
The graph passes through the points (1, 3), (5, 3.6), (8, 3.9) and (12, 4.2).
The value of n is known to be $\frac{1}{2}$.

(a)   Write an equation for y in terms of a, b and x.
(b)   By drawing an appropriate graph, find the values of a and b and hence the equation that expresses y in terms of x.

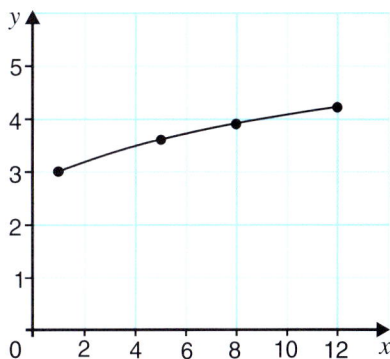

Exponential growth and decay

In some situations, quantities grow or decay according to a rule of the form $y = k \times a^t$ where y is the amount of the quantity after time t and k and a are positive constants.
This is called **exponential growth** or **decay**.

Examples of quantities growing or decaying exponentially are:
    money invested at a fixed rate of interest,
    the radioactivity of radioactive isotopes.

The table shows values of y for some values of t for $y = ka^t$.

t	0	1	2	3	4
y	k	ka	ka^2	ka^3	ka^4

The diagrams below show the general graph of the function $y = ka^t$.

Exponential growth
When $a > 1$ the value of y **grows**.

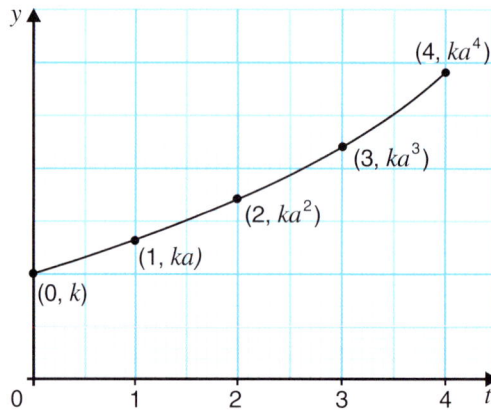

Exponential decay
When $0 < a < 1$ the value of y **decays**.

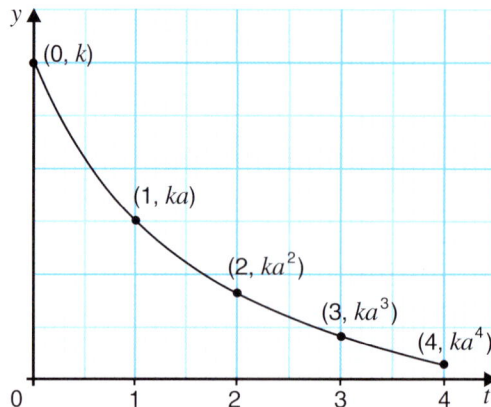

The table and diagrams show that for a function of the form $y = ka^t$:
    when $t = 0$, $y = k$,
    when t increases by 1, y becomes a times larger (or a times smaller.)

EXAMPLES

1 The following diagrams show relationships of the form $y = pq^x$.
In each case find the values of p and q.

(a)

(b)

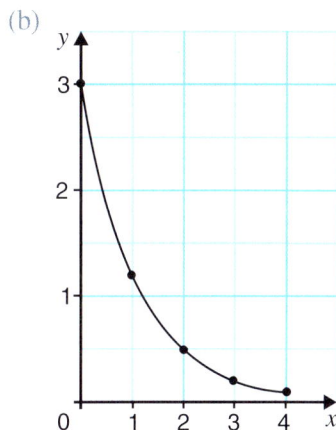

(a) $y = pq^x$
From the graph, when $x = 0$, $y = 0.6$.
$\qquad 0.6 = p \times q^0$.
So $\quad p = 0.6$

$y = pq^x$
From the graph, when $x = 1$, $y = 0.9$.
$\qquad 0.9 = p \times q^1$.
$\qquad pq = 0.9$
Substitute $p = 0.6$.
$\qquad 0.6 \times q = 0.9$
$\qquad q = 0.9 \div 0.6 = 1.5$
So $\qquad y = 0.6 \times 2.5^x$.

(b) $y = pq^x$
From the graph, when $x = 0$, $y = 3$.
$\qquad 3 = p \times q^0$.
So $p = 3$

$y = pq^x$
From the graph, when $x = 1$, $y = 1.2$.
$\qquad 1.2 = p \times q^1$.
$\qquad pq = 1.2$
Substitute $p = 3$.
$\qquad 3 \times q = 1.2$
$\qquad q = 1.2 \div 3 = 0.4$
So $\qquad y = 3 \times 0.4^x$.

2 A graph of the form $y = ka^t$ passes through the points $(1, 8)$ and $(2, 2)$.
Find the value of y when $t = 0$.

When $t = 0$, $y = k$.
So k needs to be found.

$y = ka^t$
When $t = 1$, $y = 8$.
$8 = ka$
$a = \dfrac{8}{k}$
and $a^2 = \left(\dfrac{8}{k}\right)^2 = \dfrac{64}{k^2}$

$y = ka^t$
When $t = 2$, $y = 2$.
$2 = ka^2$
$a^2 = \dfrac{2}{k}$

$a^2 = \dfrac{64}{k^2}$ and $a^2 = \dfrac{2}{k}$

Equate a^2.

$\dfrac{64}{k^2} = \dfrac{2}{k}$

Multiply both sides by k^2.
$64 = 2k$
$k = 32$

When $t = 0$, $y = k$.
So $y = 32$ when $t = 0$.

Use the value of k to calculate a.

You may use a calculator.

1 Each of these diagrams shows a relationship of the form $y = ab^x$.

(a)
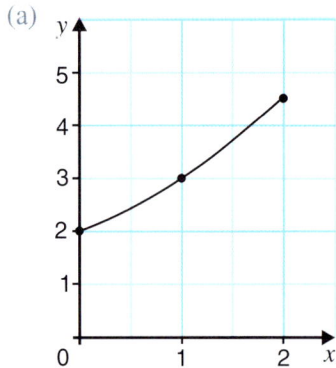

(b)
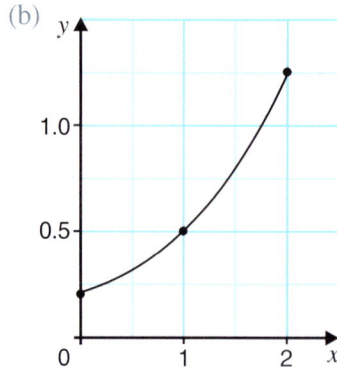

(c)
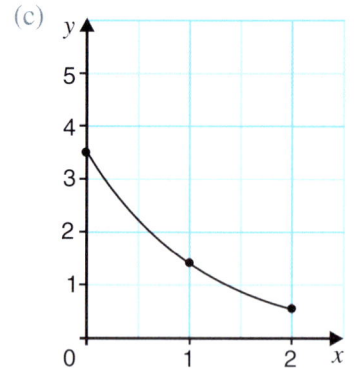

(d)
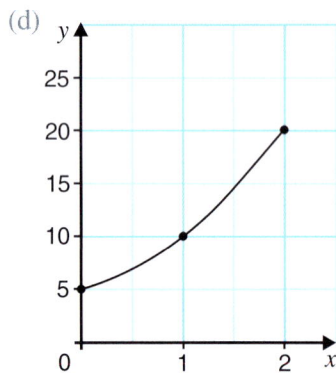

(e)
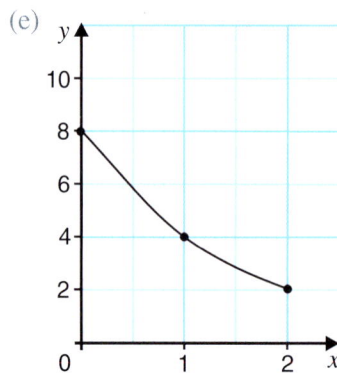

(f)
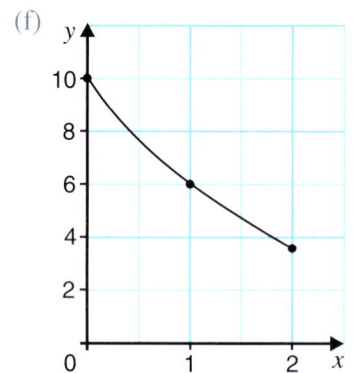

In each case find the values of a and b.

2 A graph of the form $y = ka^t$ passes through the points (1, 9.1) and (2, 31.85).
Find the value of y when: (a) $t = 0$,   (b) $t = 4$.

3 A graph of the form $y = ka^t$ passes through the points (1, 14) and (2, 9.8).
Find the value of y when: (a) $t = 0$,   (b) $t = 10$.

4 The table shows the weight, w kg, of a radioactive element during 5 successive days.

Time (t days)	0	1	2	3	4	5
Weight (w kg)	10.00	9.00	8.10	7.29	6.56	5.91

(a)   (i)   Draw a graph of this data.
      (ii)   In theory, t and w are connected by the rule $w = a \times b^t$ where a and b are
           constants.
           Does your graph support this theory?
(b)   (i)   What value of t gives the value of a?
      (ii)   Calculate the values of a and b.
(c)   After how many days is w less than half of its original weight?

- **Function notation** is a way of expressing a relationship between two variables.
  For example

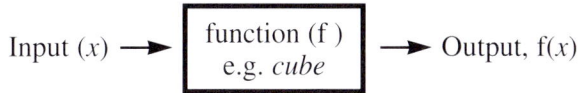

$$\text{Input } (x) \longrightarrow \boxed{\begin{array}{c} \text{function (f)} \\ \text{e.g. } cube \end{array}} \longrightarrow \text{Output, f}(x)$$

This notation gives $\text{f}(x) = x^3$

f(x) means 'a function of x'.
In the example above, $\text{f}(x) = x^3$ is equivalent to the equation $y = x^3$ where $y = \text{f}(x)$.

- **Transformations,** such as **translations** and **stretches**, can be used to change the position and size of a graph.
  The equation of the transformed (new) graph is related to the equation of the original graph.

In general

Original	New graph	Transformation	Note
$y = \text{f}(x)$	$y = \text{f}(x) + a$	**translation**, vector $\begin{pmatrix} 0 \\ a \end{pmatrix}$.	If a is **positive**, curve moves a units **up**. If a is **negative**, curve moves a units **down**.
$y = \text{f}(x)$	$y = \text{f}(x + a)$	**translation**, vector $\begin{pmatrix} -a \\ 0 \end{pmatrix}$.	If a is **positive**, curve moves a units **left**. If a is **negative**, curve moves a units **right**.
$y = \text{f}(x)$	$y = a\text{f}(x)$	**stretch**, from the x axis, parallel to the y axis, scale factor a.	The y coordinates on the graph of $y = \text{f}(x)$ are **multiplied** by a.
$y = \text{f}(x)$	$y = \text{f}(ax)$	**stretch**, from the y axis, parallel to the x axis, scale factor $\dfrac{1}{a}$.	The x coordinates on the graph of $y = \text{f}(x)$ are **divided** by a.
$y = \text{f}(x)$	$y = -\text{f}(x)$	**reflection** in the x axis.	The y coordinates on the graph of $y = \text{f}(x)$ **change signs**.
$y = \text{f}(x)$	$y = \text{f}(-x)$	**reflection** in the y axis.	The x coordinates on the graph of $y = \text{f}(x)$ **change signs**.

- **Finding relationships between variables**:
  Linear functions have straight line graphs, such as $y = ax + b$.
  From the graph of **y against x**, the gradient $= a$ and the intercept $= b$.

  Non-linear functions, such as $y = ax^n + b$, can be written as the linear function $y = az + b$ by substituting $z = x^n$.
  From the graph of **y against x^n**, the gradient $= a$ and the intercept $= b$.

- Quantities which grow or decay **exponentially** are governed by a function of the form $y = k \times a^t$, where y is the amount of the quantity after time t.
  k is the **initial value** of y and a is the **growth factor**.
  The constants k and t can be found from the graph of $y = k \times a^t$ and by using algebraic methods.

1 The graph of a function, $y = f(x)$, is shown. Copy the diagram on squared paper.
(a) On the same axes sketch the graph of the function $y = f(x) + 3$.
(b) Sketch the graph of the function $y = f(x - 2)$ on the same axes.

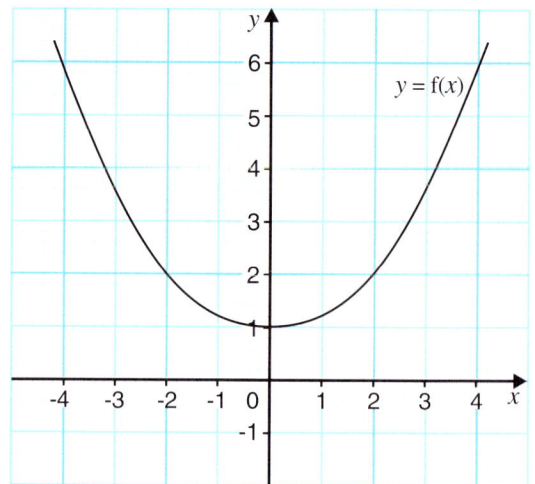

SEG 1997

2 The function $y = f(x)$ is illustrated.
(a) On separate copies of the axes sketch
(i) $y = 2f(x)$,
(ii) $y = f(x - 1)$.

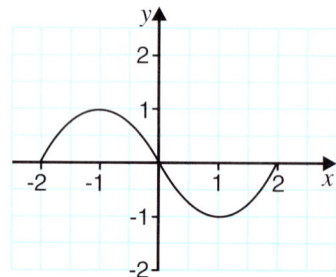

(b) Which one of the sketches below is of the form $y = f(x) + a$, where a is a constant? What is the value of a?

A

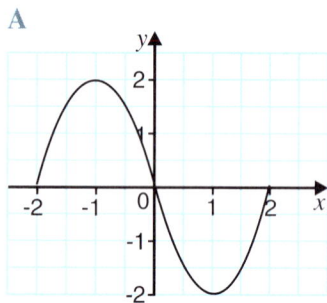

B

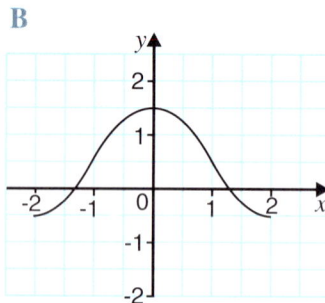

C

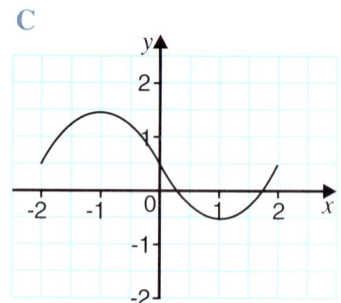

SEG 1997

3 The function $y = f(x)$ is illustrated. Sketch graphs of the functions
(a) $y = f\left(\dfrac{x}{2}\right)$;
(b) $y = f(x - 1)$.
Label each graph clearly.

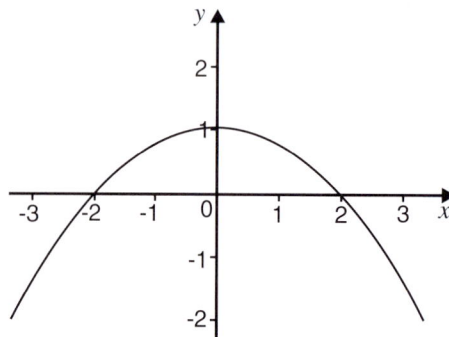

SEG 1996

240

4 The diagram shows the graph of $y = f(x)$ for $0 \leqslant x \leqslant 2$.
   On separate copies of the axes.
   (a) sketch $y = f(x) + 1$,
   (b) sketch $y = f(x - 1)$,
   (c) sketch $y = f\left(\dfrac{x}{2}\right)$.

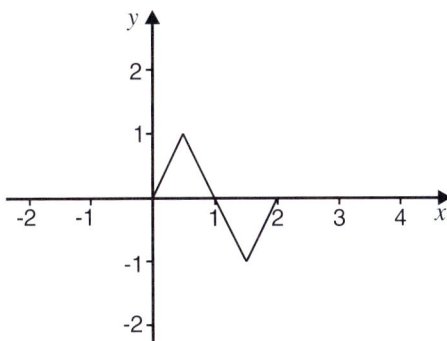

SEG 1994

5 The function $y = f(x)$ is sketched.
   Copy the diagram.
   On your diagram, sketch
   (a) $y = f(x - 1)$,
   (b) $y = 2f\left(\dfrac{x}{2}\right)$.

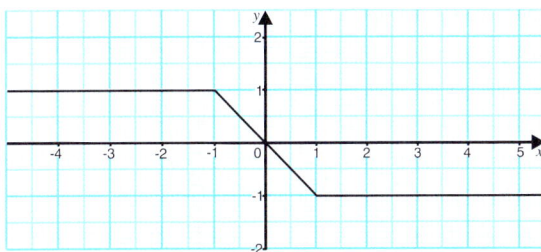

SEG 1996

6 The graph of $y = x^3 + x$ is shown.
   Copy the diagram on squared paper.
   On the same axes sketch and label the
   graphs of
   (a) $y = x^3 + x + 2$,
   (b) $y = -x^3 - x$.

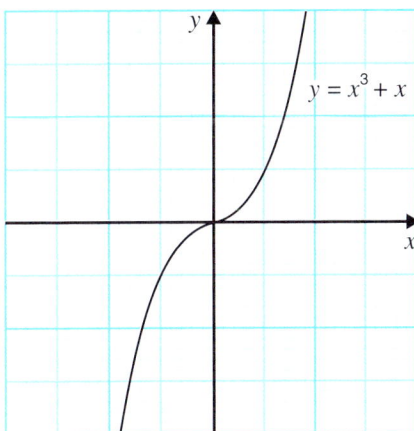

$y = x^3 + x$

SEG 1995

7 The curve of $\cos x$ for $0° \leqslant x \leqslant 360°$ is drawn.
   Copy the diagram.
   On the same axes sketch the curve of
   $3\cos x$ for $0° \leqslant x \leqslant 360°$.

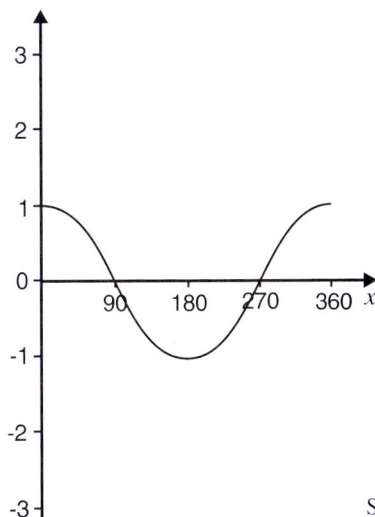

SEG 1996

241

8 The diagram shows the graph of $y = x^3$ for $-1 \leqslant x \leqslant 1$.

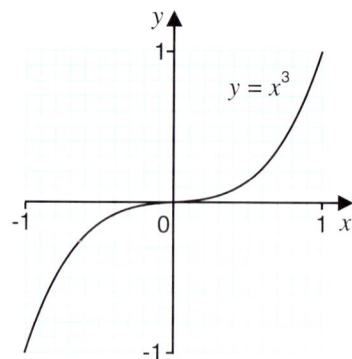

Each of the following graphs is a transformation of the graph of $y = x^3$.
Write down the equation of each graph.

(a)

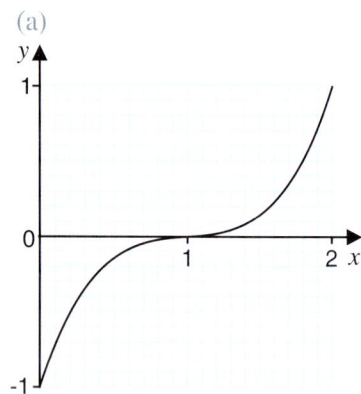

(b)

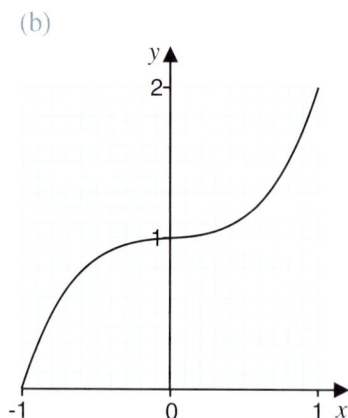

(c)

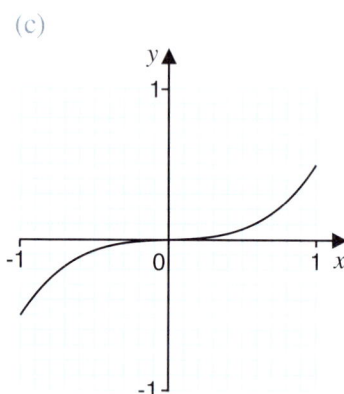

(d)

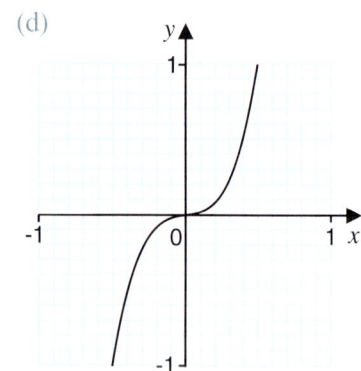

(e)

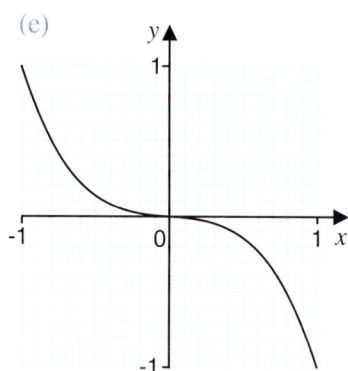

(f)

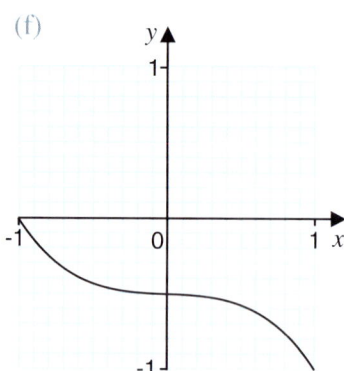

9 A manufacturing company has eight factories.
The table below gives data for a particular year for the number of serious accidents, N, and the number of production workers, P (to the nearest hundred), for each factory.

Factory	A	B	C	D	E	F	G	H
No. of production workers (P)	1200	1600	2200	3600	4200	6000	7300	8800
No. of serious Accidents (N)	6	8	8	14	18	26	27	36

(a) Illustrate these data on a graph showing that the values indicate a relationship of the form $N = aP + b$, where a and b are constants.
Use your graph to find appropriate values of a and b.

(b) Which of the eight factories has the best safety record?
Give reasons for your answer.

(c) The company takes over a ninth factory which has a production work force of 9500.
Estimate the expected yearly number of serious accidents for this factory.

SEG 1992

10 The values of x and y given in the table were obtained from an experiment.

x	0.6	1.0	1.4	1.6	1.8	2.0
y	3.7	4.0	4.7	5.2	5.9	6.8

It is known that y is approximately equal to $px^3 + q$ where p and q are constants.
Plot the graph of y against x^3.
Use your graph to estimate the values of p and q.   SEG 1998

11 In an experiment James find these values of x and y.
James suspects that the relationship connecting

x and y is of the form $y = \dfrac{a}{x} + b$.

x	1	4
y	17.2	6.4

(a) Confirm the form of the relationship by drawing an appropriate graph and find the values of a and b.
(b) Calculate x when $y = 31.6$.

12 (b) The graph of an equation of the form $y = ax^n$ passes through the points $(1, 0.4)$ and $(4, 0.8)$.
Calculate the values of a and n.
(b) The variables, x and y, are connected by a relationship of the form $y = px^n$.
When $x = 1$, $y = 5$ and when $x = 16$, $y = 40$.
Calculate the value of y when $x = 81$.

13 The diagram shows a graph with equation of the form $y = ab^x$ where a and b are constants.
Find the values of a and b.

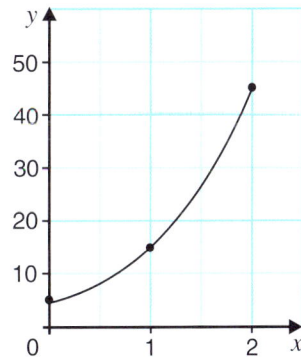

14 (a) The variables x and y are connected by an equation of the form $y = ax^n + b$ where a, b and n are constants.
When $x = 1$, $y = 5$
When $x = 4$, $y = 3.55$
When $x = 9$, $y = 3$
Calculate the values of a, b and n.
(b) The graph of a function of the form $y = ax^n + b$ passes through the points $(1, -3)$, $(8, 12)$ and $(64, 72)$.
Show that the graph passes through the point $(125, 117)$.

15 A graph with equation $y = pq^x$ passes through the points $(1, 6)$ and $(2, 3.6)$.
Find the values of p and q and the point where the graph cuts the x axis.

16 Observation suggests that the population of fish in a lake is decreasing with time according to the rule $N = nd^t$ where N is the population at time t weeks.
Initially the lake was stocked with 10 000 fish.
(a) What is the value of n?

After 2 weeks it is estimated that 6400 fish were left in the lake.
(b) Calculate the number of fish in the lake after 10 weeks.

Section Review - Algebra

⬤⬤⬤⬤⬤⬤⬤⬤⬤⬤⬤

① Solve the equation $6x + 7 = 2x - 3$.

SEG 1997

② The total cost, £C, of hiring the car can be calculated from the formula

$$C = 25d + \frac{(12m - 50d)}{100}$$

where d = number of days hired, and
$\qquad$ m = number of miles driven.
A car is hired for 7 days, and is driven 476 miles.
Calculate the total cost of hiring the car.

CAR HIRE RATES
Vauxhall Nova
per day: £25
per mile: 12p

SEG 1996

③ Amanda went for a cycle ride.
A distance-time graph of Amanda's journey
is shown.

(a) How far did Amanda cycle before she
stopped for a rest?
(b) Calculate Amanda's average speed for
the whole cycle ride.

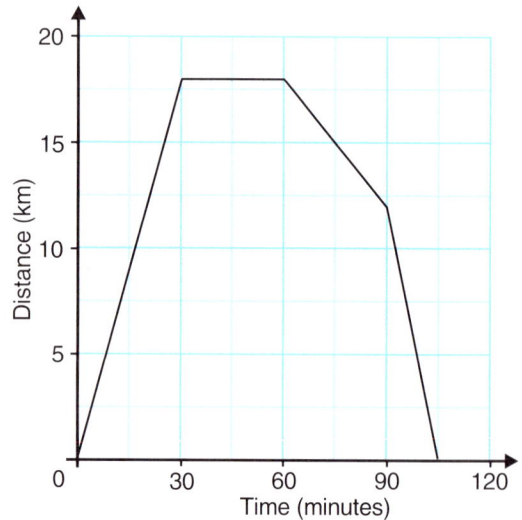

SEG 1996

④ The values of x and y are connected by the equation $x^2 + y^2 = 100$.
(a) Find the value of y when $x = 2.8$.
(b) Find the value of y when $x = y$.

SEG 1998

⑤ Jan measures the diagonal of a square field as 80 m.
The side of the field has length x m.

(a) Explain why $2x^2 = 6400$.
(b) Calculate the value of x.

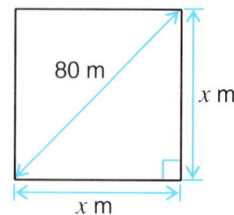

80 m

x m

Not to scale

x m

SEG 1998

⑥ (a) Simplify the expression $2(x - 3) - x$.

(b) Solve the equation $4x - 1 = x + 5$.

(c) A solution to the equation $x^3 + x = 49$ lies between 3 and 4.
Use a trial and improvement method to find this solution.
Give your answer correct to one decimal place.
You must show all your working.

SEG 1999

7 (a) Solve the equation $7(x - 1) = 3x + 2$.

(b) Multiply out and simplify $(x + 3)(2x - 1)$.

SEG 1999

8 (a) The first five terms of a sequence are shown.
$$3, 7, 11, 15, 19, \ldots .$$
Write down the nth term of the sequence.

(b) The first five terms of another sequence are shown.
$$3, 6, 11, 18, 27, \ldots .$$
(i) Write down the next term in the sequence.
(ii) Write down the nth term of the sequence.

SEG 2000 S

9 John and Sarah are each asked to continue a sequence which begins
$$2, 5, \ldots .$$
(a) John writes $2, 5, 8, 11, \ldots .$
Write down the nth term of John's sequence.

(b) Sarah writes $2, 5, 10, 17, \ldots .$
Write down the nth term of Sarah's sequence.

SEG 1998

10 Find the nth term of the sequence $2, 6, 12, 20, \ldots .$

SEG 1998

11 (a) Draw and label axes for x from -5 to 6 and for y from -3 to 6.
On your diagram draw and label the following lines.
$$y = 2x \quad \text{and} \quad x + y = 5$$

(b) Explain how to use your graph to solve the equation $2x = 5 - x$.

(c) Show clearly the single region that is satisfied by **all** of these inequalities.
$$x + y \leqslant 5 \qquad y \geqslant 2x \qquad x \geqslant 0$$
Label this region R.

SEG 1998

12 (a) Solve the equation $3(x + 2) = 4 - x$.

(b) Factorise $m^2 - 7m$.

(c) List the values of n, where n is an integer, such that $1 \leqslant n - 5 < 4$.

(d) Solve the simultaneous equations $\quad 3x + 4y = \quad 0$
$$\qquad\qquad\qquad\qquad\qquad\qquad 4x - 2y = -11.$$

SEG 2000 S

13 The diagram shows a sketch of the line $2y + x = 10$.
Copy the diagram.

(a) Find the coordinates of points G and H.

(b) (i) On your diagram, sketch the graph of $y = 2x$.
(ii) Solve the simultaneous equations
$$2y + x = 10$$
$$y = 2x.$$

(c) The equation of a straight line is $y = ax + b$.
Rearrange the equation to give x in terms of y, a and b.

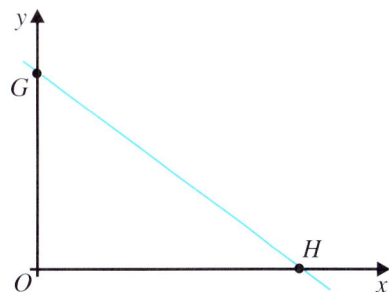

SEG 1999

14 (a) Simplify $42a^7 \div 7a^9$.

(b) What is the value of $4 + 4^{-1}$?

SEG 2000 S

15 (a) Simplify
(i) $4a^2 \times 2a^5$, (ii) $b^6 \div b^2$, (iii) $(5c^3)^2$.
(b) Factorise completely the following expression $6xy^2 - 6x^2y$.
(c) Multiply out and simplify $(m + 1)^2$.

SEG 1998

16 (a) Factorise $4xy - 2x^2y$.
(b) Multiply out and simplify $(x + 3)(x - 2)$.
(c) Solve the equation $x^2 + 5x - 24 = 0$.

SEG 2000 S

17 (a) Solve the inequality $7x + 3 > 17 + 5x$.
(b) Simplify the following.
(i) $2x^3 \times 6x^2$ (ii) $(3y^3)^2$
(c) Multiply out and simplify $(2x - 1)(x - 3)$.

SEG 1998

18 (a) (i) List all the whole number values of n which satisfy the inequality $3 < 2n \leq 11$.
(ii) Solve the inequality $2x^2 < 19$.
(b) Use trial and improvement to solve the equation $x^3 + x = 24$.
Start with $x = 3$.
Give your final answer correct to **one** decimal place.
You **must** show all your working.

SEG 1997

19 (a) List all possible values of x where x is an integer such that $-4 \leq x < 2$.
(b) Solve
(i) $4x - 5 < -3$, (ii) $y^2 \geq 25$.
(c) Rearrange this formula to express a in terms of m, c and e.
$e = m(a - c)$

SEG 1997

20 (a) Solve the equation $7x - 3 = 3x - 2$.
(b) Multiply out and simplify $(3x + 1)(x - 2)$.
(c) Solve the equation $x^2 - 8x = 0$.

SEG 1998

21 (a) Solve the equation $x^2 - 7x + 10 = 0$.
(b) Solve the inequality $3x + 7 < 25$.

SEG 1999

22 The formula connecting x and y is $\dfrac{y}{3x} = \dfrac{a}{b}$
where a and b are integers.
(a) Make x the subject of the formula.
(b) If $a : 10 = b : 1$, find the ratio $x : y$.

SEG 1997

23 A solution of the equation $x^3 + x^2 = 4$ lies between $x = 1$ and 2.
Use the method of trial and improvement to find this solution.
Give your answer correct to one decimal place.
You **must** show all your trials.

SEG 1999

24 The graph shows how the monthly pay of a salesperson depends on sales.

(a) Find the equation of the line in the form $y = ax + b$.

(b) Calculate the pay of a salesperson when sales are £5400.

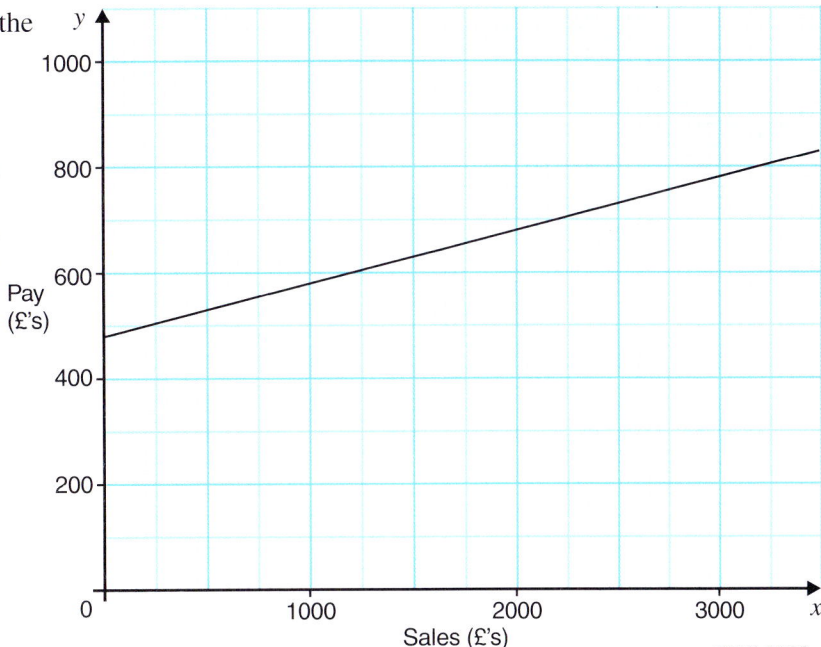

Pay (£'s)

Sales (£'s)

SEG 1999

25 (a) Rearrange the equation $2y - 5 = 2x$ in the form $y = \dots$.

(b) Write down the equation of a different line that is parallel to $2y - 5 = 2x$.

SEG 1994

26 (a) Complete the table of values for $y = x^2 - 2x - 2$.

(b) Draw the graph of $y = x^2 - 2x - 2$ for values of x from -2 to 4.

x	-2	-1	0	1	2	3	4
y	6		-2			1	

(c) (i) Use your graph to solve the equation $x^2 - 2x - 2 = 0$.

(ii) Estimate the gradient of the curve $y = x^2 - 2x - 2$ at the point where $x = 2$.

SEG 1998

27 The cross-section of a swimming pool is shown. It is filled, from empty, at a uniform rate. Copy the axes and sketch a graph of the water height against time, t, as the pool fills.

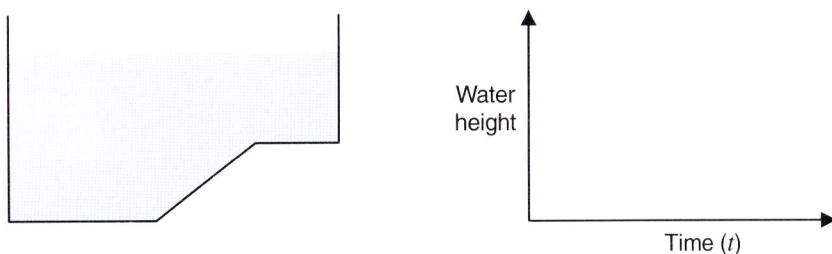

Water height

Time (t)

SEG 1997

28 (a) Complete the table of values for $y = x^3 + 5$.

(b) Draw the graph of $y = x^3 + 5$ for values of x from -3 to 3.

x	-3	-2	-1	0	1	2	3
y		-3	4			13	32

(c) Use your graph to solve the equation $x^3 + 5 = 0$.

SEG 2000 S

29 A rectangle has length $(x + 2)$ cm and width $(x + 1)$ cm. The rectangle has an area of 6 cm^2.
Form an equation and show that it can be simplified to $x^2 + 3x - 4 = 0$.

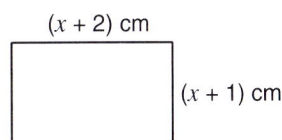

$(x + 2)$ cm

$(x + 1)$ cm

30 The diagram shows a shape, in which all the corners are right angles.
The area of the shape is 48 cm².

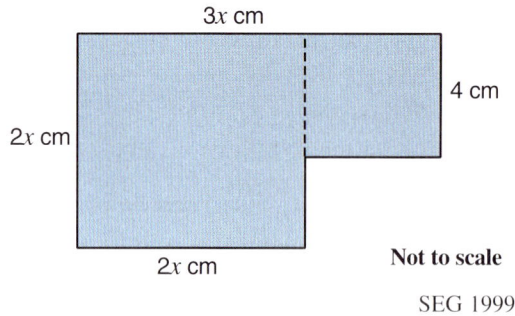

(a) Form an equation, in terms of x, for the area of the shape.
Show that it can be simplified to
$x^2 + x - 12 = 0$.

(b) By solving the equation
$x^2 + x - 12 = 0$, calculate the value of x.

3x cm

4 cm

2x cm

2x cm

Not to scale

SEG 1999

31 A rectangular lawn has a path on 3 sides as shown.
The lawn has dimensions x metres by $3x$ metres.
The path is 1 metre wide.

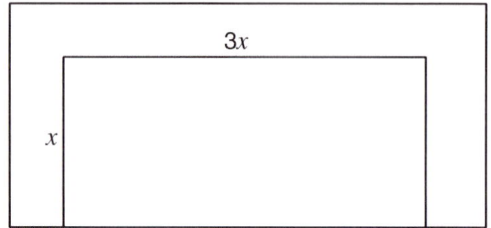

(a) The total area of the lawn and the path is 80 m².
Show that $3x^2 + 5x - 78 = 0$.

(b) By solving the equation $3x^2 + 5x - 78 = 0$ find the area of the lawn.

3x

x

Not to scale

SEG 2000 S

32 A class takes x weeks to collect £84 for charity.
The mean amount collected per week is, therefore, £$\frac{84}{x}$.
The following week the class collects £20.

(a) Write down, in terms of x, the new mean amount collected per week.
The collection of £20 increases the mean amount collected per week by £1.

(b) (i) Use your answer to part (a) to write an equation.
(ii) Show that this equation can be written as $x^2 - 19x + 84 = 0$.

(c) Solve this equation to calculate x.

SEG 1998

33 (a) The rule connecting y and x in the table below is of the form $y = 2x^c$.
What is the value of c?

(b) (i) Find the value of y when $x = 7.9$.
(ii) Find the value of x when $y = 4$.

x	1.0	2.2	3.2		6.8	7.9	9
y	2.0	3.1	3.6	4	5.2		6

SEG 1996

34 The nth term of a sequence is given by $\frac{2n}{n+1}$.

(a) Write down the value of
(i) the 20th term, (ii) the 100th term.

(b) Describe what happens to the value of the sequence as n increases in size.

SEG 1995

35 (a) Which of the following equations are illustrated by the graphs shown?

$y = -x$ $y = 2 - x$ $y = 1 - x^2$
$y = x^2$ $2y = 2 + x$ $xy = 1$

(i) y (ii) y (iii) y (iv) y

x x x x

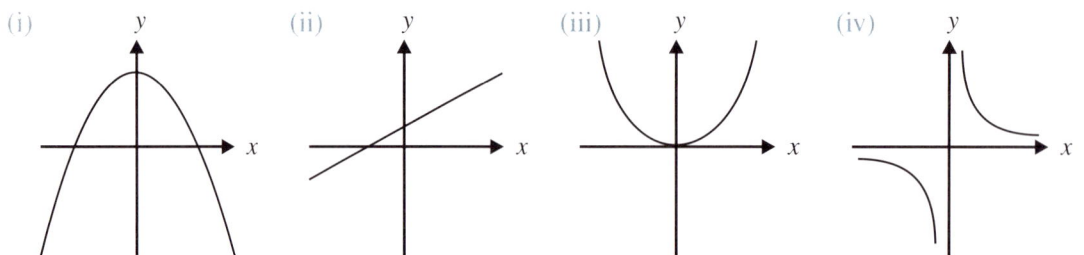

(b) Sketch a graph of the equation $y = x^3 + 1$.

SEG 1994

36 Draw the graph of $y = x^3$ over the interval $0 \leqslant x \leqslant 2$.
Use your graph to solve the equation $x^3 = 4 - 2x$.

SEG 1997

37 (a) Draw the graph of $y = x^2 - 3x$, for values of x from -1 to 4.
(b) By drawing a suitable straight line on the same diagram, estimate, correct to one decimal place, the solutions to the equation $x^2 - 2x - 1 = 0$.
(c) By drawing another straight line on the same diagram, solve the inequality $x^2 - 3x \geqslant 1$.

SEG 1998 S

38 The graph shows the journey of a cyclist.

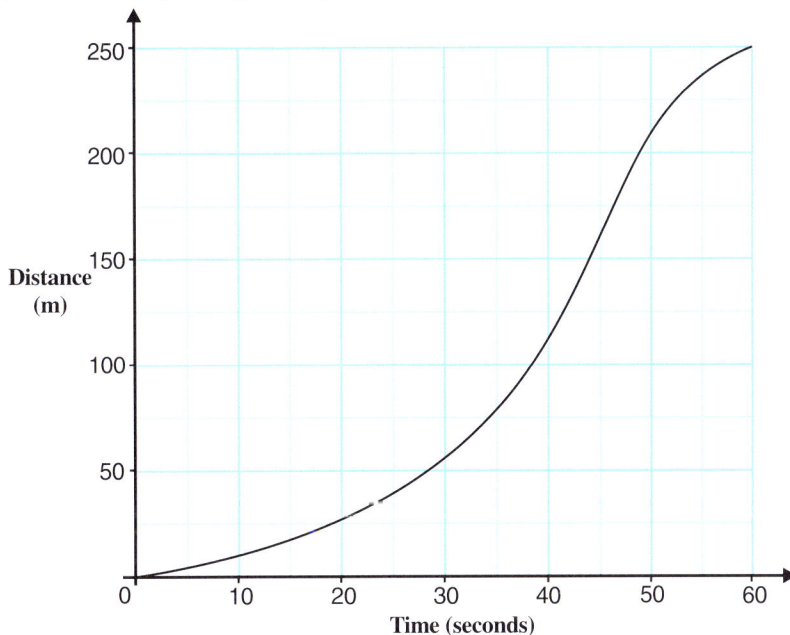

Estimate the maximum velocity of the cyclist on the journey.
State the units of your answer.

SEG 1999

39 The graph illustrates the journey of a London Underground train between two stations.
The journey takes 100 seconds.

(a) Describe how the speed of the train varies on the journey.

(b) Estimate the maximum acceleration of the train.

(c) Estimate the distance, in kilometres, between the stations.

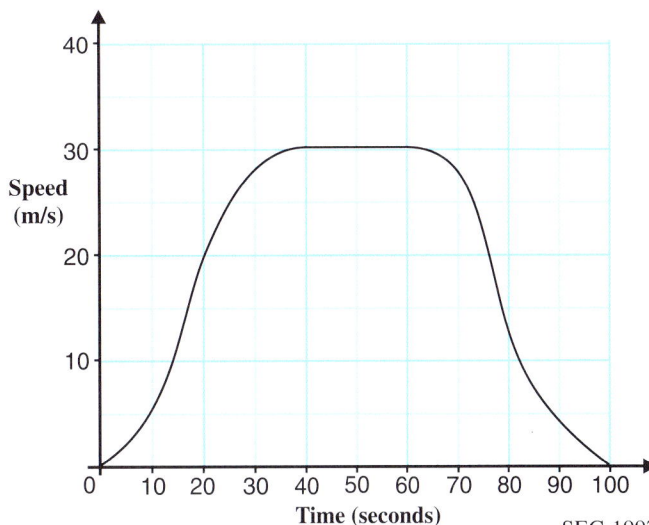

SEG 1997

40 The cross-section of a river bed is shown.
The width of the river, AB, is 12 metres and its depth is measured at 2 metre intervals from point A.

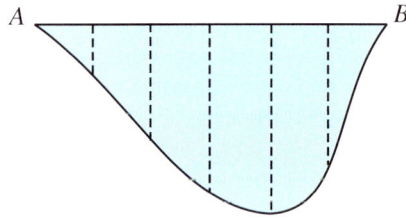

The information is recorded in the following table.

Distance from A	0	2	4	6	8	10	12
Depth	0	1.8	4.0	6.0	6.6	4.6	0

(a) Estimate the area of the cross-section of the river to the nearest square metre.
(b) The river is flowing at a speed of 0.2 m/s.
Estimate the volume of water flowing in one second.

SEG 1994

41 (a) The expression $x^2 - 6x + 7$ can be written in the form $(x + a)^2 + b$, where a and b are constants.
Determine the values of a and b and hence find the minimum value of the expression.

(b) The solutions of the equation $x^2 - 6x + 7 = 0$ can be written in the form $x = p \pm q \sqrt{2}$, where p and q are rational numbers.
Determine the values of p and q.

SEG 1996

42 A sequence is given by $x_{n+1} = \dfrac{12}{x_n + 4}$.

(a) (i) The first term of the sequence is $x_1 = 3$.
Find the next three terms.
(ii) What do you think is the value of x_n as n becomes larger? Write down this value.

(b) (i) Show that the quadratic equation which the sequence above is intended to solve is $x^2 + 4x - 12 = 0$.
(ii) Solve this quadratic equation.

SEG 1994

43 (a) You are given the formula $c(a - 5) = 2(3 - 2a)$.
Rearrange the formula to give a in terms of c.

(b) Simplify the expression $\dfrac{x}{x - 1} - \dfrac{1}{x + 1}$.

SEG 2000 S

44 (a) You are given that $(2x + b)^2 + c = ax^2 - 4x - 5$.
Calculate the values of a, b and c.
(b) You are given $q = a(p + 3)^{-3}$.
When $p = 7$, $q = 2$.
Find p when $q = \frac{1}{4}$.

SEG 2000 S

45 Solve the equation $2x^2 + 7x - 1 = 0$.

SEG 1999

46 Solve the equation $\dfrac{4}{2x - 1} - \dfrac{1}{x + 1} = 1$.

SEG 1999

47 The diagram on the right shows a sketch of the graph of $y = x^2$ for $-2 \leqslant x \leqslant 2$..

Each of the graphs below is a transformation of this graph.
Write down the equation of each graph.

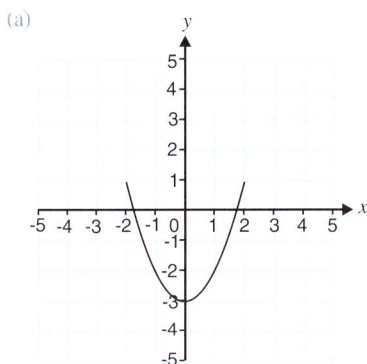

(a)

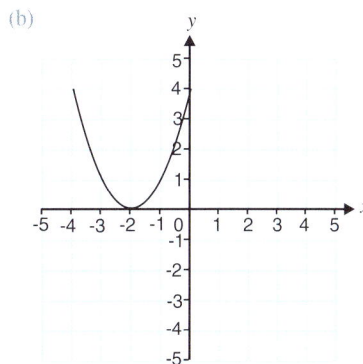

(b)

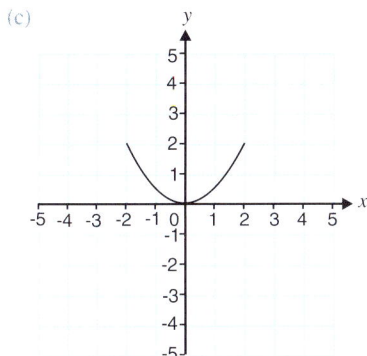

(c)

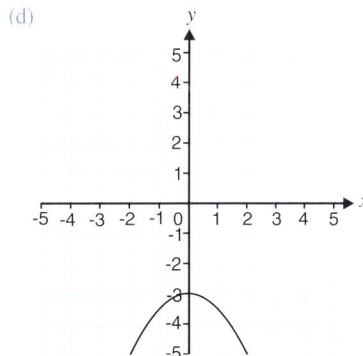

(d)

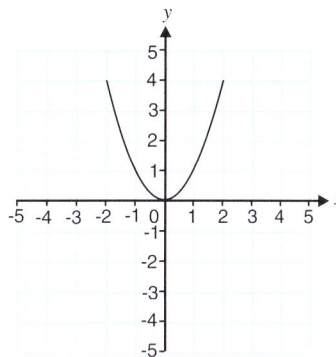

SEG 1999

48 The diagram shows a sketch of the graph of $y = f(x)$ for $-3 \leqslant x \leqslant 3$.

(a) (i) Draw the graph of $y = f(x - 2)$.
    (ii) Draw the graph of $y = f(x) - 1$.

(b) Draw the graph of $y = 1 - f(x)$.

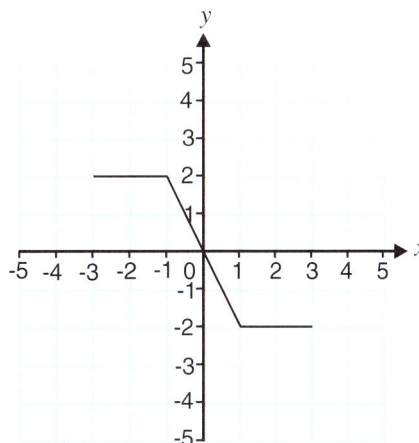

SEG 2000 S

CHAPTER 17

Angles, Parallel Lines and Polygons

An **angle** is a measure of turn.
Angles are measured in **degrees**.

Types and names of angles

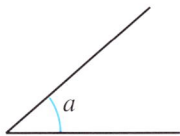

acute angle
$0° < a < 90°$

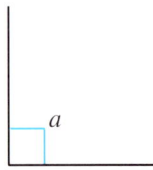

right angle
$a = 90°$

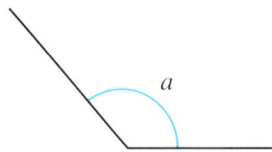

obtuse angle
$90° < a < 180°$

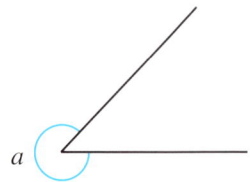

reflex angle
$180° < a < 360°$

Lines and angles

Angles at a point

When angles meet at a point, the sum of all the angles is 360°.

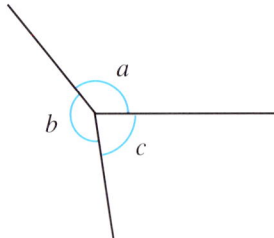

$$a + b + c = 360°$$

Complementary angles

When two angles add up to 90°, the angles are called **complementary**.

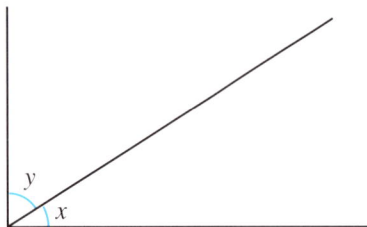

$$x + y = 90°$$

x and y are complementary angles.

Supplementary angles

Angles which can be placed together on a straight line add up to 180°.
When two angles add up to 180°, the angles are called **supplementary**.

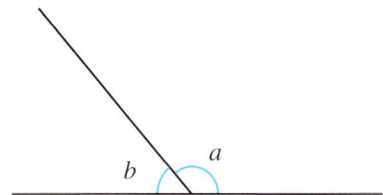

$$a + b = 180°$$

a and b are supplementary angles.

Vertically opposite angles

When two lines cross each other the angles between the lines make two pairs of equal angles.

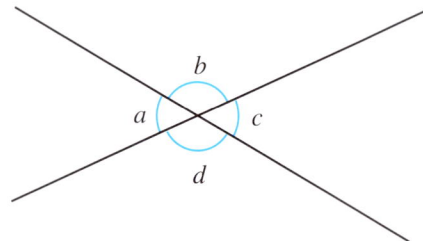

$$a = c \text{ and } b = d$$

a and c are vertically opposite angles.
b and d are vertically opposite angles.

EXAMPLES

1 Without measuring, work out the size of the angle marked a.

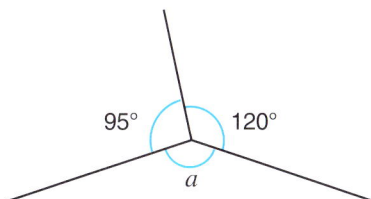

Angles at a point add up to 360°.
$a + 95 + 120 = 360$
$a = 360 - 95 - 120$
$a = 145°$

2 Calculate the sizes of the angles marked with letters.

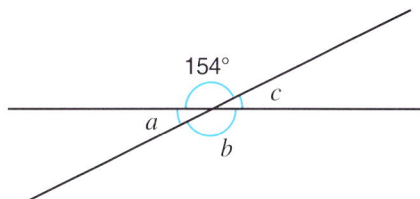

$b = 154°$ (vertically opposite angles)
$a + 154 = 180$ (supplementary angles)
$a = 180 - 154$
$a = 26°$
$c = 26°$
$a = 26°, b = 154°, c = 26°$

Parallel lines

Parallel lines are lines which never meet.

The diagram, on the right, shows two parallel lines crossed by another straight line called a **transversal**.

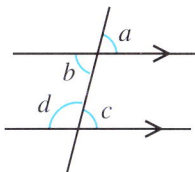

Arrowheads are used to show that lines are parallel.

Corresponding angles

Angles a and c are equal. They are called **corresponding** angles.
Corresponding angles are always equal.
Here are some examples of corresponding angles.

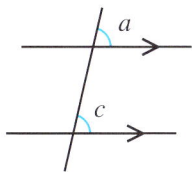

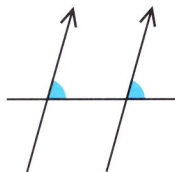

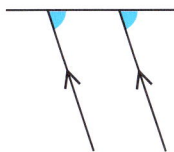

Corresponding angles are always on the same side of the transversal.

Alternate angles

Angles b and c are equal. They are called **alternate** angles.
Alternate angles are always equal.
Here are some examples of alternate angles.

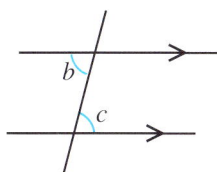

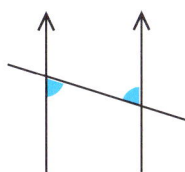

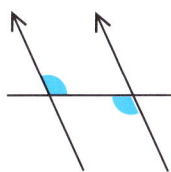

Alternate angles are always on opposite sides of the transversal.

253

Allied angles

Angles b and d add up to $180°$. They are called **allied** angles.
Allied angles are supplementary, they always add up to $180°$.
Here are some examples of allied angles.

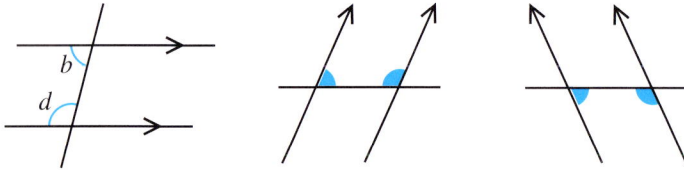

$b + d = 180°$

Allied angles are always between parallels on the same side of the transversal.

EXAMPLE

This diagram has not been drawn accurately.
(a)   Without measuring, find the sizes of the angles marked a and b.
(b)   Work out the value of c.

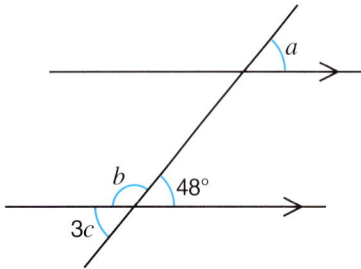

(a) $a = 48°$ (corresponding angles)

$b + 48° = 180°$ (supplementary angles)
$b = 132°$

(b) $3c = 48°$ (vertically opposite angles)
$c = 16°$

Exercise 17.1

1   Without measuring, work out the size of the angles marked with letters.

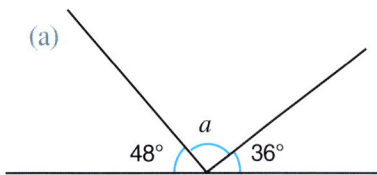

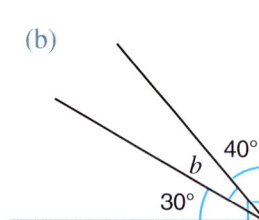

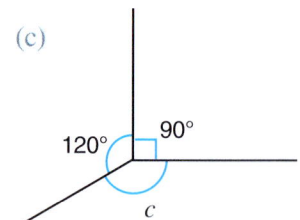

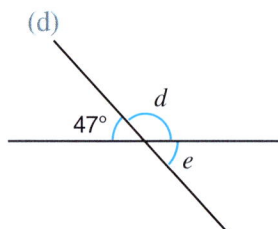

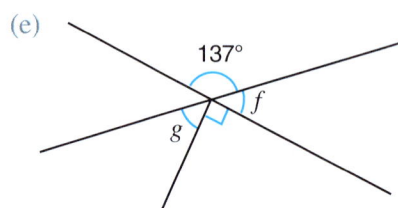

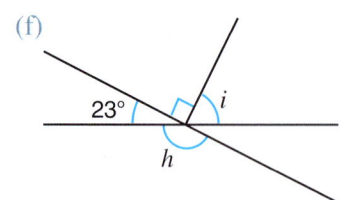

(a)

(b)

(c)

(d)

(e)

(f)

2 These diagrams are not drawn accurately. Without measuring, work out the value of *x* in each diagram.

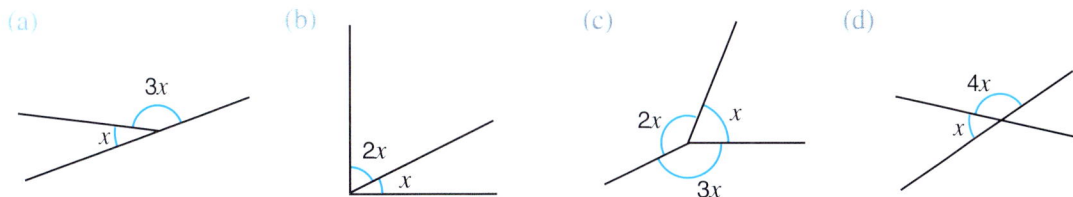

(a)   3x x

(b)   2x x

(c)   2x x 3x

(d)   4x x

3 These diagrams have not been drawn accurately. Without measuring, find the value of *a* in each diagram.

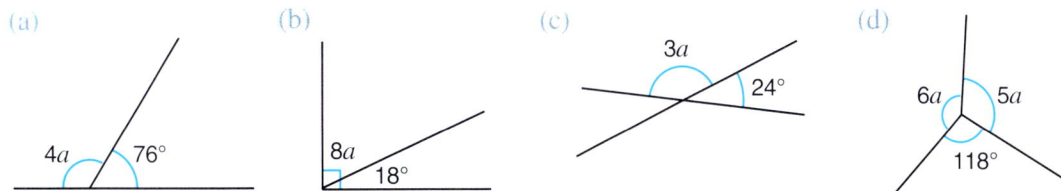

(a)   4a 76°

(b)   8a 18°

(c)   3a 24°

(d)   6a 5a 118°

4 These diagrams have not been drawn accurately. Without measuring, find the sizes of the angles marked with letters.

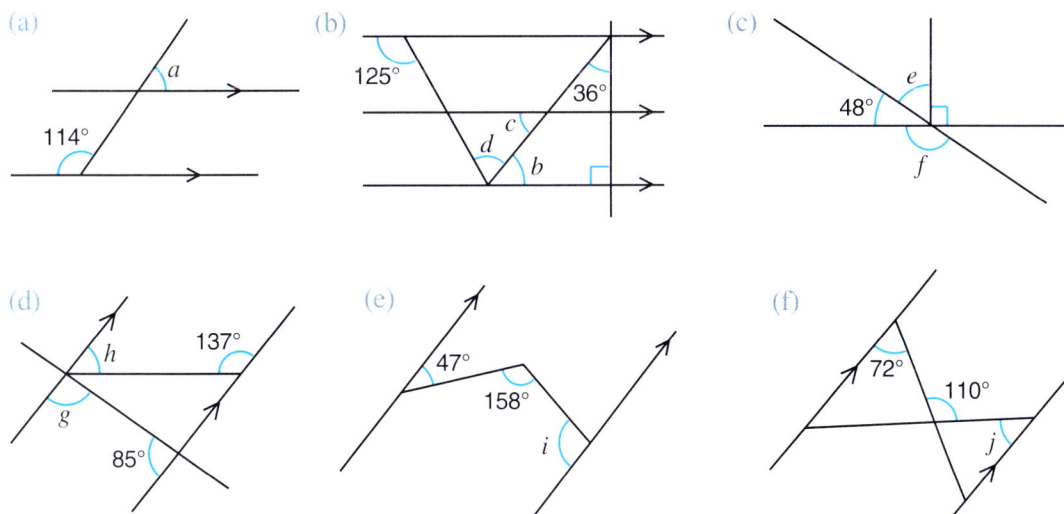

(a)   a 114°

(b)   125° 36° c d b

(c)   48° e f

(d)   h 137° g 85°

(e)   47° 158° i

(f)   72° 110° j

5 These diagrams are not drawn accurately. Work out the sizes of the required angles.

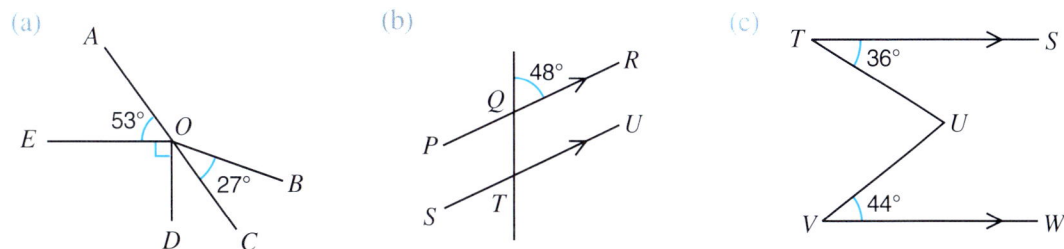

(a)   A 53° O E 27° B D C

Find ∠AOB and ∠COD.

(b)   48° R Q P U S T

Find ∠QTU and ∠QTS.

(c)   T 36° S U V 44° W

Find reflex angle *TUV*.

Types of triangle

Measure the angles in each of these triangles.

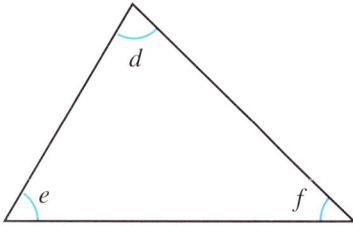

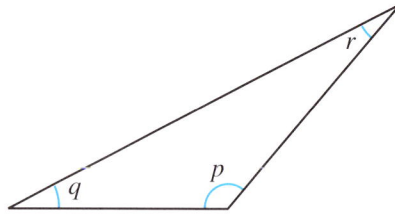

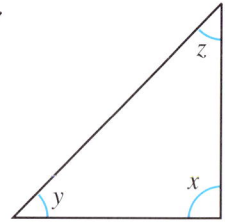

Angles d, e and f are all acute angles. Triangles with three acute angles are called **acute-angled** triangles.

Angle p is an obtuse angle. Triangles with an obtuse angle are called **obtuse-angled** triangles.

Angle x is a right angle. Triangles with a right angle are called **right-angled** triangles.

The sum of the angles in a triangle

The sum of the three angles in a triangle is 180°.

Add up the three angles d, e and f in the triangle above.
Do the same for the other two triangles.
You may not always get 180°. Can you explain why?

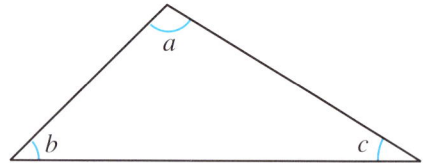

$$a + b + c = 180°$$

Exterior angle of a triangle

When one side of a triangle is extended, as shown, the angle formed is called an **exterior angle**.

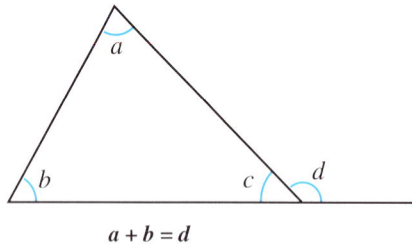

$a + b = d$

In any triangle the exterior angle is always equal to the sum of the two opposite interior angles.
Check this by measuring the angles a, b and d in the diagram.

This result can be easily proved.
$a + b + c = 180°$
(sum of angles in a triangle)
$c + d = 180°$
(supplementary angles)
$a + b + c = c + d$
$a + b = d$

EXAMPLE

Find the sizes of the angles marked a and b.

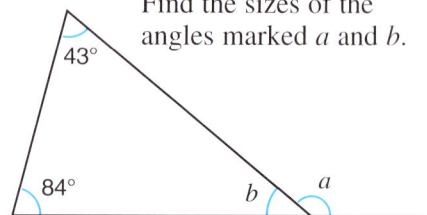

Short but fully accurate
In Geometry we often abbreviate words and use symbols to provide the reader with full details using the minimum amount of writing.

Δ is short for triangle.
ext. $\angle$ of a Δ means exterior angle of a triangle.
supp. $\angle$'s means supplementary angles.

$a = 84° + 43°$ (ext. $\angle$ of a Δ)
$a = 127°$

$b + 127° = 180°$ (supp. $\angle$'s)
$\qquad b = 180° - 127°$
$\qquad b = 53°$

256

You should be able to do this exercise without a calculator. Having completed the exercise you can use your calculator to check your working.

1 Is it possible to draw triangles with the following types of angles?
Give a reason for each of your answers.

(a) three acute angles,
(b) one obtuse angle and two acute angles,
(c) two obtuse angles and one acute angle,
(d) three obtuse angles,
(e) one right angle and two acute angles,
(f) two right angles and one acute angle.

2 Is it possible to draw a triangle with these angles?
If a triangle can be drawn, what type of triangle is it?
Give a reason for each of your answers.

(a) 95°, 78°, 7°
(b) 48°, 62°, 90°
(c) 48°, 62°, 70°
(d) 90°, 38°, 52°
(e) 130°, 35°, 15°

3 Without measuring, work out the size of the third angle in each of these triangles.

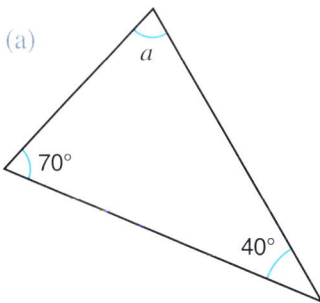

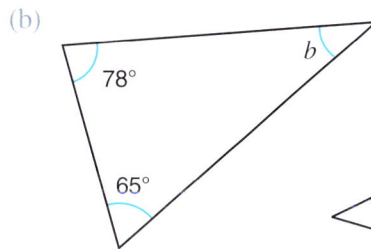

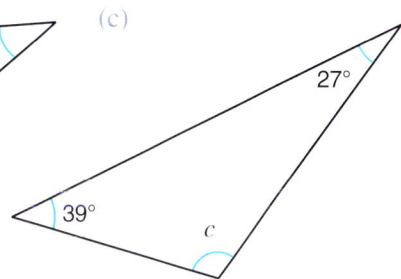

(a) *a*, 70°, 40°
(b) 78°, 65°, *b*
(c) 27°, 39°, *c*

4 The following diagrams have not been drawn accurately, work out the size of the marked angles.

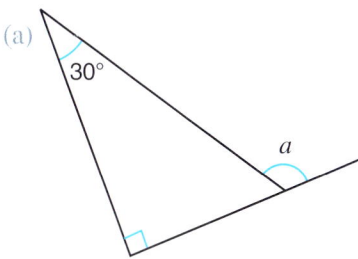

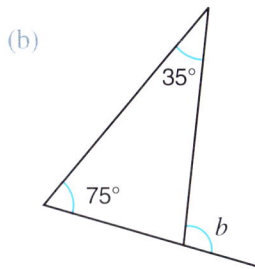

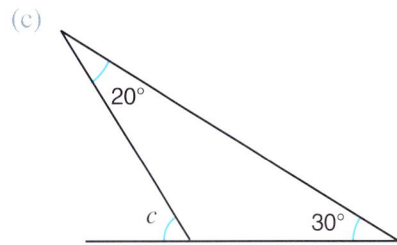

(a) 30°, *a*
(b) 35°, 75°, *b*
(c) 20°, *c*, 30°

5 In the diagram, *ABC* is an equilateral triangle and *ADC* is an isosceles triangle with side *DC* extended to *E*.
Angle *ADC* = 48°.
Calculate angle *BAD* and angle *BCE*.

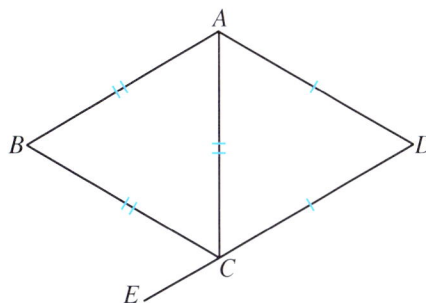

257

Special triangles

Scalene triangle

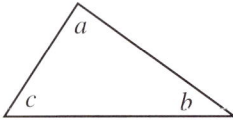

The angles are all different.
$a + b + c = 180°$.

Isosceles triangle

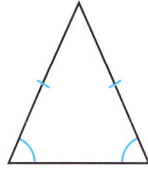

Two equal sides.
Two angles equal.

Equilateral triangle

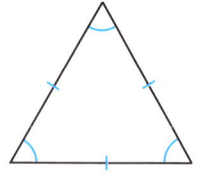

Three equal sides.
All angles are 60°.

Special quadrilaterals

Parallelogram

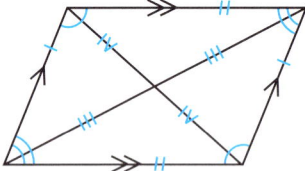

Opposite sides equal and parallel.
Opposite angles equal.
Diagonals bisect each other.

Rhombus

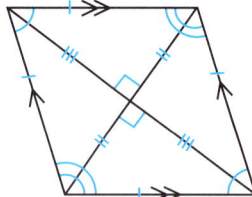

Four equal sides, opposite sides
parallel.
Opposite angles equal.
Diagonals bisect each other at 90°.

Trapezium

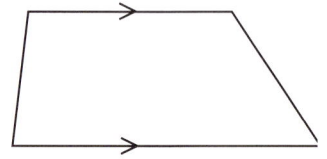

One pair of parallel sides.

Rectangle

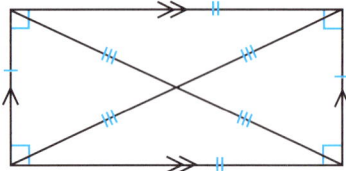

Opposite sides equal and parallel.
Angles of 90°.
Diagonals bisect each other.

Kite

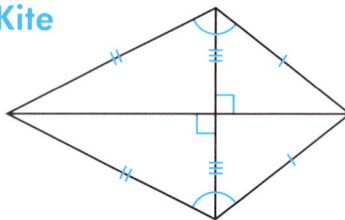

Two pairs of adjacent sides equal.
One pair of opposite angles equal.
One diagonal bisects the other at 90°.

Isosceles trapezium

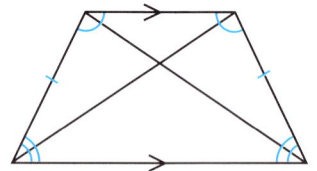

One pair of parallel sides.
Non-parallel sides equal.
Two pairs of equal angles.
Diagonals equal.

Square

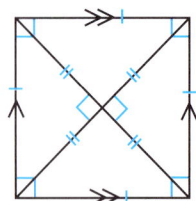

Four equal sides, opposite
sides parallel.
Angles of 90°.
Diagonals bisect each other at 90°.

Remember:
Sides of equal length are marked with
the same number of **dashes**.
Lines which are parallel are marked
with the same number of **arrowheads**.
Angles of equal size are marked with
the same number of **arcs**.

258

Lines of symmetry

These shapes are **symmetrical**.

When each shape is folded along the dashed line the left-hand side will fit exactly over the right-hand side. The dashed line is called a **line of symmetry**.

Some shapes have more than one line of symmetry.

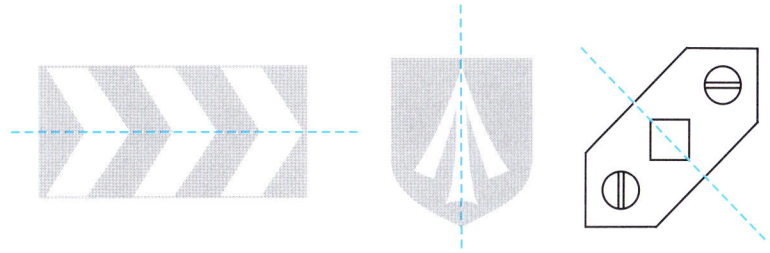
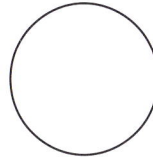
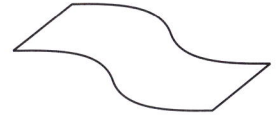

Circle
Infinite number of lines of symmetry.
Each diameter is a line of symmetry.

Shape with no lines of symmetry.

Rotational symmetry

Is this shape symmetrical?

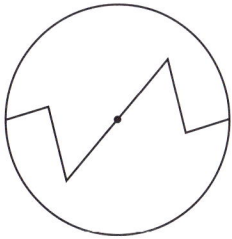

The shape does not have line symmetry.

Try placing a copy of the shape over the original and rotating it about the centre of the circle.

After 180° (a half-turn) the shape fits into its own outline.
The shape has **rotational symmetry**.
The point about which the shape is rotated is called the **centre of rotation**.
The **order of rotational symmetry** is 2. When rotating the shape through 360° it fits into its own outline twice (once after a half turn and again after a full-turn).

A shape can have both line symmetry and rotational symmetry.

Sum of the angles of a quadrilateral

The sum of the four angles of a quadrilateral is 360°.

Measure the angles of this quadrilateral.
Do the angles add up to 360°?

You may not always get 360°.
Can you explain why?

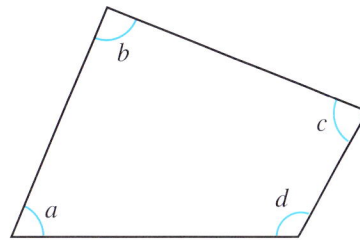

$a + b + c + d = 360°$

EXAMPLE   Without measuring, work out the size of the angle marked x.

PQ is parallel to *RS* and *PS* is parallel to *QR*.
PQRS could be either a parallelogram or a rhombus.
In both types of quadrilateral the opposite angles are equal.

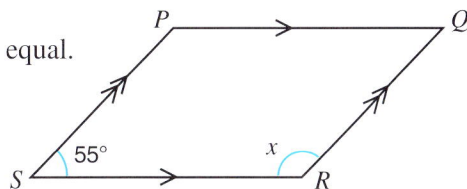

$$55° + 55° + x + x = 360°$$
$$110° + 2x = 360°$$
$$2x = 360° - 110°$$
$$2x = 250°$$
$$x = 125°$$

You should be able to do this exercise without using your calculator. Having completed the exercise you can use a calculator to check your working.

1 Triangle *ABC* is isosceles with *AC* = *CB*.
A is at (3, 0) and *B* is at (0, 3).
Give the coordinates of the possible positions of *C*.

2 Triangle *PQR* is isosceles with angle *RPQ* = angle *QRP*.
P is the point (3, 5) and *R* is the point (9, 5).
Give the coordinates of the two possible positions of *Q* so that angle *PQR* is a right angle.

3 These diagrams have not been drawn accurately.
Work out the sizes of the required angles.

(a)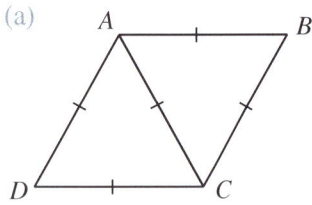

Find ∠*BCD*.

(b)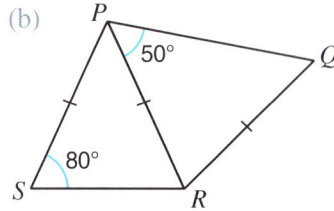

Find ∠*PRQ* and ∠*QRS*.

(c)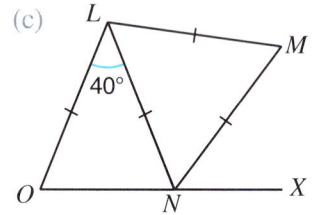

Find ∠*MNX*.

4 *PQRS* is a rectangle. *P* is the point (1, 4), *Q* (4, 6), *R* (6, 4). Find the coordinates of *S*.

5 *ABCD* is a rhombus. *A* is the point (3, 0), *B* (0, 4) and *D* (8, 0). Find the coordinates of *C*.

6 *WXYZ* is a parallelogram. *W* is the point (1, 0), *X* (4, 1), *Z* (3, 3). Find the coordinates of *Y*.

7 *OABC* is a kite. *O* is the point (0, 0), *B* (5, 5), *C* (3, 1). Find the coordinates of *A*.

8 *KLMN* is an isosceles trapezium. *K* is the point (1, 1), *M* (4, 3), *N* (5, 1).
Find the coordinates of *L*.

9 The following diagrams have not been drawn accurately. Work out the size of the angles marked with letters.

(a)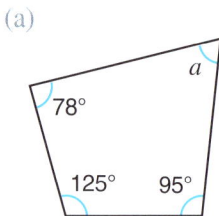

(b)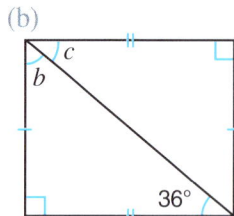

(c)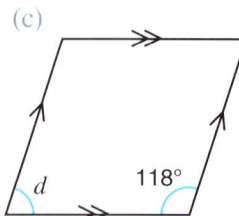

(d)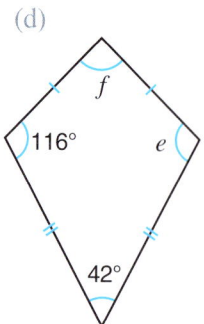

(e)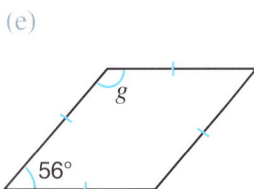

(f)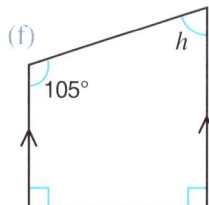

(g)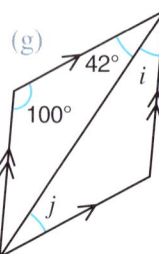

(h)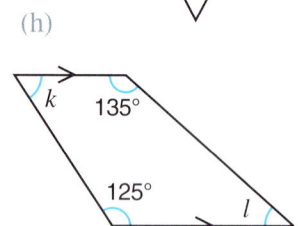

10 These quadrilaterals have been drawn on squared paper.

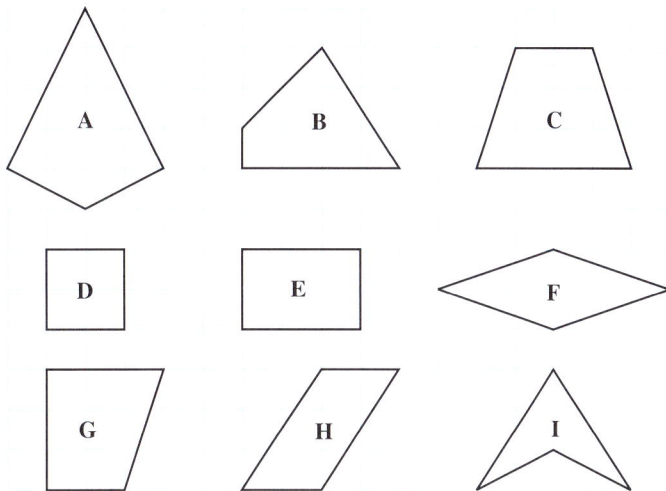

Copy and complete the table for each shape.

Shape	A	B	C	D	E	F	G	H	I
Number of lines of symmetry									
Order of rotational symmetry									

11 The flow chart is used to sort quadrilaterals.

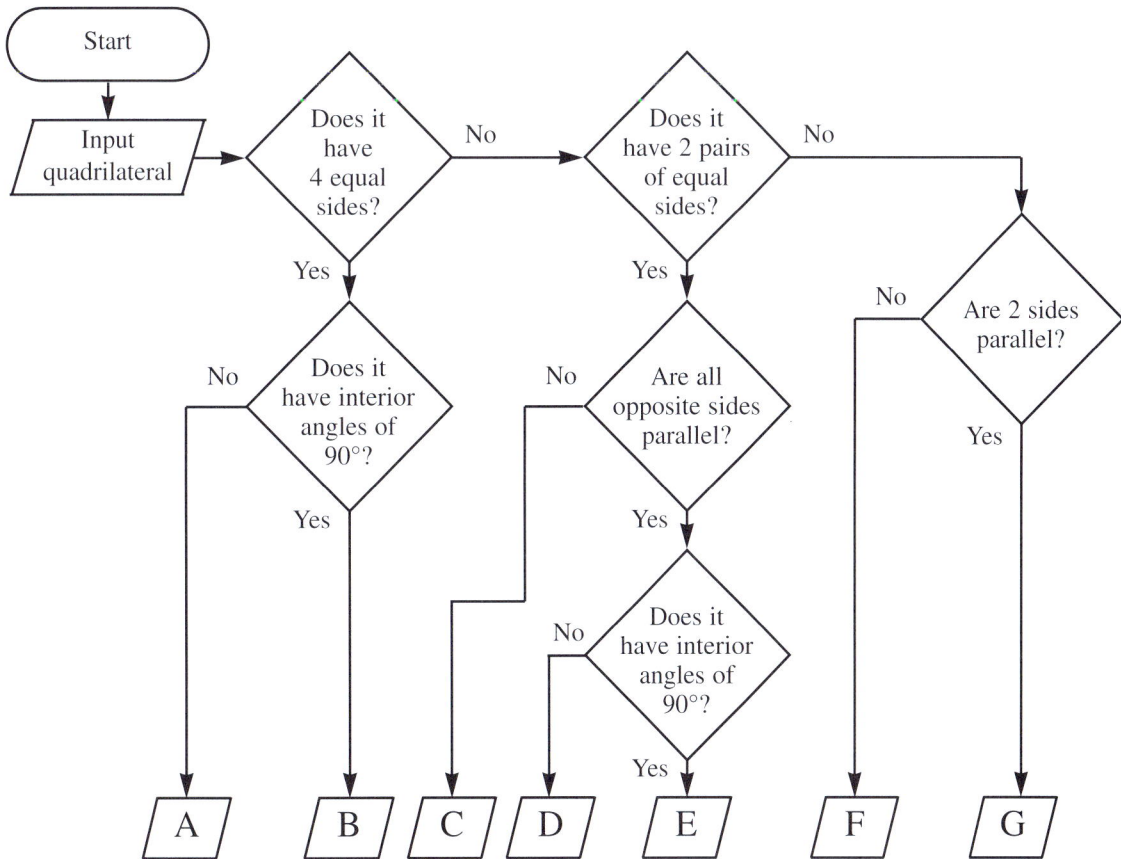

Use the flow chart to find which of the letters A to G applies to each of the following quadrilaterals.

(a) kite   (b) parallelogram   (c) rectangle
(d) rhombus   (e) square   (f) trapezium

12 The following diagrams have not been drawn accurately. Work out the size of the angles marked with letters.

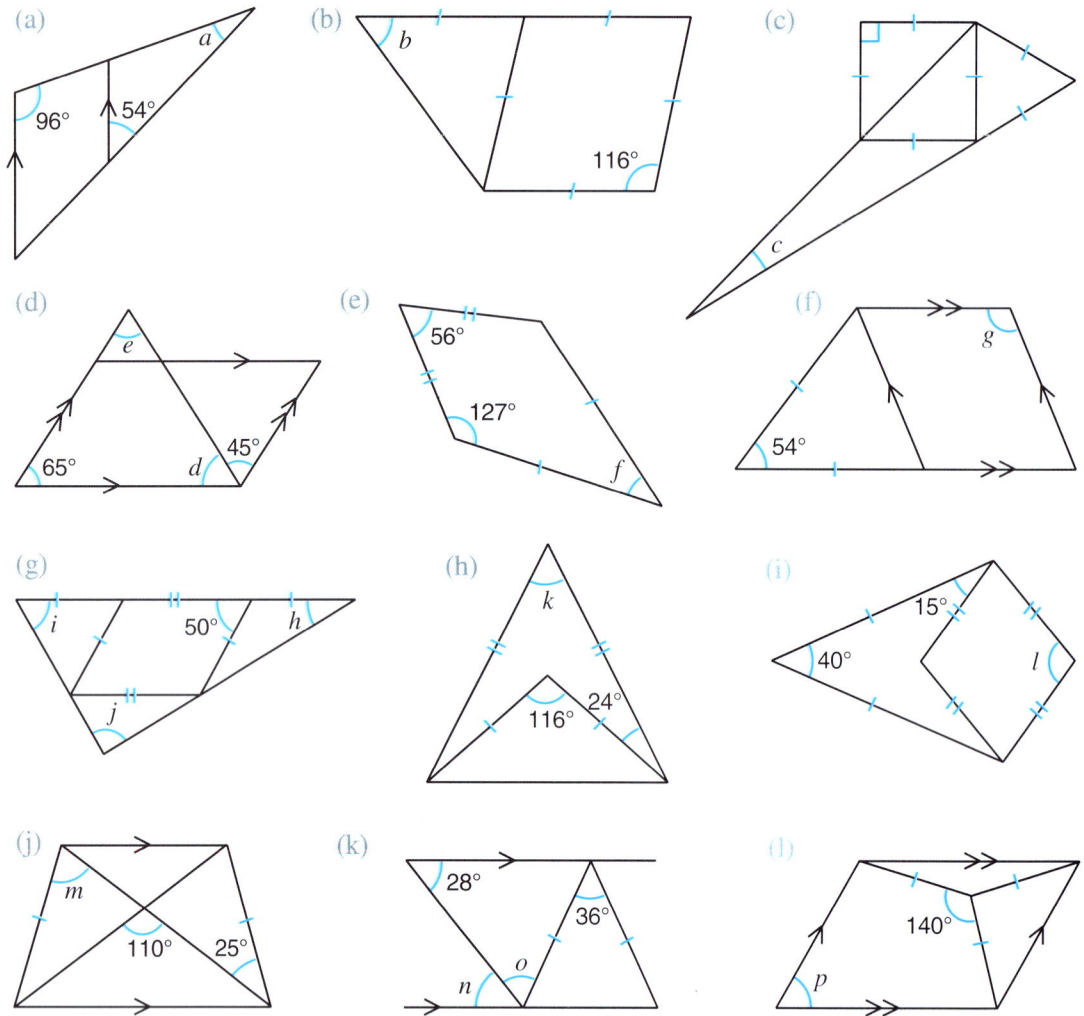

(a)

96° 54° a

(b)

b 116°

(c)

c

(d)

e 65° d 45°

(e)

56° 127° f

(f)

g 54°

(g)

i 50° h j

(h)

k 116° 24°

(i)

15° 40° l

(j)

m 110° 25°

(k)

28° 36° n o

(l)

140° p

13 In the diagram the triangles PQR and SQR are isosceles with $PQ = QR$ and $QS = SR$.
Angle $QPR = 70°$.

(a) Work out the size of angle SQR giving a reason for your answer.

(b) Work out the size of angle SQP.

Not to scale

Q

R 70° P S

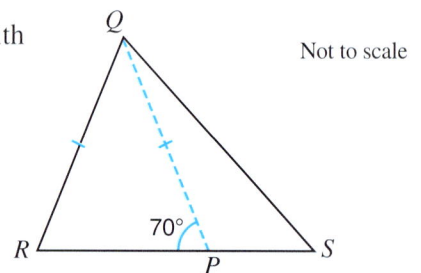

14 $PQRS$ is a rhombus. $PUST$ is a rhombus.
Angle $PTS = 80°$.
Calculate angle SQR.

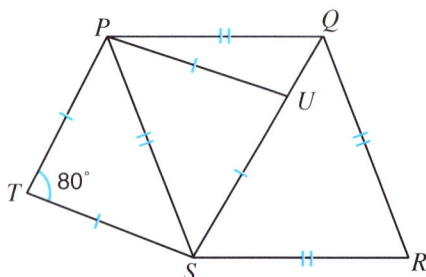

P Q U T 80° S R

15 $WXYZ$ is a square.
Find the size of the marked angles.

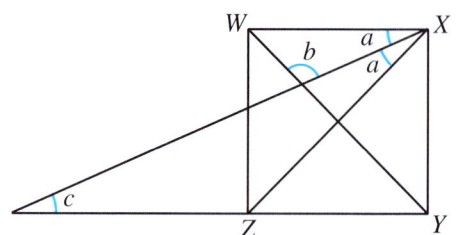

W b a X a c Z Y

262

Polygons

A **polygon** is a shape made by straight lines.
A three-sided polygon is a **triangle**.

A four-sided polygon is
called a **quadrilateral**.

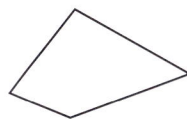

A polygon is a many-sided shape.
Look at these polygons.

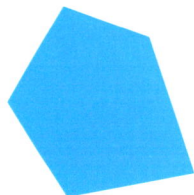

Pentagon
5 sides

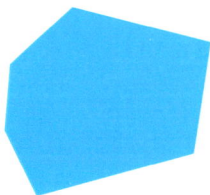

Hexagon
6 sides

Heptagon
7 sides

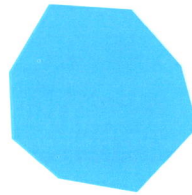

Octagon
8 sides

Interior and exterior angles of a polygon

Angles formed by sides inside a polygon are called **interior angles**.

When a side of a polygon is extended, as shown, the angle formed
is called an **exterior angle**.

At each vertex of the polygon:
    interior angle + exterior angle = 180°

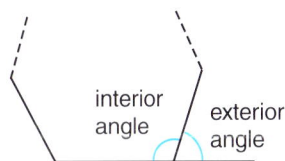

Sum of the interior angles of a polygon

The diagram shows polygons with the diagonals from one vertex drawn.

P 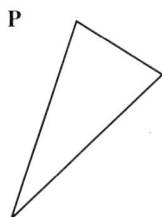 Q 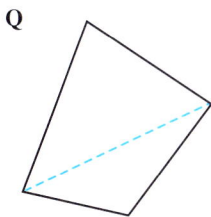 R 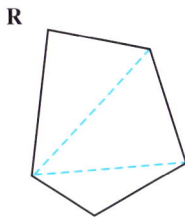 S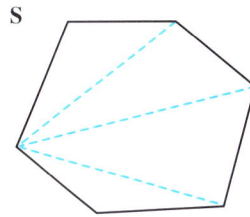

The diagonals divide the polygons into triangles.

Shape	Number of sides	Number of triangles	Sum of interior angles
P	3	1	1 × 180° = 180°
Q	4	2	2 × 180° = 360°
R	5	3	3 × 180° = 540°
S	6	4	4 × 180° = 720°

In general, for any n-sided polygon, the sum of the interior angles is $(n - 2) \times 180°$.

Sum of the exterior angles of a polygon

The sum of the exterior angles of **any** polygon is 360°.

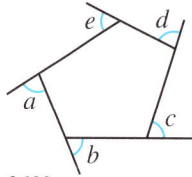

$$a + b + c + d + e = 360°$$

To find the sum of the interior angles of a pentagon substitute $n = 5$ into $(n - 2) \times 180°$.

$(5 - 2) \times 180°$
$= 3 \times 180°$
$= 540°$

EXAMPLE

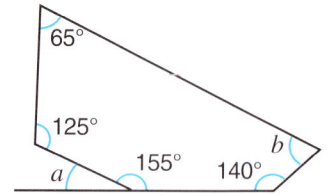

Find the sizes of the angles marked a and b.

$155° + a = 180°$ (int. angle + ext. angle = 180°)
$a = 180° - 155°$
$a = 25°$
The sum of the interior angles of a pentagon is 540°.
$b + 140° + 155° + 125° + 65° = 540°$
$b + 485° = 540°$
$\qquad b = 540° - 485°$
$\qquad b = 55°$

Regular polygons

A polygon with all sides equal and all angles equal is called a **regular polygon**.

A regular triangle is usually called an **equilateral triangle**.
A regular quadrilateral is usually called a **square**.

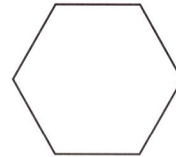

Regular hexagon

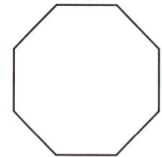

Regular octagon

Exterior angles of regular polygons

In general, for any regular n-sided polygon: exterior angle $= \frac{360°}{n}$

By rearranging the formula we can find the number of sides, n, of a regular polygon when we know the exterior angle.

$$n = \frac{360°}{\text{exterior angle}}$$

EXAMPLE

A regular polygon has an exterior angle of 30°.
(a) How many sides has the polygon?
(b) What is the size of an interior angle of the polygon?

(a) $n = \dfrac{360°}{\text{exterior angle}}$

$n = \frac{360°}{30°}$

$n = 12$

Remember:
It is a good idea to write down the formula you are using.

(b) interior angle + exterior angle = 180°
int. $\angle + 30° = 180°$
int. $\angle = 180° - 30°$
interior angle = 150°

Tessellations

Covering a surface with identical shapes produces
a pattern called a **tessellation**.

To tessellate the shape must not overlap and there must be no gaps.

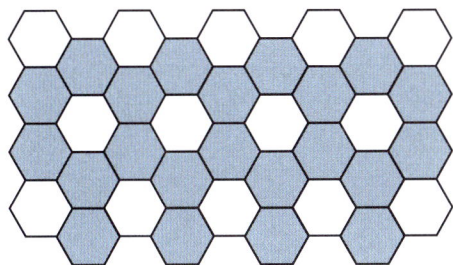

Regular tessellations

This pattern shows a tessellation of regular
hexagons.
This pattern is called a **regular tessellation** because
it is made by using a single regular polygon.

Exercise 17.4

You should be able to do this exercise without using a calculator. Having completed the exercise
you can use a calculator to check your working.

1 These diagrams have not been drawn accurately.
Work out the size of the angles marked with letters.

(a)

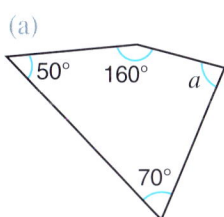

(b)

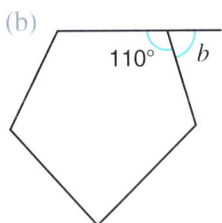

(c)

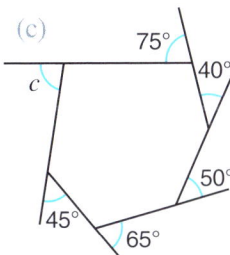

(d)

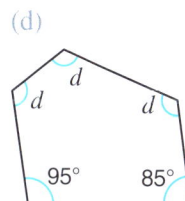

(e)

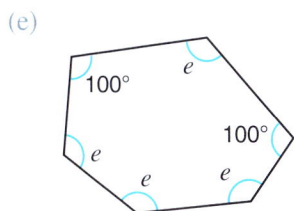

(f)

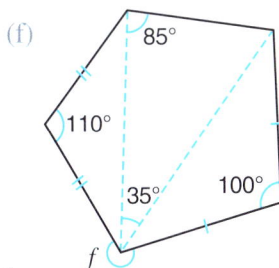

(g)

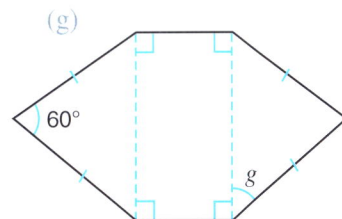

(h)

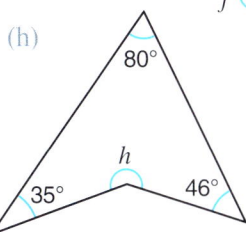

(i)

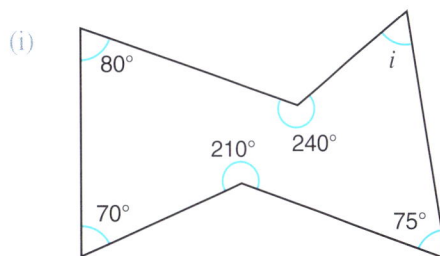

2 Work out the sum of the interior angles of these polygons.

(a)

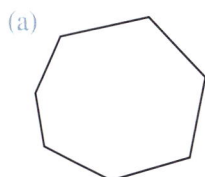

(b)

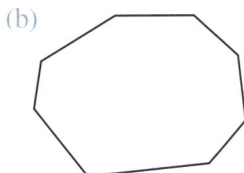

(c)

3 (a) Calculate the size of an exterior angle of a regular pentagon.
  (b) What is the size of an interior angle of a regular pentagon?

4 A regular polygon has an exterior angle of 18°.
How many sides has the polygon?

5 A regular polygon has an interior angle of 135°.
How many sides has the polygon?

6 The following diagrams are drawn using regular polygons.
Work out the values of the marked angles.

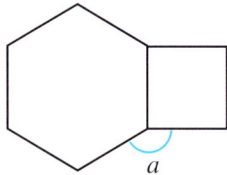

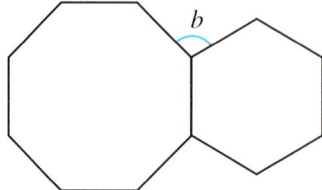

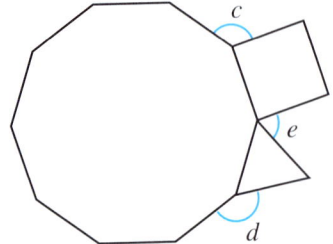

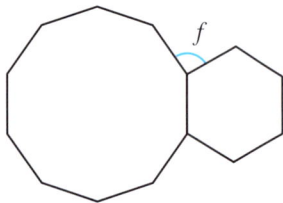

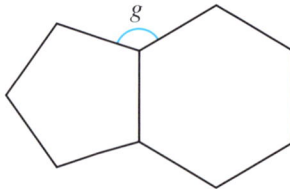

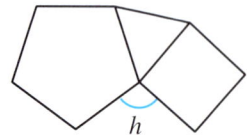

7 ABCDE is a regular pentagon.
Work out
  (a) angle x,
  (b) angle y.

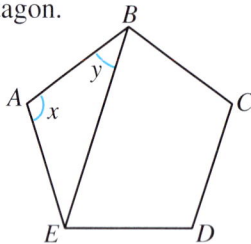

8 AB and BC are two sides of a regular octagon.
PAB is an isosceles triangle with AP = PB.
Angle APB = 36°.
Calculate angle PBC.

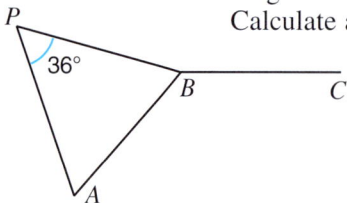

9 A regular polygon has 12 sides.
Calculate the size of an interior angle.

10 A regular polygon has x sides.
Each of its interior angles is $y°$.
Find a formula for y in terms of x.

11 Explain why regular pentagons will not tessellate.

12 Any triangle can be used to make a tessellation.
Draw a triangle of your own, make copies, and show that it will tessellate.

13 (a) Do these quadrilaterals tessellate?

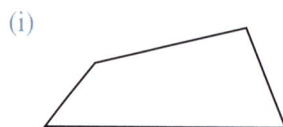

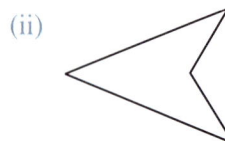

  (i)

  (ii)

Can any quadrilateral be used to make a tessellation?
  (b) Draw quadrilaterals of your own, make copies, and see if they will tessellate.

What you need to know

- An angle of 90° is called a **right angle**.
  An angle less than 90° is called an **acute angle**.
  An angle between 90° and 180° is called an **obtuse angle**.
  An angle greater than 180° is called a **reflex angle**.

- The sum of the angles at a point is 360°.

- Angles on a straight line add up to 180°.
  Angles which add up to 180° are called **supplementary angles**.
  Angles which add up to 90° are called **complementary angles**.

- These pairs of angles are equal.

Vertically opposite angles	**Corresponding angles**	**Alternate angles**

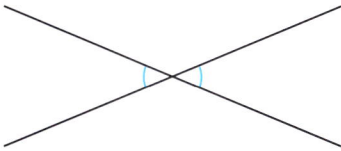

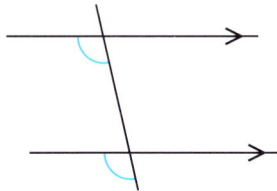

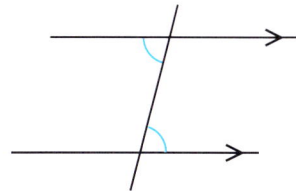

- The sum of the angles in a triangle is 180°.
$$a + b + c = 180°$$

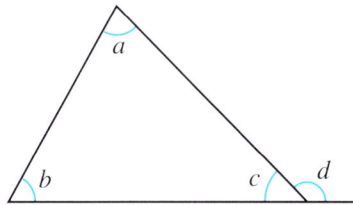

- The exterior angle is equal to the sum of the two opposite interior angles.
$$a + b = d$$

- Types of triangle:

Scalene triangle	**Isosceles triangle**	**Equilateral triangle**
All sides have different lengths.	Two equal sides. Two equal angles.	Three equal sides. Three equal angles, 60°.

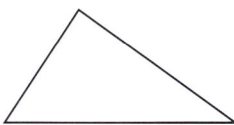

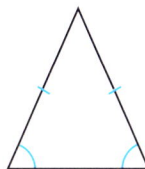

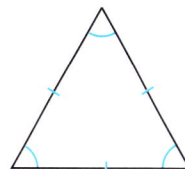

267

- The sum of the angles in a quadrilateral is 360°.

- Facts about these special quadrilaterals:

parallelogram · rectangle · square · rhombus · trapezium · isosceles trapezium · kite

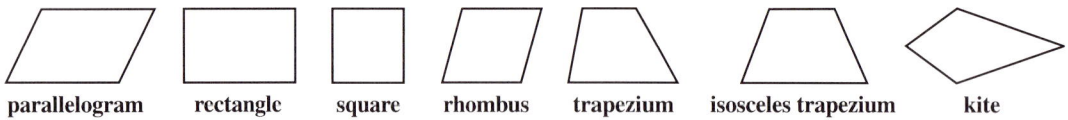

Quadrilateral	Sides	Angles	Diagonals	Line symmetry	Order of rotational symmetry	Area formula
Parallelogram	Opposite sides equal and parallel	Opposite angles equal	Bisect each other	0	2	$A = bh$
Rectangle	Opposite sides equal and parallel	All 90°	Bisect each other	2	2	$A = bh$
Rhombus	4 equal sides, opposite sides parallel	Opposite angles equal	Bisect each other at 90°	2	2	$A = bh$
Square	4 equal sides, opposite sides parallel	All 90°	Bisect each other at 90°	4	4	$A = l^2$
Trapezium	1 pair of parallel sides					$A = \frac{1}{2}(a+b)h$
Isosceles trapezium	1 pair of parallel sides, non-parallel sides equal	2 pairs of equal angles	Equal in length	1	1	$A = \frac{1}{2}(a+b)h$
Kite	2 pairs of adjacent sides equal	1 pair of opposite angles equal	One bisects the other at 90°	1	1	

- A **polygon** is a many-sided shape made by straight lines.

- A polygon with all sides equal and all angles equal is called a **regular polygon**.

- Shapes you need to know:
    A 5-sided polygon is called a **pentagon**.
    A 6-sided polygon is called a **hexagon**.
    An 8-sided polygon is called an **octagon**.

- The sum of the exterior angles of any polygon is 360°.

- At each vertex of a polygon:
    interior angle + exterior angle = 180°

- The sum of the interior angles of an n-sided polygon is given by:
    $(n - 2) \times 180°$

interior angle · exterior angle

- For a regular n-sided polygon:
    exterior angle $= \frac{360°}{n}$

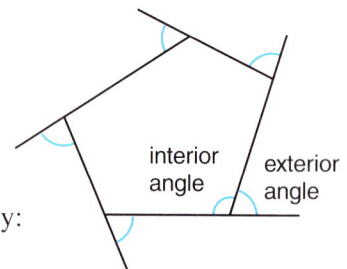

- A shape will **tessellate** if it covers a surface without overlapping and leaves no gaps.

- All triangles tessellate.

- All quadrilaterals tessellate.

Semi-regular tessellations

Tessellations can be made using more than one regular polygon.
Such patterns are called **semi-regular tessellations**.

Investigate semi-regular tessellations.

Review Exercise

1 The diagram shows two straight lines *AB* and *PQ* which cross at *O*.
The line *OT* is perpendicular to *AB*.
Angle *BOT* = 90°.
Angle *QOB* = 63°.

Work out the sizes of angle *x* and angle *y*.

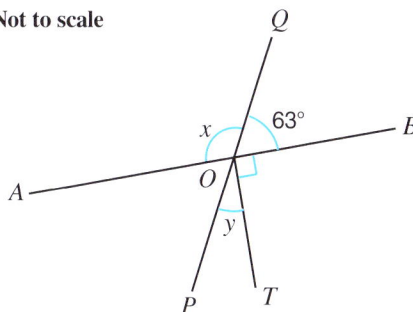

SEG 1998

2 In the diagram *PQ* = *PR* = *PS* and *SP* is parallel to *RQ*.
Angle *RPQ* = 96°.

Calculate the size of
(a) angle *PRQ*,
(b) angle *PRS*.

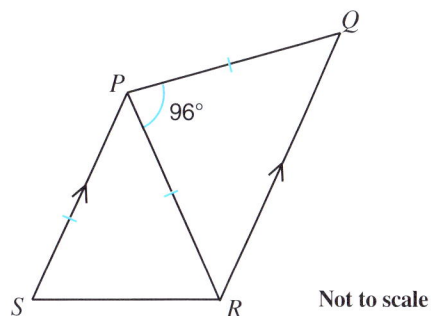

3 In the diagram *AB* is parallel to *CD*. Find *y*.

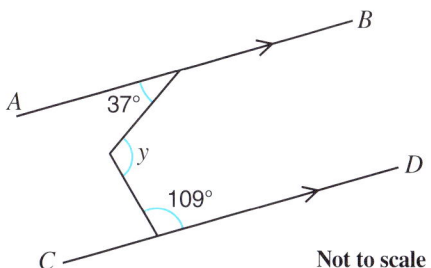

4 The diagram shows a quadrilateral with one side extended.
$CB = CD$, angle $BAD = 50°$,
angle $BCD = 40°$ and angle $ADE = 70°$.

Calculate the size of angles BDA and ABD.

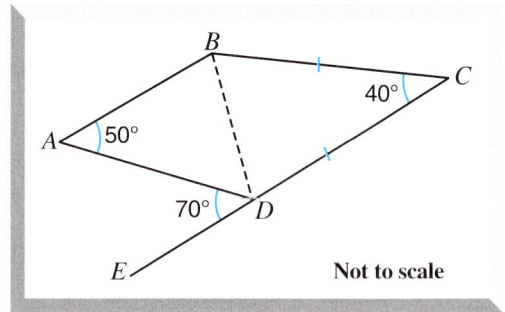

Not to scale

5 ABC is an equilateral triangle.
ACD is an isosceles triangle.
Angle $BCD = 40°$.

Work out the size of angle x giving a reason for your answer.

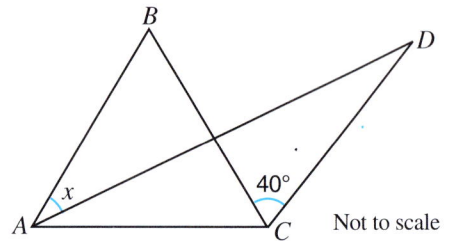

Not to scale

SEG 1995

6 The pentagon has three angles equal in size and the other two angles are each $105°$.

Calculate the size of one of the three equal angles.

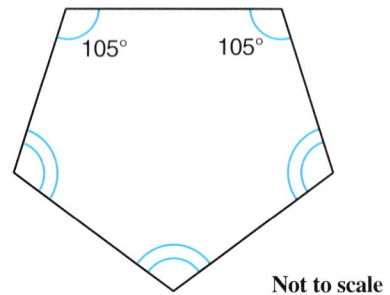

Not to scale

7 The figure $PQRS$ is a rhombus.
Find y if $x = 27°$.

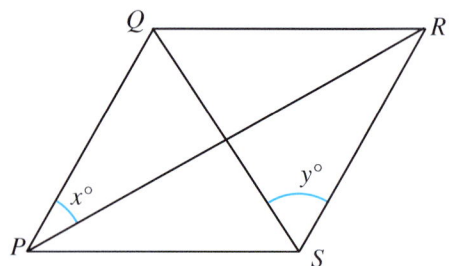

8 The figure is made up of straight lines.
Find the sum of the angles a, b, c, d, e, f, g, h.

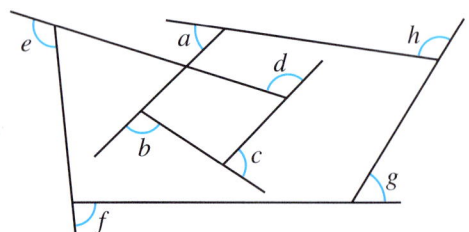

270

9 In the diagram, *PQR* is an equilateral triangle and *PT*, *TR* and *RS* are equal in length.
Angle *PRT* is 50° and *QRS* is a straight line.
Calculate angle *PTS*.

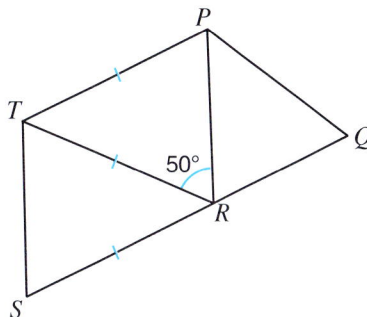

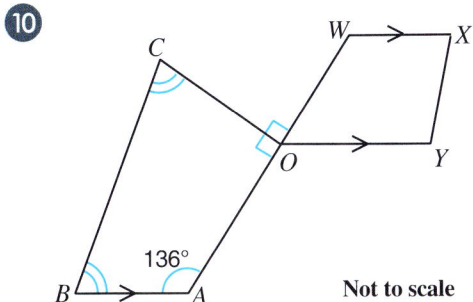

10 In the diagram the sides *BA*, *WX* and *OY* are parallel.
Angle *AOC* = angle *WOC* = 90°.
Angle *OAB* = 136°.

(a) Angle *ABC* = angle *BCO*. Work out the size of angle *BCO*.
(b) Work out the size of angle *OWX*, giving a reason for your answer.
(c) Angle *OYX* is twice the size of angle *WXY*. Work out the size of angle *WXY*.

Not to scale

SEG 1998

11 The straight lines *AB*, *CD* and *EF* are parallel.
The straight line *LHG* is at right angles to *GK*.
Angle *EKG* = 53°. Calculate angle *LHB*.

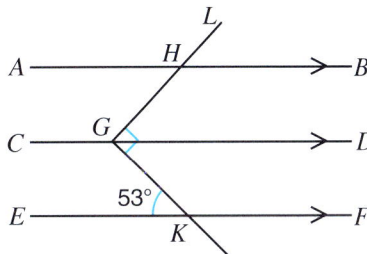

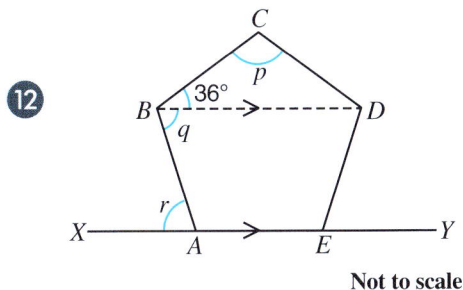

12 The diagram shows a regular pentagon *ABCDE*.
BD is parallel to *XY*. Angle *CBD* = 36°.
Work out the size of the angles *p*, *q* and *r*.

SEG 2000 S

Not to scale

13 The diagram shows two adjacent sides of a polygon.
The angle *QPR* = 15° and *PQX* is a straight line.
Calculate (a) the value of *a*,
(b) the number of sides of the polygon.

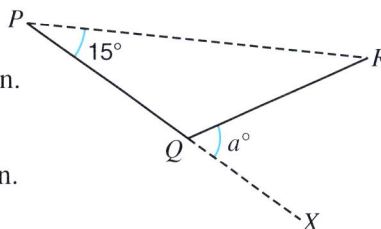

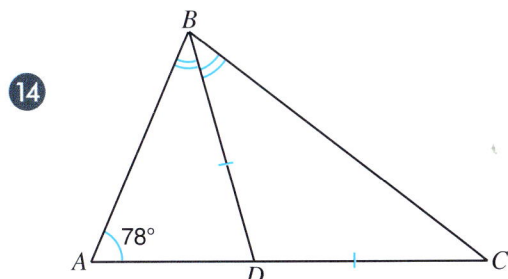

14 In the figure, the bisector of the angle *ABC* meets *AC* at *D*.
BD = *DC* and angle *BAD* = 78°.
Calculate angle *BDC*.

CHAPTER 18

Circle Properties

Circles

A **circle** is the shape drawn by keeping a pencil the same distance from a fixed point on a piece of paper. Compasses can be used to draw circles accurately.

Circumference – special name used for the perimeter of a circle.

Radius – distance from the centre of the circle to any point on the circumference.

Diameter – distance right across the circle, passing through the centre point. Notice that the diameter is twice as long as the radius.

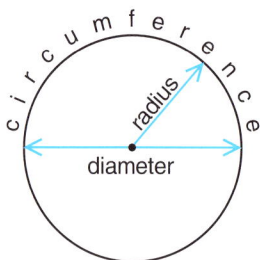

Chord – a line joining two points on the circumference. The longest chord of a circle is the diameter. A chord divides a circle into two **segments**.

Tangent – a line which touches the circumference of a circle at one point only.

Arc – part of the circumference of a circle.

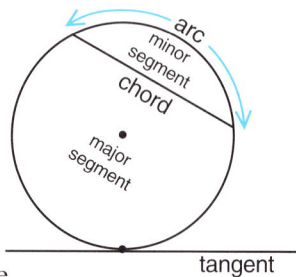

Activity

Measure the marked angles in these diagrams. *What do you notice?*

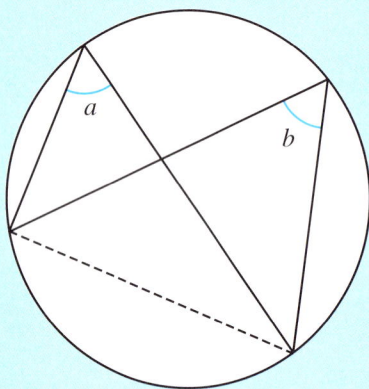

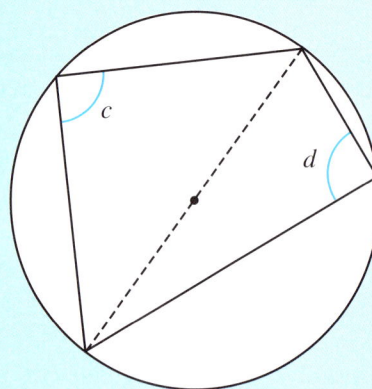

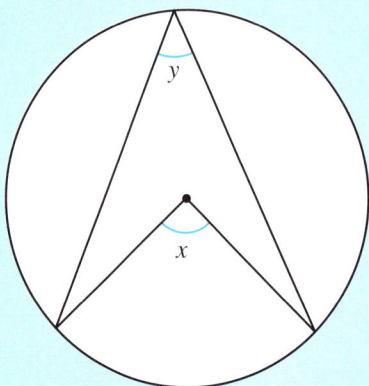

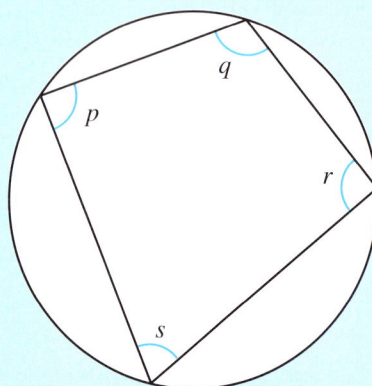

Circle properties

Angles in the same segment are equal

Angles which are:
    at the circumference,
    standing on the same chord,
    in the same segment,
are equal.

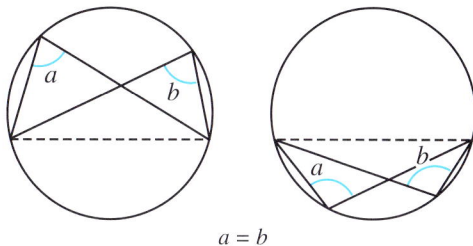

$a = b$

The angle in a semi-circle is a right angle

Angles which are:
    at the circumference,
    standing on a diameter,
are equal to 90°.

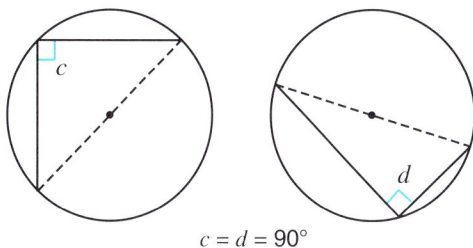

$c = d = 90°$

The angle at the centre is twice the angle at the circumference

If two angles are standing on the same chord, the angle at the centre of the circle is twice the angle at the circumference.

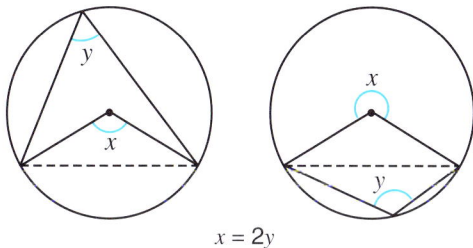

$x = 2y$

Opposite angles of a cyclic quadrilateral are supplementary

A quadrilateral whose vertices lie on the circumference of a circle is called a **cyclic quadrilateral**.

The opposite angles of a cyclic quadrilateral are supplementary (add up to 180°).

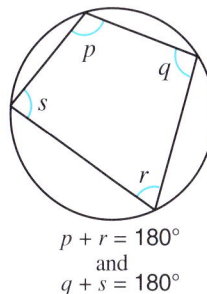

$p + r = 180°$
and
$q + s = 180°$

EXAMPLE

The diagram has not been drawn accurately.
O is the centre of the circle. Find the marked angles.

$a = 56°$ (angles in the same segment)

$b = 2 \times 56$ ($\angle$ at centre = twice $\angle$ at circum.)
$b = 112°$

$c = 180 - 56$ (opp. $\angle$s of a cyclic quad)
$c = 124°$

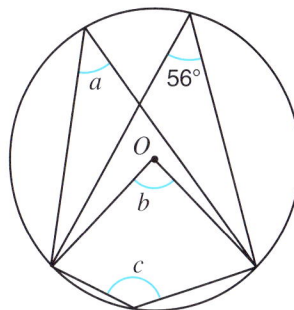

Do not use a calculator for this exercise.

1 These diagrams have not been drawn accurately.
O is the centre of the circle. Work out the size of the marked angles.

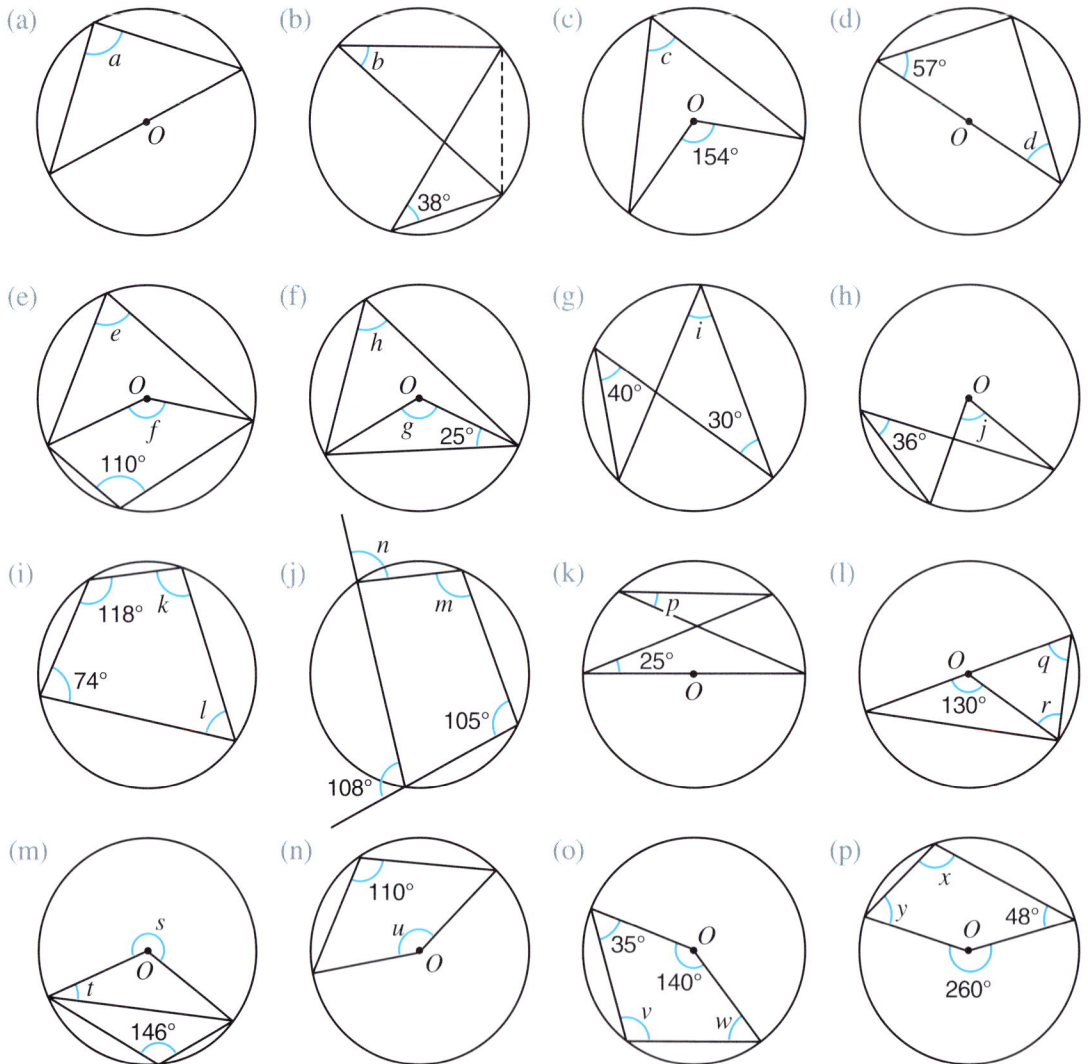

(a)

(b)
38°

(c)
c
O
154°

(d)
57°
O
d

(e)
e
O
f
110°

(f)
h
O
g
25°

(g)
40°
i
30°

(h)
O
36°
j

(i)
118° k
74°
l

(j)
n
m
105°
108°

(k)
p
25°
O

(l)
O
q
130°
r

(m)
s
O
t
146°

(n)
110°
u
O

(o)
35°
O
140°
v
w

(p)
x
y
O
48°
260°

2 In the diagram BD is a diameter.
Angle ACD = 43°.
Calculate angle x.

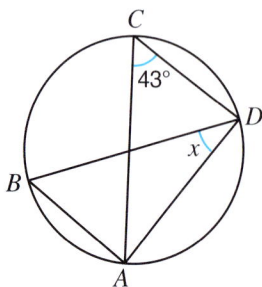

C
43°
D
x
B
A

3 ABCD is a cyclic quadrilateral, with
BA produced (extended) to E.
Angle EAD = 70° and angle CDB = 34°.
Calculate angles BCD and CAD.

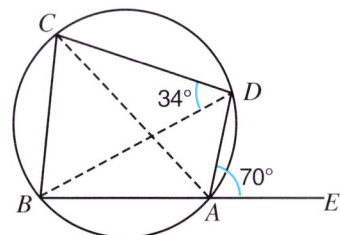

C
34°
D
B
70°
A
E

274

4 PQ is a diameter.
Angle $RPQ = 29°$.
Calculate
angle PSR.

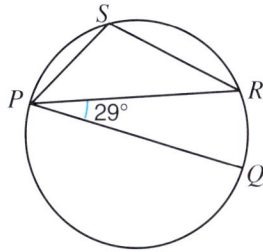

5 In the diagram, O is the
centre of the circle.
Angle $PSQ = 28°$
and angle $QSR = 47°$.
Calculate
angle PQR
and angle QRS.

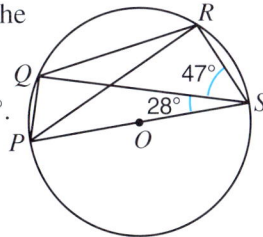

6 P, Q, R, S and T are
points on a circle.
$\angle QRS = 105°$,
$\angle PTS = 140°$,
$\angle PQR = 135°$
and $PT = TS$.
Calculate
$\angle PSR$ and $\angle TPQ$.

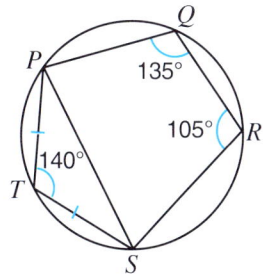

7 In the figure, O is the
centre of the circle.
Angle $ORP = 20°$.
Calculate
(a) angle POR,
(b) angle PQR.

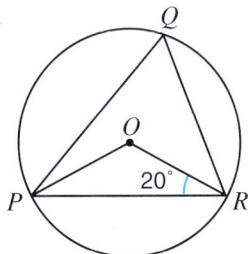

8 In the figure, O is the
centre of the circle.
$AC = CB$.
Calculate the
angles
(a) DOE,
(b) ABD,
(c) DBE.

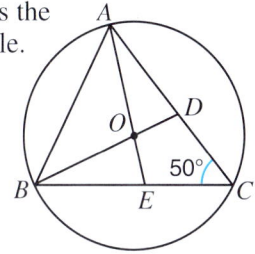

9 The centre of the circle is O.
Calculate the
value of x.

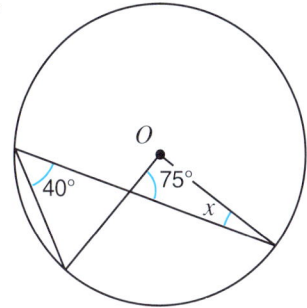

10 In the circle, centre O, QR is a diameter.
The line QS is a common chord of the
two circles and points T, S and R are
collinear. Find angle QPT.

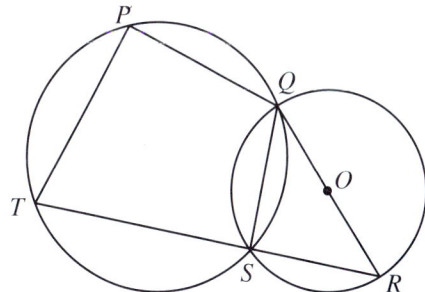

Tangents

The diagram shows a tangent drawn from a
point P to touch the circle, centre O, at T.

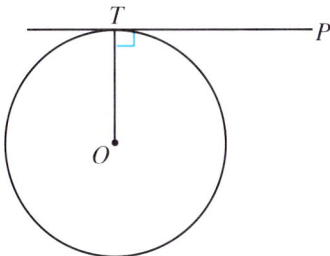

A tangent to a circle is a straight line which
touches the circumference at one point only.

A tangent is perpendicular to the radius at the
point of contact.

This diagram shows two tangents drawn from a point P to touch
the circle, centre O, at points A and B.

Tangents drawn to a circle
from the same point are
equal, $PA = PB$.
OP bisects angle APB.

*What is the name given to
the shape OAPB?*

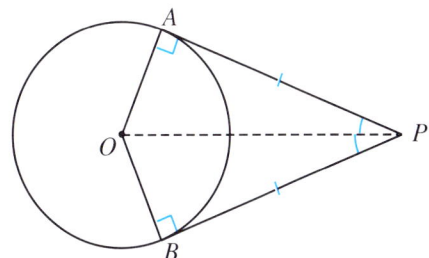

Activity

Measure the marked angles in these diagrams.
What do you notice?

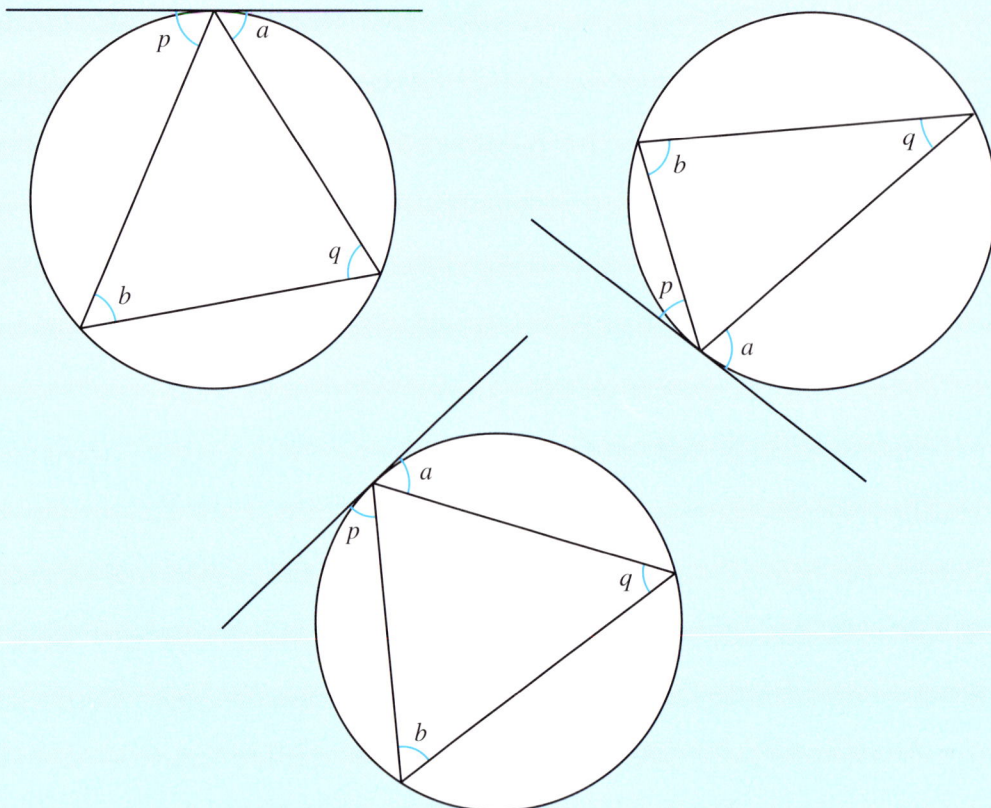

You should find that in each diagram,
angle a = angle b and   angle p = angle q.

The angle between a tangent and a chord is equal to any angle in the alternate segment, standing on the same chord.
This is known as the **alternate segment theorem**.

In each of these diagrams the shaded area shows the alternate (opposite) segment to the angle between the tangent and the chord.

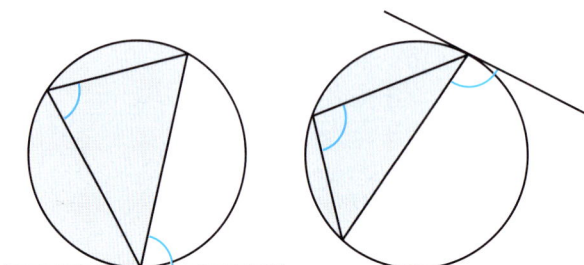

Do not use a calculator for this exercise.

1 These diagrams have not been drawn accurately.
 O is the centre of the circle. Work out the size of the marked angles.

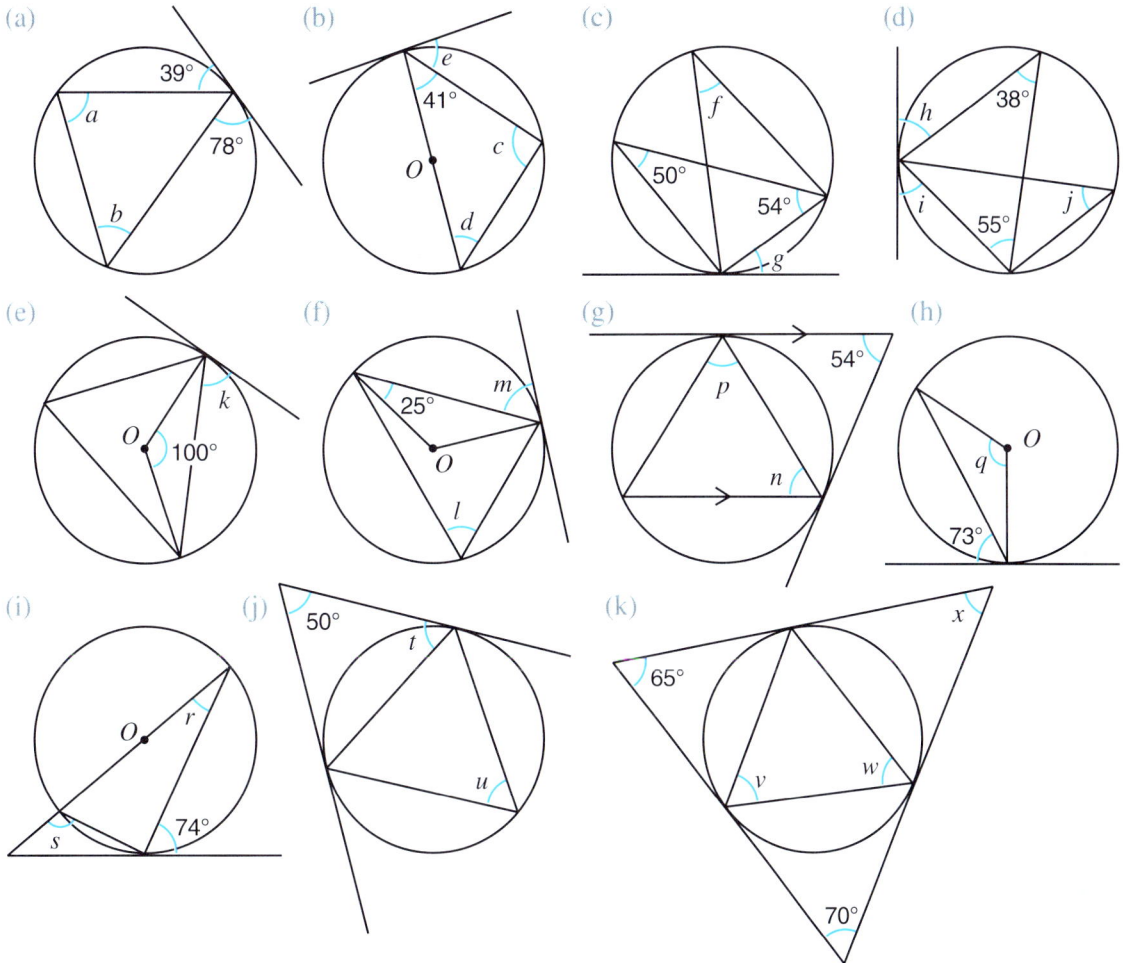

(a)

(b)

(c)

(d)

(e)

(f)

(g)

(h)

(i)

(j)

(k)

2 AB and AD are tangents to the circle centre O.
 COD is a diameter and angle $CBO = 48°$.

Calculate   (a)   angle BOC,
                  (b)   angle BDO,
                  (c)   angle BAD.

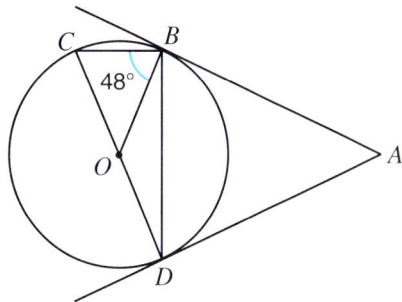

3 In the diagram, O is the centre of the circle.
 TP is a tangent.
 Angle $TPA = 42°$.

Calculate   (a)   angle PAB,
                  (b)   angle PTA.

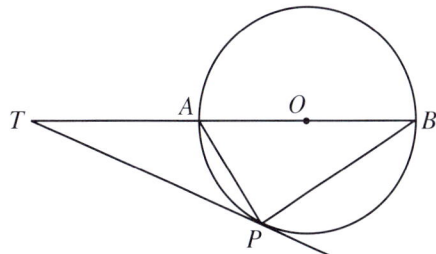

4

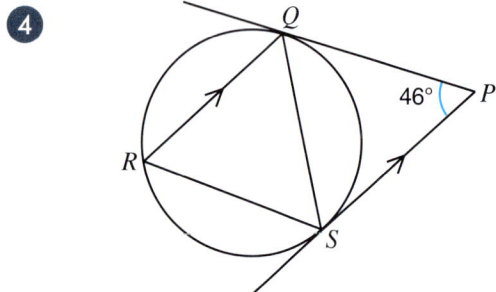

In the diagram, PQ and PS are tangents.
RQ is parallel to SP.
Angle $SPQ = 46°$.
Calculate   (a)   angle QRS,
                (b)   angle RSQ.

5

In the diagram, PQ and PS are tangents to the circle centre O.
POR is a straight line.
Angle $SRQ = 50°$.
Calculate   (a) $\angle SOQ$,
                (b) $\angle SPO$,
                (c) $\angle RSO$.

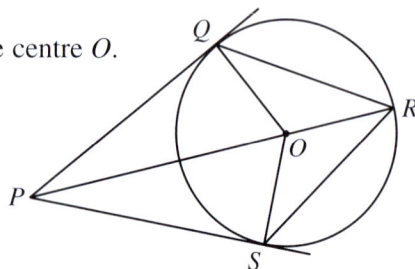

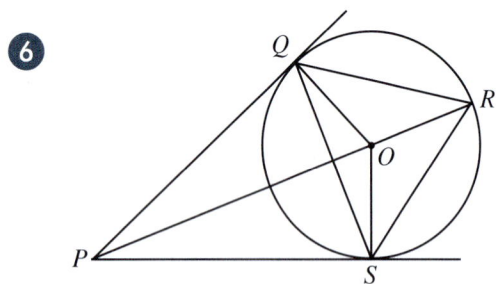

6

PQ and PS are tangents to the circle centre O.
POR is a straight line.
Angle $SPO = 18°$.
Calculate   (a) $\angle POS$,
                (b) $\angle OSR$,
                (c) $\angle SQR$.

7

In the diagram, PT is the tangent at T to the circle.
Find the sizes of the angles marked x, y and z.

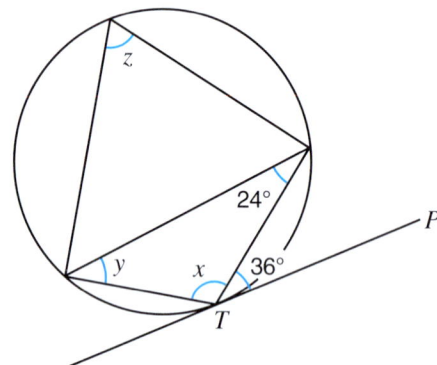

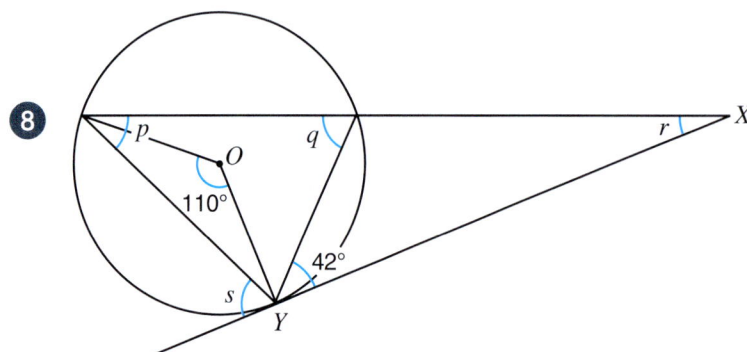

8

The line XY is a tangent to the circle and O is the centre of the circle.
Find the sizes of the angles marked p, q, r and s.

9

In the figure, AB touches the circle at T and CD is a diameter.
Write down the value of $x + 2y$.

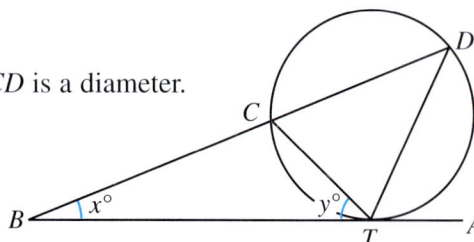

278

What you need to know

- A **chord** divides a circle into two segments.
  A chord passing through the centre of a circle is called a **diameter**.

- The vertices of a **cyclic quadrilateral** lie on the circumference of a circle.

- **Circle properties**

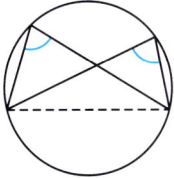

Angles in the same segment are equal.	The angle in a semi-circle is a right angle.	$x = 2y$ The angle at the centre is twice the angle at the circumference.	$p + r = 180°$ and $q + s = 180°$ Opposite angles of a cyclic quadrilateral are supplementary.

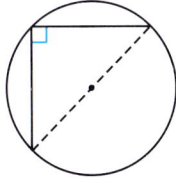

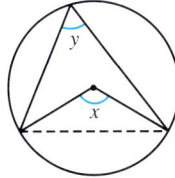

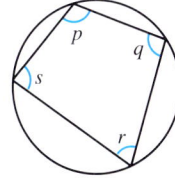

- A **tangent** to a circle touches the circumference of the circle at one point only.
  A tangent is perpendicular to the radius at the point of contact.
  Tangents drawn to a circle from the same point are equal in length.

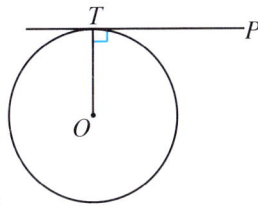

- **Alternate segment theorem**.
  The angle between a tangent and a chord is equal to any angle in the alternate (opposite) segment.

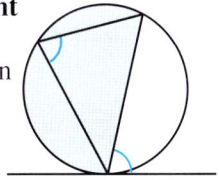

IDEAS FOR INVESTIGATION

A straight line which cuts a circle at two distinct points is called a **secant**.

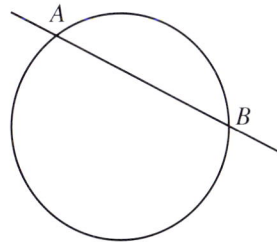

(a) In the diagram, the tangent *XT* meets the circle at *T* and the secant *XAB* cuts the circle at *A* and *B*.
Investigate the relationship between *AX*, *BX* and *TX*.

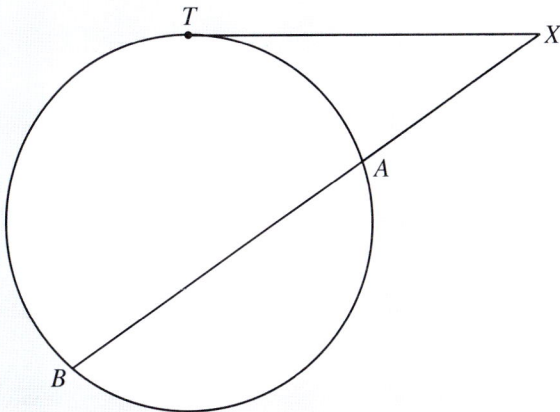

(b) In the diagram the chords *AB* and *CD* intersect at *X*.
Investigate the relationship between *AX*, *BX*, *CX* and *DX*.

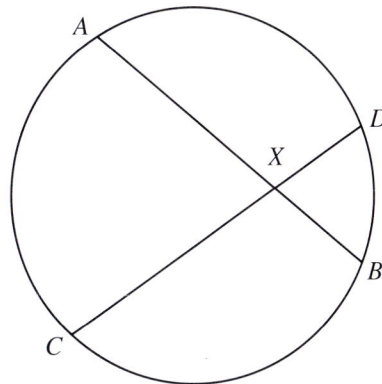

1 P, Q, R and S are four points on the circumference of a circle.
PR is a diameter of the circle and PQ is parallel to SR.
Angle $QPR = 42°$.

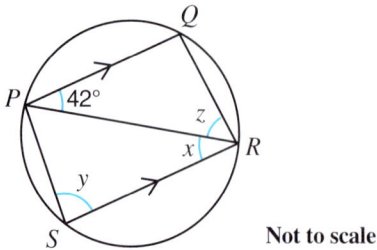

Not to scale

(a) Calculate the size of the angles marked x, y and z.

(b) The diagram is redrawn.
The points P, Q and R are marked in the same positions on the circle. The point S is marked on the circle so that QS is now perpendicular to PR.

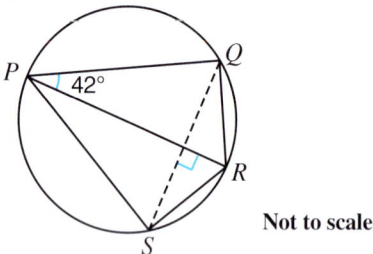

Not to scale

Calculate the size of angle RQS.

SEG 1993

2 In the diagram, O is the centre of the circle.

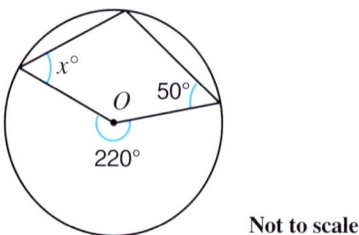

Not to scale

Find x.

3 The line AOB is a diameter of the circle, centre O.
Angle $BAC = 30°$.
Angle $BCD = 40°$.

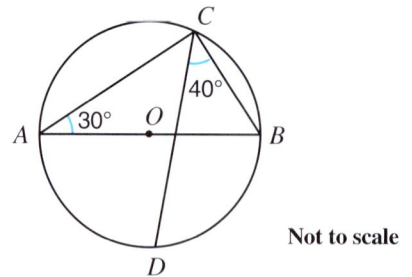

Not to scale

(a) Calculate the size of angle AOD.
(b) What is the size of angle CDB?
(c) Calculate the size of angle ODB.

SEG 1995

4 In the diagram, O is the centre of the circle and TR is the tangent to the circle at T. Calculate x.

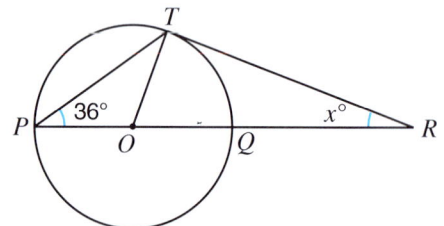

5 In the diagram, O is the centre of the circle and PQR is a tangent to the circle. Find the values of the angles marked x, y and z.

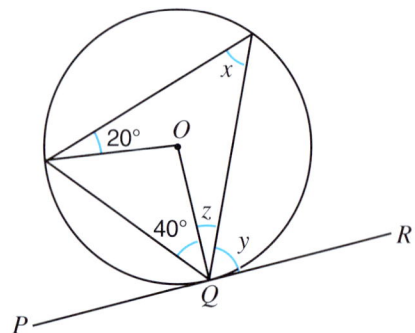

280

6 BDEF is a cyclic quadrilateral.
EFA is a straight line.
CBA is a tangent to the circle.
Angle EDB = 63° and
angle FBA = 38°.

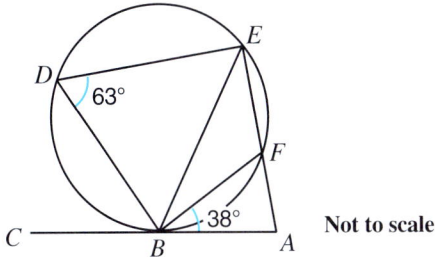

Not to scale

(a) Calculate the size of angle BAF.

(b) Calculate the size of angle EBF.

SEG 1996

7 O is the centre of the circle.
ABC is a tangent to the circle at B.

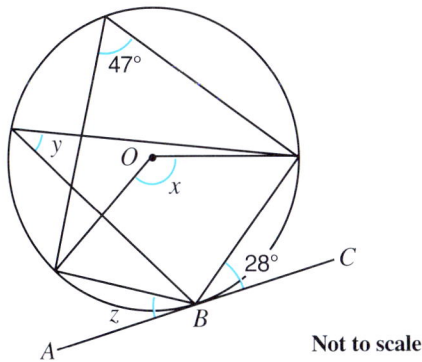

Not to scale

Work out the size of angles x, y and z.

SEG 1995

8 In the diagram, O is the centre of the circle, PT is the tangent at T and angle OPT = 25°.
Calculate angle XZT.

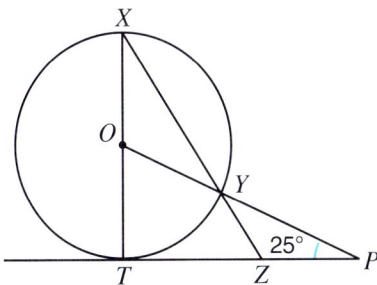

9 In the diagram, OP and OQ are tangents to the circle and QR is parallel to OP. Calculate angle x.

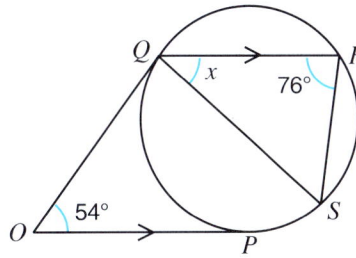

10 Angle DAT = 25°.
Angle BTA = 50°.
AT and BT are tangents to the circle.

Not to scale

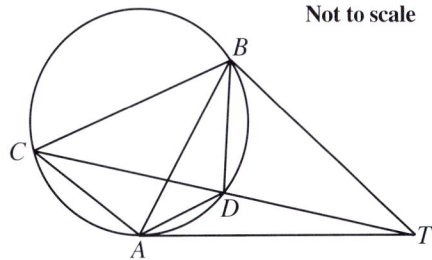

(a) Calculate the size of angle ACD.

(b) Calculate the size of angle BAD.

(c) Calculate the size of angle BDA.

SEG 1996

11 In the diagram SPT is a tangent to the circle at P.
PQ = QR and RS = SP. Angle OPQ = 50°.

Not to scale

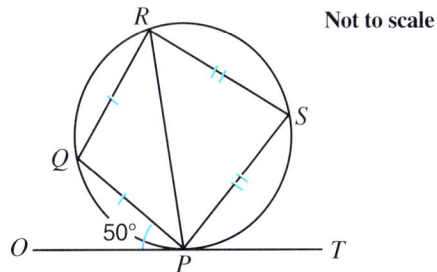

Calculate angle QRP and angle RPS.

12 Angle BAT = 55° and angle DBT = 30°.
AT and BT are tangents to the circle.
BC is a diameter of the circle.

(a) Calculate the size of angle BCT.

(b) Calculate the size of angle ABC.

(c) Calculate the size of angle ATC.

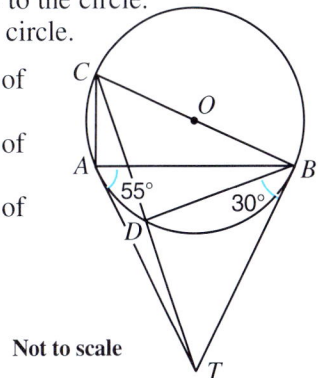

Not to scale

SEG 1998

CHAPTER 19

Circles and Other Shapes

The circle

The diagram shows a circle with radius r and diameter d.

The **circumference** of a circle can be found using the formulae:

$$C = \pi \times d$$

or $\quad C = 2 \times \pi \times r$

Remember: $\quad d = 2 \times r$

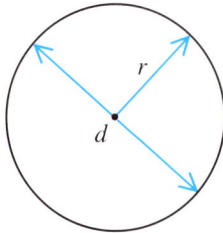

> Chapter 18 looked at angle properties of circles.
> In this chapter we look at various calculations involving lengths and areas associated with circles.

The **area** of a circle can be found using the formula: $\quad A = \pi \times r^2$

These formulae can be rearranged to find the radius when given the circumference or the area.

For $C = 2\pi r$
$$r = \frac{C}{2\pi}$$

For $A = \pi r^2$
$$r^2 = \frac{A}{\pi}$$
$$r = \sqrt{\frac{A}{\pi}}$$

In all calculations involving circles take π to be 3.14 or use the π key on your calculator.

> For more accurate calculations use the π key on your calculator.

EXAMPLES

1 The top of a tin of cat food has an area of 78.5 cm².
What is the radius of the tin?
Take $\pi = 3.14$.

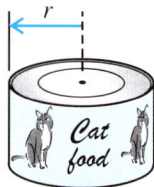

$A = \pi \times r^2$
Substitute values for A and π.
$78.5 = 3.14 \times r^2$
Solve this equation to find r.
Divide both sides of the equation by 3.14.
$$\frac{78.5}{3.14} = r^2$$
$$r^2 = 25$$
Take the square root of both sides.
$$r = 5$$
The radius of the tin is 5 cm.

2 A circle has a circumference of 28.27 cm.
Calculate (a) the radius of the circle, (b) the area of the circle.
Use the π key on your calculator.

(a) To find the radius use
$$r = \frac{C}{2\pi}$$
$$r = \frac{28.27}{2 \times \pi}$$
$$r = 4.499 \ldots$$
$$r = 4.5 \text{ cm to 1 d.p.}$$

(b) To find the area use
$A = \pi r^2$
$A = \pi \times 4.499\ldots^2$
$A = 63.59 \ldots$
$A = 63.6 \text{ cm}^2 \text{ to 3 s.f.}$

3 A circle has an area of $81\pi\,\text{cm}^2$.
Calculate the circumference of the circle, giving your answer in terms of π.

First, find the radius of the circle.
The area of a circle is given by:
$A = \pi r^2$
Substitute $A = 81\pi$.
$81\pi = \pi \times r^2$
Divide both sides by π.
$r^2 = 81$
$r = 9$
The radius of the circle is $9\,\text{cm}$.

The circumference of a circle is given by:
$C = 2\pi r$
Substitute $r = 9$.
$C = 2 \times \pi \times 9$.
$C = 18\pi$

The circumference of the circle is $18\pi\,\text{cm}$.

Exercise 19.1

Take π to be 3.14 or use the π key on your calculator.

1 Calculate (a) the circumference and (b) the area of these circles.
Give the answers correct to three significant figures.

(i)

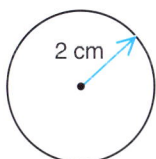

2 cm

(ii)

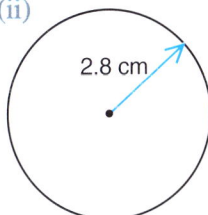

2.8 cm

(iii)

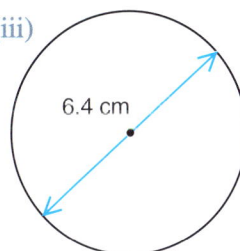

6.4 cm

2 Calculate the shaded area in each of these diagrams.

(a)

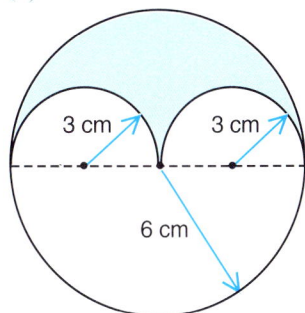

3 cm   3 cm

6 cm

(b)

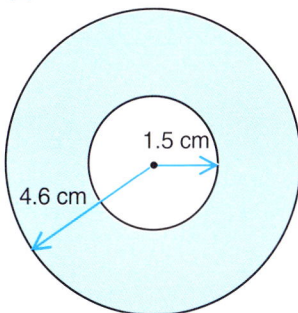

1.5 cm

4.6 cm

(c)

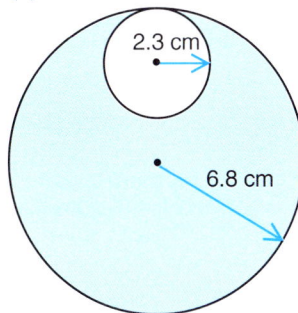

2.3 cm

6.8 cm

3 A circle has a circumference of 50 cm.
Calculate the radius of the circle.

4 A circular mug has a circumference of
24 cm. Find the radius of the mug, giving
your answer to the nearest millimetre.

5 The circumference of a copper pipe is
94 mm. Find, to the nearest millimetre,
the diameter of the pipe.

6 The wheel of a wheelbarrow
rotates 60 times when
it is pushed a
distance of 50 metres.
Calculate the radius
of the wheel, giving
your answer to the nearest millimetre.

7 A circle has an area of $50\,\text{cm}^2$.
Calculate the radius of the circle.

8 Calculate the area of a semi-circle with a diameter of 6.8 cm.

9 Calculate the perimeter of a semi-circle with a radius of 7.5 cm.

10 A circle has a circumference of 64 cm. Calculate the area of the circle.

11 A circle has an area of 128 cm². Calculate the circumference of the circle.

12 A circle has a circumference of 14π cm. Calculate the area of the circle in terms of π.

13 A circle has an area of 144π cm². Calculate the circumference of the circle in terms of π.

14 The diagram shows a small circle drawn inside a larger circle. The shaded area is 55π cm². The small circle has a radius of 3 cm. Calculate the radius of the larger circle.

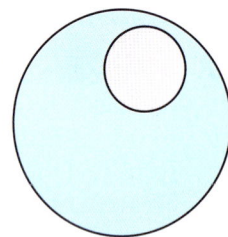

15 The diagram shows a small circle drawn inside a larger circle. The small circle has an area of 16π cm². The larger circle has a circumference of 18π cm. Calculate the shaded area. Give your answer in terms of π.

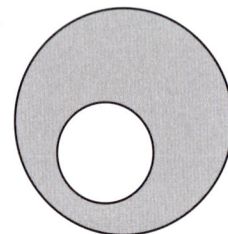

Segments and sectors

A circle can be divided up in different ways.

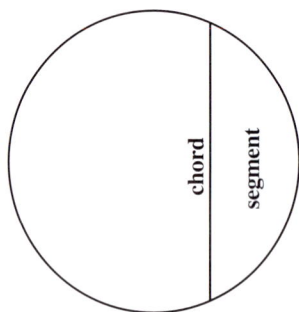

A **chord** divides a circle into two **segments**.

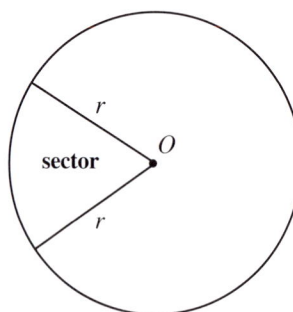

Two **radii** divide a circle into two **sectors**.

Lengths of arcs and areas of sectors

The lengths of arcs and the areas of sectors of circles are in proportion to the angle at the centre of the circle.

For a sector with angle $a°$

$$\text{Length of arc} = \frac{a}{360} \times \pi d$$

$$\text{Area of sector} = \frac{a}{360} \times \pi r^2$$

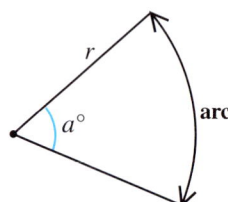

EXAMPLES

1 This shape is a sector of a circle with radius 9 cm and angle 80°.
Calculate   (a)   the length of arc AB,
           (b)   the area of sector OAB.

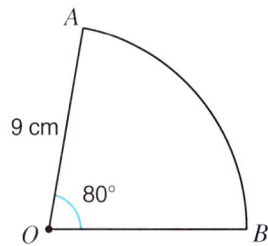

(a)   Length $AB = \frac{a}{360} \times \pi d$

$= \frac{80}{360} \times \pi \times 18$

$= 12.56 \ldots$

$= 12.6$ cm, to 3 s.f.

(b)   Area $OAB = \frac{a}{360} \times \pi r^2$

$= \frac{80}{360} \times \pi \times 9^2$

$= 56.54 \ldots$

$= 56.5$ cm², to 3 s.f.

2 The diagram shows a quadrant of a circle with radius 7 cm.
Calculate the area of the shaded segment.

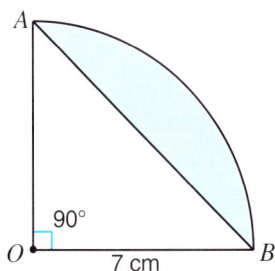

Area of segment = area of quadrant AOB − area of triangle AOB.

Area of quadrant $AOB = \frac{a}{360} \times \pi r^2$

$= \frac{90}{360} \times \pi \times 7^2$

$= 38.48 \ldots$ cm²

Area $\triangle AOB = \frac{1}{2} bh$

$= 0.5 \times 7 \times 7$

$= 24.5$ cm².

A **quadrant** is a sector in which the angle is 90°.

Area of segment = area of sector − area of triangle

$= 38.48 \ldots - 24.5$

$= 13.98 \ldots$

$= 14.0$ cm², to 3 s.f.

Exercise 19.2   Take π to be 3.14 or use the π key on your calculator.
Give answers correct to three significant figures.

1 Calculate the length of the arc of each sector.

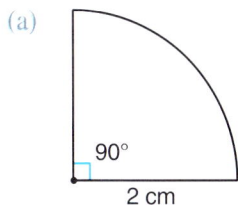

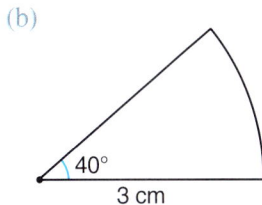

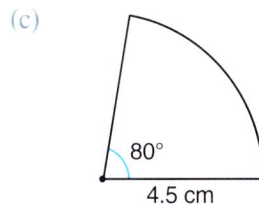

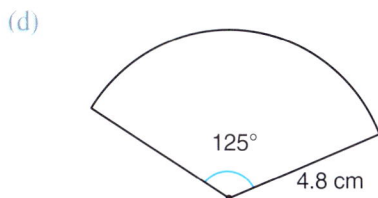

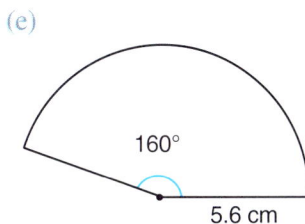

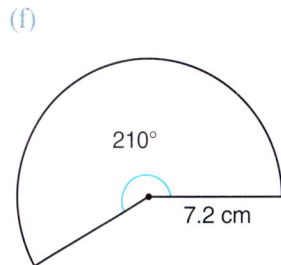

(a) 90°, 2 cm
(b) 40°, 3 cm
(c) 80°, 4.5 cm
(d) 125°, 4.8 cm
(e) 160°, 5.6 cm
(f) 210°, 7.2 cm

2 Calculate the area of each sector.

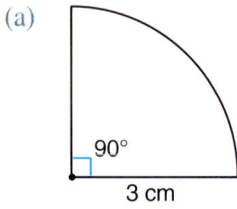

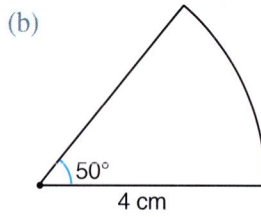

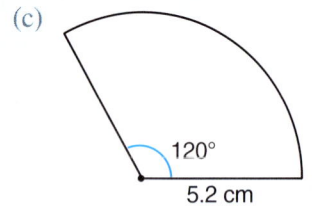

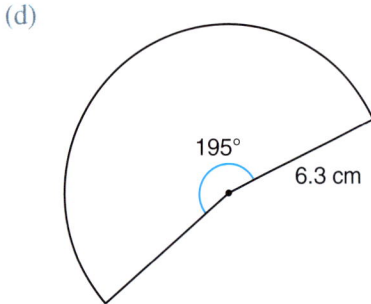

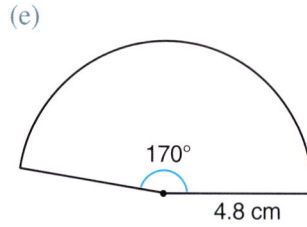

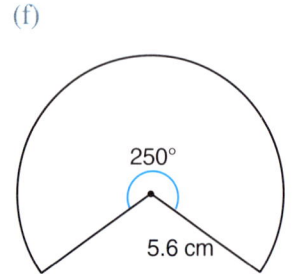

(a)

90°
3 cm

(b)

50°
4 cm

(c)

120°
5.2 cm

(d)

195°
6.3 cm

(e)

170°
4.8 cm

(f)

250°
5.6 cm

3 *OPQ* is a sector of a circle with radius 20 cm.
X is the midpoint of *OP* and *Y* is the midpoint of *OQ*.
Angle *POQ* = 65°.

Calculate
(a) the area of *XPQY*,
(b) the perimeter of *XPQY*.

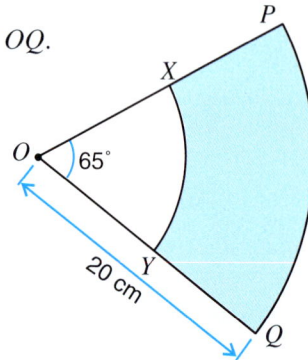

P
X
O 65°
Y
20 cm
Q

4 *OXY* is a sector of a circle, centre *O*, with radius 9 cm.
The arc length of the sector is 8.4 cm.

Calculate the size of angle *XOY*.

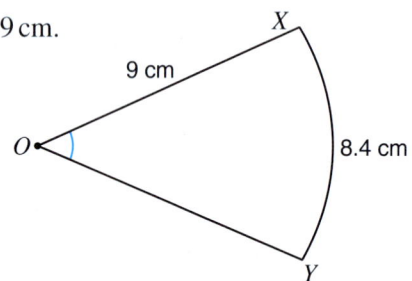

X
9 cm
O
8.4 cm
Y

5 *OPQ* is a sector of a circle, centre *O*.
The arc length of the sector is 15.6 cm.
Angle *POQ* = 135°.

Calculate the radius of the circle.

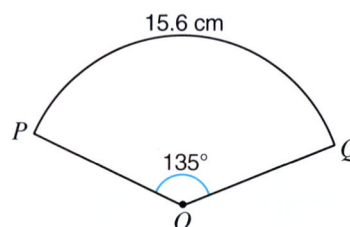

15.6 cm
P
Q
135°
O

6 *AB* and *DC* are arcs of a circle, centre *O*.
OA = 15 cm and angle *AOB* = 85°.
The area of *ABCD* is 100 cm².

Calculate
(a) the length of *OD*,
(b) the length of the arc *DC*.

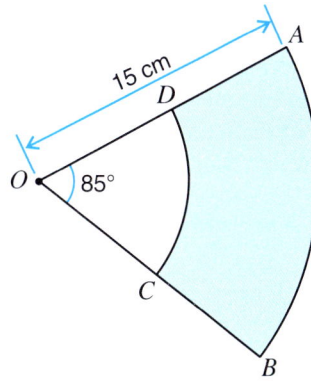

7 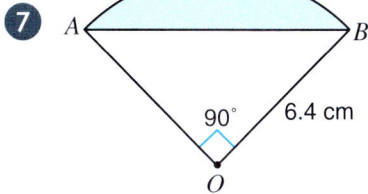 The diagram shows a sector of a circle with radius 6.4 cm.
Angle *AOB* = 90°.

Calculate the area of the shaded segment.

8 The diagram shows a sector of a circle,
centre *O*, with radius 10 cm.
M is the midpoint of *AB*. *AB* = 16 cm,
MO = 6 cm and
angle *AOM* = 53.1°.
Calculate the area of the shaded segment.

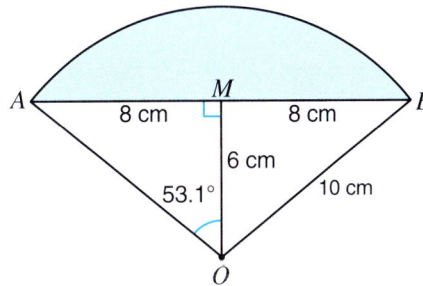

9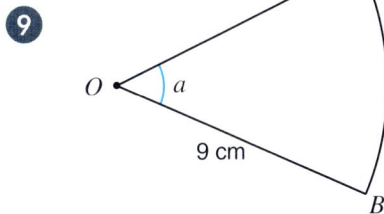

OAB is a sector of a circle, centre *O*, with radius 9 cm.
The sector has an area of 13.5 cm².

Calculate the size of angle *a*.

10 A sector of a circle has an area of 30 cm².
Angle *a* = 72°.

Calculate the radius of the circle.

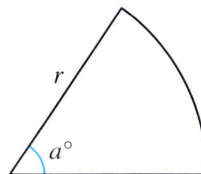

Areas of shapes

Here is a reminder of the formulae used to find the areas of other shapes.

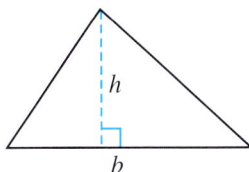

Triangle
$A = \frac{1}{2} \times b \times h$

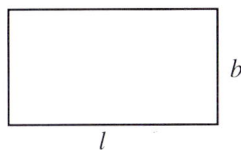

Rectangle
$A = lb$

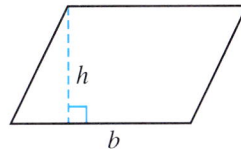

Parallelogram
$A = bh$

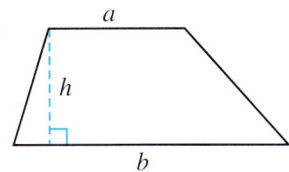

Trapezium
$A = \frac{1}{2}(a+b)h$

Compound shapes

Shapes formed by joining different shapes together are called **compound shapes**.
To find the area of a compound shape we must first divide the shape up into rectangles, triangles, circles, etc and find the area of each part.
Shapes can be divided in different ways, but they should all give the same answer.

EXAMPLE

Calculate the area of this shape.
Give the answer correct to three significant figures.

The shape can be split into: a rectangle $ABCD$,
a trapezium $BXYC$ and
a semi-circle XYZ.

Area $ABCD = 4.8 \times 3.2$
$= 15.36 \text{ cm}^2$

Area $BXYC = 0.5 (4.8 + 2.6) \times 2.5$
$= 9.25 \text{ cm}^2$

Area $XZY = 0.5 \times \pi \times 1.3^2$
$= 2.65 \dots \text{ cm}^2$

Total area $= 15.36 + 9.25 + 2.65 \dots$
$= 27.26 \dots$
$= 27.3 \text{ cm}^2$, to 3 s.f.

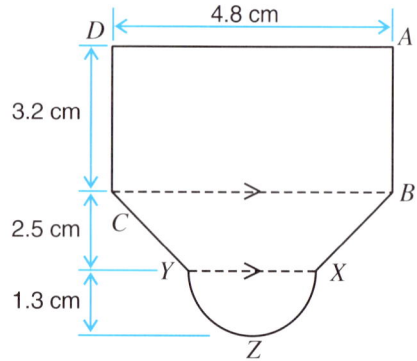

Exercise 19.3

Give answers correct to three significant figures.

1 Calculate the area of each of these shapes.

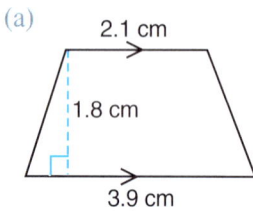

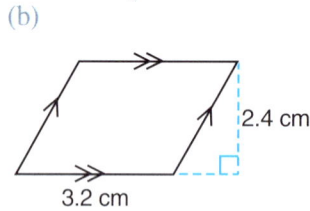

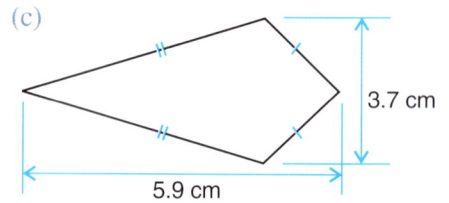

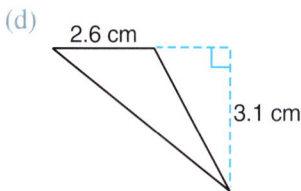

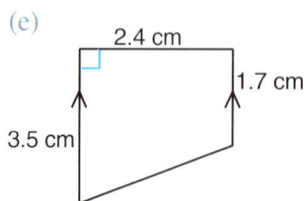

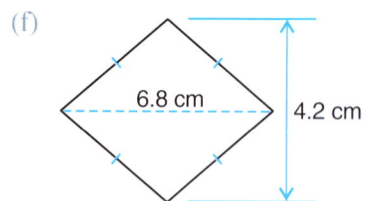

(a) 2.1 cm, 1.8 cm, 3.9 cm

(b) 2.4 cm, 3.2 cm

(c) 5.9 cm, 3.7 cm

(d) 2.6 cm, 3.1 cm

(e) 2.4 cm, 1.7 cm, 3.5 cm

(f) 6.8 cm, 4.2 cm

2 Each of these triangles has an area of 24 cm^2.
Calculate the lengths of the marked sides.

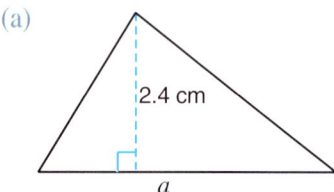

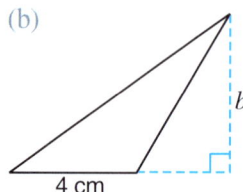

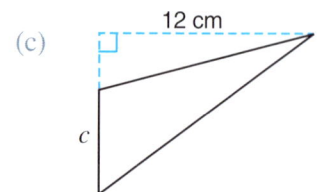

(a) 2.4 cm, a

(b) 4 cm, b

(c) 12 cm, c

288

3 This triangle has an area of $37.5\,\text{cm}^2$.
Calculate the perimeter of the triangle.

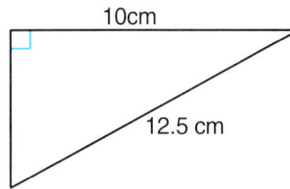

10cm

12.5 cm

4 Each of these quadrilaterals has an area of $24\,\text{cm}^2$.
Calculate the lengths of the marked sides.

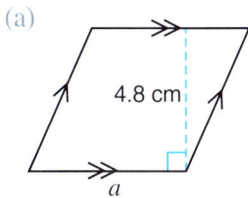

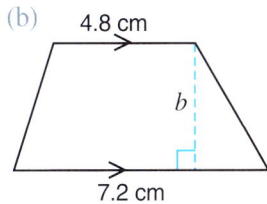

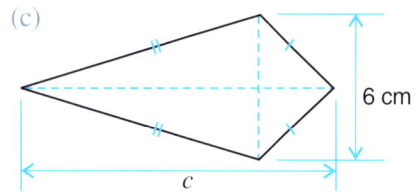

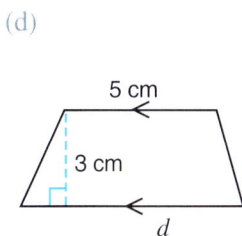

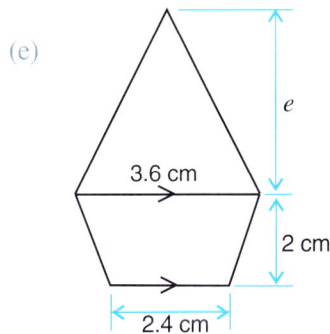

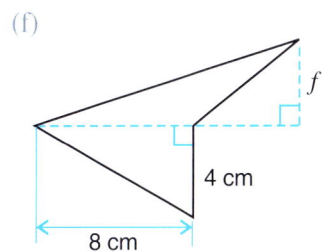

(a)

4.8 cm

a

(b) 4.8 cm

b

7.2 cm

(c)

6 cm

c

(d)

5 cm

3 cm

d

(e)

e

3.6 cm

2 cm

2.4 cm

(f)

f

4 cm

8 cm

5 A trapezium has an area of $30\,\text{cm}^2$.
The two parallel sides are 7 cm and 8 cm.
What is the perpendicular distance between the sides?

6 Calculate the shaded areas in each of these shapes.
Take π to be 3.14 or use the π key on your calculator.

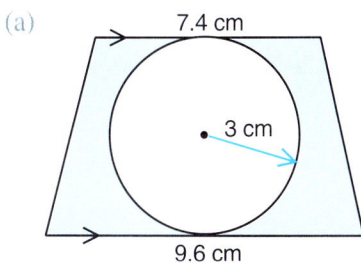

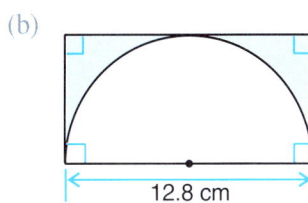

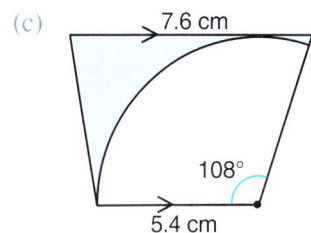

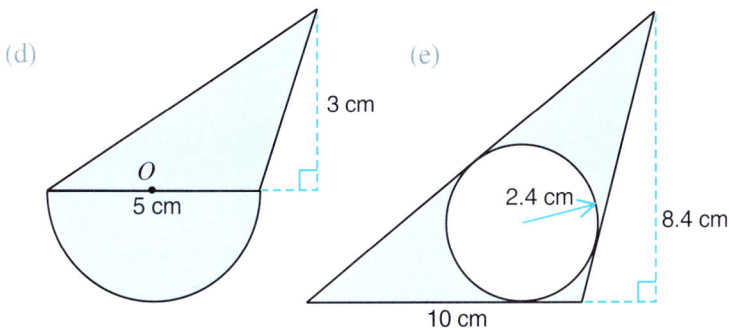

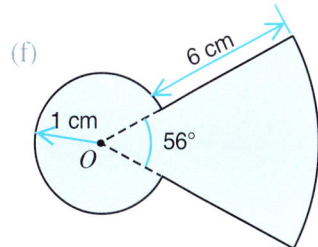

(a) 7.4 cm

3 cm

9.6 cm

(b)

12.8 cm

(c) 7.6 cm

108°

5.4 cm

(d)

3 cm

O

5 cm

(e)

2.4 cm

8.4 cm

10 cm

(f)

6 cm

1 cm

O

56°

7 In the diagram *POQ* is a sector of a circle centre *O*.
QR is parallel to *OS*.
Calculate the area of *OPQRS*.

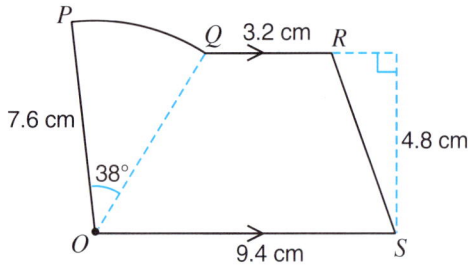

9 The diagram shows a shape *ABCDE*.
ABC and *ACE* are sectors.
AB = 8.4 cm. Angle *BAC* = angle *ACE* = 25°.
Calculate the area of the shape *ABCDE*.

8 The diagram shows a compound shape.
ABCD is a trapezium.
The arc *CD* is part of a circle centre *A*.
AD = 9 cm, *BC* = 5.8 cm, *AX* = 4.5 cm and angle *CAD* = 30°.
Calculate the area of the whole shape.

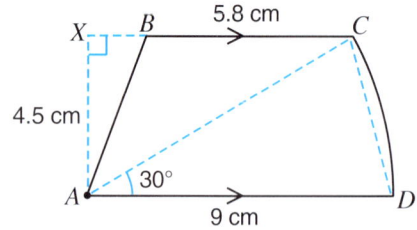

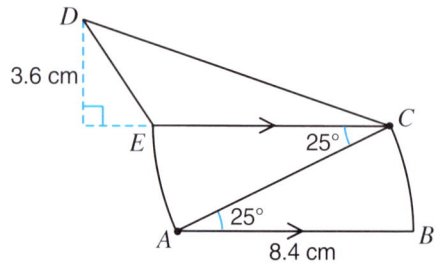

What you need to know

- The **circumference** of a circle is given by:
  $C = \pi \times d$ or $C = 2\pi \times r$

- The **area** of a circle is given by:
  $A = \pi \times r^2$

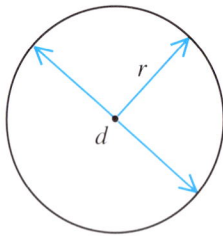

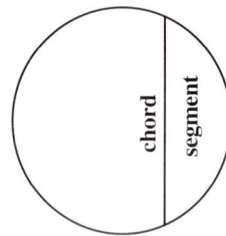

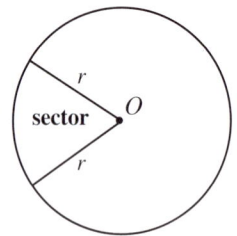

- A **chord** divides a circle into two **segments**.
  Two radii divide a circle into two **sectors**.

- The **lengths of arcs** and the **areas of sectors** are proportional to the angle at the centre of the circle.
  For a sector with angle $a°$

  $$\text{Length of arc} = \frac{a}{360} \times \pi d$$

  $$\text{Area of sector} = \frac{a}{360} \times \pi r^2$$

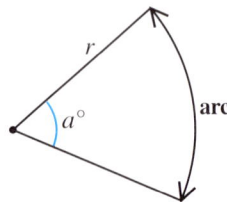

- Shapes formed by joining different shapes together are called **compound shapes**.
  To find the area of a compound shape we must first divide the shape up into rectangles, triangles, circles, etc and find the area of each part.
  Here is a reminder of the formulae used to find the areas of other shapes.

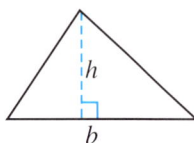

Triangle
$A = \frac{1}{2} \times b \times h$

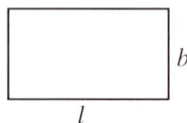

Rectangle
$A = lb$

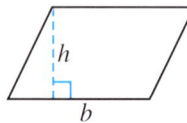

Parallelogram
$A = bh$

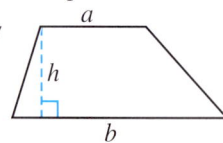

Trapezium
$A = \frac{1}{2}(a + b)h$

Take π to be 3.14 or use the π key on your calculator.

1 A rectangle measures 8 cm by 32 cm.
Four circles are drawn inside the rectangle, as shown.

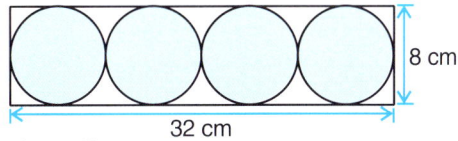

8 cm

32 cm

What area of the rectangle is not shaded?   **Not to scale**

2 A circular paddling pool is surrounded
by a concrete path of width 50 cm.
The pool has a radius of 2.5 m.
Calculate the area of the path.

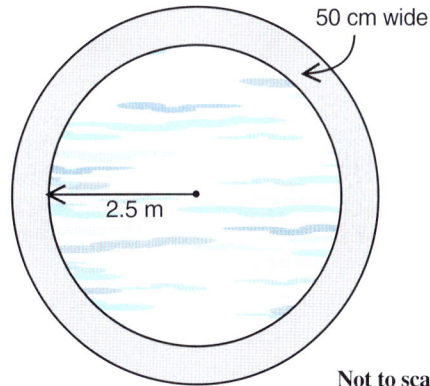

50 cm wide

2.5 m

Not to scale

SEG 1996

3 The diagram shows a circle drawn inside a trapezium, *ABCD*. *AB* is parallel to *DC*.

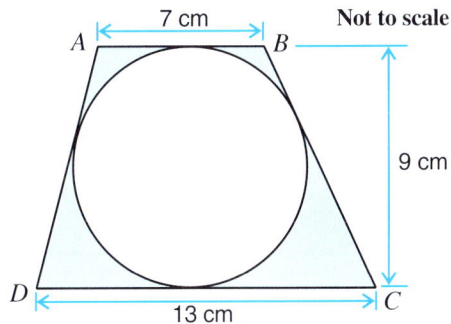

7 cm   **Not to scale**

A   *B*

9 cm

D   *C*

13 cm

What percentage of the trapezium is shaded?

4 A piece of jewellery is made from a metal square *ABCD* of side 3 cm.
The two curves are parts of circles with centres at *B* and *D*.
The piece of jewellery is formed from the
shaded area on the diagram.

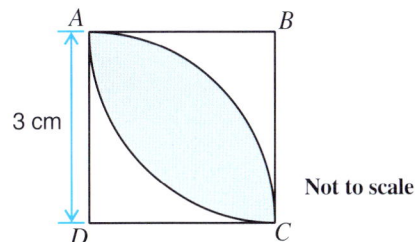

A   *B*

3 cm

Not to scale

D   *C*

Find the area of the piece of jewellery.

SEG 1997

5 (a) This earring is made from a rectangle and an isosceles triangle.
Calculate its area showing all your working.

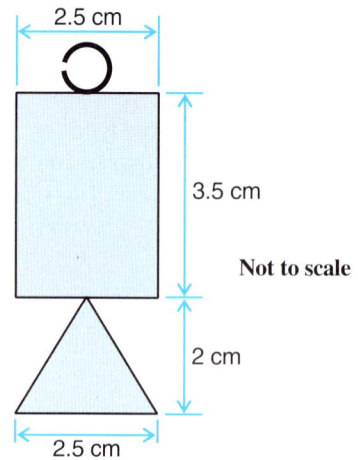

2.5 cm

3.5 cm

Not to scale

2 cm

2.5 cm

(b) Another earring is made from a sector of a circle, radius 3 cm.
The angle of the sector is 70°.
Calculate its area showing all your working.

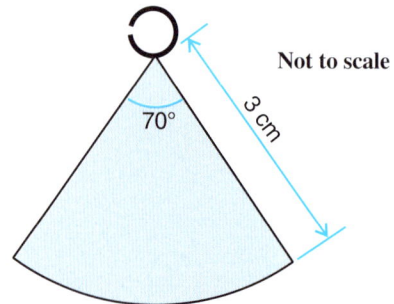

Not to scale

70°

3 cm

SEG 1994

6 The discus and hammer throwing area is made up of a circle radius 1.5 m and a sector of another circle, radius 67 m.
Both the full circle and the sector have the same centre *O*, as shown.
The length of the arc *AB* is 52 m.
The angle at the centre of the sector is *AOB*.
(a) Calculate the size of angle *AOB*.
(b) Calculate the total area enclosed by the discus and hammer throwing area.

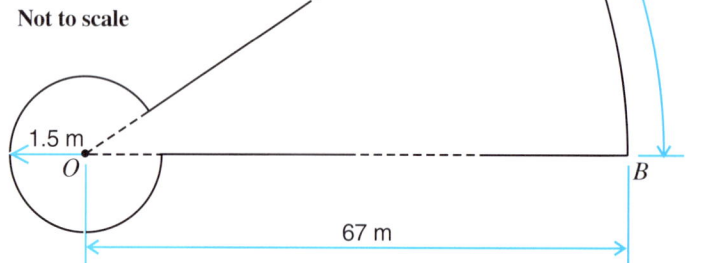

Not to scale

A

52 m

1.5 m

O

B

67 m

SEG 1996

7 The diagram shows part of the lead framework on a stained glass window.
AB and *PQ* are arcs of circles with centre *O*.
Calculate the total length of the lead.

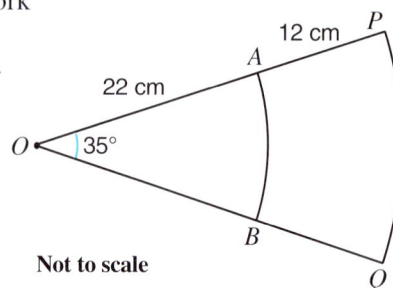

12 cm   *P*

A

22 cm

O   35°

B

Q

Not to scale

SEG 1998

292

8 A lampshade is made from a piece of material
ABCD, as shown.
Angle *AOB* = 33°, *OA* = *OB* = 55 cm,
OC = *OD* = 67 cm.
  (a) Calculate the area of the sector *OAB*.
  (b) Calculate the area of *ABCD*.
  (c) Calculate the arc length *AB*.

When the lampshade is made the ends *AD* and *BC* are
joined together.
The arcs *AB* and *CD* form two circles.
  (d) Calculate the radius of the circle formed by the
       arc *AB*.

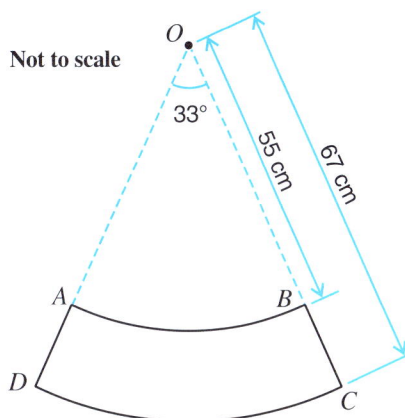

Not to scale

O
33°
55 cm
67 cm
A *B*
D *C*

SEG 1993

9 Silver pendants are made in the shape of a sector of a circle with
radius *r* cm and angle *θ*.
  (a) Calculate the **total** perimeter of the pendant when
       r = 3 cm and *θ* = 30°.
  (b) Another pendant has the same perimeter **but** *r* = 2.5 cm.
       Calculate, to the nearest degree, the angle *θ*
       required for this pendant.

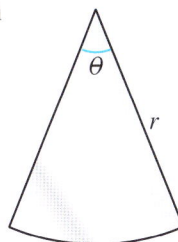

θ
r

SEG 1995

10 A wiper blade on a windscreen cleans the
clear area as shown.
Calculate the area of the windscreen
cleaned by the wiper.

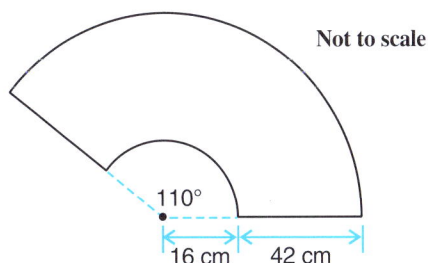

Not to scale

110°
16 cm 42 cm

SEG 1998

11 The diagram shows a segment of a circle with
radius 10 cm.
Angle *POQ* = 90°.
Calculate the area of the segment.

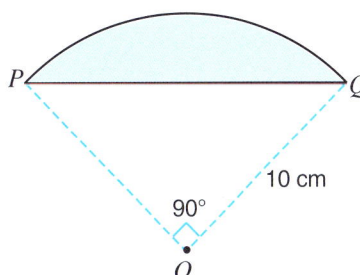

P *Q*
10 cm
90°
O

12 The diagram shows the cross-section of a building.
The roof is an arc of a circle, radius 50 m, centre *O*.
Angle *AOB* = 90°.

  (a) Calculate the arc length *AB* of the roof.
  (b) Calculate the area of the cross-section.

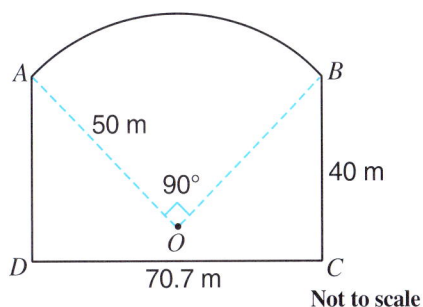

A *B*
50 m
90°
40 m
O
D 70.7 m *C*
Not to scale

CHAPTER 20

Loci and Constructions

Following rules

Three students are given rules to follow.

> **John**
> Walk so that you are always 2 metres from the lamp post.

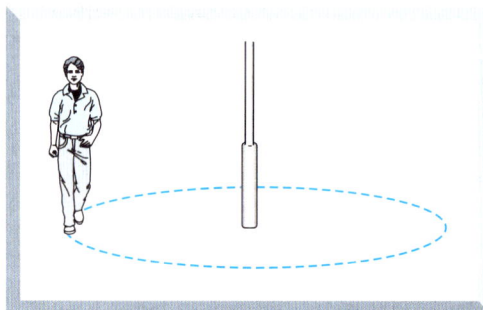

His path is a circle, radius 2 metres.

> **Hanif**
> Walk along a straight road.
> You must keep 30 cm from the edge of the road and stay on the pavement.

His path is a straight line.

> **Sarah**
> Start from the corner of the lawn.
> Walk across the lawn so that you are always the same distance from two sides.

Her path is a straight line.
The line cuts the angle in two.

Locus

The path of a point which moves according to a rule is called a **locus**.
If we talk about more than one locus we call them **loci**.

> **EXAMPLES** Draw sketches to show the loci of John, Hanif and Sarah.

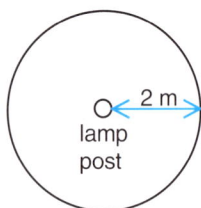

John

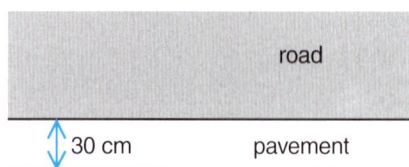

Hanif

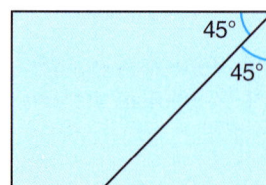

Sarah

1 Adam goes down this slide.
Make a sketch of the slide as viewed from the side and show the locus of his head.

2 A wire is stretched between two posts.
A ring slides along the wire and a dog is attached to the ring by a rope.
Make a sketch to show where the dog can go.

3 The diagram shows part of a rectangular lawn.
Starting from the wall, Sally walks across the lawn so that she is always the same distance from the hedges.
Draw a sketch to show the locus of Sally.

4 *PQRS* is a square of side 8 cm.
A point *X* is inside the square.

X is less than 8 cm from *P*.
X is nearer to *PQ* than to *SR*.

Make a sketch showing where *X* could be.

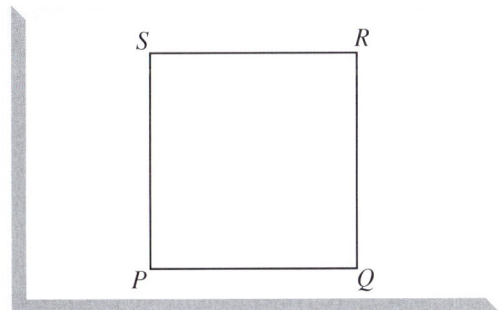

5 Sketch the locus of a point which is the same distance from *PQ* and *RS*.

[Hint: Take care to find all possible points.]

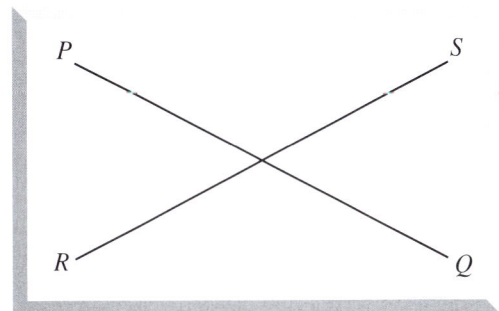

6 Mark two points 5 cm apart.
Label the points *X* and *Y*.

Place your set-square so that *X* and *Y* are on the shorter sides. Mark the point *P* where the right angle is.
Repeat this with different positions of the set-square.
What shape is the locus of *P*?

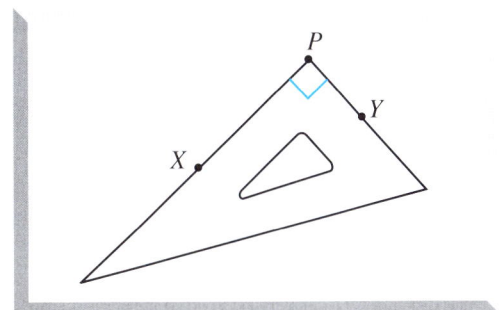

Accurate constructions

Sometimes it is necessary to construct loci accurately.
You are expected to use only a ruler and compasses.
Here are the methods for two constructions.

To draw the perpendicular bisector of a line

This means to draw a line at right angles to a given line dividing it into two equal parts.

1 Draw line AB.

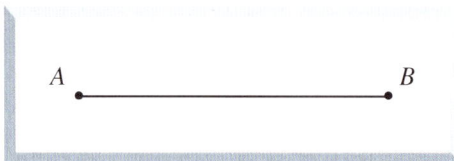

2 Open your compasses to just over half the distance AB. Mark two arcs which cross at C and D.

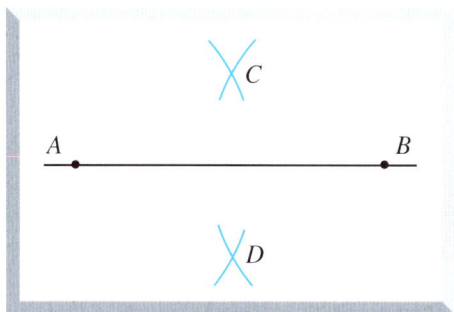

3 Draw a line which passes through the points C and D.

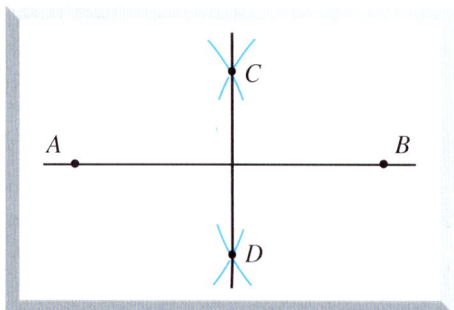

This line is the locus of a point which is the same distance from A and B.
Points on the line CD are **equidistant** (the same distance) from points A and B.
The line CD is at right angles to AB.
CD is sometimes called the **perpendicular bisector** of AB.

To draw the bisector of an angle

This means to draw a line which divides an angle into two equal parts.

1 Draw the angle A.
Use your compasses, centre A, to mark points B and C which are the same distance from A.

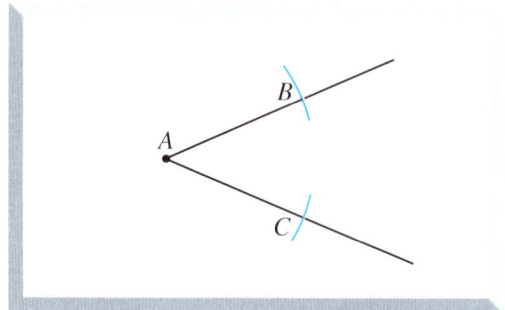

2 Use points B and C to draw equal arcs which cross at D.

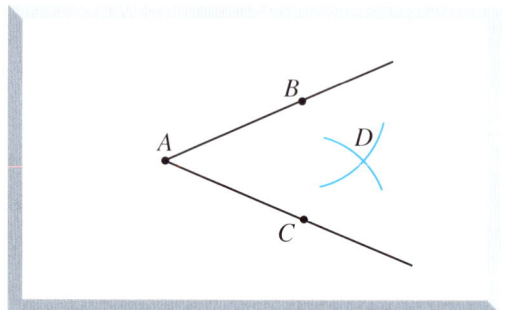

3 Draw a line which passes through the points A and D.

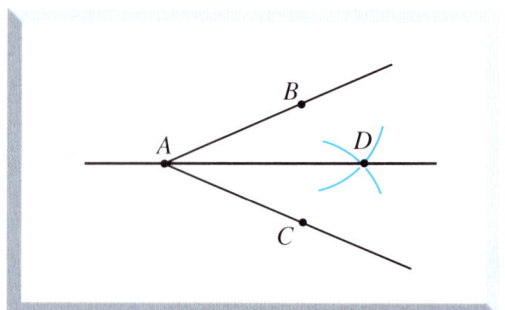

This line is the locus of a point which is the same distance from AB and BC.
Points on the line AD are **equidistant** from the lines through AB and AC.
The line AD cuts angle BAC in half.
AD is sometimes called the **bisector** of angle BAC.

1 Mark two points, A and B, 10 cm apart. Construct the perpendicular bisector of AB.

2 Use a protractor to draw an angle of 60°. Construct the bisector of the angle. Check that both angles are 30°.

3 Draw a triangle in the middle of a new page.
Construct the perpendicular bisectors of all three sides.
They should meet at a point, Y.

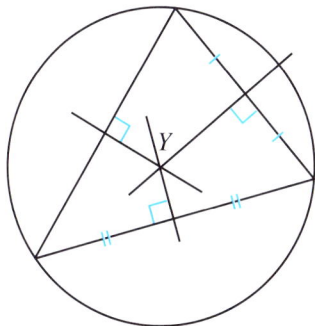

Put the point of your compasses on Y and draw the circle which goes through all three vertices of the triangle.
This construction is sometimes called the **circumscribed circle of a triangle**.

4 Draw another triangle on a new page.
Bisect each angle of the triangle.
The bisectors should meet at a point, X.

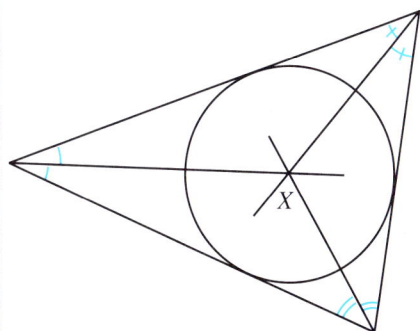

Put the point of your compasses on point X and draw the circle which just touches each side of the triangle.
This construction is sometimes called the **inscribed circle of a triangle**.

5 Using a circle of radius 4 cm, copy the diagram.
Draw the perpendicular bisectors of the chords WX and YZ.
What do you notice about the perpendicular bisectors?

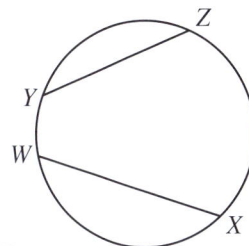

The perpendicular bisector of a chord always passes through the centre of a circle.

6 Two trees are 6 metres apart. Alan walks so that he is always the same distance from each tree. Draw a scale diagram to show his path.

7 ABC is an equilateral triangle with sides 4 cm.

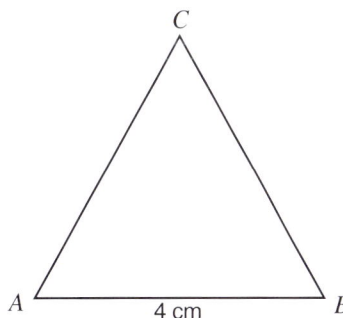

A point X is in the triangle. It is nearer to AB than to BC.
It is less than 3 cm from A.
It is less than 2 cm from BC.

Shade the region in which X could lie.

8 Draw a rectangle ABCD with AB = 6 cm and AD = 4 cm.

(a) Mark, with a thin line, the locus of a point which is 1 cm from AB.

(b) Mark, with a dotted line, the locus of a point which is the same distance from A and B.

(c) Mark, with a dashed line, the locus of a point which is 3 cm from A.

9 Draw a right-angled triangle with sides of 6 cm, 8 cm and 10 cm.

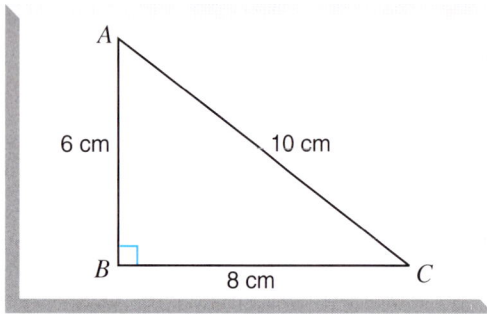

A point X is in the triangle.
It is 4 cm from B.
It is the same distance from A and B.

Mark accurately, the position of X.

10

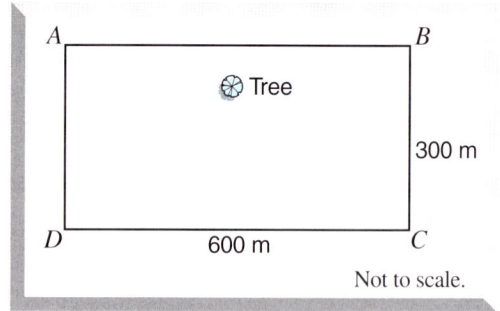

Not to scale.

(a) The diagram shows the sketch of a field.
    Make a scale drawing of the field using 1 cm to represent 100 m.

(b) A tree is 400 m from corner D and 350 m from corner C. Mark the position of the tree on your drawing.

(c) John walks across the field from corner D, keeping the same distance from AD and CD.
    Show his path on your diagram.

(d) Does John walk within 100 m of the tree in crossing the field?

What you need to know

- The path of a point which moves according to a rule is called a **locus**.

- The word **loci** is used when we talk about more than one locus.

Using a ruler and compasses you should be able to:
- Construct the **perpendicular bisector of a line**.

  Points on the line CD are **equidistant** from the points A and B.

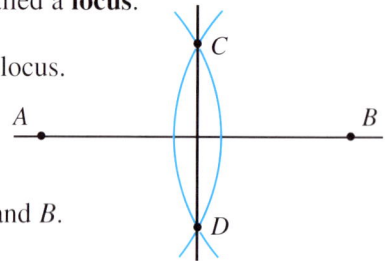

- Construct the **bisector of an angle**.

  Points on the line AD are **equidistant** from the lines AB and AC.

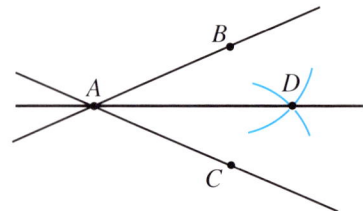

A coin is rolled along a line.
Sketch the locus of a point which starts off at the bottom.

What is the locus of the point if the coin rolls around another coin, or if the coins are not round, or … ?
Investigate.

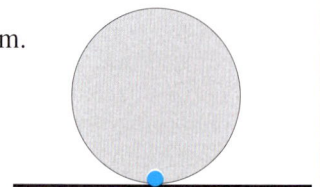

298

1 The diagram shows a rectangular field *ABCD*.
The side *AB* is 80 m long. The side *BC* is 50 m long.
Draw the diagram using a scale of 1 cm to 10 m.

Treasure is hidden in the field.
(a) The treasure is equidistant from the sides *AB* and *AD*.
Construct the locus of points for which this is true.

(b) The treasure is 60 m from corner *C*.
Construct the locus of points for which this is true.

(c) Mark with an *X* the position of the treasure.

SEG 1994

2 Building Site

The diagram shows part of a building site.
The scale is 1 cm to 1 m.
People are not allowed to walk anywhere within 2 m of the site.

Copy the diagram.
Draw accurately the edge of the region where people may **not** walk.

SEG 1995

3 The diagram shows a penguin pool at a zoo.
It consists of a right-angled triangle and a semi-circle.
The scale is 1 cm to 1 m.
Copy the diagram.

A safety fence is put up around the pool.
The fence is always 2 m from the pool.
Draw accurately the position of the fence on your diagram.

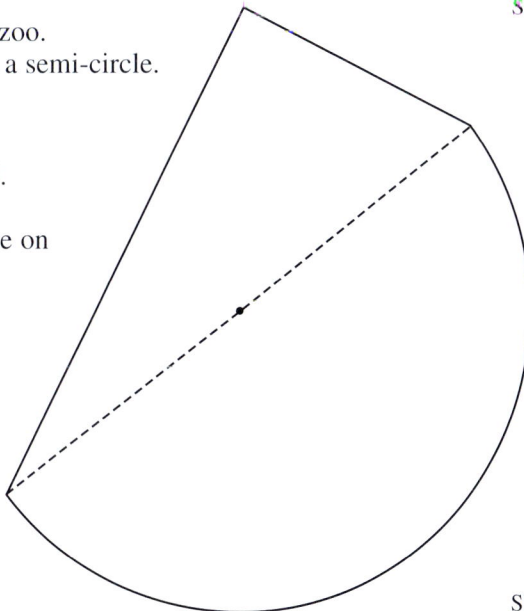

SEG 1998

4 The diagram shows the points *X* and *Y*.

Copy the diagram.

X •

(a) On your diagram mark two possible points which are the same distance from *X* as they are from *Y*.
Label them *A* and *B*.

(b) Draw the locus of the points which are the same distance from *X* as they are from *Y*.

• *Y*

SEG 1995

5 A new radio telephone mast is to be erected to provide services for the three towns, Axon, Beaver and Caxton. The position of the three towns is shown. The diagram is drawn to a scale of 1 cm to 10 km.

● Caxton

Axon ●

● Beaver

The mast is located in the triangle formed by Axon, Beaver and Caxton so that it is:

Equidistant from Axon and Beaver and 50 km from Caxton.

Construct the position of the mast on your diagram, and mark the position X.

6 A line is equidistant from $y = 1$ and $y = 5$. What is the equation of this line?

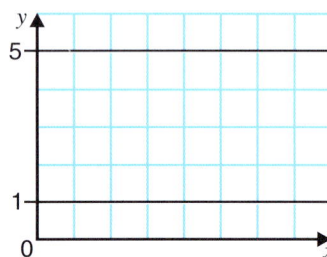

7 Beacons at O, A and B are on level ground. The beacons are used to guide aircraft landing at an airport.

The airport is equidistant from A and B.

To land at the airport an aircraft must fly directly above the line which is equidistant from OA and OB.

Copy the diagram.
On your diagram, show the line above which an aircraft must fly when landing at the airport and mark with a cross the position of the airport.

SEG 1996

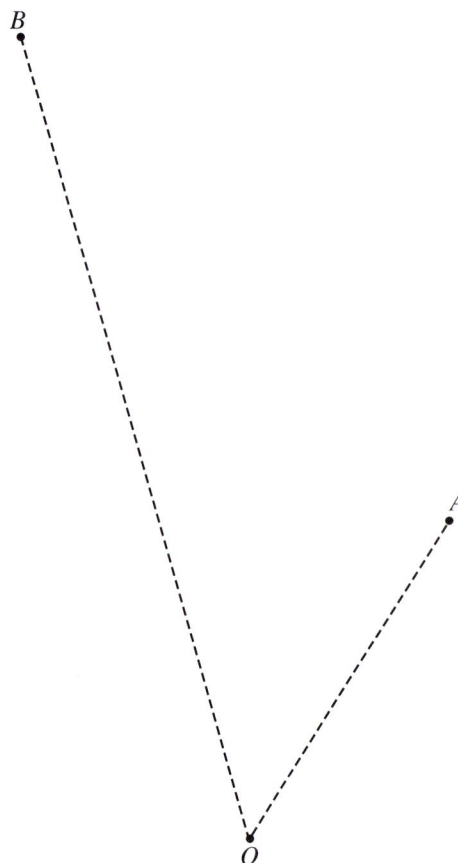

8 Three rods AB, BC, and CD are linked together to form part of a rhombus $ABCD$ of side 6 cm.
A and D are fixed points.
Make a full-sized copy of the diagram.
As the rods are moved, sketch the locus of the midpoint of BC.

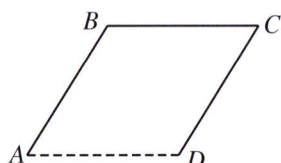

SEG 1997

CHAPTER 21

Pythagoras' Theorem

The longest side in a right-angled triangle is called the **hypotenuse**.

In any right-angled triangle it can be proved that:
"The square on the hypotenuse is equal to the sum of the squares on the other two sides."

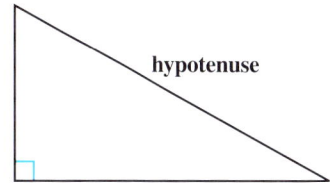

This is known as the **Theorem of Pythagoras**, or **Pythagoras' Theorem**.

Checking the Theorem of Pythagoras

Look at this triangle.

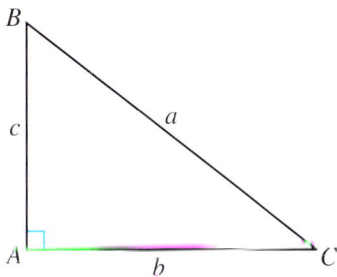

Notice that: the side opposite angle A is labelled a,
the side opposite angle B is labelled b,
the side opposite angle C is labelled c.

ABC is a right-angled triangle because $\angle BAC = 90°$.
$a = 5\,\text{cm}$, so $a^2 = 25\,\text{cm}^2$.
$b = 4\,\text{cm}$, so $b^2 = 16\,\text{cm}^2$.
$c = 3\,\text{cm}$, so $c^2 = 9\,\text{cm}^2$,

$a^2 = b^2 + c^2$

Activity

Use a ruler and a pair of compasses to draw the following triangles accurately.

(a)

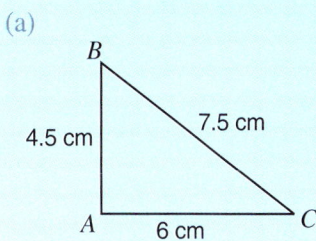

(b)

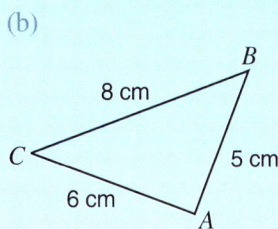

(c)

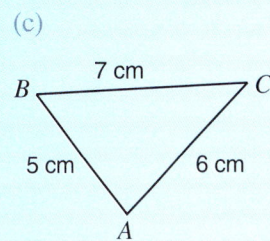

(d)

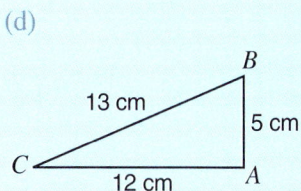

(e)

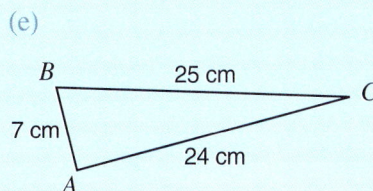

(f)

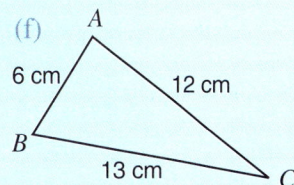

For each triangle: Measure angle BAC.
Is angle $BAC = 90°$?
Does $a^2 = b^2 + c^2$?
Explain your answers.

When we know the lengths of two sides of a right-angled triangle, we can use the Theorem of Pythagoras to find the length of the third side.

Finding the hypotenuse

EXAMPLE

The roof of a house is 12 m above the ground. What length of ladder is needed to reach the roof, if the foot of the ladder has to be placed 5 m away from the wall of the house?

Using Pythagoras' Theorem.
$$l^2 = 5^2 + 12^2$$
$$l^2 = 25 + 144$$
$$l^2 = 169$$

Take the square root of both sides.
$$l = \sqrt{169}$$
$$l = 13 \text{ m}$$

The ladder needs to be 13 m long.

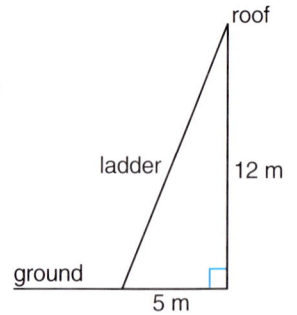

Exercise 21.1

1 These triangles are right-angled.
Calculate the length of the hypotenuse.

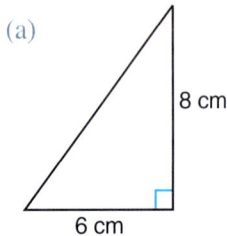

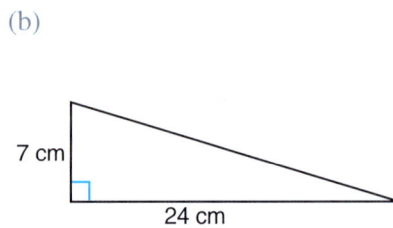

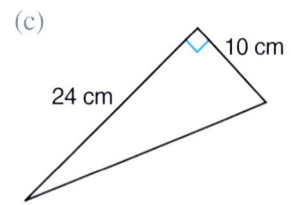

(a) 8 cm, 6 cm

(b) 7 cm, 24 cm

(c) 10 cm, 24 cm

2 These triangles are right-angled.
Calculate the length of side a to one decimal place.

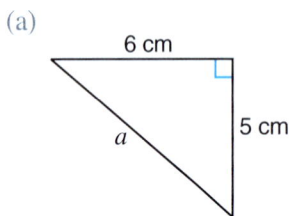

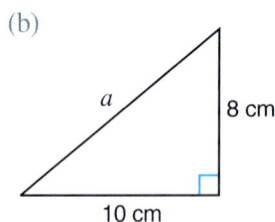

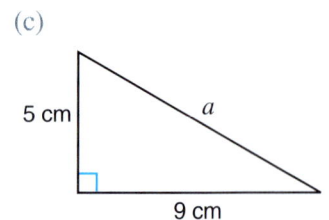

(a) 6 cm, 5 cm, a

(b) a, 8 cm, 10 cm

(c) 5 cm, a, 9 cm

3 Squares *ABXY* and *ACPQ* are drawn on the sides *AB* and *AC* of a right-angled triangle *ABC*, as shown.
ABXY has an area of 24.5 cm².
ACPQ has an area of 28.8 cm².
Calculate the length of *BC*, correct to one decimal place.

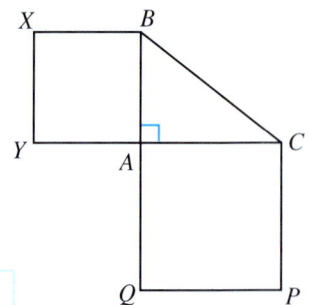

4 Lines *AB* and *CD* are drawn on a centimetre-squared grid.
Calculate the length of
(a) *AB*,
(b) *CD*.

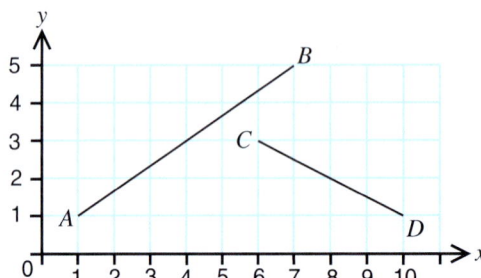

Finding one of the shorter sides

To find one of the shorter sides we can rearrange the Theorem of Pythagoras.

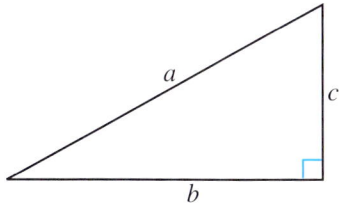

To find b we use: To find c we use:
$b^2 = a^2 - c^2$ $c^2 = a^2 - b^2$

To find the length of a shorter side of a right-angled triangle:
Subtract the square of the known short side from the square on the hypotenuse.
Take the square root of the result.

EXAMPLE

A wire used to keep a radio aerial steady is 9 metres long. The wire is fixed to the ground 4.6 metres from the base of the aerial. Find the height of the aerial, giving your answer correct to one decimal place.

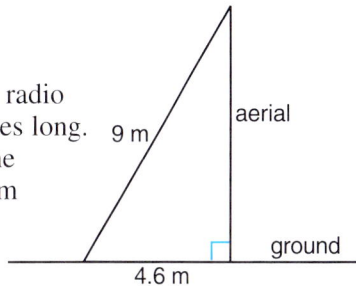

Using Pythagoras' Theorem.
$$9^2 = h^2 + 4.6^2$$
Rearranging this we get:
$$h^2 = 9^2 - 4.6^2$$
$$h^2 = 81 - 21.16$$
$$h^2 = 59.84$$
Take the square root of both sides.
$$h = \sqrt{59.84}$$
$$h = 7.735 \ldots$$
$$h = 7.7 \text{ m, correct to 1 d.p.}$$

The height of the aerial is 7.7 m, correct to 1 d.p.

Exercise 21.2

1 Work out the length of side b.

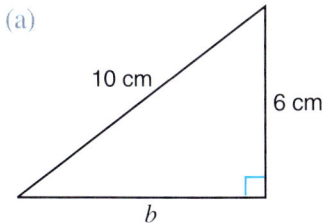

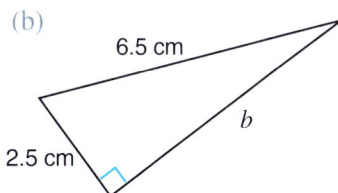

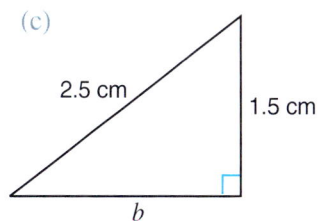

(a)
10 cm, 6 cm, b

(b)
6.5 cm, 2.5 cm, b

(c)
2.5 cm, 1.5 cm, b

2 Work out the length of side c, correct to one decimal place.

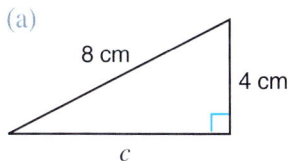

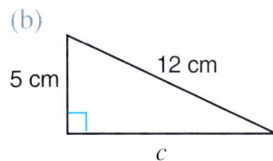

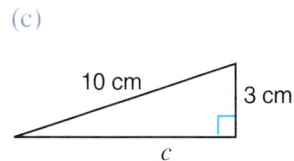

(a)
8 cm, 4 cm, c

(b)
5 cm, 12 cm, c

(c)
10 cm, 3 cm, c

3 Two boats A and B are 360 m apart.
Boat A is 120 m due east of a buoy.
Boat B is due north of the buoy.
How far is boat B from the buoy?

21 Pythagoras' Theorem

303

4 The diagram shows a right-angled triangle, *ABC*, and a square, *ACDE*.

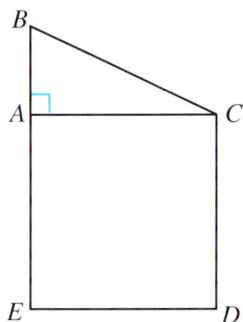

$AB = 2.5$ cm and $BC = 6.5$ cm.
Calculate the area of the square *ACDE*.

5 The diagram shows a right-angled triangle, *ABC*, and a square, *XYBA*.

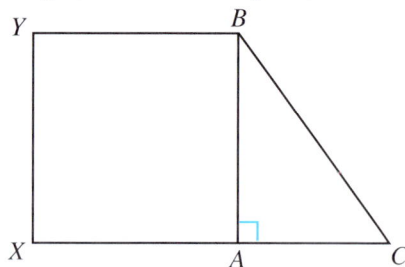

$BC = 6$ cm.
The square *XYBA* has an area of 23.04 cm².
Calculate the length of *AC*.

Problems involving the use of Pythagoras' Theorem

Questions leading to the use of Pythagoras' Theorem often involve:

Understanding the problem.
What information is given?
What are you required to find?

Drawing diagrams.
In some questions a diagram is not given.
Drawing a diagram may help you to understand the problem.

Selecting a suitable right-angled triangle.
In more complex problems you will have to select a right-angled triangle which can be used to answer the question. It is a good idea to draw this triangle on its own, especially if it has been taken from a three-dimensional drawing.

EXAMPLE

The diagram shows the side view of a swimming pool.
It slopes steadily from a depth of 1 m to 3.6 m.
The pool is 20 m long.
Find the length of the sloping bottom of the pool,
giving the answer correct to three significant figures.

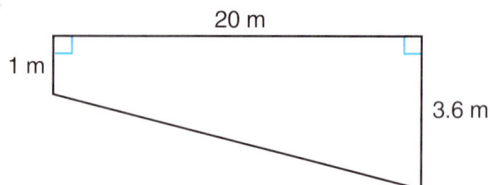

$\triangle CDE$ is a suitable right-angled triangle.
$CD = 3.6 - 1 = 2.6$ m

Using Pythagoras' Theorem in $\triangle CDE$.
$DE^2 = CD^2 + CE^2$
$DE^2 = 2.6^2 + 20^2$
$DE^2 = 6.76 + 400$
$DE^2 = 406.76$
$DE = \sqrt{406.76}$ m
$DE = 20.1682 \ldots$ m

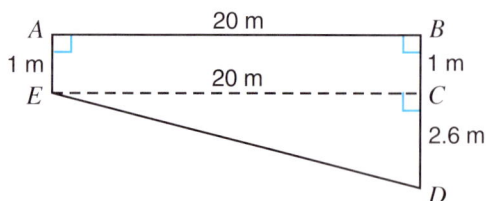

The length of the sloping bottom of the pool is 20.2 m, correct to 3 sig. figs.

1   In each of the following, work out the length of the side marked x.

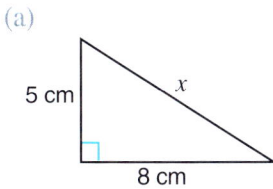

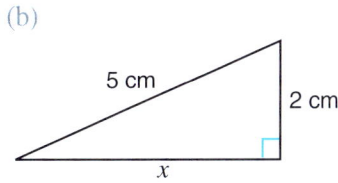

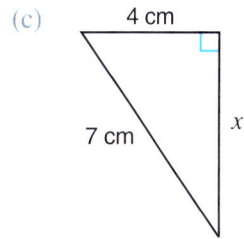

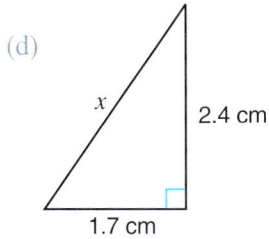

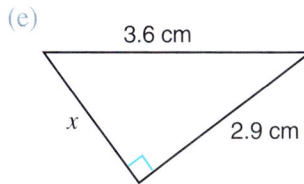

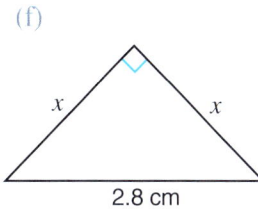

(a)

5 cm
x
8 cm

(b)

5 cm
2 cm
x

(c)

4 cm
7 cm
x

(d)

x
2.4 cm
1.7 cm

(e)

3.6 cm
x
2.9 cm

(f)

x x
2.8 cm

2   A rectangle is 8 cm wide and 15 cm long.
    Work out the length of its diagonals.

3   The length of a rectangle is 24 cm. The diagonals of the rectangle are 26 cm.
    Work out the width of the rectangle.

4   A square has sides of length 6 cm. Work out the length of its diagonals.

5   The diagonals of a square are 15 cm. Work out the length of its sides.

6   The height of an isosceles triangle is 12 cm. The base of the triangle is 18 cm.
    Work out the length of the equal sides.

7   An equilateral triangle has sides of length 8 cm.
    Work out the height of the triangle.

8   The diagram shows the side view of a car ramp.
    The ramp is 110 cm long and 25 cm high.
    The top part of the ramp is 40 cm long.
    Calculate the length of the sloping part of the ramp.

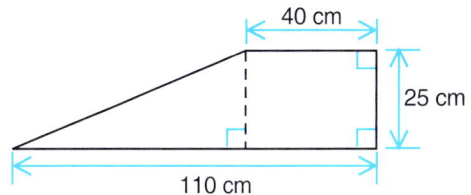

40 cm
25 cm
110 cm

9   The top of a lampshade has a diameter of 10 cm.
    The bottom of the lampshade has a diameter of 20 cm.
    The height of the lampshade is 12 cm.
    Calculate the length, l, of the sloping sides.

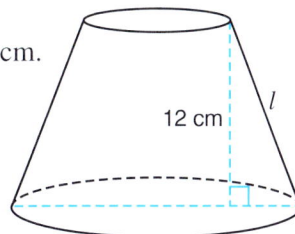

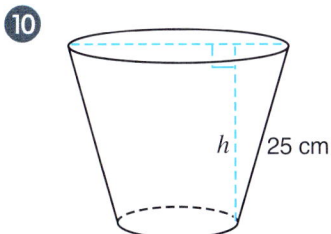

12 cm l

10

h 25 cm

The top of a bucket has a diameter of 30 cm.
The bottom of the bucket has a diameter of 16 cm.
The sloping sides are 25 cm long.
How deep is the bucket?

11 The diagram shows an isosceles trapezium *ABCD*.
AB = 6 cm and *CD* = 9 cm.
The perpendicular height is 5 cm.
Calculate the length of *BC*.

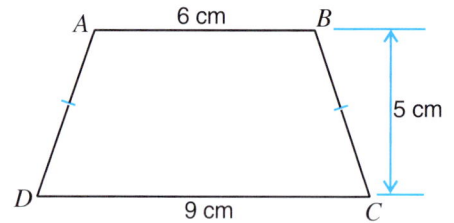

12 *ABCD* is a kite.
AB = 8.5 cm, *BC* = 5.4 cm and *BD* = 7.6 cm.
(a) Calculate the length of *AC*.
(b) Calculate the area of the kite.

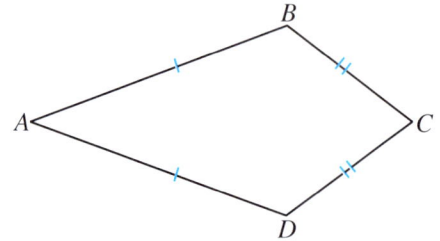

Solving problems in three dimensions

When we solve problems in three dimensions we often need to use more than one triangle to solve the problem.

EXAMPLE

This cube has sides of length 5 cm.
What is the distance from *D* to *F*?
Give the answer correct to 1 decimal place.

ΔDFH is a suitable right-angled triangle, but we only know the length of the side *DH*.
The length of *FH* can be found by using ΔFGH.

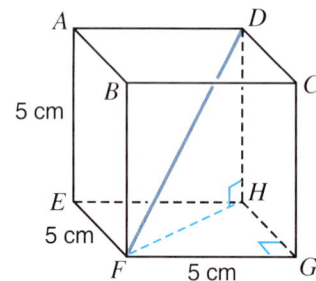

Using Pythagoras' Theorem in ΔFGH.

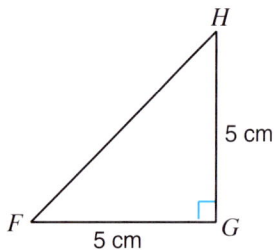

$FH^2 = FG^2 + GH^2$
$FH^2 = 5^2 + 5^2$
$FH^2 = 25 + 25$
$FH^2 = 50$
$FH = \sqrt{50}$ cm

Using Pythagoras' Theorem in ΔDFH.

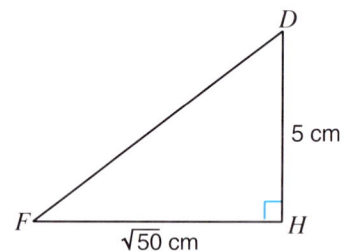

$DF^2 = DH^2 + FH^2$
$DF^2 = 5^2 + (\sqrt{50})^2$
$DF^2 = 25 + 50$
$DF^2 = 75$
$DF = \sqrt{75}$ cm
$DF = 8.66...$ cm
$DF = 8.7$ cm, correct to 1 d.p.

For accuracy, the exact value of *FH*, $(\sqrt{50})$, should be used.

1 The cube has sides of length 6 cm.
Calculate the length of the diagonal *PQ*.

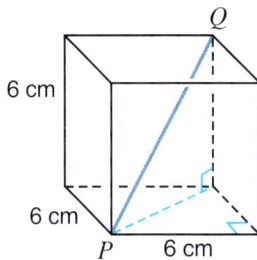

2

The diagram shows a wedge *ABCDEF*.
AD = 13 cm, *DE* = 15 cm and *EC* = 6 cm.
Calculate the length of the line *AC*.

3 *ABCDEFGH* is a cuboid.
AE = 5 cm, *EH* = 9 cm and *HG* = 6 cm.
Calculate the length of the line *AG*.

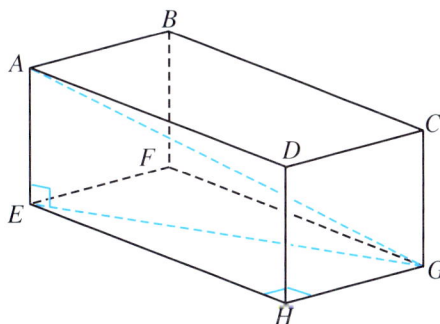

4

The diagram shows a pyramid *PABCD*.
X is at the centre of the base.
The base *ABCD* is a rectangle with
AB = *CD* = 12 cm and *BC* = *DA* = 9 cm.
The height of the pyramid, *PX*, is 18 cm.
Calculate the length of the edge *PA*.

5 The diagram of a cuboid is shown.
(a) Calculate the length of *EC*,
when *EF* = 6 cm, *FG* = 8 cm and *CG* = 5 cm.
(b) Calculate the length of *AG*,
when *AD* = 10 cm, *DC* = 8 cm and *CG* = 6 cm.
(c) Calculate the length of *FD*,
when *FG* = 7 cm, *GH* = 5 cm and *HD* = 4 cm.

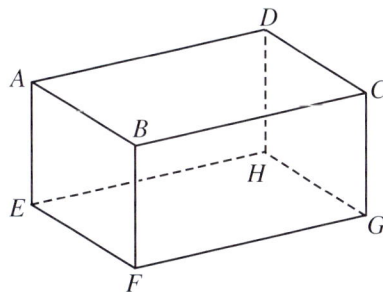

6

The diagram shows a square based pyramid.
All edges are 7 cm in length.
Calculate the height of the pyramid, *PX*.

What you need to know

- The longest side in a right-angled triangle is called the **hypotenuse**.

- The **Theorem of Pythagoras** states:
  "In any right-angled triangle the square on the hypotenuse is equal to the sum of the squares on the other two sides."

  $a^2 = b^2 + c^2$
  Rearranging gives:
  $b^2 = a^2 - c^2$
  $c^2 = a^2 - b^2$

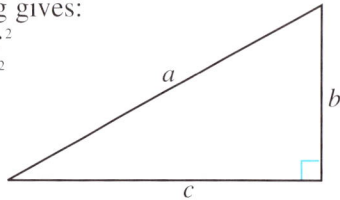

- When we know the lengths of two sides of a right-angled triangle, we can use the Theorem of Pythagoras to find the length of the third side.

IDEAS FOR INVESTIGATION

Investigate the relationship between the areas of the semi-circles A, B and C.

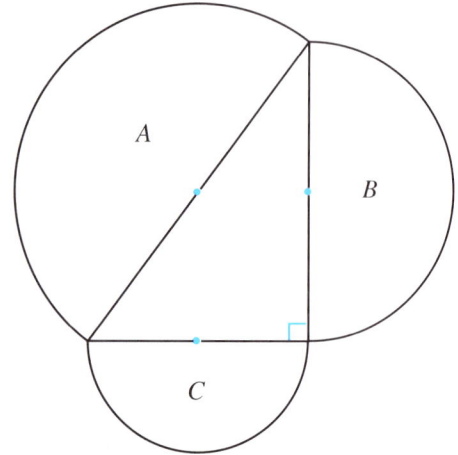

Review Exercise

1 Pauline is building a greenhouse.
The base, *PQRS* of the greenhouse should be a rectangle measuring 2.6 m by 1.4 m.

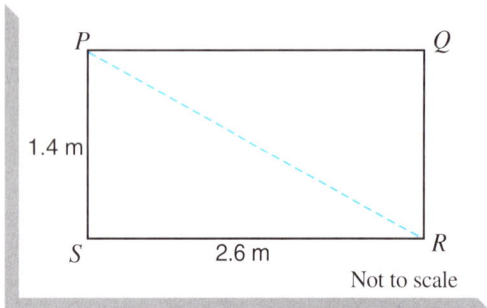

Not to scale

To check the base is rectangular Pauline has to measure the diagonal *PR*.

(a) Calculate the length of *PR* when the base is rectangular.

(b) When building the greenhouse Pauline finds angle *PSR* > 90°.
She measures *PR*.
Which of the following statements is **true**?

X: *PR* is greater than it should be.
Y: *PR* is less than it should be.
Z: *PR* is the right length.

SEG 1995

2 The diagram shows the position of a ferry sailing between Folkestone and Calais.

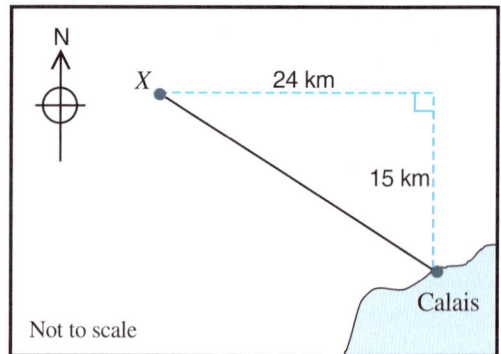

N

X ------ 24 km

15 km

Calais

Not to scale

The ferry is at *X*.
The position of the ferry from Calais is given as:

North of Calais 15 km,
West of Calais 24 km.

Calculate the distance of the ferry from Calais.
Give your answer correct to **one** decimal place.

SEG 1997

3 James plans a game.
He hides objects at X, Y and Z and marks the positions on a plan.
The plan has been drawn using a scale of 1 cm to 100 m.

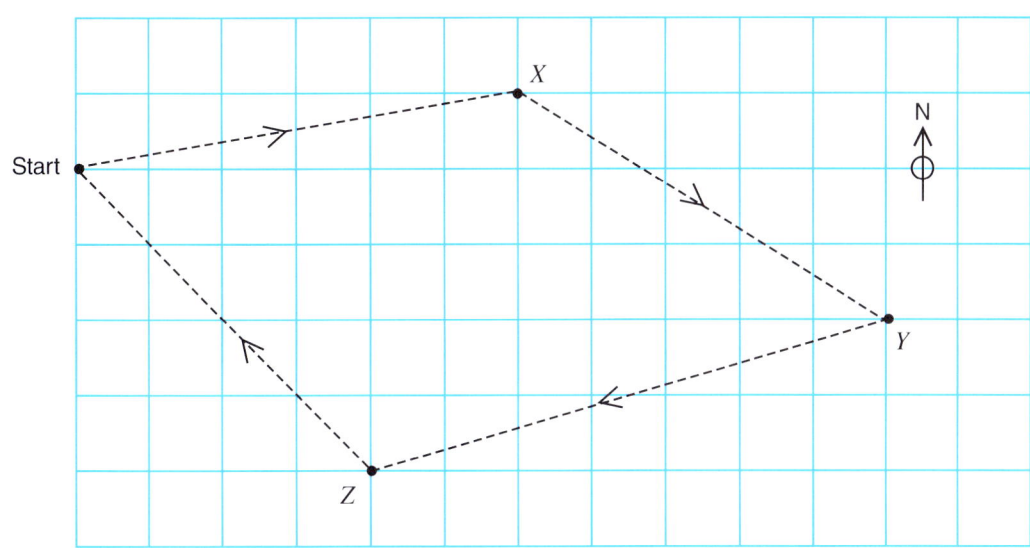

Calculate the distance a competitor must walk from Y to Z.
Give your answer to the nearest metre.

SEG 1996

4 Triangle PQR has dimensions as shown.

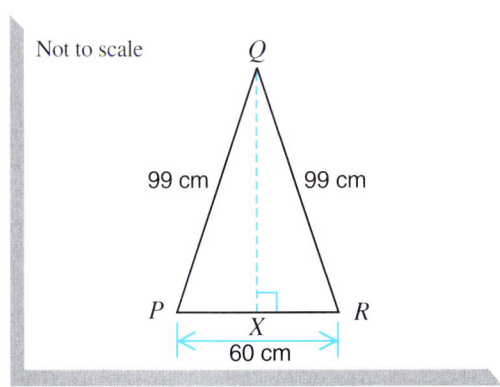

Not to scale

99 cm   99 cm

P R
X
60 cm

Calculate the height of QX.

5 This shape is a regular hexagon of side 12 cm.

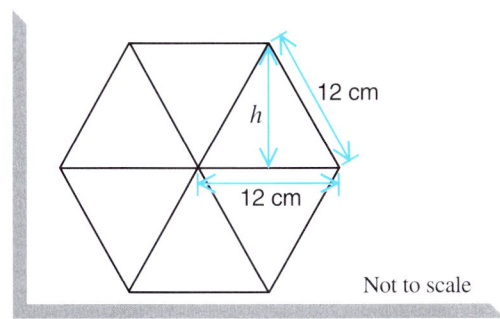

12 cm
h
12 cm

Not to scale

Calculate the height marked h.

6 The coordinates of the points A and B are $(6, 8)$ and $(1, 1)$.

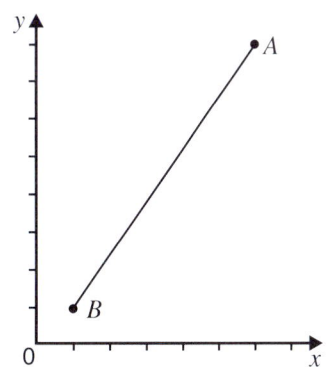

Work out the length of AB.

SEG 1996

7 A flagpole is held vertically by four wires as shown.

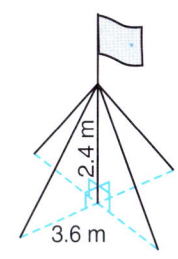

2.4 m
3.6 m

Each wire is fixed to the pole 2.4 m from the ground and to the ground 3.6 m from the foot of the pole. Calculate the total length of wire needed.

8 The diagram consists of three right-angled triangles.
$AB = 7$ cm, $BC = DE = 5$ cm and $AE = 12$ cm.

(a) Calculate the length AC.
(b) Calculate the length AD.

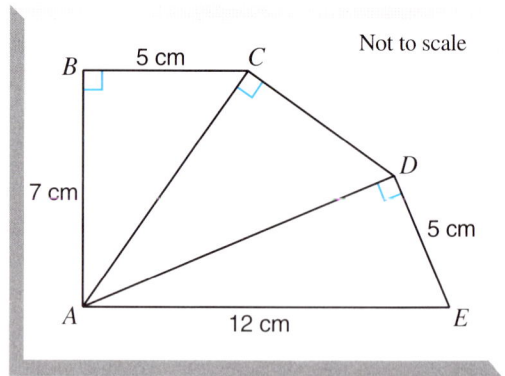

Not to scale

B   5 cm   C

7 cm

A   12 cm   E

D

5 cm

SEG 1996

9 The diagram shows a trapezium $ABCD$.

Calculate the length of the line AB.

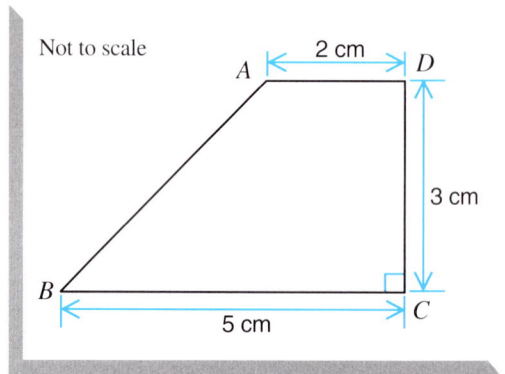

Not to scale

A   2 cm   D

3 cm

B

5 cm   C

10 John is standing 200 m due west of a power station and 300 m due north of a pylon. Calculate the distance of the power station from the pylon.

11 The quadrilateral $ABCD$ is a kite.
$DO = OB$, $DC = 104$ cm, $CO = 96$ cm and $AC = 126$ cm.

(a) Calculate the length of
  (i) DB,
  (ii) AD.
(b) Work out the area of the kite.

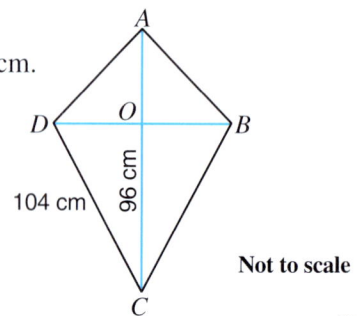

A

D   O   B

96 cm

104 cm

C

Not to scale

SEG 1995

12 The diagram shows a computer design for a ramp. Its shape is a prism. Each unit represents one metre.

Calculate the length of BD.

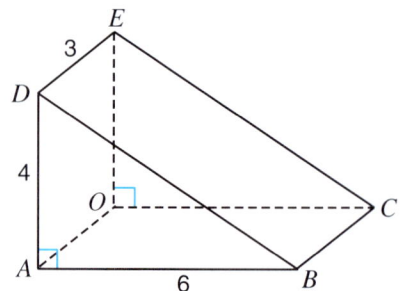

E

3

D

4

O   C

A   6   B

SEG 1995

13 The diagram shows a cuboid, where
$AB = 4$ cm, $AD = 5$ cm and $AF = 20$ cm.

Calculate the length AH.

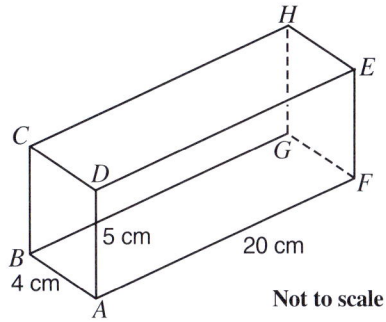

5 cm

20 cm

4 cm

Not to scale

SEG 1997

14 The cube has sides of length 10 cm.
Calculate the length of the diagonal PQ.

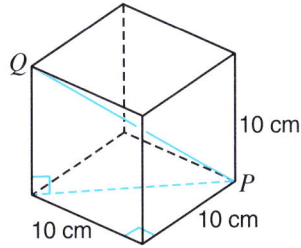

10 cm

10 cm

10 cm

15 The diagram shows a wedge $ABCDEF$.
$AC = 13$ cm, $DE = 7$ cm and $EC = 5$ cm.

Calculate the length of the line AD.

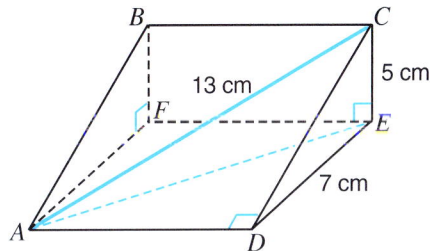

13 cm

5 cm

7 cm

16 The diagram shows a pyramid $PABCD$.
X is at the centre of the base.
The base $ABCD$ is a rectangle with
$AB = CD = 6$ cm and $BC = DA = 4.5$ cm.
The height of the pyramid, PX, is 9 cm.

Calculate the length of the edge PA.

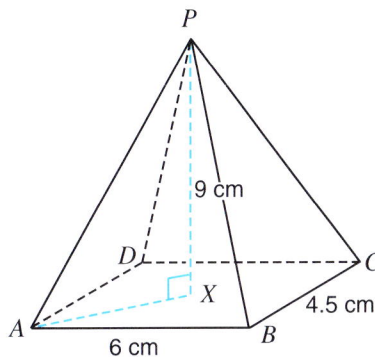

9 cm

4.5 cm

6 cm

17 The diagram shows a square based pyramid.
All edges are 8 cm in length.

Calculate the height of the pyramid, PX.

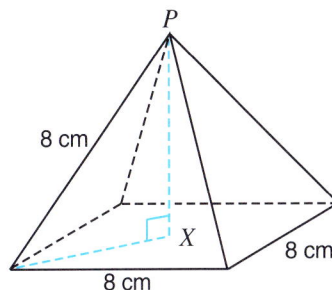

8 cm

8 cm

8 cm

CHAPTER 22

Trigonometry

We use **trigonometry** to find the lengths of sides and the sizes of angles in right-angled triangles.

We already know that the longest side of a right-angled triangle is called the **hypotenuse**.

In order to understand the relationships between sides and angles the other sides of the triangle also need to be named.

The **opposite** side is the side directly opposite the angle being used and the **adjacent** is the side next to the angle.

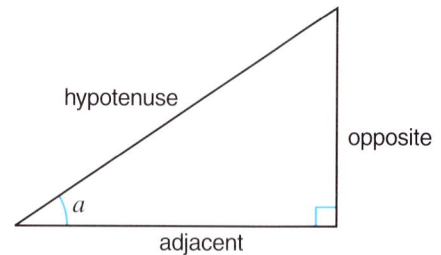

Look at this diagram.
It shows how the height of a kite changes as more and more string is let out.

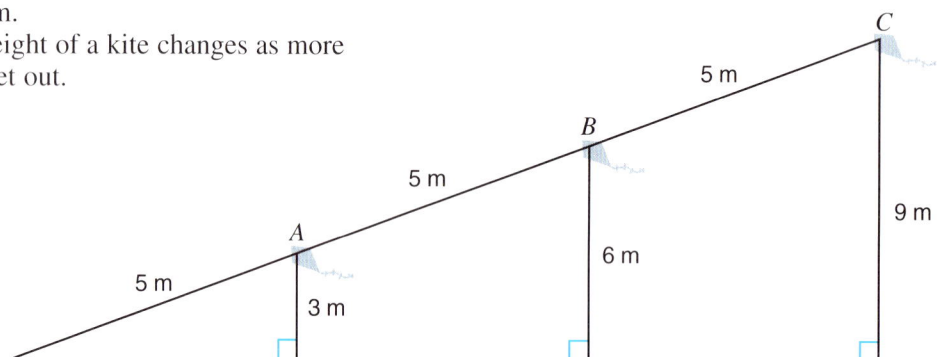

When the kite is at A, the string is 5 m long and the kite is 3 m high.

At A, the ratio $\dfrac{\text{height of kite}}{\text{length of string}}$, is therefore $\dfrac{3}{5} = 0.6$.

Calculate the value of the same ratio at B and C.
What do you notice?
When the kite is flying at angle a, the ratio $\dfrac{\text{height of kite}}{\text{length of string}}$ will always be the same whatever the length of the kite string and is called the **sine** of angle a.

Finding the length of the opposite side

The sine ratio

For any right-angled triangle:
$$\sin a = \frac{\text{opposite}}{\text{hypotenuse}}$$

The sine ratio links three pieces of information:
   the size of an **angle**,
   the length of the side **opposite** the angle,
   the length of the **hypotenuse**.
If we are given the values for two of these we can find the value of the third.

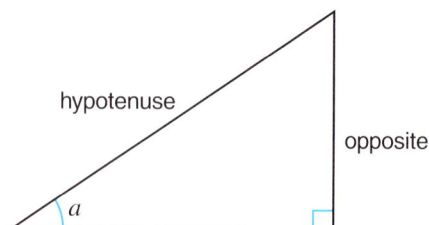

EXAMPLE

Find the height of a kite when it is flying at an angle of 40° and the kite string is 12 m long.
Give the answer correct to 3 significant figures.

$\sin a = \frac{\text{opp}}{\text{hyp}}$

Substitute known values.

$\sin 40° = \frac{h}{12}$

Multiply both sides by 12.

$h = 12 \times \sin 40°$

Using your calculator, press:

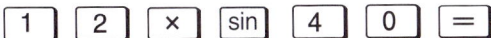

[1] [2] [×] [sin] [4] [0] [=]

$h = 7.713 \ldots$
$h = 7.71$ m, correct to 3 s.f.

The height of the kite is 7.71 m, correct to 3 s.f.

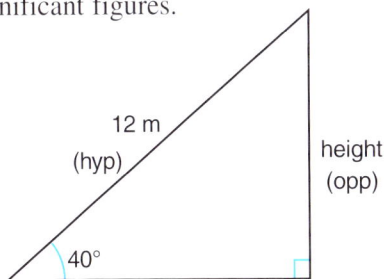

Mathematical shorthand

Word	Abbreviation
sine	sin
opposite	opp
hypotenuse	hyp

12 m (hyp)   height (opp)   40°

Exercise 22.1

1 Find the height, h, of these kites.
Give your answers correct to 3 significant figures.

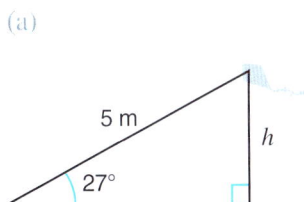

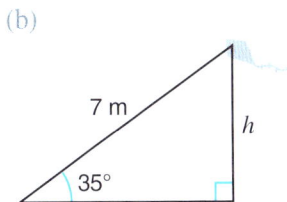

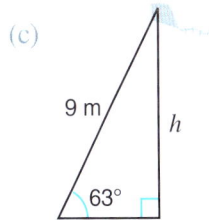

(a)   5 m h 27°

(b)   7 m h 35°

(c)   9 m h 63°

2 Calculate the lengths marked x.
Give your answers correct to 3 significant figures.

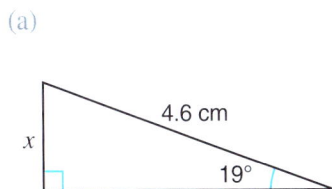

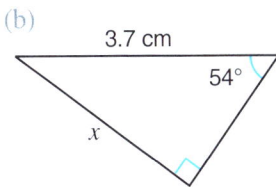

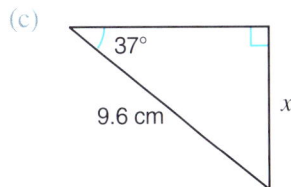

(a)   4.6 cm x 19°

(b)   3.7 cm   54° x

(c)   37°   9.6 cm x

3 In $\triangle ABC$, angle $ACB = 90°$.
  (a) If $\angle BAC = 47.5°$ and $AB = 4.6$ m find BC.
  (b) If $\angle ABC = 67.4°$ and $AB = 12.4$ m find AC.
  (c) If $\angle BAC = 15.8°$ and $AB = 17.4$ cm find BC.
  (d) If $\angle BAC = 35°$ and $AB = 8.5$ cm find the size of
        $\angle ABC$ and then find AC.
Give your answers correct to 3 significant figures.

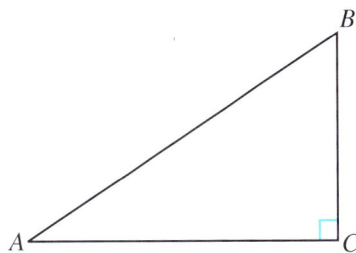

B
A   C

Finding an angle

If you are given the sine of an angle and asked to find the angle use the inverse sine function, $\sin^{-1}$, on your calculator.

Using your calculator, press: [sin] [3] [0]
The display should read 0.5.
Clear the display and press: [$\sin^{-1}$] [0] [.] [5] [=]
What do you notice?

$30° \xrightarrow{\text{sine}} 0.5$

$30° \xleftarrow[\text{sine}]{\text{inverse}} 0.5$

EXAMPLE

Find the size of angle a when the kite string is 12 m long and the kite is flying 7 m above the ground.
Give the answer correct to one decimal place.

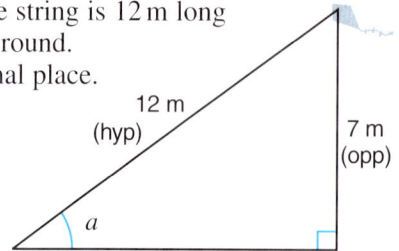

12 m (hyp)   7 m (opp)

a

$\sin a = \frac{\text{opp}}{\text{hyp}}$

Substitute known values.

$\sin a° = \frac{7}{12}$

$a = \sin^{-1} \frac{7}{12}$

Using your calculator, press: [$\sin^{-1}$] [(] [7] [÷] [1] [2] [)] [=]

$a = 35.685\ldots$

$a = 35.7°$, correct to 1 d.p.

Exercise 22.2

1 Find the size of angle a for each of these kites.
Give your answers correct to one decimal place.

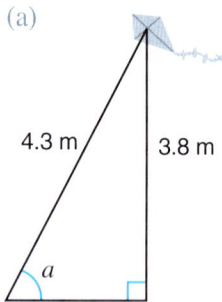

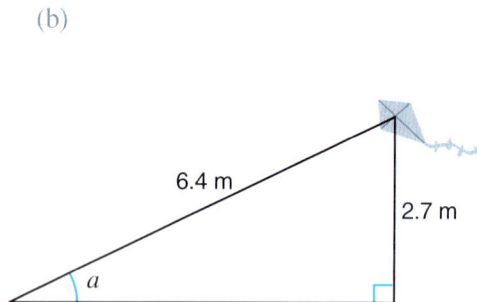

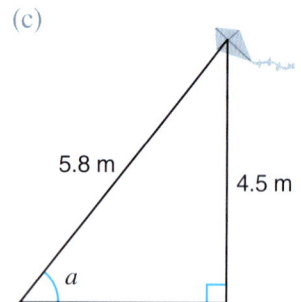

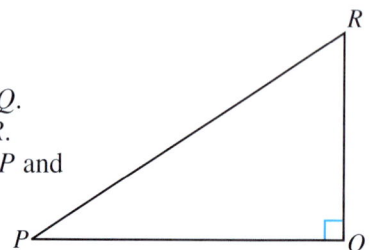

(a)

4.3 m   3.8 m

a

(b)

6.4 m

2.7 m

a

(c)

5.8 m   4.5 m

a

2 Find the size of angle x in each of these triangles.
Give your answers correct to one decimal place.

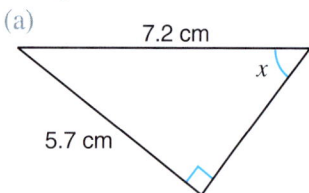

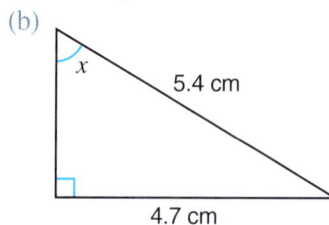

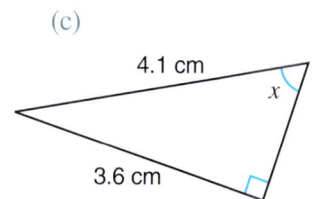

(a)

7.2 cm

x

5.7 cm

(b)

x 5.4 cm

4.7 cm

(c)

4.1 cm

x

3.6 cm

3 In $\triangle PQR$ angle $PQR = 90°$.
(a) If $QR = 4$ m and $PR = 10$ m find the size of $\angle QPR$.
(b) If $PQ = 4.7$ cm and $PR = 5.2$ cm find the size of $\angle PRQ$.
(c) If $QR = 7.2$ m and $PR = 19.4$ m find the size of $\angle QPR$.
(d) If $PQ = 3.7$ cm and $PR = 9.1$ cm find the size of $\angle QRP$ and then find the size of $\angle QPR$.
Give your answers correct to one decimal place.

R

P   Q

Finding the hypotenuse

EXAMPLE

Find the length of the string, l, when a kite is 6 m high and the string makes an angle of 50° with the ground.
Give the answer correct to 3 significant figures.

$$\sin a = \frac{\text{opp}}{\text{hyp}}$$

Substitute known values.

$$\sin 50° = \frac{6}{l}$$

Multiply both sides by l.

$$l \times \sin 50° = 6$$

Divide both sides by $\sin 50°$.

$$l = \frac{6}{\sin 50°}$$

Using your calculator, press: $\boxed{6}$ $\boxed{\div}$ $\boxed{\sin}$ $\boxed{5}$ $\boxed{0}$ $\boxed{=}$
$l = 7.832\ldots$
$l = 7.83$ m, correct to 3 s.f.

The length of the string is 7.83 m, correct to 3 s.f.

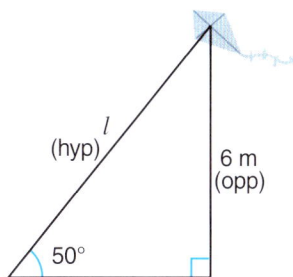

Exercise 22.3

1 Find the lengths, l, of these kite strings.
Give your answers correct to 3 significant figures.

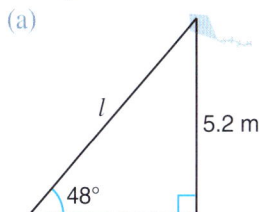

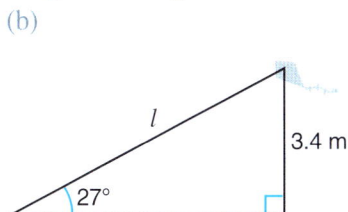

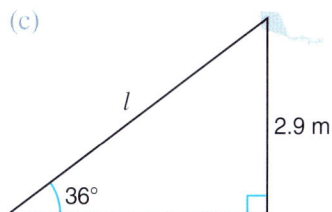

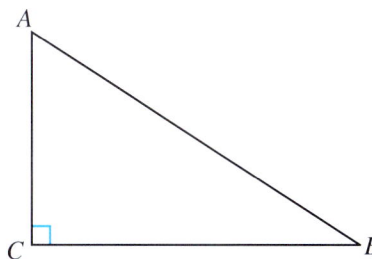

(a)

5.2 m
48°

(b)

3.4 m
27°

(c)

2.9 m
36°

2 Calculate the length of side x in each of these triangles.
Give your answers correct to two decimal places.

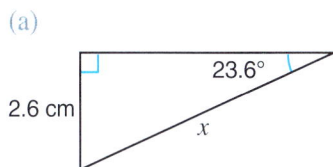

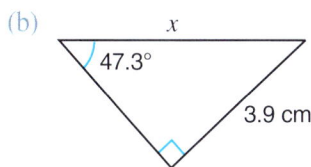

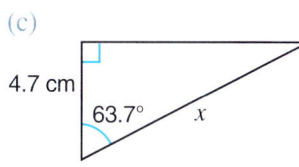

(a)

23.6°
2.6 cm
x

(b)

x
47.3°
3.9 cm

(c)

4.7 cm
63.7°
x

3 In $\triangle ABC$ angle $ACB = 90°$.
(a) If $\angle BAC = 36.2°$ and $BC = 4.5$ m find AB.
(b) If $\angle ABC = 64.7°$ and $AC = 15.8$ cm find AB.
(c) If $\angle BAC = 12.7°$ and $BC = 14.7$ cm find AB.
(d) If $\angle BAC = 72.8°$ and $AC = 7.6$ m find the size of $\angle ABC$ and then find AB.
Give your answers correct to 3 significant figures.

We have found that **sine** is the ratio $\dfrac{\text{opposite}}{\text{hypotenuse}}$.

In a similar way we can find two other ratios, the **cosine** of angle a and the **tangent** of angle a.

The cosine ratio

For any right-angled triangle:

$$\cos a = \frac{\text{adjacent}}{\text{hypotenuse}}$$

The cosine ratio links three pieces of information:
   the size of an **angle**,
   the length of the side **adjacent** to the angle,
   the length of the **hypotenuse**.
If we are given the values of two of these we can find the value of the third.

The tangent ratio

For any right-angled triangle:

$$\tan a = \frac{\text{opposite}}{\text{adjacent}}$$

The tangent ratio links three pieces of information:
   the size of an **angle**,
   the length of the side **opposite** to the angle,
   the length of the side **adjacent** to the angle.
If we are given the values of two of these we can find the value of the third.

EXAMPLE

1

Write down the sin, cos and tan ratios for angle a in the triangle.

17 cm   8 cm   15 cm

$\sin a = \dfrac{\text{opp}}{\text{hyp}} = \dfrac{8}{17}$

$\cos a = \dfrac{\text{adj}}{\text{hyp}} = \dfrac{15}{17}$

$\tan a = \dfrac{\text{opp}}{\text{adj}} = \dfrac{8}{15}$

Mathematical shorthand

Word	Abbreviation
adjacent	adj
opposite	opp
hypotenuse	hyp
sine	sin
cosine	cos
tangent	tan

How to select and use the correct ratio

There are only 3 different types of question for each of the ratios. Selecting the correct ratio is most important.
To do this:

1.   Go to the angle you know (or want to find).
2.   Name sides (opp, adj, hyp).
     If you are trying to find the length of a side, name that side first together with one other side of known length.
     If you are trying to find the size of an angle, name two sides of known length.
3.   Select the correct ratio and write it down.

   $\sin a = \dfrac{\text{opp}}{\text{hyp}}$ $\cos a = \dfrac{\text{adj}}{\text{hyp}}$ $\tan a = \dfrac{\text{opp}}{\text{adj}}$

   One way to remember the ratios is to use the initial letters, SOHCAHTOA.
   You may know another method.

4.   Substitute known values from the question.
5.   Rearrange to isolate the angle, or side, you are trying to find.
6.   Use your calculator to find the size of the angle, or side, writing down more figures than you need for the final answer.
7.   Correct to the required degree of accuracy.
8.   Give the answer, stating the degree of approximation and giving the correct units. When giving the answer to a problem you should use a short sentence.

EXAMPLES

2 Find the length, h, giving the answer to 3 significant figures

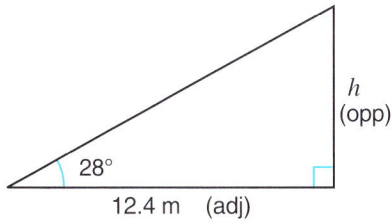

28°

12.4 m   (adj)

h (opp)

$$\tan a = \frac{\text{opp}}{\text{adj}}$$

Substitute known values.

$$\tan 28° = \frac{h}{12.4}$$

Multiply both sides by 12.4.

$$h = 12.4 \times \tan 28°$$

Using your calculator, press:

[1] [2] [.] [4] [×] [tan] [2] [8] [=]

$h = 6.593 \ldots$

$h = 6.59$ m, correct to 3 s.f.

3 Find the size of angle a, correct to one decimal place.

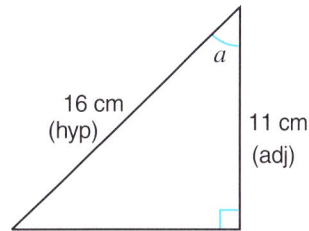

a

16 cm (hyp)

11 cm (adj)

$$\cos a = \frac{\text{adj}}{\text{hyp}}$$

Substitute known values.

$$\cos a° = \frac{11}{16}$$

$$a = \cos^{-1} \frac{11}{16}$$

Using your calculator, press:

[cos⁻¹] [(] [1] [1] [÷] [1] [6] [)] [=]

$a = 46.56 \ldots$

$a = 46.6°$, correct to 1 d.p.

Exercise 22.4

1 Write down the sin, cos and tan ratios for angle p in each of the following triangles.

(a)

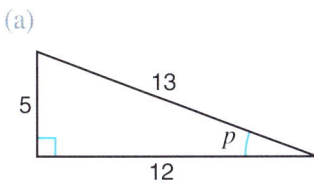

5

13

12

p

(b)

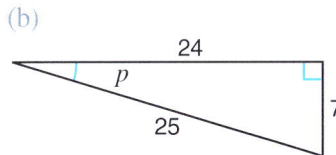

24

p

25

7

(c)

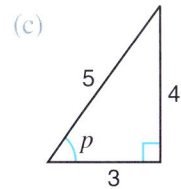

5

4

p

3

2 By choosing the correct ratio, calculate angle p in each of the following triangles. Give your answers correct to one decimal place.

(a)

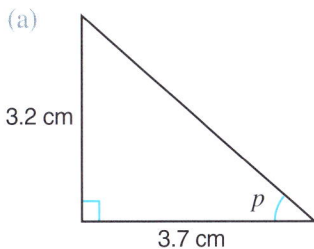

3.2 cm

3.7 cm

p

(b)

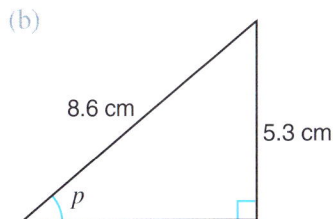

8.6 cm

5.3 cm

p

(c)

4.6 cm

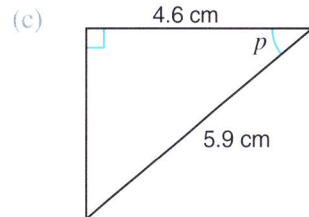

p

5.9 cm

(d)

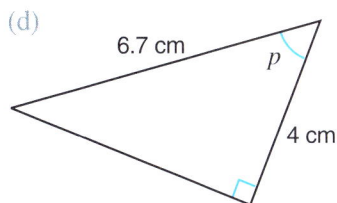

6.7 cm

p

4 cm

(e)

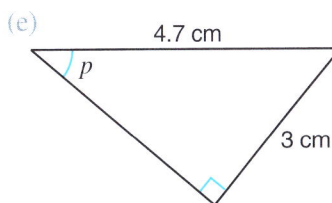

4.7 cm

p

3 cm

(f)

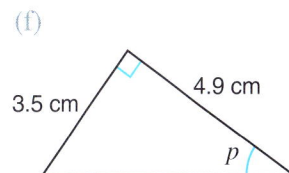

4.9 cm

3.5 cm

p

3 By choosing the correct ratio, calculate side a in each of the following triangles.

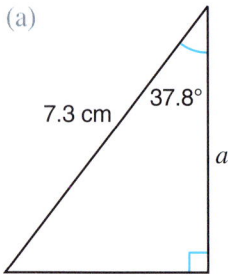

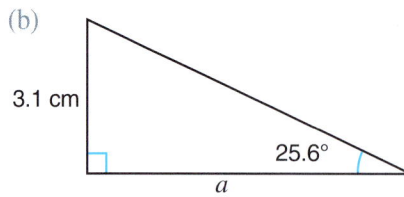

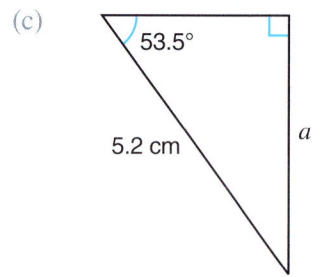

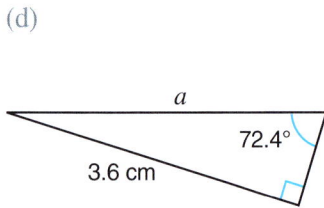

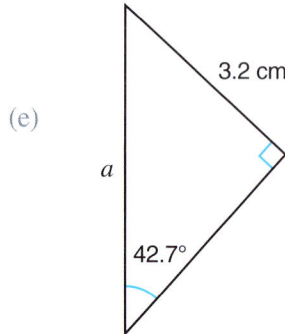

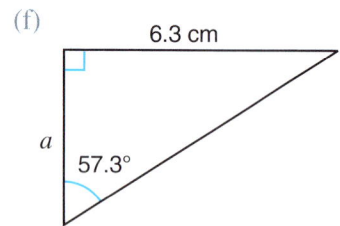

(a)

7.3 cm, 37.8°, a

(b)

3.1 cm, 25.6°, a

(c)

53.5°, 5.2 cm, a

(d)

a, 72.4°, 3.6 cm

(e)

3.2 cm, a, 42.7°

(f)

6.3 cm, a, 57.3°

4 An equilateral triangle has sides of length 5 cm. Calculate the height of the triangle.

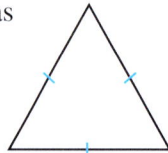

5 An isosceles triangle has sides of length 10 cm, 10 cm and 6 cm. Calculate the angles of the triangle.

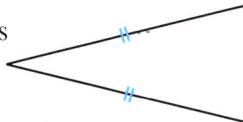

6 Calculate
  (a) the length of AC,
  (b) the length of CE.

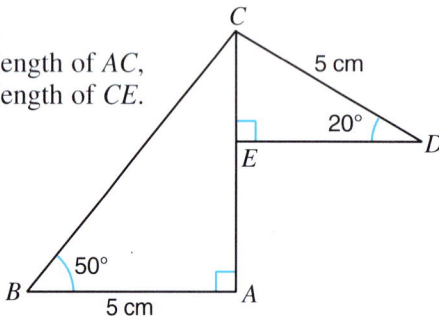

C, 5 cm, 20°, D, E, 50°, B, 5 cm, A

7
S, 3.6 cm, R, 74°, 10 cm, Q, P

Calculate
  (a) the length of RQ,
  (b) angle SPR.

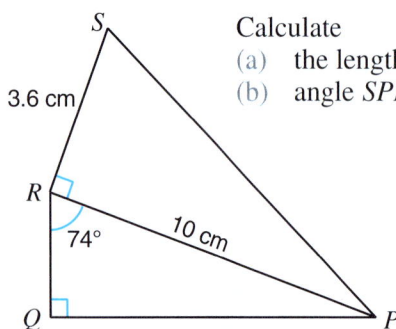

8 Calculate the length of WX.

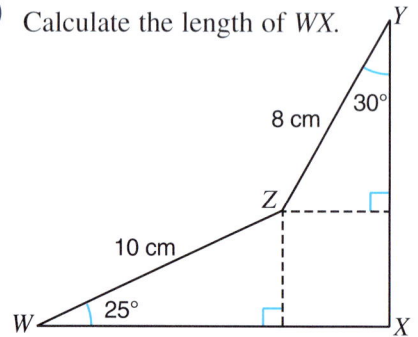

Y, 30°, 8 cm, Z, 10 cm, W, 25°, X

9 Calculate the length of PQ.

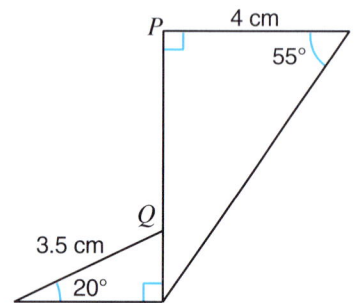

P, 4 cm, 55°, Q, 3.5 cm, 20°

10 Calculate the length of CD.

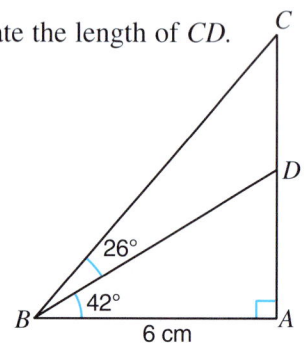

C, D, 26°, 42°, B, 6 cm, A

318

When we look **up** from the horizontal the angle we turn through is called an **angle of elevation**.

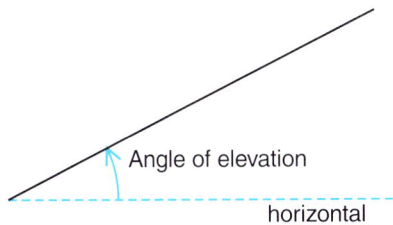

When we look **down** from the horizontal the angle we turn through is called an **angle of depression**.

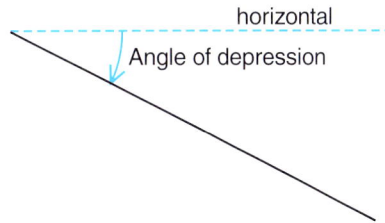

EXAMPLES

1 From a point on the ground, 30 m from the base of a pylon, the angle of elevation to the top of the pylon is 50°.

Find the height of the pylon.

$\tan a = \frac{\text{opp}}{\text{adj}}$

$\tan 50° = \frac{h}{30}$

$h = 30 \times \tan 50°$

$h = 35.75\ldots$

$h = 35.8$ m, correct to 3 s.f.

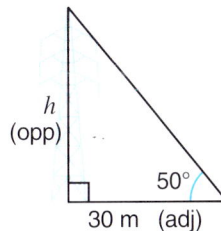

The height of the pylon is 35.8 m, correct to 3 s.f.

2 Staten Island Ferry is 270 m away from the base of the Statue of Liberty.
The ferry can be seen from a viewing point in the lantern, 85 m above the ground.

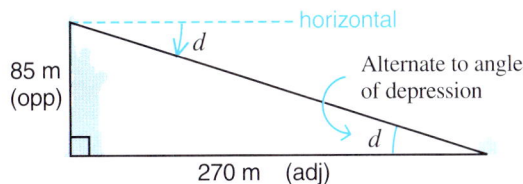

What is the angle of depression to the ferry from the viewing point?

$\tan a = \frac{\text{opp}}{\text{adj}}$

$\tan d° = \frac{85}{270}$

$d = \tan^{-1} \frac{85}{270}$

$d = 17.47\ldots$

$d = 17.5°$, correct to 1 d.p.

The angle of depression to the ferry from the viewing point is 17.5°, correct to 1 d.p.

1 From a point on the ground 20 m from the base of a tree, the angle of elevation of the top of the tree is 47°. Calculate the height of the tree.

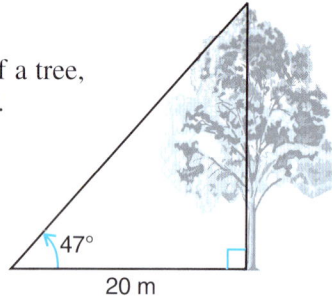

2 From a point on the ground 10 m from a block of flats, the angle of elevation of the top of the block is 76°.
Calculate the height of the block of flats.

3 A fishing boat is 200 m from the bottom of a vertical cliff.
From the top of the cliff the angle of depression to the fishing boat is 34°.
(a) Calculate the height of the cliff.
(b) A buoy is 100 m from the bottom of the cliff. Calculate the angle of depression to the buoy from the top of the cliff.

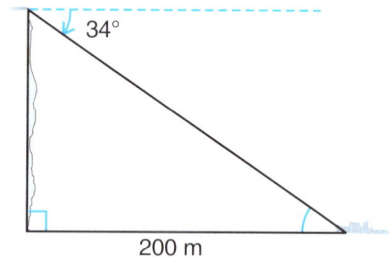

4 A yacht is 20 m from the bottom of a lighthouse.
From the top of the lighthouse the angle of depression to the yacht is 48°.
Calculate the height of the lighthouse.

5 A cat is on the ground 25 m from the foot of a house. A bird is perched on the gutter of the house 15 m from the ground.
Calculate the angle of elevation from the cat to the bird.

6 A tree, 6 m high, casts a shadow of 4.8 m on horizontal ground.
Calculate the angle of elevation of the sun.

7 From a point, A, on the ground, the angle of elevation to a hot air balloon is 9°.
The balloon is 150 m above the ground.
Calculate the distance from A to the balloon.

8 From the top of a cliff, 36 m high, the angles of depression of two boats at sea are 17° and 25°. The boats are in a straight line from the foot of the cliff. Calculate the distance between the two boats.

Three-figure bearings

Remember:
Bearings are used to describe the direction in which you must travel to get from one place to another. They are measured from the North line in a clockwise direction. A bearing can be any angle from 0° to 360° and is written as a three-figure number.

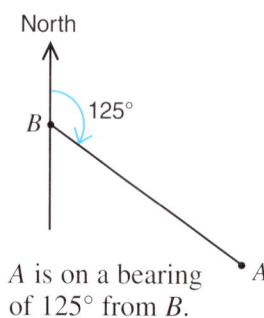

A is on a bearing of 125° from B.

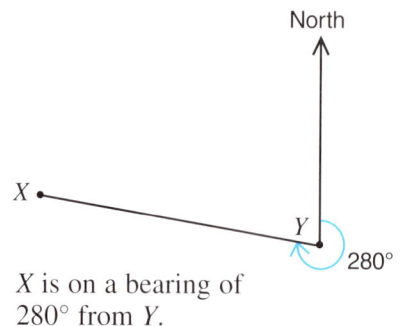

X is on a bearing of 280° from Y.

EXAMPLE

A plane flies 300 km on a bearing of 132° from an airport.
How far South and East is it from the airport?
Give the answers correct to 3 significant figures.

x is the distance South.
y is the distance East.
Using supplementary angles:
$\angle PAB = 180° - 132° = 48°$.

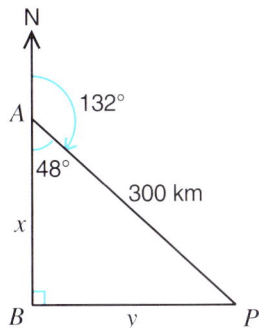

To find x

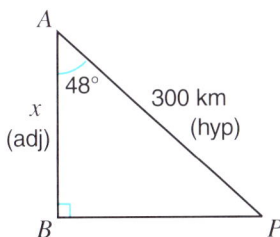

$\cos a = \frac{\text{adj}}{\text{hyp}}$

$\cos 48° = \frac{x}{300}$

$x = 300 \times \cos 48°$

$x = 200.73\ldots$ km

$x = 201$ km, correct to 3 s.f.

To find y

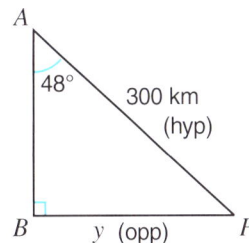

$\sin a = \frac{\text{opp}}{\text{hyp}}$

$\sin 48° = \frac{y}{300}$

$y = 300 \times \sin 48°$

$y = 222.94\ldots$ km

$y = 223$ km, correct to 3 s.f.

The plane is 201 km South and 223 km East of the airport, correct to 3 s.f.

How can you use Pythagoras' Theorem to check the answer?

Sketch diagrams

Drawing a sketch diagram may help you to understand the question.
More information can be added to the diagram as you answer the question.

Exercise 22.6

1 A plane flies 250 km on a bearing of 052.6°.
   (a) How far north is it from its original position?
   (b) How far east is it from its original position?

2 A helicopter leaves its base and flies 23 km on a bearing of 285°.
   How far west is it from its base?

3 A ship at A is 3.8 km due north of a lighthouse.
   A ship at B is 2.7 km due east of the same lighthouse.
   What is the bearing of the ship at B from the ship at A?

4 A helicopter has flown from its base on a bearing of 153°. Its distance east of base is 19 km.
   How far has the helicopter flown?

5 A fishing boat leaves port and sails on a straight course. After 2 hours its distance south of port is 24 km and its distance east of port is 7 km. On what bearing did it sail?

6 A yacht sails 15 km on a bearing of 053°, then 7 km on a bearing of 112°.
   How far north is the yacht from its starting position?

7 A plane flies 307 km on a bearing of 234°, then 23 km on a bearing of 286°.
   How far south is the plane from its starting position?

8 Jayne sails 1.5 km on a bearing of 050°. She then changes course and sails 2 km on a bearing of 140°. On what bearing must she sail to return to her starting position?

When we solve problems in three-dimensions the first task is to identify the length, or angle, we are asked to calculate.

This length, or angle, will always form part of a triangle. Having identified a suitable triangle it is a good idea to draw it in two dimensions, so that lengths of sides and sizes of angles can clearly be seen.

Most problems in three-dimensions involve:
   finding lengths,
   finding the size of an angle between two planes,
   finding the size of an angle between a line and a plane.

A suitable triangle includes the side, or angle, you are trying to calculate **and** either:
   two other sides of known length,
   or one side of known length and an angle of known size.
Sometimes we need to use more than one triangle to solve a problem.

The angle between two planes

Two planes intersect along a **common line**.

To find the angle between two planes:
   Take a point, X, on the common line.
   From X, draw a line in each plane at right angles to the common line.
The angle between the lines AX and BX (angle AXB) is the angle between the planes.

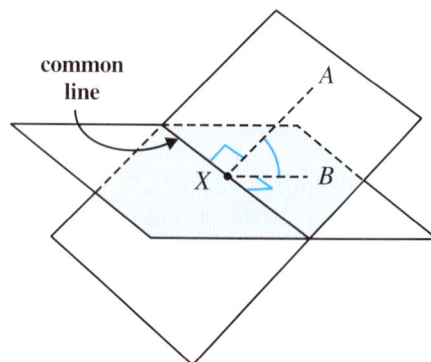

The angle between a line and a plane

A straight line meets a plane at a **point**, P.

To find the angle between a line and a plane:
   Take a point, X, on the line.
   From X, draw a line, XT, which is at right angles to the plane.
The angle XPT is the angle between the line and the plane.

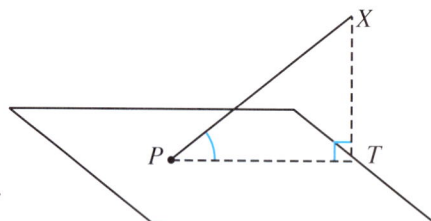

EXAMPLE

1 The diagram is a cuboid with some diagonals shown.

Name
   (a)   the angle between the planes $ABCD$ and $BCEF$,
   (b)   the angle between the planes $ABGF$ and $GBDE$,
   (c)   the angle between the line CE and the base $FGHE$,
   (d)   the angle between the line CF and the base $FGHE$.

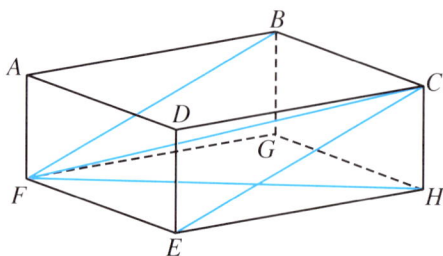

(a) $\angle ABF$ or $\angle DCE$
      BC is the common line between planes ABCD and BCEF.

(b) $\angle ABD$ or $\angle FGE$
      BG is the common line between planes ABGF and GBDE

(c) $\angle CEH$

(d) $\angle CFH$

2   *PQRST* is a pyramid. The perpendicular height, *PX*, is 10 cm.
The base is a square of side 8 cm.

Calculate:
(a)   the angle between the line *PQ* and the base *QRST*,
(b)   the angle between the face *PST* and the base *QRST*.

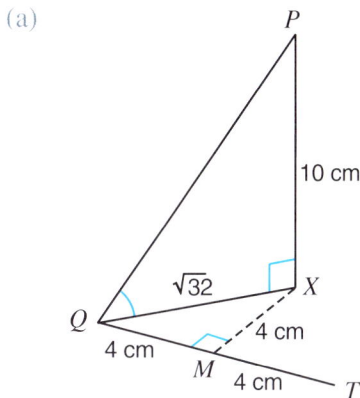

(a)

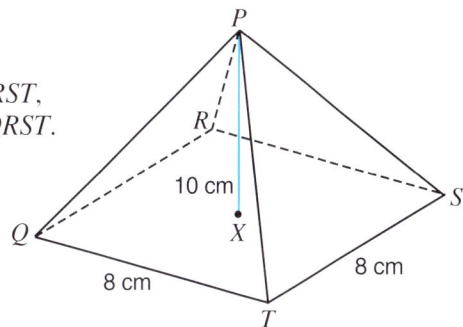

The angle between the line *PQ*
and the base *QRST* is $\angle PQX$.

ΔPQX is a suitable triangle, but we only
know the length of the side *PX*.

To find *QX* we use ΔQMX, where *M* is
the midpoint of *QT*.
Using Pythagoras' Theorem in ΔQMX.

$QX^2 = MQ^2 + MX^2$

$\qquad = 4^2 + 4^2$

$\qquad = 16 + 16$

$\qquad = 32$

$QX = \sqrt{32}$ Mark this length on your
diagram.

Using the tangent ratio in ΔPQX.

$\tan a = \dfrac{\text{opp}}{\text{adj}}$

$\tan \angle PQX = \dfrac{PX}{QX} = \dfrac{10}{\sqrt{32}}$

$\angle PQX = \tan^{-1} \dfrac{10}{\sqrt{32}}$

$\qquad = 60.503\ldots$

$\angle PQX = 60.5°$

The angle between the line *PQ* and the
base *QRST* is 60.5°, correct to 1 decimal
place.

(b)

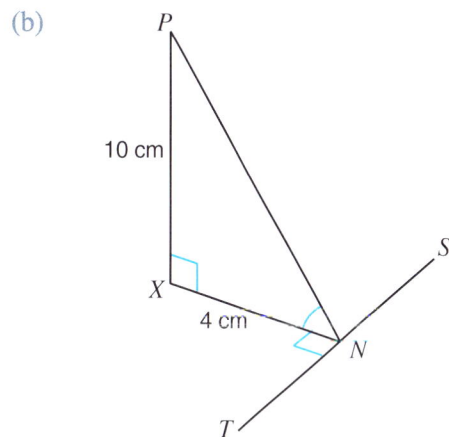

The angle between the face *PST*
and the base *QRST* is $\angle PNX$,
where *N* is the midpoint of *ST*.

NX = 4 cm (Half the width of the
base.)

Using the tangent ratio in ΔPNX.

$\tan a = \dfrac{\text{opp}}{\text{adj}}$

$\tan \angle PNX = \dfrac{PX}{NX} = \dfrac{10}{4}$

$\angle PNX = \tan^{-1} \dfrac{10}{4}$

$\qquad = 68.198\ldots$

$\angle PNX = 68.2°$

The angle between the face *PST*
and the base *QRST* is 68.2°,
correct to 1 decimal place.

1 The diagram shows a cube.

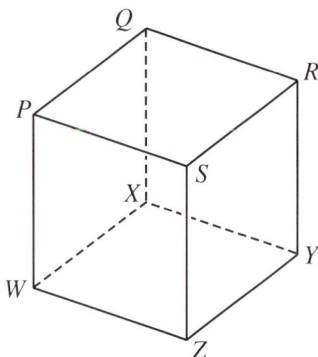

Name the angles between,
(a) the planes *WXYZ* and *QRZW*,
(b) the planes *PSZW* and *PRYW*,
(c) the planes *XRSW* and *WXYZ*,
(d) the line *RW* and the base *WXYZ*,
(e) the line *RW* and the plane *PQXW*,
(f) the line *RW* and the plane *RSZY*.

2 The diagram shows a wedge *ABCDXY*.
The base *ABCD* and the face *CBXY* are rectangles.
Angle *XAB* = 90°.
BC = 9 cm,
BA = 18 cm and
AX = 15 cm.

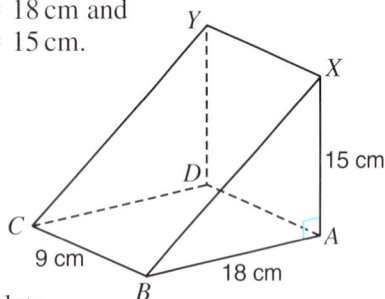

Calculate
(a) the angle between the plane *XBCY* and the base *ABCD*,
(b) the angle between the line *XC* and the base *ABCD*.

3 The diagram shows a ramp.
The ramp, *PQRS*, is 8 m wide and 10 m long.
The ramp slopes at 24° to the horizontal.
Find the slope of the diagonal *QS* to the horizontal.

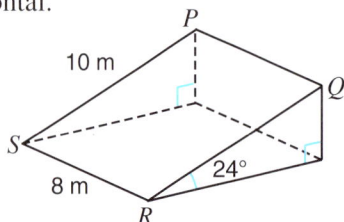

4 *PQRSTUVW* is a cuboid. *PQ* = 8 cm, *QR* = 6 cm and *RW* = 4 cm.

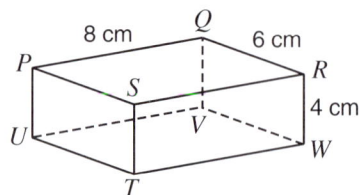

Calculate
(a) the angle between the plane *PVWS* and the base *UVWT*,
(b) the angle between the line *PW* and the base *UVWT*.

5 The diagram shows a cube *ABCDEFGH*.
AB = 6cm.

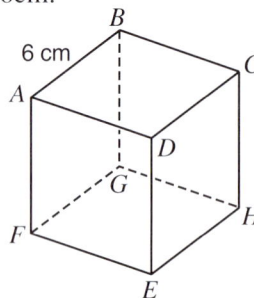

Calculate
(a) the angle between the planes *ABCD* and *BCEF*,
(b) the angle between the line *AH* and the base *EFGH*.

6 *VABCD* is a square based pyramid.
The perpendicular height, *VX*, is 8 cm.
AB = *BC* = *CD* = *DA* = 6 cm.
V is directly above the centre of the base.

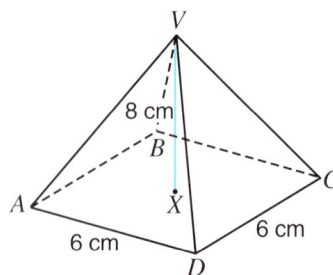

Calculate
(a) the angle between the planes *VAB* and *ABCD*,
(b) the angle between the line *VA* and the base *ABCD*.

324

7 *VWXYZ* is a pyramid of height 9 cm.
The base of the pyramid is a rectangle with
WX = *YZ* = 6cm and *XY* = *ZW* = 8 cm.
V is directly above the centre of the base.

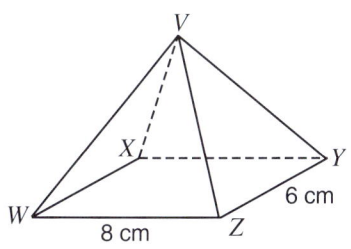

Calculate
  (a) the angle between the line *VX* and the
      base *WXYZ*,
  (b) the angle between the face *VXY* and
      the base *WXYZ*.

8 *PLMNO* is a pyramid of height 8cm.
The base of the pyramid is a square.
OL = *LM* = *MN* = *NO* = 10 cm.
P is directly above the centre of the base.

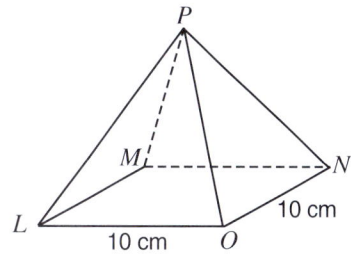

Calculate
  (a) the angle between the line *PN* and
      the base *LMNO*,
  (b) the angle between the face *PLO*
      and the base *LMNO*.

What you need to know

- **Trigonometry** is used to find the lengths of sides and the sizes of angles in right-angled triangles.

- You must learn the **sine**, **cosine** and **tangent** ratios.

$$\sin a = \frac{\text{opposite}}{\text{hypotenuse}} \qquad \cos a = \frac{\text{adjacent}}{\text{hypotenuse}} \qquad \tan a = \frac{\text{opposite}}{\text{adjacent}}$$

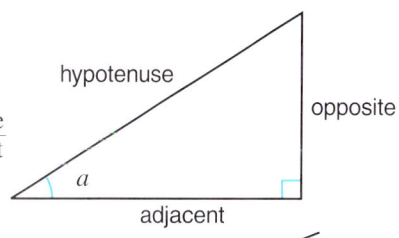

- Each ratio links the size of an angle with the lengths of two sides. If we are given the values for two of these we can find the value of the third.

- When we look **up** from the horizontal the angle we turn through is called the **angle of elevation**.

- When we look **down** from the horizontal the angle we turn through is called the **angle of depression**.

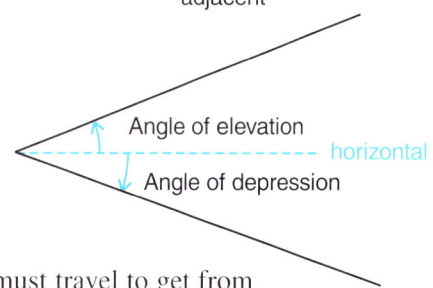

- **Three-figure bearings.**
  Bearings are used to describe the direction in which you must travel to get from one place to another. They are measured from the North line in a clockwise direction.
  A bearing can be any angle from 0° to 360° and is written as a three-figure number.

- When working in three-dimensions the first task is to identify the length, or angle, that you are trying to find. The length, or angle, will always form part of a triangle together with either:
      two other sides of known length, or
      one side of known length and an angle of known size.
  Sometimes, more than one triangle is needed to solve a problem.

- Two planes intersect along a **common line**.
  The angle between the lines *AX* and *BX*
  (angle *AXB*) is the **angle between the planes**.
  The lines *AX* and *BX* are perpendicular to the common line.

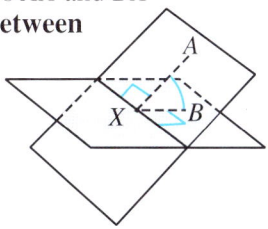

- A straight line meets a plane at a **point**.
  The angle *XPT* is the **angle between the line and the plane**.
  The line *XT* is perpendicular to the plane.

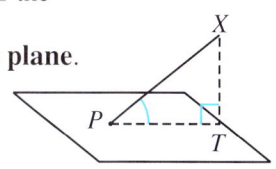

Review Exercise

1 When Jayne is 10 m from a haystack, the angle
of elevation to the top of the haystack is 18°.
Calculate *h*, the height of the haystack.

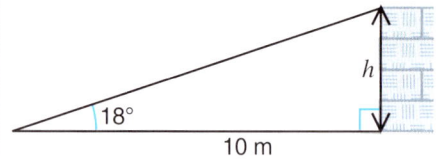

Not to scale

2 The design for a children's slide, *ABCD*, for a
playground is shown.
The height of the slide, *BD*, is 136 cm.
The distance *DC* is 195 cm.

(a) Calculate the angle *BCD*.

(b) Angle *ABD* is 28°.
Calculate the distance of *AB*.

SEG 1997

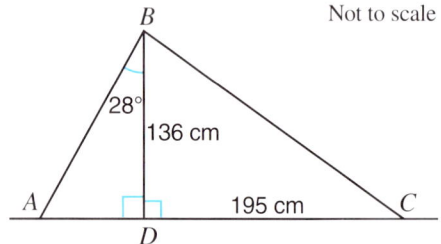

Not to scale

3 Ajit stands 30 m from the base of a tree.
From ground level he measures the angle of
elevation of the top of the tree.
He finds that this angle is 25°.
Calculate the height of the tree.

SEG 1994

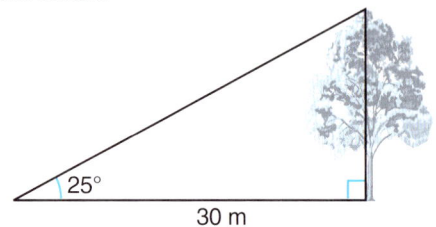

Not to scale

4 A railway tunnel has a cross-section that is part
of a circle of radius 2.1 metres.
The centre of the circle is at *O*.
Angle *AOC* = 50°.
Calculate *AB*.

SEG 1997

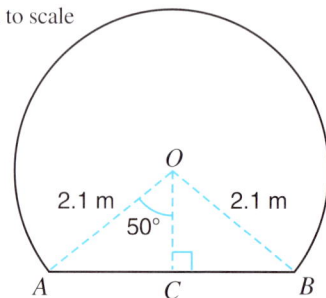

Not to scale

5 This quadrilateral is made from two right-angled
triangles.
(a) Calculate the length *x*.
(b) Calculate the angle *A*.

SEG 1995

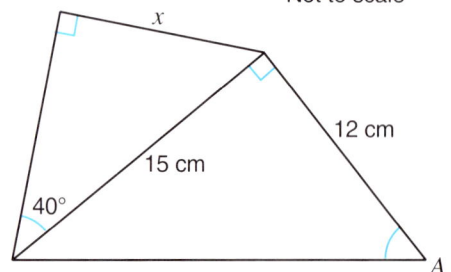

Not to scale

6 The diagram shows a river.
A boat crosses the river from P to R.
$PR = 6$ m, angle $PQR = 40°$.

Calculate the distance QR.

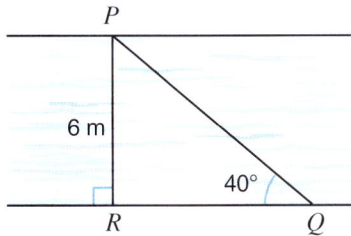

7 Triangle ABC has a right angle at B.
Angle $BAC = 50°$ and $BC = 8.3$ cm.

Calculate the length of AC.

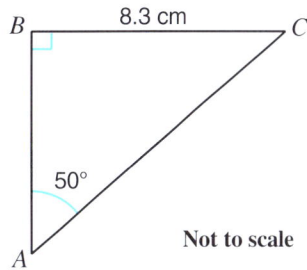

Not to scale

SEG 1998

8 The diagram shows a side view of two buildings.
The length $DE = 15$ m. Angle $FDE = 20°$.
(a) Calculate the height EF.

A telephone wire stretches from C to F.
The length $CF = 20.9$ m.
(b) Calculate the size of angle CFD.

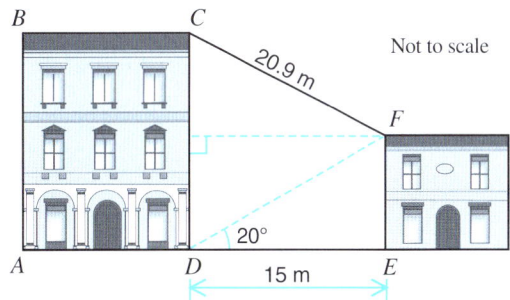

Not to scale

SEG 1998 S

9 An aircraft takes off from one end, A, of a
runway and it passes over the other end of the
runway, B, at a height of 317 m.
The angle of elevation of the aircraft from
end A of the runway is $5°$.
(a) Calculate the length of the runway AB.

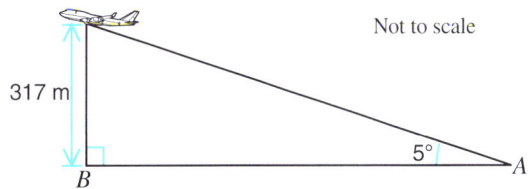

Not to scale

Another aircraft, using the same runway, passes over point B at a height of 250 m.
(b) Calculate the angle of elevation of this aircraft from end A of the runway.

SEG 1995

10 Cos $PQR = \frac{12}{13}$

(a) Find (i) tan PQR,
          (ii) sin PQR.

(b) When $QP = 2.4$ cm,
    what are the lengths of QR and PR?

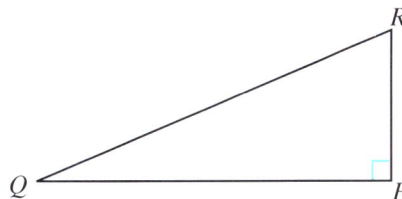

11 Do not use a calculator in this question.

A right-angled triangle LMN is drawn on one side of the square $LNOP$, as shown.

Tan $LMN = \frac{3}{4}$

(a) What is tan MLN?
(b) Find (i) sin LMN,
          (ii) cos MLN.
(c) $MN = 12$ cm.
    Calculate the area of the square.

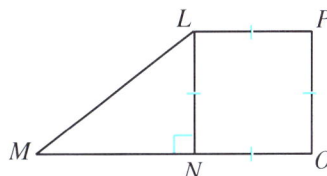

12 (a) Calculate the length, *l*, of this ladder.

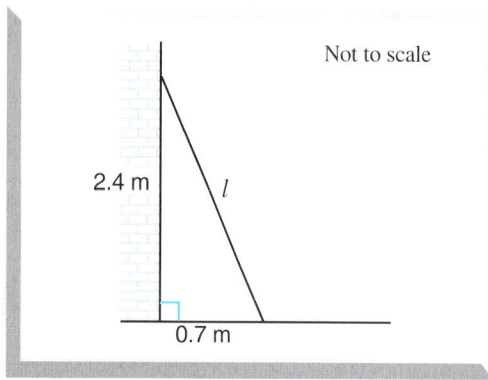

Not to scale

2.4 m

l

0.7 m

(b) A health and safety directive says:
'*A ladder must be placed at an angle of between 70° and 80° to the ground*'.

(i) A ladder is required to reach a height of 4.7 metres. Calculate the length of the longest ladder that can be used safely.

(ii) The same ladder is used to reach a height of 4.9 metres. Calculate whether or not the ladder is safe.

SEG 1996

13 A frog sits on one side of a road. Directly opposite the frog is a vertical lamp post of height 15 feet. The angle of elevation of the top of the lamp post from the frog is 31°.

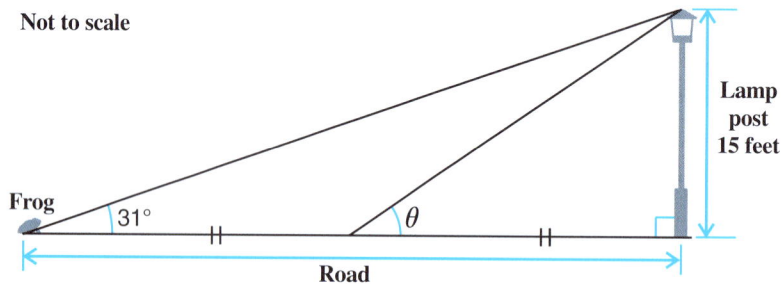

Not to scale

Frog

31°

θ

Road

Lamp post 15 feet

(a) Calculate the width of the road.
(b) Calculate the angle of elevation, *θ*, of the top of the lamp post when the frog is exactly half way across the road.

SEG 1994

14 A group of geography students need to calculate the width of a river.
They measure the angle of elevation of the top of an electricity pylon from opposite banks of the river, *P* and *L*.
The pylon is 70 metres high.

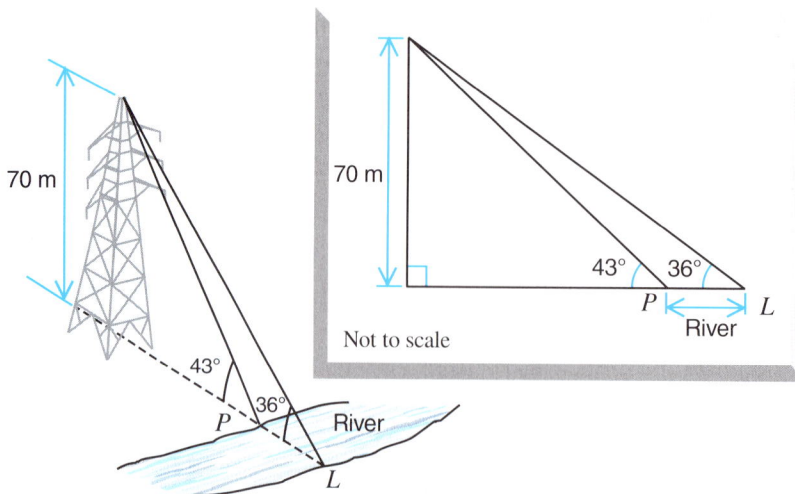

70 m

43°

36°

P

L

River

70 m

43° 36°

P *L*

River

Not to scale

Calculate the width of the river *PL*.

SEG 1996

328

15 A yacht sails from Cooktown, Australia on a bearing of 040°.
After sailing 100 km it runs aground on a coral reef.
The diagram below shows the positions of the yacht (Y) and Cooktown (C) when this happens.

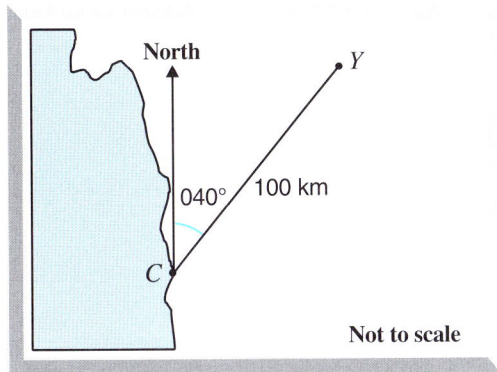

Not to scale

(a) Calculate how far the yacht (Y) is north of Cooktown (C) when it runs aground.

(b) At the time the yacht runs aground the nearest ship in the area is on a bearing of 130° from the yacht and on a bearing of 067° from Cooktown.
  (i) Draw a sketch to show the positions of the ship (S), Cooktown (C) and the yacht (Y).
  (ii) The angle CYS is 90°. Calculate the distance of the ship from the yacht.
  (iii) The ship sails towards the yacht. On what bearing does it sail?

SEG 1990

16 The diagram shows a cuboid.
$PS = 20$ cm, $SR = 30$ cm and $CR = 12$ cm.

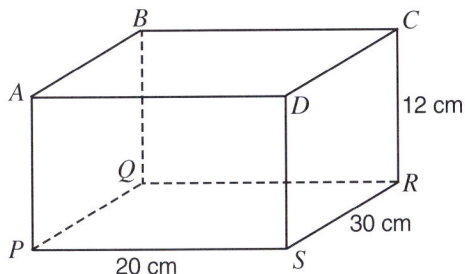

Calculate the angle between,
(a) the line SB and the base $PQRS$,
(b) the plane $PBCS$ and the base $PQRS$.

17 The diagram shows a square based pyramid. P is directly above the centre of the base. $PA = 6$ cm and $AD = 4$ cm.

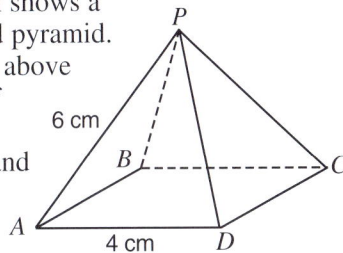

Calculate
(a) the height of the pyramid,
(b) the angle between the line PA and the base $ABCD$,
(c) the angle between the face PAB and the base $ABCD$.

18 The diagram shows a pyramid with a horizontal rectangular base $ABCD$.
$AB = 12$ cm and $BC = 10$ cm.

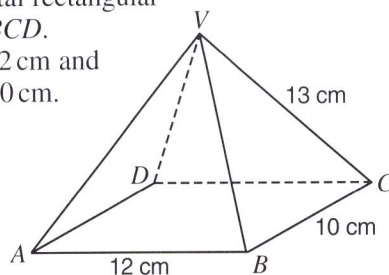

The top of the pyramid, V, is directly above the centre of the base.
$VA = VB = VC = VD = 13$ cm.

(a) Calculate the height of V above the base.
(b) Calculate the angle between VA and the base $ABCD$.
(c) Calculate the angle between the face VBC and the base $ABCD$.
(d) Calculate the angle between the face VAB and the base $ABCD$.

19 $ABCDEF$ is a triangular prism, 10cm long. ABC is an equilateral triangle of side 3 cm. P is the foot of the perpendicular from C to AB.

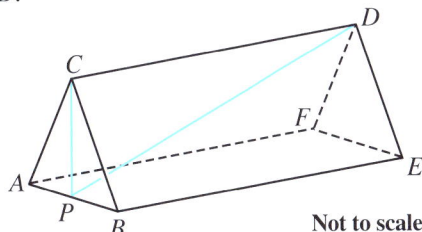

Not to scale

(a) Calculate the length of PD.
(b) Calculate the size of the angle between CE and PE.

SEG 1996

329

CHAPTER 23

Volumes and Surface Areas

3-dimensional shapes (or solids)

These are all examples of 3-dimensional shapes.

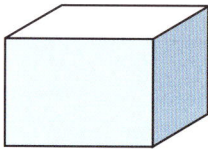 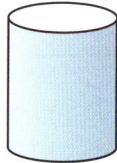  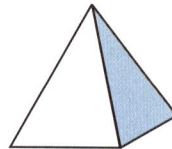 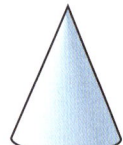

| Cuboid | Cylinder | Sphere | Pyramid with square base | Cone |

What other 3-dimensional shapes do you know?

Volume

Volume is the amount of space occupied by a three-dimensional shape.

This **cube** is 1 cm long, 1 cm wide and 1 cm high.
It has a volume of **1 cubic centimetre**.
The volume of this cube can be written as 1 cm³.

Small volumes can be measured using cubic millimetres (mm³).
Large volumes can be measured using cubic metres (m³).

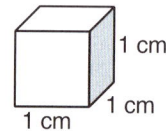

1 cm
1 cm
1 cm

Volume = 1 cm³

Volume of a cuboid

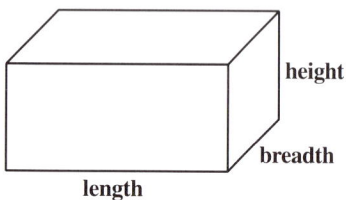

height
breadth
length

The formula for the volume of a cuboid is:
    Volume = length × breadth × height

This formula can be written using letters as:
    $V = lbh$

Volume of a cube
A cube is a special cuboid in which the length, breadth and height all have the same measurement.
Volume = length × length × length
$V = l^3$

Surface area of a cuboid

To find the surface area of a cuboid find the area of the six rectangular faces and add the answers together.
Opposite faces of a cuboid are the same shape and size.

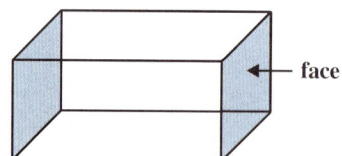

← face

Find the volume and surface area of a cuboid measuring 30 cm by 15 cm by 12 cm.

Volume $= lbh$
$= 30 \text{ cm} \times 15 \text{ cm} \times 12 \text{ cm}$
$= 5400 \text{ cm}^3$

Surface area $= (2 \times 30 \times 15) + (2 \times 15 \times 12) + (2 \times 30 \times 12)$
$= 900 + 360 + 720$
$= 1980 \text{ cm}^2$

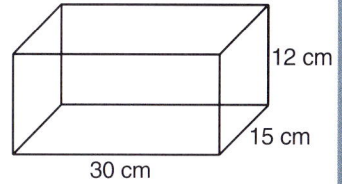

Prisms

These shapes are all **prisms**.

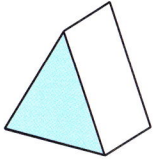 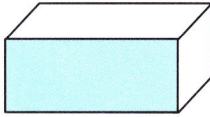  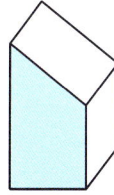 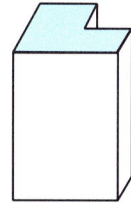

What do these 3-dimensional shapes have in common?

Volume of a prism

The formula for the volume of a prism is:
Volume = area of cross-section × length.

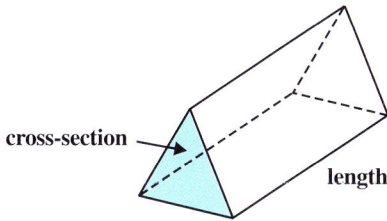

Volume of a cylinder

A **cylinder** is a prism.
The **volume of a cylinder** can be written as:
Volume = area of cross-section × height
$$V = \pi r^2 h$$

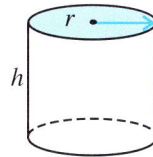

Notice that length has been replaced by height.

EXAMPLES   Find the volumes of these prisms.

(a)

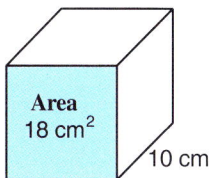

Volume = area of cross-section × length
$= 18 \times 10$
$= 180 \text{ cm}^3$

(b)

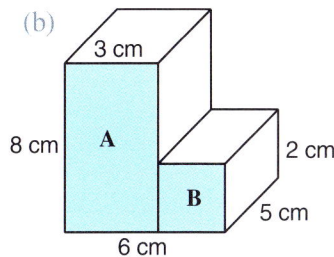

Area A $= 8 \times 3 = 24 \text{ cm}^2$
Area B $= 3 \times 2 = 6 \text{ cm}^2$
Total area $= 30 \text{ cm}^2$
Volume $= 30 \times 5 = 150 \text{ cm}^3$

(c)

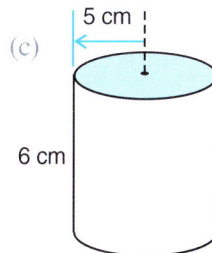

$V = \pi r^2 h$
$= \pi \times 5^2 \times 6$
$= 471.238 \ldots$
$= 471 \text{ cm}^3$, correct to 3 s.f.

You should be able to do questions 1 to 3 without using a calculator.
Having completed them you can use your calculator to check your answers.

1 Calculate the volumes and surface areas of these cubes and cuboids.

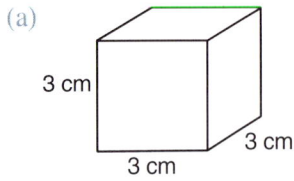

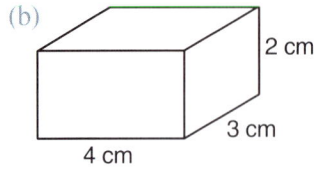

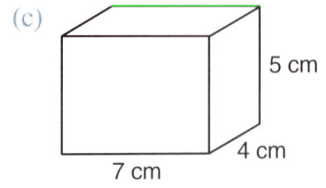

(a)

3 cm

3 cm

3 cm

(b)

2 cm

3 cm

4 cm

(c)

5 cm

4 cm

7 cm

2 Find the volumes of these prisms.

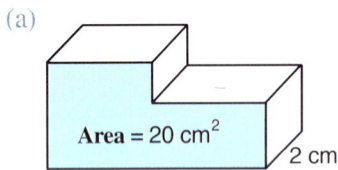

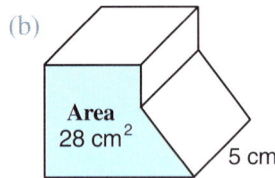

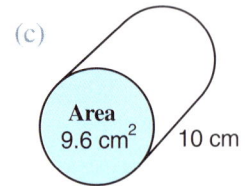

(a)

Area = 20 cm^2

2 cm

(b)

Area
28 cm^2

5 cm

(c)

Area
9.6 cm^2

10 cm

3 Calculate the shaded areas and the volumes of these prisms.

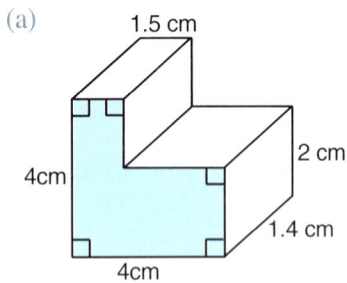

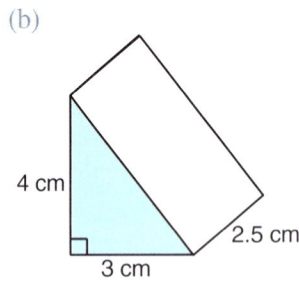

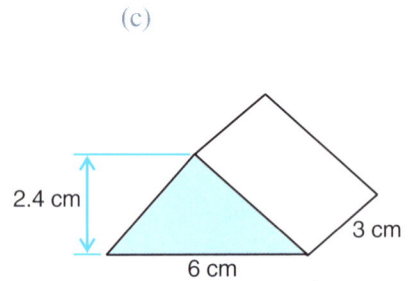

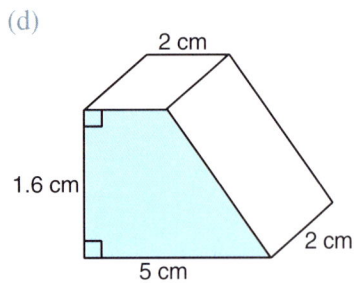

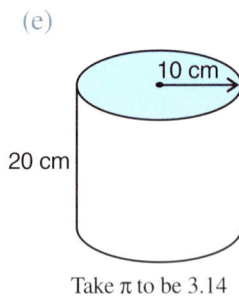

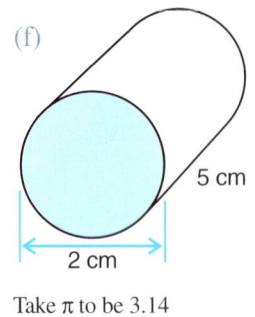

(a)

1.5 cm

2 cm

4cm

1.4 cm

4cm

(b)

4 cm

3 cm

2.5 cm

(c)

2.4 cm

6 cm

3 cm

(d)

2 cm

1.6 cm

5 cm

2 cm

(e)

10 cm

20 cm

Take π to be 3.14

(f)

5 cm

2 cm

Take π to be 3.14

4 Calculate the volumes and surface areas of these cuboids.
Where necessary give your answer to an appropriate degree of accuracy.
(a) 18 cm by 24 cm by 45 cm.
(b) 3.2 cm by 4.8 cm by 6.3 cm.
(c) 5.8 cm by 10.6 cm by 14.9 cm.

5 Find the volumes of these prisms.
Where necessary take π to be 3.14 or use the π key on your calculator.

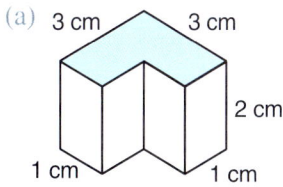

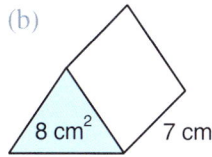

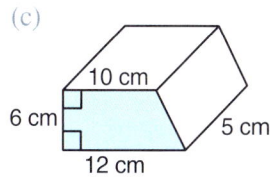

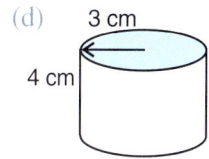

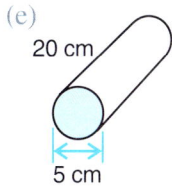

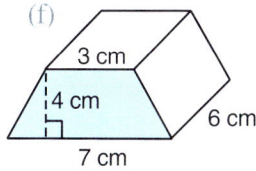

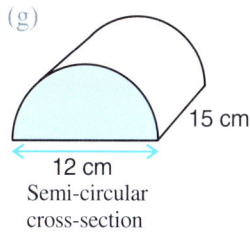

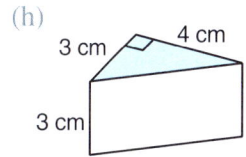

(a) 3 cm   3 cm   2 cm   1 cm   1 cm

(b) 8 cm^2 7 cm

(c) 10 cm   6 cm   5 cm   12 cm

(d) 3 cm   4 cm

(e) 20 cm   5 cm

(f) 3 cm   4 cm   6 cm   7 cm

(g) 15 cm   12 cm
Semi-circular
cross-section

(h) 4 cm   3 cm   3 cm

6 A cuboid has a volume of 2250 cm³.
The length of the cuboid is 25 cm.
The height of the cuboid is 12 cm.
Calculate the surface area of the cuboid.

7 Which tin holds more cat food?

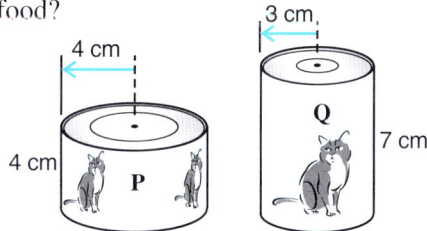

4 cm   4 cm   P

3 cm   Q   7 cm

8 A cuboid has a volume of 76.8 cm³.
The length of the cuboid is 3.2 cm.
The breadth of the cuboid is 2.4 cm.
What is the height of the cuboid?

9 A cuboid has a square base of side 3.6 cm.
The volume of the cuboid is 58.32 cm³.
Calculate the height of the cuboid.

10 The radius of a cylinder is 5 cm.
It has a volume of 900 cm³.
Calculate the height of the cylinder, giving your answer correct to 1 decimal place.

11 A cylinder is 8 cm high. It has a volume of 183 cm³.
Calculate the radius of the cylinder correct to 1 decimal place.

12 A cylinder has a diameter of 10.6 cm.
The volume of the cylinder is 1060 cm³.
Calculate the height of the cylinder.
Give your answer to an appropriate degree of accuracy.

Surface area of a cylinder

The top and bottom of a cylinder are circles.
The curved surface of a cylinder is a rectangle.

The rectangle has the same height, h, as the cylinder.
The length of the rectangle must be just long enough to "wrap around" the circle.
The lid of the cylinder has radius r and circumference $2\pi r$.
So the length of the rectangle is also $2\pi r$.

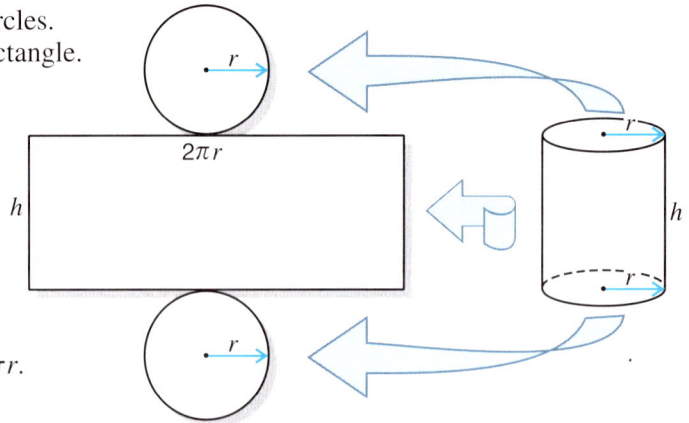

Area of lid $= \pi r^2$
Area of base $= \pi r^2$
Area of lid and base $= 2\pi r^2$

Area of rectangle $=$ length $\times$ breadth
$= 2\pi r \times h$
$= 2\pi rh$

If a cylinder has radius, r, and height, h, then the formula for the surface area is:

$$\text{Surface area} = 2\pi r^2 + 2\pi rh$$

Area of the top and bottom   Area of the rectangle

The formula for the surface area is sometimes given as:
Surface area $= 2\pi r(r + h)$

EXAMPLE

Find the surface area of a cylinder with radius 4 cm and height 6 cm. Take π to be 3.14.

$$\begin{aligned}
\text{Area} &= 2\pi rh + 2\pi r^2 \\
&= 2 \times \pi \times 4 \times 6 + 2 \times \pi \times 4^2 \\
&= 150.796 \ldots + 100.530 \ldots \\
&= 251.327 \ldots \\
&= 251.3 \text{ cm}^2, \text{ correct to 1 d.p.}
\end{aligned}$$

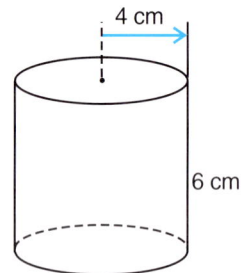

Exercise 23.2

Take π to be 3.14 or use the π key on your calculator.

1 Find the surface areas of these cylinders.

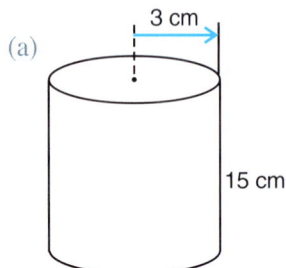

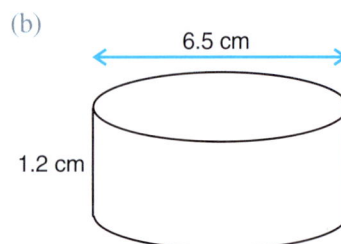

(a)

3 cm

15 cm

(b)

6.5 cm

1.2 cm

2 Show that the curved surface area of this can is approximately 75 cm².

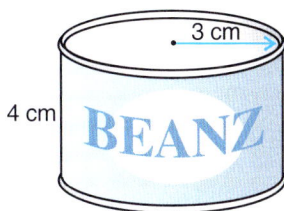

3 cm

4 cm   BEANZ

3 A bucket is in the shape of a cylinder.
  (a) Calculate the area of the bottom of the bucket.
  (b) Calculate the curved surface area of the bucket.
  (c) What is the volume of the bucket?

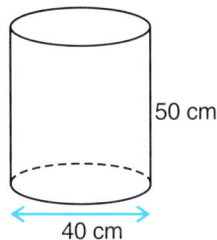

50 cm

40 cm

4 A concrete pipe is 150 cm long.
It has an internal radius of 15 cm and an external radius of 20 cm.
Calculate, giving your answers to 3 significant figures,
  (a) the area of the curved surface inside of the pipe,
  (b) the curved surface area of the outside of the pipe.

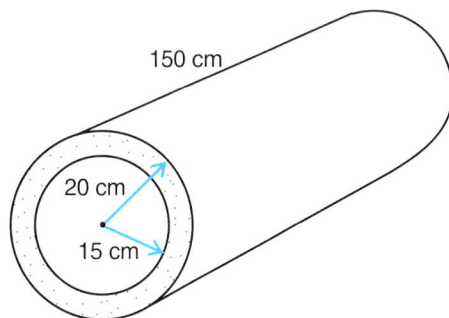

150 cm

20 cm

15 cm

5 A cylinder has a radius of 3.6 cm.
The volume of the cylinder is 346 cm³.
Calculate the total surface area of the cylinder.
Give your answer to an appropriate degree of accuracy.

Cones

The diagram shows a cone with: circular base, radius r,
                                    slant height l,
                                    perpendicular height h.

Using Pythagoras' Theorem, $l^2 = r^2 + h^2$.

Volume of a cone $= \frac{1}{3} \times$ base area $\times$ perpendicular height
The area of the circular base $= \pi r^2$.
$V = \frac{1}{3} \pi r^2 h$

Curved surface area $= \pi r l$

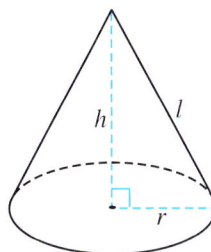

h l

r

Pyramids

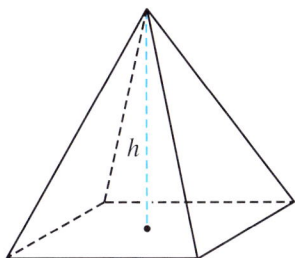

h

The volume of a pyramid is given by:
$V = \frac{1}{3} \times$ base area $\times$ perpendicular height

Spheres

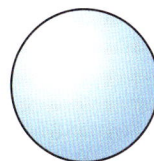

Volume $= \frac{4}{3} \pi r^3$
Surface area $= 4 \pi r^2$

1 This model was formed by joining together a pyramid and a cuboid.
The total height of the model is 5.5 cm.
Find the total volume of the model.

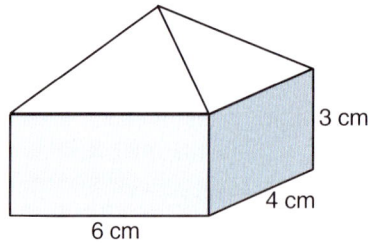

Total volume = volume of pyramid + volume of cuboid.

Volume of pyramid
$= \frac{1}{3} \times$ base area $\times$ perpendicular height
The base of the pyramid is a rectangle
measuring 6 cm by 4 cm.
The height of the pyramid = 5.5 cm − 3 cm
                                            = 2.5 cm.

$V = \frac{1}{3} \times 6 \times 4 \times 2.5$
$= 20\,\text{cm}^3$

Volume of cuboid $= lbh$
$= 6 \times 4 \times 3$
$= 72\,\text{cm}^3$

Total volume $= 20 + 72$
$= 92\,\text{cm}^3$

2 A child's toy is made from a cone with base 3 cm and height 4 cm mounted on a hemisphere with radius 3 cm.
(a) Calculate the volume of the toy.
(b) Calculate the total surface area.

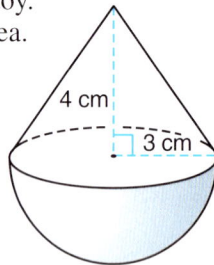

(a) Volume of hemisphere
$= \frac{1}{2} \times \frac{4}{3} \pi r^3$
$= \frac{1}{2} \times \frac{4}{3} \times \pi \times 3^3$
$= 56.548 \ldots \text{cm}^3$

Volume of cone
$= \frac{1}{3} \pi r^2 h$
$= \frac{1}{3} \times \pi \times 3^2 \times 4$
$= 37.699 \ldots \text{cm}^3$

Total volume
$= 56.548 \ldots + 37.699 \ldots$
$= 94.247 \ldots \text{cm}^3$
$= 94.2\,\text{cm}^3$, correct to 3 s.f.

(b) Surface area of hemisphere
$= \frac{1}{2} \times 4 \pi r^2$
$= \frac{1}{2} \times 4 \times \pi \times 3^2$
$= 56.548 \ldots \text{cm}^2$
Curved surface area of cone $= \pi r l$
By Pythagoras: $l^2 = r^2 + h^2$
$l^2 = 3^2 + 4^2$
$l^2 = 25$
$l = \sqrt{25} = 5\,\text{cm}$
Curved surface area of cone
$= \pi \times 3 \times 5$
$= 47.123 \ldots \text{cm}^2$
Total surface area
$= 56.548 \ldots + 47.123 \ldots$
$= 103.672 \ldots$
$= 1034\,\text{cm}^2$, correct to 3 s.f.

Use the π key on your calculator and give answers correct to 3 significant figures where appropriate.

1 Find the volumes of these solids.

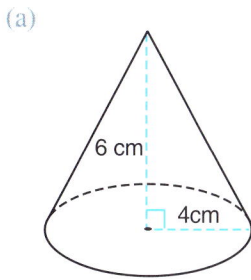

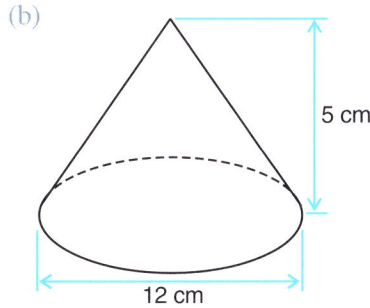

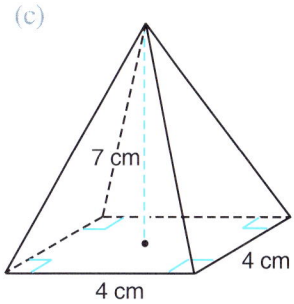

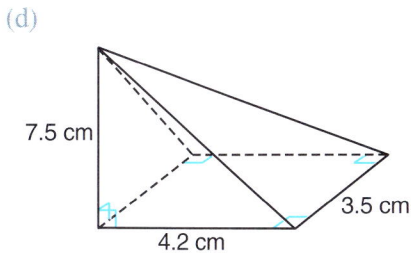

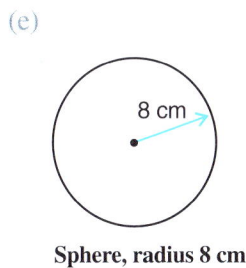

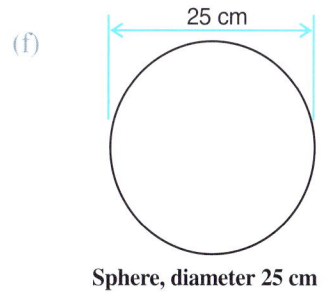

(a)

6 cm
4cm

(b)

5 cm
12 cm

(c)

7 cm
4 cm
4 cm

(d)

7.5 cm
3.5 cm
4.2 cm

(e)

8 cm

Sphere, radius 8 cm

(f)

25 cm

Sphere, diameter 25 cm

2 Find the areas of the curved surfaces for the cones below.

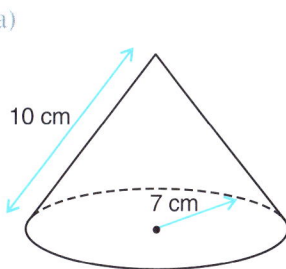

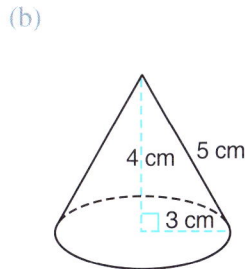

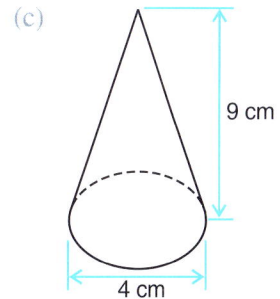

(a)

10 cm
7 cm

(b)

4 cm 5 cm
3 cm

(c)

9 cm
4 cm

3 Potato crisps are sold in different types of container.

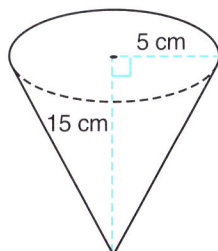

5 cm
15 cm

**A cone 15 cm high
with radius 5 cm**

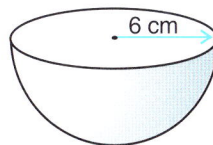

6 cm

**A hemispherical
bowl of radius 6 cm**

Which container has the greater volume?
Show all your working.

4 A pyramid with base area 20 cm² has volume 250 cm³. What is the height of the pyramid?

5 Find the surface areas of these solids.

(a)

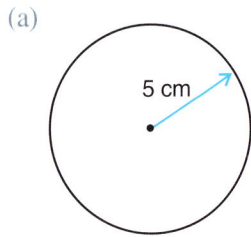

Sphere, radius 5 cm

5 cm

(b)

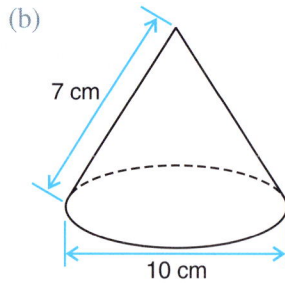

7 cm

10 cm

(c)

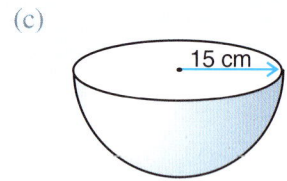

15 cm

Hemisphere, radius 15 cm

6 A quadrant of a circle is cut out of paper.
A cone is made by joining the edges
OA and *OB*, with no overlaps.

Calculate
(a) the length of the arc *AB*,
(b) the base radius of the cone,
(c) the height of the cone,
(d) the volume of the cone.

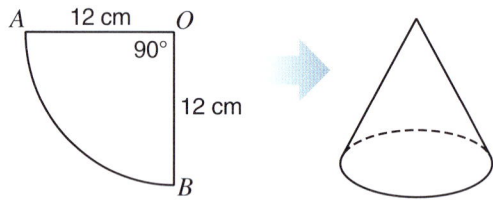

A 12 cm O

90°

12 cm

B

7 A cone is formed from a semi-circular sheet of foil.
The foil has a diameter of 10 cm.
Find
    the radius of the base of the cone,
    the volume of the cone.

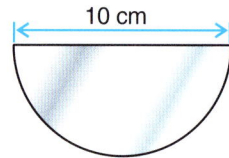

10 cm

8 For each of the solids below, find
    the total volume,
    the total surface area.

(a)

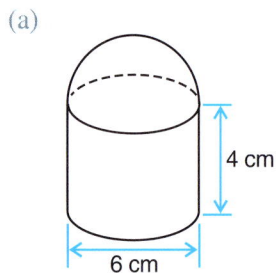

4 cm

6 cm

(b)

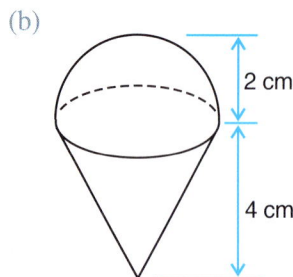

2 cm

4 cm

(c)

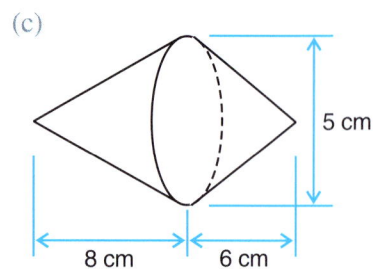

5 cm

8 cm   6 cm

9 A cone is 6.4 cm high. It has a volume of 150 cm³. Calculate the radius of the cone.

10 A sphere has a volume of 58 cm³. Calculate the radius of the sphere.

11 Rubber bungs are made by removing the tops of cones.
Starting with a cone of radius 10 cm and height 16 cm
a rubber bung is made by cutting a cone of radius 5 cm
and height 8 cm from the top.
Find the volume and total surface area of the rubber bung.

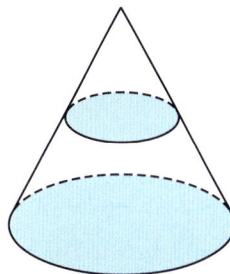

12 The dimensions of a steel bowl are shown.
Calculate
(a) the internal surface area of the bowl,
(b) the volume of the bowl.

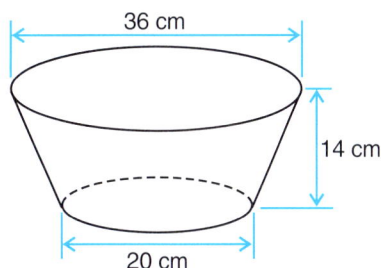

36 cm

14 cm

20 cm

13 *ABCDX* is a pyramid.
The base *ABCD* is a rectangle measuring
18 cm by 10 cm and *X* is 12 cm vertically
above the midpoint of the base.

Calculate
(a) the volume of the pyramid,
(b) the total surface area of the pyramid.

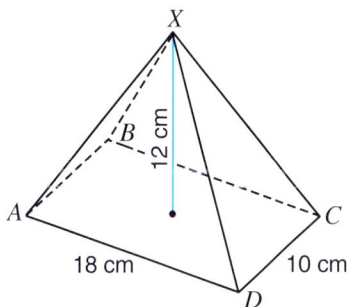

X

B

12 cm

A

C

18 cm

10 cm

D

14 A metal cylinder is melted down and made into balls for a game.
The cylinder is 15 cm high and has radius 6 cm. The balls each have radius 1 cm.
How many balls can be made?

15 One hundred ball bearings with radius 5 mm are dropped into a cylindrical can, which is half
full of oil. The height of the cylinder is 20 cm and the radius is 8 cm.
By how much does the level of the oil rise?

16 A cylinder of radius 4 cm contains water to a height of 4 cm.
A sphere of radius 3.6 cm is placed in the cylinder.
What is the percentage increase in the height of the water?

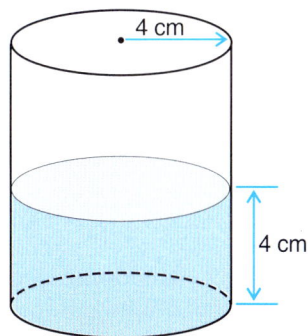

4 cm

4 cm

What you need to know

- **Faces**, **vertices** (corners) and **edges**.
  For example, a cube has 6 faces, 8 vertices and 12 edges.

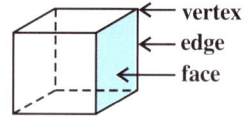

- Volume is the amount of space occupied by a 3-dimensional shape.

- The formula for the volume of a **cuboid** is:
  Volume = length × breadth × height
  $V = l\,b\,h$

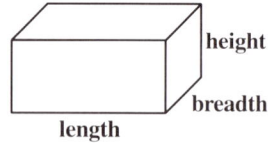

- Volume of a **cube** is:
  Volume = (length)³
  $V = l^3$

- To find the **surface area** of a cuboid find the area of the six rectangular faces and add the answers together.

- If you make a cut at right angles to the length of a **prism** you will always get the same cross-section.

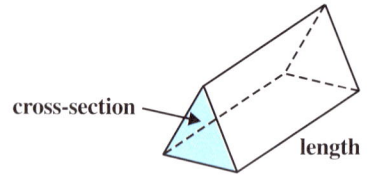

- Volume of a prism = area of cross-section × length

- A **cylinder** is a prism.
  Volume of a cylinder is:
  $V = \pi r^2 h$

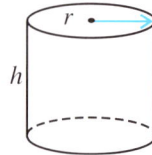

  Surface area of a cylinder is:
  Surface area = $2\pi r^2 + 2\pi rh$

- These formulae are used in calculations involving **cones, pyramids,** and **spheres.**

Cone	Pyramid	Sphere
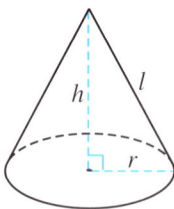	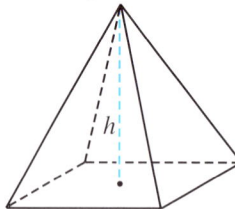	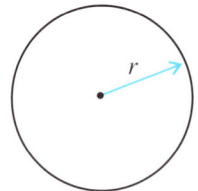

$V = \frac{1}{3} \times$ base area × height

$V = \frac{1}{3}\pi r^2 h$

Curved surface area = πrl

$V = \frac{1}{3} \times$ base area × height

Volume = $\frac{4}{3}\pi r^3$

Surface area = $4\,\pi r^2$

Review Exercise

1. The diagram shows a paint trough in the shape of a prism.
   Each shaded end of the trough is a vertical trapezium.

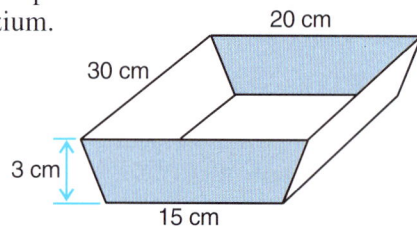

   Calculate the **volume** of paint which the trough can hold when it is full.

SEG 1995

2 A circular cable is 100 cm long with a radius of 2.5 cm.

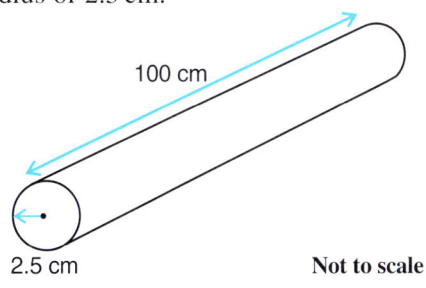

100 cm

2.5 cm   **Not to scale**

(a) What is the area of the circular end?
(b) What is the volume of the cable?

SEG 1994

3 To feed a lawn, one box of fertilizer is needed for every 9 m².
(a) How many boxes are needed to fertilize a circular lawn of radius 4 m?

The fertilizer is also sold in cylindrical drums.

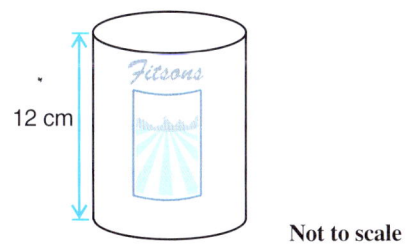

Fitsons

12 cm

Not to scale

The volume of a drum is 3060 cm³.
The height of a drum is 12 cm.
(b) Calculate the radius of a drum.

SEG 2000 S

4 The diagram shows a cuboid which is just big enough to hold six tennis balls.

Not to scale

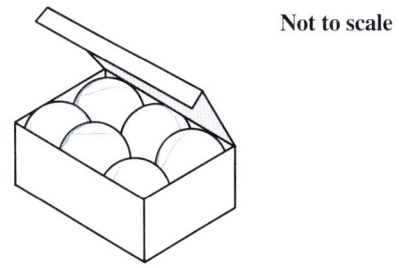

Each tennis ball has a diameter of 6.8 cm.
Calculate the volume of the cuboid.

SEG 1998

5 Tomato soup is sold in cylindrical tins. Each tin has a base radius of 3.5 cm and a height of 12 cm.

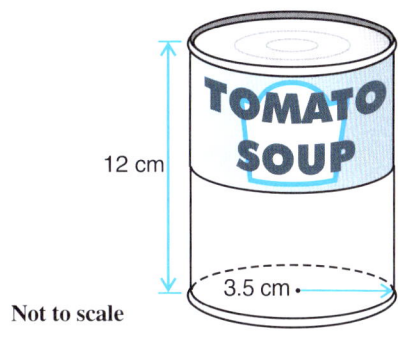

TOMATO SOUP

12 cm

3.5 cm

Not to scale

(a) Calculate the volume of soup in a full tin.
(b) Mark has a full tin of tomato soup for dinner. He pours the soup into a cylindrical bowl of radius 7 cm.

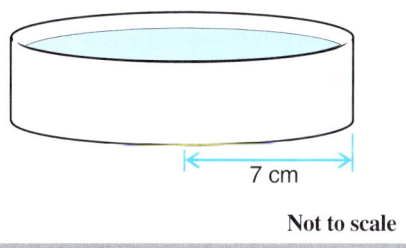

7 cm

Not to scale

What is the depth of the soup in the bowl?

SEG 1994

6 The diagram shows the uniform cross-section of a rubbish skip.

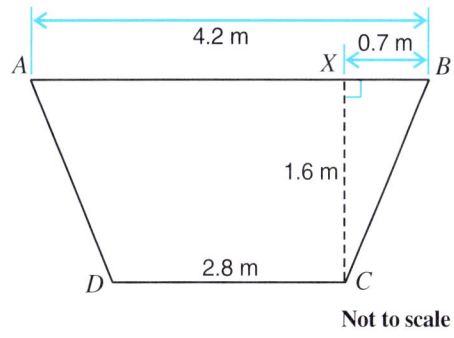

4.2 m   0.7 m

A   X   B

1.6 m

D   2.8 m   C

Not to scale

The cross-section is a trapezium.
$AB = 4.2$ m, $CD = 2.8$ m, $XB = 0.7$ m and the height $CX = 1.6$ m.

(a) Calculate the size of angle XBC.
The skip is 1.8 m wide.
(b) Calculate the volume of the skip, stating your units.

SEG 1998

7 This loaf of bread is cut into 30 slices, as shown.

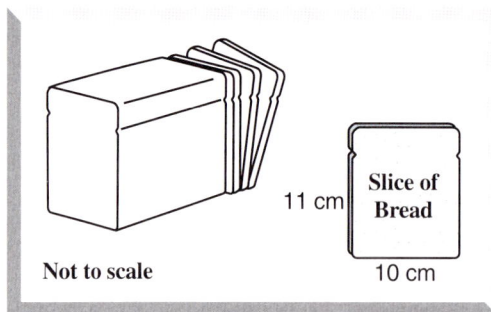

11 cm

Slice of Bread

10 cm

Not to scale

Each slice is approximately the shape of a cuboid of width 10 cm, length 11 cm and depth 8 mm.

(a) Calculate the volume of the loaf in cubic centimetres.

The same volume of bread is used to make a round loaf of length 24 cm.

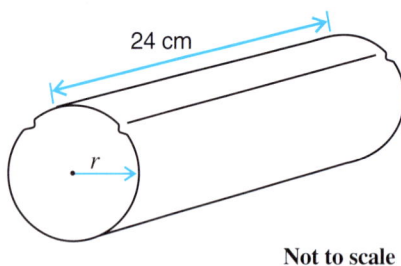

24 cm

r

Not to scale

(b) What is the radius of the round loaf?

SEG 1994

8 A gold bar is in the shape of a prism of length 10 cm.

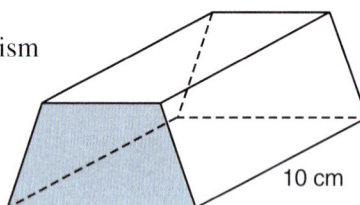

10 cm

It has a cross-section in the shape of this trapezium.

(a) Calculate the volume of the bar, stating the units of your answer.

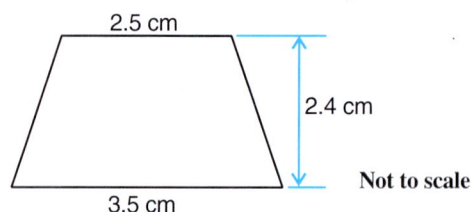

2.5 cm

2.4 cm

3.5 cm

Not to scale

The gold bar is melted down and made into twelve identical discs. No gold is wasted.
Each disc has a radius of 2.5 cm.

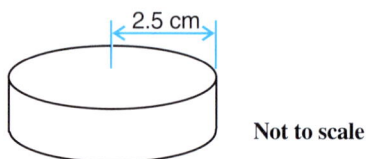

2.5 cm

Not to scale

(b) Calculate the thickness of each disc.
Give your answer to an appropriate degree of accuracy.

SEG 1999

9 A farmer's storage container is in the shape of a cylinder with a hemisphere on top.

The height of the cylinder is 9.5 m. The radius of both the cylinder and the hemisphere is 2.4 m.

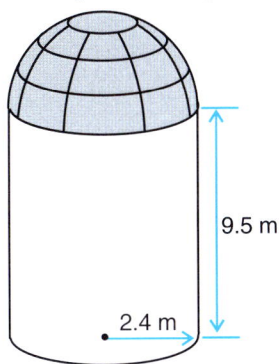

9.5 m

2.4 m

Calculate the volume of the farmer's storage container.

SEG 1996

10 A sector of a circle of radius 15 cm is cut out of card.

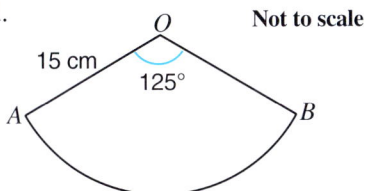

O   **Not to scale**

15 cm

125°

A   B

(a) Calculate the arc length *AB*.

The piece of card is used to create a cone by joining *OA* to *OB* with no overlap.

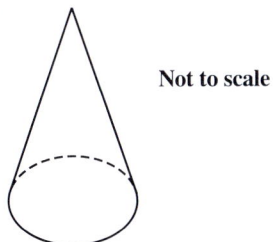

Not to scale

(b) Calculate the volume of the cone.

SEG 1996

11 A spinning top which consists of a cone of base radius 5 cm, height 9 cm and a hemisphere of radius 5cm as illustrated.

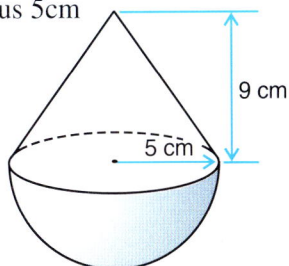

9 cm

5 cm

(a) Calculate the volume of the spinning top.
(b) Calculate the total surface area of the spinning top.

SEG 1998 S

12 (a) This diagram shows a cylinder of radius 6 cm and length 12 cm.

Not to scale

6 cm

12 cm

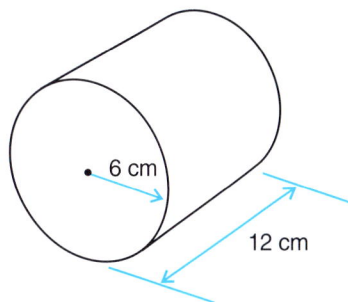

Calculate the volume of the cylinder.

(b) This diagram shows the same cylinder fitting tightly inside a box. The box is a cube.

Not to scale

12 cm

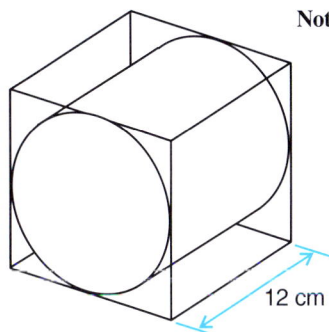

Calculate the volume of the space around the cylinder inside the cube.

(c) This diagram shows a sphere of radius 6 cm fitting tightly inside a box. The box is a cube.

Not to scale

12 cm

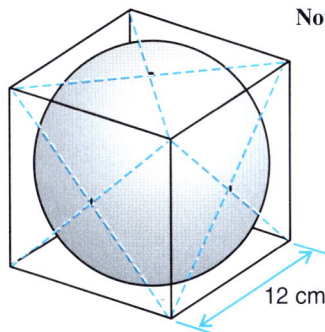

Calculate the volume of the space around the sphere, inside the cube.

(d) The **same** sized cube is tightly filled with 216 **identical** smaller spheres. What is the ratio of the radius of a small sphere to the radius of the large sphere?

SEG 1995

CHAPTER 24

Enlargements and Similar Figures

Enlargement

When a shape is enlarged:
  all **lengths** are multiplied by a **scale factor**,
  angles remain unchanged.

$$\text{Scale factor} = \frac{\text{new length}}{\text{original length}}$$

This can be rearranged to give
new length = original length $\times$ scale factor.

EXAMPLE

Enlarge this shape using a scale factor of 2.

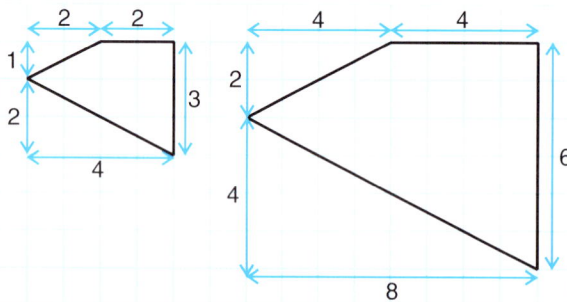

To draw an enlargement on a grid
Horizontal and vertical lines
Count the number of squares and multiply by the scale factor.

Slanting lines
Count across and up (or down) and multiply by the scale factor.

Using a centre of enlargement

A slide projector makes an enlargement of a picture.
The light bulb is the **centre of enlargement.**

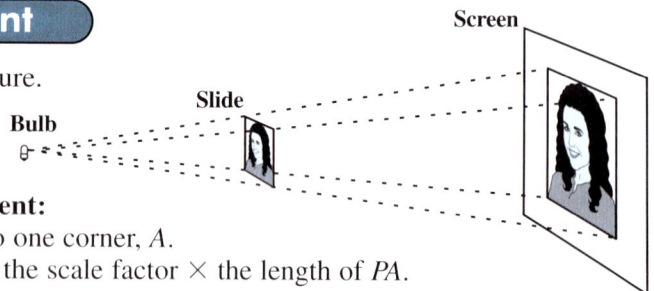

Screen
Slide
Bulb

To enlarge a shape using a centre of enlargement:
Draw a line from the centre of enlargement, *P*, to one corner, *A*.
Extend this line to *A′* so that the length of *PA′* = the scale factor $\times$ the length of *PA*.
Do the same for other corners of the shape.
Join up the corners to make the enlarged shape. Label the diagram.

EXAMPLES

1 Draw an enlargement of triangle *ABC*, centre *P* (0, 1) and scale factor 3.

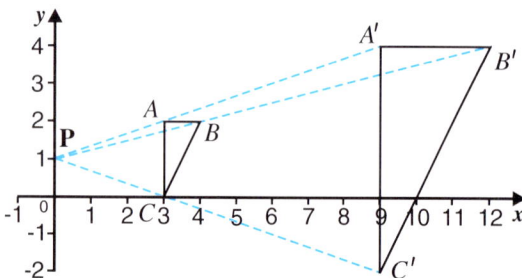

2 Use centre *P* (3, 2) and a scale factor of 2 to enlarge triangle *ABC*.

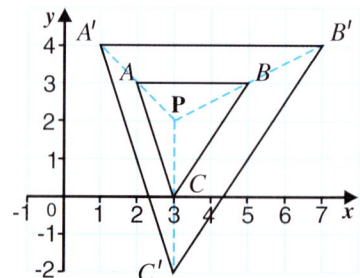

To find the centre and scale factor of an enlargement:

Join pairs of corresponding points.

Extend the lines until they meet. This point is the centre of enlargement.

Measure a pair of corresponding lengths.

Scale factor $= \dfrac{\text{new length}}{\text{original length}}$

EXAMPLE

Find the centre of enlargement and the scale factor when triangle XYZ becomes triangle $X'Y'Z'$.

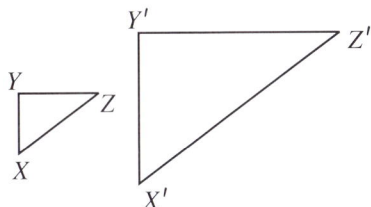

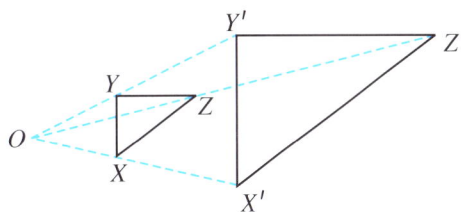

Scale factor $= \dfrac{X'Y'}{XY} = \dfrac{2.0}{0.8} = 2.5$

The centre of enlargement is the point O.

Exercise 24.1

1 Copy each diagram onto squared paper and draw an enlargement with the given scale factor.

(a) Scale factor 3

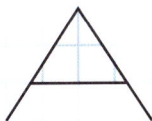

(b) Scale factor 2

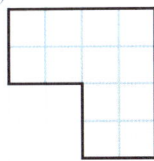

(c) Scale factor $1\frac{1}{2}$

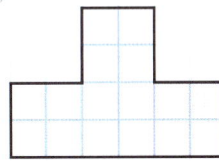

(d) Scale factor 2.5

2 Copy each diagram onto squared paper and enlarge it using the centre and scale factor given. You will need longer axes than those shown below.

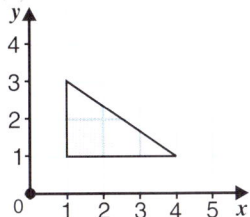

(a) Centre (0, 0), scale factor 2.

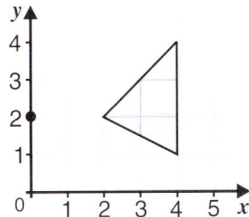

(b) Centre (0, 2), scale factor 3.

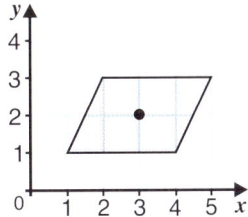

(c) Centre (3, 2), scale factor 2.

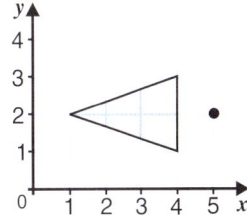

(d) Centre (5, 2), scale factor 2.5.

③ For each of the following diagrams find the scale factor and the coordinates of the centre of enlargement.

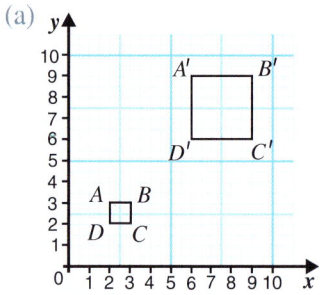

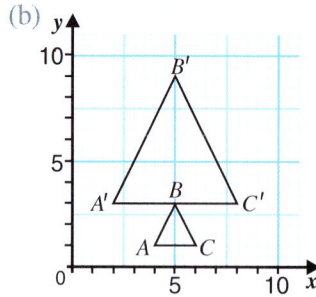

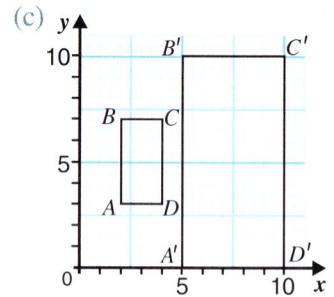

(a)

(b)

(c)

Using a scale factor which is a fraction

When the scale factor is a value between 0 and 1, such as 0.5 or $\frac{1}{3}$, the new shape is smaller than the original shape.

Even though the shape gets smaller it is still called an enlargement.

EXAMPLE

Draw an enlargement of this shape with centre (0, 1) and scale factor $\frac{1}{3}$.

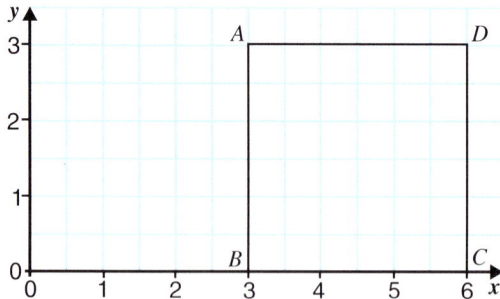

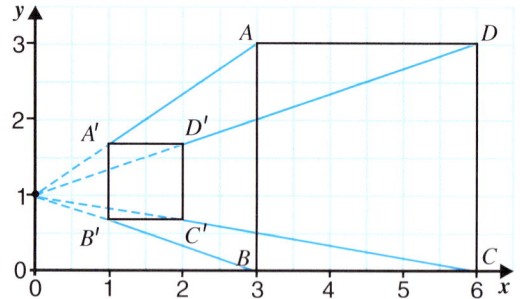

Exercise 24.2

① Copy each diagram onto squared paper and enlarge it with the centre and the scale factor given.

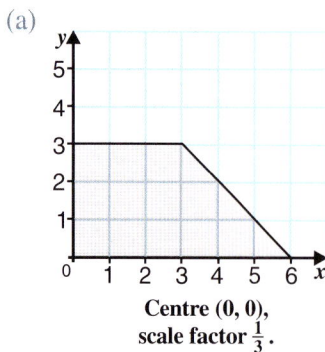

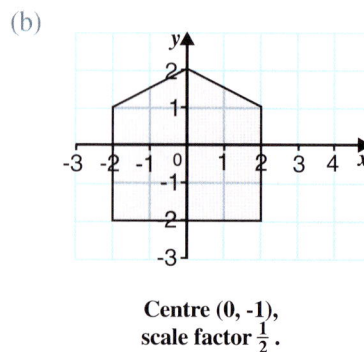

(a)

Centre (0, 0),
scale factor $\frac{1}{3}$.

(b)

Centre (0, -1),
scale factor $\frac{1}{2}$.

2 For each of the following diagrams give the centre of enlargement and the scale factor.

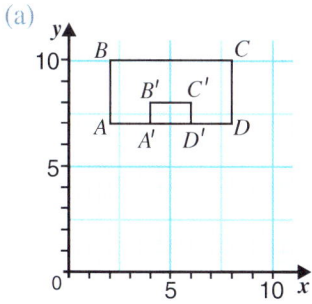

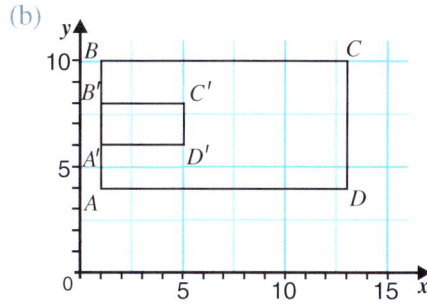

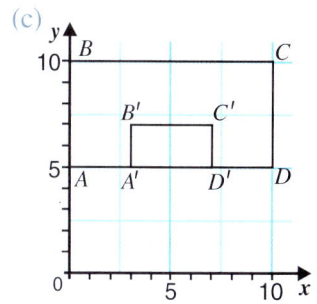

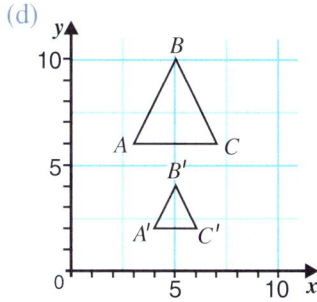

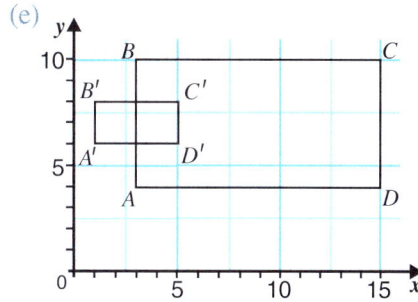

(a)

(b)

(c)

(d)

(e)

Enlargement with a negative scale factor

To enlarge a shape using a centre of enlargement:
Draw a line from one corner, A, to the centre of enlargement, P.
Extend this line to A' so that:

the length of PA' = the scale factor $\times$ the length of PA.

Do the same for other corners of the shape.
Join up the corners to make the enlarged shape.
Label the diagram.

> When a negative scale factor is used the image of the shape is **inverted**.
> *What does this mean?*

EXAMPLE

1 Draw an enlargement of triangle ABC, centre $P(-2,-1)$ and scale factor -2.

Measure the lengths of PA and PA'.

Explain how the points A', B' and C' were found from the points A, B and C.

Check that the triangle has been enlarged by the correct scale factor.

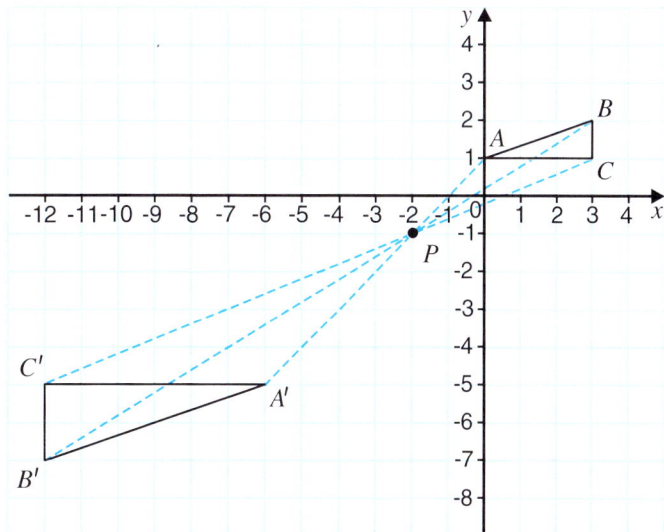

EXAMPLE

2 Find the centre of enlargement and the scale factor when triangle XYZ becomes triangle $X'Y'Z'$.

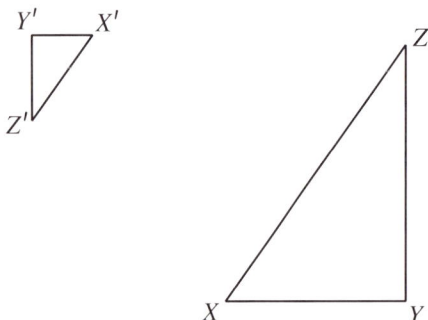

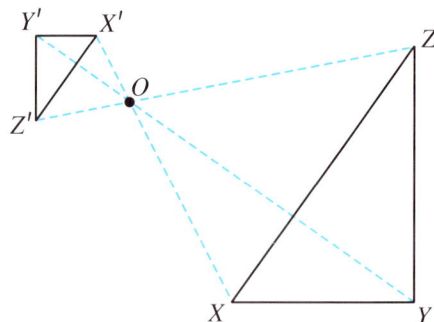

Scale factor $= \dfrac{X'Y'}{XY} = -\dfrac{0.7}{2.1} = -\dfrac{1}{3}$

The scale factor is negative because the image is inverted.
The centre of enlargement is the point O.

Exercise 24.3

1 Copy each diagram onto squared paper and enlarge it using the centre and scale factor given. You will need longer axes than those shown below.

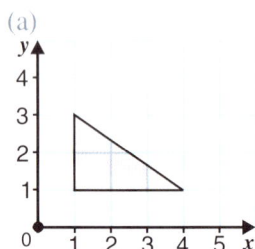

(a)

Centre (0, 0),
scale factor −2.

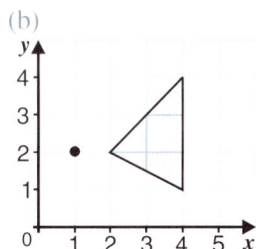

(b)

Centre (1, 2),
scale factor −3.

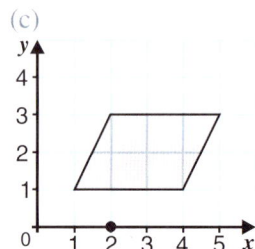

(c)

Centre (2, 0),
scale factor −1.

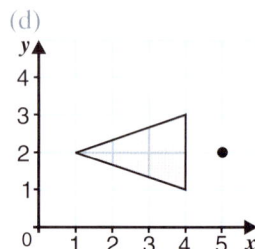

(d)

Centre (5, 2),
scale factor −2.5.

2 For each of the following diagrams give the centre of enlargement and the scale factor.

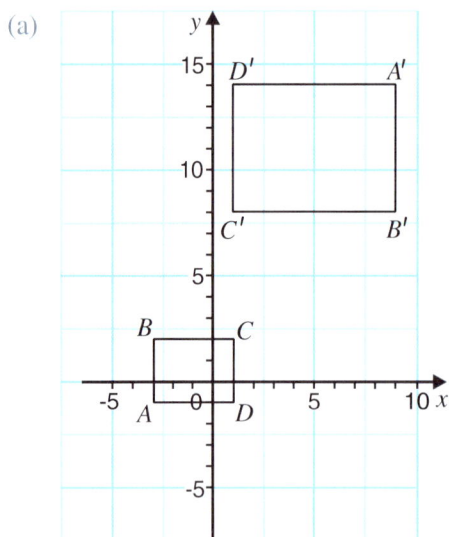

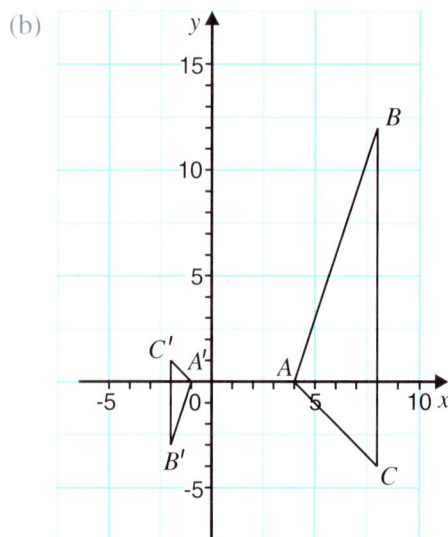

(a)

(b)

3 Describe the images of shapes which have been enlarged using:
(a) $-1 < $ scale factor < 0, (b) scale factor $= -1$, (c) scale factor < -1.

Similar figures

When one figure is an enlargement of another, the two figures are **similar**.

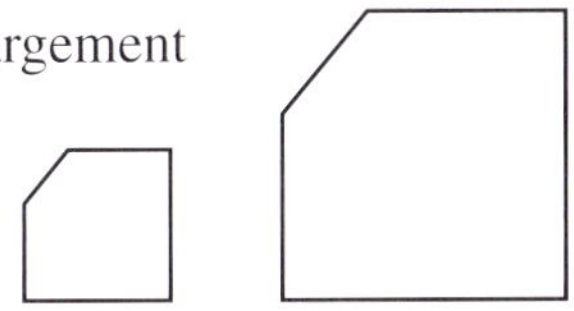

Sometimes one of the figures is rotated or reflected as well as enlarged. The two figures are still similar.

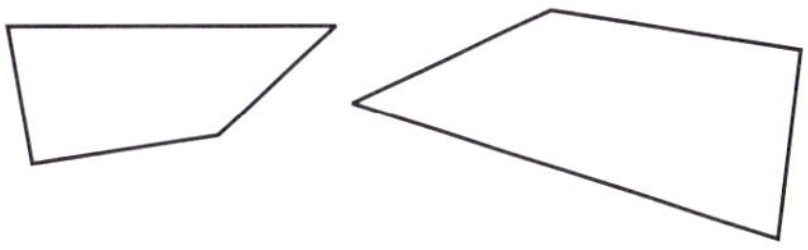

Three of these figures are similar. Which are they?

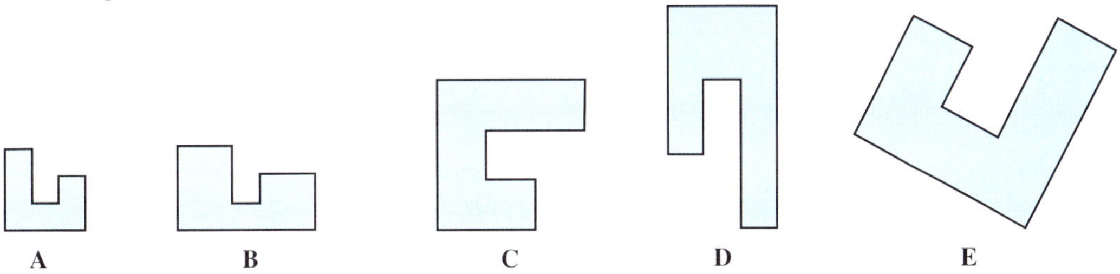

A   B   C   D   E

Figures C and E are enlargements of figure A.
Figures A, C and E are similar.

When two figures are **similar**:
their **shapes** are the same,
their **angles** are the same,
corresponding **lengths** are in the same ratio,
this ratio is the **scale factor** of the enlargement.

Activity

Figures X and Y are similar.
Y is an enlargement of X.
The ratio (or scale factor) is given

by $\dfrac{\text{new length}}{\text{original length}}$

Check that this ratio is the same for all four pairs of corresponding sides.
Check that the angles are the same in the two figures.

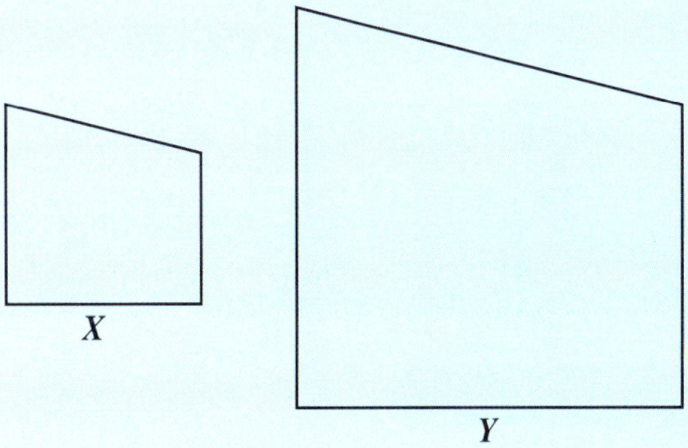

X

Y

EXAMPLE

1 A photo has width 6 cm and height 10 cm.
An enlargement is made, which has width 8 cm.
Calculate the height of the enlargement.

There are two methods for working out questions like this.
Look at each method carefully and use the one you prefer.

10

6

h

8

Method 1

$\dfrac{h}{10} = \dfrac{8}{6}$

$h = \dfrac{8}{6} \times 10$

$h = 13.3$ cm, correct to 1 d.p.

Method 2

Scale factor $= \dfrac{8}{6}$

$h = 10 \times \dfrac{8}{6}$

$h = 13.3$ cm, correct to 1 d.p.

2 These two figures are similar.
Calculate the lengths of x and y.
Write down the size of the angle marked a.

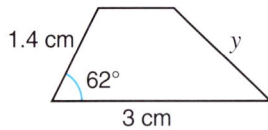

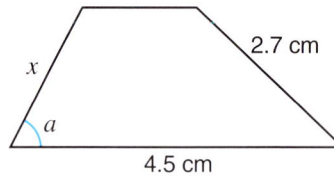

Method 1
Ratio of corresponding lengths

The corresponding sides are:

Small figure	Large figure
3	4.5
1.4	x
y	2.7

The corresponding sides are in the same ratio, so:

$\frac{x}{1.4} = \frac{4.5}{3}$

$x = \frac{4.5}{3} \times 1.4$

$x = 2.1\,\text{cm}$

$\frac{2.7}{y} = \frac{4.5}{3}$

$2.7 \times 3 = 4.5 \times y$

$y = \frac{2.7 \times 3}{4.5}$

$y = 1.8\,\text{cm}$

Method 2
Scale factor method

The scale factor $= \frac{4.5}{3} = 1.5$

Lengths in the large figure are given by:
length in small figure $\times$ scale factor
$x = 1.4 \times 1.5$
$x = 2.1\,\text{cm}$

Lengths in the small figure are given by:
length in large figure $\div$ scale factor
$y = 2.7 \div 1.5$
$y = 1.8\,\text{cm}$

The size of the angle marked a.
The angles in similar figures are the same, so
$a = 62°$.

Exercise 24.4

1 In each part, the two figures are similar. Calculate the lengths and angles marked with letters.

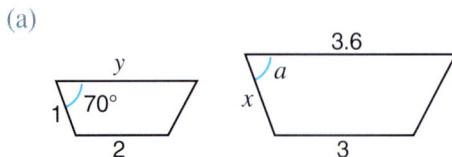

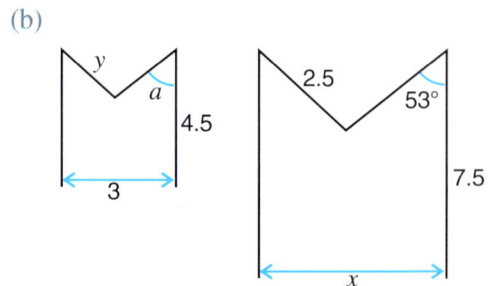

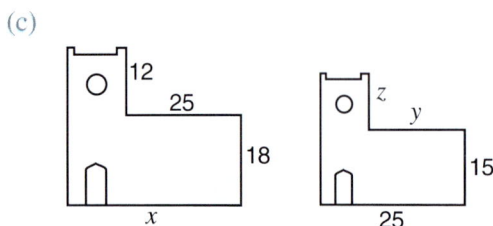

(a)

(b)

(c)

2 These two tubes are similar.

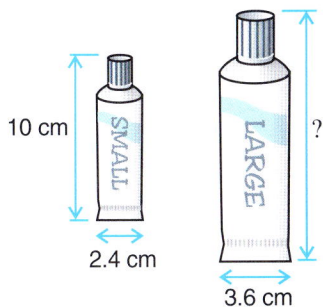

10 cm

SMALL

LARGE

?

2.4 cm

3.6 cm

The width of the small size is 2.4 cm and the height of the small size is 10 cm.
The width of the large size is 3.6 cm. Calculate the height of the large size.

3 A shape has width 0.8 cm and length 2.4 cm. It is enlarged to give a new shape with width 1 cm. Calculate the length of the new shape.

4 A castle has height 30 m. The height of the castle wall is 6 m. A scale model of the castle has height 25 cm. Calculate the height of the castle wall in the scale model.

5 The dimensions of three sizes of paper are given.

Length (cm)	24	30	y
Width (cm)	x	20	32

All the sizes are similar.
Calculate the values of x and y.

Similar triangles

For any pair of similar triangles:
   corresponding lengths are opposite equal angles,
   the scale factor is the ratio of corresponding sides.

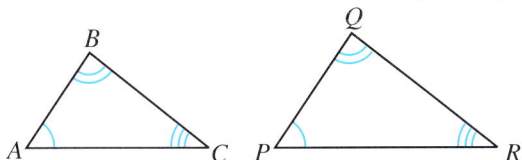

$$\frac{AB}{PQ} = \frac{BC}{QR} = \frac{CA}{RP} = \text{scale factor}$$

EXAMPLE

1 These two triangles are similar, with the equal angles marked.
Calculate the lengths x and y.

The corresponding sides are:

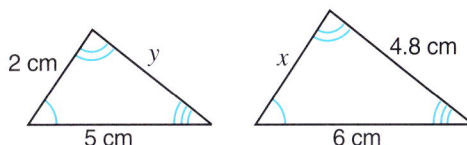

2 cm y x 4.8 cm

5 cm   6 cm

Small triangle	Large triangle
5	6
2	x
y	4.8

$\frac{x}{2} = \frac{6}{5}$

$x = \frac{6}{5} \times 2$

$x = 2.4$ cm

$\frac{4.8}{y} = \frac{6}{5}$

$4.8 \times 5 = 6 \times y$

$y = 4.8 \times \frac{5}{6}$

$y = 4$ cm

Alternative method

Scale factor $= \frac{6}{5} = 1.2$

$x = 2 \times 1.2$
$x = 2.4$ cm

$y = 4.8 \div 1.2$
$y = 4$ cm

351

EXAMPLE

2 Triangles *ABC* and *PQR* are similar. Calculate the lengths of *AC* and *PQ*.

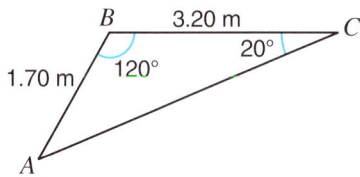

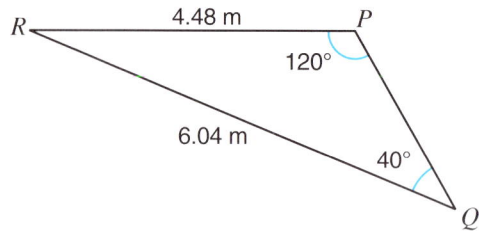

Angle *A* = 180° − (120° + 20°) = 40°
Angle *R* = 180° − (120° + 40°) = 20°

The corresponding sides are:

	Triangle *ABC*	Triangle *PQR*
Opposite 40°	3.20	4.48
Opposite 20°	1.70	*PQ*
Opposite 120°	*AC*	6.04

Alternative method

Scale factor $= \frac{4.48}{3.20} = 1.4$

$AC = 6.04 \div 1.4$
$AC = 4.31$ m, correct to 2 d.p.

$PQ = 1.70 \times 1.4$
$PQ = 2.38$ m

$\frac{6.04}{AC} = \frac{4.48}{3.20}$
$6.04 \times 3.20 = 4.48 \times AC$
$AC = \frac{6.04 \times 3.20}{4.48}$
$AC = 4.31$ m, correct to 2 d.p.

$\frac{PQ}{1.70} = \frac{4.48}{3.20}$
$PQ = \frac{4.48}{3.20} \times 1.70$
$PQ = 2.38$ m

Exercise 24.5

Question 1 should be done without a calculator.

1 In each part, the triangles are similar, with equal angles marked. Calculate lengths *x* and *y*.

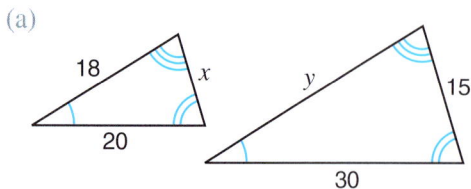

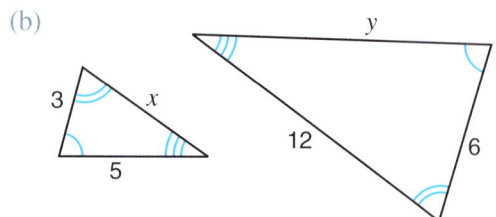

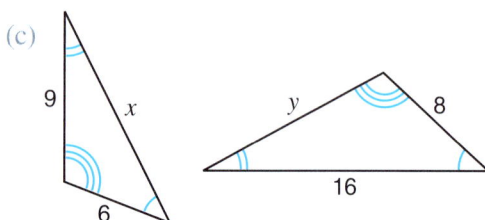

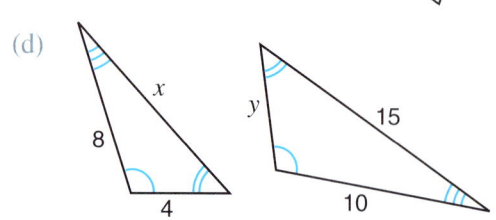

(a)

(b)

(c)

(d)

2 In each part the triangles are similar. Calculate the unknown lengths in both triangles.

(a)

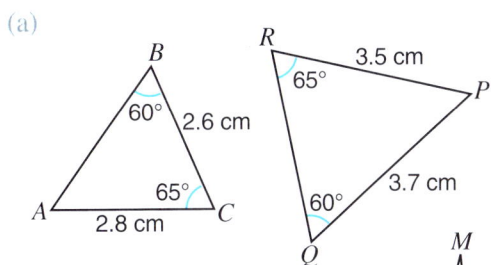

(b)

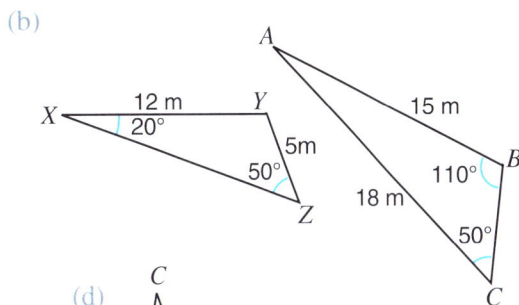

(c)

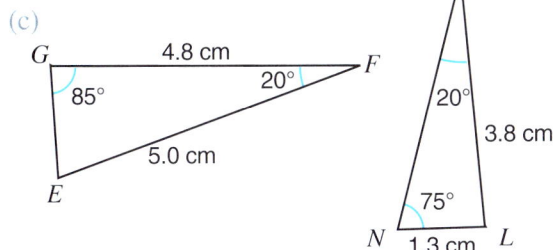

(d)

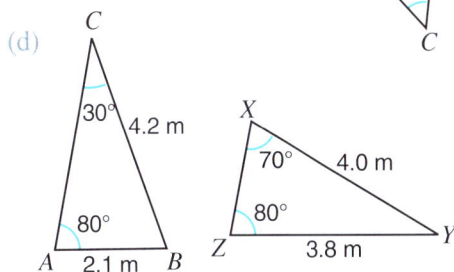

3 Triangles ABC and ADE are similar.
$\angle AED = \angle ACB$.

Calculate the lengths of AB and AE.

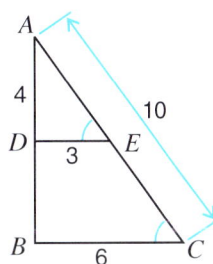

4 Triangles ABC and ADE are similar.
$\angle ADE = \angle ABC$.

(a) Write down the length of AB.
(b) Calculate the lengths of BC and AC.
(c) What is the length of EC?

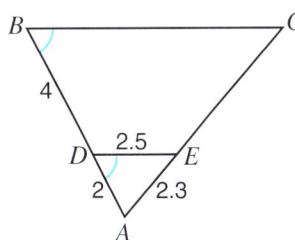

5 Triangles PST and PQR are similar.
$\angle PTS = \angle PRQ$.

(a) Write down the length of PR.
(b) Calculate QR, PQ and QS.

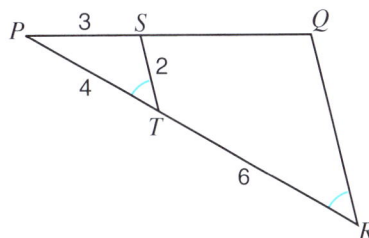

6 Triangles DEF and DGH are similar.
$\angle DGH = \angle DEF$.

Calculate GH and FH.

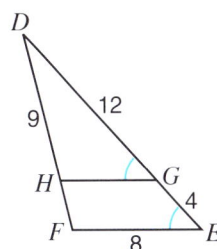

To show that two triangles are similar you have to show that:

either   they have equal angles

or   corresponding lengths are all in the same ratio.

If you can show that one of these conditions is true then the other one is also true.

EXAMPLE

AB and *CD* are parallel lines. *AD* and *BC* meet at *X*.

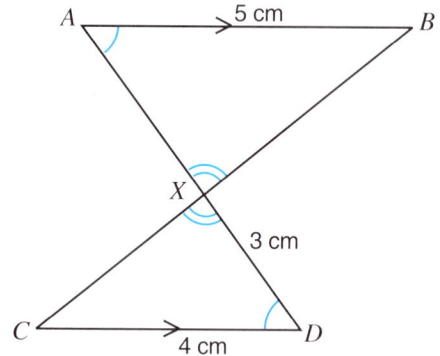

(a)   Prove that triangles *ABX* and *DCX* are similar.

(b)   Which side in triangle *DCX* corresponds to *AX* in triangle *ABX*?

(c)   Calculate the length of *AX*.

(a) $\angle BAX = \angle CDX$ (alternate angles)

$\angle AXB = \angle DXC$ (vertically opposite angles)

Triangles *ABX* and *DCX* contain two pairs of equal angles and so they are similar.

If two pairs of angles are equal then the third pair must be equal. Why?

(b) $\angle ABX = \angle DCX$.

Sides *AX* and *DX* are opposite these equal angles.

So *DX* corresponds to *AX*.

(c) $\frac{AX}{3} = \frac{5}{4}$ $\left(\text{or scale factor} = \frac{5}{4}\right)$

$AX = \frac{5}{4} \times 3$

$AX = 3.75\,\text{cm}$

You **must** give reasons for any statements you make. Alternate angles, corresponding angles and vertically opposite angles were covered in Chapter 17.

EXAMPLE

Show that these two triangles are similar.

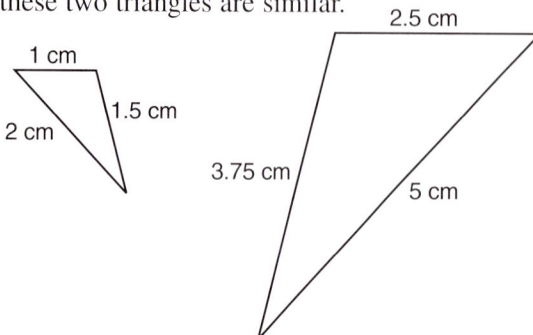

$\frac{5}{2} = 2.5$

$\frac{3.75}{1.5} = 2.5$

$\frac{2.5}{1} = 2.5$

All three pairs of corresponding sides are in the same ratio, so the triangles are similar.

354

1   BC is parallel to PQ. Show that triangles ABC and APQ are similar and calculate the required lengths.

(a)

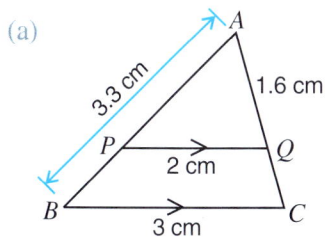

Calculate AC and AP.

(b)

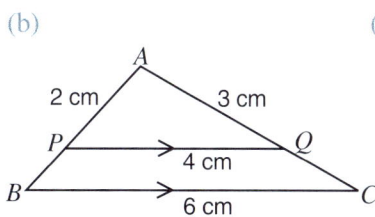

Calculate AC and BP.

(c)

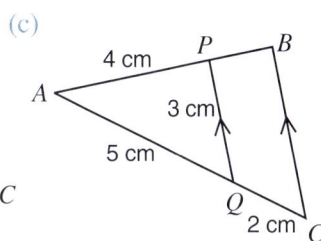

Calculate BC and BP.

(d)

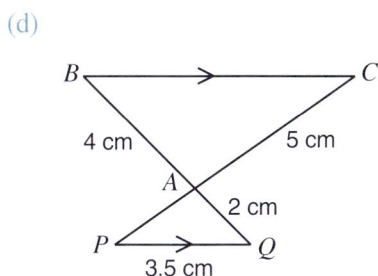

Calculate AP and BC.

(e)

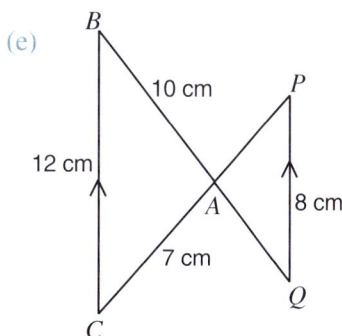

Calculate AP and BQ.

2   Show that these pairs of triangles are similar and find angle x.

(a)

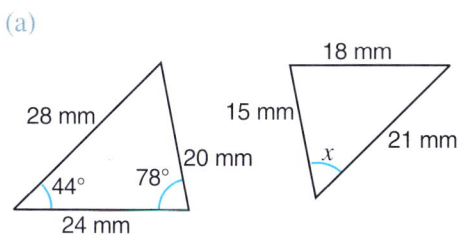

(b)

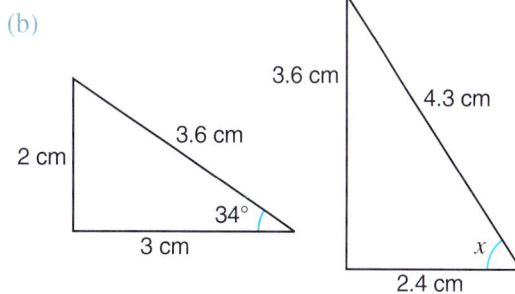

3   In each part show that triangles ABC and APQ are similar and find angle x.

(a)

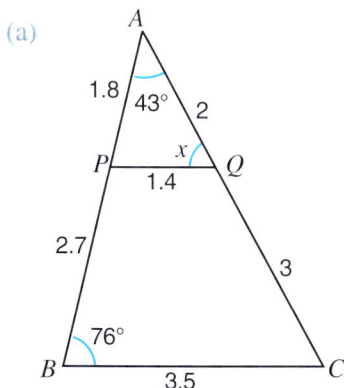

(b)

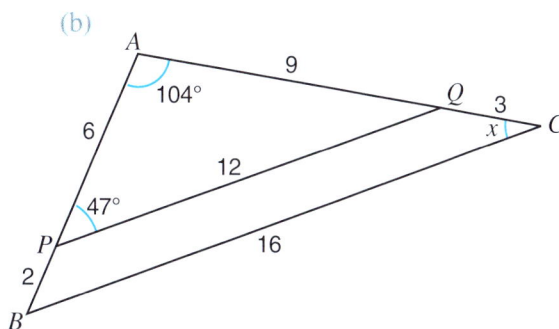

4 In each part explain why triangles *PQR* and *PYZ* are similar and calculate the required lengths.

(a)

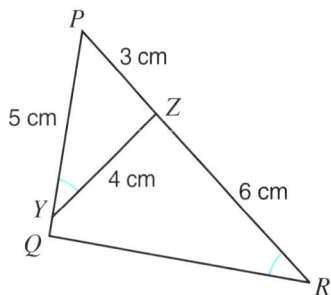

$\angle PRQ = \angle PYZ$.
Calculate *QR* and *QY*.

(b)

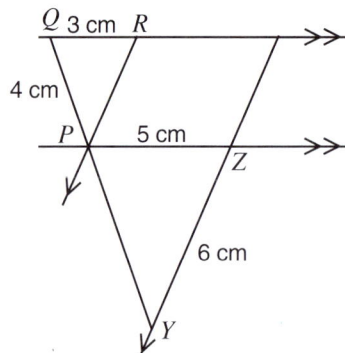

QR is parallel to *PZ* and
PR is parallel to *YZ*.
Calculate *PR* and *QY*.

(c)

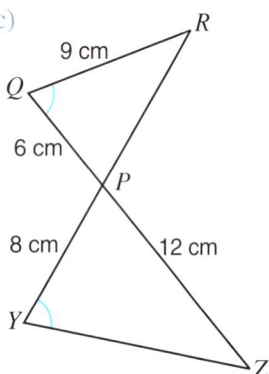

$\angle PQR = \angle PYZ$.
Calculate *YZ* and *PR*.

(d)

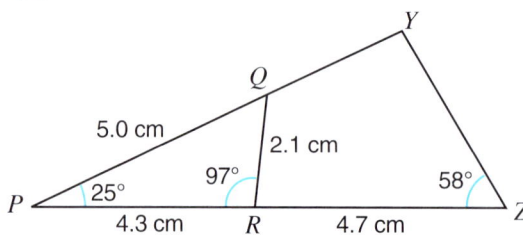

Calculate *YZ* and *QY*.

Lengths, areas and volumes of similar figures

Activity

Some cubes have side 2 cm.
They are built together to make a larger cube with side 6 cm.
This represents an enlargement with scale factor 3.

Copy and complete the table.

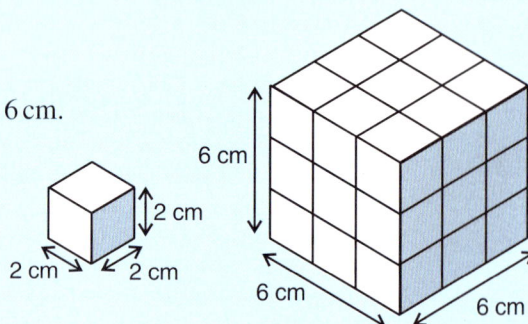

	Length of side (cm)	Area of face (cm²)	Volume of cube (cm³)
Small cube	2		8
Large cube	6	36	
Scale factor	$\dfrac{6}{2} = 3$	$\dfrac{36}{} =$	$\dfrac{}{8} =$

What do you notice about the three scale factors?

Repeat this activity with a scale factor of 4.
Now repeat it with a scale factor of *k*.

Spheres

Three spheres have radii *r* cm, 2*r* cm and 3*r* cm.
Compare the surface areas and volumes of the three spheres.

When the length scale factor $= k$
the area scale factor $= k^2$
the volume scale factor $= k^3$

For solids made of the same material, **mass is proportional to volume**.
So the mass scale factor is k^3.

EXAMPLES

1 A prototype for a new plane is made.
The real plane will be an enlargement of the prototype with scale factor 5.

(a) The area of the windows on the prototype is $0.18\,m^2$.
Find the area of the real windows.
(b) The volume of the real fuel tank is 4000 litres.
Find the volume of the fuel tank on the prototype.

It can be assumed that "scale factor" refers to the length scale factor, unless specified differently in a question.

(a) Area scale factor $= 5^2 = 25$.
Real area $= 0.18 \times 25 = 4.5\,m^2$
(b) Volume scale factor $= 5^3 = 125$.

Prototype volume $= \dfrac{4000}{125} = 32$ litres.

Corresponding lengths, areas and volumes,

Prototype plane	multiply by scale factor	Real plane
Prototype plane	divide by scale factor	Real plane

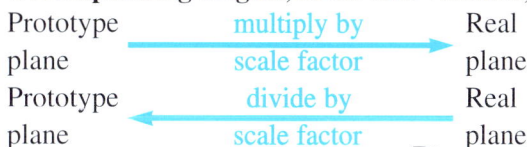

2 A scale model of a ship is made, using a scale of 1:40.
(a) The area of the real deck is $500\,m^2$.
Find, in square centimetres, the area of the deck on the model.
(b) The volume of the hold on the model is $187\,500\,cm^3$.
Find, in cubic metres, the volume of the real hold.

(a) Area scale factor $= 40^2 = 1600$.

Model deck area $= \dfrac{500}{1600}\,m^2$

$= \dfrac{500 \times 10\,000}{1600}\,cm^2$

$= 3125\,cm^2$

$1\,m^2 = 1\,m \times 1\,m$
$= 100\,cm \times 100\,cm$
$= 10\,000\,cm^2$

$1\,m^3 = 1\,m \times 1\,m \times 1\,m$
$= 100\,cm \times 100\,cm \times 100\,cm$
$= 1\,000\,000\,cm^3$

(b) Volume scale factor $= 40^3 = 64\,000$.
Volume of real hold $= 187\,500 \times 64\,000\,m^3$

$= \dfrac{187\,500 \times 64\,000}{1\,000\,000}\,m^3$

$= 12\,000\,m^3$

3 A metal ingot has volume $20\,000\,cm^3$. It is melted down and made into identical smaller ingots. Each small ingot is similar to the original ingot and has volume $25\,cm^3$. The length of the large ingot is $50\,cm$. Calculate the length of the small ingots.

Volume scale factor $= \dfrac{20\,000}{25} = 800$

Length scale factor $= \sqrt[3]{800} = 9.28\ldots$

Length of small ingot $= \dfrac{25}{\sqrt[3]{800}}$

$= 2.693\ldots$

$= 2.69\,cm$, correct to 3 s.f.

1 A model of a train is 60 cm long.
It is made on a scale of 1 to 50.
What is the length of the actual train in metres?

2 A motor car is 4.2 m long and 1.4 m high.
A scale model of the car is 8.4 cm long.
(a) What is the scale of the model?
(b) What is the height of the model?

3 A rectangular vegetable plot needs 10 kg of fertiliser.
How much fertiliser is needed for a plot with double the dimensions?

4 A company logo is printed on all its stationary.
On small sheets of paper the logo is 1.2 cm high and covers an area of 3.5 cm^2.
On large sheets of paper the logo covers an area of 14 cm^2.
What is the height of the logo on large sheets of paper?

5 The lengths of the sides of a square are halved.
What happens to its area?

6 A picture is 30 cm high and has an area of 360 cm^2. Another print of the same picture is 15 cm high. What is its area?

7 A king size photograph is 18 cm long and 12 cm wide.
A standard size photograph is 12 cm long.
(a) What is the width of a standard size photograph?
(b) What is the area of a standard size photograph?

8 A photo has length 12 cm and area 104 cm^2. Find the length and area of an enlargement with scale factor 1.2.

9 The scale of a map is 1 to 50 000.
(a) The distance between two junctions on the map is 3 cm.
What is the actual distance between the junctions in kilometres?
(b) A lake covers 20 cm^2 on the map.
How many square kilometres does the lake actually cover?

10 A map has a scale of 1 : 25 000.
(a) The length of a road is 3.5 km.
Calculate its length, in centimetres, on the map.
(b) The area of a field on the map is 12 cm^2. Calculate the true area in square metres.
(c) A park has an area of 120 000 m^2.
Calculate the area of the park on the map.

11 The measurements of a rabbit hutch are all doubled.
(a) How many times bigger is its surface area?
(b) How many times bigger is its volume?

12 A box of height 4 cm has a surface area of 220 cm^2 and a volume of 200 cm^3.
(a) What is the surface area and volume of a similar box of height 8 cm?
(b) What is the surface area and volume of a similar box of height 2 cm?

13 Two garden ponds are similar.
The dimensions of the larger pond are three times as big as the smaller pond.
The smaller pond holds 20 litres of water.
How many litres of water does the larger pond hold?

14 Two tubes of toothpaste are similar.
Copy and complete the table.

	Length (cm)	Surface area (cm^2)	Volume (cm^3)
Small	10		50
Large		50	66.6

15 Two solid spheres are made of the same material.
The smaller sphere has a radius of 4 cm and weighs 1.5 kg.
The larger sphere has a radius of 8 cm.
How much does it weigh?

16 Two fish tanks are similar.
The smaller tank is 12 cm high and has a volume of 3.6 litres.
The larger tank has a volume of 97.2 litres.
What is the height of the larger tank?

17 A tank has length 50 cm and contains a maximum of 250 kg of oil. A similar tank has length 40 cm. Calculate the maximum mass of oil which it can contain.

18 (a) A scale model of a house is made using a scale of 1 : 20.
The roof area on the model is 82 cm². Find the real roof area.
(b) The volume of the real roof space is 180 m³. Find the volume of the roof space in the model.

19 Jane makes a scale model of her village. A fence of length 12 m is represented by a length of 4 cm on her model.
(a) Calculate the scale which Jane is using.
(b) Calculate, in cubic centimetres, the volume on the model of a pool which has a volume of 20 m³.
(c) Calculate the actual area of a playground which has an area of 320 cm² on the model.

20 Joe wants to enlarge a picture so that its area is doubled.
What scale factor should he use?

21 The area of the roof of a new car is nine times the area of the roof of a model. How many times larger is the volume of the boot of the car than the volume of the boot of the model?

22 Two balls have radii of 2 cm and 5 cm.

(a) Calculate the volumes of the two balls and show that the ratio of the volumes is 8 : 125.
(b) Show that the surface area of the smaller ball is 16% of the surface area of the larger ball.

23 Pop and Fizzo come in similar cans. Cans of Pop are 8 cm tall and cans of Fizzo are 10 cm tall. A can of Pop holds 200 ml. How much does a can of Fizzo hold?

24 A bronze statue is made in two sizes.
The taller statue is 15 cm high and the shorter one is 9 cm high.
The taller statue weighs 3.75 kg.
What is the weight of the shorter statue?

25 Coffee filters are paper cones. The cones are made in these similar sizes; small, medium and large.
The slant height of a small cone is 5 cm and the surface area is 15π cm².
(a) A large cone has a surface area of 135π cm².
Calculate the length of its slant height.
(b) A medium cone has a volume of $\dfrac{81\pi}{2}$ cm³.
Calculate the surface area of a medium cone.

What you need to know

- When a shape is **enlarged**: all **lengths** are multiplied by a **scale factor**,
  angles remain unchanged.

- When a shape is enlarged using a **negative scale factor** the image is **inverted**.

- When two figures are **similar**:
  their **shapes** are the same,
  their **angles** are the same,
  corresponding **lengths** are in the same ratio,
  this ratio is the **scale factor** of
  the enlargement.

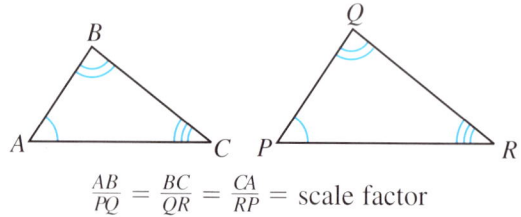

- Scale factor = $\dfrac{\text{new length}}{\text{original length}}$

- For **similar triangles**:
  corresponding lengths are opposite
  equal angles,
  the scale factor is the ratio of the
  corresponding sides.

$$\frac{AB}{PQ} = \frac{BC}{QR} = \frac{CA}{RP} = \text{scale factor}$$

- For **similar areas and volumes**:
  when the **length** scale factor $= k$
  the **area** scale factor $= k^2$
  the **volume** scale factor $= k^3$

Review Exercise

1 Draw and label an x axis from 0 to 12 and a y axis from 0 to 6.
Enlarge the shape with scale factor 2 and centre (0, 3).

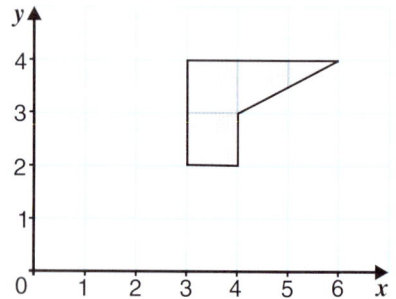

SEG 1997

2 Enlarge the shape in Question 1 with centre (0, 0) and scale factor $\frac{1}{2}$.

3 Copy each diagram onto squared paper and draw the enlargement using the centre and scale factor given.

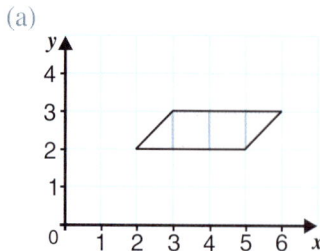

(a)

**Centre (2, 1),
scale factor −2.**

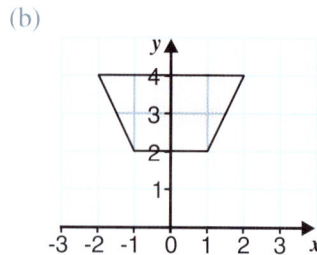

(b)

**Centre (1, 2),
scale factor −1.**

360

4 These triangles are **similar**. They are **not** drawn accurately.
Angle *A* equals angle *X*.
Angle *B* equals angle *Y*.

Calculate the length of *XY*.

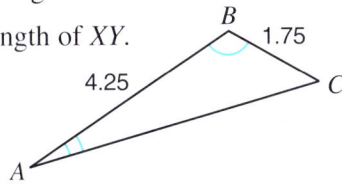
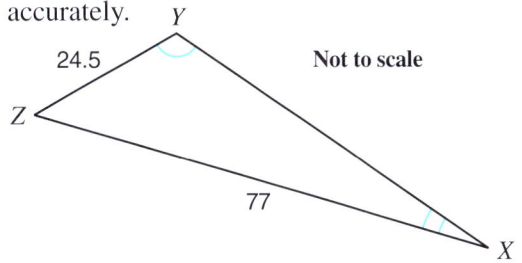

Not to scale

SEG 1996

5 All of these triangles are similar.

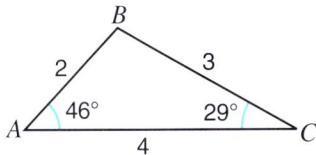
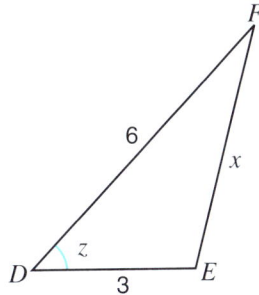
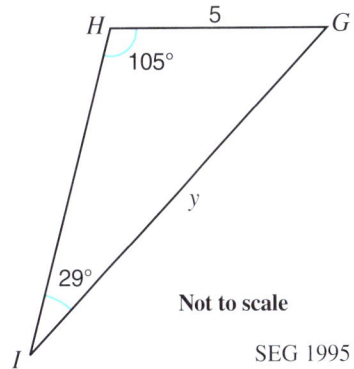

Not to scale

(a) Calculate the length *x*.
(b) Calculate the length *y*.
(c) What is the value of angle *z*?

SEG 1995

6 Duncan wants to measure the height of a tree.
He places a vertical stick of length 1.5 metres on level ground 100 metres from the base of the tree.
The lengths of the shadows of the tree and the stick are 102.4 metres and 2.4 metres respectively.

Calculate the height of the tree.

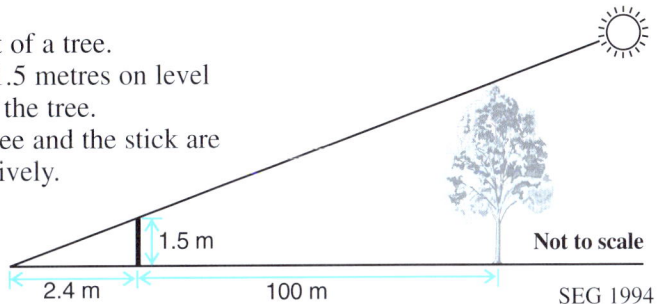

Not to scale

SEG 1994

7 State whether or not the triangles *ABC* and *XYZ* are similar.
Show working to support your answer.

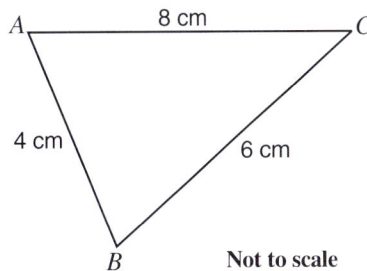
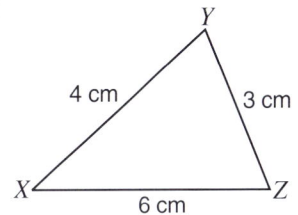

Not to scale

SEG 1995

8 The diagram shows a triangle *ABC*.
DE is parallel to *BC*.
Calculate the lengths
(a) *DE*,
(b) *AC*.

Not to scale

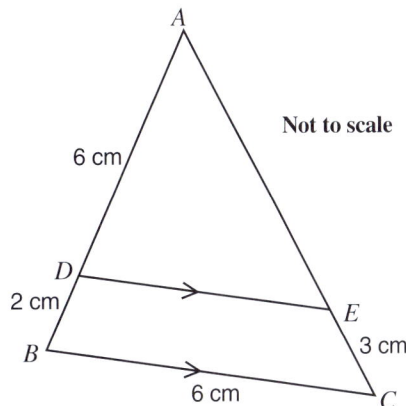

SEG 1997

9 Two similar solid shapes are made.
The height of the smaller shape is 7 cm.
The width of the smaller shape is 6 cm.
The width of the larger shape is 9.6 cm.

(a) Calculate the height of the larger shape.

(b) The volume of the larger shape is 695 cm³.
Find the volume of the smaller shape.

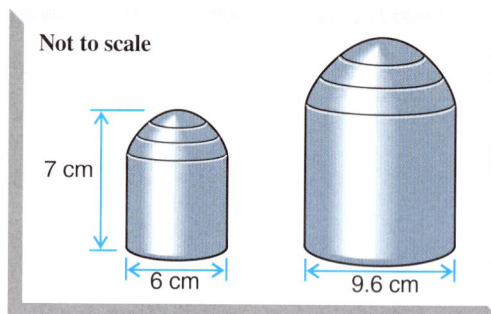

Not to scale

7 cm

6 cm   9.6 cm

SEG 2000 S

10 Two similar steam engines are cut out of a piece of card.

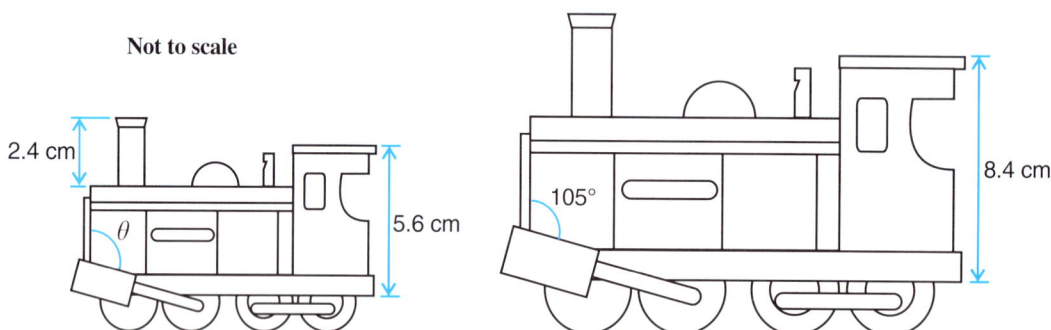

Not to scale

2.4 cm

5.6 cm

θ

105°

8.4 cm

(a) Calculate the height of the funnel on the larger steam engine.
(b) The circumference of a wheel on the larger steam engine is 5.7 cm.
Calculate the circumference of the same wheel on the smaller steam engine.
(c) What is the size of the angle marked θ on the smaller steam engine?

The area of the smaller steam engine is 16.5 cm².
(d) Calculate the area of the larger steam engine.

SEG 1994

11 The logo shown is to be enlarged for a new poster.
(a) The distance AB is 3 cm on the original shape.
On the enlarged shape AB is 13.5 cm and BC is 7.8 cm.
What is the distance BC on the original shape?

(b) The area of the original shape is 12 cm².
Calculate the area of the enlarged shape.

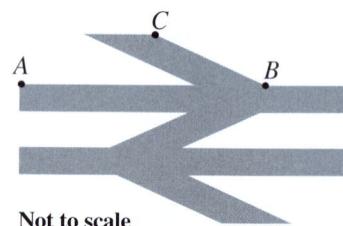

(c)

Not to scale

C

A B

Not to scale

A

2

3

E

B

2

C D

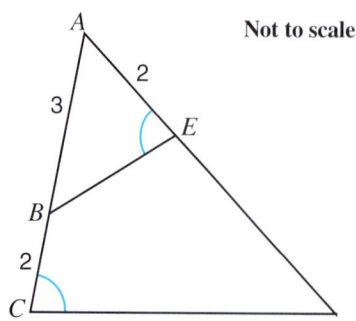

In the diagram $AB = 3$ cm, $BC = 2$ cm and $AE = 2$ cm.
Angles AEB and ACD are equal.
(i) Explain why triangle ABE is similar to triangle ADC.
(ii) Calculate the length of ED.

SEG 1996

12 **A** and **B** are two similar cones.

Not to scale

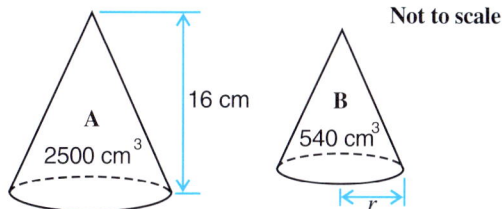

16 cm

A
2500 cm³

B
540 cm³

r

Cone **A** has a height of 16 cm and a volume of 2 500 cm³.
Cone **B** has a volume of 540 cm³.
Calculate the radius, *r*, of the base of Cone **B.**

SEG 2000 S

13 A family size tin of soup is in the shape of a cylinder.

SOUP
FAMILY
SIZE

Not to scale

10.4 cm

The diameter of the tin is 10.4 cm.
The tin is filled to a depth of 11 cm. The average portion of soup per person is 150 cm³.
(a) Calculate the number of whole portions in the family size tin.

Soup can also be bought in standard size tins and catering size tins.
The standard size tin holds two portions. The catering size tin is an enlargement of the
standard size tin by a scale factor of 2.5.
(b) How many portions does the catering size tin contain?

SEG 1997

14 (a) Pet food is sold in two sizes: Small and Regular.
The Regular size is an enlargement of the Small size.
The width and depth of the Small size are 9 cm and 4.2 cm.

Not to scale

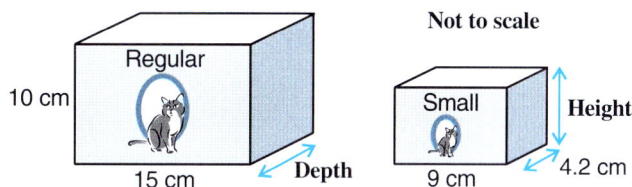

Regular
10 cm

15 cm   Depth

Small

Height

9 cm   4.2 cm

(i) Calculate the height of the Small size packet.
(ii) Calculate the depth of the Regular size packet.

(b) Two tins of pet food are similar in shape.
The small size has height 12 cm and volume 150 cm³.
The large size has height 16 cm.

Not to scale

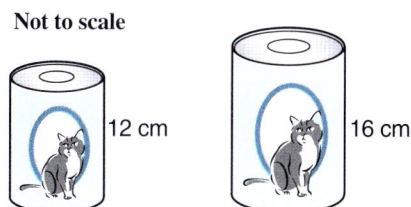

12 cm   16 cm

Calculate the volume of the large size.

SEG 1994

CHAPTER 25

Transformations

The movement of a shape from one position to another is called a **transformation**.
The change in position of the shape can be described in terms of a **reflection**, a **rotation** or a **translation**.

Reflection

Look at this diagram.
It shows the reflection of shape P in the line $x = 4$.

Shape P_1 is the **image** of P.
We also say that P is **mapped** onto P_1.

When a shape is reflected it stays the same shape and size.

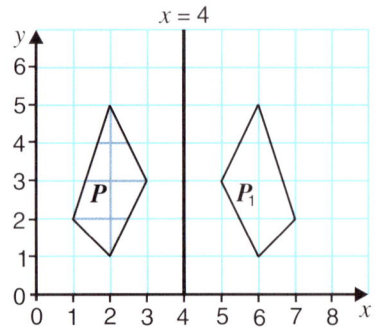

EXAMPLE

Copy the shape below onto squared paper.
Draw the reflection of triangle ABC in the line $y = x$.
Label the image $A_1 B_1 C_1$.

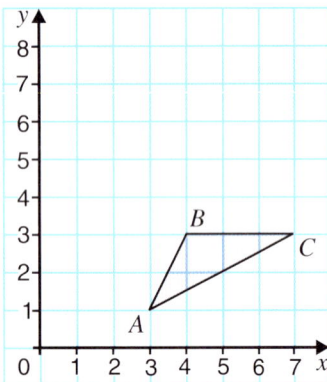

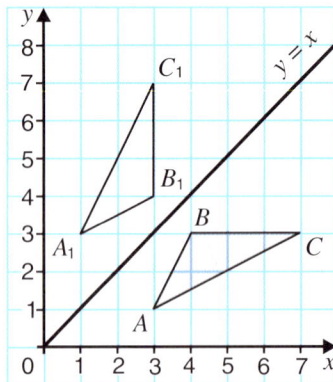

Notice that:
$A (3, 1) \rightarrow A_1 (1, 3)$
$B (4, 3) \rightarrow B_1 (3, 4)$
$C (7, 3) \rightarrow C_1 (3, 7)$
Can you see a pattern?

Exercise **25.1**

1 In the diagram P is the point $(2, 1)$.

Find the coordinates of the image of P under a reflection in
(a) the x axis,
(b) the y axis,
(c) the line $x = 1$,
(d) the line $y = -1$,
(e) the line $y = x$.

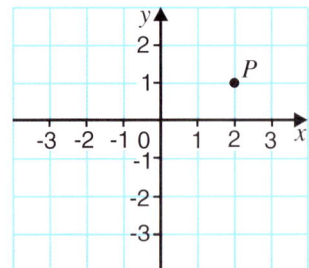

2 Copy each of the following triangles onto squared paper and then draw the reflection of each triangle in the line given.

(a) Reflect in $x = 0$.

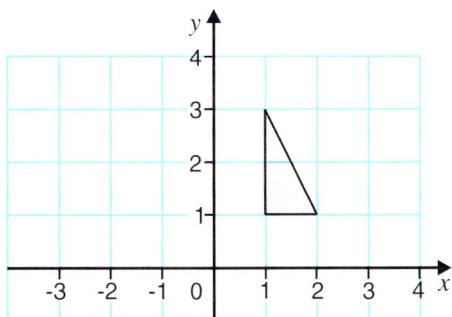

(b) Reflect in $x = 3$.

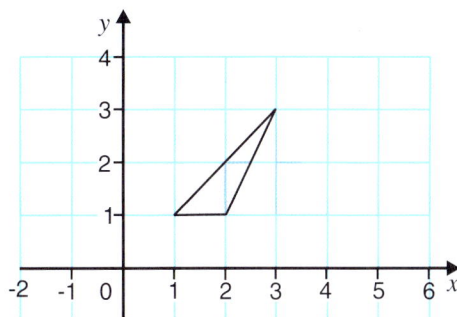

(c) Reflect in $y = 0$.

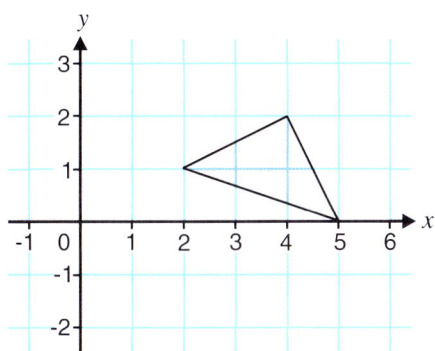

(d) Reflect in $y = -1$.

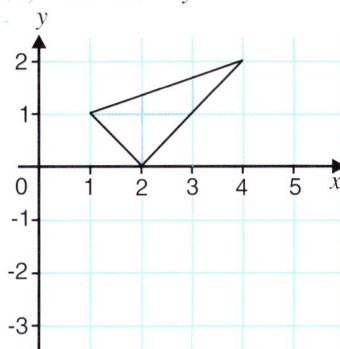

3 Copy each of the following shapes onto squared paper and then draw the reflection of each shape in the line given.

(a) Reflect in $x = -1$.

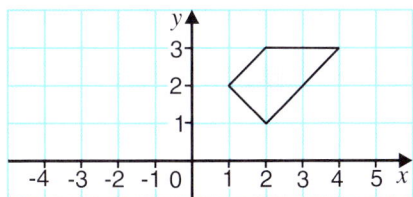

(b) Reflect in $y = 1$.

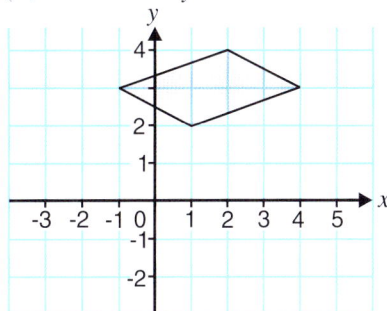

(c) Reflect in $y = x$.

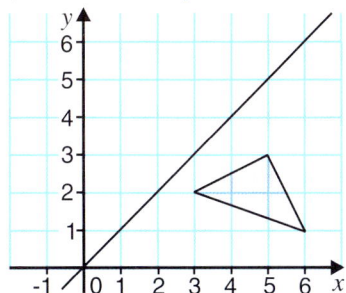

(d) Reflect in $y = -x$.

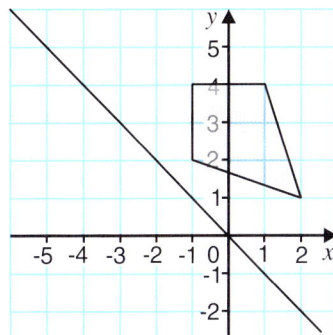

4 The diagram shows a quadrilateral $ABCD$.

Give the coordinates of B after:
(a) reflection in the x axis,
(b) reflection in the y axis,
(c) reflection in the line $x = 4$,
(d) reflection in the line $x = -1$,
(e) reflection in the line $y = x$.

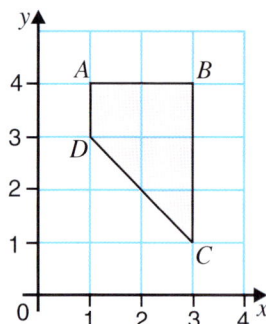

Rotation

Look at this diagram.
It shows the **rotation** of a shape through $90°$ anticlockwise about O (the origin).

The shape P_1 is the image of the shape P.
P is mapped onto P_1.

All points on the shape P are turned through the same angle about the same point.
This point is called the **centre of rotation**.

When a shape is rotated it stays the same shape and size but its **orientation** on the page changes.

For a rotation we need:
    a centre of rotation,
    an amount of turn,
    a direction of turn.

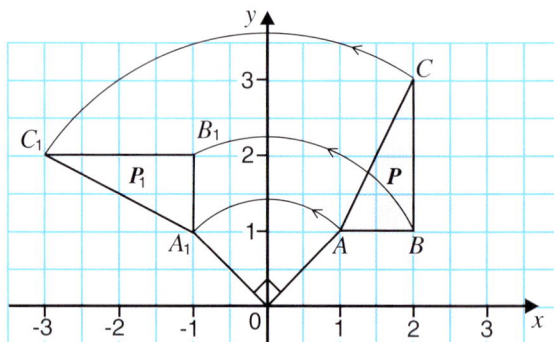

$$A \rightarrow A_1$$
$AO = A_1O$ and $\angle AOA_1 = 90°$.
What happens to points B and C?

EXAMPLE

Copy triangle ABC onto squared paper.
Draw the image of triangle ABC after it has been rotated through $90°$ clockwise about the point P $(1, 1)$.
Label the image $A_1\ B_1\ C_1$.

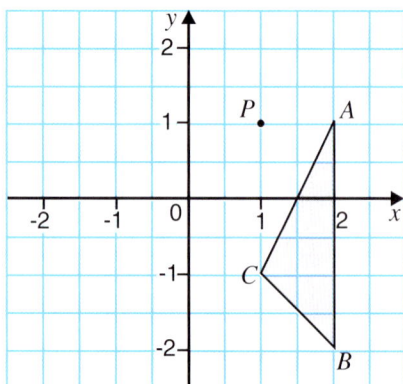

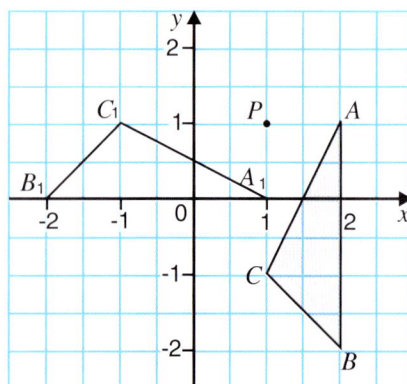

366

Exercise 25.2

1 Copy each of the following shapes onto squared paper and draw the new position of the shape after it has been rotated through 90°, clockwise about the origin (0, 0).

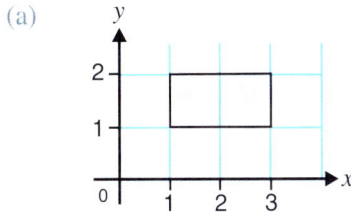

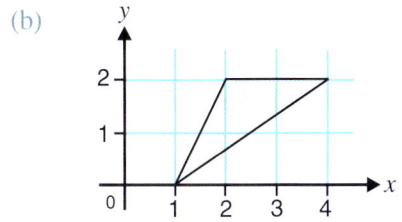

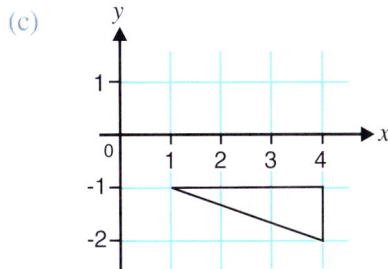

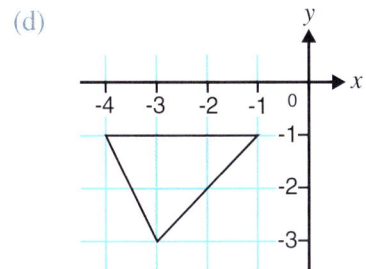

(a)

(b)

(c)

(d)

2 Copy each of the following shapes onto squared paper and then draw the new position of the shape after it has been rotated through 180°, about the point X.

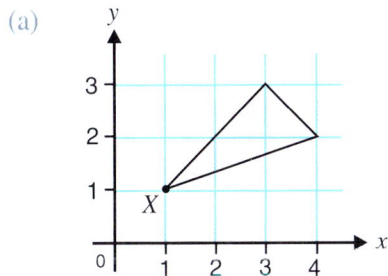

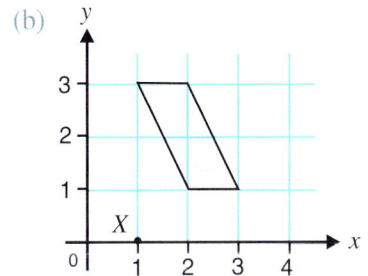

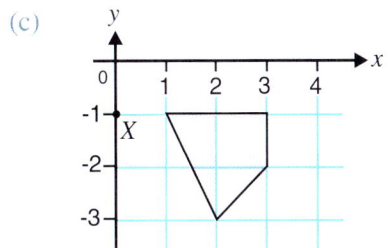

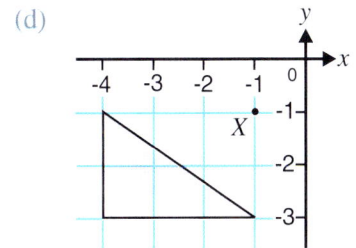

(a)

(b)

(c)

(d)

3 The diagram shows a quadrilateral ABCD.

Give the coordinates of B after:
(a) a rotation through 90°, clockwise about (0, 0),
(b) a rotation through 90°, anticlockwise about (0, 0),
(c) a rotation through 180°, about (0, 0),
(d) a rotation through 90°, clockwise about (3, 1),
(e) a rotation through 90°, anticlockwise about (3, 1),
(f) a rotation through 180°, about (3, 1).

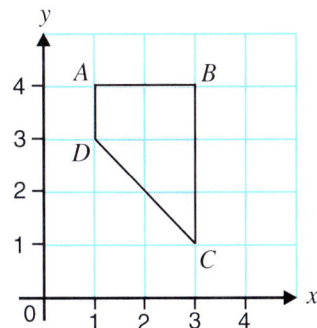

Translation

Look at this diagram.
It shows a **translation** of a shape with vector $\begin{pmatrix} 2 \\ -1 \end{pmatrix}$.

The shape P_1 is the image of the shape P.
P is mapped onto P_1.

All points on the shape P are moved the same distance in the same direction without twisting or turning.

A **vector** can be used to describe a translation.
The top number describes the **horizontal** part of the movement:

$+$ = to the right, $-$ = to the left

The bottom number describes the **vertical** part of the movement:

$+$ = upwards $-$ = downwards

When a shape is translated it stays the same shape and size and has the same orientation.

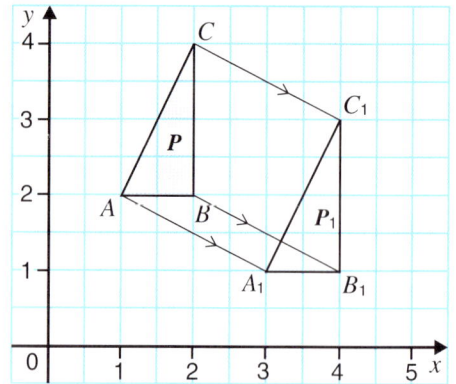

$A\ (1,\ 2) \rightarrow A_1\ (3,\ 1)$
$B\ (2,\ 2) \rightarrow B_1\ (4,\ 1)$
$C\ (2,\ 4) \rightarrow C_1\ (4,\ 3)$
Can you see a pattern?

EXAMPLE

Copy triangle ABC onto squared paper.

Draw the image of triangle ABC after it has been translated with vector $\begin{pmatrix} -3 \\ 2 \end{pmatrix}$.

Label the image $A_1\ B_1\ C_1$.

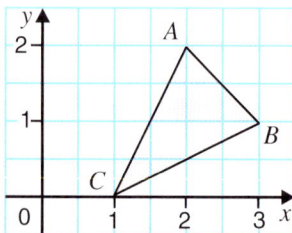

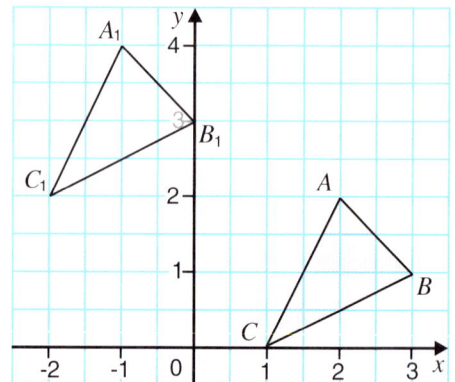

Exercise 25.3

1 Copy the shape onto squared paper.

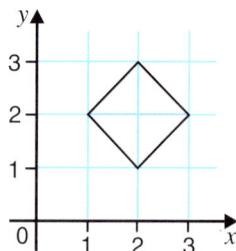

Draw the new position of the shape after each of the following translations.

(a) $\begin{pmatrix} 3 \\ 2 \end{pmatrix}$ (b) $\begin{pmatrix} 2 \\ -3 \end{pmatrix}$

(c) $\begin{pmatrix} -2 \\ 3 \end{pmatrix}$ (d) $\begin{pmatrix} -2 \\ -3 \end{pmatrix}$

2 The diagram shows a quadrilateral $ABCD$.

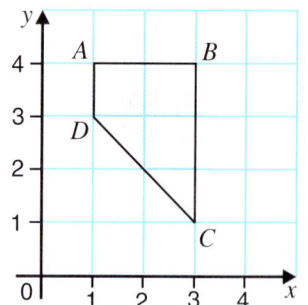

Give the coordinates of B after the shape has been translated with vector:

(a) $\begin{pmatrix} 2 \\ 1 \end{pmatrix}$ (b) $\begin{pmatrix} -2 \\ 2 \end{pmatrix}$

(c) $\begin{pmatrix} 1 \\ -3 \end{pmatrix}$ (d) $\begin{pmatrix} -2 \\ -3 \end{pmatrix}$

3 The translation $\begin{pmatrix} 2 \\ -1 \end{pmatrix}$ maps S (5, 3) onto T.

What are the coordinates of T?

4 Write down the translation which maps:
(a) X (1, 1) onto P (3, 2),   (b) X (1, 1) onto Q (2, −1),
(c) X (1, 1) onto R (−2, 2),   (d) X (1, 1) onto S (−2, −1).

5 The diagram shows quadrilateral S.
Copy S onto squared paper.

(a) The translation $\begin{pmatrix} 3 \\ 2 \end{pmatrix}$ maps S onto T.

     Draw and label T.

(b) Write down the translation which maps T onto S.

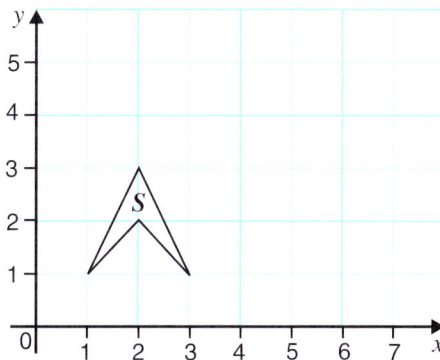

6 The translation $\begin{pmatrix} 2 \\ -1 \end{pmatrix}$ maps P(3, 2) onto Q.

The translation $\begin{pmatrix} -3 \\ 2 \end{pmatrix}$ maps Q onto R.

(a) What are the coordinates of R?
(b) Write down the translation which maps R onto P.

Enlargement

This diagram shows another transformation, called an **enlargement**.
It shows an enlargement with scale factor 2 and centre O.

The shape P_1 is the image of shape P.
P is mapped onto P_1.

When a shape is enlarged:
     angles remain unchanged,
     all **lengths** are multiplied by a **scale factor**.

Scale factor $= \dfrac{\text{new length}}{\text{original length}}$

For an enlargement we need:
     a centre of enlargement,
     a scale factor.

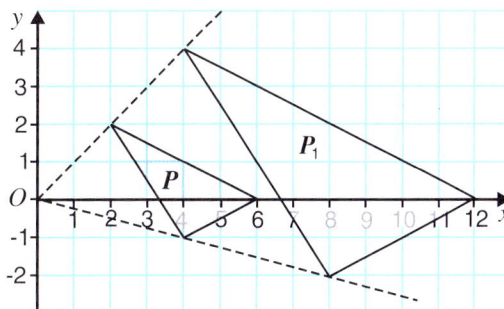

1   Copy the following triangles onto squared paper and draw the enlargement given.

    (a)   Scale factor 2, centre (2, 1).   (b)   Scale factor 3, centre (0, 1).

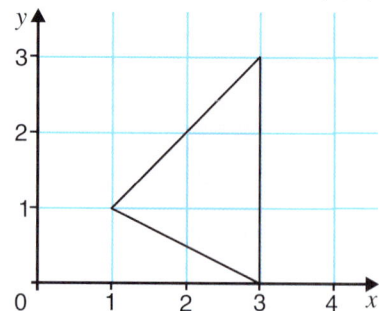

2   Copy the following shapes onto squared paper and draw the enlargement given.

    (a)   Scale factor $\frac{1}{2}$, centre (1, 2).   (b)   Scale factor $\frac{1}{3}$, centre (0, 0).

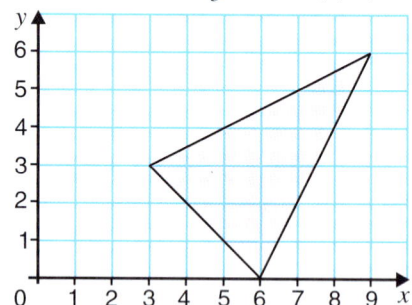

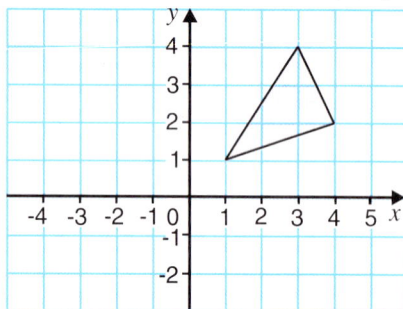

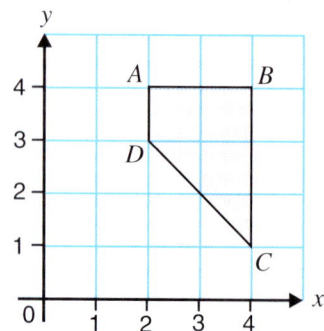

3   Copy the following shapes onto squared paper and draw the enlargement given.

    (a)   Scale factor -1, centre (0, 0).   (b)   Scale factor -2, centre $(-1, 0)$.

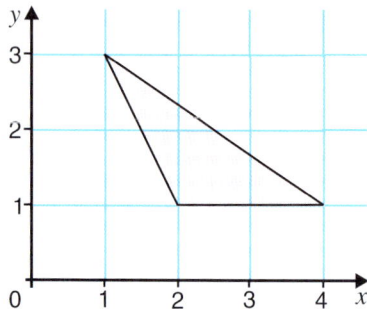

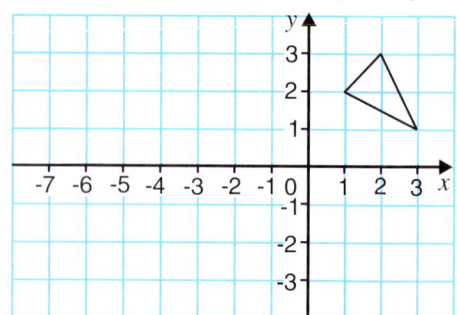

4   The diagram shows a quadrilateral *ABCD*.
      Give the coordinates of *B* after an enlargement:

    (a)   scale factor   2,   centre   (0, 0),

    (b)   scale factor $\frac{1}{2}$,   centre   (0, 0),

    (c)   scale factor -2,   centre   (0, 0),

    (d)   scale factor   3,   centre   *C*(4, 1),

    (e)   scale factor   2,   centre   *D*(2, 3),

    (f)   scale factor -2,   centre   *A*(2, 4),

    (g)   scale factor $-\frac{1}{2}$,   centre   *A*(2, 4),

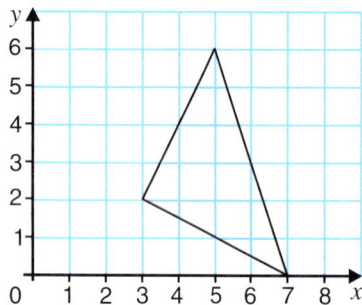

    (h)   scale factor $-\frac{1}{3}$,   centre   *C*(4, 1).

Describing transformations

Look at the shapes in this diagram.

We can describe the single transformation which maps *A* onto *B* as a **reflection** in the line $x = 3$.

We can describe the single transformation which maps *A* onto *C* as a **rotation** of 180° about (2, 1).

We can describe the single transformation which maps *A* onto *D*

as a **translation** with vector $\begin{pmatrix} 2 \\ -3 \end{pmatrix}$.

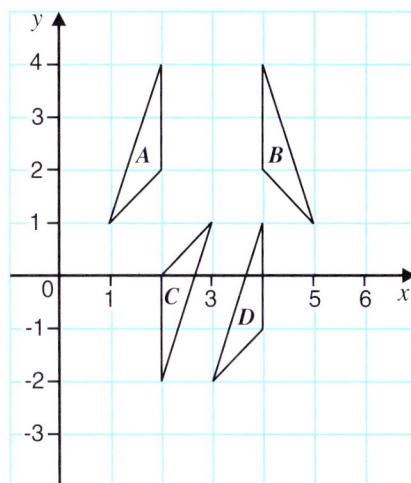

The flow chart below can be used to decide what type of transformation has taken place.
The details required to fully describe each type of transformation are also given.

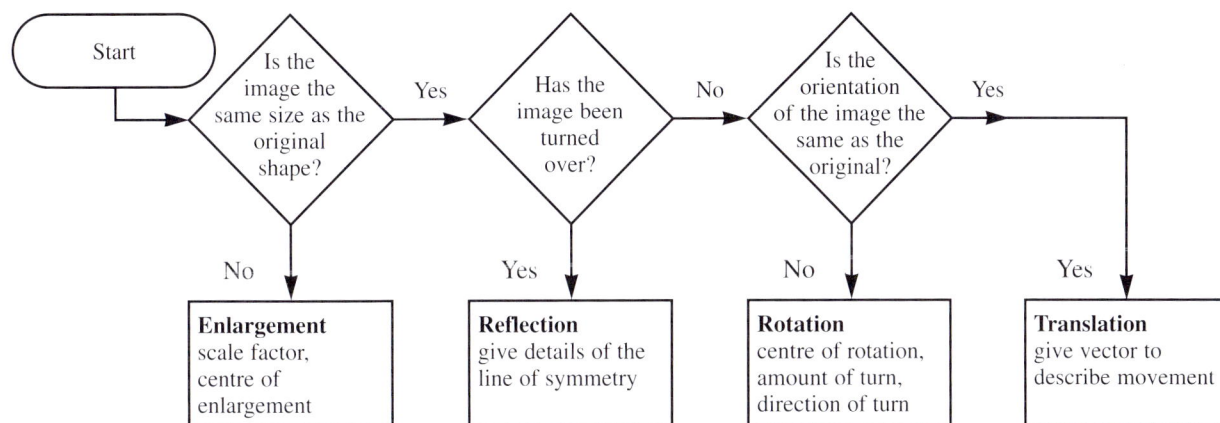

Try following the flow chart for the diagram above.

To find a line of reflection

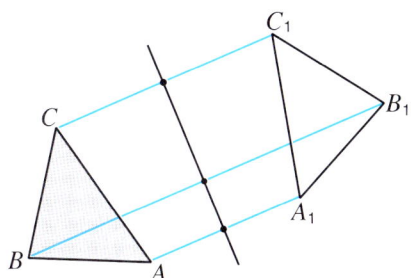

1   Join each point to its image point.
2   Put a mark halfway along each line.
3   Use a ruler to join the marks.

To find the centre and scale factor of an enlargement

This was covered in Chapter 24.
You may wish to look at this work before doing the next exercise.

To find the centre and angle of rotation

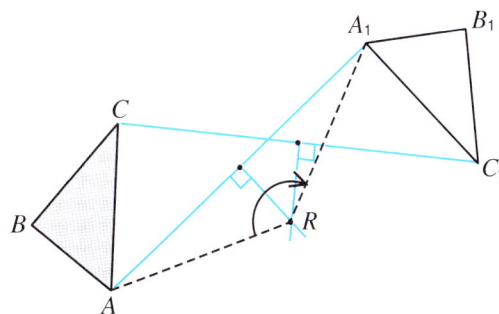

1   Join each point to its image point.
2   Put a mark halfway along each line.
3   Use a set-square to draw a line at right angles to each line. The point where the lines cross is the centre of rotation, *R*.
4   Join one point and its image to the centre of rotation.
5   The angle of rotation is given by the size of the angle ARA_1.

371

1 Describe fully the single transformations which map L onto L_1, L_2, L_3, L_4, L_5 and L_6.

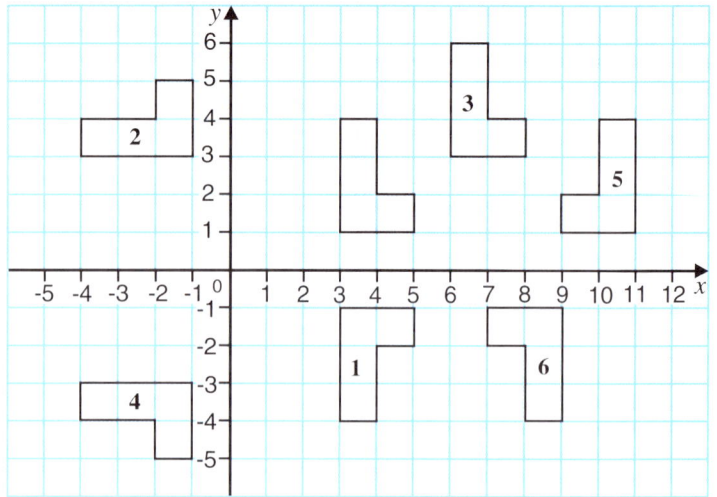

2 Describe fully the single transformation which maps
  (a) T onto U,
  (b) T onto V,
  (c) T onto W.

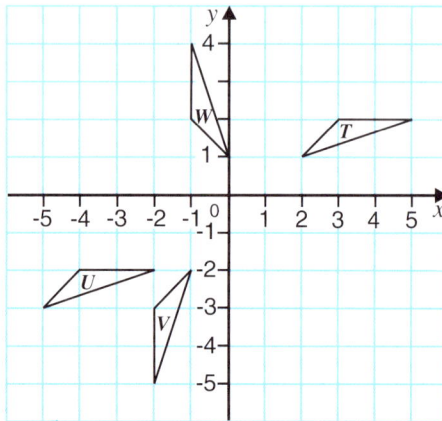

3 Describe fully the single transformation which maps
  (a) A onto B,
  (b) A onto C,
  (c) A onto D.

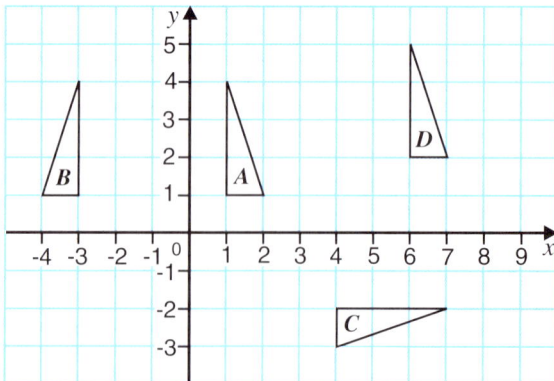

4 Describe the single transformation which maps $ABCD$ onto $PQRS$.

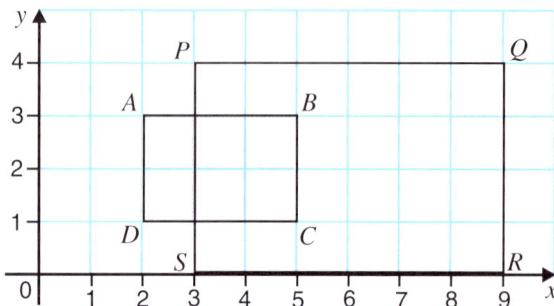

5 Describe fully the single
transformation which maps
ABC onto *XYZ*.

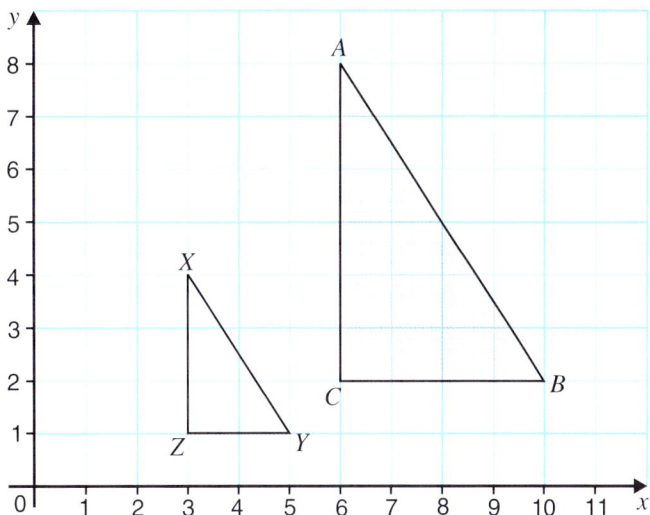

Combinations of transformations

Look at this diagram.

P has been mapped onto P_1 by a
reflection in the *x* axis.

Then P_1 has been mapped onto P_2 by
a reflection in the *y* axis.

Describe the single transformation
which maps P onto P_2.

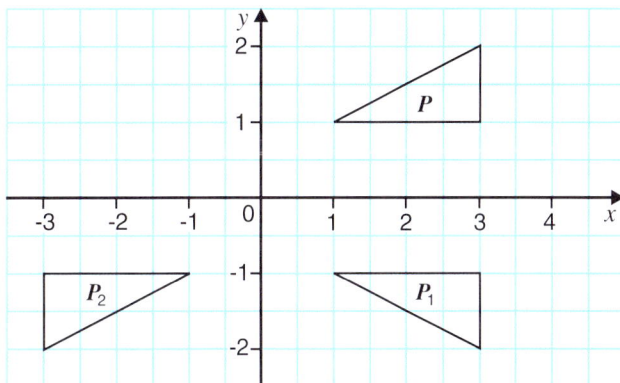

EXAMPLE Copy triangle *Q* onto squared paper.

(a) *Q* is mapped onto Q_1 by a rotation through 90°, clockwise about (0, 0). Draw and label Q_1.
(b) Q_1 is mapped onto Q_2 by a reflection in the line *y* = 0. Draw and label Q_2.
(c) Describe the single transformation which maps *Q* onto Q_2.

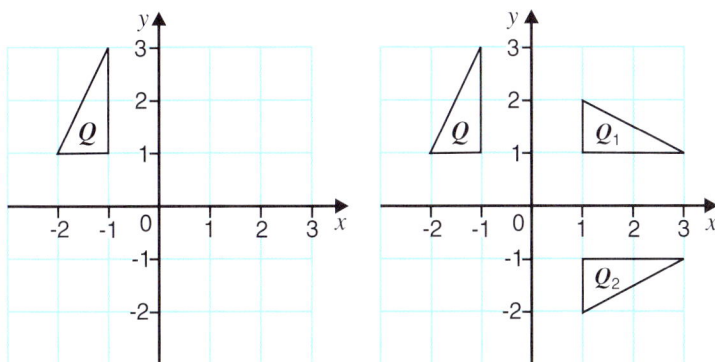

(c) Reflection in the line *y* = *x*.

1 The diagram shows a quadrilateral labelled A.
Copy the diagram onto squared paper.

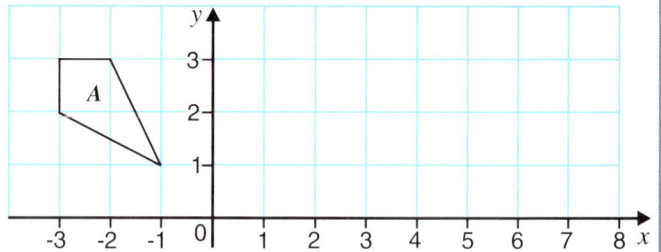

(a) A is mapped onto A_1 by a reflection in the line $x = 0$.
Draw and label A_1.

(b) A_1 is mapped onto A_2 by a reflection in the line $x = 4$.
Draw and label A_2.

(c) Describe fully the single transformation which maps A onto A_2.

2 The diagram shows a triangle labelled P.
Copy the diagram onto squared paper.

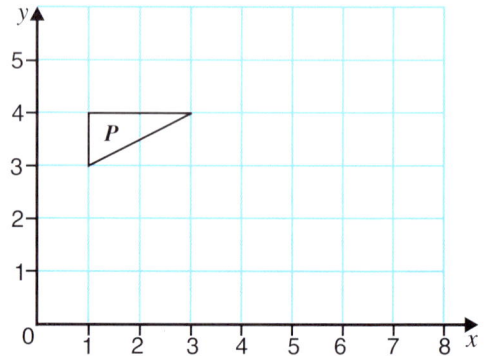

(a) P is mapped onto P_1 by a reflection in the line $y = x$.
Draw and label P_1.

(b) P_1 is mapped onto P_2 by a reflection in the line $x = 5$.
Draw and label P_2.

(c) Describe fully the single transformation which maps P onto P_2.

3 The diagram shows a triangle labelled T.
Copy the diagram onto squared paper.

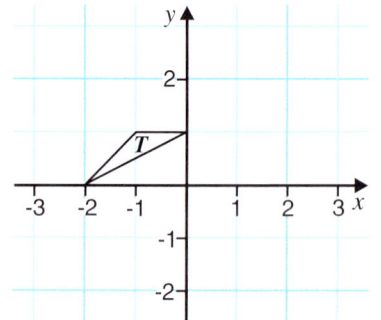

(a) Rotate T through $90°$ clockwise about $(0, 0)$ to T_1.
Draw and label T_1.

(b) Reflect T_1 in the line $y = 0$ to T_2.
Draw and label T_2.

(c) Reflect T_2 in the line $x = 0$ to T_3.
Draw and label T_3.

(d) Describe fully the single transformation which maps T onto T_3.

4 The diagram shows a quadrilateral labelled Q.
Copy the diagram onto squared paper.

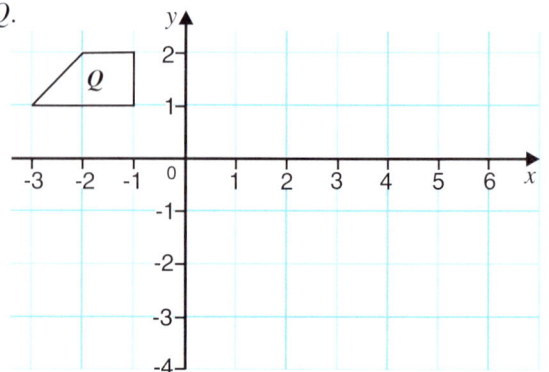

(a) Q is mapped onto Q_1 by a rotation through $90°$, anticlockwise about $(0, 0)$.
Draw and label Q_1.

(b) Q_1 is mapped onto Q_2 by a rotation through $90°$, anticlockwise about $(2, 0)$.
Draw and label Q_2.

(c) Describe fully the single transformation which maps Q onto Q_2.

5 The diagram shows a shape labelled S.
Copy the diagram onto squared paper.

(a) The translation $\begin{pmatrix} 4 \\ 2 \end{pmatrix}$ maps S onto S_1.
Draw and label S_1.

(b) The translation $\begin{pmatrix} -8 \\ 1 \end{pmatrix}$ maps S_1 onto S_2.
Draw and label S_2.

(c) Describe fully the single transformation which maps S onto S_2.

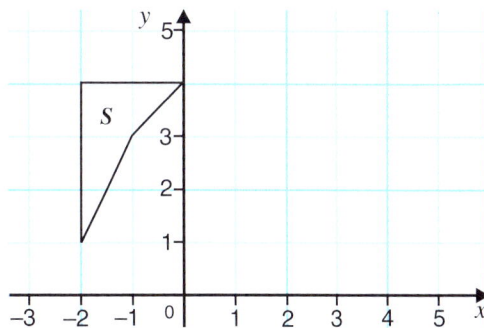

6 The diagram shows a triangle labelled R.
Copy the diagram onto squared paper.

(a) R is mapped onto R_1 by a rotation through $90°$, anticlockwise about $(0, 0)$.
Draw and label R_1.

(b) R_1 is mapped onto R_2 by a reflection in the line $y = -x$.
Draw and label R_2.

(c) R_2 is mapped onto R_3 by a reflection in the line $x = 3$.
Draw and label R_3.

(d) Describe fully the single transformation which maps R onto R_3.

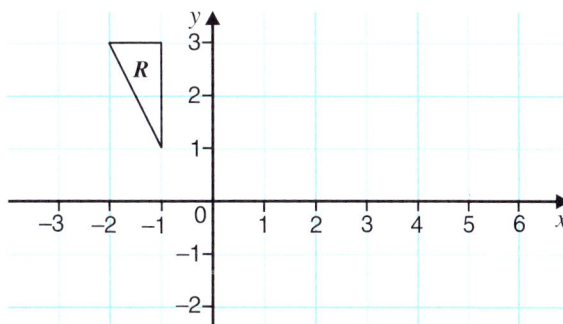

What you need to know

- The movement of a shape from one position to another is called a **transformation**.
- **Single transformations** can be described in terms of a reflection, a rotation, a translation or an enlargement.
- **Reflection**: The image of the shape is the same distance from the mirror line as the original.
- **Rotation**: All points are turned through the same angle about the same point, called a centre of rotation.
- **Translation**: All points are moved the same distance in the same direction without twisting or turning.
- **Enlargement**: This topic was first covered in Chapter 24 as an introduction to similar figures.
- How to fully describe a transformation.

Transformation	Image has equal angles?	Image same shape and size?	Details needed to describe the transformation
Reflection	Yes	Yes	Mirror line, sometimes given as an equation.
Rotation	Yes	Yes	Centre of rotation, amount of turn, direction of turn.
Translation	Yes	Yes	Vector: Top number = horizontal movement, bottom number = vertical movement.
Enlargement	Yes	No	Centre of enlargement, scale factor.

1 The position of a square, *ABCD*, is shown.

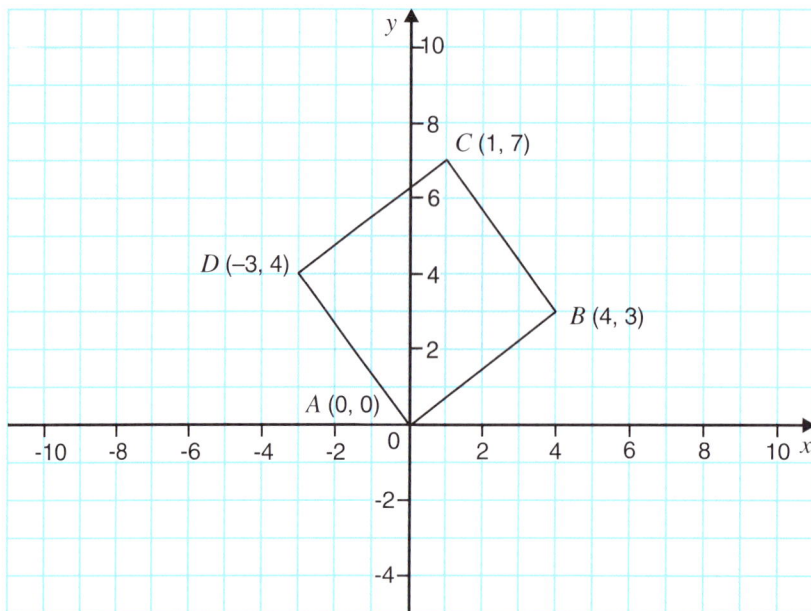

(a) *ABCD* is reflected in the line $x = 4$, to $A_1 B_1 C_1 D_1$.
What are the coordinates of C_1?

(b) *ABCD* is rotated 90° anticlockwise about *A*, to $A_2 B_2 C_2 D_2$.
What are the coordinates of B_2?

(c) The translation $\begin{pmatrix} -3 \\ -2 \end{pmatrix}$ takes *ABCD* to $A_3 B_3 C_3 D_3$.
What are the coordinates of D_3?

(d) *ABCD* is enlarged by scale factor 2, centre *A*.
What are the new coordinates of *B*?

2 The diagram shows triangles *P*, *Q*, *R*, *S* and *T*.

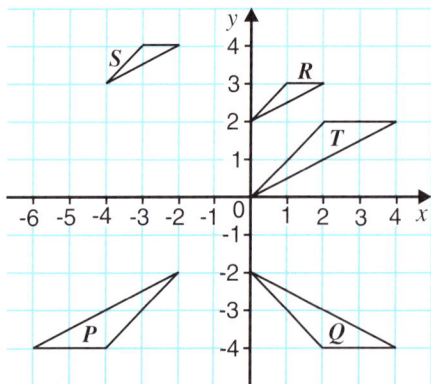

Describe fully the single transformation which maps

(a) *P* onto *Q*,   (b) *T* onto *Q*,
(c) *R* onto *S*,   (d) *S* onto *R*,
(e) *R* onto *T*,   (f) *T* onto *R*.

3 The diagram shows a kite labelled *K*.

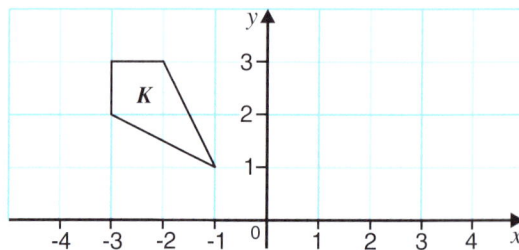

Copy the diagram onto squared paper.

(a) The translation $\begin{pmatrix} 3 \\ -1 \end{pmatrix}$ maps *K* onto K_1.
Draw and label K_1.

(b) Describe the single transformation which maps K_1 onto *K*.

4 The diagram shows a rectangle $ABCD$.

(a) The rectangle $ABCD$ is rotated about the vertex A to a new position $AB_1C_1D_1$. The coordinates of B_1 are $(-2, 1)$. What are the coordinates of C_1?

(b) The rectangle $ABCD$ is reflected in the line $x = 2$ onto $A_2 B_2 C_2 D_2$. What are the coordinates of C_2?

(c) The rectangle $ABCD$ is enlarged with scale factor 2 from the centre A (1, 1) onto $AB_3 C_3 D_3$. What are the coordinates of C_3?

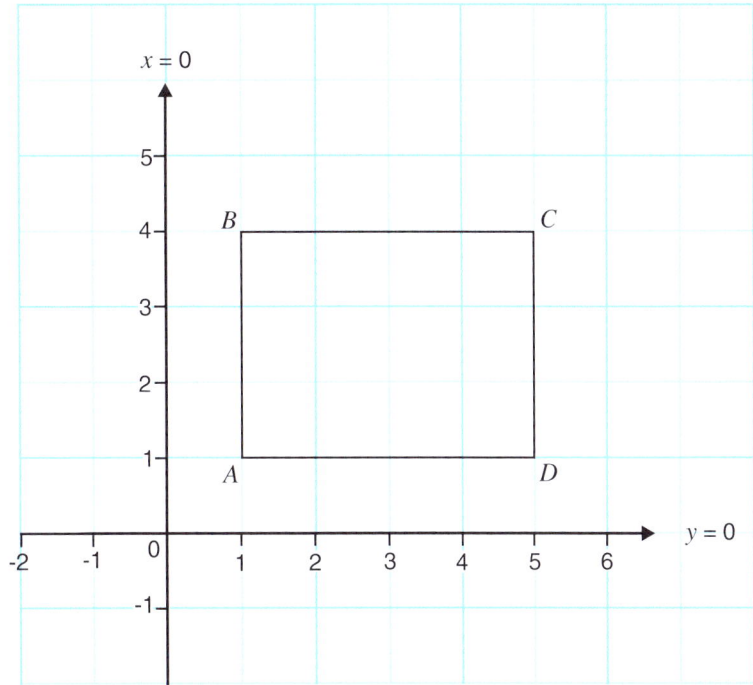

$x = 0$

$y = 0$

SEG 1991

5 The diagram shows two transformations of the shaded rectangle $PQRS$. Describe fully the single transformation which takes:

(a) $PQRS$ onto $P_1 Q_1 R_1 S_1$.

(b) $PQRS$ onto $P_2 Q_2 R_2 S_2$.

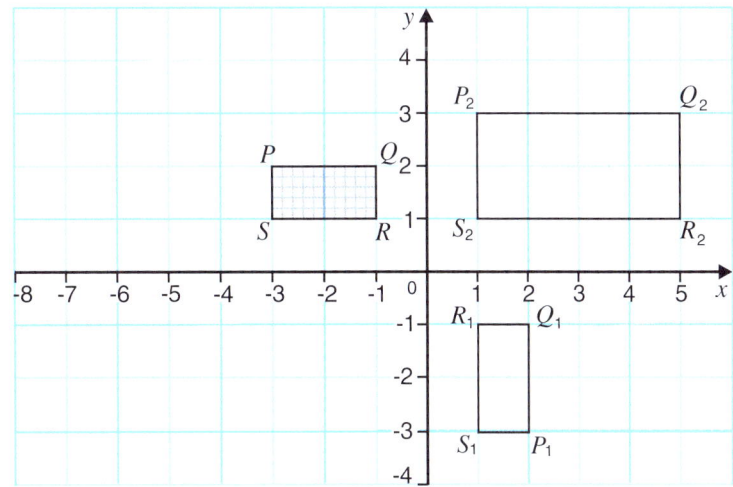

SEG 1998 S

6 The diagram shows shape A. Copy the diagram onto squared paper.

(a) Reflect shape A in the line $x = 3$. Label its new position B.

(b) Rotate shape A through $90°$ anticlockwise about centre (1, 0). Label its new position C.

(c) Another triangle, D, has vertices $(-3, 3)$, $(-5, 5)$ and $(-2, 6)$. Describe fully the **single** transformation which will take A onto D.

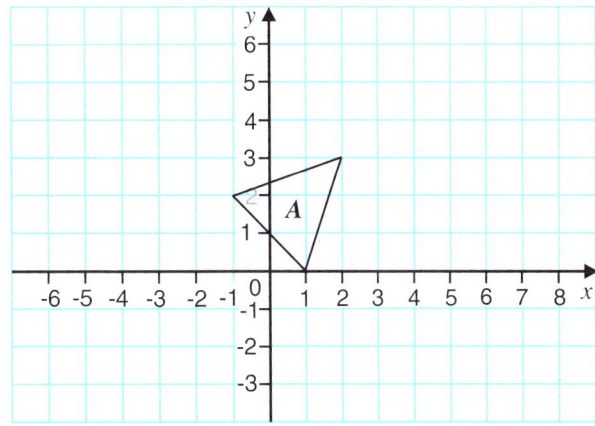

SEG 1998

7 Copy the diagram onto squared paper.
Enlarge A by a scale factor of -2, centre $(1, 2)$.

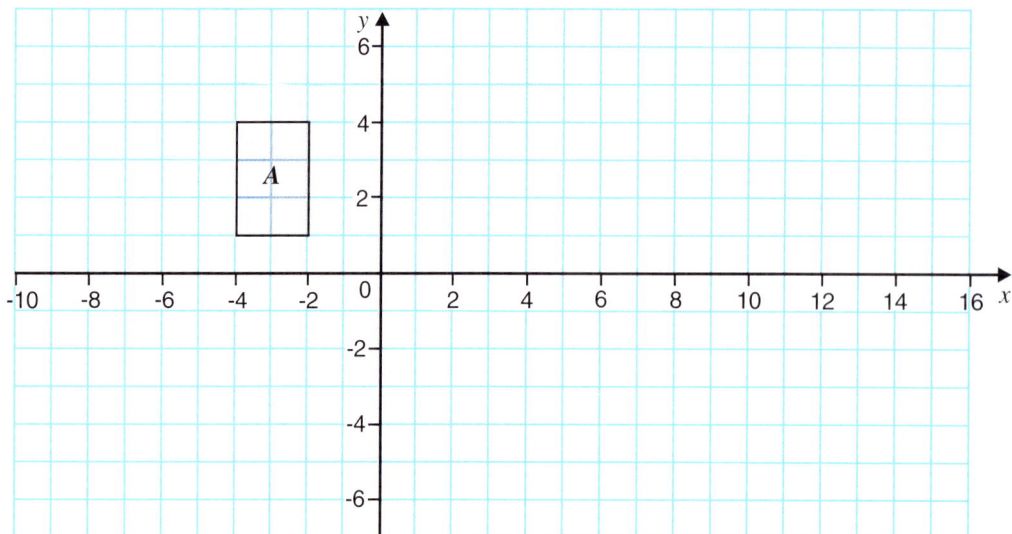

8 The diagram shows the positions of two parallelograms, $ABCD$ and $A_1 B_1 C_1 D_1$.

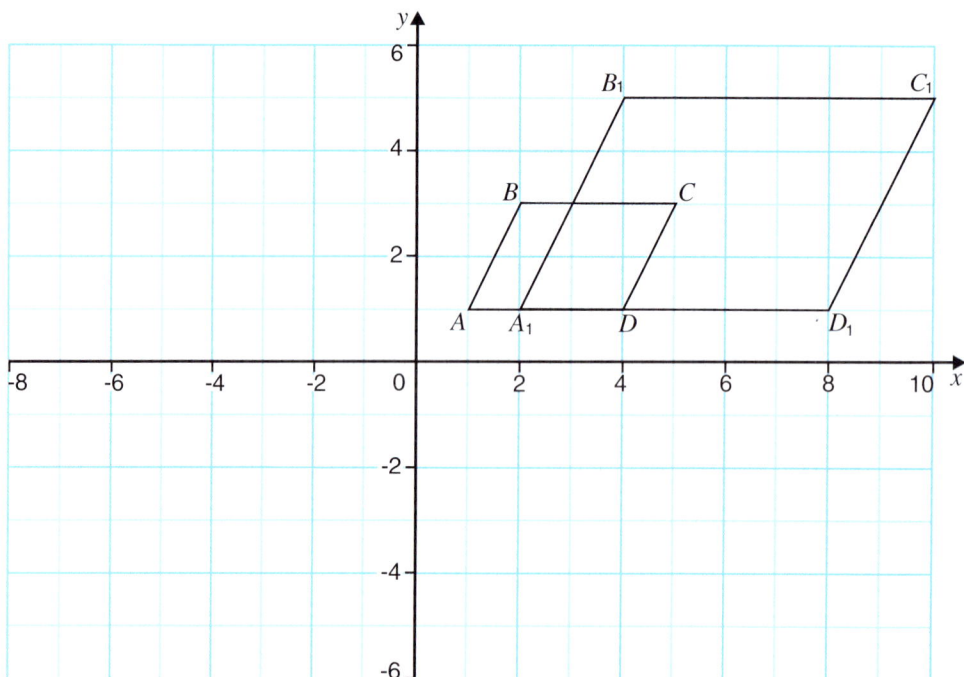

(a) Describe fully the single transformation which takes $A_1 B_1 C_1 D_1$ onto $ABCD$.

Copy the diagram onto squared paper.

(b) Rotate $ABCD$ through $180°$ about $(1, 0)$ to $A_2 B_2 C_2 D_2$.
Draw and label $A_2 B_2 C_2 D_2$.

(c) Rotate $ABCD$ through $180°$ about $(-1, 0)$ to $A_3 B_3 C_3 D_3$.
Draw and label $A_3 B_3 C_3 D_3$.

(d) Describe fully a single transformation which will take $A_3 B_3 C_3 D_3$ onto $A_2 B_2 C_2 D_2$.

9 The diagram shows a triangle labelled A. Copy the diagram onto squared paper.

(a) A is mapped onto A_1 by a reflection in the line $x = 0$. Draw and label A_1.

(b) A_1 is mapped onto A_2 by a reflection in the line $y = x$. Draw and label A_2.

(c) Describe fully the single transformation which maps A onto A_2.

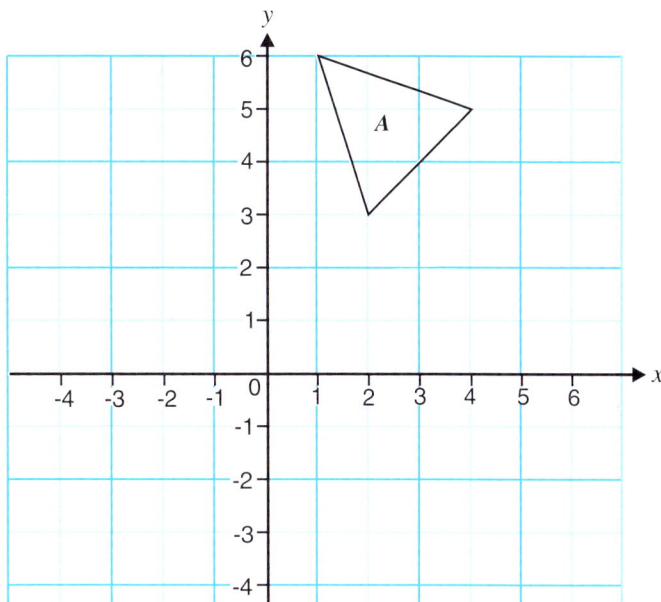

10 The diagram shows a trapezium labelled Q. Copy the diagram onto squared paper.

(a) Q is mapped onto Q_1 by a reflection in the x axis. Draw and label Q_1.

(b) Q_1 is mapped onto Q_2 by a translation with vector $\begin{pmatrix} 2 \\ 4 \end{pmatrix}$. Draw and label Q_2.

(c) Q_2 is mapped onto Q_3 by a reflection in the line $y = x$. Draw and label Q_3.

(d) Describe fully the single transformation which maps Q onto Q_3.

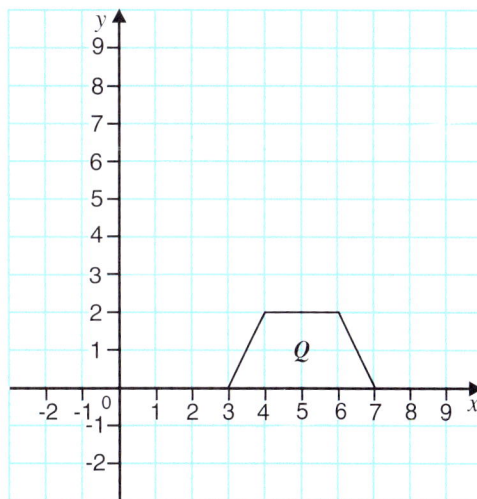

11 The diagram shows three triangles A, B and C.

(a) Describe fully the single transformation which maps triangle A onto triangle B.

(b) Describe fully the single transformation which maps triangle B onto triangle C.

(c) P is a clockwise rotation of $90°$ with centre $(3, -2)$. Q is a reflection in the line $y = x - 1$. Triangle B maps onto triangle D by P followed by Q. Draw triangle D on the diagram.

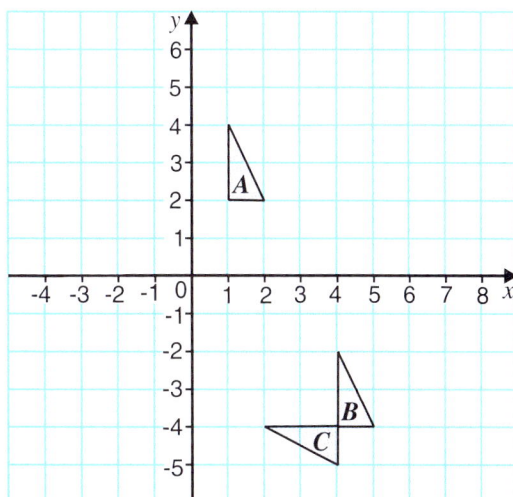

CHAPTER 26

Vectors

Activity

1 Tom and Sam start at the same point and walk in a different direction for 100 m.
They both end up exactly where they started.
Explain how.

2 Tom and Sam start at the same point and walk in different directions in a straight line for 20 m.
Explain how they end up in the same place.

Vectors and scalars

In the activity the directions in which Tom and Sam move are as important as how far they move.
Quantities which have both **size** and **direction** are called **vectors**.
Examples of vector quantities are:

Displacement	**Velocity**
A combination of distance and direction	A combination of speed and direction

Quantities which have size only are called **scalars**.
Examples of scalar quantities are: distance, area, speed, mass, volume, temperature, etc.

Vector notation

Column vectors
In Chapter 25 vectors are used to describe translations.

The diagram shows the translation of a triangle by the vector $\begin{pmatrix} 3 \\ 2 \end{pmatrix}$.

The triangle has been displaced 3 units to the right and 2 units up.

$\begin{pmatrix} 3 \\ 2 \end{pmatrix}$ gives information about the size and direction of the displacement.

The vector $\begin{pmatrix} 3 \\ 2 \end{pmatrix}$ is sometimes called a **column vector**, because it consists of one column of numbers.

Directed line segments
Vectors can be represented in diagrams using **line segments**.
The **length** of a line represents the **size of the vector**.
The **direction of the vector** is shown by an **arrow**.

Labelling vectors

The notation $\overrightarrow{AB}$, $\overrightarrow{CD}$, $\overrightarrow{OX}$, … is often used.

$\overrightarrow{AB}$ indicates the displacement from A to B.

$\overrightarrow{AB}$ should be read "vector AB".

Bold lower case letters such as **a**, **b**, **c**, … are also used.
In hand-written work **a** should be written as <u>a</u>.
a and <u>a</u> should both be read "vector a".

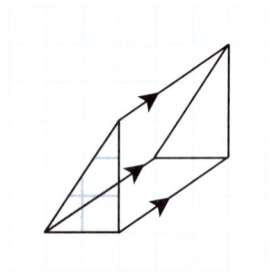

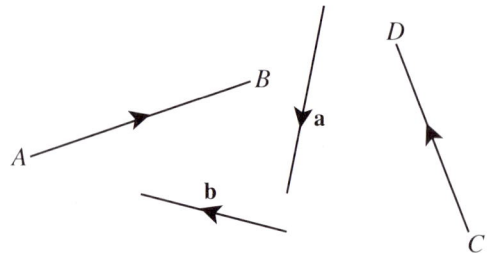

EXAMPLES

1 The points A, B and C are marked on the grid.

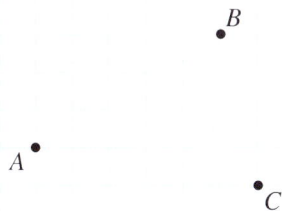

$\bullet\, B$

$A\, \bullet$

$\bullet\, C$

Write as column vectors.

(a) $\overrightarrow{AB}$ (b) $\overrightarrow{BC}$

(a) The displacement from A to B is:
$\begin{pmatrix} 5 \text{ units to the right} \\ 3 \text{ units upwards} \end{pmatrix}$

So $\overrightarrow{AB} = \begin{pmatrix} 5 \\ 3 \end{pmatrix}$

(b) The displacement from B to C is:
$\begin{pmatrix} 1 \text{ unit to the right} \\ 4 \text{ units downwards} \end{pmatrix}$

So $\overrightarrow{BC} = \begin{pmatrix} 1 \\ -4 \end{pmatrix}$

2 Draw and label the following vectors.

(a) $\mathbf{a} = \begin{pmatrix} -2 \\ 3 \end{pmatrix}$ (b) $\mathbf{b} = \begin{pmatrix} 3 \\ -2 \end{pmatrix}$

(c) $\overrightarrow{AB} = \begin{pmatrix} -4 \\ -2 \end{pmatrix}$

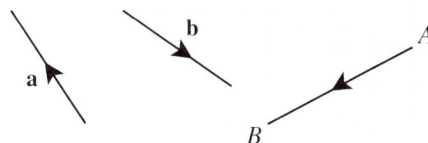

Exercise 26.1

1 On squared paper, draw and label the following vectors.

(a) $\mathbf{a} = \begin{pmatrix} -5 \\ 2 \end{pmatrix}$ (b) $\mathbf{b} = \begin{pmatrix} 5 \\ -2 \end{pmatrix}$ (c) $\mathbf{c} = \begin{pmatrix} -5 \\ -2 \end{pmatrix}$ (d) $\mathbf{d} = \begin{pmatrix} 5 \\ 2 \end{pmatrix}$

2 Mark the point O on squared paper.

(a) Draw and label the following vectors.

(i) $\overrightarrow{OA} = \begin{pmatrix} 2 \\ 4 \end{pmatrix}$ (ii) $\overrightarrow{OB} = \begin{pmatrix} 4 \\ 2 \end{pmatrix}$ (iii) $\overrightarrow{OC} = \begin{pmatrix} 4 \\ -2 \end{pmatrix}$ (iv) $\overrightarrow{OD} = \begin{pmatrix} 2 \\ -4 \end{pmatrix}$

(v) $\overrightarrow{OE} = \begin{pmatrix} -2 \\ -4 \end{pmatrix}$ (vi) $\overrightarrow{OF} = \begin{pmatrix} -4 \\ -2 \end{pmatrix}$ (vii) $\overrightarrow{OG} = \begin{pmatrix} -4 \\ 2 \end{pmatrix}$ (viii) $\overrightarrow{OH} = \begin{pmatrix} -2 \\ 4 \end{pmatrix}$

(b) Draw the polygon $ABCDEFGH$. Write each of the following as column vectors.

(i) $\overrightarrow{AB}$ (ii) $\overrightarrow{BC}$ (iii) $\overrightarrow{CD}$ (iv) $\overrightarrow{DE}$

(v) $\overrightarrow{EF}$ (vi) $\overrightarrow{FG}$ (vii) $\overrightarrow{GH}$ (viii) $\overrightarrow{HA}$

3 Write each of these vectors as column vectors.

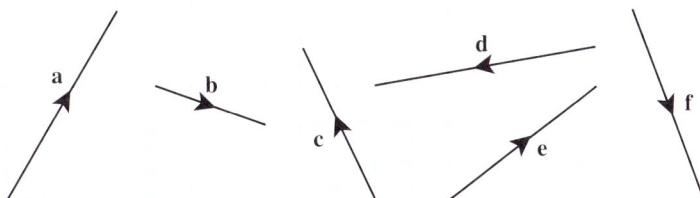

4 The diagram shows all of the different ways that a knight can move on a chess board.

(a) Describe each of the moves as a column vector.

(b) A, B, C and D are the corner squares of the chess board.
A knight starts at A and visits B, C and D and then returns to A.
Use column vectors to describe the shortest possible journey that the knight can make.

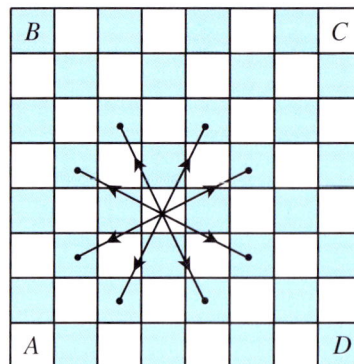

Equal vectors

The diagram shows three vectors, $\overrightarrow{AB}$, $\overrightarrow{PQ}$ and $\overrightarrow{XY}$.

$$\overrightarrow{AB} = \binom{5}{2} \qquad \overrightarrow{PQ} = \binom{5}{2} \qquad \overrightarrow{XY} = \binom{5}{2}$$

The column vectors are equal, so $\overrightarrow{AB} = \overrightarrow{PQ} = \overrightarrow{XY}$.

> Vectors are **equal** if:
> they have the same length, **and**
> they are in the same direction.

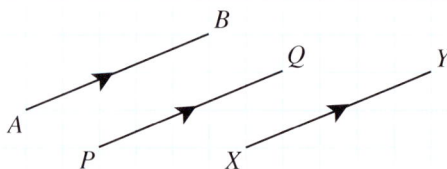

Vectors in opposite directions

The diagram shows two vectors, **a** and **b**.
The vectors are equal in length, **but** are in opposite directions.

> Vectors **a** and −**a** have the same length,
> **but** are in opposite directions.

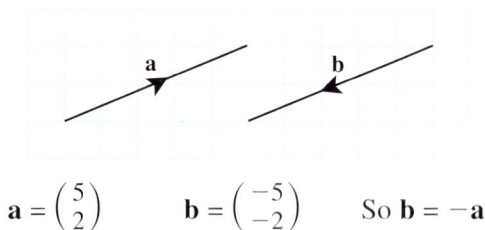

$$\mathbf{a} = \binom{5}{2} \qquad \mathbf{b} = \binom{-5}{-2} \qquad \text{So } \mathbf{b} = -\mathbf{a}$$

Multiplying a vector by a scalar

The diagram shows three vectors, **a**, **b** and **c**.

$$\mathbf{a} = \binom{4}{-2} \qquad \mathbf{b} = \binom{8}{-4} \qquad \mathbf{c} = \binom{2}{-1}$$

a and **b** are in the same direction.

$$\mathbf{b} = \binom{8}{-4} = \binom{2 \times 4}{2 \times -2}$$

This can be written as $\mathbf{b} = 2 \times \binom{4}{-2}$

So $\mathbf{b} = 2\mathbf{a}$.
This means that **b** is twice the length of **a**.

b and **c** are in the same direction.

$$\mathbf{b} = \binom{8}{-4} = 4 \times \binom{2}{-1} = 4\mathbf{c}$$

This means that **b** is 4 times as long as **c**.

a and **c** are in the same direction.
$\mathbf{c} = \frac{1}{2}\mathbf{a}$.
This means that **c** is half the length of **a**.

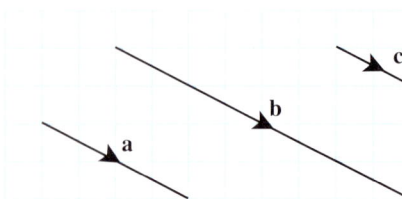

> **a** and $n\mathbf{a}$ are vectors in the same direction.
> The length of vector $n\mathbf{a} = n \times$ the length of vector **a**.

382

EXAMPLE

The diagram shows five vectors: **a**, **b**, **c**, **d** and **e**.

(a) Write each of **a**, **b**, **c**, **d** and **e** as column vectors.

(b) Express each of **b**, **c**, **d** and **e** in terms of **a**.

(a) $\mathbf{a} = \begin{pmatrix} -2 \\ 4 \end{pmatrix}$ $\mathbf{b} = \begin{pmatrix} -4 \\ 8 \end{pmatrix}$ $\mathbf{c} = \begin{pmatrix} 2 \\ -4 \end{pmatrix}$

$\mathbf{d} = \begin{pmatrix} -1 \\ 2 \end{pmatrix}$ $\mathbf{e} = \begin{pmatrix} 4 \\ -8 \end{pmatrix}$

(b) **b** is twice the length of **a** and in the same direction.

$\mathbf{b} = 2\mathbf{a}$

c is the same length as **a** but in the opposite direction.

$\mathbf{c} = -\mathbf{a}$

d is half the length of **a** and in the same direction.

$\mathbf{d} = \frac{1}{2}\mathbf{a}$

e is twice the length of **a** but in the opposite direction.

$\mathbf{e} = -2\mathbf{a}$

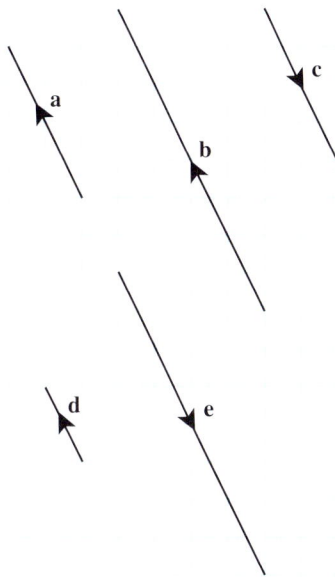

Exercise 26.2

1 The points X, Y and Z are marked on the grid.
On squared paper, draw each of the vectors **a** to **h**, where

$\mathbf{a} = 2\overrightarrow{XY},$ $\mathbf{b} = -\overrightarrow{XY},$

$\mathbf{c} = 3\overrightarrow{XY},$ $\mathbf{d} = \overrightarrow{YX},$

$\mathbf{e} = 2\overrightarrow{XZ},$ $\mathbf{f} = 2\overrightarrow{ZX},$

$\mathbf{g} = -2\overrightarrow{ZY},$ $\mathbf{h} = 3\overrightarrow{YZ}.$

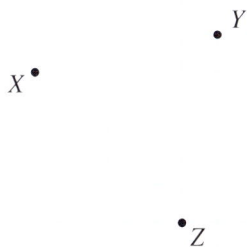

2 This diagram shows three vectors, labelled **p**, **q** and **r**.

In the diagram below which vectors
can be expressed in the form:

(i) $n\mathbf{p}$,   (ii) $n\mathbf{q}$,   (iii) $n\mathbf{r}$?
For each vector give the value of n.

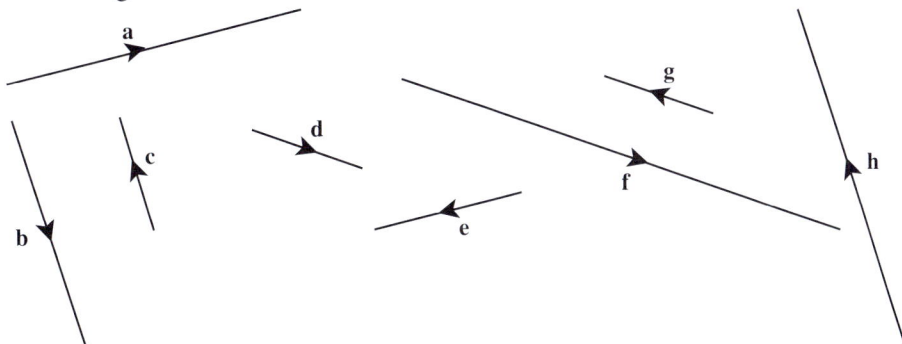

3 $\quad \mathbf{a} = \begin{pmatrix} 2 \\ -1 \end{pmatrix} \qquad \mathbf{b} = \begin{pmatrix} -1 \\ 4 \end{pmatrix} \qquad \mathbf{c} = \begin{pmatrix} -3 \\ -1 \end{pmatrix} \qquad \mathbf{d} = \begin{pmatrix} -1 \\ 2 \end{pmatrix}$

On squared paper draw vectors to represent the following.
(a) 2**a**   (b) 2**b**   (c) 3**a**   (d) −**a**
(e) 2**c**   (f) −2**d**   (g) −4**b**   (h) 5**d**

Vector addition

The diagram shows the points A, B and C.
Start at A and move to B.
Then move from B to C.

The combination of these two displacements is
equivalent to a total displacement from A to C.
This can be written using vectors as

$$\overrightarrow{AB} + \overrightarrow{BC} = \overrightarrow{AC}$$

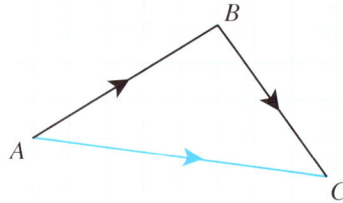

$\overrightarrow{AC}$ is called the **resultant vector**.

Using column vectors
$\overrightarrow{AB} = \begin{pmatrix} 5 \\ 3 \end{pmatrix}$, $\overrightarrow{BC} = \begin{pmatrix} 3 \\ -4 \end{pmatrix}$ and $\overrightarrow{AC} = \begin{pmatrix} 8 \\ -1 \end{pmatrix}$

The resultant vector, $\overrightarrow{AC}$, is a combination of:

$\begin{pmatrix} 5 \text{ units right followed by 3 units right} \\ 3 \text{ units up followed by 4 units down} \end{pmatrix} = \begin{pmatrix} 8 \text{ units right} \\ 1 \text{ unit down} \end{pmatrix}$

$\overrightarrow{AB} + \overrightarrow{BC} = \overrightarrow{AC}$

$\begin{pmatrix} 5 \\ 3 \end{pmatrix} + \begin{pmatrix} 3 \\ -4 \end{pmatrix} = \begin{pmatrix} 5 + 3 \\ 3 + -4 \end{pmatrix} = \begin{pmatrix} 8 \\ -1 \end{pmatrix}$

> *Use vector addition to show that:*
> $$\overrightarrow{AB} + \overrightarrow{BC} = \overrightarrow{BC} + \overrightarrow{AB} = \overrightarrow{AC}.$$

Vector diagrams

Diagrams can be drawn to show the combination of any number
of vectors.
To combine vectors when the vectors are not joined, draw equal
vectors so that the second vector joins the end of the first vector.

> **Note**
> **With** the arrow = +
> **Against** the arrow = −

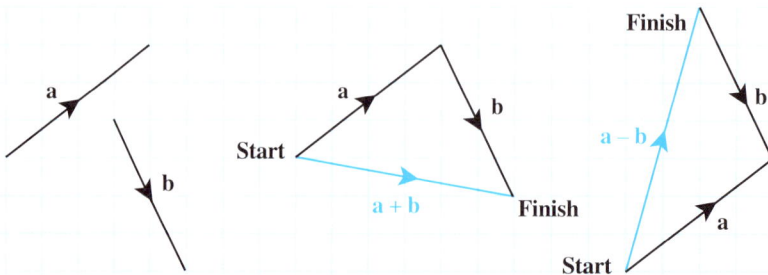

With the arrow, +**a**
With the arrow, +**b**
Resultant vector, **a** + **b**

With the arrow, +**a**
Against the arrow, −**b**
Resultant vector, **a** − **b**

EXAMPLES

1 **a**, **b** and **c** are three vectors as shown in the diagram.

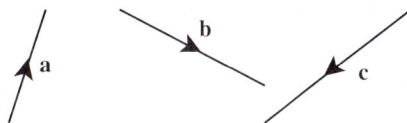

Draw diagrams to show
(a) **a + 2b** (b) **a − 2c** (c) **a + 2b − c**

(a) **a + 2b**

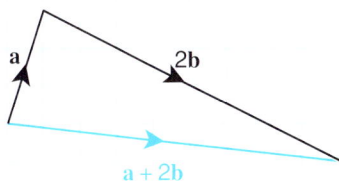

(b) **a – 2c**

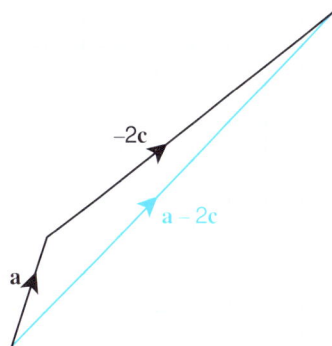

(c) **a + 2b – c**

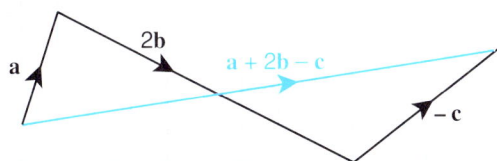

Draw a vector diagram to show that:
a + b = b + a

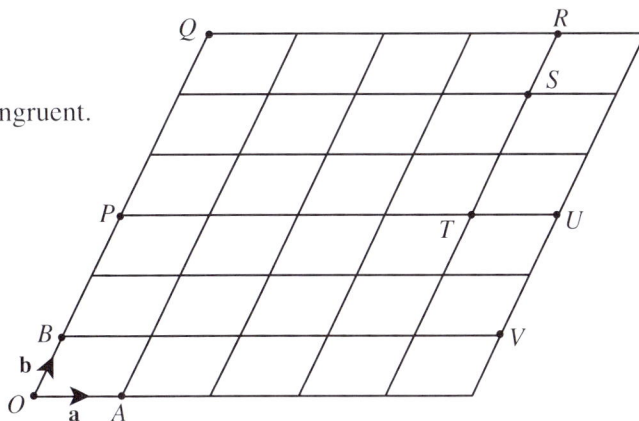

2 The parallelograms on this grid are congruent.
$\overrightarrow{OA} = $ **a** and $\overrightarrow{OB} = $ **b**.

Write in terms of **a** and **b**:

(a) $\overrightarrow{PQ}$ (b) $\overrightarrow{PT}$

(c) $\overrightarrow{TP}$ (d) $\overrightarrow{PS}$

(e) $\overrightarrow{QS}$ (f) $\overrightarrow{TS} + \overrightarrow{SV}$

(g) $\overrightarrow{PT} + \overrightarrow{SU}$

(a) $\overrightarrow{PQ}$ is in the same direction as $\overrightarrow{OB}$ and three times as long.

$\overrightarrow{PQ} = 3\mathbf{b}$

(b) $\overrightarrow{PT}$ is in the same direction as $\overrightarrow{OA}$ and four times as long.

$\overrightarrow{PT} = 4\mathbf{a}$

(c) $\overrightarrow{TP}$ is equal in length to $\overrightarrow{PT}$ but is in the opposite direction.

$\overrightarrow{TP} = -4\mathbf{a}$

(d) $\overrightarrow{PS} = \overrightarrow{PT} + \overrightarrow{TS}$
$= 4\mathbf{a} + 2\mathbf{b}$

(e) $\overrightarrow{QS} = \overrightarrow{QR} + \overrightarrow{RS}$
$= 4\mathbf{a} - \mathbf{b}$

(f) $\overrightarrow{TS} + \overrightarrow{SV}$
$\overrightarrow{SV} = \mathbf{a} - 4\mathbf{b}$
$\overrightarrow{TS} + \overrightarrow{SV} = 2\mathbf{b} + \mathbf{a} - 4\mathbf{b}$
$= \mathbf{a} - 2\mathbf{b}$

(g) $\overrightarrow{PT} + \overrightarrow{SU}$
$\overrightarrow{SU} = \mathbf{a} - 2\mathbf{b}$
$\overrightarrow{PT} + \overrightarrow{SU} = 4\mathbf{a} + \mathbf{a} - 2\mathbf{b}$
$= 5\mathbf{a} - 2\mathbf{b}$

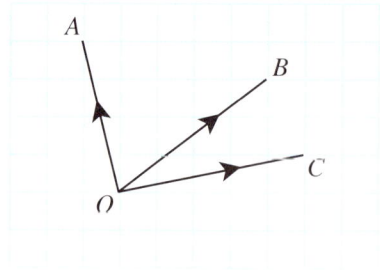

1. $\overrightarrow{OA} = \begin{pmatrix} -1 \\ 4 \end{pmatrix}$, $\overrightarrow{OB} = \begin{pmatrix} 4 \\ 3 \end{pmatrix}$, $\overrightarrow{OC} = \begin{pmatrix} 5 \\ 1 \end{pmatrix}$.

    (a) (i) Draw $\overrightarrow{OD}$ where $\overrightarrow{OD} = \overrightarrow{OA} + \overrightarrow{OB}$.

    (ii) Draw $\overrightarrow{OE}$ where $\overrightarrow{OE} = 2\overrightarrow{OA} + \overrightarrow{OC}$.

    (iii) Draw $\overrightarrow{OF}$ where $\overrightarrow{OF} = 2\overrightarrow{OB} - \overrightarrow{OC}$.

    (iv) Draw $\overrightarrow{OG}$ where $\overrightarrow{OG} = 2\overrightarrow{BO} + 3\overrightarrow{OA}$.

    (b) Draw vector diagrams to show the resultant of:

    (i) $\overrightarrow{OA} + \overrightarrow{OB}$ (ii) $\overrightarrow{OC} - \overrightarrow{OB}$

2. (a) Copy and complete the following.

    (a) $\overrightarrow{AB} + \overrightarrow{BI} = \overrightarrow{AI}$

    (b) $\overrightarrow{AB} + \overrightarrow{AO} = ?$

    (c) $\overrightarrow{TQ} - \overrightarrow{CQ} = ?$

    (d) $\overrightarrow{GR} + \overrightarrow{SW} = ?$

    (e) $\overrightarrow{HG} - \overrightarrow{SY} = ?$

    (f) $\overrightarrow{GK} + \overrightarrow{MT} = ?$

    (g) $\overrightarrow{CL} - \overrightarrow{AW} = ?$

    (h) $\overrightarrow{BP} - \overrightarrow{OV} = ?$

E	F	K	P	U
D	G	L	Q	V
C	H	M	R	W
B	I	N	S	X
A	J	O	T	Y

3. The diagram below shows vectors **a**, **b** and **c**.

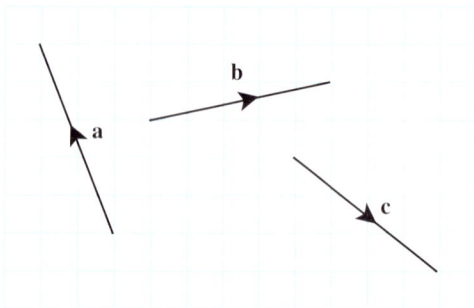

    Match the following vectors to those in the diagram opposite.

    (a) **a** + **b**
    (b) **a** − **b**
    (c) **b** + **c**
    (d) **b** − **c**
    (e) **a** + **b** − **c**
    (f) **a** + 2**b**
    (g) −2**a** − 3**c**
    (h) 2**a** + **c**

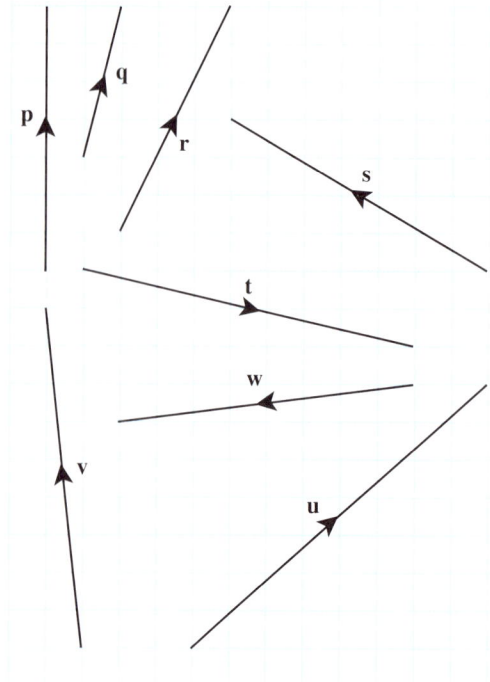

4 The rectangles on this grid are congruent.

$\overrightarrow{OA} = \mathbf{a}$ and $\overrightarrow{OE} = \mathbf{b}$.

Write each of the following vectors in terms of $\mathbf{a}$ and $\mathbf{b}$.

(a) $\overrightarrow{OQ}$ (b) $\overrightarrow{GW}$ (c) $\overrightarrow{FH}$

(d) $\overrightarrow{YV}$ (e) $\overrightarrow{OF}$ (f) $\overrightarrow{WQ}$

(g) $\overrightarrow{AE}$ (h) $\overrightarrow{RV}$ (i) $\overrightarrow{FR}$

(j) $\overrightarrow{RI}$ (k) $\overrightarrow{BU}$ (l) $\overrightarrow{TL}$

(m) $\overrightarrow{FW} + \overrightarrow{WT}$ (n) $\overrightarrow{VL} + \overrightarrow{NH}$

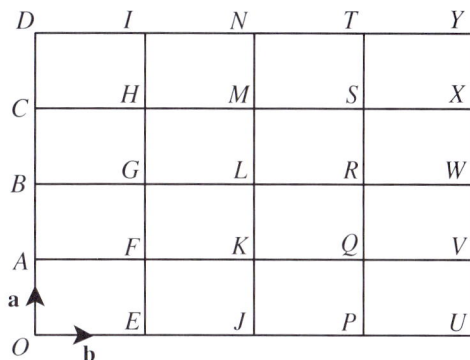

5 The parallelograms on this grid are congruent.

$\overrightarrow{OA} = \mathbf{x}$ and $\overrightarrow{OB} = \mathbf{y}$.

(a) On a copy of the grid mark each of the points C to H where:

(i) $\overrightarrow{OC} = 3\mathbf{y}$

(ii) $\overrightarrow{OD} = \mathbf{x} + 2\mathbf{y}$

(iii) $\overrightarrow{OE} = 4\mathbf{x} + 3\mathbf{y}$

(iv) $\overrightarrow{EF} = -2\mathbf{x} + \mathbf{y}$

(v) $\overrightarrow{FG} = -2\mathbf{x} - 2\mathbf{y}$

(vi) $\overrightarrow{GH} = 4\mathbf{x} + 2\mathbf{y}$

(b) Using vectors, explain why $OBHE$ is a parallelogram.

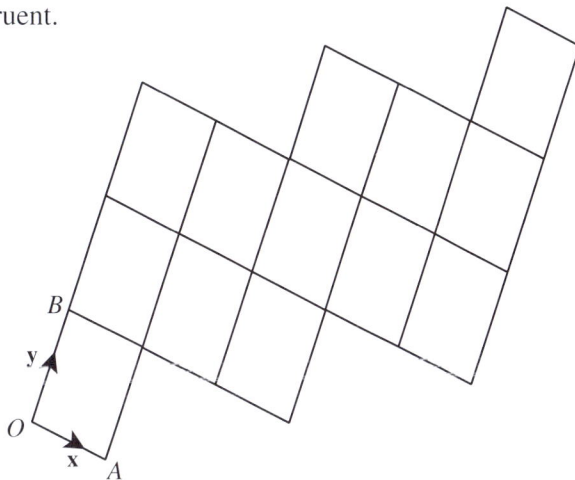

6 In the diagram $ABCD$ is a parallelogram and C is the midpoint of BE.

P, Q, R and S are the midpoints of AB, BC, CD and DA respectively.

(a) On separate copies of the diagram draw directed line segments to show:

(i) $\overrightarrow{AB} + \overrightarrow{BC}$ (ii) $\overrightarrow{AR} + \overrightarrow{RQ}$ (iii) $\overrightarrow{AP} + \overrightarrow{RC}$

(iv) $\overrightarrow{AQ} + \overrightarrow{RS}$ (v) $\overrightarrow{BC} - \overrightarrow{AB}$ (vi) $\overrightarrow{ED} - \overrightarrow{PA}$

(b) Draw vector diagrams to show the resultant vectors for:

(i) $\overrightarrow{AQ} + \overrightarrow{QR}$ (ii) $\overrightarrow{AQ} - \overrightarrow{QR}$

(iii) $\overrightarrow{PR} - \overrightarrow{RA}$ (iv) $\overrightarrow{AP} + \overrightarrow{PQ} + \overrightarrow{QR}$

$\overrightarrow{AB} = \mathbf{a}$ and $\overrightarrow{AD} = \mathbf{b}$.

(c) Write each of the following vectors in terms of $\mathbf{a}$ and $\mathbf{b}$.

(i) $\overrightarrow{PC}$ (ii) $\overrightarrow{AR}$ (iii) $\overrightarrow{AE}$

(d) What do your answers to (c) tell you about the lines:

(i) PC and AR,   (ii) PC and AE?

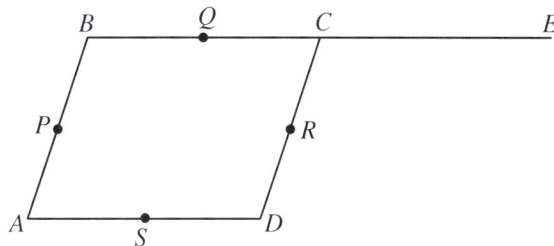

The relationships between vectors can be used to solve geometrical problems.

EXAMPLES

1 *ABCD* is a parallelogram.
E is the midpoint of the diagonal *AC*.
Show that *E* is also the midpoint of the
diagonal *BD*.

```
○○○○○○○○○○○○
```
Remember
With the arrow   = +
Against the arrow   = −

Let $\overrightarrow{AB} = \mathbf{x}$ and $\overrightarrow{AD} = \mathbf{y}$.
$$\overrightarrow{AC} = \overrightarrow{AB} + \overrightarrow{BC}$$
$$= \mathbf{x} + \mathbf{y}$$

$$\overrightarrow{AE} = \tfrac{1}{2}\ \overrightarrow{AC}$$
$$= \tfrac{1}{2}\ (\mathbf{x} + \mathbf{y})$$

$$\overrightarrow{BD} = \overrightarrow{BA} + \overrightarrow{AD}$$
$$= -\mathbf{x} + \mathbf{y}$$

$$\overrightarrow{BE} = \overrightarrow{BA} + \overrightarrow{AE}$$
$$= -\mathbf{x} + \tfrac{1}{2}\ (\mathbf{x} + \mathbf{y})$$

Multiply out brackets and simlify.
$$= -\tfrac{1}{2}\ \mathbf{x} + \tfrac{1}{2}\ \mathbf{y}$$
$$= \tfrac{1}{2}\ (-\mathbf{x} + \mathbf{y})$$

So $\overrightarrow{BE} = \tfrac{1}{2}\ \overrightarrow{BD}$.

BE is in the same direction as *BD* and is half
its length.
Because *B* is common to both *BE* and *BD*,
BED must be a straight line.
So *E* is the midpoint of *BD*.

2 *ABC* is a triangle.
P and *Q* are the midpoints of *AB* and *AC*
respectively.
Show that *PQ* is parallel to *BC* and is half
its length.

We need to show that $\overrightarrow{PQ} = \tfrac{1}{2}\ \overrightarrow{BC}$. *Why?*
$$\overrightarrow{BC} = \overrightarrow{BA} + \overrightarrow{AC}$$
$$\overrightarrow{PQ} = \overrightarrow{PA} + \overrightarrow{AQ} = \tfrac{1}{2}\ \overrightarrow{BA} + \tfrac{1}{2}\ \overrightarrow{AC}$$
$$\overrightarrow{PQ} = \tfrac{1}{2}\ (\overrightarrow{BA} + \overrightarrow{AC}) = \tfrac{1}{2}\ \overrightarrow{BC}$$

So *PQ* is parallel to *BC* and is half its length.

3 $\overrightarrow{AB} = 2\mathbf{a} + n\mathbf{b}$ $\overrightarrow{PQ} = 5\mathbf{a} - 10\mathbf{b}$
Calculate *n* if *AB* and *PQ* are parallel.

The number of **a**'s and the number of
b's in $\overrightarrow{AB}$ and $\overrightarrow{PQ}$ are in the same ratio.
$$\frac{5}{2} = -\frac{10}{n}$$
$$5n = -20$$
$$n = -4$$

```
○○○○○○○○○○○○○○○○
```
$\overrightarrow{AB}$ and $\overrightarrow{PQ}$ are parallel.
So $\overrightarrow{PQ}$ must be a multiple of $\overrightarrow{AB}$.
Why?

1 In the diagram
$\overrightarrow{OA} = \mathbf{a}$ and $\overrightarrow{OB} = \mathbf{b}$.
M is the midpoint of AB.

Express in terms of $\mathbf{a}$ and $\mathbf{b}$ in its simplest form,

(a) $\overrightarrow{AO}$,   (b) $\overrightarrow{AB}$,

(c) $\overrightarrow{MB}$,   (d) $\overrightarrow{MO}$.

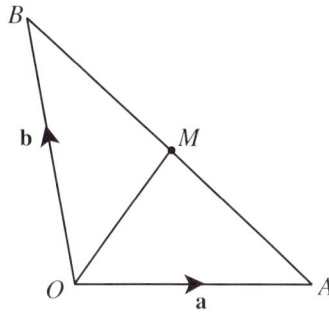

2 $OXYZ$ is a parallelogram.
P is the midpoint of OX and Q is the midpoint of OZ.
$\overrightarrow{OP} = \mathbf{p}$ and $\overrightarrow{OQ} = \mathbf{q}$

(a) Express in terms of $\mathbf{p}$ and $\mathbf{q}$ in its simplest form,

    (i) $\overrightarrow{PQ}$,   (ii) $\overrightarrow{OX}$,

    (iii) $\overrightarrow{OY}$,   (iv) $\overrightarrow{XZ}$.

(b) What can you say about the lines PQ and XZ?

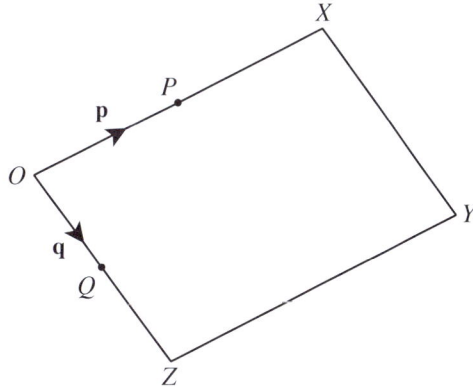

3 OXY is a triangle.
P, Q and R are the midpoints of the sides YO, OX and XY respectively.
$\overrightarrow{OP} = \mathbf{p}$ and $\overrightarrow{OQ} = \mathbf{q}$.

(a) Express in terms of $\mathbf{p}$ and $\mathbf{q}$ in its simplest form:

    (i) $\overrightarrow{OX}$ (ii) $\overrightarrow{OY}$

    (iii) $\overrightarrow{PQ}$ (iv) $\overrightarrow{XY}$

    (v) $\overrightarrow{PR}$ (vi) $\overrightarrow{RQ}$

(b) What can you say about the triangles OXY and PQR?

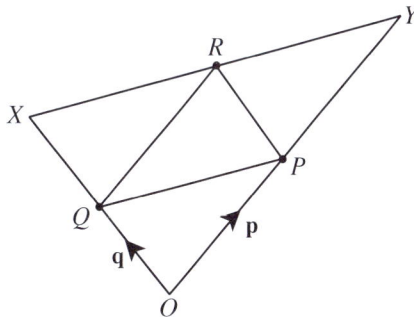

4 $OABC$ is an irregular quadrilateral.
W is the midpoint of OA.
X is the midpoint of AB.
Y is the midpoint of BC.
Z is the midpoint of CO.
$\overrightarrow{OA} = \mathbf{a}$, $\overrightarrow{OB} = \mathbf{b}$, $\overrightarrow{OC} = \mathbf{c}$.

(a) Find in terms of $\mathbf{a}$, $\mathbf{b}$ and $\mathbf{c}$.

    (i) $\overrightarrow{CB}$ (ii) $\overrightarrow{YZ}$

    (iii) $\overrightarrow{CX}$ (iv) $\overrightarrow{YX}$

    (v) $\overrightarrow{ZW}$

(b) Use your answers to (a) to show that $WXYZ$ is a parallelogram.

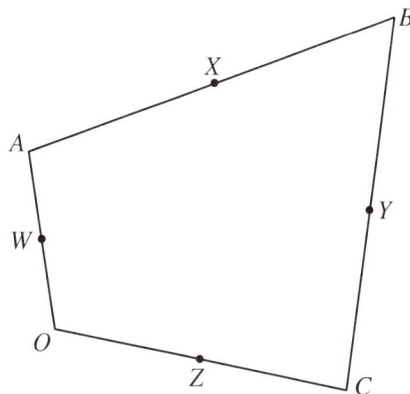

5 *OABC* is a square.

X is the midpoint of *BC*.

Y is a point on *XA* such that $\overrightarrow{XA} = 3\overrightarrow{XY}$.

$\overrightarrow{OA} = \mathbf{a}$ and $\overrightarrow{OC} = \mathbf{b}$.

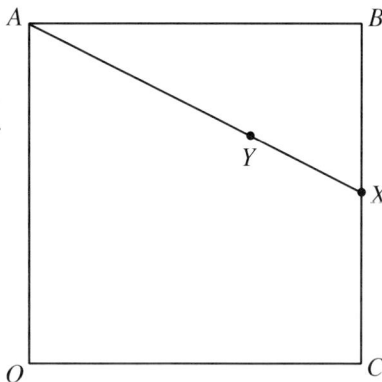

(a) Express in terms of **a** and **b**:

    (i) $\overrightarrow{CX}$ (ii) $\overrightarrow{OX}$

    (iii) $\overrightarrow{XA}$ (iv) $\overrightarrow{XY}$

    (v) $\overrightarrow{OY}$ (vi) $\overrightarrow{OB}$

(b) What does $\overrightarrow{OY}$ and $\overrightarrow{OB}$ tell you about the points *O*, *Y* and *B*?

6 In the trapezium *OABC*, *AB* is parallel to *OC*.

$\overrightarrow{OA} = -\mathbf{a} + 2\mathbf{b}$ and $\overrightarrow{OB} = 3\mathbf{a} + 4\mathbf{b}$.

(a) Calculate $\overrightarrow{AB}$ in terms of **a** and **b**.

$\overrightarrow{BC} = 3\mathbf{a} + n\mathbf{b}$.

(b) Calculate $\overrightarrow{OC}$ in terms of **a**, **b** and *n* and, hence, calculate the value of *n*.

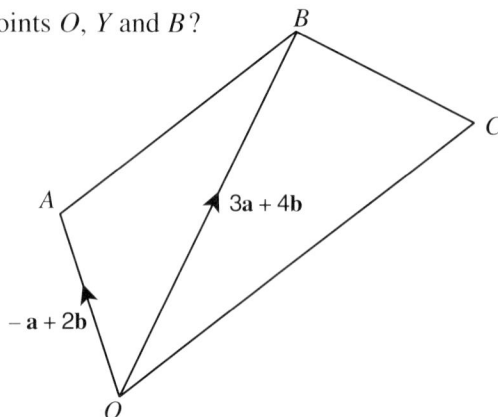

7 *ABCD* and *CDEF* are identical parallelograms.

$\overrightarrow{AB} = \mathbf{x}$ and $\overrightarrow{AD} = \mathbf{y}$.

M is the midpoint of *EF*.

Show that *AFMD* and *BCME* are trapezia.

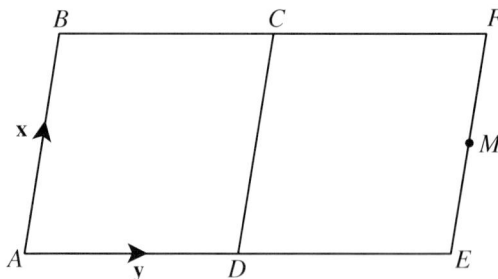

8 $\overrightarrow{OA} = -2\mathbf{a} + 4\mathbf{b}$ $\overrightarrow{OB} = -\mathbf{a} + 6\mathbf{b}$

$\overrightarrow{OD} = \mathbf{a} + 2\mathbf{b}$ $\overrightarrow{OC} = 5\mathbf{a} + 2\mathbf{b}$

(a) Find, in terms of **a** and **b**, $\overrightarrow{AD}$ and $\overrightarrow{BC}$.

(b) What do $\overrightarrow{AD}$ and $\overrightarrow{BC}$ tell you about quadrilateral *ABCD*?

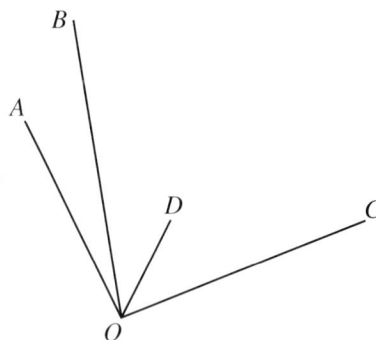

9 In triangle *OAB*, *P* and *Q* are points on *OA* such that *OP* = *PQ* = *QA*.

S and *R* are the midpoints of *PB* and *QB* respectively.

$\overrightarrow{OA} = 3\mathbf{a}$ and $\overrightarrow{OB} = \mathbf{b}$.

(a) Find in terms of **a** and **b**.

    (i) $\overrightarrow{PB}$ (ii) $\overrightarrow{QB}$ (iii) $\overrightarrow{SR}$

(b) What conclusions can you make about *OA* and *SR*?

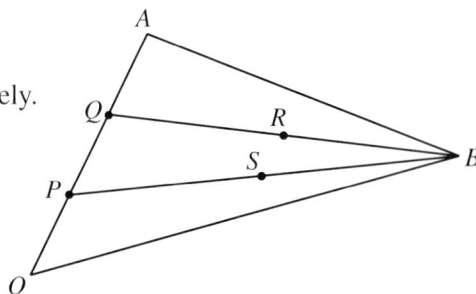

10 $\overrightarrow{OA} = -3\mathbf{a} + 5\mathbf{b}$,

$\overrightarrow{OB} = -\mathbf{a} + 4\mathbf{b}$,

$\overrightarrow{OC} = 3\mathbf{a} + 2\mathbf{b}$.

(a) Find in terms of $\mathbf{a}$ and $\mathbf{b}$.

    (i) $\overrightarrow{AB}$ (ii) $\overrightarrow{BC}$

(b) What conclusions can you make about the points A, B and C?

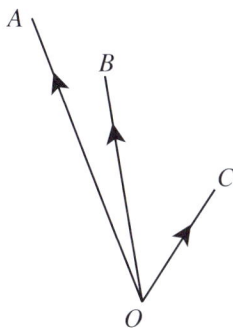

11 The lines AB, CD and EF are parallel.

$\overrightarrow{AB} = 2\mathbf{x} - \mathbf{y}$.

$\overrightarrow{CD} = 3\mathbf{x} + n\mathbf{y}$.

$\overrightarrow{EF} = m\mathbf{x} - \dfrac{5}{2}\mathbf{y}$.

(a) Calculate m and n.

$\overrightarrow{AC} = \mathbf{y}$ and $\overrightarrow{AE} = 3\overrightarrow{AC}$.

(b) Find in terms of $\mathbf{x}$ and $\mathbf{y}$.

    (i) $\overrightarrow{BD}$ (ii) $\overrightarrow{DF}$

(c) What conclusions can you make about the points B, D and F?

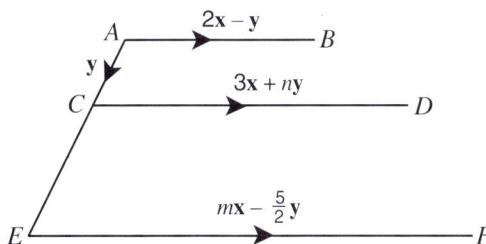

12 $ABCD$ is a parallelogram.

$\overrightarrow{AB} = \mathbf{a}$ and $\overrightarrow{AD} = \mathbf{b}$.

$\overrightarrow{AP} = \dfrac{2}{3}\overrightarrow{AD}$ and Q is the midpoint of CD.

R is a point outside $ABCD$ such that $PQRD$ is also a parallelogram.
Use vectors to show that $BPRC$ is a trapezium.

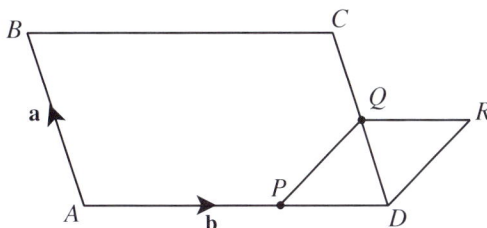

13 In triangle OAB:

$\overrightarrow{OA} = -2\mathbf{a} + 4\mathbf{b}$ and

$\overrightarrow{OB} = 7\mathbf{a} + \mathbf{b}$.

P is a point on AB such that

$\overrightarrow{OP} = 4\mathbf{a} + n\mathbf{b}$.

(a) Calculate the value of n.
(b) Use vectors to show that P lies on AB.
(c) Calculate the ratio $AP : PB$.

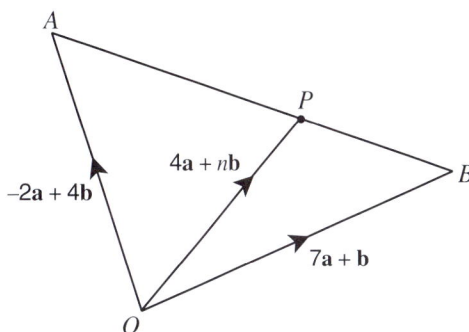

- **Vector quantities**
  Quantities which have both **size** and **direction** are called **vectors**.
  Examples of vector quantities are:

Displacement	**Velocity**
A combination of distance and direction	A combination of speed and direction

- **Vector notation**
  Vectors can be represented by **column vectors** or by **directed line segments**.
  Vectors can be labelled using:
  capital letters to indicate the start and finish of a vector,
  bold lower case letters.

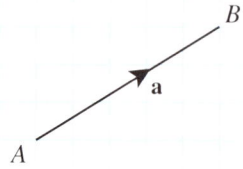

  In a **column vector:**
  The top number describes the **horizontal** part of the movement:
  + = to the right   − = to the left
  The bottom number describes the **vertical** part of the movement:
  + = upwards   − = downwards

$$\overrightarrow{AB} = \mathbf{a} = \begin{pmatrix} 5 \\ 3 \end{pmatrix}$$

- Vectors are **equal** if they have the same length **and** they are in the same direction.
  Vectors **a** and −**a** have the same length **but** are in **opposite directions**.
  The vector $n\mathbf{a}$ is parallel to the vector **a**.
  The length of vector $n\mathbf{a} = n \times$ the length of vector **a**.

- **Vector addition**
  The combination of the displacement from A to B followed by the displacement from B to C is equivalent to a total displacement from A to C.

  This can be written using vectors as $\overrightarrow{AB} + \overrightarrow{BC} = \overrightarrow{AC}$

  $\overrightarrow{AC}$ is called the **resultant vector**.

- Combinations of vectors can be shown on **vector diagrams**.

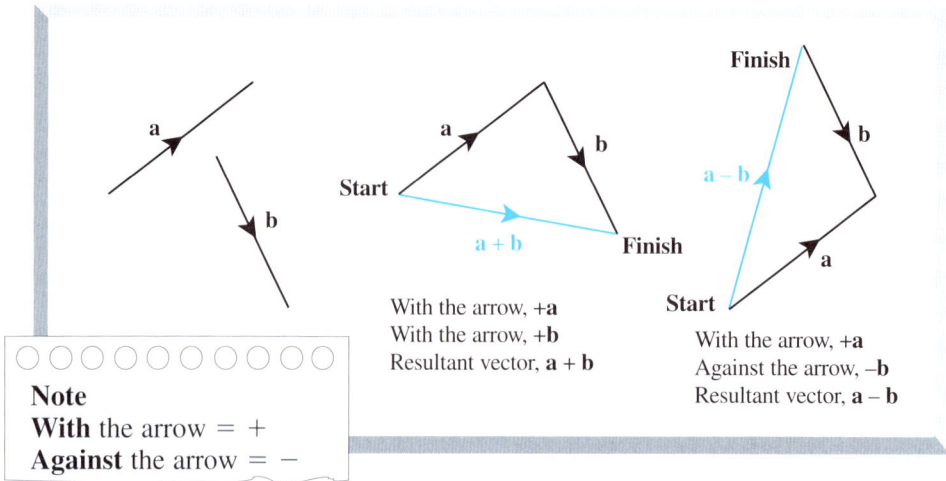

With the arrow, +**a**
With the arrow, +**b**
Resultant vector, **a** + **b**

With the arrow, +**a**
Against the arrow, −**b**
Resultant vector, **a** − **b**

Note
With the arrow = +
Against the arrow = −

- **Vector geometry** uses vectors to solve simple geometrical problems, which often involve parallel lines.

Do not use a calculator.

1 The diagram shows vectors $\overrightarrow{OA}$ and $\overrightarrow{OB}$.

$\overrightarrow{OA} = \mathbf{a}$ and $\overrightarrow{OB} = \mathbf{b}$.

$\overrightarrow{OC} = \mathbf{a} + \mathbf{b}$

$\overrightarrow{OD} = 2\mathbf{a} + \mathbf{b}$

(a) On a copy of the diagram draw $\overrightarrow{OC}$ and $\overrightarrow{OD}$.

(b) Find in terms of $\mathbf{a}$ and $\mathbf{b}$:

(i) $\overrightarrow{AB}$ (ii) $\overrightarrow{AD}$ (iii) $\overrightarrow{CD}$

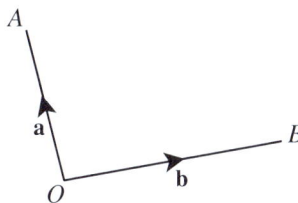

2 $\overrightarrow{AB} = \begin{pmatrix} 3 \\ 2 \end{pmatrix}$ and $\overrightarrow{OB} = \begin{pmatrix} 1 \\ 7 \end{pmatrix}$.

M is the midpoint of AB.

(a) (i) Write down $\overrightarrow{AO}$.

(ii) Calculate $\overrightarrow{AB}$.

(b) (i) Copy and complete

$\overrightarrow{OM} = \overrightarrow{OA} + \ldots$

(ii) Use this to calculate $\overrightarrow{OM}$

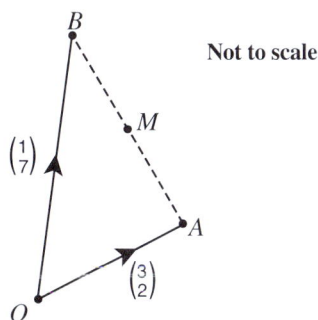

Not to scale

SEG 1994

3 OAB is a triangle. E is the midpoint of AB.

$\overrightarrow{OA} = \mathbf{a}$ and $\overrightarrow{OB} = \mathbf{b}$.

Find in terms of $\mathbf{a}$ and $\mathbf{b}$:

(a) $\overrightarrow{AB}$ (b) $\overrightarrow{AE}$ (c) $\overrightarrow{OE}$

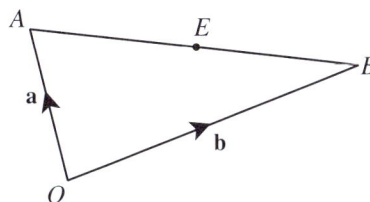

4 Vector $\mathbf{a}$, vector $\mathbf{b}$ and the point X are shown on this grid.

(a) $\overrightarrow{XY} = 3\mathbf{a} + 1\frac{1}{2}\mathbf{b}$ and $\overrightarrow{XZ} = 2\mathbf{a} - \frac{1}{2}\mathbf{b}$.

Mark Y and Z on a copy of the diagram.

(b) P is the midpoint of $\overrightarrow{YZ}$.

Express $\overrightarrow{XP}$ in terms of $\mathbf{a}$ and $\mathbf{b}$.

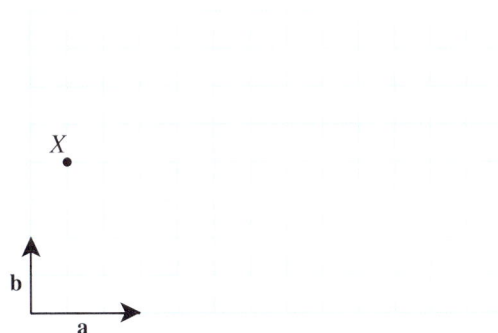

SEG 1999

5 The diagram shows two sets of parallel lines.

$\overrightarrow{BA} = \mathbf{x}$ and $\overrightarrow{DC} = \mathbf{y}$.

$\overrightarrow{AH} = \frac{1}{3}\overrightarrow{AG}$ and $\overrightarrow{AB} = \frac{1}{2}\overrightarrow{AC}$.

(a)   Write each of these vectors in terms of $\mathbf{x}$ and $\mathbf{y}$.

    (i) $\overrightarrow{DB}$ (ii) $\overrightarrow{EH}$

(b)   What can be deduced about EH and DB?

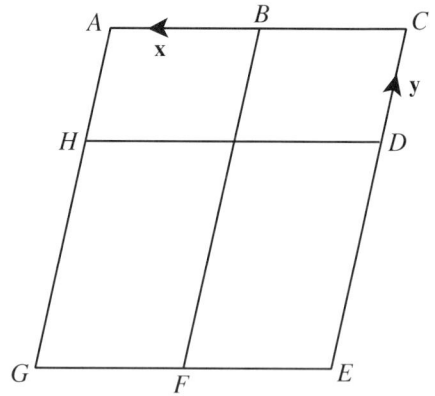

SEG 1995

6 In the diagram

$$\overrightarrow{OA} = \begin{pmatrix} 3 \\ 0 \end{pmatrix} \text{ and } \overrightarrow{OB} = \begin{pmatrix} 1 \\ 2 \end{pmatrix}.$$

The points A and B are the midpoints of OP and OQ respectively.

(a)   Calculate $\overrightarrow{OP}$.

(b)   Calculate $\overrightarrow{AB}$ and $\overrightarrow{PQ}$.

(c)   Use your answer to part (b) to give two facts about the lines AB and PQ.

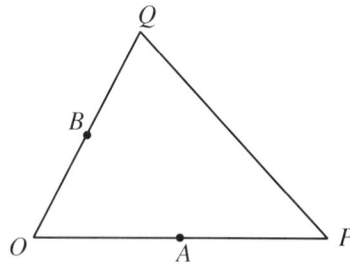

SEG 1995

7 The diagram shows a triangle ABC.
P is a point on AC.

$\overrightarrow{AP} = \mathbf{a}$ and $\overrightarrow{AP} = \frac{1}{3}\overrightarrow{AC}$.

Q is the midpoint of AB and $\overrightarrow{AQ} = \mathbf{b}$.

Write down, in terms of $\mathbf{a}$ and $\mathbf{b}$:

(a) $\overrightarrow{AC}$ (b) $\overrightarrow{AB}$ (c) $\overrightarrow{BC}$

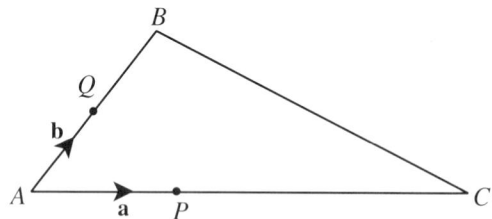

SEG 1994

8 The diagram shows the quadrilateral $OPQR$.

$\overrightarrow{OR} = \mathbf{a}$ and $\overrightarrow{OP} = \mathbf{b}$.

S is a point on OQ such that $\overrightarrow{OS} = \frac{1}{3}\overrightarrow{OQ}$.

$\overrightarrow{PQ} = 2\overrightarrow{OR}$.

(a)   Find in terms of $\mathbf{a}$ and $\mathbf{b}$:

    (i) $\overrightarrow{OQ}$ (ii) $\overrightarrow{PS}$ (iii) $\overrightarrow{RS}$

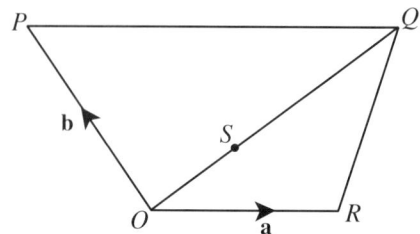

(b)   (i)   What is the ratio $PS : SR$?

    (ii)   Explain why vectors $\overrightarrow{PS}$ and $\overrightarrow{RS}$ indicate that the points P, S and R lie on a straight line.

SEG 1998

9 $\overrightarrow{OA} = 2\mathbf{a}$, $\overrightarrow{OB} = 2\mathbf{b}$ and $\overrightarrow{OC} = 3\overrightarrow{OB}$.

(a) Find $\overrightarrow{AB}$ and $\overrightarrow{AC}$, in terms of $\mathbf{a}$ and $\mathbf{b}$.

$\overrightarrow{AM} = \frac{2}{3}\overrightarrow{AB}$ and $\overrightarrow{AN} = \frac{2}{5}\overrightarrow{AC}$.

(b) Find $\overrightarrow{OM}$ and $\overrightarrow{ON}$, in terms of $\mathbf{a}$ and $\mathbf{b}$.

(c) What can you say about the points O, M and N?

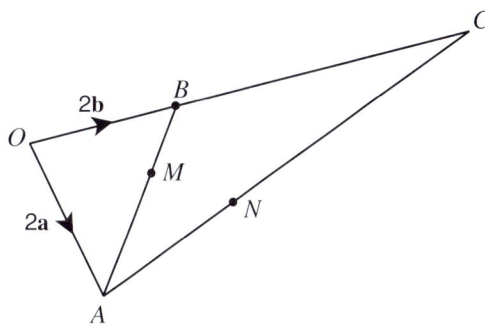

10 In the diagram:

$\overrightarrow{OA} = \overrightarrow{AC} = \overrightarrow{CE} = \mathbf{a}$,

$\overrightarrow{OB} = \overrightarrow{BD} = \overrightarrow{DF} = \mathbf{b}$,

$\overrightarrow{EG} = \overrightarrow{GH} = \overrightarrow{HF}$.

(a) Find in terms of $\mathbf{a}$ and $\mathbf{b}$.

    (i) $\overrightarrow{OE}$ (ii) $\overrightarrow{AG}$

(b) $\overrightarrow{OP} = \frac{1}{2}(\mathbf{a} + \mathbf{b})$.

Mark the position of P on a copy of the diagram.

(c) Write two statements about OP and AG.

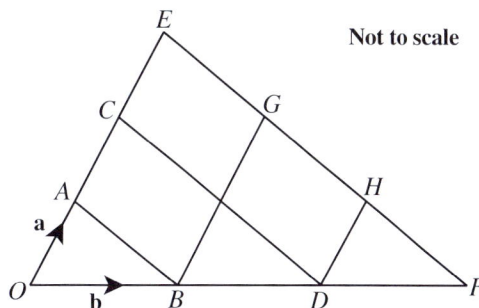

SEG 1997

11 The diagram shows the points O, A and B

where $\overrightarrow{OA} = 6\mathbf{a}$ and $\overrightarrow{OB} = 9\mathbf{b}$.

OAD is a straight line and $ABCD$ is a parallelogram.

A is the midpoint of OD.

(a) Find in terms of $\mathbf{a}$ and $\mathbf{b}$.

    (i) $\overrightarrow{AD}$ (ii) $\overrightarrow{AB}$

(b) E and F are two points such that

$\overrightarrow{AE} = \frac{1}{3}\overrightarrow{AB}$ and $\overrightarrow{DF} = \frac{2}{3}\overrightarrow{DC}$.

Find in terms of $\mathbf{a}$ and $\mathbf{b}$.

    (i) $\overrightarrow{OE}$ (ii) $\overrightarrow{OF}$

(c) What do $\overrightarrow{OE}$ and $\overrightarrow{OF}$ indicate about the points O, E and F?

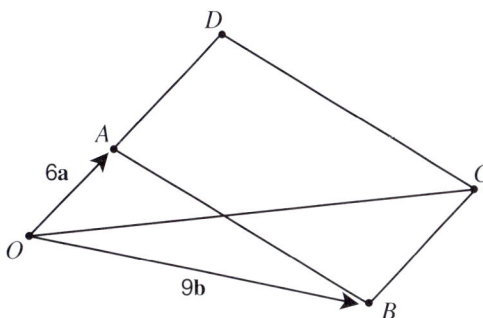

SEG 2000 S

12 $\overrightarrow{OA} = \mathbf{a} + 4\mathbf{b}$ and $\overrightarrow{OB} = 7\mathbf{a} + \mathbf{b}$.

M is a point on AB such that $\overrightarrow{AB} = 3\overrightarrow{AM}$.

(a) Express in terms of $\mathbf{a}$ and $\mathbf{b}$:

    (i) $\overrightarrow{AB}$ (ii) $\overrightarrow{OM}$

$\overrightarrow{BC} = 2\mathbf{a} + 8\mathbf{b}$

(b) (i) Express $\overrightarrow{OC}$ in terms of $\mathbf{a}$ and $\mathbf{b}$.

    (ii) What do $\overrightarrow{OM}$ and $\overrightarrow{OC}$ indicate about the points O, C and M?

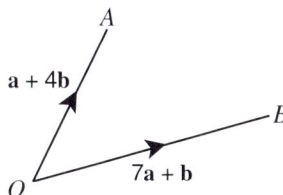

CHAPTER 27

Further Trigonometry

So far we have found sines, cosines and tangents of angles between 0° and 90°, but it is possible to find the sine, cosine and tangent of any angle.

The sine, cosine and tangent ratios were introduced in Chapter 22.

Trigonometric functions and their graphs

Activity

The sine function

Copy and complete this table. Use your calculator to find the value of $\sin x°$ correct to two decimal places, where necessary.

$x°$	0	30	60	90	120	150	180	210	240	270	300	330	360
$\sin x°$	0	0.5	0.87										

Plot these values on graph paper. Draw the graph of the sine function by joining the points with a smooth curve.

What is the maximum value of $\sin x°$?

What is the minimum value of $\sin x°$?

Describe what happens to the sine function when $x > 360°$.

Describe what happens to the sine function when $x < 0°$.

In a similar way, draw the graphs of the **cosine function** and the **tangent function**.

What do you notice about the graphs of each of these functions?

You might also try this activity using a graphical calculator, or a computer and suitable software.

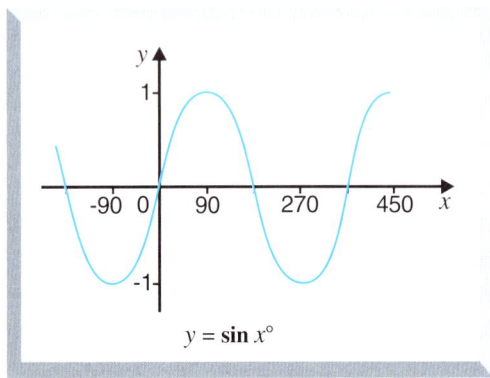

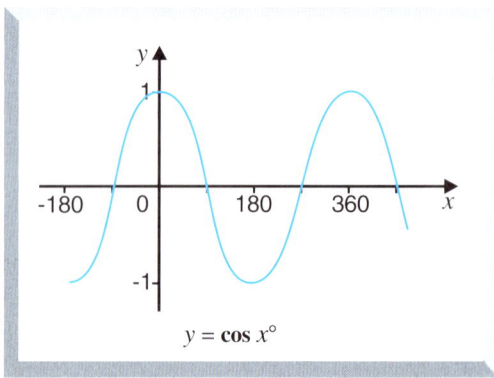

$y = \sin x°$

$y = \cos x°$

$y = \tan x°$

For every angle $x°$, the signs of $\sin x°$, $\cos x°$ and $\tan x°$ can be summarised as follows:

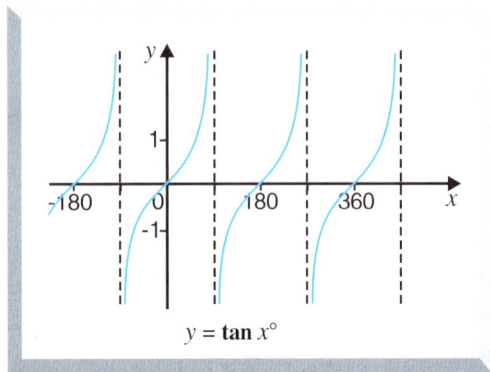

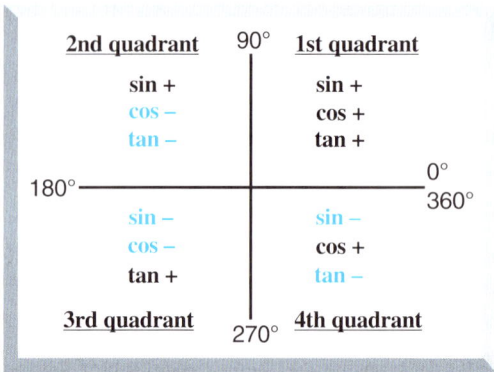

2nd quadrant	90°	1st quadrant
sin +		sin +
cos −		cos +
tan −		tan +
180°		0° 360°
sin −		sin −
cos −		cos +
tan +		tan −
3rd quadrant	270°	4th quadrant

Consider a point P. Line OP makes an angle $x°$ with line OX.
If $OP = 1$ unit, then in triangle OMP:

Positive angles are measured **anticlockwise** from the axis OX.

$\sin x° = \dfrac{\text{opp}}{\text{hyp}}$ $\cos x° = \dfrac{\text{adj}}{\text{hyp}}$ $\tan x° = \dfrac{\text{opp}}{\text{adj}}$

$\sin x° = \dfrac{PM}{OP}$ $\cos x° = \dfrac{OM}{OP}$ $\tan x° = \dfrac{PM}{OM}$

$\sin x° = \dfrac{PM}{1}$ $\cos x° = \dfrac{OM}{1}$ $\tan x° = \dfrac{\sin x°}{\cos x°}$

$PM = \sin x°$ $OM = \cos x°$ *Explain why.*

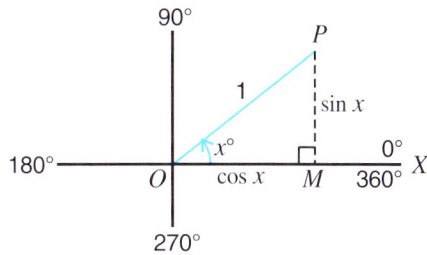

2nd quadrant

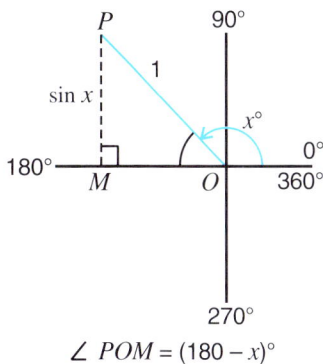

$\angle POM = (180 - x)°$

When $90° < x < 180°$,
$\sin x$ is positive.

We can write:
$\sin x° = \sin (180 - x)°$

Example
$\sin 150° = \sin (180 - 150)°$
$= \sin 30°$
$= 0.5$

3rd quadrant

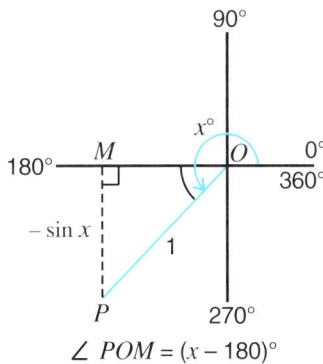

$\angle POM = (x - 180)°$

When $180° < x < 270°$,
$\sin x$ is negative.

We can write:
$\sin x° = -\sin (x - 180)°$

Example
$\sin 210° = -\sin (210 - 180)°$
$= -\sin 30°$
$= -0.5$

4th quadrant

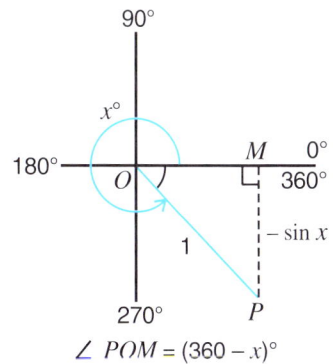

$\angle POM = (360 - x)°$

When $270° < x < 360°$,
$\sin x$ is negative.

We can write:
$\sin x° = -\sin (360 - x)°$

Example
$\sin 330° = -\sin (360 - 330)°$
$= -\sin 30°$
$= -0.5$

Activity

In a similar way investigate the values of $\cos x$ and $\tan x$ for the values of x between 0° and 360°.

EXAMPLE

Express the following in terms of the sin, cos or tan of an acute angle.
(a) $\tan 100°$ (b) $\sin 200°$ (c) $\cos 300°$ (d) $\sin (-10)°$
(e) $\cos (-20)°$ (f) $\tan 400°$ (g) $\sin 500°$

(a) $\tan 100° = -\tan (180 - 100)° = -\tan 80°$
(b) $\sin 200° = -\sin (200 - 180)° = -\sin 20°$
(c) $\cos 300° = \cos (360 - 300)° = \cos 60°$

(d) $\sin (-10)° = -\sin 10°$
(e) $\cos (-20)° = \cos 20°$

Negative angles are measured **clockwise** from the axis OX.

(f) $\tan 400° = \tan (400 - 360)° = \tan 40°$
(g) $\sin 500° = \sin (500 - 360)° = \sin 140°$
$= \sin (180 - 140)° = \sin 40°$

Angles greater than 360°
Subtract 360°, or multiples of 360°, to get the equivalent angle between 0° and 360°.

Do not use a calculator.

1 State whether the following are positive or negative.

(a) sin 50°	(b) cos 50°	(c) tan 50°	(d) sin 100°
(e) cos 100°	(f) tan 100°	(g) cos 150°	(h) sin 200°
(i) tan 250°	(j) cos 300°	(k) sin 350°	(l) tan 87°
(m) cos 143°	(n) sin 117°	(o) tan 162°	(p) cos 296°
(q) tan 321°	(r) cos 196°	(s) sin 218°	(t) cos 400°
(u) tan 500°	(v) sin 500°	(w) cos (−30)°	(x) sin (−100)°
(y) cos (−100)°	(z) tan (−100)°		

2 Express each of the following in terms of the sin, cos or tan of an acute angle.

(a) tan 100°	(b) cos 150°	(c) sin 200°	(d) tan 250°
(e) cos 300°	(f) sin 120°	(g) tan 170°	(h) cos 210°
(i) sin 290°	(j) tan 330°	(k) cos 370°	(l) sin 260°
(m) tan 370°	(n) sin 480°	(o) cos 600°	(p) sin (−50)°
(q) cos (−100)°	(r) tan (−150)°		

3 The exact values of sin 45°, cos 45° and tan 45° can be found by using this triangle.

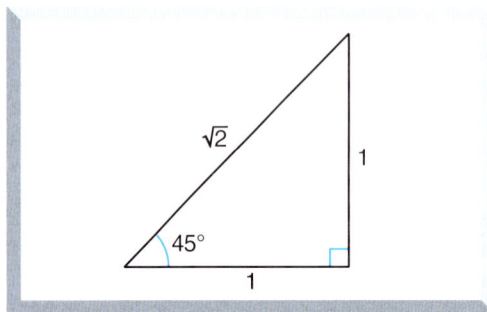

eg $\sin 45° = \dfrac{1}{\sqrt{2}}$

(a) Write down the exact value of (i) cos 45°, (ii) tan 45°.

(b) Hence write down the exact values of
 (i)   cos 135°,   (ii)   tan 225°,   (iii) sin 315°,
 (iv) sin 135°,   (v)   cos 225°,   (vi) tan 315°.

4 The exact values of sin 30°, cos 30°, tan 30° and sin 60°, cos 60°, tan 60° can be found by using this triangle.

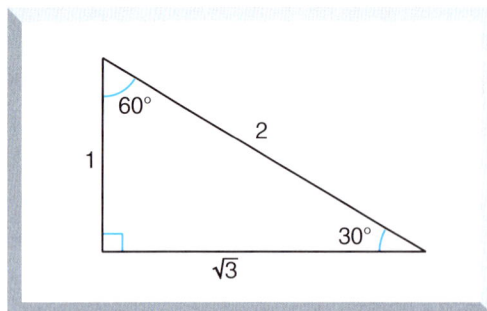

(a) Write down the exact values of sin 30°, cos 30°, tan 30° and hence give the exact values of
 (i)   sin 150°,   (ii) cos 210°,   (iii) tan 330°,   (iv) cos 330°.

(b) Write down the exact values of sin 60°, cos 60°, tan 60° and hence give the exact values of
 (i)   cos 120°,   (ii) tan 240°,   (iii) cos 240°,   (iv) sin 300°.

Finding angles

For which angles, between 0° and 360°, is cos p = 0.412?

cos p = 0.412
cos p is positive, so possible angles are
in the 1st and 4th quadrants.
This can be shown on a diagram.
$p = \cos^{-1}(0.412)$
Using a calculator.
p = 65.669 ...
p = 65.7°, to 1 d.p.

Positive angles are measured clockwise.
p = 65.7°, and
p = 360° − 65.7° = 294.3°

So p = 65.7° and 294.3°, correct to 1 d.p.

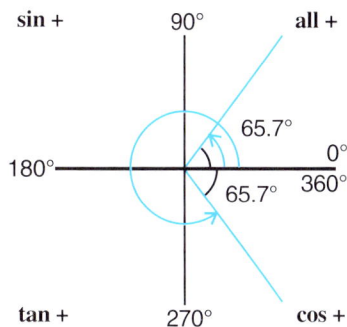

Note
Because of the symmetries of the
graphs of trigonometric functions,
angles formed between the lines
and the horizontal axis are
always **equal**.
Explain why.

EXAMPLE

For which angles, between 0° and 360°, is tan p = −1.5?

tan p = −1.5

tan p is negative, so possible angles are
in the 2nd and 4th quadrants.
$p = \tan^{-1}(-1.5)$
p = − 56.309 ...
p = − 56.3°, to 1 d.p.

p = 180° − 56.3° = 123.7°, and
p = 360° − 56.3° = 303.7°

So p = 123.7° and 303.7°, correct to 1 d.p.

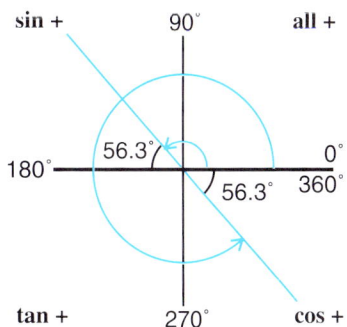

Exercise 27.2

Use your calculator to find the values of the following.
Give your answers correct to three decimal places.

1
(a) sin 100°	(b) cos 150°	(c) tan 200°	(d) sin 250°
(e) cos 300°	(f) tan 350°	(g) tan 187°	(h) cos 187°
(i) cos 143°	(j) sin 117°	(k) tan 162°	(l) cos 296°
(m) tan 321°	(n) cos 196°	(o) sin 218°	(p) cos 400°
(q) tan 500°	(r) sin 500°	(s) cos (−30)°	(t) sin (−100)°

2 For each of the following, find all the values of p between 0° and 360°.
(a) cos p = 0.5	(b) sin p = −0.5	(c) tan p = 1
(d) sin p = 0.5	(e) tan p = −1	(f) cos p = −0.5
(g) sin p = −0.766	(h) cos p = 0.766	(i) sin p = 0.866
(j) tan p = −2.050	(k) tan p = 0.193	(l) cos p = 0.565
(m) sin p = 0.342	(n) cos p = −0.866	(o) tan p = 0.700

At the beginning of the chapter we looked at the graphs of the sine, cosine and tangent functions. Each of the functions is called a **periodic function**.

After a **period** (distance along the x axis) each graph repeats itself.

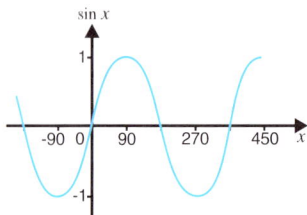

The **sine function** is a periodic function with period 360°.
$$-1 \leqslant \sin x \leqslant 1$$

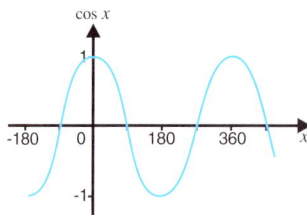

The **cosine function** is a periodic function with period 360°.
$$-1 \leqslant \cos x \leqslant 1$$

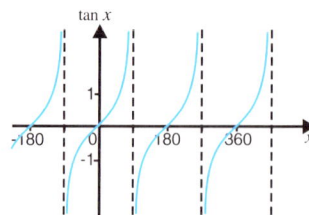

The **tangent function** is a periodic function with period 180°.
Tan x is undefined at 90°, 270°, ...

EXAMPLE

Compare the following graphs: $y = \sin x$, $y = 2\sin x$, $y = \sin 2x$.

x	0	45	90	135	180	225	270	315	360
$y = \sin x$	0	0.71	1	0.71	0	-0.71	-1	-0.71	0
$y = 2\sin x$	0	1.41	2	1.41	0	-1.41	-2	-1.41	0
$y = \sin 2x$	0	1	0	-1	0	1	0	-1	0

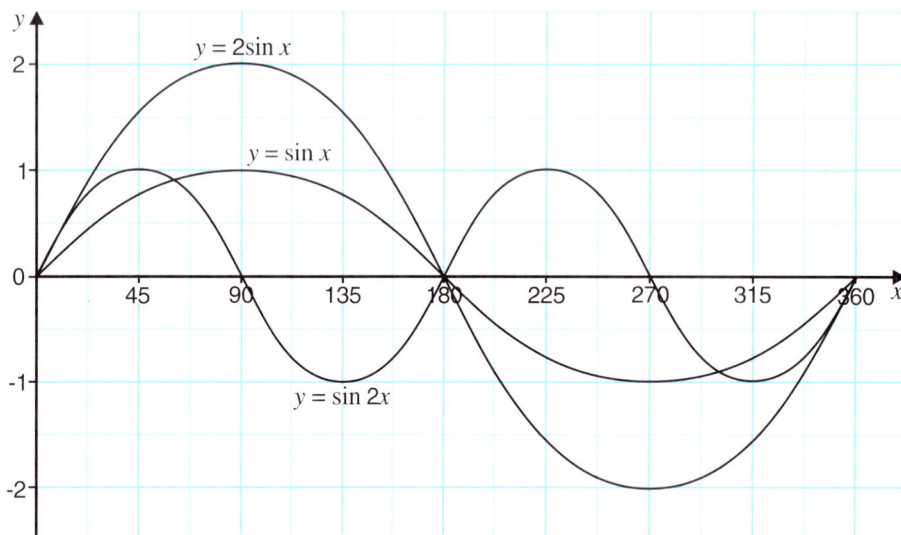

$y = \sin x$
Period: 360°
$-1 \leqslant \sin x \leqslant 1$

$y = 2\sin x$
Period: 360°
$-2 \leqslant 2\sin x \leqslant 2$

$y = \sin 2x$
Period: 180°
$-1 \leqslant \sin 2x \leqslant 1$

Exercise 27.3

1 Use the graphs of the sine function and the cosine function, to find the values of x, between 0° and 360°, when

(a) (i) $\sin x = 1$ (ii) $\sin x = 0$ (iii) $\sin x = -1$

(b) (i) $\cos x = 1$ (ii) $\cos x = 0$ (iii) $\cos x = -1$

2 Given that tan 45° = 1, use the graph of the tangent function to find all the values of x, between 0° and 360°, when   (a)   tan x = 1   (b)   tan x = 0   (c)   tan x = −1

3   (a)   Draw the graph of $y = 3 \sin x$ for values of x between 0° and 360°.
     (b)   Use your graph to find   (i) x when y = 1.50,   (ii) y when x = 240°.

4   (a)   Draw the graph of $y = 3 \cos x$ for values of x between 0° and 360°.
     (b)   Use your graph to solve the equation $3 \cos x = 0.6$.

5 Compare the graph of $y = 3 \sin x$ with $y = \sin x$ and the graph of $y = 3 \cos x$ with $y = \cos x$.
What do you notice?
Hence sketch the graphs of
  (a) (i) $y = 2 \sin x$ (ii) $y = 5 \sin x$ (iii) $y = \frac{1}{2} \sin x$
  (b) (i) $y = 2 \cos x$ (ii) $y = 5 \cos x$ (iii) $y = \frac{1}{2} \cos x$

6   (a)   Draw the graph of $y = \sin 2x$.
     (b)   Compare this graph with the graph of $y = \sin x$.
           What do you notice?
     (c)   Hence sketch the graph of $y = \sin 3x$.

7   (a)   Draw the graph of $y = \cos 2x$.
     (b)   Compare this graph with the graph of $y = \cos x$.
           What do you notice?
     (c)   Hence sketch the graph of $y = \cos 3x$.

8 Draw graphs of the following.
  (a) $y = \sin x + 1$ (b) $y = \sin x - 2$
  (b)   Compare these graphs with the graph of $y = \sin x$.
         What do you notice?
  (c)   Hence sketch the graphs of   (i) $y = \cos x + 2$ (ii) $y = \cos x - 1$

Questions 9 to 12.
Use a graphical calculator to check your answers.

9   (a)   On the same diagram, draw the graphs of $y = 2\cos x$ and $y = 4\sin x$ for values of x from 0° to 360°.
     (b)   Use your graph to find the solutions to the equation $4\sin x = 2\cos x$ for the interval $0° \leqslant x \leqslant 360°$.

10   (a)   On the same diagram, draw the graphs of $y = 5\cos x$ and $y = \sin x + 2$ for values of x from 0° to 360°.
     (b)   Use your graph to find the solutions to the equation $5\cos x = \sin x + 2$ for the interval $0° \leqslant x \leqslant 360°$.

11   (a)   On the same diagram, draw the graphs of $y = 3\sin x$ and $y = 1 - \cos x$ for values of x from 0° to 360°.
     (b)   Use your graph to find the solutions to the equation $3\sin x = 1 - \cos x$ for the interval $0° \leqslant x \leqslant 360°$.

12   (a)   On the same diagram, draw the graphs of $y = 3\cos x$ and $y = 1 - \sin x$ for values of x from 0° to 360°.
     (b)   Use your graph to find the solutions to the equation $3\cos x = 1 - \sin x$ for the interval $0° \leqslant x \leqslant 360°$.

In Chapter 22 we used trigonometry to find sides and angles in right-angled triangles. However, not all triangles are right-angled and to solve problems involving acute-angled and obtuse-angled triangles we need to know further rules.

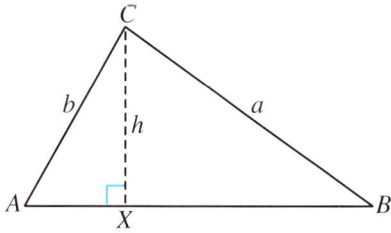

Remember
Angles are labelled with **capital letters** and the **sides** opposite the angles with **lower case letters**.

The **altitude**, or height of the triangle, is shown by the line CX.
The line CX divides triangle ABC into two right-angled triangles.

In triangle CAX.
$$\sin A = \frac{h}{b}$$
This can be rearranged to give:
$h = b \sin A$

In triangle CBX.
$$\sin B = \frac{h}{a}$$
This can be rearranged to give:
$h = a \sin B$

$h = b \sin A$ and $h = a \sin B$, so
$b \sin A = a \sin B$,
which can be rearranged as:
$$\frac{a}{\sin A} = \frac{b}{\sin B}$$

Activity

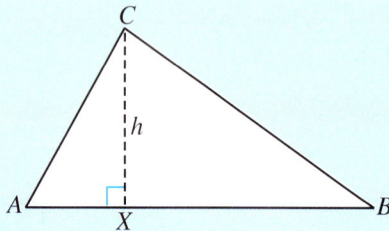

Find rules to connect:
$\sin A$ and $\sin C$,
$\sin B$ and $\sin C$.

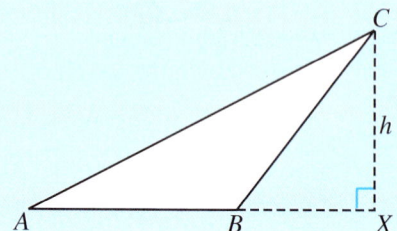

Can you find similar rules for obtuse-angled triangles?

The Sine Rule

In any triangle labelled ABC it can be proved that:
$$\frac{a}{\sin A} = \frac{b}{\sin B} = \frac{c}{\sin C}$$

The Sine Rule can also be written as:
$$\frac{\sin A}{a} = \frac{\sin B}{b} = \frac{\sin C}{c}$$

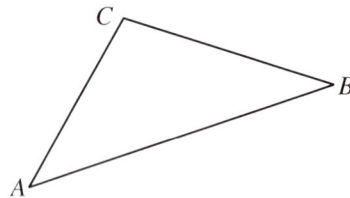

Finding sides

To find a side using the Sine Rule you need:
  two angles of known size, **and**
  the length of a side which is opposite one of the known angles.

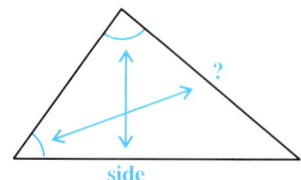

EXAMPLE

In triangle ABC, angle $A = 37°$, angle $C = 72°$ and $b = 12\,cm$.
Calculate a, correct to 3 significant figures.

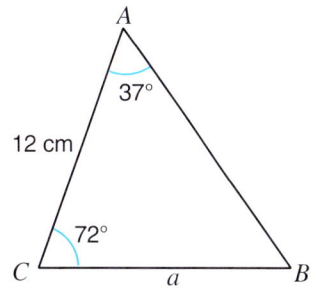

Using the Sine Rule:
$$\frac{a}{\sin A} = \frac{b}{\sin B} = \frac{c}{\sin C}$$

Substitute known values.

$$\frac{a}{\sin 37°} = \frac{12}{\sin 71°} = \frac{c}{\sin 72°}$$

Using:
$$\frac{a}{\sin 37°} = \frac{12}{\sin 71°}$$

Multiply both sides by $\sin 37°$.

$$a = \frac{12 \times \sin 37°}{\sin 71°}$$

$$= 7.637 \ldots$$
$$a = 7.64\,cm, \text{ correct to 3 s.f.}$$

To find angle B:
$$\angle A + \angle B + \angle C = 180°$$
$$37° + \angle B + 72° = 180°$$
$$\angle B = 71°$$

Alternative method
First rearrange the equation,
then substitute known values.

Use $\dfrac{a}{\sin A} = \dfrac{b}{\sin B}$

Rearrange to give $\quad a = \dfrac{b \sin A}{\sin B}$

Substitute $\quad a = \dfrac{12 \times \sin 37°}{\sin 71°}$

Exercise 27.4

1 Find the side marked a in each of the following triangles.

(a)

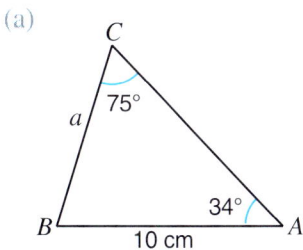

(b)

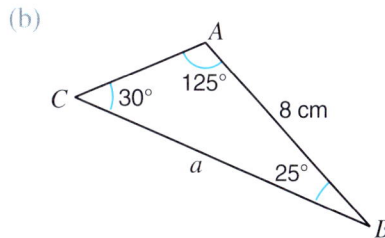

(c)

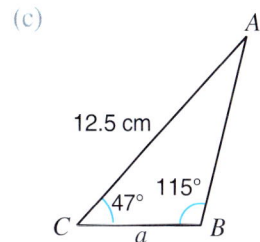

2 Find the marked side in each of these triangles.

(a)

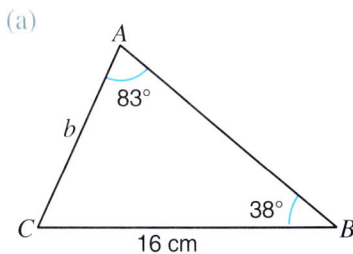

(b)

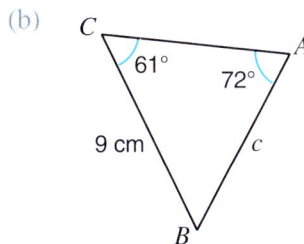

(c)

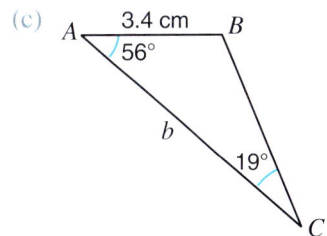

(d)

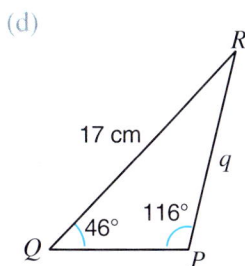

(e)

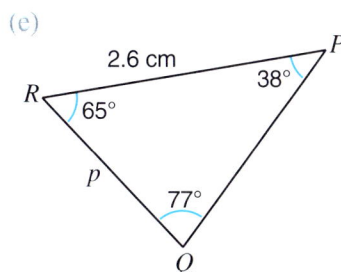

(f)

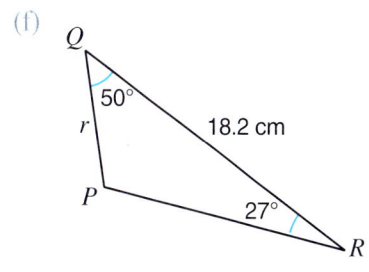

3 Find the remaining angles and sides of these triangles.

(a) $\triangle ABC$, when $\angle BAC = 57°$, $\angle ABC = 68°$ and $BC = 6.7\,\text{cm}$.

(b) $\triangle LMN$, when $\angle LMN = 33.2°$, $\angle LNM = 75.6°$ and $LN = 3.3\,\text{cm}$.

(c) $\triangle PQR$, when $\angle PQR = 62.8°$, $\angle PRQ = 47.4°$ and $PQ = 12.3\,\text{cm}$.

(d) $\triangle STU$, when $\angle TSU = 94.9°$, $\angle STU = 53.3°$ and $SU = 19.4\,\text{cm}$.

(e) $\triangle XYZ$, when $\angle XYZ = 108.6°$, $\angle YXZ = 40.2°$ and $XZ = 13.8\,\text{cm}$.

Finding angles

To find an angle using the Sine Rule you need:

the length of the side opposite the angle you are trying to find, **and**

the length of a side opposite an angle of known size.

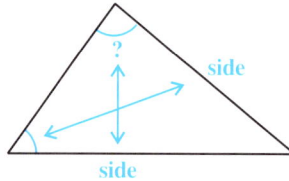

EXAMPLE

Angle $A = 42°$, $a = 6\,\text{cm}$ and $c = 4\,\text{cm}$.
Calculate angle C, correct to one decimal place.

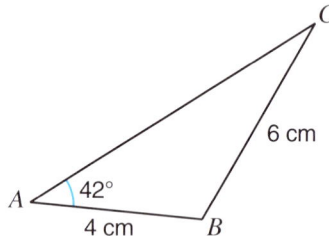

Using the Sine Rule:
$$\frac{\sin A}{a} = \frac{\sin B}{b} = \frac{\sin C}{c}$$

Substitute known values.
$$\frac{\sin 42°}{6} = \frac{\sin B}{b} = \frac{\sin C}{4}$$

Using:
$$\frac{\sin 42°}{6} = \frac{\sin C}{4}$$

Multiply both sides by 4.
$$\sin C = \frac{4 \times \sin 42°}{6}$$

$\sin C = 0.446\ldots$

$C = \sin^{-1}(0.446\ldots)$

$C = 26.49\ldots$

$C = 26.5°$, correct to 1 d.p.

$C = \sin^{-1}(0.446\ldots)$ gives possible angles of $26.5°$ and $153.5°$.
$C \neq 153.5°$ since in an obtuse-angled triangle, the obtuse angle is always opposite the longest side of the triangle.

The ambiguous case

There are two angles between $0°$ and $180°$ which have the same sine.
When we use the sine rule to find an angle we must therefore look at the information to see if there are two possible values for the angle.

404

EXAMPLE

In triangle PQR, $PQ = 8\,cm$, $QR = 6\,cm$ and angle $QPR = 38°$.
Find the size of angle QRP.

Using this information **two** triangles can be drawn.
Use a ruler and compasses to construct the triangles.

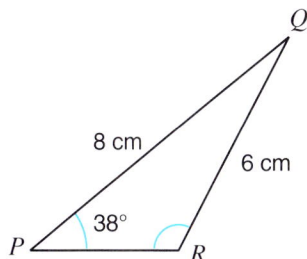

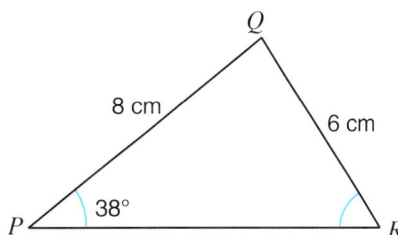

Using the Sine Rule:
$$\frac{\sin P}{p} = \frac{\sin Q}{q} = \frac{\sin R}{r}$$
Substitute known values.
$$\frac{\sin 38°}{6} = \frac{\sin Q}{q} = \frac{\sin R}{8}$$
Using:
$$\frac{\sin 38°}{6} = \frac{\sin R}{8}$$
Multiply both sides by 8.
$$\sin R = \frac{8 \times \sin 38°}{6}$$

$\sin R = 0.820\ ...$
$R = \sin^{-1}(0.820\ ...)$
$R = 55.17\ ...$
$R = 55.2°$
Also, $R = 180° - 55.2° = 124.8°$

$\angle QPR = 55.2°$ or $124.8°$, correct to 1 d.p.

Exercise 27.5

1 Find angle A in each of these acute-angled triangles.

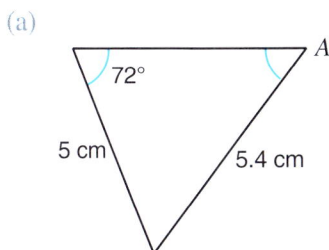

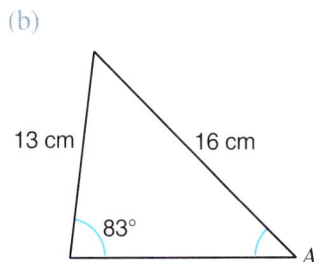

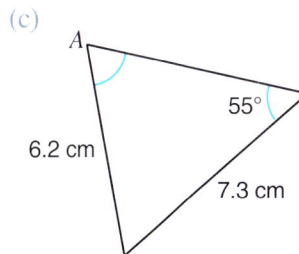

(a)

(b)

(c)

2 Find angle A in each of these obtuse-angled triangles.

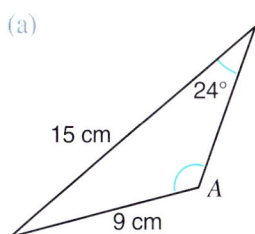

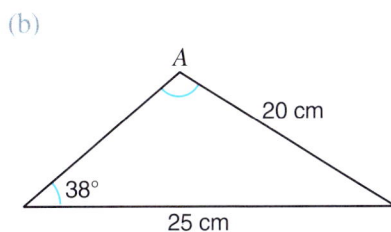

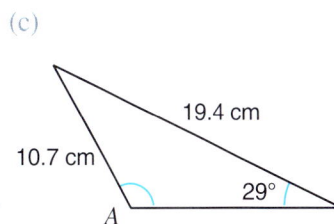

(a)

(b)

(c)

3 In triangle ABC, $AB = 6$ cm, $BC = 4$ cm and angle $BAC = 30°$.
There are two possible triangles that can be constructed.
Calculate the two possible values of angle BCA.

4 In triangle PQR, $QR = 7.5$ cm, $RP = 7$ cm and angle $PQR = 60°$.
There are two possible triangles that can be constructed.
Find the missing sides and angles of both triangles.

5 Find the missing sides and angles in each of the following triangles.
(a) $\triangle ABC$, when $AB = 8.3$ cm, $AC = 8.9$ cm and angle $ABC = 69.3°$.
(b) $\triangle DEF$, when $DE = 8.5$ cm, $DF = 16.34$ cm and angle $DEF = 125°$.

Deriving the Cosine Rule

$AB = c$
Let $AX = x$
So, $BX = c - x$

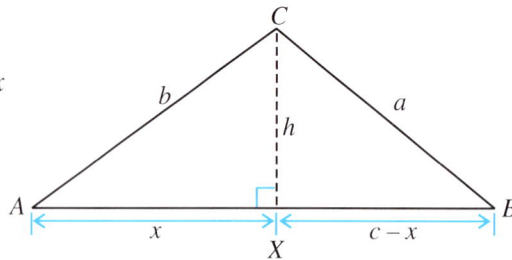

On page 402, starting with the triangle ABC, we derived the Sine Rule.

In triangle ACX.
Using Pythagoras' Theorem.
$b^2 = x^2 + h^2$

Using the cosine ratio.
$\cos A = \dfrac{\text{adj}}{\text{hyp}}$

$\cos A = \dfrac{x}{b}$

$x = b \cos A$

In triangle BCX.
Using Pythagoras' Theorem.
$a^2 = (c - x)^2 + h^2$
$a^2 = c^2 - 2cx + x^2 + h^2$
Replace: $x^2 + h^2$ by b^2, and x by $b \cos A$.
$a^2 = c^2 - 2c(b \cos A) + b^2$
This can be rearranged as:
$a^2 = b^2 + c^2 - 2bc \cos A$,
and is called the **Cosine Rule.**

The Cosine Rule

In any triangle labelled ABC it can be proved that:
$\qquad a^2 = b^2 + c^2 - 2bc \cos A$
In a similar way, we can find the Cosine Rule for b^2 and c^2.
$\qquad b^2 = a^2 + c^2 - 2ac \cos B$
$\qquad c^2 = a^2 + b^2 - 2ab \cos C$

When using the Cosine Rule to find the size of an angle it is sometimes easier to rearrange the above formulae as:
$$\cos A = \frac{b^2 + c^2 - a^2}{2bc} \qquad \cos B = \frac{a^2 + c^2 - b^2}{2ac} \qquad \cos C = \frac{a^2 + b^2 - c^2}{2ab}$$

Finding sides

To find a side using the Cosine Rule you need:
two sides of known length, **and**
the size of the angle between the known sides.

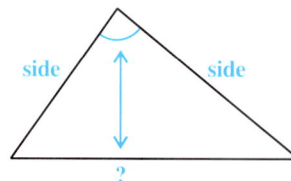

406

EXAMPLE

Calculate the length of side a.

Using the Cosine Rule:
$a^2 = b^2 + c^2 - 2bc \cos A$
Substitute known values.
$a^2 = 20^2 + 16^2 - 2 \times 20 \times 16 \times \cos 56°$
$\quad = 400 + 256 - 357.88 \ldots$
$\quad = 298.116 \ldots$
Take the square root.
$a = 17.266 \ldots$
$a = 17.3 \, \text{cm}$, correct to 3 s.f.

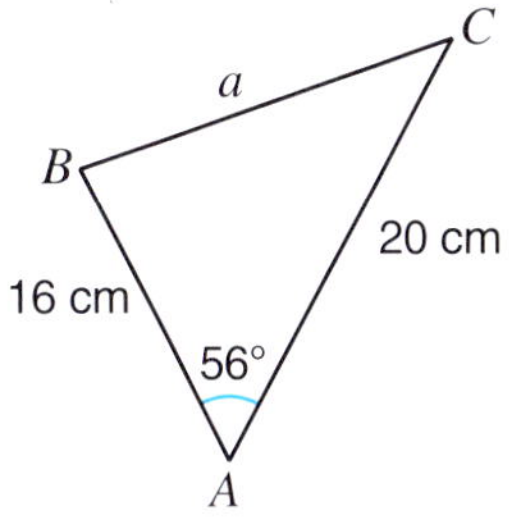

Exercise 27.6

1 Calculate the lengths of the sides marked a.
Give your answers correct to three significant figures.

(a)

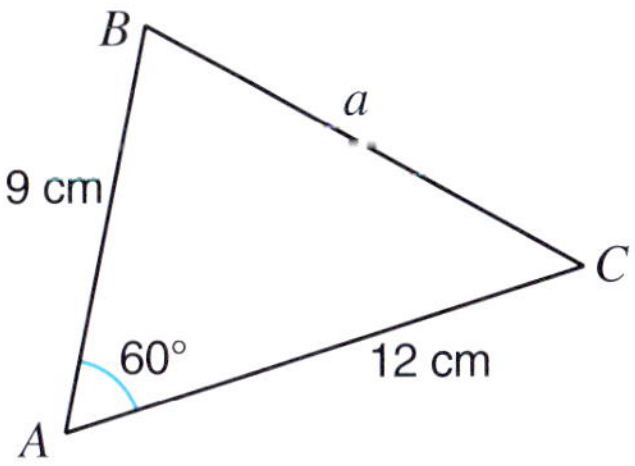

(b)

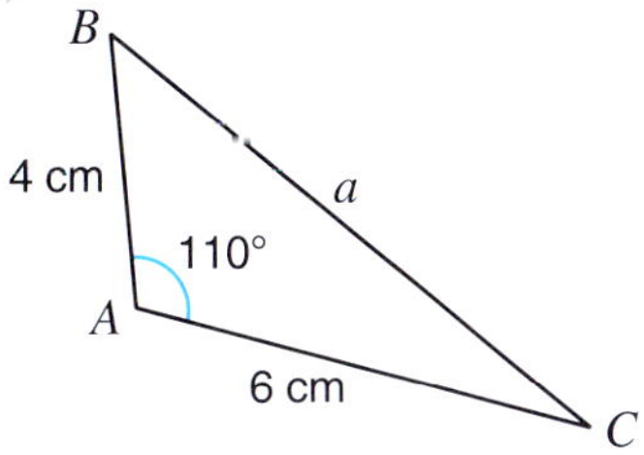

(c)

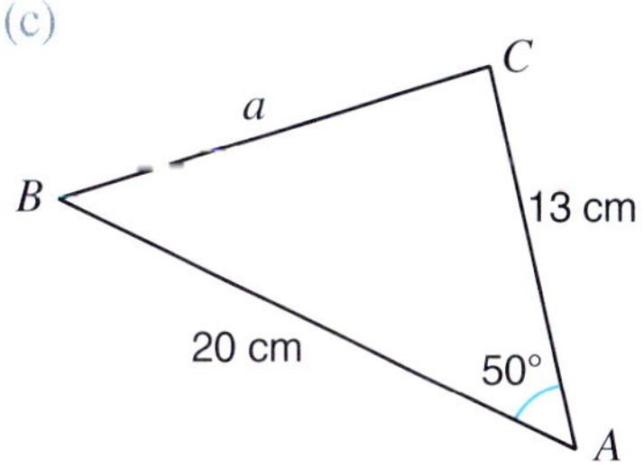

2 Calculate the lengths of the sides marked with letters.
Give your answers correct to three significant figures.

(a)

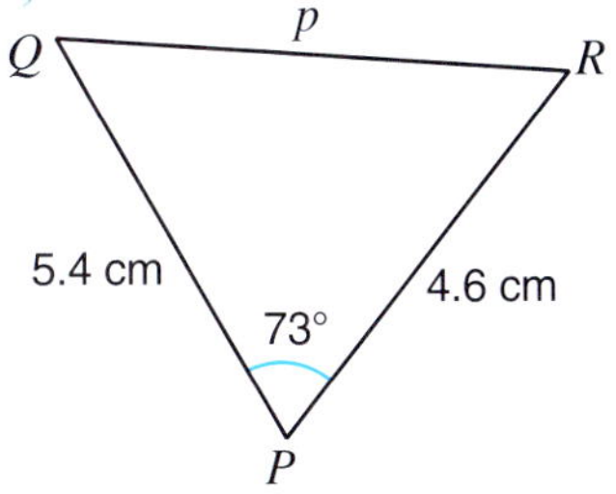

(b)

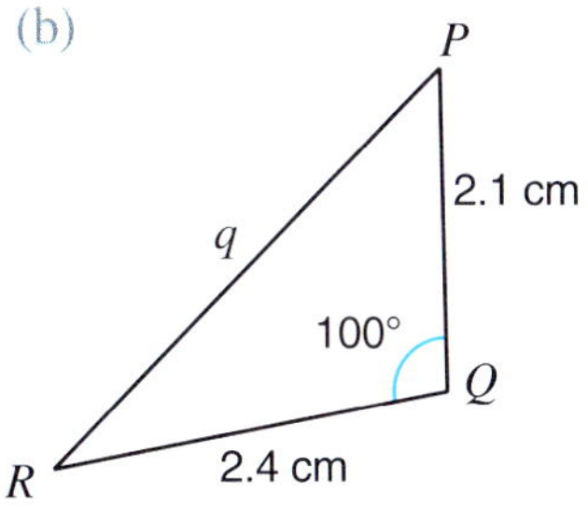

(c)

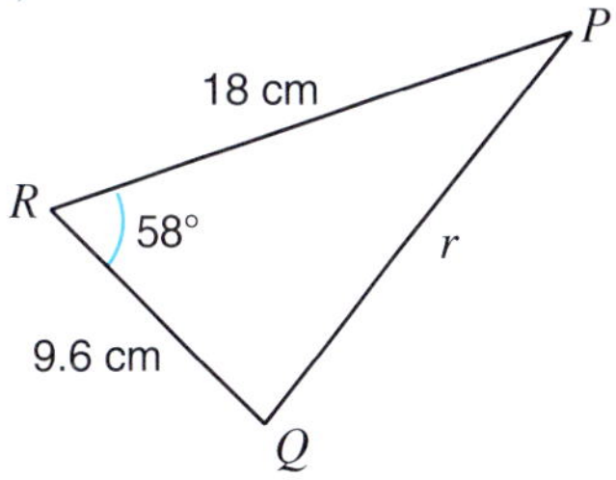

3 In triangle ABC, $AB = 8$ cm, $AC = 13$ cm and $\angle BAC = 70°$. Calculate BC.

4 In triangle LMN, $LM = 16$ cm, $MN = 9$ cm and $\angle LMN = 46.8°$. Calculate LN.

5 In triangle PQR, $PQ = 9$ cm, $PR = 5.4$ cm and $\angle RPQ = 135°$. Calculate QR.

6 In triangle XYZ, $XY = 7.5$ cm, $YZ = 13$ cm and $\angle XYZ = 120°$. Calculate XZ.

Finding angles

To find an angle using the Cosine Rule you need:
   three sides of known length.

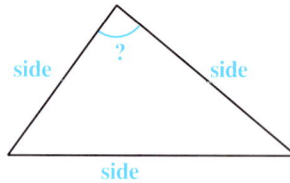

EXAMPLE

Calculate the size of angle A.

Using the Cosine Rule:

$$\cos A = \frac{b^2 + c^2 - a^2}{2bc}$$

Substitute known values

$$\cos A = \frac{5^2 + 4^2 - 6^2}{2 \times 5 \times 4}$$

$\cos A = 0.125$

$A = \cos^{-1}(0.125)$

$A = 82.819 \dots$

$A = 82.8°$, correct to 1 d.p.

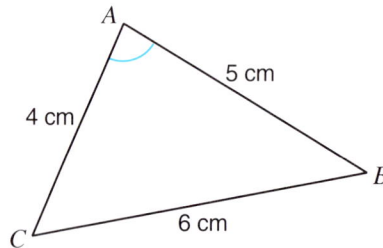

Exercise 27.7

1 Calculate angle A in each of the following.
    Give your answers correct to one decimal place.

(a)

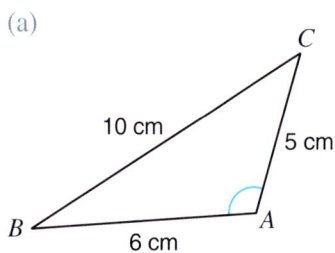

(b)

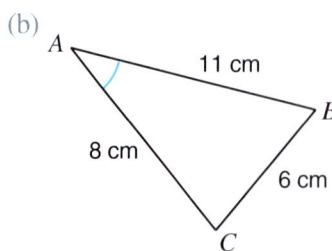

(c)

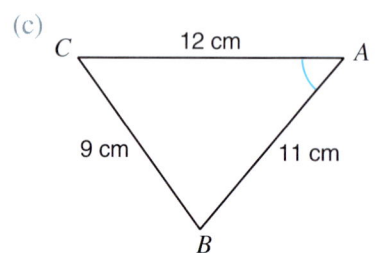

2 In this question give your answers correct to one decimal place.

(a) Calculate $\angle B$.

(b) Calculate $\angle C$.

(c) Calculate $\angle P$.

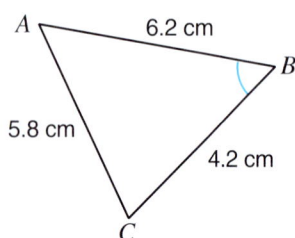

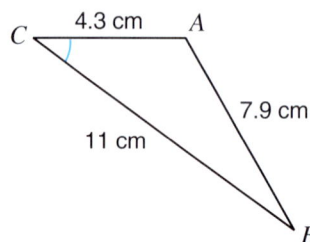

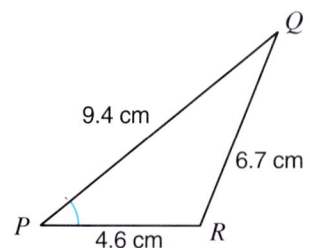

3 In triangle ABC, $AB = 18\,\text{cm}$, $BC = 23\,\text{cm}$ and $CA = 24\,\text{cm}$. Calculate $\angle ACB$.

4 In triangle PQR, $PQ = 10\,\text{cm}$, $QR = 12\,\text{cm}$ and $RP = 20\,\text{cm}$. Calculate $\angle PQR$.

5 In triangle LMN, $LM = 8\,\text{cm}$, $MN = 6\,\text{cm}$ and $NL = 11\,\text{cm}$. Calculate $\angle LMN$.

6 In triangle XYZ, $XY = 9.6\,\text{cm}$, $YZ = 13.4\,\text{cm}$ and $XZ = 20\,\text{cm}$. Calculate $\angle XYZ$.

Area of a triangle

Look at these triangles. Both are labelled ABC.

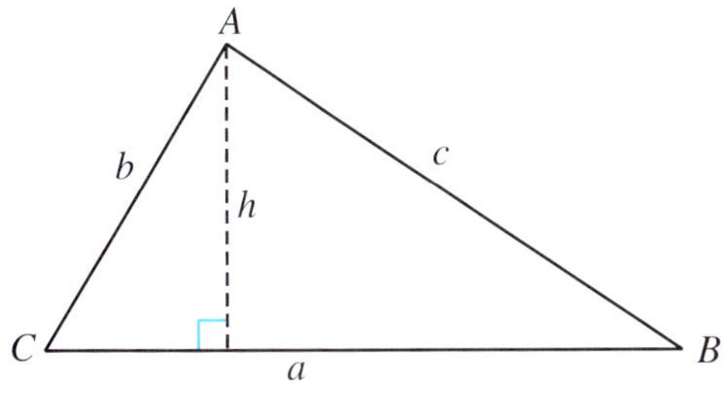

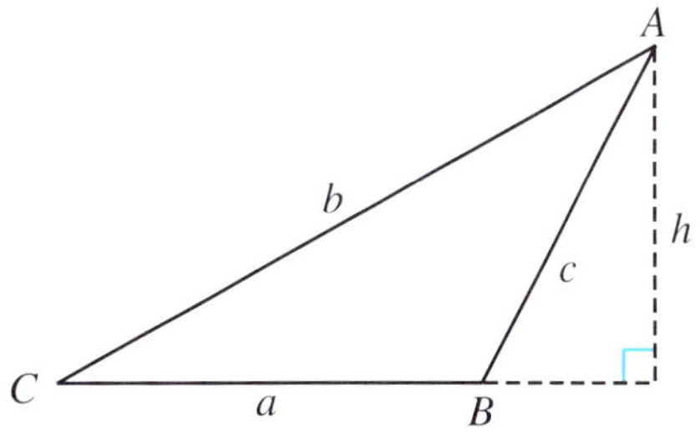

The height of each triangle is labelled h.
In both triangles $h = b \sin C$.

The area of triangle $ABC = \frac{1}{2} \times$ base $\times$ height
$$= \frac{1}{2} \times a \times b \sin C$$
$$= \frac{1}{2} ab \sin C$$

base $= a$
height $= b \sin C$

For any triangle ABC:
Area $= \frac{1}{2} ab \sin C$

To use this formula to find the area of a triangle we need:
two sides of known length, **and**
the size of the angle between the known sides.

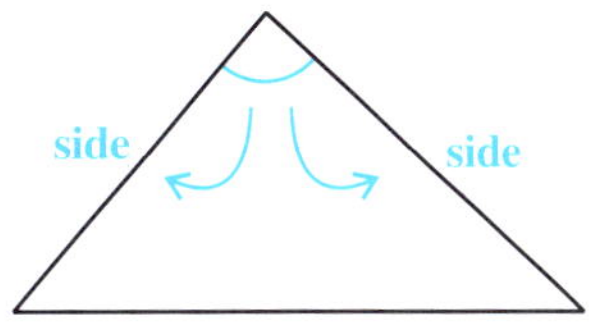

side   side

In a similar way write down a formula to find the area of triangle ABC using a, c and angle B.

Can you find a rule which gives the area of a parallelogram?

EXAMPLE

Calculate the area of triangle PQR.

Area $PQR = \frac{1}{2} \times p \times q \times \sin R$
$$= 0.5 \times 2.4 \times 4.5 \times \sin 67°$$
$$= 4.9707 \ldots$$
$$= 4.97\,\text{cm}^2, \text{ correct to 3 s.f.}$$

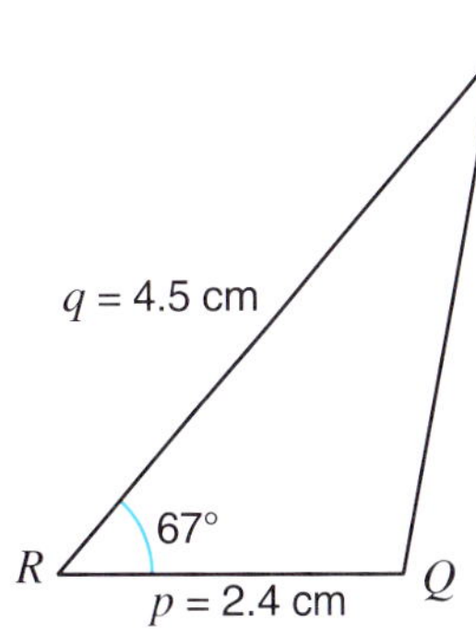

$q = 4.5\,\text{cm}$

$67°$

$p = 2.4\,\text{cm}$

1 Calculate the areas of these triangles.
Give your answers correct to three significant figures.

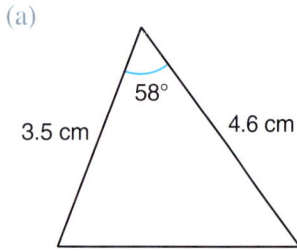

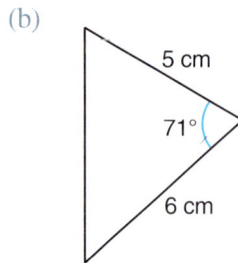

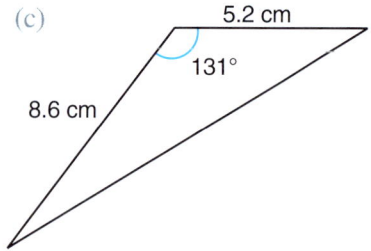

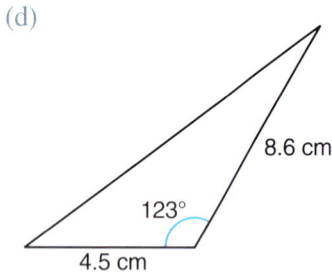

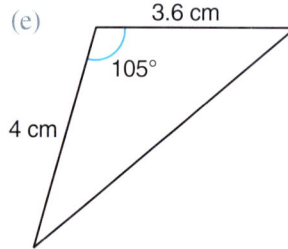

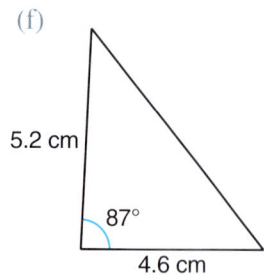

(a)

3.5 cm   58°   4.6 cm

(b)

5 cm   71°   6 cm

(c)

5.2 cm   131°   8.6 cm

(d)

8.6 cm   123°   4.5 cm

(e)

3.6 cm   105°   4 cm

(f)

5.2 cm   87°   4.6 cm

2 PQRS is a parallelogram.
PQ = 9.2 cm, PS = 11.4 cm and angle QPS = 54°.
Calculate the area of the parallelogram.

3 ABCD is a quadrilateral.

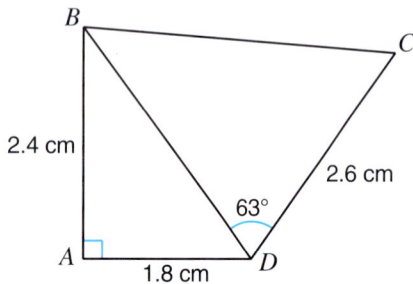

B   C
2.4 cm
2.6 cm
63°
A   1.8 cm   D

(a) Calculate the length of BD.
(b) Calculate the area of ABCD.

6 PQRS is a kite.

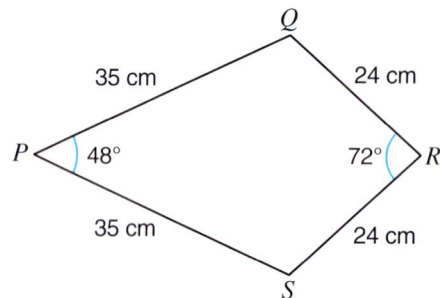

Q
35 cm   24 cm
P   48°   72°   R
35 cm   24 cm
S

PQ = SP = 35 cm.
QR = RS = 24 cm.
Angle QPS = 48°, angle QRS = 72°.
Calculate the area of the kite.

4 A regular hexagon has sides of length 5 cm.
Calculate the area of the hexagon.

5 The area of triangle PQR is 31.7 cm².
PQ = 9.6 cm and angle PQR = 48°.
Calculate the length of QR.
Give your answer correct to one decimal place.

7 Triangle XYZ is isosceles, with XY = YZ.
Angle XYZ = 54°.
The area of triangle XYZ is 22 cm².
Calculate the lengths of XY and YZ.

8 The area of triangle ABC is 25.6 cm².
AB = 6.7 cm, AC = 9.2 cm.
Calculate the two possible sizes of angle A.

Right-angled triangles
Use the **trigonometric ratios** (sin, cos and tan) or **Pythagoras' Theorem**.

Triangles which are not right-angled

The Sine Rule

To find a **side** you need:
two angles of known size, **and**
the length of a side which is opposite
one of the known angles.

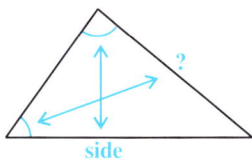

To find an **angle** you need:
the length of the side opposite the angle
you are trying to find, **and** the length of
a side opposite an angle of known size.

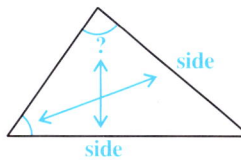

The Cosine Rule

To find a **side** you need:
two sides of known length, **and**
the size of the angle between the known sides.

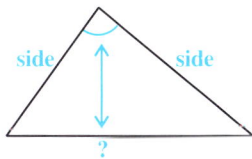

To find an **angle** you need:
three sides of known length.

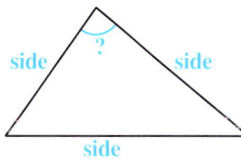

To find the **area of a triangle**, when you know two sides and the angle between the sides, use:

Area of triangle $= \frac{1}{2} ab \sin C$

EXAMPLE

Find the unknown sides and angles in this triangle.

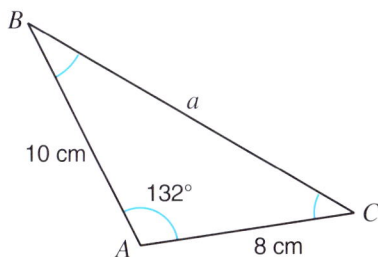

Using the Cosine Rule to find a.
$a^2 = b^2 + c^2 - 2bc \cos A$
$a^2 = 8^2 + 10^2 - 2 \times 8 \times 10 \times \cos 132°$
$a^2 = 271.06 ...$
$a = 16.46 ...$
Store this accurate value of a in the memory of
your calculator.
$a = 16.5$ cm, correct to 3 s.f.

Now use the Sine Rule to find angle C.
$\frac{\sin A}{a} = \frac{\sin B}{b} = \frac{\sin C}{c}$
$\frac{\sin 132°}{16.46 ...} = \frac{\sin B}{8} = \frac{\sin C}{10}$

Using:
$\frac{\sin 132°}{16.46 ...} = \frac{\sin C}{10}$
$\sin C = \frac{10 \times \sin 132°}{16.46 ...}$
$\sin C = 0.451 ...$
$C = \sin^{-1}(0.451 ...)$
$C = 26.83 ...$
$C = 26.8°$, correct to 1 d.p.

$B = 180° - 26.8° - 132°$
$B = 21.2°$

1 (a) Find the unknown sides and angles in these triangles.
(b) Calculate the area of each triangle.

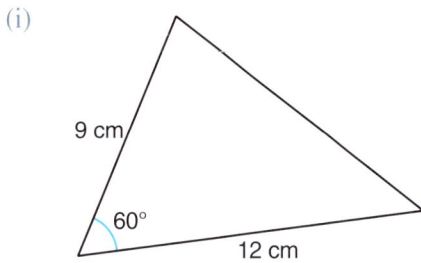

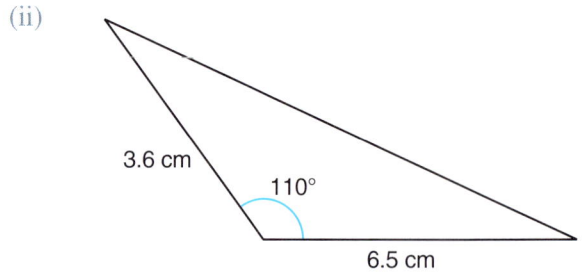

(i)

9 cm
60°
12 cm

(ii)

3.6 cm
110°
6.5 cm

2 The diagram shows the positions of a tree, at T, and at a pylon, at P, on opposite sides of a river. Two bridges cross the river at X and Y.

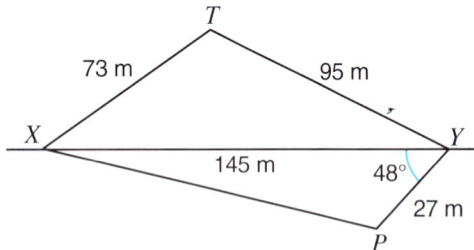

T
73 m   95 m
X
145 m   48°
27 m
P
Y

Remember:
The **longest side** is opposite the **largest angle**.
The **shortest side** is opposite the **smallest angle**.

$XY = 145$ m, $XT = 73$ m, $TY = 95$ m, $YP = 27$ m and $\angle XYP = 48°$.
(a) Calculate the angles of triangle XTY.
(b) Calculate XP and $\angle XPY$.

3 Two ships, P and Q, leave port at 2 pm.
P travels at 24 km/h on a bearing of 085°.
Q travels at 32 km/h on a bearing of 120°.
Calculate the distance between the ships at 2.30 pm.

4 The diagram shows a tower.
At A the angle of elevation to the top of the tower is 43°.
At B the angle of elevation to the top of the tower is 74°.
The distance AB is 10m.
Calculate the height of the tower.

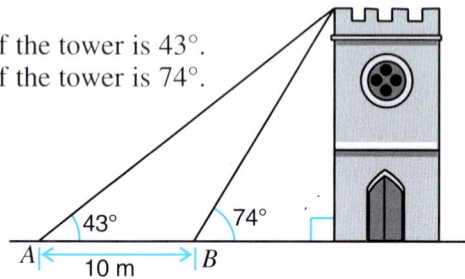

43°   74°
A 10 m B

5 The diagram shows part of a steel framework, ABC.
B is on horizontal ground. A is 10m vertically above B.
$BC = 16$ m. Angle $ABC = 23°$.
(a) Calculate the length of AC.
(b) Calculate angle BCA.
(c) Calculate the vertical height of C above B.

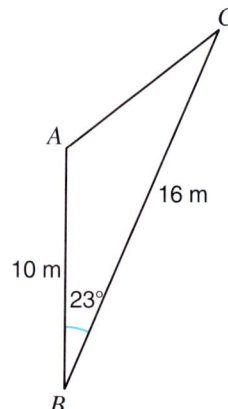

C
A
16 m
10 m
23°
B

6 In triangle LMN, $MN = 7.5\,$cm, angle $MLN = 104°$ and angle $LMN = 34°$.
   (a) Calculate the length of LM.
   (b) Calculate the area of the triangle.

7 The diagram shows a quadrilateral $PQRS$.
$PQ = 4\,$cm, $QR = 5\,$cm, $RS = 7\,$cm,
$QS = 8\,$cm and angle $SPQ = 110°$.

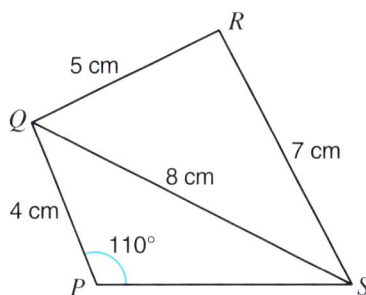

   (a) Calculate angle QSP.
   (b) Calculate angle QSR.
   (c) Calculate the area of $PQRS$.

8 An isosceles triangle has an area of $25.6\,$cm².
The two equal sides are $8.4\,$cm long.
Calculate the two possible lengths of the third side.

What you need to know

- The graphs of the trigonometric functions.

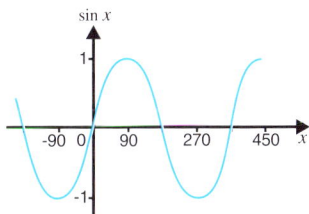

The **sine function** is a periodic function with period $360°$.
$-1 \leqslant \sin x \leqslant 1$

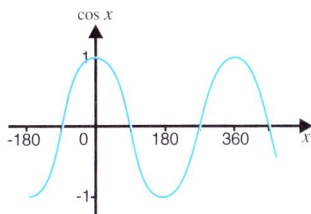

The **cosine function** is a periodic function with period $360°$.
$-1 \leqslant \cos x \leqslant 1$

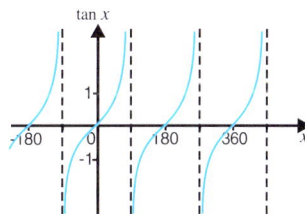

The **tangent function** is a periodic function with period $180°$.
Tan x is undefined at $90°$, $270°$, ...

- For every angle $x°$, the signs of $\sin x°$, $\cos x°$ and $\tan x°$ can be shown on a diagram.

   Positive angles are measured **anticlockwise.**
   Negative angles are measured **clockwise.**

For angles greater than $360°$: subtract $360°$, or multiples of $360°$, to get the equivalent angle between $0°$ and $360°$.

- The **exact values** of the trigonometric ratios for the angles $30°$, $45°$ and $60°$ can be found from the triangles below.

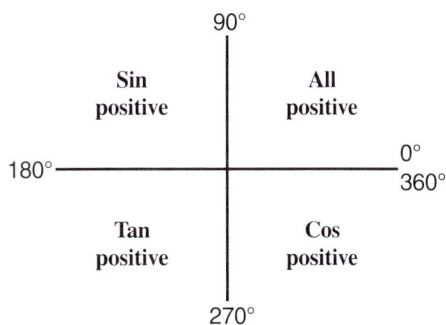

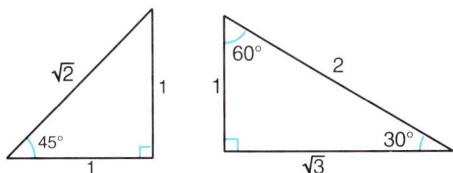

	$30°$	$45°$	$60°$
sin	$\frac{1}{2}$	$\frac{1}{\sqrt{2}}$	$\frac{\sqrt{3}}{2}$
cos	$\frac{\sqrt{3}}{2}$	$\frac{1}{\sqrt{2}}$	$\frac{1}{2}$
tan	$\frac{1}{\sqrt{3}}$	1	$\sqrt{3}$

- **The Sine Rule**.

  $$\frac{a}{\sin A} = \frac{b}{\sin B} = \frac{c}{\sin C}$$

  This can be also written as:

  $$\frac{\sin A}{a} = \frac{\sin B}{b} = \frac{\sin C}{c}$$

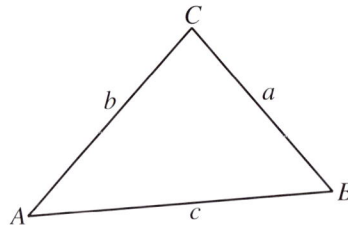

- **The Cosine Rule**

  $a^2 = b^2 + c^2 - 2bc \cos A$
  $b^2 = a^2 + c^2 - 2ac \cos B$
  $c^2 = a^2 + b^2 - 2ab \cos C$

  When using the Cosine Rule to find the size of an angle it is sometimes easier to rearrange the above formulae as:

  $$\cos A = \frac{b^2 + c^2 - a^2}{2bc} \qquad \cos B = \frac{a^2 + c^2 - b^2}{2ac} \qquad \cos C = \frac{a^2 + b^2 - c^2}{2ab}$$

- To find the **area of a triangle** when you know two sides and the angle between the two sides use:

  Area of triangle $= \frac{1}{2} ab \sin C$

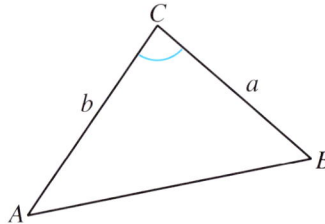

- Solving problems involving triangles.

  Right-angled triangles
  Use the **trigonometric ratios** (sin, cos and tan) or **Pythagoras' Theorem.**

  Triangles which are not right-angled
  The Sine Rule
  To find a **side** you need:
  two angles of known size, **and** the length of a side which is opposite one of the known angles.

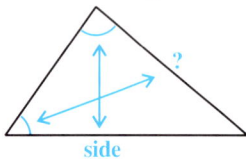

  To find an **angle** you need:
  the length of the side opposite the angle you are trying to find, **and** the length of a side opposite an angle of known size.

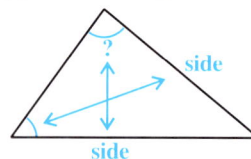

  The Cosine Rule
  To find a **side** you need:
  two sides of known length, **and** the size of the angle between the known sides.

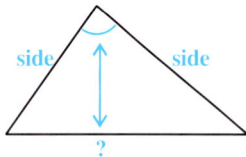

  To find an **angle** you need:
  three sides of known length.

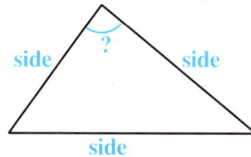

IDEAS FOR INVESTIGATION

Investigate graphs of the form $y = a \sin bx$ and $y = a \cos bx$.

What can you say about the values of a and b and the graphs of the functions?

Do not use a calculator in questions 1 to 3.

1 State whether the following are positive or negative.
  (a) cos 100°   (b) tan 100°   (c) sin 100°
  (d) cos 200°   (e) tan 200°   (f) sin 200°
  (g) cos 300°   (h) tan 300°   (i) sin 300°

2 Sin 30° = 0.5
  (a) Write down the value of sin 150°.
  (b) If sin x = −0.5, write down the possible values of x between 0° and 360°.

3 Cos 30° = $\frac{\sqrt{3}}{2}$
  (a) Write down the value of cos 150°.
  (b) Cos x = cos 30°, 0° ⩽ x ⩽ 360° and x ≠ 30°. Write down the value of x.
  (c) Cos y = − $\frac{\sqrt{3}}{2}$. Write down the possible values of y between 0° and 360°.

4 (a) The diagram shows part of the graph of y = cos x.
    (i) Write down the value of a.
    (ii) Copy the diagram and sketch the rest of the graph of y = cos x as far as x = 4a.
  (b) The angle y is between 0° and 360°. Work out accurately the two solutions of the equation cos y = −0.5.

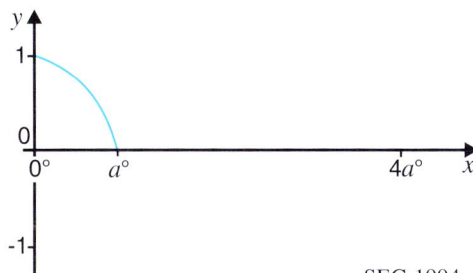

SEG 1994

5 The graph of y = sin x for 0° ⩽ x ⩽ 360° is drawn below.

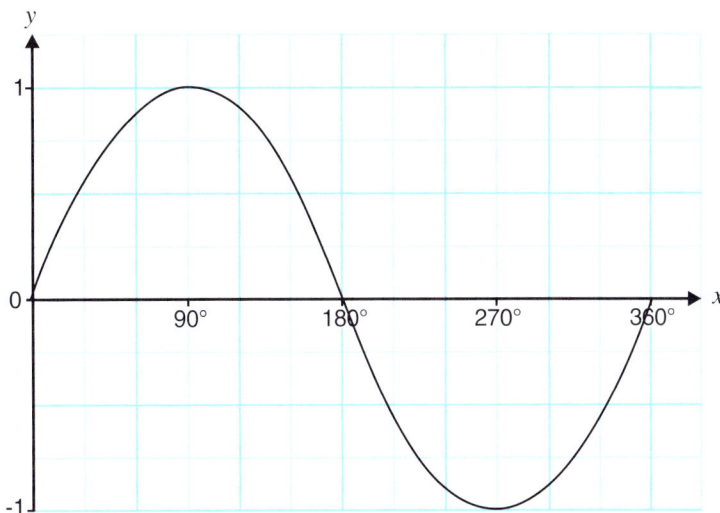

  (a) Angle p satisfies the equation sin p = sin 210°. Angle p is not equal to 210°. What is the value of p?
  (b) Copy the graph and on the same axes as y = sin x, draw the graph of y = $\frac{1}{2}$ cos x for 0° ⩽ x ⩽ 360°.
  (c) Use the graphs to solve the equation sin x = $\frac{1}{2}$ cos x for the range of x that the graphs allow.

SEG 1995

6 On a particular day the height, h metres, of the tide at Weymouth, relative to a certain point, can be modelled by the equation $h = 5\sin(30t)°$, where t is the time in hours after midnight.

(a) Copy the axes and sketch the graph of h against t for $0 \leqslant t \leqslant 12$.

(b) At what time is low tide?

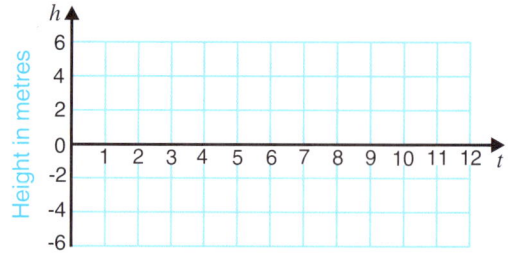

SEG 1994

7 A fairground ride consists of seats fastened onto a big wheel. The height, H metres, of a seat above the ground at any time, t seconds, after the start of the ride is given by the equation $H = 9.7 - 8\cos(20t)°$.

(a) What is the maximum height of the seat above the ground?

(b) At what time is the seat 7 m above the ground for the first time?

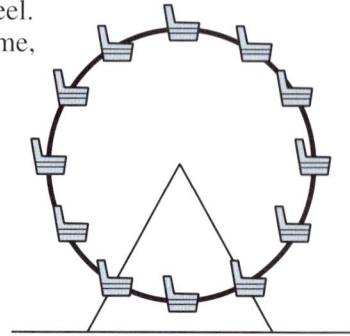

SEG 1997

8 Two dogs are taking a boy for a walk!
Fido's lead is 2 metres long and Rover's lead is 2.5 metres long.
They are pulling in different directions at an angle of 35° to each other.
Calculate the distance between the two dogs.

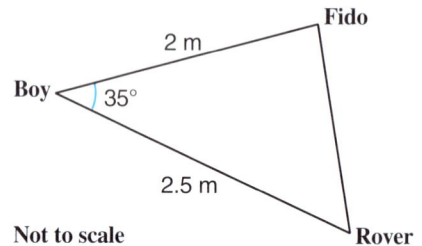

Not to scale

SEG 1994

9 In the triangle ABC, $AB = 6$ cm, $BC = 5$ cm and angle $BAC = 45°$.
There are two possible triangles that can be constructed.
Calculate the **two** possible values of the angle BCA.

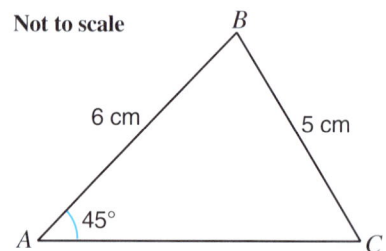

Not to scale

SEG 1995

10 In the Olympic sailing regatta one of the courses is in the shape of a triangle.
Buoys are fixed at the three corners of the triangle PQR.
$PQ = 1.8$ km. $PR = 2.5$ km.
Q is due north of P. Angle $PQR = 60°$.
Calculate the bearing of P from R.

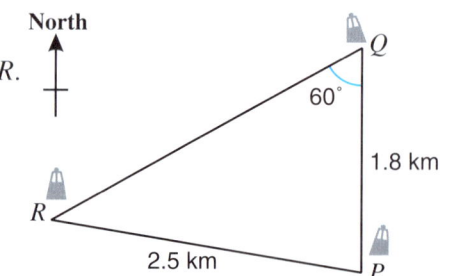

Not to scale

SEG 1996

11 Two ships, *A* and *B*, leave Dover Docks at the same time.
Ship *A* travels at 25 km/h on a bearing of 120°.
Ship *B* travels at 30 km/h on a bearing of 130°.
Calculate how far apart the two ships are after 1 hour.

SEG 1994

12 A flag pole stands on the side of a hill supported by two cables.
(a) Calculate the length of the lower cable *a*.
(b) Calculate the angle *x* between the upper cable and the flagpole.

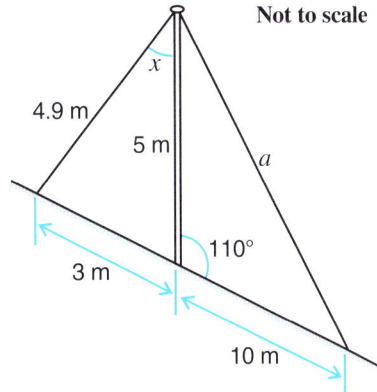

Not to scale

4.9 m

5 m

x

a

3 m

110°

10 m

SEG 1995

13 A surveyor wishes to measure the height of a church.
Measuring the angle of elevation, she finds that the angle increases from 30° to 35° after walking 20 metres towards the church.
What is the height of the church?

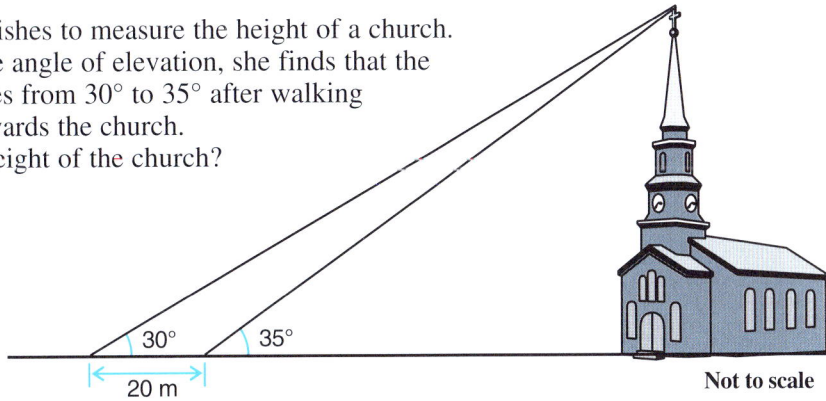

30°   35°

20 m

Not to scale

SEG 1994

14 In triangle *ABC*, *AC* = 4 cm, *AB* = 7 cm and angle *ACB* = 100°.
Calculate the area of the triangle.

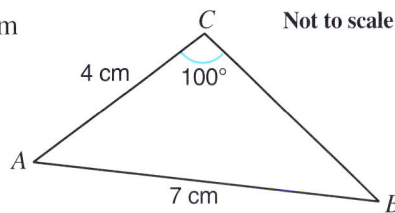

C   Not to scale

4 cm   100°

A

7 cm   *B*

SEG 1998

15 In this cuboid *AB* = 12 cm, *BC* = 7 cm and *P* is the mid-point of *BC*.
(a) Calculate the length of *AP*.

Q is a point on *EF* such that *AQ* = 8 cm and *QP* = 7 cm.
(b) Calculate the size of angle *AQP*.

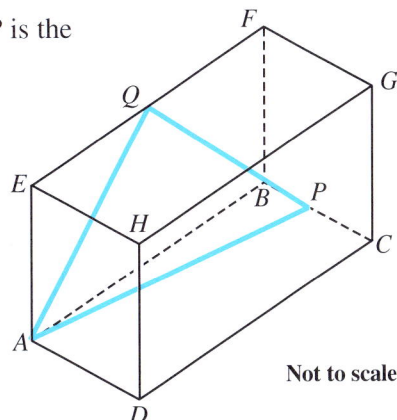

F

G

Q

E

H

B   *P*

C

A

D

Not to scale

SEG 1995

Section Review – Shape, Space and Measures

1 OW, OX and OY meet at O, as shown.

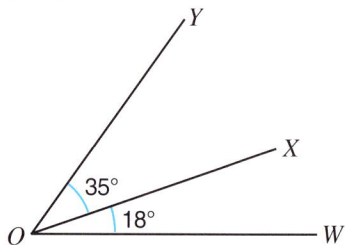

Reflection in OW followed by reflection in OX followed by reflection in OY gives the same transformation as a reflection in a line OZ. Find the angle WOZ.

2 These regular polygons are similar.

Not to scale

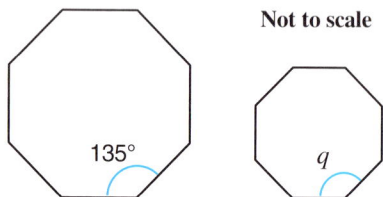

The lengths of the sides are in the ratio 4 : 3.
The larger polygon has a perimeter of 48 cm.
Find the perimeter of the smaller polygon and the size of angle q.

SEG 1999

3 A regular pentagon is drawn below. Use angles to explain why you cannot make a tessellation from regular pentagons.

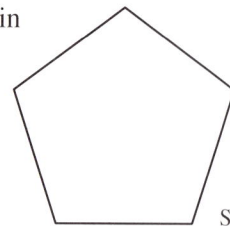

SEG 1999

4 The diagram shows a window. The arc AB is a semicircle. $BC = AD = 75$ cm, $DC = 80$ cm.

Calculate the area of the window.

Not to scale

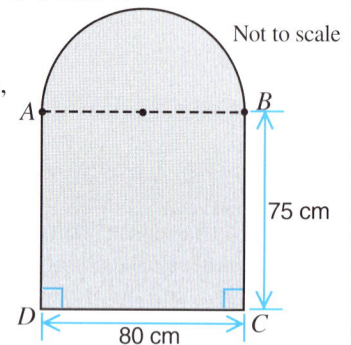

SEG 1996

5 A parallelogram $ABCD$ has vertices at (6, 3), (9, 3), (12, 9) and (9, 9) respectively.
(a) An enlargement scale factor $\frac{2}{3}$ and centre (0, 0) transforms parallelogram $ABCD$ onto parallelogram $A_1 B_1 C_1 D_1$. Draw the parallelogram $A_1 B_1 C_1 D_1$.
(b) The parallelogram $A_1 B_1 C_1 D_1$ can be transformed back onto the parallelogram $ABCD$ by a single transformation. Describe fully this transformation.

SEG 1998 S

6 Two straight roads are shown on the diagram.
A new gas pipe is to be laid from Bere equidistant from the two roads.
The diagram is drawn to a scale of 1 cm to 1 km.
(a) Copy the diagram and construct the path of the gas pipe.
(b) The gas board needs a construction site depot.
The depot must be equidistant from Bere and Cole.
The depot must be less than 4 km from Alton.
Draw loci on the diagram to represent this information.

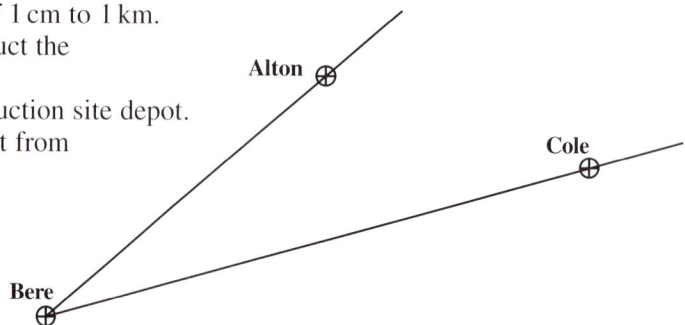

(c) The depot must be nearer the road through Cole than the road through Alton.
Mark on your diagram, with a cross, a possible position for the site depot which satisfies all these conditions.

418

7 (a) The diagram shows a rectangle with its diagonals drawn.

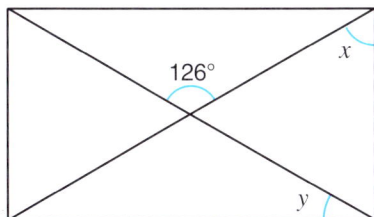

126°

x

y

Not to scale

Work out the size of angle x and the size of angle y.

(b) The diagram shows a triangle ABC.

Not to scale

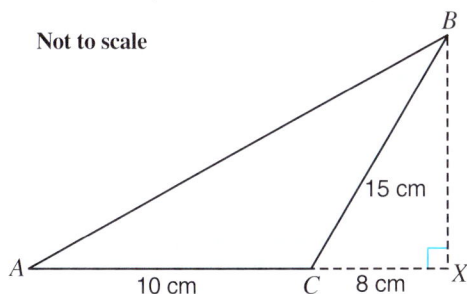

B

15 cm

A

10 cm C 8 cm X

Angle $BXA = 90°$, $BC = 15$ cm and $CX = 8$ cm.

(i) Calculate BX.

(ii) $AC = 10$ cm.
Calculate the area of triangle ABC.   SEG 1999

8 The diagram shows a zig-zag path which joins the upper and lower gardens at a holiday resort.

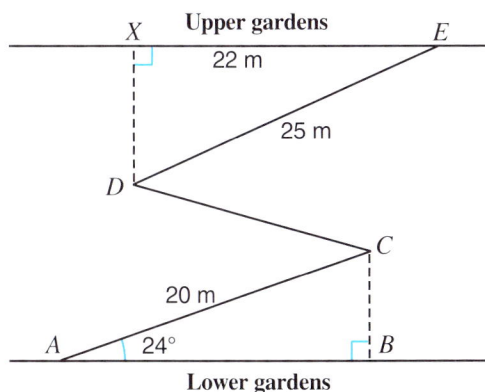

X **Upper gardens** E
22 m
25 m
D
C
20 m
A 24° B
Lower gardens

Not to scale

The path DE is 25 m long and $XE = 22$ m.

(a) Calculate XD.

The path AC is 20 m long and slopes at 24° to the horizontal.

(b) Calculate BC.   SEG 2000 S

9 The diagram shows a kite, $ABCD$.

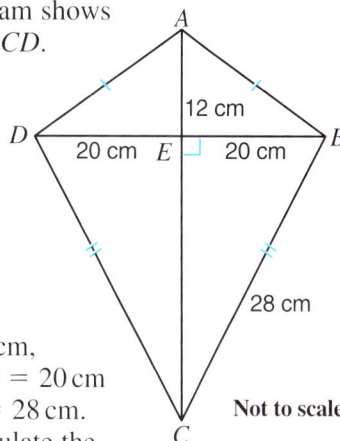

A
12 cm
D 20 cm E 20 cm B
28 cm
C **Not to scale**

$AE = 12$ cm, $DE = EB = 20$ cm and $BC = 28$ cm.

(a) Calculate the size of angle EBC.

(b) Calculate the length of EC and hence find the area of the kite.   SEG 1998

10 Do not use a calculator in this question.
Tan $XYZ = \frac{4}{3}$

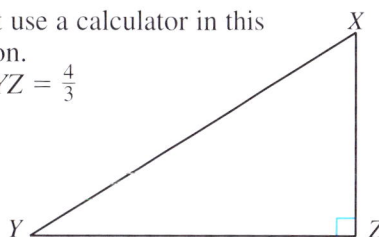

X
Y Z

(a) Find

(i) sin XYZ,

(ii) cos XYZ.

(b) When $XZ = 10$ cm, what are the lengths of XY and YZ?

11 The diagram shows a right-angled triangle ABC and a trapezium $ACDE$.
Angle $BAC = 36°$ and $AC = 7.9$ cm.

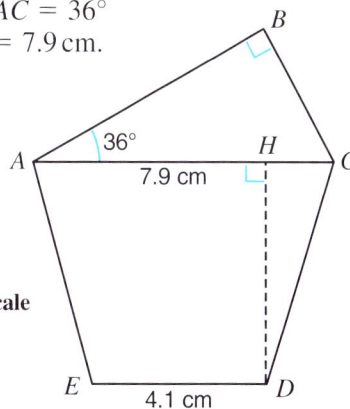

B
A 36° H C
7.9 cm
E 4.1 cm D

Not to scale

(a) Calculate the length of AB.

The area of the trapezium is 52 cm².
$ED = 4.1$ cm.

(b) Calculate DH, the height of the trapezium.   SEG 1999

419

12 The diagram shows triangle T.
Copy the diagram.

(a) Draw the image of triangle T after a reflection in the *x* axis.
Label the image R.

(b) Draw the image of triangle T after a translation $\begin{pmatrix} 4 \\ -2 \end{pmatrix}$.
Label the image S.

(c) Triangle R can be transformed onto triangle S by a rotation about the point (4, *p*) followed by a reflection in the line *x* = 6.
Find (i) the value of *p*,
(ii) the angle through which R is rotated.

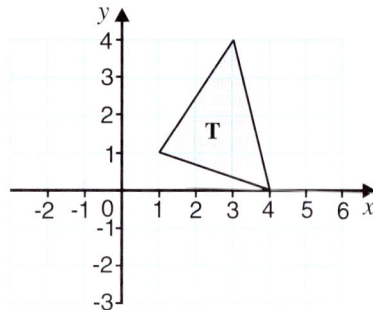

13 Describe fully the **single** transformation which maps triangle *A* onto triangle *B*.

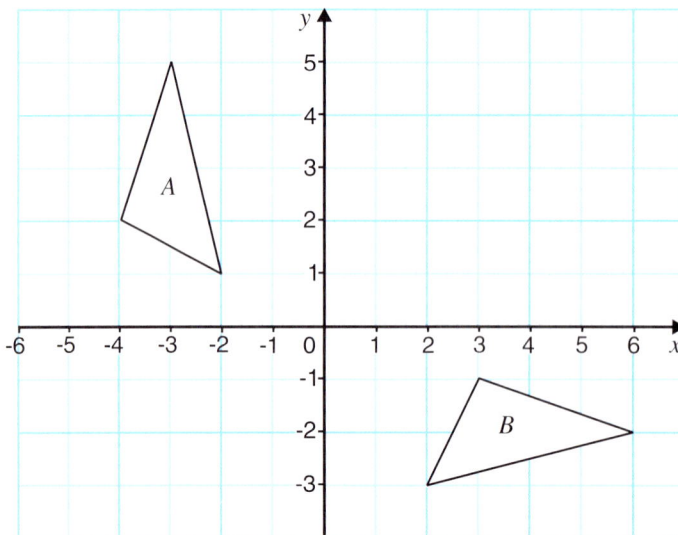

SEG 1999

14 A quadrilateral *PQRS* has vertices at *P*(−2, 1), *Q*(−4, 1), *R*(−4, 4) and *S*(−2, 4).

(a) Plot *PQRS* on squared paper.

(b) Draw the enlargement of *PQRS* with scale factor −3, centre (0, 0).

15 A piece of land is bounded by three straight roads *PQ*, *QR* and *RP*, as shown.

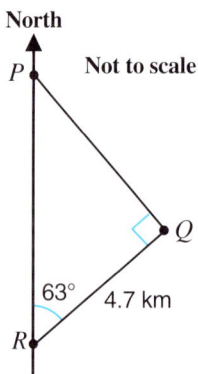

P is due north of *R*.
Q is on a bearing of 063° from *R*.
PQR is a right angle.

(a) What is the bearing of *P* from *Q*?
The length of *QR* is 4.7 km.

(b) Calculate the area of the piece of land.

SEG 1999

16 In the diagram *AB* is parallel to *DE*.
ACE is a straight line and angle *ABC* = 110°.

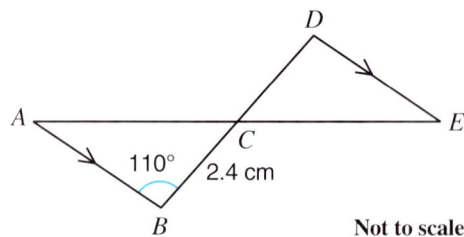

Triangle *ABC* is similar to triangle *CDE*.
AC : *CE* is 3 : 4.
BC = 2.4 cm.

(a) Write down the size of angle *CDE*.

(b) Calculate *CD*.

SEG 2000 S

17 Not to scale

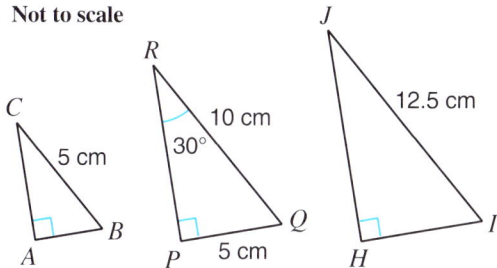

Triangles *ABC*, *PQR* and *HIJ* are all similar.
(a) Calculate the length of *AB*.
(b) What is the size of angle *B*?
(c) Calculate the length of *HJ*.

SEG 1994

18 On the diagram, the shaded rectangle *ABCD* represents a ski-slope.
Rectangle *ABEF* is at right angles to rectangle *ECDF*.

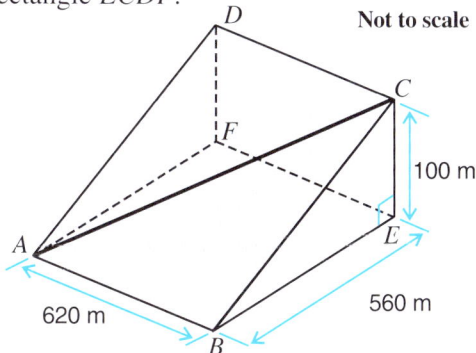

Not to scale

Alison skis in a straight line from *C* to *A*.
Her average speed is 12 metres per second.
How long, in seconds, does it take her to ski from *C* to *A*?

SEG 1998

19 *VABCD* is a square based pyramid.
The vertical height, *VX*, is 12 cm.
V is directly above the centre of the base.
AB = BC = CD = DA = 5 cm.

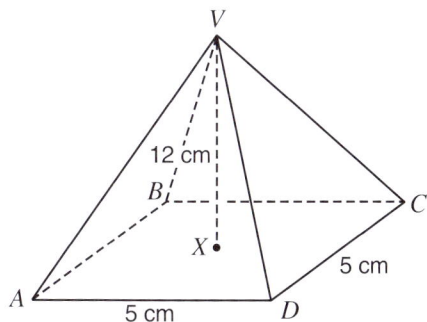

Calculate
(a) the angle between the planes *VAB* and *ABCD*,
(b) the angle between the line *VA* and the base *ABCD*.

20 *OAB* is a sector of angle 50°.

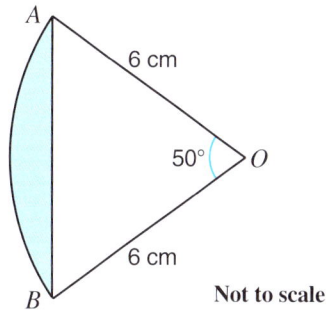

Not to scale

Calculate the area of the shaded segment.

SEG 2000 S

21 The diagrams show pieces of cheese. Each piece of cheese is cut from a cylinder, radius 8 cm and height 2.5 cm.

(a) Calculate the volume of this piece of cheese.

Camembert

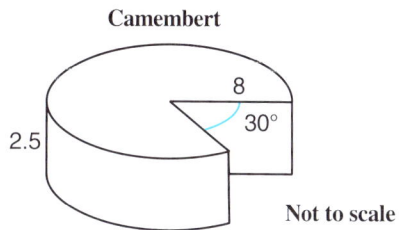

Not to scale

(b) Calculate the angle *x* on this piece of cheese.

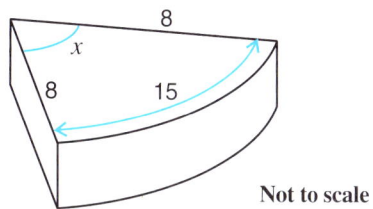

Not to scale

(c) Calculate the arc length *AB*.
The straight line distance *AB* is 10 cm.

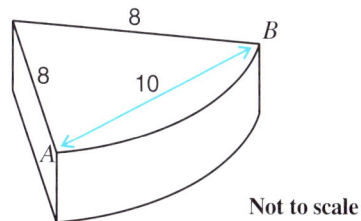

Not to scale

SEG 1996

22 *ABCD* is a rectangle.
AXY is the sector of a circle with centre *A*.
AB = 80 cm, *AD* = 25 cm and
DY = 60 cm.

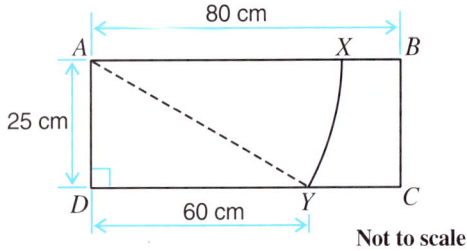

80 cm

25 cm

60 cm

Not to scale

(a) Calculate the length of *AY*, the radius of the sector *AXY*.
(b) Calculate angle *DAY*.
(c) Calculate the shaded area.

SEG 1999

23 The diagram shows a model of an ice cream cone outside a sweetshop.
The lower section is an inverted cone of slant height 78 cm and radius 31 cm.

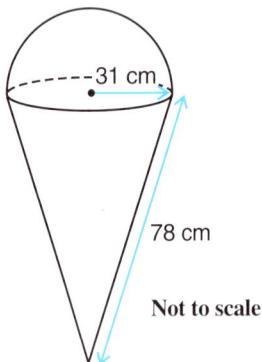

---31 cm.

78 cm

Not to scale

(a) Calculate the volume of the cone. Take π to be 3.14 or use the π key on your calculator.
(b) The ice cream dome is a perspex hemisphere of uniform thickness 1 cm. The internal radius is 30 cm and the weight of the perspex is 0.002 kg per cm³.

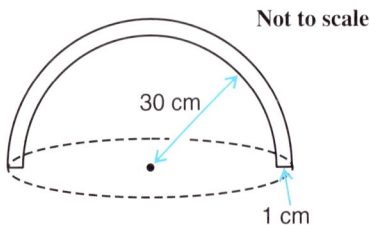

Not to scale

30 cm

1 cm

Calculate the weight of the ice cream dome.

SEG 1994

24 A scale model of the proposed Millennium Tower is shown. The model is a cone of height 2 m and base radius 0.1 m. The angle between the slanting side and the vertical is θ.

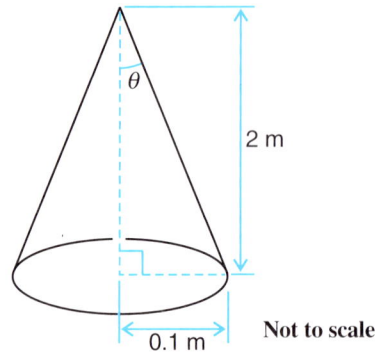

θ

2 m

Not to scale

0.1 m

(a) What is the value of θ, to the nearest degree?
(b) The proposed Millennium Tower is 1000 m high.
What is its base radius?
(c) Calculate, in cubic metres, the volume of the scale model.
(d) How many times larger than the scale model is the volume of the proposed Millennium Tower?

SEG 1997

25 Tan 45° = 1.
(a) Write down the value of tan 135°.
(b) Tan *x* = tan 45°, *x* ≠ 45°.
Write down the value of *x*.
(c) Tan *y* = −1.
Write down the possible values of *y* between 0° and 360°.

26 $\sin 60° = \dfrac{\sqrt{3}}{2}$.
(a) Write down the exact value of sin 120°.
(b) $\sin y = -\dfrac{\sqrt{3}}{2}$.
Write down the possible values of *y* between 0° and 360°.

27 (a) cos *x* = 0.5 for 0° ≤ *x* ≤ 360°.
Write down all the possible values of *x*.
(b) cos *y* = cos 210° for 0° ≤ *y* ≤ 360°.
Angle *y* is not equal to 210°.
Find the value of *y*.

28 The diagram shows a sketch of the graph of $y = \sin x$ for $-360° \leqslant x \leqslant 360°$.

(a) How many solutions are there to the equation $\sin x = 0.25$ between $-360°$ and $360°$?

(b) Solve the equation $\sin x = -0.8$ for $-360° \leqslant x \leqslant 360°$. Give your solutions to the nearest degree.

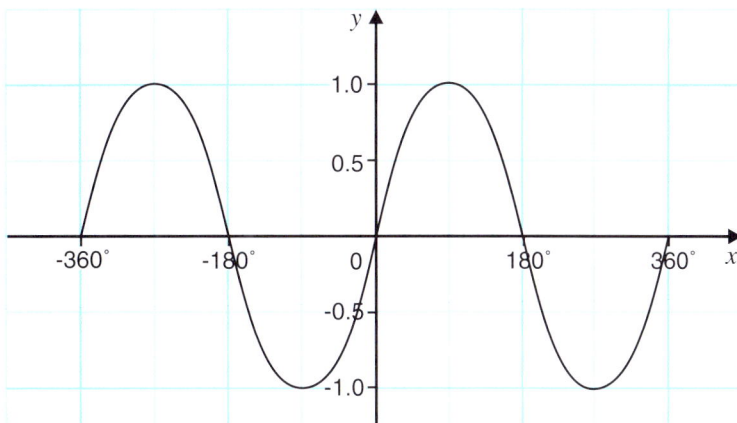

SEG 2000 S

29 The graph of $y = 2.5 \cos x$ is drawn below.

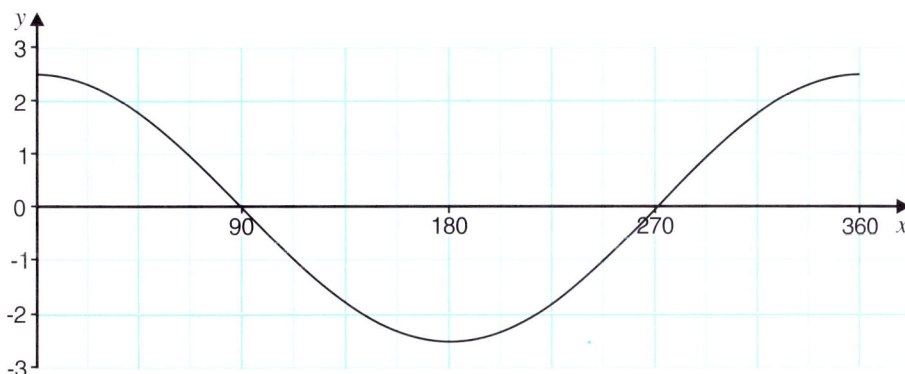

Copy the graph.

(a) Complete this table of values and use it to draw the graph of $y = 5 \sin x$ on the same axes.

Angle $x°$	0	45	90	135	180	225	270	315	360
$5 \sin x$									

(b) Use your graph to find the solutions to the equation $5 \sin x = 2.5 \cos x$, for the interval $0 \leqslant x \leqslant 360$.

SEG 1997

30 In each diagram, O is the centre of a circle.

(a) Calculate the value of angle a.

(b) Calculate the value of angle b.

(c) Calculate the length of the minor arc AB. The radius of this circle is 5 cm.

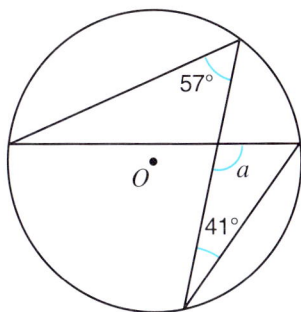

Not to scale

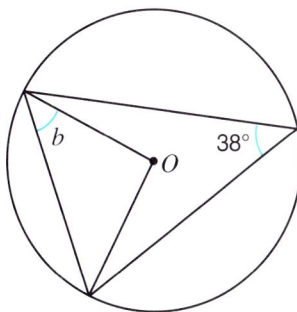

Not to scale

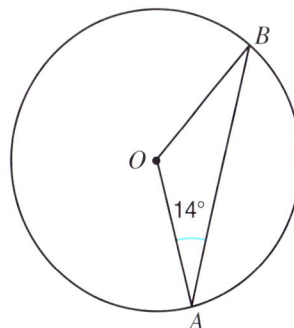

Not to scale

SEG 1998

31 In the diagram, O is the centre of the circle and BA and BC are tangents to the circle. Angle $ABC = 34°$.

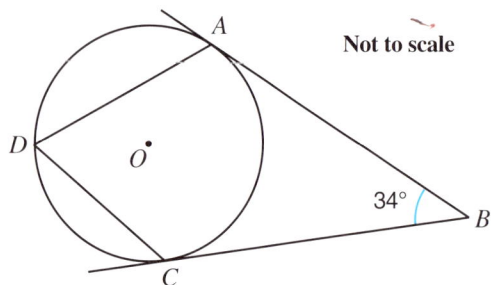

Not to scale

(a) Find the obtuse angle AOC.
(b) Find angle ADC.
(c) The points D, O and B lie on a straight line.
What is the size of angle DCB?

SEG 1993

32 A, B, C and D are points on the circumference of a circle, centre O. PQ is the tangent to the circle at B. Angle $OBA = 40°$ and angle $CBQ = 60°$.

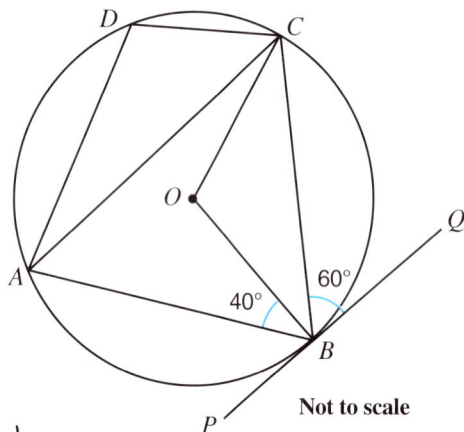

Not to scale

(a) Find angle BAC.
(b) Find angle ADC.

SEG 2000 S

33 Two planes leave an airport at the same time.
Plane A flies on a bearing of 330° with a speed of 800 km/h.
Plane B flies due East at 1200 km/h.
(a) Calculate their distance apart after one hour.
(b) Calculate the bearing of A from B after one hour.

SEG 1997

34 $ABCD$ is a cyclic quadrilateral.

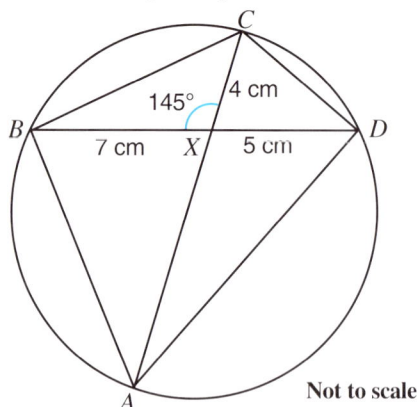

Not to scale

The diagonals AC and BD intersect at X. $BX = 7$ cm, $CX = 4$ cm, $DX = 5$ cm and angle $CXB = 145°$.
(a) Explain why triangles BXC and AXD are similar.
(b) Calculate the length of AX.
(c) Calculate the length of BC.

SEG 1998

35 A door wedge is in the shape of a triangular prism.

Not to scale

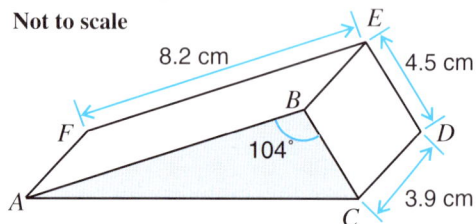

$AB = FE = 8.2$ cm, $BC = ED = 4.5$ cm and $AF = BE = CD = 3.9$ cm.
Angle ABC is 104°.
(a) Calculate the length AC.
(b) Find the volume of the door wedge.

SEG 1998

36 The diagram shows the plan view of a field with dimensions as shown.

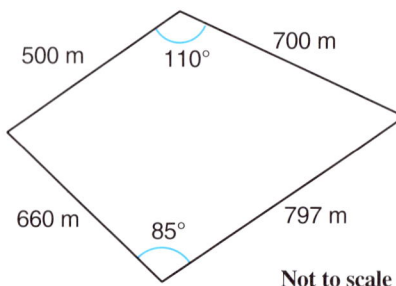

Not to scale

(a) Calculate the total area of the field.
(b) Calculate the length of the longer diagonal of the field.

SEG 1997

424

37 In triangle ABC the length of AB is 8.3 cm and angle ABC is $20°$.
D is a point on BC such that the length of DC is 6.1 cm and angle ADB is $105°$.

Not to scale

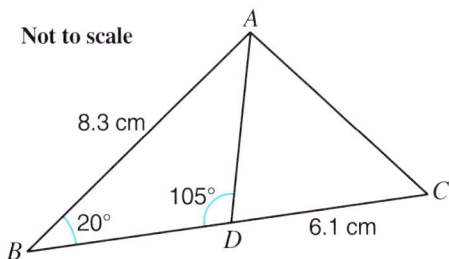

Calculate the length of AC.   SEG 1999

38 $ABCD$ is a quadrilateral with diagonal AC.

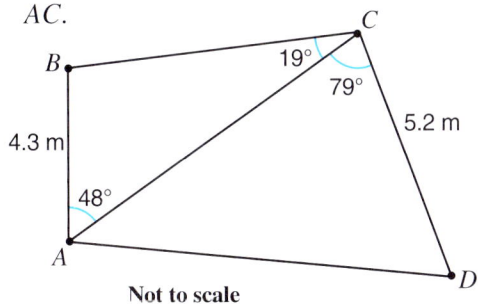

Not to scale

$AB = 4.3$ m and $CD = 5.2$ m.
Angle $BAC = 48°$, angle $BCA = 19°$ and angle $ACD = 79°$.
Calculate the length of AD.   SEG 2000 S

39 $ABCD$ is a parallelogram with $\overrightarrow{AB} = \mathbf{a}$ and $\overrightarrow{AD} = \mathbf{b}$.

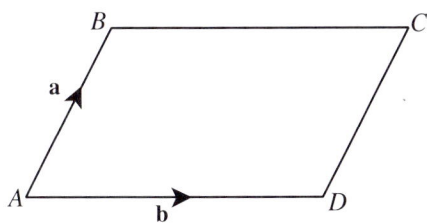

Find $\overrightarrow{AM}$ and $\overrightarrow{BM}$ where M is the midpoint of AC, in terms of $\mathbf{a}$ and $\mathbf{b}$.
     SEG 1997

40 $ABCDEF$ is a regular hexagon.

$\overrightarrow{AB} = \begin{pmatrix} 2 \\ 0 \end{pmatrix}$,

$\overrightarrow{BC} = \begin{pmatrix} 1 \\ -1.73 \end{pmatrix}$.

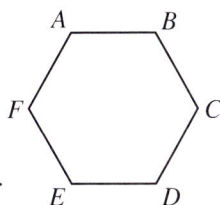

Find the vector $\overrightarrow{DF}$.
     SEG 1997

41 OAB is a triangle with $\overrightarrow{OA} = 2\mathbf{a} + 2\mathbf{b}$ and $\overrightarrow{OB} = 4\mathbf{a} + 4\mathbf{b}$.

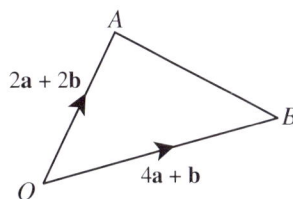

C is the midpoint of AB.
$\overrightarrow{OC} = x\mathbf{a} + y\mathbf{b}$.
Calculate the values of x and y.

42 Solids A and B are each made from a cone and a hemisphere.

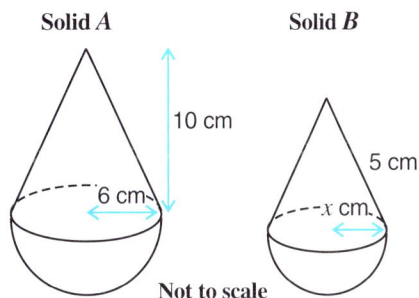

Not to scale

In solid A, the cone has a height of 10 cm.
The radius of the base of the cone and the hemisphere is 6 cm.

(a) Calculate, in terms of π, the volume of solid A.

(b) The total surface area of solid B is 33π cm².

   (i) The total surface area of solid B is given by the expression $2\pi x^2 + 5\pi x$, where x is the radius of the base of the cone and the hemisphere.
   Form and solve an equation to calculate x.

   (ii) Solid C is similar to solid B and has a total surface area of 132π cm².
   The slant height of the cone in solid B is 5 cm.
   Calculate the slant height of solid C.
     SEG 2000 S

CHAPTER 28

Data Collection and Sampling

To answer questions such as:

Which is the most popular colour of car?

Is it going to rain tomorrow?

Which team won the World Cup in 1998?

we need to collect data.

Data is continually being collected.
Governments collect data to assist in the planning of roads, schools, hospitals, housing, etc.
Manufacturers collect data to plan future production.
Organisations collect data about sporting achievements, investments and spending.
People collect data to plan DIY projects, holidays and diets.

Types of data

Data is made up of a collection of **variables**.
Each variable can be described, numbered or measured.

Data which can only be **described** in words is **qualitative**. Such data is often organised into categories, such as make of car, colour of hair, etc.

Data which is given **numerical** values, such as shoe size or height, is **quantitative**.
Quantitative data is either **discrete** or **continuous**.

Discrete data can only take certain values, usually whole numbers, but may include fractions (e.g. shoe sizes).

Continuous data can take any value within a range and is measurable (e.g. height, weight, temperature, etc.).

EXAMPLES

The taste of an orange is a qualitative variable.

The number of pips in an orange is a discrete quantitative variable.

The surface area of an orange is a continuous quantitative variable.

Exercise 28.1

State whether the following data is qualitative or quantitative.
If the data is quantitative state whether it is discrete or continuous.

1. The colours of cars in a car park.

2. The weights of eggs in a carton.

3. The numbers of desks in classrooms.

4. The names of students in a class.

5. The sizes of spanners in a toolbox.

6. The depths that fish swim in the sea.

7. The number of goals scored by football teams on a Saturday.

8. The brands of toothpaste on sale in supermarkets.

9. The sizes of ladies dresses in a store.

10. The heights of trees in a wood.

Collection of data

Data can be collected in a variety of ways; by observation, by interviewing people and by using questionnaires. The method of collection will often depend on the type of data to be collected.

Data collection sheets

Data collection sheets are used to record data.
To answer the question, "Which is the most popular colour of car?", we could draw up a simple data collection sheet and record the colours of passing cars by observation.

EXAMPLE

A **data collection sheet** for colour of car is shown, with some cars recorded.

Colour of car	Tally	Frequency
Black	||	2
Blue	⽶⽶⽶ |||	13
Green	||||	4
Red	⽶⽶⽶⽶ |	
Silver	⽶⽶⽶ ||	
White	⽶⽶⽶⽶ ||||	
	Total	

> The colour of each car is recorded in the **tally** column by a single stroke.
>
> To make counting easier, groups of 5 are recorded as ⽶⽶⽶.

How many red cars are recorded?
How many cars are recorded altogether?

Colour is a discrete variable. The total number of times each colour appears is called its **frequency**. A table for discrete data with the totals included is called a **frequency distribution**.

For large amounts of discrete data, or for continuous data, we organise the data into **groups** or **classes**. When data is collected in groups it is called a **grouped frequency distribution** and the groups you put the data into are called **class intervals**.

EXAMPLE

The weights of 20 boys are recorded in the grouped frequency table shown below.

Weight w kg	Tally	Frequency
$50 \leqslant w < 55$	|	1
$55 \leqslant w < 60$	|||	3
$60 \leqslant w < 65$	⽶⽶⽶⽶ ||||	9
$65 \leqslant w < 70$	⽶⽶⽶ |	6
$70 \leqslant w < 75$	|	1
	Total	20

> Weights are grouped into class intervals of equal width.
>
> $55 \leqslant w < 60$ means 55 kg, or more, but less than 60 kg.

John weighs 54.9 kg. *In which class interval is he recorded?*
David weighs 55.0 kg. *In which class interval is he recorded?*

What is the width of each class interval?

If we need to collect data for more than one type of information, for example; the make, colour, registration letter and mileage of cars; we will need to collect data in a different way.

We could create a **data collection card** for each car.

Car	1
Make	Vauxhall
Colour	Grey
Registration letter	P
Mileage	18 604

Alternatively, we could use a data collection sheet and record all the information about each car on a separate line.

This is an example of a simple **database**.

Car	Make	Colour	Registration letter	Mileage
1	Vauxhall	Grey	P	18 604
2	Ford	Blue	M	33 216
3	Ford	White	N	27 435
4	Nissan	Red	L	32 006

When all the data has been collected, separate frequency or grouped frequency tables can be drawn up.

Exercise 28.2

1 The days of the week on which some students were born are recorded.

Monday	Monday	Sunday	Wednesday	Thursday
Friday	Saturday	Tuesday	Monday	Friday
Thursday	Sunday	Monday	Friday	Tuesday
Thursday	Wednesday	Tuesday	Monday	Wednesday
Friday	Monday	Saturday	Friday	Thursday
Tuesday	Thursday	Monday	Sunday	Tuesday
Saturday	Wednesday	Friday	Thursday	Tuesday
Monday	Wednesday	Friday	Sunday	Thursday
Tuesday	Wednesday	Sunday		

(a) Make a frequency table for the data.
(b) On which day of the week did most births occur?

2 The heights, in centimetres, of 36 girls are recorded as follows.

148	161	175	156	155	160	178	159	170
163	147	150	173	169	170	174	166	163
162	158	155	165	168	154	156	163	167
172	170	165	160	164	172	157	173	161

(a) Copy and complete the grouped frequency table for the data.

Height h cm	Tally	Frequency
$145 \leqslant h < 150$		
$150 \leqslant h < 155$		

(b) What is the width of each class interval?
(c) How many girls are in the class interval $155 \leqslant h < 160$?
(d) How many girls are less than 160 cm?
(e) How many girls are 155 cm or taller?

3 A database of cars is shown.

Car	Make	Colour	Mileage
1	Vauxhall	Grey	18 604
2	Ford	Blue	33 216
3	Ford	White	27 435
4	Nissan	Red	32 006
5	Vauxhall	Blue	31 598
6	Ford	Green	37 685
7	Vauxhall	Red	21 640
8	Nissan	White	28 763
9	Ford	White	30 498
10	Vauxhall	White	9 865
11	Nissan	Red	7 520
12	Vauxhall	Grey	16 482

(a) (i) Draw up separate frequency tables for make and colour.
    (ii) Draw up a grouped frequency table for mileage.
        Use class intervals of 5000 miles, starting at $0 \leqslant m < 5000$, $5000 \leqslant m < 10\,000$, . . .

(b) (i) Which make of car is the most popular?
    (ii) Which colour of car is the most popular?
    (iii) What percentage of cars have a mileage of 30 000 or more?

4 (a) By using copies of the data collection card for cars or by using a copy of the data collection sheet, record information about the cars in your school car park.

(b) Draw up frequency tables for make and colour and a grouped frequency table for mileage.

(c) (i) Which make of car is the most popular?
    (ii) Which colour of car is the most popular?
    (iii) What percentage of cars have a mileage of 30 000 or more?

(d) Compare your data with the data in question 3.
    What differences do you find?

Data Collection and Sampling

5 The following database gives information about a group of 16 year old students.

Student	Gender	Height (cm)	Shoe size	Pulse rate (beats/min)
Mary	F	162	6	72
Alan	M	170	8	64
Jim	M	186	10	72
Tony	M	180	10	68
Laura	F	172	8	70
Jane	F	168	7	82
Wendy	F	155	5	72
Mark	M	180	9	68
Peter	M	168	8	62
Beryl	F	166	7	72

Investigate the data for males and females separately.
What differences do you find?

6 Use data collection cards to collect information about students in your class. Include gender, height, shoe size and pulse rate.
Investigate the data for males and females separately.
What differences do you find?

Questionnaires

Questionnaires are frequently used to collect data.
In business they are used to get information about products or services and in politics they are frequently used to test opinion on a range of issues and personalities.

When constructing questions for a questionnaire you should:

(1) use simple language, so that everyone can understand the question;

(2) ask short questions which can be answered precisely, with a "yes" or "no" answer, a number; or a response from a choice of answers;

(3) provide tick boxes, so that questions can be answered easily;

(4) avoid open-ended questions, like: "What do you think of education?" which might produce long rambling answers which would be difficult to collate or process;

(5) avoid leading questions, like: "Don't you agree that there is too much bad language on television?" and ask instead:
"Do you think that there is too much bad language on television?"

Yes ☐   No ☐

(6) ask questions in a logical order.

Multiple-response questions

In many instances a choice of responses should be provided.

Instead of asking "How old are you?" which does not indicate the degree of accuracy required and many people might consider personal, we could ask instead:

Which is your age group?

under 18 ☐   18 to 40 ☐

41 to 65 ☐   over 65 ☐

Notice there are no gaps and only **one** response applies to each person.

Sometimes we invite **multiple responses** by asking questions, such as:

Which soaps do you watch?

Coronation Street ☐

Eastenders ☐

Emmerdale ☐

Brookside ☐

Hollyoaks ☐

Tick as many as you wish.

Hypothesis

A **hypothesis** is a statement that may or may not be true.
To test a hypothesis we can construct a questionnaire, carry out a survey and analyse the results.

EXAMPLE A questionnaire to test the hypothesis, "People think it is better to give than to receive." could include questions like these.

1. **Gender:** male ☐   female ☐

2. **Age:**   11 - 16 ☐   17 - 21 ☐   22 - 59 ☐   60 & over ☐

3. **Do you think it is better to give than to receive?**
    Yes ☐   No ☐

4. **To which of the following have you given in the last year?**
    School ☐   Charities ☐   Church ☐
    Hospital ☐   Special appeals ☐   Homeless ☐

    Other (please list) _____

Suggest another question which could be included.

Exercise 28.3

1 In preparing the questions for a questionnaire on radio listening habits the following questions were rejected.

(a) When do you listen to the radio?
(b) What do you like about radio programmes?
(c) Don't you agree that the radio gives the best news reports.

Explain why each question is unsuitable and rewrite the question so that it could be included in the questionnaire.

2 In preparing questions for a survey on the use of a library the following questions were considered. Explain why each question in its present form is unsuitable and rewrite the question.

(a) How old are you?
(b) How many times have you used the library?
(c) Which books do you read?
(d) How could the library be improved?

3 Design a questionnaire to test the hypothesis:
"Most people take regular exercise."

4 Design a questionnaire to test the hypothesis:
"Children have too much homework."

5 Design a questionnaire to test the hypothesis:
"Children watch more television than adults."
Consider:
(a) does gender affect people's opinions?
(b) do people's opinions change with age?

6 Design a questionnaire to test the hypothesis:
"Boys are better at estimating than girls."
Consider:
(a) suitable tests,
(b) does the ability to estimate change with age?

Two-way tables

We have already seen that the results of a survey can be recorded on data collection sheets and then collated using frequency or grouped frequency tables. We can also illustrate data using **two-way tables**.

A two-way table is used to illustrate the data for two different features (variables) in a survey.

EXAMPLE

The following two-way table shows the results of a survey.

Wear	Glasses	
	Yes	No
Boys	4	14
Girls	3	9

How many boys wear glasses?
How many children wear glasses?
How many children were surveyed?

Do the results of the survey prove or disprove the hypothesis, "More boys wear glasses than girls"?
Explain your answer.

Exercise 28.4

1 The two-way table shows the results of a survey.

	A			1	2	2
Grade in Mathematics	B		1	2	5	2
	C		1	8	3	
	D		3	3	2	
	E	2	1	2		
		E	D	C	B	A

Grade in English

Do the results prove or disprove the hypothesis: "Students get better grades in English than Mathematics"? Explain your answer.

2 The two-way table shows the number of boys and girls in families taking part in a survey.

	4					
Number of girls	3	1		2		
	2	1	2	3		
	1	5	9		1	1
	0		3		2	
		0	1	2	3	4

Number of boys

(a) (i) How many families have two children?
   (ii) Does the data support the hypothesis: "More families have less than 2 children than more than 2 children"? Explain your answer.

(b) (i) How many girls are included in the survey?
   (ii) Does the data support the hypothesis: "More boys are born than girls"? Explain your answer.

3 The two-way table shows the results of a survey to test the hypothesis: "More girls are left-handed than boys." Do the results prove or disprove the hypothesis? Explain your answer.

	Left-handed	
	Yes	No
Boys	3	18
Girls	2	12

4 The table shows information about houses in a street.

	Garage	No garage
Semi-detached houses	16	4
Detached houses	27	9

Does the information support the hypothesis: "More detached houses have garages than semi-detached houses"? Explain your answer.

5 The two-way table shows the age and gender of people taking part in a survey.

	Age				
	Under 18	18 to 25	26 to 40	41 to 64	65 and over
Female	0	2	7	9	7
Male	0	4	17	19	10

Give a reason why the data collected may not be representative of the whole population.

Sampling

When information is required about a small group of people it is possible to survey everyone.
When information is required about a large group of people it is not always possible to survey everyone and only a **sample** may be asked. The sample chosen should be large enough to make the results meaningful and representative of the whole group or the results may be **biased**.
For example; to test the hypothesis: "Girls are more intelligent than boys," you would need to ask equal numbers of boys and girls from various age groups.

Sampling methods

In a **simple random sample** everyone has an equal chance of being selected.
For example, the names of the whole group could be written on identical pieces of paper and placed in a hat. Names could then be taken from the hat, without looking, until the sample is complete.

In a **systematic random sample** people are selected according to some rule.
For example, names could be listed in alphabetical order and every tenth person selected.

However, samples chosen using these methods may not be representative of the whole group.
For example, a sample taken from a school population may consist of girls only, or pupils from Year 10 only.

A **stratified random sample** is used to overcome the possible bias of random samples by taking into account the composition of all the people in the original group.
The original group is divided up into separate categories or strata, such as male/female, age group, etc, before a random sample is taken. A simple random sample is then taken from each category in proportion to the size of the category.

A **census** is when the whole of a population is surveyed.
The only true sample is when 100% of the population is surveyed.
A large sample allows more reliable inferences to be made about the whole population.

Quota samples are often used in market research.
The population is divided into groups (gender, age, etc). A given number (quota) are surveyed from each group.
This type of sample is not random, but is cheap to carry out and can be done quickly.
How reliable are such samples?

Jayne is investigating the spending habits of girls in her school.
The table shows the numbers of girls in each part of the school.

Year Group	Lower School	Upper School	Sixth Form
Number of girls	140	100	60

Jayne wants a stratified random sample of 30 girls.
How many girls should be chosen from each part of the school?

Sample size   Lower School: $\frac{140}{300} \times 30 = 14$

Upper School: $\frac{100}{300} \times 30 = 10$

Sixth Form: $\frac{60}{300} \times 30 = 6$

Exercise 28.5

1 In a school there are 320 pupils in the lower school and 240 pupils in the upper school. How many pupils from each part of the school should be included in a stratified random sample of size 40?

2 A college wants to do a survey of the smoking habits of its students.
Explain how you would take
(a) a random sample of 100 students,
(b) a stratified random sample of 100 students.

SEG 1994

3 The number of pupils in each year group at a boys school is shown.
The school carries out a homework survey.
(a) Explain why a simple random sample of pupils should not be used.
(b) Calculate how many pupils should be included from each year group in a stratified random sample of size 50.

Year Group	Number of boys
7	90
8	110
9	110
10	100
11	90

4 The table shows the numbers of employees in each section of a company.

Department	Managerial	Clerical	Technical	Manual
Number of employees	26	65	637	572

A survey on job satisfaction is to be carried out.
(a) Explain why a simple random sample of employees is unsuitable.
(b) A stratified random sample of size 100 is used. How many employees from the technical department will be included?

5 State one advantage and one disadvantage of a postal survey.

6 The table shows the types of houses on an estate.
A survey on life in the community is to be carried out.
Explain how a stratified random sample of size 50 is obtained.

Type of housing	Number of houses
Housing Association	450
Privately owned	270
Flats for the elderly	180

434

7 The table shows the age distribution of a club's membership.

How many members should be included from each of these age groups in a stratified random sample of 25?

Age (years)	Number
Under 21	49
21 to 65	76
Over 65	13

8 An industrial concern employs personnel as shown in the table.

How many employees from each section should be included in a stratified random sample of 60 employees?

Management	Sales	Shop floor
48	261	2691

9 The number of people living in three villages is given in the table.

A sample of 240 people is to be taken by Mr James. He selects, at random, 80 from each village.

Village	Population
Atford	3000
Beeham	4000
Calbridge	5000

(a) Explain why this might be an inappropriate sampling method.

(b) Show how Mr James could select a more representative sample of 240 people from the three villages.

(c) Suggest another method of sampling he might use.

SEG 1994

What you need to know

- **Qualitative** data – Data which can only be described in words.

- **Quantitative** data – Data that has a numerical value. Quantitative data is either **discrete** or **continuous**. **Discrete** data can only take certain values. **Continuous** data has no exact value and is measurable.

- **Data Collection Sheets** – Used to record data during a survey.

- **Tally** – A way of recording each item of data on a data collection sheet. A group of five is recorded as ⊞.

- **Frequency Table** – A way of collating the information recorded on a data collection sheet.

- **Grouped Frequency Table** – Used for continuous data or for discrete data when a lot of data has to be recorded.

- **Database** – A collection of data.

- **Class Interval** – The width of the groups used in a grouped frequency distribution.

- **Two-way Tables** – A way of illustrating two features of a survey.

- **Questionnaire** – A set of questions used to collect data for a survey. Questionnaires should:
  (1) use simple language,
  (2) ask short questions which can be answered precisely,
  (3) provide tick boxes,
  (4) avoid open-ended questions,
  (5) avoid leading questions,
  (6) ask questions in a logical order.

- **Hypothesis** – A hypothesis is a statement which may or may not be true.

- When information is required about a large group of people it is not always possible to survey everyone and only a **sample** may be asked. The sample chosen should be large enough to make the results meaningful and representative of the whole group (population) or the results may be **biased**.

- In a **simple random sample** everyone has an equal chance of being selected.

- In a **systematic random sample** people are selected according to some rule.

- In a **stratified random sample** the original group is divided up into separate categories or strata, such as male/female, age group, etc, before a random sample is taken. A simple random sample is then taken from each category in proportion to the size of the category.

1 State whether each of the following examples of data is discrete or continuous.
  (a) The distance travelled by a car on a particular journey.
  (b) The average speed of a car for the same journey.

2 In a survey of community life on a new housing estate the following question is suggested.
  (a) "What do you most like about living here?"

An alternative is proposed.
  (b) "Tick the box which describes why you most like living here."

Design of houses ☐

Friendliness of neighbours ☐

More open space ☐

Give one advantage of each form of question.

SEG 1995

3 Rosemary wants to know how people in her neighbourhood spend their leisure time.
She has produced a questionnaire to help her gather the information she needs.
Two of the questions that Rosemary used on her questionnaire are shown.

Question 1. How old are you?

Question 2. What is your favourite sport?

Rewrite each question so that there are 3 possible responses.
Each question must be in a more appropriate form for a questionnaire.

SEG 1996

4 Lorraine is writing a questionnaire for a survey about her local Superstore.
She thinks that the local people visit the store more often than people from further away.
She also thinks that local people spend less money per visit.
Write three questions which would help her to test these ideas.
Each question should include three responses from which people choose one.

SEG 1994

5 A bus company wants to carry out a survey.
It wants to find out the distribution of the age of its passengers and the frequency with which they use buses.
The bus company intends to use a questionnaire.
Write **two** questions and responses that will enable the bus company to carry out the survey.

SEG 1995

6 The table shows the age and gender of people taking part in a survey to test the hypothesis "Children have too much homework".

	Age				
	Under 11	11 to 16	17 to 25	26 to 50	Over 50
Male	0	4	6	5	5
Female	0	0	0	0	0

Give three reasons why the sample is biased.

7 The following questionnaires were designed to find out how pupils travelled to school.

A
Please complete.

All answers should be put in the space provided.

Name .... Age..........

1. How do you come to school?

....

2. When do you leave home?

....

3. How long is your journey?

....

Thank you.

B
This questionnaire is part of a GCSE project.

1. How do you travel to school?

Walk	Bus	Car	Bicycle

2. How far do you travel to school?

0 - 1	1 - 2	2 - 3	Over 3 km

3. How long does your journey take?

....

(a) Write down one strength of questionnaire A and one weakness of questionnaire B.

(b) The following question was written to replace question 3 in both questionnaires.

How long is your journey to school?

Under 5	5 - 10	10 - 15	15 - 20

Rewrite this question in a more suitable form.

SEG 1996

8 The table shows the number of people working different shifts at a factory.

Sex	Age (years)	Shift		
		Morning	Afternoon	Evening
Men	Under 30	6	8	9
	30 and over	7	12	17
Women	Under 30	8	11	18
	30 and over	6	15	23

John thinks that the proportion of people aged 30 years and over who work the evening shift is greater than the proportion of people who are under 30 years of age who work the evening shift.
Is he correct? You must show all your working.

SEG 1996

9 Each student in Year 10 and 11 was asked to select one sport.
The choices made are shown in the table.

		Outdoor Sports		Indoor Sports	
		Hockey	Tennis	Badminton	Squash
Year 11	Girls	12	10	15	5
	Boys	10	15	7	19
Year 10	Girls	14	9	17	3
	Boys	15	12	11	13

(a) How many students chose hockey?

(b) How many more girls chose tennis than squash?

(c) One girl says that boys usually prefer outdoor sports.

Do the figures in the table support this view? Explain your answer.

SEG 1994

10 (a) Some students are conducting a survey to see if there should be a tuck shop in their school.
This is a suggestion for the first question.

> *Question*   *Response*
> *"Don't you think the shop over the road is*   *YES/NO*
> *very expensive and it would be better to*
> *have a tuck shop in school?"*

    (i) Give **one** reason why this is not a suitable first question.

    (ii) Suggest a better question.
Your question should have at least three responses to choose from.

(b) The students want a representative sample for their survey.

Manjit suggested
We don't need to ask any Year 11's, because they will be leaving soon.
Let's just ask Year 8.

Tom suggested
Let's just ask the people who use the drinks machine at breaktime.

    (i) Choose **one** of these suggestions, and explain why it would **not** give a representative sample.

    (ii) Suggest a better way of selecting a representative sample of students.

SEG 1995

11 Lorraine investigates the spending habits of students at her school.
The number of students in each year group is shown.

Year Group	9	10	11	12	13
Number of students	200	200	200	120	80

Total 800

Explain, with calculations, how Lorraine obtains a stratified random sample of 100 students for her survey.

SEG 1994

12 A street contains 36 houses.
The income earned in each house is as follows.

House number	£	House number	£	House number	£
1	10 400	13	4250	25	6200
2	11 500	14	19 700	26	9800
3	11 200	15	5750	27	8700
4	5750	16	47 500	28	9300
5	4250	17	75 600	29	12 700
6	32 500	18	77 500	30	6800
7	17 500	19	47 500	31	8500
8	20 400	20	79 400	32	4200
9	16 540	21	28 500	33	4200
10	36 500	22	67 500	34	5200
11	4250	23	48 500	35	5800
12	4750	24	36 200	36	10 900

Houses numbered 1–15 belong to a Housing Association.
Houses numbered 16–24 belong to a Private Development of large houses.
Houses numbered 25–36 are Sheltered Housing for old age pensioners.
A sample of 12 houses is chosen to estimate the mean income, per house, for the whole street.
The sample is chosen by selecting the first four in each column.

(a) Why is this sample of 12 not suitable?

(b) Copy and complete this table to show how many houses, from each type of housing, you require for a stratified sample of 12.

Type of housing	Number required
Housing Association	
Private Development	
Sheltered Housing	

SEG 1995

13 In a school there are 420 pupils in the lower school, 310 pupils in the middle school and 130 pupils in the upper school.

(a) How many pupils from each part of the school should be included in a stratified random sample of size 100?

(b) Explain briefly in what circumstances a stratified random sample might be taken rather than a simple random sample.

SEG 2000 S

14 The table shows the number of people in each age group in a certain club.

Mehmet wants to choose a sample of 25 people from the club using stratified sampling.
How many people from each age group should he choose?

Age (years)	Number
Under 18	52
18 - 60	68
Over 60	23
Total	143

SEG 1996

15 A school is carrying out a survey about the sporting activities of pupils.
The numbers of pupils in each year are shown on the right.

Year	Number
8	212
9	176
10	183
11	143
Total	714

(a) Give **one** reason why a simple random sample of pupils may not be representative of the whole school.

The school decides to interview a stratified sample of 40 pupils.

(b) How many pupils from Year 11 should be selected?
(c) One of the questions asked was:

	Answer 'Yes' or 'No'
Do you often take part in any of the following sports?	ATHLETICS ☐
	FOOTBALL ☐
	CRICKET ☐
	TENNIS ☐

Suggest **one** way in which this question could be improved.

SEG 1997

16 The table shows the number of people working in different sections of a paint manufacturing company.

Work Section	Number of men	Number of women
Manufacturing workshop	500	100
Storage and Distribution	200	100
Purchasing	30	50
Marketing and management	10	10

The owner wants to question 200 workers on how to improve production.
He proposes to allocate each person a number and then select 200 numbers at random.
(a) State **one** disadvantage of such a selection process.

It was suggested that a Stratified Sample would be more representative of the workers in the company.
(b) (i) Calculate the number of people in a Stratified Sample of 200 who would represent the purchasing section.
   (ii) How many women should be included within the people chosen from the purchasing section?

SEG 1994

CHAPTER 29

Presentation of Data

Most people find numerical information easier to understand if it is presented in pictorial form. For this reason, television reports, newspapers and advertisements frequently use graphs and diagrams to present and compare information.

Information can be presented and compared in many ways. In statistics, scatter graphs, histograms and frequency polygons are all used to present and compare information.

Scatter graphs

When we investigate statistical information we often find there are connections between sets of data, for example height and weight. In general taller people weigh more than shorter people.

To see if there is a connection between two sets of data we can plot a **scatter graph**. This scatter graph shows information about the heights and weights of ten boys.

The diagram shows that taller boys generally weigh more than shorter boys.

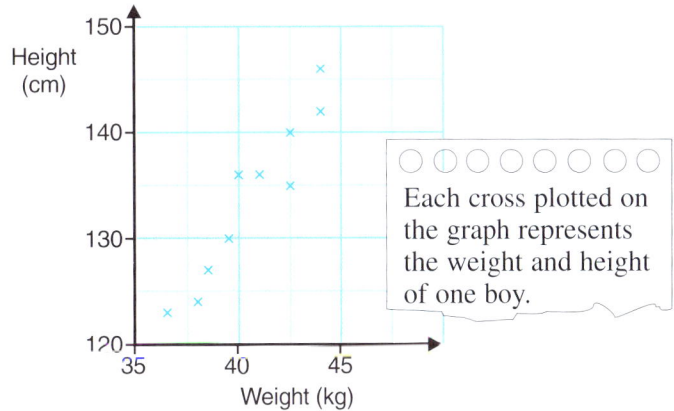

Each cross plotted on the graph represents the weight and height of one boy.

Correlation

The relationship between two sets of data is called **correlation**.

In general the scatter graph of the heights and weights, shows that as height increases, weight increases. This type of relationship shows there is a **positive correlation** between height and weight.

But if as the value of one variable increases the value of the other variable decreases, then there is a **negative correlation** between the variables.

When no relationship exists between two variables there is **zero correlation**.

The following graphs show types of correlation.

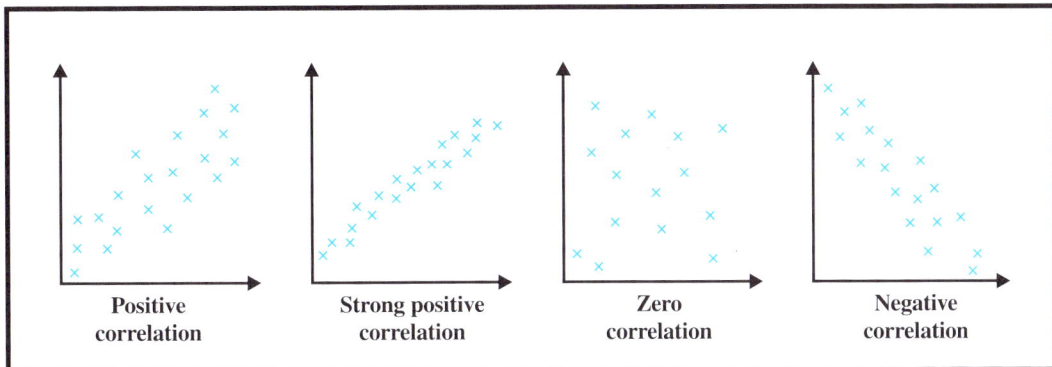

| Positive correlation | Strong positive correlation | Zero correlation | Negative correlation |

As points get closer to a straight line the stronger the correlation.
Perfect correlation is when all the points lie on a straight line.

1 The scatter graph shows the shoe sizes and heights of a group of girls.

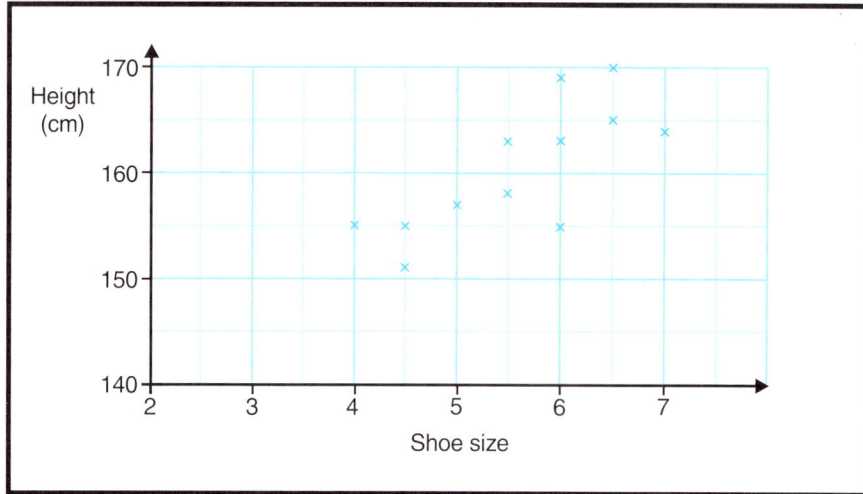

(a) How many girls wear size $6\frac{1}{2}$ shoes?
(b) How tall is the girl with the largest shoe size?
(c) Does the shortest girl wear the smallest shoes?
(d) What do you notice about the shoe sizes of taller girls compared to shorter girls?

2 (a) Which of these graphs shows the strongest positive correlation?
(b) Which of these graphs shows perfect negative correlation?
(c) Which of these graphs shows the weakest correlation?

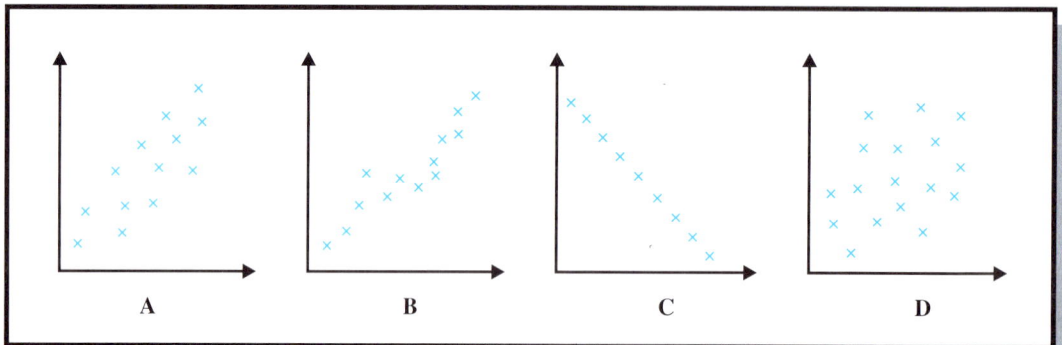

3 Describe the type of correlation you would expect between:
(a) the age of a car and its secondhand selling price,
(b) the heights of children and their ages,
(c) the shoe sizes of children and the distance they travel to school,
(d) the number of cars on the road and the number of road accidents,
(e) the engine size of a car and the number of kilometres it can travel on one litre of fuel.

4 The table shows the distance travelled and time taken by motorists on different journeys.

Distance travelled (km)	30	45	48	80	90	100	125
Time taken (hours)	0.6	0.9	1.2	1.2	1.3	2.0	1.5

(a) Draw a scatter graph for the data.
(b) What do you notice about distance travelled and time taken?
(c) Give one reason why the distance travelled and the time taken are not perfectly correlated.

5 Tyres were collected from a number of different cars. The table shows the distance travelled and depth of tread for each tyre.

Distance travelled (1000 km)	4	5	9	10	12	15	18	25	30
Depth of tread (mm)	9.2	8.4	7.6	8	6.5	7.4	7	6.2	5

(a) Draw a scatter graph for the data.
(b) What do you notice about the distance travelled and the depth of tread?
(c) Give one reason why the distance travelled and the depth of tread are not perfectly correlated.

Line of best fit

We have seen that **scatter graphs** can be used to illustrate two sets of data and from the distribution of points plotted an indication of the relationship which exists between the data can be seen.

The scatter graph of heights and weights has been redrawn below and a **line of best fit** has been drawn, by eye, to show the relationship between height and weight.

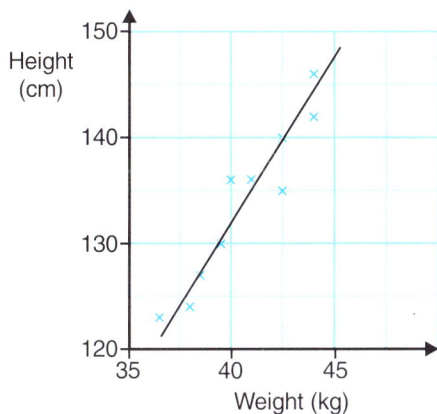

Lines of best fit
- The slope of the line shows the trend of the points.
- A line is only drawn if the correlation (positive or negative) is strong.
- The line does not have to go through the origin of the graph.

Where there is a relationship between the two sets of data the line of best fit can be used to estimate other values.

A boy is 132 cm tall.
Using the line of best fit an estimate of his weight is 40 kg.

In a similar way we can use the line to estimate the height of a boy when we know his weight.
A boy weighs 43 kg. Estimate his height.

Exercise 29.2

1 The table shows the ages and weights of ten babies.

Age (weeks)	2	4	9	7	13	5	6	1	10	12
Weight (kg)	3.5	3.3	4.2	4.7	5	3.8	4	3	5	5.5

(a) (i) Use this information to draw a scatter graph.
    (ii) Draw a line of best fit by eye.

(b) Mrs Wilson's baby is 11 weeks old.
    Use the graph to estimate the weight of her baby.

2 The table shows the sales and profits for eight shops.

Sales (£)	400	570	340	530	500	290	370	560
Profit (£)	80	110	72	100	106	55	65	116

(a) (i) Use this information to draw a scatter graph.
    (ii) Draw a line of best fit by eye.

(b) Use the graph to estimate:
    (i) the profit for a shop whose sales were £480,
    (ii) the sales for a shop whose profit was £60.

3 The table shows the weights and fitness factors for a number of women.
The higher the fitness factor the fitter a person is.

Weight (kg)	45	48	50	54	56	60	64	72	99	112
Fitness Factor	41	48	40	40	35	40	34	30	17	15

(a) (i) Use this information to draw a scatter graph.
    (ii) Draw the line of best fit by eye.

(b) Use the graph to estimate:
    (i) the fitness factor for a woman whose weight is 80 kg,
    (ii) the weight of a woman whose fitness factor is 22.

4 The table shows the marks obtained by students in examinations in statistics at Easter and in the summer.

Mark at Easter	30	19	59	39	67	15	70	11	56	44
Mark in the summer	41	29	77	50	84	24	89	16	71	59

(a) (i) Use this information to draw a scatter graph.
    (ii) Draw the line of best fit by eye.

(b) Another student scored 35 marks in the Easter examination but did not sit the summer examination. What mark would you predict for this student in the summer examination?

5 The following table gives the marks obtained by some candidates taking examinations in French and German.

Mark in French	53	35	39	53	50	59	36	43
Mark in German	64	32	44	70	56	68	40	48

(a) (i) Use this information to draw a scatter graph.
    (ii) Draw the line of best fit by eye.

(b) Use the graph to estimate:
    (i) the mark in German for a candidate who got 70 in French,
    (ii) the mark in French for a candidate who got 58 in German.

(c) Which of the two estimates in (b) is likely to be more reliable?
Give a reason for your answer.

Histograms with equal class width intervals

Histograms are used to present information contained in **grouped frequency distributions**.
Histograms can have equal or unequal class width intervals.
In a histogram with equal class intervals, **frequency** is proportional to the **heights** of the bars.

> A histogram with equal class width intervals looks like a bar chart with no gaps.

Frequency polygons

Frequency polygons are often used instead of histograms to compare two, or more, sets of data.
A frequency polygon is drawn by plotting the frequencies at the midpoint of each class interval and then joining successive points with straight lines.
To compare data, frequency polygons for different groups of data can be drawn on the same diagram.

EXAMPLE

The frequency distribution of the heights of some boys is shown.

Height (cm)	130 -	140 -	150 -	160 -	170 -	180 -
Frequency	1	7	12	9	3	0

> **Note:**
> 130 - means 130 or more but less than 140.

Draw a histogram and a frequency polygon to illustrate the data.

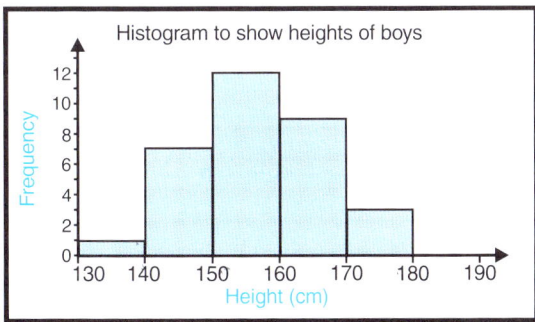

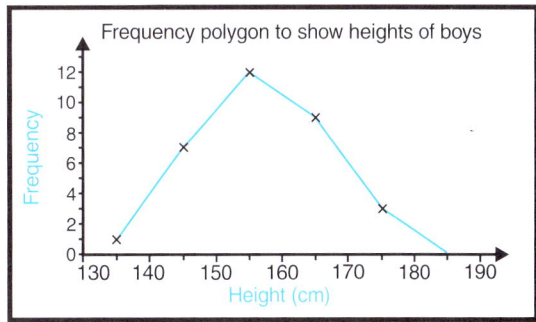

Individual bars are not labelled because the horizontal axis represents a **continuous** variable.

Exercise 29.3

1 A frequency distribution of the heights of some girls is shown.

Height (cm)	130 -	140 -	150 -	160 -	170 -	180 -	190 -
Frequency	3	5	12	4	1	0	0

Draw a histogram to illustrate the data.

2 The table shows the times taken by 200 students to complete a puzzle.

Time (seconds)	1 -	10 -	20 -	30 -	40 -	50 -	60 -	70 -	80 - 90
Number of students	0	2	16	24	44	50	35	20	9

Draw a histogram to show these results.

3 The table shows the distances travelled to school by 100 children.

Distance (km)	0 -	2 -	4 -	6 -	8 -	10 -	12 -	14 - 16
Frequency	26	32	22	10	6	3	1	0

Draw a frequency polygon to illustrate this information.

4 The frequency distribution of the weights of some students is shown.

Weight (kg)	40 -	50 -	60 -	70 -	80 -	90 - 100
Number of males	0	6	11	5	2	1
Number of females	3	14	8	0	0	0

(a) On the same diagram draw a frequency polygon for the males and a frequency polygon for the females.
(b) Compare and comment on the weights of male and female students.

5 The table shows the results for competitors in the 1997 and 1998 Schools' Javelin Championship.
Only the best distance thrown by each competitor is shown.

Distance thrown (*m* metres)	Number of competitors 1997	Number of competitors 1998
$10 \leqslant m < 20$	0	1
$20 \leqslant m < 30$	3	4
$30 \leqslant m < 40$	14	19
$40 \leqslant m < 50$	21	13
$50 \leqslant m < 60$	7	11
$60 \leqslant m < 70$	0	2

(a) On the same diagram draw a frequency polygon for the 1997 results and then a frequency polygon for the 1998 results.
(b) Compare and comment on the results.

Histograms with unequal class width intervals

Data is sometimes grouped using **unequal** class width intervals.
In a histogram with unequal class intervals the vertical axis is labelled **frequency density**.
Frequency is proportional to the **areas** of the bars.

$$\text{frequency} = \text{frequency density} \times \text{class width interval}$$

1 The table shows the frequency distribution of the heights of some women. Draw a histogram for the data.

Height	150 -	165 -	175 -	180 -	185 - 195
Frequency	15	20	20	10	4

The data has unequal class intervals.
Before a histogram can be drawn, the height of each bar must be calculated.
The height of each bar is given by the frequency density for each group, where:

Frequency density = $\dfrac{\text{frequency}}{\text{class width interval}}$

Frequency	15	20	20	10	4
Class width interval	15	10	5	5	10
Frequency density	1	2	4	2	0.4

The histogram is shown below.

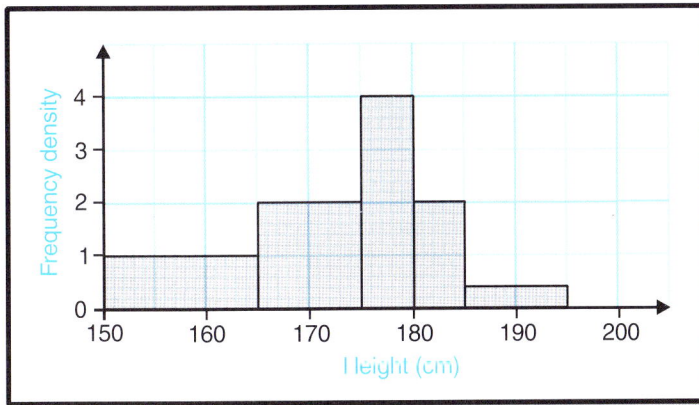

When drawing histograms mark a **continuous scale** on the horizontal axis. Draw bars, between the lower and upper class boundaries, for each class interval.

Remember
The **area** of each bar is proportional to the **frequency**.

2 The histogram represents the heights of some plants.

Five plants are less than 20 cm high.
(a) How many plants are at least 30 cm high?
(b) How many plants are there altogether?

Find the frequency density for the plants $10 \leqslant h < 20$.

Frequency density is given by:

$\dfrac{\text{frequency}}{\text{class width interval}}$

$= \frac{5}{10} = 0.5$

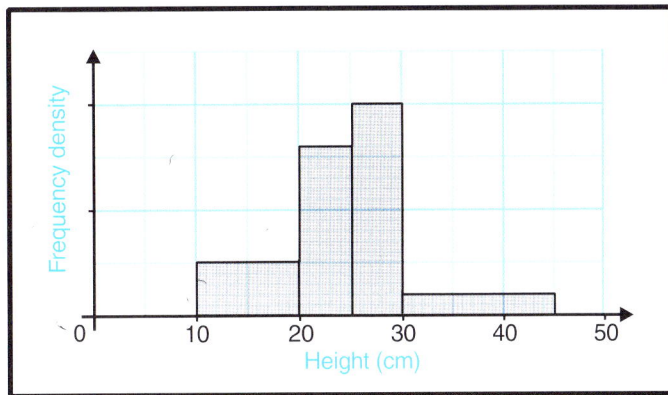

The frequency density axis can now be labelled.

(a) Plants at least 30 cm high are in the interval $30 \leqslant h < 45$.
Frequency = frequency density × class width interval
Frequency density = 0.2 (from vertical axis)
Class width interval = 45 − 30 = 15 (from horizontal axis)
Frequency = 0.2 × 15 = 3
3 plants are at least 30 cm high.

(b) Total frequency = 5 + 1.6 × 5 + 2 × 5 + 3
= 5 + 8 + 10 + 3 = 26
There are 26 plants altogether.

1 The ages of people in a coach party is shown.

Age (years)	10 -	20 -	40 -	45 -	50 - 60
Frequency	4	16	13	9	6

Draw a histogram for the data.

2 The frequency distribution of the weights of some children is shown in the table.

Weight (kg)	40 -	50 -	55 -	60 -	65 -	75 - 85
Frequency	9	10	17	32	28	4

Draw a histogram for the data.

3 The frequency distribution of the annual wages of all the employees of a small firm is shown in the table.

Annual Wage (£1000's)	6 -	10 -	15 -	20 -	30 - 45
Frequency	6	8	13	17	3

Represent this information as a histogram.

4 A group of students were asked how long they spent watching television on a particular Sunday.
The results are shown in the table.

Time (hours)	0 -	2 -	6 -	10 -	12 - 15
Frequency	7	6	19	5	3

Show the results as a histogram.

5 The histogram shows the distribution of the ages of a sample of cars.

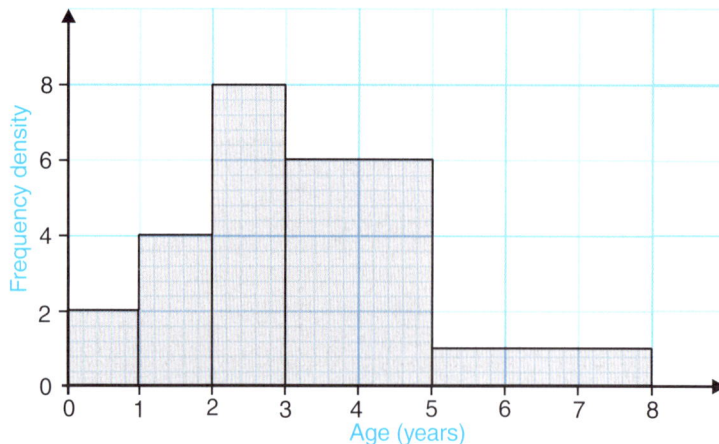

(a) How many cars in the sample were between 2 and 3 years of age?
(b) How many cars in the sample were between 3 and 5 years of age?

6 The histogram shows the age distribution of students delivering newspapers in a town in 1999.

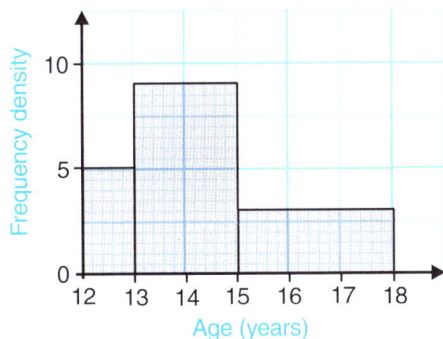

How many students delivered newspapers in the town in 1999?

7 The histogram shows the distribution of the prices paid for houses sold in a town in 1998.

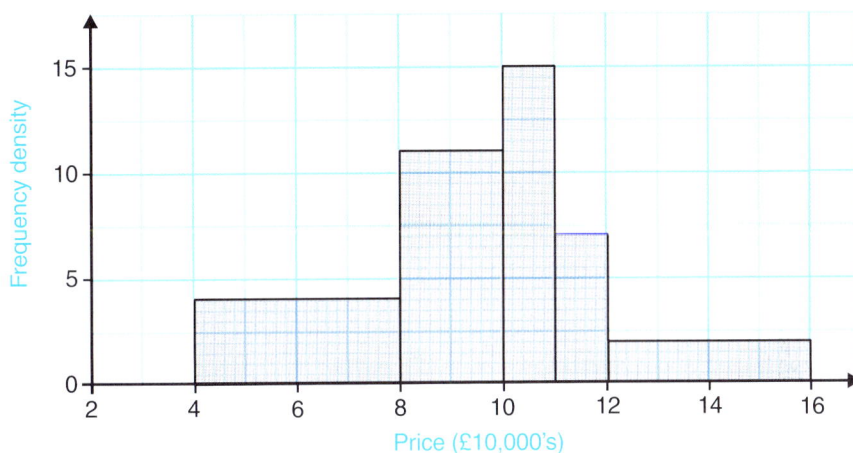

How many houses were sold altogether?

8 The histogram represents the age distribution of the employees in a small company.

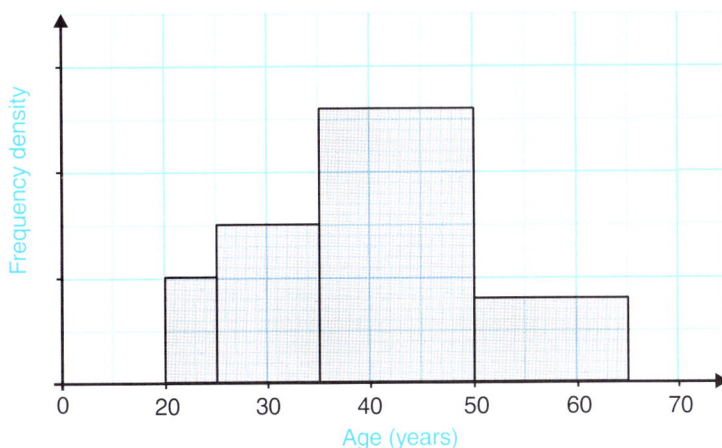

There are 5 employees in the 20 to 25 age range.
(a) How many employees are in the 50 to 65 age range?
(b) How many employees has the company?

9 The histogram shows the distribution of distances thrown by competitors in a throwing competition.

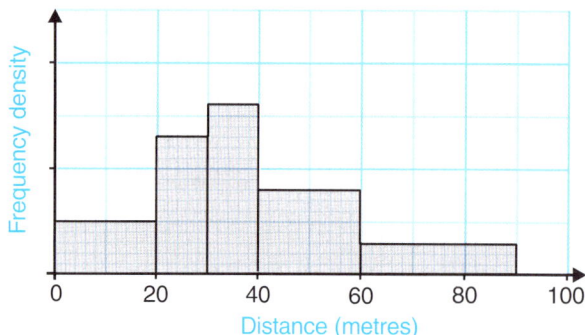

Nine competitors threw 60 metres or more.
(a)   How many competitors threw less than 20 metres?
(b)   How many competitors took part in the competition?

10 The table shows the distribution of the heights of all the sixth formers in a school.

Height (h cm)	Number of students
$150 \leqslant h < 165$	75
$165 \leqslant h < 175$	100
$175 \leqslant h < 180$	100
$180 \leqslant h < 185$	50
$185 \leqslant h < 195$	20

Represent this information as a histogram.

11 The table shows the distribution of the heights of some plants.
The heights were measured to the nearest centimetre.

Height (cm)	1 - 5	6 - 10	11 - 15
Frequency	0	15	10

(a)   (i)   What is the height of the smallest plant that could be placed in the 6 - 10 class?
      (ii) What is the width of the 6 - 10 class?

(b)   Draw a histogram of the distribution.

12 The table below shows the amount of milk, measured to the nearest litre, produced by some cows on a given day.

Milk (litres)	5 - 14	15 - 19	20 - 24	25 - 34
Number of cows	5	10	7	3

Draw a histogram to represent these data.

Note
When the classes have gaps between them the upper class boundary is halfway between the end of one class and the beginning of the next.

450

What you need to know

- A **scatter graph** can be used to show the relationship between two sets of data.

- The relationship between two sets of data is referred to as **correlation**.

- You should be able to recognise **positive** and **negative** correlation.

Positive correlation

Negative correlation

- When there is a relationship between two sets of data a **line of best fit** can be drawn on the scatter graph.
  The correlation is stronger as points get closer to a straight line.
  Perfect correlation is when all the points lie on a straight line.

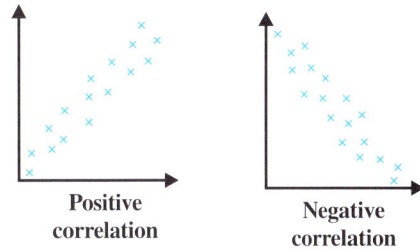

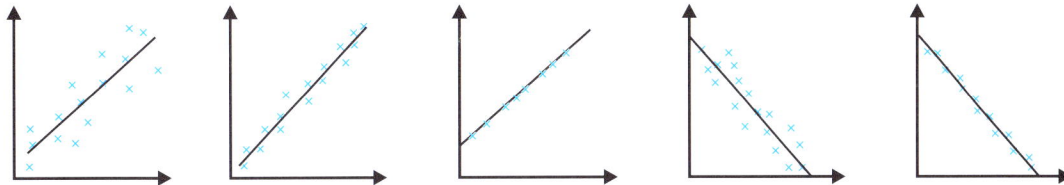

- The line of best fit can be used to **estimate** the value from one set of the data when the corresponding value of the other set is known.

- **Frequency polygon**. Used to illustrate grouped frequency distributions.
  Often used to compare two or more distributions on the same diagram.
  Frequencies are plotted at the midpoints of the class intervals and joined with straight lines.
  The horizontal axis is a continuous scale.

- **Histograms**. Used to illustrate grouped frequency distributions.
  The horizontal axis is a continuous scale.
  Bars are drawn between the lower and upper class boundaries for each class interval.
  When the classes have gaps between them the upper class boundary is halfway between the end of one class and the beginning of the next

- Histograms can have equal or unequal class width intervals.
  With **equal** class width intervals: **frequency** is proportional to the **heights** of the bars.
  With **unequal** class width intervals: **frequency** is proportional to the **areas** of the bars.
  frequency = frequency density × class width interval

- Before a histogram can be drawn, the height of each bar must be calculated.
  The height of each bar is given by the **frequency density** for each group, where:

$$\text{frequency density} = \frac{\text{frequency}}{\text{class width interval}}$$

IDEAS FOR INVESTIGATION

1 Record the resting pulse rates for 10 members of your class.
Ask them to run on the spot for one minute and then take their pulse rate again, call this the exercise rate.
Plot a scatter graph of "resting" pulse rate against "exercise" pulse rate and draw a line of best fit.
What type of correlation exists between the resting pulse rates and the exercise pulse rates for these pupils?
Take the resting pulse rate of someone else.
Can you use your graph to estimate their exercise pulse rate?
Ask them to run on the spot and comment on the results.

2 Investigate the statement: "Taller people have bigger feet".
You might like to consider age and gender separately.

1 The table shows a record of the temperature at midday and the number of ice creams sold each Sunday between 1 pm and 2 pm.

Temperature (°C)	5	10	25	26	20	18	15
Number of ice creams	23	25	45	44	40	35	35

(a) Draw a scatter diagram of this information.
Label the horizontal axis **Temperature (°C)**, from 0 to 30.
Label the vertical axis **Number of ice creams**, from 0 to 50.

(b) What type of correlation is shown on the scatter diagram?

(c) Draw a line of best fit and use it to predict the number of ice creams sold on a Sunday when the temperature is 30°C.

SEG 1997

2 Dr Malik wants to buy a car. She collects information about engine capacity and fuel economy.
She draws a scatter graph as shown.

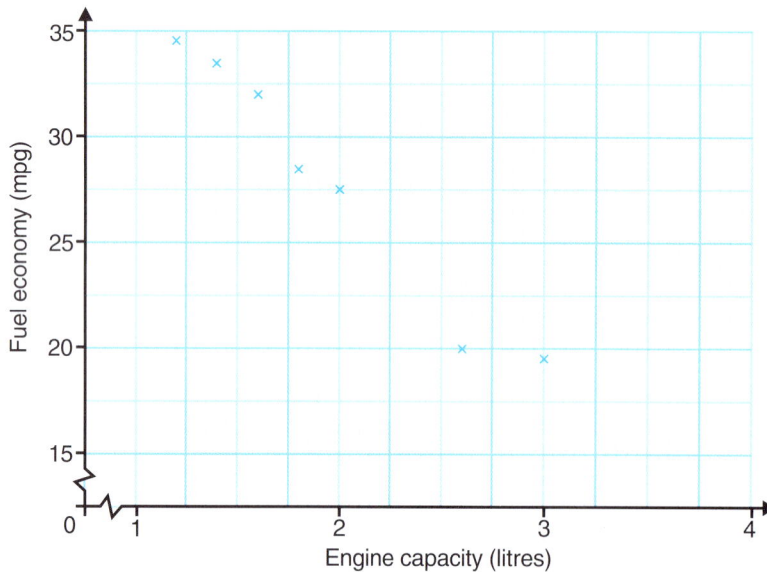

(a) Copy the scatter graph.
Draw a line of best fit on your scatter graph.

(b) Use your graph to estimate the fuel economy of a car with an engine capacity of:
(i) 2.3 litres,
(ii) 3.5 litres.

(c) Which of the two estimates in (b) is more reliable?
Give a reason for your answer.

Dr Malik decides to buy a car with a fuel economy of at least 30 mpg.
(d) Use your graph to estimate the largest engine capacity that she should consider.

SEG 1998 S

3 The scatter diagram shows the heights of some plants, d days after germinating.

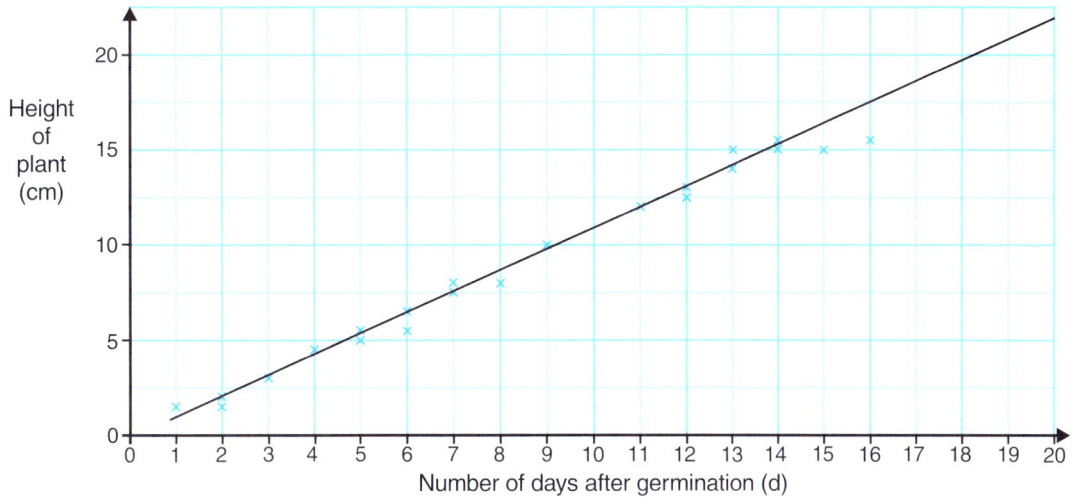

A line of best fit has been drawn on the diagram.
(a) Use the line of best fit to estimate the height of a plant:
    (i)   10 days after germination,
    (ii) 20 days after germination.

(b) Which of your two answers in (a) is likely to be more reliable?
    Give a reason for your answer.

SEG 1998

4 The scatter diagram shows the number of books that have been read by ten children and the reading ages of these children.

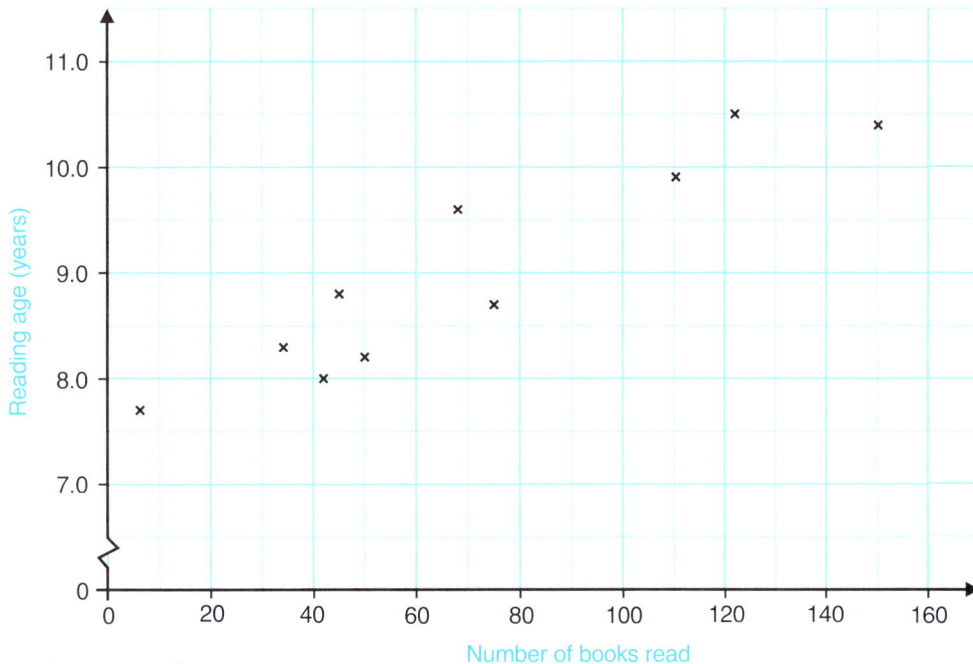

Copy the scatter diagram.
(a) Draw a line of 'best fit' on the scatter diagram.
(b) Paul has read 100 books. Use your line of 'best fit' to predict his reading age.
(c) Paul's reading age is 8.0 years. Calculate the difference between this and your prediction from part (b).
(d) By referring to the scatter diagram, comment on whether the value calculated in part (c) is unusual.

SEG 1997

5 The number of road accidents involving male drivers of various ages is represented by the scatter graph.

(a) Copy the scatter graph and draw a line of best fit.

(b) Use your line of best fit to estimate the number of accidents that would involve male drivers of age 25 years.

The line already drawn on the scatter graph represents the line of best fit for the number of accidents involving female drivers of various ages.

(c) Describe the differences illustrated by these two lines of best fit.

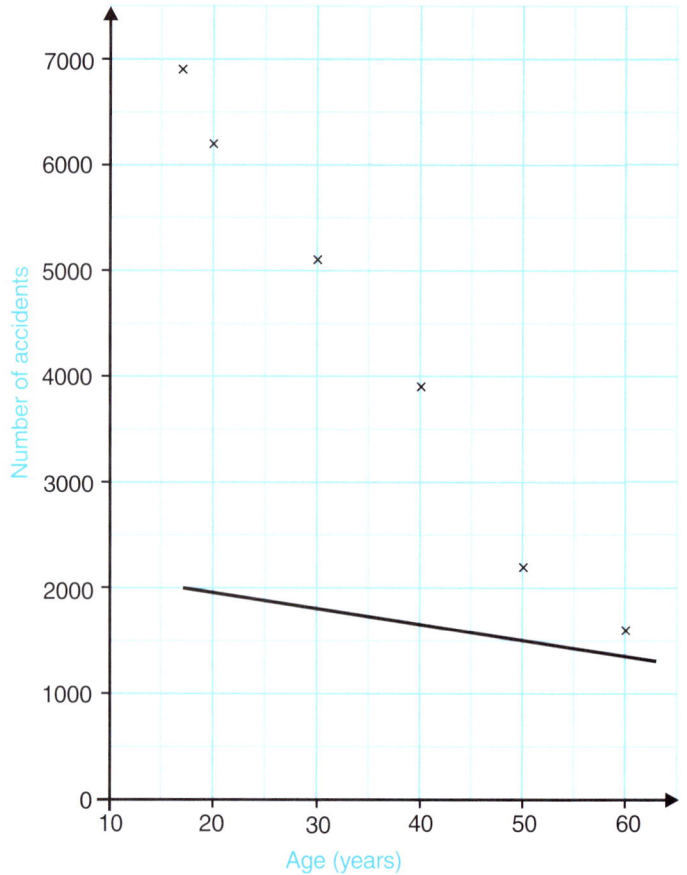

SEG 1995

6 The graph shows the results of a survey of the times at which pupils arrived at school one day.

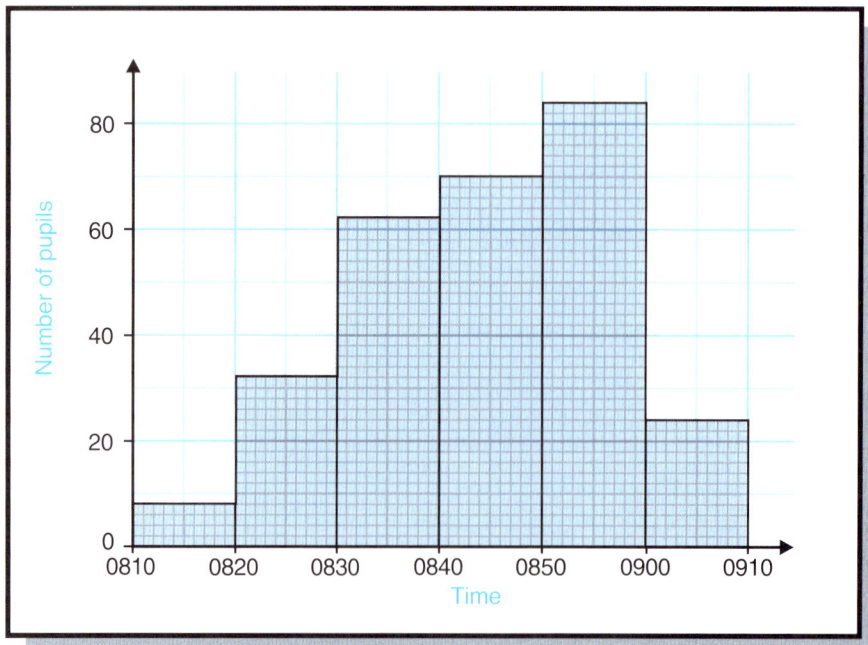

(a) How many pupils arrived for school between 0830 and 0850?

(b) How many pupils attended school that day?

SEG 1995

454

7 The grouped frequency table shows the results of a survey about the distance travelled to work by people each day.

Distance (km)	0 -	4 -	8 -	12 -	16 -	20 - 24
Number of people	10	24	30	8	7	1

(a) Draw a histogram to illustrate this information.
(b) How many people travelled less than 8 kilometres?

8 The table shows the length of time taken by some children to complete a puzzle.

(a) Draw a frequency polygon to show the data.

(b) How many children took 30 minutes or more to complete the puzzle?

Time (minutes)	Number of children
0 -	0
10 -	10
20 -	25
30 -	18
40 -	7
50 - 60	0

9 The graph gives information about the weight of cucumbers produced from 100 seeds of two different varieties, type x and type y.

(a) Which variety of seed has more variation in the weight of cucumbers produced?

(b) Give a reason for your answer.

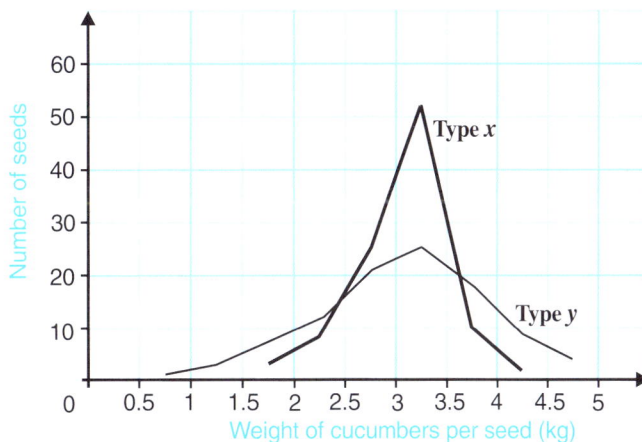

SEG 1995

10 The table gives information about the weight of the potato crop produced by 100 potato plants of two different types.

Weight of potatoes per plant w kg	Number of plants Type X	Number of plants Type Y
$0 \leqslant w < 0.5$	0	0
$0.5 \leqslant w < 1.0$	3	0
$1.0 \leqslant w < 1.5$	12	6
$1.5 \leqslant w < 2.0$	55	39
$2.0 \leqslant w < 2.5$	23	32
$2.5 \leqslant w < 3.0$	7	23
$3.0 \leqslant w < 3.5$	0	0

(a) On the same diagram draw a frequency polygon for each type of potato.

(b) Which type of potato produces the heavier crop?

(c) (i) Which type of potato has more variation in the weight of the crop?
    (ii) Give a reason for your answer.

SEG 1994

11 The height of each of 60 plants of type *A* was measured and recorded.

Height of plant (cm)	8 -	10 -	12 -	14 -	16 -	18 -	20 - 22
Number of plants	0	2	3	18	19	18	0

(a) On graph paper, draw a frequency polygon to show these results.

The frequency polygon of 60 plants of type *B* is shown.

(b) Write down **two** differences between the two types of plant shown by the frequency polygons.

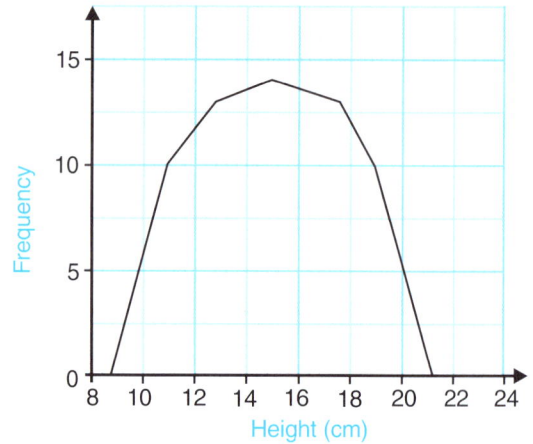

SEG 1994

12 The age of each person in a coach party is illustrated in the histogram.

There are 6 people in the 70 - 80 age range.

(a) How many people are there in the 45 - 50 age range?

(b) How many people are there in the 50 - 70 age range?

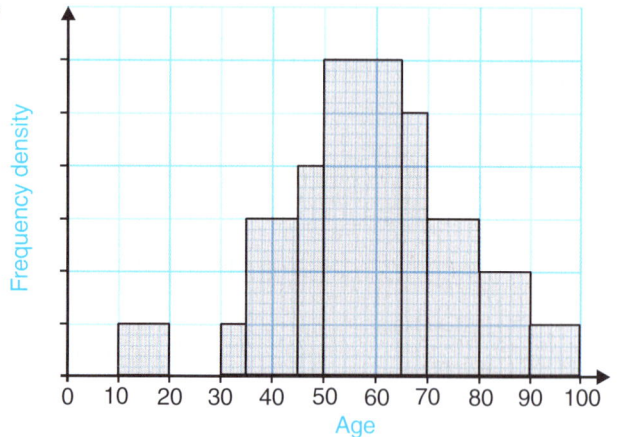

SEG 1994

13 In a survey 50 people were asked how many hours of television they watched in one week.
The histogram shows the results of the survey.

No one watched more than 40 hours of television in one week

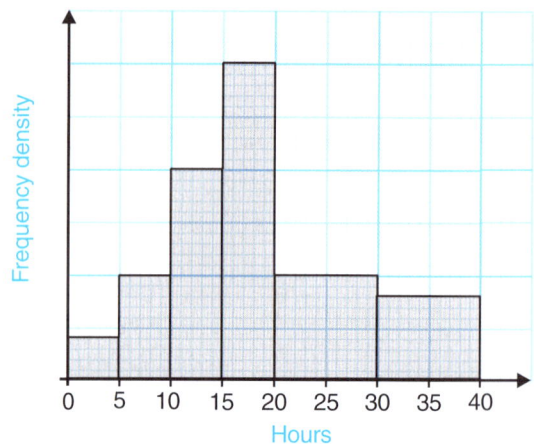

Use the histogram to complete the table of values.

Number of hours	0 -	5 -	10 -	15 -	20 -	30 - 40
Frequency	2					

SEG 1996

14 In a survey 110 people were asked how many hours of radio they listened to in a week. The results were as shown. Draw a histogram to illustrate the data.

Number of hours	0 -	5 -	10 -	20 -	30 -	50 - 100
Number of people	10	6	18	24	32	20

SEG 1995

15 (a) The weights of new born babies in a country are recorded as shown. Construct a histogram to display the data.

Weight (w kg)	Frequency
$0 \leqslant w < 1.5$	9000
$1.5 \leqslant w < 2.5$	24 000
$2.5 \leqslant w < 5$	65 000
$5 \leqslant w < 7$	2000

(b) This histogram shows the weights of new born babies in another country. How many new born babies were there in this country?

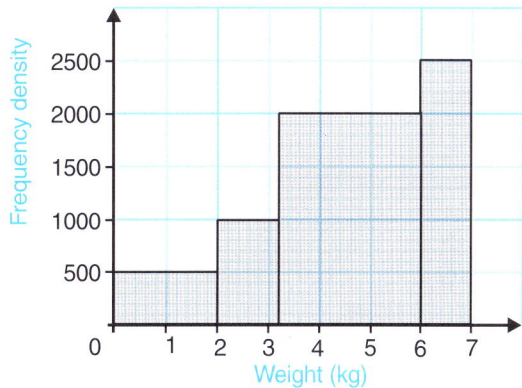

SEG 1997

16 This table shows the age of teachers in Castle School.

Teachers' age (in years)	21 - 25	26 - 35	36 - 45	46 - 65
Frequency	6	14		2
Frequency density	1.2	1.4	0.4	

(a) Copy and complete the table by calculating the frequency for the age range 36 - 45 and the frequency density for the age range 46 - 65.

(b) Draw a histogram to show the age distribution of the teachers in Castle School.

(c) This histogram represents the age distribution of teachers in Berry School. There are 4 teachers in the 21 - 25 age range.

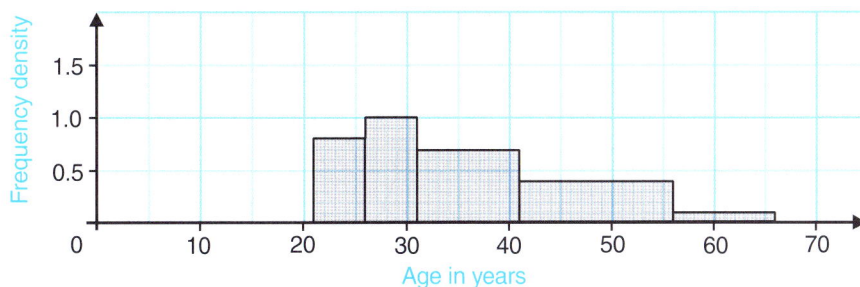

(i) Use this histogram to calculate how many teachers are in the 31 - 40 age range in Berry School.

(ii) Use this histogram to estimate how many teachers are age 51 or over in Berry School.

(iii) What do the two histograms tell you about the difference between the age distributions of teachers in Castle School and Berry School?

SEG 1994

CHAPTER 30

Measures of Average and Spread

In statistics measures of average and spread are used to compare data.

Types of average

There are three types of average, the **mode**, the **median** and the **mean**.

The **mode** is the most common amount.
The **median** is found by arranging the data in order of size and taking the middle amount.
The **mean** is found by finding the total of all the data and dividing the total by the number of data values.

EXAMPLE

The price, in pence, of a can of cola in different shops is shown.

    33,   34,   31,   33,   30,   31,   31,   35.

Find   (a)   the mode,
           (b)   the median,
           (c)   the mean price.

(a)   The most common price is 31.
       The mode is 31 pence.
       We sometimes say the modal price is 31p.

(b)   Arrange the data in order of size.
       30,   31,   31,   31,   33,   33,   34,   35.

       The middle amount is $\dfrac{31 + 32}{2} = 31.5$

       The median is 31.5 pence.

> Where there are an even number of values the median is the average of the middle two.

(c)   Add the data.
       $33 + 34 + 31 + 33 + 30 + 31 + 31 + 35 = 258$

       The mean $= \dfrac{258}{8} = 32.25$

       The mean is 32.25 pence.

Frequency distributions

To find measures of average for **frequency distributions** we have to take into account the frequency of each amount.

EXAMPLE

The table shows the boot sizes of players in a rugby team.

Boot size	8	9	10	11
Frequency	3	5	6	1

Find (a) the mode, (b) the median, (c) the mean boot size.

(a) The mode is the boot size with the largest frequency.
The modal boot size is 10.

(b) The median is the boot size of the middle player.
There are 15 players altogether.
The middle one is the 8th player.
The first 3 players wear boot size 8,
the next 5 wear boot size 9.
So the 8th player wears boot size 9.
The median boot size is 9.

> **Mathematical shorthand**
> Σ is the Greek letter 'sigma'.
> Σf means the sum of frequencies.
> Σfx means the sum of the values of fx.
> Mean $= \dfrac{\Sigma fx}{\Sigma f}$

(c) The mean $= \dfrac{\text{Total of all boot sizes}}{\text{Total number of players}} = \dfrac{8 \times 3 + 9 \times 5 + 10 \times 6 + 11 \times 1}{3 + 5 + 6 + 1} = \dfrac{140}{15} = 9.333\ldots$

The mean boot size is 9.3, correct to 1 d.p.

Grouped frequency distributions

When there is a lot of data, or the data is continuous, **grouped frequency distributions** are used.

Calculating the mean
For a grouped frequency distribution the true value of the mean cannot be found as the actual values of the data are not known.

To **estimate the mean**, we assume that all the values in each class are equal to the midpoint of the class.

$$\text{Estimated mean} = \frac{\Sigma\,(\text{frequency} \times \text{midpoint})}{\text{Total frequency}} = \frac{\Sigma fx}{\Sigma f}$$

Modal class
For a grouped frequency distribution with equal class width intervals, the **modal class** is the class (or group) with the highest frequency.

EXAMPLE

The table shows the masses of a group of children.
(a) Calculate an estimate of the mean mass.
(b) Find the modal class.

Mass (kg)	Frequency
40 -	3
50 -	10
60 -	6
70 - 80	12

(a)

Mass (kg)	Midpoint x	Frequency f	Frequency × Midpoint $f \times x$
40 - 50	45	3	135
50 - 60	55	10	550
60 - 70	65	6	390
70 - 80	75	12	900
	Totals	$\Sigma f = 31$	$\Sigma fx = 1975$

> Midpoint of 40 - 50 kg class is given by:
> $\dfrac{40 + 50}{2} = \dfrac{90}{2} = 45$

Estimate of mean $= \dfrac{\Sigma fx}{\Sigma f} = \dfrac{1975}{31} = 63.709\ldots$

Estimate of mean mass $= 63.7$ kg, correct to 3 sig. figs.

(b) The modal class is 70 - 80 kg.

Do not use a calculator in questions 1 to 3. Show your working clearly.

1 Find the mode, median and mean of these lengths.
4 m, 5 m, 3 m, 6 m, 6 m, 6 m, 3 m, 7 m.

2 The mean of seven numbers is 6. Six of the numbers are 2, 5, 7, 3, 7 and 10. What is the other number?

3 The mean length of 8 rods is 75 cm. An extra rod is added. The mean length of the 9 rods is 81 cm. What is the length of the extra rod?

4 Find the mean and median of these weights.
2.3 kg, 8.0 kg, 4.5 kg, 3.7 kg, 5.2 kg, 2.3 kg, 3.1 kg.

5 During a certain week, a saleswoman sold the following numbers of various sizes of a particular style of shoe.

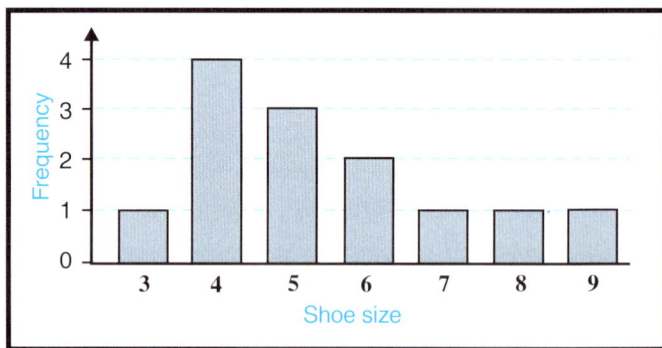

(a) Show the data in a frequency distribution table.
(b) She decides to display the median size in the window. Which size is this?
(c) Her assistant says it would be better to display the modal size. Which size is this?
(d) Calculate the mean size. Comment on your answer.

6 Find the mode, median and mean for the following data.

(a)

Number of letters delivered	1	2	3	4	5	6
Number of days	6	9	6	6	2	1

(b)

Number of siblings	0	1	2	3	4	5
Frequency	1	4	10	4	1	1

7 Give the modal class and calculate an estimate of the mean for each of the following.

(a)

Time spent watching TV per week (hours)	0 -	10 -	20 -	30 -	40 - 50
Number of students		2	8	5	14	7

(b)

Salary (s) (£000's)	$10 \leqslant s < 15$	$15 \leqslant s < 20$	$20 \leqslant s < 25$	$25 \leqslant s < 30$	$30 \leqslant s < 35$
Number of employees	79	32	14	0	2

8 Calculate an estimate of the mean height.

Height in metres (to nearest 0.1 m)	Number of trees
3.0 - 3.4	12
3.5 - 3.9	10
4.0 - 4.4	23
4.5 - 4.9	18
5.0 - 5.4	13

9 Calculate an estimate of the mean mark. Notice that the class intervals are not all equal.

Mark	Number of students
0 - 19	12
20 - 29	23
30 - 34	25
35 - 39	14
40 - 50	3

10 Some women walked one mile. The time taken by each was recorded. The results are as follows.

Time t minutes	$12 \leqslant t < 16$	$16 \leqslant t < 20$	$20 \leqslant t < 24$	$24 \leqslant t < 28$	$28 \leqslant t < 32$
Number of women	1	9	43	22	5

(a) What is the modal class for the time taken?
(b) Calculate an estimate of the mean time taken.

SEG 1998

Which is the best average to use?

Many questions in mathematics have definite answers. This one does not.
Sometimes the mean is best, sometimes the median and sometimes the mode. It all depends on the situation and what you want to use the average for.

EXAMPLE

A youth club leader gets a discount on cans of drinks if she buys all one size. She took a vote on which size people wanted. The results were as follows:

Size of can (ml)	100	200	330	500
Number of votes	9	12	19	1

Mode = 330 ml
Median = 200 ml
Mean = 245.6 ml, correct to one decimal place.

Which size should she buy?

The mean is no use at all because she can't buy cans of size 245.6 ml. Even if the answer is rounded to the nearest whole number (246 ml), it's still no use.
The median is possible because there is an actual 200 ml can. However, only 12 out of 41 people want this size.
In this case the **mode** is the best average to use, as it is the most popular size.

In questions 1 to 3 find all the averages possible.
State which is the most sensible and why.

1 On a bus: 23 people are wearing trainers,
                10 people are wearing boots,
                 8 people are wearing lace-up shoes.

2 20 people complete a simple jigsaw. Their times, in seconds, are recorded.
5, 6, 8, 8, 9, 10, 11, 11, 12, 12, 12, 15, 15, 15, 15, 18, 19, 20, 22, 200.

3 Here are the marks obtained by a group of 11 students in an exam. The exam was marked out of 100.
5, 6, 81, 81, 82, 83, 84, 85, 86, 87, 88.

4 The times for two swimmers to complete each of ten 25m lengths are shown below.

Swimmer A	30.1	30.1	30.1	30.6	30.7	31.1	31.1	31.5	31.7	31.8
Swimmer B	29.6	29.7	29.7	29.9	30.0	30.0	30.1	30.1	30.1	44.6

Which is the better swimmer? Explain why.

5 The table shows the number of runs scored by two batsmen in several innings.

Batsman A	0	0	10	12	20	22	50	51	81	104		
Batsman B	0	24	25	27	28	30	33	34	44	45	46	96

Which is the better batsman? Explain why.

Cumulative frequency tables

This **frequency table** shows the masses of some stones recorded during an experiment.

Mass (kg)	20 -	30 -	40 -	50 -	60 - 70
Number of stones	3	5	10	8	4

The first class is $20 - 30$ kg.
The **upper class boundary** of this class is 30 kg.
What are the upper class boundaries of the other groups?

The information given in a frequency table can be used to make a **cumulative frequency table**.

Mass (kg), less than	20	30	40	50	60	70
Cumulative frequency	0	3	8	18	26	30

> **Note**
> If the question does not give the upper class boundaries, then the upper class boundary of each class is equal to the lower class boundary of the next class.

Mass of stone (less than)	Number of stones
20 kg	0
30 kg	0 + 3 = 3
40 kg	0 + 3 + 5 = 8
50 kg	0 + 3 + 5 + 8 + 10 = 18

Cumulative frequency graph

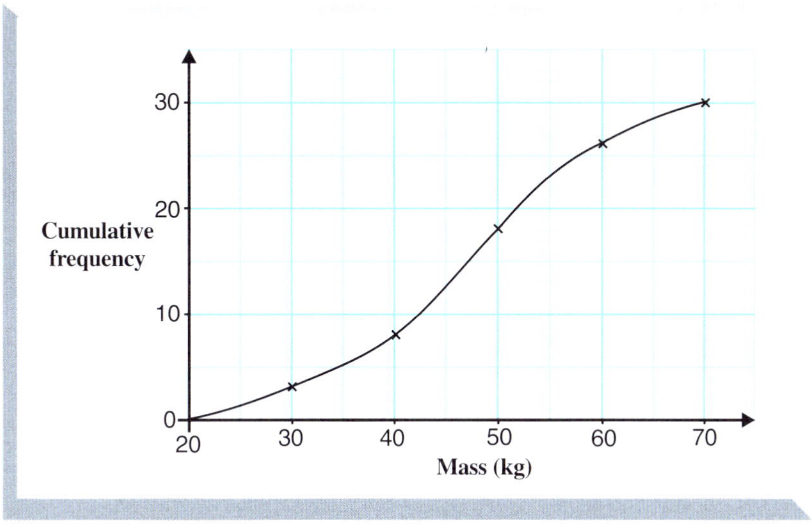

To draw a **cumulative frequency graph**:
1. Draw and label:
   the **variable** on the horizontal axis,
   cumulative frequency on the vertical axis.

2. Plot the cumulative frequency against the upper class boundary of each class.

3. Join the points with a smooth curve.

Using a cumulative frequency graph

Median

The median of 13 numbers is the 7th number.
The median of 14 numbers is between the 7th and
8 th numbers.
We could call this the "$7\frac{1}{2}$ th" number.
For n numbers, the rule for finding the median is:

Median $= \frac{1}{2}(n + 1)$th number

> The median of a frequency distribution is
> the value of the middle number.
> On a cumulative frequency graph this
> value is read from the horizontal axis.

Interquartile range

The **range** of a set of data measures how spread out the data is.
Range = highest value − lowest value.
The range is influenced by extreme high or low values of data and can be misleading.

A better way to measure spread is to find the range of the
middle 50% of the data.
This is called the **interquartile range**.
Interquartile range (IQR) = Upper Quartile − Lower Quartile

For n numbers the rules for finding the quartiles are:

Lower Quartile $= \frac{1}{4}(n + 1)$th number

Upper Quartile $= \frac{3}{4}(n + 1)$th number

> On a cumulative frequency
> graph the values of the
> Upper Quartile and the
> Lower Quartile are read
> from the horizontal axis.

Using the cumulative frequency graph from the previous page, estimate:
(a) the median mass of the stones,
(b) the interquartile range of the masses of the stones.

When n is large
When the total frequency, n, is 'large' you need not bother with '+1' in the rules for the median, lower quartile and upper quartile.
Instead use: median $= \frac{1}{2}n$ th number
lower quartile $= \frac{1}{4}n$ th number
upper quartile $= \frac{3}{4}n$ th number
'Large' means greater than 50. *Explain why.*

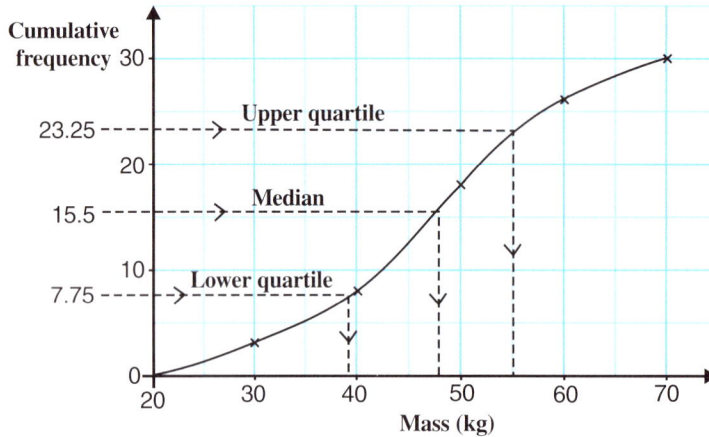

(a) There are 30 stones.
$\frac{1}{2}(30+1)=15.5$, so the median is the mass of the 15.5th stone.
Read along from 15.5 on the vertical axis and down to the horizontal axis.
This is shown on the graph.
Median = 48 g.

Why are the values for the median and interquartile range only estimates?

(b) $\frac{1}{4}(30+1)=7.75$, so the lower quartile is the mass of the 7.75th stone.
$\frac{3}{4}(30+1)=23.25$, so the upper quartile is the mass of the 23.25th stone.
Read these values from the graph.

IQR = Upper Quartile − Lower Quartile
= 55 − 39
= 16 g
The interquartile range is 16 g.

Some variables are discrete and can only take certain values.
In many cases these are whole numbers. For these variables there are gaps between the classes.

For example, this frequency distribution table shows the number of spelling mistakes found in some essays.

Number of mistakes	0 - 5	6 - 10	11 - 15	16 - 20
Number of essays	9	17	8	3

The first class ends at 5. The highest number of spelling mistakes in the class 0 - 5 is 5.
The second class starts at 6.
We take the upper class boundary for the class 0 - 5 to be halfway between 5 and 6, at 5.5.
What are the upper class boundaries for the other classes?

In the following example there are gaps between the classes, because the lengths are measured to the nearest centimetre.

464

EXAMPLE

In an experiment Sophie measured and recorded the longest roots of plants.

Length (to nearest cm)	0 - 2	3 - 5	6 - 8	9 - 11	12 - 14
Number of plants	0	14	35	23	10

(a)   Make a cumulative frequency table for the data Sophie collected.
(b)   Draw a cumulative frequency graph for the data.
(c)   Use your graph to find:
    (i)   the median length,
    (ii)   the interquartile range of lengths.
(d)   How many plants had roots at least 11.2 cm long?

> The class 3 - 5 includes measurements from 2.5 cm to 5.5 cm. The upper class boundary is 5.5.

(a)

Length (cm) less than	2.5	5.5	8.5	11.5	14.5
Cumulative frequency	0	14	47	70	80

(b)

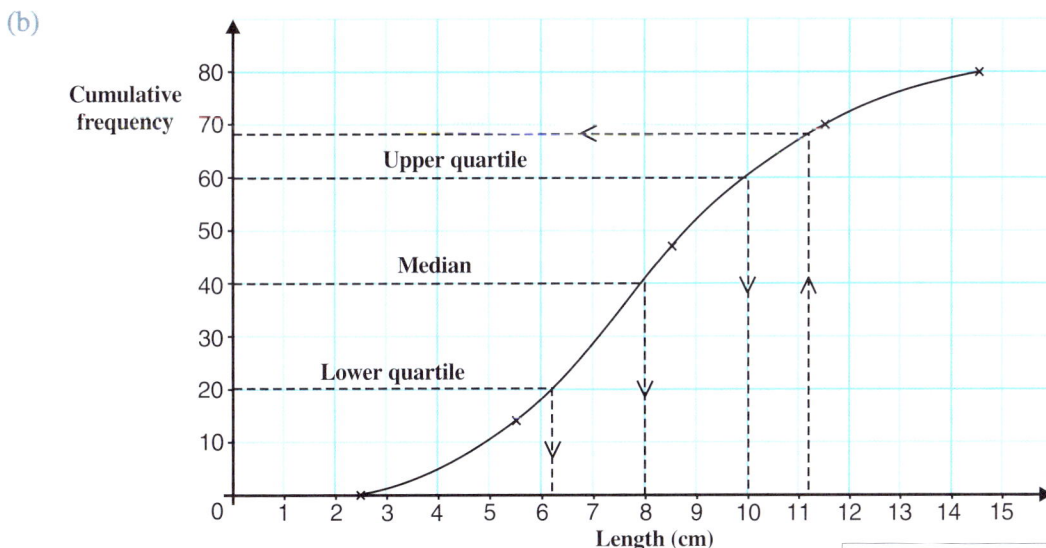

(c)   (i)   There are 80 plants.
$\frac{1}{2}$ of 80 = 40, so the median is the length of the roots of the 40th plant.
Median = 8.0 cm.

(ii)   For the lower quartile use $\frac{1}{4}$ of 80 = 20.
Lower quartile = 6.2 cm
For the upper quartile use $\frac{3}{4}$ of 80 = 60.
Upper quartile = 10.0 cm
IQR = Upper Quartile − Lower Quartile
= 10.0 − 6.2
= 3.8 cm

> **Remember**
> Cumulative frequency is plotted against the upper class boundary for each class.

(d)   From 11.2 on the horizontal axis read upwards to the graph and across to the vertical axis.
There are 68 plants of length less than 11.2 cm.
So the number of plants with roots at least 11.2 cm long is 80 − 68 = 12 plants.

1 Silvia made a record of the times students took to walk to school in the morning.

Time (minutes)	0 -	5 -	10 -	15 -	20 -	25 - 30
Number of students	3	8	12	10	5	2

(a) Copy and complete this cumulative frequency table.

Time (minutes), less than	0	5	10	15	20	25	30
Cumulative frequency							

(b) Draw a cumulative frequency graph for the data.
(c) Use your graph to find:
    (i) the median time,
    (ii) the upper quartile time,
    (iii) the lower quartile time.
(d) Calculate the interquartile range of the times.

2 A secretary weighed a sample of letters to be posted.

Mass (g)	20 -	30 -	40 -	50 -	60 -	70 -	80 - 90
Number of students	2	4	12	7	8	17	3

(a) How many letters were in the sample?
(b) Draw a cumulative frequency graph for the data.
(c) Use your graph to find:
    (i) the median weight of a letter,
    (ii) the interquartile range of the weights.

3 The times taken by competitors to complete the crossword in an annual competition were recorded to the nearest minute.

Time (minutes)	10 - 14	15 - 19	20 - 24	25 - 29	30 - 34
Frequency	7	21	37	12	3

(a) Copy and complete the cumulative frequency table.

Time (minutes)	< 9.5	< 14.5	< 19.5	< 24.5	< 29.5	< 34.5
Cumulative frequency						

(b) Draw a cumulative frequency graph for the data.
(c) Use your graph to find:
    (i) the interquartile range of times,
    (ii) the number of competitors who took less than last year's winning time of
       16 minutes to complete the crossword.

4 Draw a cumulative frequency graph for the results shown in this table.

Number of marks	0 - 20	21 - 25	26 - 30	31 - 40
Number of students	5	9	12	8

(a) Find the median mark.
(b) Find the interquartile range of marks.
(c) The minimum mark for a Grade A is 33. What percentage of students gained Grade A?
(d) 10% of students failed. What was the minimum mark for a pass?

5 A survey was made of the heights of plants produced by a batch of seed.

Height (cm)	80 -	85 -	90 -	95 -	100 - 105
Frequency	20	35	15	11	14

(a) How many plants were measured in the survey?
(b) Draw a cumulative frequency graph for the data.
Label the horizontal axis from 70 cm to 110 cm.
(c) Use your graph to estimate:
  (i) the median height,
  (ii) the interquartile range of heights,
  (iii) the number of plants taller than 97.5 cm.
(d) The shortest 10 plants are used for testing. Estimate the height of the tallest of these 10 plants.

6 The times spent listening to the radio last week by some students is shown.

Time (t hours)	$0 \leqslant t < 5$	$5 \leqslant t < 10$	$10 \leqslant t < 15$	$15 \leqslant t < 20$	$20 \leqslant t < 30$	$30 \leqslant t < 40$
Number of students	7	15	18	24	12	4

(a) Draw a cumulative frequency graph for the data.
(b) Use your graph to find the interquartile range of times.
(c) What percentage of the students spent more than 25 hours per week listening to the radio?

7 The heights of a number of men are shown in this table.
Draw a cumulative frequency graph for the data.
Use your graph to find:
(a) the median and interquartile range of heights,
(b) the number of men whose heights were less than 155 cm,
(c) the number of men whose heights were at least 163 cm,
(d) the maximum height of the shortest 20 men,
(e) the minimum height of the tallest 10% of men.

Height (cm)	Number of men
140 -	1
150 -	6
160 -	8
170 -	21
180 - 190	14

Comparing distributions

EXAMPLE

A firm tested a sample of electric motors produced by an assembly line. They kept a running total of the numbers of motors which had failed at any time. This cumulative frequency graph was plotted using the data collected.

(a)   Find the median lifetime of a motor.

(b)   Find the interquartile range of lifetimes.

(c)   A sample of motors, produced by another assembly line, was tested and found to have:
Median lifetime = 1900 hours
Upper quartile = 2000 hours
Lower quartile = 1700 hours
Compare the two samples of motors.

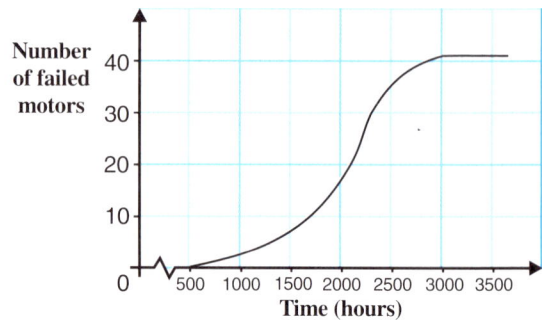

(a)   Median lifetime = 2100 hours

(b)   IQR = Upper Quartile − Lower Quartile
= 2300 − 1700
= 600 hours

(c)   For the second sample:
Median = 1900 hours
IQR = 2000 − 1700 = 300 hours
The first sample has a greater median time. On average, they lasted 200 hours longer than motors in the second sample.

The spread of the second sample (given by the IQR) is much smaller. It is 300 hours, compared with 600 hours for the first sample.

Exercise 30.4

1   The heights of a group of boys and a group of girls were recorded separately.
The results are shown by the cumulative frequency graphs.

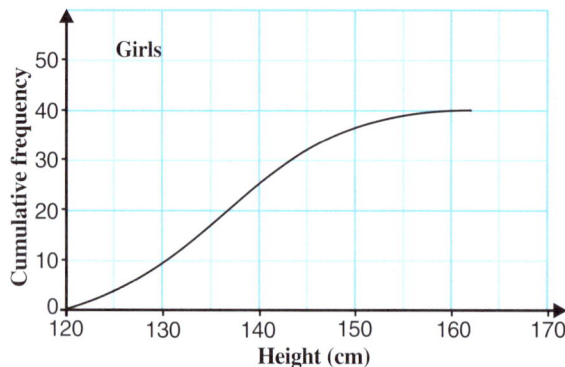

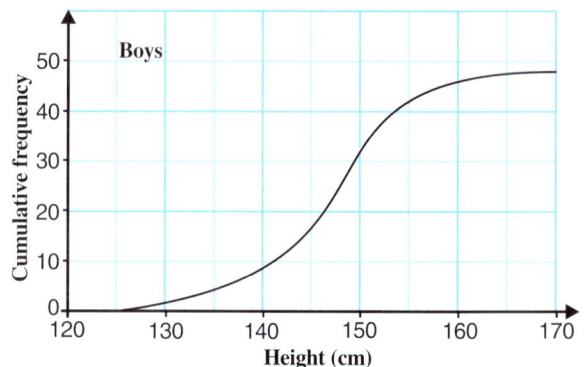

(a)   How many girls were measured?
(b)   Find the interquartile range of heights of the girls.
(c)   Find the interquartile range of heights of the boys.

(d)   Use your answers to parts (b) and (c) to comment on the heights of the girls compared with the boys.
(e)   How many boys are taller than the tallest girl?

468

2 The milk yields of a herd of cows is shown in the table below.

Milk yield (litres)	$5 \leq x < 10$	$10 \leq x < 15$	$15 \leq x < 20$	$20 \leq x < 25$	$25 \leq x < 30$
Number of cows	15	28	37	26	25

(a) Use the data to draw a cumulative frequency graph.
(b) Use your graph to estimate:
    (i)   the median milk yield,
    (ii) the interquartile range of milk yields.
(c) A neighbouring farmer calculated the following results for his herd of cows.
Median yield = 22 litres, Lower quartile = 9 litres, Upper quartile = 28 litres.
Compare and comment on the data for the two herds.

3 A record is kept of the number of people arriving at a meeting, measured from the time the doors are opened.

Time (minutes)	0 -	10 -	20 -	30 -	40 -	50 -	60 - 70
Frequency	2	5	6	7	8	4	4

(a) Copy and complete the cumulative frequency table and draw the cumulative frequency graph.

Time (minutes)	≤ 10	≤ 20	≤ 30	≤ 40	≤ 50	≤ 60	≤ 70
Cumulative frequency							

(b) People are late for the meeting if they arrive more than 35 minutes after the doors are opened.
How many people were late for the meeting?
(c) The same number of people attended a second meeting.
The following results were recorded.
        Median time of arrival   31 minutes
        Interquartile range   11 minutes
Make **two** comparisons between the times of arrival at the first meeting and the second meeting.

SEG 1997

4 The length of life of 100 batteries of a certain make was recorded.
The table shows the results.

Length of life (hours)	< 10	< 15	< 20	< 25	< 30	< 35	< 40
Cumulative frequency	0	2	9	50	86	96	100

(a) Draw a cumulative frequency graph to illustrate these data.
(b) How many batteries had a life of more than 32 hours?
(c) Use your graph to estimate:
    (i)   the median,
    (ii) the interquartile range.
(d) Another make of battery has a median length of life of 25 hours and an interquartile range of 7 hours.
Is this make of battery likely to be more reliable than the first?
Give a reason for your answer.

SEG 1998

You have already met two measures of spread.
The **range** measures the spread of all the data. It is influenced by extreme high or low values of data and can be misleading.

Range = highest value − lowest value

The **interquartile range** measures the spread of the middle 50% of the data.

Interquartile range = Upper quartile − Lower quartile

A third measure of spread, called **standard deviation**, is more precise.
Standard deviation measures the average deviation (difference) of each piece of data from the mean.
Every piece of data is involved in the calculation of standard deviation.

Standard deviation is given by the formulae:
$$s = \sqrt{\frac{\Sigma(x - \bar{x})^2}{n}} \quad \text{or} \quad s = \sqrt{\frac{\Sigma x^2}{n} - \left\{\frac{\Sigma x}{n}\right\}^2}$$
where n = the number of pieces of data,
$\bar{x} = \dfrac{\Sigma x}{n}$ = the mean of the data.

EXAMPLE

(Method 1)
Find the mean and standard deviation of the numbers 1, 2, 3, 4.

The mean value of the numbers is given by $\bar{x}$, where $\bar{x} = \dfrac{\Sigma x}{n} = \dfrac{1 + 2 + 3 + 4}{4} = \dfrac{10}{4} = 2.5$

x	$x - \bar{x}$	$(x - \bar{x})^2$
1	−1.5	2.25
2	−0.5	0.25
3	0.5	0.25
4	1.5	2.25
	$\Sigma(x - \bar{x}) = 0$	$\Sigma(x - \bar{x})^2 = 5$

Notice that:

$\Sigma(x - \bar{x}) = 0$

This is a useful check.

$$s = \sqrt{\frac{\Sigma(x - \bar{x})^2}{n}} = \sqrt{\frac{5}{4}} = \sqrt{1.25} = 1.1180 \ldots$$

The standard deviation = 1.12, to 3 sig. figs.

Method 1 is rather time consuming so we generally use another method which is quicker and gives the same result.

Activity   Copy and complete this table.

Values of x	Mean of x $\bar{x} = \dfrac{\Sigma x}{n}$	Values of x^2	Mean of x^2 $\dfrac{\Sigma x^2}{n}$	Mean of x^2 − (Mean of x)^2 $\dfrac{\Sigma x^2}{n} - \left(\dfrac{\Sigma x}{n}\right)^2$	Standard deviation $\sqrt{\dfrac{\Sigma x^2}{n} - \left(\dfrac{\Sigma x}{n}\right)^2}$
1, 2, 3, 4	2.5	1, 4, 9, 16	7.5	$7.5 - 2.5^2 = 1.25$	1.12
1, 1, 2, 2	1.5	1, 1, 4, 4			
1, 1, 4, 4					
1, 4, 5, 6, 9					
1, 2, 5, 8, 9					
51, 52, 55, 58, 59					

As the values of x become more spread out, the difference between "The mean of x^2" and "(The mean of x)^2" increases. The standard deviation is the square root of this difference.

$$s = \sqrt{\frac{\Sigma x^2}{n} - \left\{\frac{\Sigma x}{n}\right\}^2}$$

It can be shown that this formula is equivalent to the one used in method 1.

EXAMPLE

(Method 2)
Find the mean and standard deviation of these two sets of marks. Compare the two classes.

Class A	4, 8, 6, 10
Class B	5, 8, 7, 6, 5

For Class A:
$n = 4$, $\Sigma x = 28$, $\Sigma x^2 = 216$

$\bar{x} = \dfrac{28}{4} = 7$

$s = \sqrt{\dfrac{216}{4} - \left(\dfrac{28}{4}\right)^2} = 2.24$, to 3 sig. figs.

For Class B:
$n = 5$, $\Sigma x = 31$, $\Sigma x^2 = 199$

$\bar{x} = \dfrac{31}{5} = 6.2$

$s = \sqrt{\dfrac{199}{5} - \left(\dfrac{31}{5}\right)^2} = 1.17$, to 3 sig. figs.

Class A did better overall (higher mean mark).
Class B were more consistent (lower spread of marks).

Standard deviation for a frequency distribution

Standard deviation for a **frequency distribution** is given by the formulae:

$s = \sqrt{\dfrac{\Sigma f(x - \bar{x})^2}{\Sigma f}}$ or $s = \sqrt{\dfrac{\Sigma fx^2}{\Sigma f} - \left(\dfrac{\Sigma fx}{\Sigma f}\right)^2}$

Grouped data
It is assumed that all values in a **group**, or **class**, are equal to the value of the midpoint. Answers will only be **estimates** of the standard deviation.
Explain why.

EXAMPLE

Calculate an estimate of the standard deviation for the following data.

Volume (x cm^3)	$0 \leqslant x < 10$	$10 \leqslant x < 20$	$20 \leqslant x < 25$	$25 \leqslant x < 30$
Frequency	8	10	12	10

Class	Midpoint, x	Frequency, f	fx	fx^2
0 - 10	5	8	40	200
10 - 20	15	10	150	2250
20 - 25	22.5	12	270	6075
25 - 30	27.5	10	275	7562.5
	Totals	$\Sigma f = 40$	$\Sigma fx = 735$	$\Sigma fx^2 = 16087.5$

$s = \sqrt{\dfrac{\Sigma fx^2}{\Sigma f} - \left(\dfrac{\Sigma fx}{\Sigma f}\right)^2}$

$= \sqrt{\dfrac{16087.5}{40} - \left(\dfrac{735}{40}\right)^2}$

$= 8.03 \text{ cm}^3$, correct to 3 sig. figs.

Note
The units of standard deviation are the same as the units of the variable.

Using the statistical functions on a calculator

In examinations you are expected to use a calculator with statistical functions to find the mean and standard deviation. This will enable you to analyse data quickly.

If your calculator works in a different way refer to the instruction booklet supplied with the calculator or ask someone for help.

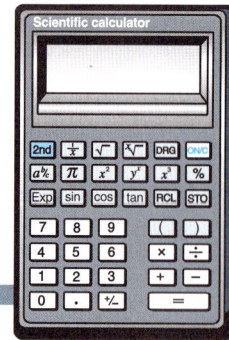

EXAMPLES

1 Calculate the mean and standard deviation of 1, 3, 5, 2.

Set the calculator to SD mode. [MODE] [2]

Clear statistical memory. [SHIFT] [SCL] [=]

Enter data. [1] [DT] [3] [DT] [5] [DT] [2] [DT]

Mean [SHIFT] [$\bar{x}$] [=] (2.75)

Standard deviation [SHIFT] [$x\sigma_n$] [=] (1.47901 …)

Standard deviation = 1.47, to 3 sig. figs.

2 Calculate the mean and standard deviation for this frequency distribution.

x	0 -	10 -	20 -	30 - 40
f	6	8	9	5

Set the calculator to SD mode.

[MODE] [2]

Clear statistical memory.

[SHIFT] [SCL] [=]

Enter data.

[5] [×] [6] [DT] [1] [5] [×] [8]

[DT] [2] [5] [×] [9] [DT] [3] [5]

[×] [5] [DT]

Notice that the frequency is entered after the value of the variable.

Mean [SHIFT] [$\bar{x}$] [=] (19.642 …)

Mean = 19.6, to 3 sig. figs.

Standard deviation [SHIFT] [$x\sigma_n$] [=] (10.170 …)

Standard deviation = 10.2, to 3 sig. figs.

When you have finished, remember to change your calculator out of standard deviation mode by pressing [MODE] [1] (or the appropriate keys on your calculator).

Exercise 30.5

Use a calculator to answer the questions in this exercise.

1 Calculate the mean and standard deviation of the following.
   (a)   3, 5, 6, 2.
   (b)   27, 38, 29, 31, 35.
   (c)   108 cm, 120 cm, 97 cm, 105 cm, 118 cm, 112 cm.
   (d)   1.2 kg, 3.2 kg, 3.9 kg, 1.7 kg.

2 Calculate the mean and standard deviation for each of these sets of data.

(a)

Mark	0	1	2	3	4
Frequency	1	2	6	2	1

(b)

Boot size	5	6	7	8	9
Number of pairs sold	2	4	7	6	1

(c)

Dress size	10	12	14	16	18
Number of dresses	9	13	17	8	3

3 Calculate estimates of the mean and standard deviation for the following data.

Mass (kg)	0 -	10 -	20 -	30 - 40
Number of children	2	3	5	3

4 The students in two classes had a spelling test.
Use the mean and standard deviation to compare the marks scored.

```
Class A   4   6   5   5   4   5   4   4   8   7
          4   5   7   5   8   7   4   8   4   5
          5   6   5   8   8   8   5   4   5   7

Class B   6   7   7   8   7   7   7   5   7   6
          7   7   7   9   7   7   7   8   7   7
          7   8   7   9   7
```

5 A round of golf is made up of 18 holes.
The fewer the number of shots taken,
the better the score.
The score cards of two golfers are shown.

Chris		
4	5	4
4	5	3
7	5	8
6	4	5
4	8	5
5	7	4

Robert		
3	4	5
3	4	2
4	3	5
3	3	4
4	4	3
4	3	4

Use the mean and standard deviation to compare the performance of the two golfers.

6 The times, in seconds, taken by some boys and some girls to swim one length of a pool are shown.

Boys:	28.3	25.6	29.4	26.5	32.7	27.3	26.2	24.8
Girls:	33.3	29.7	32.5	29.4	30.6	33.2		

Use the mean and standard deviation to compare the swimming times of the boys and girls.

7 Use the mean and standard deviation to compare the sizes of stones on Beach A and Beach B.

Diameter of stone (cm)		0 -	1 -	2 -	3 -	4 - 5
Frequency:	Beach A	2	7	42	44	5
	Beach B	26	25	21	18	10

8 Which of the following results show more consistency?
Give a reason for your answer.

Chemistry mark	$0 \leqslant x < 20$	$20 \leqslant x < 30$	$30 \leqslant x < 40$	$40 \leqslant x < 50$	$50 \leqslant x < 60$	60 or more
Number of students	5	6	3	5	4	0

Physics mark	$0 \leqslant x < 10$	$10 \leqslant x < 20$	$20 \leqslant x < 30$	$30 \leqslant x < 40$	$40 \leqslant x < 50$	$50 \leqslant x < 60$	60 or more
Number of students	2	11	5	3	0	1	0

Adding extra items to a set of data

EXAMPLE

The mean and standard deviation of the masses of a group of students are 52.3 kg and 4.7 kg respectively. Another student, of mass 54.2 kg joins the group. Without calculation, describe the effects on the mean and the standard deviation of the masses of the group.

Mean: The student's mass is greater than the old mean so the mean will **increase**.

Standard deviation: The difference between the new student's mass and the old mean is only 1.9 kg. This difference is less than the old standard deviation (4.7 kg) so the standard deviation will **decrease**.

Transforming a whole set of data

Mr Jones recorded a score for each candidate he interviewed. The mean score was 37 and the standard deviation was 5. Later it was found that he had been too harsh in assessing candidates.
One colleague suggested adding 20 to each of the recorded scores.
Another colleague suggested multiplying each score by 2.
Find the new mean and standard deviation when each of these suggestions is carried out separately.

The results would be as follows.

Can you explain why?

	New mean	New standard deviation
Adding 20	57	5
Multiplying by 2	74	10

474

The effects of transforming a whole set of data can be summarised in a table.

Old mean	Old standard deviation	Transformation applied to each item of data	New mean	New standard deviation
$\bar{x}$	s	Add a	$\bar{x} + a$	s
$\bar{x}$	s	Subtract a	$\bar{x} - a$	s
$\bar{x}$	s	Multiply by a	$a\bar{x}$	as
$\bar{x}$	s	Divide by a	$\dfrac{\bar{x}}{a}$	$\dfrac{s}{a}$

Exercise 30.6

1 The lengths of 8 worms have mean 12.5 cm and standard deviation 3.4 cm.
   (a) Another worm, of length 11.2 cm is added to the group.
       Without calculation describe the effect on the mean and standard deviation.
   (b) It was later discovered that the length of the extra worm was actually 21.2 cm.
       Without calculation describe the effect on the mean and standard deviation.

2 Describe the effect on the mean and standard deviation (s.d.) for each of the following.

	Original mean	Original s.d.	Extra item(s)	
(a)	28.4 kg	3.2 kg	19.3 kg	
(b)	1.75 m	0.12 m	1.76 m,	1.78 m
(c)	1.5 km	0.2 km	1.4 km,	1.5 km
(d)	0.76 g	0.04 g	0.82 g,	0.70 g
(e)	278 cm³	32 cm³	245 cm³,	285 cm³

3 (a) Calculate the mean and standard deviation of these numbers.
       2,   4,   6,   8,   10

   (b) Without further calculation, use your answer to part (a) to write down the mean and
       standard deviation of these sets of numbers.
       (i)   3,   5,   7,   9,   11.   (ii)   1,   3,   5,   7,   9.
       (iii) 4,   8,   12, 16, 20.   (iv)   1,   2,   3,   4,   5.

4 A general knowledge test is marked out of 50.
The results for a group of people are shown.

30   25   38   45   36   40   27   43   39
   (a) Calculate the mean and standard deviation of these results.
   (b) The results are reported as percentages.
       Find the mean and standard deviation of the percentages.

5 The times, in seconds, recorded for the runners in a race are shown.
   13.9   15.6   14.8   13.2   15.3   14.5   15.1   14.7

   (a) Calculate the mean and standard deviation of these times.
   (b) The times recorded were all 2 seconds slower than the actual times. Find the mean and
       standard deviation of the actual times.

6 (a) Find the mean and standard deviation of the data given in the table.

Width (metres)	Number of roads
$0 \leqslant w < 5$	23
$5 \leqslant w < 10$	34
$10 \leqslant w < 20$	45
$20 \leqslant w < 30$	14

Later three more roads, of widths 11.4 m, 12.7 m and 4.7 m were added to the list.
  (b) (i) State whether the mean would be decreased, increased or remain the same.
      (ii) State whether the standard deviation would be decreased, increased or remain the same.
  (c) Give reasons for your answers to part (b).

7 A history test is marked out of 80. The results of the test have a mean of 48 and a standard deviation of 8.
  (a) Find the new mean and standard deviation if 20 marks are added to each score.
  (b) Find the new mean and standard deviation if each score is multiplied by 1.25.
  (c) The teacher gives the results of the test as percentages.
      What are the mean and standard deviation of the percentages?

8 The marks in a geography test have mean 12.4 and standard deviation 3.8.
The marks are scaled by first adding 2 to each mark and then multiplying the results by 4.
Find the new mean and standard deviation.

9 The marks in a science assessment have mean 45 and standard deviation 8.
The marks are scaled by first subtracting 5 from each mark and then multiplying by 1.25.
Find the mean and standard deviation of the final set of marks.

What you need to know

- There are three types of **average**: the **mode**, the **median** and the **mean**.

  The **mode** is the most common amount.

  The **median** is the middle amount (or the mean of the two middle amounts) when the amounts are arranged in order of size.

  Mean $= \dfrac{\text{Total of all amounts}}{\text{Number of amounts}}$

- The **range** is a measure of **spread**.
  Range = highest amount − lowest amount

- To find the mean of a **frequency distribution** use:
  Mean $= \dfrac{\text{Total of all amounts}}{\text{Number of amounts}} = \dfrac{\Sigma fx}{\Sigma f}$

- To find the mean of a **grouped frequency distribution**, first find the value of the midpoint of each class. Then use:
  Estimated mean $= \dfrac{\text{Total of all amounts}}{\text{Number of amounts}} = \dfrac{\Sigma fx}{\Sigma f}$

- Choosing the best average to use:
    When the most **popular** value is wanted use the **mode**.
    When **half** of the values have to be above the average use the **median**.
    When a **typical** value is wanted use either the **mode** or the **median**.
    When all the **actual** values have to be taken into account use the **mean**.
    When the average should not be distorted by a few very small or very large values do **not** use the mean.

- The information given in a frequency table can be used to make a **cumulative frequency table**.

- To draw a **cumulative frequency graph**:

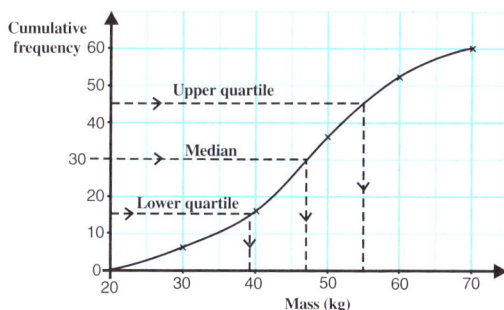

1. Draw and label: the variable on the horizontal axis,
   cumulative frequency on the vertical axis.
2. Plot the cumulative frequency against the upper class boundary of each class.
3. Join the points with a smooth curve.

- If the question does not give the upper class boundaries, then the upper class boundary of each class is equal to the lower class boundary of the next class.

- When the classes have gaps between them then the upper class boundary is halfway between the end of one class and the beginning of the next.

- The **median** is the value of the middle number.
  The **lower quartile** is the value located at $\frac{1}{4}$ of the total frequency.
  The **upper quartile** is the value located at $\frac{3}{4}$ of the total frequency.
  The **interquartile range** measures the spread of the middle 50% of the data.
  Interquartile range $=$ Upper Quartile $-$ Lower Quartile

- **Standard deviation** is a measure of **spread**. It can be calculated by using a formula or by using the statistical functions on a calculator.
  The standard deviation of a set of numbers with a mean of $\overline{x}$ is given by:

$$s = \sqrt{\frac{\Sigma(x - \overline{x})^2}{n}} \quad \text{or} \quad s = \sqrt{\frac{\Sigma x^2}{n} - \left\{\frac{\Sigma x}{n}\right\}^2}$$

- Adding an extra item to a set of data:
  increases the mean if it is larger than the mean of the original data,
  decreases the mean if it is smaller than the mean of the original data,
  increases the standard deviation if its difference from the mean of the original data is greater than the standard deviation,
  decreases the standard deviation if its difference from the mean of the original data is less than the standard deviation.

- The effects of transforming a whole set of data can be summarised in a table.

Old mean	Old standard deviation	Transformation applied to each item of data	New mean	New standard deviation
$\overline{x}$	s	Add a	$\overline{x} + a$	s
$\overline{x}$	s	Subtract a	$\overline{x} - a$	s
$\overline{x}$	s	Multiply by a	$a\overline{x}$	as
$\overline{x}$	s	Divide by a	$\dfrac{\overline{x}}{a}$	$\dfrac{s}{a}$

1 (a) Pauline measures the length of some English cucumbers.
The lengths in centimetres are:
27, 28, 29, 30, 31, 31, 32, 33, 35, 37, 39.

    (i) What is the range of the lengths of these cucumbers?
    (ii) What is the mean length of these cucumbers?

(b) Pauline measures the lengths of some Spanish cucumbers. The range of the lengths of these cucumbers is 6 cm and the mean is 30 cm.
Comment on the differences in these two varieties of cucumber.

SEG 1998

2 The weekly wages of employees are recorded.

Wage (£)	100 -	200 -	300 -	400 -	500 -	600 - 1000
Frequency	2	13	4	0	2	12

(a) Which is the modal group?
(b) In which group is the median value?
(c) Without calculating, state which of the mean, mode or median is the largest.
Explain your answer.

SEG 1997

3 In an experiment 50 people were asked to estimate the length of a rod to the nearest centimetre.
The results were recorded.

Length (cm)	20	21	22	23	24	25	26	27	28	29
Frequency	0	4	6	7	9	10	7	5	2	0

(a) Find the value of the median.
(b) Calculate the mean length.
(c) In a second experiment another 50 people were asked to estimate the length of the same rod.
The most common estimate was 23 cm.
The range of the estimates was 13 cm.
Make **two** comparisons between the results of the two experiments.

SEG 1995

4 David is playing cricket.
The table shows the number of runs he has scored off each ball so far.

Number of runs	0	1	2	3	4	5	6
Number of balls	3	8	4	3	5	0	2

(a) (i) What is the median number of runs per ball?
    (ii) Calculate the mean number of runs per ball.

Off the next five balls, David scores the following runs:
4, 4, 5, 3 and 6.
(b) (i) Calculate the new median.
    (ii) Calculate the new mean.

(c) Give a reason why the mean is used, rather than the median, to give the average number of runs scored per ball.

SEG 1998

5 This cumulative frequency diagram shows information about the distances travelled to work each day by a group of adults.

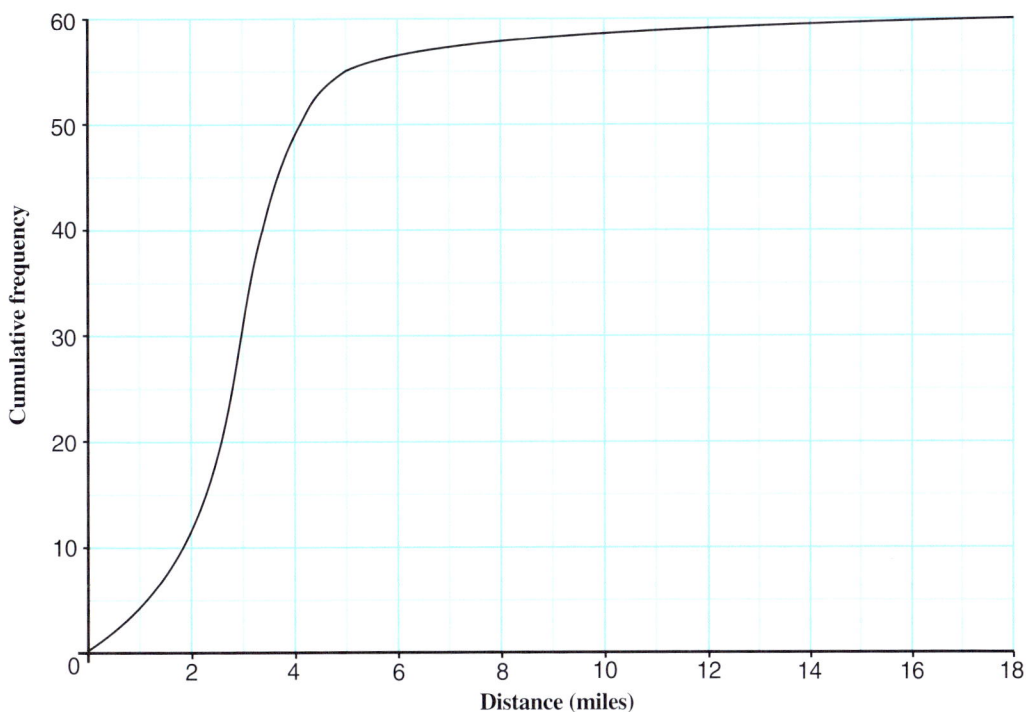

(a) What is the median distance travelled?
(b) Find the interquartile range.
    Explain how you obtain your answer.
(c) Give a reason why the interquartile range is a better measure of spread than the range for this data.

SEG 2000 S

6 A sample of 40 trout is taken at a fish farm.

Mass (g)	40 -	50 -	60 -	70 -	80 -	90 - 100
Frequency	2	3	8	9	13	5

(a) Copy and complete the cumulative frequency table.

Mass (g)	< 50	< 60	< 70	< 80	< 90	< 100
Cumulative frequency						

(b) Draw the cumulative frequency graph.
(c) Find the median mass of the trout.
(d) Find the interquartile range of the mass of the trout.
(e) A second sample of trout has a median mass of 75 g, an upper quartile of 93 g and a lower quartile of 55 g.
    Compare and comment on the spread of the data in these two samples.

SEG 1997

7 A researcher has timed how long it took each of 140 children to complete a puzzle.

(a) Copy and complete the table below and use it to draw a cumulative frequency curve.

Time (in minutes)	Frequency	Cumulative frequency
0 and less than 9.5	12	
9.5 and less than 19.5	25	
19.5 and less than 29.5	42	
29.5 and less than 39.5	35	
39.5 and less than 49.5	18	
49.5 and less than 59.5	8	

(b) Use your graph to find the median time taken by the children.
(c) Use your graph to calculate the interquartile range of the times of the children.
(d) The interquartile range of the times for a second group of children was 13 minutes. What can you conclude from this about the times of the two groups of children?

SEG 1995

8 Two types of leaves were collected and their lengths measured.
The results are shown by the cumulative frequency curves.

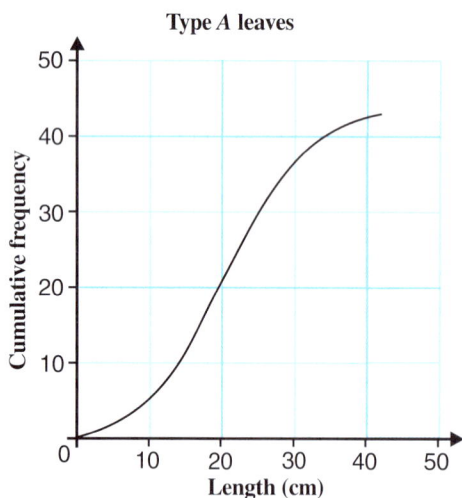

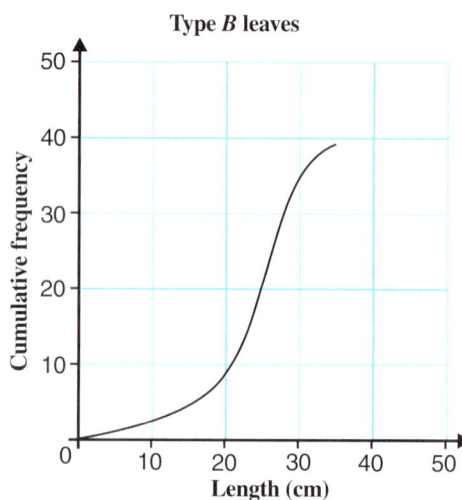

(a) How many type *A* leaves were collected?
(b) (i) Find the interquartile range for the type *B* leaves.
   (ii) The interquartile range for the type *A* leaves was 12 cm.
      What does this show about the length of the type *A* leaves compared with the type *B* leaves?
(c) How many type *A* leaves were longer than the longest type *B* leaf?

SEG 1995

9 The times for 160 adults to complete an exercise schedule are shown on the frequency diagram.

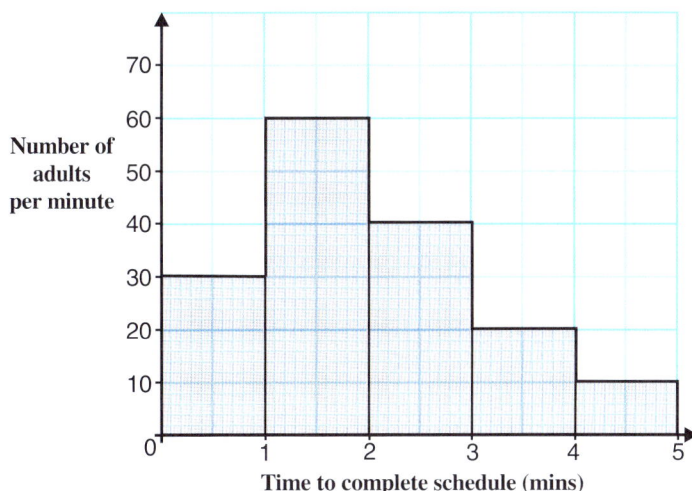

(a) Construct a cumulative frequency table for the data.

(b) Draw the cumulative frequency curve.

(c) Use your graph to estimate the time it would take 40% of the adults to complete the exercises.

(d) Use your graph to find the number of adults who took more than 3.5 minutes to complete the exercises.

Time in minutes	Cumulative frequency
⩽ 1	
⩽ 2	
⩽ 3	
⩽ 4	
⩽ 5	

SEG 1995

10 A company records the number of enquiries about its products.
The monthly numbers for 1994 and 1995 are given.

	Jan	Feb	Mar	Apr	May	Jun	Jul	Aug	Sep	Oct	Nov	Dec
1994	10	1	6	22	5	3	3	1	4	8	10	16
1995	10	10	30	2	2	3	5	2	1	1	10	17

The mean and standard deviation for 1994 are given.
Copy the table.
Complete the entries for 1995.
Comment on these results.

	mean	standard deviation
1994	7.42	6.06
1995	......	......

SEG 1997

11 A set of examination scores has a mean of 27.2 marks and standard deviation of 7.82 marks.

(a) If 5 marks are added to each score, what are the mean and the standard deviation?

(b) If all the original examination scores are doubled, what are the mean and the standard deviation?

SEG 1996

12 The maximum daily temperatures in degrees Centigrade (°C) at Sandy Bay during the first two weeks in July are shown.

19   19   19   20   20   20   20   21   21   21   21   23   24   26

The mean maximum daily temperature is 21 °C.
(a) Calculate the standard deviation of the maximum daily temperatures at Sandy Bay.

The maximum daily temperatures during the first two weeks in July at Longsands have a mean of 21.6°C and a standard deviation of 3.02 °C.
(b) Comment on the difference between the maximum daily temperatures at Sandy Bay and Longsands during the first two weeks in July.

The maximum daily temperatures during the first two weeks in May at Longsands were 5 °C lower than those in July.
(c) Write down the mean and standard deviation of the maximum daily temperatures at Longsands during the first two weeks in May.

SEG 1998

13 There are twenty pupils in class *A* and twenty pupils in class *B*.
All the pupils in class *A* were given an I.Q. test.
Their scores on the test are given below.

100,   104,   106,   107,   109,   110,   113,   114,   116,   117,
118,   119,   119,   121,   124,   125,   127,   127,   130,   134.

(a) The mean of their scores is 117.
Calculate the standard deviation.

(b) Class *B* take the same I.Q. test.
They obtain a mean of 110 and standard deviation of 21.
Compare the data for class *A* and class *B*.

(c) Class *C* has only 5 pupils.
When they take the I.Q. test they all score 105.
What is the value of the standard deviation for class *C*?

SEG 1995

14 Sixty four adults had their pulse taken at the start of an exercise session. The results are given in the table.

Pulse (beats per minute)	Mid-point	Frequency
50 - 54	52	1
55 - 59	57	4
60 - 64	62	12
65 - 69	67	14
70 - 74	72	16
75 - 79	77	12
80 - 84	82	5

(a) Calculate an estimate of the mean and the standard deviation.
(b) After two minutes of exercise, the sixty four adults had their pulse taken again.
Describe the effect on the values of the mean and standard deviation if
(i)   each pulse had increased by exactly 10 beats per minute;
(ii) each pulse was exactly 1.2 times its original value.

SEG 1996

CHAPTER 31

Probability

Probability

How likely or unlikely it is that an event will occur can be calculated or estimated using the idea of **probability**.

Probabilities have numerical values between 0 and 1.
A **probability of 0** means that an event is **impossible**.
A **probability of 1** means that an event is **certain**.
Probabilities are written either as a fraction, a decimal or a percentage.

Probability words
In any situation involving uncertainty there are a number of possibilities or **outcomes** that may occur. Outcomes which are of particular interest are called **events**.

Calculating probabilities using equally likely outcomes

Probabilities can be **calculated** in situations where each outcome is **equally likely** to occur.

In such situations, the probability of an event, X, occurring is given by:

$$P(X) = \frac{\text{Number of possible outcomes in the event}}{\text{Total number of possible outcomes}}$$

In this book P(X) stands for the probability of X.

Probability words
In many probability situations things are taken or picked at **random**.
For example:
A boy is picked at random from a group.
This means that any boy in the group is equally likely to be picked.

EXAMPLES

1 A card is taken at random from a full pack of playing cards with no jokers. What is the probability that the card:
(a) is a red King,
(b) has an odd number on it?

A card is taken at **random** from the pack so there are 52 possible **equally likely** outcomes.

(a) There are 2 red kings in the pack so there are 2 possible outcomes in the event 'taking a red King'.
P(red King) $= \frac{2}{52} = \frac{1}{26}$

(b) There are 20 cards with odd numbers in a pack so there are 20 possible outcomes in the event 'taking a card with an odd number on it'.

P(odd) $= \frac{20}{52} = \frac{5}{13}$

2 This table shows how 100 counters are coloured red or blue and numbered 1 or 2.

	Red	Blue
1	23	19
2	32	26

One counter is taken from the bag at random. Calculate the probability:
(a) that the counter is red and numbered 1,
(b) that the counter is red or numbered 1.

There are 100 possible **equally likely** outcomes.

(a) 23 of these possible outcomes are in the event 'taking a counter that is red and numbered 1'.

P(red and numbered 1) $= \frac{23}{100}$

(b) 74 (23 + 32 + 19) of these possible outcomes are in the event 'taking a counter that is red or numbered 1'.
P(red or numbered 1) $= \frac{74}{100} = \frac{37}{50}$

1 A bag contains 4 red counters, 3 white counters and 3 blue counters.
A counter is taken from the bag at random.
What is the probability that the counter is:
(a)   red,
(b)   not red,
(c)   white or blue,
(d)   red, white or blue,
(e)   green?

2 500 tickets are sold in a raffle.
Elaine buys one ticket.
(a)   What is the probability that Elaine wins first prize?

Sam says that the probability that a girl wins first prize is 50%.
(b)   Explain why Sam might be wrong.

3 There are 6 red counters and 4 green counters in a box.
Counters are taken from the box at random and are not put back.
(a)   What is the probability that the first counter taken out is red?
(b)   If the first counter taken out is red, what is the probability that the second counter taken out is red?
(c)   If the first counter taken out is green, what is the probability that the second counter taken out is red?

4 In a hat there are twelve discs numbered from 43 to 54.
Nina takes a disc from the hat at random.
What is the probability that Nina takes a disc:
(a)   with at least one 4 on it,
(b)   that has not got a 4 on it,
(c)   that has a 3 or a 4 on it?

5 This table shows the way that fifty red and blue counters are numbered either 1 or 2.

	Red	Blue
1	12	8
2	8	22

One of the counters is chosen at random.
What is the probability that the counter is:
(a)   a 1,   (b)   blue,   (c)   blue and a 1?

A blue counter is chosen at random.
(d)   What is the probability that it is a 1?

A counter numbered 1 is chosen at random.
(e)   What is the probability that it is blue?

6 The table shows the way that 120 pupils from Year 7 travel to Linfield School.

	Boys	Girls
Walk	23	17
Bus	15	20
Car	12	8
Bike	20	5

A pupil from Year 7 is chosen at random.
What is the probability that the pupil:
(a)   walks to school,
(b)   is a girl who travels by car,
(c)   is a boy who does not travel by bus?

A girl from Year 7 is chosen at random.
What is the probability that:
(d)   she walks to school,
(e)   she does not travel by car?

A Year 7 pupil who travels by bike is chosen at random.
(f)   What is the probability that the pupil is a boy?

7 The table shows the number of boys and girls in a class of 30 pupils who wear glasses.

	Boy	Girl
Wears Glasses	3	1
Does not wear glasses	11	15

A pupil from the class is picked at random.
(a)   What is the probability that it is a boy?
(b)   What is the probability that it is a girl who does not wear glasses?
A girl from the class is picked at random.
(c)   What is the probability that she wears glasses?
A pupil who wears glasses is picked at random.
(d)   What is the probability that it is a boy?

8 Tim plays a friend at Noughts and Crosses.
He says: 'I can either win, draw or lose, so the probability that I will win must be $\frac{1}{3}$.'
Explain why Tim is wrong.

In question 8 in Exercise 31.1, probabilities **cannot** be calculated using equally likely outcomes.
In such situations probabilities can be estimated using the idea of **relative frequency**.

The relative frequency of an event, X, occurring is given by:

$$R(X) = \frac{\text{Number of times the event occurs in an experiment (or is observed)}}{\text{Total number of trials in the experiment (or total number of observations)}}$$

It is not always necessary to perform an experiment or make observations.
Sometimes the information required can be found in past records.

> In this book R(X) stands for the relative frequency of X.

EXAMPLES

1 In an experiment a drawing pin is dropped for 100 trials. The drawing pin lands point side up 37 times. What is the relative frequency of the drawing pin landing point side up?

$R(\text{lands point side up}) = \frac{37}{100}$
$= 0.37$

2 50 cars are observed passing the school gate. 14 red cars are observed. What is the relative frequency of a red car passing the school gate?

$R(\text{a red car passes}) = \frac{14}{50}$
$= 28\%$

> **Probability words**
> Probability experiments are made up of a lot of repeated parts called **trials**.
> For example, in Example 1 each trial is carried out by dropping the drawing pin once.
>
> **Relative frequency** is the frequency of an event occurring related to the total number of trials (or observations).

3 Rainfall records show that in April it rained in Newcastle on 24 days in 1998.
Estimate the probability of rain in Newcastle on a day in April.

The number of times the event is observed is 24.
There are 30 days in April.
So the total number of observations = 30.
$R(\text{rain on a day in April}) = \frac{24}{30} = 0.8$
An estimate of the probability of rain in Newcastle on a day in April is 0.8.

4 Jamie does the following experiment with a bag containing 2 red and 8 blue counters.

> Take a counter from the bag at random. Record the colour then put the counter back in the bag.
> Repeat this for 100 trials.

Jamie calculates the relative frequency of getting a red counter every 10 trials and shows his results on a graph.
Draw a graph showing the results that Jamie might get.

This is the sort of graph that Jamie might get.

> $P(\text{Red}) = \frac{2}{10} = 0.2$
> This is shown on the graph by the dotted line.

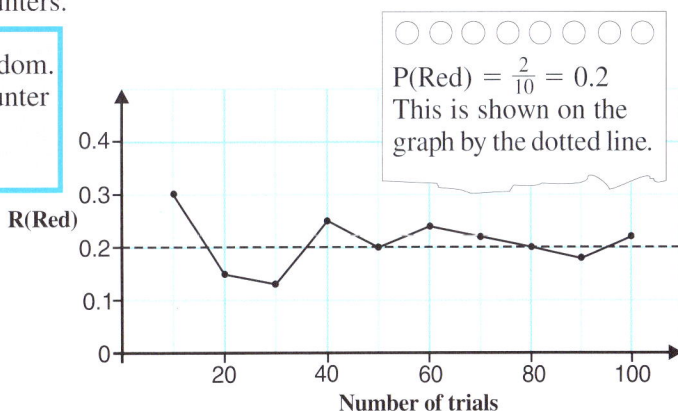

Jamie's graph illustrates: As the number of trials increases R(Red) gets closer to P(Red). Relative frequency gives a better estimate of probability the larger the number of trials.

Try Jamie's experiment yourself and see what sort of results you get.

5 Three faces of a dice are red, two faces are green and one face is blue.
Sadiq and Helen do an experiment with the dice to test how fair it is when it is rolled.
Their results are shown in the table.
Sadiq says "My results show that the dice is fair".

(a) Explain why Sadiq might be wrong.

(b) Is the dice fair? Explain your answer.

Student	Number of trials	R(Red)	R(Green)	R(Blue)
Sadiq	20	0.5	0.3	0.2
Helen	300	0.46	0.29	0.25

Using equally likely outcomes:
P(Red) = 0.5, P(Green) = 0.33 and P(Blue) = 0.17
to an accuracy of two decimal places.
The dice is **fair** if the relative frequencies are close
to the probabilities after a large number of trials.

(a) Sadiq might be wrong because he uses too few trials in his experiment.

(b) Although Sadiq's results suggest that the dice might be fair, Helen's results are more reliable because of the larger number of trials.
Her results suggest that it is more likely that the dice is **unfair**.

Probability words
Situations where all the possible outcomes are equally likely are said to be **fair**.
Another word for this is **unbiased**.
When all the possible outcomes are not equally likely the situation is said to be **unfair** or **biased**.

Exercise 31.2

1 A gardener plants 40 daffodil bulbs of which 36 grow into daffodil plants.
What is the relative frequency that a bulb grows into a plant?

2 A bag of counters contains red (R), green (G), white (W) and blue (B) counters.
In an experiment James takes a counter from the bag at random and then replaces it.
He repeats this trial 30 times and gets these results.

W R R W G R B G W R B W W G G
R R W B G B B W G R R W B R W

(a) Calculate the relative frequency of James taking a white counter from the bag.
James continues the experiment for **another** 270 trials. He gets **another** 111 white counters.

(b) Estimate the probability of James taking a white counter from the bag.

3 Gemma keeps the results of her chess games with Helen.
Out of the first 10 games, Gemma wins 6. Out of the first 30 games Gemma wins 21.
Estimate the probability that Gemma will win her next game of chess with Helen.

4 The results of games of chess played by four children at a chess club is shown in this table.

(a) Calculate the relative frequency of a win for each player.

(b) Which of these relative frequencies is most likely to give the best estimate of the probability that the child will win their next game? Explain your answer.

(c) If Tom plays Pam, who do you think is the most likely to win? Explain your answer.

Player	Games won	Games drawn	Games lost
Tom	4	2	6
Sam	8	1	7
Kim	3	0	1
Pam	9	2	9

5 Sally stood at her school gate and recorded the colour of 50 passing cars.

This table shows her results.

Colour	Frequency
Red	14
White	19
Blue	6
Green	5
Other	6

What is the relative frequency of a white car passing?
How likely is this to be a good estimate of the probability of a white car passing?
Explain your answer.

6 A counter is taken from a bag at random.
Its colour is recorded and the counter is then put back in the bag.
This is repeated 300 times.
The number of red counters taken from the bag after every 100 trials is shown in the table.

Number of trials	Number of red counters
100	52
200	102
300	141

(a) Calculate the relative frequency after each 100 trials.
(b) Estimate the probability of taking a red counter from the bag.

7 Five students do an experiment to test the fairness of this spinner.

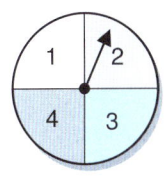

This table shows the data the students collect.

Student	Number of trials	Faces landed on 1	2	3	4
Peter	20	6	5	4	5
Sam	60	22	21	8	9
Daron	250	90	85	35	40
Tracy	40	15	15	6	4
Peter	150	48	54	22	26

(a) Peter looks at his data and decides that the spinner is likely to be fair.
Why could he be wrong?
(b) Which student's data gives the best test of fairness of the spinner?
Explain your answer.
(c) Use the data from **all** the experiments to estimate the probability of the spinner landing on each number.

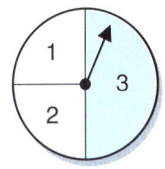

8 The diagram shows a spinner which is spun a number of times.
The graph shows the relative frequency of the spinner landing on the number 1 plotted against the number of times the spinner is spun.

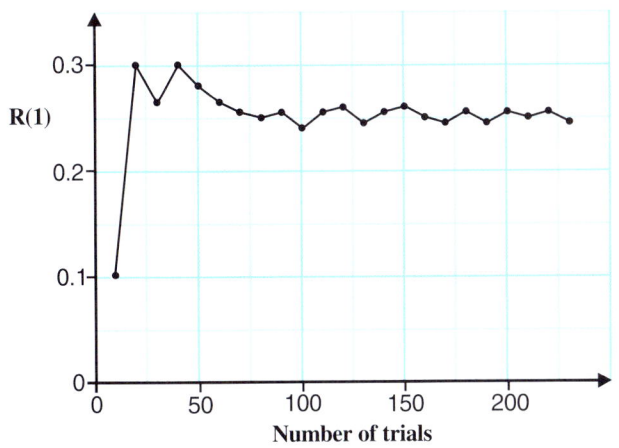

(a) The spinner is a fair spinner.
How can you tell from the graph?

(b) How might the relative frequency of the spinner landing on the number 3 change with the number of trials?
Show your answer on a graph with relative frequency plotted after every 20 trials.

1 Estimate the number of Heads you would get if you tossed a fair coin 1000 times?

For a large number of trials R(Head) is a good estimate of P(Head).
So … after a large number of trials R(Head) = 0.5.

$$R(Head) = \frac{Number\ of\ Heads}{Total\ number\ of\ trials} \quad so \quad 0.5 = \frac{Number\ of\ Heads}{1000}$$

So, estimate of number of Heads = $1000 \times 0.5 = 500$.

2 A counter was taken at random from a bag of counters and then replaced.
This was repeated 1000 times.
The relative frequency of getting a red counter was found to be 0.147.
There are 20 counters in the bag. Estimate the number of red counters.

Because of the large number of trials it can be assumed that a good estimate of P(red) is 0.147.

$$0.147 = \frac{Number\ of\ red\ counters}{20} \quad \text{which gives an estimate of } 0.147 \times 20 \text{ red counters} = 2.94$$

There must be a whole number of red counters, so the most likely number in the bag is 3.

Exercise 31.3

1 The relative frequency of a switch being faulty is 0.02. James buys 300 switches.
Estimate the number of faulty switches that he buys.
Explain why this is only an approximation.

2 Tony rolled a dice a large number of times and got 150 ones.
How many times do you think he rolled the dice?

3 The manager of a restaurant analyses all the meals ordered from the lunchtime menu.
He works out that the relative frequency of a customer ordering soup as a starter is 0.63.
800 customers order from the lunchtime menu each month.
Estimate how many of them are likely to order soup.

4 A ball is taken at random from a bag containing 50 coloured balls. Its colour is noted and the ball is put back in the bag.
In an experiment, this trial was carried out 300 times. The colours obtained were:
Red 77, Blue 91 and White 132.
Estimate the number of each coloured ball in the bag.

5 Here are some instructions for an experiment.

> Take a bead at random from a bag containing 500 beads.
> Record the colour of the bead and then put it back in the bag.
> Repeat this a number of times.

Two sets of results from the experiment are shown in the table.

Result set	Number of beads taken	Number of red beads taken	Relative frequency of picking a red bead	Estimated number of red beads in the bag
A	35	8		
B	300	78		

(a) Copy and complete the table.
(b) Which set of results should give the more accurate estimate of the number of red beads in the bag?
Explain your answer.

SEG 1998

Mutually exclusive events

When a coin is tossed the event 'heads' cannot occur at the same time as the event 'tails'.
When a person is picked at random the event 'girl' cannot occur at the same time as the event 'boy'.
When a card is taken at random from a pack of cards the event 'the Ace of Hearts' cannot occur at the same time as the event 'a black card'.

Events which **cannot occur at the same time** are called **mutually exclusive events**.

*Why are the events pick a red card from a pack of cards and pick the Ace of Hearts from the same pack of cards **not** mutually exclusive?*

> When a dice is rolled you must either get a six (6) or not get a six (not 6).
> This pair of events are **mutually exclusive**.
> The event rolling a dice and either getting a six **or** not getting a six is **certain** to occur.
>
> So …   P(6 or not 6) = 1
>
> Now …   P(6) = $\frac{1}{6}$ and P(not 6) = $\frac{5}{6}$ so …   P(6) + P(not 6) = 1
>
> So …   P(6 or not 6) = P(6) + P(not 6)

This example illustrates the following rules.

When A and B are mutually exclusive events:
    P(A or B) = P(A) + P(B)

Because the events A and not A are certain to occur and must be mutually exclusive:
    P(not A) = 1 − P(A)

EXAMPLE

The spinner has a ring of numbers inside a ring of colours.
These tables show some of the probabilities of the arrow stopping
on each colour and number when the spinner is spun.

Red(R)	Yellow(Y)	Blue(B)
0.25	0.5	

1	2	3
0.375	0.5	

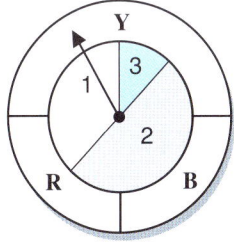

Safia spins the spinner once.
(a) What is the probability of the arrow stopping on blue?
(b) What is the probability of the arrow stopping on blue or 1?

(a) The arrow stopping on R, Y or B is certain to occur.
    P(R) + P(Y) + P(B) = 1
    0.25 + 0.5 + P(B) = 1
    0.75 + P(B) = 1
    P(B) = 1 − 0.75
    P(B) = 0.25

(b) The arrow stopping on B and the arrow stopping on 1 are mutually exclusive.
    P(B or 1) = P(B) + P(1)
    = 0.25 + 0.375
    = 0.625

Show that the probability of the arrow stopping on red or blue or 3 is 0.625.
*Can you explain why P(B or 2) = 0.5 and **not** P(B) + P(2)?*

1 A fish is taken at random from a tank containing only red fish and black fish. The probability that the fish is black is $\frac{2}{5}$. What is the probability that the fish is red?

2 The probability of a switch working is 0.96. What is the probability of a switch not working?

3 Six out of every 100 men are taller than 1.85 m.
A man is picked at random.
What is the probability that he is not taller than 1.85 m?

4 A bag contains red, white and blue balls.
A ball is taken from the bag at random.
The probability of taking a red ball is 0.4.
The probability of taking a white ball is 0.35.
What is the probability of taking a white ball or a blue ball?

5 A spinner can land on red, white or blue.
The probability of the spinner landing on red is 0.2.
The probability of the spinner landing on red or on blue is 0.7.
The spinner is spun once.
What is the probability that the spinner lands:
(a)   on blue,   (b)   on white?

6 The table gives the probabilities of the scorer of the first goal in a mixed hockey match.

A man over 1.8 metres tall   0.2
A woman over 1.6 metres tall 0.4
A man over 25 years old   0.5
A woman over 25 years old   0.3
A man who wears glasses   0.2
A woman who wears glasses   0.1

The first goal is scored by:
Event A
either a man who wears glasses **or** a woman over 25.

Event B
either a woman over 1.6 metres tall **or** a woman over 25.

Event C
a person who wears glasses.

Where possible, use the table to calculate the probability of each of events A, B and C.
If it is not possible explain why.

7 A bag contains red, green, blue, yellow and white counters.
The table shows the probabilities of obtaining each colour when a counter is taken from the bag at random.

Red	Green	Blue	Yellow	White
30%	25%	20%	20%	10%

(a)   (i)   How can you tell that there is a mistake in the table?
      (ii)   The probability of getting a white counter is wrong. What should it be?

A counter is taken from the bag at random.
(b)   (i)   What is the probability that it is either green or blue?
      (ii)   What is the probability that it is either red, green or blue?
      (iii)   What is the probability that it is not yellow?

8 Some red, white and blue cubes are numbered 1 and 2.
The table shows the probabilities of obtaining each colour and number when a cube is taken at random.

	Red	White	Blue
1	0.1	0.3	0
2	0.3	0.1	0.2

A cube is taken at random.
(a)   What is the probability of taking a red cube?
(b)   What is the probability of taking a cube numbered 2?
(c)   State whether or not the following pairs of events are mutually exclusive.
      Give a reason for each answer.
      (i)   Taking a cube numbered 1 and taking a blue cube.
      (ii)   Taking a cube numbered 2 and taking a blue cube.
(d)   (i)   What is the probability of taking either a blue cube or a cube numbered 1 (or both)?
      (ii)   What is the probability of taking either a blue cube or a cube numbered 2 (or both)?

EXAMPLES

1 A fair coin is thrown twice.
Identify all of the possible outcomes and write down their probabilities.

Method 2
Use a **possibility space diagram**.

	H & T	T & T
	H & H	T & H

2nd throw — T (top), H (bottom)
1st throw — H, T

Method 1
List the outcomes systematically.

1st throw	2nd throw
Head (H)	Head (H)
Head (H)	Tail (T)
Tail (T)	Head (H)
Tail (T)	Tail (T)

Method 3
Use a **tree diagram**.

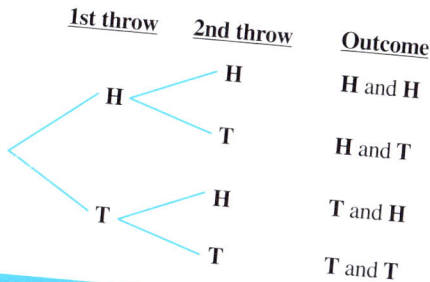

1st throw	2nd throw	Outcome
H	H	H and H
H	T	H and T
T	H	T and H
T	T	T and T

The lines are called the **branches** of the tree diagram.

When a fair coin is tossed twice, there are four possible outcomes.
Because the coin is fair all the possible outcomes are **equally likely**.
Because all the outcomes are equally likely their probabilities can be worked out.

P(H and H) = P(H and T) = P(T and H) = P(T and T) = $\frac{1}{4}$.

2 A fair dice is rolled twice.
Use a possibility space diagram to show all the possible outcomes.
What is the probability of getting a 'double six'?
What is the probability of getting any 'double'?
What is the probability that exactly one 'six' is obtained?

2nd roll

6	1 and 6	2 and 6	3 and 6	4 and 6	5 and 6	6 and 6
5	1 and 5	2 and 5	3 and 5	4 and 5	5 and 5	6 and 5
4	1 and 4	2 and 4	3 and 4	4 and 4	5 and 4	6 and 4
3	1 and 3	2 and 3	3 and 3	4 and 3	5 and 3	6 and 3
2	1 and 2	2 and 2	3 and 2	4 and 2	5 and 2	6 and 2
1	1 and 1	2 and 1	3 and 1	4 and 1	5 and 1	6 and 1
	1	2	3	4	5	6

1st roll

The dice is fair so there are 36 equally likely outcomes.

P(double 6)
There is one outcome in the event (6 and 6).
P(double 6) = $\frac{1}{36}$

P(any double)
The 6 outcomes in the event are shaded blue.
P(any double) = $\frac{6}{36} = \frac{1}{6}$

P(exactly one six)
The 10 outcomes in the event are shaded grey.
P(exactly one six) = $\frac{10}{36} = \frac{5}{18}$

1 Two fair dice are rolled and the numbers obtained are added.
  (a) Draw a possibility space diagram to show all of the possible outcomes.
  (b) Use your diagram to work out:
     (i) the probability of obtaining a total of 10,
     (ii) the probability of obtaining a total greater than 10,
     (iii) the probability of obtaining a total less than 10.
  (c) Explain why the probabilities you worked out in (b) should add up to 1.

2 A fair coin is tossed and a fair dice is rolled.
Copy and complete the table to show all the possible outcomes.

Dice

		1	2	3	4	5	6
	H		H2				
Coin	T						

What is the probability of obtaining:
  (a) a head and a 5,   (b) a tail and an even number,
  (c) a tail and a 6,   (d) a tail and an odd number,
  (e) a head and a number more than 4,   (f) an odd number?

3 Sanjay has to travel to school in two stages.
Stage 1: he can go by bus or train or he can get a lift.
Stage 2: he can go by bus or he can walk.

  (a) List all the different ways that Sanjay can travel to school.

Sanjay decides the way that he travels on each stage at random.
  (b) What is the probability that he goes by bus in both stages?

Sanjay travels to school 200 times in a year.
  (c) On how many days is he likely to travel by bus on at least one of the stages?

4 To help Whitley Rovers choose a new football strip, 800 fans were asked to choose the colour they preferred.
280 fans chose a red strip, 320 chose a white strip and 200 chose a blue strip.

One fan was chosen at random.
  (a) Estimate the probability that he did not choose white.

Two fans were chosen at random.
  (b) Make a list of the 9 possible pairs of colours that the two fans might have chosen.
  (c) Jimmy looked at the list of 9 possible pairs of colours and said:
      'The probability that the two fans both picked a red strip must be $\frac{1}{9}$'.
      Explain why Jimmy was wrong.

5 The diagram shows an unbiased spinner.
It is divided into four equal sections numbered as shown.
The spinner is spun twice and the numbers the arrow lands
on each time are added.
Calculate the probability of getting:
  (a) a total of 2,   (b) a total of 3,   (c) a total of 6.

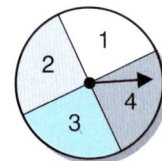

6 Bag A contains 2 red balls and 1 white ball.
Bag B contains 2 white balls and 1 red ball.
A ball is drawn at random from each bag.

(a) Copy and complete the table to show all possible
pairs of colours.

(b) Explain why the probability of each outcome is $\frac{1}{9}$.

(c) Calculate the probability that the two balls are the
same colour.

Bag A

		R	R	W
	W	RW		
Bag B	W			
	R			

Two balls are drawn from another bag.
The probability that they are the same colour is 0.6.

(d) What is the probability that the balls are a different colour?

7 The diagram shows two sets of cards A and B.

One card is taken at random from set A. One card is taken at random from set B.

(a) List all the possible outcomes.

The two numbers are added together.

(b) (i) What is the probability of getting a total of 5?
(ii) What is the probability of getting a total that is not 5?

All the cards are put together and one of them is taken at random.

(c) What is the probability that it is labelled A or 2 (or both)?

8 Students at a college must choose to study two subjects from the list:

Maths   English   Science   Art

(a) Write down all the possible pairs of subjects that the students can choose.

David chooses both subjects at random.

(b) What is the probability that one of the subjects he chooses is Maths?

James chooses Maths and one other subject at random.

(c) What is the probability that he chooses Maths and Science?

9 A spinner has an equal probability of landing on either red, green, blue, yellow or white.
The spinner is spun twice.

(a) List all the possible outcomes.

(b) (i) What is the probability that, on both spins, the spinner lands on white?
(ii) What is the probability that, on both spins, the spinner lands on white at least
once?
(iii) What is the probability that, on both spins, the spinner lands on the same colour?

10 The diagram shows two unbiased spinners.
Each spinner is divided into equal sections
and numbered as shown.
Each spinner is spun and the numbers that
each arrow lands on are added together.

(a) Calculate the probability of getting a
total of 2.

(b) Calculate the probability of getting a
total of 6.

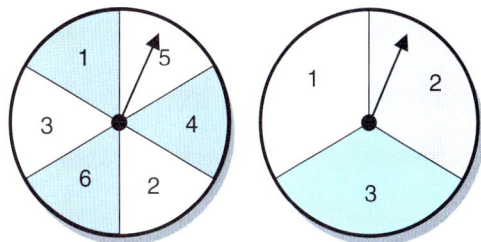

A **tree diagram** can be used to find all the possible outcomes when two or more events are combined. It can also be used to help calculate probabilities when outcomes are not equally likely.

EXAMPLE

1 **Box A** contains 1 red ball (R) and 1 blue ball (B).
Box B contains 3 red balls (R) and 2 blue balls (B).
A ball is taken at random from Box A.
A ball is then taken at random from Box B.

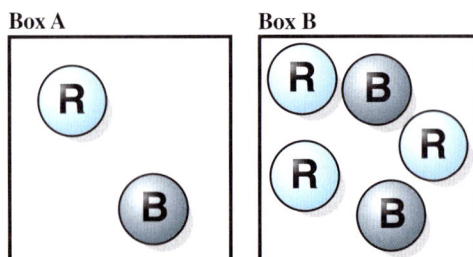

Box A Box B

(a) Draw a tree diagram to show all the possible outcomes.

(b) Calculate the probability that two red balls are taken.

(a)

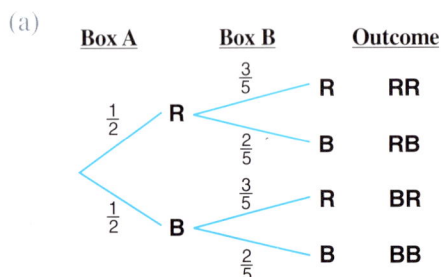

Box A	Box B	Outcome

Remember:
When drawing a tree diagram probabilities must be put on the branches.
Using equally likely outcomes:
In Box A
$P(R) = \frac{1}{2}$ $P(B) = \frac{1}{2}$
In Box B
$P(R) = \frac{3}{5}$ $P(B) = \frac{2}{5}$

(b) The numbers of Red and Blue balls are unequal in Box B.
This means that the outcomes RR, RB, BR and BB are not equally likely.

Method

Multiply the probabilities along the branches of the tree diagram.

$P(RR) = \frac{1}{2} \times \frac{3}{5} = \frac{1 \times 3}{2 \times 5} = \frac{3}{10}$

The probability that two red balls are taken is $\frac{3}{10}$.

Why the method works

On $\frac{3}{5}$ of the occasions that a ball is taken from Box B it will be R.
On $\frac{1}{2}$ of these occasions the ball taken from Box A will also be R.
So on $\frac{1}{2} \times \frac{3}{5}$ occasions the balls taken from Box A and Box B will be RR.

By completing the table solve the above problem using equally likely outcomes.

		Box B				
		R	R	R	B	B
Box A	R					
	B					

EXAMPLE

2 The probability that Amanda is late for school is 0.4.
Use a tree diagram to find the probability that on two days running:
(a) she is late twice, (b) she is late exactly once.

Day 1	Day 2	Probability

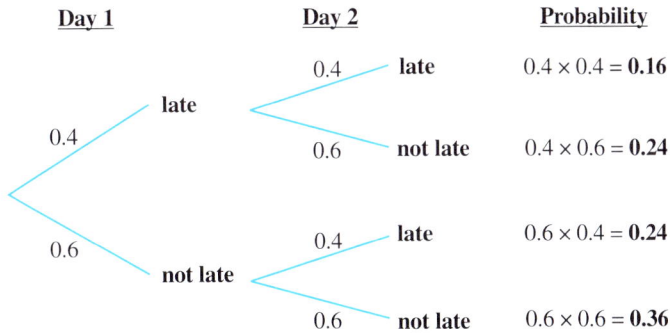

$$0.4 \times 0.4 = \textbf{0.16}$$
$$0.4 \times 0.6 = \textbf{0.24}$$
$$0.6 \times 0.4 = \textbf{0.24}$$
$$0.6 \times 0.6 = \textbf{0.36}$$

(a) The probability that Amanda is late twice.

The outcome included in this event is:
(late **and** late)
P(late twice) = 0.16

(b) The probability that Amanda is late exactly once.

The outcomes included in this event are:
(late **and** not late) **or** (not late **and** late)
These outcomes are mutually exclusive.
P(late exactly once) = 0.24 + 0.24 = 0.48

Exercise 31.6

1 A bag contains 3 red counters and 2 blue counters.
A counter is taken at random from the bag and then replaced.
Another counter is taken at random from the bag.

(a) Copy and complete the tree diagram to show all the possible outcomes. Write the probability of each of the events on the branches of the tree diagram.

(b) (i) Calculate the probability that both counters taken are blue.
(ii) Calculate the probability that at least one counter taken is blue.

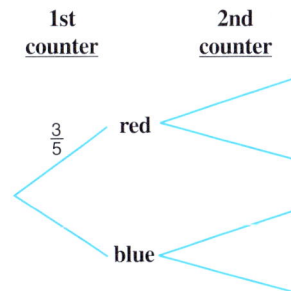

2 A manufacturer makes an electrical circuit which contains two switches. The probability that a switch is faulty is 0.1.

(a) Copy and complete the tree diagram. Write the probability of each of the events on the branches of the tree diagram.

(b) (i) Calculate the probability that both switches are faulty.
(ii) Calculate the probability that exactly one switch is faulty.

The circuit works if both switches are not faulty.
(c) The manufacturer makes 1000 circuits. Estimate the number that work.

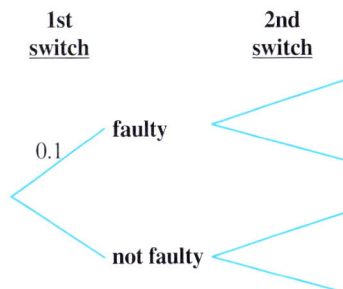

3 Five people in a group of 50 people are left handed.
There are 20 females in the group.
A person is picked at random from the group.

   (a)   (i)   What is the probability that the person is
            left handed?
       (ii)   What is the probability that the person is
             right handed?
     (iii)   What is the probability that the person is female?
     (iv)   What is the probability that the person is male?

   (b)   Copy and complete the tree diagram.
       Write the probability of each of the events on the branches of the tree diagram.

   (c)   (i)   Calculate the probability that the person picked is a left handed female.
       (ii)   Calculate the probability that the person picked is a left handed female or is a
            right handed male.

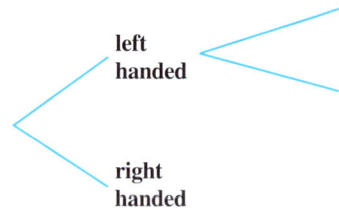

4 Bag A contains 3 blue counters, 5 red counters and 2 white counters.
Bag B contains 2 blue counters and 3 red counters.
Tom takes a ball at random from Bag A.
Sam takes a ball at random from Bag B.

   (a)   Copy and complete the tree diagram to show the
       possible pairs of colours that Tom and Sam can take.
       Write the probability of each of the events on the
       branches.

   (b)   Calculate the probability that Tom takes a blue counter
       from Bag A and Sam takes a red counter from Bag B.

   (c)   Calculate the probability that the counter taken by Tom
       is the same colour as the counter taken by Sam.

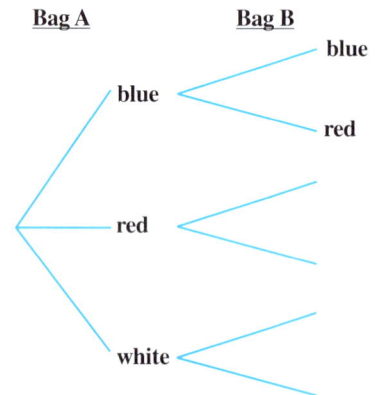

5 Seema and Dario play a game on a network with two fair spinners.
In the game, Seema and Dario each have a counter which they move between A and B on
the network.
They move their counters by taking turns to spin one of the spinners.
If their counter is at A, they spin spinner 1.
If their counter is at B, they spin spinner 2.
After each spin, they move their counter
depending on where the arrow on the
spinner lands.
The player whose counter is at B after a
given number of turns is the winner.

Dario starts at A and Seema starts at B.
Use tree diagrams to find the most likely
winner:

   (a)   in a game in which each player has
       two spins,

   (b)   in a game in which each player has
       three spins.

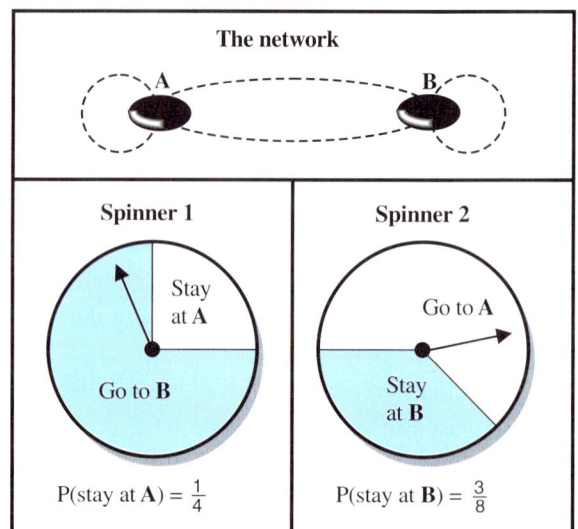

The network

Spinner 1 — Stay at **A** / Go to **B**

Spinner 2 — Go to **A** / Stay at **B**

$P(\text{stay at } \textbf{A}) = \frac{1}{4}$

$P(\text{stay at } \textbf{B}) = \frac{3}{8}$

Independent events

When two coins are tossed, the outcome of the first toss has no affect on the outcome of the second toss.
One person being left handed does not influence another person being left handed.
These are examples of events which can happen together but which do not affect each other.
Events like this are called **independent** events.
All of the examples in Exercise 38.6 involved independent events.

When A and B are **independent** events then the probability of A and B occurring is given by:
P(A and B) = P(A) × P(B)

This rule can be extended to any number of independent events. For example:
P(A and B and C) = P(A) × P(B) × P(C)

EXAMPLES

1 A fair spinner has four equal sections.
The sections are coloured blue (B), red (R), white (W) and green (G).
The arrow on the spinner is spun twice.
(a) Are the outcomes from each of these spins independent?
(b) Find the probability of the arrow landing on red and green in any order.
The arrow on the spinner is spun three times.
(c) Find the probability of the arrow landing on the same colour.

(a) Yes. The events are independent as the outcome from one spin does not affect the next spin.
$P(B) = P(R) = P(W) = P(G) = \frac{1}{4}$

Try answering part (b) using equally likely outcomes.

(b) P((R and G) or (G and R)) = P(R and G) + P(G and R)
= P(R) × P(G) + P(G) × P(R)
= $(\frac{1}{4} \times \frac{1}{4}) + (\frac{1}{4} \times \frac{1}{4}) = \frac{1}{16} + \frac{1}{16}$
The probability of the arrow landing on red and green in any order is $\frac{1}{8}$.

(c) P((R and R and R) or (B and B and B) or (G and G and G) or (W and W and W))
= P(R and R and R) + P(B and B and B) + P(G and G and G) + P(W and W and W)
= $(\frac{1}{4} \times \frac{1}{4} \times \frac{1}{4}) + (\frac{1}{4} \times \frac{1}{4} \times \frac{1}{4}) + (\frac{1}{4} \times \frac{1}{4} \times \frac{1}{4}) + (\frac{1}{4} \times \frac{1}{4} \times \frac{1}{4}) = 4 \times \frac{1}{64}$
The probability that the arrow lands on the same colour is $\frac{1}{16}$.

2 Bob has three 50p coins and two 20p coins.
Sam has four 50p coins and one 20p coin.
Bob picks one of his coins at random and gives it to Kim.
Sam picks one of his coins at random and gives it to Kim.
(a) What is the probability that Bob and Sam give Kim a total of £1?
(b) What is the probability that Bob and Sam give Kim a total of 70p?

(a) Both Bob and Sam give 50p.
P(50p and 50p) = P(50p) × P(50p)
= $\frac{3}{5} \times \frac{4}{5} = \frac{12}{25}$

(b) Tom gives 50p and Sam 20p, or Sam gives 20p and Tom 50p.
P(50p and 20p or 20p and 50p)
= P(50p and 20p) + P(20p and 50p)
= P(50p) × P(20p) + P(20p) × P(50p)
= $\frac{3}{5} \times \frac{1}{5} + \frac{2}{5} \times \frac{4}{5} = \frac{11}{25}$

You are not asked to use a tree diagram in any of the questions in this exercise. However, you can do so if you think it will help.

1 Which of the following pairs of events are likely to be independent?
(a) A: The sun shines today.
   B: The sun shines tomorrow.
(b) A: It rains on August Bank Holiday.
   B: It rains on Spring Bank Holiday.
(c) Tom and Sam are brothers.
   A: Tom has blue eyes.
   B: Sam has blue eyes.
(d) Tom and Sam are in the same class at school.
   A: Tom has blue eyes.
   B: Sam has blue eyes.
(e) Mr. Rice drives to work.
   A: His car breaks down.
   B: Mr. Rice is late for work.
(f) A red dice and a blue dice are rolled.
   A: The red dice lands on an even number.
   B: The blue dice lands on an even number.

2 A fair spinner can land on either black or white.
The probability that it lands on white when it is spun is 0.3.
(a) What is the probability that it lands on black when it is spun?

The spinner is spun twice.
(b) Find the probability of getting two blacks or two whites.

3 In box A there are 3 red and 5 blue counters.
In box B there are 2 red and 3 blue counters.
In box C there are 7 red and 3 blue counters.
A counter is chosen at random from each box.
Calculate the probability that:
(a) all of the counters are red.
(b) at least one of the counters is red.

4 Each of two identical spinners can stop on red, yellow or blue.
The probability of it landing on red is 0.1.
The probability of it landing on blue is 0.3.
Both spinners are spun.
(a) What is the probability that both spinners land on blue?

Jane and Sally play a game with the spinners.
Jane spins both spinners.
If they land on the same colour she wins.
If they don't she loses.
(b) Who is more likely to win the game? Show **all** your working.

5 Samantha takes examinations in Maths and in English,
The probability that she passes Maths is 0.7.
The probability that she passes English is 0.8.
The results in each subject are independent of each other.
Calculate the probability that:
(a) Samantha passes Maths and fails English,
(b) Samantha fails both subjects.

6 The probability that it rains on a Monday is $\frac{3}{8}$.
The probability that there is a Maths test on a Monday is $\frac{1}{3}$.
These two events are independent.
(a) What does the term independent mean?
(b) Calculate the probability that there is a Maths test on a rainy Monday.
(c) In a school year there are 39 Mondays.
How many Maths tests are likely to take place in a school year on a Monday when it doesn't rain?

7 Dice A and Dice B are two normal dice.
Dice A is a fair dice.
Dice B is biased so that the probability of getting an even number is $\frac{2}{3}$.
Both of the dice are tossed.

Find the probability that:
(a) an odd number is scored on dice A and an even number on dice B,
(b) an odd number is scored on one dice and an even number on the other.

8 A bag contains red, white and blue cubes.
The cubes are numbered 1, 2, 3 and 4.
The probabilities of taking cubes from the box at random are shown in the table.

Colour of cube

	Red	White	Blue
1	0.1	0	0
2	0.1	0.1	0.1
3	0	0.2	0.2
4	0.1	0	0.1

(Number on cube)

A single cube is taken from the box at random.
(a) What is the probability that:
   (i)   the cube is white,
   (ii) the cube is red and numbered 4,
   (iii) the cube is white or numbered 1 (or both),
   (iv) the cube is white or numbered 3 (or both)?

A cube is taken from the box at random and then replaced.
Another cube is then taken from the box at random.
(b) Calculate the probability that the cubes are a different colour.

9 A box contains cubes which are coloured red (R), white (W) or blue (B) and numbered 1, 2 or 3.
The table shows the probabilities of obtaining each colour and each number when a cube is taken from the box at random.

Colour of cube

	R	W	B
1	0.2	0	0.1
2	0.1	0.3	0
3	0	0.1	0.2

(Number on cube)

A single cube is taken from the box at random.
(a) What is the probability that the cube is:
   (i)   red and numbered 2,
   (ii) white or numbered 1 (or both),
   (iii) white or numbered 3 (or both)?

A cube is taken from the box at random and then replaced.
Another cube is then taken from the box at random.
(b) Calculate the probability that:
   (i)   both cubes are blue and numbered 1,
   (ii) both cubes are blue or numbered 1,
   (iii) both cubes are blue or both cubes are numbered 1.

10 The tables give some information about the members of two clubs.

Club A

	Male	Female
Wears glasses	22	8
Does not wear glasses	48	22

Club B

	Male	Female
Wears glasses	8	37
Does not wear glasses	12	43

(a) A male from club A is picked at random and a male from club B is picked at random.
   What is the probability that:
   (i)   both of them wear glasses,
   (ii) one of them wears glasses?

(b) A member of club A is picked at random and a member of club B is picked at random.
   What is the probability that:
   (i)   both members picked are female,
   (ii) one male and one female is picked?

In some situations the probability of a particular event occurring can be affected by other events.
For example:
If it rains, the probability of a particular driver winning a Formula 1 Grand Prix might change.
When probabilities depend on other events they are called **conditional probabilities.**

EXAMPLE

1 A bag contains six red counters and four blue counters.
Three counters are taken from the bag at random and put in a box.
(a) What is the probability that the **second** counter put in the box is blue:
   (i) if the **first** counter put in the box is red,
   (ii) if the **first** counter put in the box is blue?
(b) What is the probability that the **third** counter put in the box is red:
   (i) if the **first two** counters put in the box are red,
   (ii) if the **first** counter put in the box is blue and the **second** counter put in the box is red?
(c) Show all the possible ways that the counters can be put in the box on a tree diagram.
   Label the branches of the tree diagram with their probabilities.
(d) What is the probability that there are at least two blue counters in the box?

(a) (i) If the first counter put in the box is red,
   then 4 of the 9 counters left in the bag are blue.   So P(Blue) $= \frac{4}{9}$
   (ii) If the first counter put in the box is blue,
   then 3 of the 9 counters left in the bag are blue.   So P(Blue) $= \frac{3}{9} = \frac{1}{3}$

(b) (i) If the first two counters put in the box are red,
   then 4 of the 8 counters left in the bag are red.   So P(Red) $= \frac{4}{8} = \frac{1}{2}$
   (ii) If the first counter put in the box is blue and the
   second counter put in the box is red,
   then 5 of the 8 counters left in the bag are red.   So P(Red) $= \frac{5}{8}$

(c)

1st counter	2nd counter	3rd counter	Outcome

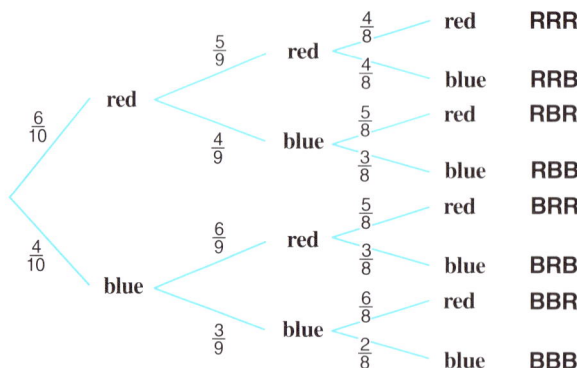

(d) The outcomes included in the event at least two blue counters in the box are:

Red (R) and Blue (B) and Blue (B)   P(R and B and B) $= \frac{6}{10} \times \frac{4}{9} \times \frac{3}{8} = \frac{1}{10}$

Blue (B) and Red (R) and Blue (B)   P(B and R and B) $= \frac{4}{10} \times \frac{6}{9} \times \frac{3}{8} = \frac{1}{10}$

Blue (B) and Blue (B) and Red (R)   P(B and B and R) $= \frac{4}{10} \times \frac{3}{9} \times \frac{6}{8} = \frac{1}{10}$

Blue (B) and Blue (B) and Blue (B)   P(B and B and B) $= \frac{4}{10} \times \frac{3}{9} \times \frac{2}{8} = \frac{1}{30}$

So P(at least two blue counters) $= \frac{1}{10} + \frac{1}{10} + \frac{1}{10} + \frac{1}{30}$

$= \frac{1}{3}$

2 A box contains 20 counters which are coloured either red or blue and numbered either 1 or 2. The table shows how the counters are coloured and numbered.

	Number	
	1	2
Colour Red	5	3
Blue	5	7

Two counters are taken from the box at random **without replacement**.

(a) Find the probability that the sum of the numbers on the counters is an odd number **and** that the counters are a different colour.

(b) Find the probability that the sum of the numbers on the counters is an even number **and** that the counters are the same colour.

(a) The outcomes included in the event are:
Red 1 and Blue 2   (R1 and B2)
Blue 2 and Red 1   (B2 and R1)
Blue 1 and Red 2   (B1 and R2)
Red 2 and Blue1   (R2 and B1)

$P(\text{R1 and B2}) = \frac{5}{20} \times \frac{7}{19} = \frac{7}{76}$

$P(\text{B2 and R1}) = \frac{7}{20} \times \frac{5}{19} = \frac{7}{76}$

$P(\text{B1 and R2}) = \frac{5}{20} \times \frac{3}{19} = \frac{3}{76}$

$P(\text{R2 and B1}) = \frac{3}{20} \times \frac{5}{19} = \frac{3}{76}$

$\frac{7}{76} + \frac{7}{76} + \frac{3}{76} + \frac{3}{76} = \frac{5}{19}$

So the required probability is $\frac{5}{19}$.

(b) The outcomes included in the event are:
Red 1 and Red 1   (R1 and R1)
Blue 1 and Blue 1   (B1 and B1)
Red 2 and Red 2   (R2 and R2)
Blue 2 and Blue 2   (B2 and B2)

$P(\text{R1 and R1}) = \frac{5}{20} \times \frac{4}{19} = \frac{1}{19}$

$P(\text{B1 and B1}) = \frac{5}{20} \times \frac{4}{19} = \frac{1}{19}$

$P(\text{R2 and R2}) = \frac{3}{20} \times \frac{2}{19} = \frac{3}{190}$

$P(\text{B2 and B2}) = \frac{7}{20} \times \frac{6}{19} = \frac{21}{190}$

$\frac{1}{19} + \frac{1}{19} + \frac{3}{190} + \frac{21}{190} = \frac{22}{95}$

So the required probability is $\frac{22}{95}$.

3 Mr Smith passes through two sets of traffic lights on his journey to work.
On any one day, the probability that Mr Smith is delayed by the first set of traffic lights is 0.3 and the probability that he is delayed by the second set of traffic lights is 0.6.
If he is not delayed by either set of traffic lights the probability that Mr Smith is late for work is 0.01.
If he is delayed by exactly one set of traffic lights the probability that Mr Smith is late for work is 0.05.
If he is delayed by both sets of traffic lights the probability that Mr Smith is late for work is 0.1.
Calculate the probability that, on any one day, Mr Smith is late for work.

Step 1 Work out the probabilities of Mr Smith being delayed by the traffic lights.
P(not delayed by either set of traffic lights) $= 0.7 \times 0.4 = 0.28$
P(delayed by exactly one set of traffic lights) $= 0.3 \times 0.4 + 0.7 \times 0.6 = 0.54$
P(delayed by both sets of traffic lights) $= 0.3 \times 0.6 = 0.18$

Step 2 Work out the probabilities of Mr Smith being late for each possible delay.
P(late if not delayed by either set of traffic lights) $= 0.28 \times 0.01 = 0.0028$
P(late if delayed by exactly one set of traffic lights) $= 0.54 \times 0.05 = 0.027$
P(late if delayed by both sets of traffic lights) $= 0.18 \times 0.1 = 0.018$

Step 3 P(Mr Smith being late for work on any one day) $= 0.0028 + 0.027 + 0.018$
$= 0.0478$

On how many days is Mr Smith likely to be late during a year in which he works 200 days?

1 Tom takes blocks at random from a bag containing 7 red (R) and 3 white (W) blocks.
As he takes them from the bag, he puts the blocks one on top of the other.
Here are some examples of possible piles of blocks that Tom could make.

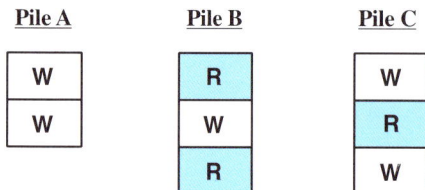

Pile A   Pile B   Pile C

W
W

R
W
R

W
R
W

The tree diagram shows the ways that the first two blocks can be taken from the bag.

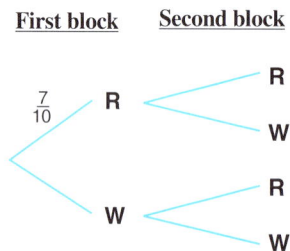

First block   Second block

$\frac{7}{10}$ R —— R

R —— W

W —— R

W —— W

(a) (i) Copy the tree diagram and complete the probabilities on the branches.
(ii) Calculate the probability that Tom makes **Pile A** with the first two blocks that he takes.

(b) Calculate the probability that Tom makes either **Pile B** or **Pile C** with the first three blocks that he takes.

SEG 1998

2 A bag contains 4 red balls and 6 blue balls.
One ball is taken from the bag at random. It is **not** put back in the bag.
A second ball is taken from the bag at random.
(a) Draw a tree diagram to show the possible pairs of colours taken from the bag.
Fill in the probabilities on the branches of the tree diagram.
(b) (i) Find the probability that the two balls taken from the bag are both red.
(ii) Find the probability that the balls taken from the bag are red and blue.

SEG 1994

3 A club has 15 girls and 6 boys.
Two of these members were chosen at random to join a national committee.
(a) Copy and complete the probability tree.
Label each branch with its probability.

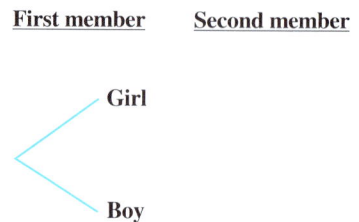

First member   Second member

Girl

Boy

(b) Calculate the probability that a boy and a girl were chosen.

SEG 1994

4 Boris and John play three sets of tennis.
The probability of Boris winning the first set is 0.4.
If Boris wins a set the probability of his winning the next set is 0.7.
If John wins a set the probability of his winning the next set is 0.8.
(a) Copy and complete the tree diagram to show all the possible outcomes. Label each branch with its probability.

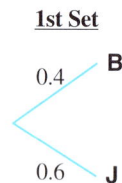

1st Set

0.4 B

0.6 J

(b) Calculate the probability that John wins all **three** sets.
(c) Calculate the probability that Boris wins **at least** two sets.

SEG 1995

5 Andre has a box of tennis balls.
It contains 3 white, 4 green and 5 yellow tennis balls.
Andre chooses a ball at random and does not replace it.
He then chooses a second ball at random.
(a) Draw a tree diagram to show Andre's choices.
Label each branch with its probability.
(b) What is the probability that Andre chooses at least one white ball?

SEG 1997

6 A tube of fruit gums contains 3 red gums, 4 black gums and 3 green gums.
Two gums are chosen at random and not replaced.
What is the probability that they are both the same colour?
SEG 1995

7 The probability that Simon passes his driving test at the first attempt has been estimated to be about $\frac{1}{3}$.
If a test is failed, the probability of passing the next test is $\frac{7}{12}$.
Calculate the probability that Simon passes his driving test at his third attempt.
SEG 1995

8 An aeroplane has two engines. From past experience the probability of failure of an engine on any journey is $\frac{1}{1000}$.
A plane can safely land with just one engine working with a probability of $\frac{9}{10}$.
It will always land safely if both engines are working.
Calculate the probability that a plane will safely finish a journey.
SEG 1995

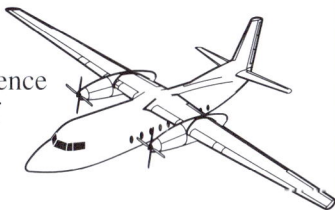

9 Kitty has 6 black socks, 4 red socks and 2 white socks in a drawer.
She goes to the drawer, in the dark, and takes two socks from the drawer at random.
(a) Calculate the probability that the first sock is black and the second sock is white.
(b) Calculate the probability that the two socks are **both** red.
SEG 1995

10 A bag contains packets of crisps of different flavours: 5 chicken, 3 beef and 2 plain.
Abigail takes **three** packets of crisps from the bag at random.
(a) Calculate the probability that she takes:
  (i) three packets of chicken flavoured crisps,
  (ii) both packets of plain crisps.
(b) Abigail gives, at random, two of her packets to her sister.
Calculate the probability that Abigail's sister receives both packets of plain crisps.
SEG 1998

11 A box contains 25 counters which are either coloured black or white.
Each counter is numbered 1, 2 or 3.
This table shows how the counters are coloured and numbered.

		Colour	
		Black	White
	1	6	5
Number	2	4	3
	3	2	5

Tom and Sam use the box of counters to play a game.
In the game, they each take one counter at random from the box and place it on the table in front of them.
If Tom's counter has the same colour as Sam's counter **and** a different number to Sam's counter then Tom wins.
If Sam's counter has a different colour to Tom's counter **and** the same number as Tom's counter then Sam wins.
Otherwise the game is a draw.
What is the most likely result of this game?

12 In a game Aldijana and James take turns to throw one dart at this target.
The winner is the first player to hit the centre of the target.
Each time Aldijana throws a dart at the target the probability of hitting the centre is 0.4.
Each time James throws a dart at the target the probability of hitting the centre is 0.3.
Aldijana and James toss a fair coin to decide who throws the first dart.
(a) (i) Calculate the probability that James wins the toss **and** wins the game with his first throw.
  (ii) Calculate the probability that James loses the toss **and** wins the game with his first throw.
(b) Calculate the probability that Aldijana wins with **her** first throw of the game.
SEG 1999

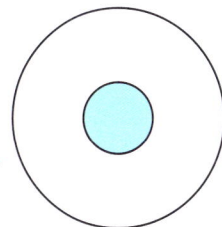

13 Bag A contains 6 red and 4 blue counters.
Bag B contains 5 red and 4 blue counters.
Bag C contains 5 red and 3 blue counters.
One counter is taken at random from bag A and **put in** bag B.
Two more counters are then taken at random from bag A and **put in** bag C.

Calculate the probability that:

(a) there are more red counters in bag B than in bag C,

(b) there are more red counters in bag C than in bag B,

(c) bags B and C each contain the same number of red and blue counters.

The counters are returned to their original bags.
One counter is taken at random from bag A and **put in** bag B.
Two counters are then taken from bag B **without replacement**.

(d) Calculate the probability that the number of red counters and the number of blue counters in bags B and C are the same.

14 A restaurant offers a choice of a free bottle of red or white wine with lunchtime special meals of chicken, fish or beef.
Analysis of orders over a month shows that:
if a customer orders chicken then the probability of choosing white wine is 0.7,
if a customer orders fish then the probability of choosing white wine is 0.8,
if a customer orders beef then the probability of choosing red wine is 0.9.

The probability that a customer orders chicken is 0.5 and the probability that a customer orders fish is 0.3.
In any one week approximately 800 customers order a lunchtime meal.
Estimate the number of bottles of white wine that are required.

15 A boy is learning to skate.
He tries to skate over a five metre section without falling over.
The probability that he succeeds on his first attempt is $\frac{1}{4}$.

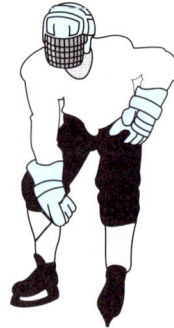

If he succeeds on any attempt, the probability of success on his next attempt is doubled.
If he fails, the probability that he fails his next attempt is $\frac{3}{4}$.

(a) Draw a tree diagram showing the outcomes of his first three attempts. Label each branch with its probability.

(b) Calculate, the probability that the boy is successful at least twice in his first three attempts.

SEG 1996

16 An experiment was carried out with a bag containing twenty-five coloured counters. In the experiment the following trial was repeated a large number of times.

> Take three counters from the bag at random, without replacement, and record their colours.

These relative frequencies were calculated.

Outcome	Relative frequency
Red, Red, Red	0.054
Red, Red, Blue	0.052
Green, Green, Blue	0.026

(a) Calculate an estimate of the number of each coloured counter in the bag.

(b) Estimate the probability that in a trial the three counters have a different colour.

What you need to know

- You need to know the meaning of these terms:

  outcome, event   fair, unbiased, biased, taken at random

  equally likely outcomes   trial

- **Probability** describes how likely or unlikely it is that an event will occur.
  Probability is measured on a scale of 0 (**impossibility**) to 1 (**certainty**).
  Probability **must** be written as a fraction, a decimal or a percentage.

- How to determine probabilities using **equally likely outcomes**.
  The probability of an event X occurring is given by:

$$P(X) = \frac{\text{Number of possible outcomes in an event}}{\text{Total number of possible outcomes}}$$

- How to estimate probabilities using **relative frequency.**
  The relative frequency of an event X occurring is given by:

$$R(X) = \frac{\text{Number of times an event occurs in an experiment (or is observed)}}{\text{Total number of trials in the experiment (or observations)}}$$

  Relative frequency gives a better estimate of probability the larger the number of trials.

- How to use probabilities to **estimate** the number of times an event occurs in an **experiment** or **observation**.
  Estimate = total number of trials (or observations) $\times$ probability of event

- How to determine probabilities of **mutually exclusive** events.
  Mutually exclusive events cannot occur at the same time.

  When A and B are mutually exclusive events …   P(A or B) = P(A) + P(B).

  The events A and not A are mutually exclusive.
  A or not A is certain to occur. So …   P(not A) = 1 − P(A).

- How to find all the possible outcomes when two events are combined.
  By **listing** the outcomes systematically.
  By using a **possibility space diagram**.
  By using a **tree diagram**.

- How to find the probability of a combined event by:
  finding all the equally likely outcomes in simple situations,
  using a tree diagram.

- How to determine probabilities of two or more **independent** events.
  The outcomes of independent events do not influence each other.

  When A and B are independent events …   P(A and B) = P(A) × P(B).

- How to determine probabilities and solve problems involving **conditional probability**.
  Conditional probabilities arise when the probabilities of particular events occurring are affected by other events.

The network game

The game is about moving about this network.

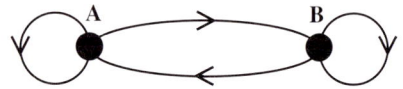

At A roll a dice
>   If it lands on an odd number, stay at A.
>   If it lands on an even number, move to B.

At B roll a dice
>   If it lands on a 1 or 2, stay at B.
>   If it lands on a 3, 4, 5 or 6, move to A.

Where are you most likely to end up if you …

… start at A and throw the dice twice?   … start at B and throw the dice 5 times?
… start at B and throw the dice twice?   … start at A and throw the dice 10 times?
… start at A and throw the dice 5 times?   … start at B and throw the dice 10 times?

Analyse the game using probability.

Investigate network games for different networks and different probabilities **a, b, c** …

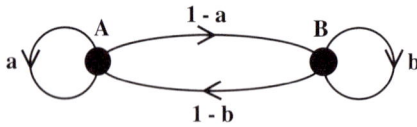

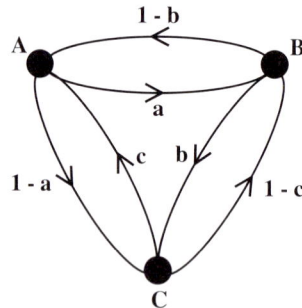

Review Exercise

1   A bead is taken at random from a bag and its colour is recorded. The bead is then replaced. This is repeated 400 times.

The relative frequencies of taking each colour are shown on this graph.

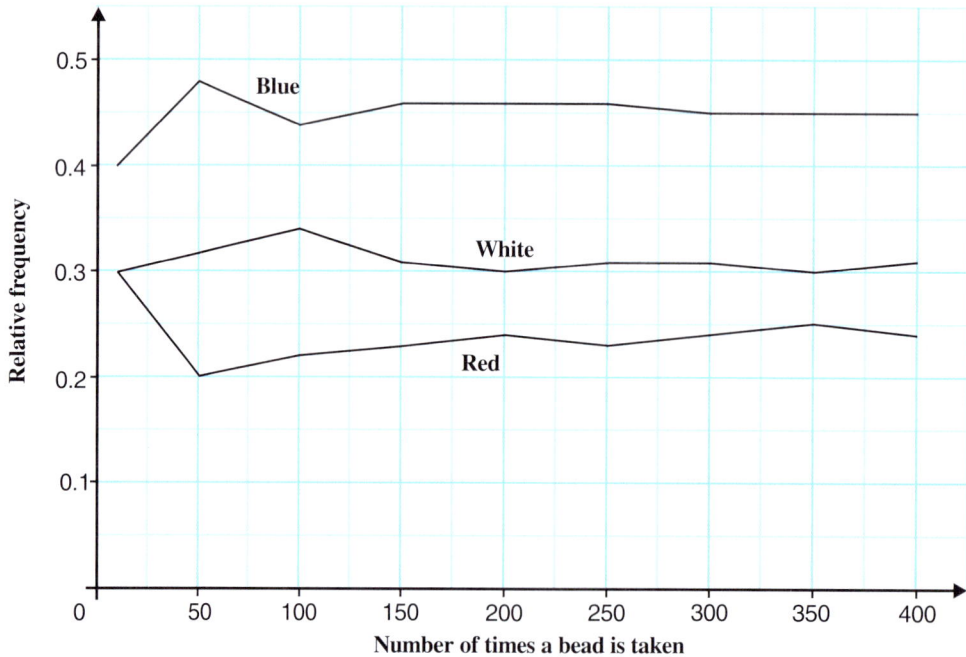

(a)   Approximately how many times was a blue bead taken from the bag?

The bag contains a total of 20 beads.

(b)   Estimate how many of each colour are in the bag.

SEG 1999

2 (a) A fair spinner is labelled as shown.

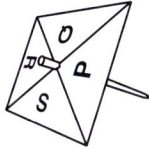

The results of the first ten spins are:
P Q R P Q S R R S Q
  (i) Write down the relative frequency of the letter *R* for these results.
  (ii) As the number of results increases, what do you expect to happen to the relative frequency of the letter *R*?

(b) Another spinner has four unequal sides coloured red, green, white and blue.
The probability of getting a blue is $\frac{7}{24}$.
The probability of getting a blue or a green is $\frac{11}{24}$.
What is the probability of getting a green?

SEG 1997

3 The diagram shows two sets of cards.

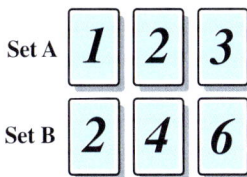

Set A   **1 2 3**

Set B   **2 4 6**

(a) A card is taken at random from set A and another card is taken at random from set B.
The numbers on the cards are added together to give a score.
What is the probability of getting a score that is an odd number?

(b) The cards in set A are red.
The cards in set B are blue.
All the cards are shuffled together.
  (i) One card is taken at random. What is the probability that it is a red or 2 or both?
  (ii) One card is taken at random and is then replaced. Another card is then taken at random.
  What is the probability that both cards are red or 2 or both?

SEG 1998

4 The diagram shows a fun slide at a leisure pool.

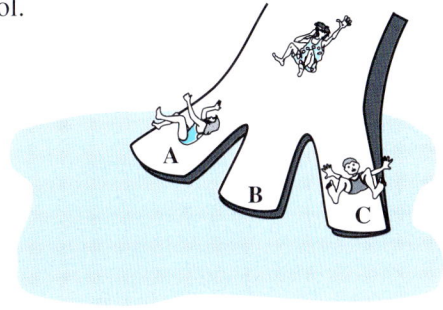

There is one entrance to the fun slide, and three different exits A, B and C.
The choice of exit is mutually exclusive.
The following information was obtained after observing the fun slide in use.
Probability of using exit A = 0.2
Probability of using exit A or B = 0.7
Probability of using exit B or C = 0.8
A child on the water slide is observed at random.
What is the probability that the child uses exit C?

SEG 1995

5 David and Sita each hold a green flag in their left hand and a black flag in their right hand.
David and Sita each raise one flag.
The probability that a black flag is raised by Sita is 0.4 and by David is 0.3.
(a) Copy and complete this tree diagram.

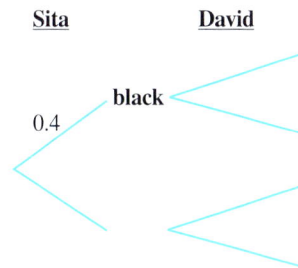

(b) Calculate the probability that:
  (i) two green flags are raised,
  (ii) one flag of each colour is raised.

6 Arrows are fired at a target.
Each arrow either hits or misses the target.
Each time Andy fires an arrow the probability that he hits the target is $\frac{3}{5}$.

Andy fires two arrows.
(a) Calculate the probability that both shots hit the target.
(b) Calculate the probability that Andy hits the target exactly once with his two shots.

SEG 1994

7 The diagram shows a fair six sided spinner.
The spinner has three blank sectors, two sectors with a 1 and one sector with a 2.

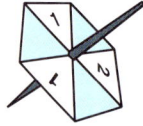

(a) The spinner is spun twice.
  (i) Copy and complete the tree diagram.

First go	Second go

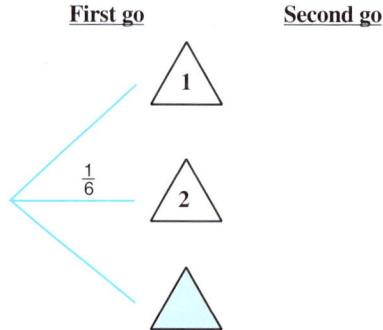

$\frac{1}{6}$

  (ii) What is the probability of getting two blanks?

The spinner is used to play a game called 'Double your money'.
In the game:

getting a △ means you lose

getting a /1\ means you get your money back

getting a /2\ means you get double your money back

(b) Tom has two goes. He pays £1 for each go.
What is the probability that after two goes Tom has **at least** £1 more than he started with?

SEG 1998

8 A bag contains 7 red counters, 8 white counters and 5 blue counters.
Anna takes a counter at random from the bag and, without replacing it, takes a second counter at random.
What is the probability that Anna
(a) has **two** red counters,
(b) has exactly **one** red counter,
(c) has **two** counters the same colour?

SEG 1995

9 (a) Packet A contains 20 pens of which 5 do not work.
Packet B contains 10 pens of which 3 do not work.
One pen is drawn at random from packet A and one pen is drawn at random from packet B.
What is the probability that both pens work?
(b) Packet C contains 18 pens of which 6 do not work.
Two pens are drawn at random **without replacement** from packet C.
  (i) What is the probability that both pens work?
  (ii) What is the probability that one pen works and the other pen does not?

SEG 1997

508

10 A door has a latch lock, *A*, and a mortice lock, *B*, both locked.
The porter has a key ring with three latch keys and four mortice keys on it.

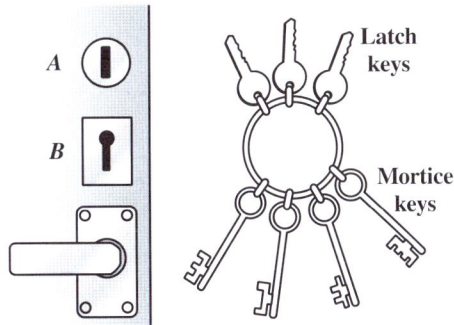

The porter does not know which latch key fits lock *A* or which mortice key fits lock *B*.
He is equally likely to choose any latch key for lock *A* and any mortice key for lock *B*.
(a) What is the probability that the first latch key he chooses will open lock *A* **and** the first mortice key he chooses will open lock *B*?

If he chooses the wrong key he will now select from the others.
(b) (i) What is the probability that the first latch key he chooses does not work and the second latch key he chooses will open lock *A?*
(ii) What is the probability that he chooses exactly four keys to open both locks?

SEG 1996

11 A drinks machine dispenses cups of coffee and cups of tea but **not** always as requested.
If tea is selected then the probability of getting tea is 0.6.
If coffee is selected then the probability of getting coffee is 0.7.
100 people select a drink from the machine at random.
How many of them are likely **not** to get the drink they select?

SEG 1997

12 The probability of a person passing their driving test at the first attempt is 0.7.
If the person fails the test at the first attempt then the probability that they pass at the second attempt is 0.6.
The probability that a person passes their driving test at their first, second or third attempt is 0.934.
Calculate the probability that a person passes their third test after two failures.

SEG 1994

13 The table shows how 50 counters are coloured red, white or blue and numbered 1 or 2.

		Number	
		1	2
	Red	3	11
Colour	White	7	13
	Blue	4	12

Three counters are taken at random from the box **without replacement**.
(a) Calculate the probability that the counters have the same colour and that the sum of their numbers is even.
(b) Calculate the probability that the counters have different colours and different numbers.

14 Tom has six 10p coins, three 20p coins and two 50p coins in his pocket.
Tom takes coins from his pocket at random, one at a time and gives them to Sam.
He stops when Sam has **at least** 30p.
(a) What is the most likely number of coins that Tom gives to Sam?
(b) Calculate the probability that Sam receives exactly 30p.

Section Review - Handling Data

1 Keith is investigating what proportion of children are left-handed.
He conducts a survey in his class at school.
The results of the survey are shown.

(a) How many children were included in the survey?

(b) Keith says 'More boys than girls are left-handed'.
Give one reason why he may be wrong.

(c) Keith says 'The probability that a child is left-handed is $\frac{1}{7}$'.
Give one reason why he may be wrong.

(d) The school has 385 children.
If Keith is correct, estimate how many would be left-handed.

	Right-handed	Left-handed
Boys	⊦⊦⊦⊦ ⊦⊦⊦⊦ ⊦⊦⊦⊦ |||	Boys |||
Girls	⊦⊦⊦⊦ ⊦⊦⊦⊦ ||	Girls ||

SEG 1996

2 The two-way table shows the connection between the number of cars owned and the number of adults in thirty different families.

Number of cars owned

		0	1	2	3	4
Number of adults	1	4	5	0	0	0
	2	1	5	3	0	0
	3	0	2	2	3	0
	4	0	0	1	1	1
	5	0	0	1	1	0

For example, there are four families with one adult and no cars.

(a) How many of the thirty families have one car for each adult?

(b) Find the modal number of cars owned by the thirty families.

(c) Calculate the total number of adults in the thirty families.

(d) Calculate the total number of cars owned by the thirty families.

SEG 1997

3 The table shows the results for a group of students taking a first aid test.
Carol says "Girls are more likely to pass a first aid test than boys".
Do the results of this test support this hypothesis?

	Passed	Failed
Boys	19	4
Girls	49	13

4 Ross keeps a record of the number of miles that he drives and the amount of petrol used, in litres.

Distance travelled (miles)	300	370	410	420	440	450
Petrol used (litres)	36	41	45	46	51	51

(a) Plot a scatter graph of these results.

(b) What relationship does the scatter graph show?

(c) (i) Draw the line of best fit on the scatter graph, and use it to estimate the amount of petrol, in litres, needed to travel 600 miles.

(ii) Comment on the reliability of this estimate.

SEG 1996

5 A group of students take a Maths test and an English test.
This scatter diagram shows their scores.

A line of best fit has been drawn.

(a) James missed the Maths test. He scored 66 in the English test. Use the scatter diagram to estimate what James might have scored in the Maths test.

(b) Give a reason why James' Maths score is only an estimate.

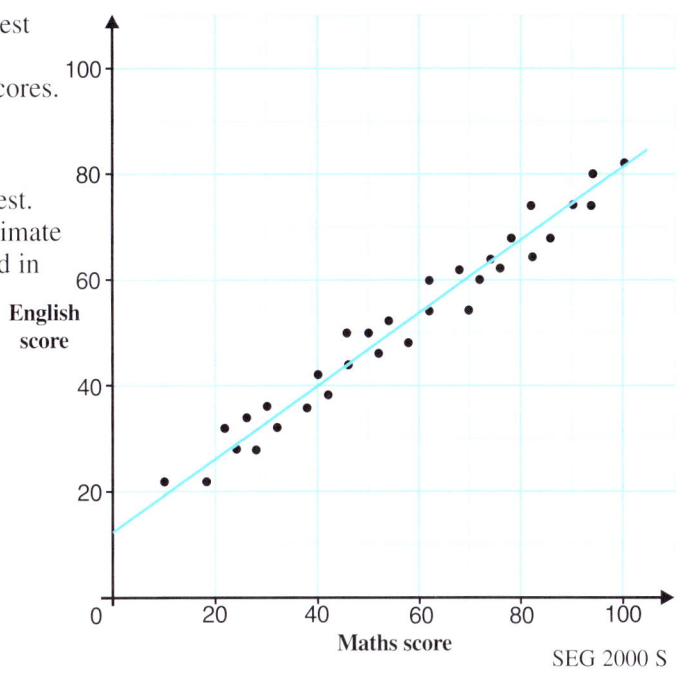

SEG 2000 S

6 A fair dice was thrown 60 times and the scores were recorded.

(a) Write down the relative frequency of the score of 4.

(b) When the same fair dice is thrown a large number of times, what would you expect to happen to the relative frequency of the score of 4?

Score	1	2	3	4	5	6
Frequency	9	12	10	7	11	11

SEG 1995

7 Four dice each have 3 red faces, 2 blue faces and 1 green face.
Three students each pick one of these dice and throw it a number of times.
Their results are summarised in this table.

Student's Name	Number of throws	Frequency		
		Red	Blue	Green
Seema	20	10	7	3
Keith	300	126	84	90
Bryn	400	195	140	65

(a) What is the relative frequency of Bryn throwing red?

(b) Which student's dice is most likely to be biased? Explain your answer.

SEG 2000 S

8 The results of a survey of 100 households are given in the table.

(a) Calculate the mean number of people per household.

One hundred years ago the mean number of people per household was 4.3.

(b) Use the results above to comment on the hypothesis that household size has decreased.

Number of people in household	Frequency
1	11
2	28
3	21
4	25
5	10
6	5

SEG 1998

511

9 The table shows the time, in seconds, it took each of forty students to drink a can of lemonade.

(a) Calculate an estimate of the mean of these times.
(b) Draw a frequency polygon for this frequency distribution.

Time (seconds)	Frequency
0 and less than 8	4
8 and less than 16	9
16 and less than 24	11
24 and less than 32	6
32 and less than 40	8
40 and less than 48	2

SEG 1996

10 The table shows the grouped frequency distribution of the speeds of 80 vehicles on a main road.

(a) Calculate an estimate of the mean speed of these vehicles.

The frequency polygon shows the speeds of 80 vehicles on a motorway. Copy the graph.

Speed S km/h	Frequency
$50 \leqslant S < 60$	15
$60 \leqslant S < 70$	48
$70 \leqslant S < 80$	17

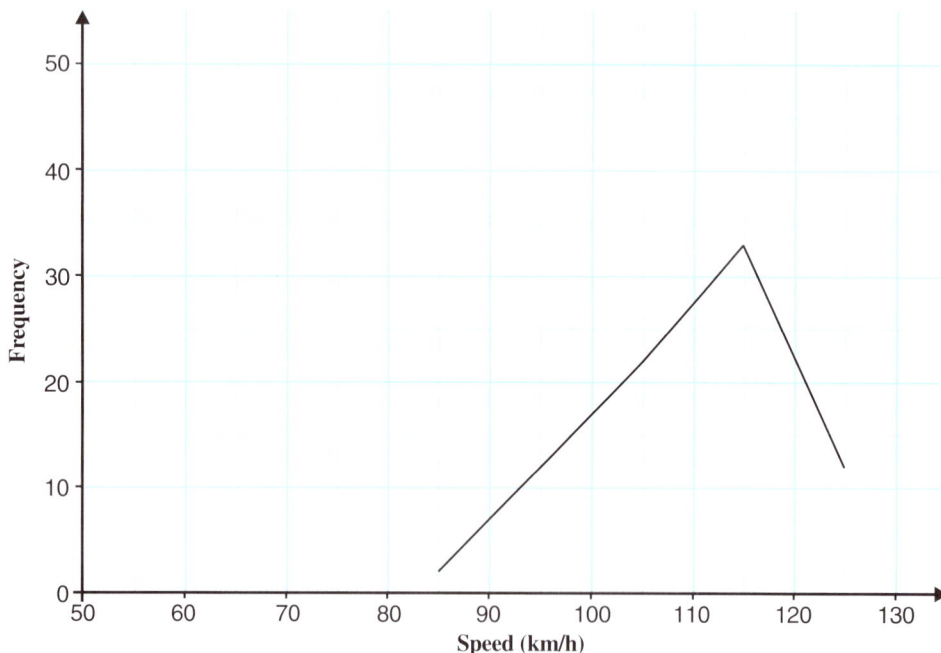

(b) On the same diagram draw a frequency polygon for the speeds of vehicles on the main road.
(c) Compare and comment on the speeds of vehicles on these two roads.

SEG 2000 S

11 Kathryn is conducting a survey on television viewing habits. She thinks of two questions for the questionnaire.

Question 1. How old are you?
Question 2. When do you watch television?

(a) Explain why each of these questions is unsuitable.
(b) Rewrite each of these questions so that she could include them in her questionnaire.

SEG 1996

12 In an opinion poll, 2000 men in Birmingham are asked how they intend to vote in a General Election.
  (a) Give two reasons why this is an unreliable way of predicting the outcome of a General Election.
  (b) Give three ways in which the opinion poll could be improved.

  SEG 1994

13 The letters of the word C R E A M are written on separate red cards and shuffled together.
  (a) A card is taken at random. What is the probability of getting an R?

  The letters of the word C R A C K E R are written on separate blue cards.
  The red and blue cards are shuffled together.
  (b) A card is then taken at random.
    (i) What is the probability of getting an R?
    (ii) What is the probability of getting a red card or an R (or both)?

  All the cards are shuffled.
  (c) A red card is taken at random and a blue card is taken at random.
    What is the probability of getting a red R and a blue R?

    SEG 1999

14 A charity sells scratch cards. The probability of winning a cash prize is 0.15 with each card.
  (a) Draw and label a probability tree diagram to show the possible outcomes when two scratch cards are bought.
  (b) Calculate the probability that **at least one** of the two cards wins a cash prize.

  SEG 1998

15 The probability of the arrow stopping on each number when it is spun is given in the table.
  In a game a player spins the arrow twice.
  The numbers obtained on each spin are added to give the player's score.

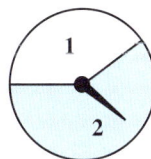

Number on spinner	Probability
1	0.4
2	0.6

  (a) (i) Calculate the probability of scoring 4.
      (ii) Calculate the probability of scoring 3.
  (b) In the game two players each spin the arrow twice.
      To win, a player must score **exactly one more** than their opponent.
      Calculate the probability that the second player wins.

      SEG 1998

16 The diagram shows a network of roads.

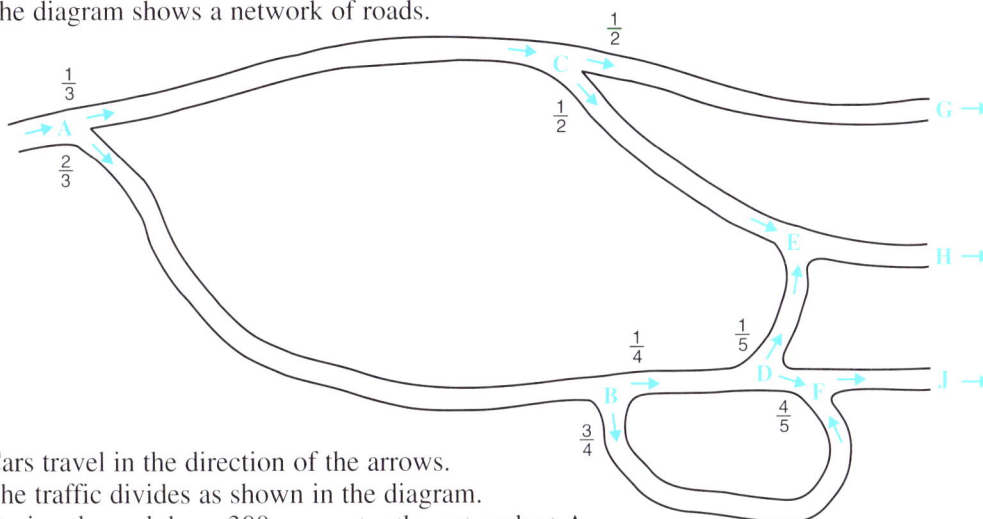

  Cars travel in the direction of the arrows.
  The traffic divides as shown in the diagram.
  During the rush hour 300 cars enter the network at A.
  (a) (i) How many cars would you expect to take the road from A to C?
      (ii) How many cars would you expect to pass through G?
  (b) Calculate the probability of a car passing through J.

  SEG 1996

17 The graph shows the cumulative frequency curve for the lengths of telephone calls to a hospital ward.

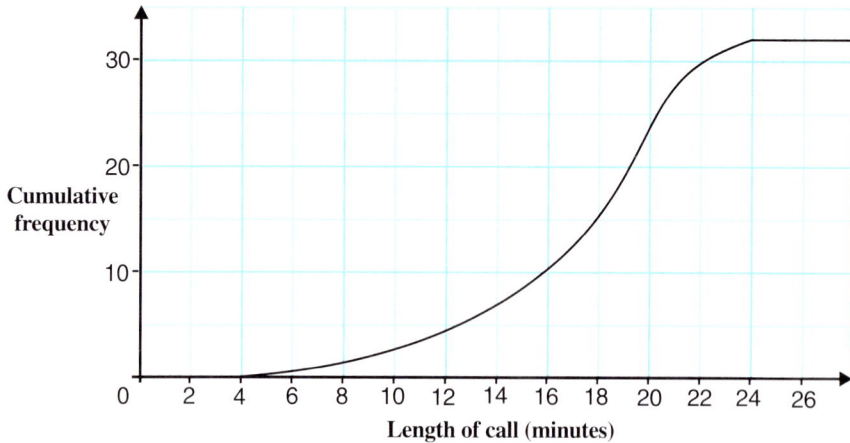

(a) Write down the lower and upper quartile for the lengths of the telephone calls.
(b) How many calls lasted between 12 and 18 minutes?
(c) Use the graph to estimate the probability that a call lasts 16 minutes or more. SEG 1998

18 The frequency distribution of the weights of 100 baking potatoes is given in the table.

(a) Draw a cumulative frequency curve to represent the data.

Weight (g)	Frequency
$0 \leqslant g < 100$	0
$100 \leqslant g < 200$	0
$200 \leqslant g < 300$	0
$300 \leqslant g < 400$	20
$400 \leqslant g < 500$	60
$500 \leqslant g < 600$	20

A cumulative frequency distribution of the weights of 100 economy potatoes is given opposite.

(b) On the same diagram draw a cumulative frequency curve for economy potatoes.
(c) By comparing the interquartile ranges, comment on the spread of weights of economy and baking potatoes.
You must show all your working.

Weight (g)	Cumulative Frequency
$0 \leqslant g < 50$	0
$0 \leqslant g < 100$	8
$0 \leqslant g < 200$	37
$0 \leqslant g < 300$	72
$0 \leqslant g < 400$	89
$0 \leqslant g < 500$	100

SEG 1999

19 The mass of each of 60 apples was recorded to the nearest gram.

Mass	80 -	85 -	90 -	95 -	100 -	105 -	110 - 115
Frequency	3	7	13	15	12	8	2

(a) Calculate the values of the cumulative frequencies.

Mass	< 80	< 85	< 90	< 95	< 100	< 105	< 110	< 115
Cumulative frequency								

(b) Draw the cumulative frequency curve.
(c) Use your graph to estimate the interquartile range of the mass of the apples.
(d) Use your graph to estimate the number of apples that have a mass of less than 106 g.
(e) Seventeen of the apples are rejected as they are too heavy.
What is the maximum weight of the apples that are accepted? SEG 1996

514

20 The number of pupils in each of three schools is given in the table. A stratified random sample of 200 pupils is to be taken. Calculate the number of pupils that should be chosen from each of the schools.

School	Number of pupils
Ashworth Comprehensive School	1500
Brigholm Grammar School	640
Corchester School	360

SEG 1998

21 The speeds of 100 cars travelling along a road are shown in this table.

Speed (s km/h)	$20 \leqslant s < 35$	$35 \leqslant s < 45$	$45 \leqslant s < 55$	$55 \leqslant s < 65$	$65 \leqslant s < 85$
Frequency	6	19	34	26	15

(a) Draw a histogram to show this information.
(b) The speed limit along this road is 48 km/h.
Estimate the number of cars exceeding the speed limit.

SEG 1999

22 The histogram summarises the marks out of 100 obtained on a test by a group of students.

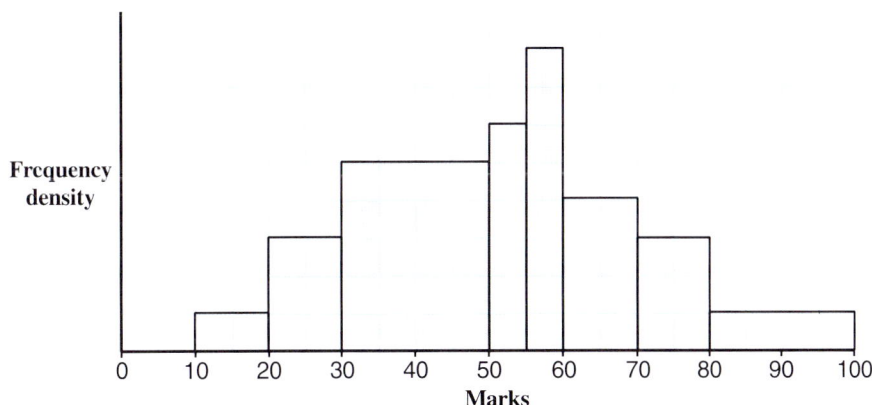

Twelve students scored between 70 and 80 marks.
(a) How many students scored between 80 and 100 marks?
(b) How many students took the test?
(c) Estimate the mean score of the students on this test.

SEG 1997

23 The names of eight competitors are put in a bag: five are female and three are male.
Three names are drawn at random from the bag to determine who wins prizes. A name is not replaced in the bag after it has been chosen.
(a) Draw a tree diagram to show all possible outcomes.
(b) Calculate the probability that the first two names are female.
(c) Calculate the probability that all three names are male.
(d) Calculate the probability that at least one name is female.

SEG 1997

24 A bag contains 4 black balls, 5 white balls and 6 red balls.
Three balls are drawn at random without replacement.
(a) What is the probability that the colours of the three balls are all the same?
(b) What is the probability that the colours of the three balls are all different?

SEG 1996

25 Moira has a set of cards numbered 1, 2 and 4. She has six cards altogether.

She has three cards numbered '1', two cards numbered '2' and one card numbered '4'.
Moira chooses two cards, at random, **without replacement**.
(a) (i) What is the probability that the first card is numbered '2'?
    (ii) Given that the first card is numbered '2', what is the probability that the second card is also numbered '2'?
(b) Draw a probability tree diagram to show the three possible outcomes for Moira's first card and, for each of these, the possible outcomes for her second card.
    Fill in the probabilities on the branches of your tree diagram.

Moira adds the numbers on her two cards together to get a total score.
(c) Find the probability that Moira gets:
    (i) a total score of 2,
    (ii) a total score of 3.
(d) What is the probability that Moira gets the same number on both cards?

SEG 1999

26 A bag contains packets of crisps of different flavours: 5 chicken, 3 beef and 2 plain.
Abigail takes **three** packets of crisps from the bag at random.
(a) Calculate the probability that she takes:
    (i) three packets of chicken flavoured crisps,
    (ii) both packets of plain crisps.
(a) Abigail gives, at random, two of her packets to her sister.
    Calculate the probability that Abigail's sister receives both packets of plain crisps.

SEG 1998

27 The delivery times in days of a sample of 20 first class letters are shown.

$$1 \quad 1 \quad 3 \quad 1 \quad 1 \quad 1 \quad 1 \quad 1 \quad 2 \quad 1$$
$$1 \quad 2 \quad 4 \quad 1 \quad 1 \quad 1 \quad 1 \quad 1 \quad 2 \quad 1$$

(a) Calculate the mean and the standard deviation of the delivery times.

The delivery times of a sample of 20 second class letters have a mean of 3.1 days and a standard deviation of 1.2 days.
(b) Comment on the differences between the delivery times for first and second class letters.

During bad weather delivery times for second class letters are increased by one day.
(c) How does bad weather change the mean and the standard deviation of the delivery times for second class letters?

SEG 1998

28 The heights of 38 bean plants from crop **A** are given in the table.
(a) Calculate estimates of the mean and the standard deviation for the heights of these plants.

(b) A different crop, **B**, of bean plants was grown in pre-warmed soil. This crop has a mean height of 39 cm and a standard deviation of 10 cm.
    Compare the heights of crop **A** and crop **B**.

Height, h, (cm)	Frequency
$0 \leq h < 20$	6
$20 \leq h < 30$	10
$30 \leq h < 40$	14
$40 \leq h < 50$	8

SEG 1997

516

29 A group of students were investigating the time it took to solve some puzzles.
Ten students recorded their solving times for two puzzles, A and B.

(a) The results, in seconds, for puzzle A are shown below.

    12   23   42   35   27   51   25   42   34   15

Calculate the standard deviation of these solving times.

(b) The **range** of the solving times for puzzle B was 5 seconds.
    Is the standard deviation of the solving times for puzzle B higher or lower than that for puzzle A?
    Explain your answer.

These histograms show the solving times for 100 boys doing three puzzles, A, B and C.

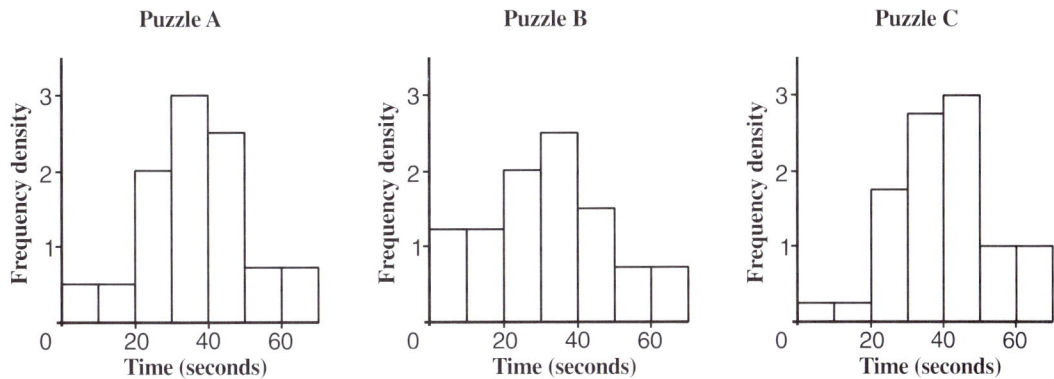

(c) Which puzzle has the greatest standard deviation of solving times?
    Use the histograms to explain your answer.

(d) This histogram shows the solving times for 100 girls doing puzzle A.

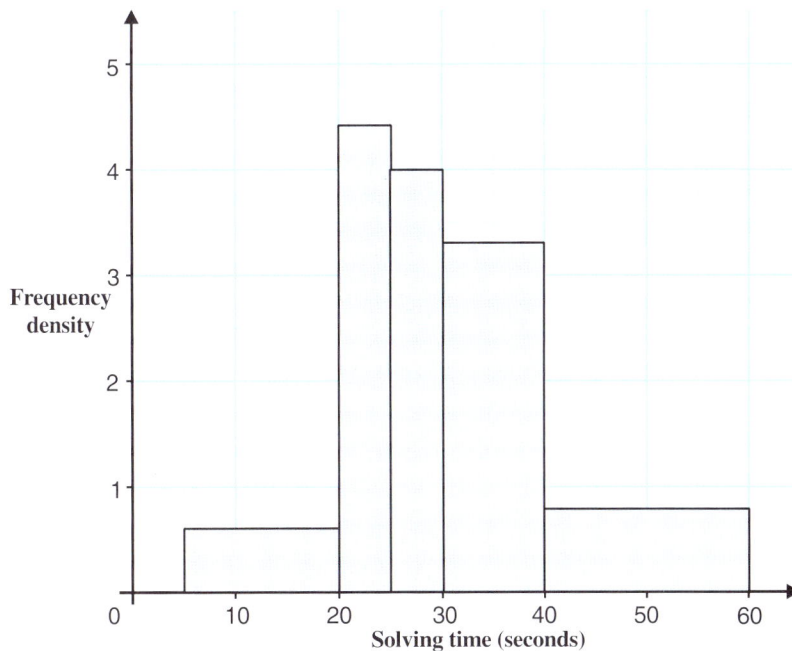

Use the histogram to complete this table.

Solving times (seconds)	5 - 20	20 - 25	25 - 30	30 - 40	40 - 60
Frequency		22	20		

SEG 1999

Exam Practice - Non-calculator Paper

1 Sam and Tom share 100 counters in the ratio 2 : 3.
They use the counters to keep score in a game.
At the end of the game Sam and Tom have counters in the ratio 7 : 13.
Calculate the change in the number of Sam's counters.

SEG 1999

2 (a) Find an approximate value of the expression $19.7 \times 41.2 \div 0.0483$.

(b) All six faces of this cuboid are to be painted.
There is enough paint to cover $5\,m^2$.

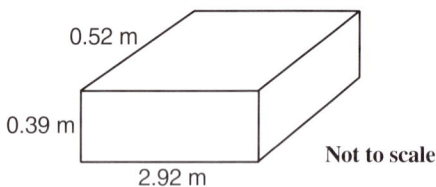

0.52 m

0.39 m

2.92 m

Not to scale

Use approximations to estimate whether there is enough paint to paint the cuboid.
You **must** show all your working.

SEG 2000 S

3 (a) Sticks are arranged to form a sequence of patterns as shown.

Pattern 1   Pattern 2   Pattern 3

Write an expression, in terms of n, for the number of sticks needed to form the nth pattern.

(b) Squares are arranged to form a sequence of rectangular patterns as shown.

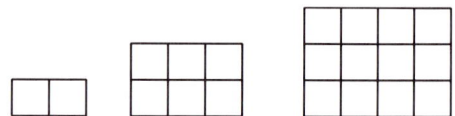

Pattern 1   Pattern 2   Pattern 3

Write an expression, in terms of n, for the number of squares needed to form the nth pattern.

SEG 1999

4 The graph shows the weekly pocket money of 100 children aged 10 years.

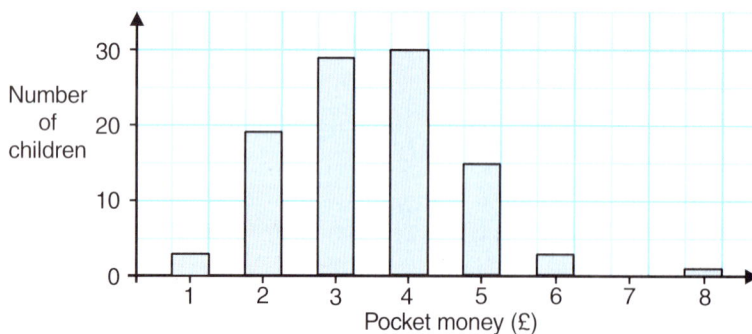

(a) (i) What is the median amount of pocket money?
(ii) Calculate the mean amount of pocket money.

The table shows the weekly pocket money of 100 students aged 16 years.

Pocket money (£)	0 -	5 -	10 -	15 -	20 - 25
Number of students	19	18	21	19	23

(b) Do the 10 years olds or the 16 year olds have the larger range in pocket money?
Give a reason for your answer.

SEG 1999

5 In the diagram, *WA* is a straight line and *ZX* is parallel to *BD*.

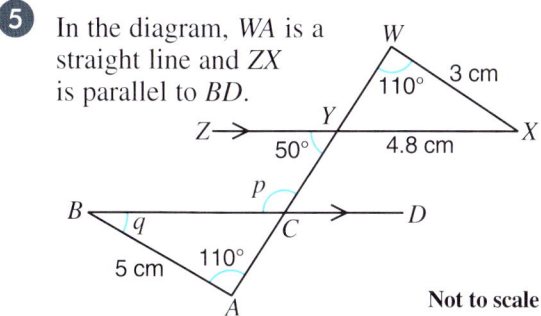

Not to scale

(a) Work out the size of angle *p* and the size of angle *q*.

Triangle *ABC* is similar to triangle *WXY*. *AB* = 5 cm, *WX* = 3 cm and *YX* = 4.8 cm.

(b) Calculate the length of *BC*. SEG 1999

6 (a) These polygons are similar.

Not to scale

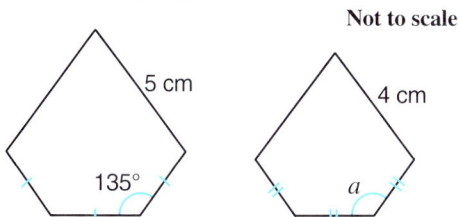

What is the size of angle *a*?

(b) Part of a regular polygon is shown.

Not to scale

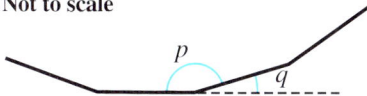

The complete polygon has *n* sides, where $n = \dfrac{360}{q}$ and $p + q = 180°$.

(i) Calculate the value of *n*, when *p* = 168°.

(ii) Write down a formula for *n* in terms of *p*. SEG 1999

7 *PQRS* is a parallelogram with vertices at *P*(1, 1), *R*(7, 8) and *S*(5, 3).

(a) Write down the coordinates of *Q*.

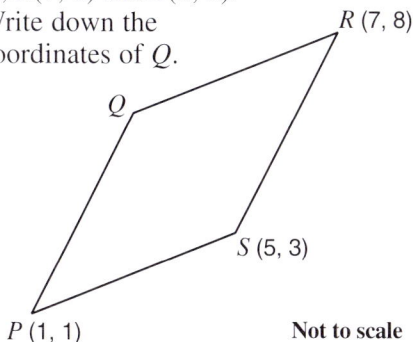

Not to scale

(b) The parallelogram is enlarged with scale factor $\frac{1}{2}$, centre *P*(1, 1). Write down the new coordinates of *S*. SEG 1999

8 By writing down the prime factors of 126 and 210, find the highest common factor of 126 and 210. You **must** show all your working. SEG 1998

9 A car travels at 28 metres per second. What is its speed in kilometres per hour? Give your answer to an appropriate degree of accuracy. SEG 1997

10 The table shows the ages and weights of chickens.

Age (days)	10	20	40	50	70	80	100
Weight (g)	100	300	1000	1300	2000	2000	2400

(a) Use this information to draw a scatter graph.

(b) Draw a line of best fit on the diagram.

(c) (i) Use the line of best fit to estimate the weight of a chicken aged 140 days.

(ii) Give a reason why your answer may not be very reliable. SEG 1999

11 (a) The dimensions of a cylinder are given. The following formulae represent certain quantities connected with the cylinder.

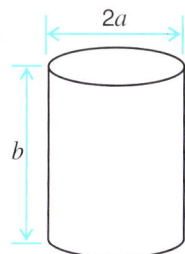

πa^2 $2\pi a$
$2\pi ab$ $\pi a^2 b$ $\pi a(a + 2b)$

Which of these formulae represents length?

(b) Water is poured into a cylinder at a constant rate. Sketch the graph of the depth of water against time.

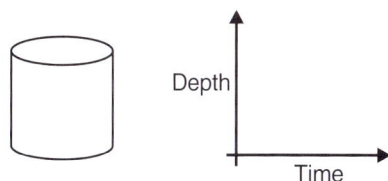

SEG 2000 S

12 The following formulae represent certain quantities connected with containers, where a, b and c are dimensions.

$$\pi a^2 b \qquad 2\pi a(a + b) \qquad 2a + 2b + 2c \qquad \tfrac{1}{2}(a + b)c \qquad \sqrt{a^2 + b^2}$$

(a) Which of these formulae represent area?

(b) Which of these formulae represent volume?

SEG 1999

13 The table shows the distribution of the weights of a sample of 80 fish.

Weight (g)	100 -	120 -	140 -	160 -	180 -	200 -	220 -	240 -
Frequency	5	8	17	23	12	9	6	0

(a) Complete the cumulative frequency table for the data and use it to draw a cumulative frequency graph.

Weight (g)	< 120	< 140	< 160	< 180	< 200	< 220	< 240
Cumulative Frequency							

(b) Use your graph to estimate
   (i) the median weight,
   (ii) the interquartile range.

(c) Another sample of 80 fish have a median weight of 340 g and an interquartile range of 10 g.
   Compare and comment on the weights of these two samples of fish.

SEG 2000 S

14 The table below illustrates the age distribution in a village of 360 people.

Age	0 -	10 -	20 -	30 -	40 -	50 -	60 -	70 -	80 - 100
Frequency	44	51	59	68	50	35	31	18	4

(a) By completing the cumulative frequency table, draw a cumulative frequency diagram to illustrate these data.

Age (less than)	0	10	20	30	40	50	60	70	80	100
Cumulative frequency										

(b) Use your graph to estimate
   (i) the median,
   (ii) the interquartile range.

(c) The age distribution of another village has a median age of 45 years and interquartile range equal to 20 years.
   Compare the distributions of the age of people in these two villages.

SEG 1998 S

15 A dice is biased as follows:
   the probability of scoring a 6 is 0.4;
   the probability of scoring a 5 is 0.2.

(a) The dice is thrown once.
   Calculate the probability of scoring a 5 or a 6.

(b) The dice is thrown twice and the scores are added together.
   Calculate the probability of getting a total of 11.

SEG 2000 S

16 A bag contains ten counters which are either coloured red or blue.
Each counter is numbered either 1, 2 or 3.
This table shows how the counters are coloured and numbered.

		Number		
		1	2	3
Colour	Red	3	0	2
	Blue	1	4	0

One counter is taken from the bag at random.

(a) (i) Calculate the probability that the counter is red or numbered 1.
(ii) Calculate the probability that the counter is red and numbered 1 or blue and numbered 2.

The counter is put back in the bag.
Two counters are then taken from the bag at random.

(b) Find the probability that the sum of the numbers on the counters is 4 **and** that the counters have the same colour.   SEG 2000 S

17 The diagram shows two spinners.
Spinner A has four equal sectors and spinner B has six equal sectors.
The sectors are numbered as shown.

Spinner A   **Spinner B**

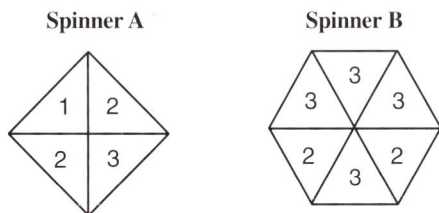

Each spinner is spun once, spinner A followed by spinner B.

(a) Copy and complete the tree diagram for both spinners.

Spinner A   **Spinner B**

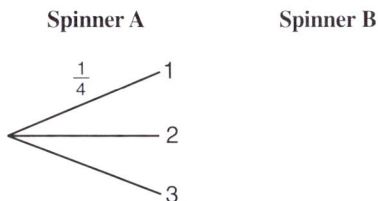

(b) What is the probability of getting a score of 3 with each spinner?
(c) The scores on the two spinners are added.
What is the probability of getting a total score of 5?   SEG 1999

18 ABC is a right-angled triangle.

Not to scale

$\cos ACB = \frac{4}{5}$.
$AC = 15$ cm.
Calculate AB.

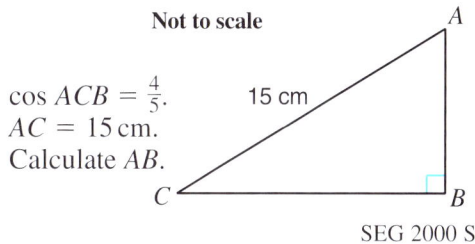

SEG 2000 S

19 (a) A number sequence begins
3,   6,   11,   18,   27,   … .
Write an expression, in terms of n, for the nth term of this sequence.
(b) Factorise completely $4a^2 - 2ab$.
(c) Multiply out and simplify
$(x + 2)(2x - 1)$.   SEG 1999

20 (a) Solve the equation
$4x - 1 = 2(x + 4)$.
(b) Solve the simultaneous equations
$2x + 3y = 5$
$3x - 2y = 14$.
You **must** show all your working.
(c) Solve the equation
$x^2 - 11x + 24 = 0$.   SEG 1999

21 (a) Solve these equations.
(i) $4(x - 1) = 9$
(ii) $3x + 2 = \frac{x}{3}$
(b) Solve the simultaneous equations.
$x + 3y = 29$
$2x - y = 23$
You **must** show all your working.   SEG 1998

22 (a) Complete the table of values for
$y = x^2 - x - 1$.

x	-2	-1	0	1	2	3
y		1	-1			5

(b) Draw the graph of $y = x^2 - x - 1$ for the values of x from -2 to 3.
(c) (i) Use your graph to solve the equation $x^2 - x - 1 = 2$.
(ii) Use your graph to solve the equation $x^2 - x - 1 = x$.
(d) The graph of $y = x^2 - x - 1$ and a graph of the form $y = ax^2 + b$ can be used to solve the equation
$2x^2 - x - 6 = 0$.
Find the values of a and b.   SEG 1999

Practice Exam Questions

23 (a) Calculate the value of 0.2^3.
(b) Calculate the value of $5^{-3} \times 8^{\frac{1}{3}}$.
Give your answer as a decimal.

SEG 2000 S

24 (a) Write the number $0.\dot{2}\dot{1}$ as a fraction in its simplest form.
(b) A rational number, R, is given by the formula $R = (3 - \sqrt{2})^2 + x$.
Calculate a possible value of x.

SEG 1999

25 (a) (i) Find a fraction that is equal to the recurring decimal $0.12222 \ldots$
(ii) Which of the following are rational?

$0.12222 \ldots,$

$(0.1222 \ldots)^2,$

$\sqrt{0.12222 \ldots}$

When π is used in a calculation, only an approximate value is used.
(b) Explain why it is only possible to use an approximate value for π.

SEG 1996

26 Simplify the following expressions, leaving your answer in surd form.
(a) $\sqrt{8} + \sqrt{18}$.
(b) $\sqrt{32} \times \sqrt{27}$.

SEG 1999

27 Cho Oyu, a mountain in Nepal, is 26 900 feet high, to the nearest 100 feet. Snowdon, a mountain in Britain, is 3550 feet high, to the nearest 50 feet. What is the lower bound of the difference in height between Cho Oyu and Snowdon?

SEG 2000 S

28 A GCSE student is planning a statistics project to investigate the proportion of left-handed students at his school.
(a) Describe how the student could obtain a stratified random sample of 60 pupils from his school of 380 girls and 320 boys.
(b) State **one** advantage of stratified random sampling over simple random sampling.

SEG 1997

29 AB, BC and CA are tangents to the circle at P, Q and R respectively.
The centre of the circle is at O.
AC is parallel to PO and angle ACB is $40°$.

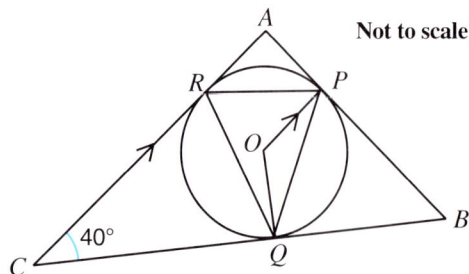

Work out angle POQ.

SEG 1999

30 Alena and Ben design a questionnaire about the reading habits of pupils in their school.
(a) One of their questions is:
"How often do you read each week?"
Give **one** reason why this question is unsatisfactory.

(b) Ben asks pupils in the school library at lunchtime to complete the questionnaire.
Give **one** reason why this is unsatisfactory.

(c) Alena wants to investigate the reading habits of boys and girls of different ages.
Describe how she could obtain a stratified sample to do this.

SEG 1998

31 Carol has a bag of sweets. The bag contains two toffees, three candies and five mints.
She picks a sweet, at random, and eats it. She then picks a second sweet, at random.
(a) What is the probability that both sweets are toffees?
(b) Draw a probability tree diagram to show all the possible outcomes for the two sweets.
Fill in the probabilities on the branches of your tree diagram.
(c) What is the probability that the second sweet that Carol picks will be a toffee?

SEG 1999

32 These triangles are similar. The lengths are measured in centimetres.

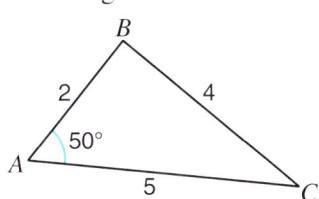

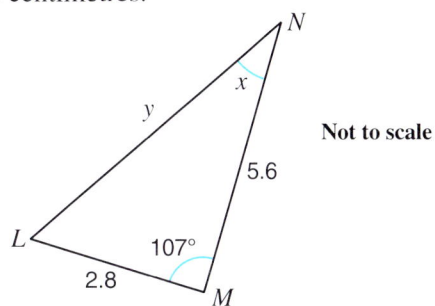

Not to scale

(a) Calculate the angle x.

(b) Calculate the length y.

(c) (i) Which of triangles **X**, **Y** and **Z** are **definitely** congruent to triangle ABC?

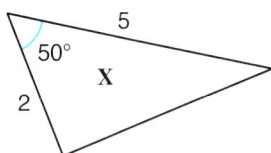

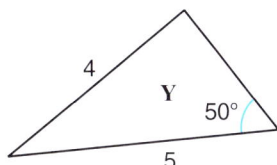

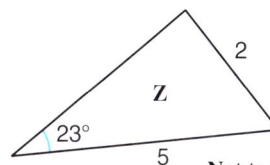

Not to scale

(ii) Explain your answer.

SEG 2000 S

33 One hundred females were asked how many hours of television they watched in one week.

(a) This histogram shows the results.

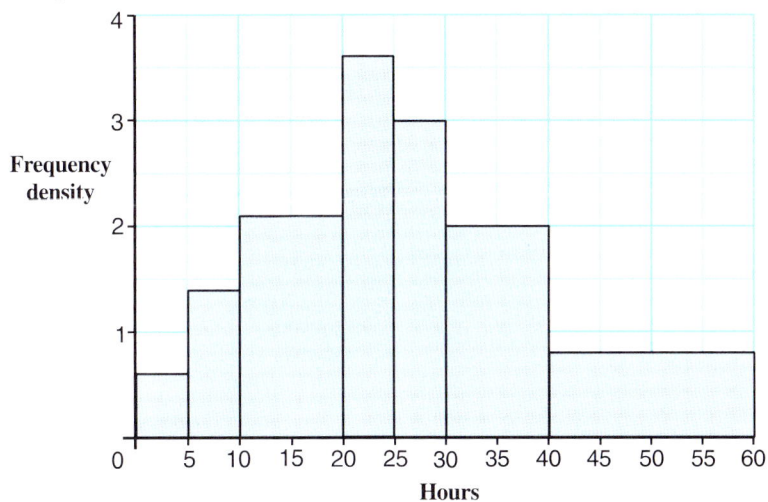

(i) How many of the females watched television for between 10 and 25 hours in the week?

(ii) Estimate the number of females who watched television for more than 35 hours in the week.

The one hundred females were chosen, at random, from customers leaving a supermarket on a Saturday morning.

(b) Give one reason why this method of choosing a sample is unsatisfactory.

SEG 2000 S

34 (a) A sketch of the graph of $y = \sin x$ for $0° \leqslant x \leqslant 720°$ is shown. Find all the values of x in the interval $0° \leqslant x \leqslant 720°$ that satisfy $\sin x = \frac{1}{2}$.

(b) Find all the values of x which satisfy the equation $\cos x = -\cos 30°$ in the interval $0° \leqslant x \leqslant 720°$.

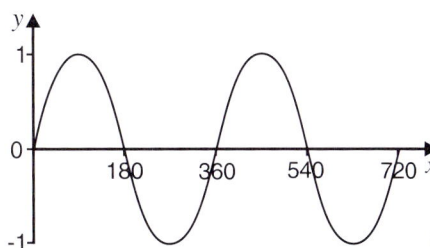

SEG 1997

35 The graph of $y = x^2$ is sketched on the axes.
Copy the diagram.
On the same axes sketch and label the graphs of
(a) $y = (x - 2)^2$,
(b) $y = x^2 - 2$.

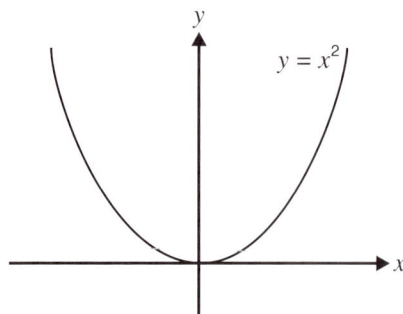

$y = x^2$

SEG 1994

36 (a) The pupils in classes 8A and 8B in a school take a test.
This table shows the means and standard deviations of their marks.

	Mean	Standard Deviation
Class 8A	33.8	8.6
Class 8B	29.6	9.2

(i) Which class has the greater variation in marks?
Explain your answer.
(ii) One page was missing from the test paper taken by class **8B**.
To allow for this each mark is increased by 5.
What is the new mean and standard deviation for class **8B**'s marks?

(b) These histograms show the distribution of marks for classes **8A** and **8B** in a **different** test.

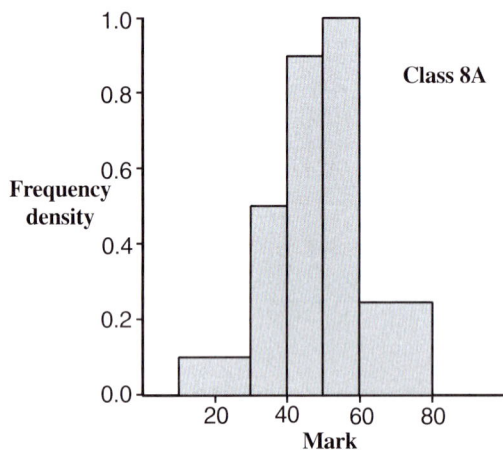

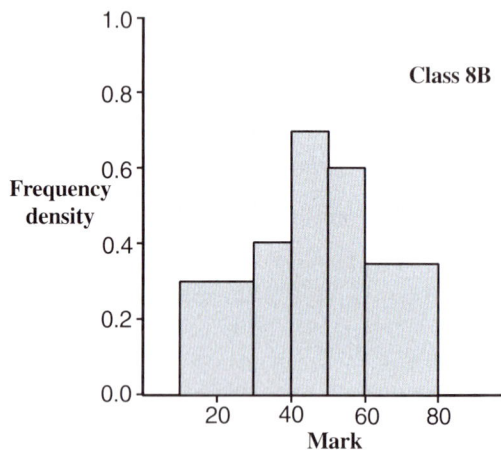

Which class has the smaller standard deviation of marks?
Give a reason for your answer.

SEG 2000 S

37 (a) Multiply out $(2x + 3)(x - 4)$. Simplify your answer.
(b) $x^2 - 8x + a = (x - b)^2$
Find the numerical value of a.
(c) Write as a single fraction $\dfrac{1}{x - 3} + \dfrac{1}{x + 4}$.
(d) The expression $\dfrac{1}{\sqrt{a}} = a^n$ is true for all values of a. Find the value of n.

SEG 1998 S

38 Simplify fully the expression $\dfrac{7x + 21}{2x^2 + 5x - 3}$.

SEG 1999

39 If $\dfrac{1}{x - 1} - \dfrac{1}{x + 5} = 2$ show that $x^2 + 4x - 8 = 0$.

SEG 1999

40 $ABCD$ is a rectangular, horizontal yard. AP and BQ are vertical poles. PQ is a straight wire between P and Q.

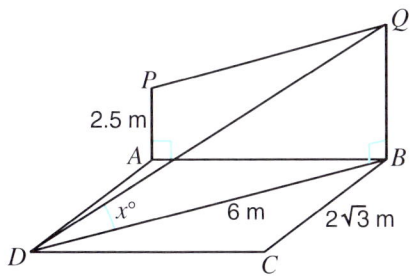

$AP = 2.5$ metres, $BD = 6$ metres and $BC = 2\sqrt{3}$ metres.

Sin $x = 0.6$
Cos $x = 0.8$
Tan $x = 0.75$

$x°$ is the angle of elevation of Q from D.

The length of the wire, PQ, can be written in the form $a\sqrt{b}$ where a and b are prime numbers.

Calculate the values of a and b.

SEG 2000 S

41 The diagram shows two sets of parallel lines.

Vector $\overrightarrow{AB} = \mathbf{x}$ and vector $\overrightarrow{AH} = \mathbf{y}$.

$AC = 4AB$ and $AH = \frac{1}{2}AG$.

Not to scale

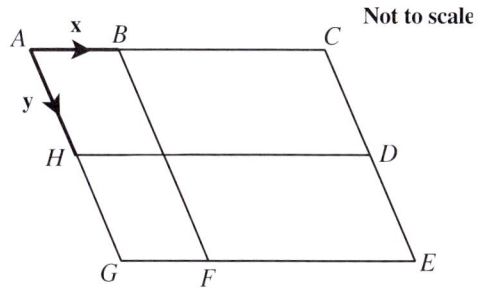

(a) Write the vector $\overrightarrow{AF}$ in terms of $\mathbf{x}$ and $\mathbf{y}$.

(b) Write the vector $\overrightarrow{BG}$ in terms of $\mathbf{x}$ and $\mathbf{y}$.

(c) Find **two** different vectors that can be written as $\mathbf{y} + 4\mathbf{x}$.

(d) Write down **two** statements about line segments which have the same vector.

SEG 1998

42 The coordinates of the points in the region **R** satisfy the inequalities:

$y > (x - 1)(x + 2)$
$2y > 3x + 6$
$x + 2y \leqslant 2$

By representing these inequalities on a graph find the maximum value of $2x + y$ in **R**, where x and y are integers.

SEG 2000 S

43 (a) One of these formulae represents the shaded area. Use dimensions to decide which one.

$A = \pi a^2 b^2$
$A = \pi (ab)^2$
$A = 2\pi (b - a)$
$A = \pi (b + a)(b - a)$

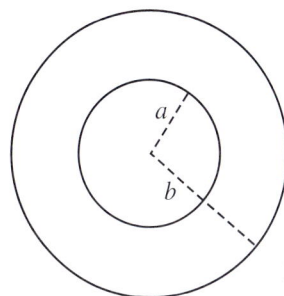

Not to scale

(b) One of these formulae represents the volume of the shape drawn on the right. Use dimensions to decide which one.

$V = \frac{1}{2}\pi c^2 d^2$

$V = \frac{1}{2}\pi cd^2$

$V = \frac{1}{2}\pi (cd)^2$

$V = \frac{1}{2}\pi cd$

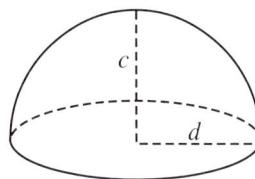

Not to scale

SEG 1998

Exam Practice - Calculator Paper

1 Find the value of $\dfrac{3.92^2}{19.2 - 0.87}$.

Give your answer to an accuracy of 2 significant figures.

SEG 1999

2 This formula gives R in terms of a, b and c.

$$R = \sqrt{\dfrac{2a + b}{c}}$$

Sam wants to find the value of R when $a = 6.87$, $b = 11.31$ and $c = 6.109$.

(a) (i) Write down the numbers Sam could use to estimate the value of R.

(ii) Use these numbers to estimate R **without using a calculator**. You **must** show all your working.

(b) Use your calculator to find the value of R correct to 3 significant figures.

SEG 1998

3 ABCDE is a regular pentagon. ABO and DCO are straight lines which intersect at O.

Not to scale

Calculate angle x.

SEG 2000 S

4 One hundred children were asked to complete a jigsaw puzzle.
The table shows the distribution of the time taken to complete the puzzle by the children.

Time (minutes)	0 -	4 -	8 -	12 -	16 -	20 -	24 -
Frequency	0	13	19	30	26	12	0

(a) Draw a frequency polygon to show this information.

(b) Calculate an estimate of the mean time taken by these children to complete the puzzle.

SEG 2000 S

5 A dice is thrown.

(a) The table shows the results for the first 30 throws.

Number on dice	1	2	3	4	5	6
Frequency	8	5	6	5	4	2

What is the relative frequency of getting a 1?

The dice continues to be thrown.

(b) The following table shows the results for the first 60 throws.

Number on dice	1	2	3	4	5	6
Frequency	17	11	10	9	10	3

What is the relative frequency of getting a 1?

(c) Do you think the dice is biased? Give a reason for your answer.

(d) Estimate the number of times a 1 or 6 will occur when the dice is thrown 600 times.

SEG 2000 S

6 Four balls, each of radius 5 cm, are packed tightly inside a cylinder of height 10 cm.

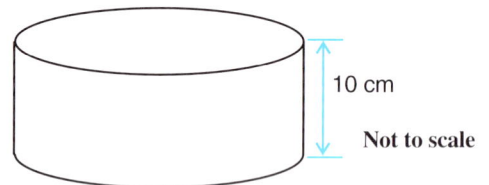

10 cm

Not to scale

This diagram shows a plan view of the balls inside the cylinder.

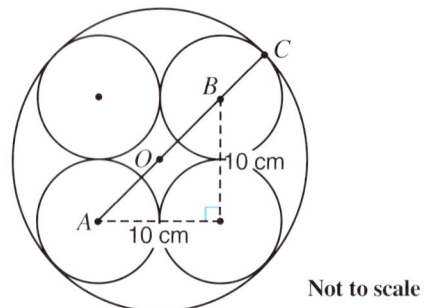

Not to scale

O is the centre of the cylinder.
A and B are the centres of balls.

(a) By calculating the length AB, find the radius of the cylinder, OC.

(b) Calculate the volume of wasted space inside the cylinder.

SEG 1999

526

7 The diagram shows a circle with diameter *AB*.
C is a point on the circumference and angle *ABC* = 90°.
AB = 6.25 cm and *BC* = 6.0 cm.

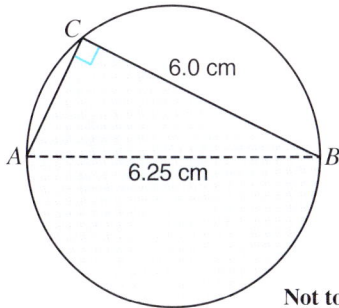

6.0 cm

A ------- 6.25 cm ------- *B*

Not to scale

(a) Calculate the length of *AC*.
(b) Calculate the area of the shaded shape.

SEG 1998

8 The diagram shows the end view of a building.

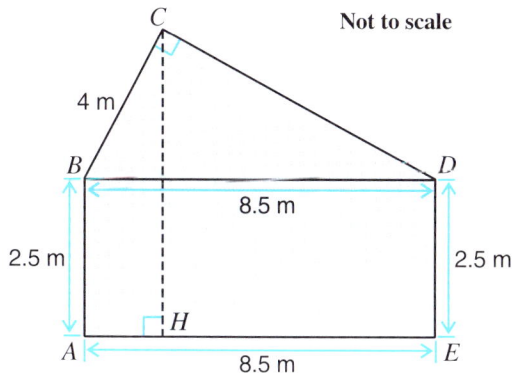

Not to scale

4 m

8.5 m

2.5 m   2.5 m

H

A ◄—— 8.5 m ——► *E*

BCD is a right-angled triangle.
Angle *BCD* = 90°.
BC = 4 m and *BD* = 8.5 m.
(a) Calculate angle *CBD*.

CH is perpendicular to *AE*.
AB = *ED* = 2.5 m.
(b) Calculate *CH*, the height of the building.

SEG 1999

9 The area of the United Kingdom is 244 018 square kilometres.
(a) Write 244 018 in standard form, correct to three significant figures.

The area of the Earth is 5.09×10^8 square kilometres.
(b) Calculate the area of the United Kingdom as a percentage of the area of the Earth.

SEG 1999

10 Not to scale

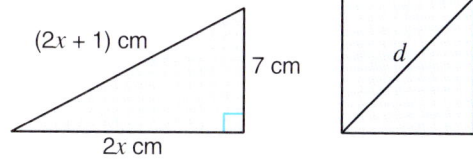

(2x + 1) cm   7 cm   *d*

2x cm

The square has the same perimeter as the triangle.
The triangle is right-angled and has an area of 84 cm².
Calculate the length, *d*, of the diagonal of the square.
Give your answer correct to one decimal place.

SEG 1998 S

11 Evaluate 0.07^4, giving your answer in standard form.

SEG 1998

12 Asif invested £7200 for three years.
During the first two years his investment grew at the rate of 14% per year. In the third year the investment lost 45% of its value.
Calculate the final value of Asif's investment.

SEG 1998

13 Sanjay gets a 4.5% wage increase.
His new wage is £8.36 per hour.
How much did he earn per hour before his wage increase?

SEG 1999

14 A train travels from Hiroshima to Kokura in 44 minutes.
The distance is 120 miles.
(a) Find the average speed of the train in miles per hour.
(b) Another train has an average speed 20% lower than this.
What is the percentage increase in the time taken?

SEG 1999

15 An aeroplane flies from New York to Los Angeles, a distance of 2475 miles, at an average speed of 427 miles per hour.
How long does the flight take in hours and minutes?

SEG 1997

527

16 You are given the formula $P = \dfrac{V^2}{R}$.

    (a)   Work out the value of P when $V = 3.85$ and $R = \frac{8}{5}$.

    (b)   Rearrange the formula to give V in terms of P and R.

SEG 1999

17 A solution of the equation $x^3 - 5x = 21$ lies between $x = 3$ and $x = 4$.
Use trial and improvement to find this solution.
Give your answer correct to 2 decimal places.
You **must** show all your trials.

SEG 1999

18 The diagram shows part of a roof structure.

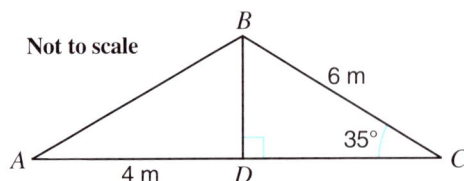

$AD = 4\,\text{m}$, $BC = 6\,\text{m}$ and angle $BCD = 35°$.
BD is perpendicular to AC.
    (a)   Calculate the height of BD.
    (b)   Calculate angle BAC.

SEG 2000 S

19   (a)   Use the formula $v = \sqrt{u^2 + 2as}$ to find the value of v when $u = 24$, $a = -9.8$ and $s = 10\frac{1}{4}$.

    (b)   **Without using a calculator**, use approximation to check that your answer to (a) is of the correct order of magnitude.
You **must** show all your working.

SEG 1996

20 A lorry moving ore in a gold mine carries 3.19×20^4 kilograms of ore.
The ore contains 1.89×10^2 grams of gold. What percentage of the ore is gold?
Give your answer in standard form.

SEG 1998

21 George passes three sets of traffic lights on his way to work.
The lights work independently of each other.
The probability that he has to stop at any set of traffic lights is 0.35.
What is the probability that George stops at two or three sets of traffic lights?

SEG 1998

22 In a survey of one hundred shoppers the amount of money that they spent at shop A is recorded.

Amount spent (£)	0 -	20 -	40 -	60 -	80 -	100 -	120 - 100
Frequency	8	8	18	26	20	12	8

Calculate an estimate of the mean amount of money spent at shop A.

SEG 1999

23 The weights of a sample of 100 cooking apples from an orchard are shown in this table.

Weight w (grams)	$50 \leqslant w < 100$	$100 \leqslant w < 150$	$150 \leqslant w < 200$	$200 \leqslant w < 250$	$250 \leqslant w < 300$
Frequency	11	21	32	27	9

   (a) Calculate an estimate of the mean weight of the cooking apples in the sample.

   (b) (i) Copy and complete this cumulative frequency table for the weights of the cooking apples.

Weight, w (grams)	< 100	< 150	< 200	< 250	< 300
Cumulative frequency					

       (ii) Draw a cumulative frequency diagram for the sample of cooking apples.

   (c) Estimate the median weight of the cooking apples in the sample.

There are approximately 12 500 cooking apples in the orchard.

   (d) (i) Should the median weight or the mean weight be used to estimate the total weight of apples in the orchard?
Give a reason for your answer.

      (ii) All cooking apples weighing more than 210 g each are sold to a company who make apple pies.
Estimate the **total** number of cooking apples sold to this company.

SEG 1999

24 (a) The volume of a cone is given by the formula $V = \frac{1}{3}\pi r^2 h$.
Rearrange the formula to give r, in terms of V and h.

   (b) These cones are similar.

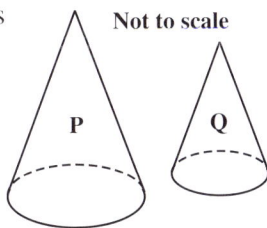

Not to scale

P   Q

The ratio of the height of P to the height of Q is 3 : 2.
The volume of P is 5.4 cm^3.
Calculate the volume of Q.

SEG 1998

25 Cone A has a height of 10 cm and a volume of 1280 cm^3.

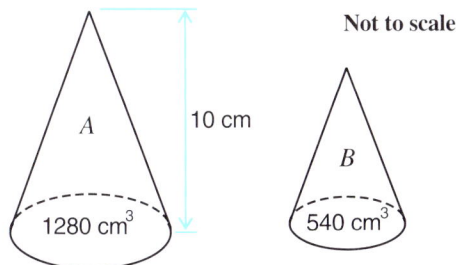

Not to scale

A   10 cm

B

1280 cm³   540 cm³

   (a) Calculate the radius of cone A.

Cone B is similar to cone A.
Cone B has a volume of 540 cm^3.

   (b) Calculate the height of cone B.

SEG 1999

26 The probability that a seedling will grow is 0.9.
Two seedlings are chosen at random and planted.

   (a) What is the probability that neither seedling will grow?

   (b) What is the probability that at least one of the seedlings will grow?

SEG 2000 S

27 The diagram shows a pyramid with a horizontal rectangular base $ABCD$.
$AB = 6$ cm and $BC = 5$ cm.
The top of the pyramid, V, is directly above the centre of the base.
$VA = VB = VC = VD = 8$ cm.

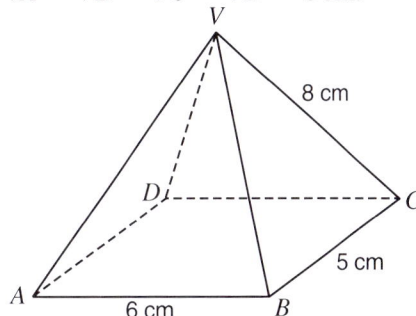

V

8 cm

D   C

A   6 cm   B   5 cm

   (a) Calculate the height of V above the base.

   (b) Calculate the angle between VA and the base $ABCD$.

   (c) Calculate the angle between the face VBC and the base $ABCD$.

   (d) Calculate the angle between the face VAB and the base $ABCD$.

28 (a) A solution of the equation $x^3 - 3x = 72$ lies between $x = 4$ and 5.
Use the method of trial and improvement to find this solution. Give your answer to one decimal place. You **must** show all your trials.
(b) Solve the equation $x^2 + 3x = 0$.
(c) Solve the inequality $-1 \leqslant 3x + 2 < 5$.

SEG 2000 S

29 Angles x and y lie between 0° and 360°.
(a) Find the **two** values of x which satisfy the equation $\cos x = 0.5$.
(b) Solve the equation $\sin y = \cos 240°$.

SEG 1999

30 The diagram shows a circle, centre O. The chord BA is parallel to the tangent QC.
PBQ and QCR are tangents.
Angle $PBA = 63°$. $QC = 6\,\text{cm}$.

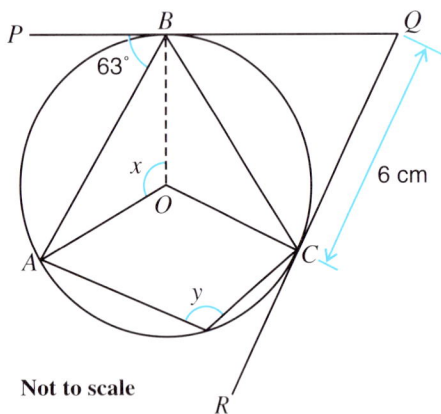

Not to scale

(a) **Calculate** the value of angle x and angle y.
(b) Write down the value of angle PQR and hence calculate the area of triangle BQC.

SEG 1998 S

31 The diagram shows triangle ABC.
$AB = 8.6\,\text{cm}$, $BC = 3.1\,\text{cm}$ and $AC = 9.7\,\text{cm}$.

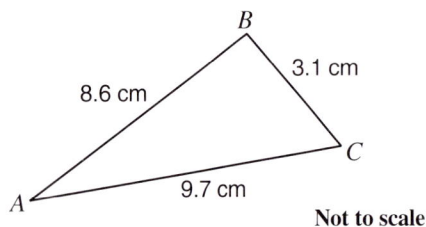

Not to scale

Calculate angle ABC.

SEG 1999

32 The diagram shows a window in the shape of a segment, ABC, of a circle of radius 48 cm, centre O.
The lower edge of the window is 90 cm wide.

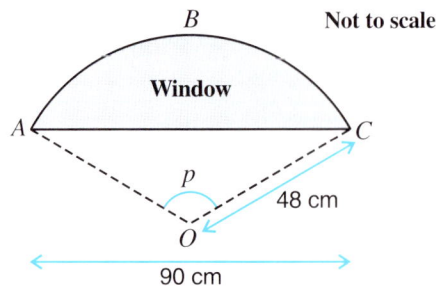

(a) Calculate the size of angle p.
(b) Calculate the area of the window.

SEG 1999

33 X and Y are two points on the bank of a river. Z is a third point on the opposite bank of the river.
$XY = 50\,\text{m}$.
Angle $XYZ = 40°$.
Angle $XZY = 84°$.

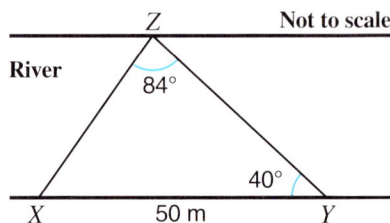

Assuming that the river banks are straight and parallel, calculate the width of the river.

SEG 2000 S

34 The table shows the number of students in years 7 and 8 of a school.
A sample of 100 of these students are asked some questions about sport.
The students are part of a stratified random sample.
There are 125 boys in year 7.

Year	Students
7	226
8	273

(a) How many boys and how many girls from year 7 should be included in the sample?
(b) What is the advantage in choosing a stratified random sample rather than a simple random sample for this survey?

SEG 2000 S

35 The table shows the annual salaries of employees of a certain firm.

Salaries (£ x thousands)	$10 \leqslant x < 15$	$15 \leqslant x < 20$	$20 \leqslant x < 30$	$30 \leqslant x < 40$	$40 \leqslant x < 50$
Number of employees	20	60	13	0	6

(a) (i) By using the midpoint of each class interval, calculate an estimate of the mean salary.
   (ii) Calculate an estimate of the median salary.
   (iii) A trade union representative at the firm claims that salaries are too low. In order to support this claim he quotes the average salary. Should he use the mean or the median?
       Explain your answer.

(b) Draw a histogram for the data in the table.

SEG 1997

36 In a strength competition Jan has up to three attempts to lift a weight.
The probability that he lifts the weight on his first attempt is 0.8.
As he gets tired, the probability that he lifts the weight on his second attempt is 0.4 and on his third attempt is 0.3.
Calculate the probability that Jan fails to lift the weight.

SEG 1997

37 An atlas gives the population of Singapore as 2 690 000 and its land area as 4290 km².
The population density, in people/km², of a country is defined by

$$\text{population density} = \frac{\text{population}}{\text{land area}}.$$

(a) Find the population density for Singapore, giving your answer in standard form.

(b) The population has been given to the nearest 10 000 and the land area to the nearest 10 km².
   (i) By considering the maximum and minimum possible values for the population and land area of Singapore, determine the maximum possible population density.
   (ii) The population density is predicted to reach 700 by the year 2000. By taking this predicted population density of 700, find the maximum percentage growth in population that this represents.

SEG 1997

38 The marks in a History test taken by class 10A are shown.

50   54   56   57   59   60   63
64   66   67   68   69   69   71
74   75   77   77   80   84

(a) The mean of these marks is 67. Calculate their standard deviation.

Twenty pupils in class 10B also take the test.
Their marks have a mean of 60 and standard deviation of 21.

(b) Comment on the differences between the marks for class 10A and class 10B.

(c) Five pupils in class 10C take the test.
   Each of them obtains the same score of 55 marks.
   Explain why the standard deviation of these marks is zero.

SEG 2000 S

39 ABCD is a rectangular region of length 10.2 m and area 55.25 m².

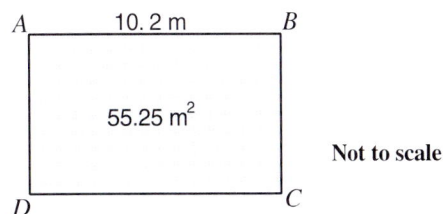

The length is given to the nearest 10 cm.
The area is given to the nearest 0.05 m².
Calculate the lower bound of the width of the region.

SEG 2000 S

40 Cylinder A has radius y and height $2x$.
Sphere B has radius x.

    (a) The total surface area of cylinder A is
given by the expression $2\pi y^2 + 4\pi xy$.
Factorise this expression completely.

    (b) Cylinder A has the same surface area as
sphere B.
Show that $y^2 = 2x(x - y)$.

    (c) Calculate the value of x when $y = 3$.
Give your answer to an accuracy of 1 decimal place.

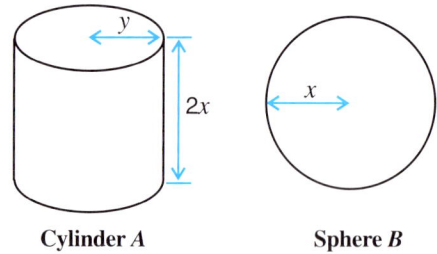

Cylinder A   **Sphere B**

SEG 1998

41 (a) Show that the equation $2x^2 + 6x - 32 = 0$ can be rearranged to give $x = \dfrac{16}{x + 3}$.

    (b) Use the equation $x = \dfrac{16}{x + 3}$

    and an iterative method to find the **positive** solution of $2x^2 + 6x - 32 = 0$.
Give your answer correct to one decimal place.
You **must** show all your iterations.

SEG 1999

42 Solve the equation $\dfrac{6}{2x - 1} - \dfrac{3}{x + 1} = 1$

SEG 2000 S

43 In the formula $y = ab^x$, a and b are positive rational numbers.
When $x = 0$, $y = 10$ and when $x = -2$, $y = 40$.
Calculate the value of x when $y = 160$.

SEG 1999

44 Jane goes for a bicycle ride.
Her journey goes down and then up a hill.
This graph shows her speed during her journey.

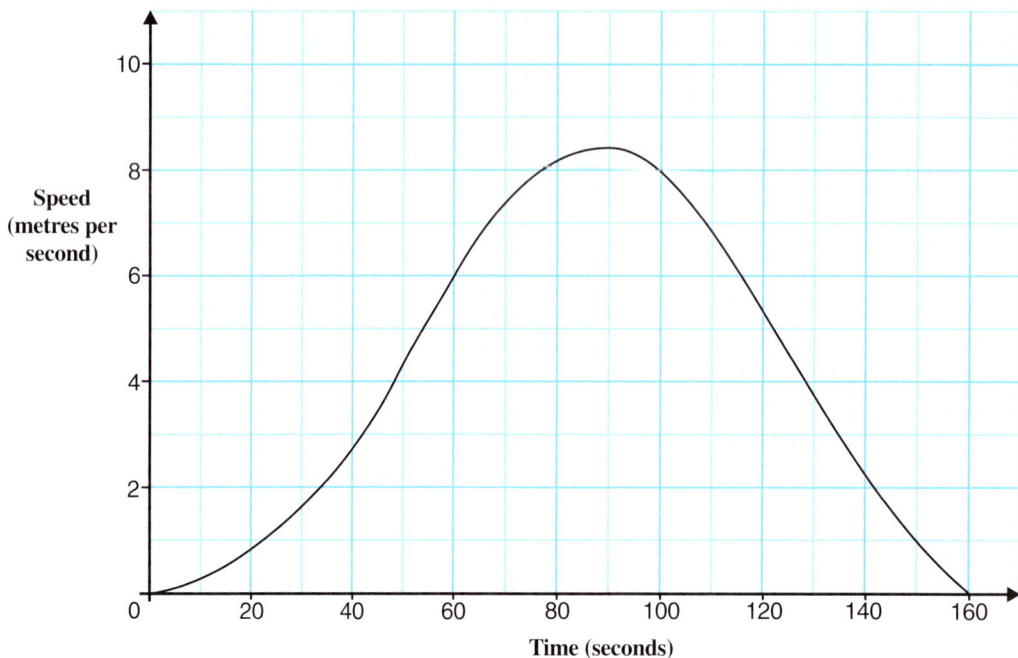

    (a) Use the graph to estimate Jane's acceleration 70 seconds after the start of her journey.

    (b) Use an appropriate method, with intervals of 20 seconds, to estimate the distance that
Jane travels.

SEG 1999

45 The expression $x^2 - 10x + 14 + a$, where a is an integer, can be written in the form $(x - b)^2$, where b is an integer.
   (a) Calculate the values of a and b.
   (b) Solve the equation $x^2 - 10x + 14 = 0$.

46 The number of fish, F, needed to stock a lake is proportional to the cube of the width, W metres, of the lake. The number of fish needed to stock a lake of width 100 m is 2700.
   (a) Find the equation connecting F and W.
   (b) Find the number of fish when the width of the lake is 200 metres.
   (c) Find the width of the lake when 4800 fish are needed.

SEG 1999

47 The illumination, L, provided by a light bulb is inversely proportional to the square of the distance, d, from the bulb.
When $L = 40$, $d = 5$.
   (a) Find an equation expressing L in terms of d.
   (b) Find the value of L when d is 20.

SEG 2000 S

48 The graph of $y = \dfrac{12}{x} + 5$ is shown.
Copy the graph.
Draw another graph for values of x where $-3 \leqslant x \leqslant 3$ and, hence, solve the
equation $x^3 - 2x - \dfrac{12}{x} - 5 = 0$.

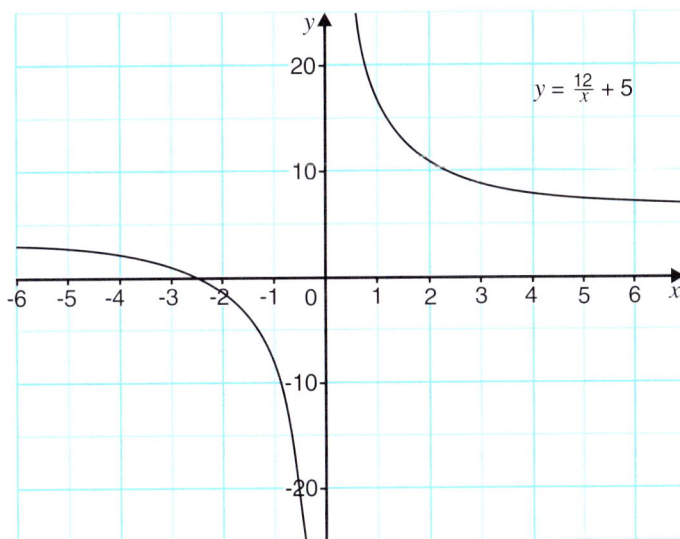

SEG 1999

49 Gary has produced this set of experimental data in his science lesson.
Gary knows that the two variables are connected by a formula $y = ax^2 + b$ where a and b are constants.

x	1.2	2.5	3.6	4.0	5.2
y	-3	7	20	26	48

   (a) Calculate the values of x^2 and plot the graph of y against x^2.
   (b) Use your graph to estimate the values of a and b.

SEG 1999

50 In an experiment, Tim obtains these values of x and y.
Tim knows that the relationship connecting x and y is of the form $y = \dfrac{a}{x} + b$.
By plotting an appropriate graph, find the values of a and b.

x	1	5
y	65	17

SEG 2000 S

GCSE Mathematics Coursework   ●●●●●●

All GCSE mathematics courses include a coursework component to test your ability to use and apply mathematics. The coursework component is worth 20% of the overall marks in examinations in mathematics. The style of coursework depends on the syllabus you are taking.

Why do I have to do coursework?

Coursework gives you the opportunity to use and apply a range of mathematical knowledge and skills. With coursework, you have the chance to be a 'real-life mathematician'.
Another important reason is that you may suffer from examination anxiety. Coursework gives you the opportunity to demonstrate the knowledge and skills which you possess.

How is coursework marked?

Coursework is marked against a set of assessment criteria which are common to all examination boards. Whilst administrative procedures may differ between boards the same coursework criteria are used by all. These criteria are divided into three strands:
1. Making and monitoring decisions to solve problems
2. Communicating mathematically
3. Developing skills of mathematical reasoning

How each strand is used to assess different aspects of your work

1. Making and monitoring decisions to solve problems
This strand is about deciding what needs to be done then doing it. You will need to select an appropriate method, obtain information and introduce your own questions to develop the task further.

> For the higher marks you will need to analyse alternative approaches, coordinate a number of variables and apply independently a range of appropriate mathematical techniques.

2. Communicating mathematically
This strand is about communicating what you are doing using words, tables, diagrams and symbols. You will need to consider how you present your mathematics, decide whether it is appropriate and amend as necessary.
For example, you might consider whether your chosen table of results allows you to find a rule or whether it might be better to draw a graph or to express your findings using symbols.

> For the higher marks you will need to use mathematical symbols accurately, concisely and efficiently in presenting a reasoned argument.

3. Developing skills of mathematical reasoning
This strand is about testing, explaining and justifying what you have done. You will need to search for patterns or rules and provide generalisations. Generalisations (or hypotheses in the case of statistics) will need to be tested, justified, explained, modified and proved.

> For the higher marks you will need to provide a sophisticated and rigorous justification, argument or proof which demonstrates a mathematical insight into the problem.

What do I have to do to get a particular grade in coursework?

Information on what you have to do to get a particular grade is provided under the heading of 'Grade Descriptors'. The following grade descriptors are provided to give a general indication of the standards of achievement you will need to show in order to achieve the given grades:

Grade F
In order to carry through tasks and solve mathematical problems, you identify and obtain necessary information; you check your results, considering whether these are sensible. You show understanding of situations, by describing them mathematically using symbols, words and diagrams. You make general statements of your own, based on evidence you have produced, and give an explanation of your reasoning.

Grade C
Starting from problems or contexts that have been presented, you introduce questions of your own which generate a fuller solution. You examine critically and justify your choice of mathematical presentation, considering alternative approaches and explaining improvements you have made. You justify your generalisations or solutions, showing some insight into the mathematical structure of the situation being investigated. You appreciate the difference between a mathematical explanation and experimental evidence.

Grade A
You give reasons for the choices you make when investigating within mathematics itself or when using mathematics to analyse tasks; these reasons explain why particular lines of enquiry are followed and others are rejected. You apply the mathematics you know in familiar and unfamiliar contexts. You use mathematical language and symbols effectively in presenting a convincing reasoned argument. Your report includes mathematical justifications and explains your solutions to problems involving a number of features or variables.

How will each strand be marked?

Each strand will be marked out of 8 according to the following criteria which have been interpreted for you to make them easier to understand.

Making and monitoring decisions to solve problems

Comment	Mark
You have tried simple approaches to solve the problem	1
You have developed and used your own strategy to solve the problem	2
You have identified and obtained the necessary information to solve the problem	3
You have broken down the given task to solve it in a methodical fashion	4
You have introduced your own relevant questions beyond that given	5
You have developed and followed through alternative approaches involving high level mathematics (beyond that required for grade C)	6
You have analysed and given reasons for your approach which involves a number of mathematical features or variables	7
You have explored independently and extensively an area of mathematics with which you were originally unfamiliar	8

Communicating mathematically

Comment	Mark
You explained your thinking and organised your work	1
You presented information in a clear and organised way	2
You showed your understanding by illustrating information using symbols, words and diagrams	3
You used appropriate forms of presentation with linking explanation and interpretation	4
You considered alternative approaches to your presentation which enabled you to make further progress with the task	5
You used mathematical symbols consistently (implying the use of algebra in a conventional way)	6
You used mathematical symbols and language accurately in presenting a reasoned argument	7
You used mathematical symbols concisely and efficiently	8

Developing skills and mathematical reasoning

Comment	Mark
You showed some understanding of the task by finding particular examples	1
You gathered further data in an attempt to find a pattern that applied to more than one case	2
You made a generalisation from your own evidence	3
You confirmed the generalisation by testing further examples	4
You provided a justification for the generalisation by showing mathematical insight into the problem	5
You examined the generalisation or solution constructively and made further progress on the task	6
You provided a sophisticated justification which coordinated a number of mathematical features or variables	7
You provided a mathematically rigorous justification, argument or proof which included the conditions for its validity	8

How will my coursework be graded?

Each of the three strands will be marked out of 8 to give a total of 24 marks.
This can then be converted into a GCSE grade by the examination board.
The table shows the link between the grade descriptors and the coursework mark.

Total	Grade
20	A
14	C
8	F

Types of coursework

There are three main types of coursework.

Investigational coursework

Investigational coursework will involve solving a problem by exploring different approaches and asking appropriate questions. You will usually be given a starting point for the investigation and this will give you some idea of the approach to explore. By asking appropriate questions you can extend the task and explore some different approaches which will lead you to ask further questions.

In answering the questions, it is useful to see if you can provide some generalisation which can be tested on further examples. You should also try to explain why your generalisation works and see if you can justify or prove it using some graphical, geometrical or algebraic proof.

When undertaking **investigational coursework** you should …

- Introduce the task so that the reader is clear what you are trying to do.
- Indicate how you intend to proceed with the investigation.
- Be systematic rather than haphazard.
- Keep things simple by changing only one variable at a time.
- Provide diagrams, tables and graphs to highlight possible relationships and generalisations.
- Consider the best way to present your findings and explain why you think that this is the best way.
- Test generalisations on further examples.

- Include information on generalisations that didn't work and say why they didn't work.
- Check your work and ensure that it is accurate.
- Use a computer where appropriate but explain how you programmed it to support your work.
- Provide information on how your task has been developed and the mathematical thinking behind this development.
- Reflect on the results at frequent stages and see if these pose further questions.
- Provide a conclusion which relates to the original task and any extension work undertaken.

Practical coursework

Practical coursework will involve solving some practical or real-life problem involving:

   the use of practical equipment (ruler, protractor, compasses, etc.)
   construction and measurement skills (nets, scale drawings, trigonometry, etc.)
   statistical work (see next section)
   estimation and calculation of probabilities
   simulating real-life problems using mathematics
   modelling with a computer (including databases and spreadsheets)

When undertaking **practical coursework** you should …

- Introduce the task so that the reader is clear what you are trying to do.
- Indicate how you intend to proceed with the work and what you will need.
- Provide diagrams, tables and graphs to highlight aspects of the work.
- Consider the best way to present your findings and explain why you think that this is the best way.
- Check your work and ensure that it is accurate (lengths to the nearest millimetre and angles to the nearest degree).

- Explain any measurements undertaken and detail steps to ensure their accuracy.
- Use a computer where appropriate but explain how you programmed it to support your work.
- Provide information on how your task has been developed and the mathematical thinking behind this development.
- Reflect on the results at frequent stages and see if these pose further questions.
- Provide a conclusion which relates to the original task and any extension work undertaken.

Statistical coursework

Statistical coursework is a useful vehicle for helping you to use and understand the statistics work associated with the GCSE examination. Statistical coursework can be based on 'primary' data supplied by you or else 'secondary' data which can be found in reference information such as that provided by government, business or commerce. Your statistical work should include a hypothesis which should be formulated in advance of the task being started.

Before undertaking any statistical work you should plan your work and decide what you are going to investigate. In statistical coursework, the planning stage is the most important and you need to decide:

   what you want to investigate and why you want to investigate it
   how you are going to collect the information for your investigation
   how you intend to ensure that this data is representative and free from bias
   what presumptions, if any, you are making in your investigation

The use of secondary data and comparing this with your own data is particularly recommended as an extension to your work which will allow access to the higher grades.

When undertaking **statistical coursework** you should …

- Introduce the task so that the reader is clear what you are trying to do.
- Provide a hypotheses which you intend to investigate.
- Indicate how you intend to proceed with the work, what data you will need and how you will collect it.
- Not be too ambitious and concentrate on one area of investigation at a time.
- Give reasons for the format of data collection sheets and state any assumptions you have made.
- Explain the thinking behind questions on questionnaires and include details of any improvements made.
- Provide diagrams, tables and graphs to highlight aspects of the work.
- Consider the best way to present your findings and explain why you think that this is the best way.
- Include information to explain and justify your hypothesis.
- Check your work and ensure that it is accurate (especially calculation and graph work).
- Use a computer where appropriate but explain how you programmed it to support your work.
- Provide information on how your task has been developed and the mathematical thinking behind this development.
- Reflect on the results at frequent stages and see if these pose further hypotheses..
- Provide a conclusion which relates to the original hypothesis and any extension work undertaken.

IDEAS FOR INVESTIGATION

Some chapters include ideas for investigational, practical and statistical tasks and give you the opportunity to improve and practice your skills of using and applying mathematics. You might like to refer to the advice given about the different types of coursework when trying any of the ideas for investigation.

Coursework tasks

SEG provides a variety of options to help students meet the requirements of the coursework component of the syllabuses. Centres can opt to use:
- their own tasks,
- set tasks produced by SEG.

Four examples of tasks set by SEG appear below.

Triangle rows

A triangle of side 3 units is drawn on triangular paper.
Numbers are written in each triangle as shown.

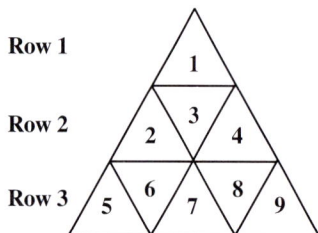

Row 1
Row 2
Row 3

The first number in Row 1 is 1.
The first number in Row 2 is 2.
The first number in Row 3 is 5.

A triangle of side 4 units is now drawn.
Numbers are written in each triangle as shown.

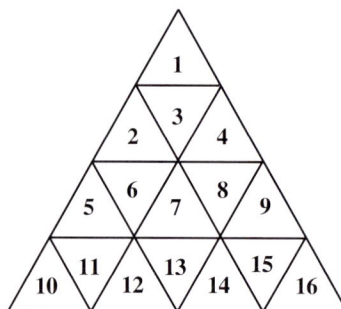

What is the first number in each row?
What patterns do you notice?
Investigate further.

SEG 1999

Number chains

A number chain is formed using the following steps.

Step 1: Choose a number.
Step 2: Add 20 to this number.
Step 3: Divide this number by 11.
Step 4: Go back to Step 2.

Investigate the number chain.

Investigate further.

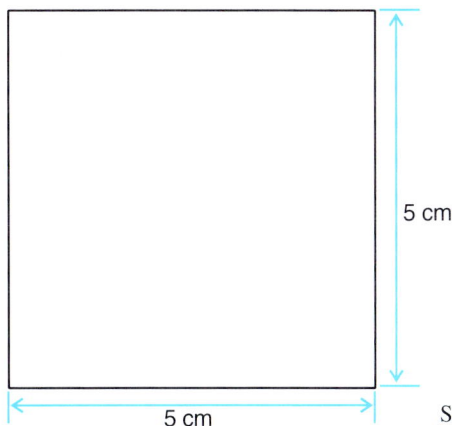

SEG 1999

Q scores

The Q score of a shape is defined by:

$$Q = \frac{4\pi A}{P^2}$$

where A is the area of the shape and
P is the perimeter of the shape.

Use the formula to find the Q score of this square.

Investigate the Q scores of different shapes.

Investigate further.

5 cm

5 cm

SEG 1999

Foot length

The foot lengths of 30 primary school children were measured as shown in Table 1 and Table 2.

Table 1 - Girls

Age (months)	Foot length (cm)
90	18.0
86	17.5
105	20.2
91	18.4
87	17.4
102	20.5
88	17.5
95	18.1
106	20.4
104	21.3
94	18.3
89	17.9
100	19.0

Table 1 - Boys

Age (months)	Foot length (cm)
110	21.3
107	20.1
98	19.3
100	19.5
95	18.2
106	20.3
97	18.4
109	21.1
97	17.6
100	19.2
94	18.8
99	19.5
106	20.0
102	20.4
95	18.4
104	20.7
108	20.0

It is stated that:

"The older you are, the longer your foot length."

Use the information provided in the tables to investigate this statement.

Investigate further. You may wish to collect data of your own.

SEG 1999

Answers

CHAPTER 1

Exercise **1.1** — Page 1

1. (a) 80% (b) 48% (c) 65%
2. (a) $\frac{13}{25}$ (b) $\frac{1}{8}$ (c) $\frac{29}{40}$
3. (a) 45% (b) 7% (c) 1.5%
4. (a) 0.15 (b) 0.47 (c) 0.875
5. (a) $66\frac{2}{3}\%$ (b) $22\frac{2}{9}\%$ (c) $37\frac{7}{9}\%$
6. 0.42, $\frac{17}{40}$, 43%, $\frac{13}{30}$
7. 28%, 0.2805, $\frac{57}{200}$, $\frac{2}{7}$
8. (a) 90% (b) 85% (c) 88% (d) 80%
9. Maths (85%) 10. Team A

Exercise **1.2** — Page 2

1. (a) 1 : 2 (b) 3 : 4 (c) 2 : 5
   (d) 1 : 2 : 3 (e) 3 : 7 (f) 2 : 3 : 4
   (g) 4 : 9 (h) 11 : 13 : 15
2. (a) 12 (b) 28 (c) 100 (d) 20
3. 198 cm 4. 400 g 5. 64
6. 18 years 7. 40 : 9 8. 1 : 250
9. 1 : 1500
10. (a) 11 : 2 (b) 5 : 2 (c) 40 : 17
    (d) 9 : 20 (e) 3 : 4 (f) 5 : 1
11. (a) 100 ml (b) 4 : 1

Exercise **1.3** — Page 4

1. (a) £64.35, £17.55 (b) £37.50, £60
   (c) £64.75, £46.25 (d) £34.65, £19.80
2. 50 3. £4900
4. 5 5. 170 000 km²
6. £1500, £2500, £4000 7. 200 kg
8. 40°, 60°, 80° 9. 8 cm, 12 cm, 18 cm
10. 80

Exercise **1.4** — Page 5

1. (a) $3\frac{3}{4}$ (b) $4\frac{3}{5}$ (c) $2\frac{1}{8}$
2. (a) $\frac{8}{5}$ (b) $\frac{35}{6}$ (c) $\frac{41}{9}$
3. (a) 9 (b) 26 (c) 21
   (d) 25 (e) 68 (f) 55
   (g) 119 (h) 207
4. £92 5. £743.75 6. £132.50

---

7. (a) (i) 20 squares (ii) 25 squares
   (b) $\frac{19}{20}$

Exercise **1.5** — Page 6

1. (a) $\frac{5}{8}$ (b) $\frac{9}{20}$ (c) $\frac{5}{8}$
   (d) $\frac{1}{2}$ (e) $\frac{29}{35}$ (f) $1\frac{5}{12}$
   (g) $\frac{29}{30}$ (h) $\frac{29}{36}$ (i) $2\frac{13}{60}$
   (j) $1\frac{1}{18}$
2. (a) $\frac{5}{8}$ (b) $\frac{1}{8}$ (c) $\frac{1}{12}$
   (d) $\frac{8}{15}$ (e) $\frac{5}{8}$ (f) $\frac{17}{45}$
   (g) $\frac{5}{24}$ (h) $\frac{19}{48}$
3. (a) $4\frac{1}{4}$ (b) $3\frac{5}{6}$ (c) $4\frac{3}{8}$
   (d) $5\frac{17}{20}$ (e) $6\frac{13}{20}$ (f) $5\frac{9}{20}$
4. (a) $1\frac{1}{10}$ (b) $\frac{5}{12}$ (c) $\frac{5}{8}$
   (d) $3\frac{3}{10}$ (e) $1\frac{27}{40}$ (f) $\frac{47}{48}$
5. (a) $\frac{7}{20}$ (b) $\frac{17}{20}$
6. $\frac{7}{60}$
7. (a) $\frac{27}{80}$ (b) Andy
8. $\frac{7}{30}$

Exercise **1.6** — Page 6

1. (a) $\frac{1}{12}$ (b) $\frac{1}{30}$ (c) $\frac{1}{3}$
   (d) $\frac{2}{35}$ (e) $\frac{1}{4}$ (f) $\frac{1}{6}$
   (g) $\frac{1}{6}$ (h) $\frac{3}{7}$
2. (a) $1\frac{1}{8}$ (b) $3\frac{3}{4}$ (c) $3\frac{17}{20}$
   (d) $4\frac{7}{8}$ (e) $1\frac{13}{15}$ (f) $13\frac{1}{2}$
   (g) $\frac{1}{3}$ (h) $5\frac{19}{20}$
3. (a) $2\frac{3}{5}$ (b) $3\frac{1}{2}$ (c) $5\frac{2}{5}$
   (d) $1\frac{1}{3}$ (e) $3\frac{4}{7}$ (f) $1\frac{1}{3}$
4. (a) $\frac{4}{15}$ (b) 15

Exercise **1.7** — Page 7

1. (a) $\frac{3}{5}$ (b) $2\frac{2}{5}$ (c) $1\frac{1}{3}$
   (d) $\frac{2}{3}$ (e) $1\frac{1}{2}$ (f) $\frac{2}{3}$
   (g) $1\frac{1}{6}$ (h) $1\frac{4}{5}$
2. (a) $\frac{2}{3}$ (b) $1\frac{3}{8}$ (c) $1\frac{1}{7}$
   (d) $4\frac{2}{3}$ (e) $13\frac{1}{2}$ (f) $\frac{4}{5}$
   (g) $1\frac{1}{2}$ (h) $1\frac{1}{4}$ (i) $2\frac{2}{27}$
   (j) $3\frac{6}{25}$

3. (a) 21, $\frac{17}{20}$ cm   (b) 23, $\frac{1}{2}$ cm

4. (a) $\frac{32}{45}$ (b) $2\frac{2}{5}$

5. $\frac{16}{21}$

Exercise 1.8 — Page 8

1. £3.20   **2.** 70 km   **3.** £3.20

4. £5   **5.** 96 cm   **6.** 189

7. £200   **8.** Neither   **9.** Yes

Exercise 1.9 — Page 9

1. (a) 37   (b) 3   (c) 9
(d) 58   (e) 6   (f) 30
(g) 0   (h) 56   (i) 56
(j) 6   (k) 28   (l) 0

2. (a) $5 \times 6 + 7$ (b) $5 + 6 \times 7$
(c) $15 + 8 \times 9$ (d) $15 \times 8 + 9$
(e) $15 \times 8 - 9$ (f) $15 \div 5 + 3$
(g) $5 - 24 \div 6$ (h) $19 \div 19 + 7 \times 0$
(i) $4 \times 4 + 7 \times 2$ or $4 + 4 \times 7 - 2$

3. Many answers, for example:
$6 \div 3 + 2 - 1 = 3$
$6 \div 3 + 2 \div 1 = 4$
$6 \div 3 + 2 + 1 = 5$
$6 - 3 + 2 + 1 = 6$
$6 + 3 - 2 \div 1 = 7$
$6 + 3 - 2 + 1 = 8$
$(6 - 3) \times (2 + 1) = 9$
$6 + 3 + 2 - 1 = 10$

Exercise 1.10 — Page 10

1. (a) 0.077 836 …   (b) 0.355 960 …
(c) 11.045 …   (d) 3.421 98 …
(e) 1.061 22 …   (f) 2.367 18 …
(g) −386   (h) 0.155

2. (a) 4.768

(b) (2 . 7 6 + 3 . 2)
÷ 1 . 2 5 =

3. (a) 0.5

(b) √ ((5 . 7 6 ÷ 3
. 6) ÷ 6 . 4) =

4. (a) **C**   (b) **B**   (c) **D**   (d) **A**

5. (a) ((2 . 6 x^2 + 2 . 4
8) ÷ 1 . 5) x^2 =

(b) 37.9456

7. (a) 15   (b) 10
(c) 10, 11, 12, 13   (d) 1 and 12, 9 and 10
(e) 18

Review Exercise 1 — Page 12

1. $\frac{2}{5}$, 0.405, 0.41, 41.05%, $\frac{83}{200}$

2. (a) 24   (b) 10   (c) 4

3. (a) $\frac{2}{7}$ (b) $3\frac{1}{3}$ (c) $1\frac{4}{35}$
(d) $\frac{1}{2}$ (e) $\frac{3}{49}$

4. £10.20   **5.** £80   **6.** $\frac{7}{10}$

7. (a) $2\frac{1}{12}$ m   (b) $\frac{1}{4}$ m^2

8. 326 480

9. (a) £15   (b) 40%

10. Sam £69.30, Anna £25.20

11. (a) 37.5%   (b) 24

12. (a) 45p   (b) $\frac{1}{30}$

13. No. 14 and 6 are not doubled.

14. 4.292 …

15. (a) 4.8 is not divided by 1.2.
(b) 25.586 …

16. (a) Question 3   (b) Question 2

17. (a) Brackets around $(50 - 30)$
(b) (i) £149.40   (ii) £4.92

CHAPTER 2

Exercise 2.1 — Page 14

1. (a) £16   (b) £15   (c) £66
(d) £52.50   (e) £25   (f) 27 kg
(g) £11.25   (h) 12 m

2. (a) £80   (b) £13
(c) £16.50   (d) 57.50

3. (a) £510   (b) £5.50
(c) £33.60   (d) £40.95

4. 270   **5.** £1.95   **6.** 40 pence per minute

7. 24 g   **8.** 759 g   **9.** £215

10. (a) 660   (b) 198

11. 8400 cm^2

Exercise 2.2 — Page 15

1. (a) 32%   (b) $12\frac{1}{2}$%   (c) 50%
(d) 90%   (e) 30%

2. 20%   **3.** 30%

4. $12\frac{1}{2}$%   **5.** $37\frac{1}{2}$%

6. (a) $33\frac{1}{3}$%   (b) $66\frac{2}{3}$%   (c) $11\frac{1}{9}$%
(d) $42\frac{1}{2}$%   (e) $56\frac{1}{2}$%

7. 9.5%   **8.** 8%   **9.** 25%

Exercise 2.3 — Page 16

1. £18.45
2. (a) £244.64 (b) £4706 (c) £2372.50
3. $83\frac{1}{3}\%$
4. (a) 6.27 cm² (b) 6.15%
5. (a) £14 541.75 (b) 113.10
6. (a) £10 530 (b) 17.3%
7. (a) 36.3% (b) 23.7% (c) 37.8%

Exercise 2.4 — Page 17

1. £313.60 2. £272 3. £203.40
4. £15 600 5. £23 220 6. £1100
7. (a) £42 (b) £132.98

Exercise 2.5 — Page 18

1. £881 2. £809 3. £67.08
4. £15.06 5. £4357.15 6. £228.92
7. £413.69 8. £2549.00

Exercise 2.6 — Page 19

1. (a) £300 (b) £25
2. £74.84 3. 810 4. £6.30
5. £112 6. £46.76
7. (a) £57 (b) £81 (c) £83 000
   (d) £92.50 (e) £222.50 (f) £67.50

Exercise 2.7 — Page 21

1. (a) £59.50 (b) £399.50
2. (a) £15.75 (b) £105.75
3. £170.37 4. £291.40
5. (a) £8.97 (b) £188.50
6. £216.20 7. £44.13
8. £428.87 9. £69.32

Exercise 2.8 — Page 23

1. £20 2. (a) £280 (b) £560
3. £242 4. £330.75
5. (a) earns 78p more interest.
6. (a) £70 (b) £48
   (c) £225 (d) £225
7. (a) £63.05 (b) £675.13
8. 10.99 m 9. 81 m

10. (a) (i) £8268.73 (ii) 63.6%
    (b) (i) £12 721.12 (ii) 63.6%
    (c) Same percentage reduction.
11. (a) £2420 (b) £1938.66
12. 8 years
13. (a) 49 days (b) Never

Exercise 2.9 — Page 24

1. 20% 2. 20%
3. 25% 4. 16.7%
5. Becky
   Sam's increase = 32%
   Becky's increase = 40%
6. (a) $12\frac{1}{2}\%$ (b) 12%
   Rent went up by a greater percentage.
7. 12% 8. Car A 13.8%, Car B 18.2%
9. 19.5% 10. 1995 - 1996 (9.2%)
11. 18.6%

Exercise 2.10 — Page 26

1. 600 ml 2. £600 3. £220
4. (a) 50 (b) 90
5. 67.5 mg 6. £293.75 7. £1420
8. School A 425, School B 450 9. £1600
10. (a) £45 000, £30 000, £20 000, £12 5000
    (b) 3.75%

Review Exercise 2 — Page 27

1. Alan £2500, Brenda £900, Christine £1200, David £800, Ellie £600
2. 4825 Escudos
3. (a) £1.96 (b) £118.80
4. £57.23 5. £944.40
6. £538.20 7. £4480.11
8. (a) £116.53 (b) 1916
9. £679.04 10. £275.40
11. $2\frac{3}{4}$ hours
12. (a) 1261.21 Guilders (b) £26.34
13. £16.83 14. £5683.33
15. £824.24 16. £3206.25
17. 46.2% 18. 36 000
19. £4 20. £9
21. £12 000 22. £1.60

Exercise **3.1** — Page 31

1.

980	1000	1000
61 120	61 100	61 000
9710	9700	10 000
620	600	1000
9950	9900	10 000
5760	5800	6000
7500	7500	8000
7500	7500	8000
7500	7500	7000

2.
(a) 19 000, nearest 1000
(b) 260, nearest 10
(c) 140, nearest 10
(d) £50, nearest £10
(e) 130, nearest 10
(f) 24 000, nearest 1000
(g) 310 000 km², nearest 10 000 km²
(h) 190 km, nearest 25 km
(i) £50, nearest £10
(j) 700, nearest 50

3.
(a) 745 − 749
(b) 750 − 754
(c) 8450 − 8499
(d) 8500 − 8549

4. 42 500   **5.** 135, 144   **6.** 2749

Exercise **3.2** — Page 32

1. 4   **2.** 5
3. Depends on the classroom
4. 10   **5.** 5   **6.** 9
7. 24   **8.** 29   **9.** 19
10. 5

Exercise **3.3** — Page 33

1. 0.96, 0.97, 3.962, 3.96, 4.0, 0.06, 567.65, 567.7, 4.99, 5.00

2.
(a) 46.1, 59.7, 569.4, 17.1, 0.7
(b) 46.14, 59.70, 569.43, 17.06, 0.66
(c) 46.145, 59.697, 569.434, 17.059, 0.662

3.
(a) £12.16, nearest p
(b) £3.57, nearest p
(c) £2.37, nearest p
(d) 35.7 cm, nearest mm
(e) £1.33, nearest p

Exercise **3.4** — Page 35

1. 450 000, 7 980 000, 8 000 000, 1300, 0.000 57, 0.094, 0.0937, 0.093 75, 0.010, 0.030

2.
(a) 83 000, 83, 1000, 0.0073, 0.0019
(b) 82 700, 82.7, 1000, 0.007 28, 0.001 90
(c) 82 660, 82.66, 1001, 0.007 281, 0.001 899

3.
(a) 51 cm² (2 s.f.)   (b) 157 cm² (3 s.f.)
(c) 6100 m² (2 s.f.)   (d) 1.23 m (nearest cm)
(e) 154 000 m² (3 s.f.)

Exercise **3.5** — Page 36

1.
(a) 8, 7.56   (b) 27, 27.59
(c) 200, 202.02   (d) 300, 299.86

2.
(a) 2, 2.2   (b) 5, 4.8
(c) 10, 9.5   (d) 40, 39.9

3.
(a) 6.4, 6.41875   (b) 20, 18.709677 …
(c) 20, 20.45631 …

4. 5

5.
(a) 2, 2.041 737 …   (b) 8, 6.912 637 …
(c) 1, 0.936 692 …

6.
(a) Meadow View 66 m², Park View 61 m²
(b) Meadow View 65.72 m², Park View 60.07 m²

7. 52 cm²   **8.** 24 cm²

9.
(a) 2.047 009 …
(b) $(50 + 10) \div (10 \times 3) = 2$

10.
(a) 5.165 624 …
(b) $\sqrt{(500 \div 20)} = 5$

Review Exercise **3** — Page 38

1. 3499, 2450

2.
(a) 245 000
(b) (i) 26 000 000   (ii) Nearest million

3. (a) 9.2   (b) 9.18   (c) 9.177

4. (a) 1   (b) 1.5   (c) 1.49

5. $\frac{6^2 - 2}{3} + 2 = \frac{34}{3} + 2 = 13$

6. $0.4 \times 90 \div 6 = 6$, not correct

7.
(a) 2.784 m, nearest millimetre
(b) 180 miles, nearest 10 miles

8.
(a) 37.8226 m²
(b) (i) 38 m²
(ii) Carpet sold in whole m²

9.
(a) 2, 1.99972 …
(b) 10, 9.85276 …
(c) 6, 5.6283 …

10. (a) 31.284 …
(b) $(90 \times 10) \div (20 + 10) = 30$

11. $200 \times 0.5 \div 10 = 10$, not correct

12. 390

13. (a) 1.92525 kg
(b) (i) 1.93 kg

14. £67.60

15. Not correct, $(900 \times 0.2) + (200 \times 1) = £380$

16. Not likely, 37 km $\div$ 20 000 = 1.85 m

CHAPTER 4

Exercise 4.1 — Page 43

1. (a) 2^9 (b) $2^3 \times 3^4$
(c) $5^5 \times 7^4$ (d) $3^2 \times 7^3$

2. (a) 6 (b) 5 (c) 4
(d) 5 (e) 0 (f) 2
(g) 4 (h) 4 (i) 3
(j) 0 (k) 1 (l) 2

3. (a) 8 (b) 7 (c) 11
(d) 3 (e) 1 (f) 4
(g) 6 (h) 20 (i) 2
(j) 8 (k) 6 (l) 3

4. (a) $x = 2$, $y = 4$ (b) $x = 3$, $y = 5$
(c) $x = 3$, $y = 2$ (d) $x = 2$, $y = 3$
(e) $x = 2$, $y = 3$ (f) $x = 3$, $y = 2$

5. (a) $a = 2$, $b = 3$ (b) $a = 2$, $b = 3$
(c) $a = 2$, $b = 3$ (d) $a = 2$, $b = 5$
(e) $a = 2$, $b = 5$ (f) $a = 3$, $b = 5$
(g) $a = 3$, $b = 2$ (h) $a = 2$, $b = 7$

6. (a) (i) $2^2 \times 3$ (ii) 2×3^2
(iii) $2^3 \times 5$ (iv) $2 \times 3 \times 5$
(v) $2^4 \times 3^2$ (vi) $2^2 \times 3^2 \times 5$
(b) (i) LCM = 36, HCF = 6
(ii) LCM = 720, HCF = 8
(iii) LCM = 90, HCF = 6
(iv) LCM = 720, HCF = 6

7. (a) 5 (b) 10 (c) 30

8. (a) $3 \times 7 = 21$ (b) $2^2 \times 11 = 44$
(c) $3^3 \times 5^2 = 675$

9. (a) 0.125 (b) 134.4 (c) 9.953 28
(d) 0.125 (e) 3.375 (f) 112
(g) 40 (h) 1250 (i) 2.5

Exercise 4.2 — Page 45

1. (a) (i) $\frac{1}{2}$ (iii) $\frac{1}{7}$ (iii) $\frac{1}{20}$
(b) (i) 7^{-3} (ii) 7^3 (iii) 3^{-5}

2. (a) $\frac{1}{16}$ (b) $\frac{1}{125}$ (c) $\frac{1}{100}$
(d) $\frac{1}{16}$ (e) $\frac{1}{3}$ (f) $\frac{1}{400}$

3. (a) $11\frac{1}{10}$ (b) $2\frac{7}{8}$ (c) $1\frac{6}{25}$
(d) $\frac{5}{6}$ (e) $\frac{29}{100}$ (f) $\frac{1}{100}$
(g) $\frac{4}{25}$ (h) $1\frac{7}{30}$

4. (a) -4 (b) -2 (c) -2
(d) -3 (e) -1 (f) -2
(g) -3 (h) -1

5. (a) (i) 1 (ii) 1 (iii) 1 (iv) 1

Exercise 4.3 — Page 46

1. Missing entries:
7.5×10^4
800 000 000
80×10^8
35 000 000 000 000
$3.5 \times 10\,000\,000\,000\,000$
$6.23 \times 10\,000\,000\,000\,000$
6.23×10^{13}

2. (a) 3×10^{11} (b) 8×10^7
(c) 7×10^8 (d) 6.3×10^2
(e) 3.219×10^9

3. (a) 600 000 (b) 2000
(c) 50 000 000 (d) 3 700 000 000
(e) 28 (f) 71 000

4. Missing entries:
7.5×10^{-3}
8.75×10^{-6}
$3.5 \times 0.000\,000\,001$
3.5×10^{-9}
$6.2 \times 0.000\,000\,000\,001$
6.2×10^{-12}

5. (a) 0.35
(b) 0.0005
(c) 0.000 005 5
(d) 0.000 000 062 5
(e) 0.000 000 000 031 67
(f) 0.000 115

6. (a) 7×10^{-3} (b) 4×10^{-2}
(c) 5×10^{-9} (d) 8×10^{-4}
(e) 2.3×10^{-6} (f) 4.5×10^{-8}

7. (a) Mercury 5.8×10^7 km
Venus 1.08×10^8 km
Earth 1.49×10^8 km
Mars 2.28×10^8 km
(b) A.Centauri 40 350 000 000 000 km
A.Cygni 105 300 000 000 000 km

8. Blood cell 7.5×10^{-4} cm
Hydrogen atom 2×10^{-7} mm
Mumps virus 2.25×10^{-4} mm

Exercise 4.4 Page 48

1. (a) 9.38×10^{19} (b) 1.6×10
   (c) 2.25×10^{26} (d) 1.25×10^{-37}
   (e) 2.4×10^{20} (f) 5×10^{-2}

2. (a) 3.74×10^5 (b) 2.44×10^5
   (c) 3×10^{-1} (d) 5.08×10^{20}
   (e) 1.52×10^{-3} (f) 2.50×10

3. (a) 2.088×10^9 (b) 32.95%

4. (a) 6.495×10^{13} km   5. $30\ 000$

6. (a) 4.55×10^9 years   (b) 0.0152%

7. 3.616×10^{14} square metres

8. (a) 2.1% (b) 30.21

Exercise 4.5 Page 49

1. (a) 1.5×10^0 (b) 2.7×10^{13}
   (c) 4.5×10^4 (d) 1.25×10^{-13}
   (e) 6.25×10^{-17} (f) 1.5×10^4

2. (a) $5\ 500\ 000$ (b) $5\ 000\ 000$
   (c) $0.006\ 15$ (d) $1\ 700\ 000$
   (e) 0.7 (f) 0.0005

3. (a) 2.4×10^8 (b) 1.5×10^5
   (c) 6×10^{11} (d) 8×10^{-5}
   (e) 3.2×10^9 (f) 1.08×10^{-3}
   (g) 5×10^1 (h) 1×10^6

4. (a) 9.94×10^{19} (b) 1.25×10^{-37}
   (c) 2.4×10^{20} (d) 3×10^{-4}
   (e) 4×10^8 (f) 12.5

5. (a) $8\ 400\ 000$ (b) $7\ 600\ 000$
   (c) 1.5×10^{-5} (d) 1.6×10^{11}
   (e) 3.2×10^{12} (f) 5×10^{-2}
   (g) 1.25×10^{-4} (h) 1.6×10^{11}
   (i) 8×10^6 (j) 1.6×10^8

Exercise 4.6 Page 51

1. (a) 20 (b) 5 (c) 3 (d) 10
   (e) 2 (f) 2.5 (g) 2 (h) 4
   (i) 0.5 (j) 7

2. (a) 10 (b) 6 (c) 8 (d) 4
   (e) 2 (f) 3 (g) 2 (h) 5
   (i) 2 (j) 5

3. (a) $\frac{1}{10}$ (b) $\frac{1}{3}$ (c) $\frac{1}{7}$ (d) $\frac{1}{3}$ (e) $\frac{1}{2}$
   (f) $\frac{1}{2}$ (g) $\frac{1}{5}$ (h) $\frac{1}{4}$ (i) $\frac{1}{3}$ (j) $\frac{1}{4}$

4. (a) 100 (b) 27 (c) 8 (d) 4
   (e) 32 (f) 243 (g) 25 (h) 32
   (i) 81 (j) 216

5. (a) $\frac{1}{100}$ (b) $\frac{1}{64}$ (c) $\frac{1}{4}$ (d) $\frac{1}{8}$ (e) $\frac{1}{8}$
   (f) $\frac{1}{100\ 000}$ (g) $\frac{1}{125}$ (h) $\frac{1}{8}$ (i) $\frac{1}{32}$ (j) $\frac{1}{25}$

6. (a) 3 (b) 4 (c) 5 (d) $\frac{1}{2}$
   (e) $\frac{2}{3}$ (f) $\frac{1}{4}$ (g) $\frac{3}{4}$ (h) 256
   (i) 125 (j) 1.5

7. (a) $\frac{3}{4}$ (b) $\frac{1}{2}$ (c) 3
   (d) $\frac{15}{56}$ (e) $6\frac{3}{4}$

Exercise 4.7 Page 52

1. (a) a^7 (b) x^6 (c) $\frac{1}{b^3}$
   (d) t^3 (e) $\frac{1}{x^2}$ (f) $8b^7$
   (g) $6t^6$ (h) $8x^2$ (i) $\frac{25}{y^2}$
   (j) $12x^5$ (k) x^6y^5 (l) $\frac{z^4}{y^2}$
   (m) $\frac{y}{x}$ (n) $\frac{6r^9}{s^2}$ (o) $3p^7$
   (p) $18x^8$

2. (a) b^8 (b) $\frac{1}{x^6}$ (c) $25p^6q^8$
   (d) $\frac{x^{12}}{8}$ (e) $\frac{1}{4y^2}$ (f) $8a^3$
   (g) x^2y (h) $3a^2b$ (i) $2x^2y$
   (j) $\frac{125r^3t^9}{s^6}$

3. (a) a (b) x^{16} (c) $\frac{1}{x^3}$
   (d) 1 (e) $\frac{1}{a^2}$ (f) $4b^3$
   (g) $2y^2$ (h) $5z^4$ (i) $3x^8$
   (j) $\frac{4}{t^5}$ (k) x^4 (l) p^2q^7
   (m) $4rs^6$ (n) $3x$ (o) r

4. (a) $\frac{4a}{c^3}$ (b) xy^3
   (c) 2 (d) $\frac{2x^7}{y^6}$

Exercise 4.8 Page 53

1. (a) $x = \frac{1}{4}$ (b) $x = \frac{2}{3}$ (c) $x = -\frac{3}{2}$
   (d) $x = -\frac{2}{3}$ (e) $x = \frac{10}{3}$ (f) $x = -\frac{3}{4}$
   (g) $x = -2$ (h) $x = -\frac{3}{2}$

2. (a) $x = 8$ (b) $x = 18$ (c) $x = -1$
   (d) $x = -1$ (e) $x = \frac{5}{2}$ (f) $x = 2$
   (g) $x = -2$ (h) $x = -2$ (i) $x = -2$
   (j) $x = -3$

3. (a) (i) 2 (ii) $\frac{1}{8}$ (iii) $\frac{1}{8}$ (iv) $\frac{5}{3}$
   (b) $x = \left(\frac{y}{2}\right)^{\frac{1}{n}}$

545

4. (a) The number of bacteria at the start of the experiment ($t = 0$ hours).
(b) 25   (c) 3 hours

5. (a) Decrease (0.81 is less than 1)
(b) (i) 10% decrease
(ii) 10% decrease
(iii) 10% decrease

Review Exercise 4 Page 55

1. (a) $x = 7$ (b) $x = 4$ (c) $x = 0$
(d) $x = 3$ (e) $x = 2$ (f) $x = 4$

2. (a) $x = 5$ (b) $x = 1$
(c) $x = 6$ (d) $x = 6$

3. (a) (i) $2 \times 3^2 \times 7$
(ii) $2 \times 3^2 \times 5$
(iii) $2 \times 3 \times 5 \times 7$
(b) 630   (c) 18

4. (a) 3   (b) $2^3 \times 7$ (c) 168

5. 90

6. (a) 2^0 (b) 2^6 **7.** (a) 5   (b) 200

8. (a) (i) 2.1×10^3 (ii) $2^2 \times 3 \times 5^2 \times 7$
(b) 2

9. (a) 57 024   (b) $2^9 \times 3^4 \times 11$
(c) 4.56192×10^5

10. (a) 9.6×10^{-3} cm
(b) (i) 1.188×10^8 (ii) 1 140 480 cm

11. 1.672×10^{-24} grams   **12.** 22.09 m

13. (a) 209 953   (b) 3830.32 …

14. (a) (i) 810 000   (ii) 8.1×10^5 (iii) 4
(b) 3.24×10^6

15. (a) 2   (b) $\frac{1}{16}$ (c) $\frac{1}{3}$

16. (a) $w = 0$ (b) $x = -2$
(c) $y = \frac{1}{5}$ (d) $z = -4$

17. (a) (i) x^{-3} (ii) $6x^8$ (iii) 3^{a-b}
(b) $a^{\frac{3}{2}}$

18. (a) x^8 (b) x^{-1} (c) $8x^6$

19. (a) 5   (b) $\frac{1}{2}$ (c) $x = \left(\frac{y}{5}\right)^{\frac{1}{n}}$

20. $a = 10,\ b = \frac{2}{3}$

CHAPTER 5

Exercise 5.1 Page 59

1. (a) True, $a : b = 2 : 5$
(b) True, $c : d = 20 : 1$
(c) False, $e : f$ not the same
(d) True, $h : g = 200 : 7$

2. (a)

w	0.5	2	5	10	50
x	1.5	6	15	30	150
y	0.45	1.8	4.5	10	45
z	0.99	3.96	9.9	22	99

(b) (i) True, $w\ \alpha\ y$, $w : y$ always 10 : 9
(ii) True, $w\ \alpha\ z$, $w : z$ always 50 : 99
(iii) True, $x\ \alpha\ z$, $x : z$ always 50 : 33

(c) $w\ \alpha\ x, k = \frac{1}{3}$ $w\ \alpha\ y, k = 0.9$
$w\ \alpha\ z, k = 1.98$ $x\ \alpha\ y, k = \frac{10}{3}$
$x\ \alpha\ z, k = \frac{50}{33}$ $y\ \alpha\ z, k = \frac{5}{11}$

3. (a) (i) 1 : 2   (ii) 1 : 5   (iii) 6 : 35
(b) $a = 2,\ b = 60,\ c = 8,\ d = 350$

4. (a) $q = 0.625p$ (or $p = 1.6q$)
(b) $a = 7.5,\ b = 32$

5. (a) $y = 0.05x$ (b) $a = 5,\ b = 400$

6. (a) $C = 10.5A$ (b) £577.50
(c) 68.75 m

7. (a) $d = 5n$ (b) 1 km   (c) 600 times

8. (a) (i) $e = 30w$ (ii) 159 mm
(iii) 3.22 kg
(b) 5 : 16

Exercise 5.2 Page 61

1. (a) (i) False   (ii) True, $ab = 10$
(b) (i) True, $c = 30d$ (ii) False
(c) (i) False   (ii) True, $ef = 1.6$
(d) (i) False   (ii) True, $hg = 30$

2. (a) $k = 5$

a	2	5	10	25	50
b	10	25	50	125	250

(b) $k = 20$

a	2	5	10	25	50
b	10	4	2	0.8	0.4

(c) $k = 0.02$

p	2	5	10	25	50
q	0.04	0.1	0.2	0.5	1

(d) $k = 12.5$

p	2	5	10	25	50
q	6.25	2.5	1.25	0.5	0.25

3. (a) $y = \dfrac{48}{x}$ or $xy = 48$ (b) $a = 4,\ b = 96$

4. (a) $LM = 14.4$ or $M = \dfrac{14.4}{L}$
(b) $a = 1.2,\ b = 16$

5. (a) $y = 9$ (b) $r = 25$

6. $lw = 200$, $k = 200$,
k represents the constant area

7. (a) $nt = 12$ or $t = \dfrac{12}{n}$ (b) 2 days
(c) 3 workers

Exercise 5.3 Page 64

1. (a) V is proportional to the square of t.
(b) L is inversely proportional to a.
(c) y is proportional to the cube of x.
(d) p is inversely proportional to the square of q.
(e) L is proportional to the square root of n.
(f) b is inversely proportional to the cube of c.

2. (a) y is multiplied by 4.
(b) x is multiplied by 5.

3. (a) y is divided by 4 (is 4 times smaller).
(b) x is divided by 5 (is 5 times smaller).

4. (a) h is divided by 4 (is 4 times smaller).
(b) r is divided by 4 (is 4 times smaller).

5. (a) $y = kx^3$ (b) $1:64$ (c) $4:5$

6. (a) $y = k\sqrt{x}$ (b) $1:4$

7. (a) $y = \dfrac{k}{x^2}$ (b) $25:1$ (c) $5:6$

8. (a) $V = 5t^2$ (b) $R = \dfrac{320}{s^3}$
(c) $y = 10\sqrt{x}$ (d) $A = \dfrac{100}{b}$
(e) $L = 3.125p^3$ (f) $Q = 12.5\sqrt{P}$

9. (a) 80 (b) $y = 5$ (c) $x = 4$

10. (a)

a	1	2	4	10
b	3	12	48	300

(b)

a	1	2	4	10
b	10	2.5	0.625	0.1

(c)

a	1	2	4	10
b	10	5	2.5	1

(d)

a	1	2	4	10
b	0.5	4	32	500

(e)

a	1	2	4	10
b	0.2	0.141	0.1	0.063

11. (a) (i) 1.6 (ii) 0.016
(b) (i) 10 (ii) 16

12. (a) $h = 0.05s^2$ (b) 20 (c) 125

13. (a) 0.001 (b) 8 (c) 17.1

14. (a) $q = \dfrac{40}{p^2}$, $a = 0.4$, $b = 20$
(b) $q = \dfrac{160}{p^3}$, $c = 0.16$, $d = 2$
(c) $q = 0.15625p^2$, $e = 15.625$, $f = 8$

15. $z = \dfrac{640}{x^3}$ **16.** 0.32

17. (a) 16 (b) $\sqrt{\dfrac{\text{Volume}}{\pi}}$

18. (a) $t = 4\sqrt{l}$ (b) 80 (c) 225

19. (a) 70.0 kg (b) 701.2 km

Exercise 5.4 Page 67

1. (a) (i) 3 (ii) -1 (iii) $-\tfrac{1}{2}$
(b) (i) (ii) (iii)

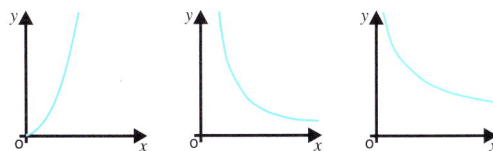

(c) (i) Less steep, steeper, steeper.
(ii) Steeper, less steep, less steep.

2. (a) 2 (b) 0.25
$k = 10$, $n = -2$

3. $q = 0.2p^3$ **4.** $s = \dfrac{20}{\sqrt{t}}$

5. (a) **B** (b) **A** (c) **D** (d) **C**

Review Exercise 5 Page 69

1. (a) q is proportional to the square of p.
(b) A is inversely proportional to the cube of x.
(c) y is proportional to x.

2. (a) (i) $\times 4$ (ii) $\times \tfrac{1}{2}$ (iii) $\times 8$
(iv) $\times 2$ (v) $\times \sqrt{2}$ (vi) $\times \tfrac{1}{4}$
(b) (i) $\times 9$ (ii) $\times \tfrac{1}{3}$ (iii) $\times 27$
(iv) $\times 3$ (v) $\times \sqrt{3}$ (vi) $\times \tfrac{1}{9}$
(c) (i) $\times \tfrac{1}{4}$ (ii) $\times 2$ (iii) $\times \tfrac{1}{8}$
(iv) $\times \tfrac{1}{2}$ (v) $\times \dfrac{1}{\sqrt{2}}$ (vi) $\times 4$

3. (a)

p	1	2	4	10
q	3	6	12	30

(b)

p	1	2	4	10
q	10	5	2.5	1

(c)

p	1	2	4	10
q	10	40	160	1000

4. (a) $NL^2 = 320$ or $N = \dfrac{320}{L^2}$ (b) 889

5. (a)

x	5	10	20
y	45	180	720

6. $pv = k$ or $p = \dfrac{k}{v}$

7. (a) $W = BH^2$ (b) 100 kg

8. (a) $V - k\sqrt{h}$ (b) 2 : 1

9. $I = \dfrac{k}{x^2}$,   1 : 16

10. (a) 2300 hours on 19th March.
    (b) 200 hours after the leak started.

11. $T = 4$ minutes, 12 seconds, 31 seconds

12. (a) $d = 3.58\sqrt{h}$ (b) 32 km

13. (a) $N = k\sqrt{H}$ (b) 2   (c) 5

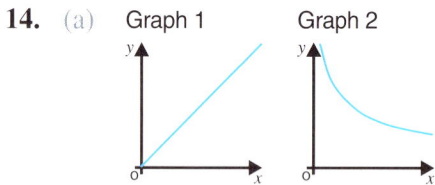

14. (a) Graph 1   Graph 2

Graph 3   Graph 4

  (b) Graph 2
  (c) Graph 1 : $y = kx$
     Graph 2 : $y = \dfrac{k}{\sqrt{x}}$
     Graph 3 : $y = kx^2$ or $y = kx^3$
     Graph 4 : $y = k\sqrt{x}$

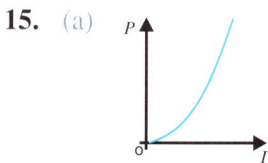

15. (a)

17. (a) (i) C
       (ii) $v = kr^2$
    (b) $v = 1000r^2$

CHAPTER 6

Exercise 6.1   Page 72

1. (a) $\dfrac{7}{9}$ (b) $\dfrac{1}{9}$ (c) $\dfrac{8}{9}$ (d) $\dfrac{4}{11}$
  (e) $\dfrac{82}{99}$ (f) $\dfrac{5}{37}$ (g) $\dfrac{8}{37}$ (h) $\dfrac{425}{999}$
  (i) $\dfrac{6}{37}$ (j) $\dfrac{2}{7}$

2. (a) $\dfrac{1}{6}$ (b) $\dfrac{1}{30}$ (c) $\dfrac{11}{18}$ (d) $\dfrac{7}{15}$
  (e) $\dfrac{7}{30}$ (f) $\dfrac{5}{6}$ (g) $\dfrac{181}{990}$ (h) $\dfrac{3}{22}$
  (i) $\dfrac{31}{36}$ (j) $\dfrac{17}{22}$

3. $\dfrac{2}{17}$ **4.** 2, 4, 5, 8, 10, 16, 20

Exercise 6.2   Page 73

1. (a) $\dfrac{1}{2}$ (b) $\dfrac{9}{20}$ (c) $\dfrac{3}{10}$ (d) $\dfrac{5}{8}$
  (e) $\dfrac{9}{4}$ (f) $-\dfrac{1}{4}$ (g) $\dfrac{3}{11}$ (h) 7
  (i) $\dfrac{7}{20}$ (j) $\dfrac{25}{111}$ (k) 2   (l) $-\dfrac{1}{5}$
  (m) 4   (n) $\dfrac{3}{4}$ (o) $\dfrac{11}{90}$

2. Rational: a, b, d, f, i, j, k, l
  Irrational: c, e, g, h, m

3. (a) Irrational   (b) Rational, $\dfrac{157}{50}$
  (c) Irrational   (d) Rational, $\dfrac{1}{2}$
  (e) Rational, $\dfrac{8}{3}$ (f) Rational, $\dfrac{3}{4}$
  (g) Irrational   (h) Rational, $\dfrac{4}{3}$
  (i) Rational, $\dfrac{5}{2}$ (j) Irrational

4. (a) Irrational   (b) Rational, $\dfrac{5}{4}$
  (c) Rational, $\dfrac{3}{2}$ (d) Rational, $\dfrac{7}{9}$

5. (a) e.g. $\sqrt{5}$ (b) e.g. $\sqrt{20}$
  (c) e.g. $\sqrt{41}$

6. (a) e.g. $3 = 4 = 7$
  (b) (i)   e.g. $(\pi + 4) + (5 - \pi) = 9$
     (ii)   e.g. $\sqrt{2} + \sqrt{5}$

7. (a) e.g. $\sqrt{2} \times \sqrt{18} = \sqrt{36} = 6$
  (b) e.g. $\sqrt{3} \times \sqrt{2} = \sqrt{6}$
  (c) e.g. $\sqrt{8} \div \sqrt{2} = \sqrt{4} = 2$
  (d) e.g. $\sqrt{3} \div \sqrt{2} = \sqrt{\dfrac{3}{2}}$

Exercise 6.3   Page 75

1. a, d, e, i, k, m, n, o

2. (a) $2\sqrt{2}$ (b) $3\sqrt{2}$ (c) $2\sqrt{3}$
  (d) $3\sqrt{3}$ (e) $3\sqrt{5}$ (f) $2\sqrt{5}$
  (g) $4\sqrt{3}$ (h) $4\sqrt{2}$ (i) $5\sqrt{2}$
  (j) $3\sqrt{6}$ (k) $2\sqrt{6}$ (l) $7\sqrt{2}$
  (m) $5\sqrt{3}$ (n) $6\sqrt{2}$ (o) $4\sqrt{5}$
  (p) $3\sqrt{7}$ (q) $10\sqrt{2}$ (r) $8\sqrt{2}$
  (s) $4\sqrt{7}$ (t) $5\sqrt{7}$

3. (a) $2\sqrt{2}$ (b) $\sqrt{5}$ (c) $7\sqrt{3}$
  (d) $2\sqrt{2}$ (e) $5\sqrt{5}$ (f) $5\sqrt{3}$
  (g) $5\sqrt{2}$ (h) $\sqrt{2}$ (i) $7\sqrt{5}$
  (j) $3\sqrt{3}$ (k) $6\sqrt{3}$ (l) $6\sqrt{2}$
  (m) $12\sqrt{5}$ (n) $14\sqrt{3}$ (o) $5\sqrt{5}$
  (p) $10\sqrt{2}$ (q) $5\sqrt{3}$ (r) $6\sqrt{2}$

4. (a) $\dfrac{3}{2}$ (b) $\dfrac{5}{4}$ (c) $\dfrac{3}{2}$ (d) $\dfrac{2\sqrt{6}}{3}$

5. (a) 3 (b) 6 (c) 6
(d) 30 (e) 4 (f) 6
(g) 6 (h) $5\sqrt{2}$ (i) $3\sqrt{2}$
(j) $3\sqrt{5}$ (k) $6\sqrt{2}$ (l) $10\sqrt{2}$
(m) 12 (n) $6\sqrt{6}$ (o) $8\sqrt{6}$
(p) $12\sqrt{6}$

6. (a) $2 + \sqrt{2}$ (b) $3\sqrt{2} - 3$
(c) $2\sqrt{3} + 2$ (d) $5\sqrt{2} - 5$
(e) 1 (f) 3
(g) $5 + 2\sqrt{6}$ (h) 4
(i) $4\sqrt{3} - 8$ (j) -3

Exercise 6.4 — Page 76

1. (a) $\frac{\sqrt{3}}{3}$ (b) $\frac{\sqrt{5}}{5}$ (c) $\frac{\sqrt{7}}{7}$
(d) $\sqrt{2}$ (e) $\sqrt{5}$ (f) $2\sqrt{2}$
(g) $2\sqrt{3}$ (h) $2\sqrt{7}$ (i) $\frac{\sqrt{6}}{2}$
(j) $3\sqrt{5}$ (k) $3\sqrt{3}$ (l) $\frac{\sqrt{15}}{3}$
(m) $3\sqrt{6}$ (n) $7\sqrt{5}$ (o) $\frac{\sqrt{21}}{3}$
(p) $\frac{\sqrt{22}}{2}$ (q) $\frac{\sqrt{30}}{3}$ (r) $\frac{3\sqrt{14}}{2}$
(s) $\frac{2\sqrt{35}}{5}$ (t) $\frac{3\sqrt{10}}{2}$

2. (a) $\frac{3\sqrt{2}}{2}$ (b) $\sqrt{3}$ (c) $\frac{\sqrt{6}}{2}$
(d) $\sqrt{2}$ (e) $\frac{3\sqrt{2}}{2}$ (f) $\frac{\sqrt{2}}{2}$
(g) $\sqrt{3}$ (h) 2 (i) 2
(j) 3 (k) $\frac{1}{2}$ (l) 4
(m) $\frac{\sqrt{3}}{2}$ (n) 1 (o) $\sqrt{3}$
(p) $2\sqrt{2}$ (q) 1 (r) $\sqrt{5}$
(s) $\frac{\sqrt{2}}{2}$ (t) $\frac{\sqrt{3}}{3}$

Review Exercise 6 — Page 78

1. (a) $0.\dot{7}$ (b) $\frac{5}{18}$
2. (a) $0.\dot{1}\dot{8}$ (b) $\frac{7}{22}$
3. (a) $\frac{5}{11}$ (b) $\frac{71}{110}$
4. rational: $(2.2)^3$, 0.66666, $\sqrt{16}$
   irrational, $\sqrt{2}$, π
5. (a) e.g. $\sqrt{2} \times \sqrt{8} = \sqrt{16} = 4$
   (b) 2^{-2}, $4^{\frac{1}{2}}$, 4^{-2}
6. (a) e.g. 5.2 (b) e.g. $\sqrt{26}$ (c) e.g. 9
   (d) e.g. 7 (e) π (f) $\frac{7}{15}$

7.

	Rational	Irrational
$\frac{7}{3}$	YES	NO
π	NO	YES
$4\sqrt{2}$	NO	YES

8. (a) $\frac{36}{11}$

(b)

$x + y$	Always irrational	Always rational	Some-times
x rational, y rational	✗	✓	✗
x irrational, y rational	✓	✗	✗
x irrational, y irrational	✗	✗	✓

9. (a) $\sqrt{400}$, $\sqrt{441}$, $\sqrt{484}$, $\sqrt{529}$, $\sqrt{576}$
(b) $\sqrt{8} \times \sqrt{18}$

10. (a) (i) e.g. $\pi + \sqrt{2}$
   (ii) e.g. $\sqrt{3} \times \sqrt{12} = \sqrt{36} = 6$
   e.g. $\sqrt{2} \times \sqrt{3} = \sqrt{6}$ irrational
(b) Irrational
(c) $\sqrt[3]{27}$, $\left(2^6\right)^{\frac{1}{3}}$, $\left(\frac{1}{16}\right)^{-\frac{1}{4}}$

11. (a) (i) $\sqrt{2}$ m, irrational
   (ii) 1 m, rational
   (iii) $\pi\sqrt{2}$ m, irrational
   (iv) 1 m², rational
(b) e.g. 8 (c) $\frac{3}{11}$

12. (a) (i) $\sqrt{125}$, irrational
   (ii) 3, rational
(b) e.g. $a = 2$, $b = \sqrt{5}$
   $a = 1$, $b = \sqrt{3}$

13. (a) $3\sqrt{2}$ (b) $11\sqrt{3}$
14. (a) $\frac{\sqrt{5}}{3}$ (b) $10\sqrt{3}$
15. (a) $\frac{5}{3}$ (b) $6 + 3\sqrt{3} + 2\sqrt{2} + \sqrt{6}$
(c) $\frac{\sqrt{10}}{4}$

CHAPTER 7

Exercise 7.1 — Page 80

1. 75 **2.** 200 **3.** 25 **4.** 250 miles
5. 22 pounds **6.** 170 cm **7.** 66.4 kg
8. (a) 610 m (b) 4.8 km
   (c) 5.57 feet (d) 2.75 pounds
9. 6.6 m³, 1 d.p. **10.** 3.35 kg, nearest 10 g

Exercise **7.2** Page 81

2. 6.4 m, nearest 0.1 m

3. 72 kg, nearest kilogram

4. 175 ml, nearest 10 ml

5. (a) 12 m, nearest metre
  5.9 m, nearest 10 cm
  5 l, nearest litre
  500 m², nearest 50 m²
 (b) 1200 cm, nearest 100 cm
  5900 mm, nearest 100 mm
  5000 ml, nearest 1000 ml
  500 000 000 mm², nearest 50 000 000 mm²

Exercise **7.3** Page 83

1. 10.30 am **2.** 6 km

3. (a) $2\frac{1}{2}$ hours (b) 50 minutes

4. (a) 8 m/s (b) 100 km (c) 12 cm
 (d) 1 hour (e) 1 s

5. B 4 hours, C 70 km/hour, D 100 km/hour

6. 10 km/hour

7. (a) 48 km/hour (b) 80 km/hour
 (c) 108 km/hour

8. (a) 37.5 miles per hour
 (b) 90 miles per hour

9. (a) 12.8 km/litre (b) 30 miles per gallon

10. (a) 8.86 m/s, 8.95 m/s, 8.96 m/s, 9.04 m/s
 (b) 8.95 m/s

11. (a) 56 km/hour (b) 60 km/hour

12. 11.09 am **13.** 4.81 m/s

14. 0.23 km/min **15.** 3×10^8 m/s

16. (a) Coach B, by 30 km
 (b) Coach A, by 16 minutes
 (c) Coach B, by 17.9 km/hour

Exercise **7.4** Page 86

1. 2.1 g/cm³ **2.** 8 g/cm³

3. 9 g/cm³ **4.** 28.6 g/cm³

5. 7200 g **6.** 9360 g

7. 2000 cm³ **8.** Steel 2.5 g/cm³, Foam 200 g

9. 5×10^7 kg/m³

10. 100 g

11. 118.3 people/km²

12. (a) 30 350 km² (b) 104.2 people/km²
 (c) 5.74×10^7

13. 11 500 g

Exercise **7.5** Page 89

1. (a) continuous (b) discrete
 (c) discrete (d) continuous
 (e) discrete (f) continuous

2. (a) exact (b) 4.5 mins $\leqslant t <$ 5.5 mins
 (c) exact (d) 62.5 kg $\leqslant w <$ 63.5 kg
 (e) 152.5 cm $\leqslant$ J $<$ 153.5 cm

3. (a)
 (b)

4. (a) 12.5 s $\leqslant t <$ 13.5 s
 (b) 82.55 s $\leqslant t <$ 82.65 s

5. (a) nearest 0.01 m (centimetre)
 (b) 1.525 m $\leqslant h <$ 1.535 m

6. (a) 61.5 kg (b) 2.25 m (c) 12.625 s

7. (a) nearest 10 m (b) nearest 50 m
 (c) nearest 100 m

8. (a) 10 499, 9500 (b) 10 049, 9950
 (c) 10 024, 9975 (d) 549, 450
 (e) 504, 495

9. (a) 94.5 s (b) 67.685 s, 67.695 s
 (c) Dan's time could be between 67.5 s
  and 68.5 s

Exercise **7.6** Page 91

1. 98.5° **2.** 1260 cm

3. (a) 247.5 miles (b) 157.5 miles

4. (a) 505 kg (b) 3.4 kg

5. (a) 87 998, 86 000 (b) 11 999, 10 001

6. 10

7. 39.208 cm³ (3 d.p.)

8. 0.159 g/cm³ (3 d.p.)

9. (a) 503 (b) 96

10. (a) 162 minutes (3 s.f.)
 (b) 226 minutes (3 s.f.)

11. 7.428 cm (3 d.p.) **12.** 68 330.58 g (2 d.p.)

13. (a) 2.195 km
 (b) (i) 26.595 km, 26.485 km
  (ii) 3.03 km/h (3 s.f.)

14. 5.741 cm² (3 d.p.)

15. (a) 34.575, 33.465
 (b) -11.425, -12.805
 (c) 615.729, 580.123 (3 d.p.)
 (d) 3.70125, 2.28325
 (e) 8.98875, 8.04075
 (f) 1.0419, 0.9797 (4 d.p.)

Exercise 7.7
Page 94

1. (a) area   (b) length   (c) length
   (d) length   (e) volume   (f) area
   (g) volume   (h) area

2. (a) perimeter   (b) area   (c) volume
   (d) none   (e) area   (f) perimeter
   (g) perimeter   (h) none   (i) volume
   (j) volume   (k) none   (l) area

3. (a) (i) $2\pi(x + y)$
   (b) (ii) $\pi(x^2 + y^2)$, πxy

5. $\frac{1}{2}pqs$, volume

$$2\left(p + q + r + \frac{3s}{2}\right),\text{ edge length}$$

$s(p + q + r) + pq$, surface area

6. (a) correct   (b) correct   (c) correct
   (d) wrong   (e) correct   (f) wrong

7. (a), (b), (c), (e)

Review Exercise 7
Page 96

1. 55

2. (a) Clara: 5 foot 2 inches = 157.36 cm
     Clara is taller
   (b) 156.5 cm

3. Any volume from 645 ml up to, but not including 650 ml.

4. (a) (i) 950 m, 1050 m
     (ii) 995 m, 1005 m
     (iii) 999.5 m, 1000.5 m
     (iv) 999.95 m, 1000.05 m
   (b) (i) 4500 gallons, 5500 gallons
     (ii) 4950 gallons, 5050 gallons
     (iii) 4995 gallons, 5005 gallons
     (iv) 4999.5 gallons, 5000.5 gallons
   (c) (i) 19.5 s, 20.5 s
     (ii) 19.95 s, 20.05 s
     (iii) 19.995 s, 20.005 s
   (d) (i) 750 kg, 1250 kg
     (ii) 975 kg, 1025 kg
     (iii) 997.5 kg, 1002.5 kg
     (iv) 990 kg, 1010 kg
     (v) 900 kg, 1100 kg

5. Erica: 2 s.f. (nearest 10 cm)
   Asif: 3 s.f. (nearest 1 cm)

6. 3255 g, 3245 g   7. 11.615 s, 11.605 s

8. 1.195 m   9. £324.99

10. (a) Maximum cost £92.49,
     minimum cost £91.50
   (b) £18.99

11. 25 km/h

12. (a) 9.46×10^{12} km (3 s.f.)
   (b) 4.23 light years (3 s.f.)
   (c) 187 500 miles/second

13. $4\frac{3}{4}$ hours or 5 hours

14. (a) (i) 0.2 kg   (ii) kg/cm^3
   (b) 2.29 kg (3 s.f.)

15. Europe: 0.065 people/km^2,
   Asia: 0.068 people/km^2, Asia

16. (a) 25.25 kg, 25.15 kg   (b) 574.75 kg

17. (a) (i) 6.25 cm   (ii) 101 cm   (iii) 256
   (b) 225

18. 163.9 people/km^2 (1 d.p.)   19. 6.7%

21. In order: length, volume, area

22. (a) ab, $4\pi rl$

23. (a) area   (b) length   (c) volume

24. $11.2r^2$

Section Review
Page 100

1. 6 694, 500 m

2. (a) 23p   (b) 20%   (c) 50 g

3. 36 km/h

4. (a) £552   (b) £24 000

5. (a) $x = 504$, $y = 756$ (b) $2^5 \times 3^5 \times 7^2$
   (c) $2^3 \times 3^2 \times 7^2$ (d) $2^2 \times 3^5 \times 7$
   (e) $2^4 \times 3^2 \times 7^2$, all powers are even

6. (a) (i) 5   (ii) 30
   (b) $x = 14, 21$ $y = 77, 91$

7. (a) 1.5×10^3 (b) 6×10^5

8. 23% decrease

9. (a) $\sqrt{\dfrac{40\,095}{(9.87)^2}} \approx \sqrt{\dfrac{40\,000}{10^2}} = 20$
   (b) (i) 1.5×10^4 (ii) 6×10^6

10. (a) $2^2 \times 5$
   (b) (i) $a = 2$, $b = 5$ (ii) $x = -\frac{1}{2}$

11. (a) 3.43×10^5 (b) 2

12. (a) $\frac{1}{64}$ (b) $\frac{3}{5}$ (c) $\frac{1}{16}$

13. (a) $\sqrt{5}$, π, $\left(\sqrt{3}\right)^3$
   (b) E.g. $\sqrt{5} \times \sqrt{20}$

14. (a) (i) (ii) (v)
   (b) E.g. $\frac{1}{2} + \frac{1}{3} = \frac{5}{6}$
   (c) (i) $\frac{5}{9}$ (ii) $\frac{4}{11}$

15. (a) (i) rational, $\frac{3}{11}$
     (ii) irrational
     (iii) rational, $1\frac{5}{16}$
   (b) E.g. $b = 50$ (c) a

551

16. (a) 2.4735 kg   (b) 1.62805 kg, 1.62795 kg

17. 2152.5 m, 2167.5 m

18. 12 feet 7 inches = 151 inches = 3.87 m
Bus will go under the bridge

19. 968 ml

20. (a) 2.07 (3 s.f.)
(b) (i) £229.08
(ii) $C = 20 + 0.5 (2 \times 50 + 200)$
$C = 170$
Sarah's answer is wrong

21. (a) 3 906 250
(b) (i) 0.111 (3 s.f.)
(ii) Accuracy of numbers in the question only 3 sig.figs.
(c) 0.153 (3 s.f.)

22. 76.7 million

23. (a) $2.346\,549 \times 10^6$
(b) £2.47 million (3 s.f.)

24. (a) 2 hours 51 minutes   (b) 530 mph

25. (a) 43 minutes   (b) $\frac{500 \times 10^6}{200\,000 \times 60} \approx 40$

26. 93.75%

27. (a) £11.52   (b) £955.08

28. 14.4% (3 s.f.)   **29.** £391

30. £17.34   **31.** 50.9 lb/cu.ft. (3 s.f.)

32. (a) 1   (b) 6.28×10^5 (3 s.f.)

33. 5.2×10^5 kilowatt hours

34. (a) 161 000   (b) 17.9% (3 s.f.)

35. (a) $\sqrt{85}$, irrational   (b) $\sqrt{5}$, irrational
(c) 4, rational

36. (a) $\frac{7}{33}$ (b) $\frac{271}{330}$

37. (a) 575.25 cm²
(b) $(x + 0.5)^2 - (x - 0.5)^2 = 2x$ cm²

38. (a) 1505 g
(b) maximum cost = 28.76p
minimum cost = 27.24p

39. (a) 0.155 cm
(b) Yes. Maximum radius of rod (5.505 cm) is less than the minimum radius of the cylinder (5.55 cm)

40. (a) 16.52 cm³ to 16.62 cm³ (4 s.f.)
(b) 1.47 g/cm³ (3 s.f.)

41. (a) $d = \frac{1}{20} v^2$ or $20d = v^2$
(b) 125 feet   (c) 64.8 mph (3 s.f.)

42. (a) $F = \frac{66.73}{d^2}$ or $Fd^2 = 66.73$
(b) 1.10 Newtons (3 s.f.)   (c) 13.3 m (3 s.f.)

552

CHAPTER 8

Exercise 8.1   Page 106

1. $12e$ **2.** $b - 3$

3. (a) $(a + 1)$ years   (b) $(a - 4)$ years
(c) $(a + n)$ years

4. $(h + 12)$ cm

5. (a) $2d$ (b) $2d + 5$

6. (a) $P = y + 5$ (b) $P = y - 2$
(c) $P = 2y$ (d) $P = 2y + 3$
(e) $P = 3y - 1$

7. Ben $d - 2$, Charlotte $2d$, Erica $\frac{1}{2} d$
Frank $3d - 5$, Gillian $3d - 1$

Exercise 8.2   Page 107

1. (a) $3c$ (b) $5x$ (c) $7p$ (d) $5y$
(e) $10g$ (f) $13z$ (g) $8m$ (h) $2r$
(i) $5t$ (j) $3j$ (k) $4c$ (l) w
(m) 0 (n) $-5x$ (o) $-14a$

2. (a) $4x$ (b) $6a$ (c) $9y$ (d) $2u + 2v$

3. (a) $3a + 5$ (b) $2x + 3y$
(c) $3m + 2n$ (d) cannot be simplified
(e) $3p + 3q$ (f) $d + 3$
(g) $-2a$ (h) 7
(i) $c - d + 11$ (j) 0
(k) $3v - 2w$ (l) $-2 - 5t$

4. (a) $P = 4x + 2$ (b) $P = 4a + 6b$
(c) $P = 3x$ (d) $P = 6y + 9$

5. (a) $4p^2$ (b) $ac - ab$ (c) $6a^2$
(d) $3a + 2a^2$ (e) $4ab$ (f) $-y^2$

6. (a) $3y$ (b) $5p$ (c) xy (d) a^2
(e) $2a^2$ (f) $4a^2$ (g) h^3 (h) w^3
(i) $2d^3$ (j) $2m^3$ (k) $6x^3$ (l) $6a^2$

7. (a) $4x^2$ (b) $10y^2$ (c) $24a^2$ (d) $15a^2$

8. (a) $3x^3$ (b) $6d^3$ (c) $60t^3$

9. (a) fg (b) $20c$ (c) $4de$
(d) $2ab$ (e) $12xy$ (f) $8ab$
(g) $2h^2j$ (h) $5wy$ (i) $14mp^2$
(j) $6x^3y$ (k) $21a^3b^3$ (l) $12e^2f^4g^2$

10. (a) $2v$ (b) $4p$ (c) $\dfrac{ac^3}{2}$
(d) $\dfrac{4}{m}$ (e) $\dfrac{16}{w^2}$ (f) 1

Exercise 8.3   Page 109

1. (a) $3a - 12$ (b) $bc - 3b$
(c) $d^2 + 2d$ (d) $3e^2 - 3e$
(e) $6f - 4f^2$ (f) $2g^2 + 3gh$
(g) $15jk - 20j^2$ (h) $6m - 8m^2$
(i) $6p^2 + 9pq - 12p$ (j) $r^2s + rs^2 + 2rs$

2. (a) $2x + 5$ (b) $3a + 11$
     (c) $6w + 31$ (d) $5z + 8$
     (e) $8t + 15$ (f) $2c - 6$
     (g) $8a + 23$ (h) $6x - 20$
     (i) $2p - 11$

3. (a) $5x + 8$ (b) $5a + 13$
     (c) $9y + 23$ (d) $3a$
     (e) $26t + 30$ (f) $5z + 13$
     (g) $2q - 44$ (h) $33 - x$
     (i) $12e$ (j) $8d + 10$

4. (a) $5a + b$ (b) $17x + 14$
     (c) $5d^2 + 4de$ (d) $2u + 6v$
     (e) x (f) $2x^2 - x + 4$

Exercise 8.4   Page 110

1. (a) $4(a + b)$ (b) $5(c - d)$
     (c) $e(f + g)$ (d) $j(h + k)$
     (e) $l(l - 1)$ (f) $m(1 + m)$
     (g) $5(n + 2p)$

2. (a) $2(a + b)$ (b) $7(c + d)$
     (c) $2(4e - f)$ (d) $7(g + 2h)$
     (e) $8(3j - 2k)$ (f) $a(b - 1)$
     (g) $d(c + e)$ (h) $f(g + h)$
     (i) $2j(2k + 1)$ (j) $3l(2 - 3m)$
     (k) $a(a - 1)$ (l) $b(1 - b)$
     (m) $cd(d + 1)$ (n) $e(ef - 1)$
     (o) $gh(h - g)$

3. (a) $2a(2 + 9b)$ (b) $b^2(a - c)$
     (c) $4x(5 + y)$ (d) $a^2(a + a^3 + 1)$
     (e) $\pi r(2 + r)$ (f) $4ab(5a + 3b)$
     (g) $2a(2a - 1)$ (h) $3pq(1 - 3p)$

Exercise 8.5   Page 112

1. (a) $x = 2$ (b) $n = 3$ (c) $a = 0$
     (d) $d = 7.5$ (e) $c = 1\frac{1}{2}$ (f) $a = -10$
     (g) $p = 1\frac{1}{2}$ (h) $w = -1$ (i) $m = -1\frac{1}{2}$
     (j) $z = 10$ (k) $t = 20$ (l) $x = -18$

2. (a) $p = 4$ (b) $t = 3$ (c) $h = 7$
     (d) $d = 10$ (e) $b = 6$ (f) $x = 10$
     (g) $y = 5$ (h) $z = 8$ (i) $n = 24$

3. (a) $p = -10$ (b) $a = 2\frac{1}{2}$ (c) $t = 7$
     (d) $n = 4$ (e) $c = -0.5$ (f) $h = -4$
     (g) $x = 3$ (h) $y = -8$ (i) $y = 12$
     (j) $m = -3$ (k) $t = -18$ (l) $v = -9$

4. (a) $x = 2$ (b) $a = 1$ (c) $p = 2$
     (d) $m = 2$ (e) $y = 3$ (f) $t = 3$
     (g) $n = 1$ (h) $c = 7$ (i) $h = 2$
     (j) $d = 4\frac{1}{2}$ (k) $k = 1$ (l) $x = 6$
     (m) $a = -1$ (n) $x = 1$

5. (a) $c = 7$ (b) $p = 3$ (c) $a = 3$
     (d) $t = 2$ (e) $h = 4$ (f) $u = 2$
     (g) $b = 1$ (h) $d = -2\frac{1}{2}$ (i) $n = -1$
     (j) $x = 3$

6. (a) $t = -5$ (b) $y = 2$ (c) $s = \frac{1}{2}$
     (d) $q = 3$ (e) $a = 1.8$ (f) $c = 0.11$
     (g) $p = 5$ (h) $x = -6$

Exercise 8.6   Page 114

1. (a) $x = 3$ (b) $a = 2$ (c) $c = 6$
     (d) $p = 5$ (e) $d = 3$ (f) $t = 3$
     (g) $a = 1$ (h) $t = -1$

2. (a) $n = 2$ (b) $z = 6$ (c) $w = 3$
     (d) $m = 4$ (e) $h = 2$ (f) $x = -3$
     (g) $w = 3$ (h) $y = 1\frac{1}{2}$ (i) $v = -8$
     (j) $c = -1\frac{1}{2}$

3. (a) Multiply both sides by 12.
     (b) Multiply both sides by 8.
     (c) Multiply both sides by 7.
     (d) Multiply both sides by 15.

4. (a) $x = 6$ (b) $w = 8$ (c) $n = 24$
     (d) $a = \frac{15}{32}$ (e) $p = \frac{16}{21}$ (f) $b = \frac{5}{6}$

5. (a) $y = 28$ (b) $a = 24$ (c) $a = 24$
     (d) $t = 8$ (e) $h = 11$ (f) $x = -4$
     (g) $x = -3$ (h) $a = 5$ (i) $x = \frac{7}{9}$
     (j) $x = 4$ (k) $x = -5$ (l) $x = 3$
     (m) $a = 7$ (n) $x = -1$

Exercise 8.7   Page 116

1. (a) $(7x - 4)$ cm   (b) $7x - 4 = 59$, $x = 9$
     (c) 13 cm, 17 cm, 29 cm

2. (a) $18x = 540$ (b) $150°$

3. (a) $(6x + 16)$ cm   (b) $x = 2$
     (c) 28 cm

4. (a) (i) $6x$ years   (ii) $(x + 20)$ years
       (iii) $(6x + 20)$ years
     (b) 5 years

5. (a) (i) $x - 10$ (ii) $x - 8$
     (b) (i) $x + 2 = 3(x - 8)$
       (ii) $x = 13$ (iii) 5

Review Exercise 8   Page 117

1. (a) $(n - 2)$ years   (b) $3n$ years
     (c) $(3n + 4)$ years   (d) $8n + 2$

2. (a) Cost $= 25n$ (b) $6n$ pence

3. (a) $3x - 5$ (b) 1

4. (a) $q = -2$ (b) $s = -1\frac{1}{2}$
     (c) $p = 2$ (d) $t = 1\frac{1}{2}$
     (e) $p = 6$ (f) $x = 10\frac{1}{2}$

5. $x = 20$

6. (a) $x = 2$ (b) $x = 1\frac{1}{2}$

7. $x = -0.8$ **8.** $x = 1.25$

9. (a) $(3x + 1)$ cm
  (b) (i) $3x + 1 = 22$ (ii) 7 cm, 5 cm, 10 cm

10. (a) $(4x + 20)°$
  (b) (i) $4x + 20 = 180$ (ii) $44°$

11. (a) $8x$ cm²
  (b) (i) $x = \frac{3}{4}$ (ii) 11 cm

12. $x = 2$
  4 cm, 3 cm; 2 cm, 6 cm

13. (a) (i) $(x + 9)$ years (ii) $(3x + 9)$ years
  (b) 9 years

14. (a) $3n$ pence (b) $4(n - 5)$ pence
  (c) (i) $3n + 4(n - 5) = 85$ (ii) 15

15. (a) $(5c + 1)$ kg
  (b) (i) $2c + 10 = 5c + 1$ (ii) 3 kg

16. (a) (i) $(x + 7)$ pence (ii) $(4x + 7)$ pence
  (b) 67p

17. (a) $10x + 10y$ (b) $11(10x + y)$

CHAPTER 9

Exercise 9.1 — Page 122

1. (a) 13, 21, 24 (b) 144
2. (a) 49, 97 (b) 1537
3. (a) 16, linear (b) 21, quadratic
  (c) 31, linear (d) 4, linear
  (e) 50, quadratic (f) 21, linear
4. (a) $4n$ (b) $2n - 1$ (c) $4n + 3$
  (d) $5n - 3$ (e) $4n + 4$ (f) $8 - 2n$
5. (a) $n^2 - 1$ (b) $n^2 + 3$ (c) $2n^2$
  (d) $n^2 + n$ (e) $\frac{1}{n^2}$ (f) $\frac{n^2}{(n + 1)^2}$
6. (a) $3n + 2$ (b) $n^2 + 4$ (c) $6n + 2$
  (d) $3n^2$ (e) $5n - 2$ (f) $n^2 + 2$
  (g) $n^2 - n$ (h) $\frac{n}{n + 1}$

Exercise 9.2 — Page 124

1. (a) 5 (b) 15 (c) 28
2. (a) 20 (b) 56 (c) 10
3. (a) 11 (b) 21 (c) 3
4. (a) 3 (b) 11 (c) 6.6
5. (a) $S = 18$ (b) $S = 18$
6. (a) $S = 36$ (b) $S = 36$
7. $F = 4100$ **8.** $F = 144$
9. 138 minutes   **10.** 0.3
11. £40.14

12. (a) $C = 15$ (b) $-15°C$
13. (a) $x = 38$ (b) $x = 8$
  (c) $x = -172$ (d) $x = 2240$
14. (a) $x = 8$ (b) $x = 22$
  (c) $x = -5$ (d) $x = -10$
  (e) $x = -2.5$ (f) $x = -5$
15. (a) $T = 1.80$ (b) $T = 2.46$
16. (a) $v = 6.3$ (b) $v = 7.4$

Exercise 9.3 — Page 125

1. (a) $x = y - 5$ (b) $x = y + 2$
  (c) $x = \frac{y}{4}$ (d) $x = 2y$
  (e) $x = \frac{y}{2} - 3$ (f) $x = \frac{y}{3} + 3$
  (g) $x = 2y + \frac{5}{2}$ (h) $x = \frac{2y}{3} - 2$

2. $K = \frac{20P}{9}$ **3.** $C = \frac{5F - 160}{9}$

4. $y = x + 3, \quad x = y - 3$
  $y = 3x + 1, \quad x = \frac{1}{3}(y - 1)$
  $y = \frac{1}{3}x, \quad x = 3y$
  $y = 3x, \quad x = \frac{1}{3}y$
  $y = 3x - 1, \quad x = \frac{1}{3}y + \frac{1}{3}$

5. (a) $v = u - 3$ (b) $v = r + u$
  (c) $v = \frac{r}{2}$ (d) $v = \frac{u}{i}$
  (e) $v = tx$ (f) $v = u + at$
  (g) $v = \frac{p - d}{m}$ (h) $v = \sqrt{\frac{F}{m}}$

6. (a) £107 (b) 9 days

7. $a = \frac{2A}{h} - b$

8. (a) $V = IR$ (b) $m = \frac{E}{c^2}$
  (c) $x = \sqrt{\frac{y - b}{a}}$ (d) $v = \sqrt{\frac{2e}{m}}$

9. (a) $a = b - c^2$ (b) $a = \sqrt{b}$
  (c) $a = 2b + \frac{c}{4}$ (d) $a = \frac{b}{3}$
  (e) $a = \frac{4b}{15}$ (f) $a = \frac{3b}{2}$
  (g) $a = 2\sqrt{b}$ (h) $a = \sqrt{\frac{3b + 5}{2}}$

10. (a) $x = b - 2a$ (b) $x = \frac{b - a}{2}$
  (c) $x = \frac{1}{2}b - a$ (d) $x = 6b - 2a$
  (e) $x = ab + ac$ (f) $x = \frac{b}{a + 2}$
  (g) $x = \frac{c}{a} - b$ (h) $x = a - \frac{1}{2}b$

(i) $x = 4a - 2b^2$ (j) $x = \dfrac{a}{b}$

(k) $x = \dfrac{a}{c} - b$

11. (a) $t = \sqrt{\dfrac{x}{3}}$ (b) $t = \sqrt{\dfrac{V}{a}}$

(c) $t = \sqrt{\dfrac{b-a}{2}}$ (d) $t = \sqrt{a-b}$

(e) $t = \sqrt{\dfrac{c-a}{b}}$ (f) $t = \sqrt{\dfrac{a-c}{b}}$

(g) $t = \sqrt{ab}$ (h) $t = \sqrt{ab} - 1$

12. (a) $r = \dfrac{mv^2}{F}$ (b) $c = \sqrt{\dfrac{E}{m}}$ (c) $g = \dfrac{l}{4\pi^2 T^2}$

13. (a) $x = a^2 - 3$
(b) $x = 9a^2 - 2$
(c) $x = 8b^2 + \frac{1}{2}a$

14. (a) $a = \dfrac{3x}{2}$ (b) $a = \dfrac{b}{1-x}$

(c) $a = \dfrac{b+2}{1-x}$ (d) $a = \dfrac{3x-2}{1-x}$

(e) $a = \dfrac{5y+3}{1+y}$ (f) $a = \dfrac{2b+x}{x-b}$

(g) $a = \dfrac{6+y}{y+3}$ (h) $a = \dfrac{5x}{3}$

(i) $a = \dfrac{4x^3}{1+4x^2}$

Review Exercise 9 Page 127

1. (a) $5n + 2$ (b) $n(n+1)$

2. (a) $\frac{1}{10}n$ (b) $n^2 - 1$ (c) 2^n

3. (a) $n + 3$ (b) $2n^2$

4. (a) $100 - n$ (b) $\dfrac{2n}{100-n}$

5. (a) $\dfrac{n+1}{n}$

(b) (i) $\dfrac{1}{2^{n-1}}$ (ii) Terms get close to zero

6. (a) $2n^2 = 450$, $n = 15$ (b) $2n^2 + n$

7. A: n^2 B: $2n^2$ C: $2n^2 + n$

8. (a) $2n^2$ (b) $n = 10$

9. (a) $4n - 1$ (b) $n^2 + 2$ **10.** 2×3^{-n}

11. (a) n^3 (b) $\dfrac{n^2}{n^3} = \dfrac{1}{n} = n^{-1}$

12. $-31.7°C$ **13.** $T = -14$ **14.** $u = 6.74$

15. (a) $s = -14.95$ (b) $u = 17.2$

16. (a) $T = 1.42$
(b) T is a multiple of π (irrational)

17. (a) $D = 101.6$ (b) $v = 68.7$

18. $R = 9.375$

19. (a) $19.4°F$ (b) -40 (c) $C = \dfrac{5F - 160}{9}$

20. $h = \dfrac{A - 2\pi r^2}{\pi r}$

21. (a) 9.2 (b) $t = \dfrac{v-u}{a}$

22. (a) $y = 5$ (b) $n = \frac{1}{2}$ (c) $x = \left(\dfrac{y}{5}\right)^{\frac{1}{n}}$

23. (a) $r = \sqrt[3]{\dfrac{3V}{4\pi}}$ (b) $r = 2.62$

24. (a) 66 (b) $y = 9C^2 - 25$

25. (a) (i) $p = 4n + 4$ (ii) 37

(b) $n = \sqrt{\dfrac{A-4}{5}}$

CHAPTER 10

Exercise 10.1 Page 132

1. (1) $y = 4$ (2) $x = -3$ (3) $x = 1$
(4) $y = -1$ (5) $y = x$

2.

x	1	2	3
(a) y	3	4	5
(b) y	2	4	6
(c) y	4	2	0

3. (a)   (b)   (c)

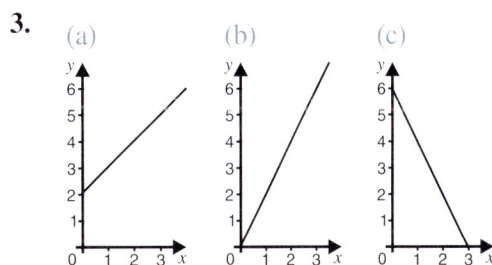

4.

x	-2	-1	0	1	2	3
(a) y	-3	-2	-1	0	1	2
(b) y	-8	-5	-2	1	4	7

5. Entries are: 6, 4, 3

7. (b) Same slope, parallel y intercept is different

8. (b) Same slope, parallel y intercept is different

9. (b) Same y intercept, 3 Different slope

Exercise 10.2 Page 134

1. (a) Gradient 3, Intercept -1

2. $y = 3x$, $y = 3x + 2$

3. Gradients: $4, 3, 2, -2, \frac{1}{2}, 2, 0, -\frac{1}{2}$
Intercepts: $3, 5, -3, 4, 3, 0, 3, 4$

4. (1) C (2) D (3) B (4) A

5. (a) $y = 5x - 4$ (b) $y = -\frac{1}{2}x + 6$

6. (a) $y = x - 2$ (b) $y = -2x - 2$

7. (c) 1 (d) $(0, -4)$ (e) $y = x - 4$

8. (c) $y = -2x - 1$

Exercise **10.3** — Page 136

1. $y = \dfrac{3x}{2} + 3$

2. (a) $y = -\frac{4}{5}x + 4$ (b) $y = \frac{2}{7}x - 2$

(c) $y = -\frac{2}{3}x + \frac{4}{3}$ (d) $y = x + \frac{2}{3}$

3. $y = -\frac{3}{2}x + $ (any number)

4. (a) $\frac{4}{5}$ (b) 2

(c) $y = $ (any number)$x + 2$

5. (a) $(0, 5)$ (b) $(3, 0)$

6. (a) $(0, 4), (5, 0)$ (b) $(0, -2), (0.5, 0)$

(c) $(0, 5), (7.5, 0)$

Exercise **10.4** — Page 137

1. (a)

x	1	2	3
$y = x + 2$	3	4	5
$y = 5 - x$	4	3	2

(c) $x = 1.5$

2. (b) $x = 2.5$

3. (a) $x = 8$ (b) $x = 2$ (c) $x = 3$

4. (b) $y = 9$ (c) $x = 3$

5. (c) The number of hours for which the two firms charge the same amount.

6. (d) B (e) A (f) 6 days

Exercise **10.5** — Page 139

1. B **2.** (a)

3.

4. (a) (b) (c) (d)

5. (a) **1.** D **2.** A **3.** C **4.** B

Review Exercise **10** — Page 141

1. S

2. (a) $x = 4.2$ (c) $x = 2$

3. (a) $y = 2x + $ (any number)

(b) $y - $ (any number)$x = 5$

4. $a = -\frac{3}{5}, \; b = 3$

5. (a) (i) -2

(ii)

6. (a) £32.50

(b) (i) 0.5

(ii) Charge for each extra minute

(c) $C = 0.5t + 10$

(d) 148 minutes

7. $y = 0.5 - 0.5x$

8. (a) Entries for b:10, 7.5, 6, 5, 3.75, 3.33, 3

(b) Amy: 8 years 5 months
Ben: 3 years 7 months

9. (a) 12 cm (b) 2 (c) 10 kg

10. **1.** C **2.** B **3.** E **4.** A

11. $A : W, B : Z, C : X$

12. (a) (i) (ii) (b)

13. (a) $A : G, B : H, C : E, D : F$ (b)

CHAPTER 11

Exercise **11.1** — Page 147

1. $x = 4, \; y = 2$ **2.** $x = 3, \; y = 5$

3. $x = 2, \; y = 3$ **4.** $x = 2, \; y = 3$

5. $x = 3, \; y = 1$ **6.** $x = 4, \; y = 3$

Exercise **11.2** — Page 148

1. (a) Both sides have gradient -1.

(b) Both sides have gradient 4.

(c) Both lines are the same.

(d) Both lines have gradient 0.4.

2. (a) $y = -2x + 6, \; y = -2x + 3$

(b) $y = 2x + 3.5, \; y = 2x + 2$

(c) $y = 2.5x - 4, \; y = 2.5x + 1.75$

(d) $y = -3x + 1.25, \; y = -3x + 0.5$

556

3. (b) and (d) have no solution.
　　(a)　$x = 0.4,\ \ y = 4$
　　(c)　$x = -0.125,\ \ y = 1.875$

Exercise 11.3　　　Page 150

1. $x = 1,\ \ y = 2$　　　**2.** $x = 3,\ \ y = 4$
3. $x = 2,\ \ y = 1$　　　**4.** $x = 1,\ \ y = 7$
5. $x = 3,\ \ y = 1$　　　**6.** $x = 2,\ \ y = 3$
7. $x = 5,\ \ y = 2$　　　**8.** $x = 4,\ \ y = 2$
9. $x = 5,\ \ y = 4$　　　**10.** $x = 3,\ \ y = 2$
11. $x = 4,\ \ y = 1$　　　**12.** $x = 4,\ \ y = 2$
13. $x = 2,\ \ y = 3$　　　**14.** $x = 4,\ \ y = -2$
15. $x = 2,\ \ y = -1.5$　**16.** $x = -1,\ \ y = 3$
17. $x = -5,\ \ y = 6$　　**18.** $x = 2.5,\ \ y = -1$
19. $x = -6,\ \ y = 2.5$　**20.** $x = 3,\ \ y = -1.5$

Exercise 11.4　　　Page 151

1. $x = 2,\ \ y = 1$　　　**2.** $x = 2,\ \ y = 3$
3. $x = 3,\ \ y = 1$　　　**4.** $x = 4,\ \ y = 2$
5. $x = 2,\ \ y = 1$　　　**6.** $x = 4,\ \ y = -3$
7. $x = 4,\ \ y = 0.5$　　**8.** $x = -3,\ \ y = 0.5$
9. $x = 4,\ \ y = 1$　　　**10.** $x = 2.2,\ \ y = 5.6$
11. $x = 1.5,\ \ y = 2$　　**12.** $x = 1,\ \ y = 2$
13. $x = 5,\ \ y = 2$　　　**14.** $x = 1,\ \ y = -2$
15. $x = -1,\ \ y = 2$　　**16.** $x = 2,\ \ y = 1$
17. $x = -1,\ \ y = 1$　　**18.** $x = -2,\ \ y = 3$
19. $x = -1,\ \ y = 7$　　**20.** $x = 4,\ \ y = -1$
21. $x = 2.5,\ \ y = 3$　　**22.** $x = 2,\ \ y = -1$
23. $x = 1,\ \ y = -2$　　**24.** $x = -2,\ \ y = 0.5$

Exercise 11.5　　　Page 152

1. $x = 2,\ \ y = 6$　　　**2.** $x = 9,\ \ y = 18$
3. $x = 8,\ \ y = 2$　　　**4.** $x = 3,\ \ y = 6$
5. $x = 2,\ \ y = 13$　　**6.** $x = 0,\ \ y = 2$
7. $x = 2,\ \ y = 4$　　　**8.** $x = 7,\ \ y = 6$
9. $x = 4,\ \ y = 8$　　　**10.** $x = 10.5,\ \ y = 0.5$
11. $x = -68,\ \ y = -122$　**12.** $x = 8,\ \ y = 6$

Exercise 11.6　　　Page 153

1. (a)　$40s + 30d = 1500$
　　(b)　$s = 18,\ \ d = 26$

2. $x = 95,\ \ y = 82$　　**3.** 32 children, 3 adults
4. $x = 100,\ \ y = 70$　　**5.** Coffee 50p, Tea 40p
6. $x = 160,\ \ y = 120$

Review Exercise 11　　　Page 154

1. (a)　$x = 3,\ y = 7$　　(b)　$x = 7.5,\ y = 0.5$
　　(c)　$x = 4.5,\ y = 1.25$　(d)　$x = 2,\ y = -6$

2. (a)　$x = 0.5,\ y = 1.5$　(b)　$x = 3,\ y = 2$
　　(c)　$x = 1,\ y = 4$　　(d)　$x = 3,\ y = 2$
　　(e)　$x = -1,\ y = 2$　　(f)　$x = 5,\ y = -1$
　　(g)　$x = 3,\ y = -2$　　(h)　$x = 2,\ y = -0.5$
　　(i)　$x = 2,\ y = 3$　　(j)　$x = 3,\ y = -1$
　　(k)　$x = 2,\ y = -1$　　(l)　$x = 1,\ y = 2$
　　(m)　$x = 3,\ y = 4$　　(n)　$x = -7,\ y = 4$
　　(o)　$x = 22,\ y = 20$　　(p)　$x = -2,\ y = 1$

3. (a)　Same gradient, 2
　　　　$y = 2x - 2,\ \ y = 2x - \frac{3}{2}$
　　(b)　Same gradient, $\frac{1}{4}$
　　　　$y = \frac{1}{4}x + \frac{1}{4},\ \ y = \frac{1}{4}x + \frac{3}{8}$
　　(c)　$a = 3$, $b =$ any number
　　(d)　Any values where $p = -3q$

4. $x = 1.2,\ \ y = 1.4$

5. (a)　$2x + 3y = 67,\ \ 5x + y = 86$
　　(b)　Pen 15p, pencil 11p

6. (a)　$2x + 3y = 10.75,\ \ x + 2y = 6$
　　(b)　$x = 3.5,\ \ y = 1.25$

CHAPTER 12

Exercise 12.1　　　Page 156

1. (a)　2, 3, 4　　　　(b)　$-1, 0, 1, 2, 3$
　　(c)　$-4, -3, -2, -1$　(d)　$-1, 0, 1, 2$

2. (a)　$x \geqslant 2$　　　(b)　$-6 \leqslant x < -2$
　　(c)　$-2 < x < 1$　　(d)　$x < 5$ and $x \geqslant 8$

3. (a)
　　(b)
　　(c)

Exercise 12.2　　　Page 157

1. $d > 4$　　　**2.** $e \geqslant 2$　　　**3.** $f < -2$
4. $g \leqslant \frac{1}{2}$　　**5.** $h < 2$　　　**6.** $j \geqslant 2\frac{1}{2}$
7. $k > -4$　　**8.** $m > -6\frac{1}{2}$　**9.** $n \leqslant 2$
10. $p > 8$　　**11.** $q > 1$　　　**12.** $r \geqslant -1\frac{1}{2}$
13. $t > 13$　　**14.** $u \leqslant 9$　　　**15.** $v < 1\frac{1}{2}$
16. $w > 8$　　**17.** $x \geqslant -6$　　**18.** $a < 2\frac{1}{3}$
19. $b \leqslant 1\frac{1}{7}$　**20.** $c < \frac{3}{8}$　　　**21.** $x \leqslant -\frac{1}{3}$
22. $x < 1\frac{1}{2}$　**23.** $x \geqslant \frac{4}{5}$　　　**24.** $x \leqslant -1\frac{9}{13}$
25. $x < \frac{4}{9}$　　**26.** $x > 11\frac{1}{2}$　　**27.** $x \geqslant \frac{3}{31}$

Exercise **12.3** — Page 158

1. $a < -2$ 2. $b \geqslant 3$ 3. $c \leqslant -4$
4. $d > -1$ 5. $e \geqslant 2$ 6. $f < 1$
7. $g > -4$ 8. $h \geqslant 2$ 9. $j \leqslant 1$
10. $k > -\frac{1}{3}$ 11. $m < -3$ 12. $n > -4$
13. $p \geqslant \frac{5}{9}$ 14. $q > -2\frac{1}{5}$

Exercise **12.4** — Page 159

1. (a) $1 < x \leqslant 5$ (b) $-1 \leqslant x < 9$
   (c) $-7 < x \leqslant 4$ (d) $1 < x \leqslant 3$
   (e) $-2 \leqslant x < 4$ (f) $3 < x < 4\frac{1}{2}$
   (g) $-\frac{1}{3} \leqslant x \leqslant 4$ (h) $2 < x \leqslant 5$
   (i) $-3 \leqslant x < 6$ (j) $-2 < x < 2$
   (k) $3 \leqslant x < 6$ (l) $-4\frac{1}{2} \leqslant x \leqslant -1$

2. (a) 6, 7, 8   (b) $-2, -1, 0, 1, 2, 3, 4$
   (c) 0, 1, 2   (d) 4, 5, 6, 7
   (e) 5   (f) 2, 3
   (g) $-2, -1, 0$ (h) $-1, 0, 1, 2, 3$
   (i) $-4, -3, -2, -1, 0, 1, 2, 3, 4, 5, 6$
   (j) 8, 9, 10, 11, 12, 13, 14, 15, 16
   (k) $-4, -3, -2, -1, 0, 1, 2, 3$
   (l) -6

Exercise **12.5** — Page 159

1. (a) $x \leqslant -3$ and $x \geqslant 3$
   (b) $-6 < x < 6$
   (c) $x < -1$ and $x > 1$
   (d) $-5 \leqslant x \leqslant 5$
   (e) $-2 < x < 2$
   (f) $x \leqslant -7$ and $x \geqslant 7$
   (g) $x < -1$ and $x > 1$
   (h) $-2 \leqslant x \leqslant 2$

2. (a) $-1, 0, 1$
   (b) $-4, -3, -2, -1, 0, 1, 2, 3, 4$
   (c) $\ldots, -5, -4$ and $4, 5, \ldots$
   (d) $\ldots, -8, -7$ and $7, 8, \ldots$
   (e) $-2, -1, 0, 1, 2$
   (f) $\ldots, -4, -3$ and $3, 4, \ldots$
   (g) $-6, -5, -4, -3, -2, -1, 0, 1, 2, 3, 4, 5, 6$
   (h) $\ldots, -4, -3$ and $3, 4, \ldots$

Exercise **12.7** — Page 162

3. $y \geqslant 1$, $y \leqslant x$
4. $y < 4$, $x \leqslant 3$, $y \leqslant 2x$ and $y > x$
5. $x \leqslant 2$, $x + y > 3$, $y \leqslant 3 - x$

Exercise **12.8** — Page 164

1. (a) There are at most 40 tram units
   (b) $x + y \leqslant 32$

---

2. (a) (i) $12A + 8B \leqslant 100$ $(3A + 2B \leqslant 25)$
       (ii) $2A + 3B \leqslant 20$
   (b) Possible production options
   (c) 6   (d) 9

3. (a) $1000x + 1500y \leqslant 18\,000$
       $(2x + 3y \leqslant 36)$
       $x + 2y \leqslant 20$
   (b) 6   (c) 18

4. (a) 10 batches

Review Exercise **12** — Page 166

1. (a) $x \geqslant -5$ (b) $x < 3$
   (c) $x \leqslant 6$ (d) $x \geqslant -2$

2. (a) $-1, 0, 1, 2, 3, 4$
   (b) $-3, -2, -1, 0, 1$ (c) $-2, -1$

3. (a) $a < -3$ and $a > 3$
   (b) $-10 \leqslant a \leqslant 10$ (c) $-4 \leqslant a \leqslant 4$

4. (a) $-4, -3, -2, -1, 0, 1, 2, 3, 4$
   (b) $\ldots, -7, -6$ and $6, 7, \ldots$
   (c) $-3, -2, -1, 0, 1, 2, 3$

5. (a) $-3, -2, -1, 0, 1$
   (b) (i) $x > 7$ (ii) $x \leqslant -\frac{2}{3}$

6. $-1 \leqslant x < 1$ 7. $-1, 0, 1$ 8. $a > 5$

9. (a) $-4, -3, -2, -1, 0, 1$
   (b) (i) $x < \frac{1}{2}$ (ii) $y \leqslant -5$ and $y \geqslant 5$

10. $x = 3$, $y = 1$; $x = 3$, $y = 2$;
    $x = 4$, $y = 1$; $x = 4$, $y = 2$; $x = 5$, $y = 1$

11. (a) $x < -\frac{1}{3}$
    (b)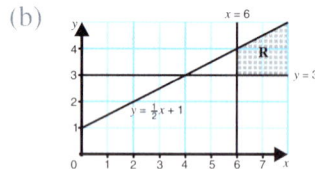

12. (a)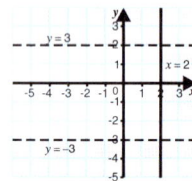
    (b)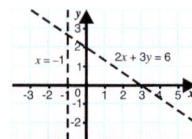
    (c)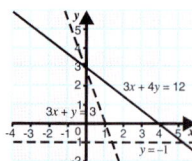

13. (a)

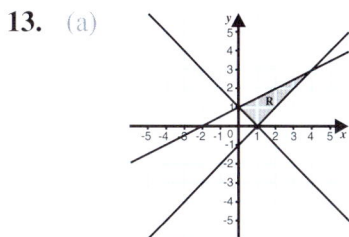

(b) $(0, 1), (1, 0), (1, 1), (2, 1), (2, 2), (3, 2),$
$(4, 3)$

14. (a) (i) $0 \leqslant y \leqslant 5$
(ii) $25x + 15y \geqslant 90 \, (5x + 3y \geqslant 18)$
(b) $x = 3, \quad y = 1$

CHAPTER 13

Exercise 13.1 — Page 169

1. $x^2 + 7x + 12$
2. $x^2 + 6x + 5$
3. $x^2 - 3x - 10$
4. $2x^2 - 3x - 2$
5. $3x^2 - 20x + 12$
6. $6x^2 + 7x + 2$
7. $x^2 + 6x - 16$
8. $x^2 + 3x - 10$
9. $x^2 + 2x - 3$
10. $x^2 - 5x + 6$
11. $x^2 - 5x + 4$
12. $x^2 - 5x - 14$
13. $2x^2 + x - 3$
14. $3x^2 + 14x - 5$
15. $12x^2 + 14x - 10$
16. $x^2 - 9$
17. $x^2 - 25$
18. $x^2 - 49$
19. $x^2 - 100$
20. $x^2 + 6x + 9$
21. $x^2 + 10x + 25$
22. $x^2 - 6x + 9$
23. $x^2 - 14x + 49$
24. $4x^2 - 12x + 9$

Exercise 13.2 — Page 171

1. (a) $x(x + 5)$ (b) $x(x - 7)$
   (c) $y(y - 6)$ (d) $t(5 - t)$
   (e) $y(8 + y)$ (f) $x(x - 20)$

2. (a) $(x - 3)(x + 3)$ (b) $(x - 9)(x + 9)$
   (c) $(y - 5)(y + 5)$ (d) $(y - 1)(y + 1)$
   (e) $(x - 8)(x + 8)$ (f) $(10 - x)(10 + x)$
   (g) $(6 - x)(6 + x)$ (h) $(x - a)(x + a)$

3. (a) $(x + 5)(x + 1)$ (b) $(x + 7)(x + 2)$
   (c) $(x + 2)(x + 4)$ (d) $(x + 3)(x + 6)$
   (e) $(x - 5)(x - 1)$ (f) $(x - 5)(x - 2)$
   (g) $(x - 4)(x - 3)$ (h) $(x + 4)(x - 1)$
   (i) $(x + 7)(x - 2)$ (j) $(x - 5)(x + 1)$

4. (a) $(x + 1)(x + 2)$ (b) $(x + 1)(x + 7)$
   (c) $(x + 3)(x + 5)$ (d) $(x + 2)(x + 6)$
   (e) $(x + 1)(x + 11)$ (f) $(x + 4)(x + 5)$
   (g) $(x + 4)(x + 6)$ (h) $(x + 4)(x + 9)$

5. (a) $(x - 3)^2$ (b) $(x - 4)(x - 2)$
   (c) $(x - 10)(x - 1)$ (d) $(x - 15)(x - 1)$
   (e) $(x - 5)(x - 3)$ (f) $(x - 8)(x - 2)$
   (g) $(x - 10)(x - 2)$ (h) $(x - 8)(x - 3)$

6. (a) $(x - 3)(x + 2)$ (b) $(x - 6)(x + 1)$
   (c) $(x - 4)(x + 6)$ (d) $(x - 3)(x + 8)$
   (e) $(x - 5)(x + 3)$ (f) $(x - 3)(x + 6)$
   (g) $(x - 8)(x + 5)$ (h) $(x - 6)(x + 2)$

7. (a) $(x - 2)^2$ (b) $(x + 5)(x + 6)$
   (c) $(x - 2)(x + 4)$ (d) $(x - 7)(x + 3)$
   (e) $(x - 4)(x + 5)$ (f) $(x + 3)(x + 4)$
   (g) $(x + 4)^2$ (h) $(x - 1)^2$
   (i) $(x - 7)(x + 7)$ (j) $t(t + 12)$
   (k) $(x - 2)(x - 7)$ (l) $(x - 6)(x - 1)$
   (m) $(x + 2)(x + 9)$ (n) $(x + 3)(x + 8)$
   (o) $(x + 1)(x + 18)$ (p) $(x - y)(x + y)$
   (q) $(x + 3)(x - 2)$ (r) $y(y + 4)$
   (s) $(y - 5)^2$ (t) $(x - 6)^2$

Exercise 13.3 — Page 172

1. (a) $x(7x + 5)$ (b) $x(5x - 4)$
   (c) $x(x + 1)$ (d) $y(y - 2)$
   (e) $5y(2 - y)$ (f) $3y(3 - 2y)$
   (g) $2x(3x + 4)$ (h) $t(1 + 5t)$
   (i) $x(5x - 4)$ (j) $4(3x^2 - 2)$

2. (a) $(2x - 1)(2x + 1)$
   (b) $(3x - 7)(3x + 7)$
   (c) $(5 - 2x)(5 + 2x)$
   (d) $(3x - 4)(3x + 4)$
   (e) $(3t - 2s)(3t + 2s)$
   (f) $(10x - 9)(10x + 9)$
   (g) $(11 - 4y)(11 + 4y)$
   (h) $(s - 2t)(s + 2t)$
   (i) $2(5 - x)(5 + x)$
   (j) $3(2x - 3y)(2x + 3y)$

3. (a) 27.2 (b) 50 (c) 79.74

4. (a) $(2x + 3)(x + 4)$
   (b) $(2x + 1)(x + 12)$
   (c) $(2x + 1)^2$
   (d) $(3x + 4)(2x + 3)$
   (e) $(11x + 1)(x + 1)$
   (f) $(3x + 2)(x + 5)$

5. (a) $(2y - 7)(y - 1)$
   (b) $(2x - 1)^2$
   (c) $(3x - 2)(x - 1)$
   (d) $(2x - 1)(x - 1)$
   (e) $(2x - 5)(x - 3)$
   (f) $(3y - 2)^2$

6. (a) $(2x - 3)(x + 2)$
   (b) $(3x + 1)(x - 5)$
   (c) $(3x - 1)(x + 5)$
   (d) $(2y - 7)(y + 1)$
   (e) $(3x + 2)(3x - 1)$
   (f) $(10x - 3)(x + 3)$

559

7. (a) $(3x + 1)(x + 10)$
  (b) $(8x + 7)(8x - 7)$
  (c) $(3x + 5)(x + 2)$
  (d) $(6x + 5)(x - 5)$
  (e) $(5x - 3)(x - 3)$
  (f) $(4x - 5)(2x + 3)$

8. (a) $(5 - 2x)(x - 4)$
  (b) $(3x - 1)^2$
  (c) $(7x - 5)(2 - x)$
  (d) $2(2x + 3)(x + 4)$
  (e) $3(2x - 3)(x + 2)$
  (f) $2(3x - 1)(x + 5)$

Exercise **13.4**   Page 174

1. (a) $x = 2$ or 3 (b) $x = -4$ or -6
  (c) $x = 3$ or -1 (d) $x = 0$ or 5
  (e) $x = 0$ or 4 (f) $x = 0$ or -2

2. (a) $x = 1$ or 2 (b) $y = -3$ or -4
  (c) $m = 4$ or -2 (d) $a = 3$ or -4
  (e) $n = 9$ or -4 (f) $z = 6$ or 3
  (g) $k = -3$ or -5 (h) $c = -7$ or -8
  (i) $b = 4$ or -5 (j) $v = 12$ or -5
  (k) $w = 4$ or -12 (l) $p = 9$ or -8

3. (a) $x = 0$ or 5 (b) $y = 0$ or -1
  (c) $p = 0$ or -3 (d) $a = 0$ or 4
  (e) $t = 0$ or 6 (f) $g = 0$ or 4
  (g) $x = 0$ or -7 (h) $x = 0$ or $\frac{3}{4}$
  (i) $x = 0$ or $\frac{1}{5}$

4. (a) $x = \pm 2$ (b) $y = \pm 12$
  (c) $a = \pm 3$ (d) $d = \pm 4$
  (e) $x = \pm 10$ (f) $x = \pm 6$
  (g) $x = \pm 7$ (h) $x = \pm 1.5$
  (i) $x = \pm 3$ (j) $x = \pm 4$

5. (a) $x = -2\frac{1}{2}$ or -1 (b) $x = -\frac{1}{2}$ or -5
  (c) $x = -1\frac{1}{3}$ or 7 (d) $y = -\frac{2}{3}$ or $-\frac{1}{2}$
  (e) $x = \frac{2}{3}$ or -3 (f) $z = -\frac{1}{3}$ or 2

6. (a) $y = 5$ or -1 (b) $x = -\frac{1}{3}$ or $\frac{1}{2}$
  (c) $x = 7$ or 8 (d) $y = 0$ or 1
  (e) $x = 4$ (f) $z = 3$ or $\frac{1}{6}$
  (g) $x = -3\frac{1}{2}$ or 3 (h) $x = -\frac{2}{3}$ or $\frac{1}{2}$
  (i) $y = -1\frac{1}{4}$ or 2

Exercise **13.5**   Page 175

1. (a) Entries are: 8, 2, 0, 2, 8
  (c) $x = \pm 0.9$

2. (a) Entries are: 6, 2, 0, 0, 2, 6
  (c) $x = -1.6$ or 0.6 (d) $\left(-\frac{1}{2}, -\frac{1}{4}\right)$

3. (a) Entries are: 5, 1, -1, -1, 1, 5
  (c) $x = -0.6$ or 1.6

4. (a) $x = -3$ or 1

5. (a) Entries are: -6, 1, 6, 9, 9, 6, 1, -6
  (c) $x = \pm 2.2$

6. $x = \pm 2.8$

7. (a) $x = \pm 2.8$
  (b) $x = \pm 2.2$
  (c) $x = \pm 1.5$
  (d) $x = \pm 2.4$

Exercise **13.6**   Page 177

1. (a) $x = -0.586$ or -3.41
  (b) $x = -1.62$ or 0.618
  (c) $x = 0.232$ or 1.43
  (d) $x = 0.791$ or 2.78
  (e) $x = -7.30$ or -0.365
  (f) $x = -0.786$ or 2.12
  (g) $z = -2.37$ or -0.634
  (h) $x = -2.72$ or 2.94
  (i) $x = -6.45$ or -1.55

2. (a) $x = -0.851$ or 2.35
  (b) $x = -0.740$ or 0.540
  (c) $x = -3.81$ or 1.31
  (d) $x = 0.148$ or 4.52
  (e) $x = -0.581$ or 2.58
  (f) $x = -3.48$ or 0.479

3. (a) $x = -1.7$ or -0.3,
    $x = -1$, no solutions
  (b) $x = -1.71$ or -0.293,
    $x = -1$, no solutions

4. (a) $b^2 - 4ac > 0$
  (b) $b^2 - 4ac = 0$
  (c) $b^2 - 4ac < 0$
  (d) $\sqrt{b^2 - 4ac}$ rational

Exercise **13.7**   Page 179

1. (a) 8 cm and 15 cm
  (b) 3.2 cm and 6.8 cm

2. (a) $3(8 + 2x)(5 + 2x) = (15 + 2x)(14.5 + 2x)$
  (b) 2.5 m

3. 9.3 cm and 4.3 cm

4. 24 cm by 7 cm

5. 7.24 m by 2.76 m

6. (a) 13 and 18   (b) 3.55 and 8.45

7. 9, 12 and 15; -3, 0 and 3

8. (a) $x^2 - 8x - 20 = 0$
  (b) 10, 11, 13 and 17; -2, -1, 1 and 5

9. (a) 11th
  (b) 15th

10. 3 and 8

1. (b) $x = 4.30$

   (c) $x_{n+1} = \dfrac{5x_n - 3}{x_n}$ is much faster.

2. (b) $x = 1.40$

   (c) $x_{n+1} = \dfrac{7x_n + 2}{6x_n}$ is quicker.

3. $x_2 = 1.7320 \ldots$, x_3 does not exist.

4. E.g. $x_{n+1} = \sqrt{100 - 7x_n}$ with $x_1 = 7$ leads
   to $x = 7.09$

5. E.g. $x_{n+1} = \dfrac{8 - 3x_n}{x_n}$ leads to $x = -4.70$
   Other root is $x = 1.70$

1. (a) $3p^2 - 11p - 4$ (b) $p(3p + 5)$

2. (a) $x^2 - a^2$, $(x - 5)(x + 5)$
   (b) $2x^2(x^3 + 2)$

3. $x(x - 2)(x + 2)$ 4. $x = -3$ or $\frac{1}{2}$

5. $\frac{1}{2}(2x - 1)(x + 1) = 52$,
   height of triangle $= 8\,\text{cm}$

6. (a) $x(x + 3) = 2(x + 1)$
   (b) $BC = 1\,\text{cm}$

7. (a) $x = 5$ or 15

8. (a) $(60 - 2x)\,x = 300$
   (b) $x = 6.34$ or 23.7

9. (a) Entries for y: 6, 1, -2, -3, -2, 1, 6
   (c) $x = -0.7$ or 2.7

10. (a) $x_2 = 3.3166 \ldots$ $x_3 = 3.2119 \ldots$
    $x_4 = 3.1956 \ldots$
    (b) $x = 3.193$ (or -2.193)

11. (a) $x(6 - x) = 7$
    (b) Entries for y: 7, 2, -1, -2, -1, 2, 7
    (c) $4.4\,\text{cm}$ by $1.6\,\text{cm}$

12. (a) $2x^2 + 5x + 3$ (b) $40.5\,\text{m}^2$ (c) $8.2\,\text{m}$

CHAPTER 14

1. (a) $2x^2 - 3x + 34$
   (b) $3x^2 - 2x + 5$
   (c) 1
   (d) $-14x^2 + 66x - 18$

2. (a) $-6x + 29y - 24z$
   (b) 0
   (c) $10x^2 + 12xy + 10y^2$
   (d) $13x^2 + 24xy + 13y^2$

1. (a) $x = \pm 2.8$
   (b) $x = \pm 2$,   draw $y = 4$
   (c) $x = -2.7$ or 2.2,   draw $y = \frac{1}{2}x + 2$
   (d) $x = -2.4$ or 3.4,   draw $y = -x$

2. $x = -1.4$ or 2.9

3. (a) $x = -2, 0$ or 2
   (b) $x = -1.5, -0.7$ or 2.3,   draw $y = 1$
   (c) $x = -2.5, 0$ or 2.5,   draw $y = x$
   (d) $x = -1.1$ or 2.2,   draw $y = 3 - x$

4. (a) $y = -x - 1$ (b) $y = 1 - x^2$
   (c) $y = x^3 + 2$

5. $x = 1.6$ 6. $x = 0.7$

1. (a) $\dfrac{4}{x - 3}$ (b) $\dfrac{x + 2}{3}$

   (c) $\dfrac{2x - 3}{x + 5}$ (d) $\dfrac{17 - x}{x + 3}$

   (e) $\dfrac{x + 2y + 3z}{2x - 3y + z}$ (f) $\dfrac{8x + 9}{3x + 2}$

   (g) $\dfrac{x + 2}{3x + 2}$ (h) $-\dfrac{1}{2}$

2. (a) **E**   (b) **C**   (c) **B**   (d) **A**   (e) D

3. (a) $\dfrac{x + 5y}{3 + 4xy}$ (b) $\dfrac{x + y + 2z}{2x - 3y + z}$

   (c) $\dfrac{ab - 3}{b + a}$ (d) $\dfrac{x + b + y}{ab - 2y}$

4. (a) $\dfrac{x}{x + 1}$ (b) $\dfrac{x + 2}{x + 3}$

   (c) $\dfrac{x}{x + 3}$ (d) $\dfrac{x - 5}{x + 3}$

   (e) $\dfrac{x - 2}{x - 3}$ (f) $\dfrac{x - 5}{x + 4}$

   (g) $\dfrac{x - 5}{x - 4}$ (h) $\dfrac{2x - 5}{3x - 1}$

1. (a) $\frac{2}{3}$ (b) $-1\frac{1}{4}$ (c) $\dfrac{y}{2}$

2. (a) $\frac{2}{3}$ (b) $-\frac{1}{2}$ (c) $-\dfrac{2}{x}$

3. (a) $\dfrac{7x + 8}{(x + 5)(x - 4)}$ (b) $\dfrac{37x + 3}{(2x + 3)(5x - 3)}$

   (c) $\dfrac{3x^2 + 4x - 14}{(x + 2)(x - 3)}$

4. (a) $\dfrac{x - 31}{(x + 5)(x - 4)}$ (b) $\dfrac{13x - 33}{(2x + 3)(5x - 3)}$

   (c) $\dfrac{x^2 + 2x + 10}{(x - 3)(x + 2)}$

5. (a) $\dfrac{7x-12}{x(2x-6)}$ (b) $\dfrac{7-x}{2x}$

(c) $\dfrac{x^2-3x+9}{x(2x-6)}$ (d) $\dfrac{4}{x-3}$

(e) $\dfrac{3}{4x}$ (f) $\dfrac{x-3}{4}$

Exercise 14.5 — Page 191

2. (b) $x=-0.2$ or 6

3. (a) $x=-1.5$ or 0.25 (b) $x=-2$ or 0.8
(c) $x=-0.721$ or 1.39 (d) $x=-\frac{5}{7}$ or 6

4. (a) $\dfrac{60}{x}+\dfrac{90}{x+6}=5\frac{1}{2}$ (c) $24\,\text{km/h}$

5. (d) $23\,\text{cm}\times 28\,\text{cm}$

Exercise 14.6 — Page 194

1. (a) $(x+3)^2+11$ (b) $(x+3)^2-4$
(c) $(x+5)^2-29$ (d) $(x-2)^2+1$
(e) $(x-2)^2-2$ (f) $(x-2)^2-8$
(g) $(x-3)^2-5$ (h) $(x-4)^2-16$
(i) $(x+6)^2-36$

2. (a) $a=3,\ b=6$
(b) $a=5,\ b=-20$
(c) $a=-3,\ b=-14$
(d) $a=-4,\ b=-12$
(e) $a=6,\ b=-32$
(f) $a=3,\ b=0$

3. (a) $(2x+4)^2-11$;
$p=2,\ q=4,\ r=-11$
(b) $(3x+2)^2-1$;
$p=3,\ q=2,\ r=-1$
(c) $(5x-4)^2-19$;
$p=5,\ q=-4,\ r=-19$
(d) $(4x+4)^2-21$;
$p=4,\ q=4,\ r=-21$
(e) $(10x+3)^2-6$;
$p=10,\ q=3,\ r=-6$
(f) $(4x-5)^2-16$;
$p=4,\ q=-5,\ r=-16$

4. (a) $x=-3.45$ or -1.45
(b) $x=-2.90$ or 6.90
(c) $x=-2$ or 8
(d) $x=-6$ or -2
(e) $x=-2$ or 6
(f) $x=-1.5$ or 2.5

Exercise 14.7 — Page 195

1. $x=9.4$

2. (a) $x=6.2$ (b) $x=6.22$

3. (a) $2x^2(x+2)$ (b) $x=5.3$

4. $x=1.82$

Review Exercise 14 — Page 196

1. (a) x^2+xy
(b) (i) $2x^2+5xy-3y^2$ (ii) $x^2+2xy+y^2$

2. $x+2y$ **3.** $y=2x+1$

4. $x=2.1$ **5.** $x=1.3$

6. $\dfrac{6}{x-2}$ **7.** $\dfrac{3}{(2x+1)(x+1)}$

8. $x=-1.66$ or 0.906

9. (b) $x=-0.781$ or 1.28

10. (b) $=-70$ or 50

11. (a) $\dfrac{2x-1}{x+2}$ (b) $p=4,\ q=1$

12. (a) $(x-5)^2-18$ (b) $x=0.757$ or 9.24

13. (a) $(x-2)^2-2$; $a=-2,\ b=-2$
minimum value $=-2$
(b) $x=0.59$ or 3.41

14. $x=2.59$

15. $x=3.7$

CHAPTER 15

Exercise 15.1 — Page 199

1. a and c

2. (a) C, D (b) A, F, G (c) B, E (d) F

3. (b) (ii) yes
(c) (i) yes (ii) no

4. $P:0.75, Q:0, R:-1.5$ **5.** 0.6 **6.** -0.5

7. (b) (i) 0 (ii) 2 (iii) 4
(iv) 5 (v) 6 (vi) 8
(c) graph getting steeper as x increases

8. (b) (i) 18.8 (ii) 12 (iii) 6.8
(iv) 3 (v) 0.8 (vi) 0
(vii) 0.8 (viii) 3 (ix) 6.8
(x) 12 (xi) 18.8
(c) symmetrical about $(0, 0)$

Exercise 15.2 — Page 202

1. (b) $-2\leqslant x<1$
(c) (i) -4 (ii) 2

2. (b) 0.4, Jane is increasing in weight at the rate of $0.4\,\text{kg/week}$ at the age of 5 weeks.

3. (b) $0.07\,\text{cm/s}$ **4.** (b) $0.9\,\text{m/s}$

5. (b) $2\,\text{cm/min}$

6. (a) 3
(b) The oil slick is increasing in area at a rate of $3\,\text{km}^2/\text{hour}$

Exercise 15.3 — Page 205

1. (a) (i) A and B, C and D, D and E, E and F
   (ii) C and D, E and F
   (iii) D and E
   (iv) A and B, C and D, D and E, E and F
   (b) (i) 1.2 m/s   (ii) 2.2 m/s

2. (a) (i) B and C, D and E
   (ii) A and B, E and F
   (iii) F and G
   (iv) A and B
   (v) B and C, D and E
   (vi) F and G

3. (a) 0.5 km/min (= 30 km/h)
   (b) 0.3 km/min (= 20 km/h)
   (c) 0.4 km/min (= 24 km/h)

4. (a) (i) 40 seconds   (ii) 900 m
   (iii) 22.5 m/s
   (b) 30 m/s   (c) 21 m/s

5. (a) 2 minutes   (b) 1 minute   (c) 0.8 m/s²

6.

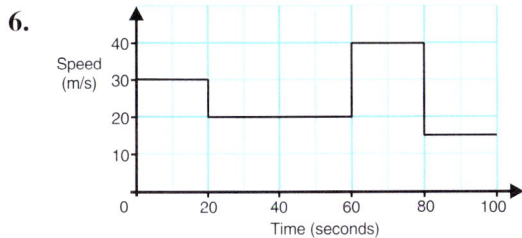

7. 2.8 m/s

8. (a) Tom accelerates at a constant rate for the first 75 seconds of his ride. His acceleration is then non-uniform until he reaches a maximum speed of 7 m/s. Tom then slows down to stop at 260 seconds.
   (b) 0.06 m/s²
   (c) 0.05 m/s²
   (d) 155 seconds

Exercise 15.4 — Page 210

1. (b) 21 sq. units

2. (a) 28 sq. units   (b) 30 sq. units
   (c) 30.5 sq. units

3. (a) 20 sq. units   (b) 19 sq. units
   (c) 18.75 sq. units

4. (b) 11 sq. units   5. 20 sq. units

6. 40 sq. units   7. 100 sq. units

Exercise 15.5 — Page 212

1. (a) 52.5, 51
   (b) (i) flow, distance
       (ii) litres, kilometres

2. (a) 55.6 sq. units
   (b) Distance travelled in metres

3. (a) The bus accelerates at a constant rate for the first 30 seconds, then travels at a constant speed of 15 m/s.
   (b) 640 m

4. 120 m

5. 26 seconds

6. 160 420 cm³   (160 000 cm³)

7. 15 500 litres, amount of oil escaped in the 5 hours after the collision.

8. (b) 26.6 sq. units   (c) 73.4°C

9. (a) (ii) $A = 2x$
   (b) (i) $A = x$ (ii) $A = 3x$
       (iii) $A = 4x$ (iv) $A = 10x$
       In general $A = yx$
   (c) (i) $A = \frac{1}{2}x^2$ (ii) $A = x^2$
       (iii) $A = \frac{3}{2}x^2$ (iv) $A = 2x^2$
       In general $A = \frac{1}{y}x^y$

Review Exercise 15 — Page 216

1. (a) 4.17 m/s
   (b)

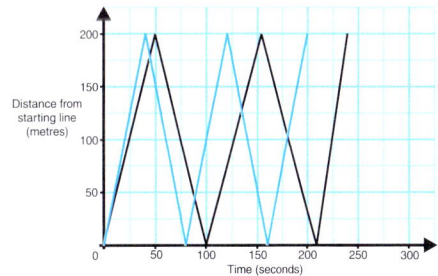

2. (a) 80 seconds   (b) 10 m
   (c) Robert, gradient steeper

3. (a) B and C, F and G (b) E and F
   (c) H and K

4. 1.2 cm/s

5. (a) 0.3 m/s²   (b) 2.2 km

6. (a) 1000 km/h   (b) 1600 km/h²
   (c) 2970 km

7. (a) 4 minutes
   (b) The train slowed down from 80 mph to 40 mph over a two-minute period, travelled at a constant speed of 40 mph for 1 minute before slowing to a stop at 20 minutes.
   (c) 600 m/h²   (d) 15 miles

8. (a) 7.2 km   (b) 50 seconds

9. (a) 0.35 m/s²   (b) 1100 m

10. (a) $1.6 \, \text{m/s}^2$
(b) (i) $153.75 \, \text{m}$
(ii) distance travelled in the first 10 seconds.

11. (a) (i) 0.03 (ii) 0.02 (iii) 0.03
(b) The rate at which the depth of liquid gas changes in the tank

12. $347.5 \, \text{mm}$ (35 cm)

CHAPTER 16

Exercise 16.1   Page 223

1. (a)

x	-2	-1	0	1	2
y	-8	-1	0	1	8

(b)

x	-2	-1	0	1	2
y	-6	1	2	3	10

(c)

x	1	2	3	4	5
y	-8	-1	0	1	8

(d)

x	-2	-1	0	1	2
y	-16	-2	0	2	16

(c) (i) Translation, vector $\begin{pmatrix} 0 \\ 2 \end{pmatrix}$

(ii) Translation, vector $\begin{pmatrix} 3 \\ 0 \end{pmatrix}$

(iii) Stretch, from x parallel to y axis, scale factor 2

(d) (i) $y = x^3 - 5$ (ii) $y = (x - 2)^3$

2. **a:** $y = x^2 + 1$ **b:** $y = x^2 - 4$
c: $y = (x - 1)^2$ **d:** $y = (x + 1)^2$

3. (a) Translation, vector $\begin{pmatrix} 0 \\ 3 \end{pmatrix}$

(b) Translation, vector $\begin{pmatrix} 2 \\ 0 \end{pmatrix}$

(c) Stretch, from x axis, parallel to y axis, scale factor 2

(d) Stretch, from y axis, parallel to x axis, scale factor 2

4. **a:** $y = 4x^2$ **b:** $y = \frac{1}{2}x^2$
c: $y = (4x)^2$ **d:** $y = -2x^2$

5. (a) $y = 9 - x^2$ (b) $y = 2(4 - x^2)$

(c) $y = 4 - \left(\frac{1}{2}x\right)^2$

6. (a) $y = x^4 - x^3 - 5$

(b) $y = (x - 3)^4 - (x - 3)^3$

(c) $y = \frac{1}{2}(x^4 - x^3)$

(d) $y = \left(\frac{1}{2}x\right)^4 - \left(\frac{1}{2}x\right)^3$

Exercise 16.2   Page 227

1. (a)
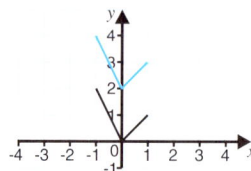

(b) Translation, vector $\begin{pmatrix} 0 \\ 2 \end{pmatrix}$

(c) (i)
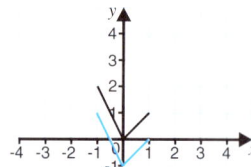

Translation, vector $\begin{pmatrix} 0 \\ -1 \end{pmatrix}$

(ii)
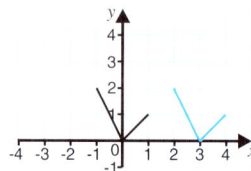

Translation, vector $\begin{pmatrix} 3 \\ 0 \end{pmatrix}$

(iii)
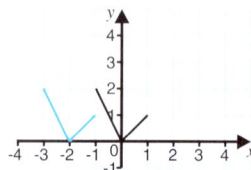

Translation, vector $\begin{pmatrix} -2 \\ 0 \end{pmatrix}$

(iv)
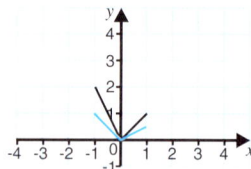

Stretch, from x axis, parallel to y axis, scale factor 0.5

(v)
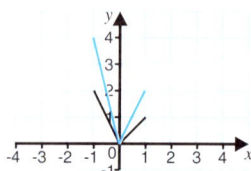

Stretch, from x axis, parallel to y axis, scale factor 2

(vi)
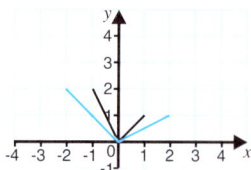

Stretch, from y axis, parallel to x axis, scale factor 2

(vii)

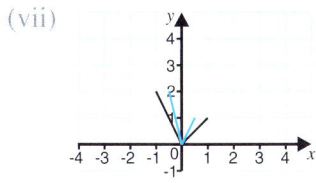

Stretch, from y axis, parallel to x axis, scale factor 0.5

(viii)

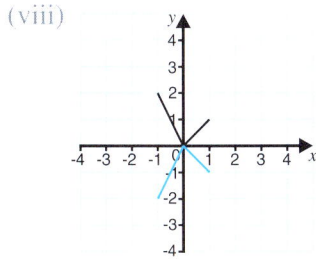

Reflection in x axis

(ix)

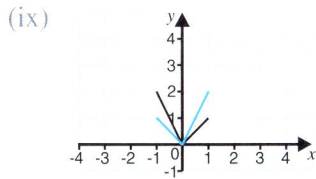

Reflection in y axis

(x)

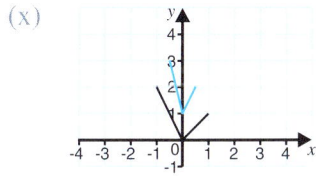

Stretch, from y axis, parallel to x axis, scale factor 0.5, followed by, translation, vector $\begin{pmatrix} 0 \\ 1 \end{pmatrix}$

(xi)

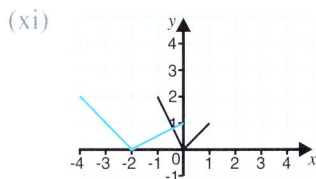

Translation, vector $\begin{pmatrix} -1 \\ 0 \end{pmatrix}$, followed by, stretch, from y axis, parallel to x axis, scale factor 2

(xii)

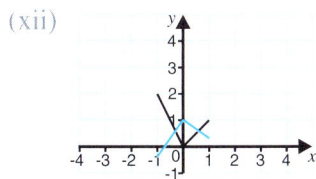

Reflection in x axis, followed by, translation, vector $\begin{pmatrix} 0 \\ 1 \end{pmatrix}$

2. (a)

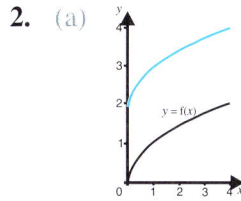

(b)

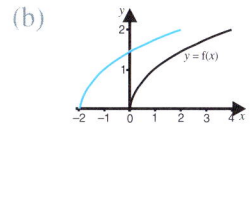

(c)

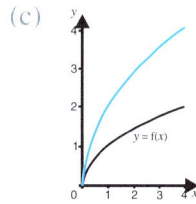

(d)

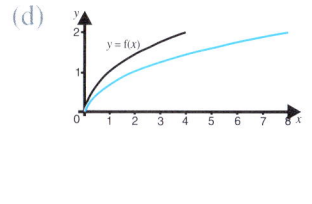

(e)

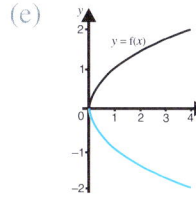

3. (a)

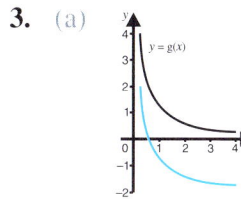

(b)

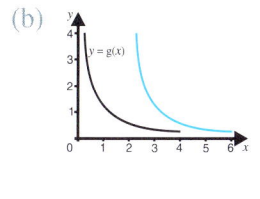

(c)

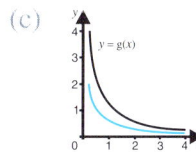

(d)

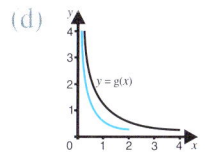

(e)

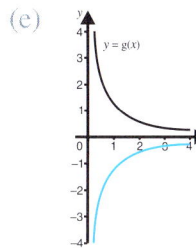

4. (a)

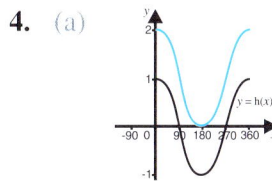

(b)

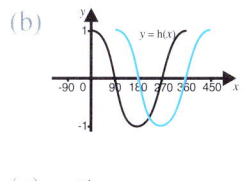

(c)

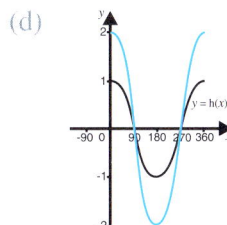

(d)

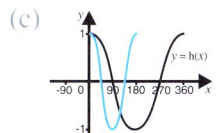

(e)

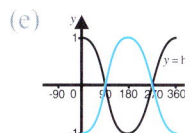

5. (a) (i)

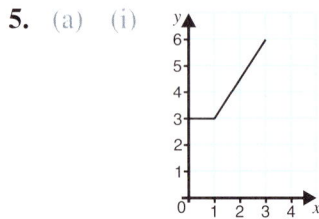

(ii) $g(x) = 3f(x)$

(b) (i)

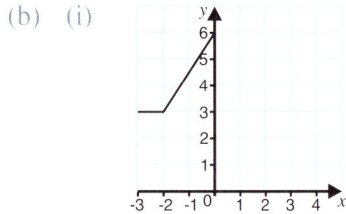

(ii) $h(x) = g(x + 3)$
(iii) $h(x) = 3f(x + 3)$

(c) (i)

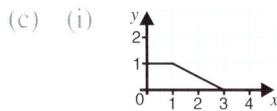

(ii)

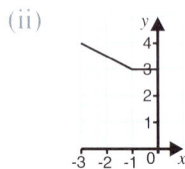

(d)

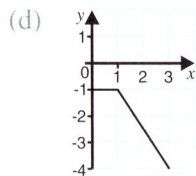

$y = 2 - 3f(x)$

6. **a:** $y = 2f(x)$ **b:** $y = f(x - 2)$
   c: $y = f(x) - 5$ **d:** $y = f(-x)$
   e: $y = 2f(x + 5) - 7$

7. $A(x) = f(2x)$

$B(x) = f(2x + 5)$

$C(x) = 1 - f(x)$

8. (a) Reflection in x axis.
   (b) Stretch, from y axis, parallel to x axis, scale factor $\frac{1}{2}$.
   (c) Reflection in x axis.
   (d) Reflection in x axis, followed by, stretch, from y axis, parallel to x axis, scale factor $\frac{1}{2}$. (Transformations in either order.)
   (e) **a:** $y = -\sin x$
      b: $y = \sin 2x$
      c: $y = -\sin 2x$

Exercise 16.3   Page 231

1. (a) $y = 28x + 13$, $q = 40.3 - 12.8p$
   (b) (i) $y = 88.6$ (ii) $p = 2.55$

2. (a) $l = 0.0625w + 20$
   (b) (i) $l = 51.25$ (ii) $w = 560$

3. $a = 0.1$, $b = 2.4$

4. 2.1 m/s^2

5. (a) Non-linear graph
   (b) Linear graph, $y = 25x^3 + 22.7$,
      $a = 25$, $b = 22.7$

6. $a = 0.05$, $b = 2.4$ **7.** $a = 0.2$, $b = 5$

8. $n = 3$, $a = -0.2$, $b = 10.3$

Exercise 16.4   Page 234

1. $1 \rightarrow$ (c), $2 \rightarrow$ (a), $3 \rightarrow$ (b)

2. (a) $f(x) = 0.5x^2 + 1.6$

   (b) $f(x) = 0.5\sqrt{x} + 1.6$

   (c) $f(x) = 0.5x^3 + 1.6$

   (d) $f(x) = \dfrac{0.5}{x} + 1.6$

   (e) $f(x) = \dfrac{0.5}{x^2} + 1.6$

   (f) $f(x) = \dfrac{0.5}{\sqrt{x}} + 1.6$

3. (a) $n = 2$, $a = 0.04$, $b = 8$
   (b) $n = -1$, $a = 6.2$, $b = 4.7$
   (c) $n = -0.5$, $a = 12$, $b = 3.6$
   (d) $n = 0.5$, $a = 5.7$, $b = -4.8$
   (e) $n = -2$, $a = 2.4$, $b = 2.2$

4. (a) $k = 2$, $n = -0.5$ (b) $k = 8$, $n = 0.5$

5. (a) $y = ax^{\frac{1}{2}} + b$

   (b) $a = 0.49$, $b = 2.51$,
      $y = 0.49x^{\frac{1}{2}} + 2.51$

Exercise 16.5   Page 238

1. (a) $a = 2$, $b = 1.5$
   (b) $a = 0.2$, $b = 2.5$
   (c) $a = 3.5$, $b = 0.4$
   (d) $a = 5$, $b = 2$
   (e) $a = 8$, $b = 0.5$
   (f) $a = 10$, $b = 0.6$

2. (a) $y = 2.6$ (b) $y = 390.1625$

3. (a) $y = 20$ (b) $y = 0.565$ (3 sig. fig.)

4. (a) (i) Graph shows experimental decay. Yes.
   (b) (i) $t = 0$ (ii) $a = 10$, $b = 0.9$
   (c) 7 days

1. (a) (b)

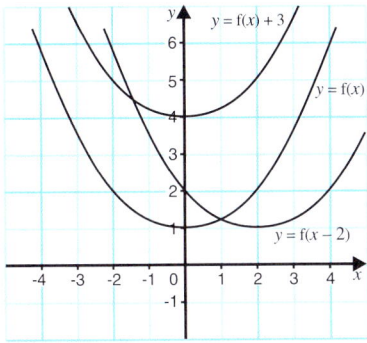

2. (a) (i)

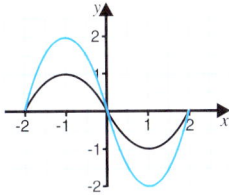

(ii)

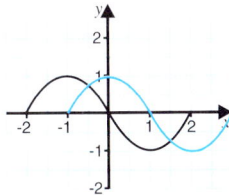

(b) **C**, $a - 0.5$

3. (a)

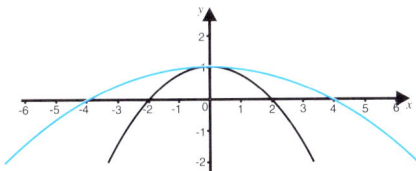

(b)

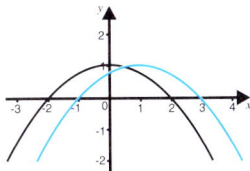

4. (a)

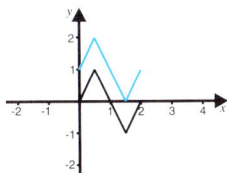

(b)

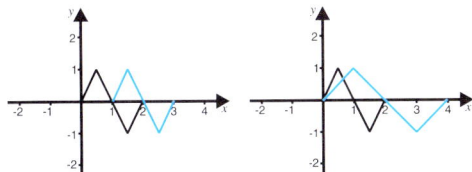

5. (a)

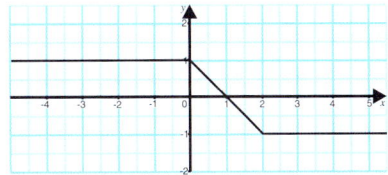

(b)

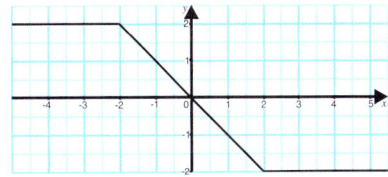

6.

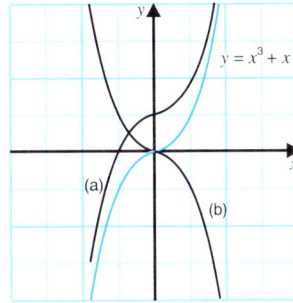

7.

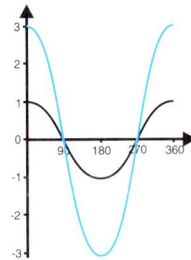

8. (a) $y = (x - 1)^3$

(b) $y = x^3 + 1$

(c) $y = \frac{1}{2} x^3$

(d) $y = (2x)^3$

(e) $y = (-x)^3$

(f) $y = \frac{1}{2}(-x)^3 - 0.5$

9. (a) $a = 4.1$, $b = 0$

(b) G, furthest below line

(c) 39

10. $p = 0.4$, $q = 3.6$

11. (a) $a = 14.4$, $b = 2.8$ (b) $x = 0.5$

12. (a) $a = 0.4$, $n = 0.5$ (b) $y = 135$

13. $a = 5$, $b = 3$

14. (a) $a = 3, b = 2, n = -\frac{1}{2}$

(b) Graph has equation $y = 5x^{\frac{2}{3}} - 8$

15. $p = 10, q = 0.6, (0, 10)$

16. (a) $n = 10\,000$ (b) 1070

Section Review   **Page 244**

1. $x = -2\frac{1}{2}$ **2.** £228.62

3. (a) 18 km   (b) 20.6 km/h

4. (a) $y = 9.6$ (b) $y = 7.07$

5. (a) By Pythagoras, $x^2 + x^2 = 80^2$,
so $2x^2 = 6400$ (b) $x = 56.6$

6. (a) $x - 6$ (b) $x = 2$ (c) $x = 3.6$

7. (a) $x = 2\frac{1}{4}$ (b) $2x^2 + 5x - 3$

8. (a) $4n - 1$ (b) (i) 38 (ii) $n^2 + 2$

9. (a) $3n - 1$ (b) $n^2 + 1$

10. $n^2 + n$

11. (b) $x = 1.7$, value of x at point where $y = 2x$ and $x + y = 5$ intersect. (c)

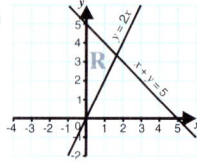

12. (a) $x = -\frac{1}{2}$ (b) $m(m - 7)$
(c) 6, 7, 8 (d) $x = -2$, $y = 1.5$

13. (a) $G\,(0, 5)$, $H\,(10, 0)$

(b) (i)

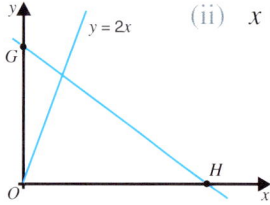

(ii) $x = 2$, $y = 4$

(c) $x = \dfrac{y - b}{a}$

14. (a) $6a^{-2}$ (b) $4\frac{1}{4}$

15. (a) (i) $8a^7$ (ii) b^4 (iii) $25c^6$
(b) $6xy\,(y - x)$ (c) $m^2 + 2m + 1$

16. (a) $2xy\,(2 - x)$ (b) $x^2 + x - 6$
(c) $x = -8$ or 5

17. (a) $x > 7$
(b) (i) $12x^5$ (ii) $9y^6$
(c) $2x^2 - 7x + 3$

18. (a) (i) 2, 3, 4, 5
(ii) $-3.08 < x < 3.08$ (3 s.f.)
(b) $x = 2.8$

19. (a) $-4, -3, -2, -1, 0, 1$
(b) (i) $x < \frac{1}{2}$ (ii) $y \leqslant -5$ and $y \geqslant 5$
(c) $a = \dfrac{e + mc}{m}$ or $a = \dfrac{e}{m} + c$

20. (a) $x = \frac{1}{4}$ (b) $3x^2 - 5x - 2$
(c) $x = 0$ or 8

21. (a) $x = 2$ or 5 (b) $x < 6$

22. (a) $x = \dfrac{by}{3a}$ (b) $1 : 30$

23. $x = 1.3$

24. (a) $y = 0.1x + 480$ (b) £1020

25. (a) $y = x + 2.5$
(b) E.g. $y = x +$ (any number)

26. (a)

x	-2	-1	0	1	2	3	4
y	6	1	-2	-3	-2	1	6

(c) (i) $x = -0.7$ or 2.7 (ii) 2

27.

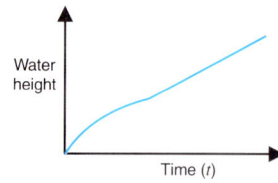

28. (a)

x	-3	-2	-1	0	1	2	3
y	-22	-3	4	5	6	13	32

(c) $x = -1.7$

29. $(x + 2)(x + 1) = 6$
$x^2 + 3x + 2 = 6$
$x^2 + 3x - 4 = 0$

30. (a) $(2x)^2 + 4x = 48$
$4x^2 + 4x - 48 = 0$
$x^2 + x - 12 = 0$
(b) $x = 3$ $(x \neq -4)$

31. (a) $(3x + 2)(x + 1) = 80$
$3x^2 + 5x - 78 = 0$
(b) $x = 4\frac{1}{3}$, area of lawn $= 56.3\,\text{m}^2$

32. (a) $£\left(\dfrac{104}{x + 1}\right)$

(b) (ii) $\dfrac{104}{x + 1} = \dfrac{84}{x} + 1$
$104x = 84(x + 1) + x(x + 1)$
$x^2 - 19x + 84 = 0$
(c) $x = 7$ or 12

33. (a) $c = \frac{1}{2}$
(b) (i) $y = 5.6$ (ii) $x = 4$

34. (a) (i) $\frac{40}{21}$ (ii) $\frac{200}{101}$
(b) The value gets closer to 2

35. (a) (i) $y = 1 - x^2$ (ii) $2y = 2 + x$
(iii) $y = x^2$ (iv) $xy = 1$

(b)

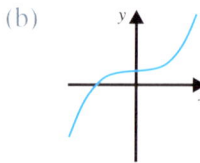

36. $x = 1.2$

37. (b) Draw the line $y = 1 - x$
$x = -0.4$ or 2.4
(c) Draw the line $y = 1$
$x \leqslant -0.3$ and $x \geqslant 3.3$

38. $10\,\text{m/s}$

39. (a) The train accelerates from rest to $30\,\text{m/s}$, travels at a constant speed before slowing to stop after a total of 100 seconds.
(b) $2\,\text{m/s}^2$ (c) $1.9\,\text{km}$

40. (a) $46\,\mathrm{m^2}$ (b) $9.2\,\mathrm{m^3}$

41. (a) $a = -3$, $b = -2$, minimum value $= -2$
     (b) $p = 3$, $q = 1$

42. (a) (i) $x_2 = 1.71$, $x_3 = 2.10$, $x_4 = 1.97$
        (ii) $x_n \approx 2$

     (b) (i) $x = \dfrac{12}{x + 4}$

           $x(x + 4) = 12$
           $x^2 + 4x - 12 = 0$
        (ii) $x = -6$ or 2

43. (a) $a = \dfrac{5c + 6}{c + 4}$

     (b) $\dfrac{x^2 + 1}{(x - 1)(x + 1)}$

44. (a) $a = 4$, $b = -1$, $c = -6$
     (b) $p = 17$

45. $x = -3.6$ or 0.14 (2 d.p.)

46. $x = -1\frac{1}{2}$ or 2

47. (a) $y = x^2 - 3$ (b) $y = (x + 2)^2$
     (c) $y = \frac{1}{2}x^2$ (d) $y = -\frac{1}{2}x^2 - 3$

48. (a) (i)

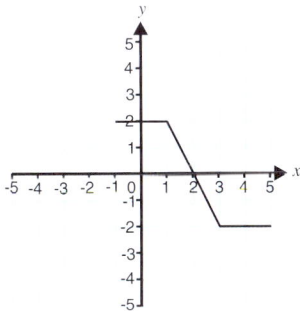

       (ii)

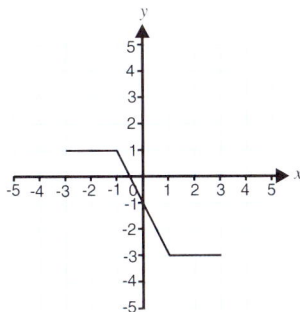

     (b)

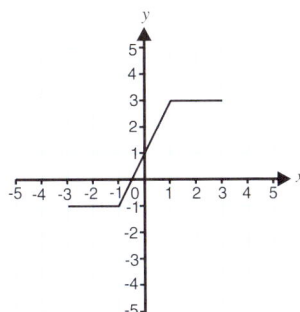

CHAPTER 17

Exercise 17.1   Page 254

1. (a) $a = 96°$
     (b) $b = 20°$
     (c) $c = 150°$
     (d) $d = 133°$, $e = 47°$
     (e) $f = 43°$, $g = 47°$
     (f) $h = 157°$, $i = 67°$

2. (a) $45°$ (b) $30°$ (c) $60°$ (d) $36°$

3. (a) $26°$ (b) $9°$ (c) $52°$ (d) $22°$

4. (a) $a = 66°$
     (b) $b = 54°$, $c = 54°$, $d = 71°$
     (c) $e = 42°$, $f = 132°$
     (d) $g = 95°$, $h = 43°$
     (e) $i = 69°$
     (f) $j = 38°$

5. (a) $\angle AOB = 153°$, $\angle COD = 37°$
     (b) $\angle QTU = 48°$, $\angle QTS = 132°$
     (c) $\angle TUV = 280°$

Exercise 17.2   Page 257

1. (a) yes   (b) yes   (c) no
     (d) no   (e) yes   (f) no

2. (a) yes, obtusc-angled
     (b) no
     (c) yes, acute-angled
     (d) yes, right-angled
     (e) yes, obtuse-angled

3. (a) $a = 70°$ (b) $b = 37°$ (c) $c = 114°$

4. (a) $a = 120°$ (b) $b = 110°$ (c) $c = 50°$

5. $\angle BAD = 126°$, $\angle BCE = 54°$

Exercise 17.3   Page 260

1. Any point on the line $y = x$, except $(1.5, 1.5)$

2. $(6, 2)$, $(6, 8)$

3. (a) $\angle BCD = 120°$
     (b) $\angle PRQ = 80°$, $\angle QRS = 160°$
     (c) $\angle MNX = 50°$

4. $S\,(3, 2)$ **5.** $C\,(5, 4)$ **6.** $Y\,(6, 4)$

7. $A\,(1, 3)$ **8.** $L\,(2, 3)$

9. (a) $a = 62°$
     (b) $b = 54°$, $c = 36°$
     (c) $d = 62°$
     (d) $e = 116°$, $f = 86°$
     (e) $g = 124°$
     (f) $h = 75°$
     (g) $i = 38°$, $j = 42°$
     (h) $k = 55°$, $l = 45°$

10.

A	B	C	D	E	F	G	H	I
1	0	1	4	2	2	0	0	1
1	1	1	4	2	2	1	2	1

11. (a) C (b) D (c) E
(d) A (e) B (f) G

12. (a) $a = 30°$
(b) $b = 58°$
(c) $c = 15°$
(d) $d = 70°$, $e = 45°$
(e) $f = 50°$
(f) $g = 117°$
(g) $h = 25°$, $i = 65°$, $j = 90°$
(h) $k = 68°$
(i) $l = 70°$
(j) $m = 85°$
(k) $n = 28°$, $o = 80°$
(l) $p = 70°$

13. (a) 70° (b) 30°

14. 50°

15. (a) $22\frac{1}{2}°$ (b) $112\frac{1}{2}°$ (c) $22\frac{1}{2}°$

Exercise 17.4 Page 265

1. (a) $a = 80°$ (b) $b = 70°$
(c) $c = 85°$ (d) $d = 120°$
(e) $e = 130°$ (f) $f = 250°$
(g) $g = 60°$ (h) $h = 199°$
(i) $i = 45°$

2. (a) 900° (b) 1080° (c) 1260°

3. (a) 72° (b) 108° (c) 540°

4. 20   **5.** 8

6. $a = 150°$ $b = 105°$ $c = 126°$
$d = 156°$ $e = 66°$ $f = 96°$
$g = 132°$ $h = 102°$

7. (a) $x = 108°$ (b) $y = 36°$

8. 153°   **9.** 150°   **10.** $y = 180 - \dfrac{360}{x}$

11. At any vertex, sum of angles cannot equal 360°.

13. Yes, all quadrilaterals tessellate.
(a) (i) Yes (ii) Yes

Review Exercise 17 Page 269

1. $x = 117°$, $y = 27°$

2. (a) 42° (b) 69°

3. $y = 108°$

4. $\angle BDA = 40°$, $\angle ABD = 90°$

5. $x = 20°$
$\angle ACD = 100°$, $\angle CAD = 40°$, $AC = CD$,
$\angle BAD = 60° - 40° = 20°$

6. 110°   **7.** $y = 63°$

8. 720°   **9.** $\angle PTS = 135°$

10. (a) $\angle BCO = 67°$ (b) $\angle OWX = 136°$
(c) $\angle WXY = 60°$

11. $\angle LHB = 37°$

12. $p = 108°$, $q = 72°$, $r = 72°$

13. (a) $a = 30$ (b) 12

14. $\angle BDC = 34°$

CHAPTER 18

Exercise 18.1 Page 274

1. (a) $a = 90°$
(b) $b = 38°$
(c) $c = 77°$
(d) $d = 33°$
(e) $e = 70°$, $f = 140°$
(f) $g = 130°$, $h = 65°$
(g) $i = 40°$
(h) $j = 72°$
(i) $k = 106°$, $l = 62°$
(j) $m = 108°$, $n = 105°$
(k) $p = 25°$
(l) $q = 65°$, $r = 65°$
(m) $s = 292°$, $t = 56°$
(n) $u = 140°$
(o) $v = 110°$, $w = 75°$
(p) $x = 130°$, $y = 82°$

2. 47°

3. $\angle BCD = 70°$, $\angle CAD = 76°$

4. 119°

5. $\angle PQR = 105°$, $\angle QRS = 118°$

6. $\angle PSR = 45°$, $\angle TPQ = 95°$

7. (a) 140° (b) 70°

8. (a) 100° (b) 40° (c) 25°

9. 25°   **10.** 90°

Exercise 18.2 Page 277

1. (a) $a = 78°$, $b = 39°$
(b) $c = 90°$, $d = 49°$, $e = 49°$
(c) $f = 50°$, $g = 50°$
(d) $h = 55°$, $i = 38°$, $j = 38°$
(e) $k = 50°$
(f) $l = 65°$, $m = 65°$
(g) $n = 63°$, $p = 54°$
(h) $q = 146°$
(i) $r = 16°$, $s = 106°$
(j) $t = 65°$, $u = 65°$
(k) $v = 67\frac{1}{2}°$, $w = 57\frac{1}{2}°$, $x = 45°$

2. (a) 84° (b) 42° (c) 84°

3. (a) 48° (b) 6°

4. (a) 67° (b) 46°

5. (a) 100° (b) 40° (c) 25°

6. (a) 72° (b) 36° (c) 54°

7. $x = 120°$, $y = 36°$, $z = 60°$

8. $p = 42°$, $q = 55°$, $r = 13°$, $s = 55°$

9. 90

Review Exercise 18 — Page 280

1. (a) $x = 42°$, $y = 90°$, $z = 48°$ (b) 42°

2. 60°

3. (a) 100° (b) 30° (c) 50°

4. 18° **5.** $x = 50°$, $y = 28°$, $z = 30°$

6. (a) 79° (b) 25°

7. $x = 94°$, $y = 28°$, $z = 19°$

8. $57\frac{1}{2}°$ **9.** 50°

10. (a) 25° (b) 40° (c) 115°

11. $\angle QRP = 50°$, $\angle RPS = 40°$

12. (a) 30° (b) 35° (c) 10°

CHAPTER 19

Exercise 19.1 — Page 283

1. (a) (i) 12.6 cm (ii) 17.6 cm (iii) 20.1 cm
(b) (i) 12.6 cm² (ii) 24.6 cm² (iii) 32.2 cm²

2. (a) 28.3 cm² (b) 59.4 cm² (c) 128.6 cm²

3. 7.96 cm **4.** 3.8 cm **5.** 30 mm

6. 13.3 cm **7.** 3.99 cm **8.** 18.2 cm²

9. 38.6 cm **10.** 326 cm² **11.** 40.1 cm²

12. 49π cm² **13.** 24π cm **14.** 8 cm

15. 65π cm²

Exercise 19.2 — Page 285

1. (a) 3.14 cm (b) 2.09 cm (c) 6.28 cm
(d) 10.5 cm (e) 15.6 cm (f) 26.4 cm

2. (a) 7.07 cm² (b) 6.98 cm² (c) 28.3 cm²
(d) 67.5 cm² (e) 34.2 cm² (f) 68.4 cm²

3. (a) 170 cm² (b) 54 cm

4. 53.5° **5.** 6.62 cm

6. (a) 9.5 cm (b) 14.1 cm

7. 11.7 cm² **8.** 44.7 cm²

9. 19.1° **10.** 6.91 cm

Exercise 19.3 — Page 288

1. (a) 5.4 cm² (b) 7.68 cm² (c) 10.9 cm²
(d) 4.03 cm² (e) 6.24 cm² (f) 14.3 cm²

2. (a) $a = 20$ cm (b) $b = 12$ cm
(c) $c = 4$ cm

3. 30 cm

4. (a) $a = 5$ cm (b) $b = 4$ cm
(c) $c = 8$ cm (d) $d = 11$ cm
(e) $e = 10$ cm (f) $f = 2$ cm

5. 4 cm

6. (a) 22.7 cm² (b) 17.6 cm² (c) 7.62 cm²
(d) 17.3 cm² (e) 23.9 cm² (f) 26.6 cm²

7. 49.4 cm² **8.** 34.3 cm² **9.** 45.9 cm²

Review Exercise 19 — Page 291

1. 54.9 cm² **2.** 8.64 m²

3. 29.3% **4.** 5.14 cm²

5. (a) 11.25 cm² (b) 5.5 cm²

6. (a) 44.5° (b) 1749 m²

7. 102 cm

8. (a) 871 cm² (b) 422 cm²
(c) 31.7 cm (d) 5.04 cm

9. (a) 7.57 cm (b) 58.9°

10. 2983 cm²

11. 28.5 cm²

12. (a) 78.5 m (b) 3541 m²

CHAPTER 20

Exercise 20.1 — Page 295

6. Circle

Exercise 20.2 — Page 297

5. Perpendicular bisectors pass through the centre of the circle.

7.

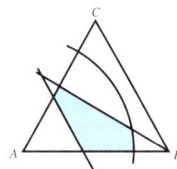

8.

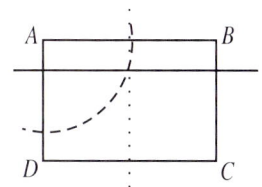

9.

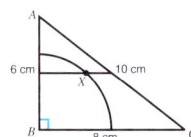

10.

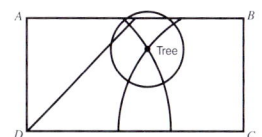

Review Exercise 20 — Page 299

1.
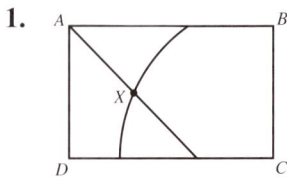

2.
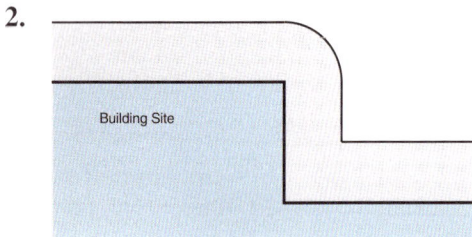

3.
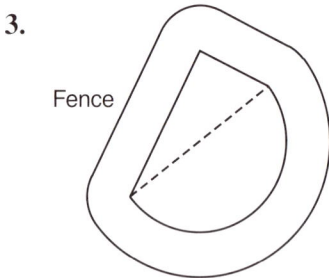

Fence

4.
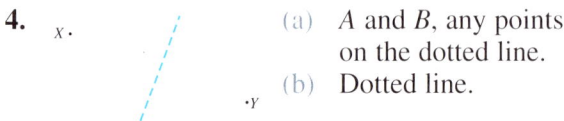

(a) *A* and *B*, any points on the dotted line.
(b) Dotted line.

5.
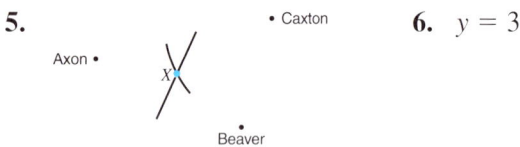

6. $y = 3$

7.
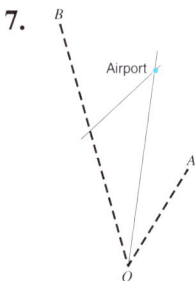

8.
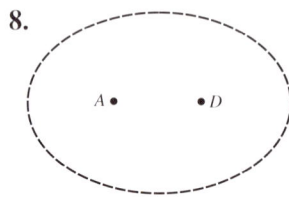

CHAPTER 21

Exercise 21.1 — Page 302

1. (a) 10 cm   (b) 25 cm   (c) 26 cm
2. (a) 7.8 cm   (b) 12.8 cm   (c) 10.3 cm
3. 7.3 cm
4. (a) 7.21 cm   (b) 4.47 cm

Exercise 21.2 — Page 303

1. (a) 8 cm   (b) 6 cm   (c) 2 cm
2. (a) 6.9 cm   (b) 10.9 cm   (c) 9.5 cm
3. 339 cm   **4.** 36 cm^2 **5.** 3.6 cm

Exercise 21.3 — Page 305

1. (a) 9.4 cm   (b) 4.6 cm   (c) 5.7 cm
(d) 2.9 cm   (e) 2.1 cm   (f) 2.0 cm
2. 17 cm   **3.** 10 cm   **4.** 8.5 cm
5. 10.6 cm   **6.** 15 cm   **7.** 6.9 cm
8. 74.3 cm   **9.** 13 cm   **10.** 24 cm
11. 5.22 cm   **12.** (a) 11.4 cm   (b) 43.5 cm^2

Exercise 21.4 — Page 307

1. 10.4 cm   **2.** 20.7 cm
3. 11.9 cm   **4.** 19.5 cm
5. (a) 11.2 cm
(b) 14.1 cm
(c) 9.49 cm
6. 4.95 cm

Review Exercise 21 — Page 308

1. (a) 2.95 m
(b) X
2. 28.3 km   **3.** 728 m   **4.** 94.3 cm
5. 10.4 cm   **6.** 8.60   **7.** 17.3 m
8. (a) 8.60 cm   (b) 10.9 cm
9. 4.24 cm
10. 361 m
11. (a) (i) 80 cm   (ii) 50 cm
(b) 5040 cm^2
12. 7.21   **13.** 21 cm   **14.** 17.3 cm
15. 9.75 cm   **16.** 9.75 cm   **17.** 5.66 cm

CHAPTER 22

Exercise 22.1 — Page 313

1. (a) $h = 2.27$ m   (b) $h = 4.02$ m
(c) $h = 8.02$ m
2. (a) $x = 1.50$ cm   (b) $x = 2.99$ cm
(c) $x = 5.78$ cm
3. (a) $BC = 3.39$ m
(b) $AC = 11.4$ m
(c) $BC = 4.74$ cm
(d) $\angle ABC = 55°$, $AC = 6.96$ cm

Exercise **22.2** — Page 314

1. (a) $a = 62.1°$
   (b) $a = 25.0°$
   (c) $a = 50.9°$

2. (a) $x = 52.3°$
   (b) $x = 60.5°$
   (c) $x = 61.4°$

3. (a) $\angle QPR = 23.6°$
   (b) $\angle PRQ = 64.7°$
   (c) $\angle QPR = 21.8°$
   (d) $\angle QRP = 24.0°$, $\angle QPR = 66.0°$

Exercise **22.3** — Page 315

1. (a) $l = 7.00$ m
   (b) $l = 7.49$ m
   (c) $l = 4.93$ m

2. (a) $x = 6.49$ cm
   (b) $x = 5.31$ cm
   (c) $x = 10.61$ cm

3. (a) $AB = 7.62$ m
   (b) $AB = 17.5$ cm
   (c) $AB = 66.9$ cm
   (d) $\angle ABC = 17.2°$, $AB = 25.7$ m

Exercise **22.4** — Page 317

1.

	sin p	cos p	tan p
(a)	$\frac{5}{13}$	$\frac{12}{13}$	$\frac{5}{12}$
(b)	$\frac{7}{25}$	$\frac{24}{25}$	$\frac{7}{24}$
(c)	$\frac{4}{5}$	$\frac{3}{5}$	$\frac{4}{3}$

2. (a) $p = 40.9°$ (b) $p = 38.0°$
   (c) $p = 38.8°$ (d) $p = 53.3°$
   (e) $p = 39.7°$ (f) $p = 35.5°$

3. (a) $a = 5.77$ cm   (b) $a = 6.47$ cm
   (c) $a = 4.18$ cm   (d) $a = 3.78$ cm
   (e) $a = 4.72$ cm   (f) $a = 4.04$ cm

4. 4.33 cm   5. 72.5°, 72.5°, 34.9°

6. (a) 5.96 cm   (b) 1.71 cm

7. (a) 2.76 cm   (b) 19.8°

8. 13.06 cm   9. 4.52 cm   10. 9.45 cm

Exercise **22.5** — Page 320

1. 21.4 m   2. 40.1 m

3. (a) 135 m   (b) 53.5°

4. 22.2 m   5. 31.0°

6. 51.3°   7. 959 m

8. 40.5 m

Exercise **22.6** — Page 321

1. (a) 152 km   (b) 199 km

2. 22.2 km   3. 145°   4. 41.9 km

5. 164°   6. 6.40 km   7. 174 km

8. 283°

Exercise **22.7** — Page 324

1. (a) $\angle RZY$ or $\angle QWX$ (b) $\angle RPS$ or $\angle YWZ$
   (c) $\angle SWZ$ or $\angle RXY$ (d) $\angle RWY$
   (e) $\angle RWQ$ (f) $\angle WRZ$

2. (a) 39.8°   (b) 36.7°

3. 18.5°

4. (a) 26.6°   (b) 21.8°

5. (a) 45°   (b) 35.3°

6. (a) 69.4°   (b) 62.1°

7. (a) 60.9°   (b) 71.6°

8. (a) 48.5°   (b) 58°

Review Exercise **22** — Page 326

1. 3.25 m

2. (a) 34.9°   (b) 154 cm

3. 14.0 m   4. 3.22 m

5. (a) 9.64 cm   (b) 51.3°

6. 7.15 cm   7. 10.8 m

8. (a) 5.46 m   (b) 64.1°

9. (a) 3620 m   (b) 3.9°

10. (a) (i) $\frac{5}{12}$ (ii) $\frac{5}{13}$
    (b) $QR = 2.6$ cm, $PR = 1$ cm

11. (a) $\frac{4}{3}$
    (b) (i) $\frac{3}{5}$ (ii) $\frac{3}{5}$
    (c) 81 cm²

12. (a) 2.5 m
    (b) (i) 5.00 m   (ii) Safe, 78.5°

13. (a) 25 feet   (b) 50.2°

14. 21.3 m

15. (a) 76.6 km
    (b) (i) 51 km   (ii) 310°

16. (a) 18.4°   (b) 21.8°

17. (a) 5.29 cm   (b) 61.9°   (c) 69.3°

18. (a) 10.4 cm   (b) 53.1°
    (c) 60°   (d) 64.3°

19. (a) 10.3 cm   (b) 14.4°

CHAPTER 23

Exercise 23.1 Page 332

1. (a) 27 cm³, 54 cm²   (b) 24 cm³, 52 cm²
   (c) 140 cm³, 166 cm²

2. (a) 40 cm³   (b) 140 cm³   (c) 96 cm³

3. (a) 11 cm², 15.4 cm²
   (b) 6 cm², 15 cm³
   (c) 7.2 cm², 21.6 cm³
   (d) 5.6 cm², 11.2 cm³
   (e) 314 cm², 6280 cm³
   (f) 3.14 cm², 15.7 cm³

4. (a) 19 440 cm³, 4644 cm²
   (b) 96.8 cm³, 131.5 cm²
   (c) 916.1 cm³, 611.7 cm²

5. (a) 16 cm³   (b) 56 cm³   (c) 330 cm³
   (d) 113 cm³   (e) 393 cm³   (f) 120 cm³
   (g) 848 cm³   (h) 48 cm³

6. 1155 cm²   7. P   8. 10 cm

9. 4.5 cm   10. 11.5 cm   11. 2.7 cm

12. 12.0 cm

Exercise 23.2 Page 334

1. (a) 339 cm²   (b) 90.9 cm²

3. (a) 1260 cm²   (b) 6280 cm²
   (c) 62 800 cm³

4. (a) 14 100 cm²   (b) 18 800 cm²

5. 274 cm²

Exercise 23.3 Page 337

1. (a) 101 cm³   (b) 188 cm³
   (c) 37.3 cm³   (d) 36.8 cm³
   (e) 2140 cm³   (f) 8180 cm³

2. (a) 220 cm²   (b) 47.1 cm²   (c) 57.9 cm²

3. cone 393 cm³, hemisphere 452 cm³;
   hemispherical bowl has greater volume.

4. 37.5 cm

5. (a) 314 cm²   (b) 188 cm²   (c) 2120 cm²

6. (a) 18.8 cm   (b) 3 cm
   (c) 11.6 cm   (d) 110 cm³

7. (a) 2.5 cm   (b) 28.3 cm³

8. (a) 170 cm³, 160 cm²
   (b) 33.5 cm³, 53.2 cm²
   (c) 91.6 cm³, 117 cm²

9. 4.73 cm   10. 2.40 cm

11. 1470 cm³, 837 cm³

12. (a) 1730 cm²   (b) 8860 cm³
13. (a) 720 cm³   (b) 564 cm²
14. 405   15. 2.6 mm   16. 97.2%

Review Exercise 23 Page 340

1. 1575 cm³

2. (a) 19.6 cm²   (b) 1960 cm³

3. (a) 6   (b) 9 cm

4. 1890 cm³

5. (a) 462 cm³   (b) 3 cm

6. (a) 66.4°   (b) 10.1 m³

7. (a) 2640 cm³   (b) 5.9 cm

8. (a) 72 cm³   (b) 3.0 mm

9. 201 m³

10. (a) 32.7 cm   (b) 400 cm³

11. (a) 497 cm³   (b) 319 cm²

12. (a) 1360 cm³   (b) 371 cm³
    (c) 823 cm³   (d) 1 : 6

CHAPTER 24

Exercise 24.1 Page 345

3. (a) scale factor 3, centre (0, 0)
   (b) scale factor 3, centre (5, 0)
   (c) scale factor 2.5, centre (0, 5)

Exercise 24.2 Page 346

2. (a) scale factor $\frac{1}{3}$, centre (5, 7)
   (b) scale factor $\frac{1}{3}$, centre (1, 7)
   (c) scale factor $\frac{2}{5}$, centre (5, 5)
   (d) scale factor $\frac{2}{5}$, centre (5, 0)
   (e) scale factor $\frac{1}{3}$, centre (0, 7)

Exercise 24.3 Page 348

2. (a) centre (1, 4), scale factor -2
   (b) centre (0, 0), scale factor $-\frac{1}{4}$

3. (a) inverted and smaller
   (b) inverted and same size
   (c) inverted and larger

Exercise 24.4 Page 350

1. (a) $x = 1.5$, $y = 2.4$, $a = 70°$
   (b) $x = 5$, $y = 1.5$, $a = 53°$
   (c) $x = 30$, $y = 20.8$, $z = 10$

2. 15 cm   **3.** 3 cm

4. 5 cm   **5.** $x = 16$, $y = 48$

Exercise 24.5   Page 352

1. (a) $x = 10$, $y = 27$ (b) $x = 6$, $y = 10$
    (c) $x = 12$, $y = 12$ (d) $x = 12$, $y = 5$

2. (a) $AB = 2.96$ cm, $QR = 3.25$ cm
    (b) $XZ = 14.4$ m, $BC = 6.25$ m
    (c) $EG = 1.6$ cm, $MN = 4.0$ cm
    (d) $AC = 4.0$ m, $XZ = 2.0$ m

3. $AB = 8$, $AE = 5$

4. (a) $AB = 6$ (b) $BC = 7.5$, $AC = 6.9$
    (c) $EC = 4.6$

5. (a) $PR = 10$
    (b) $QR = 5$, $PQ = 7.5$, $QS = 4.5$

6. $GH = 6$, $FH = 3$

Exercise 24.6   Page 355

1. (a) $AC = 2.4$ cm, $AP = 2.2$ cm
    (b) $AC = 4.5$ cm, $BP = 1$ cm
    (c) $BC = 4.2$ cm, $BP = 1.6$ cm
    (d) $AP = 2.5$ cm, $BC = 7$ cm
    (e) $AP = 4\frac{2}{3}$ cm, $BQ = 16\frac{2}{3}$ cm

2. (a) $x = 58°$ (b) $x = 56°$

3. (a) $61°$ (b) $29°$

4. (a) $QR = 7.2$ cm, $QY = 0.4$ cm
    (b) $PR = 3.6$ cm, $QY = 10.7$ cm
    (c) $YZ = 12$ cm, $PR = 9$ cm
    (d) $YZ = 3.8$ cm, $QY = 2.7$ cm

Exercise 24.7   Page 358

1. 30 m

2. (a) $1 : 50$ (b) 2.8 cm

3. 40 kg   **4.** 2.4 cm

5. area is quartered   **6.** 90 cm²

7. (a) 8 cm   (b) 96 cm²

8. 14.4 cm, 149.76 cm²

9. (a) 1.5 km   (b) 5 km²

10. (a) 14 cm   (b) 750 000 m²
    (c) 1.92 cm²

11. (a) 4   (b) 8

12. (a) 880 cm²   (b) 55 cm², 25 cm³

13. 540 litres   **14.** Entries are: 41.3 cm², 11 cm

15. 12 kg   **16.** 36 cm   **17.** 128 kg

18. (a) 3.28 m²   (b) 22 500 cm³

19. (a) $1 : 300$ (b) 0.741 cm³   (c) 2880 m²

20. 1.41   **21.** 27

22. (a) 33.5 cm³, 524 cm³

23. 391 ml   **24.** 0.81 kg

25. (a) 15 cm   (b) 33.75π

Review Exercise 24   Page 360

4. $XY = 59.5$

5. (a) $x = 4.5$ (b) $y = 10$ (c) $z = 46°$

6. 64 m

7. No. Not *all* corresponding lengths are in the
same ratio.

8. (a) $DE = 4.5$ cm   (b) $AC = 12$ cm

9. (a) 11.2 cm   (b) 170 cm³

10. (a) 3.6 cm   (b) 3.8 cm
    (c) $\theta = 105°$ (d) 37.125 cm²

11. (a) $BC = 1.73$ cm   (b) 243 cm²
    (c) (i) $\angle A$ is common
          $\angle AEB = \angle ACD$ (given)
          Triangles AEB and ACD are similar,
          equal angles.
      (ii) $ED = 5.5$ cm

12. $r = 7.33$ cm

13. (a) 6   (b) 31

14. (a) (i) 6 cm   (ii) 7 cm
    (b) 356 cm³

CHAPTER 25

Exercise 25.1   Page 364

1. (a) $(2, -1)$ (b) $(-2, 1)$ (c) $(0, 1)$
    (d) $(2, -3)$ (e) $(1, 2)$

4. (a) $(3, -4)$ (b) $(-3, 4)$ (c) $(5, 4)$
    (d) $(-5, 4)$ (e) $(4, 3)$

Exercise 25.2   Page 367

3. (a) $(4, -3)$ (b) $(-4, 3)$
    (c) $(-3, -4)$ (d) $(6, 1)$
    (e) $(0, 1)$ (f) $(3, -2)$

Exercise 25.3   Page 368

2. (a) $(5, 5)$ (b) $(1, 6)$
    (c) $(4, 1)$ (d) $(1, 1)$

3. $T(7, 2)$

4. (a) $\begin{pmatrix} 2 \\ 1 \end{pmatrix}$ (b) $\begin{pmatrix} 1 \\ -2 \end{pmatrix}$
    (c) $\begin{pmatrix} -3 \\ 1 \end{pmatrix}$ (d) $\begin{pmatrix} -3 \\ -2 \end{pmatrix}$

5. (b) $\begin{pmatrix} -3 \\ -2 \end{pmatrix}$

6. (a) (2, 3) (b) $\begin{pmatrix} 1 \\ -1 \end{pmatrix}$

Exercise 25.4 Page 370

4. (a) (8, 8) (b) (2, 2) (c) $(-8, -8)$
(d) (4, 10) (e) (6, 5) (f) $(-2, 4)$
(g) (1, 4) (h) (4, 0)

Exercise 25.5 Page 372

1. L_1 reflection in the x axis ($y = 0$)
L_2 rotation, 90° anticlockwise, about (0, 0)

L_3 translation $\begin{pmatrix} 3 \\ 2 \end{pmatrix}$

L_4 reflection in $y = -x$
L_5 reflection in $x = 7$
L_6 rotation, 180°, about (6, 0)

2. (a) translation $\begin{pmatrix} -7 \\ -4 \end{pmatrix}$
(b) reflection in $y = -x$
(c) rotation, 90° anticlockwise, about (1, 0)

3. (a) reflection in $x = -1$
(b) rotation, 90° clockwise, about $(1, -2)$
(c) translation $\begin{pmatrix} 5 \\ 1 \end{pmatrix}$

4. enlargement, scale factor 2, centre (1, 2)
5. enlargement, scale factor $\frac{1}{2}$, centre (0, 0)

Exercise 25.6 Page 374

1. (c) translation $\begin{pmatrix} 8 \\ 0 \end{pmatrix}$
2. (c) rotation, 90° anticlockwise, about (5, 5)
3. (d) rotation, 90° anticlockwise, about (0, 0)
4. (c) rotation, 180°, about $(1, -1)$
5. translation $\begin{pmatrix} -4 \\ 3 \end{pmatrix}$

6. translation $\begin{pmatrix} 6 \\ 0 \end{pmatrix}$

Review Exercise 25 Page 376

1. (a) (7, 7) (b) $(-3, 4)$
(c) $(-6, 2)$ (d) (8, 6)

2. (a) reflection in $x = -1$
(b) reflection in $y = -1$
(c) translation $\begin{pmatrix} -4 \\ 1 \end{pmatrix}$
(d) translation $\begin{pmatrix} 4 \\ -1 \end{pmatrix}$
(e) enlargement, scale factor 2, centre (0, 4)
(f) enlargement, scale factor $\frac{1}{2}$, centre (0, 4)

3. translation $\begin{pmatrix} -3 \\ 1 \end{pmatrix}$
4. (a) $C_1 (-2, 5)$ (b) $C_2 (-1, 4)$
(c) $C_3 (9, 7)$
5. (a) reflection in $y = x$
(b) enlargement, scale factor 2, centre $(-7, 1)$
6. (c) translation $\begin{pmatrix} -4 \\ 3 \end{pmatrix}$

8. (a) enlargement, scale factor $\frac{1}{2}$, centre (0, 1)
(b) translation $\begin{pmatrix} 4 \\ 0 \end{pmatrix}$
9. (a) rotation, 90° clockwise, about (0, 0)
10. (a) rotation, 90° anticlockwise, about (1, 3)
11. (a) translation $\begin{pmatrix} 3 \\ -6 \end{pmatrix}$
(b) reflection in $y = -x$

CHAPTER 26

Exercise 26.1 Page 381

2. (b) (i) $\begin{pmatrix} 2 \\ -2 \end{pmatrix}$ (ii) $\begin{pmatrix} 0 \\ -4 \end{pmatrix}$ (iii) $\begin{pmatrix} -2 \\ -2 \end{pmatrix}$

(iv) $\begin{pmatrix} -4 \\ 0 \end{pmatrix}$ (v) $\begin{pmatrix} -2 \\ 2 \end{pmatrix}$ (vi) $\begin{pmatrix} 0 \\ 4 \end{pmatrix}$

(vii) $\begin{pmatrix} 2 \\ 2 \end{pmatrix}$ (viii) $\begin{pmatrix} 4 \\ 0 \end{pmatrix}$

3. $\mathbf{a} = \begin{pmatrix} 3 \\ 5 \end{pmatrix}$ $\mathbf{b} = \begin{pmatrix} 3 \\ -1 \end{pmatrix}$

$\mathbf{c} = \begin{pmatrix} -2 \\ 4 \end{pmatrix}$ $\mathbf{d} = \begin{pmatrix} -6 \\ -1 \end{pmatrix}$

$\mathbf{e} = \begin{pmatrix} 4 \\ 3 \end{pmatrix}$ $\mathbf{f} = \begin{pmatrix} 2 \\ -5 \end{pmatrix}$

4. (a) $\begin{pmatrix} 1 \\ 2 \end{pmatrix}, \begin{pmatrix} 2 \\ 1 \end{pmatrix}, \begin{pmatrix} 2 \\ -1 \end{pmatrix}, \begin{pmatrix} 1 \\ -2 \end{pmatrix}, \begin{pmatrix} -1 \\ -2 \end{pmatrix},$
$\begin{pmatrix} -2 \\ -1 \end{pmatrix}, \begin{pmatrix} -2 \\ 1 \end{pmatrix}, \begin{pmatrix} -1 \\ 2 \end{pmatrix}$
(b) 20 moves

Exercise 26.2 Page 383

2. (i) $\mathbf{a} = 2\mathbf{p},$ $\mathbf{e} = -\mathbf{p}$
(ii) $\mathbf{b} = 2\mathbf{q},$ $\mathbf{c} = -\mathbf{q},$ $\mathbf{h} = -3\mathbf{q}$
(iii) $\mathbf{d} = \frac{1}{2}\mathbf{r},$ $\mathbf{f} = 2\mathbf{r},$ $\mathbf{g} = -\frac{1}{2}\mathbf{r}$

Exercise 26.3 Page 386

2. Any vector equal to the following.
(b) $\overrightarrow{AN}$ (c) $\overrightarrow{TC}$ (d) $\overrightarrow{GV}$
(e) $\overrightarrow{HE}$ (f) $\overrightarrow{GR}$ (g) $-\overrightarrow{CL}$
(h) $\overrightarrow{BI}$

3. (a) r   (b) s   (c) t   (d) q
    (e) v   (f) u   (g) w   (h) p

4. (a) $\mathbf{a} + 3\mathbf{b}$ (b) $3\mathbf{b}$
   (c) $2\mathbf{a}$ (d) $-3\mathbf{a}$
   (e) $\mathbf{a} + \mathbf{b}$ (f) $-\mathbf{a} - \mathbf{b}$
   (g) $-\mathbf{a} + \mathbf{b}$ (h) $-\mathbf{a} + \mathbf{b}$
   (i) $\mathbf{a} + 2\mathbf{b}$ (j) $2\mathbf{a} - 2\mathbf{b}$
   (k) $-2\mathbf{a} + 4\mathbf{b}$ (l) $-2\mathbf{a} - \mathbf{b}$
   (m) $3\mathbf{a} + 2\mathbf{b}$ (n) $-3\mathbf{b}$

5. (a)

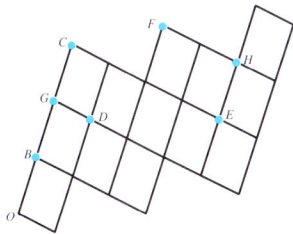

   (b) $\overrightarrow{OB} = \overrightarrow{EH} = \mathbf{y}$

   OB is parallel and equal to EH,
   so $OBHE$ is a parallelogram.

6. (c) (i) $\frac{1}{2}\mathbf{a} + \mathbf{b}$ (ii) $\frac{1}{2}\mathbf{a} + \mathbf{b}$
    (iii) $\mathbf{a} + 2\mathbf{b}$

   (d) (i) $\overrightarrow{PC} = \overrightarrow{AR}$, so PC is parallel and
       equal in length to AR.

     (ii) $\overrightarrow{AE} = 2\overrightarrow{PC}$, so PC is parallel to AE
       and AE is $2 \times$ length of PC.

Exercise 26.4   Page 389

1. (a) $-\mathbf{a}$ (b) $\mathbf{b} - \mathbf{a}$
   (c) $\frac{1}{2}(\mathbf{b} - \mathbf{a})$ (d) $-\frac{1}{2}(\mathbf{a} + \mathbf{b})$

2. (a) (i) $\mathbf{q} - \mathbf{p}$ (ii) $2\mathbf{p}$
     (iii) $2\mathbf{p} + 2\mathbf{q}$ (iv) $2\mathbf{q} - 2\mathbf{p}$
   (b) parallel, $PQ = \frac{1}{2}XZ$

3. (a) (i) $2\mathbf{q}$ (ii) $2\mathbf{p}$
     (iii) $\mathbf{q} - \mathbf{p}$ (iv) $2\mathbf{p} - 2\mathbf{q}$
     (v) $\mathbf{q}$ (vi) $-\mathbf{p}$
   (b) similar triangles

4. (a) (i) $\mathbf{b} - \mathbf{c}$ (ii) $-\frac{1}{2}\mathbf{b}$
     (iii) $\frac{1}{2}\mathbf{a} + \frac{1}{2}\mathbf{b} - \mathbf{c}$ (iv) $\frac{1}{2}\mathbf{a} - \frac{1}{2}\mathbf{c}$
     (v) $\frac{1}{2}\mathbf{a} - \frac{1}{2}\mathbf{c}$

5. (a) (i) $\frac{1}{2}\mathbf{a}$ (ii) $\frac{1}{2}\mathbf{a} + \mathbf{b}$
     (iii) $\frac{1}{2}\mathbf{a} - \mathbf{b}$ (iv) $\frac{1}{6}\mathbf{a} - \frac{1}{3}\mathbf{b}$
     (v) $\frac{2}{3}\mathbf{a} + \frac{2}{3}\mathbf{b}$ (vi) $\mathbf{a} + \mathbf{b}$
   (b) OYB is a straight line

6. (a) $4\mathbf{a} + 2\mathbf{b}$
   (b) $\overrightarrow{OC} = 6\mathbf{a} + (4 + n)\mathbf{b}$
     $n = -1$

7. $\overrightarrow{AF} = 2\mathbf{y} + \mathbf{x}$, $\overrightarrow{DM} = \mathbf{y} + \frac{1}{2}\mathbf{x}$
   So AF is parallel to DM and $AF = 2DM$
   $\overrightarrow{BE} = -\mathbf{x} + 2\mathbf{y}$, $\overrightarrow{CM} = -\frac{1}{2}\mathbf{x} + \mathbf{y}$
   So BE is parallel to CM and $BE = 2CM$

8. (a) $\overrightarrow{AD} = 3\mathbf{a} - 2\mathbf{b}$ $\overrightarrow{BC} = 6\mathbf{a} - 4\mathbf{b}$
   (b) $ABCD$ is a trapezium

9. (a) (i) $\mathbf{b} - \mathbf{a}$ (ii) $\mathbf{b} - 2\mathbf{a}$ (iii) $\frac{1}{2}\mathbf{a}$
   (b) parallel, $OA = 6SR$

10. (a) (i) $2\mathbf{a} - \mathbf{b}$ (ii) $4\mathbf{a} - 2\mathbf{b}$
   (b) ABC is a straight line
     $BC = 2AB$

11. (a) $m = 5, n = -\frac{3}{2}$
   (b) (i) $\mathbf{x} + \frac{1}{2}\mathbf{y}$ (ii) $2\mathbf{x} + \mathbf{y}$
   (c) BDF is a straight line
     $DF = 2BD$

12. $\overrightarrow{BP} = -\mathbf{a} + \frac{2}{3}\mathbf{b}$, $\overrightarrow{CR} = -\frac{1}{2}\mathbf{a} + \frac{1}{3}\mathbf{b}$
   BP is parallel to CR and $BP = 2CR$

13. (a) $n = 2$
   (b) $\overrightarrow{AB} = 9\mathbf{a} - 3\mathbf{b}$, $\overrightarrow{AP} = 6\mathbf{a} - 2\mathbf{b}$
     $\overrightarrow{AP} = \frac{2}{3}\overrightarrow{AB}$, so ABP is a straight line
   (c) $2 : 1$

Review Exercise 26   Page 393

1. (a)   (b) (i) $\mathbf{b} - \mathbf{a}$
                     (ii) $\mathbf{a} + \mathbf{b}$
                     (iii) $\mathbf{a}$

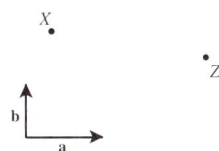

2. (a) (i) $\begin{pmatrix} -3 \\ -2 \end{pmatrix}$ (ii) $\begin{pmatrix} -2 \\ 5 \end{pmatrix}$

   (b) (i) $\overrightarrow{OM} = \overrightarrow{OA} + \overrightarrow{AM}$

     (ii) $\begin{pmatrix} 2 \\ 4.5 \end{pmatrix}$

3. (a) $\mathbf{b} - \mathbf{a}$ (b) $\frac{1}{2}(\mathbf{b} - \mathbf{a})$ (c) $\frac{1}{2}(\mathbf{a} + \mathbf{b})$

4. (a)

   (b) $2\frac{1}{2}\mathbf{a} + \frac{1}{2}\mathbf{b}$

5. (a) (i) **x** + **y**
       (ii) 2**x** + 2**y**
   (b) *EH* is parallel to *DB*, and *EH* = 2*DB*

6. (a) $\begin{pmatrix} 6 \\ 0 \end{pmatrix}$

   (b) $\overrightarrow{AB} = \begin{pmatrix} -2 \\ 2 \end{pmatrix}$, $\overrightarrow{PQ} = \begin{pmatrix} -4 \\ 4 \end{pmatrix}$

   (c) *AB* is parallel to *PQ* and *PQ* = 2*AB*

7. (a) 3**a**   (b) 2**b**   (c) 3**a** − 2**b**

8. (a) (i) 2**a** + **b**

      (ii) $\frac{2}{3}$ (**a** − **b**)

      (iii) $\frac{1}{3}$ (**b** − **a**)

   (b) (i) 2 : 1
      (ii) *PS* and *RS* are parallel
         S is a common point

9. (a) $\overrightarrow{AB}$ = −2**a** + 2**b**, $\overrightarrow{AC}$ = −2**a** + 6**b**
   (b) $\overrightarrow{OM} = \frac{2}{3}$ (**a** + 2**b**), $\overrightarrow{ON} = \frac{6}{5}$ (**a** + 2**b**)
   (c) $\overrightarrow{ON}$ = 1.8 $\overrightarrow{OM}$, *OMN* is a straight line

10. (a) (i) 3**a**   (ii) **a** + **b**
   (b) *P* is the midpoint of *EF*
   (c) *OP* is parallel to *AG* and *OP* = 1.5*AG*

11. (a) (i) 6**a**   (ii) 9**b** − 6**a**
   (b) (i) 4**a** + 3**b**   (ii) 8**a** + 6**b**
   (c) $\overrightarrow{OF} = 2\overrightarrow{OE}$
      OEF is a straight line
      E is the midpoint of *OF*

12. (a) (i) 6**a** − 3**b** (ii) 3**a** + 3**b**
   (b) (i) 9**a** + 9**b** (ii) $\overrightarrow{OC} = 3\overrightarrow{OM}$
      OCM is a straight line

CHAPTER 27

Exercise 27.1   Page 398

1. (a) positive   (b) positive   (c) positive
   (d) positive   (e) negative   (f) negative
   (g) negative   (h) negative   (i) positive
   (j) positive   (k) negative   (l) positive
   (m) negative   (n) positive   (o) negative
   (p) positive   (q) positive   (r) negative
   (s) negative   (t) positive   (u) negative
   (v) positive   (w) positive   (x) negative
   (y) negative   (z) positive

2. (a) −tan 80° (b) −cos 30° (c) −sin 20°
   (d) tan 70° (e) cos 60° (f) sin 60°
   (g) −tan 10° (h) −cos 30° (i) −sin 70°
   (j) −tan 30° (k) cos 10° (l) −sin 80°
   (m) tan 10° (n) sin 60° (o) −cos 60°
   (p) −sin 50° (q) −cos 80° (r) tan 30°

3. (a) (i) $\frac{1}{\sqrt{2}}$ (ii) 1

   (b) (i) $-\frac{1}{\sqrt{2}}$ (ii) 1

      (iii) $-\frac{1}{\sqrt{2}}$ (iv) $\frac{1}{\sqrt{2}}$

      (v) $-\frac{1}{\sqrt{2}}$ (vi) −1

4. (a) $\frac{1}{2}$, $\frac{\sqrt{3}}{2}$, $\frac{1}{\sqrt{3}}$

      (i) $\frac{1}{2}$ (ii) $-\frac{\sqrt{3}}{2}$

      (iii) $-\frac{1}{\sqrt{3}}$ (iv) $\frac{\sqrt{3}}{2}$

   (b) $\frac{\sqrt{3}}{2}$, $\frac{1}{2}$, $\sqrt{3}$

      (i) $-\frac{1}{2}$ (ii) $\sqrt{3}$

      (iii) $-\frac{1}{2}$ (iv) $-\frac{\sqrt{3}}{2}$

Exercise 27.2   Page 399

1. (a) 0.985   (b) −0.866   (c) 0.364
   (d) −0.940   (e) 0.5   (f) −0.176
   (g) 0.123   (h) −0.993   (i) −0.799
   (j) 0.891   (k) −0.325   (l) 0.438
   (m) −0.810   (n) −0.961   (o) −0.616
   (p) 0.766   (q) −0.839   (r) 0.643
   (s) 0.866   (t) −0.985

2. (a) *p* = 60°, 300°   (b) *p* = 210°, 330°
   (c) *p* = 45°, 225°   (d) *p* = 30°, 150°
   (e) *p* = 135°, 315°   (f) *p* = 120°, 240°
   (g) *p* = 230°, 310°   (h) *p* = 40°, 320°
   (i) *p* = 60°, 120°   (j) *p* = 116°, 296°
   (k) *p* = 10.9°, 190.9° (l) *p* = 55.6°, 304.4°
   (m) *p* = 20°, 160°   (n) *p* = 150°, 210°
   (o) *p* = 35°, 215°

Exercise 27.3   Page 400

1. (a) (i) *x* = 90°
      (ii) *x* = 0°, 180°, 360°
      (iii) *x* = 270°
   (b) (i) *x* = 0°, 360°
      (ii) *x* = 90°, 270°
      (iii) *x* = 180°

2. (a) *x* = 45°, 225°
   (b) *x* = 0°, 180°, 360°
   (c) *x* = 135°, 315°

3. (a) (i) *x* = 30°, 150°
      (ii) *y* = −2.6

4. (b) *x* = 78.5°, 281.5°

9. (b) $x = 26.6°, 206.6°$

10. (b) $x = 56°, 282°$

11. (a) $x = 0°, 143°, 360°$

12. (b) $x = 90°, 307°$

Exercise **27.4**   Page 403

1. (a) $a = 5.79\,\text{cm}$ (b) $a = 13.1\,\text{cm}$
(c) $a = 4.26\,\text{cm}$

2. (a) $b = 9.92\,\text{cm}$ (b) $c = 8.28\,\text{cm}$
(c) $b = 10.1\,\text{cm}$ (d) $q = 13.6\,\text{cm}$
(e) $p = 1.64\,\text{cm}$ (f) $r = 8.48\,\text{cm}$

3. (a) $\angle ACB = 55°,\ AC = 7.41\,\text{cm},$
$AB = 6.54\,\text{cm}$
(b) $\angle MLN = 71.2°,\ LM = 5.84\,\text{cm},$
$AB = 5.71\,\text{cm}$
(c) $\angle RPQ = 69.8°,\ QR = 15.7\,\text{cm},$
$PR = 14.9\,\text{cm}$
(d) $\angle SUT = 31.8°,\ ST = 12.8\,\text{cm},$
$UT = 24.1\,\text{cm}$
(e) $\angle XYZ = 31.2°,\ XY = 7.54\,\text{cm},$
$ZY = 9.4\,\text{cm}$

Exercise **27.5**   Page 405

1. (a) $61.7°$ (b) $53.7°$ (c) $74.7°$

2. (a) $137.3°$ (b) $129.7°$ (c) $118.5°$

3. $48.6°, 131.4°$

4. $\angle QPR = 68.1°,\ \angle PRQ = 51.9°,$
$PQ = 6.36\,\text{cm}$
$\angle QPR = 111.9°,\ \angle PRQ = 8.1°,$
$PQ = 1.14\,\text{cm}$

5. (a) $\angle ACB = 60.7°,\ \angle BAC = 50°,$
$BC = 7.29\,\text{cm}$
(b) $\angle DFE = 25.2°,\ \angle EDF = 29.8°,$
$EF = 9.91\,\text{cm}$

Exercise **27.6**   Page 407

1. (a) $a = 10.8\,\text{cm}$ (b) $a = 8.27\,\text{cm}$
(c) $a = 15.3\,\text{cm}$

2. (a) $p = 5.98\,\text{cm}$ (b) $q = 3.45\,\text{cm}$
(c) $r = 15.3\,\text{cm}$

3. $12.7\,\text{cm}$ **4.** $11.8\,\text{cm}$

5. $13.4\,\text{cm}$ **6.** $18\,\text{cm}$

Exercise **27.7**   Page 408

1. (a) $A = 130.5°$ (b) $A = 32.2°$
(c) $A = 45.8°$

2. (a) $B = 64.5°$ (b) $C = 35.4°$
(c) $P = 41.6°$

3. $45°$ **4.** $130.5°$

5. $102.6°$ **6.** $119.9°$

Exercise **27.8**   Page 410

1. (a) $6.83\,\text{cm}^2$ (b) $14.2\,\text{cm}^2$ (c) $16.9\,\text{cm}^2$
(d) $16.2\,\text{cm}^2$ (e) $6.95\,\text{cm}^2$ (f) $11.9\,\text{cm}^2$

2. $84.8\,\text{cm}^2$

3. (a) $3\,\text{cm}$ (b) $5.63\,\text{cm}^2$

4. $65\,\text{cm}^2$ **5.** $8.9\,\text{cm}$

6. $729\,\text{cm}^2$ **7.** $XY = YZ = 7.37\,\text{cm}$

8. $56.2°, 123.8°$

Exercise **27.9**   Page 412

1. (a) (i) $10.8\,\text{cm}, 73.9°, 46.1°$
(ii) $8.44\,\text{cm}, 46.4°, 23.6°$
(b) (i) $46.8\,\text{cm}^2$
(ii) $11\,\text{cm}^2$

2. (a) $118.7°, 35.1°, 26.2°$
(b) $XP = 128.5\,\text{m},\ \angle XPY = 123°$

3. $9.24\,\text{km}$ **4.** $12.7\,\text{m}$

5. (a) $7.84\,\text{m}$ (b) $29.9°$ (c) $14.7\,\text{m}$

6. (a) $5.17\,\text{cm}$ (b) $10.8\,\text{cm}^2$

7. (a) $28°$ (b) $38.2°$ (c) $28\,\text{cm}^2$

8. $6.63\,\text{cm}, 15.4\,\text{cm}$

Review Exercise **27**   Page 415

1. (a) negative   (b) negative
(c) positive   (d) negative
(e) positive   (f) negative
(g) positive   (h) negative
(i) negative   (j) negative

2. (a) 0.5 (b) $210°, 330°$

3. (a) $-\dfrac{\sqrt{3}}{2}$ (b) $x = 330°$ (c) $y = 150°, 210°$

4. (a) (i) $a = 90°$
(ii)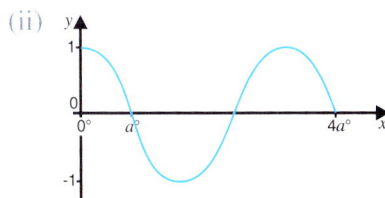

(b) $y = 120°, 240°$

5. (a) $p = 330°$ (c) $x = 27°, 207°$

6. (b) $9\,\text{a.m.}$

7. (a) $17.7\,\text{m}$ (b) $3.51\,\text{seconds}$

8. $1.43\,\text{m}$ **9.** $58.1°, 121.9°$

10. 098.6° **11.** 6.91 km

12. (a) 12.6 m (b) 35.3°

13. 65.8 m **14.** 10 cm²

15. (a) 12.5 cm (b) 112.7°

Section Review   Page 418

1. 53°

2. 36 cm, $q = 135°$

3. Angles are 108°.
360 does not divide exactly by 108.

4. 8510 cm² (3 s.f.)

5. (a) A_1 (4, 2), B_1 (6, 2), C_1 (8, 6), D_1 (6, 6)
(b) Enlargement, centre (0, 0), scale factor $\frac{3}{2}$.

6. (a)

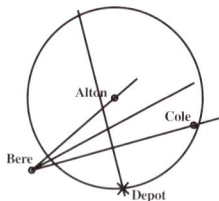

7. (a) $x = 63°$, $y = 27°$
(b) (i) 12.7 cm (3 s.f.)
(ii) 63.4 cm² (3 s.f.)

8. (a) 11.9 m (3 s.f.) (b) 8.13 m (3 s.f.)

9. (a) 44.4° (b) $EC = 19.6$ cm, 632 cm²

10. (a) (i) $\frac{4}{5}$ (ii) $\frac{3}{5}$
(b) $XY = 12.5$ cm, $YZ = 7.5$ cm

11. (a) 6.39 cm (b) 8.67 cm

12. (a) (b)

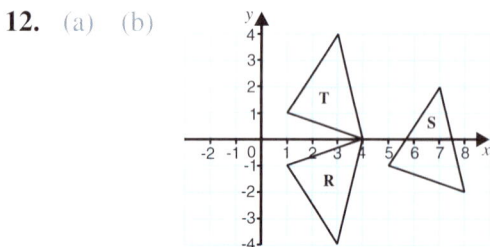

(c) (i) $p = -1$ (ii) 180°

13. Rotation, 90° clockwise,
about the point $(-2, -3)$

14. (b) P_1 (6, −3), Q_1 (12, −3), R_1 (12, −12),
S_1 (6, −12)

15. (a) 333° (b) 21.7 km²

16. (a) 110° (b) 3.2 cm

17. (a) 2.5 cm (b) 60° (c) 10.8 cm

18. 70.1 seconds

19. (a) 78.2° (b) 73.6°

20. 1.92 cm²

21. (a) 461 cm³ (b) 107.4° (c) 11.4 cm

22. (a) 65 cm (b) 67.4° (c) 416 cm²

23. (a) 134 000 cm³ (3 s.f.) (b) 11.7 kg (3 s.f.)

24. (a) 3° (b) 50 m
(c) 0.0209 m³ (3 s.f.) (d) 1.25×10^8

25. (a) −1 (b) 225°
(c) 135°, 315°

26. (a) $\frac{\sqrt{3}}{2}$ (b) 240°, 300°

27. (a) 60°, 300° (b) 150°

28. (a) 4 (b) $x = -127°, -53°, 233°, 307°$

29. (b) $x = 27°, 207°$

30. (a) 82° (b) 52° (c) 13.3 cm

31. (a) 146° (b) 73° (c) 126.5°

32. (a) 60° (b) 110°

33. (a) 1740 km (3 s.f.) (b) 293°

34. (a) $BXC = \angle AXD$ (vert. opp $\angle$'s)
$\angle CBX = \angle DXA$ ($\angle$'s in same segment)
$\angle BCX = \angle ADX$ ($\angle$'s in same segment)
Triangles BXC and AXD are similar,
same angles.
(b) 8.75 cm (c) 10.5 cm

35. (a) 10.3 cm (b) 69.8 cm³

36. (a) 426 000 m² (3 s.f.) (b) 990 m (3 s.f.)

37. 6.05 cm **38.** 12.3 cm

39. $\overrightarrow{AM} = \frac{1}{2}(\mathbf{a} + \mathbf{b})$, $\overrightarrow{BM} = \frac{1}{2}(\mathbf{b} - \mathbf{a})$

40. $\overrightarrow{DF} = \begin{pmatrix} -3 \\ 1.73 \end{pmatrix}$ **41.** $x = 3$, $y = 1\frac{1}{2}$

42. (a) 264π cm³
(b) (i) $2\pi x^2 + 5\pi x = 33\pi$
$x = 3$
(ii) 10 cm

CHAPTER 28

Exercise 28.1   Page 426

1. qualitative

2. quantitative, continuous

3. quantitative, discrete

4. qualitative

5. quantitative, discrete

6. quantitative, continuous

7. quantitative, discrete

8. qualitative

9. quantitative, discrete

10. quantitative, continuous

Exercise 28.2

Page 428

1. (a)

Day	Frequency
Monday	8
Tuesday	7
Wednesday	6
Thursday	7
Friday	7
Saturday	3
Sunday	5
Total	43

(b) Monday

2. (a)

Height h cm	Frequency
$145 \leqslant h < 150$	2
$150 \leqslant h < 155$	2
$155 \leqslant h < 160$	7
$160 \leqslant h < 165$	9
$165 \leqslant h < 170$	6
$170 \leqslant h < 175$	8
$175 \leqslant h < 180$	2
Total	36

(b) 5 cm
(c) 7
(d) 11
(e) 32

3. (a) (i)

Make	Frequency
Ford	4
Nissan	3
Vauxhall	5
Total	12

Colour	Frequency
Blue	2
Green	1
Grey	2
Red	3
White	4
Total	12

(ii)

Mileage (m)	Frequency
$0 \leqslant m < 5000$	0
$5000 \leqslant m < 10\,000$	2
$10\,000 \leqslant m < 15\,000$	0
$15\,000 \leqslant m < 20\,000$	2
$20\,000 \leqslant m < 25\,000$	1
$25\,000 \leqslant m < 30\,000$	2
$30\,000 \leqslant m < 35\,000$	4
$35\,000 \leqslant m < 40\,000$	1
Total	12

(b) (i) Vauxhall
(ii) white
(ii) 41.7%

Exercise 28.3

Page 431

1. (a) Too open
(b) Too open
(c) Leading

2. (a) Too personal (b) Too open
(c) Too open (d) Too open

Exercise 28.4

Page 432

1. Prove, Maths better 7, English better 13
English > Maths

2. (a) (i) 10
(ii) No. Less 8, More 12
(b) (i) 37
(ii) No. Girls 37, Boys 37, same

3. Disprove, Boys $\frac{3}{21} = \frac{1}{7}$, Girls $\frac{2}{14} = \frac{1}{7}$,
same proportion

4. Disprove; Semi-detached $\frac{16}{20} = 80\%$
Detached $\frac{27}{36} = 75\%$
% semi-detached > % detached

5. Fewer females than males, no-one under 18.

Exercise 28.5

Page 434

1. Lower school 23, Upper school 17

2. (a) Allocate each student a number.
Select 100 numbers at random.
(b) Group students by age and sex.
Select from each group, at random, in
proportion to group size.

3. (a) Pupils from one year group only may be
chosen.
(b) 9, 11, 11, 10, 9

581

4. (a) May not sample all departments.
(b) 49

5. Advantage: confidential, wider circulation, etc
Disadvantage: slow, non-response, etc

6. 50 (sample size) ÷ 900 (total) gives 1 in 18 to be chosen at random.
Housing Association 25, Private 15, Flats 10

7. 9, 14, 2   **8.** 1, 5, 54

9. (a) Does not take the size of the village into account.
(b) Stratified random sample.
(c) Quota or systematic sample.

Review Exercise **28**   Page 436

1. (a) continuous   (b) continuous

2. A: People can express any opinion.
B: Easier to collect and analyse information.

3. For example:
Question 1, Which age group are you in?
Under 18   18 to 50   Over 50

Question 2: Which type of sport do you prefer?
Team games   Racket sports   Swimming

4. For example:
How often do you visit the superstore each week?
Once   2 or 3 times   More than 3 times

How far from the superstore do you live?
Less than 2 miles   2 to 5 miles
More than 5 miles

How much do you spend per visit?
Less than £5   £5 to £20   More than £20

5. For example:
Which is your age group?
0 - 11   12 - 18   19 - 30   31 - 60   Over 60

How many times per week do you use a bus?
1 or 2   3 to 5   6 to 10   More than 10

6. Only males asked.
No-one under 11.
Mainly adults surveyed.

7. (a) A Strength: can give information to own degree of accuracy

B Weakness: classes overlap

(b) How many minutes is your journey to school?

Less than 5   ☐

5 but less than 10 ☐

10 but less than 15 ☐ ...

8. Yes. Over 30: $\frac{40}{80} = 0.5$ Under 30: $\frac{27}{60} = 0.45$

9. (a) 51   (b) 11
(c) Yes. 52 chose outdoor sports,
50 chose indoor sports

10. (a) (i) Leading **and** long
(ii) Do you think the school should have a tuck shop?   Yes☐   No☐
(b) (i) Manjit. Bias. Students in different age groups will have different needs and different spending habits.
(ii) Stratified random sample by age and sex of school population.

11. 25, 25, 25, 15, 10

12. (a) Not representative of all incomes
Only one private house included.
(b) Housing Association 5, Private 3, Sheltered 4

13. (a) 49, 36, 15

14. 9, 12, 4

15. (a) Pupils from one year group only or same sex may be chosen.
(b) 8

16. (a) All sections may not be represented.
People of one sex may not be included.
(b) (i) 16   (ii) 10

CHAPTER 29

Exercise **29.1**   Page 442

1. (a) 2   (b) 164 cm   (c) No
(d) Taller girls usually have larger shoe sizes than shorter girls.

2. (a) B   (b) C   (c) D

3. (a) negative   (b) positive
(c) zero   (d) positive
(e) negative

4. (b) positive correlation
(c) Different conditions, types of road, etc.

5. (b) negative correlation
(c) Different road surfaces, driving styles, etc.

Exercise **29.2**   Page 443

1. (b) 4.8 - 4.9 kg

2. (b) (i) £96 - £98   (ii) £310 - £320

3. (b) (i) 27 - 28   (ii) 91 - 92 kg

4. (b) 46 - 48

5. (b) (i) 88 - 89   (ii) 49 - 50
(c) (ii), as estimated value is within the range of known values.

4. (b) Females have less variation in height than males.

5. (b) 1998 results are more spread, 1997 mode is higher

5. (a) 8   (b) 12

6. 32   7. 68

8. (a) 12   (b) 71

9. (a) 10   (b) 64

11. (a) (i) 5.5 cm   (ii) 5

1. (b) positive   (c) 49 - 51

2. (b) (i) 24.5 - 25.5 mpg   (ii) 13 - 14 mpg
    (c) (b) (i). (b) (ii) is beyond know values.
    (d) 1.7 litres

3. (a) (i) 10 to 12 cm   (ii) 21 to 23 cm
    (b) (i), as estimated value is between known values

4. (b) 9.7 years   (c) 1.7 years
    (d) Unusual as most values are closer to line of best fit.

5. (b) 5700 - 5800
    (c) Less variation in the number of accidents by age for females.

6. (a) 132   (b) 280

7. (b) 34

8. (b) 25

9. (a) Type y
    (b) Weights spread over greater range.

10. (b) Type Y
     (c) (i) Type X
          (ii) Weights spread over more weight class intervals.

11. (b) Less variation in height in type A. Type A has higher mean height.

12. (a) 4   (b) 23

13.

No of hours	0 -	5 -	10 -	15 -	20 -	30 - 40
Frequency	2	5	10	15	10	8

15. (b) 10 300

16. (a) Missing entries: 4, 0.1
     (c) (i) 7   (ii) 3
          (iii) More younger teachers at Castle School.

CHAPTER 30

1. 6 m, 5.5 m, 5 m   2. 8

3. 129 cm   4. 3.7 kg, 4.16 kg

5. (a)

Shoe size	3	4	5	6	7	8	9
Frequency	1	4	3	2	1	1	1

    (b) 5   (c) 4
    (d) 5.38. No shoe of this size, could display size 5 or 6.

6. (a) 2, 2.5, 2.73   (b) 2, 2, 2.1

7. (a) 30 - 40 hours, 29.4 hours, 30 - 40 hours
    (b) £10 000 $\leq s <$ £15 000, £15 200, £10 000 $\leq s <$ £15 000

8. 4.27 m   9. 27.7

10. (a) $20 \leq t < 24$ minutes   (b) 23 minutes

1. Mode trainers. Cannot calculate others

2. Mode 15 s, median 12 s, mean 22.15 s. Median most sensible, not affected by 200 as is mean, mode not much use.

3. Mode 81, median 83, mean 69.8 Median most sensible, not affected by 5 & 6 as is mean, mode not much use.

4. Swimmer A.
    Mean is lower (A 30.88 s, B 31.38 s), range less (A 1.7 s, B 15 s), median is higher (A 30.9 s, B 30.0 s)

5. Batsman B
    Higher median (B 31.5, A 21)

1. (a) Entries are: 0, 3, 11, 23, 33, 38, 40
    (c) (i) 14 mins   (ii) 18.5 mins
         (iii) 9.5 mins
    (d) 9 mins

2. (a) 53
    (c) (i) 62 g   (ii) 30 g

3. (a) Entries are: 0, 7, 28, 65, 77, 80
    (c) (i) 6 minutes   (ii) 12

4. (a) 26.5   (b) 8   (c) 15   (d) 17

5. (a) 95
    (c) (i) 89 cm   (ii) 10 cm   (iii) 19
    (d) 83 cm

6. (b) 9.5 hours   (c) 9

7. (a) 175 cm, 14.5 cm   (b) 3   (c) 41
    (d) 172.5 cm   (e) 185.5 cm

Exercise 30.4   Page 468

1. (a) 40
    (b) 13 cm
    (c) 8 cm
    (d) Girls heights are more varied, etc.
    (e) 1

2. (b) (i) 18 litres   (ii) 10 litres
    (c) Neighbour's cows have higher average yield, but the yield is more varied, etc.

3. (a) Entries are: 2, 7, 13, 20, 28, 32, 36
    (b) 19
    (c) Median lower for second meeting and the times were less varied, etc.

4. (b) 9
    (c) (i) 25 hours   (ii) 5.5 hours
    (d) No. Greater spread means that some batteries will have shorter life, etc.

Exercise 30.5   Page 473

1. (a) 4, 1.58   (b) 32, 4
    (c) 110 cm, 7.81 cm   (d) 2.5 kg, 1.09 kg

2. (a) 2, 1   (b) 7, 1.05
    (c) 13.32, 2.25

3. (a) 21.9 kg, 9.91 kg

4. Class A: mean 5.67, s.d. 1.49
Class B: mean 7.12, s.d. 0.82
Class B: had higher mean and lower standard deviation.

5. Chris: mean 5.17, s.d. 1.42
Robert: mean 3.61, s.d. 0.75
Robert had lower mean and standard deviation

6. Boys: mean 27.6 s, s.d. 2.37 s
Girls: mean 31.5 s, s.d. 1.61 s
The boys had a lower mean, but the girls had a lower standard deviation.

7. Beach A: mean 2.93 cm, s.d. 0.78 cm
Beach B: mean 2.11 cm, s.d. 1.31 cm
Beach A: has a higher mean but lower standard deviation

8. Chemistry: mean 32.6, s.d. 15.7
Physics: mean 20.9, s.d. 11.1
Physics more consistent, lower standard deviation

Exercise 30.6   Page 475

1. (a) lower mean, lower s.d.
    (b) higher mean, higher s.d.

2. (a) lower mean, higher s.d.
    (b) higher mean, lower s.d.
    (c) lower mean, lower s.d.
    (d) same mean, higher s.d.
    (e) lower mean, lower s.d.

3. (a) 6, 2.83
    (b) (i) 7, 2.83   (ii) 5, 2.83
        (iii) 12, 5.66   (iv) 3, 1.41

4. (a) 35.9, 6.64   (b) 71.8%, 13.3%

5. (a) 14.6 s, 0.728 s   (b) 16.6 s, 0.728 s

6. (a) 11.5 m, 6.89 m
    (b) (i) decreased   (ii) decreased
    (c) (i) mean width of 3 extra roads is less than 11.5 m
       (ii) difference from 11.5 of all 3 extra values is less than 6.89

7. (a) 68, 8   (b) 60, 10   (c) 60, 10

8. 57.6, 15.2

9. 50, 10

Review Exercise 30   Page 478

1. (a) (i) 12 cm   (ii) 32 cm
    (b) English cucumbers are longer on average and slightly more varied in length.

2. (a) £200 - £300   (b) £300 - £400
    (c) Mean, influenced by 12 people earning £600 - £1000.

3. (a) 24 cm   (b) 24.32 cm
    (c) 1st group had higher mode (1st 25, 2nd 23), but lower range (1st 7, 2nd 13).

4. (a) (i) 2   (ii) 2.28
    (b) (i) 2.5   (ii) 2.63
    (c) The calculation for the mean involves the number of runs scored off every ball.

5. (a) 3 miles   (b) 0.5 miles
    (c) Range is affected by a few long journeys, etc.

6. (a) Entries are: 2, 5, 13, 22, 28, 35, 40
    (c) 78.5 g   (d) 19 g
    (e) The spread of the second sample is greater (1QR 38 g compared with 19 g), etc.

7. (a) Entries are: 12, 37, 79, 114, 132, 140
    (b) 27.5 minutes   (c) 18 minutes
    (d) The times of the second group are less varied, etc.

8. (a) 43
    (b) (i) 7   (ii) more varied
    (c) 2

9. (a) Entries are: 30, 90, 130, 150, 160
    (c) 1.55 mins   (d) 18

10. Entries for 1995: 7.75, 8.24
Higher mean and standard deviation in 1995

11. (a) 32.2, 7.82   (b) 54.4, 15.64

12. (a) 1.96°C
(b) Warmer (higher mean) at Longsands, but more variation (higher standard deviation) in temperatures.
(c) 16.6°C, 3.02°C

13. (a) 8.98
(b) Class A has a higher mean but lower standard deviation

14. (a) 69.5 beats/min, 7.13 beats/min
(b) (i) mean increased by 10 beats/min standard deviation the same (7.13 beats/min)
(ii) mean multiplied by 1.2 (83.4 beats/min) standard deviation multiplied by 1.2 (8.55 beats/min)

CHAPTER 31

Exercise 31.1   Page 484

1. (a) $\frac{4}{10} = \frac{2}{5}$ (b) $\frac{6}{10} = \frac{3}{5}$ (c) $\frac{6}{10} = \frac{3}{5}$
(d) $\frac{10}{10} = 1$ (e) 0

2. (a) $\frac{1}{500}$
(b) Depends how many tickets are bought by girls.

3. (a) $\frac{6}{10} = \frac{3}{5}$ (b) $\frac{5}{9}$ (c) $\frac{6}{9} = \frac{2}{3}$

4. (a) $\frac{8}{12} = \frac{2}{3}$ (b) $\frac{4}{12} = \frac{1}{3}$ (c) $\frac{9}{12} = \frac{3}{4}$

5. (a) $\frac{20}{50} = \frac{2}{5}$ (b) $\frac{30}{50} = \frac{3}{5}$ (c) $\frac{8}{50} = \frac{4}{25}$
(d) $\frac{8}{30} = \frac{4}{15}$ (e) $\frac{8}{20} = \frac{2}{5}$

6. (a) $\frac{40}{120} = \frac{1}{3}$ (b) $\frac{8}{120} = \frac{1}{15}$ (c) $\frac{55}{120} = \frac{11}{24}$
(d) $\frac{17}{50}$ (e) $\frac{42}{50} = \frac{21}{25}$ (f) $\frac{20}{25} = \frac{4}{5}$

7. (a) (i) $\frac{14}{30} = \frac{7}{15}$ (ii) $\frac{15}{30} = \frac{1}{2}$
(b) $\frac{1}{16}$ (c) $\frac{3}{4}$

8. Depends on the ability of the players.

Exercise 31.2   Page 486

1. $\frac{36}{40} = \frac{9}{10}$

2. (a) $\frac{9}{30} = \frac{3}{10}$ (b) $\frac{120}{300} = \frac{2}{5}$

3. $\frac{21}{30} = \frac{7}{10}$

4. (a) Tom $\frac{4}{12} = \frac{1}{3}$ Kim $\frac{3}{4}$
Sam $\frac{8}{16} = \frac{1}{2}$ Pam $\frac{9}{20}$
(b) Pam. Most games played.
(c) Pam. $\frac{9}{20} > \frac{1}{3}$

5. $\frac{19}{50}$

6. (a) $\frac{52}{100} = 0.52$ $\frac{102}{200} = 0.51$ $\frac{141}{300} = 0.47$
(b) 0.47

7. (a) Only 20 trials
(b) Daron, most trials
(c) 1. $\frac{181}{520}$ 2. $\frac{180}{520} = \frac{9}{26}$
3. $\frac{75}{520} = \frac{15}{104}$ 4. $\frac{84}{520} = \frac{21}{130}$

8. (a) R(1) is about 0.25
(b) Varies around 0.5

Exercise 31.3   Page 488

1. 6; e.g. 0.02 may not be exact, there may be a run of faulty switches, etc.

2. 900   **3.** 500

4. Red 13, Blue 15, White 22

5. (a) Missing entries: $\frac{8}{35}$, 114; $\frac{78}{300}$, 130
(b) Set B. Larger number of trials.

Exercise 31.4   Page 490

1. $\frac{3}{5}$ **2.** 0.04   **3.** $\frac{94}{100} = \frac{47}{50}$

4. 0.6   **5.** (a) 0.5   (b) 0.3

6. A 0.5
B not possible, not mutually exclusive
C 0.3

7. (a) (i) Probabilities add to more than 100%
(ii) 5%
(b) (i) 45%   (ii) 75%   (iii) 80%

8. (a) 0.4   (b) 0.6
(c) (i) Yes   (ii) No
(d) (i) 0.6   (ii) 0.6

Exercise 31.5   Page 492

1. (a)

		1	2	3	4	5	6
	6	7	8	9	10	11	12
	5	6	7	8	9	10	11
2nd	4	5	6	7	8	9	10
die	3	4	5	6	7	8	9
	2	3	4	5	6	7	8
	1	2	3	4	5	6	7

1st die

(b) (i) $\frac{3}{36} = \frac{1}{12}$ (ii) $\frac{3}{36} = \frac{1}{12}$ (iii) $\frac{30}{36} = \frac{5}{6}$
(c) Total must be less than, equal to, or greater than 10.

2.

Coin	Dice	1	2	3	4	5	6
	H	H1	H2	H3	H4	H5	H6
	T	T1	T2	T3	T4	T5	T6

(a) $\frac{1}{12}$ (b) $\frac{3}{12} = \frac{1}{4}$ (c) $\frac{1}{12}$

(d) $\frac{3}{12} = \frac{1}{4}$ (e) $\frac{2}{12} = \frac{1}{6}$ (f) $\frac{6}{12} = \frac{1}{2}$

3. (a)
Stage 1	Stage 2
Bus	Bus
Bus	Walk
Train	Bus
Train	Walk
Lift	Bus
Lift	Walk

(b) $\frac{1}{6}$ (c) 133

4. (a) $\frac{480}{800} = \frac{3}{5}$

(b)
1st fan	2nd fan
Red	Red
Red	White
Red	Blue
White	Red
White	White
White	Blue
Blue	Red
Blue	White
Blue	Blue

(c) Events not equally likely.

5. (a) $\frac{1}{16}$ (b) $\frac{2}{16} = \frac{1}{8}$ (c) $\frac{3}{16}$

6. (a)

Bag A

Bag B	R	R	W
W	RW	RW	WW
W	RW	RW	WW
R	RR	RR	WR

(c) $\frac{4}{9}$ (d) 0.4

7. (a)

A	1	1	2	2	3	3
B	2	3	2	3	2	3

(b) (i) $\frac{2}{6} = \frac{1}{3}$ (ii) $\frac{4}{6} = \frac{2}{3}$

(c) $\frac{4}{5}$

8. (a) Maths, English
Maths, Science
Maths, Art
English, Science
English, Art
Science, Art

(b) $\frac{3}{6} = \frac{1}{2}$ (c) $\frac{1}{3}$

9. (a)

2nd spin	W	RW	GW	BW	YW	WW
	Y	RY	GY	BY	YY	WY
	B	RB	GB	BB	YB	WB
	G	RG	GG	BG	YG	WG
	R	RR	GR	BR	YR	WR
		R	G	B	Y	W

1st spin

(b) (i) $\frac{1}{25}$ (ii) $\frac{9}{25}$ (iii) $\frac{5}{25} = \frac{1}{5}$

10. (a) $\frac{1}{15}$ (b) $\frac{3}{15} = \frac{1}{5}$

Exercise 31.6 — Page 495

1. (a)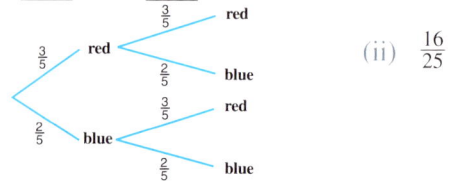

(b) (i) $\frac{4}{25}$

(ii) $\frac{16}{25}$

2. (a)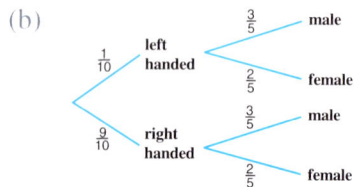

(b) (i) 0.01 (ii) 0.18

(c) 810

3. (a) (i) $\frac{5}{50} = \frac{1}{10}$ (ii) $\frac{45}{50} = \frac{9}{10}$

(iii) $\frac{20}{50} = \frac{2}{5}$ (iv) $\frac{30}{50} = \frac{3}{5}$

(b)
(tree diagram)

(c) (i) $\frac{2}{50} = \frac{1}{25}$ (ii) $\frac{29}{50}$

4. (a)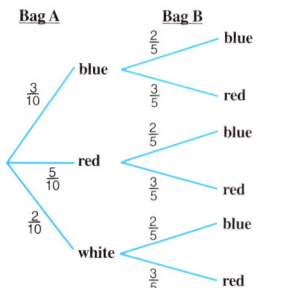

(b) $\frac{9}{50}$

(c) $\frac{21}{50}$

5. (a) Seema. P(Dario ends on B) $= \frac{30}{64}$

P(Seema ends on B) $= \frac{39}{64}$

(b) Dario P(Dario ends on B) $= \frac{294}{512}$

P(Seema ends on B) $= \frac{267}{512}$

Exercise 31.7   Page 498

1. (a) not   (b) independent
(c) not   (d) independent
(e) not   (f) independent

2. (a) 0.7   (b) 0.58

3. (a) $\frac{21}{200}$ (b) $\frac{71}{80}$

4. (a) 0.09   (b) Sally (0.54)

5. (a) 0.14   (b) 0.06

6. (a) The events do not influence each other.
(b) $\frac{1}{8}$ (c) 8

7. (a) $\frac{1}{3}$ (b) $\frac{1}{2}$

8. (a) (i) 0.3   (ii) 0.1
(iii) 0.4   (iv) 0.5
(b) 0.66

9. (a) (i) 0.1   (ii) 0.7   (iii) 0.6
(b) (i) 0.01   (ii) 0.25   (iii) 0.18

10. (a) (i) $\frac{22}{175}$ (ii) $\frac{81}{175}$
(b) (i) $\frac{24}{100} = \frac{6}{25}$ (ii) $\frac{31}{50}$

Exercise 31.8   Page 502

1. (a) (i) 1st block / 2nd block tree diagram   (ii) $\frac{1}{15}$ (b) $\frac{7}{30}$

2. (a) tree diagram   (b) (i) $\frac{12}{90} = \frac{2}{15}$ (ii) $\frac{8}{15}$

3. (a) (i) 1st member / 2nd member tree diagram   (b) $\frac{3}{7}$

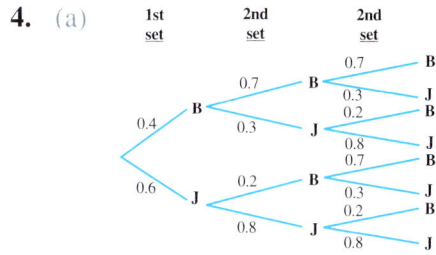

4. (a) tree diagram   (b) 0.384   (c) 0.388

5. (a) tree diagram   (b) $\frac{5}{11}$

6. $\frac{4}{15}$ **7.** $\frac{35}{216}$

8. 0.9997992   **9.** (a) $\frac{1}{11}$ (b) $\frac{1}{11}$

10. (a) (i) $\frac{1}{12}$ (ii) $\frac{1}{45}$
(b) $\frac{1}{45}$

11. P(Tom wins) $= \frac{33}{100}$

P(Sam wins) $= \frac{52}{300}$

P(Draw) $= \frac{149}{300}$

So Draw most likely

12. (a) (i) 0.15   (ii) 0.09
(b) 0.34

13. (a) $\frac{1}{10}$ (b) $\frac{8}{15}$ (c) $\frac{11}{30}$ (d) $\frac{92}{225}$

14. 488

15. (a) tree diagram   (b) $\frac{1}{4}$

16. (a) 10 Red, 8 Blue, 7 Green   (b) 0.243

1. (a) 180 (b) Blue 9, White 6, Red 5

2. (a) (i) $\frac{3}{10}$ (ii) Approaches $\frac{1}{4}$

   (b) $\frac{1}{6}$

3. (a) $\frac{2}{3}$ (b) (i) $\frac{2}{3}$ (ii) $\frac{4}{9}$

4. 0.3

5. (a)

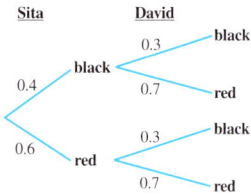

   (b) (i) 0.42
      (ii) 0.46

6. (a) $\frac{9}{25}$ (b) $\frac{12}{25}$

7. (a) (i)

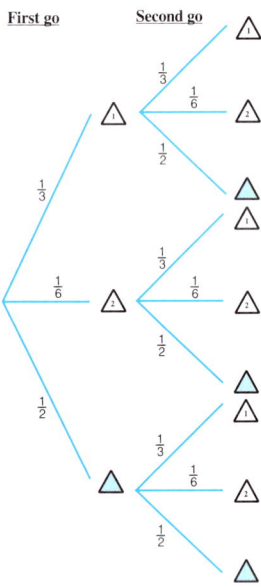

(ii) $\frac{1}{4}$

   (b) $\frac{5}{36}$

8. (a) $\frac{21}{190}$ (b) $\frac{91}{190}$ (c) $\frac{59}{190}$

9. (a) $\frac{21}{40}$ (b) (i) $\frac{22}{51}$ (ii) $\frac{8}{17}$

10. (a) $\frac{1}{12}$ (b) (i) $\frac{1}{3}$ (ii) $\frac{1}{4}$

11. 35

12. 0.45

13. (a) $\frac{229}{1225}$ (b) $\frac{332}{1225}$

14. (a) 2 coins (b) $\frac{17}{30}$

1. (a) 35
   (b) More boys than girls were included in the survey.
   (c) Survey is based on a small sample.
   (d) 55

2. (a) 12 (b) 1 (c) 30 (d) 45

3. (a) No. Boys more likely to pass, $\frac{19}{23} > \frac{49}{62}$

4. (b) Positive correlation between distance travelled and amount of fuel used.
   (c) (i) 65 litres
      (ii) Not very reliable, graph plotted using a small number of points.

5. (a) 78
   (b) E.g. May be better at Maths than English.

6. (a) $\frac{7}{60}$ (b) Gets closer to $\frac{1}{6}$

7. (a) $\frac{195}{400} = \frac{39}{80}$
   (b) Keith, e.g. there are twice as many blue faces on each dice, so ratio of blue : green $\approx$ 2 : 1

8. (a) 3.1
   (b) Hypothesis is supported by the survey, the mean has reduced.

9. (a) 22.2 seconds

10. (a) 65.25 km/h
   (c) E.g. higher speeds possible on a motorway

11. (a) Qn. 1: Too personal, Qn. 2: Too open
   (b) E.g. use multiple-response questions and provide boxes to tick

12. (a) Only men surveyed
      Local issues may affect voting.
   (b) Survey people from different parts of the country.
      Survey equal numbers of men and women.
      Survey more people.

13. (a) $\frac{1}{5}$
   (b) (i) $\frac{3}{12} = \frac{1}{4}$ (ii) $\frac{7}{12}$
   (c) $\frac{2}{35}$

14. (a)

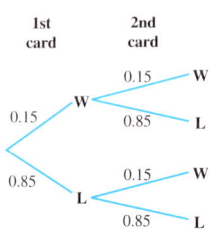

(b) 0.2775

15. (a) (i) 0.36 (ii) 0.48
   (b) 0.2496

16. (a) (i) 100 (ii) 50 (b) $\frac{19}{30}$

17. (a) 15 minutes, 20 minutes (to the nearest minute)
   (b) 11 (c) $\frac{22}{32} = \frac{11}{16}$

18. (c) Economy: 1QR ≈ 170 g
  Baking: 1QR ≈ 80 g
  E.g. Economy more spread

19. (a) Entries are: 0, 3, 10, 23, 38, 50, 58, 60
  (c) 11 g   (d) 52   (e) 102 g

20. Ashworth 120, Brigholm 51, Corchester 29

21. (a)   (b) 65

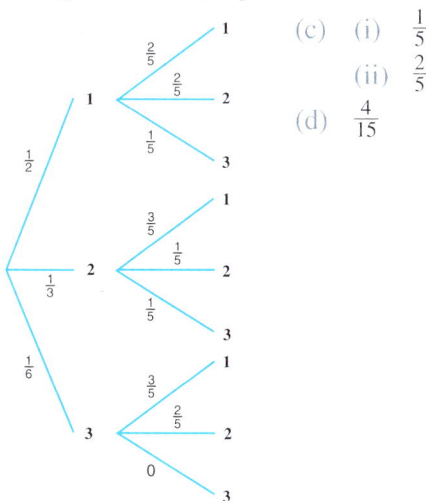

22. (a) 8   (b) 120   (c) 51.4

23. (a)   (b) $\frac{5}{14}$
                                         (c) $\frac{1}{56}$
                                         (d) $\frac{55}{56}$

24. (a) $\frac{34}{455}$ (0.0747 to 3 s.f.)
  (b) $\frac{24}{91}$ (0.264 to 3 s.f.)

25. (a) (i) $\frac{1}{3}$ (ii) $\frac{1}{5}$
  (b)   (c) (i) $\frac{1}{5}$
                                  (ii) $\frac{2}{5}$
                             (d) $\frac{4}{15}$

26. (a) (i) $\frac{1}{12}$ (ii) $\frac{1}{15}$
  (b) $\frac{1}{45}$

27. (a) mean 1.4, standard deviation 0.8
  (b) higher mean (longer delivery time) and
    higher standard deviation (more varied
    length of delivery).
  (c) mean : increased by 1 day to 4.1 day's.
    standard deviation : no change

28. (a) mean 30.5 cm, s.d. 11.2 cm (3 s.f.)
  (b) Crop B has a higher mean (taller) but a
    lower standard deviation (more
    consistent in height).

29. (a) 11.8 seconds
  (b) Lower. The differences between each
    time and the mean time will be lower for
    puzzle B.
  (c) Puzzle B. Times not 'bunched' around
    the mean, as for Puzzles A and C.
  (d) Missing entries: 9, 33, 16

Non-calculator Paper   Page 518

1. 5 fewer

2. (a) 16 000   (b) not enough paint

3. (a) $4n + 1$ (b) $n^2 + n$

4. (a) (i) £3   (ii) £3.49
  (b) 16 year olds
    Range 10 year olds = 8 − 1 = 7
    Range 16 year olds = 25 − 0 = 25

5. (a) $p = 130°, q = 20°$ (b) 8 cm

6. (a) 135°
  (b) (i) 30   (ii) $n = \dfrac{360}{180 - p}$

7. (a) Q (3, 6)   (b) (3, 2)

8. 42

9. 100.8 km/h

10. (c) (i) 3600 g
    (ii) 140 days is beyond known values

11. (a) $2\pi a$ (b)

12. (a) $2\pi a (a + b), \ \frac{1}{2}(a + b) c$
  (b) $\pi a^2 b$

13. (a) Entries are: 5, 13, 30, 53, 65, 74, 80
  (b) (i) 168 g   (ii) 40 g
  (c) Second sample has higher median weight
    and lower interquartile range of weights

14. (a) Entries are: 0, 44, 95, 154, 222, 272,
    307, 338, 356, 360
  (b) (i) 34 years   (ii) 30 years
  (c) Second village has a higher median age
    and lower interquartile range of ages.

15. (a) 0.6   (b) 0.16

16. (a) (i) $\frac{3}{5}$ (ii) $\frac{7}{10}$
  (b) $\frac{24}{90} = \frac{4}{15}$

17. (a)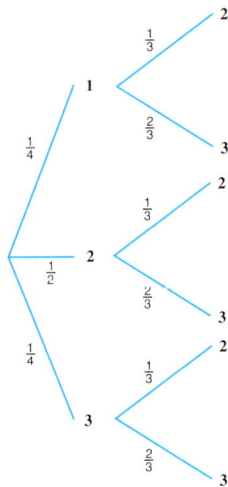

(b) $\frac{1}{6}$

(c) $\frac{5}{12}$

18. 9 cm

19. (a) $n^2 + 2$ (b) $2a(2a - b)$ (c) $2x^2 + 3x - 2$

20. (a) $x = 4\frac{1}{2}$ (b) $x = 4, y = -1$ (c) $x = 3$ or 8

21. (a) (i) $x = 3\frac{1}{4}$ (ii) $x = -\frac{3}{4}$

(b) $x = 14, \ y = 5$

22. (a) Missing entries are: $5, -1, 1$

(c) (i) $x = -1.3$ or 2.3

(ii) $x = -0.4$ or 2.4

(d) $a = -1, b = 5$

23. (a) 0.008   (b) 0.016

24. (a) $\frac{7}{33}$ (b) $6\sqrt{2}$

25. (a) (i) $\frac{11}{90}$ (ii) $0.12222\ldots, (0.12222\ldots)^2$

(b) π is irrational

26. (a) $5\sqrt{2}$ (b) $12\sqrt{6}$ **27.** 23 275 feet

28. (a) Select 60 girls and boys in the ratio $380 : 320 = 19 : 16$ 33 girls, 27 boys

(b) Stratified sample ensures representative numbers of boys and girls are surveyed.

29. $130°$

30. (a) Too open   (b) Not representative sample

(c) Find the ratio of boys to girls in each age group and survey using the same ratio.

31. (a) $\frac{1}{45}$ (b) 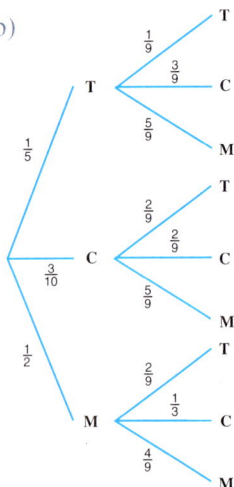   (c) $\frac{1}{5}$

32. (a) $23°$ (b) 7 cm

(c) (i) X

(ii) X : SAS - two sides and the included angle.

33. (a) (i) 39

(ii) 26

(b) Not representative sample of TV watchers.

34. (a) $x = 30°, 150°, 390°, 510°$

(b) $x = 150°, 210°, 510°, 570°$

35.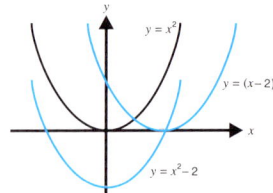

36. (a) (i) 8B, higher standard deviation

(ii) mean 34.6, standard deviation 9.2

(b) 8A, marks more clustered about centre of diagram.

37. (a) $2x^2 - 5x - 12$

(b) 16

(c) $\dfrac{2x + 1}{(x - 3)(x + 4)}$

(d) $-\frac{1}{2}$

38. $\dfrac{7}{2x - 1}$

40. $a = 2, \ b = 7$

41. (a) $x + 2y$ (b) $2y - x$

(c) $\overrightarrow{AD}$ and $\overrightarrow{HE}$

(d) parallel, equal length

42. -2

43. (a) $A = \pi(b + a)(b - a)$

(b) $V = \pi cd^2$

Calculator Paper   Page 526

1. 0.84

2. (a) (i) $a = 7, \ b = 10, \ c = 6$

(ii) $R = \sqrt{\dfrac{2 \times 7 + 10}{6}} = \sqrt{\dfrac{24}{6}} = \sqrt{4} = 2$

(b) 2.02

3. $36°$

4. (b) 14.2 minutes

5. (a) $\frac{4}{15}$ (b) $\frac{17}{60}$

(c) Yes, frequency of each number should be approximately equal.

(d) 200

6. (a) $AB = 14.1\,\text{cm}$, $OC = 12.1\,\text{cm}$
    (b) $2480\,\text{cm}^3$

7. (a) $1.75\,\text{cm}$ (b) $20.6\,\text{cm}^2$

8. (a) $61.9°$ (b) $6.0\,\text{m}$

9. (a) 2.44×10^5 (b) 0.048%

10. $19.8\,\text{cm}$

11. 2.401×10^{-5}

12. £5146.42

13. £8

14. (a) 164 miles per hour (b) 25%

15. 5 hours 48 minutes

16. (a) 9.26 (b) $V = \sqrt{PR}$

17. $x = 3.36$

18. (a) $3.44\,\text{m}$ (b) $40.7°$

19. (a) 19.4
    (b) $v = \sqrt{20^2 - 2 \times (-10) \times 10}$
        $= \sqrt{200} \approx 14$

    Answer to (a) is of the correct magnitude.

20. $(5.92 \times 10^{-4})\%$

21. 0.28175

22. £72

23. (a) $176\,\text{g}$
    (b) (i) Entries are: 11, 32, 64, 91, 100
    (c) $180\,\text{g}$
    (d) (i) Median. The mean can be distorted by unusually small or high values.
        (ii) 1800

24. (a) $r = \sqrt{\dfrac{3V}{\pi h}}$ (b) $1.6\,\text{cm}^3$

25. (a) $11.1\,\text{cm}$ (b) $7.5\,\text{cm}$

26. (a) 0.01 (b) 0.99

27. (a) $6.98\,\text{cm}$ (b) $60.8°$
    (c) $66.7°$ (d) $70.3°$

28. (a) $x = 4.4$ (b) $x = 0$ or -3
    (c) $-1 \leqslant x < 1$

29. (a) $60°, 300°$ (b) $210°, 330°$

30. (a) $x = 126°$, $y = 121.5°$
    (b) $63°$ (c) $16.0\,\text{cm}^2$

31. $101.4°$

32. (a) $139.3°$ (b) $2049\,\text{cm}^2$

33. $26.8\,\text{m}$

34. (a) Boys 25; girls 20
    (b) Boys and girls in years 7 and 8 will be represented in proportion.

35. (a) (i) £19 140
       (ii) £17 500
       (iii) Median. The median is lower than the mean, which is distorted by the 6 people with the highest wages.
    (b)

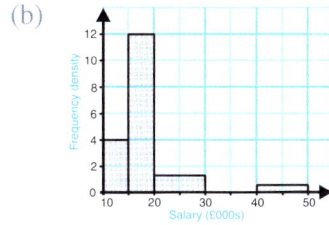

36. 0.084

37. (a) 6.270×10^2 people/km^2
    (b) (i) 6.289×10^2 people/km^2
       (ii) 12%

38. (a) 8.98
    (b) 10B has a lower mean mark and greater standard deviation (variation in marks).
    (c) There is no spread so the standard deviation is zero.

39. $5.4\,\text{m}$

40. (a) $2\pi y\,(y + 2x)$
    (b) $2\pi y^2 + 4\pi xy = 4\pi x^2$
       Divide each term by π
       $y^2 + 2xy = 2x^2$
       $y^2 = 2x^2 - 2xy$
       $y^2 = 2x\,(x - y)$
    (c) $x = 4.1$ ($x \neq -1.1$)

41. (a) $2x^2 + 6x - 32 = 0$
       $x^2 + 3x - 16 = 0$
       $x(x + 3) = 16$
       $x = \dfrac{16}{x + 3}$
    (b) $x = 2.8$

42. $x = -2.5$ or 2

43. $x = -4$

44. (a) $0.1\,\text{m/s}^2$ (b) $664\,\text{m}$

45. (a) $a = 11$, $b = 5$
    (b) $x = 1.68$ or 8.32

46. (a) $F = 0.0027W^3$
    (b) 21 600
    (c) $121\,\text{m}$

47. (a) $L = \dfrac{1000}{d^2}$ (b) 2.5

48. Draw the graph of $y = x^3 - 2x$
    $x = -1.7$ or 2.5

49. (b) $a = 2$, $b = -5.7$

50. Draw the graph of y against $\dfrac{1}{x}$
    $a = 60$, $b = 5$

Index